NEW YORK PRACTICE LIBRARY

New York Landlord and Tenant

Rent Control and Rent Stabilization
Second Edition

by

Joseph Rasch
of the New York Bar

Author of
New York Landlord and Tenant
including Summary Proceedings
and
New York Law and Practice of Real Property

1987

THE LAWYERS CO-OPERATIVE PUBLISHING CO.
Aqueduct Building
Rochester, New York 14694

Copyright © 1969-1986
by
THE LAWYERS CO-OPERATIVE PUBLISHING CO.

Copyright © 1987
by
THE LAWYERS CO-OPERATIVE PUBLISHING CO.

Library of Congress Catalog Card Number 87-80713

PREFACE

This is a unique sourcebook containing, in a single volume, all the statutes and administrative materials pertinent to New York's Rent Control and Rent Stabilization.

The materials herein have been divided into five basic parts: The Emergency Housing Rent Control Law; New York City's Housing Rent Control; Rent Stabilization; Emergency Tenant Protection; and Miscellaneous Laws affecting rent control and stabilization.

The markings on the page borders facilitate access to these materials, as do the Table of Contents at the front and the Index at the back of the volume.

The predecessor of this volume was published 15 years ago. It did not include Rent Stabilization in its title, and its pocket part supplementation had become unwieldy and spine-breaking. Hence, this new edition.

This volume, like its predecessor, will also be supplemented annually.

JOSEPH RASCH

TABLE OF CONTENTS

PAGE

PART I: EMERGENCY HOUSING RENT CONTROL
Emergency Housing Rent Control Law......... 1
Rent and Eviction Regulations of the Office of Rent Administration of the Division of Housing and Community Renewal................ 49
Advisory Bulletins of the State Rent Administrator 130

PART II: NEW YORK CITY HOUSING RENT CONTROL
Local Emergency Housing Rent Control Law ... 223
New York City Rent and Eviction Regulations . 247
New York City Rent and Rehabilitation Law ... 378
Rent Administrator's Interpretations 457
Rent Administrator's Operational Bulletins 581
Rent Administrator's Information and Instruction Sheets 652
Exemption from Rent Increases for Low Income Elderly Persons 713

PART III: RENT STABILIZATION
Rent Stabilization Law 725
Rent Stabilization Code for Rent Stabilized Apartments in New York City 764
Rent Stabilization Regulations of the Housing and Development Administration............ 863
Orders of the Rent Guidance Board............ 871
Hotel Orders................................. 981

PART IV: EMERGENCY TENANT PROTECTION
Emergency Tenant Protection Act of 1974 995
State Tenant Protection Regulations........... 1024
State Tenant Protection Bulletins 1072

PART V: MISCELLANEOUS LAWS
Rules of Practice for the Office of Rent Administration Adjudicatory Proceeding.............. 1155
Omnibus Housing Act of 1983................. 1174

v

Private Housing Finance Law (§§ 607, 608, 706-a)
.... 1188
Increase of Rentals, Department of HPD Supervisory Agency............................. 1192
Public Authorities Law (§ 2429) 1193
Destabilization Provisions of Real Property Tax Law (§§ 421-a, 489) J51 Housing 1194
Unlawful Evictions........................... 1199

INDEX 1203

TOTAL CLIENT-SERVICE LIBRARY® REFERENCES

50 Am Jur 2d, Landlord and Tenant §§ 1248–1252 (Emergency Rental Legislation)

New York Jur 2d, Landlord and Tenant (1st Edition §§ 326.5–326.10, Supplement, Emergency Rent Control)

New York CLS, Unconsolidated Laws, Chapters 249–249A; NYC Administrative Code §§ Y51-5.0 et seq.

New York Forms, Leases—Real Property §§ 8:181–8:183, Form 8:184 (Rent Controlled Housing)

VERALEX™: Cases and annotations pertinent to these materials can be further researched through the VERALEX electronic retrieval system's two services, **Auto-Cite®** and **SHOWME™**. Use Auto-Cite to check citations for form, parallel references, prior and later history, and annotation references. Use SHOWME to display the full text of cases and annotations.

ANNOTATION REFERENCES

Tenant's rights, under due process clause of Federal Constitution, to notice and hearing prior to imposition of higher rents or additional service charges for government-owned or government-subsidized housing. 28 ALR Fed 739.

Validity and construction of statute or ordinance establishing rent control benefit or rent subsidy for elderly tenants. 5 ALR4th 922.

Federal Housing and Rent Act of 1947 and amendments. 10 ALR2d 249.

Enforceability of option to purchase, consideration for which is payment of rentals exceeding rent control maximum. 28 ALR2d 1204.

To quickly locate major components of this work, follow the guide bar shown below to the black strips appearing on the side of the volume.

PART I: EMERGENCY HOUSING RENT CONTROL

PART II: NEW YORK CITY HOUSING RENT CONTROL

PART III: RENT STABILIZATION

PART IV: EMERGENCY TENANT PROTECTION

PART V: MISCELLANEOUS LAWS

PART I: EMERGENCY HOUSING RENT CONTROL
Emergency Housing Rent Control Law
Rent and Eviction Regulations of the
    Office of Rent Administration of the
    Division of Housing and Community Renewal
Advisory Bulletins of the State
    Rent Administrator

PART I

EMERGENCY HOUSING RENT CONTROL

EMERGENCY HOUSING RENT CONTROL LAW

§ 1. Declaration and findings; termination.
§ 2. Definitions.
§ 3. Temporary state housing rent commission.
§ 4. General powers and duties of the commission.
§ 5. Evictions.
§ 6. Investigations; records; reports.
§ 7. Cooperation with other governmental agencies.
§ 8. Procedure.
§ 9. Judicial review.
§ 10. Prohibitions.
§ 11. Enforcement.
§ 12. Application.
§ 13. Pending proceedings.
§ 14. Intent.
§ 15. Separability.
§ 16. Existing rights preserved.
§ 17. Short title.

§ 1. Declaration and findings; termination. 1. The legislature hereby finds that a serious public emergency continues to exist in the housing of a considerable number of persons in the state of New York which emergency was created by war, the effects of war and the aftermath of hostilities; that such emergency necessitated the intervention of federal, state and local government in order to prevent speculative, unwarranted and abnormal increases in rents; that there continues to exist an acute shortage of dwellings; that unless residential rents and evictions continue to be regulated and controlled, disruptive practices and abnormal conditions will produce serious threats to the public health, safety and general welfare; that to prevent such perils to health, safety and welfare, preventive action by the legislature continues to be imperative; that such action is necessary in order to prevent exactions of unjust, unreasonable and oppressive rents and rental agreements and to forestall profiteering, speculation and other disruptive practices tending to produce threats to the public health; that the transition from regulation to a normal market of free bargaining between landlord and tenant, while still the objective of state policy, must be administered with due regard for such emergency; that in order to prevent uncertainty, hardship and dislocation, the provisions of this act are declared to be necessary and designed to protect the public health, safety and general welfare.

2. The provisions of this act, and all regulations, orders and requirements thereunder shall remain in full force and effect until and including May 14, 1987 [Am L 1983, ch 403, § 60, eff June 30, 1983, Am L 1985, ch 172, § 2, eff June 5, 1985, Am L 1985, ch 248, § 3, eff June 19, 1985].

§ 2. Definitions. When used in this act, unless a different meaning clearly appears from the context, the following terms shall mean and include:

1. "Commission." Prior to July first, nineteen hundred sixty-four, the temporary state housing rent commission created by this act. On and after July first, nineteen hundred sixty-four, the division of housing and community renewal in the executive department.

2. "Housing accommodation." Any building or structure, permanent or temporary, or any part thereof, occupied or intended to be occupied by one or more individuals as a residence, home, sleeping place, boarding house, lodging house or hotel, together with the land and buildings appurtenant thereto, and all services, privileges, furnishings, furniture and facilities supplied in connection with the occupation thereof, including (a) entire structures or premises as distinguished from the individual housing accommodations contained therein, wherein twenty-five or less rooms are rented or offered for rent by any lessee, sublessee or other tenant of such entire structure or premises, and (b) housing accommodations which were previously exempt, or not subject to control as a result of a conversion or a change from a non-housing to a housing use and which have subsequently been certified by a municipal department having jurisdiction to be a fire hazard or in a continued dangerous condition or detrimental to life or health but only so long as such illegal or hazardous condition continues and further certification

with respect thereto shall not be required notwithstanding any inconsistent provision of this act, and any plot or parcel of land which had been rented prior to May first, nineteen hundred fifty, for the purpose of permitting the tenant thereof to construct or place his own dwelling thereon, unless exempt or excluded from control pursuant to any other provision of this act, except that it shall not include structures in which all of the housing accommodations are exempt or not subject to control under this act or any regulation issued thereunder; or

(a) a hospital, convent, monastery, asylum, public institution, or college or school dormitory or any institution operated exclusively for charitable or educational purposes on a non-profit basis; or

(b) notwithstanding any previous order, finding, opinion or determination of the commission, housing accommodations in any establishment which on March first, nineteen hundred fifty, was and still is commonly regarded as a hotel in the community in which it is located and which customarily provides hotel services such as maid service, furnishing and laundering of linen, telephone and secretarial or desk service, use and upkeep of furniture and fixtures, and bellboy service, provided, however, that the term hotel shall not include any establishment which is commonly regarded in the community as a rooming house, nor shall it include any establishment not identified or classified as a "hotel", "transient hotel" or "residential hotel" pursuant to the federal act, irrespective whether such establishment provides either some services customarily provided by hotels, or is represented to be a hotel, or both; and provided further that housing accommodations in hotels only within the cities of Buffalo and New York which have been and still are occupied by a tenant who has resided in such hotel continuously since December second, nineteen hundred forty-nine, so long as such tenant occupies the same, shall continue to remain subject to control under this act; or

(c) any motor court, or any part thereof; any trailer, or trailer space used exclusively for transient occupancy or any part thereof; or any tourist home serving transient guests exclusively, or any part thereof; or

(d) nonhousekeeping, furnished housing accommodations, located within a single dwelling unit not used as a rooming or boarding house, but only if (1) no more than two tenants for whom rent is paid (husband and wife being considered one tenant for this purpose), not members of the landlord's immediate family live in such dwelling unit, and (2) the remaining portion of such dwelling unit is occupied by the landlord or his immediate family; or

(e) housing accommodations operated by the United States, the state of New York, or any political subdivision thereof, or by any municipal or public authority, only so long as they are so operated; or housing accommodations in buildings in which rentals are fixed by or subject to the supervision of the commissioner of housing and community renewal pursuant to powers granted under laws other than the emergency housing rent control law; or

(f) housing accommodations in buildings operated exclusively for charitable purposes on a non-profit basis; or

(g) housing accommodations which were completed on or after February first, nineteen hundred forty-seven, provided, however, that maximum rents established under the veterans emergency housing act for priority constructed housing accommodations completed on or after February first, nineteen hundred forty-seven, shall continue in full force and effect, if such accommodations are being rented to veterans of world war II or their immediate families, who, on June thirtieth, nineteen hundred forty-seven, either occupied such housing accommodations or had a right to occupy such housing accommodations at any time on or after July first, nineteen hundred forty-seven, under any agreement whether written or oral; or which are (1) housing accommodations created by a change from a non-housing to a housing use on or after February first, nineteen hundred forty-seven, or which are (2) additional housing accommodations, other than rooming house accommodations, created by conversion on or after February first, nineteen hundred forty-seven; provided, however, that any housing accommodations created as a result of any conversion of housing accommodations on or after May first, nineteen hundred fifty, shall continue to be subject to rent control as provided for herein unless the commission issues an order decontrolling them which it shall do if there has been a structural change involving substantial alterations or remodeling and such change has resulted in additional housing accommodations consisting of self-contained family units as defined by regulations issued by the commission; provided further, however, that such order of decontrol shall not apply to that portion of the original housing accommodation occupied by a tenant in possession at the time of the conversion but only so long as that tenant continues in occupancy; and provided further, that no such order of decontrol shall be issued unless such conversion occurred after the entire structure, or any lesser portion thereof as may have been thus converted, was vacated by voluntary surrender of possession or in the manner provided in section five of this act; or

(h) housing accommodations which are rented after April first, nineteen hundred fifty-three, and have been continuously occupied by the owner thereof for a period one year prior to the date of renting; provided, however, that this paragraph shall not apply where the owner acquired possession of the housing accommodation after the issuance of a certificate of eviction under subdivision two of section five of this act within the two year period immediately preceding the date of such renting, and provided further, that this exemption shall remain effective only so long as the housing accommodations are not occupied for other than single family occupancy; or

(i) housing accommodations which become vacant provided, however, that this exemption shall not apply or become effective where the commission determines or finds that the housing accommodations became vacant because the landlord or any person acting on his behalf, with intent to cause the tenant to vacate, engaged in any course of conduct (including, but not limited to, interruption or discontinuance of essential services) which interfered with or disturbed or was intended to interfere with or disturb the comfort, repose, peace or quiet of the tenant in his use or occupancy of the housing accommodations; and further provided that housing accommodations as to which a housing emergency has been declared pursuant to the emergency tenant protection act of nineteen seventy-four shall be subject to the provisions of such act for the duration of such emergency; or

(j) housing accommodations (not otherwise exempt or excluded from control) in two family houses occupied in whole or in part by the owner thereof, and in one family houses whether or not so occupied, on and after July first, nineteen hundred fifty-five, in the counties of Monroe, Nassau, Oneida, Onondaga and Schenectady, and, on and after July first, nineteen hundred fifty-seven, any housing accommodations in the county of Onondaga containing four rental units or less, provided, however, that this exemption with respect to one and two family houses shall remain effective only so long as the housing accommodations are not occupied for other than single family occupancy, and provided further, however, that this exemption shall become or remain effective in any city or town within the counties of Monroe, Oneida or Schenectady subject to the provisions of subdivision four of section twelve hereof providing for the continuance or reestablishment of controls with respect to such housing accommodations therein; or

(k) housing accommodations (not otherwise exempt or excluded from control) elsewhere than in the city of New York, except housing accommodations used as boarding houses or rooming houses in the county of Westchester, which are or become vacant on or after July first, nineteen hundred fifty-seven, provided, however, that this exemption shall not apply or become effective in any case where the vacancy in the housing accommodation occurred or occurs because of the removal of the tenant to another housing accommodation in the same building, or because of the eviction of the tenant after the issuance of a final order in a summary proceeding to recover possession of the housing accommodation, whether after a trial of the issues or upon the consent or default of the tenant or otherwise without a trial, and provided, further, however that this exemption shall become effective in any city or town subject to the provisions of subdivision five of section twelve hereof providing for the continuance of control with respect to such housing accommodations, and provided further, that this exemption shall remain effective only so long as the housing accommodations are not occupied for other than single family occupancy.

(l) housing accommodations which are not occupied by

the tenant in possession as his primary residence provided, however, that any such housing accommodation shall continue to be subject to rent control as provided herein unless the commission issues an order decontrolling such accommodation which the commission shall do upon application by the landlord, whenever it is established by any facts and circumstances which, in the judgment of the commission, may have a bearing upon the question of residence, that the tenant maintains his primary residence at some place other than at such housing accommodation. (Added L 1971, ch 373, eff May 1, 1972)

2-a. The landlord of a housing accommodation specified in paragraph (h) or (i) or (j) or (k) of subdivision two of this section shall file a report with the commission within thirty days following the date of first rental of such accommodation after decontrol. No copy of such report shall be required to be served upon the new tenant of such housing accommodation.

3. "Rent." Consideration, including any bonus, benefit or gratuity demanded or received for or in connection with the use or occupancy of housing accommodations or the transfer of a lease of such housing accommodations.

4. "Maximum rent." The maximum lawful rent for the use of housing accommodations. Maximum rents may be formulated in terms of rents and other charges and allowances.

5. "Person." An individual, corporation, partnership, association, or any other organized group of individuals or the legal successor or representative of any of the foregoing.

6. "Landlord." An owner, lessor, sublessor, assignee, or other person receiving or entitled to receive rent for the use or occupancy of any housing accommodation or an agent of any of the foregoing.

7. "Tenant." A tenant, subtenant, lessee, sublessee, or other person entitled to the possession or to the use or occupancy of any housing accommodation.

8. "Documents." Records, books, accounts, correspondence, memoranda and other documents, and drafts and copies of any of the foregoing.

9. "Municipality." A city, town or village.

10. "Local governing body."

   a. In the case of a city, the council, common council or board of aldermen and the board of estimate, board of estimate and apportionment or board of estimate and contract, if there be one.

   b. In the case of a town, the town board.

   c. In the case of a village, the board of trustees.

11. "Local laws." The local laws specified in chapter one of the laws of nineteen hundred fifty, namely local laws numbers twenty-one, twenty-three, twenty-four, twenty-five and seventy-three of the local laws of the city of New York for the year nineteen hundred forty-nine; and local law number three of the city of Buffalo for the year nineteen hundred forty-seven.

12. "Federal act." The emergency price control act of nineteen hundred forty-two, and as thereafter amended and as superseded by the housing and rent act of nineteen hundred forty-seven, and as the latter was thereafter amended prior to May first, nineteen hundred fifty, and regulations adopted pursuant thereto.

§ 3. **Temporary state housing rent commission.** 1. There is hereby created a temporary state commission, to be known as the temporary state housing rent commission. Such commission shall consist of one commissioner, to be known as the state rent administrator, who shall be appointed by the governor, by and with the advice and consent of the senate, and who shall serve during the pleasure of the governor. He shall receive an annual salary to be provided by law. He shall also be entitled to his expenses actually and necessarily incurred by him in the performance of his duties.

2. The commission shall establish and maintain such offices within the state as the commission may deem necessary, and shall designate one of them as its principal office. The commission may appoint such officers, counsel, employees and agents as the commission may deem necessary, fix their compensation within the limitations provided by law, and prescribe their duties. All employees of the commission shall be appointed in accor-

dance with the provisions of the civil service law and rules.

3. Any officer or employee under federal or municipal civil service selected by the commission may, with the consent of the appropriate governmental agency by which he is or has been employed, be transferred without further examination or qualification to comparable offices, positions and employment under the commission. Any such officer or employee who has been appointed to an office or position under the rules and classifications of the state or any municipal civil service commission, shall retain, upon such transfer, the civil service classification and status which he had prior to such transfer. Any such officer or employee who at the time of transfer has a temporary or provisional appointment shall be subject to removal, examination or termination as though such transfer had not been made. The commission may, by agreement with the appropriate federal agency and state civil service commission, make similar provision for any federal officer or employee so transferred. Notwithstanding the provisions of any other law, any such officer or employee so transferred, pursuant to the provisions of this section, who is a member or beneficiary under any existing municipal pension or retirement system, shall continue to have all rights, privileges, obligations and status with respect to such fund, system or systems as are now prescribed by law, but during the period of his employment by the commission, all contributions to any pension or retirement fund or system to be paid by the employer on account of such officer or employee, shall be paid by the commission. The commission may by agreement with the appropriate federal agency, make similar provisions relating to retirement for any federal officer or employee so transferred.

§ 4. General powers and duties of the commission. 1. At the time this act shall become effective, the commission shall establish maximum rents which shall be

(a) for housing accommodations outside the city of New York, the maximum rent which was established on March first, nineteen hundred fifty, pursuant to the federal act, and shall not include adjustments granted by orders issued under the federal act after that date, regardless of whether they were made effective as of, or retroactive to, that date or a date prior thereto; and

(b) for housing accommodations within the city of New York, the maximum rent which was established on March first, nineteen hundred fifty, pursuant to the federal act, and shall not include either, (1) adjustments granted by orders issued under the federal act after that date, regardless of whether they were made effective as of, or retroactive to, that date or a date prior thereto, or (2) adjustments granted by orders increasing the maximum rent, issued after March first, nineteen hundred forty-nine, under the federal act, regardless of whether the order of increase was made effective as of, or retroactive to, March first, nineteen hundred forty-nine, or a date prior thereto, but shall include adjustments for new or additional services or facilities provided by the landlord while the housing accommodations were not rented or where tenant-occupied, to which the tenant then in possession had agreed, either expressly or impliedly; and

(c) for housing accommodations within the cities of New York and Buffalo which on March first, nineteen hundred fifty, had no maximum rent established pursuant to the federal act, but which were subject to a maximum rent established pursuant to the local laws of the cities of New York and Buffalo, the maximum rent which was established on March first, nineteen hundred fifty, pursuant to such local laws.

2. Whenever the commission determines that such action is necessary to effectuate the purposes of this act, it may also establish maximum rents for housing accommodations, as that term is defined herein, in municipalities in which no maximum rent was in effect on March first, nineteen hundred fifty. Any housing accommodation for which a maximum rent is so established shall be deemed a housing accommodation for all the purposes, and subject to all the provisions of this act.

2-a. For housing accommodations created by a change from a non-housing to a housing use or by conversion on or after February first, nineteen hundred forty-seven, including those decontrolled by order, and certified by a municipal department having jurisdiction to be a fire hazard or in a continued dangerous condition or detrimental to life or health, the maximum rent shall be the rent charged on January first, nineteen hundred fifty-seven, or the date of first rental, whichever is later. Any housing accommodations for which a maximum rent is so established shall be deemed a housing accommodation for all the purposes, and subject to all the provisions of this act, but only so long as such illegal or hazardous condition continues and further certification with respect thereto shall not be required notwithstanding any inconsistent provision of this act.

2-b. Provision shall be made pursuant to regulations prescribed by the commission for the establishment, adjustment and modification of maximum rents in rooming houses, which shall include those housing accommodations subject to control pursuant to the provisions of paragraph (b) of subdivision two of section two of this act, having regard for any factors bearing on the equities involved, consistent with the purposes of this act to correct speculative, abnormal and unwarranted increases in rent.

3. Whenever the foregoing standard is not susceptible of application to a housing accommodation to which this act applies, and for which no maximum rent was established on March first, nineteen hundred fifty, or where no registration statement had been filed as had been required by the federal act, the maximum rent thereof shall be fixed by the commission, having regard to the maximum rents for comparable housing accommodations or any other factors bearing on the equities involved, consistent with the purposes of this act.

3-a. Notwithstanding the foregoing provisions of this section, on and after May first, nineteen hundred fifty-three, the maximum rent for any housing accommodation shall not be less than the maximum rent in effect on March first, nineteen hundred forty-three (or if there was no such maximum rent then in effect, the maximum rent first established pursuant to the federal act prior to July first, nineteen hundred forty-seven) plus fifteen per centum thereof as such sum is adjusted to reflect:

(1) the amount of any decreases in maximum rent required by order because of decreases in dwelling space, services, furniture, furnishings or equipment, or substan-

tial deterioration or failure to properly maintain such housing, and

(2) the amount of increases in maximum rent authorized by order because of increases in dwelling space, services, furniture, furnishings or equipment, or major capital improvements.

Nothing contained in this subdivision, however, shall have the effect of increasing the maximum rent of any housing accommodation more than fifteen per centum above the maximum rent in effect on April thirtieth, nineteen hundred fifty-three.

4. (a) The commission may from time to time adopt, promulgate, amend or rescind such rules, regulations and orders as it may deem necessary or proper to effectuate the purposes of this act, including practices relating to recovery of possession; provided that such regulations can be put into effect without general uncertainty, dislocation and hardship inconsistent with the purposes of this act; and provided further that such regulations shall be designed to maintain a system of rent controls at levels which, in the judgment of the commission, are generally fair and equitable and which will provide for an orderly transition from and termination of emergency controls without undue dislocations, inflationary price rises or disruption. Provision shall be made pursuant to regulations prescribed by the commission, for individual adjustment of maximum rents where the rental income from a property yields a net annual return of less than seven and one-half percentum of the valuation of the property. Such valuation shall be the current assessed valuation established by a city, town or village, which is in effect at the time of the filing of the application for an adjustment under this subparagraph properly adjusted by applying thereto the ratio which such assessed valuation bears to the full valuation as determined by the state board of equalization and assessment on the basis of assessment rolls of cities, town and villages for the year nineteen hundred fifty-four and certified for such year by such board pursuant to section forty-nine-d of the tax law; provided, however, that where at the time of the filing of the application for an adjustment under the subparagraph such board has computations for such year indicat-

ing a different ratio for subclasses of residential property in a city, town or village, the commission shall give due consideration to such different ratio except ratios in excess of one hundred percent, provided, further, that where such board has not determined and certified any ratio pursuant to such section of such law for a city, town or village for such year, the commission shall apply the ratio determined or certified by such board pursuant to sections twelve hundred twelve of the real property tax law for the most recent year; except where there has been a bona fide sale of the property within the period between March fifteenth, nineteen hundred fifty-seven, and the time of filing of the application, as the result of a transaction at arms' length, on normal financing terms at a readily ascertainable price and unaffected by special circumstances such as a forced sale, exchange of property, package deal, wash sale or sale to cooperative; provided, however, that where there has been more than one such bona fide sale within a period of two years prior to the date of the filing of such application the commission shall disregard the most recent of such sales if a prior sale within such two-year period was adopted as the valuation of the property in a proceeding under this subparagraph. In determining whether a sale was on normal financing terms, the commission shall give due consideration to the following factors:

(i) The ratio of the cash payment received by the seller to (a) the sales price of the property and (b) the annual gross income from the property;

(ii) The total amount of the outstanding mortgages which are liens against the property (including purchase money mortgages) as compared with the equalized assessed valuation of the property;

(iii) The ratio of the sales price to the annual gross income of the property, with consideration given to the total amount of rent adjustments previously granted, exclusive of rent adjustments because of changes in dwelling space, services, furniture, furnishings or equipment, major capital improvements, or substantial rehabilitation:

(iv) The presence of deferred amortization in purchase money mortgages, or the assignment of such mortgages at a discount;

(v) Any other facts and circumstances surrounding such sale which, in the judgment of the commission, may have a bearing upon the question of financing.

No application for adjustment of maximum rent based upon a sales price valuation shall be filed by the landlord under this subparagraph prior to six months from the date of such sale of the property. In addition, no adjustment ordered by the commission based upon such sales price valuation shall be effective prior to one year from the date of such sale. Where, however, the assessed valuation of the land exceeds four times the assessed valuation of the buildings thereon, the commission may determine a valuation of the property equal to five times the equalized assessed valuation of the buildings, for the purposes of this subparagraph. The commission may make a determination that the valuation of the property is an amount different from such equalized assessed valuation where there is a request for a reduction in such assessed valuation currently pending; or where there has been a reduction in the assessed valuation for the year next preceding the effective date of the current assessed valuation in effect at the time of the filing of the application. Net annual return shall be the amount by which the earned income exceeds the operating expenses of the property, excluding mortgage interest and amortization, and excluding allowances for obsolescence and reserves, but including an allowance for depreciation of two per centum of the value of the buildings exclusive of the land, or the amount shown for depreciation of the buildings in the latest required federal income tax return, whichever is lower; provided, however, that no allowance for depreciation of the buildings shall be included where the buildings have been fully depreciated for federal income tax purposes or on the books of the owner; or (2) the landlord who owns no more than four rental units within the state has not been fully compensated by increases in rental income sufficient to offset unavoidable increases in property taxes, fuel, utilities, insurance and repairs and maintenance, excluding mortgage interest and amortization, and excluding allowances for depreciation, obsolescence and reserves, which have occurred since the federal date determining the maximum rent or the date the property was acquired by the present owner, whichever is later; or (3) the landlord operates a hotel or rooming house or owns a cooperative apartment and has not been fully compensated by increases in rental income from the controlled housing accommodations sufficient to offset unavoidable increases in property taxes and other costs as are allocable to such controlled housing accommodations, including costs of operation of such hotel or rooming house, but excluding mortgage interest and amortization, and excluding allowances for depreciation, obsolescence and reserves, which have occurred since the federal date determining the maximum rent or the date the landlord commenced the operation of the property, whichever is later; or (4) the landlord and tenant voluntarily enter into a valid written lease in good faith with respect to any housing accommodation, which lease provides for an increase in the maximum rent not in excess of fifteen per centum and for a term of not less than two years except that where such lease provides for an increase in excess of fifteen per centum, the increase shall be automatically reduced to fifteen per centum; or (5) the landlord and tenant by mutual voluntary written agreement, subject to the approval of the commission, agree to a substantial increase or decrease in dwelling space or a change in the services, furniture, furnishings or equipment provided in the housing accommodations; or (6) there has been, since March first, nineteen hundred fifty, an increase in the rental value of the housing accommodations as a result of a substantial rehabilitation of the building or housing accommodation therein which materially adds to the value of the property or appreciably prolongs its life, excluding ordinary repairs, maintenance and replacements; or (7) there has been since March first, nineteen hundred fifty, a major capital improvement required for the operation, preservation or maintenance of the structure; or (8) there has been since March first, nineteen hundred fifty, in structures containing more than four housing accommodations, other improvements made with the express consent of the tenants in occupancy of at least seventy-five per centum of the housing accommodations, provided, however, that no adjustment granted hereunder shall exceed fifteen per centum unless the tenants have agreed to a higher percentage of increase, as herein provided; or (9) there has been, since March first, nineteen hundred fifty, a subletting without written consent from the landlord or an increase in the number of adult occupants who are not members of the immediate family of the tenant, and the landlord has not been compensated therefor by adjustment of the maximum rent by lease or order of the commission or pursuant to the federal act; or (10) the presence of unique or peculiar circumstances materially affecting the maximum rent has resulted in a maximum rent which is substantially lower than the rents generally prevailing in the same area for substantially similar housing accommodations.

In addition to the filing of written statements setting forth the final rate of equalization concerning assessment rolls of cities, towns and villages, after determination thereof by the state board of equalization and assessment, with the appropriate officials as now required by law, such board shall also file a copy of each such statement, duly certified, in so far as they relate to cities, towns and villages subject to rent control pursuant to this act, with the state rent administrator and the chairman of the temporary state commission to study rents and rental conditions. Where such board has made computations indicating a different ratio for subclasses of residential property, such information shall also be filed with such rent administrator and the chairman of such temporary state commission.

(b) The total of all adjustments ordered by the commission pursuant to (1) and (3) of paragraph (a) of subdivision four hereof for any individual housing accommodation shall not exceed fifteen per centum for any twelve month period; provided, however, that in ordering an adjustment pursuant to (1), the commission may waive this limitation where a greater increase is necessary to make the earned income of the property equal to its operating expense; provided further, however, that the maximum rents subject to the allocation requirement of paragraph (c) hereof shall be increased by such further additional amount during each succeeding twelve-month period, not exceeding fifteen per centum of the maximum rent in effect on the effective date of the original order of adjustment, until the maximum rents for the property shall reflect the net annual return provided for pursuant to (1) hereof, but in no event, however, shall the total increase ordered for a succeeding twelve-month period be more than an additional three per centum of the maximum rent in effect on the effective date of the original order of adjustment unless a new application be filed by the landlord.

The commission shall compile and make available for public inspection at reasonable hours at its principal office and at each appropriate local office, and shall file with the chairman of the temporary state commission to study rents and rental conditions the manual of accounting procedures and advisory bulletins applicable to applications under (1), (2) and (3) hereof, and all amendments thereto.

(c) Any increase in maximum rent shall be apportioned equitably among all the controlled housing accommodations in the property. In making such apportionment and in fixing the increases in maximum rents the commission shall give due consideration (1) to all previous adjustments or increases in maximum rents by lease or otherwise; and (2) to all other income derived from the property, including income from space and accommodations not controlled, or the rental value thereof if vacant or occupied rent-free, so that there is allocated to the controlled housing accommodations therein only that portion of the amount of increase necessary pursuant to (1), (2) or (3) of paragraph (a) of subdivision four hereof, as is properly attributable to such controlled accommodations.

(d) No landlord shall be entitled to any increase in the maximum rent unless he certifies that he is maintaining all essential services furnished or required to be furnished as of the date of the issuance of the order adjusting the maximum rent and that he will continue to maintain such services so long as the increase in such maximum rent continues in effect; nor shall any landlord be entitled to any increase in the maximum rent in any case where a municipal department having jurisdiction certifies that the housing accommodation is a fire hazard or is in a continued dangerous condition or detrimental to life or health, or is occupied in violation of law.

(e) Before ordering any adjustment in maximum rents, a reasonable opportunity to be heard thereon shall be accorded the tenant and the landlord.

5. (a) Whenever in the judgment of the commission such action is necessary or proper in order to effectuate the purposes of this act, the commission may, by regulation or order, regulate or prohibit speculative or manipulative practices or renting or leasing practices, including practices relating to recovery of possession, which in the judgment of the commission are equivalent to or are likely to result in rent increases inconsistent with the purposes of this act.

(b) Whenever in the judgment of the commission such action is necessary or proper in order to effectuate the purposes of this act, the commission may provide regulations to assure the maintenance of the same living space, essential services, furniture, furnishings and equipment as were provided on the date determining the maximum rent, and the commission shall have power by regulation or order to decrease the maximum rent for any housing accommodation with respect to which a maximum rent is in effect pursuant to this act if it shall find that the living space, essential services, furniture, furnishings or equipment to which the tenant was entitled on such date has been decreased.

(c) Whenever any municipal department having jurisdiction certifies that any housing accommodation is a fire hazard or is in a continued dangerous condition or detrimental to life or health, or is occupied in violation of law, the commission may issue an order decreasing the maximum rent of such housing accommodation in such amount as it deems necessary or proper, until the said municipal department has certified that the illegal or hazardous condition has been removed.

6. Any regulation or order issued pursuant to this section may be established in such form and manner, may contain such classifications and differentiations, and may provide for such adjustments and reasonable exceptions as in the judgment of the commission are necessary or proper in order to effectuate the purposes of this act. No increase or decrease in maximum rent shall be effec-

Housing Rent Control

tive prior to the date on which the order therefor is issued.

7. Regulations, orders, and requirements under this act may contain such provisions as the commission deems necessary to prevent the circumvention or evasion thereof.

8. The powers granted in this section shall not be used or made to operate to compel changes in established rental practices, except where such action is affirmatively found by the commission to be necessary to prevent circumvention or evasion of any regulation, order, or requirement under this act.

§ 5. **Evictions.** 1. So long as the tenant continues to pay the rent to which the landlord is entitled, no tenant shall be removed from any housing accommodation with respect to which a maximum rent is in effect pursuant to this act by action to evict or to recover possession, by exclusion from possession, or otherwise, nor shall any person attempt such removal or exclusion from possession notwithstanding the fact that the tenant has no lease or that his lease, or other rental agreement has expired or otherwise terminated, notwithstanding any contract, lease agreement or obligation heretofore or hereafter entered into which provides for surrender of possession, or which otherwise provides contrary hereto, except on one or more of the following grounds, or unless the landlord has obtained a certificate of eviction pursuant to subdivision two of this section:

(a) the tenant is violating a substantial obligation of his tenancy other than the obligation to surrender possession of such housing accommodation and has failed to cure such violation after written notice by the landlord that the violation cease within ten days, or within the three month period immediately prior to the commencement of the proceeding the tenant has wilfully violated such an obligation inflicting serious and substantial injury to the landlord; or

(b) the tenant is committing or permitting a nuisance in such housing accommodation; or is maliciously or by reason of gross negligence substantially damaging the housing accommodations; or his conduct is such as to interfere substantially with the comfort or safety of the landlord or of other tenants or occupants of the same or other adjacent building or structure; or

(c) occupancy of the housing accommodations by the tenant is illegal because of the requirements of law, and the landlord is subject to civil or criminal penalties therefor, or both; or

(d) the tenant is using or permitting such housing accommodation to be used for an immoral or illegal purpose; or

(e) the tenant who had a written lease or other written rental agreement which terminates on or after May first, nineteen hundred fifty, has refused upon demand of the landlord to execute a written extension or renewal thereof for a further term of like duration not in excess of one year but otherwise on the same terms and conditions as the previous lease except in so far as such terms and conditions are inconsistent with this act; or

(f) the tenant has unreasonably refused the landlord access to the housing accommodations for the purpose of making necessary repairs or improvements required by law or for the purpose of inspection or of showing the accommodations to a prospective purchaser, mortgagee or prospective mortgagee, or other person having a legitimate interest therein; provided, however, that in the latter event such refusal shall not be ground for removal or eviction if such inspection or showing of the accommodations is contrary to the provisions of the tenant's lease or other rental agreement.

2. No tenant shall be removed or evicted on grounds other than those stated in subdivision one of this section unless on application of the landlord the commission shall issue an order granting a certificate of eviction in accordance with its rules and regulations, designed to effectuate the purposes of this act, permitting the landlord to pursue his remedies at law. The commission shall issue such an order whenever it finds that:

(a) the landlord seeks in good faith to recover possession of housing accommodations because of immediate and compelling necessity for his own personal use and occupancy or for the use and occupancy of his immediate family; provided, however, this subdivision shall not ap-

Housing Rent Control

and would not be likely to result in the circumvention or evasion thereof; provided, however, that no such order shall be required in any action or proceeding brought pursuant to the provisions of subdivision one of this section.

The commission on its own initiative or on application of a tenant may revoke or cancel an order granting such certificate of eviction at any time prior to the execution of a warrant in a summary proceeding to recover possession of real property by a court whenever it finds that:

(a) the certificate of eviction was obtained by fraud or illegality; or

(b) the landlord's intentions or circumstances have so changed that the premises, possession of which is sought, will not be used for the purpose specified in the certificate.

The commencement of a proceeding by the commission to revoke or cancel an order granting a certificate of eviction shall stay such order until the final determination of the proceeding regardless of whether the waiting period in the order has already expired. In the event the commission cancels or revokes such an order, the court having jurisdiction of any summary proceeding instituted in such case shall take appropriate action to dismiss the application for removal of the tenant from the real property and to vacate and annul any final order or warrant granted or issued by the court in the matter.

4. Notwithstanding the preceding provisions of this section, the state, any municipality, or housing authority may nevertheless recover possession of any housing accommodations operated by it where such action or proceeding is authorized by statute or regulations under which such accommodations are administered.

5. Any order of the commission under this section granting a certificate of eviction shall be subject to judicial review only in the manner prescribed by sections eight and nine.

6. Where after the commission has granted a certificate of eviction certifying that the landlord may pursue his remedies pursuant to local law to acquire possession, and a tenant voluntarily removes from a housing accommoda-

tion or has been removed therefrom by action or proceeding to evict from or recover possession of a housing accommodation upon the ground that the landlord seeks in good faith to recover possession of such accommodation (1) for his immediate and personal use, or for the immediate and personal use by a member or members of his immediate family, and such landlord or members of his immediate family shall fail to occupy such accommodations within thirty days after the tenant vacates, or such landlord shall lease or rent such space or permit occupancy thereof by a third person within a period of one year after such removal of the tenant, or (2) for the immediate purpose of withdrawing such housing accommodations from the rental market and such landlord shall lease or sell the housing accommodation or the space previously occupied thereby, or permit use thereof in a manner other than contemplated in such eviction certificate within a period of one year after such removal of the tenant, or (3) for the immediate purpose of altering or remodeling such housing accommodations, and the landlord shall fail to start the work of alteration or remodeling of such housing accommodations within ninety days after such removal on the ground that he required possession of such accommodations for the purpose of altering or remodeling the same, or if after having commenced such work shall fail or neglect to prosecute the work with reasonable diligence, or (4) for the immediate purpose of demolishing such housing accommodations and constructing a new building or structure for a greater number of housing accommodations in accordance with approved plans, or reasonable amendment thereof, and the landlord has failed to complete the demolition within six months after the removal of the last tenant or, having demolished the premises, has failed or neglected to proceed with the new construction within ninety days after the completion of such demolition or (5) for some purpose other than those specified above for which the removal of the tenant was sought and the landlord has failed to use the vacated premises for such purpose, such landlord shall unless for good cause shown, be liable to the tenant for three times the damages sustained on account of such removal plus reasonable attorney's fees and costs as determined by the court;

Housing Rent Control

provided, however, that subparagraph (4) herein shall not apply to any action which does not constitute a violation of any local law providing for penalties upon failure to demolish or comply with state rent control eviction certificates. In addition to any other damage, the cost of removal of property shall be a lawful measure of damage.

7. Any statutory tenant who vacates the housing accommodations, without giving the landlord at least thirty days' written notice by registered or certified mail of his intention to vacate, shall be liable to the landlord for an amount not exceeding one month's rent except where the tenant has been removed or vacates pursuant to the provisions of this section or of subdivision four of section ten of this act. Such notice shall be postmarked on or before the last day of the rental period immediately prior to such thirty-day period.

8. Where after the commission has granted a certificate of eviction authorizing the landlord to pursue his remedies pursuant to local law to acquire possession for any purpose stated in subdivision two of section five or in subdivision four of section ten of this act or for some other stated purpose, and a tenant voluntarily removes from a housing accommodation or has been removed therefrom by action or proceeding to evict from or recover possession of a housing accommodation and the landlord or any successor landlord of the premises does not use the housing accommodation for the purpose specified in such certificate of eviction, the vacated accommodation or any replacement or subdivision thereof shall, unless the commission approves such different purpose, be deemed a housing accommodation subject to control, notwithstanding any definition of that term in this act to the contrary. Such approval shall be granted whenever the commission finds that the failure or omission to use the housing accommodation for the purpose specified in such certificate was not inconsistent with the purposes of this act and would not be likely to result in the circumvention or evasion thereof. The remedy herein provided for shall be in addition to those provided for in subdivision one of section eleven of this act and to the tenant's action for damages provided for in subdivision six of this section.

§ 6. Investigations; records; reports.

1. The commission is authorized to make such studies and investigations, to conduct such hearings, and to obtain such information as the commission deems necessary or proper in prescribing any regulation or order under this act or in the administration and enforcement of this act and regulations and orders thereunder.

2. The commission is further authorized, by regulation or order, to require any person who rents or offers for rent or acts as broker or agent for the rental of any housing accommodations to furnish any such information under oath or affirmation or otherwise, to make and keep records and other documents, and to make reports, and the commission may require any such person to permit the inspection and copying of records and other documents and the inspection of housing accommodations. The administrator or any officer or agent designated by the commission for such purposes, may administer oaths and affirmations and may, whenever necessary, by subpoena require any such person to appear and testify or to appear and produce documents, or both, at any designated place.

3. For the purpose of obtaining any information under subdivision one, the commission may by subpoena require any other person to appear and testify or to appear and produce documents, or both, at any designated place.

4. The production of a person's documents at any place other than his place of business shall not be required under this section in any case in which, prior to the return date specified in the subpoena issued with respect thereto, such person either has furnished the commission with a copy of such documents certified by such person under oath to be a true and correct copy, or has entered into a stipulation with the commission as to the information contained in such documents.

5. In case of contumacy by, or refusal to obey a subpoena served upon, any person referred to in subdivision three, the supreme court in or for any judicial district in which such person is found or resides or transacts business, upon application by the commission, shall have jurisdiction to issue an order requiring such person to appear and give testimony or to appear and produce

documents, or both; and any failure to obey such order of the court may be punished by such court as a contempt thereof. The provisions of this subdivision shall also apply to any person referred to in subdivision two, and shall be in addition to the provisions of subdivision one of section ten.

6. Witnesses subpoenaed under this section shall be paid the same fees and mileage as are paid witnesses under article eighty of the civil practice law and rules.

7. Upon any such investigation or hearing, the commission or an officer duly designated by the commission to conduct such investigation or hearing, may confer immunity in accordance with the provisions of section 50.20 of the Criminal Procedure Law.

8. The commission shall not publish or disclose any information obtained under this act that the commission deems confidential or with reference to which a request for confidential treatment is made by the person furnishing such information, unless the commission determines that the withholding thereof is contrary to the public interest.

9. Any person subpoenaed under this section shall have the right to make a record of his testimony and to be represented by counsel.

§ 7. Cooperation with other governmental agencies.

1. The commission shall cooperate with the federal government and other appropriate governmental agencies in effectuating the purposes of this act, and shall endeavor to procure and may accept from the federal housing expediter and other officers and agencies of the federal government and from the temporary city housing rent commission of the city of New York such cooperation, information, records and data as will assist the commission in effectuating such purposes.

2. The commission may request and shall receive cooperation and assistance in effectuating the purposes of this act from all departments, divisions, boards, bureaus, commissions or agencies of the state and political subdivisions thereof. The commissioner and state rent administrator shall be deemed to be an officer included within the provisions of section one hundred sixty-one of the execu-

tive law, and shall be accorded all the rights and privileges of the officers specified in subdivision one of said section.

§ 8. **Procedure.** 1. After the issuance of any regulation or order by the commission any person subject to any provision of such regulation or order may, in accordance with regulations to be prescribed by the commission, file a protest against such regulation or order specifically setting forth his objections to any such provisions and affidavits or other written evidence in support of such objections. Statements in support of any such regulation or order may be received and incorporated in the record of the proceedings at such times and in accordance with such regulations as may be prescribed by the commission. Within a reasonable time after the filing of any protest under this subdivision the commission shall either grant or deny such protest in whole or in part, notice such protest for hearing, or provide an opportunity to present further evidence in connection therewith. In the event that the commission denies any such protest in whole or in part, the commission shall inform the protestant of the grounds upon which such decision is based, and of any economic data and other facts of which the commission has taken official notice.

2. In the administration of this act the commission may take official notice of economic data and other facts, including facts found by the commission as a result of action taken under section four.

3. Any proceedings under this section may be limited by the commission to the filing of affidavits, or other written evidence, and the filing of briefs.

4. Any protest filed under this section shall be granted or denied by the commission, or granted in part and the remainder of it denied, within a reasonable time after it is filed. If the commission does not act finally within a period of ninety days after the protest is filed, the protest shall be deemed to be denied. However, the commission may grant one extension not to exceed thirty days with the consent of the party filing such protest; any further extension may only be granted with the consent of all parties to the protest. No proceeding may be brought

Housing Rent Control

pursuant to article seventy-eight of the civil practice law and rules to challenge any order or determination which is subject to such protest unless such review has been sought and either (1) a determination thereon has been made or (2) the ninety-day period provided for determination of the protest (or any extension thereof) has expired. If the commission does not act finally within a period of ninety days after the entry of an order of remand to the commission by the court in a proceeding instituted pursuant to section nine, the order previously made by the commission shall be deemed reaffirmed. However, the commission may grant one extension not to exceed thirty days with the consent of the petitioner; any further extension may only be granted with the consent of all parties to the petition. [Subd 4 am L 1984, ch 102, § 5, eff April 1, 1984.]

5. The commission shall compile and make available for public inspection at reasonable hours at its principal office and at each appropriate local office a copy of each decision hereafter rendered by it upon granting, or denying, in whole or in part, any protests filed under this section.

§ 9. **Judicial review.** 1. Any person who is aggrieved by the final determination of a protest may, in accordance with article seventy-eight of the civil practice law and rules, within sixty days after such determination, commence a proceeding in the supreme court praying that the regulation or order protested be enjoined or set aside in whole or in part. Such proceeding may at the option of the petitioner be instituted in the county where the commission has its principal office or where the property is located. The answer shall include a statement setting forth, so far as practicable, the economic data and other facts of which the commission has taken official notice. Upon the filing of such petition the court shall have jurisdiction to set aside such regulation or order, in whole or in part, to dismiss the petition, or to remit the proceeding to the commission; provided, however, that the regulation or order may be modified or rescinded by the commission at any time notwithstanding the pendency of such proceeding for review. No objection to such regulation or order, and no evidence in support of any objection thereto, shall be considered by the court, unless such objection shall have been set forth by the petitioner in the protest or such evidence shall be contained in the return. If application is made to the court by either party for leave to introduce additional evidence which was either offered and not admitted, or which could not reasonably have been offered or included in such proceedings before the commission, and the court determines that such evidence should be admitted, the court shall order the evidence to be presented to the commission. The commission shall promptly receive the same, and such other evidence as the commission deems necessary or proper, and thereupon the commission shall file with the court the original or a transcript thereof and any modification made in regulation or order as a result thereof; except that on request by the commission, any such evidence shall be presented directly to the court. Upon final determination of the proceeding before the court, the original record, if filed by the commission with the court, shall be returned to the commission. [Subd 1 am L 1984, ch 102, § 6, eff April 1, 1984.]

2. No such regulation or order shall be enjoined or set aside, in whole or in part, unless the petitioner shall establish to the satisfaction of the court that the regulation or order is not in accordance with law, or is arbitrary or capricious. The effectiveness of an order of the court enjoining or setting aside, in whole or in part, any such regulation or order shall be postponed until the expiration of thirty days from the entry thereof. The jurisdiction of the supreme court shall be exclusive and its order dismissing the petition or enjoining or setting aside such regulation or order, in whole or in part, shall be final, subject to review by the appellate division of the supreme court and the court of appeals in the same manner and form and with the same effect as provided by law for appeals from a judgment in a special proceeding. Notwithstanding any provision of section thirteen hundred four of the civil practice act to the contrary, any order of the court remitting the proceeding to the commission may, at the election of the commission, be subject to review by the appellate division of the supreme court and the court of appeals in the same manner and form and with the same effect as provided in the civil practice

act for appeals from a final order in a special proceeding. All such proceedings shall be heard and determined by the court and by any appellate court as expeditiously as possible and with lawful precedence over other matters. All such proceedings for review shall be heard on the petition, transcript and other papers, and on appeal shall be heard on the record, without requirement of printing.

3. (a) Within thirty days after arraignment, or such additional time as the court may allow for good cause shown, in any criminal proceeding, and within five days after judgment in any civil or criminal proceeding, brought pursuant to section eleven involving alleged violation of any provision of any regulation or order, the defendant may apply to the court in which the proceeding is pending for leave to file in the supreme court a petition setting forth objections to the validity of any provision which the defendant is alleged to have violated or conspired to violate. The court in which the proceeding is pending shall grant such leave with respect to any objection which it finds is made in good faith and with respect to which it finds there is reasonable and substantial excuse for the defendant's failure to present such objection in a protest filed in accordance with section eight. Upon the filing of a petition pursuant to and within thirty days from the granting of such leave, the supreme court shall have jurisdiction to enjoin or set aside in whole or in part the provision of the regulation or order complained of or to dismiss the petition. The court may authorize the introduction of evidence, either to the commission or directly to the court, in accordance with subdivision one of this section. The provisions of subdivision two of this section shall be applicable with respect to any proceedings instituted in accordance with this subdivision.

(b) In any proceeding brought pursuant to section eleven of this act involving an alleged violation of any provision of any such regulation or order, the court shall stay the proceeding:

(1) during the period within which a petition may be filed in the supreme court pursuant to leave granted under paragraph (a) of this subdivision with respect to such provision;

(2) during the pendency of any protest properly filed by the defendant under section eight prior to the institution of the proceeding under section eleven of this act, setting forth objections to the validity of such provision which the court finds to have been made in good faith; and

(3) during the pendency of any judicial proceeding instituted by the defendant under this section with respect to such protest or instituted by the defendant under paragraph (a) of this subdivision with respect to such provision, and until the expiration of the time allowed in this section for the taking of further proceedings with respect thereto.

(c) Notwithstanding the provisions of paragraph (b) of this subdivision, stays shall be granted thereunder in civil proceedings only after judgment and upon application made within five days after judgment. Notwithstanding the provisions of paragraph (b) of this subdivision, in the case of a proceeding under subdivision one of section eleven the court granting a stay under paragraph (b) of this subdivision shall issue a temporary injunction or restraining order enjoining or restraining, during the period of the stay, violations by the defendant of any provision of the regulation or order involved in the proceeding. If any provision of a regulation or order is determined to be invalid by judgment of the supreme court which has become effective in accordance with subdivision two of this section, any proceeding pending in any court shall be dismissed, and any judgment in such proceeding vacated, to the extent that such proceeding or judgment is based upon violation of such provision. Except as provided in this subdivision, the pendency of any protest under section eight, or judicial proceeding under this section, shall not be grounds for staying any proceeding brought pursuant to section eleven; nor, except as provided in this subdivision, shall any retroactive effect be given to any judgment setting aside a provision of a regulation or order.

4. The method prescribed herein for the judicial review of a regulation or order shall be exclusive.

§ 10. **Prohibitions.** 1. It shall be unlawful, regardless of any contract, lease or other obligation heretofore or hereafter entered into, for any person to demand or receive any rent for any housing accommodations in excess of the maximum rent or otherwise to do or omit to do any act, in violation of any regulation, order or requirement hereunder, or to offer, solicit, attempt or agree to do any of the foregoing.

2. It shall be unlawful for any person to remove or attempt to remove from any housing accommodations the tenant or occupant thereof or to refuse to renew the lease or agreement for the use of such accommodations, because such tenant or occupant has taken, or proposes to take, action authorized or required by this act or any regulation, order or requirement thereunder.

3. It shall be unlawful for any officer or employee of the commission, or for any official adviser or consultant to the commission, to disclose, otherwise than in the course of official duty, any information obtained under this act, or to use any such information for personal benefit.

4. Nothing in this act shall be construed to require any person to offer any housing accommodations for rent, but housing accommodations already on the rental market may be withdrawn only after prior written approval of the state rent commission, if such withdrawal requires that a tenant be evicted from such accommodations.

5. It shall be unlawful for any landlord or any person acting on his behalf, with intent to cause the tenant to vacate, to engage in any course of conduct (including, but not limited to, interruption or discontinuance of essential services) which interferes with or disturbs or is intended to interfere with or disturb the comfort, repose, peace or quiet of the tenant in his use or occupancy of the housing accommodations. (Added L 1971, ch 371, eff June 11, 1971)

§ 11. **Enforcement.** 1. Whenever in the judgment of the commission any person has engaged or is about to engage in any acts or practices which constitute or will constitute a violation of any provision of section ten of this act, the commission may make application to the supreme court for an order enjoining such acts or practices, or for an order enforcing compliance with such provision, or for an order directing the landlord to correct the violation, and upon a showing by the commission that such person has engaged or is about to engage in any such acts or practices a permanent or temporary injunction, restraining order, or other order shall be granted without bond. Jurisdiction shall not be deemed lacking in the supreme court because the defense is based upon an order of an inferior court.

2. Any person who wilfully violates any provision of section ten of this act, and any person who makes any statement or entry false in any material respect in any document or report required to be kept or filed under this act or any regulation, order, or requirement thereunder, and any person who wilfully omits or neglects to make any material statement or entry required to be made in any such document or report, shall, upon conviction thereof, be subject to a fine of not more than five thousand dollars, or to imprisonment for not more than two years in the case of a violation of subdivision three of section ten and for not more than one year in all other cases, or to both such fine and imprisonment. Whenever the commission has reason to believe that any person is liable to punishment under this subdivision, the commission may certify the facts to the district attorney of any county having jurisdiction of the alleged violation, who shall cause appropriate proceedings to be brought.

3. Any court shall advance on the docket and expedite the disposition of any criminal or other proceedings brought before it under this section.

4. No person shall be held liable for damages or penalties in any court, on any grounds for or in respect of anything done or omitted to be done in good faith pursuant to any provision of this act or any regulation, order, or requirement thereunder, notwithstanding that subsequently such provision, regulation, order, or requirement may be modified, rescinded, or determined to be invalid. In any action or proceeding wherein a party relies for ground of relief or defense or raises issue or brings into question the construction or validity of this act or any regulation, order, or requirement thereunder, the court having jurisdiction of such action or proceeding may at any stage certify such fact to the commission. The commission may intervene in any such action or proceeding.

5. If any landlord who receives rent from a tenant violates a regulation or order prescribing the maximum rent with respect to the housing accommodations for which such rent is received from such tenant, the tenant paying such rent may, within two years from the date of the occurrence of the violation, except as hereinafter provided, bring an action against the landlord on account of the overcharge as hereinafter defined. In such action, the landlord shall be liable for reasonable attorney's fees and costs as determined by the court, plus whichever of the following sums is the greater: (a) Such amount not more than three times the amount of the overcharge, or the overcharges, upon which the action is based as the court in its discretion may determine, or (b) an amount not less than twenty-five dollars nor more than fifty dollars, as the court in its discretion may determine; provided, however, that such amount shall be the amount of the overcharge or overcharges or twenty-five dollars, whichever is greater, if the defendant proves that the violation of the regulation or order in question was neither wilful nor the result of failure to take practicable precautions against the occurrence of the violation. As used in this section, the word "overcharge" shall mean the amount by which the consideration paid by a tenant to a landlord exceeds the applicable maximum rent. If any landlord who receives rent from a tenant violates a regulation or order prescribing maximum rent with respect to the housing accommodations for which such rent is received from such tenant, and such tenant either fails to institute an action under this subdivision within thirty days from the date of the occurrence of the violation or is not entitled for any reason to bring the action, the commission may institute an action on behalf of the state within such two-year period. If such action is instituted by the commission, the tenant affected shall thereafter be barred from bringing an action for the same violation or violations. Any action under this subdivision by either the tenant or the commission, as the case may be, may be brought in any court of competent jurisdiction. Recovery, by judgment or otherwise, in an action for damages under this subdivision shall be a bar to the recovery under this subdivision of any recovery, by judgment or otherwise, in

any other action against the same landlord on account of the same overcharge or overcharges prior to the institution of the action in which such recovery of damages was obtained. Where recovery by judgment or otherwise is obtained in an action instituted by the commission under this subdivision, there shall be paid over to the tenant from the moneys recovered, one-third of such recovery, exclusive of costs and disbursement or the amount of the overcharge or overcharges, whichever is the greater.

6. If any landlord who receives rent from a tenant violates any order containing a directive that rent collected by the landlord in excess of the maximum rent be refunded to the tenant within thirty days, the commission may, within one year after the expiration of such thirty day period or after such order shall become final by regulation of the commission, bring an action against the landlord on account of the failure of the landlord to make the prescribed refund. In such action, the landlord shall be liable for reasonable attorney's fees and costs as determined by the court, plus whichever of the following sums is the greater: (a) Such amount not more than three times the amount directed to be refunded, or the amount directed to be refunded, upon which the action is based as the court in its discretion may determine, or (b) an amount not less than twenty-five dollars nor more than fifty dollars, as the court in its discretion may determine; provided, however, that such amount shall be the amount directed to be refunded or twenty-five dollars, which ever is greater, if the defendant proves that the violation of the order in question was neither wilful nor the result of failure to take practical precautions against the occurrence of the violation. If the commission fails to institute such action within thirty days from the date of the occurrence of the violation, the tenant paying such rent may thereafter institute an action for the same violation within such one year period, and the liability of the landlord in such action by the tenant shall be the same as if such action were brought by the commission. If such action is instituted by the commission, the tenant affected shall thereafter be barred from bringing an action for the same violation. Any action under this subdivision by either the commission or the tenant, as the case may be,

Housing Rent Control

may be brought in any court of competent jurisdiction. Recovery by judgment or otherwise in an action under this subdivision based on the failure of the landlord to make the prescribed refund, shall be a bar to recovery under this subdivision of any recovery, by judgment or otherwise, from the same landlord in any other action instituted on account of the same violation, prior to the institution of the action in which such recovery is obtained. Where recovery by judgment or otherwise, is obtained in an action instituted by the commission under this subdivision, there shall be paid over to the tenant from the moneys recovered one-third of such recovery, exclusive of costs and disbursements, or the amount of the prescribed refund, whichever is greater.

7. Any tenant who has vacated his housing accommodations because the landlord or any person acting on his behalf, with intent to cause the tenant to vacate, engaged in any course of conduct (including, but not limited to, interruption or discontinuance of essential services) which interfered with or disturbed or was intended to interfere with or disturb the comfort, repose, peace or quiet of the tenant in his use or occupancy of the housing accommodations may, within ninety days after vacating, apply to the commission for a determination that the housing accommodations were vacated as a result of such conduct, and may, within one year after such determination, institute a civil action against the landlord by reason of such conduct. In such action the landlord shall be liable to the tenant for three times the damages sustained on account of such conduct plus reasonable attorney's fees and costs as determined by the court. In addition to any other damages the cost of removal of property shall be a lawful measure of damages. (Added L 1971, ch 371, eff June 11, 1971)

§ 12. Application. 1. Whenever the commission shall find that, in any municipality specified by the commission, (a) the percentage of vacancies in all or any particular class of housing accommodations is five per centum or more, or, (b) the availability of adequate rental housing accommodations and other relevant factors are such as to make rent control unnecessary for the purpose of eliminating speculative, unwarranted, and abnormal increases in rents and of preventing profiteering and speculative and other disruptive practices resulting from abnormal market conditions caused by congestion, the controls imposed upon rents by authority of this act in such municipality or with respect to any particular class of housing accommodations therein shall be abolished in the manner hereinafter provided; provided however, that, except as otherwise provided in this section, no controls shall be abolished by the commission unless the commission shall hold a public hearing or hearings on such proposal at which interested persons are given a reasonable opportunity to be heard. Notice of such hearing shall be provided by publication in a daily newspaper published or having general circulation in the municipality affected not less than fifteen days prior to the date of the hearing. (As am L 1971, Ch 374, eff June 1, 1971)

2. Notwithstanding the provisions of this section or any other provision of this act, the local governing body of a city, town or village, upon a finding that decontrol in such city, town or village is warranted after a public hearing upon notice by publication in a daily or weekly newspaper published or having general circulation in the city or town not less than twenty days prior to the date of hearing, and after notice to the commission, may adopt a resolution to decontrol all or any specified class of housing accommodation in such city, town or village. Such resolution shall thereafter be filed with the division. Upon receipt of any such resolution the controls imposed by authority of this act shall be abolished in the city, town or village affected with respect to housing accommodations specified in such resolution in the manner hereinafter specified. Notwithstanding the foregoing provisions of this paragraph, a city, town or village any portion of which is within the limits of an area designated as a critical defense housing area by the federal government at the time of adoption of the decontrol resolution, shall not become decontrolled without the approval of the commission. (As am L 1971, ch 374, eff June 1, 1971, and L 1971, ch 599, eff June 22, 1971)

2-a. Upon the issuance of an order of decontrol or upon the filing of a resolution resulting in decontrol of a housing accommodation pursuant to subdivision two, such decontrol shall take place:

(a) if the landlord and tenant execute a written lease for a term of not less than two years wherein the landlord agrees to maintain the same services and equipment required by this act and which provides for an increase in the maximum rent not in excess of fifteen percent for the first year and not more than a second five percent increase for the second year and otherwise continues the terms and conditions of the existing tenancy; upon the execution of such lease;

(b) if the landlord offers the tenant a lease in accordance with the terms provided in paragraph (a) and the tenant fails to execute such lease, six months from the date that the commission issued the order or the date the municipality filed the resolution, provided that the landlord has notified the tenant in writing by certified mail that his failure to execute the lease within thirty days of such notification will result in the decontrol of the housing accommodation on the date set forth therein, such date to be the expiration of such thirty days or such six months, whichever is later; or

(c) if the landlord does not offer the tenant a lease in accordance with the terms provided in paragraph (a), two years from the date the commission issued the order or the municipality filed the resolution. (Subd 2-a added L 1971, ch 374, eff June 1, 1971)

3. (a) Notwithstanding the provisions of section four or of any other inconsistent provision of this act, housing accommodations subject to rent control as provided for in this act on June thirtieth, nineteen hundred fifty-five, in any city or town within the counties of Cattaraugus, Chautauqua, Columbia, Dutchess, Erie, Fulton, Herkimer, Montgomery, Niagara, Ontario, Oswego, Saratoga, Seneca, Steuben, Suffolk, Ulster and Yates shall, subsequent to such date, be no longer subject to such rent control, except as hereinafter in this subdivision provided.

(b) The governing body of any such city or town, as hereinafter specified, may, and it is hereby authorized and empowered to, by resolution duly adopted for such purpose not later than June thirtieth, nineteen hundred fifty-five, and declaring the continuance of emergency conditions therein, elect to be excluded from the operation of the provisions of this subdivision providing for the termination of rent control therein, to the extent specified in such resolution.

In the case of any such city or town elsewhere than within the counties of Erie and Niagara, such resolution may provide for such exclusion with respect to all or any particular class of such housing accommodations within such city or town; and in the case of any such city or town within the counties of Erie or Niagara, such resolution may provide for such exclusion with respect to all or any particular class of such housing accommodations in such city or town, except (1) one family houses and (2) two family houses occupied in whole or in part by the owner.

In the event of the adoption of such a resolution in any such city or town, the provisions of this subdivision providing for the termination of rent control therein shall not apply with respect to such housing accommodations within such city or town as specified in the resolution so adopted. Any such resolution, upon adoption, shall forthwith be transmitted to the commission.

(c) The governing body of any city or town elsewhere than in the counties of Columbia, Dutchess and Erie, as hereinafter specified, with respect to which the provisions of this subdivision providing for the termination of rent control therein are applicable and in effect subsequent to June thirtieth, nineteen hundred fifty-five, may, and it is hereby authorized and empowered to, by resolution duly adopted for such purpose at any time subsequent to such date and declaring the existence of emergency conditions therein, request the commission to reestablish the regulation of rents on housing accommodations therein, to the extent specified in such resolution.

In the case of any such city or town elsewhere than within the county of Niagara, such resolution may request such reestablishment with respect to all or any particular class of such housing accommodations in such city or town; and in the case of any such city or town within the county of Niagara, such resolution may request such reestablishment with respect to all or any particular class of such housing accommodations in such city or town, except (1) one family houses and (2) two family houses occupied in whole or in part by the owner.

Any such resolution, upon adoption, shall forthwith be transmitted to the commission. Upon receipt of such resolution, the commission shall by regulation or order reestablish the same maximum rents for such housing accommodations within such city or town specified in such resolution as last previously established by the commission and in force and effect therein immediately prior to decontrol pursuant to this subdivision. Any such regulation or order shall take effect on the date specified in such resolution, and thereafter such maximum rents shall be and continue in force and effect as to such housing accommodations within such city or town until changed or abolished in accordance with the applicable provisions of this act, and all the provisions of this act applying generally with respect to maximum rents on such housing accommodations shall apply with respect thereto within such city or town.

(d) Notwithstanding the provisions of section four or of any other inconsistent provision of this act, housing accommodations subject to rent control as provided for in this act on June thirtieth, nineteen hundred fifty-seven, in any city or town within the counties of Columbia, Dutchess or Erie shall, subsequent to such date, be no longer subject to such rent control, except as hereinafter in this subdivision provided.

The governing body of any such city or town, as hereinbefore or hereinafter specified, may, and it is hereby authorized and empowered to, by resolution adopted for such purpose not later than June thirtieth, nineteen hundred fifty-seven, and declaring the continuance of emergency conditions therein, elect to be excluded from the operation of the provisions of this paragraph (d) providing for the termination of rent control therein, to the extent specified in such resolution. Such resolution may provide for such exclusion with respect to all or any particular class of housing accommodations subject to such rent control within such city or town. In the event of the adoption of such a resolution in any such city or town, the provisions of this paragraph (d) providing for the termination of rent control therein shall not apply with respect to such housing accommodations within such city or town as specified in the resolution so adopted. Any such resolution, upon adoption, shall forthwith be transmitted to the commission.

4. (a) Notwithstanding any inconsistent provision of this act, the local governing body of any city or town within the county of Monroe, the county of Oneida, the county of Onondaga or the county of Schenectady wherein housing accommodations are or shall be subject to rent control as provided for in this act, by resolution duly adopted for such purpose not later than June thirtieth, nineteen hundred fifty-five, may, and it is hereby authorized and empowered to, elect that the provisions of paragraph (j) of subdivision two of section two hereof excepting housing accommodations in one family houses, and in two family houses occupied in whole or in part by the owner thereof, in such counties from the classifications of housing accommodations subject to rent control shall not apply in such city or town; and in the event of the adoption of such a resolution in any such city or town, such housing accommodations specified in such subdivision within such city or town shall continue to be subject to rent control. Any such resolution, upon adoption, shall forthwith be transmitted to the commission.

(b) Notwithstanding any inconsistent provision of this act, the local governing body of any city or town within the county of Monroe, the county of Oneida or the county of Schenectady wherein housing accommodations are or shall be subject to rent control as provided for in this act, and wherein the provisions of paragraph (j) of subdivision two of section two hereof excepting housing accommodations in one family houses, and in two family houses occupied in whole or in part by the owner thereof, in such city or town, from the classifications of housing accommodations subject to rent control are in force and effect subsequent to June thirtieth, nineteen hundred fifty-five, by resolution duly adopted for such purpose at any time subsequent to such date, may, and it is hereby authorized and empowered to, request the commission to reestablish the regulation of rents on such housing accommodations therein.

Any such resolution, upon adoption, shall forthwith be transmitted to the commission. Upon receipt of such resolution, the commission shall by regulation or order

Housing Rent Control

reestablish the same maximum rents for such housing accommodations within such city or town as last previously established by the commission and in force and effect therein immediately prior to decontrol pursuant to the provisions of paragraph (j) of subdivision two of section two hereof. Any such regulation or order shall take effect on the date specified in such resolution, and thereafter such maximum rents shall be and continue in force and effect as to such housing accommodations within such city or town until changed or abolished in accordance with the applicable provisions of this act, and all the provisions of this act applying generally with respect to maximum rents on such housing accommodations shall apply with respect thereto within such city or town.

5. Notwithstanding any inconsistent provision of this act, the local governing body of any city or town other than the city of New York, wherein housing accommodations are or shall be subject to rent control as provided for in this act, by resolution duly adopted for such purpose not later than June thirtieth, nineteen hundred fifty-seven, may, and it is hereby authorized and empowered to, elect that the provisions of paragraph (k) of subdivision two of section two hereof excepting housing accommodations, other than housing accommodations used as boarding houses or rooming houses in the county of Westchester, which are or become vacant therein from the classifications of housing accommodations subject to rent control shall not apply in such city or town; and in the event of the adoption of such a resolution in any such city or town, such housing accommodations specified in such subdivision within such city or town shall continue to be subject to rent control in like manner as before. Any such resolution, upon adoption, shall forthwith be transmitted to the commission.

6. Notwithstanding any inconsistent provision of this act, the local governing body of the city of Albany, by resolution duly adopted for such purpose not later than June thirtieth, nineteen hundred sixty-five, determining the existence of a public emergency requiring the regulation and control of residential rents and evictions within such city, which determination shall follow a survey

which such city shall have caused to be made of the supply of housing accommodations within such city, the condition of such accommodations and the need for re-establishing the regulation and control of residential rents and evictions within such city may, and it is hereby authorized and empowered to request the commission to re-establish the regulations of rents with respect to all or any particular class of housing accommodations in the city of Albany, to the extent specified in such resolution.

Any such resolution, upon adoption, shall forthwith be transmitted to the commission. Upon receipt of such resolution, the commission shall forthwith by regulation or order fix as the maximum rents therefor the rents which were lawfully chargeable therefor on April first, nineteen hundred sixty-two, in accordance with the request contained in such resolution. Any such regulation or order recontrolling rents shall take effect on the date specified in such resolution, and thereafter the maximum rents established thereby shall be and continue in force and effect as to such housing accommodations within such city until changed or abolished in accordance with the applicable provisions of this act and the regulations adopted thereunder, and all the provisions of this act applying generally with respect to maximum rents on such housing accommodations and evictions therefrom shall apply with respect thereto within such city.

[The provisions of subd 6, § 12 shall remain in full force and effect until and including May 14, 1987 (L 1985, ch 248, § 2).]

7. Notwithstanding any inconsistent provision of this act, the local governing body of the city of Mount Vernon, by resolution duly adopted for such purpose not later than sixty days after the effective date of this subdivision (June 24, 1983), determining the existence of a public emergency requiring the regulation and control of residential rents and evictions within such city and the need for re-establishing the regulation and control of residential rents and evictions within such city for housing accommodations subject to the provisions of this act on the first day of June, nineteen hundred eighty-three, may, and it is hereby authorized and empowered to request the division of housing and community control to re-establish

the regulations of rents with respect to such housing accommodations in the city of Mount Vernon, to the extent specified in such resolution.

Any such resolution, upon adoption, shall forthwith be transmitted to the division of housing and community renewal. Upon receipt of such resolution, the division of housing and community renewal shall forthwith by regulation or order fix as the maximum rents therefor the rents which were lawfully chargeable therefor on June first, nineteen hundred eighty-three, in accordance with the request contained in such resolution. Any such regulation or order recontrolling rents shall be deemed to have been in full force and effect on and after the first day of June, nineteen hundred eighty-three, and thereafter the maximum rents established thereby shall be and continue in force and effect as to such housing accommodations within such city until changed or abolished in accordance with the applicable provisions of this act and the regulations adopted thereunder, and all the provisions of this act applying generally with respect to maximum rents on such housing accommodations and evictions therefrom shall apply with respect thereto within such city. (Subd 7 added L 1983, ch 353, § 1, eff June 24, 1983).

§ 13. **Pending proceedings.** The commission may provide for and authorize the continued processing of any application or proceeding pending at the time this act becomes effective, provided, however, that the final determination of the commission in such pending application or proceeding shall not be inconsistent with this act.

§ 14. **Intent.** 1. It is the intention of this act to subject to control only those housing accommodations, as that term is defined herein, which were subject to rent control and for which a maximum rent was in effect on March first, nineteen hundred fifty, pursuant to federal or local laws, and in the discretion of the commission those housing accommodations for which a maximum rent was thereafter established, pursuant to the provisions of section four hereof.

2. Any reference made in this act to the local laws specified in chapter one of the laws of nineteen hundred

fifty shall be deemed to be solely for purposes of identification, and if any of such laws shall be held invalid, the reference made herein and any maximum rent established hereunder shall not be affected thereby.

3. The provisions of this section shall be deemed to supersede any other inconsistent provisions of this act.

4. Notwithstanding the decontrol of housing accommodations therein pursuant to this act, unless otherwise provided herein, no municipality shall have the power to adopt local laws with respect to the regulation or control of rents or evictions or otherwise to the subject matter of this act.

§ 15. Separability. If any provision of this act or the application of such provision to any person or circumstances shall be held invalid, the validity of the remainder of the act and the applicability of such provision to other persons or circumstances shall not be affected thereby.

§ 16. Existing rights preserved. Except for matters pending before the commission, no action or proceeding, civil or criminal, pending at the time when this act as amended shall take effect, brought by or against the commission, shall be affected or abated by the enactment or this act or by anything therein contained. No existing right or remedy of any character shall be lost or impaired or affected by such enactment.

§ 17. Short title. This act shall be known and may be cited as the emergency housing rent control law.

[This act shall take effect June, 30 1961.]

RENT AND EVICTION REGULATIONS

of the

OFFICE OF RENT ADMINISTRATION OF THE DIVISION OF HOUSING AND COMMUNITY RENEWAL

[Section numbers refer to the designation of these Regulations as published in the State of New York Official Compilation of the Codes, Rules, and Regulations, Volume 9, Executive (C), Subtitle S (Housing), Chapter VII (Emergency Housing Rent Control), Subchapter B]

PART

2100 —SCOPE.
2101 —MAXIMUM RENTS.
2102 —ADJUSTMENTS.
2103 —REGISTRATION AND RECORDS.
2104 —EVICTIONS.
2105 —PROHIBITIONS.
2106 —ENFORCEMENT.
2107 —PROCEEDINGS BEFORE LOCAL RENT ADMINISTRATOR.
2108 —PROTESTS.
2109 —MISCELLANEOUS PROCEDURAL MATTERS.
FORM OF NOTICE OF APPEARANCE BY ATTORNEY AT LAW

PART 2100

SCOPE

Section 2100.1 Statutory authority. [Additional statutory authority: L. 1964, ch. 244, as amd.] (a) These regulations [Subchapter B] are adopted and promulgated pursuant to the powers granted to the Temporary State Housing Rent Commission, by the Emergency Housing Rent Control Law, chapter 250 of the laws for the year 1950, as last amended by chapters 371, 373, and 383 of the laws of New York, 1971, and transferred to the Division of Housing and Community Renewal in the Executive Department by chapter 244 of the laws of New York 1964. As used in this Subchapter the term "Act" shall mean the Emergency Housing Rent Control Law, as amended by chapter 250 of the Laws of 1950, and as further amended by chapters 36 and 443 of the Laws of 1951, chapters 320 and 321 of the Laws of 1953, chapter 685 of the Laws of 1955, chapter 755 of the Laws of 1957, chapter 695 of the

Laws of 1959, chapter 337 of the Laws of 1961, chapters 21, 126 and 973 of the Laws of 1962, chapters 329, 347 and 805 of the Laws of 1963, chapters 423 and 486 of the Laws of 1965, chapters 68 and 649 of the Laws of 1967, chapters 480 and 509 of the Laws of 1969, and chapters 371, 373, 374 and 383 of the Laws of 1971 and chapters 355 and 420 of the Laws of 1973. This Subchapter shall supersede all regulations previously promulgated and in effect prior to March 15, 1951.

(b) Effective July 1, 1964, whenever the Temporary State Housing Rent Commission is referred to or designated in this Subchapter such reference or designation shall be deemed to refer to the Division of Housing and Community Renewal in the Executive Department.

(c) The Division of Housing and Community Renewal shall be deemed and held to constitute the continuation of the Temporary State Housing Rent Commission, and not a different agency or authority.

(d) All rules, regulations, acts, determinations and decisions of the Temporary State Housing Rent Commission in force on July 1, 1964, shall continue in force and effect as rules, regulations, acts, determinations and decisions of the Division of Housing and Community Renewal until duly modified or abrogated by the Division of Housing and Community Renewal.

(e) Any proceeding or other business or matter undertaken or commenced by or before the Temporary State Housing Rent Commission, and pending on July 1, 1964, may be conducted and completed by the Division of Housing and Community Renewal in the same manner and under the same terms and conditions and with the same effect as if conducted and completed by the Temporary State Housing Rent Commission.

(f) Effective July 1, 1964, whenever the State Rent Administrator or the Administrator is referred to or designated in this Subchapter, such reference or designation shall be deemed to refer to the Commissioner of Housing and Community Renewal in the Executive Department.

2100.2 Statutory definitions. [Additional statutory authority: L. 1964, ch. 244] When used in this Subchapter, unless a different meaning clearly appears from the context, the following terms shall mean and include:

(a) *Commission.* Prior to July 1, 1964, the Temporary State Housing Rent Commission created by the Act. Effective July 1, 1964, the Division of Housing and Community Renewal.

(b) *Housing accommodation.* Any building or structure, permanent or temporary, or any part thereof, occupied or intended to be occupied by one or more individuals as a residence, home, sleeping place, boarding house, lodging house or hotel, together with the land and buildings appurtenant thereto, and all services, privileges, furnishings, furniture and facilities supplied in connection with the occupation thereof, including (1) entire structures or premises as distinguished from the individual housing accommodations contained therein, wherein 25 or less rooms are rented or offered for rent by any lessee, sublessee or other tenant of such entire structure or premises and (2) housing accommodations which were previously exempt, or not subject to control as a result of conversion or a change from a nonhousing to a housing use and which have subsequently been certified by a municipal department having jurisdiction to be a fire hazard or in a continued dangerous condition or detrimental to life or health but only so long as such illegal or hazardous condition continues and without further certification with respect thereto, and any plot or parcel of land which had been rented prior to May 1, 1950, for the purpose of permitting the tenant thereof to construct or place his own dwelling thereon, unless exempt or excluded from control pursuant to any other provision of this Subchapter.

(c) *Rent.* Consideration, including any bonus, benefit or gratuity demanded or received for or in connection with the use or occupancy of housing accommodations or the transfer of a lease of such housing accommodations.

(d) *Maximum rent.* The maximum lawful rent for the use of housing accommodations. Maximum rents may be formulated in terms of rents and other charges and allowances.

(e) *Person.* An individual, corporation, partnership, association, or any other organized group of individuals or the legal successor or representative of any of the foregoing.

(f) *Landlord.* An owner, lessor, sublessor, assignee, proprietary lessee of a housing accommodation in a structure or premises owned by a co-operative corporation or association, or other person receiving or entitled to receive rent for the use or occupancy of any housing accommodation or an agent of any of the foregoing.

(g) *Tenant.* A tenant, subtenant, lessee, sublessee, or other person entitled to the possession or to the use or occupancy of any housing accommodation.

(h) *Documents.* Records, books, accounts, correspondence, memoranda and other documents, and drafts and copies of any of the foregoing.

(i) *Municipality.* A city, town or village.

(j) *Local governing body.* (1) In the case of a city, the council, common council or board of aldermen and the board of estimate, board of estimate and apportionment or board of estimate and contract, if there be one.

(2) In the case of a town, the town board.

(3) In the case of a village, the board of trustees.

(k) *Federal Act.* The Emergency Price Control Act of 1942, and as thereafter amended and as superseded by the Housing and Rent Act of 1947, and as the latter was thereafter amended prior to May 1, 1950, and regulations adopted pursuant thereto.

(l) *Local laws.* Local Law No. 3 of the City of Buffalo for the year 1947.

(m) *Final order.* An order shall be deemed to be final on the date of its issuance by the local rent administrator unless a protest is filed against such order as provided in section 2108.2, *infra*. Where a protest is filed, it shall be deemed to be final on the date of issuance of an order by the Administrator either denying or granting the protest, in whole or in part. Notwithstanding the filing of a protest by either the landlord or the tenant an order adjusting, fixing or establishing a maximum rent shall continue to remain in effect until further order of the Administrator.

2100.3 Additional definitions. [Additional statutory

authority: L. 1964, ch. 244; L. 1971, ch. 371, 373, 374, 383, and 599.] (a) *Administrator.* Prior to July 1, 1964, the State Rent Administrator or such other person or persons as the Administrator may designate to carry out the powers and duties delegated to him by the Act. Effective July 1, 1964, the Commissioner of Housing and Community Renewal or such other person or persons as he may designate to carry out the powers and duties previously delegated to the State Rent Administrator by the Act and now delegated to the Division of Housing and Community Renewal by chapter 244 of the Laws of 1964.

(b) *Office of Rent Administration.* The office of the Division of Housing and Community Renewal established by the Commissioner of Housing and Community Renewal to administer rent control under this Subchapter.

(1) *State Rent Administrator of the Office of Rent Administration of the Division of Housing and Community Renewal.* The person designated by the Commissioner of Housing and Community Renewal to administer rent control under the regulations and to carry out any of the duties delegated to him by the Commissioner of Housing and Community Renewal.

(2) *Director of Litigation and Review of the Office of Rent Administration of the Division of Housing and Community Renewal.* The person designated by the Commissioner of Housing and Community Renewal to carry out the duties related to protests, judicial review, appeals, and enforcement of this Subchapter in the administration of rent control.

(3) *Director of Operations of the Office of Rent Administration of the Division of Housing and Community Renewal.* The person designated by the Commissioner of Housing and Community Renewal to supervise the operations of the local rent offices and local rent administrators in the administration of rent control under this Subchapter.

(4) *Local Rent Administrator.* The person designated by the Commissioner of Housing and Community Renewal to administer rent control in a local rent area set forth in section 2100.8.

(c) *Local rent office.* The office of the commissioner for a particular rent area as set forth in section 2100.8.

(d) *Essential services.* Those essential services which the landlord was providing, or which he was obligated to provide, on March 1, 1950, and which were included with the maximum rent for the housing accommodations on that date. These may include, for example, any or all of the following: repairs, decorating and maintenance, the furnishing of light, heat, hot and cold water, telephone, elevator service, kitchen, bath and laundry facilities and privileges, maid service, linen service, janitor service and removal of refuse.

(e) *Apartment.* A room or rooms providing facilities commonly regarded in the community as necessary for a self-contained family unit but not including housing accommodations located in a rooming house or hotel.

(f) *Rooming house.* In addition to its customary usage, a building or portion of a building, other than an apartment rented for single-room occupancy, in which housing accommodations are rented on a short term basis of daily, weekly or monthly occupancy to more than two paying tenants, not members of the landlord's immediate family provided that the landlord has satisfied all of the requirements of the authorities having jurisdiction over such establishments. The term shall include boarding houses, dormitories, trailers not a part of a motor court, residence clubs, tourist homes and all other establishments of a similar nature, except a hotel or a motor court. Where a landlord has not satisfied all of the requirements of the authorities having jurisdiction over such establishments, none of the housing accommodations within such establishment shall be deemed rooming house accommodations within the purview of this Subchapter.

(g) *Hotel.* Notwithstanding any order, finding, opinion or determination made or issued by the Administrator at any time prior to June 30, 1959, any establishment which complies with the requirements for hotels of the public authorities having jurisdiction over such establishments, and which on March 1, 1950 was and still is commonly regarded as a hotel and in which at least an appreciable number of its occupants were and still are provided with customary hotel services such as maid service, furnishing and laundering of linen, telephone and secretarial or desk service, use and upkeep of furniture and fixtures, and bellboy service, or which services were and still are available with or without cost; provided, however, that the term hotel shall not include any establishment which is commonly regarded in the community as a rooming house, irrespective whether such establishment provides some services customarily provided by hotels, or is represented to be a hotel, or both. Any establishment not identified or classified as a "hotel", "transient hotel" or "residential hotel" pursuant to the Federal Act shall not be deemed to be a hotel.

(h) *Hotel tenant.* A tenant, subtenant, lessee, sublessee or other person entitled to the possession or to the use or occupancy of any housing accommodation within a hotel in the city of Buffalo who has resided in such hotel continuously for 90 days or more prior to March 1, 1950.

2100.4 Effective date. This Subchapter shall become effective March 15, 1951.

2100.5 Amendment or revocation. [Additional statutory authority: L. 1964, ch. 244] Any provision of this Subchapter may be amended or revoked by the commissioner at any time.

2100.6 Filing of amendments. Such amendment or revocation shall be filed with the Secretary of State and shall take effect upon the date of filing unless otherwise specified therein.

2100.7 Separability. If any provision of this Subchapter or the application of such provisions to any persons or circumstances shall be held invalid, the validity of the remainder of this Subchapter and the applicability of such provisions to other persons or circumstances shall not be affected thereby.

2100.8 Local areas subject to control. [Additional statutory authority: L. 1964, ch. 244] Except as hereinafter provided in sections 2100.9 and 2100.10 of this Subchapter (which describe housing accommodations not subject to rent control and housing accommodations exempted by this Subchapter), this Subchapter shall apply to all housing accommodations located in the counties, cities, towns and villages listed below, and as same may be hereafter amended.

Local rent administration office	Local rent areas
Albany	In Albany County, the Cities of Albany and Watervliet, the following towns: Bethlehem, Green Island and New Scotland, and the following villages: Green Island, Voorheesville.
	In Rensselaer County, the City of Rensselaer, the following towns: Hoosick and North Greenbush and the Village of Hoosick Falls.
	In Schenectady County, the Towns of Niskayuna and Princetown.
Buffalo	In Erie County, the City of Buffalo, the Town of Cheektowaga, and the Villages of Depew and Sloan.
Hempstead	Nassau County—all cities, towns, and villages—except the Villages of East Rockaway, Garden City, Great Neck Estates, Great Neck Plaza, Island Park, Lynbrook, Rockville Centre, Thomaston, and Woodsburgh.
	To June 1, 1974:
Syracuse Branch Office	In Monroe County, the Towns of Brighton, Greece and Irondequoit.
	In Oneida County, the City of Sherrill and the following towns: Bridgewater, Deerfield, Floyd, Marcy, Marshall, Sangerfield, Trenton, Vernon, Verona and Westmoreland.
	Onondaga County.
White Plains	In Westchester County, the Cities of Mount Vernon, New Rochelle, White Plains and Yonkers, the following towns: Cortlandt, Eastchester, Greenburgh, Harrison, Mamaroneck, Ossining, Rye, and Yorktown and the following villages: Ardsley, Croton-on-Hudson, Dobbs Ferry, Hastings-on-Hudson, Larchmont, Mamaroneck, North Pelham, North Tarrytown, Pelham Manor, Port Chester, Tarrytown, and Tuckahoe.

2100.9 Housing accommodations not subject to rent control. [Additional statutory authority: L. 1964, ch. 244] This Subchapter shall not apply to the following:

(a) Housing accommodations owned and operated by the United States, the State of New York or any political subdivision thereof, or by a municipal or public authority, only so long as they are so owned and operated or operated; or housing accommodations in buildings in which rentals are fixed by or subject to the supervision of the Commissioner of Housing and Community Renewal pursuant to the powers granted under laws other than the Emergency Housing Rent Control Law.

(b) A hospital, convent, monastery, asylum, public institution, or college or school dormitory or any institution operated exclusively for charitable or educational purposes on a nonprofit basis.

(c) Housing accommodations which were completed on or after February 1, 1947, provided, however, that maximum rents established under the Veterans' Emergency Housing Act for priority constructed housing accommodations completed on or after February 1, 1947, shall continue in full force and effect, if such accommodations are being rented to veterans of World War II or their immediate families who, on June 30, 1947, either occupied such housing accommodations, or had a right to occupy such housing accommodations at any time on or after July 1, 1947, under any agreement whether written or oral.

(d) Housing accommodations created by a change from a nonhousing to a housing use on or after February 1, 1947, provided, however, that where a municipal department having jurisdiction has certified or certifies the housing accommodations to be a fire hazard or in a continued dangerous condition or detrimental to life or health, such housing accommodations shall be subject to this Subchapter, but only so long as such illegal or hazardous condition continues and without further certification with respect thereto.

(e) Additional housing accommodations, other than rooming house accommodations, created by conversion on or after February 1, 1947 and prior to May 1, 1950, provided, however, that where a municipal department having jurisdiction has certified or certifies the housing accommodations to be a fire hazard or in a continued dangerous condition or detrimental to life or health, such housing accommodations shall be subject to this Subchapter, but only so long as such illegal or hazardous condition continues and without further certification with respect thereto.

(f) Rooms or other housing accommodations in hotels except that a room or housing accommodation occupied by a hotel tenant as herein defined in the city of Buffalo is subject to this Subchapter so long as such tenant occupies the same.

(g) Any motor court, or any part thereof; any trailer, or trailer space used exclusively for transient occupancy or any part thereof; or any tourist home serving transient guests exclusively, or any part thereof.

(h) Nonhousekeeping, furnished housing accommodations, located within a single dwelling unit not used as a rooming or boarding house, but only if:

(1) no more than two tenants for whom rent is paid (husband and wife being considered one tenant for this purpose), not members of the landlord's immediate family, live in such dwelling unit, and

(2) the remaining portion of such dwelling unit is occupied by the landlord or his immediate family.

(i) Housing accommodations in buildings operated exclusively for charitable purposes on a nonprofit basis.

(j) Structures subject to underlying leases. Leases for entire structures or premises as distinguished from the individual housing accommodations therein contained, wherein more than 25 rooms are rented or offered for rent by any lessee, sublessee or other tenant of such entire structure or premises; leases for entire structures or premises as distinguished from the individual housing accommodations therein wherein 25 or less rooms are rented or offered for rent by any lessee or other tenant of such entire structure or premises and such lessee, sublessee or other tenant does not occupy any portion of the structure or premises as his dwelling and sublets, as an entrepreneur for his own profit, the individual rooms to subtenants; or structures in which all of the housing accommodations are exempt or not subject to control under this Subchapter.

(k) Housing accommodations which are rented after April 1, 1953 and have been continuously occupied by the owner thereof for a period of one year prior to the date of renting; provided, however, that this subdivision shall not apply where the owner acquired possession of the housing accommodation after the issuance of a certificate of eviction pursuant to this Subchapter within the two-year period immediately preceding the date of such renting, and provided further, that this exemption shall remain effective only so long as the housing accommodations are not occupied for other than single family occupancy.

RENT AND EVICTION REGULATIONS

(l) Housing accommodations in one- or two-family houses which are or become vacant on or after April 1, 1953, provided, however, that this exemption shall remain effective only so long as the housing accommodations are not occupied for other than single family occupancy.

(m) Housing accommodations (not otherwise exempt or excluded from control) in two-family houses occupied in whole or in part by the owner thereof, and in one-family houses whether or not so occupied, on and after July 1, 1955, in the county of Nassau, provided, however, that this exemption shall remain effective only so long as the housing accommodations are not occupied for other than single family occupancy.

(n) Housing accommodations (not otherwise exempt or excluded from control) in two-family houses occupied in whole or in part by the owner thereof, and in one-family houses whether or not so occupied, on and after July 1, 1955, in the counties of Monroe, Oneida, Onondaga and Schenectady, and, on and after July 1, 1957, any housing accommodations in the county of Onondaga containing four rental units or less, provided, however, that this exemption with respect to one- and two-family houses shall remain effective only so long as the housing accommodations are not occupied for other than single family occupancy, and provided further, however, that this exemption shall become or remain effective only in those cities and towns within said counties other than Onondaga County which have not elected to continue or reestablish controls over such housing accommodations.

(o) All housing accommodations (not otherwise exempt or excluded from control) in the counties of Cattaraugus, Chautauqua, Columbia, Dutchess, Erie, Fulton, Herkimer, Montgomery, Niagara, Ontario, Oswego, Saratoga, Seneca, Steuben, Suffolk, Ulster and Yates, except housing accommodations in the following communities which shall continue to remain subject to rent control:

(1) in *Erie County* (other than in one-family houses and in two-family houses occupied in whole or in part by the owner, provided, however, that such exemption from control shall remain effective only so long as the housing accommodations are not rented for other than

single family occupancy), the city of Buffalo and the town of Cheektowaga.

(p) Housing accommodations (not otherwise exempt or excluded from control) except housing accommodations used as boarding houses or rooming houses in the county of Westchester, which are or become vacant on or after July 1, 1957, provided, that this exemption shall not apply or become effective in any case where the vacancy in the housing accommodation occurred or occurs because of the removal of the tenant to another housing accommodation in the same building, or because of the eviction of the tenant after the issuance of a final order in a summary proceeding to recover possession of the housing accommodation, whether after a trial of the issues or upon consent or default of the tenant or otherwise without a trial, and provided further, that this exemption shall remain effective only so long as the housing accommodations are not occupied for other than single family occupancy, and provided further, however, that this exemption shall not apply to housing accommodations in the following cities or towns:

(1) in *Albany County,* the cities of Albany and Watervliet and the towns of Bethlehem and Green Island;

(2) in *Erie County,* the city of Buffalo and the town of Cheektowaga;

(3) in *Nassau County,* the city of Long Beach;

(4) in *Onondaga County,* the towns of Otisco and Pompey;

(5) in *Rensselaer County,* the city of Rensselaer; and

(6) in *Westchester County,* the cities of Mount Vernon, New Rochelle, White Plains and Yonkers and the towns of Cortlandt, Eastchester, Greenburgh, Mamaroneck, Mount Pleasant, Ossining and Yorktown.

(q) Individual housing accommodations in the city of Albany, other than rooming houses as defined in subdivision (f) of section 2100.3, *supra,* the rent for which exceeded $80 per month on April 1, 1962, or where an individual housing accommodation was vacant on said date, the first rent thereafter charged exceeded $80 per month.

RENT AND EVICTION REGULATIONS

(r) Housing accommodations in the village of Larchmont, county of Westchester, which are or become vacant on or after November 1, 1964, and in the unincorporated area of the town of Mamaroneck, county of Westchester, which are or become vacant on or after February 1, 1965, provided that these exemptions shall remain effective only so long as the housing accommodations are not occupied for other than single family occupancy.

(s) Housing accommodations in the city of Mount Vernon, county of Westchester, contained in one and two family houses effective January 1, 1969, and effective April 1, 1969, housing accommodations contained in three family houses and in structures containing four or more family dwelling units which are vacant or become vacant on or after January 1, 1969, provided, however, that such decontrol shall take effect only after inspection by the Department of Buildings of the City of Mount Vernon and certification by said department that the dwelling unit or units to be decontrolled are free of building violations.

(t) Housing accommodations which become vacant effective June 30, 1971, provided, however, that this exemption shall not apply or become effective where the Administrator, following proceedings commenced within 90 days after the date of vacating, determines or finds that the housing accommodations became vacant because the landlord or any person acting on his behalf, with intent to cause the tenant to vacate, engaged in any course of conduct (including, but not limited to, interruption or discontinuance of essential services) which interfered with or disturbed or was intended to interfere with or disturb the comfort, repose, peace or quiet of the tenant in his use or occupancy of the housing accommodations.

(u) Housing accommodations which are decontrolled by order of the Administrator, or by resolution of the local governing body of a city or town or village duly filed with the Administrator, as authorized and provided for in section 2100.19.

2100.10 Housing accommodations subject to rent control, but exempted from control by this Subchapter. This Subchapter shall not apply to the following housing accommodations only so long as they meet the specific requirements hereinafter set forth:

(a) *Farming tenants.* Housing accommodations situated on a farm and occupied by a tenant who is engaged for a substantial portion of his time in farming operations thereon.

(b) *Service employees.* Dwelling space occupied by domestic servants, superintendents, caretakers, managers, or other employees to whom the space is provided as part or all of their compensation without payment of rent and who are employed for the purpose of rendering services in connection with the premises of which the dwelling space is a part.

(c) *Summer resort housing.* Housing accommodations located in a resort community and customarily rented or occupied on a seasonal basis prior to October 1, 1945, which were not rented during any portion of the period beginning on November 1, 1943 and ending on February 29, 1944. This exemption shall apply only as long as the housing accommodations continue to be rented on a seasonal basis and shall be effective only from June 1 to September 30, inclusive.

(d) *Nonprofit clubs.* Rooms in a bona fide club certified by the Administrator as exempt. The Administrator may so certify if on written request of the landlord the club establishes that it is a nonprofit organization and is recognized as such by written statement of the Bureau of Internal Revenue; that it rents rooms only to members, bona fide guests of members, and members of bona fide clubs with which the club has reciprocal arrangements for the exchange of privileges; and that it is otherwise operated as a bona fide club.

(e) *College fraternity or sorority houses.* Rooms in a bona fide college fraternity or sorority house certified by the Administrator as exempt. The Administrator may so certify if, the landlord establishes that the fraternity or sorority is a bona fide organization operated for the benefit of students and not for profit as a commercial or business enterprise. This exemption shall not apply when the rooms are rented to persons who are not members of the fraternity or sorority.

2100.11 Conversions after May 1, 1950. (a) Any housing accommodations resulting from conversion of housing accommodations created on or after May 1, 1950 shall continue to be subject to rent control unless the Administrator issues an order decontrolling them which he shall do if there has been a structural change in a residential unit or units involving substantial alterations or remodeling; and such change has resulted in additional housing accommodations consisting of self-contained family units, provided, however, that such order of decontrol shall not apply to that portion of the original housing accommodations occupied by a tenant in possession at the time of the conversion, only so long as such tenant continues in occupancy. Such order shall be effective as of the date of the completion of such conversion. Where the date of first renting is prior to the date of completion the landlord may make application for an order establishing a maximum rent pursuant to subdivision (a) of section 2102.6, *infra*. Such maximum rent shall remain in effect until further order of the Administrator pursuant to this section.

(1) The term *self-contained family unit* shall mean a housing accommodation with private access, containing two or more rooms, consisting of at least one bedroom and a living room-dining space area in addition to a kitchen (with cooking and refrigeration facilities and a sink), having a minimum total area of 410 square feet for the foregoing rooms, and a private bathroom (with a wash basin, toilet and bathtub or enclosed shower). Such accommodation shall also contain at least one closet plus an additional closet for each bedroom which shall not be included in the computation of the total floor area. In lieu of a kitchen the accommodation may include an enclosed kitchenette or an area in the living room which is either recessed or semienclosed provided that all of the above-specified kitchen facilities and equipment are within such recessed or semi-enclosed area. Where, however, the landlord establishes that either the two-room or total floor area requirement, or both, cannot be complied with because of unique or peculiar circumstances, the Administrator may waive this requirement where he finds that such waiver is not inconsistent with the purposes of the Act or this Sub-

chapter and would not be likely to result in the circumvention or evasion thereof.

(b) No order of decontrol shall be issued under this section unless such conversion occurred after the entire structure, or any lesser portion thereof as may have been thus converted, was vacated by voluntary surrender of possession or in the manner provided in Part 2104 of this Subchapter and unless the Administrator shall find that the landlord has satisfied all of the requirements of the authorities having jurisdiction over such conversion and over the occupancy of the newly created housing accommodations.

(c) Where housing accommodations were or are decontrolled by an order issued pursuant to this section and a municipal department having jurisdiction thereafter certifies the housing accommodations to be a fire hazard or in a continued dangerous condition or detrimental to life or health, such housing accommodations shall be subject to this Subchapter, but only so long as such illegal or hazardous condition continues and without further certification with respect thereto.

(d) No order of decontrol shall be issued by the Administrator where there is a conversion of occupied housing accommodations unless and until the landlord obtains an order authorizing subdivision or a certificate of eviction in accordance with the provisions of section 2104.7.

2100.12 Withdrawal from rental market. Nothing in this Subchapter shall be construed to require any person to offer any housing accommodations for rent, but housing accommodations already on the rental market may be withdrawn only after an order is issued by the Administrator under section 2104.9, if such withdrawal requires that a tenant be evicted from such accommodations.

2100.13 Commercial or professional renting of controlled housing accommodations on or after May 1, 1955. Any housing accommodation subject to this Subchapter which may be rented on or after May 1, 1955 for commercial or professional use shall continue to be subject to control and the landlord may not collect more than the maximum rent until an order is issued by the Administrator exempting the housing accommodation from this Subchapter during the period of occupancy by the tenant. Such order shall be issued by the Administrator where he finds that the renting was made in good faith without any intent to evade the Act or this Subchapter and shall be effective as of the date of the commercial or professional renting.

2100.14 Effect of this Subchapter on leases and other rental agreements. The provisions of any lease or other rental agreement shall remain in force pursuant to the terms thereof, except insofar as those provisions are inconsistent with the Act or this Subchapter.

2100.15 Receipt for rent paid. No payment of rent need be made unless the landlord tenders a receipt for the amount to be paid when so requested by a tenant.

2100.16 Waiver of benefit void. An agreement by the tenant to waive the benefit of any provision of the Act or this Subchapter is void.

2100.17 Substitution of applicable dates. Parts 2100 to 2109, inclusive, of this Subchapter are applicable to housing accommodations within the city of Albany; provided, however, that wherever March 1, 1950 appears therein, April 1, 1962 shall be substituted, and wherever May 1, 1950 appears therein, June 30, 1963 shall be substituted.

2100.18 Housing accommodations which are not the primary residence of the tenant in possession. Any housing accommodations on or after May 1, 1972 which are not occupied by the tenant in possession as his primary residence shall continue to be subject to rent control unless the administrator issues an order decontrolling such accommodation, which the administrator shall do upon application by the landlord, whenever it is established by any facts and circumstances which, in the judgment of the administrator, may have a bearing upon the question of residence, that the tenant maintains his primary residence at some place other than at such housing accommodation.

2100.19 Application. (a) Whenever the administrator shall find that, in any municipality specified by the administrator, (1) the percentage of vacancies in all or any particular class of housing accommodations is five *per centum* or more, or (2) the availability of adequate rental housing accommodations and other relevant factors are such as to make rent control unnecessary for the purpose of eliminating speculative, unwarranted, and abnormal increases in rents and of preventing profiteering and speculative and other disruptive practices resulting from abnormal market conditions caused by congestion, the controls imposed upon rents by authority of the act in such municipality or with respect to any particular class of housing accommodations therein shall be abolished in the manner hereinafter provided; provided, however, that except as otherwise provided in this section, no controls shall be abolished by the administrator unless the administrator shall hold a public hearing or hearings on such proposal at which interested persons are given a reasonable opportunity to be heard. Notice of such hearing shall be provided by publication in a daily newspaper published or having general circulation in the municipality affected not less than 15 days prior to the date of the hearing.

(b) Notwithstanding the provisions of this section or any other provision of the act, the local governing body of a city or town or village, upon a finding that decontrol in such city or town or village is warranted after a public hearing upon notice by publication in a daily or weekly newspaper published or having general circulation in the city or town or village not less than 20 days prior to the date of hearing, and after notice to the administrator, may adopt a resolution to decontrol all or any specified class of housing accommodation in such city or town or village. Such resolution shall thereafter be filed with the administrator. Upon receipt of any such resolution, the controls imposed by authority of the act shall be abolished in the city or town or village affected with respect to housing accommodations specified in such resolution in the manner hereinafter specified. Notwithstanding the foregoing provisions of this subdivision, a city or town or village any portion of which is within the limits of an area designated as a critical defense housing area by the

Federal government at the time of adoption of the decontrol resolution, shall not become decontrolled without the approval of the administrator.

(c) Upon the issuance of an order of decontrol pursuant to subdivision (a) of this section or upon the filing of a resolution resulting in decontrol of a housing accommodation pursuant to subdivision (b) of this section, such decontrol shall take place in the manner hereinafter specified:

(1) If the landlord and tenant execute a written lease for a term of not less than two years wherein the landlord agrees to maintain the same services and equipment required by the act and which provides for an increase in the maximum rent not in excess of 15 percent for the first year and not more than an additional five percent increase for the second year, and otherwise continues the terms and conditions of the existing tenancy, decontrol shall take place upon the execution of such lease;

(2) If the landlord offers the tenant a lease in accordance with the terms provided in paragraph (1) of this subdivision and the tenant fails to execute such lease, and if the landlord notifies the tenant in writing by certified mail that his failure to execute the lease within 30 days of such notification will result in the decontrol of the housing accommodations, decontrol shall take place on the expiration of six months from the date the administrator abolished controls pursuant to subdivision (a) of this section or the date the municipality filed the resolution with the administrator pursuant to subdivision (b) of this section, whichever is applicable, or the expiration date of the 30-day period, if it is later than the applicable six-month date.

(3) If the landlord does not offer the tenant a lease in accordance with the terms provided in paragraph (1) of this subdivision or does not serve the notice provided in paragraph (2) of this subdivision, decontrol shall take place two years from the date the administrator issued the order pursuant to paragraph (1) or the municipality filed the resolution with the administrator pursuant to paragraph (2), whichever is applicable.

PART 2101

MAXIMUM RENTS

(Statutory authority: L. 1950, ch. 250, as amd.; L. 1964, ch. 244;
Emergency Housing Rent Control Law, §§ 4[4][a], 12[7])

Section 2101.1 Maximum rents for housing accommodations, except in hotels.

(a) Except as otherwise provided in this section, the maximum rent for housing accommodations outside the City of New York shall be the maximum rent which was established on March 1, 1950 pursuant to the Federal act, and shall not include adjustments granted by orders issued under the Federal act after that date, regardless of whether they were made effective as of, or retroactive to, that date or a date prior thereto.

(b) For housing accommodations within the City of Buffalo which on March 1, 1950 had no maximum rent established pursuant to the Federal act, but which were subject to a maximum rent established pursuant to the local laws of the City of Buffalo, the maximum rent shall be the rent established on March 1, 1950 pursuant to such local laws.

(c) For housing accommodations first rented after March 1, 1950, or where there has been a change thereafter in rooming houses in the number of occupants or terms of occupancy, the maximum rent shall be the first rent for such accommodations, provided the landlord shall register the accommodations by May 15, 1950, or within 15 days from the time of first renting, whichever is later, as provided in section 2103.3 of this Title. The administrator may order a decrease in the maximum rent, as provided in section 2102.4(a) of this Title where said maximum rent is substantially higher than the maximum rents for comparable housing accommodations, giving due consideration to any factors bearing on the equities involved. If the landlord fails to file a proper registration statement within the time specified, such renting shall not constitute the establishment of a maximum rent and the administrator may fix the maximum rent as provided in section 2102.6 of this Title. For the purposes of this subdivision, the term "housing accommodations first rented after March 1, 1950" shall not include an accommodation changed from unfurnished to furnished, or an apartment, in whole or in part, changed into a rooming house or rented, in whole or in part, to more than one tenant, in which cases the prior maximum rent for such accommodation shall be the maximum rent, unless and until the administrator shall grant an adjustment in or fix such maximum rent as provided in Part 2102 of this Title.

(d) For housing accommodations in rooming houses, where the number of occupants or the term of occupancy for housing accommodations rented prior to March 1, 1950 was thereafter changed and no registration statement has been filed for such number of occupants or term of occupancy under the Federal act, the maximum rent shall be the rent charged for such changed term of occupancy or for the changed number of occupants but not more than the maximum rent for similar housing accommodations for the same term or number of occupants in the same establishment provided the landlord shall file a proper and timely registration statement by May 15, 1950, or within 15 days from the date of such renting, whichever is later, as required by section 2103.3 of this Title. The administrator may order a decrease in the maximum rent so established in accordance with the provisions of section 2102.4(a) of this Title. If the landlord fails to file such proper and timely registration statement, the administrator may establish the maximum rent as provided in section 2102.6 of this Title.

(e) Any tenant in a rooming house on a daily term of occupancy who has resided in such rooming house on such daily basis continuously for a period of more than seven days shall, upon written request to the landlord, be permitted by the landlord to change to a weekly term of occupancy. Such written request shall be sent to the landlord by registered mail, return receipt requested.

(f) For housing accommodations in rooming houses no maximum rent may be established upon the basis of renting to more than three occupants in a single room.

(g) For housing accommodations in rooming houses created by conversion on or after February 1, 1974, including those decontrolled by order pursuant to the Federal act or this Subchapter, the maximum rent shall be the rent charged on January 1, 1959, or the date of first renting, whichever is later, subject, however, to reduction as provided in section 2102.4 of this Title. Any housing accommodations for which a maximum rent is established by this subdivision shall on and after June 30, 1959 be deemed a housing accommodation for all the purposes of this Subchapter.

(h) For housing accommodations created by a change from a nonhousing to a housing use or by conversion on or after February 1, 1947, including those decontrolled by order pursuant to the Federal act or this Subchapter, and which are certified by a municipal department having jurisdiction to be a fire hazard or in a continued dangerous condition or detrimental to life or health, the maximum rent shall be the rent charged on January 1, 1957, or the date of first renting, whichever is later, subject, however, to reduction as provided in section 2102.4(c) of this Title. Any housing accommodations for which a maximum rent is established by this subdivision shall be deemed a housing accommodation for all the purposes of this Subchapter, but only so long as such illegal or hazardous condition continues and without further certification with respect thereto.

(i) For housing accommodations in any establishment which had been deemed to be a hotel by reason of an order, finding, opinion or determination made or issued by the administrator at any time prior to June 30, 1959 and which is found by the administrator not be a hotel as defined by section 2100.3(g) of this Title the maximum rent shall be the rent charged on July 1, 1959 or the date of first renting, whichever is later, notwithstanding the prior establishment of a maximum rent for such housing accommodations pursuant to the Federal act or this Subchapter, subject, however, to reduction as provided in section 2102.4(e) of this Title.

(j) For housing accommodations which were not subject to rent control because they were located in an establishment which was a hotel on March 1, 1950, the maximum rent shall be established by order of the administrator pursuant to section 2102.6(e) of this Title, where the administrator finds the establishment is no longer a hotel.

(k) For housing accommodations within the City of Albany, the maximum rent shall be that rent which was lawfully chargeable therefor on April 1, 1962, or where the accommodation was vacant on said date, the first rent thereafter lawfully charged.

(l) For housing accommodations within the City of Mount Vernon, which were subject to the provisions of the Federal act on June 1, 1983 and not decontrolled thereafter by reason of a vacancy. The maximum rent shall be that rent which was lawfully chargeable therefor on June 1, 1983 and thereafter the maximum rents shall be and continue in force and effect for such housing accommodations within the city until changed, abolished, or decontrolled in accordance with the applicable provisions of the Federal act and this Subchapter. All provisions of the Federal act and this Subchapter applying generally with respect to maximum rents for such housing accommodations and evictions therefrom shall apply with respect thereto.

2101.2 Maximum rents for housing accommodations in hotels. In the City of Buffalo, the maximum rent payable by any hotel tenant is the rent established on March 1, 1950 by Local Law No. 3 of the City of Buffalo for the year 1947. This shall include any adjustment granted by the Temporary City Housing Rent Commission of the City of Buffalo pursuant to the provisions of the said local law; except that where there was no maximum rent established by such local law on March 1, 1950, the maximum rent payable by any hotel tenant shall be the amount of rent payable on that date.

2101.3 Maximum rents for housing accommodations, including equalization adjustment effective May 1, 1953. (a) Notwithstanding the provisions of sections 2101.1 and 2101.2 of this Part, on and after May 1, 1953, the maximum rent for any housing accommodations shall be not less than the maximum rent in effect on March 1, 1943, pursuant to the Federal act but, if no such maximum rent for a housing accommodation was in effect on March 1, 1943, then the maximum rent shall be the maximum rent first established pursuant to the Federal act prior to July 1, 1947, plus 15 percent thereof as such sum is adjusted to reflect:

(1) the amount of any decreases in maximum rent required by order because of decreases in dwelling space, services, furniture, furnishings or equipment or because of substantial deterioration or failure to properly maintain such housing accommodation; and

(2) the amount of any increases in maximum rent authorized because of increases in dwelling space, services, furniture, furnishings or equipment or because of major capital improvements.

(b) Nothing contained in this section, however, shall have the effect of increasing the maximum rent of any housing accommodation more than 15 percent above the maximum rent in effect on April 30, 1953.

2101.4 Maximum rents on and after June 30, 1961 for housing accommodations where rent adjustments were ordered pursuant to section 2102.3(b)(5). Any adjustments in maximum rents ordered by the administrator on and after June 30, 1961, and resulting in an increase thereof solely by reason of the amendments made by chapter 337 of the Laws of 1961 to paragraph (a) of subdivision (4) of section 4 of the Act which provided for the application of the most recent equalization rate, rather than the equalization rate for the year 1954, are hereby rescinded and nullified, provided, however, that no right is conferred by this section to recover any such increase heretofore paid.

2101.5 Services included in the maximum rent. Every landlord shall provide with housing accommodations, the same dwelling space and the same essential services, furniture, furnishings and equipment as were provided, or were required to be provided, on March 1, 1950 or any subsequent date determining the maximum rent.

PART 2102

ADJUSTMENTS

(Statutory authority: L. 1950, ch. 250, as amd.)

Section 2102.1 Maximum rents. Maximum rents may be increased or decreased only by order of the Administrator except as hereinafter specified.

2102.2 Effective date of orders adjusting rents. No order increasing or decreasing a maximum rent previously established pursuant to this Subchapter shall be effective prior to the date on which the order is issued.

2102.3 Grounds for increase of maximum rent.

(a) (1) This section sets forth specific standards for the increase of a maximum rent. In applying these standards and entering an order adjusting a maximum rent, the Administrator shall take into consideration all factors bearing on the equities involved, subject to the general limitation that the adjustment can be put into effect without dislocation and hardship inconsistent with the purposes of the Act.

(2) The Administrator shall have the power to revoke or modify any adjustment granted hereunder if there has been a substantial change in the basis upon which such adjustment was granted.

(3) No landlord shall be entitled to any increase in the maximum rent under this section unless he certifies that he is maintaining all essential services provided or required to be provided with the housing accommodations involved as of the date of the issuance of the order adjusting the maximum rent and that he will continue to maintain such services so long as the increase in such maximum rent continues in effect; nor shall any landlord be entitled to any increase in the maximum rent in any case where a municipal department having jurisdiction certifies that the housing accommodation is a fire hazard, or is in a continued dangerous condition or detrimental to life or health, or is occupied in violation of law.

(4) The total of all adjustments for any individual housing accommodation granted under paragraphs (5) and (7) of subdivision (b) below shall not exceed 15 per cent for any 12-month period, except as provided in subparagraph (iv) of paragraph (5) of subdivision (b) of this section.

(5) That portion of the amount of increase computed under paragraphs (5), (6) and (7) of subdivision (b) below as is properly attributable to the controlled housing accommodations shall be apportioned among them so that each bears an equitable portion thereof. In making such apportionment and in fixing the increases in maximum rents the Administrator shall give due consideration to all previous adjustments or increases in maximum rents by lease or otherwise. Each controlled housing accommodation shall bear no more than that portion of the amount of increase as is properly attributable to such housing accommodation, whether or not the amount so attributed shall be fully collectible by reason of existing lease.

(b) Any landlord may file an application to increase the maximum rent otherwise allowable, on forms prescribed by the Administrator, only on one or more of the following grounds:

(1) *Increased service or facilities, substantial rehabilitation, major capital or other improvements.* The Administrator may grant an appropriate adjustment of a maximum rent where he finds that:

(i) the landlord and tenant by mutual voluntary written agreement, subject to the approval of the Administrator, agree to a substantial increase in dwelling space or an increase in the services, furniture, furnishings or equipment provided in the housing accommodations; or the tenant has accepted and is obtaining the benefit of increased services, furniture, furnishings or equipment; or

(ii) there has been since March 1, 1950 an increase in the rental value of the housing accommodations as a result of a substantial rehabilitation of the building or housing accommodations therein which materially adds to the value the property or appreciably prolongs its life, excluding ordinary repairs, maintenance and replacements; or

(iii) there has been since March 1, 1950 a major capital improvement required for the operation, preservation or maintenance of the structure; or

(iv) there has been since March 1, 1950 in structures containing more than four housing accommodations, other improvements made with the express consent of the tenants in occupancy of at least 75 per cent of the housing accommodations, provided, however, that no adjustment for any individual housing accommodation shall exceed 15 per cent of the maximum rent prescribed on the date the order is issued under this subparagraph unless the tenant has agreed to a higher percentage of increase.

(2) *Voluntary written agreements.* The landlord and tenant have voluntarily entered into a valid written lease in good faith with respect to any housing accommodation, which lease provides for an increase in the maximum rent then in effect under this Subchapter. The maximum rent established by the execution of such lease for the housing accommodation may not thereafter be increased by a subsequent lease executed pursuant to this paragraph except where the rent provided by such subsequent lease does not result in an increase of more than 15 per cent over the maximum rent in effect prior to the execution of the original lease, exclusive of adjustments ordered by the Administrator; *or* where after the expiration of the term of such lease, or in a case where such lease is terminated after the expiration of the first two years of its term, a new written lease may be entered into by the landlord and tenant for a term of not less than two years and providing for an increase not in excess of 15 per cent over the maximum rent then in effect; *or* where such lease is terminated on or after December 15, 1955 and after the expiration of 12 months of its term a new written lease may be entered into by the landlord and tenant for a term of not less than the unexpired remainder of the first two years of the original lease plus two years and providing for an increase, commencing with the expiration of the first two years of the original lease, not in excess of 15 per cent over the maximum rent then in effect. The maximum rent shall be automatically increased by the execution of such lease to the amount specified in such lease except that where such lease provides for an increase in excess of 15 per cent, the increase shall be automatically reduced to 15 per cent provided such lease:

(i) takes effect on or after March 15, 1951 for a term of not less than two years from the effective date thereof;

(ii) contains a certification by the landlord that he is maintaining all essential services furnished, or required to be furnished, as of the date determining the maximum rent and will continue to maintain such services so long as the increase in the maximum rent continues in effect;

(iii) gives the landlord no right of cancellation of said lease inconsistent with the provisions of this Subchapter;

(iv) does not provide for the payment by the tenant of any rent in excess of the amount therein provided, unless the maximum rent is thereafter increased by order of the Administrator to which the tenant has consented pursuant to paragraph (1) of this subdivision; and

(v) if the lease is for a vacant housing accommodation and is for longer than a two-year term, gives the tenant the right of cancellation of said lease at any time after the expiration of the first two years of such lease by giving the landlord at least 30 days' notice in writing of his intention to cancel such lease and surrender possession of the housing accommodation.

Within 30 days after the date of delivery of such lease by the tenant to the landlord, the landlord shall file a report of such lease upon forms prescribed by the Administrator, which shall include a statement of any additional services or equipment furnished to the tenant as a consideration for the execution of the lease.

(3) *Increased subtenants or occupants.* (i) There has been since March 1, 1950 a subletting without the written consent of the landlord or an increase in the number of adult occupants who are not members of the immediate family of the tenant, and the landlord has not been compensated therefor by adjustment of the maximum rent by lease or order of the Administrator or pursuant to the federal Act.

(ii) The Administrator may grant an appropriate adjustment by reason of such change. Such adjustment shall be effective only during the period of subletting or increase in the number of occupants.

(4) *Unique or peculiar circumstances.* (i) Because of unique or peculiar circumstances which materially affected the maximum rent thereof, the maximum rent is substantially lower than the rents generally prevailing in the same area for substantially similar housing accommodations.

(ii) The Administrator may grant an appropriate adjustment of the maximum rent in the amount requested provided that the adjustment shall not result in a maximum rent higher than the rents generally prevailing in the same area for substantially similar housing accommodations.

(5) *Net annual return.* (i) The net annual rental income from a property yields a net annual return of less than seven and one-half percent of the valuation of the property, as hereinafter defined. Such valuation shall be the current assessed valuation established by a city, town or village, which is in effect at the time of the filing of the application for an adjustment under this paragraph, properly adjusted by applying thereto the ratio which such assessed valuation bears to the full valuation as determined by the State Board of Equalization and Assessment on the basis of the assessment rolls of cities, towns and villages for the year 1954 and certified for such year by such board pursuant to section 49-d of the Tax Law; provided, however, that where at the time of the filing of the application for an adjustment under this paragraph such board has computations for such year indicating a different ratio for subclasses of residential property in a city, town or village, the Administrator shall give due consideration to such different ratio except ratios in excess of 100 percent, provided, however, that where such board has not determined and certified any ratio pursuant to such section of such law for a city, town or village for such year, the Administrator shall apply the ratio determined or certified by such board pursuant to section 12(12) of the Real Property Tax Law for the most recent year except where there has been a bona fide sale of the property within the period between March

15, 1957, and the time of filing of the application, as a result of a transaction at arms' length, on normal financing terms at a readily ascertainable price and unaffected by special circumstances such as a forced sale, exchange of property, package deal, wash sale or sale to a co-operative; provided, however, that where there has been more than one such bona fide sale within a period of two years prior to the date of filing of such application the Administrator shall disregard the most recent of such sales if a prior sale within such two-year period was adopted as the valuation of the property in a proceeding under this paragraph. In determining whether a sale was on normal financing terms, the Administrator shall give due consideration to the following factors:

(a) the ratio of the cash payment received by the seller to the sales price of the property *and* the annual gross income from the property;

(b) the total amount of the outstanding mortgages which are liens against the property (including purchase money mortgages) as compared with the equalized assessed valuation of the property;

(c) the ratio of the sales price to the annual gross income of the property, with consideration given to the total amount of rent adjustments previously granted, exclusive of rent adjustments because of changes in dwelling space, services, furniture, furnishings or equipment, major capital improvements, or substantial rehabilitation;

(d) the presence of deferred amortization in purchase money mortgages, or the assignment of such mortgages at a discount; and

(e) any other facts and circumstances surrounding such sale which, in the judgment of the Administrator, may have a bearing upon the question of financing.

No application for adjustment of maximum rent based upon a sales price valuation shall be filed by the landlord under this paragraph prior to six months from the date of such sale of the property. In addition, no adjustment ordered by the Administrator based upon such sales price valuation shall be effective prior to one year from the date of such sale. Where, however, the assessed valuation of the land exceeds four times the assessed valuation of the buildings thereon the Administrator may determine a valuation of the property equal to five times the equalized assessed valuation of the buildings, for the purpose of this paragraph. The Administrator may make a determination that the valuation of the property for the purposes of this paragraph is an amount different from such equalized assessed valuation where there is a request for a reduction in such assessed valuation currently pending; or where there has been a reduction in the assessed valuation for the year next preceding the effective date of the current assessed valuation in effect at the time of the filing of the application.

(ii) For the purposes of this paragraph the following terms shall mean and include:

(a) *Property.* Any structure or group of structures including the land containing housing accommodations having either common facilities, or which are contiguous, or which are operated as a single enterprise and which the Administrator shall in his discretion find appropriate to be considered as a single operation for the purpose of this paragraph. The term property also includes a housing accommodation allocated to a proprietary lessee in a structure or premises owned by a co-operative corporation or association.

(b) *Net annual return.* The amount by which the earned income exceeds the operating expenses of the property.

(c) *Earned income.* The current maximum rents on an annual basis from all controlled housing accommodations; the current rents on an annual basis from all decontrolled and uncontrolled housing accommodations, commercial and business space, and other rented or rentable space; any other income earned from the operation of the property. Where a housing accommodation without a maximum rent is vacant or is occupied without payment of any rent or with payment of a partial rent, the rent generally prevailing for substantially similar controlled housing accommodations shall be deemed the rent for the purposes of the application. Where commercial or business or other rentable space is vacant or is occupied without paying of any rent or with payment of a partial rent, the rent generally prevailing for substantially similar space shall be deemed the rent for the purposes of the application. Where the Administrator finds in considering an application under this paragraph that a present tenant is paying a rent less than the maximum rent, the Administrator, upon request of the landlord, may reduce the maximum rent of the housing accommodation to the amount actually being paid, or to the highest maximum rent for comparable controlled housing accommodations in the structure, whichever is higher.

(d) Operating expenses. All operating expenses necessary in the operation and maintenance of the property and properly allocable to the test year, excluding mortgage interest and amortization, but including an allowance for depreciation of two per cent of the valuation of the buildings exclusive of the land, as defined in subparagraph (i) above, or the amount shown for depreciation of the buildings in the latest required federal income tax return, whichever is lower; provided, however, that no allowance for depreciation of the buildings shall be included where the buildings have been fully depreciated for federal income tax purposes or on the books of the owner. Increases or decreases in real estate taxes, water or sewage charges and wages currently in effect may be projected in computing operating expenses.

(e) Test year. The most recent full calendar year or fiscal year, or any 12 consecutive months ending not more than 90 days prior to the filing of the application.

(iii) If, as determined by the Administrator, a property is earning a net annual return of less than six per cent of the valuation of the property, the Administrator shall grant an adjustment in the maximum rents.

Rent and Eviction Regulations

(iv) No adjustment under this paragraph for any individual housing accommodation shall exceed 15 per cent of the maximum rent in effect on the date the order is issued under this paragraph; provided, however, that the Administrator may waive this limitation where a greater increase is necessary to make the earned income of the property equal to its operating expenses; provided further, however, that the maximum rents, subject to the allocation requirement of paragraph (5) of subdivision (a) of this section, shall be increased by such further additional amount during each succeeding 12-month period, not exceeding 15 per cent of the maximum rent in effect on the effective date of the original order of adjustment, until the maximum rents for the property shall reflect the net annual return provided for in this paragraph, but, in no event, however, shall the total increase ordered for a succeeding 12-month period be more than an additional three per cent of the maximum rent in effect on the effective date of the original order of adjustment unless a new application is filed by the landlord.

(v) no further application may be filed under this paragraph sooner than one year from the date of filing a prior application under this paragraph if an increase had previously been granted thereunder to establish a net annual return of six per cent of the valuation of the property. No order increasing a maximum rent shall be issued on a subsequent application sooner than one year from the effective date, or the earlier effective date if there are dual effective dates, of the order granting an increase on the prior application. The Administrator may waive these limitations where the property has been affected by a significant increase in operating costs which applied to a substantial segment of housing accommodations in the community.

(6) *Unavoidable increases in operating costs in small structures.* (i) The landlord owns no more than four rental units within the State and has incurred unavoidable increases in property taxes, fuel, utilities, insurance and repairs and maintenance which have occurred

since the federal date determining the maximum rent or the date the property was acquired by the present owner, whichever is later.

(ii) Where the Administrator finds in considering an application under this paragraph that a present tenant is paying a rent less than the maximum rent, the Administrator, upon request of the landlord, may reduce the maximum rent of the housing accommodation to the amount actually being paid, or to the highest maximum rent for comparable controlled housing accommodations in the structure, whichever is higher. If, as determined by the Administrator, the landlord has not been fully compensated by increases in rental income sufficient to offset such increases in operating costs the Administrator shall grant an adjustment in the maximum rents.

(iii) No further application may be filed under this paragraph sooner than one year from the date of filing a prior application under this paragraph if an increase had previously been granted thereunder. No order increasing a maximum rent shall be issued on a subsequent application sooner than one year from the effective date, or the earlier effective date if there are dual effective dates, of the order granting an increase on the prior application. The Administrator may waive these limitations where the property has been affected by a significant increase in operating costs which applied to a substantial segment of housing accommodations in the community.

(7) *Unavoidable increases in operating costs in other specified structures.*

(i) The landlord operates a hotel or rooming house or owns a co-operative apartment and has incurred unavoidable increases in property taxes and other costs, including costs of operation of such hotel or rooming house, but excluding mortgage interest and amortization, and excluding allowances for depreciation obsolescence and reserves, which have occurred since the federal date determining the maximum rent or the date the landlord commenced the operation of the property, whichever is later.

(ii) Where the Administrator finds in considering

an application under this paragraph that a present tenant is paying a rent less than the maximum rent, the Administrator, upon request of the landlord, may reduce the maximum rent of the housing accommodation to the amount actually being paid, or to the highest maximum rent for comparable controlled housing accommodations in the structure, whichever is higher. If, as determined by the administrator, the landlord has not been fully compensated by increases in rental income from the controlled housing accommodations sufficient to offset such increases in operating costs as are allocable to such controlled housing accommodations the administrator shall grant an adjustment in the maximum rents.

(iii) No further application may be filed under this paragraph sooner than one year from the date of filing a prior application under this paragraph if an increase had previously been granted thereunder. No order increasing a maximum rent shall be issued on a subsequent application sooner than one year from the effective date, or the earlier effective date if there are dual effective dates, of the order granting an increase on the prior application. The administrator may waive these limitations where the property has been affected by a significant increase in operating costs which applied to a substantial segment of housing accommodations in the community.

(8) Other necessary adjustments of maximum rents not inconsistent with the purposes of the act or regulations. Where the administrator finds in considering an application of the landlord, that adjustments of maximum rents on grounds other than those set forth in paragraph (1), (2), (3), (4), (5), (6) or (7) are not inconsistent with the purposes of the act or these regulations, and such adjustments are necessary to maintain a system of rent controls at levels which are generally fair and equitable, the administrator may issue orders increasing the maximum rents by the amounts of such adjustments. The total adjustments of maximum rents for any housing accommodation in any 12-month period under this paragraph shall not exceed 15 percent of the maximum rent in effect on the date of the first order

granting an adjustment in said 12-month period. The administrator may waiver this limitation because of unique and peculiar circumstances, where he finds such waiver is not inconsistent with the purposes of the act or this Part.

(9) Validation of increases legally authorized pursuant to the Emergency Tenant Protection Act in the City of Mount Vernon prior to the effectuation of the reimposition of regulation pursuant to the Emergency Housing Rent Control Law. A landlord who was authorized to collect a rental adjustment by lease offered prior to July 15, 1983 pursuant to the Emergency Tenant Protection Act in accordance with the rent guidelines authorized by the Westchester County Rent Guidelines Board for guideline year 1982-1983, may continue to collect such rental increases provided that the landlord was not at the same time collecting an increase pursuant to paragraph (8) of this subdivision, and provided further that he makes a valid and authorized application in accordance with paragraph (8) of this subdivision as implemented by operational bulletin 110 on or before September 1, 1983. The rental adjustment received pursuant to paragraph (8) of this subdivision will be inclusive of those increases received pursuant to this section and shall not be in addition thereto.

2102.4 Grounds for decrease of maximum rent. The administrator at any time, on his own initiative, or on application of the tenant, may order a decrease of the maximum rent otherwise allowable, only on the grounds that:

(a)(1) Where a maximum rent has been established for a housing accommodation, other than in a rooming house, pursuant to section 2101.1(d) of this Title, and the landlord has filed a proper and timely registration statement pursuant to section 2103.3 of this Title, the administrator may order a decrease in the maximum rent where such maximum rent is substantially higher than the maximum rents for comparable housing accommodations, giving due consideration to any factors bearing on the equities involved.

(2) Where a maximum rent has been established for

housing accommodations in rooming houses pursuant to section 2101.1(d), (e) or (h) of this Title, and the landlord has filed a proper and timely registration statement pursuant to section 2103.3 of this Title, the administrator may order a decrease in the maximum rent where such maximum rent is substantially higher than the maximum rents for comparable accommodations. Such comparability shall be limited to comparable accommodations in the same establishment, if any. The administrator may also order a decrease in the maximum rent where such maximum rent is based on a change in the number of occupants or the terms of occupancy and is higher than the amount by which the landlord customarily varied the rent for such number of occupants or terms of occupancy as reflected by the maximum rents for such rooms or units and terms of occupancy in effect on March 1, 1950, and where the landlord had no such customary variation and the maximum rent established upon a change in the number of occupants or the terms of occupancy is more than the rental value of such changed occupancy. In all such cases the administrator may take into consideration any factors bearing on the equities involved.

(b) There has been a substantial deterioration of the housing accommodations because of the failure of the landlord to properly maintain the same, or there has been a decrease in the dwelling space, essential services, furniture, furnishings or equipment required under section 2101.5 of this Title. It shall be no defense to an application to decrease the maximum rent that furniture or furnishings were removed on or after May 1, 1955 from a furnished housing accommodation with the consent of the tenant.

(c) A municipal department having jurisdiction certifies that the housing accommodation is a fire hazard or is in a continued dangerous condition or detrimental to life or health, or is occupied in violation of law.

(d) Under subdivision (b) of this section, the maximum rent of the housing accommodations shall be decreased by that amount which the administrator finds to be the reduction in the rental value of the housing accommodations because of the substantial deterioration or decrease in dwelling space, essential services, furniture, furnishings or equipment. The administrator may, however, take into consideration all factors bearing on the equities involved.

(e) Notwithstanding any other provision of this Subchapter, where a maximum rent has been established for a housing accommodation in a rooming house, the administrator may order a decrease in the maximum rent, having regard for any factors bearing on the equities involved, consistent with the purposes of the act to correct speculative, abnormal and unwarranted increases in rent.

(f) (1) No increase in maximum rent pursuant to these regulations shall be collected from a tenant to whom there has been issued a tax abatement certificate pursuant to section 467-b of the Real Property Tax Law as amended by Chapter 689, Laws of New York, 1972 (tax abatement for rent controlled property occupied by senior citizens) except as may be prescribed in such certificate.

(2) The Administrator, upon application by the tenant on prescribed forms shall issue such tax abatement certificate where he finds that the tenant is eligible. A tenant shall be eligible for such tax abatement certificate if the requirements of section 467-b of the Real Property Tax Law amended by chapter 689 are complied with, and the governing body of the city, town, or village wherein the housing accommodations are located has adopted a local law, ordinance, or resolution in accordance with the provisions of said section.

2102.5 Decrease of services: application, order or report. (a) (1) Until the accommodations become vacant the landlord shall maintain the same dwelling space, essential services, furniture, furnishings and equipment as required under section 2101.5 unless and until he has filed an application to decrease the dwelling space, essential services, furniture, furnishings, or equipment and an order permitting a decrease has been entered thereon by the Administrator.

(2) On or after May 1, 1955 the removal of furniture or furnishings from housing accommodations rented as furnished, whether or not such removal is consented to by the tenant, shall constitute a decrease in service.

(b) When the accommodations become vacant the landlord may prior to renting to a new tenant decrease the dwelling space, essential services, furniture, furnishings, or equipment. Within 10 days after so renting, the landlord shall file a written report with the local rent administrator showing such decrease.

(c) The order on any application under subdivision (a) of this section may require an appropriate decrease in the maximum rent. Any maximum rent for which a report is required by subdivision (b) of this section may be decreased in accordance with the provisions of section 2102.4.

(d) If the landlord shall have failed to file an application or a proper and timely report, as required by subdivisions (a) or (b) of this section, the maximum rent shall be deemed in doubt and the Administrator may issue an order fixing the maximum rent pursuant to section 2102.6.

2102.6 Orders where the maximum rent or other facts are in dispute, in doubt, or not known, or where maximum rent must be fixed. (a) Where the maximum rent or any fact necessary to the determination of the maximum rent, or the dwelling space, essential services, furniture, furnishings or equipment required to be provided with the accommodation, is in dispute between the landlord and the tenant, or is in doubt, or is not known, or is prescribed by subdivisions (i) or (j) of section 2101.1, the Administrator at any time upon written request of either party, or on his own initiative, may issue an order determining the facts including the amount of the maximum rent, the dwelling space, essential services, furniture, furnishings and equipment, required to be provided with the accommodations. Such order shall determine such facts or establish the maximum rent as of May 1, 1950 or the date of first renting, whichever is later, except where the maximum rent is prescribed by subdivisions (i) or (j) of section 2101.1, *supra.* Where such order establishes the maximum rent it may contain a directive that all rent collected by the landlord in excess of the maximum rent established under this subdivision for a period not exceeding two years prior to the date of its issuance shall be refunded to the tenant within 30 days after such order shall become final. Where the maximum rent is prescribed by subdivision (i) of section 2101.1, *supra,* the Administrator shall determine the date upon which the housing accommodations became subject to this Subchapter and establish the maximum rent on the basis of the rent charged on January 1, 1957 or the date of first renting, whichever is later.

(b) Where the landlord has failed to file an application or report required by subdivisions (a) and (b) of section 2102.5, the Administrator at any time upon written request of either party, or on his own initiative, may issue an order establishing the maximum rent by decreasing the previous maximum rent of the housing accommodations by that amount which the Administrator finds to be the reduction in the rental value of the housing accommodations because of the decrease in dwelling space, essential services, furniture, furnishings or equipment. The Administrator may take into consideration all factors bearing on the equities involved. Such order shall establish the maximum rent as of the date of decrease of such dwelling space, essential services, furniture, furnishings or equipment or as of May 1, 1950, whichever is later, and may contain a directive that all rent collected by the landlord in excess of the maximum rent established under this subdivision for a period not exceeding two years prior to the date of its issuance shall be refunded to the tenant within 30 days after such order shall become final.

(c) Where no registration statement had been filed prior to May 1, 1950 under the federal Act, or after that date as is required by this Subchapter, the Administrator at any time upon written request of either party, or on his own initiative, may, when he cannot determine the maximum rent pursuant to subdivision (a) herein, issue an order fixing a maximum rent which may be established on the basis of the maximum rent for comparable housing accommodations. Where there are maximum rents in effect in the same establishment, these may be used as comparable housing accommodations, in the discretion of the Administrator. In cases of a change in the number of occupants or terms of occupancy in rooming houses, the maximum rent may be established upon the basis of the amount by which the landlord has customarily varied his rent for such change in the number of occupants or terms of occupancy as reflected in the maximum rents in effect on March 1, 1950. Where the landlord has no customary variation the Administrator may issue an order fixing the maximum rent for such rooms, units or occupancy based upon the rental value of the change in occupancy or in terms of occupancy, after taking into consideration the previous maximum rent therefor. The Administrator may take into consideration all factors bearing on the equities involved. Such order shall fix the maximum rent as of May 1, 1950, or the date of first renting, whichever is later, and may contain a directive that all rent collected by the landlord in excess of the maximum rent established under this subdivision for a period not exceeding two years prior to the date of its issuance shall be refunded to the tenant within 30 days after such order shall become final.

(d) Where no proper or timely registration statement has been filed as is required by this Subchapter, the Administrator may issue an order fixing a maximum rent on the basis of the maximum rents for comparable housing accommodations, as set forth more specifically in subdivision (c) of this section, after taking into consideration all other factors bearing on the equities involved. Such order shall be effective as of May 1, 1950, or the date of such first renting, whichever is later, and may contain a directive that all rent collected by the landlord in excess of the maximum rent established under this subdivision for a period not exceeding two years prior to the date of its issuance shall be refunded to the tenant within 30 days after such order shall become final, provided the Administrator shall have instituted a proceeding to establish such maximum rent by May 1, 1952, or within three months from the time of filing of such registration statement, whichever is later. If the Administrator fails to institute a proceeding to establish such maximum rent by May 1, 1952 or within three months from the time of filing of such registration statement, whichever is later, any order issued fixing the maximum rent under this subdivision shall be effective as of the date of the issuance of the order.

(e) Where it is necessary for the Administrator to determine whether an establishment which was a hotel on March 1, 1950 is still a hotel, the Administrator shall issue an order determining such fact. Where the Administrator finds that an establishment is no longer a hotel, he shall issue orders fixing maximum rents for the housing accommodations within such establishment which were not subject to rent control. The maximum rents so fixed shall be based upon the maximum rents for comparable housing accommodations taking into consideration all factors bearing upon the equities. Such orders shall be effective as of the date of issuance.

2102.7 Order where an apartment is rented to more than one tenant. (a) On and after February 1, 1952, where an apartment, in whole or in part, is rented or sought to be rented to more than one tenant, a landlord shall file an application with the Administrator to fix maximum rents for the units or portions of such apartment. Such application shall set forth the present maximum rent for the apartment, the furniture, furnishings, facilities, equipment and other services added or proposed to be added, the number of occupants, and the space to be occupied by each tenant in such apartment, the terms and conditions of occupancy, and all other data which may be required by the Administrator. In fixing the maximum rent the Administrator shall apportion the previous maximum rent for the entire apartment among the tenants in proportion to the space they occupy, and shall add thereto the increased rental value of any furniture, furnishings, facilities and equipment added by the landlord. Where the landlord has satisfied all of the requirements of the authorities having jurisdiction over the physical conversion and over the occupancy of the changed housing accommodations the Administrator, in fixing maximum rents for individual tenants, shall also take into consideration all factors bearing on the equities involved including the cost of any physical conversion or alteration. If there was no previous maximum rent for the entire apartment, the Administrator shall establish a maximum rent for the entire apartment based upon the rents generally prevailing for comparable housing accommodations prior to apportioning the maximum rent for the entire apartment among the tenants as hereinbefore provided. Unless and until an order is issued by the Administrator fixing maximum rents for the individual tenants of the apartment, the aggregate maximum rent for all of the tenants in the apartment shall be the maximum rent previously established for the apartment. All orders issued under this section shall be effective as of the date of first renting.

(b) Where no application has been made under this section the Administrator at any time upon written request of a tenant, or on his own initiative, may issue an order pursuant to this section fixing a maximum rent for each of the individual tenants in the apartment effective as of the date of such renting. In fixing such maximum rents for the individual tenants, the Administrator shall use the standards prescribed in subdivision (a) of this section. Such order may contain a directive that all rent collected by the landlord in excess of the maximum rent established under this subdivision for a period not exceeding two years prior to the date of its issuance shall be refunded to the tenant within 30 days after such order shall become final.

PART 2103

REGISTRATIONS AND RECORDS

(Statutory authority: L. 1950, ch. 250, as amd.)

Section 2103.1 Registration of housing accommodations. Except as otherwise specifically provided by this Subchapter, every landlord of housing accommodations rented or offered for rent shall file a written statement on the form provided therefor, containing such information as the Administrator may require, to be known as a registration statement, unless a registration statement was heretofore filed in accordance with the rent regulations promulgated pursuant to the federal Act or unless the maximum rent for such housing accommodations is prescribed by subdivisions (i) or (j) of section 2101.1, *supra*.

2103.2 Report on decontrol of certain housing accommodations. [Additional statutory authority: L. 1964, ch. 244] The landlord of a housing accommodation specified in subdivisions (k), (l), (m), (n), (p), (r), (s), and (t) of section 2100.9, *supra,* shall file a report of such decontrol upon forms prescribed by the commissioner within 30 days following the date of first rental of such accommodations after decontrol.

2103.3 First rents. (a) For housing accommodations first rented after March 1, 1950, or where there has been a change thereafter in a rooming house in the number of occupants or terms of occupancy, such registration statement shall be filed by May 15, 1950, or within 15 days after first renting, whichever is later.

(b) For housing accommodations in rooming houses created by conversion on or after February 1, 1947, including those decontrolled by order pursuant to the Federal Act or this Subchapter, such registration statement shall be filed by July 31, 1959, or within 15 days after first renting, whichever is later.

2103.4 Change of ownership. Where, since the filing of the registration statement for any housing accommodations, there has been a change in the identity of the landlord, by transfer of title or otherwise, and no notice of such change has been filed, the successor landlord shall file a notice on a form provided for that purpose on or before May 15, 1950 or within 15 days after the change, whichever is later.

2103.5 Service of papers. Any notice, order or other process or paper directed to the person named in the registration statement as the landlord at the address given therein, or where a notice of change in identity has been filed, to the person named as landlord and at the address given in the most recent such notice, shall constitute notice to the person who is then the landlord.

2103.6 Notices to attorneys at law. (a) Whenever a person is involved in a proceeding before the Administrator and an attorney at law has filed a notice of appearance in such proceeding, all subsequent written communications or notices to such person (other than subpoenas) shall be sent to such attorney at law at the address designated in such notice of appearance. The notice of appearance to be filed by an attorney at law who represents a party in a proceeding before the Administrator shall be on a form prescribed by the Administrator unless proceedings are instituted before the Administrator by formal application pursuant to this Subchapter and the representation of such attorney at law and his mailing address are stated in such application in the space allotted for the mailing address of the represented party. The service of written communications and notices upon such attorney at law shall be deemed full and proper service upon the party or parties so represented.

(b) Whenever an attorney at law shall represent the same party or parties in more than one proceeding before the commission, separate notices of appearance shall be filed in each proceeding. For the purposes of this section a protest against an order of the local rent administrator shall be deemed a separate proceeding.

(c) This section shall not apply to preliminary investigations conducted by the Administrator.

2103.7 Failure to file. Where the landlord has failed to file a proper and timely registration statement as required by this Part 2103, the Administrator may establish the maximum rent pursuant to section 2102.6.

2103.8 Records and record-keeping. (a) Every landlord of a rooming house or hotel subject to this Subchapter, rented or offered for rent, shall keep, preserve, and make available for examination by the Administrator, records showing the rents received for each housing accommodation, the particular term and number of occupants for which such rents were charged, and the name and address of each occupant.

(b) Every other landlord shall keep, preserve, and make available for examination by the Administrator, records of the same kind as he has customarily kept relating to the rents received for housing accommodations.

2103.9 Registration of housing accommodations within the city of Albany. Within the city of Albany, every landlord of housing accommodations subject to this Subchapter, rented or offered for rent on June 30, 1963, shall file with the Administrator a written statement on the form provided therefor, to be known as a registration statement. This form shall identify each housing accommodation and shall specify therein the maximum rent provided by this Subchapter for such housing accommodation and shall contain such other information as the Administrator shall require. This registration statement shall be filed pursuant to instructions appearing on the form, on or before July 31, 1963.

PART 2104

EVICTIONS

(Statutory authority: L. 1950, ch. 250, as amd.)

Section 2104.1 Restrictions on removal of tenant, including hotel tenants. [Additional statutory authority: L. 1964, ch. 244] (a) So long as the tenant continues to pay the rent to which the landlord is entitled, no tenant shall be removed from any housing accommodations by action to evict or to recover possession, by exclusion from possession, or otherwise, nor shall any person attempt such removal or exclusion from possession, notwithstanding that such tenant has no lease or that his lease, or other rental agreement has expired or otherwise terminated, notwithstanding any contract, lease agreement or obligation heretofore or hereafter entered into which provides for surrender of possession, or which otherwise provides contrary hereto, except on one or more of the grounds specified in section 2104.2, *infra,* or unless the landlord has obtained a certificate of eviction as hereinafter provided.

(b) It shall be unlawful for any person to remove or attempt to remove any tenant or occupant from any housing accommodations or to refuse to renew the lease or agreement for the use of such accommodations, because such tenant or occupant has taken, or proposes to take, action authorized or required by the Act or any regulation, order or requirement thereunder.

(c) (1) No tenant of any housing accommodation shall be removed or evicted unless and until such removal or eviction has been authorized by a court of competent jurisdiction.

(2) Except as hereinafter provided this subdivision shall not apply where the removal or eviction is for nonpayment of rent and involves a tenant of a hotel or rooming house who occupies his accommodations on a daily or weekly basis, provided the landlord shall give written notice thereof to the tenant at least three days prior to the date specified therein for the surrender of possession and prior to any action for removal or eviction. In computing the three-day period, the day of service and any intervening Sunday shall be excluded. Every such notice shall include therein a statement of the rent due and the rental period or periods for which said rent is due. An exact copy of every such notice together with an affidavit of service shall be filed with the local rent office within 48 hours after such notice is given to the tenant. Should the tenant tender the rent due within the three-day period, the landlord may not remove or evict the tenant.

(d) Any statutory tenant who vacates the housing accommodations, without giving the landlord at least 30 days' written notice by registered or certified mail of his intention to vacate, shall be liable to the landlord for an amount not exceeding one month's rent, except where the tenant has been removed or vacates pursuant to the provisions of Part 2104 of this Subchapter. Such notice shall be postmarked on or before the last day of the rental period immediately prior to such 30-day period.

2104.2 Proceedings for eviction without certificate. An action or proceeding to recover possession of any housing accommodation shall be maintainable after service and filing of the notice required by section 2104.3, *infra*, only upon one or more of the following grounds:

(a) The tenant is violating a substantial obligation of his tenancy other than the obligation to surrender possession of such housing accommodation and has failed to cure such violation after written demand by the landlord that the violation cease within 10 days; or within the three-month period immediately prior to the commencement of the proceeding the tenant has wilfully violated such an obligation inflicting serious and substantial injury to the landlord.

(b) The tenant is committing or permitting a nuisance in such housing accommodations; or is maliciously or by reason of gross negligence substantially damaging the housing accommodations; or his conduct is such as to interfere substantially with the comfort or safety of the landlord or of other tenants or occupants of the same or other adjacent building or structure.

(c) Occupancy of the housing accommodations by the tenant is illegal because of the requirements of law, and the landlord is subject to civil or criminal penalties therefor, or both.

(d) The tenant is using or permitting such housing accommodation to be used for an immoral or illegal purpose.

(e) The tenant who had a written lease or other written rental agreement which terminates on or after May 1, 1950, has refused upon demand of the landlord to execute a written extension or renewal thereof for a further term of like duration not in excess of one year but otherwise on the same terms and conditions as the previous lease except insofar as such terms and conditions are inconsistent with the Act.

(f) The tenant has unreasonably refused the landlord access to the housing accommodations for the purpose of making necessary repairs or improvements required by law or for the purposes of inspection or of showing the accommodations to a prospective purchaser, mortgagee or prospective mortgagee, or other person having a legitimate interest therein; provided, however, that in the latter event such refusal shall not be ground for removal or eviction if such inspection or showing of the accommodations is contrary to the provisions of the tenant's lease or rental agreement.

2104.3 Notices required in proceedings under section 2104.2. [Additional statutory authority: L. 1964, ch. 244] (a) Except where the ground for removal or eviction of a tenant is nonpayment of rent, no tenant shall be removed or evicted from housing accommodations by court process and no action or proceeding shall be commenced for such purpose upon any of the grounds permitted in section 2104.2, *supra,* unless and until the landlord shall have given written notice to the tenant and the local rent office as hereinafter provided.

(b) Every notice to a tenant to vacate or surrender possession of housing accommodations shall state the ground under section 2104.2 upon which the landlord relies for removal or eviction of the tenant, the facts necessary to establish the existence of such ground, and the date when the tenant is required to surrender possession.

(c) Within 48 hours after the notice is served upon the tenant, an exact copy thereof together with an affidavit of service shall be filed with the local rent office.

(d) Every such notice shall be served upon the tenant within the period of time hereinafter set forth prior to the date specified therein for the surrender of possession and prior to the commencement of any proceeding for removal or eviction:

(1) Where the notice specifies one or more of the grounds stated in subdivisions (b), (c) and (d) of section 2104.2 for such removal or eviction, not less than 10 days unless the tenant is a weekly tenant in which case the notice required shall be not less than two days.

(2) Where the notice specifies one or more of the grounds stated in subdivisions (a), (e) and (f) of section 2104.2 for such removal or eviction, not less than one month unless the tenant is a weekly tenant in which case the notice required shall not be less than seven days.

2104.4 Proceedings for eviction with certificate. (a) No tenant shall be removed or evicted on grounds other than those stated in section 2104.2 unless on application of the landlord (or where the housing accommodations are located in a structure or building owned by two or more persons not constituting a co-operative corporation or association, the application shall be consented to by all the co-owners) the Administrator shall issue a certificate permitting the landlord to pursue his remedies at law at the expiration of the waiting period hereinafter specified in subdivision (b) of this section. The Administrator may issue an order granting a certificate if the removal or eviction meets the requirements of sections 2104.5,

2104.6, 2104.7, 2104.8, or 2104.9, *infra*. The Administrator may also issue orders granting certificates in other cases if the requested removal or eviction is not inconsistent with the purposes of the Act or this Subchapter and would not be likely to result in the circumvention or evasion thereof.

(b) Certificates issued pursuant to this section or sections 2104.5, 2104.6, 2104.7, or 2104.9, *infra,* shall authorize the landlord to commence proceedings to remove or evict the tenant at the expiration of three months from the date of issuance of the certificate by the Administrator. Certificates issued pursuant to section 2104.8, *infra,* shall authorize the landlord to commence proceedings to remove or evict the tenant at the expiration of six months from the date of issuance of the certificate by the Administrator. Where the Administrator finds (1) that equivalent accommodations are available for rent into which the tenant can move without substantial hardship or loss, or (2) that undue hardship would result to the landlord, a certificate may be issued and may authorize the landlord to pursue his remedies for removal or eviction of the tenant at the expiration of a period shorter than such maximum waiting period.

(c) No certificate shall be used in connection with any action or proceeding to remove or evict a tenant unless such removal or eviction is sought for the purpose specified in the certificate.

(d) In the event that the landlord's intentions or circumstances so change that the premises, possession of which is sought, will not be used for the purpose specified in the certificate, the certificate shall thereupon be null and void. The landlord shall immediately notify the local rent administrator in writing and surrender the certificate for cancellation.

(e) Wherever relocation of a tenant at the same rent is required as a condition for the granting of a certificate of eviction, the administrator may, in his discretion, substitute a requirement that the landlord pay to the tenant a sum equivalent to the difference for two years between the present rent for the housing accommodations and the rent payable for the offered accommodations, plus reasonable moving expenses.

(f) The provisions of this section shall apply to all certificates issued pursuant to this Subchapter.

2104.5 Occupancy by landlord or immediate family.

(a) (1) A certificate shall be issued where the landlord seeks in good faith to recover possession of housing accommodations because of immediate and compelling necessity for his own personal use and occupancy or for the use and occupancy of his immediate family. As used in this subdivision, the term *immediate family* includes only a son, daughter, stepson, stepdaughter, father, mother, father-in-law, or mother-in-law. Provided, however, that where the housing accommodations are located in a building containing 12 or less housing accommodations and the landlord does not reside in the building or is a housing accommodation located in a structure or premises owned by a cooperative corporation or association which is allocated to an individual proprietary lessee, and the landlord seeks to recover possession for his own personal use, an immediate and compelling necessity need not be established.

(2) The provisions of this subdivision shall not apply where a tenant or the spouse of a tenant lawfully occupying the housing accommodation is sixty-two years of age or older, or has an impairment which results from anatomical, physiological or psychological conditions, other than addiction to alcohol, gambling, or any controlled substance, which are demonstrable by medically accepted clinical and laboratory diagnostic techniques, and which are expected to be permanent and which prevent such person from engaging in any substantial gainful employment, unless the landlord offers to provide and, if requested, provides an equivalent or superior housing accommodation at the same or ower regulated rent in a closely proximate area.

(b) Where the housing accommodations are located in a structure or premises which contain more than two housing accommodations and the housing accommodations or structure or premises are owned by two or more persons not constituting a cooperative corporation or association (husband and wife as owners being considered one owner for this purpose), no certificate shall be issued under this section for occupancy of any housing accommodation in such structure or premises where two housing accommodations are already owner-occupied as a result of certificates of eviction. The prohibition contained in this subdivision shall not apply where the co-owners stand in the relationship of immediate family as defined in subdivision (a) of this section.

(c) (1) In the case of a housing accommodation in a structure or premises owned by a cooperative corporation or association, a certificate shall be issued by the Administrator to a purchaser of stock where (i) the tenant originally obtained possession of the housing accommodation by virtue of a rental agreement with the tenant-owner; or (ii) the stock was acquired by the purchaser prior to July 1, 1955 and more than two years prior to the date of the filing of the application; or (iii) the stock was acquired by the purchaser on or after July 1, 1955 and more than two years had expired since the date of filing the notice of sale with the local rent office as hereafter provided in subparagraph (v) of paragraph (3) of this subdivision; or (iv) the stock was acquired less than two years prior to the date of filing of the application and on that date stock in the cooperative has been purchased by persons who are tenant-owners of at least 80 percent of the housing accommodations in the structure or premises and are entitled by reason of stock ownership to proprietary leases of housing accommodations in the structure or premises; or (v) the cooperative was organized and acquired its title or leasehold interest in the structure or premises before February 17, 1945 and on that date stock in the cooperative allocated to 50 percent or more of the housing accommodations in the structure or premises was held by individual tenant-owners, who are or whose assignees or subtenants are in occupancy of such housing accommodations in the structure or premises at the date of the filing of the application.

(2) No certificate of eviction shall be issued under paragraph (1) of this subdivision unless the applicant shall establish that he has complied with the requirements of subdivisions (a) and (d) of this section; provided, however, that where the applicant seeks to recover possession for his own personal use, he need not ablish an immediate and compelling necessity.

(3) No certificate of eviction shall be issued under paragraph (1) of this subdivision, except as provided in paragraph (4) of this subdivision, unless the applicant shall also establish that the cooperative corporation or association has complied with the following requirements:

(i) On the date the cooperative plan was first presented to the tenants, each tenant in occupancy of a controlled housing accommodation in the premises was furnished with a copy of the plan and notified in writing that he had the exclusive right for a period of 60 days to purchase the stock allocated to his housing accommodation at the specified price, and that the plan would not be declared effective, unless on or before December 31, 1955 or within six months from the time the cooperative plan was presented to such tenants, whichever date is later, stock in the cooperative had been sold in good faith without fraud or duress, and with no discriminatory repurchase agreement or other discriminatory inducement, to at least 35 percent of the tenants in occupancy of controlled housing accommodations at the time of the presentation of the plan. Housing accommodations vacant on the date the plan is presented or subsequently vacated, shall not be included in the computation of the 35 percent requirement except when the vacant housing accommodation is purchased for personal occupancy by a tenant of a controlled housing accommodation.

(ii) Subsequent to the date the cooperative plan had been declared effective, the tenants of controlled housing accommodations had been served with a written notice that the plan had been declared effective, setting forth the terms of sale and the names of the tenants of the controlled housing accommodations who had purchased the stock allocated to their own housing accommodations or to vacant housing accommodations and the names and addresses of other purchasers of vacant housing accommodations; and that the tenants of controlled housing accommodations who had not as yet purchased, still had the exclusive right, for a period of 30 days from the date of service of the notice, to purchase the stock allocated to their housing accommodations on the terms previously offered to the tenants; except where *(a)* the cooperative plan had been declared effective prior to July 1, 1955, and *(b)* prior to that date the tenant of a controlled housing accommodation in the premises had received written notice or notices that for a period of not less than 30 days he had the right to purchase the stock allocated to his housing accommodation at the price and terms specified in said plan, and *(c)* on July 1, 1955 such stock was held or was thereafter reacquired by the cooperative or by a sponsor, nominee of the cooperative or by any other person associated with the formulation of the plan, and *(d)* such stock was offered after July 1, 1955 for sale for personal occupancy at the same or different terms than previously offered to the tenant of such controlled housing accommodation, the latter was given a written notice of the offer to sell and the right for a period of 30 days to purchase the stock on the terms specified in such offer.

(iii) Within 10 days from the date of service of the notice provided by subparagraph (ii) the co-operative had filed with the local rent office having jurisdiction a copy of the co-operative plan; a copy of the first notice served upon all tenants of controlled housing accommodations; a copy of the notice required by subparagraph (ii), and a statement, duly verified by an officer of the co-operative and where the sale was made on or after July 1, 1955, a statement duly verified by each purchaser, that the sales had been made in good faith pursuant to the terms set forth in the co-operative plan without fraud or duress and with no discriminatory repurchase agreement or other discriminatory inducement and whether for personal occupancy by the purchaser. A duplicate set of the above specified papers shall also be kept available in the building for inspection by a tenant of controlled housing accommodations or his authorized representative.

(iv) In the event that the stock allocated to a controlled housing accommodation shall be offered for sale by the co-operative, its sponsor, nominees or other persons associated with the formulation of the plan to a purchaser in good faith for his personal occupancy at terms more favorable than those previously offered to the tenant of such controlled housing accommodation, the latter must first be given a written notice of the new terms and 15 days within which to elect to purchase stock at such new terms.

(v) Within 10 days after any sale or resale of stock subsequent to the effective date of the plan, all tenants who had not yet purchased had been served with written notices by the co-operative setting forth the names and addresses of each of the purchasers, the designation of the housing accommodations, and in those cases where the stock had been sold for personal occupancy of the purchaser, the terms of the sales. Copies of these notices, together with proof of service upon each such tenant, must be filed with the local rent office within five days of the date of service. Copies of these notices shall also be kept available in the building for inspection.

(4) Where the co-operative plan was declared effective prior to July 1, 1955, the Administrator shall issue a certificate of eviction to a purchaser who acquired the stock prior to July 1, 1955, if he finds that the requirements of the former subdivision (c) of this section have been met and that the purchaser had served the tenant of the controlled housing accommodation before December 31, 1955, with a written notice setting forth the name and address of the purchaser, designation of the housing accommodation and the terms of the sale. A copy of this notice, together with proof of service upon such tenant, must be filed with the local rent office within five days of the date of service. Where, however, stock allocated to a controlled housing accommodation occupied by a tenant has not in fact been sold prior to July 1, 1955, to a purchaser in good faith for personal occupancy, no certificate of eviction shall be issued unless such tenant had been afforded the rights conferred by subparagraphs (ii), (iii), (iv) and (v) of paragraph (3) of this subdivision. The co-operative must file all documents required in the preceding subparagraphs

of paragraph (3) no later than December 31, 1955 or such later date as is applicable.

(5) As used herein, the term *tenant-owner* includes only

(i) a person who purchased the stock allocated to a vacant housing accommodation excluding, however, any housing accommodations which had been vacated after the filing of an application for a certificate of eviction or an order of subdivision pursuant to this Subchapter within the one-year period preceding the presentation of the co-operative plan to the tenants; or

(ii) a person who while he was a tenant in occupancy in the building, purchased the stock allocated to his housing accommodation; or

(iii) a person who purchased the stock allocated to a housing accommodation which was occupied by a tenant who obtained his possession from said purchaser of the stock; or

(iv) a person who purchased the stock allocated to a housing accommodation from an owner of such stock who was in occupancy of such housing accommodation; or

(v) a person who purchased the stock allocated to a housing accommodation while it was occupied by a tenant and which thereafter became vacant after voluntary removal by the tenant.

(6) As used herein, the term *housing accommodation* shall not include servants' rooms which are nonhousekeeping and located in the service portion of the building or apartments not subject to this Subchapter; and the term *tenant* shall not include the persons occupying such servants' rooms or apartments not subject to this Subchapter.

(7) As used herein, the term *stock* shall also include other evidence of interest in the co-operative corporation or association with the right to possession of a housing accommodation by virtue of a proprietary lease or otherwise.

(8) As used herein, the term *co-operative corporation or association* shall also include the sponsor of a co-operative plan.

(9) Where a co-operative plan and any amendments thereof presented to the tenants of controlled housing accommodations is not declared effective and filed with the local rent office pursuant to subparagraphs (ii) and (iii) of paragraph (3) of this subdivision, a period of 18 months from the date of the presentation of the first plan must elapse before another co-operative plan may be presented to the tenants of the structure.

(d) Where the landlord purchased and thereby acquired title to the premises on or after May 1, 1950, or where the landlord acquired his rights in the housing accommodations (other than in a structure or premises owned by a co-operative corporation or association) through an enforceable contract of sale of the real property which meets the minimum requirements of this subdivision, no certificate shall be issued under subdivisions (a), (b) or (c) of this section unless the landlord on or before the date of the filing of the application has made a payment or payments totaling at least 20 per cent of the purchase price or the assessed valuation of the premises, whichever is the greater; provided, however, that where the Administrator finds that equivalent accommodations are available for rent into which the tenant can move without substantial hardship or loss, or that undue hardship would result to the landlord, a certificate may be issued although less than 20 per cent has been paid. This requirement shall not apply where the landlord is a former member of the armed forces of the United States of America who obtained a loan for use in purchasing housing accommodations guaranteed in whole or part by the Administrator of Veterans Affairs. The contract of sale of the real property referred to in this subdivision shall

(1) give the purchaser the right of immediate possession and assign all of the rents and income from the property to the purchaser;

(2) not give the purchaser the right to cancel because of failure to secure occupancy of the premises;

(3) provide that the risk of damage to or destruction to the building on the premises by fire or other cause or casualty shall be the risk of the purchaser, and any such damage or destruction shall not excuse such pur-

chaser from paying the price for the premises nor from performing the other conditions and covenants of the contract;

(4) require the purchaser at all times to keep the buildings on the premises insured for the benefit of the seller in an amount equal to at least the unpaid balance owing under the contract to the seller;

(5) require the purchaser to pay all taxes, assessments, and water rents which shall thereafter be taxed or assessed upon or placed against the property.

(e) A certificate shall be issued where the landlord establishes that it is an organization exempt from taxation under the Federal Internal Revenue Code, and that it seeks in good faith to recover possession of the housing accommodations for the immediate and personal use and occupancy as housing accommodations by members of its staff.

2104.6 Tenant not using premises for own dwelling.

(a) A certificate shall be issued for the eviction of the tenant and subtenants where the landlord seeks in good faith to recover possession of housing accommodations for which the tenant's lease or other rental agreement has expired or otherwise terminated, and at the time of termination the occupants of the housing accommodations are subtenants or other persons who occupied under a rental agreement with the tenant, and no part of the accommodations is used by the tenant as his dwelling.

(b) No tenant shall be evicted under this section where the premises are operated as a rooming house and the eviction of the tenant will result in the removal of the furniture and furnishings used by the occupants, unless the landlord establishes that substantially similar furniture and furnishings will be provided at the time of the removal and that arrangements will be made for the occupants to remain in occupancy under substantially the same terms and conditions as those existing on the date of the issuance of the certificate.

(c) No occupant of housing accommodations, other than the tenant, shall be evicted under this section, where the rental agreement between the landlord and tenant contemplated the subletting by the tenant of the entire accommodations or a substantial portion thereof.

RENT AND EVICTION REGULATIONS

(d) No occupant of housing accommodations shall be evicted under this section where the occupant is either the surviving spouse of the deceased tenant or some other member of the deceased tenant's family who has been living with the tenant.

2104.7 Subdivision by alteration or remodeling. A certificate or an order authorizing subdivision shall be issued where the landlord seeks in good faith to recover possession of housing accommodations for the immediate purpose of substantially altering or remodeling them, provided that the landlord shall have secured such approval therefor as is required by law. No certificate or order authorizing subdivision involving alteration or remodeling shall be granted under this section unless the administrator shall find:

(a) That such alteration or remodeling is for the purpose of subdividing an under-occupied housing accommodation containing six or more rooms, exclusive of bathrooms and kitchen, into a greater number of housing accommodations consisting of self-contained family units which meet the requirements of section 2100.11 of this Title. An apartment may be deemed under-occupied when there is less than one occupant for each room, exclusive of bathrooms, kitchen and three additional rooms. Roomers or boarders who are not members of the tenant's family shall not be counted as occupants.

(b) Upon approval of plans by the local authorities having jurisdiction thereof, where such approval is required, and before proceeding with such alteration or remodeling, application shall be made to the administrator for an order directing the tenant occupying such housing accommodation to remain in possession of an adequate portion thereof, as determined by the administrator, and to surrender possession of the remainder of said housing accommodation, within a time to be fixed by the administrator. Where it is not practicable for the tenant to remain in possession of a portion of the housing accommodation, the administrator may require the landlord to furnish suitable temporary housing accommodations to the tenant during the alteration. The order so granted shall be conditioned on the right of such tenant to first occupancy of any housing accommodation resulting from such alteration or remodeling of such subdivided housing accommodation.

(c) Where the tenant cannot be adequately housed in any portion of the subdivided housing accommodation, the landlord may secure a certificate or an order authorizing subdivision where he shows that he is willing and able to relocate the tenant in other suitable housing accommodations within the same city, village or town not unreasonably distant from the premises being altered, and available at a rent not greater than the rent now being paid by such tenant.

(d) The administrator shall establish the terms and conditions under which such alteration or remodeling may be made and shall establish the maximum rent to be paid by the tenant occupying such suitable portion of such housing accommodation during the alteration, and shall establish the maximum rent to be paid by such tenant for the first occupancy of any housing accommodation selected by him in such subdivided housing accommodation after it has been altered or remodeled. The administrator shall, pursuant to subdivision (a) of section 2102.6 of this Title, establish the maximum rent on the basis of the maximum rents for comparable housing accommodations after taking into consideration all other factors bearing on the equities involved. The landlord shall file an application under section 2100.11 of this Title for an order of decontrol, provided, however, that such order of decontrol shall not apply to that portion of the original housing accommodations occupied by a tenant in possession at the time of the conversion but only so long as such tenant continues in occupancy.

(e) Where the housing accommodation to be subdivided had a maximum monthly rent of $200 or more as of March 1, 1943, or the date of first renting thereafter, there shall be no requirement that the tenant be relocated or given occupancy of any of the housing accommodations created by the alteration or subdivision.

(f) In the case of housing accommodations in a structure or premises owned by a cooperative corporation or association where the landlord is the individual owner of stock allocated to a housing accommodation, no certificate or order shall be granted under this section unless the administrator shall also find that the landlord has met the requirements of section 2104.5(c) of this Part.

(g) The order in all such cases shall grant the landlord permission to recover possession of the housing accommodations without further application should the tenant fail to abide by the order of subdivision issued by the administrator.

2104.8 Demolition. A certificate shall be issued where the landlord seeks in good faith to recover possession of housing accommodations for the immediate purpose of demolishing them, provided that the landlord shall have secured such approval therefor as is required by law. No certificate involving demolition will be granted under this section unless the administrator shall find:

(a) that such demolition is to be made for the purpose of constructing new buildings or structures containing at least 20 percent more housing accommodations consisting of self-contained family units (as defined in section 2100.11 of this Title) than are contained in the structure to be demolished; provided, however, where as a result of conditions detrimental to life or health of the tenants, violations have been placed upon the structure containing the housing accommodations by the local authorities having jurisdiction over such matters and the cost of removing such violations would substantially equal or exceed the assessed valuation of the structure, the new buildings or structures shall only be required to make provision for a greater number of housing accommodations consisting of self-contained family units than are contained in the structure to be demolished; or

(b) that such demolition is to be made for the purpose of carrying out a program of clearance, replanning, reconstruction, and neighborhood rehabilitation of substandard and insanitary areas pursuant to and under the conditions imposed by article 15 of the General Municipal Law; or

(c) that such demolition is to be made for the purpose of constructing other than housing accommodations.

2104.9 Withdrawal of occupied housing accommodations from rental market. [Additional statutory authority: L. 1964, ch. 244] A certificate shall be issued where the landlord establishes that he seeks in good faith to permanently withdraw occupied housing accommodations from both the housing and non-housing rental markets without any intent to rent or sell all or any part of the land or structure and (a) that he requires the entire structure containing the housing accommodations or the land for his own immediate use in connection with a business which the landlord owns and operates in the immediate vicinity of the property in question, or (b) that substantial violations affecting the health and safety of the tenants have been placed on the structure containing the housing accommodations by the local authorities having jurisdiction over such matters and that the cost of removing these violations would substantially equal or exceed the assessed valuation of the structure established by the city, town or village wherein it is located, as adjusted by applying thereto the ratio which such assessed valuation bears to the full valuation as determined by the State Board of Equalization and Assessment on the basis of the assessment rolls of such city, town or village for the most recent year and certified for such year be* such board pursuant to section 1212 of the Real Property Tax Law; provided, however, that where at the time of filing of the application, such board has computations indicating a different ratio for subclasses of residential property in a city, town or village, the commissioner shall give due consideration to such different ratio, or (c) where the landlord is a hospital, convent, asylum, public institution, college, school or any institution operated exclusively for charitable or educational purposes on a nonprofit basis and requires the housing accommodations or the land for its own immediate use in connection with its charitable or educational purposes, or (d) that the continued operation of the housing accommodations would impose other undue hardship upon him. No certificate shall be issued under this section where the granting of the certificate is inconsistent with the purposes of the Act.

---

* So in original. Apparently should read "by".

PART 2105
PROHIBITIONS

(Statutory authority: L. 1950, ch. 250, as amd.)

Section 2105.1 General prohibitions. It shall be unlawful, regardless of any contract, lease or other obligation heretofore or hereafter entered into, for any person to demand or receive, any rent for any housing accommodations in excess of the maximum rent, or otherwise to do or omit to do any act, in violation of any regulation, order or requirement under the Act or this Subchapter, or to offer, solicit, attempt or agree to do any of the foregoing.

(a) The term *rent* as hereinbefore defined shall also include the payment by a tenant of a fee or rental commission to a landlord or to any person or real estate broker where such person or real estate broker is an agent or employee of the landlord or is employed by the landlord in connection with the operation of the building, or where such person or real estate broker manages the building in which the housing accommodation is located, or where the landlord or his employee refer the tenant to such person or real estate broker for the purpose of renting the housing accommodation. Where the landlord has listed the housing accommodation with such person or real estate broker for rental purposes such fact shall be prima facie evidence of the existence of an agency relationship between such other person or real estate broker and the landlord for the purposes of this section.

2105.2 Evasion. The maximum rents and other requirements provided in this Subchapter shall not be evaded, either directly or indirectly, in connection with the renting or leasing or the transfer of a lease of housing accommodations by requiring the tenant to pay, or obligate himself for membership or other fees, or by modification of the practices relating to payment of commissions or other charges, or by modification of the services furnished or required to be furnished with the housing accommodations, or otherwise.

2105.3 Purchase of property as condition of renting. (a) No person shall require a tenant or prospective tenant to purchase or agree to purchase furniture or any other property as a condition of renting housing accommodations.

(b) The term *person* as used in this section shall include an agent or any other employee of a landlord acting with or without the authority of his employer.

(c) The term *person* as used in this section shall also include a tenant in occupancy of housing accommodations who attempts to sell furniture or any other property to an incoming tenant.

2105.4 Term of occupancy. No tenant shall be required to change his term of occupancy; for example, a tenant on a monthly basis shall not be required to change to a weekly basis, and a tenant on a weekly basis shall not be required to change to a daily basis.

2105.5 Security deposits. [Additional statutory authority: L. 1964, ch. 244] Regardless of any contract, agreement, lease or other obligation heretofore or hereafter entered into, no person shall demand, receive or retain a security deposit for or in connection with the use and occupancy of housing accommodations, except (a) if the demand, collection, or retention of such security deposit was permitted under the rent regulations promulgated pursuant to the federal Act, and said security deposit does not exceed the rent for one month in addition to the authorized collection of rent; or (b) if the demand, collection, or retention of such security deposit was pursuant to a rental agreement with the tenant and said security deposit does not exceed the rent for one month (or for one week where the rental payment period is for a term of less than one month) in addition to the authorized collection of rent and provided (1) that said security deposit shall be deposited in an interest-bearing account in a banking organization on and after September 1, 1970; (2) the person depositing such security money shall be entitled to receive, as administration expenses, a sum equivalent to one percent per annum upon the security money so deposited; (3) the balance of the interest paid by the banking organization shall be held in trust until repaid or applied for the rental of the housing accommodations, or annually paid to the tenant; and (4) so long as the landlord complies with the provisions of section 7-103 of the General Obligations Law.

2105.6 Lease with option to buy. (a) Where a lease of housing accommodations was entered into prior to May 1, 1950, and the tenant, as a part of such lease or in connection therewith, was granted an option to buy the housing accommodations which were the subject of the lease, with the further provision that some or all of the payments made under the lease should be credited toward the purchase price in the event such option is exercised, the landlord, notwithstanding any other provision of this Subchapter, may be authorized to receive payment made by the tenant in accordance with the provisions of such lease and in excess of the maximum rent for such housing accommodations.

(1) Such authority may be secured only by a written request of the tenant to the local rent office and may be granted by order of the Administrator if he finds that such payments in excess of the maximum rent will not be inconsistent with the purposes of the Act or this Subchapter and would not be likely to result in the circumvention or evasion thereof.

(2) After entry of such order the landlord shall be authorized to demand, receive and retain, and the tenant shall be authorized to offer payments provided by the lease in excess of the maximum rent for periods commencing on or after May 1, 1950. After entry of such order, the provisions of the lease may be enforced in accordance with law, notwithstanding any other provision of this Subchapter.

(3) Nothing in this section shall be construed to authorize the landlord to demand or receive or the tenant to offer payments in excess of the maximum rent in the absence of an order of the Administrator as herein provided.

(b) Where a lease of housing accommodations has been entered into on or after May 1, 1950 and the tenant as a part of such lease or in connection therewith has been granted an option to buy the housing accommodations which are the subject of the lease, the landlord prior to the exercise by the tenant of the option to buy, shall not demand or receive nor shall the tenant offer payments in excess of the maximum rent, whether or not such lease allocates some portion or portions of the periodic payments therein provided as payment on or for the option to buy.

2105.7 Disclosure by employees. It shall be unlawful for any officer or employee of the commission, or for any official adviser or consultant to the commission, to disclose, otherwise than in the course of official duty, any information obtained under the Act, or to use any such information for personal benefit.

2105.8 Conduct with intent to cause the tenant to vacate. It shall be unlawful for any landlord or any person acting on his behalf, with intent to cause the tenant to vacate, to engage in any course of conduct (including, but not limited to, interruption or discontinuance of essential services) which interfere with or disturbs or is intended to interfere with or disturb the comfort, peace, repose or quiet of the tenant in his use or occupancy of the housing accommodations. (See section 10, subdivision 5 of the Act.)

PART 2106

ENFORCEMENT

(Statutory authority: L. 1950, ch. 250, as amd.)

Section 2106.1 Criminal penalties and civil actions.
(a) Any person who willfully violates any provision of section 10 of the Act, and any person who makes any statement or entry false in any material respect in any document or report required to be kept or filed under the Act or any regulation, order, or requirement thereunder, and any person who wilfully omits or neglects to make any material statement or entry required to be made in any such document or report, shall, upon conviction thereof, be subject to a fine of not more than $5,000, or to imprisonment for not more than two years in the case of a violation of subdivision 3 of section 10 of the Act and for not more than one year in all other cases, or to both such fine and imprisonment. (See Emergency Housing Rent Control Law, § 11, subd. 2.)

(b) If any landlord who receives rent from a tenant

violates a regulation or order prescribing a maximum rent with respect to the housing accommodations for which such rent is received from such tenant, the tenant paying such rent may, within two years from the date of the occurrence of the violation, bring an action against the landlord on account of the overcharge pursuant to subdivision 5 of section 11 of the Act. Under circumstances specified in that section of the Act, the Administrator may bring an action against the landlord for such overcharge. Where judgment is rendered in favor of the Administrator in such action, there shall be paid over to the tenant from the moneys recovered one third of such recovery, exclusive of costs and disbursements.

(c) If any landlord who receives rent from a tenant violates any order containing a directive that rent collected by the landlord in excess of the maximum rent be refunded to the tenant within 30 days, the Administrator may, within one year after the expiration of such 30-day period or after such order shall become final as such term is defined in subdivision (m) of section 2100.2, *supra*, bring an action against the landlord on account of the failure of the landlord to make the prescribed refund pursuant to subdivision 6 of section 11 of the Act. Under circumstances specified in that section of the Act, the tenant may bring an action against the landlord for such failure to refund. Where judgment is rendered in favor of the Administrator in such action, there shall be paid over to the tenant from the moneys recovered one third of such recovery, exclusive of costs and disbursements.

(d) Where after the Administrator has granted a certificate of eviction certifying that the landlord may pursue his remedies pursuant to local law to acquire possession, and a tenant voluntarily removes from a housing accommodation or has been removed therefrom by action or proceeding to evict from or recover possession of a housing accommodation upon the ground that the landlord seeks in good faith to recover possession of such accommodations (1) for his immediate and personal use, or for the immediate and personal use by a member or members of his immediate family, and such landlord or members of his immediate family shall fail to occupy such accommodations within 30 days after the tenant vacates, or such landlord shall lease or rent such space or permit occupancy thereof by a third person within a period of one year after such removal of the tenant, or (2) for the immediate purpose of withdrawing such housing accommodations from the rental market and such landlord shall lease or sell the housing accommodation or the space previously occupied thereby, or permit use thereof in a manner other than contemplated in such eviction certificate within a period of one year after such removal of the tenant, or (3) for the immediate purpose of altering or remodeling such housing accommodations, and the landlord shall fail to start the work of alteration or remodeling of such housing accommodations within 90 days after such removal on the ground that he required possession of such accommodations for the purpose of altering or remodeling the same, or if after having commenced such work shall fail or neglect to prosecute the work with reasonable diligence, or (4) for the immediate purpose of demolishing such housing accommodations and constructing a new building or structure for a greater number of housing accommodations in accordance with approved plans, or reasonable amendment thereof, and the landlord has failed to complete the demolition within six months after the removal of the last tenant or, having demolished the premises, has failed or neglected to proceed with the new construction within 90 days after the completion of such demolition or (5) for some purpose other than those specified above for which the removal of the tenant was sought and the landlord has failed to use the vacated premises for such purpose, such landlord shall unless for good cause shown, be liable to the tenant for three times the damages sustained on account of such removal plus reasonable attorney's fees and costs as determined by the court; provided, however, that paragraph (4) herein shall not apply to any action which does not constitute a violation of any local law providing for penalties upon failure to demolish or comply with State rent control eviction certificates. In addition to any other damage, the cost of removal of property shall be a lawful measure of damage. (See Emergency Housing Rent Control Law, § 5, subd. 6.)

RENT AND EVICTION REGULATIONS

(e) (1) Any tenant who has vacated his housing accommodations because the landlord or any person acting on his behalf, with intent to cause the tenant to vacate, engaged in any course of conduct (including, but not limited to, interruption or discontinuance of essential services) which interfered with or disturbed or was intended to interfere with or disturb the comfort, repose, peace or quiet of the tenant in his use or occupancy of the housing accommodations may, within 90 days after vacating, apply to the Administrator for a determination that the housing accommodations were vacated as a result of such conduct, and may, within one year after such determination, institute a civil action against the landlord by reason of such conduct. In such action the landlord shall be liable to the tenant for three times the damages sustained on account of such conduct plus reasonable attorney's fees and costs as determined by the court. In addition to any other damages the cost of removal of property shall be a lawful measure of damages (See section 11 subdivision 7 of the Act.)

(2) The State Rent Administrator shall institute a proceeding to determine that housing accommodations were vacated because the landlord or any person acting on his behalf engaged in such course of conduct as is described in the preceding paragraph of this subdivision by forwarding to all parties affected, a notice setting forth the proposed action. A person who has been served with notice in such a proceeding shall have seven days from the date of mailing of the notice in which to answer. Every answer must be verified, and an original and one copy shall be filed with the State Rent Administrator. The State Rent Administrator may thereafter issue an appropriate order determining whether the housing accommodations were vacated as a result of such course of conduct, and whether the housing accommodations are subject to control. A copy of any order issued shall be forwarded to all parties to the proceeding.

2106.2 Inspection and records. (a) Any person who rents or offers for rent, or acts as a broker or agent for the rental of any housing accommodations shall, as the Administrator may from time to time require, furnish information under oath or affirmation or otherwise, permit inspection and copying of records and other documents and permit inspection of any such housing accommodations.

(b) Any person who rents or offers for rent, or acts as a broker or agent for the rental of any housing accommodations shall, as the Administrator may from time to time require, make and keep records and other documents and make reports.

PART 2107

PROCEEDINGS BEFORE LOCAL RENT ADMINISTRATOR

(Statutory authority: L. 1950, ch. 250, as amd.)

Section 2107.1 Proceedings instituted by landlord or tenant in the local rent office. A proceeding is instituted in a local rent office by a landlord or a tenant with the filing of an application for adjustment of rent, for a certificate of eviction, or for other relief provided by the Act or this Subchapter. Such application shall be verified by the applicant and filed with the local rent administrator for the area within which the housing accommodation is located upon the appropriate form issued by the Administrator in accordance with the instructions contained in such forms.

2107.2 Proceedings instituted by the local rent administrator on his own initiative. The local rent administrator may institute a proceeding on his own initiative whenever he deems it necessary or appropriate pursuant to the Act or this Subchapter.

2107.3 Notice to the parties affected. (a) Where the application is made by a landlord or tenant the local rent administrator shall forward, as promptly as possible, a copy of such application by mail to the person or persons affected thereby.

(b) Where the proceeding is instituted by the local rent administrator on his own initiative, he shall forward to all parties affected thereby a notice setting forth the proposed action.

Rent and Eviction Regulations

2107.4 Answer. A person who has been served with a copy of an application or a notice of a proceeding shall have seven days from the date of mailing in which to answer, except that a tenant shall have 15 days from the date of mailing within which to answer where the application was made pursuant to paragraph (5) of subdivision (b) of section 2102.3, *supra*. Every answer must be verified, and an original and one copy shall be filed with the local rent administrator.

2107.5 Action by local rent administrator. At any stage of a proceeding the local rent administrator may:

(a) reject the application if it is insufficient or defective;

(b) make such investigation of the facts, hold such conferences, and require the filing of such reports, evidence, affidavits, or other material relevant to the proceeding;

(c) forward to or make available for inspection by either party any relevant evidence and afford an opportunity to file rebuttal thereto;

(d) for good cause shown accept for filing any papers, even though not filed within the time required by this Subchapter;

(e) require any person to appear or produce documents or both pursuant to a subpoena issued by the Administrator;

(f) consolidate two or more applications or proceedings which have at least one ground in common;

(g) forward to either party a notice of action proposed to be taken by the local rent administrator;

(h) grant or order a hearing.

2107.6 Final determination by the local rent administrator. (a) The local rent administrator, on such terms and conditions as he may determine, may:

(1) dismiss the application if it fails substantially to comply with the provisions of the Act or this Subchapter;

(2) grant or deny the application, in whole or in part;

(3) issue an appropriate order in a proceeding instituted on his own initiative.

(b) A copy of any order issued shall be forwarded to all parties to the proceeding.

2107.7 Pending proceedings. Where a section is amended during the pendency of a proceeding before the local rent administrator, the determination shall be in accordance with the amended section unless the proceeding is to determine an adjustment of maximum rent and was remanded to the local rent administrator for further action as provided in section 2108.9, *infra*. In such event the local rent administrator shall determine the remanded proceeding in accordance with the section in effect on the date of issuance of the original order by the local rent administrator.

2107.8 Modification or revocation of orders. [Additional statutory authority: L. 1964, ch. 244] (a) Except as provided in subdivisions (a) or (b) of this section or except pursuant to an order of remand issued by the State Rent Administrator, the local rent administrator may not modify, supersede or revoke any order issued under these or previous sections unless he finds that such order was the result of illegality, irregularity in vital matters, or fraud. Where an order is modified, superseded or revoked by the local rent administrator he may also direct that rent collected by the landlord in excess of the maximum rent be refunded to the tenant within 30 days after his action shall become final.

(b) The local rent administrator on his own initiative or on application of a tenant may revoke or cancel an order granting a certificate of eviction at any time prior to the execution of a warrant in a summary proceeding to recover possession of real property by a court whenever he finds that:

(1) the certificate of eviction was obtained by fraud or illegality; or

(2) the landlord's intentions or circumstances have so changed that the premises, possession of which is sought, will not be used for the purpose specified in the certificate.

(c) The commencement of a proceeding by the local rent administrator to revoke or cancel an order granting a certificate of eviction shall stay such order until the final determination of the proceeding regardless of whether the waiting period in the order has already expired.

Rent and Eviction Regulations

(d) The local rent administrator shall give notice to the persons affected of his intention to modify, supersede or revoke an order, in which event the provisions of sections 2107.2 through 2107.6, inclusive, shall apply.

PART 2108

PROTESTS

(Statutory authority: L. 1950, ch. 250, as amd.)

Section 2108.1 Persons who may file protests. (a) Any person aggrieved by this Subchapter or by an order issued by a local rent administrator may file a protest to the Administrator in the manner provided in this Subchapter.

(b) A joint protest, verified by each person joining therein, may be filed by two or more landlords or tenants, where at least one ground is common to all persons so filing. The Administrator, in his discretion, may treat such protest as joint or several.

(c) The Administrator may, in his discretion, consolidate two or more protests which have at least one ground in common.

2108.2 Time for filing protests. (a) A protest against any provision of this Subchapter may be filed at any time after the effective date thereof.

(b) A protest against an order of a local rent administrator must be filed with the Administrator within 33 days after the date such order is issued unless subdivision (c) of this section is applicable. A protest served by mail, postmarked not more than 33 days after the date of such order, shall be compliance with this subdivision.

(c) A protest may be filed by a tenant against an order of a local rent administrator granting a certificate of eviction relating to a housing accommodation other than in a one- or two-family house after the expiration of the 33-day period provided for in subdivision (b) of this section and prior to the date of the issuance of a final order by a court in summary dispossess proceedings, where there has been a change of circumstances due to the fact that other suitable housing accommodations subject to landlord's control have become vacant since the date of the order granting the certificate of eviction.

2108.3 Time of filing answer to protests. Where a protest against an order issued by a local rent administrator has been filed by a landlord or tenant, the other party or parties shall be afforded a period of 15 days from the date of service of such protest within which to serve and file an answer to the protest.

2108.4 Form and content of protest against this Subchapter or portion thereof. [Additional statutory authority: L. 1964, ch. 244] No printed form of protest is provided or prescribed. Each protest against this Subchapter or portion thereof must be clearly designated "Protest to the Commissioner of Housing and Community Renewal re Section .... (or Sections ....) of the Rent and Eviction Regulations", and shall set forth the following:

(a) the name and post-office address of the party filing the protest, and whether he is a landlord or tenant, or representative;

(b) a complete identification of the provision or provisions protested, citing the section or sections of this Subchapter to which the objection is made;

(c) a simple, concise statement of the objections to this Subchapter or portion thereof protested;

(d) a specific statement of the relief requested;

(e) each protest shall be verified by the party filing the protest.

2108.5 Form and content of protest against an order of the local rent administrator. [Additional statutory authority: L. 1964, ch. 244] No printed form of protest is provided or prescribed. Each protest must be clearly designated "Protest to the Commissioner of Housing and Community Renewal re Order bearing docket number ....", and shall set forth the following:

(a) the name and post-office address of the party filing the protest, and whether he is the landlord or tenant of the accommodations involved or a representative;

(b) a complete identification of the order to which

objection is made, the date of issuance thereof, the docket number, and the name of the local rent office;

(c) the location by post-office address of all housing accommodations involved in the protest;

(d) the names and post-office addresses of all other parties affected by the protest;

(e) a simple, concise statement of the objections to the order protested;

(f) a specific statement of the relief requested;

(g) a statement informing the person served with the protest that he may within 15 days from the date of such service, file thereto a verified answer by filing the same with the Commissioner of Housing and Community Renewal, Office of Rent Administration, 393 Seventh Avenue, New York 1, New York, together with proof of service of the copy of the answer upon the party filing the protest;

(h) each protest shall be verified by the party filing the protest;

(i) each such protest shall contain proof of service of (1) a copy of the protest and (2) copies of all accompanying papers upon the local rent administrator and and upon all parties affected by the protest.

2108.6 Service and filing of protests. [Additional statutory authority: L. 1964, ch. 244] (a) Each protest shall be filed in an original and one copy at the Division of Housing and Community Renewal, Office of Rent Administration, 393 Seventh Avenue, New York 1, New York.

(b) Where the protest is against an order issued by the local rent administrator, a copy of the protest shall also be served on the local rent administrator issuing the order being protested, and upon each party affected by the protest.

(c) A protest under section 2108.5 will not be accepted for filing unless accompanied by an affidavit or other proof of such service.

2108.7 Time of filing answer to protest. Any person served with a protest as provided in subdivision (b) of section 2108.6 may, within 15 days from the date of service, file a verified answer thereto, by filing the same with the Administrator, together with proof of service of a copy thereof upon the party filing the protest. The Administrator may, in his discretion, and for good cause shown, extend the time within which to answer.

2108.8 Action by Administrator. Within a reasonable time after the filing of the protest and the answers, if any, the Administrator may:

(a) reject the protest if it is insufficient or defective;

(b) make such investigation of the facts, hold such conferences, and require the filing of such reports, evidence, affidavits, or other material relevant to the proceeding;

(c) forward to or make available for inspection by either party any relevant evidence and afford an opportunity to file rebuttal thereto;

(d) for good cause shown accept for filing any papers, even though not filed within the time required by this Subchapter;

(e) require any person to appear or produce documents or both pursuant to a subpoena issued by the Administrator;

(f) grant or order a hearing.

2108.9 Final determination by the Administrator. The Administrator, on such terms and conditions as he may determine, may:

(a) dismiss the protest if it fails substantially to comply with the provisions of the Act or this Subchapter;

(b) grant or deny the protest, in whole or in part, or remand the proceeding to the local rent administrator for further action;

(c) in the event that the Administrator denies any such protest in whole or in part, the Administrator shall inform the party or parties filing the protest of the grounds upon which such decision is based, and of any economic data and other facts of which the Administrator has taken official notice.

2108.10 Pending protests and remit proceedings. Where a section is amended during the pendency of a protest or a proceeding remitted by a court after judicial review, the determination shall be in accordance with the amended section unless it is a determination of an adjustment of maximum rent, in which event the determination shall be in accordance with the section in effect on the date of issuance of the original order by the local rent administrator.

2108.11 Time within which the Administrator shall take final action. (a) If the Administrator does not act finally within a period of 90 days after a protest if* filed, or within such extended period as may be fixed by the Administrator with the consent of the party filing the protest, the protest shall be deemed to be denied.

(b) If the Administrator does not act finally within a period of 90 days after the entry of an order of remand to the Administrator by the court in a proceeding pursuant to section 2108.13, *infra,* or within such extended period as may be fixed by the Administrator with the consent of the party filing the petition for review under article 78 of the Civil Practice Act, the order previously made by the Administrator shall be deemed reaffirmed.

2108.12 Stays. (a) The filing of a protest against an order, other than an order adjusting, fixing or establishing a maximum rent, within 33 days after the date of the issuance of such order shall stay such order until the final determination of the protest by the Administrator. Where the protest is against an order granting a certificate of eviction it shall stay such order as herein provided regardless of whether the waiting period provided in the order has already expired.

(b) The commencement of a proceeding by the Administrator to revoke or cancel an order granting a certificate of eviction shall stay such order until the final determination of the proceeding regardless of whether the waiting period in the order has already expired.

2108.13 Judicial review. [Additional statutory authority: L. 1964, ch. 244] The filing and determination of a protest is a prerequisite to obtaining judicial review of any provision of this Subchapter or any order issued

---

* So in original. Apparently should read "is".

thereunder, except as provided by section 8 of the Act. A proceeding for review may be instituted under article 78 of the Civil Practice Law and Rules provided the petition is filed within 30 days after the final determination of the protest. Service of the petition upon the Division of Housing and Community Renewal shall be made by leaving a copy thereof with the division's Office of Rent Administration at 393 Seventh Avenue, New York 1, New York.

2108.14 Modification or revocation of orders on protest. [Additional statutory authority: L. 1964, ch. 244] The commissioner, on application of either party or on his own initiative, and upon notice to all parties affected, may, prior to the date that a petition for judicial review has been commenced in the Supreme Court pursuant to article 78 of the Civil Practice Law and Rules, modify, supersede or revoke any order issued by him under these or previous regulations where he finds that such order was the result of illegality, irregularity in vital matters, or fraud. Where an order is modified, superseded or revoked by the commissioner he may also direct that all rent collected by the landlord and/or by predecessor and successor landlords in excess of the maximum rent be refunded to the tenant within 30 days.

2108.15 Protests against an order of the State Rent Administrator. Any person aggrieved by an order issued under this Subchapter by the State Rent Administrator may file a protest to the State Commissioner of Housing and Community Renewal in the same manner as provided in this Subchapter for the filing of a protest against an order of a Local Rent Administrator.

PART 2109

MISCELLANEOUS PROCEDURAL MATTERS

(Statutory authority: L. 1950, ch. 250, as amd.)

Section 2109.1 When a notice or paper shall be deemed served. (a) Notices, orders, protests, answers and other papers may be served personally or by mail. When service is made personally or by mail an affidavit by the person making the service or mailing shall constitute sufficient proof of service. When service is by registered mail the return post office receipt shall constitute sufficient proof of service.

(b) In any proceedings under this Subchapter any notice, order or other process or paper directed to the person named as landlord on the registration statement on file in the local rent office, at the mailing address given thereon, or where a notice of change of identity has been filed in the local rent office, to the person named therein as landlord and at the address given in such notice of change of identity most recently filed, shall constitute notice to such landlord.

(c) Where a notice of appearance has been filed by an attorney, service on the attorney shall be deemed proper service as if made on the party or parties represented.

2109.2 Power of subpoena. The Administrator or any officer or agent designated by the Administrator, may administer oaths and affirmations and may, whenever necessary, by subpoena require any person to appear and testify or to appear and produce documents, or both, at any designated place.

2109.3 Production of documents. The production of a person's documents at any place other than his place of business shall not be required in any case in which, prior to the return date specified in the subpoena issued with respect thereto, such person either has furnished the Administrator with a copy of such documents certified by such person under oath to be a true and correct copy, or has entered into a stipulation with the Administrator as to the information contained in such documents.

2109.4 Action by commission on failure to obey subpoena. In case of contumacy or refusal to obey a subpoena served upon any person, the supreme court in, or for any judicial district in which such person is found or resides or transacts business upon application by the Administrator, shall have jurisdiction to issue an order requiring such person to appear and give testimony or to appear and produce documents, or both; and any failure to obey such order of the court may be punished by such court as a contempt thereof.

2109.5 Privilege against self-incrimination. No person shall be excused from attending and testifying or from producing documents or other evidence in obedience to the subpoena of the Administrator or of any duly authorized officer or agent thereof, on the ground that the testimony or evidence required of him may tend to incriminate him or subject him to a penalty or forfeiture, but no person shall be prosecuted or subjected to any penalty or forfeiture for or on account of any transaction, matter or thing concerning which he is compelled, after having claimed his privilege against self-incrimination, to testify or produce evidence, except that such person so testifying shall not be exempt from prosecution and punishment for perjury committed in so testifying. The immunity herein provided shall extend only to natural persons so compelled to testify.

2109.6 Disclosure of information by the Administrator. The Administrator shall not publish or disclose any information obtained under the Act or this Subchapter that the Administrator deems confidential or with reference to which a request for confidential treatment is made by the person furnishing such information, unless the Administrator determines that the withholding thereof is contrary to the public interest.

2109.7 Delegation of authority. The Administrator may delegate in writing to the local rent administrator, or any other person or persons, the authority to carry out any of the duties and powers granted to him by the Act or this Subchapter.

2109.8 Opinions and official interpretations. (a) Official interpretations of general applicability with respect to the provisions of the Act or this Subchapter shall be issued only by the Administrator. No interpretation shall be given in response to any hypothetical question.

(b) Any person desiring an opinion as to the applicability of the Act or this Subchapter to a specific factual situation, shall make a request in writing for such opinion to the local rent administrator for the locality within which the housing accommodations involved are situated. Such request shall set forth in full the facts out of which the question arises and shall state the name and post-office address of the person or persons making the request and the location of the housing accommodations involved. If there is a pending or closed proceeding in the particular office, or if the inquirer has previously requested an opinion on the same or substantially the same facts, his request shall so indicate. No opinion shall be given in response to any hypothetical question.

(c) Any opinion or official interpretation shall remain in full force and effect unless and until revoked or modified in writing by the official issuing it or by the Administrator.

ADVISORY BULLETINS OF THE STATE RENT ADMINISTRATOR

These Bulletins were issued and published prior to the filing of the Rent and Eviction Regulations with the Secretary of State, and accordingly, the section numbers of the Regulations referred to in the Bulletins are different from the section numbers of the filed Regulations. To enable the reader to find the Regulation referred to in the Bulletin, the following chart gives the corresponding section number in the filed Regulations with the section number in the Bulletins.

Bulletin Section Number	Filed Section Number
2(2)	2100.2
2(3)	2100.2(c)
2(7)	2100.2(g)
3	2100.3
3(8)	2100.3(h)
9	2100.9
9(1)	2100.9(a)
9(8)	2100.9(h)
9(10)	2100.9(j)
9(11)	2100.9(k)
9(12)	2100.9(l)
9(13)	2100.9(m)
9(14)	2100.9(n)
9(15)	2100.9(o)
10	2100.10
10(2)	2100.10(b)
10(3)	2100.10(c)
12(3)	2100.12
13	2100.13
15	2100.15
21	2101.1
21(1)	2101.1(c)
21(2)	2101.1(b)
21(4)	2101.1(d)
23	2101.3
24	2101.4

ADVISORY BULLETINS

Bulletin Section Number	Filed Section Number
33	2102.3
33(1)	2102.3(a)
33(1)(c)	2102.3(b)(1)(iii)
33(1)(d)	2102.3(b)(1)(iv)
33(2)	2102.3(b)(2)
33(2)(b)	2102.3(b)(2)(ii)
33(3)	2102.3(b)(3)
33(4)	2102.3(b)(4)
33(5)	2102.3(b)(5)
33(6)	2102.3(b)(6)
33(7)	2102.3(b)(7)
34	2102.4
34(2)	2102.4(b)
34(3)	2102.4(c)
35	2102.5
35(1)	2102.5(a)
36	2102.6
36(a)	2102.6(c)
42	2103.2
43	2103.3
51	2104.1
51(2)	2104.1(b)
52	2104.2
52(1)	2104.2(a)
52(3)	2104.2(c)
53	2104.3
54	2104.4
54(2)	2104.4(b)
54(4)	2104.4(d)
54(5)	2104.4(e)
55	2104.5
55(1)	2104.5(a)
55(3)	2104.5(c)
55(4)	2104.5(d)
56	2104.6
57	2104.7
59	2104.9
59(2)	2104.9(b)
61	2105.1
62	2105.2
63	2105.3
95	2108.5

ADVISORY BULLETIN No. 1

(Issued April 16, 1956)

INSTRUCTIONS TO LANDLORDS FOR THE PREPARATION OF APPLICATIONS AND REPORTS

General Instructions

(1) **Use the right form.** In order to simplify the selection of the right form the Commission has keyed the form number to the section of the Regulations under which the application is made. An application for an increase of maximum rent pursuant to Section 33(3) of the Regulations should be made on Form 33(3). An application for a prior opinion pursuant to Section 33(1) of the Regulations should similarly be made on Form 33(1)PO. The "PO" is an added key that the form deals with prior opinions. In other situations descriptive symbols are used to indicate the use to which the form should be made.

As a further aid in the selection of the proper form a description of its use is set forth in the title. Form 33(1) is entitled "Landlord's Application for Increase of Maximum Rent (Substantial Rehabilitation; Major Capital Improvements; or Other Improvements)". This indicates that it is to be used for applications pursuant to Section 33(1) of the Regulations where the requested increase is based upon either a substantial rehabilitation, major capital improvement or other improvement.

If you will be guided by the fact that the form number is keyed to the section of the Regulations involved and that the title of the form is descriptive of its use, you will have little difficulty in selecting the form that fits your needs.

(2) **Supply all required information.** Applications are rejected if essential information is lacking. This not only delays you because you will be required to refile a proper application; but, in addition wastes our time. Use care in

Advisory Bulletins

preparing your applications in order that we may be able to serve you better.

Particular attention should be given to the blank spaces on the form. Complete all required information. In all cases the address and description of the housing accommodations involved must be clearly stated. The identification or description of the housing accommodations must correspond with the identification used on the registration statement on file with the Local Rent Office. It is also imperative to complete the information concerning the name and mailing address of both the landlord and tenant. In addition each form contains instructions. Read these instructions carefully and supply the information required. Remember care used at the outset will reduce delays to a minimum—the result will be an expeditious determination of your application.

(3) **Notarize your application before filing.** Before filing your application you are required to sign the original and all copies. Only the original application need be sworn to before a Notary Public or other person authorized to administer oaths. The Commission has assigned personnel to each Local Rent Office for your convenience who are authorized to administer oaths. No charge is made for this service.

(4) **File the correct number of copies.** The original application and at least one extra copy, together with accompanying documents, if any, must be filed. In addition the landlord is required to file an additional copy of the application for each housing accommodation affected by the application. *There are filing instructions on each form. Check these instructions carefully before filing.*

(5) **File at the correct Local Rent Office.** File the application either by delivery or mailing to the Local Rent Office servicing the premises involved in the application. You will avoid delay by filing in the proper office. Section 8 of the Regulations defines the areas under the jurisdiction of the indicated Local Rent Offices.

Applications under Section 33(1) of the Regulations for Increased Services, etc.

(6) **Use the right form.** Application for rent increases pursuant to Section 33(1) of the Regulations are based

upon different grounds. This particular section has four subdivisions. Where it is based upon a substantial increase in dwelling space, or an increase in the services, furniture, furnishings or equipment provided in the housing accommodations, or where the tenant has accepted and is obtaining the benefit of increased services, furniture, furnishings or equipment, you should use Form 33(1)C—"Landlord's Application for Increase of Maximum Rent (Increased Services or Facilities)". On the other hand, where it is based upon a substantial rehabilitation, major capital improvements or other improvements, you should use Form 33(1)—"Landlord's Application for Increase of Maximum Rent (Substantial Rehabilitation, Major Capital Improvements, or Other Improvements)". Where a prior opinion as to whether specified work would result in a major capital improvement or a substantial rehabilitation, within the meaning of Section 33(1) (b or c) of the Regulations, is desired, Form 33(1)PO—"Landlord's Application for Prior Opinion (Substantial Rehabilitation or Major Capital Improvement)"—should be used.

(7) **File application after the work is done.** The Commission no longer grants rent increases on an agreement to install or on an offer to install a new service or equipment item. Unless you are making an application for a prior opinion, the new service or facility must be added or installed before the application is filed. The only exception to the requirement that the work must be completed before the application is filed is the case where there has been a major capital improvement or a substantial rehabilitation of the property and the work has been substantially completed. In such a case the applications will be accepted prior to final completion of the work and the issuance of any required certificate from the local authorities having jurisdiction.

(8) **Specify the added service or facility.** On the application, in the space provided for the landlord's statement, give enough information to justify the relief requested. If the present maximum rent includes a sink, for example, it is not enough just to say that you have installed a sink. You should also show that you are installing a new modern sink in place of an old or obsolete sink. Specify the type of sink previously supplied

Advisory Bulletins

and the new sink in order to show that you have now given your tenant a larger or better grade sink. It is not enough merely to state the name of the new equipment that you install. You must state the date of installation, size or dimensions of the equipment where this bears upon the rental value, and the cost.

(9) **Check the Commission's Schedule of Rental Values.** The Commission has published a Schedule of Rental Values which covers the usual items of equipment supplied to tenants by landlords. From time to time this schedule is revised. Make sure that you have the latest issue of this important table; and refer to it before preparing your application. In some instances the rent increase is based upon size, capacity, cost, or other variable factors.

Other Applications

(10) **Eviction Certificate Applications.** There are six different forms of applications for eviction certificates (Forms 54, 55, 56, 57, 58 and 59), corresponding to the six separate sections of the Regulations which relate to these certificates. The form number on the application form that you use is keyed to the section number of the Regulations. Make sure that you use the right form. Additional statements may be added to any of these forms. If you file under more than one ground, you can use the form that primarily covers your situation, and add a rider which covers the other ground for relief. In applying for eviction certificates, sufficient copies of the application must be filed, according to the number of tenants and subtenants against whom you want to bring eviction proceedings. This may be a larger number than the actual number of apartments involved. Check the form for filing instructions. Adherence to these instructions will facilitate the processing of your application.

(11) **Increases on Financial Grounds.** Applications for increases on the ground of insufficient annual return [Form 33(5)], or on the ground of unavoidable increases in operating costs in small structures [Form 33(6)], or on the ground of increased costs in hotels, rooming houses, or cooperative apartments [Form 33(7)], require detailed financial data. In preparing the figures you should consult

the separate instruction booklet issued by the Commission with the application form. The booklet gives instructions by item numbers corresponding to the items on the application blank.

(12) **Lease Reports.** No application is needed to obtain an increase resulting from the execution of a two-year lease. But you must file a Report of Lease [Form 33(2)] to record the increased rent at the Local Rent Office of the Rent Commission. *The report is to be filed within 30 days after the tenant delivers the signed lease to the landlord.*

(13) **Report of Statutory Decontrol.** In 1953 two additional grounds for decontrol were added to the Rent Law. One of these applies to the rental of a vacant unit in a one- or two-family house on or after April 1, 1953. The other applies to the rental after April 1, 1953 of a unit which had been occupied by the owner himself, for at least one year before renting, or at least two years if the owner obtained possession by a certificate of eviction. In either case an application for decontrol is not required, but a report (Form 42) must be filed with the Local Rent Office within thirty days after the date of first rental after decontrol. The report is helpful in that it shows the essential conditions necessary for decontrol in each case. Filing the report with the Local Rent Office may also avoid unnecessary processing of tenant complaints.

(14) **Decontrol Application.** The application for decontrol (Form 11) is used when a structural change has been made on or after May 1, 1950 to alter housing units into a greater number of self-contained units. This is the only ground for permanent decontrol that requires an application by the landlord. When you file the application, you can save time by submitting the substantiating evidence. This includes details of the construction work; a copy of the approved plans or a sketch to show the layout before and after the alteration; and a copy of the certificate of occupancy or other approval from the City Department of Housing and Buildings. If you claim decontrol on another ground you may still apply for an order from the Rent Commission pursuant to Section 36(a) of the Regulations, to avoid uncertainty and the possibility of an adverse court decision. No printed application form is available in such a case. Use ordinary paper and follow Form 11 as a

Advisory Bulletins

guide. If you claim exemption from control by reason of a commercial or professional renting of controlled housing accommodations on or after May 1, 1955, you must first obtain an order from the Rent Commission pursuant to Section 13 of the Regulations. Use Form 13—"Application for Order Exempting Housing Accommodations from Control." The housing accommodations need not be rented prior to the filing of the application. The application must be executed by both the landlord and the prospective tenant. Follow all instructions indicated on this form.

(15) **To discontinue a service.** You must obtain permission in advance from the Rent Commission to discontinue a service in an occupied housing accommodation. An application for such approval is filed on Form 35(1). For example, to discontinue the service of manual operation of elevators by installing automatic elevators, it is necessary to first obtain permission by filing on Form 35(1).

You may discontinue providing a service or equipment item before renting a vacant apartment. It is unnecessary to get permission from the Commission, but you must file a report (Form 35) within 10 days after renting. The Commission will then decide whether to order a rent reduction. If you rent the apartment under a two-year lease which provides for a rent increase, you must certify that all essential services required to be furnished are actually furnished and will be furnished so long as the increase remains in effect.

If a landlord discontinues a service in a vacant apartment without filing the report on time, or if a landlord discontinues a service in an occupied housing accommodation without first obtaining permission, the Rent Commission may reduce the rent *retroactively* to the time of discontinuance of the service.

(16) **First renting after employee occupancy.** If an apartment has been occupied rent-free by an employee, manager or stockholder ever since the beginning of rent control, it may now be rented as a "first-rent." This means that the first controlled rent for the apartment can be set by the landlord. This rent may be reduced if considered unreasonably high by the Commission. The landlord files a "first-rent" Registration Statement (Form

S-1) within 15 days after first renting. Neither an application nor a Report of Lease is filed since there is no existing maximum rent to be increased. On the Registration Statement the landlord indicates the reason that the apartment was never before under rent control. If the Registration Statement is not filed on time, the Rent Commission may fix a rent retroactively to the date of renting under Section 36 of the Regulations.

(17) **Report of change of landlord.** The Rent Commission requires a report to be filed whenever there is a change in identify of landlord (Form 44). If the new landlord does not file the report, the Rent Commission may send notices of tenant complaints to the last landlord indicated by its records. Any reduction order issued in that way may be binding on the present landlord. By filing the report, the new landlord may also obtain from the Rent Commission a certification of the legal rents as they appear in the records of the Local Rent Office. To obtain the certification, file with the report a rent roll in duplicate, listing each apartment, the name of the tenant, and the present rent charged. The Local Rent Office will then certify one copy of this rent roll and return it to you.

Grounds for an Increase in Maximum Rent

The following highlights important grounds for increase of maximum rent to small landlords, and mentions others. If you find you have a ground for an increase, obtain the necessary forms from the Local Rent Office and request any Advisory Bulletin published by the Rent Commission in respect thereto.

All grounds for an increase are contained in Section 33 of the Regulations, and the forms for applications for increase are numbered to correspond with the paragraph number in which the ground appears.

(1) Increased Services—Major Capital Improvements; Substantial Rehabilitation.

Section 33(1) gives a landlord a right to obtain an increase in maximum rent when he has increased the services or facilities to the tenant, or has made major capital improvements required for the operation, preservation or maintenance of the structure, or has substantially rehabilitated the property, thus adding to its rental value or appreciably prolonging its life.

Obtain the most recent Rental Value Schedule from your Local Rent Office which shows the maximum amounts allowed for increases of those items having fixed rental values. For those items where there has been a major capital improvement in an entire structure or a substantial rehabilitation, the rental value in many cases is determined by amortizing the cost over seven years and allowing rent increases to cover the yearly amortization.

(2) Voluntary Leases.

Section 33(2) gives a landlord the right to obtain up to a 15% increase over the existing maximum rent, by granting a tenant a lease for two years. However, where a prior voluntary lease was executed which provided for a full 15% rent increase no further voluntary lease may be entered into until at least the first year of the previous lease has expired. In such a case a new lease may be entered into for the unexpired remainder of the first two years of the original lease plus two years. The further rent increase may not become effective before the expiration of the first two years of the original lease. For instance, if a housing unit had a maximum rent of $100.00 per month and this was increased by a voluntary lease to $115.00 per month with a term which began on March 1, 1955 and was to terminate on February 28, 1957, no new lease increase could be obtained prior to March 1, 1956. On or after March 1, 1956 a landlord could enter into a new lease for a term expiring no sooner than February 28, 1959 with the rent remaining at $115.00 per month until February 28, 1957 and the 15% increase, or whatever lesser amount the tenant agreed to pay, would become effective on March 1, 1957.

If the prior lease did not provide for a full 15% increase, but only for a 10% increase, and increased the maximum rent from $100.00 per month to $110.00 per month, the landlord and tenant can enter into a new voluntary lease which would increase the maximum rent to $115.00 per month until February 28, 1957 and then provide for an additional increase of not more than 15% above the $110.00 maximum rent for the two years commencing March 1, 1957. If the prior lease did not provide for a full 15% increase, but only for a 10% increase, and increased the maximum rent from $100.00 per month to $110.00 per month, the only voluntary lease that the landlord and tenant could enter into before the expiration of the first year of the original lease would be one which would increase the rent from $110.00 to $115.00 and which would provide for a minimum term of two years.

If increased services are given at the time a lease is made and are part of one transaction, the landlord is not entitled to obtain a 15% increase on top of an increase for the additional services. For example, where the maximum rent is $40.00 and is to be increased by lease by 15% to $46.00, and the landlord is also going to supply a new refrigerator for $3.00, the lease should be for $49.00. The lease report filed on Form 33(1)CL will show the facts, and an order will be made increasing the rent for the increased services appearing thereon. The lease should contain a clause that the rent of $49.00 includes a new refrigerator or any other service included in a lease rent. The Rent Commission's Advisory Bulletin No. 12 further clarifies the provisions of this section.

(3) Subletting and Increased Occupancy.

Section 33(3) permits an increase for subletting and increased occupancy—specifically, where (a) there has been an increase in the number of subtenants since March 1, 1950 or (b) there has been an increase in the number of adult occupants since March 1, 1950 who are not members of the immediate family of the tenant. Those who may be considered members of the immediate family are mother, father, son, step-son, son-in-law, daughter, step-daughter, daughter-in-law, father-in-law and mother-in-law.

(4) Peculiar Circumstances.

Section 33(4) permits an increase where the maximum rent in effect on March 1, 1950 was below comparable rents because of unique or peculiar circumstances. For example, a mother who owned a house may have rented a $100.00 apartment to a son for $50.00. It would be unfair to compel the landlord to rent this apartment to a stranger for $50.00. This type of case is now rare because

Advisory Bulletins

such a provision was in the Federal Law and has been in effect for five years under the State Law. (See Advisory Bulletin No. 8.)

(5) Net Annual Return.

Section 33(5) authorizes a landlord to apply for a rent adjustment to bring the return on his property to an amount equal to 6% of the valuation of the property. "Valuation" for the purposes of this section is the full valuation, determined by applying to the assessed valuation of the property the equalization rate for the particular city or town as determined by the State Board of Equalization and Assessment for the year 1953. There are four specific situations set forth in the statute where the Administrator may use a valuation other than the current equalized assessed valuation; the most important of these is the right to use a price established by a sale occurring subsequent to March 15, 1951.

For New York City the following are the equalization rates used by the Rent Commission:

Bronx	96%
Brooklyn	98%
Manhattan	100%
Queens	93%
Richmond	96%

In determining the return being earned on the property no consideration is given to mortgage interest as an expense, but the 6% return is allowed on the total valuation. In this way, landlords are treated alike without regard for differences in financing. For example, two identical houses standing side by side are each assessed at $25,000.00. One property is owned free and clear, while the other is held subject to a 60% mortgage. It would manifestly be unfair to establish different maximum rents for the two properties solely because of the difference in mortgage interest payments.

A 2% depreciation allowance based upon the valuation of the building is permitted in determining the total expenses of the property. Certain items of expense which normally do not recur annually are allocated over a period of years. For example, where a new roof is installed in the "test year" (the one-year period chosen by the landlord to set forth his income and expenses) it would be improper to allow the full amount as a yearly expense, when a new roof may be installed only once in twenty years. The amount allowed for any such major item is the cost divided by the number of years of estimated useful life. The landlord is permitted to claim not only those major items installed in the "test year" but similarly those incurred since 1943 or the date he acquired the property, whichever is later. Advisory Bulletin No. 7, published by the commission, contains detailed instructions to be followed by landlords wishing to make application under Section 33(5) of the Regulations.

(6) Increased Costs for Small Structures.

Section 33(6) is designed to permit small home owners, who own no more than four units, to obtain an increase in rent where there have been increased costs to the landlord which have not been compensated by increased rents.

This type of increase is of importance to the small landlord where the cost of fuel, insurance, painting or taxes has increased.

An application under this section is filed on Form 33(6), which contains all necessary instructions.

(7) Increases in Hotels.

Section 33(7) provides for increases in rent for hotels and rooming houses; it is similar in purpose to Section 33(6) in that it provides for rent increases based on increased costs. See Advisory Bulletin No. 11.

The attention of all landlords is called to the fact that all essential services must be maintained in order to qualify for an increase in the Maximum Rent.

CONSULT YOUR LOCAL OFFICE

If you have read the grounds for increase and believe you are entitled to an increase, apply to your Local Rent Office. Study the Advisory Bulletins and the forms which you can obtain there, and then file the forms if you think that you qualify.

ADVISORY BULLETIN No. 2
(Issued April 1, 1953)
(This revokes Advisory Bulletin No. 2 revised March 15, 1951)
APPLICATION AND COMPUTATION OF EQUALIZATION ADJUSTMENT SECTION 4(3-A) OF THE ACT

Section 4(3-a) of the Emergency Housing Rent Control Act reads as follows:

3-a. Notwithstanding the foregoing provisions of this section, on and after May first, nineteen hundred fifty-three, the maximum rent for any housing accommodation shall not be less than the maximum rent in effect on March first, nineteen hundred forty-three (or if there was no such maximum rent then in effect, the maximum rent first established pursuant to the federal act prior to July first, nineteen hundred forty-seven) plus fifteen per centum thereof as such sum is adjusted to reflect:

(1) the amount of any decreases in maximum rent required by order because of decreases in dwelling space, services, furniture, furnishings or equipment, or substantial deterioration or failure to properly maintain such housing, and

(2) the amount of increases in maximum rent authorized by order because of increases in dwelling space, services, furniture, furnishings or equipment, or major capital improvements.

Nothing contained in this subdivision, however, shall have the effect of increasing the maximum rent of any housing accommodation more than fifteen per centum above the maximum rent in effect on April thirtieth, nineteen hundred fifty-three.

1. Q. What is the 15 per cent rent increase granted under the 1953 Act?
   A. It is an increase primarily of those rents which have remained the same since 1943.
2. Q. What is this increase called?
   A. It is called an equalization adjustment.
3. Q. When does the equalization adjustment go into effect?

ADVISORY BULLETINS

  A. It goes into effect on May 1st, but all other sections of the law go into effect on April 1st.
4. Q. How can a tenant know whether his rent is affected?
  A. If his rent has been the same since March 1, 1943, then he knows that his landlord is now permitted a 15 per cent increase by the new law.
5. Q. Why is this increase being granted?
  A. Because over the last ten years there have been very substantial increases in costs of operating buildings, such as fuel, taxes, water charges, etc. Those tenants who have paid increases have contributed their share of the increased costs, but the others are not carrying their share. The Legislature therefore deemed it equitable to require them to pay this increase. This additional income will help to avert further rent increases for tenants who already are paying 15 per cent or more above the March 1943 rent.
6. Q. Must the landlord obtain an order from the Local Rent Administrator increasing the maximum rent of the housing accommodation to get this increase?
  A. No. The Legislature granted an equalization adjustment and therefore, as of May 1, 1953, the equalized rent becomes the new ceiling rent.
7. Q. Supposing that a tenant gave his landlord an increase of 10 per cent for a lease, or that the rent authorities granted a 10 per cent increase for other than services. How is that rent affected?
  A. In either case, the landlord would be entitled to an additional 5 per cent on the basic rent. Thus, if the rent has been $50 when the lease was given, that 10 per cent or $5 increases the rent to $55. Under the new law, the new rent would be 15 per cent above the original $50, or an increase of $7.50, making a total of $57.50. The landlord would now be entitled to $2.50 more. Of course, if the lease is still in effect, he cannot collect the additional $2.50 until the lease expires.

ADVISORY BULLETINS

8. Q. Would the same answer apply to ANY increase for other than for services of less than 15 per cent?

A. Yes. The new law provides that the landlord is entitled to an increase of 15 per cent over the 1943 rental. Any increase the landlord has received by way of a lease, or by way of an official order (other than for increased services, such as a new stove, etc.), of less than 15 per cent for a particular housing accommodation is now equalized up to 15 per cent.

9. Q. Supposing that the rent has been the same except for an increase for a new stove, or an increase for a new refrigerator, or a television antenna, etc., how does that figure in the new equalization adjustment?

A. The Act applies the 15 per cent increase only to the basic rent and does not affect—neither increases or decreases—the additional payments for refrigerators, stoves, television antennae, etc. For instance, if your rent was frozen at $40 monthly and you have since paid an additional $3 monthly for the new stove, etc., your new rent would be $40 plus 15 per cent, or $6, which makes $46, plus the same $3 or a total of $49 instead of $43.

10. Q. Supposing that the rent has been the same except for a 15 per cent increase by a two-year lease which conforms with the requirements of Section 33(2) of the Regulations and which also provides for a replacement of the refrigerator, gas range and the kitchen sink as a consideration for the execution of the lease, how does that figure in the new equalization adjustment?

A. The Act applies the 15 per cent increase only to the basic rent. The amount of increases because of increase in services, etc., may only be added where the increase in rent was authorized by order. In the instant situation the increase was obtained by means of a statutory lease. Under the circumstances the application of the equalization adjustment does not result in any change in the maximum rent.

ADVISORY BULLETINS

11. Q. If a housing accommodation was not rented on March 1, 1943, but was first rented at some later date, is it affected?

A. Yes, provided it was rented prior to July 1, 1947; if it was not rented until after that date the rent is not increased by the equalization provision.

12. Q. Suppose that a tenant has moved into a housing accommodation at some time later than 1943 and does not know what the frozen rent was—or suppose that a landlord purchased property recently, and does not know what the frozen rents were—how can they easily find out for certain what the rent should be under the equalization adjustment?

A. The Rent Commission has provided a printed form entitled "Request for Information to Compute Equalization Adjustment." These forms may be obtained by calling at your Local Rent Office *in person*. Either a landlord or a tenant requiring this information must file this form in triplicate with the Local Rent Office. The request may be filed either by mail or in person. Replies will be mailed, as in many instances it will require some time to check all the facts.

13. Q. May a landlord collect the increased rent before such requests are returned by the Local Rent Office?

A. Yes, the law makes the new equalization adjustment effective on May 1, 1953. Adjustments between landlords and tenants may be made later. The Local Rent Offices will supply information as fast as humanly possible, but the time required cannot be foretold as it is impossible to forecast how many requests may be received.

14. Q. What does the landlord do to obtain an equalization adjustment?

A. He presents the correct bill to the tenant. Since an equalization adjustment does not require an order from the Commission, there is no prescribed form for the landlord to serve upon his tenant.

15. Q. Supposing the landlord makes an overcharge?

ADVISORY BULLETINS

 A. If he makes an overcharge, whether by error or intent, the tenant who has paid the overcharge can get it back.

ADVISORY BULLETIN No. 4
(Revised Jan. 1, 1970)
EVICTIONS

1. Q. Is a tenant protected against eviction by the New York State Emergency Housing Rent Control Law of 1969?

 A. Yes. A tenant who pays his rent is protected against eviction. The Regulations now spell out the manner in which occupants of any controlled rental units may be evicted. For additional detailed information consult Part V of the Regulations which deals with evictions.

2. Q. How may a tenant be evicted under the Regulations?

 A. There are two types of eviction actions and the law therefore sets up different methods of proceeding under them. The first is that in which the landlord seeks the tenant's eviction because of some special need to recover possession of the housing accommodations. The landlord cannot proceed in the local court unless and until he obtains a certificate of eviction from the Local Rent Administrator. In the second type of case it is the tenant's own improper conduct or the illegal occupancy which makes him subject to eviction. In the latter cases, set forth in question 3, the landlord need not obtain a certificate of eviction.

3. Q. Do the Regulations set forth exactly what conduct by the tenant is considered wrongful?

 A. Yes. Section 52 of the Regulations sets forth six grounds where a tenant may be evicted on application of his landlord to a court or a justice of the peace without a certificate from the Local Rent Administrator. The six grounds are:

  (1) The tenant is violating a substantial obligation of his tenancy other than the obligation to surrender possession of the housing accommo-

Advisory Bulletins

dation and has failed to cure such violation after written demand by the landlord that the violation cease within ten days; or within the three month period immediately prior to the commencement of the court proceeding the tenant has wilfully violated such an obligation inflicting serious and substantial injury to the landlord.

(2) The tenant is committing or permitting a nuisance in the housing accommodations; or is maliciously or by reason of gross negligence substantially damaging the housing accommodations; or his conduct is such as to interfere substantially with the comfort or safety of the landlord or of other tenants or occupants of the same or other adjacent building or structure.

(3) Occupancy of the housing accommodations by the tenant is illegal because of the requirements of law, and the landlord is subject to civil or criminal penalties therefor, or both.

(4) The tenant is using or permitting the housing accommodation to be used for an immoral or illegal purpose.

(5) The tenant who had a written lease or other written rental agreement, which terminates on or after May 1, 1950, has refused upon demand of the landlord to execute a written extension or renewal thereof for a further term of like duration not in excess of one year but otherwise on the same terms and conditions as the previous lease except insofar as such terms and conditions are inconsistent with the State law.

(6) The tenant has unreasonably refused the landlord access to the housing accommodations for the purpose of making necessary repairs or improvements required by law or for the purposes of inspection or of showing the accommodations to a prospective purchaser, mortgagee or prospective mortgagee, or other person having a legitimate interest therein; provided,

however, that in the latter event such refusal shall not be ground for removal or eviction if such inspection or showing of the accommodations is contrary to the provisions of the tenant's lease or rental agreement.

4. Q. How is a tenant protected when a landlord seeks eviction under one of the above six grounds?

   A. Section 53 of the Regulations provides that the landlord must first serve a written notice upon the tenant setting forth the facts. Within 48 hours after the notice is served upon the tenant, a copy of this notice together with an affidavit of service must be filed with the Local Rent Office.

   The landlord must wait one month from the date of service of this notice upon the tenant before commencing his court action to evict unless the tenant is a weekly tenant in which case the notice required shall be seven days. However, in cases of nuisance, or use of the premises for an immoral or illegal purpose, or where the occupancy is illegal, the waiting period need only be ten days unless the tenant is a weekly tenant in which case the notice required shall be two days. During this waiting period, where the tenant has convincing proof that the landlord is not proceeding in good faith and is seeking merely to harass or annoy him, he may complain to the Local Rent Office.

   Where there is a legitimate dispute as to the facts the issues will be left to the local court for decision.

   No action can be taken by the landlord to exclude the tenant from possession unless there is a judgment of a court or a justice of the peace awarding possession to the landlord.

5. Q. May a landlord lock out or otherwise exclude a tenant from possession on a claim that the tenant has not paid his rent?

   A. A judgment of a court or a justice of the peace awarding possession must first be obtained before any tenant may be evicted.

ADVISORY BULLETINS

6. Q. What are the types of cases where the landlord must obtain a certificate of eviction from the Local Rent Administrator?

   A. The Regulations provide that, except for the instances set forth in Question 3, no tenant may be evicted unless on application of a landlord, the Administrator issues a certificate, permitting the landlord to apply for a court order of eviction thereafter. In all such cases the Local Rent Administrator will give the tenant an opportunity to present his answer and objections to the application together with such data as may be relevant.

   The Regulations provide five general classes of cases where certificates are required to be issued by the Administrator before a landlord may commence a court action to evict a tenant. These classes are:

   (1) Occupancy by landlord or immediate family.
   (2) Tenant not using premises for own dwelling.
   (3) Subdivision by alteration or remodeling.
   (4) Demolition.
   (5) Withdrawal of occupied housing accommodations from the rental market.

   There are detailed provisions as to each, and for exact provisions consult Sections 54-59 of the Regulations.

7. Q. How much time will be allowed the tenant when a certificate of eviction is issued by the Local Rent Administrator?

   A. In most cases there will be a waiting period of three months from the date of issuance of the certificate before the landlord will be permitted to commence his court action for eviction. This does not affect the right of the tenant to request the local court for a stay of the final warrant for whatever period the court may deem proper.

8. Q. Does the Local Rent Administrator ever evict a tenant?

   A. No. A judgment awarding possession of housing accommodations to a landlord may only be granted by the local court.

9. Q. A tenant dies leaving his wife in possession of the apartment. May the landlord evict her on the theory that the tenant being dead no longer occupies the premises?
A. No. Section 56 of the Regulations provides that no occupant of housing accommodations shall be evicted under that section where the occupant is either the surviving spouse of the deceased tenant or some other member of the deceased tenant's family who has been living with the tenant.

ADVISORY BULLETIN No. 5
(Revised December 1, 1961)
PROHIBITIONS AND ENFORCEMENT

When a tenant pays more than the maximum legal rent which is established by the Rent Commission for his housing accommodation he is being overcharged and should report that fact to the Local Rent Office on Form 60SP [Tenant's Statement of Violations]. There are several situations where a tenant may be unaware of the fact that he has paid any excess rent to his landlord because his landlord may have camouflaged the payment by calling it a bonus, gift, broker's commissions, or the purchase price of furniture or any other property which the tenant is required to buy as a condition of renting the apartment. No matter what "gimmick" is used the amount paid by the tenant in furtherance of such scheme is excess "rent" and its collection is a violation.

There are cases where a landlord may have unwittingly collected more rent from his tenant than the Rent Commission permits. However, in those cases there is no attempt by the landlord to conceal its collection. When a tenant reports this type of violation to the Local Rent Office, the landlord is notified that the violation has been reported to it and a copy of the tenant's statement is mailed to him. The landlord is given an opportunity to file his answer to the complaint of violation. A conference may be held with the landlord and tenant present. Usually the landlord voluntarily refunds the excess rent collected by him when he becomes aware of his transgression. Where the rent increase was based upon additional services or equipment for which the landlord failed to apply for a Commission order so increasing the rent, this factor will receive appropriate consideration in determining the maximum rent and such refund as may be directed.

Serious Violations

Violations of a more serious nature are referred by the Local Rent Office to the Enforcement Division of the Rent Commission. These include the cases where the landlord uses an evasive method to circumvent the Act or the Rent Regulations, i.e. bonus payments, payment of brokerage commissions by the tenant, tie-in-furniture sales, etc. In addition the Local Rent Office refers violations to the Enforcement Division where the landlord is known to be a repeat violator. Local Rent Offices maintain indices of violators for the purpose of ascertaining whether the landlord had previously been found to have been in violation. A referral to the Enforcement Division is made for the purpose of the Commission's making a full investigation which is not necessarily limited to the individual violation disclosed by the tenant's individual complaint. The Enforcement Division may refer the matter after investigation to the District Attorney for criminal prosecution, bring civil suit on behalf of the Commission, or both.

Treble Damage Suit

The Emergency Housing Rent Control Law gives a tenant who has been overcharged the right to sue for damages based upon the excess rent paid by him during the two-year period prior to the commencement of the lawsuit. If the overcharge was a wilful violation of law, the tenant may collect as much as three times the total amount of such overcharge, plus attorney's fees and court costs [see § 11(5) of the Act]. If the tenant fails to take action within 30 days from the date of the violation and the tenant has not already commenced suit, the Commission may file suit on behalf of the State. If judgment in such action is rendered in favor of the Commission, the tenant will be entitled to one-third of the recovery, exclusive of costs and disbursements. Generally the Commission will not institute the action unless the issue involved is significant to the rent control program. Individual tenants are assisted in bringing suit by the provision for an allowance for attorney's fees coupled with the right to retain all damages awarded by the Court.

Failure to Comply With Refund Directive

Where the Local Rent Office establishes a maximum rent by order and directs the refund of excess rent collected by the landlord within 30 days from the date when the order becomes final, the failure of the landlord to make the refund creates a cause of action for damages [see § 11(6) of the Act]. Suit to recover such damages may be brought by the Commission on behalf of the State within one year from the date of the violation. If the violation was wilful, three times the amount of the excess rent, plus attorney's fees and costs, may be awarded by the Court. If judgment is rendered in favor of the Commission in such action, the tenant will be entitled to one-third of the recovery, exclusive of costs and disbursements. No action is normally taken by the Commission under this section unless it would be significant to the rent control program. The tenant may, however, bring his own suit where no action has been taken by the Commission and 30 days have expired since the refund order became final.

Criminal Penalties

In addition to the civil penalties referred to above, the law prescribes a criminal penalty for the violation of the Emergency Housing Rent Control Law. A person who wilfully submits false records to the Commission or who wilfully charges more than the maximum rent may be fined up to $5,000.00, or imprisoned for as much as one year, or both [see § 11(2) of the Act].

Rent and Eviction Regulations

Section 2(3). **"Rent."** Consideration, including any bonus, benefit or gratuity demanded or received for or in connection with the use or occupancy of housing accommodations or the transfer of a lease of such housing accommodations.

Section 61. **General prohibitions.** It shall be unlawful, regardless of any contract, lease or other obligation heretofore or hereafter entered into, for any person to demand or receive any rent for any housing accommodations in excess of the maximum rent, or otherwise to do or omit to do any act, in violation of any regulation, order or requirement under the Act or these Regulations, or to offer, solicit, attempt or agree to do any of the foregoing.

The term *"rent"* as hereinbefore defined shall also include the payment by a tenant of a fee or rental commission to a landlord or to any person or real estate broker where such person or real estate broker is an agent or employee of the landlord or is employed by the landlord in connection with the operation of the building, or where such person or real estate broker manages the building in which the housing accommodation is located, or where the landlord or his employee refer the tenant to such person or real estate broker for the purpose of renting the housing accommodation. Where the landlord has listed the housing accommodation with such person or real estate broker for rental purposes such fact shall be prima facie evidence of the existence of an agency relationship between such other person or real estate broker and the landlord for the purposes of this section.

Section 62. **Evasion.** The maximum rents and other requirements provided in these Regulations shall not be evaded, either directly or indirectly, in connection with the renting or leasing or the transfer of a lease of housing accommodations by requiring the tenant to pay, or obligate himself for membership or other fees, or by modification of the practices relating to payment of commissions or other charges, or by modification of the services furnished or required to be furnished with the housing accommodations, or otherwise.

Section 63. **Purchase of property as condition of renting.**

1. No person shall require a tenant or prospective tenant to purchase or agree to purchase furniture or any other property as a condition of renting housing accommodations.

2. The term "person" as used in this section shall include an agent or any other employee of a landlord acting with or without the authority of his employer.

3. The term "person" as used in this section shall also include a tenant in occupancy of housing accommodations

Advisory Bulletins

who attempts to sell furniture or any other property to an income tenant.

ADVISORY BULLETIN No. 6
(Revised June 1, 1960)
PAINTING AND OTHER MAINTENANCE COMPLAINTS IN NEW YORK CITY

1. Q. Has the tenant the same right to painting services that he had under Federal law?

   A. Yes. The landlord must continue to provide the same painting and decorating service as he was required to provide under the Federal regulations which were in effect on March 1, 1950. However, this will not require the landlord to paint any more frequently than was the custom in the period immediately prior to March 1, 1943, nor will the landlord in any case be required to paint more frequently than at two year intervals.

2. Q. My apartment hasn't been painted in over two years. Am I entitled to get my apartment painted?

   A. Yes, if your landlord previously had a custom of painting every two years.

3. Q. My apartment was painted every three years prior to March 1943. More than two years have elapsed since the last painting. Can I demand that my landlord paint?

   A. No. If your landlord had a three year custom previous to March 1, 1943, he may continue painting at three year intervals without being in violation of the regulations.

4. Q. Prior to March 1, 1943 my landlord had a practice of painting my whole apartment every two years, and the kitchen and the bathroom every year. My apartment was painted and decorated a year and one-half ago. Can I make him paint the kitchen and bathroom now?

   A. No. The painting of kitchen and bathroom alone cannot be compelled. It must be done as part of the entire painting of the apartment, which is due at the end of two years.

ADVISORY BULLETINS

5. Q. My landlord has always painted one or two rooms at a time. Can I now make him paint the entire apartment at one time?

   A. No. In this particular case, the obligation of the landlord is to continue the same painting service that was provided on and prior to March 1, 1943.

6. Q. What steps must a tenant take in order to get his apartment painted?

   A. Ask your landlord to paint the apartment. If he fails to do so, you may obtain two copies of the Tenant's Application Form 34(2) N.Y.C. from your Local Rent Office. These forms may be obtained by requesting them through the mail. After carefully reading the instructions, complete each copy of the form making certain to answer all questions. File two copies of the form with your Local Rent Office.

7. Q. What do I do after that?

   A. Nothing. The Local Rent Office will forward a copy of your application to the landlord, together with a notice that the maximum rent may be reduced because of the landlord's alleged failure to comply with his obligation to paint and decorate. Should the landlord recognize this obligation he will be given one month to paint your apartment and file proof of the completion of the work. However, if he does not paint during this one month period, an order reducing the maximum rent will be issued unless the landlord disputes the obligation to paint. In such case he will be given an opportunity to submit his evidence. Should the Local Rent Office, after a study of the record, determine that the landlord has an obligation to paint and that he has failed to comply with this obligation, a notice will be sent to both the landlord and the tenant advising them that unless the landlord paints within seven days of the date of the notice, and submits written proof thereof to the Local Rent Office within that period, an order reducing the maximum rent will be issued.

8. Q. A landlord had a practice of painting a particular apartment every two years. He painted the apart-

Advisory Bulletins

ment two years ago. The tenant now in possession moved into this apartment a year ago and at that time paid for his own painting. The tenant now claims that the two-year interval has run and that the landlord is now obligated to paint and decorate. The landlord had advised the tenant that since the apartment was painted only a year ago by the tenant, he will not paint for another year, and the tenant has, therefore, filed an application for a rent reduction based upon the landlord's failure to paint. What disposition will be made of this application?

A. The application will be accepted for processing. In computing the time period, the date when the landlord last painted the apartment determines whether or not he is in default of his obligation to maintain the painting and decorating service.

9. Q. But I don't want a rent reduction, I want my apartment painted.

A. The Local Rent Administrator will notify the landlord of his obligation to paint, but if he fails to do so an order will be issued reducing the rent. Thereafter, you can make your own arrangements to have your apartment painted since the reduced rent reflects the elimination of the landlord's obligation to continue painting your apartment.

10. Q. Do I have to remove my furniture from the walls and place it in the middle of each room to be painted?

A. While you do not have to remove heavy pieces of furniture, such as a piano or a very heavy combination radio-phonograph, the landlord's request that you place other pieces of furniture in the middle of the room is a reasonable one which you must comply with. It then becomes the obligation of the landlord to properly cover and protect your furniture while he is painting the apartment.

11. Q. I have wall to wall carpeting. My landlord insists that I must lift my carpeting and roll it to the center of the room, or otherwise remove it.

A. You are not obligated to do this. If the carpeting has not been tacked down you may be requested to roll it up so as to facilitate the job of the painters.

12. Q. Some of the rooms in my apartment have wallpaper. The landlord does not want to give me new wallpaper but is willing to paint those rooms instead. Must he give me wallpaper?

    A. No. The landlord has the option of either giving you new wallpaper *or* painting those rooms.

13. Q. The landlord insists that I must remove the wallpaper, and also that I must then prepare the surface of the walls for painting by "sizing" the walls. Must I do this?

    A. That depends upon the facts. If the landlord previously either hung the wallpaper or paid for the wallpaper, then it is his obligation to both remove the wallpaper and "size" the walls, if he now wishes to paint.

14. Q. My landlord is willing to paint my apartment; but, insists that all of the woodwork and walls shall be painted a buff color since he wants uniformity of colors in his building. My apartment was last painted by my landlord with a variety of colors and the colors used in each room blends in with the decorative scheme for each of the rooms. For that reason, I have refused to permit my landlord to paint my apartment. I have requested him to repaint with the existing colors. Do I have to permit my landlord to change the color scheme of the rooms in my apartment?

    A. No. The landlord must repaint with the existing color scheme unless he obtains the consent of the tenant.

15. Q. My landlord insists that I sign a paper or a release, agreeing to free both him and his painters from any damage done to my furniture which may occur as a result of the painting of my apartment. Do I have to sign such a paper?

    A. No. This office takes the position that the tenant is under no obligation to sign such a paper. Should the landlord refuse to proceed with the

Advisory Bulletins

painting and decorating unless a release is executed, the Local Rent Administrator will consider there has been a failure to provide the customary painting and decorating service.

16. Q. I rented a vacant apartment last month and upon my landlord's refusal to paint and decorate the apartment, I painted it at my expense. Can I get my rent reduced?

    A. If less than one year has expired since the tenant rented the apartment, he can file an application for a rent reduction pursuant to Section 34(2) of the Regulations. The landlord will be required to produce his books and records if he claims that at the time of the renting the painting was not due. Should the landlord fail to establish this, it would follow that there had been a reduction in the service of painting and decorating. The landlord will be given an opportunity to promptly refund the actual cost to the tenant of painting and decorating providing the cost is reasonable. Should the landlord fail to do this, the Local Rent Office will issue an order reducing the maximum rent.

17. Q. My apartment has a structural defect and also it is a health hazard. Where can I file my complaint?

    A. For complaints other than painting and decorating which involve deterioration and other structural, maintenance, or health services or repairs in New York City, tenants may apply to the appropriate New York City Agency as indicated below:

IN MULTIPLE DWELLINGS (Occupied by 3 or more families), rooming houses or furnished rooms.

Sanitary, Maintenance, or Structural Defects may be reported to the Complaint Bureau of Housing in the Department of Housing and Buildings:

    Bronx   — 1932 Arthur Avenue (LUdlow 3-9567)
    Brooklyn — 8th Floor, Municipal Building (MAin 4-5650)

Manhattan — 18th Floor, Municipal Bldg. (WHitehall 3-3535)
Queens — 120-55 Queens Blvd., Kew Gardens, L. I. (BOulevard 8-6918)
Richmond — Borough Hall, St. George, S. I. (GIbraltar 7-1000)

IN ONE AND TWO FAMILY HOUSES—These are regulated by the Sanitary Code and the Building Code and are not covered by the Multiple Dwelling Law.

Health and Sanitary Conditions—defective plumbing, furnaces, stoves or equipment supplied by landlord; filth, rats and vermin; defective paint or plaster; dampness; water in cellar; etc.—may be reported to the Sanitary Bureau of the Borough Office of the Health Department:

Bronx — 1826 Arthur Avenue (LUdlow 3-5500)
Brooklyn — 295 Flatbush Avenue Extension (TRiangle 5-9400)
Manhattan — 125 Worth Street (WOrth 4-3800)
Queens — 90-37 Parsons Blvd., Jamaica (OLympia 8-6600)
Richmond — 51 Stuyvesant Pl., St. George, S. I. (SAint George 7-6000)

Structural Defect—Wall, supports, beams, reefs, chimneys, etc., dangerous, defective or in bad repair—may be reported to the Complaint Bureau of Buildings, in the Building Bureau of the Department of Housing and Buildings:

Bronx — 1932 Arthur Avenue (LUdlow 3-9567)
Brooklyn — 8th Floor, Municipal Building (MAin 4-5650)
Manhattan — 20th Floor, Municipal Bldg. (WHitehall 3-3535)
Queens — 120-55, Queens Blvd., Kew Gardens, L. I. (BOulevard 8-6918)
Richmond — Borough Hall, St. George, S. I. (GIbraltar 7-1000)

ADVISORY BULLETIN NO. 7
(Revised May 1, 1969)
INCREASE OF MAXIMUM RENT (FAIR RETURN) —
SECTION 33(5) OF THE REGULATIONS

ADVISORY BULLETINS

1. INSTRUCTIONS FOR FILING APPLICATION

An original and one copy of Forms 33(5)s or 33(5) and 33(5)A, together with an original and one copy of all required schedules, must be filed with the Local Rent Office by delivery or mailing. The landlord is also required to file an additional copy of Forms 33(5)s or 33(5) and 33(5)A for each housing accommodation affected by the application, with the name and mailing address of the tenant inserted in Item 2 of Form 33(5). These copies will be served upon the tenants by the Administrator.

Where the present owner acquired title to the property since March 15, 1957, the landlord is also required to file a supplemental statement (Form 33(5) Supplement) with the application. An original and two copies of this form must be filed together with all riders.

Where a property contains more than 12 rental units, the requirement to serve a copy of the rent roll (Form 33(5)A) upon each tenant may be waived upon application to the Local Rent Administrator. If a waiver is granted, the landlord must be prepared to make the rent roll available to the tenants at such places and at such times as the Local Rent Administrator deems to be reasonable in the particular circumstances. The application for a waiver of individual service of Form 33(5)A should be made by letter addressed to the Local Rent Administrator, giving the property address and the number of rental units, and requesting the Local Rent Administrator to establish the conditions necessary for such waiver.

No application may be filed by the landlord based upon a sale price valuation prior to six months from the date of the sale of the property to the landlord.

Before filing the application be sure to sign all copies and have the original sworn to before a Notary Public or other person authorized to administer oaths. The application must be signed by an individual owner, partner or corporate officer.

2. SPECIFIC INSTRUCTIONS FOR COMPLETION OF APPLICATION'S OPERATING STATEMENT

Test Year, Item 7.

You may select as your "TEST YEAR" one of the following:

(a) The most recent calendar year (January 1st to December 31st).

(b) Your most recent fiscal year (one year ending on the last day of a month other than December 31st,) provided that books of account are maintained and closed accordingly.

(c) Any 12 consecutive months ending within 90 days prior to the date of filing of this application. Such period must end on the last day of a month.

Rental Income, Item 8.

Enter in Item 8 the total annual rental income from Column 6 of Form 33(5)A. It is to be noted that this total should include the annual rental income from all sources, i.e., dwelling units, stores, units for professional or business use and garages.

Miscellaneous Income (Other Than Rents), Item 9.

List income received from the operation of washing machines and other laundry equipment, vending machines, sign rentals, etc. during the "test year". Receipts or reimbursements for the use of water, gas, electricity, telephone, fuel or other special services should not be included in this item, but should be reflected as credits in reduction of the costs incurred to provide such services. If there is no "Miscellaneous Income", enter "None" in Item 9.

Fuel, Item 11.

Enter the cost of all fuel used during the "test year" for the operation of the property. Attach to the application a schedule showing the following:

Date of Delivery   Vendor   Tons or Gallons   Type   Amount

Utilities, Item 12.

Enter the cost, for the "test year", of water and sewer charges and of all gas, electric and telephone service supplied for the tenants and for the operation of the building. Receipts or reimbursements for the use of such services are to be credited as reductions of these costs. Water and sewer charges may be presented at the rates in effect at the time of filing of the application, in lieu of the actual costs incurred for the "test year". Attach to the application a schedule showing the following:

Period From	To	Type of Service	Amount

Payroll and Related Costs; or Owner's Janitorial Allowance, Item 13.

Salaries and wages and related payroll costs for employees, or janitorial allowance claimed by the owner for his own services, should be entered under this item.

Any landlord who personally performs the janitorial services (such as cleaning halls, attending to heating system, cleaning of walks, etc.) may claim an allowance for such services computed at $6.00 per month per unit including any apartments occupied by the owner.

This computed claim for "Owner's Janitorial Allowance" should be accompanied by a statement describing the nature of the janitorial services that he performs.

Where a property has a payroll of one or more employees required for its servicing and operation, (such as superintendent, elevator operators, doorman, porters and handymen), the amount of salaries and wages paid to such employees for the "test year", plus the amount of rental allowance for apartments occupied by employees should be entered under this item and schedule attached as follows:

Employees Name	Regular or Part Time	Services Performed	Wage Rate (Monthly or Weekly)	Amount Paid For Test Year

Payroll and Related Costs; or Owner's Janitorial Allowance, Item 13. (continued)

Expenditures directly related to the amount of salaries and wages paid for the "test year", such as social security and unemployment taxes, welfare benefits, and disability and workmen's compensation insurance expenses are to be added to the salaries and wages scheduled.

Salaries and wages and directly related costs paid for the "test year" period for repairs and maintenance work (such as wages of painters, carpenters, etc.) or for executive or administrative services should not be entered under this item.

The applicant can enter under this item a "projected" amount of payroll and related costs. He may compute this amount by adjusting his "test year's" experience so as to reflect the annual new levels of wages or other payroll changes which are in effect at the time of filing the application.

Insurance, Item 15.

Enter the annual costs either of premiums allocable to the "test year" or of premiums for policies in effect at the time of filing the application for insuring the building and contents for fire, tornado, sprinkler leakage, boiler, plate glass and public liability, etc.

The gross annual premium costs are to be reduced by all credits which have been or may be received, such as dividends, rate adjustments, etc.

The schedule attached should show the following:

Type of Insurance	Amount of Coverage	From: (Date)	To: (Date)	Term (No. of Years)	Total Premium	Annual Cost

Management Expense or Owner's Management Allowance, Item 16.

Enter all management fees chargeable to the operation of the property. For agent-managed buildings compute this cost by applying to the Total Income shown on Line 10 of Form 33(5) the percentage or rate which was the basis for the management fees paid for the "test year". For owner-managed properties an allowance may be claimed. Such allowance is in lieu of payment to an agent for management and leasing services and is in recognition of management work performed by the landlord such as collecting rents, negotiating leases, purchasing supplies and equipment, exercising supervision over employees, and over the maintenance of the property. The amount of allowance is to be computed at 6% of the first $100,000.00 of rental income shown on Line 10 of Form 33(5)s or Form 33(5). Excess over $100,000.00 will be computed at rates prevailing in the area.

The schedule attached should show the following:

Managed By	Basis of Computation	Annual Amount

Repairs and Maintenance Replacements and Improvements Form 33(5)s only Item 17 & 18

Instructions For Use of Optional Short Form

(the blue Optional Form 33(5)s must be used)

Advisory Bulletins

Where a building contains 12 or less residential units the landlord may use 17.5% of the "Annual Rental Income", Item 8, for the combined Items 17 and 18 ("Repairs and Maintenance" and "Replacements and Improvements") in lieu of preparing and substantiating Schedules in detail.

Where a building contains 13 or more residential units, inclusive, the landlord may use 15% for "walk-up" buildings or 12% for "elevator" buildings of the "Annual Rental Income", Item 8, for the combined Items 17 and 18 ("Repairs and Maintenance" and "Replacements and Improvements") in lieu of preparing and substantiating Schedules in detail.

Where the landlord elects to use the appropriate ratio the total annual expense shall be computed by applying such ratio to the amount indicated for Item 8. Enter the resulting computation as Item 17.

Repairs and Maintenance—Form 33(5) Only, Item 17.

(to be followed when optional allowance is not used)

Enter the annual cost of repair and maintenance expenses (such as painting and decorating, plumbing repairs, carpentry, electrical and general repairs, and supplies, including also wages and related costs paid to employees for services relating to the above). Do not include items of the nature described in Instruction for Item 18.

The amount of such annual cost is to be computed by taking the one year average or one-fourth of the landlord's expenses for four years ending with the last month of the "test year".

This average of a four-year cycle of "repair and maintenance" expenses is for the purpose of establishing for the "test year" an annual amount which would be normally recurrent. Where applicant is unable to present such costs for a four-year period, he should submit an explanation.

Where the applicant has been the owner of the property for less than four years, the bills and data of the previous owner of the property should be used to complete the four years' experience.

Advisory Bulletins

The schedule in support of this item should list in detail all invoices covering the expenses claimed for each of the four years. The totals for each year should be summarized and the one year average shown. The itemization for each of the four years should be arranged to show the following:

Date of Invoice	Vendor	Type of Repair	Location (Apt. No. Lobby, etc.)	Amount

Any credits which reduce the costs itemized in these schedules are to be noted and deducted from the total for the period covered (such as allowances in price, returns of merchandise, proceeds from the sale of materials and supplies, and any payments received from insurance carriers for damages, etc.)

In cases where the building consists of 40 or more residential units it is optional for the applicant to set forth in Schedule 1, in lieu of all invoices covering the expenses claimed for each of the four years or whatever period is presented in the application, the following:

> The net amounts, per the general ledger or books of account, of the various categories which make up the TOTAL of "REPAIRS and MAINTENANCE"—such as painting (within apartments), painting (within building—lobby, halls, etc.), exterior painting (windows, sashes, fire escapes, etc.), carpentry repairs, plumbing repairs, electrical repairs, mechanical repairs, supplies, misc., repairs, etc.

Replacements and Improvements—Form 33(5) Only, Item 18.
(to be followed when optional allowance is not used)

Enter one year's proration of the cost of all improvements and replacements made since the date the property was acquired by the present owner and not fully depreciated.

The schedule for this item should show the following:

Date Acquired	Vendor	Item	Where Used (Apt. No.)	Cost	Useful Life	Charge to Test Year

Where, however, the maximum rent had been increased on or after April 1, 1953 pursuant to § 33(1)(b) (substantial rehabilitation) or § 33(1)(c) (major capital improvement) charge an amount to the "test year" equal to 12 times the monthly rental increase ordered by the administrator. But, where the rental increase was on the basis of the improvement as well as for an increase in service (such as central heating system plus heat) the cost of the improvement should be allocated so that the cost

Advisory Bulletins

will be recouped within the appropriate number of years. (In the given example the cost of furnishing heat will be reflected as a "fuel" expense.)

Miscellaneous, Item 19.

Enter all expenses incurred in "test year" necessary to the operation of the property and not otherwise classified, such as exterminating, upkeep of uniforms. Mortgage interest and amortization are not to be included as operating expenses of the building.

Professional fees may be included only for that part which applies to the operation of the building rather than to the financial or personal affairs of the ownership. Such costs should be shown for a three year period ending with the last month of the "test year" and the one year average entered under this item. Where fees claimed on a subsequent application are in connection with the filing of prior applications, and for the representation of the landlord in those cases, the amounts to be accepted for inclusion in the three year average shall be the amounts paid for increases effective in the "test year" and the two years prior thereto, limited, however, to 25% of the "Actual Amount of Grant" of each of the respective increases ordered. The schedule should show the following:

Date of Invoice   Vendor   Type of Expense   Amount

Depreciation—Form 33(5)s or 33(5), Item 20.

Enter the lower of the following:

(1) The amount of depreciation claimed for the building in the latest Federal Income Tax Return.

(2) 2% of the equalized assessed valuation of the building exclusive of the land or, where the purchase price is being claimed as the "valuation-basis", 2% on that part of the purchase price which will represent the building value. To establish such building value one must apply to the total purchase price the same ratio that the assessed valuation of the building bears to the total of the current assessed valuation. Example: Assume the property's total assessed to be $10,000.00 of which the building valuation is $8,000.00. This establishes 80% as the ratio of the

ADVISORY BULLETINS

building's valuation. Accordingly 80% would be the ratio to be applied to whatever purchase price is claim as the "valuation-basis". The 2% depreciation allowance is to be computed on the amount thus established.

The schedule for this item should show the applicant's computation for the depreciation allowance claimed.

Determination of Valuation, Items 23 & 24

Part A—The equalized assessed valuation of the property is to be used as the "valuation-basis" (Item 23—Form 33(5)) is to be based on the assessed valuation of the village, city or town by which the property is assessed and in effect at the time of the filing of the application; it is to be determined by dividing the village, city or town assessed valuation by the appropriate equalization rate as determined by the New York State Board of Equalization and Assessment. A Table of Equalization Rates for the village, city or town in which your property is located can be obtained at your Local Rent Office. The rate is to be selected by you from such "Table" is to be the one cited for your type or class of property. For example, the equalization rate for an apartment house in a city is 93%. The equalized assessed valuation of that property, if assessed at $10,000.00, would be $10,000.00 divided by .93, or $10,752.69. On this same property, the building represents $8,000.00 of the $10,000.00 assessed valuation. Hence, the valuation of the building to be used in computing the depreciation allowance is $8,000.00 divided by .93, or $8,602.15.

Part B—Where the present landlord acquired the property by a bona-fide purchase since March 15, 1957, the purchase price, in the absence of any special factors or circumstances, may generally be used instead of the equalized assessed valuation as the basis for the net annual return. The purchase price should be inserted in Item 24 on Form 33(5).

ADVISORY BULLETINS

3. SPECIFIC INSTRUCTION FOR COMPLETION OF FORM 33(5)A—RENTAL INCOME

All controlled, decontrolled, uncontrolled and commercial units in the property are to be listed at the rent in effect at the time this application is filed (Units with seasonal, alternate, or other varying rents are to be entered at the average earned in the "test year".) Rents in Column 5 are to be converted to an annual basis by multiplying weekly rates by 52 and monthly rates by 12. For commercial units which have a percentage rental, show in Column 5 and 6 the actual amount earned in the last lease year prior to the end of the "test year" used in the application. If any housing accommodation is vacant, or is occupied in whole or in part rent free, use the maximum rent in effect for such accommodation, if any. If there is no maximum rent therefor or if commercial or business or other rentable space in the property is vacant or is occupied in whole or in part rent free, its full rental value shall be entered on this schedule. This includes any units occupied by the landlord or his employees. Indicate in Column 2 by a check-mark all uncontrolled, decontrolled, business and commercial space. Information should be furnished as to the rental in effect for business and commercial space at the time of the first Federal rent freeze.

4. INSTRUCTIONS FOR THE SUBMISSION OF EVIDENCE WITH APPLICATION

The supporting evidence you submit is a significant factor for determining whether the property qualifies for increases in maximum rents under this provision of the Regulations. The following preparatory steps are suggested for assembling the evidence to support your application:

(a) Assemble this evidence for submission with your application.

(b) Insert the evidence relating to each "Item" of Form 33(5) or 33(5)s into separate envelopes or packets, together with a copy of the schedule, if any, to which the evidence relates. Where the evidence is not complete indicate such fact on the schedule and explain its absence.

(c) Identify each envelope or packet and each copy of the enclosed schedule. This identification must include the address of the property and the "Item" number.

(d) Be ready to submit any General Ledger and books of original entry which relate to the "test year" used in your application—if requested during the processing of your application.

(e) Assemble all cancelled checks in support of the items which must be so verified. These cancelled checks may be assembled in either of the following ways:

(1) Attach the cancelled check to the bill which was paid by the check; or

(2) Retain the cancelled checks in their monthly packets together with the monthly bank statement. The checks should be arranged in either numerical sequence or in the order of the dates of their issuance. Include cancelled checks for the full "test year", and those relating to expenses which are properly chargeable to the "test year" and to items listed in the schedules for "Repairs and Maintenance" and "Replacements and Improvements" if optional allowance is not used. Where the cancelled checks are not attached to the bills, the bills must be marked with the number and the date of the check by which it was paid.

(f) Pack all of the above described material into a secure package.

(g) Mark the outside of the package as follows: "RETURN TO .... (insert your name and address);

(h) Deliver this package by mail, or in person to the Local Rent Office with your application.

ADVISORY BULLETIN NO. 8
(Revised March 15, 1951)
SECTION 33(4). UNIQUE OR PECULIAR CIRCUMSTANCES

Section 33(4) is designed to give relief to a landlord who is suffering severe hardship because unique or peculiar factors in the rental transaction materially influenced the amount of the rent received by the landlord, resulting in a rent substantially out of line with the rents generally prevailing for comparable controlled housing units. This section does not permit adjustments solely because there are variations in rents for similar housing accommodations.

There are two prerequisites to an adjustment under this section. First, the landlord must establish the existence of unique or peculiar circumstances which materially affected the maximum rent of the housing accommodations. Second, the landlord must establish that the maximum rent of the housing accommodations is substantially out of line with the rents generally prevailing in the same area for substantially similar controlled housing accommodations.

Examples of Unique or Peculiar Circumstances.

A. **Renting to a relative.** The son of the landlord occupied the top floor of a two-family house on the Federal date determining the maximum rent. The son paid $25.00 per month even though similar housing accommodations on that date were renting for between $50.00 and $55.00 per month. The son has vacated and the apartment is now rented by, or the landlord desires to rent it to, a stranger.

B. **Renting under unusual pressure or necessity.** Two months prior to the Federal date determining the maximum rent the owner of a one-family house received notice from his employer that he was being transferred to Los Angeles within a week, and that this transfer would be for a one year period. In order to dispose quickly of his home he rented it to the first applicant for an amount substantially below the prevailing level of rents for comparable houses.

C. **Factors with respect to management.** 1. On the Federal date determining the maximum rent a house was owned and managed by a landlord who was senile. Being incapable of normal business judgment he rented the accommodations prior to that date for an amount substantially below the prevailing level of rent for comparable houses.

2. Some months prior to the Federal date determining the maximum rent a house had been forfeited to the city for non-payment of taxes. Under local law, a temporary receiver was appointed to collect rents and pay taxes until the property was either redeemed or sold. The property was rented by the tax receiver for an amount substantially below the prevailing rent for comparable accommodations. Subsequently the premises were sold to a new owner.

Examples Not Constituting Unique or Peculiar Circumstances.

D. **Concession.** A maximum rent in New York City had been reduced by the Federal authorities because of the existence of a concession. The landlord claims that his maximum rent is therefore substantially below comparable rents within the house and desires an increase. Since this maximum rent had been established pursuant to the Federal laws then in effect, it cannot be deemed unique or peculiar circumstances which would warrant application by the landlord for an increase in maximum rent.

E. **Entire Building below comparability.** A landlord claims that housing accommodations in a structure completed in 1941 were rented for less than the rents generally prevailing for similar housing accommodations because it was opened for rental in an off-season period. Since these maximum rents represent the free bargains of the parties in a competitive rental market, the circumstances cannot be considered unique or peculiar and the landlord cannot therefore obtain a rent adjustment pursuant to this section.

Standards for Comparison

In a multi-family structure comparison of rents will usually be restricted to the controlled rents in that structure. There will generally be no comparison made between apartments in different multi-dwelling structures because of the widely varying factors which affect rental value. The United States Emergency Court of Appeals in London Terrace, Inc. v. Creedon, 162 F. (2d) 722, 725, held that it was proper for the Housing Expediter to limit comparability not only to the building but to the tier in the building. The Court said: "Generally speaking, in apartment buildings, the only units that may be said to be identical are those in the same tier, for apartment units in other tiers vary in many tangible and intangible respects."

Where one or two-family houses are involved it is proper to broaden the inquiry to include the maximum rents of similar controlled housing accommodations within the neighborhood.

Only maximum rents in effect on March 1, 1950, excluding adjustments by voluntary increase leases under Section 204(b) of the Housing and Rent Acts of 1947 and 1948, or by order of the Housing Expediter under Section 5(a)(19) of the Federal regulations then in effect may be considered in determining the rent generally prevailing. The rents of uncontrolled or decontrolled housing accommodations cannot be considered in determining the generally prevailing rents. Isolated high or low maximum rents will not be considered as a basis for comparison, since these are not determinative of rents generally prevailing for similar housing accommodations.

The application must be filed upon Form 33(4). Complete instructions for the preparation of this form appear thereon. The landlord must be sure to state the facts which he claims establish the existence of unique or peculiar circumstances, and the landlord should further set forth the housing accommodations which he alleges are comparable controlled housing accommodations with substantially higher maximum rents.

ADVISORY BULLETIN No. 10
(Revised October 1, 1961)
INCREASE OF MAXIMUM RENT (INCREASED COSTS—SMALL STRUCTURES)—SECTION 33(5) OF THE REGULATIONS

Section 33(6) is designed to give relief to the so-called "non-professional" landlord who owns no more than four rental units (excluding any unit personally occupied by him) within the State, and who for lack of detailed records may not be in a position to establish his right to rent increases based upon a return on the valuation of the property under Section 33(5) of the Regulations. Application Form 33(6) has been prepared for use by landlords wishing to file under this section, which reads as follows:

Section 33(6). Unavoidable increases in operating costs in small structures.

a. The landlord owns no more than four rental units within the State and has incurred unavoidable increases in property taxes, fuel, utilities, insurance and repairs and maintenance which have occurred since the Federal date determining the maximum rent or the date the property was acquired by the present owner, whichever is later.

b. Where the Administrator finds in considering an application under this paragraph that a present tenant is paying a rent less than the maximum rent, the Administrator, upon request of the landlord, may reduce the maximum rent of the housing accommodation to the amount actually being paid, or to the highest maximum rent for comparable controlled housing accommodations in the structure, whichever is higher. If, as determined by the Administrator, the landlord has not been fully compensated by increases in rental income sufficient to offset such increases in operating costs the Administrator shall grant an adjustment in the maximum rents.

c. No further application may be filed under this paragraph sooner than one year from the date of filing a prior application under this paragraph if an increase had previously been granted thereunder. No order increasing a maximum rent shall be issued on a subsequent application sooner than one year from the effective date, or the earlier effective date if there are dual effective dates, of the order granting an increase on the prior application. The Administrator may waive these limitations where the property has been affected by a significant increase in operating costs which applied to a substantial segment of housing accommodations in the community.

Section 33 also contains the following provision:

That portion of the amount of increase computed under paragraph . . . (6) . . . as is properly attributable to the

Advisory Bulletins

controlled housing accommodations shall be apportioned among them so that each bears an equitable portion thereof. In making such apportionment and in fixing the increases in maximum rents the Administrator shall give due consideration to all previous adjustments or increases in maximum rents by lease or otherwise. Each controlled housing accommodation shall bear no more than that portion of the amount of increase as is properly attributable to such housing accommodation, whether or not the amount so attributed shall be fully collectible by reason of existing lease or otherwise.

Instructions for preparing and filing an application under this paragraph are printed on Form 33(6) and should be read in conjunction with this Advisory Bulletin before application is completed and filed at the Local Rent Office.

On the face of the form is entered general information concerning the property and the rental income derived therefrom. On the reverse side of the form information is entered concerning the specific items of expense which will be considered in this application. All bills relating to such expenses should accompany the application.

Increases granted under this paragraph will reflect only the *increase* in each item of expense, that is, the difference between the cost of the item for the current period and the cost for the base period. The base period will be either the year when Federal rent control took effect or the year in which the landlord acquired the property, *whichever is later.*

As a result of a survey conducted by the Commission, indexes have been established for the various items of expense in the different areas of the State. These indexes show the change in the costs of the different items of expense for each year since Federal rent control first took effect. By applying the appropriate index to current expenses, the increase in the cost of the various items will be determined by the Local Rent Administrator. For example, if a landlord has spent $200 for fuel during the current year and the base period index is 60, it means that the base period cost was 60 percent of the current cost. Therefore the base period expense for fuel would be $120 and the increased cost would be $80. The other allowable items of expense will be processed in the same manner, except where the landlord's base year's expense is specifically requested.

Increases to which the landlord is entitled as a result of the 15% equalization adjustment permitted under Section 4, Subdivision 3(a) of the Act (commonly referred to as the "Equalization Adjustment") are considered to be part of his compensatory income. If the landlord has not received rental increases sufficient to offset the total increases in expenses during the period of his ownership of the property, he will be entitled to an adjustment under this paragraph.

In adjusting rents consideration will be given to all previous adjustments in the maximum rents of the individual housing accommodations by lease or otherwise. *In no event will a landlord be entitled to an adjustment under this section where he is not maintaining all essential services required to be provided with the housing accommodations.*

ADVISORY BULLETIN No. 11
INCREASE OF MAXIMUM RENT (INCREASED COSTS—HOTELS, ROOMING HOUSES AND COOPERATIVES) SECTION 33(7) OF THE REGULATIONS

Section 33(7) of the Regulations may be used by operators of rooming-houses, controlled rooms in hotels in New York City and Buffalo, and by owners of cooperative apartments instead of the net return procedure under Section 33(5).

Section 33(7). **Unavoidable increases in operating costs in other specified structures.**

a. The landlord operates a hotel or rooming house or owns a cooperative apartment and has incurred unavoidable increases in property taxes and other costs, including costs of operation of such hotel or rooming house, but excluding mortgage interest and amortization, and excluding allowances for depreciation, obsolescence and reserves, which have occurred since the Federal date determining the maximum rent or the date the present landlord commenced the operation of the property, whichever is later.

ADVISORY BULLETINS

b. If, as determined by the Administrator, the landlord has not been fully compensated by increases in rental income sufficient to offset such increases in operating costs, the Administrator shall grant an adjustment in the maximum rents in the manner and subject to the provisions of subdivision c. of this paragraph.

c. That portion of the increased operating costs applicable to the controlled housing accommodations shall be apportioned equitably among all the controlled housing accommodations in the property. In making such apportionment and in fixing the increases in maximum rent the Administrator shall give due consideration to all previous adjustments or increases in maximum rents by lease or otherwise, provided, however, that no adjustment for any individual housing accommodation shall exceed 15 percent of the maximum rent prescribed on the date the order is issued under this paragraph.

d. No further application may be filed under this paragraph until one year from the date an increase is granted hereunder. The test year used in any subsequent application shall begin after the end of the test year used in the last previous application. The Administrator may waive these limitations where the property has been affected by a significant increase in operating costs which applied to a substantial segment of housing accommodations in the community.

General: Detailed instructions for the preparation of the forms, which are to be used by operators of hotels and rooming houses and owners of cooperative apartments, are set forth in the following paragraphs. Where the instructions for a particular item on the form differ in respect to hotels and to rooming houses, this difference will be indicated by the captions—"For Hotels" and "For Rooming-Houses".

Owners of cooperative apartments are required to complete only items 1, 2, 3 and 5 on Form 33(7) and to submit a schedule showing the present rents and the number of shares allocated to the housing accommodations for which the increase is requested and the total number of shares in the building. They must also submit the operating statement of the cooperative organization for the base period and for the current period.

Preparation of Form 33(7)

Instruction 1—Name and Mailing Address of Landlord—Form 33(7), Item 1.

Enter in the proper spaces the name, telephone number, and address of landlord. If the subject property is a hotel with a name different from the landlord's, the name of the hotel is to be noted above the name of landlord.

Instruction 2—Name and Mailing Address of Tenant—Form 33(7), Item 2.

On the original form and duplicate, this item is to be left blank. Instruction 22 indicates the use of this item for those copies which the landlord is required to prepare for service upon the tenants.

Instruction 3—Address of Property—Form 33(7), Item 3.

Enter the address of the property for which the increase is requested.

Instruction 4—Units—Form 33(7), Item 4.

For Hotels:

Enter on line (a) the number of units and the number of rooms contained therein, presently occupied by controlled tenants. Enter on line (b) the number of all other units and the number of rooms contained therein. Enter on line (c) the totals of both units and rooms. (Note that the totals for units and rooms to be used here should be the entire number of units and rooms in the hotel less the number of units and rooms devoted to employees' use.)

Divide the number of units on line (a) by the number of units on line (c). This will establish the percentage ratio of controlled units to the total number of units.

Repeat the same procedure for rooms. This will establish the percentage ratio of controlled rooms to the total number of rooms.

Add the percentage ratios of units and rooms and divide the sum by 2. This will establish the "Ratio of Controlled to Total" which is to be entered in Item 4(d).

For Rooming Houses:

Complete Items 4a, 4b, and 4c only. Leave Item 4d blank.

ADVISORY BULLETINS

Instruction 5—**Acquisition Data—Form 33(7), Item 5.**

Enter the date the subject property was acquired by the present owner, the manner in which the property was acquired and the cost. If the property was acquired by private sale or foreclosure, check appropriate item; if acquired in some other manner, check "otherwise", and explain in space in Item 5.

Instruction 6—**"Base Year" and "Current Year"—Form 33(7), Item 6.**

The "Base Year" is the calendar or fiscal year which included the Federal date determining the maximum rent, or the first complete calendar or fiscal year which commenced subsequent to the acquisition of the property by the landlord, whichever is later. The landlord may select as his "Current Year" one of the following: the most recent calendar year; the most recent fiscal year; any 12 consecutive months ending within 90 days prior to the date of filing of this application.

Instruction 7—**Salaries and Wages—Form 33(7), Item 7.**

Enter the cost of salaries and wages, and the cost of all items directly related thereto, such as social security and unemployment taxes, hospital benefits, and compensation insurance. Projection of the current year's payroll to an annual amount, based on wage-schedules in effect at the time of filing the application, will be allowed. Do not include in this item any wages for repair and maintenance work, or executive or administrative salaries. The payroll-allocations used in the landlord's books may be followed. Where payroll is reported as part of any other item of this form (for example as part of "heat, light and power" in Item 10), it may also be projected as indicated above.

Attach to the application a schedule (to be designated by the landlord as Schedule E) showing the following:

Schedule of Salaries & Wages

Based on Payroll of

(Date)

Department or Duties	No. of Employees Regular Part-Time	Current Wage Rate Monthly or Weekly	Amount of Annual Wages

After listing all the wages, show the amount of social security and unemployment taxes, hospital benefits and compensation insurance which apply to the annualized amounts listed.

Where the applicant is the operator of a rooming-house, the salaries and wages item may include the value of services actually performed by the operator in the operation of the rooming-house.

Instruction 8—Insurance—Form 33(7), Item 8.

Enter premiums properly allocable to the base year and to the current year for (a) fire insurance on building and contents and (b) all other forms of insurance, such as innkeepers' liability, public liability, tornado, sprinkler leakage, boiler, plate glass, etc. Compensation premiums are not to be included but should be allocated to the payroll items to which they apply. Attach to the application a schedule (to be designated by the landlord as Schedule F) showing for the "Current Year" the following:

Type of Insurance	Amount of Coverage	Effective Date	Expiration Date	Total Term Premium	Allocable To Current Year

Instruction 9—General Expenses—Form 33(7), Item 9.

Prepare a schedule (to be designated by the landlord as Schedule G) with columns for the "Base Year" and for the "Current Year", enumerating: (a) all the "Administrative and General" categories of expense not separately furnished elsewhere on this form; (b) all the categories of "Advertising and Business Promotion" expenses; (c) rooms-expenses; and (d) miscellaneous expenses not otherwise classified.

Salaries of officers of corporations connected with the ownership or operation of the property and salaries of partners and individual proprietors or operators are to be shown as a separate item.

Where the applicant is the lessee of the property the lease rental should be listed separately.

ADVISORY BULLETINS

Instruction 10—**Heat, Light and Power**—**Form 33(7), Item 10.**

Prepare a schedule for the "Current Year" (to be designated by the landlord as Schedule H) showing separately in detail the expenses for heating fuel, gas, electricity and water. Projection of water charges on the basis of rates in effect at the time of filing the application will be allowed.

Instruction 11—**Repairs and Maintenance**—**Form 33(7), Item 11.**

Enter the cost of all repair and maintenance expenses (including all painting and decorating and any wages applicable to this category and not included in other items). No equipment costs or capital improvements are to be included in this item. Attach a schedule (to be designated by the landlord as Schedule I) showing by categories or types of expense the details of this item for both the "Base Year" and the "Current Year".

Instruction 12—**Real Estate Taxes**—**Form 33(7), Item 12.**

Enter for the "Base Year" the real estate taxes chargeable to that period. Enter for the "Current Year" the amount of real estate taxes payable for the tax year in effect at the time the application is filed. Attach to the application the current tax bill or copy (to be designated by the landlord as Schedule J).

Instruction 13—**Replacements and Improvements**—**Form 33(7), Item 13.**

Enter the properly allocable portion of the cost of all improvements and replacements chargeable to the "Base Year" and to the "Current Year" made by the present landlord.

Attach to the application a schedule (to be designated by the landlord as Schedule K) showing for the "Base Year" and for the "Current Year", the following:

Date Acquired	Item	Cost	Useful Life	One Year Charge

Instruction 14—**Total Expenses**—**Form 33(7), Item 14.**

Enter the total of Items 7 through 13.

Instruction 15—**All Income Other than Room-Rents**—**Form 33(7), Item 15.**

Attach a schedule (to be designated by the landlord as Schedule D) summarizing the net results of departmental operations and showing income from sources other than room-rents for both the "Base Year" and the "Current Year". The total of this item for each period to be entered in Item 15 must be detailed as follows:

(a) Profit or (Loss) of Food and Beverage Department, should be itemized as follows: Sales of Food and Beverages, Costs of Food and Beverages, Gross Profit, Allocable Payroll, and Other Expenses.

(b) Profit or (Loss) of Telephone Department, should be itemized as follows: Telephone Receipts, Costs of Calls (including taxes and facilities), Allocable Payroll, and Expenses.

(c) Profit or (Loss) of other operated departments, should be itemized showing Receipts, Allocable Payrolls and Expenses.

(d) Store Rentals.

(e) Public Room Rentals.

(f) Concession Rentals.

(g) Miscellaneous Income.

Allocable payrolls and expenses shown in Schedule D must be applicable to the particular department and are not to be included in this item if they have already been included elsewhere.

Instruction 16—**Net Cost of Operations**—**Form 33(7), Item 16.**

Enter the amounts obtained by subtracting Item 15 from Item 14.

Instruction 17—**Increase in Cost of Operations**—**Form 33(7), Item 17.**

Enter the amount obtained by subtracting Item 16, Column 1, from Item 16, Column 2.

Instruction 18—**Controlled Tenants' Share of Cost-Increase**—**Form 33(7), Item 18.**

For Hotels

Enter the amount obtained by multiplying Item 17 by the percentage ratio in Item 4(d).

Advisory Bulletins

For Rooming-Houses

No entry required for this item.

Instruction 19—**Compensatory Income—Form 33(7), Item 19.**

For Hotels

Enter the amount obtained by subtracting the total of Column 7, Form 33(7)H, from the total of Column 5, Form 33(7)H.

For Rooming-Houses

Enter the amount shown in Item (c) of Form 33(7)R.

Instruction 20—**Increased Costs not Previously Compensated—Form 33(7), Item 20.**

For Hotels

Enter the amount obtained by subtracting Item 19 from Item 18.

For Rooming-Houses

Enter the amount obtained by subtracting Item 19 from Item 17.

Preparation of Rental Schedules

Instruction 21

For Hotels

Landlords are to fill out Form 33(7)H, the instructions for the preparation of which are contained on the form itself. They are also to submit a schedule (to be designated by the landlord as Schedule B) showing the rooms income earned in both the "Base Year" and the "Current Year" classified as "Income From Permanent Tenants" and "Income From Transient Tenants".

For Rooming-Houses

Landlords are to fill out Form 33(7)R, the instructions for the preparation of which are contained on the form itself. Be sure to list all controlled, decontrolled, uncontrolled and commercial units. If not controlled, indicate by check (√) in Column 2.

Filing Application

Instruction 22—**Filing**

For Hotels

An original and one copy of Forms 33(7) and 33(7)H, together will all required documents and schedules, must be filed with the Local Rent Office by delivery or mailing. The landlord is also required to file an additional copy of Forms 33(7) and 33(7)H for each housing accommodation affected by the application, with the name and mailing address of the tenant inserted in Item 2 of Form 33(7). These copies will be served upon the tenants by the Administrator.

Before filing the application forms be sure to sign all copies and have the original sworn to before a Notary Public or other person authorized to administer oaths.

For Rooming-Houses

An original and one copy of Forms 33(7) and 33(7)R, together with all required documents and schedules, must be filed with the Local Rent Office by delivery or mailing. The landlord is also required to file an additional copy of Forms 33(7) and 33(7)R for each housing accommodation affected by the application, with the name and mailing address of the tenant inserted in Item 2 of Form 33(7). These copies will be served upon the tenants by the Administrator.

Before filing the application forms be sure to sign all copies and have the original sworn to before a Notary Public or other person authorized to administer oaths.

For Cooperatives

An original and one copy of Form 33(7) together with the required statements must be filed with the Local Rent Office by delivery or mailing. The landlord is also required to file an additional copy of Form 33(7) and of the statement showing the income, for each housing accommodation affected by the application. These copies will be served upon the tenants by the Administrator.

Before filing the application forms be sure to sign all copies and have the original sworn to before a Notary Public or other person authorized to administer oaths.

ADVISORY BULLETIN No. 12
(Revised July 12, 1965)
VOLUNTARY LEASE AGREEMENTS—SECTION 33(2) OF THE REGULATIONS

Under Section 33(2) of the Rent and Eviction Regulations landlords and tenants are permitted to enter into voluntary leases which may provide for an increase in rent not in excess of 15% above the maximum rent in effect for a controlled housing accommodation where the conditions specified in Section 33(2) are met.

The tenant, by executing such a lease, secures himself against having to pay more than the amount agreed upon during the term of the lease. Similarly, by executing such a lease, the landlord commits himself to charging no more than the amount agreed upon during the term of the lease.

As a condition for the increase in the maximum rent, the landlord must certify that he is maintaining and will continue to maintain all essential services together with any additional services which the tenant may secure in his bargaining for the lease.

The maximum rent is automatically increased by the execution of such a voluntary lease. The tenant will continue to have substantially the same protection afforded by the present Rent and Eviction Regulations so long as they continue in effect.

The following questions and answers clarify these provisions:

1. Q. A landlord requests a tenant to enter into a two year lease providing for an increase of not more than 15 percent in the maximum rent. Must the tenant sign a lease?

    A. No. The tenant need not sign a lease unless he wishes to. The maximum rent cannot be increased merely because the tenant does not sign a lease.

2. Q. May a tenant be evicted if he does not enter into a lease providing for some increase in the maximum rent?

    A. No. The tenant may not be evicted under the present law and regulations for refusing to enter into such a lease and he will continue to have such protection while the regulations remain in force, whether he has a lease or not.

3. Q. Is it possible for a landlord to obtain an increase in the maximum rent if the tenant does not have the protection of a lease?

   A. Yes. A landlord may be able to obtain an increase in the maximum rent if he can prove the necessary facts under certain sections of the Regulations.

4. Q. If a tenant declines to accept the landlord's terms for a lease, or does not enter into any lease, may the landlord decrease the essential services which he gave, or which he was required to give for the maximum rent?

   A. No. Should the landlord for any reason refuse to provide such services the tenant may file a complaint with the local Rent Administrator. If the landlord refuses to restore the services, the maximum rent may be reduced.

5. Q. What does the tenant gain by signing such a voluntary lease agreement?

   A. (1) The contractual right to remain in the leased premises, subject to the conditions in the lease and subject to the Regulations, at the rent agreed upon in the lease for the duration of the lease; (2) If the landlord were eligible for a greater increase in rent during the period of the proposed lease through some adjustment section of the Regulations, he will not be able to compel the tenant to pay the increase during the lease term without the tenant's written consent.

6. Q. The tenant is agreeable to having a lease but prefers a three year lease instead of a two year lease. Would this be proper under the Regulations?

   A. Yes. The lease may be for as long a period as the tenant and the landlord may agree upon, provided it is for a minimum period of two years. However, the Regulations provide that if the lease is with a new tenant and is for longer than a two year

Advisory Bulletins

term, the new tenant must be given the right to cancel the lease at any time after the expiration of the first two years of the lease by giving the landlord at least thirty days' notice in writing of his intention to cancel the lease and surrender possession of the apartment. If the tenant elects to cancel his lease, he must vacate the apartment.

7. Q. The tenant would like to have the right to cancel the lease upon thirty days' notice to the landlord at any time prior to the expiration of the first two years of the lease. Is this permissible?

   A. Yes. The lease may give the tenant the right to cancel or terminate sooner. This would apply to any lease, whether for a minimum period of two years or for a longer term. However, this option may only be given a tenant and a landlord cannot have this right of cancellation.

8. Q. The tenant wishes to pay only a 10 percent increase and the landlord is willing to accept this. Is this permissible?

   A. Yes. The rent increase may be in any amount not exceeding 15 percent.

9. Q. The tenant is willing to sign a lease but he wishes a new stove, or a new refrigerator, or the right to put up a television antenna, or some other increase or improvement in the services as a consideration for the execution of the lease. May this be part of the lease agreement?

   A. Yes. This is a matter of bargaining between landlord and tenant. It is important to remember that the lease should specifically include a statement of such additional services and state that they are included in the lease rent and are being provided by the landlord on the effective date of the lease term.

10. Q. If a tenant signs a lease which provides for additional services or equipment, and the landlord fails to furnish such additional services or equipment, what may the tenant do?

    A. He may file a complaint with the Local Rent Administrator and the new maximum rent may be reduced.

Advisory Bulletins

11. Q. If a landlord enters into such a lease and his expenses afterwards are increased, may he obtain an additional increase above that established in the voluntary lease agreement?

    A. Yes. However, since the landlord and tenant are both bound by the terms of the lease, the landlord will not be able to compel the tenant to pay any rent in excess of the lease rent until the lease expires.

12. Q. If a tenant signs such a lease may the landlord, or a purchaser of the property, have him evicted for personal occupancy or to subdivide the apartment during the term of the lease?

    A. No. The tenant is protected from eviction for such purposes by his lease agreement until the lease expires.

13. Q. Will the housing accommodations be decontrolled if the tenant signs such a lease?

    A. No. The tenant continues to receive the protection of the Regulations as well as the benefits of the lease.

14. Q. A tenant is not agreeable to entering into a voluntary lease agreement, but he does want a new refrigerator, or a new stove, or a new service. How may he obtain it?

    A. The tenant and the landlord must come to an agreement about the additional service. A form is provided on which the landlord can apply for an increase based upon this agreement. The amount of the increase of the maximum rent for the additional service will be determined by the Local Rent Administrator.

15. Q. If the landlord and tenant sign such a voluntary lease agreement, what remains to be done for it to become effective?

    A. The new maximum rent takes effect automatically in accordance with the terms of the lease if the lease complies with the requirements of Section 33(2) of the Regulations. Within thirty days after the date of delivery of the signed lease to the landlord the landlord must file a report of it upon prescribed forms with the Local Rent Administrator. This must include a statement of any additional services or equipment furnished to the tenant as a consideration for the execution of the lease.

16. Q. Will the Local Rent Administrator advise either a tenant or a landlord to execute such a lease?

A. No. The Local Rent Administrator has no authority to give such advice, nor would it be proper for him to do so. It is for each tenant and each landlord, respectively, to use his own judgment and come to his own conclusion.

17. Q. When may the landlord and the tenant enter into a voluntary lease?

A. The landlord and tenant may enter into and execute a voluntary lease at any time provided the increase in the maximum rent did not take effect prior to March 15, 1951. Under Amendment No. 53 to Section 33(2) of the Rent and Eviction Regulations a new voluntary written lease may be entered into provided that at least twelve months of the prior voluntary lease had already expired. The new voluntary lease must be for a period including the unexpired portion of the first two years of the prior lease plus two years. Where the prior lease provided for a full 15% rent increase, the new lease may not provide for a further rent increase prior to the expiration of the first two years of the prior lease.

For instance, if a housing unit had a maximum rent of $100.00 per month and this was increased by a voluntary lease to $115.00 per month with a term which began on March 1, 1959 and was to terminate on February 28, 1961, no new lease increase could be obtained prior to March 1, 1960. On or after March 1, 1960 a landlord could enter into a new lease for a term expiring no sooner than February 28, 1963 with the rent remaining at $115.00 per month until February 28, 1961 and the 15% increase, or whatever lesser amount the tenant agreed to pay, would become effective on March 1, 1961. If the prior lease did not provide for a full 15% increase, but only for a 10% increase, and increased the maximum rent from $100.00 per month to $110.00 per month, the landlord and tenant can enter into a new voluntary lease which would increase the maximum rent to $115.00 per month until February 28, 1961 and then provide for an additional increase of not more than 15% above the $110.00 maximum rent for the two years commencing March 1, 1961. If the prior lease did not provide for a full 15% increase, but only a 10% increase, and increased the maximum rent from $100.00 per month to $110.00 per month, the only voluntary lease that the landlord and tenant could enter into before the expiration of the first year of the original lease would be one which would increase the rent from $110.00 per month to no more than $115.00 per month and which would provide for a minimum term of two years.

18. Q. A landlord proposes to include a so-called "escalator clause" in the lease to provide for an additional increase in rent during the term of the lease in the event that such increase is permitted by new rent regulations, or in the event that State rent control terminates. Is such a clause proper under the Rent and Eviction Regulations?

A. No. A lease containing such a clause does not ordinarily comply with the requirements of Section 33(2) of the Regulations. It would be proper for a lease to contain a provision that the maximum rent resulting from the execution of the lease may be further increased by order of the Administrator based upon additional services or equipment installed by the landlord at or prior to the execution of the lease to which the tenant has consented in writing or based upon a major capital improvement which is either completed or in progress at the time of the execution of the lease. The lease may in such cases provide that the additional amount as determined by the Administrator may then become payable under the lease agreement.

ADVISORY BULLETINS

19. Q. May a lease validly provide that during the first year the maximum rent is increased by 10% and during the second year by an additional 5% over the original maximum rent?

A. Yes. Such a clause is valid under the Regulations since it does not require the payment of more than 15% over the former maximum rent at any time during the term of the lease.

20. Q. Is it possible for a landlord to obtain an increase in the maximum rent for an increase in services, etc. in addition to the permissible 15% statutory lease increase?

A. Yes. It is proper for a statutory lease to provide for a further rent increase where the tenant has consented to the increase in services, etc. and the Administrator has issued an order increasing the maximum rent on the basis of such increase in services, etc. Where the consent to the increase in services, etc. is a part of the same agreement which provided for the statutory lease increase, it would be proper for the landlord to file a combination form (Form 33(1)(CL)) which reports the lease increase and makes application for a further rent adjustment based upon the increased services, etc.

ADVISORY BULLETIN NO. 13

[This Bulletin, issued July 6, 1956, was revoked on June 15, 1961, with the issuance of the revision of Administrator's Opinion No. 95 relative to § 33(1).]

ADVISORY BULLETIN No. 14

(Revised June 1969)

FORM AND CONTENT OF PROTEST AGAINST AN ORDER OF THE LOCAL RENT ADMINISTRATOR

There is no official form for a protest. **Section 95** of the Rent and Eviction Regulations specifies the content of a protest against an order of the Local Rent Administrator. In order to assist both landlords and tenants in the preparation of a protest, the Commission has prepared the following guide:

PROTEST FORM

This is a form for a Protest against an order of the Local Rent Administrator, pursuant to Section 95 of the Rent and Eviction Regulations, which specifies the content of a Protest against an order of the Local Rent Administrator.

Protest to the Commissioner of Housing & Community Renewal by .... (landlord) (tenant) from an order of the Local Rent Administrator issued .... 19 .. and bearing Local Rent Office Docket No. .....

(1) I, the undersigned, am the (landlord) (tenant) and (own) (occupy) premises (No.) .... (Street) .... (Apt. No.) .... located in the County of ...., State of New York. My post-office address is (No.) .... (Street) .... (Apt. No.) .... (City) ....

(2) The specific address of the Local Rent Office involved is (No.) .... (Street) .... County of ...., State of New York.

(3) The housing accommodation involved in this Protest is located at (No.) .... (Street) .... (City) ...., State of New York.

(4) The names and post-office addresses of all other parties affected by this Protest are as follows (attach additional sheets, if necessary): ....

(5) Said Local Rent Administrator's Order should be (revoked) (modified) and my specific objections are as follows (attach additional sheets, if necessary): ....

(6) Notice is hereby served on the (landlord) (tenant) that he may within 15 days from the date of service of this Protest, file a verified answer thereto, by filing the same with the Division of Housing and Community Renewal at 393 Seventh Avenue, New York, New York 10001, together with proof of service of a copy of the answer upon the party filing the Protest.

Dated .... 19 ..

....
Petitioner

VERIFICATION

State of New York } ss:
County of ....

........, being duly sworn, deposes and says: That (s)he is the petitioner in the above-entitled proceeding; that (s)he has read the foregoing petition and knows the contents thereof; that the same is true to (his) (her) own knowledge except as to the matters therein stated to be alleged on information and belief, and that as to those matters (s)he believes it to be true.

....
Petitioner

Sworn to before me this .... day of .... 19..

....
Notary Public or Comm. of Deeds

AFFIDAVIT OF SERVICE

State of New York } ss:
County of ....

........, being duly sworn, deposes and says: That (s)he is the petitioner herein. That (s)he resides at (No.) .... (Street) .... County of ...., State of New York and that (s)he is over 21 years of age.

That on the .... day of ...., 19.., (s)he served upon the following named person(s): ...., ..., a copy of the annexed Protest by depositing the same, properly enclosed in a post-paid wrapper, in the post-office letter box, regularly maintained at (No.) .... (Street) .... (City) .... directed to the Local Rent Office at (No.) .... (Street) .... (City) .... and to the following named person(s):

........, ..., ... at the addresses within the State designated by them for that purpose or the place where they then kept an office, between which places there then was and now is a regular communication by mail.

....

Sworn to before me this .... day of .... 19..

....
Notary Public or Comm. of Deeds

ADVISORY BULLETIN A

KEY POINTS TO RENT CONTROL COVERAGE

Under New York State law, rent controls are in effect in many sections of the State where acute housing short-

193

ages still exist. As of May 1, 1969, some 115,000 housing accommodations were rent controlled in twelve cities, fifty-three towns, and some one hundred and one villages. In general, rental accommodations erected before February 1, 1947 are rent controlled. Those built after that date are not. A number of exceptions to control are also stipulated in the law. For example, vacancies in one- and two-family houses and, in even larger structures in some counties are not rent controlled. Neither are subdivided apartments or those rented for professional or business use.

Rent controls are ordered lifted in any area when the housing emergency ceases, by either the finding of the Commissioner of Housing and Community Renewal that a five percent vacancy rate has been reached, or pursuant to a request of the governing body of the city, town, or village.

Consult your local rent administration office on any rent control problem you may have. It is there to serve you. A list of the offices is attached to this bulletin. In New York City rent control is under municipal administration and law. In the City of Albany housing accommodations which rented at $80.00 per month or less on April 1, 1962 are under rent control.

MAINTENANCE OF SERVICES

Tenants may obtain a rent reduction where there is any decrease in normal essential services, or if equipment (refrigerators, stoves, etc.) is not maintained, or if the building deteriorates. Forms for filing single or multiple complaints may be obtained at local rent administration offices. Where the facts sustain a complaint, the landlord is given an opportunity to correct conditions. If he fails to do so, rent reductions are imposed.

RENT ADJUSTMENTS

Landlords may obtain rent adjustments on a number of grounds specified in the state law. Installation of new equipment with the consent of tenants, failure to earn a return of six percent on property valuation, voluntary lease agreements, major capital improvements and rehabilitation of a building are the principal grounds for rent adjustment grants. A careful check is made of all applications. A rent adjustment may not be granted, however, unless essential services are being maintained.

EVICTIONS

While the law protects tenants from unwarranted evictions—it does permit landlords to recover possession on proper grounds.

A certificate of eviction must be obtained from the local rent administration office before a landlord may go to court for the eviction of a tenant who pays his rent and commits no nuisance or other wrongful act on the premises.

Some of the circumstances under which the Rent Law authorizes the issuance of a certificate are: proposed occupancy of an apartment by the landlord or a member of his immediate family; demolition of the building in order to erect a new one with more apartments; and subdivision of a large underoccupied apartment, thereby increasing the housing supply. Ample opportunity is afforded tenants to oppose an eviction application if they believe it fails to meet the strict provisions of the law.

Even after a certificate is issued, the landlord must usually wait at least three months before going to court for the actual eviction proceedings against a tenant; the interval is intended to afford the tenant reasonable time to find other housing.

OVERCHARGES

The great majority of landlords operate their property within the Rent Law. A few, either deliberately or unintentionally collect higher rents than are legally permitted. Overcharges take other forms too, viz: compelling a tenant to pay a bonus or to purchase furniture as a condition to renting an apartment.

Tenants who are victims of overcharges are entitled to refunds and may also recover, by court action, up to three times the overcharge for a two year period, plus costs and counsel fees.

Flagrant violators are subject to civil action by the state, and also criminal prosecution. If found guilty, they are liable to fine and imprisonment.

A tenant in occupancy or his landlord will be informed of the legal maximum rent for an apartment by filing a request at the local rent administration office.

HOW TO APPLY

The local rent administration offices are the clearing house for all landlord-tenant applications. It is there that forms are obtained for the filing of applications for evictions, rent reductions or increases. Be sure to fill out the proper form correctly. Assistance is available upon request at each office. The local rent offices handle many applications a month. This means that it may take time to process your application. It will be handled in the order of its receipt, unless special circumstances demand emergency action.

PROCEDURE

Both landlord and tenant are afforded a full opportunity of submitting their side of the case before a decision is rendered. Where necessary, an inspection of the building is made, and a hearing or conference is held so that the parties or their representatives may present their case in person. Either a landlord or tenant, who questions a decision of the Local Rent Administrator in a case, has the right under the Rent Law to file a protest within 33 days after such decision is issued. Two copies of the protest must be sent to the Division of Housing and Community Renewal, Office of Rent Administration, 393 Seventh Avenue, New York, NY 10001, one to the Local Rent Administrator, and one to the opposing party in the dispute. After reviewing the facts, the Commissioner within 90 days may grant or deny the protest in whole or in part. Thereafter a party may take the case within 30 days to the State Supreme Court for review.

ADVISORY BULLETIN B
SCHEDULE OF RENTAL VALUES
July 1, 1969

The Schedule of Rental Values herein shall apply to adjustments of maximum rents pursuant to Section 33(1) of the Rent and Eviction Regulations. Where application is made by the landlord for a rent increase under Section 33(1) (a or d) the landlord must obtain the requisite

Advisory Bulletins

consent of the tenant. Where the application is made under Section 33(1)(b or c) the consent of the tenant is not required. All rent adjustments are monthly. Application forms are available at the local rent administration offices.

The rental values shown shall apply to specific items of Equipment or Service and are to serve as a guide except where it is found that because of a unique and peculiar combination of factors, the following allowances may not be appropriate.

For items that do not appear and which have a rental value, the rent adjustment, will be established by use of the actual cost and the application of a reasonable and appropriate period of amortization.

Item of Equipment or Service

HEAT AND HOT WATER—NONE BEFORE   Monthly Adjustment
- (1) per radiator-heated room (excluding bathrooms), with floor area of at least 70 sq. feet and containing one or more windows and one or more radiators $4.00
- (2) per windowless heated room (excluding bathrooms) of any size and heated by either radiator, riser or ceiling coil.... 1.75
- (3) per heated room (excluding bathrooms) with floor area of less than 70 sq. feet, containing one or more windows and heated by either radiator, riser or ceiling coil 1.75*
- * where room is on top floor or faces either the street or rear open court and is heated either by a 3″ riser, a 2″ riser with a ceiling coil, or by a radiator...................... 2.75
- (4) hot water (per room, including bathrooms)................ 1.25
- (5) in addition to the above, the cost of installation of a modern central heating system will be amortized (none before).

AUTOMATIC GAS OR ELECTRIC WATER HEATER
   with minimum tank capacity of 20 gallons................... 1.75
   [Tenant's consent required if in replacement of hot water heater which complies with the requirements of the local governing authority.]

REFRIGERATORS (installed)   Monthly
   Used mechanical refrigerators (none before) 2.00
   Replacement of old refrigerator with a new mechanical refrigerator [according to National Electrical Mfgrs. Ass'n (NEMA) standards]

Net Capacity (in Cubic Feet)	Conventional or Semi-Automatic Defroster	Full Automatic Defroster	Zero-Degree Freezer
up to and including 7.5	$3.00	$4.00	
7.6 - 8.9	$3.50	$4.50	
9.0 - 10.9	$4.00	$5.00	
10.0 - 12.4	....	....	$5.75
11.0 - 12.9	$4.50	$5.50	
12.5 and over	....	....	$6.25

Where a previous order had been issued for a replacement of a mechanical refrigerator more than 5 years

Advisory Bulletins

prior to the date of a new application, a subsequent replacement with a new late model shall have the full rental value indicated above. Where a prior order had been issued less than 5 years from the date of a new application, a subsequent replacement with a new late model shall have a rental value of the difference between the amount of the previous adjustment and the rental value for the new replacement. This time limitation shall not apply if application is filed at request of tenant in occupancy, for a period of two years or more.

New mechanical refrigerator (none before)

Net Capacity (in Cubic Feet)	Conventional or Semi-Automatic Defroster	Full Automatic Defroster	Zero-Degree Freezer
up to and including 7.5	$5.00	$6.00	
7.6 - 8.9	$5.50	$6.50	
9.0 - 10.9	$6.00	$7.00	
10.0 - 12.4	....	....	$7.75
11.0 - 12.9	$6.50	$7.50	
12.5 and over	....	....	$8.25

[Landlord is required to supply the following information in his application: name of manufacturer, year, model number, cu. ft. capacity, and actual cost. If with "fully automatic defroster" or with "zero-degree freezer", indicate that fact in the application.]

GAS RANGE AND COOKING STOVES (installed)

New modern domestic model gas range or stove
(none before) $3.00*

New modern domestic model gas range or stove
(replacing existing equipment) $2.00*
  * plus 25 cents for each $15 (exclusive of sales tax) or fraction thereof (minimum $5) actual cost above $100 (exclusive of sales tax)

Where a previous order had been issued for a replacement of a gas range or cooking stove more than 5 years prior to the date of a new application, a subsequent replacement with a new late model shall have the full rental value indicated above. Where a prior order had been issued less than 5 years from the date of a new application, a subsequent replacement with a new late model shall have a rental value of the difference between the amount of the previous adjustment and the rental value for the new replacement. This time limitation shall not apply if application is filed at request of tenant in occupancy, for a period of two years or more.

Used gas range or stove (none before) $1.00

Advisory Bulletins

SINKS   Monthly
 (a) Kitchen
  Combination sink and tub (porcelain enamel on iron or steel) $3.00
  Combination sink and tub with metal cabinet (porcelain enamel on iron or steel) 4.00
  Combination sink and drain board (porcelain enamel on iron or steel) with drawers and metal cabinet 4.00
 (b) Bathroom
  Sinks or wash basins (vitreous china or porcelain on iron or steel)
   (replacement) (with new mixing faucets and pop-up waste)... 1.50
   (without mixing faucets and pop-up waste) 1.00
  (none before) the above rental value plus plumbing costs amortized

PLUMBING
 Plumbing replacements—(New Brass or Copper Plumbing Improvements)
  Basement Piping without new Water Service installation . 1.00
  Basement Piping with new Water Service installation 1.25
  Risers (concealed)....................................... 2.75
   (exposed replacing exposed) 1.50
  Branches to Fixtures (concealed) 3.00
   (exposed replacing exposed) 1.00
  Trim in Kitchen and one Bathroom [includes modern faucets for all sinks and tubs together with modernization of shower (new head, body, arm and concealed brass supply)] 1.00
  The above plumbing replacement rental values are in accordance with Administrator's Opinion No. 121 which governs increases due to plumbing replacements and are subject to the conditions and modifications indicated in Administrator's Opinion No. 121.
  Other Rental Values for Concealed Brass Plumbing; Additional Bathroom or Toilet; Previous Installation of Bathtub, Kitchen Sink or Washbasin[1]
  Set of concealed risers (hot and cold water)[2] 1.50
  Basement piping (with set of additional risers) .... .25
  Concealed branches per fixture[3]........................ .60
  In lieu of branches[4] .... .25
  New trim
   Wash Basin Faucets .... .15

[1] These allowances are for fixtures in excess of normal installation for one master bathroom and one kitchen. Additional adjustments are only for existing plumbing being replaced with brass. Fixtures which have been removed at some prior date are not counted, and may not be installed without tenant consent.

[2] Normal installation grant, of $2.75 is considered to include two complete sets of risers. Therefore, $1.50 is allowed for one additional set. No adjustment for additional risers is warranted where there is a common wall between two plumbing installations (i.e. back-to-back). Basement piping is adjusted by $.25 per set of risers. (2 sets of risers at $.25 plus common piping $.50-$1.00.) New water service adjustment is not affected.

[3] Normal adjustment for five concealed branches is $3.00, or $.60 each. (Kitchen sink—with or without tub, bathtub, concealed shower, wash basin and toilet.)

[4] Allowance is made in lieu of branch for any single fixture backing on an existing riser which requires less than 3 feet piping.

199

ADVISORY BULLETINS

Bathtub Faucets	.25
Kitchen Sink Faucets	.25
Shower Head, Body, Arm with concealed brass supply and faucets	.50

SCREENS AND STORM WINDOWS   Monthly

Screens (new and full length only—none before)	.25
Combination screens and storm windows	.50
Combination screen and storm door (each)	1.00

ELECTRICITY AND GAS

Current for operation of TV	.75
Current for operation of refrigerator	1.25
Current for operation of refrigerator with zero-degree freezer	1.75
Current for operation of air-conditioner	

For each air-conditioning unit installed, a monthly allowance of $.33 per 1000 B.T.U.'s (British Thermal Units) of cooling capacity per hour.

Electricity (per room, including bathroom)	1.00
Gas (per room, excluding bathroom)	.50

REWIRING

Rewiring of entire building—per apartment:
(a) Monthly rental adjustment where all units are contained in one building 3.25
(b) Monthly rental adjustment where units are contained in two or more buildings and are connected from the same entrance service 3.75

This rewiring rental value is in accordance with Administrator's Opinion No. 117 revised which governs rent increases due to rewiring. The indicated rental values are subject to modification as indicated in Administrator's Opinion No. 117 revised.

Each air-conditioner circuit and outlet installed at tenant's request (including necessary wiring within the apartment from the fuse panel box to the tenant's air conditioning unit) 1.00

MISCELLANEOUS

Shower—pipes concealed	1.50
Bathroom modernization, including tile, plumbing and all fixtures	Amortized
Flushometer (formerly high tank)	1.00
New low-tank with toilet bowl	1.00
Vinyl linoleum or composition tile	
per room	1.00
Bathroom	.50
Lighting fixtures [new (none before)—per room] including complete installation with wall switch or combination wall switch and outlet	.50
Additional electrical outlets (per duplex outlet receptacle)	.25*

*Provided that the distance between all receptacles is no less than 12 feet measured horizontally along the wall at the floor of the room.

Electric wall switches (per room—none before)	.25
Television antenna (any part of landlord's property)	2.00
Washing machines (installed by tenant)	
Permanently attached to the plumbing or floor	1.00
Kitchen cabinets	Amortized
Clothes closet—built-in	1.00
Air-conditioner installed by tenant—protrusion beyond window line or attachment to exterior of building	2.00

Advisory Bulletins

OPERATIONAL BULLETIN NO. 105
(Issued January 31, 1975)
Standards for determining applications under Section 33-8 of Rent and Eviction Regulations to compensate for unavoidable increased costs of operation.

Effective immediately, applications by landlords for rent adjustments under Section 33-8 of the Rent and Eviction Regulations, Emergency Housing Rent Control Law, to compensate for unavoidable increased costs of operation shall be determined in accordance with the following standards:

1. There have been no prior increases in the maximum rent of the housing accommodations for a period of two years preceding the date of filing of the landlord's application under either the provisions of Section 33-2 Voluntary Written Agreements, 33-4 Unique or Peculiar Circumstances, 33-5 Net Annual Return, 33-6 Unavoidable Increases in Operating Costs in Small Structures, 33-7 Unavoidable Increases in Operating Costs in Other Specified Structures, or 33-8 Other Necessary Adjustments of Maximum Rents not inconsistent with the purposes of the Act or Regulations.

2. The amount of the rent adjustment for a housing accommodation to compensate for unavoidable increased costs of operation shall not exceed 15% of the maximum rent in effect on the date of the filing of the landlord's application, or the rate of the guideline in effect for the municipality wherein the property is located as last filed by the County Rent Guidelines Board under the Emergency Tenant Protection Act of 1974 for two year leases on the housing accommodations in the same or a comparable building which are subject to that Act, whichever is the lower percentage.

3. The application by the landlord shall request the amount of adjustment as allocated to each housing accommodation in the building and establish the requested adjustment to be necessary by clear evidence that there has been in the preceding two years a significant unavoidable increase in the operating costs of real estate taxes,

heating fuel, utility charges, and/or labor pursuant to a collective bargaining contract for which the rent has not been previously adjusted, and which cost increase is contemplated to continue in effect, and further that in the event the cost increase does not continue in effect, or is substantially reduced the landlord will thereupon notify the Local Rent Administrator to adjust the maximum rent by an appropriate reduction. Where the cost increase is discontinued or substantially reduced on a community-wide or industry-wide basis, the Local Rent Administrator may issue appropriate rent reduction orders on his own initiative.

OPERATIONAL BULLETIN NO. 106
(Issued September 1, 1975)
Change in rental value for electric current for operation of air conditioner.

The schedule of rental values is hereby amended to increase the allowance for current for operation of air conditioners so as to reflect the increased cost of operation. Based upon an analysis made by Con Edison in June–July, 1975, the approximate costs of the most popular sized air conditioner units on an all-year round basis is as follows:

4000 BTU	$ 3.33	per month
5000 BTU	3.75	" "
6000 BTU	4.17	" "
9000 BTU	6.25	" "
12000 BTU	9.17	" "
15000 BTU	10.83	" "
18000 BTU	12.50	" "

Effective immediately all applications filed for rent increase for the operation of an air conditioner shall be determined by this schedule. If the size of the air conditioner is not set forth, the rental value shall be computed on a mathematical basis in proportion to the amounts which are set forth.

Advisory Bulletins

OPERATIONAL BULLETIN NO. 107
(Issued October 15, 1975)

Revised standards for determining applications for rent adjustments under Section 33-8 of Regulations to compensate for unavoidable increased costs of operation at two-year intervals by an adjustment at the rate of 15%.

Applications by landlords filed hereafter for rent adjustments under Section 33-8 of the Regulations to compensate for unavoidable increased costs of operation shall be determined in accordance with the following standards:

1. There have been no prior rent adjustments totalling 15% or more in the maximum rents of the rent controlled housing accommodations in the building for a period of two years under Section 33-2 Voluntary Written Agreements, 33-4 Unique or Peculiar Circumstances, 33-5 Net Annual Return, 33-6 Unavoidable Increases in Operating Costs in Small Structures, 33-7 Unavoidable Increases in Operating Costs of Other Structures, or 33-8 Other Necessary Adjustments of Maximum Rents Not Inconsistent with the Purposes of the Act or Regulations.

2. The amount of the rent adjustment for each rent controlled housing accommodation in the building shall be 15% of the maximum rent in effect on the filing date of the landlord's application, or in those cities, towns or villages in the Counties of Nassau and Westchester which have adopted resolutions under the Emergency Tenant Protection Act, the rate of the Guideline in effect as last filed by the County Rent Guidelines Board for two year leases on housing accommodations in the same or a comparable building which are subject to that Act, whichever is the lower percentage, and except where there have been prior rent adjustments within the preceding two year period totalling less than 15%, the adjustment may only be for the difference to bring the total adjustment up to the 15%.

3. The application by the landlord shall be on the prescribed form and shall request the amount of adjustment for each rent controlled housing accommodation in the building. The landlord shall certify that he is main-

taining all essential services provided or required to be provided with the housing accommodations and that he will continue to maintain such services so long as the increase in maximum rent continues in effect. The landlord shall establish the requested rent increase to be necessary by certifying that there has been in the preceding two years a significant unavoidable increase in the operating costs, including real estate taxes, heating fuel, utility charges, repairs, replacements, and labor for which the rent has not been previously adjusted by the rate of 15%, and which costs increase is contemplated to continue in effect, and further that in the event the costs increase does not continue in effect, or is substantially reduced, the landlord will notify the Rent Administrator to adjust the maximum rent by an appropriate reduction. The Rent Administrator may at any time require a landlord to submit clear evidence of the validity of this certification. Where the cost increase is discontinued or substantially reduced on a building, community or industry-wide basis, the Rent Administrator may issue rent reduction orders on his own initiative effective as of the date of such discontinuance or reduction, with a refund directive.

4. No other applications by the landlord for rent adjustments shall be pending under Sections 33-4, 5, 6, or 7 of the Regulations or shall be filed for a period of two years.

5. The rent adjustment pursuant to Section 33-8 necessary to compensate for unavoidable increased costs of operation shall be a separate increased cost charge which will be collectible for a period of two years, unless changed by order prior thereto, or the landlord thereupon files a further application establishing that an adjustment continues to be warranted.

The rent adjustment for a two year period at the rate of 15% has been found to be generally necessary and appropriate based upon the records of analysis of statements of Income and Expenses for a representative number of apartment buildings containing housing accommodations subject to regulation under the Emergency Housing Rent Control Law or the Emergency Tenant Protection Act. The rate has been further found to be consistent with the purpose and intent of the Law and not excessive, it being the prescribed maximum rate for rent adjustments by voluntary two year leases.

OPERATIONAL BULLETIN NO. 107 SUPPLEMENT NO. 1.

(Issued July 1, 1976)

Use of Two Year Lease Guideline Rates as rate of rent adjustment under Section 33-8, Rent and Eviction Regulations, in counties of Nassau and Westchester.

Under the standards of paragraph 2 of this Bulletin issued October 15, 1975, the rate of rent adjustment is 15% of the maximum rent or the rate of the guideline in effect for two year leases on housing accommodations in the same or comparable buildings which are subject to the Emergency Tenant Protection Act, whichever rate is the lower, in the counties of Nassau and Westchester.

By reason of the guideline rates for two year leases on all apartments which are initially entered under the Emergency Tenant Protection Act's requirements on and after July 1, 1976 being lower than 15%, commencing July 1, 1976 such lower rates shall apply to the adjustments pursuant to Section 33-8 of the Rent and Eviction Regulations on all rent controlled housing in Nassau and Westchester, namely:

Nassau County 12%
Westchester County 5%

OPERATIONAL BULLETIN NO. 107 SUPPLEMENT NO. 2.

(Issued July 19, 1976)

Modification of Use of Two Year Lease Guideline Rate as the rate of rent adjustment under Section 33-8 Rent and Eviction Regulations in the County of Westchester for rent controlled apartments.

It is deemed necessary and proper that the compensatory rent adjustments on rent controlled apartments in Westchester pursuant to Section 33-8 which are to be effective for a two year period shall be at the rate of 10%, and not at the County's Guideline Rate of 5% for two year leases for apartments under the Emergency Tenant Protection Act.

An examination of the rates of increase in expenses for the operation of apartment buildings from 1974 to 1975 reported in the Westchester County Rent Guidelines Board's findings shows the rate to have been 11.4% for buildings containing both rent controlled apartments and apartments under the Emergency Tenant Protection Act, and 2.2% for buildings containing only apartments covered by the Emergency Tenant Protection Act, and no rent controlled apartments.

Therefore, Supplement No. 1 to Operational Bulletin No. 107 dated July 1, 1976, and the Bulletin are modified to provide that rent adjustments pursuant to Section 33-8 shall be at the rate of 10% for rent controlled apartments in Westchester County.

The use of the Nassau County Two Year Guideline Rate of 12% continues without change for rent controlled apartments in Nassau County.

All other procedures under Operational Bulletin No. 107 continue without change. However, it should be further noted that adjustments may not be granted hereunder to a building which has received a determination under Section 33-5 following an accounting analysis of the income and expenses for the preceding year. The landlord of such building may either file a further application under Section 33-5 upon the expiration of one year, or under Section 33-8 upon the expiration of a two year period from the date of the last adjustment. Also, since the adjustments under the Bulletin are compensatory for unavoidable increases in operating expenses in the preceding two years, a landlord who has not owned and operated a building for such a period is generally unable to meet these requirements. If such a new owner can establish such facts and circumstances to show that he does meet the requirements, adjustments may then be determined to be warranted.

ADVISORY BULLETINS

OPERATIONAL BULLETIN NO. 108

(Issued November 13, 1975)

Designation of Director, Rent Operations Bureau, Local Rent Administrator for Westchester Local Rent Administration Office, and Assistant Director, Tenant Protection Bureau.

Mrs. Geraldine Waggoner has been reassigned from the Tenant Protection Bureau and designated Director, Operations Bureau, and Local Rent Administrator for the Westchester Local Rent Administration Office at 99 Church Street, White Plains, effective this date, succeeding Mr. Harold Grosberg, who has retired from State service.

Mr. Christopher Caleca has also been designated to act as Assistant Director of the Tenant Protection Bureau, to carry out supervisory assignments in the Bureau in addition to his other duties.

OPERATIONAL BULLETIN NO. 109

(Issued February 9, 1976)

Revised Rental Values for new Refrigerators, Cooking Stoves, and other miscellaneous equipment.

The following indicated monthly rental values are a guide for the adjustments of maximum rents pursuant to Section 33-1 of the Rent and Eviction Regulations, where the equipment is installed with the consent of the tenant and application is filed by the landlord for the adjustment of the maximum rent, reciting a full description of the equipment including size, make and model where applicable, and date of installation. Where it is found that a unique and peculiar combination of factors exists, these allowances may not be appropriate for use as a guide to the adjustment. These allowances supersede the allowances set forth in Advisory Bulletin B, July 1, 1969, for the indicated equipment. The other items in Advisory Bulletin B which are not listed in this Bulletin have not have been the subject of recent applications, and therefore no action has been taken to determine the current costs thereof and such new rental values as may be appropriate as a guide.

REFRIGERATORS

Replacement with new modern model installed

Net Capacity in Cu. Ft.	Conventional Defrost	Automatic Defrost
9.5 – 11.8	$4.50	$5.50
11.9 – 13.9	5.00	6.00
14 – 15.5	—	6.50
15.6 – 17.5	—	7.00
17.6 up	—	7.50

GAS RANGES

Replacement with new modern model installed

Size in inches	
20	$2.50
24	3.00
30	3.50
36	3.75

MISCELLANEOUS EQUIPMENT

Bath Sink Faucets installed	$ .50
Bathtub Faucets installed	.50
Kitchen Sink Faucets installed	.50
Shower Head and Body Faucets installed (concealed supply)	.75
Bathroom Low Tank and Bowl installed	2.00
Electric Dishwasher (new replacement)	5.00
" " installed (none before)	7.00
Combination Screens/Storms (fully installed in window)	1.00

OPERATIONAL BULLETIN NO. 109
SUPPLEMENT NO. 1

(Issued February 1, 1979)

Determination of Rental Value for new equipment in amount other than the fixed allowance set forth or where there is no such allowance in the Bulletin— (Section 33-1a Rent and Eviction Regulations).

In any case where new equipment is installed by a landlord at the tenant's request under a written mutual agreement to a rent increase subject to the Division's approval of the landlord's application for the rent adjustment, if the actual cost paid to a regular vendor of the equipment will not be obtained within a 40 month period by the collection of the rent adjustment in the amount set forth in this Bulletin, the written mutual agreement of landlord and tenant may be to a rent increase based upon a 40 month allocation of the actual cost, exclusive of interest or other carrying charges. The application by the landlord for approval of the rent adjustment shall include the tenant's written consent, and be accompanied by the evidence of the cost—i.e. paid bill and check or certified copies thereof.

The 40 month standard will also be applied in determining the rent adjustment for new equipment having no fixed rental value under this Bulletin.

OPERATIONAL BULLETIN NO. 110
(Issued July 15, 1977)

Revised procedure for rent adjustments to compensate for unavoidable increased costs of operation at two year intervals.

Effective immediately the following procedure shall be operative for rent adjustments to compensate owners for unavoidable increased costs of operation at two year intervals. This procedure supersedes that set forth in Operational Bulletin No. 107, October 15, 1975, and supplements thereto. All pending applications under the prior procedure will be terminated in order to provide the applicant landlord an opportunity to proceed under this Bulletin, except in the Albany and Buffalo local rent areas where the maximum rate of rent adjustment has been 15%. It continues to be necessary that there be compensatory rent increases by reason of unavoidable increased costs of operation on rent controlled apartments pursuant to the Law and Section 33-8 of the Regulations thereunder.

An examination of the rates of increase in the costs of operation of 156 apartment buildings with both rent controlled apartments and decontrolled apartments subject to the Emergency Tenant Protection Act in Westchester County, where the largest number of rent controlled housing accommodations are located, shows the rate of increase in expenses to have been 14.7% from 1975 to 1976, excluding interest and depreciation. Specifically, the total income in thousands for 1975 was $7,676 and for 1976, $8,281, while expenses increased from $7,195 to $8,124, which figures clearly show a compensatory increase in income to be warranted.

In Nassau County the rate of increase for 46 buildings with apartments subject to the Emergency Tenant Protection Act, and also an unreported number of rent controlled apartments in some of such buildings is 20%. Since many of the cost factors are common throughout the state, these rates are believed prevalent in the Albany and Buffalo areas as well.

Therefore, it is found appropriate and consistent with the intent and purpose of the law to permit rent adjustments at the rate of *15%* for rent controlled apartments in all areas under the law where unavoidable increased costs of operation have been sustained and the building is operated in compliance with all requirements of law, if there has been no compensatory rent increase for such apartments in the prior two year period under either Section 33-2, 5, 6, 7 or 8 of the Regulations.

In order to provide a clear and simplified procedure for a landlord and tenant to proceed and be heard on the implementation of such rent adjustments where warranted, the landlord must now complete and serve a sixty day notice form on the tenant by certified mail certifying that a rent adjustment is authorized under this Bulletin and that the rent will be changed not to exceed the authorized rate on the next rent payment date following sixty days from the service of the notice on the tenant, unless the Division shall issue a notice or order changing such rent. A copy of the notice must be filed by the landlord with the State Division's local rent office where it will be placed in a building file record for such further proceedings, if any, as may be commenced. The notice forms will be provided without charge at all State Division offices.

The landlord is further required to certify that essential services are maintained and no violations of law to his knowledge are in effect under state, municipal, and federal codes concerning such required services, and/or that an agreement is in effect with the enforcement authority, and such an agreement is being complied with, to maintain and improve the building in compliance with the requirements of such laws.

Also, the landlord must certify that the maximum rent is on record with the Division and that the rent adjustment will be terminated or reduced in the event there is a significant reduction in operating expenses, by written notice to the tenant with a copy to the Division.

The sixty day notice shall be effective to increase the maximum rent where there is compliance with this Bulletin and all other requirements of law unless the State Division shall thereafter issue an order or notice determining that the adjustment is not warranted. The Notice form provides for the tenant to return one copy to the landlord either acknowledging receipt and that the adjusted rent will be paid or objecting to and/or questioning the Notice. The landlord must respond to the tenant's question and/or objection. Thereafter the tenant may file a complaint with the State Division of Housing and Community Renewal by completing Part B of the form and mailing or delivering it to the State Division of Housing and Community Renewal, if the landlord has failed to respond to the tenant, or the landlord's response is not satisfactory.

The rent adjustment which goes into effect will normally be operative for the next two year period. The landlord may not obtain a further rent increase *under this procedure* for a two year period.

If a building is operated at a loss as defined in Section 33-5 of the Regulations, despite these rent adjustments, the owner may submit an application for an additional rent adjustment in an amount necessary to eliminate such loss, which application will be granted as the evidence may warrant.

Furthermore, where a building does not provide a 7½% return on the property's valuation as defined in the law and Section 33-5 of the Regulations, despite the rent adjustments hereunder, an application with evidence establishing this fact may be granted upon the expiration of one year from the date of the rent adjustments hereunder to the extent authorized by Section 33-5, which further rent adjustments may not exceed 15% for the next year (except where the owner is sustaining a loss, as defined in the law).

No landlord may proceed under this Bulletin unless he is the legal owner of the property for a period of at least two years.

OPERATIONAL BULLETIN NO. 110
SUPPLEMENT NO. 1
(Issued August 22, 1977)

Revised procedure for rent adjustments to compensate for unavoidable increased costs of operation at two-year intervals.

Action by Local Rent Administrator following examination of copy of Landlord's Sixty Day Notice of Maximum Rent Adjustment, and tenant's objections thereto.

1. Examination to determine compliance with specific requirements of Operational Bulletin No. 110.

Where the examination of the Landlord's Sixty Day Notice, the tenant's objection, and/or other available data, establishes that there has not been compliance with the following specific requirements:

    a. That maximum rent has not been increased for two years;

    b. That landlord has not been the legal owner for a two year period;

    c. That the rent increase shall not exceed 15%,

the Local Rent Administrator will issue an Advice of Defective Notice of Maximum Rent Adjustment and Notice of Non-Collectability (Form RAS 33-8-86).

2. Examination of Certifications in Landlord's Sixty Day Notice

    a. Certification relating to increase in operating costs:

If evidence is on record or is filed by an objecting tenant that there is reason to question that the particular building did not in fact sustain the increase in costs, the Local Rent Administrator will proceed to determine the question with appropriate notice of the commencement of the proceeding to the landlord and tenant on the prescribed form (RAS 33-8-10). In the course of the proceeding the landlord may be required or provided the opportu-

Advisory Bulletins

nity of submitting records relating to the operating costs and maximum rents. If a finding is not made before the rent payment date in the Sixty Day Notice, the rent increases will be collectable unless the Local Rent Administrator shall direct to the contrary, subject to refunds of any amount of increase determined to be unwarranted. The final determination will be issued on the prescribed form (RAS 33-8-30).

b. Certification relating to maintenance of essential services and/or non-existence of violations of law:

(1) If the tenant files objection to the Sixty Day Notice with proof that violation(s) of law are in effect, inquiry will immediately be made to the appropriate municipal enforcement authority to obtain an official statement or copy of the record showing whether violation(s) are so in effect. If the tenant is in error, written notice thereof will be given to the tenant and landlord. If the municipal enforcement authority states violations exist, this may be contrary to the landlord's certification which, if false, may subject him to penalties as well as render the Sixty Day Notice defective. Therefore, the Local Rent Administrator will refer the file for investigation and further findings to the State Rent Administrator, Attention: Chief Enforcement Attorney, with a notice to the landlord and tenant that an investigation is being made (Form No. RAS 33-8-85). Upon completion of the investigation, notice of the findings and thereafter an order with a determination of whether the Sixty Day Notice is or is not effective, and of such further action, if any, which is being taken under the requirements of law, will be issued (Forms RAS 33-8-10 and 30).

(2) Where the tenant files an objection to the Sixty Day Notice relating to a complaint that a particular essential service, such as painting, has not been maintained, if there is evidence on record to show that the tenant had previously notified the landlord to provide the service and the landlord had failed to do so for no lawful reason and/ or that the Local Rent Administrator in a prior proceeding within the two year period had determined that the landlord failed to provide such a required service, the Local Rent Administrator will issue an Advice of Defective Notice of Maximum Rent Adjustment and Notice of

ADVISORY BULLETINS

Non-Collectability (RAS 33-8-86), otherwise the tenant's objection must be acted upon in a subsequent proceeding under Section 34-2 of the Regulations, wherein rent reduction may be ordered in such amounts as are appropriate. In the latter situation, the Local Rent Administrator will notify the tenant to file the prescribed application form (i.e. Form 34-2), and that the Landlord's Sixty Day Notice continues in effect, subject to such later order as may reduce the rent.

c. Certification relating to rent:

If the tenant files objection to the Sixty Day Notice with the claim that the stated Maximum Rent is higher than the rent paid or otherwise in effect, and the registration record shows the Maximum Rent on the date of the Sixty Day Notice to be in a lower amount than stated in the Notice, the Local Rent Administrator will issue the Advice of Defective Notice of Maximum Rent Adjustment and Notice of Non-Collectability (Form RAS 33-8-86) reciting the amount of the Maximum Rent which is on record.

3. General Procedures After Examination.

Copies of the Sixty Day Notices which appear to be duly executed and served and to otherwise conform to the Law, Section 33-8 of the Regulations and Operational Bulletin No. 110 thereunder will be maintained in an address file for record purposes. All inquiries, objections and notices related thereto will thereafter be maintained in that file.

**OPERATIONAL BULLETIN NO. 110
SUPPLEMENT NO. 3**

(Issued July 16, 1975)

Changes in Costs of Operation Last Two Calendar Years—1976 to 1978—and Costs of Heating Fuel in 1979—as basis of Authorized Rent Adjustments at rate of 15% + 3% for a two year period for eligible rent controlled apartments.

The analysis of costs of operation received for buildings with rented housing accommodations has disclosed the following changes in the last two calendar years:

1. That in Westchester County in 242 buildings with 6,989 apartments, of which 4,062 are under Emergency

Advisory Bulletins

Tenant Protection Act and the balance—2,927—therefore under Emergency Housing Rent Control Law, the increase in expenses exclusive of interest and depreciation from 1976 to 1977 was 6.3% and from 1977 to 1978, 4.1%, for a total increase of 10.4% for the two year period 1976 to 1978.

2. That in Nassau County, in 65 buildings with 4,098 apartments under the Emergency Tenant Protection Act and an undetermined number of apartments under the Emergency Housing Rent Control Law in an undetermined number of such buildings, the increase in expenses excluding interest and depreciation from 1976 to 1977 was 7% and from 1977 to 1978, 5.7%, for a total increase of 12.7% for the two year period 1976 to 1978.

The rate of rent adjustment at two year intervals to compensate owners for unavoidable increased costs of operation has been in effect at 15%. Based upon the foregoing data, no decrease in this rate is warranted.

However, additional consideration is also required to be given to the expense items of fuel oil, gas and electricity for buildings with apartments under the rent control law in the four areas of Albany, Buffalo, Westchester, and Nassau. The Consumer Price Index reported an increase in the price of "fuel oil, coal, and bottled gas" at the rate of 27.0%, and "gas (piped) and electricity" at the rate of 9.4% in the New York-Northeastern New Jersey region from May 1978 to May 1979, with increases of 3.2% and 3.7% in the one month period from April to May, 1979. In the Buffalo area, the corresponding changes for a 12 month period to April, 1979 were 16.1% and 8.2%, and for the February, 1979–April, 1979 period, 8.9% and 2.9%. Reported economic forecasts are that the prices will continue to accelerate for an indeterminate period. By reason of the curtailment of petroleum supplies as well as the rising costs, conservation programs are also being developed which will in part reduce the impacts of the cost increases. Nevertheless, the continuing high rates of increases in the costs are unique and peculiar to the current and projected period of the next two years.

Therefore, the authorized maximum rate of rent adjustment at two year intervals to compensate owners for unavoidable increased costs of operation will be at 15%

plus an additional 3%—total 18%—in all local rent areas. The use of this rate of rent adjustment by owners is subject to the requirements and limitations in Operational Bulletin No. 110 dated July 15, 1977 and Supplement No. 1 thereto dated August 1, 1977, and the applicable sections of the Rent and Eviction Regulations including Section 33-8. The landlord, thereunder, must execute and serve the prescribed sixty day notice and certificate on the tenant and Division and make available all records upon receipt of a notice to do so.

Furthermore, no rent may be adjusted hereunder to exceed the rent in effect for any comparable apartment in the building or complex which is not subject to the rent control law (including apartments subject to the Tenant Protection Act). In such event, the maximum rent may only be adjusted at an appropriate lower rate for the two year period to equal the rent for such a non-rent controlled comparable apartment. This limitation will bar adjustments under the authority of the rent control law which would result in a level of maximum rent in excess of the Fair Market Rent for that class of apartment.

OPERATIONAL BULLETIN NO. 110 SUPPLEMENT NO. 4
(Issued November 10, 1980)

Changes in Costs of Operation Last Two Calendar Years—1977 to 1979—as basis of Authorized Rent Adjustments at a rate of 15% for the first year and 10% for the second year (§ 33-8, Regulations).

The analysis of costs of operation received for buildings with rented housing accommodations has disclosed the following changes in the last two calendar years:

1. That in Westchester County in 469 buildings with 13,345 apartments, of which 7,699 are under Emergency Tenant Protection Act and the balance—5,646—therefore under Emergency Housing Rent Control Law, the increase in expenses exclusive of interest and depreciation from 1977 to 1978 was 5.3% and from 1978 to 1979, 11%, for a total increase of 16.3% for the two year period 1977 to 1979.

2. That in Nassau County, in 120 buildings with 7,243

Advisory Bulletins

apartments under the Emergency Tenant Protection Act and an undetermined number of apartments under the Emergency Housing Rent Control Law in an undetermined number of such buildings, the increase in expenses excluding interest and depreciation from 1977 to 1978 was 6.7%, and from 1978 to 1979, 8.8%, for a total increase of 15.5% for the two year period 1977 to 1979.

The rate of rent adjustment to be in effect for a two year period has been 15% + 3%—or 18%—pursuant to Supplement No. 3, July 16, 1979. In the 12 month period prior thereto, the rate had been at 15% for two years, as set forth in Supplement No. 2 issued June 30, 1978. The apartments which received increases at the 15% rate for the most part will be eligible for further increase during 1980–81 pursuant to the findings set forth herein.

Based upon the foregoing factors and the further reported changes in the Consumer Price Index, as well as the findings by the Westchester County and Nassau County Rent Guidelines Boards for classes of buildings which include both apartments subject to rent control and apartments subject to tenant protection, the rate of rent adjustment hereafter, subject to the requirements and limitations in Operational Bulletin No. 110, dated July 15, 1977, Supplements No. 1 dated August 1, 1977, No. 2 dated June 30, 1978, and No. 3 dated July 16, 1979, except as changed by this Supplement No. 4, shall be 15% for the first year, and an additional 10% for the second year, above the maximum rent in effect at the commencement of each year.

In view of the varying higher levels of rents which are currently in effect for apartments no longer subject to rent control but regulated pursuant to the Emergency Tenant Protection Act in municipalities located in Nassau and Westchester Counties, the limitation that no rent controlled maximum rent shall be adjusted to exceed the rent in effect on the date of adjustment for any comparable apartment in the building or complex not subject to rent control is modified to provide that where the non-rent controlled apartments are regulated under ETPA, the rent controlled apartment rent shall not be adjusted to exceed the average of the legal regulated rents for apartments with the same number of rooms in the building or complex which are under ETPA. This will continue to limit rent increases to the Fair Market Rent levels for apartments of the same size in the building or complex.

The prescribed form (33-8) entitled "Landlord's Sixty Day Notice of Maximum Rent Adjustment and Certificate of Unavoidable Increased Costs of Operation With No Increase In Maximum Rent For Past Two Year Period" has been revised to incorporate the provisions of this Supplement, and a copy is attached hereto.

In all instances where the landlord has served the Notice and Certificate prior to the issuance date of this Supplement, but the Notice has not yet become effective to increase the rent, the landlord may elect to serve a second notice on the revised form pursuant to this Supplement, which may then be effective on the same date as the initial notice, provided that the second notice clearly recites, "This Notice revises the rent adjustment in the prior Notice bearing date of _____, 1980, and the rent adjustment is therefore effective sixty days from that date."

Advisory Bulletins

STATE OF NEW YORK
DIVISION OF HOUSING & COMMUNITY RENEWAL
OFFICE OF RENT ADMINISTRATION

LANDLORD'S SIXTY DAY NOTICE OF MAXIMUM RENT ADJUSTMENT
and
CERTIFICATE OF UNAVOIDABLE INCREASED COSTS OF OPERATION WITH NO INCREASE IN MAXIMUM RENT FOR PAST TWO YEAR PERIOD

1. MAILING ADDRESS OF LANDLORD:

NAME _____ TEL. NO. _____
NUMBER AND STREET _____
CITY, STATE & ZIP CODE NO. _____

2. MAILING ADDRESS OF TENANT:

NAME _____ TEL. NO. _____
NUMBER AND STREET _____
CITY, STATE & ZIP CODE NO. _____

3. ADDRESS OF HOUSING ACCOMMODATIONS: _____
(NUMBER AND STREET) (APT. OR RM. NO.) (CITY, STATE & ZIP CODE NO.)

PART A

To: _____, Tenant   (Serve original and 1 copy by certified mail or personal delivery)
    Full name(s)

Copy to: NYS Division of Housing and Community Renewal. (Serve by mail or personal delivery)

PLEASE TAKE NOTICE THAT:

1. The Maximum Rent will be adjusted not to exceed the authorized rates and changed from $ _____ to $ _____ per month for the first year (twelve month period) and from $ _____ to $ _____ per month for the second year, commencing on the next rent payment date following sixty days from the date of mailing of this Notice by certified mail or personal service on the tenant, unless the New York State Division of Housing and Community Renewal shall issue a further notice or order changing said rents.

2. This Notice is authorized by the New York State Division of Housing and Community Renewal pursuant to the Emergency Housing Rent Control Law, and as provided in Operational Bulletin No. 110, under section 33-8 Rent and Eviction Regulations.

3. The landlord certifies:
   (1) There has been in the preceding two year period a significant unavoidable increase in the operating costs, including real estate taxes, heating fuel, utility charges, repairs, replacements, and labor, with no increase in the maximum rent to compensate for that cost increase, and that he will make available to the New York State Division of Housing and Community Renewal all records of such operating costs upon receipt of a notice to do so.
   (2) That he is maintaining all essential services which are required by law and that there are no violations in effect of municipal, county, state, or federal laws to his knowledge which relate to the maintenance of such services, and that he will continue to so maintain the essential services and/or that an agreement suspending any such violation is in effect with the enforcement authority to maintain, restore, and improve the building, and is being complied with.
   (3) That the Maximum Rent for this housing accommodation is the rent on record with the New York State Division of Housing and Community Renewal and that the adjustment of said rent under this Notice will be terminated or reduced in the event that there is a significant reduction in the operating expenses, and notice thereof will be given to the tenant in writing with a copy to the New York State Division of Housing and Community Renewal.
   (4) That the Maximum Rents for this housing accommodation as adjusted under this Notice do not exceed the average of the legal regulated rents for apartments with the same number of rooms, services, equipment, and improvements in the building or complex which are not subject to the Emergency Housing Rent Control Law and are subject to the Emergency Tenant Protection Act, or the rent for any such apartment which is not subject to either of such laws.

AFFIRMATION

I affirm that the information herein is true and I understand that this Notice will be accepted for all purposes as an affidavit, and if it contains a material false statement shall subject me to the same penalties for perjury as if I has been duly sworn.

Date of Mailing or Delivery _____   _____
                                                Signature of owner, agent, or officer with title.

See Instructions and Part B on reverse side of this Notice

219

ADVISORY BULLETINS

INSTRUCTIONS

Prepare original and three copies of this form

The landlord should complete and sign Part A and then deliver the <u>original</u> and <u>one copy</u> to the tenant by certified mail or personal service, and <u>one copy</u> by mail or hand delivery to the State Division of Housing and Community Renewal local office for the area where the property is locate sixty days prior to the rent payment date on which the rent adjustment is to be paid. The landlord retains the fourth copy.

The tenant should sign and complete the appropriate part(s) of Part B of this form and return one copy to the landlord within 7 days from date of delivery to the tenant.

If the Notice has been questioned or objected to upon the receipt of the landlord's reply or the failure of the landlord to reply within the 7 day prescribed period, the tenant may submit the original of this Notice to the State Division of Housing and Community Renewal for its action upon his objections or questions after completing and signing Part C.

The Law, Regulations and Operational Bulletin No. 110 are available for examination at all offices of the State Division of Housing and Community Renewal.

* * * * * * *

The maximum rent, as adjusted by this Notice, not to exceed the authorized rate, is payable unless changed by Notice or Order issued by the State Division of Housing and Community Renewal. A refund may be ordered if a Notice is found not to conform to the requirements of law, and the landlord may be subject to the penalties of law.

PART B

Tenant acknowledgment to Landlord:

☐ Receipt of this Notice is acknowledged and the Maximum Rent as adjusted by this Notice will be paid on the next rent payment date following sixty days from the date of mailing of this Notice.

Date of Mailing or Delivery: _____   _____
                                                Signature of Tenant

Tenant objection or question to Landlord:

☐ Receipt of this Notice is acknowledged but the Rent Adjustment is questioned and/or objected to because: (State objection and/or question)

Date of Mailing or Delivery: _____   _____
                                                Signature of Tenant

Landlord is required to reply in writing to the tenant within 7 days from the date of mailing or personal delivery of this objection and/or question.

A failure to reply to the tenant may render this Notice subject to cancellation by the State Division of Housing and Community Renewal.

PART C

Tenant Complaint to State Division of Housing and Community Renewal:

(File only after submission of question or objection to landlord)

I have received this Notice from the Landlord, and have served the Landlord with objection(s) or question(s) but (I do not agree with the Landlord's reply) or (I have received no reply) - (strike out one). My question or objection is:

(State facts and attach any supporting documents or copies thereof.)

Date of Mailing or Delivery: _____   _____
                                                Signature of Tenant

-2-

OPERATIONAL BULLETIN NO. 111

(Issued July 9, 1979)

See Tenant Protection Bulletin No. 22, infra, under Emergency Tenant Protection Act of 1974.

PART II: NEW YORK CITY HOUSING RENT CONTROL
Local Emergency Housing Rent Control Law
New York City Rent and Eviction Regulations
New York City Rent and Rehabilitation Law
Rent Administrator's Interpretations
Rent Administrator's Operational Bulletins
Rent Administrator's Information and
 Instruction Sheets
Exemption from Rent Increases for Low
 Income Elderly Persons

PART II

NEW YORK CITY HOUSING RENT CONTROL

LOCAL EMERGENCY HOUSING RENT CONTROL LAW
[STATE ENABLING ACT]

Section 1. The regulation and control of residential rents and evictions within cities having a population of one million or more on and after May first, nineteen hundred sixty-two shall be governed by the provisions of this section, notwithstanding the provisions of the emergency housing rent control law:

1. Short title. This section shall be known and may be cited as the "local emergency housing rent control act".

2. Legislative finding. The legislature hereby finds that a serious public emergency continues to exist in the housing of a considerable number of persons in the state of New York which emergency was created by war, the effects of war and the aftermath of hostilities; that such emergency necessitated the intervention of federal, state and local government in order to prevent speculative, unwarranted and abnormal increases in rents; that there continues to exist an acute shortage of dwellings; that unless residential rents and evictions continue to be regulated and controlled, disruptive practices and abnormal conditions will produce serious threats to the public health, safety and general welfare; that to prevent such perils to health, safety and welfare, preventive action by the legislature continues to be imperative; that such action is necessary in order to prevent exactions of unjust, unreasonable and oppressive rents and rental agreements and to forestall profiteering, speculation and other disruptive practices tending to produce threats to the public health; that in order to prevent uncertainty, hardship and dislocation, the provisions of this section are necessary and designed to protect the public health,

safety and general welfare, that the transition from regulation to a normal market of free bargaining between landlord and tenant, while still the objective of state policy, must be administered with due regard for such emergency; and that the policy herein expressed should now be administered locally within cities having a population of one million or more by an agency of the city itself.

3. Local determination as to continuation of emergency. The continuation, after May thirty-first, nineteen hundred sixty-seven, of the public emergency requiring the regulation and control of residential rents and evictions within cities having a population of one million or more shall be a matter for local determination within each such city. Any such determination shall be made by the local legislative body of such city on or before April first, nineteen hundred sixty-seven and at least once in every third year thereafter following a survey which the city shall cause to be made of the supply of housing accommodations within such city, the condition of such accommodations and the need for continuing the regulation and control of residential rents and evictions within such city. Such survey shall be submitted to such legislative body not less than thirty nor more than sixty days prior to the date of any such determination. [Am L 1965, ch 318, eff May 28, 1965; L 1966, ch 13, eff March 1, 1966; L 1967, ch 657, eff June 1, 1967]

4. Establishment of city housing rent agency. On or before April first, nineteen hundred sixty-two, the mayor of each city having a population of one million or more shall establish or designate an official, bureau, board, commission or agency of such city (referred to in this section as the "city housing rent agency") to administer the regulation and control of residential rents and evictions within such city unless such city, acting through its local legislative body, shall have enacted, prior to April first, nineteen hundred sixty-two, a local law or ordinance pursuant to subdivision five of this section, prescribing a different method of establishing or designating a city housing rent agency and in such case such agency shall be established or designated in accordance with said local law or ordinance.

Rent Control Law

5. [As am L 1971, ch 371, eff June 30, 1971] Authority for local rent control legislation. At any time after the effective date of this act, each city having a population of one million or more, acting through its local legislative body, is hereby authorized and empowered to adopt and amend local laws or ordinances in respect of the establishment or designation of a city housing rent agency. When it deems such action to be desirable or necessitated by local conditions in order to carry out the purposes of this section, such city, except as hereinafter provided, is hereby authorized and empowered to adopt and amend local laws or ordinances effective on or after May first, nineteen hundred sixty-two in respect of the regulation and control of residential rents, including but not limited to provision for the establishment and adjustment of maximum rents, the classification of housing accommodations, the regulation of evictions, and the enforcement of such local laws or ordinances. The validity of any such local laws or ordinances, and the rules or regulations promulgated in accordance therewith, shall not be affected by and need not be consistent with the provisions of the state emergency housing rent control law or with the rules and regulations of the temporary state housing rent commission thereunder.

Notwithstanding any local law or ordinance, housing accommodations which became vacant on or after July first, nineteen hundred seventy-one or which hereafter become vacant shall be subject to the provisions of the emergency tenant protection act of nineteen seventy-four, provided, however, that this provision shall not apply or become effective with respect to housing accommodations which, by local law or ordinance, are made directly subject to regulation and control by a city housing rent agency and such agency determines or finds that the housing accommodations became vacant because the landlord or any person acting on his behalf, with intent to cause the tenant to vacate, engaged in any course of conduct (including but not limited to, interruption or discontinuance of essential services) which interfered with or disturbed or was intended to interfere with or disturb the comfort, repose, peace or quiet of the tenant in his use or occupancy of the housing accommodations.

The removal of any housing accommodation from regulation and control of rents pursuant to the vacancy exemption provided for in this paragraph shall not constitute or operate as a ground for the subjection to more stringent regulation and control of any housing accommodation in such property or in any other property owned by the same landlord, notwithstanding any prior agreement to the contrary by the landlord. The vacancy exemption provided for in this paragraph shall not arise with respect to any rented plot or parcel of land otherwise subject to the provisions of this act, by reason of a transfer of title or possession occurring on or after July first, nineteen hundred seventy-one of a dwelling located on such plot or parcel and owned by the tenant where such transfer of title or possession is made to a member of the tenant's immediate family regardless of whether the member of the tenant's immediate family occupies the dwelling with the tenant prior to the transfer of title or possession or thereafter took occupancy pursuant to such transfer of title or possession.

The term "immediate family" shall include a husband, wife, son, daughter, stepson, stepdaughter, father, mother, father-in-law or mother-in-law. [Am L 1974, ch 576, § 2; L 1980, ch 69, § 2, which added concluding paragraph]

5. [As am L 1971, ch 372, eff June 1, 1971] Authority for local rent control legislation. Each city having a population of one million or more, acting through its local legislative body, may adopt and amend local laws or ordinances in respect of the establishment or designation of a city housing rent agency. When it deems such action to be desirable or necessitated by local conditions in order to carry out the purposes of this section, such city, except as hereinafter provided, acting through its local legislative body and not otherwise, may adopt and amend local laws or ordinances in respect of the regulation and control of residential rents, including but not limited to provision for the establishment and adjustment of maximum rents, the classification of housing accommodations, the regulation of evictions, and the enforcement of such local laws or ordinances. The validity of any such local laws or ordinances, and the rules or regulations promul-

gated in accordance therewith, shall not be affected by and need not be consistent with the state emergency housing rent control law or with rules and regulations of the state division of housing and community renewal.

Notwithstanding the foregoing, no local law or ordinance shall hereafter provide for the regulation and control of residential rents and eviction in respect of any housing accommodations which are (1) presently exempt from such regulation and control or (2) hereafter decontrolled either by operation of law or by a city housing rent agency, by order or otherwise. No housing accommodations presently subject to regulation and control pursuant to local laws or ordinances adopted or amended under authority of this subdivision shall hereafter be by local law or ordinance subjected to more stringent or restrictive provisions of regulation and control than those presently in effect.

5. [As am L 1971, ch 373, eff May 1, 1972] Authority for local rent control legislation. At any time after the effective date of this act, each city having a population of one million or more, acting through its local legislative body, is hereby authorized and empowered to adopt and amend local laws or ordinances in respect of the establishment or designation of a city housing rent agency. When it deems such action to be desirable or necessitated by local conditions in order to carry out the purposes of this section, such city, except as hereinafter provided, is hereby authorized and empowered to adopt and amend local laws or ordinances effective on or after May first, nineteen hundred sixty-two in respect of the regulation and control of residential rents, including but not limited to provision for the establishment and adjustment of maximum rents, the classification of housing accommodations, the regulation of evictions, and the enforcement of such local laws or ordinances. The validity of any such local laws or ordinances, and the rules or regulations promulgated in accordance therewith, shall not be affected by and need not be consistent with the provisions of the state emergency housing rent control law or with the rules and regulations of the temporary state housing rent commission thereunder.

Notwithstanding the foregoing, no local law or ordinance shall subject to such regulation and control any housing accommodation which is not occupied by the tenant in possession as his primary residence; provided, however, that such housing accommodation not occupied by the tenant in possession as his primary residence shall continue to be subject to regulation and control as provided for herein unless the city housing rent agency issues an order decontrolling such accommodation, which the agency shall do upon application by the landlord whenever it is established by any facts and circumstances which, in the judgment of the agency, may have a bearing upon the question of residence, that the tenant maintains his primary residence at some place other than at such housing accommodation.

5. [As am L 1971, ch 1012, eff July 2, 1971] Authority for local rent control legislation. Each city having a population of one million or more, acting through its local legislative body, may adopt and amend local laws or ordinances in respect of the establishment or designation of a city housing rent agency. When it deems such action to be desirable or necessitated by local conditions in order to carry out the purposes of this section, such city, except as hereinafter provided, acting through its local legislative body and not otherwise, may adopt and amend local laws or ordinances in respect of the regulation and control of residential rents, including but not limited to provision for the establishment and adjustment of maximum rents, the classification of housing accommodations, the regulation of evictions, and the enforcement of such local laws or ordinances. The validity of any such local laws or ordinances, and the rules or regulations promulgated in accordance therewith, shall not be affected by and need not be consistent with the state emergency housing rent control law or with rules and regulations of the state division of housing and community renewal.

Notwithstanding the foregoing, no local law or ordinance shall hereafter provide for the regulation and control of residential rents and eviction in respect of any housing accommodations which are (1) presently exempt from such regulation and control or (2) hereafter decontrolled either by operation of law or by a city housing rent agency, by order or otherwise. No housing accommoda-

Rent Control Law

tions presently subject to regulation and control pursuant to local laws or ordinances adopted or amended under authority of this subdivision shall hereafter be by local law or ordinance or by rule or regulation which has not been theretofore approved by the state commissioner of housing and community renewal subjected to more stringent or restrictive provisions of regulation and control than those presently in effect.

6. Succession of city agency to state rent control functions within city. All the functions and powers possessed by and all the obligations and duties of the temporary state housing rent commission and the state rent administrator under the provisions of the state emergency housing rent control law and the rules and regulations of the commission thereunder, insofar as they relate to the regulation and control of residential rents and evictions within a city having a population of one million or more, shall be transferred to the city housing rent agency of such city on May first, nineteen hundred sixty-two, subject to the provisions of any local laws, ordinances, rules or regulations adopted pursuant to this subdivision or subdivision five of this section. On and after such date, and until the adoption of a local law or ordinance in respect of the regulation and control of residential rents within such city pursuant to subdivision five of this section, such city housing rent agency is hereby authorized and empowered, from time to time, to adopt, promulgate, amend or rescind rules, regulations and orders under the state emergency housing rent control law and the validity of such rules, regulations and orders shall not be affected by and need not be consistent with the rules, regulations and orders of the temporary state housing rent commission under such law. All acts, orders, determinations, decisions, rules and regulations of the temporary state housing rent commission relating to the regulation and control of residential rents and eviction within such city which are in force at the time of such transfer shall continue in force and effect as acts, orders, determinations, decisions, rules and regulations of such city housing rent agency until duly modified, superseded or abrogated pursuant to such local laws, ordinances, rules or regulations.

7. *Investigations.* The city housing rent agency is authorized to make such studies and investigations, to conduct such hearings, and to obtain such information as it deems necessary or proper in prescribing any regulation or order under a local law adopted pursuant to subdivision five of this section or in administering and enforcing such local law and the regulations and orders thereunder or the state emergency housing rent control law and the regulations and orders thereunder.

The city housing rent agency is further authorized, by regulation or order, to require any person who rents or offers for rent or acts as broker or agent for the rental of any housing accommodations to furnish any such information under oath or affirmation, or otherwise, to make and keep records and other documents, and to make reports, and the city housing rent agency may require any such person to permit the inspection and copying of records and other documents and the inspection of housing accommodations. Any officer or agent designated by the city housing rent agency for such purposes may administer oaths and affirmations and may, whenever necessary, by subpoena, require any such person to appear and testify or to appear and produce documents, or both, at any designated place.

For the purpose of obtaining any information under this subdivision, the city housing rent agency may by subpoena require any other person to appear and testify or to appear and produce documents, or both, at any designated place.

The production of a person's documents at any place other than his place of business shall not be required under this subdivision in any case in which, prior to the return date specified in the subpoena issued with respect thereto, such person either has furnished the city housing rent agency with a copy of such documents certified by such person under oath to be a true and correct copy, or has entered into a stipulation with the city housing rent agency as to the information contained in such documents.

In case of contumacy by, or refusal to obey a subpoena served upon, any person referred to in this subdivision, the supreme court in or for any judicial district in which such person is found or resides or transacts business, upon application by the city housing rent agency, shall have jurisdiction to issue an order requiring such person to appear and give testimony or to appear and produce documents, or both; and any failure to obey such order of the court may be punished by such court as a contempt thereof. The provisions of this paragraph shall be in addition to the provisions of paragraph (a) of subdivision nine of this section.

Witnesses subpoenaed under this subdivision shall be paid the same fees and mileage as are paid witnesses under article eighty of the civil practice law and rules.

Upon any such investigation or hearing, the city housing rent agency, or an officer duly designated by the city housing rent agency to conduct such investigation or hearing, may confer immunity in accordance with the provisions of section 50.20 of the Criminal Procedure Law.

The city housing rent agency shall not publish or disclose any information obtained under this section that the city housing rent agency deems confidential or with reference to which a request for confidential treatment is made by the person furnishing such information, unless the city housing rent agency determines that the withholding thereof is contrary to the public interest.

Any person subpoenaed under this section shall have the right to make a record of his testimony and to be represented by counsel.

8. Judicial Review. Any person who is aggrieved by the final determination of the city housing rent agency in an administrative proceeding protesting a regulation or order of such agency may, in accordance with article seventy-eight of the civil practice law and rules, within sixty days after such determination, file a petition with the supreme court specifying his objections and praying that the regulation or order protested be enjoined or set aside in whole or in part. Such proceeding may at the option of the petitioner be instituted in the county where the city housing rent agency has its principal office or where the property is located. A copy of such petition shall forthwith be served on the city housing rent agency, and the city housing rent agency shall file with such court the

original or a transcript of such portions of the proceedings in connection with the determination as are material under the petition. Such return shall include a statement setting forth, so far as practicable, the economic data and other facts of which the city housing rent agency has taken official notice. Upon the filing of such petition the court shall have jurisdiction to set aside the regulation or order protested, in whole or in part, to dismiss the petition, or to remit the proceeding to the city housing rent agency; provided, however, that the regulation or order may be modified or rescinded by the city housing rent agency at any time notwithstanding the pendency of such proceeding for review. No objection to such regulation or order, and no evidence in support of any objection thereto, shall be considered by the court, unless such objection shall have been presented to the city housing rent agency by the petitioner in the proceedings resulting in the determination or unless such evidence shall be contained in the return. If application is made to the court by either party for leave to introduce additional evidence which was either offered and not admitted, or which could not reasonably have been offered or included in such proceedings before the city housing rent agency, and the court shall order the evidence to be presented to the city housing rent agency. The city housing rent agency shall promptly receive the same, and such other evidence as the city housing rent agency deems necessary or proper, and thereupon the city housing rent agency shall file with the court the original or a transcript thereof and any modification made in such regulation or order as a result thereof; except that on request by the city housing rent agency, any such evidence shall be presented directly to the court. Upon final determination of the proceeding before the court, the original record, if filed by the city housing rent agency with the court, shall be returned to the city housing rent agency. [Opening Paragraph of subd 8 am L 1984, ch 102, § 7, eff April 1, 1984.]

No regulation or order of the city housing rent agency shall be enjoined or set aside, in whole or in part, unless the petitioner shall establish to the satisfaction of the court that the regulation or order is not in accordance with law, or is arbitrary or capricious. The effectiveness of an order of the court enjoining or setting aside, in whole or in part, any such regulation or order shall be postponed until the expiration of thirty days from the entry thereof. The jurisdiction of the supreme court shall be exclusive and its order dismissing the petition or enjoining or setting aside such regulation or order, in whole or in part, shall be final, subject to review by the appellate division of the supreme court and the court of appeals in the same manner and form and with the same effect as provided in the civil practice act for appeals from a final order in a special proceeding. Notwithstanding any provision of section thirteen hundred four of the civil practice act to the contrary, any order of the court remitting the proceeding to the city housing rent agency may, at the election of the city housing rent agency, be subject to review by the appellate division of the supreme court and the court of appeals in the same manner and form and with the same effect as provided in the civil practice act for appeals from a final order in a special proceeding. All such proceedings shall be heard and determined by the court and by any appellate court as expeditiously as possible and with lawful precedence over other matters. All such proceedings for review shall be heard on the petition, transcript and other papers, and on appeal shall be heard on the record, without requirement of printing.

Within thirty days after arraignment, or such additional time as the court may allow for good cause shown, in any criminal proceeding, and within five days after judgment in any civil or criminal proceeding, brought pursuant to subdivision ten of this section involving alleged violation of any provision of any regulation or order of the city housing rent agency, the defendant may apply to the court in which the proceeding is pending for leave to file in the supreme court a petition setting forth objections to the validity of any provision which the defendant is alleged to have violated or conspired to violate. The court in which the proceeding is pending shall grant such leave with respect to any objection which it finds is made in good faith and with respect to which it finds there is reasonable and substantial excuse for the defendant's failure to present such objection in an administrative proceeding before the city housing rent agency. Upon the filing of a petition pursuant to and within thirty days from the granting of such leave, the supreme court shall have jurisdiction to enjoin or set aside in whole or in part the provision of the regulation or order complained of or to dismiss the petition. The court may authorize the introduction of evidence, either to the city housing rent agency or directly to the court, in accordance with the first paragraph of this subdivision. The provisions of the second paragraph of this subdivision shall be applicable with respect to any proceedings instituted in accordance with this paragraph.

In any proceeding brought pursuant to subdivision ten of this section involving an alleged violation of any provision of any such regulation or order, the court shall stay the proceeding:

(1) during the period within which a petition may be filed in the supreme court pursuant to leave granted under the third paragraph of this subdivision with respect to such provision;

(2) during the pendency of any administrative proceeding before the city housing rent agency properly commenced by the defendant prior to the institution of the proceeding under subdivision ten of this section, setting forth objections to the validity of such provision which the court finds to have been made in good faith; and

(3) during the pendency of any judicial proceeding instituted by the defendant under this subdivision with respect to such administrative proceeding or instituted by the defendant under the third paragraph of this subdivision with respect to such provision, and until the expiration of the time allowed in this subdivision for the taking of further proceedings with respect thereto.

Notwithstanding the provisions of the immediately preceding paragraph, stays shall be granted thereunder in civil proceedings only after judgment and upon application made within five days after judgment. Notwithstanding the provisions of the third paragraph of this subdivision, in the case of a proceeding under the first paragraph of subdivision ten of this section the court granting a stay under the immediately preceding paragraph of this subdivision shall issue a temporary injunction or restraining order enjoining or restraining, during the period of the stay, violations by the defendant of any provision of the regulation or order involved in the proceeding. If any provision of a regulation or order is determined to be invalid by judgment of the supreme court which has become effective in accordance with the second paragraph of this subdivision, any proceeding pending in any court shall be dismissed, and any judgment in such proceeding vacated, to the extent that such proceeding or judgment is based upon violation of such provision. Except as provided in this paragraph, the pendency of any administrative proceeding before the city housing rent agency or judicial proceeding under this subdivision shall not be grounds for staying any proceeding brought pursuant to subdivision ten of this section; nor, except as provided in this paragraph, shall any retroactive effect be given to any judgment setting aside a provision of a regulation or order.

The method prescribed herein for the judicial review of a regulation or order of the city housing rent agency shall be exclusive.

9. Prohibitions. (a) It shall be unlawful, regardless of any contract, lease or other obligation heretofore or hereafter entered into, for any person to demand or receive any rent for any housing accommodations in excess of the maximum rent established therefor by the temporary state housing rent commission or the city housing rent agency or otherwise to do or omit to do any act, in violation of any regulation, order or requirement of the city housing rent agency hereunder or under any local law adopted pursuant to subdivision five of this section or to offer, solicit, attempt or agree to do any of the foregoing.

(b) It shall be unlawful for any person to remove or attempt to remove from any housing accommodations the tenant or occupant thereof or to refuse to renew the lease or agreement for the use of such accommodations, because such tenant or occupant has taken, or proposes to take, action authorized or required by the state emergency housing rent control law or any local law adopted pursuant to subdivision five of this section or any regulation, order or requirement thereunder.

(c) It shall be unlawful for any officer or employee of the city housing rent agency or for any official adviser or consultant to the city housing rent agency to disclose, otherwise than in the course of official duty, any information obtained under this section, or to use any such information for personal benefit.

(d) It shall be unlawful for any landlord or any person acting on his behalf, with intent to cause the tenant to vacate, to engage in any course of conduct (including, but not limited to, interruption or discontinuance of essential services) which interferes with or disturbs or is intended to interfere with or disturb the comfort, repose, peace or quiet of the tenant in his use or occupancy of the housing accommodations. (Added L 1971, ch 371, eff June 11, 1971)

10. Enforcement. (a) Whenever in the judgment of the city housing rent agency any person has engaged or is about to engage in any acts or practices which constitute or will constitute a violation of any provision of subdivision nine of this section, the city housing rent agency may make application to the supreme court for an order enjoining such acts or practices, or for an order enforcing compliance with such provision, or for an order directing the landlord to correct the violation, and upon a showing by the city housing rent agency that such person has engaged or is about to engage in any such acts or practices a permanent or temporary injunction, restraining order, or other order shall be granted without bond. Jurisdiction shall not be deemed lacking in the supreme court because the defense is based upon an order of an inferior court.

(b) Any person who wilfully violates any provision of subdivision nine of this section, and any person who makes any statement or entry false in any material respect in any document or report required to be kept or filed under any local law adopted pursuant to subdivision five of this section or any regulation, order, or requirement thereunder, and any person who wilfully omits or neglects to make any material statement or entry required to be made in any such document or report, shall, upon conviction thereof, be subject to a fine of not more than five thousand dollars, or to imprisonment for not more than two years in the case of a violation of paragraph (c) of subdivision nine of this section and for not more than one year in all other cases, or to both such fine and imprisonment. Whenever the city housing rent agency has reason to believe that any person is liable to punishment under this paragraph, the city housing rent agency may certify the facts to the district attorney of any county having jurisdiction of the alleged violation, who shall cause appropriate proceedings to be brought.

(c) Any court shall advance on the docket and expedite the disposition of any criminal or other proceedings brought before it under this subdivision.

(d) No officer or employee of the city housing rent agency shall be held liable for damages or penalties in any court, on any grounds for or in respect of anything done or omitted to be done in good faith pursuant to any provision of the state emergency housing rent control law or any local law adopted pursuant to subdivision five of this section or any regulation, order, or requirement thereunder, notwithstanding that subsequently such provision, regulation, order, or requirement may be modified, rescinded, or determined to be invalid. In any action or proceeding wherein a party relies for ground of relief or defense or raises issue or brings into question the construction or validity of such local law or any regulation, order, or requirement thereunder, the court having jurisdiction of such action or proceeding may at any stage certify such fact to the city housing rent agency. The city housing rent agency may intervene in any such action or proceeding.

(e) If any landlord who receives rent from a tenant violates a regulation or order of the temporary state housing rent commission or the city housing rent agency prescribing the maximum rent with respect to the housing accommodations for which such rent is received from such tenant, the tenant paying such rent may, within two years from the date of the occurrence of the violation, except as hereinafter provided, bring an action against the landlord on account of the overcharge as hereinafter defined. In such action, the landlord shall be liable for reasonable attorney's fees and costs as determined by the court, plus whichever of the following sums is the greater: (a) such amount not more than three times the amount of the overcharge, or the overcharges, upon which the action is based as the court in its discretion may determine, or (b) an amount not less than twenty-five dollars nor more than fifty dollars, as the court in its discretion may determine; provided, however, that such amount shall be the amount of the overcharge or overcharges or twenty-five dollars, whichever is greater, if the defendant proves that the violation of the regulation or order in question was neither wilful nor the result of failure to take practicable precautions against the occurrence of the violation. As used in this section, the word "overcharge" shall mean the amount by which the consideration paid by a tenant to a landlord exceeds the applicable maximum rent. If any landlord who receives rent from a tenant violates a regulation or order of the temporary state housing rent commission or the city housing rent agency prescribing maximum rent with respect to the housing accommodations for which such rent is received from such tenant, and such tenant either fails to institute an action under this paragraph within thirty days from the date of the occurrence of the violation or is not entitled for any reason to bring the action, the city housing rent agency may institute an action within such two-year period. If such action is instituted by the city housing rent agency, the tenant affected shall thereafter be barred from bringing an action for the same violation or violations. Any action under this paragraph by either the tenant or the city housing rent agency, as the case may be, may be brought in any court of competent jurisdiction. A judgment in an action for damages under this subdivision shall be a bar to the recovery under this paragraph of any damages in any other action against the same landlord on account of the same overcharge prior to the institution of the action in which such judgment was rendered. Where judgment is rendered in favor of the city housing rent agency in such action, there shall be paid over to the tenant from the moneys recovered one-third of such recovery, exclusive of costs and disbursements.

(f) If any landlord who receives rent from a tenant violates any order of the city housing rent agency containing a directive that rent collected by the landlord in excess of the maximum rent be refunded to the tenant within thirty days, the city housing rent agency may, within one year after the expiration of such thirty day period or after such order shall become final by regulation of the city housing rent agency, bring an action against the landlord on account of the failure of the landlord to make the prescribed refund. In such action, the landlord shall be liable for reasonable attorney's fees and costs as determined by the court, plus whichever of the following sums is the greater: (a) such amount not more than three times the amount directed to be refunded, or the amount directed to be refunded, upon which the action is based as the court in its discretion may determine, or (b) an amount not less than twenty-five dollars nor more than fifty dollars, as the court in its discretion may determine; provided, however, that such amount shall be the amount directed to be refunded or twenty-five dollars, whichever is greater, if the defendant proves that the violation of the order in question was neither wilful nor the result of failure to take practical precautions against the occurrence of the violation. The tenant paying such rent may also institute an action under this section if the city housing rent agency fails to institute an action within thirty days from the date of occurrence of the violation. If an action is instituted by the city housing rent agency, the tenant affected shall thereafter be barred from bringing an action for the same violation. Any action under this section by either the city housing rent agency or the tenant, as the case may be, may be brought in any court of competent jurisdiction. A judgment in an action for damages under this section shall be a bar to recovery under this subdivision of any damages in any other action against the same landlord on account of the same violation prior to the institution of the action in which such judgment was rendered. Where an action is brought by the tenant the damages which shall be awarded to the tenant shall be the same as if such action was brought by the city housing rent agency. Where judgment is rendered in favor of the city housing rent agency in such action, there shall be paid over to the tenant from the moneys recovered one-third of such recovery, exclusive of the costs and disbursements.

(g) Where after the city housing rent agency has granted a certificate of eviction certifying that the landlord may pursue his remedies pursuant to local law to acquire possession, and a tenant voluntarily removes from a housing accommodation or has been removed therefrom by action or proceeding to evict from or recover possession of a housing accommodation upon the ground that the landlord seeks in good faith to recover possession of such accommodation for any purpose specified in a local law adopted pursuant to subdivision five of this section and such landlord shall lease or sell the housing accommodation or the space previously occupied thereby, or permit use thereof in any manner other than contemplated in such eviction certificate, such landlord shall, unless for good cause shown, be liable to the tenant for three times the damages sustained on account of such removal plus reasonable attorney's fees and costs as determined by the court; in addition to any other damage, the cost of removal of property shall be a lawful measure of damage.

(h) Any tenant who has vacated his housing accommodations because the landlord or any person acting on his behalf, with intent to cause the tenant to vacate, engaged in any course of conduct (including but not limited to, interruption or discontinuance of essential services) which interfered with or disturbed or was intended to interfere with or disturb the comfort, repose, peace or quiet of the tenant in his use or occupancy of the housing accommodations may, within ninety days after vacating, apply for a determination that the housing accommodations were vacated as a result of such conduct, and may, within one year after such determination, institute a civil action against the landlord by reason of such conduct. Application for such determination may be made to the city housing rent agency with respect to housing accommodations which, by local law or ordinance, are made directly subject to regulation and control by such agency. For all other housing accommodations subject to regulation and control pursuant to the New York city rent stabilization law of nineteen hundred sixty-nine, applica-

Rent Control Law

tion for such determination may be made to the New York city conciliation and appeals board. For the purpose of making and enforcing any determination of the New York city conciliation and appeals board as herein provided, the provisions of sections seven, eight and ten, whenever they refer to the city housing rent agency, shall be deemed to refer to such board. In such action the landlord shall be liable to the tenant for three times the damages sustained on account of such conduct plus reasonable attorney's fees and costs as determined by the court. In addition to any other damages the cost of removal of property shall be a lawful measure of damages. (Added L 1971, ch 371; Am L 1974, ch 576, § 3.)

11. Transfer of certain pending matters. Except as provided in subdivision thirteen of this section, any matter, application, proceeding or protest undertaken, filed or commenced by, with or before the temporary state housing rent commission or the state rent administrator relating to the regulation and control or residential rents and evictions within a city having a population of one million or more and pending on May first, nineteen hundred sixty-two, shall be transferred to, conducted by, and completed or determined by the city housing rent agency. In discharging such responsibilities the city housing rent agency shall act in conformity with the provisions of the state emergency housing rent control law, and the rules and regulations promulgated thereunder, governing such matters, applications or proceedings, unless at the time such action is taken, such state law, and the rules and regulations promulgated thereunder, have been amended or superseded by local laws, ordinances, rules or regulations adopted pursuant to subdivision five of this section, and in such event, in conformity therewith to the extent such local law, ordinances, rules or regulations are made expressly applicable to such matters, applications or proceedings.

12. Termination of state regulation and control. On and after May first, nineteen hundred sixty-two, the temporary state housing rent commission and the state rent administrator shall have no jurisdiction over the regulation and control of residential rents and evictions within any city having a population of one million or more.

13. Pending court proceedings. All appeals or other court proceedings relating to the regulation and control of residential rents and evictions in a city having a population of one million or more to which the temporary state housing rent commission or the state rent administrator is a party and which is pending on May first, nineteen hundred sixty-two or thereafter prosecuted shall be prosecuted or defended by the temporary state housing rent commission and the state rent administrator pursuant to the state emergency housing rent control law to a final determination or other disposition by the court in accordance with law. If the court remits any such matter to the temporary state housing rent commission, the commission may transfer such matter to the city housing rent agency for disposition pursuant to subdivision eleven of this section.

14. Civil service. Upon the transfer of the functions of the temporary state housing rent commission to the city housing rent agency pursuant to subdivision six of this section, the officers, and employees of such commission, other than those certified for retention by the state rent administrator to the state department of civil service prior to April first, nineteen hundred sixty-two, as required for the continued operations of such commission, shall be transferred as of May first, nineteen hundred sixty-two, to the city housing rent agency for the continued performance of their functions. Such officers and employees shall be transferred to similar or corresponding positions in such city housing rent agency, without further examination or qualification, and shall retain their respective civil service jurisdictional classifications and status. If the city housing rent agency determines that it will not accept for transfer all such officers and employees, the city housing rent agency shall certify to the state department of civil service those officers and employees whom it will not accept for transfer and in such event, the determination of those to be transferred shall be made by selection of the city housing rent agency from among officers and employees holding permanent appointments in competitive class positions in the order of their respective dates of original appointments in the service of the state, with due regard to the right of

preference in retention of disabled and nondisabled veterans and blind persons.

Notwithstanding the provisions of any general, special or local law, code or charter requiring officers and employees of a city having a population of one million or more to be residents of such city at the time of their entry into city service or during the continuance of such service, officers and employees of the temporary state housing rent commission shall be transferred to and shall be retained by the city housing rent agency pursuant to this subdivision without regard to local residence.

Officers and employees holding permanent appointments in competitive class positions, other than those certified by the state rent administrator for retention in the service of the state, who are not accepted for transfer by the city housing rent agency or who request to be excepted from such transfer shall have their names entered on an appropriate preferred list for reinstatement to the same or similar positions in the service of the state.

Officers and employees transferred to the city housing rent agency pursuant to this subdivision shall be entitled to full seniority credit for all purposes, including the determination of their city salaries and increments, for service in the state government rendered prior to such transfer, as though such service had been service in the city government. Such transferees shall retain their earned unused sick leave and vacation credits, but not in excess of maximum accumulations permitted under such municipal rules as may be applicable.

Officers and employees transferred pursuant to this subdivision shall thereafter be subject to the rules and jurisdiction of the municipal civil service commission having jurisdiction over the city housing rent agency to which such transfer is made. The state department of civil service shall transfer to such municipal civil service commission on May first, nineteen hundred sixty-two, or as soon thereafter as may be practicable, all eligible lists, records, documents and files pertaining to the officers and employees so transferred and to their positions. Examinations for positions in the temporary state housing rent commission which are in process on May first, nineteen hundred sixty-two, shall be completed by the state civil service commission and eligible lists established. Such lists shall be included among the eligible lists transferred to the municipal civil service commission. Any such eligible list shall continue to be used by such municipal civil service commission and shall be certified by it in accordance with the provisions of its rules and regulations for filling vacancies in appropriate positions in the city housing rent agency exercising the functions transferred pursuant to this section; provided, however, that such certifications from promotion eligible lists shall be limited to eligibles transferred to such city housing rent agency pursuant to this subdivision. Promotions in the temporary state housing rent commission shall be made from among eligibles on appropriate lists who are not transferred to the city housing rent agency. All other matters which relate to the administration of the civil service law with respect to the officers and employees transferred pursuant to this subdivision, and with respect to their positions, and which at the time of such transfer are pending before the state department of civil service or the state civil service commission, shall be transferred to such municipal civil service commission, and any action theretofore taken on such matters by such state department or commission shall have the same force and effect as if taken by such municipal civil service commission.

15. Intergovernmental cooperation. The temporary state housing rent commission and the state rent administrator shall cooperate with the city housing rent agency in effectuating the purposes of this act and shall make available to the city housing rent agency such cooperation, information, records and data as will assist the city housing rent agency in effectuating such purposes.

Upon the request of the city housing rent agency, all such information, records and data relating to the regulation and control of residential rents and evictions within such city shall be transferred to the city housing rent agency on May first, nineteen hundred sixty-two or as soon thereafter as may be practicable.

Subject to the approval of the state rent administrator, the state commissioner of general services is hereby authorized to sublease or otherwise make available, in part or in whole, to the city housing rent agency, upon such terms and conditions as the said commissioner may prescribe, any premises leased to the state and occupied on or prior to May first, nineteen hundred sixty-two by the temporary state housing rent commission.

Notwithstanding the provisions of section one hundred seventy-eight of the state finance law, the state commissioner of general services is hereby authorized to sell, lease or otherwise make available to the city housing rent agency, upon such terms and conditions as the said commissioner may prescribe and subject to the approval of the state rent administrator, any or all personal property used on or prior to May first, nineteen hundred sixty-two by the temporary state housing rent commission.

16. Saving clause. If any local law or ordinance in respect of the regulation and control of residential rents and evictions adopted pursuant to subdivision five of this section shall be held wholly or partially invalid by final decree of a court of competent jurisdiction, the city housing rent agency shall administer the provisions of the state emergency housing rent control law to the extent of any such invalidity.

17. Separability. If any subdivision, paragraph, sentence, clause or provision of this section shall be held wholly or partially invalid by final decree of a court of competent jurisdiction, to the extent that it is not invalid, it shall be valid and no other subdivision, paragraph, sentence, clause or provision shall on account thereof be deemed invalid.

Section 2. Promptly after the effective date of this act, the mayor of each city having a population of one million or more shall transmit to the governor, in such form and detail as the governor may prescribe, his request, if any, for an appropriation from the state treasury to defray the reasonable and necessary expenses of such city for personal service and for maintenance and operation in respect of the regulation and control of residential rents within such city pursuant to this act. Any such request shall be in sufficient detail to justify the reasonableness and necessity of the amount requested.

If a request is received from the mayor of any such city after the final adjournment of the regular session of the legislature in nineteen hundred sixty-two, the state director of the budget is authorized to transfer to such city from time to time a portion of any outstanding appropriation made to the temporary state housing rent commission after filing a certificate of such transfer with the state comptroller, the chairman of the senate finance committee and the chairman of the assembly ways and means committee. Any amount so transferred shall be paid from the general fund to the credit of the local assistance fund on the audit and warrant of the state comptroller on vouchers requisitioned by the mayor of such city or by an official of such city designated by the mayor.[1]

Section 5. Any adjustments in maximum rents ordered by the temporary state housing rent commission on and after June thirtieth, nineteen hundred sixty-one, and resulting in an increase thereof solely by reason of the amendments made by chapter three hundred thirty-seven of the laws of nineteen hundred sixty-one to paragraph (a) of subdivision four of section four of the emergency housing rent control law which provided for the application of the most recent equalization rate, rather than the equalization rate for the year nineteen hundred fifty-four, are hereby rescinded and nullified, provided, however, that no right is conferred by this act to recover any such increase paid prior to the effective date of this act.

Section 6. Notwithstanding any provision of chapter three hundred thirty-seven of the laws of nineteen hundred sixty-one, maximum rents established in any city having a population of one million or more pursuant to the emergency housing rent control law, as last amended by such chapter, shall not be increased during the period between the effective date of this act and May first, nineteen hundred sixty-two, except with the voluntary written consent of the tenant affected.

---

[1] § 3 of the Emergency Housing Rent Control Act repeats § 12-a of the Emergency Housing Rent Control Law; § 4 amends paragraph a of subd 4 of § 4 of the Emergency Housing Rent Control Law.

NEW YORK CITY RENT AND EVICTION REGULATIONS

Part

2200 Scope
2210 Maximum Rents
2202 Adjustments; Determination of Rents and Services
2203 Registration and Records
2204 Evictions
2205 Prohibitions
2206 Enforcement
2207 Proceedings before District Rent Administrator
2208 Administrative Review
2209 Miscellaneous Procedural Matters
2210 Housing Accommodations Covered by Title YY of the New York City Administrative Code

[Section numbers refer to the designation of these Regulations as published in the State of New York Official Compilation of the Codes, Rules, and Regulations, volume 9, Executive (C), Subtitle S (Housing), Chapter VII (Emergency Housing Rent Control), Subchapter D.]

Section 2200.1 Statutory authority. These regulations are adopted and promulgated by the Division of Housing and Community Renewal pursuant to the City Rent and Rehabilitation Law (title Y of chapter 51 of the Administrative Code of the City of New York, formerly being chapter 41 and renumbered by chapter 100 of the Laws of 1963, as amended) and the Local Emergency Housing Rent Control Act (chapter 21 of the Laws of 1962) and the Omnibus Housing Act (chapter 403 of the Laws of 1983). As used in these regulations, the term *Rent Law* shall mean the Rent and Rehabilitation Law of the City of New York.

2200.2 Statutory definitions. When used in these regulations, unless a different meaning clearly appears from the content, the following terms shall mean and include:

(a) *Administrator.* The commissioner of the Division of Housing and Community Renewal.

(b) *City.* The City of New York or an administrative agency of the City of New York.

(c) *Documents.* Records, books, accounts, correspondence, memoranda and other documents, and drafts and copies of any of the foregoing.

(d) *Federal Act.* The Emergency Price Control Act of 1942, and as thereafter amended and as superseded by the Housing and Rent Act of 1947, and as the latter was thereafter amended prior to May 1, 1950, and the regulations adopted pursuant thereto.

(e) *Housing accommodations.* Subject to the provisions of subdivisions (f) and (g) of this section, any building or structure, permanent or temporary, or any part thereof, occupied or intended to be occupied by one or more individuals as a residence, home, sleeping place, boarding house, lodging house or hotel, together with the land and buildings appurtenant thereto, and all services, privileges, furnishings, furniture and facilities supplied in connection with the occupation thereof, and any plot or parcel of land (as distinguished from any building constructed or placed thereon) which is not owned by the city and which was rented prior to May 1, 1950, for the purpose of permitting the tenant thereof to construct thereon his own building or structure designed exclusively for residential occupancy by not more than two families, and on which there exists such a building or structure owned and occupied by a tenant of such plot or parcel, including:

(1) entire structures or premises, as distinguished from the individual housing accommodations contained therein, wherein 25 or fewer rooms are rented or offered for rent by any lessee, sublessee or other tenant of the entire structure or premises, and where such lessee, sublessee or other tenant occupies a portion of the structure or premises as his dwelling;

(2) housing accommodations in any multiple dwelling aided by a loan made by the city under article 8 of the Private Housing Finance Law, provided that where any such housing accommodations were not subject to rent control immediately prior to the first date on which moneys are advanced to the landlord under the loan, or the occupancy date as defined in such article 8, whichever is earlier:

(i) rent control hereunder as to such housing accommodations shall begin on such earlier date; and

(ii) such control shall continue only so long as is required by such article 8;

(3) housing accommodations in any multiple dwelling with respect to which tax exemption and tax abatement under section J51-2.5 of the Administrative Code of the City of New York begin after April 30, 1962, notwithstanding that immediately prior to the date when such tax exemption and tax abatement begin, such housing accommodations may not have been subject to control. Where any such housing accommodations were not controlled immediately prior to such date:

(i) they shall become subject to control when tax exemption and tax abatement begin; and

(ii) they shall remain subject to control until the date on which such tax exemption or tax abatement terminates, whichever is later; and

(4) housing accommodations which become subject to control pursuant to the provisions of paragraph (5), (9), (10), (11), (12), (13) or (14) of subdivision (f) of this section or section 2200.9 of this Part.

(f) *Housing accommodations not subject to control.* Notwithstanding the foregoing definition of housing accommodations, these regulations shall not apply to the following:

(1)(i) Leases for entire structures or premises as distinguished from the individual housing accommodations therein contained, wherein more than 25 rooms are rented or offered for rent by any lessee, subleasee or other tenant of such entire structure or premises;

(ii) leases for entire structures or premises as distinguished from the individual housing accommodations therein, wherein 25 or fewer rooms are rented or offered for rent by any lessee, sublessee or other tenant of such entire structure or premises, where such lessee, sublessee or other tenant does not occupy any portion of the structure or premises as his dwelling and sublets, as an entrepreneur for his own profit, the individual rooms to subtenants; or

(iii) leases for entire structures or premises in which all of the housing accommodations are exempt or not subject to control under these regulations.

(2) A hospital, convent, monastery, asylum, public institution, or college or school dormitory or any institution operated exclusively for charitable or educational purposes on a nonprofit basis.

(3) Rooms or other housing accommodations in hotels, except that a room or housing accommodation occupied by a hotel tenant as defined in these regulations, is subject to these regulations so long as such tenant occupies the same.

(4)(i) Any motor court, or any part thereof; any trailer or trailer space used exclusively for transient occupancy or any part thereof; or any tourist home serving transient guests exclusively, or any part thereof.

(ii) The term *motor court* shall mean an establishment renting rooms, cottages or cabins, supplying parking or storage facilities for motor vehicles in connection with such renting, and other services and facilities customarily supplied by such establishments, and commonly known as a motor, auto or tourist court in the city.

(iii) The term *tourist home* shall mean a rooming house which caters primarily to transient guests and is known as a tourist home in the city.

(5) Nonhousekeeping, furnished housing accommodations, located within a single dwelling unit not used as a rooming or boarding house, but only if:

(i) no more than two tenants for whom rent is paid (husband and wife being considered one tenant for this purpose), not members of the landlord's immediate family, live in such dwelling unit; and

(ii) the remaining portion of such dwelling unit is occupied by the landlord or his immediate family.

(6) Housing accommodations owned and operated by the United States, the State of New York, the City of New York, or the New York City Housing Authority; or owned by the city and under the supervision of the City Department of Housing Preservation and Development pursuant to section 1802, subdivision 8 of chapter 61 of the City Charter; or housing accommodations in buildings in which rentals are fixed by or subject to the

supervision of the commissioner of the Division of Housing and Community Renewal.

(7) Housing accommodations in buildings operated exclusively for charitable purposes on a nonprofit basis.

(8) Housing accommodations which were completed on or after February 1, 1947, except:

(i) accommodations resulting from substantial demolition, as defined in section 2200.10(c) of this Part, which shall continue to be subject to control unless the administrator shall issue an order decontrolling them pursuant to section 2200.10; or

(ii) where the former structure, or any lesser portion thereof, was vacated on or after November 22, 1963 other than by voluntary surrender of possession or in the manner provided by Part 2204 of this Title; provided, however, that maximum rents established under the Veterans' Emergency Housing Act, for priority-constructed housing accommodations completed on or after February 1, 1947, shall continue in full force and effect if such accommodations are being rented to veterans of World War II or their immediate families who, on June 30, 1947 either occupied such housing accommodations or had a right to occupy such accommodations at any time on or after July 1, 1947, under any agreement whether written or oral.

(9) Housing accommodations created by a change from a nonhousing use to a housing use on or after February 1, 1947, but only if the space comprising such accommodations was devoted to a nonhousing use on February 1, 1947; provided that any such housing accommodations shall become subject to control if, while in such decontrolled status, it is certified, by a city agency having jurisdiction, to be a fire hazard or in a continued dangerous condition or detrimental to life or health; and once subject to control, it shall continue to be subject to control, notwithstanding the subsequent removal of the conditions on which such certification was based. Such housing accommodations shall remain decontrolled only so long as the housing accommodations are not occupied for other than single-family occupancy.

(10) Additional housing accommodations, other than rooming house accommodations, created by conversion on or after February 1, 1947; provided, however:

(i) that any housing accommodations created as a result of any such conversion on or after May 1, 1950 shall continue to be subject to control unless the State Rent Commission issued an order decontrolling them, or the administrator shall issue an order decontrolling them pursuant to section 2200.9 of this Part;

(ii) that such accommodations shall remain decontrolled only so long as the housing accommodations are not occupied for other than single-family occupancy; and

(iii) that any such housing accommodation shall become subject to control if, while in such decontrolled status, it is certified, by a city agency having jurisdiction, to be a fire hazard or in a continued dangerous condition or detrimental to life or health; and once subject to control it shall continue to be subject to control, notwithstanding the subsequent removal of the conditions on which such certification was based.

(11) Housing accommodations rented after April 1, 1953, which were or are continuously occupied by the owner thereof for a period of one year prior to the date of renting; provided, however, that this paragraph shall not apply:

(i) where, within the two-year period immediately preceding the date of such renting, the owner acquired possession of the housing accommodations after the issuance of an eviction certificate by the State Rent Commission, pursuant to section 5(2) of the State Rent Act, or by the administrator pursuant to Part 2204 of this Title; and

(ii) to any housing accommodation rented on or after May 1, 1962, where decontrol as previously obtained under section 2(2)(h) of the State Rent Act or under this subdivision for any housing accommodation in the same building. Such housing accommodations shall remain decontrolled only so long as the housing accommodations are not occupied for other

RENT REGULATIONS

than single-family occupancy. Any such housing accommodation shall become subject to control if, while in such decontrolled status it is certified, by a city agency having jurisdiction, to be a fire hazard or in a continued dangerous condition or detrimental to life or health; and once subject to control, it shall continue to be subject to control, notwithstanding the subsequent removal of the conditions on which such certification was based.

(12) Housing accommodations in one- and two-family houses which were or shall become vacant on or after April 1, 1953; provided, however, that such accommodations shall remain decontrolled only so long as the housing accommodations are not occupied for other than single-family occupancy. Any such housing accommodation shall become subject to control if, while in such decontrolled status, it is certified, by a city agency having jurisdiction, to be a fire hazard or in a continued dangerous condition or detrimental to life or health; and once subject to control, it shall continue to be subject to control, notwithstanding the subsequent removal of the conditions on which such certification was based.

(13)(i) Housing accommodations which are not subject to rent control by reason of the provisions of Decontrol Order No. 51 of the State Rent Commission and section 9(18) of the Rent and Eviction Regulations adopted by the State Rent Administrator, as continued in effect by the Rent Law.

(ii) Such housing accommodations shall remain decontrolled only so long as the housing accommodations are not occupied for other than single-family occupancy.

(iii) Any such housing accommodation shall become subject to control if, while in such decontrolled status, it is certified, by a city agency having jurisdiction, to be a fire hazard or in a continued dangerous condition or detrimental to life or health; and once subject to control, it shall continue to be subject to control, notwithstanding the subsequent removal of the conditions on which such certification was based.

(14)(i) Individual housing accommodations having un-

253

furnished maximum rents of $250 or more per month as of April 1, 1960, or furnished maximum rents of $300 or more per month as of April 1, 1960, which are or become vacant on or after March 26, 1964; or

(ii) On and after October 1, 1964 individual housing accommodations having unfurnished maximum rents of $300 or more per month as of April 1, 1960, or furnished maximum rents of $360 or more per month as of April 1, 1960; provided, however, that where such housing accommodation is occupied by a tenant whose household contains one or more children attending an elementary or secondary school, such housing accommodation shall continue to remain subject to control under the Rent Law and these regulations until June 30, 1965; and provided, further, that where such housing accommodation is occupied on March 26, 1964 by a tenant whose household contains four or more related persons, it shall continue to remain subject to control under the Rent Law and these regulations so long as such tenant remains in occupancy; or

(iii) On and after April 1, 1965, individual housing accommodations having unfurnished maximum rents of $250 to $299.99, inclusive, per month as of April 1, 1960, or furnished maximum rents of $300 to $359.99, inclusive, per month as of April 1, 1960; provided, however, that where such housing accommodation is occupied by a tenant whose household contains one or more children attending an elementary or secondary school, such housing accommodation shall continue to remain subject to control under the Rent Law and these regulations until June 30, 1965; and provided, further, that where such housing accommodation is occupied on March 26, 1964 by a tenant whose household contains four or more related persons, it shall continue to remain subject to control under the Rent Law and these regulations so long as such tenant remains in occupancy.

(iv) The exemptions provided for in this paragraph shall remain effective only so long as the housing accommodations are not occupied for other than single-family occupancy.

(v) The term *related persons* as used in this paragraph shall be limited to the tenant and a parent, grandparent, child, stepchild, grandchild, brother or sister of the tenant or of the tenant's spouse, or the spouse of any of the foregoing, who customarily occupied the housing accommodation on and before March 26, 1964. An unmarried child or grandchild of the tenant or the tenant's spouse who temporarily resided elsewhere on such date because of attendance at an educational institution or service in the Armed Forces of the United States shall be deemed to be a related person in occupancy.

(vi) Any such housing accommodation shall become subject to control if, while in such decontrolled status, it is certified, by a city agency having jurisdiction, to be a fire hazard or in a continued dangerous condition or detrimental to life or health; and once subject to control, it shall continue to be subject to control, notwithstanding the subsequent removal of the conditions on which such certification was based.

(15)(i) Individual housing accommodations having unfurnished maximum rents of $250 or more per month as of April 1, 1965, or furnished maximum rents of $300 or more per month as of April 1, 1965, which are or become vacant after January 29, 1968 by voluntary surrender of possession or in the manner provided by Part 2204 of this Title; or

(ii) On and after October 1, 1968, individual housing accommodations consisting of less than three rooms having unfurnished maximum rents of $250 or more per month as of April 1, 1965, or furnished maximum rents of $300 or more per month as of April 1, 1965; or

(iii) On and after October 1, 1968, individual housing accommodations consisting of at least three rooms and less than four rooms having unfurnished maximum rents of $250 or more per month as of April 1, 1965, or furnished maximum rents of $300 or more per month as of April 1, 1965, provided that such housing accommodation shall continue to remain subject to control until it becomes vacant as provided in subparagraph (i) of this paragraph, where it was occupied on January 29, 1968 by a tenant whose household then consisted of four or more related persons, as such term is defined (a single parent or a single head of the household being deemed to be two persons, for the purpose of this provision, when residing with one or more dependent children); and provided, further, that such housing accommodation shall also continue to remain subject to control where occupied by less than four related persons on January 29, 1968 until October 1, 1969, unless a written lease has been executed, or the landlord has offered such lease to the tenant by certified mail prior to June 1, 1968 or between September 1, 1968 and September 15, 1968, both dates inclusive, which lease:

(a) shall be for a term of at least one year commencing October 1, 1968, or commencing from the date of expiration of any existing lease expiring on or after October 1, 1968;

(b) may provide for a monthly rent not exceeding 10 percent above the maximum rent in effect on the date of its execution;

(c) shall contain a certification by the landlord that he will continue to maintain all essential services furnished or required by the Rent Law to be furnished on the date of execution of the lease during the lease term; and

(d) shall give the tenant an option to cancel the lease by giving the landlord at least 30 days' written notice by certified mail prior to the date when such cancellation shall take effect; or

(iv) On and after October 1, 1968 individual housing accommodations consisting of four or more rooms having unfurnished maximum rents of $250 or more per month as of April 1, 1965, or furnished maximum rents of $300 or more per month as of April 1, 1965, provided that such housing accommodation shall continue to remain subject to control until it becomes vacant as provided in subparagraph (i) of this paragraph, where it was occupied on January 29, 1968 by a tenant whose household then consisted of four or more related persons, as such term is herein defined (a single parent or a single head of the household being deemed to be two persons, for the purpose of this provision, when residing with one or more dependent children); and provided, further, that such housing accommodations shall also continue to remain subject to control where occupied by less than four related persons on January 29, 1968 until October 1, 1970, unless a written lease has been executed, or the landlord has offered such lease to the tenant by certified mail prior to June 1, 1968 or between September 1, 1968 and September 15, 1968, both dates inclusive, which lease:

(a) shall be for a term of at least two years commencing October 1, 1968, or from the date of expiration of any existing lease expiring on or after October 1, 1968;

(b) may provide for a monthly rental not exceeding 10 percent above the maximum rent in effect on the date of its execution during the first year of its term, and for an additional 10 percent, above the rent payable during the first year, for the second year of its term;

(c) shall contain a certification by the landlord that he will continue to maintain all essential services furnished or required by the Rent Law to be furnished on the date of execution of the lease during the lease term; and

(d) shall give the tenant an option to cancel the lease by giving the landlord at least 30 days' written notice by certified mail prior to the date when such cancellation shall take effect.

(v) The exemption provided for in this paragraph shall not apply to entire structures rented by means of an underlying lease, and shall remain effective only so long as the housing accommodations are not occupied for other than single-family occupancy.

(vi) The term *related person,* as used in this paragraph, shall be limited to the tenant and a parent, grandparent, child, stepchild, grandchild, brother or sister of the tenant or the tenant's spouse, or the spouse of any of the foregoing, who customarily occupied the housing accommodations on January 29,

1968, except that a child of the tenant born or legally adopted on or before July 1, 1968 shall be deemed to have been in occupancy on January 29, 1968, and that an unmarried child or grandchild of the tenant or the tenant's spouse, who temporarily resided elsewhere on January 29, 1968 because of attendance at an educational institution or service in the Armed Forces or in the Peace Corps of the United States, shall be deemed to be a related person in occupancy for the purpose of this paragraph.

(vii) For the purpose of this paragraph, the term *maximum rent* shall not include any conditional rent increase applicable solely to a tenant in occupancy.

(viii) In computing the number contained in a housing accommodation, such computation shall not include bathrooms, foyers and windowless rooms and shall be limited to living rooms, kitchens (other than an enclosed kitchenette or an area in the living room which is either recessed or semienclosed), dining rooms (other than dinettes or dining alcoves) and bedrooms.

(ix) Notwithstanding any provision of this paragraph to the contrary, where the total number of related persons in occupancy shall become less than four, by means other than the demise of any such related person, and results from the permanent moving of any related person other than the tenant or his or her spouse, the landlord may make application after the effective date of this paragraph, and not more than once in any succeeding year, for an order decontrolling such housing accommodations on the basis of such change in occupancy. In the event that such application shall be granted, the administrator shall prescribe the effective date of decontrol, which shall contain conditions consistent with those imposed in this paragraph under similar circumstances.

(16) No more than two housing accommodations in any one-year period, in a structure containing six or fewer housing accommodations in which at least one housing accommodation is occupied by an owner as his residence and which are to become vacant on or after August 1, 1970 by voluntary surrender of possession or

pursuant to Part 2204 of this Title; provided, however, that this exemption shall remain effective only so long as the housing accommodations are not occupied for other than single-family occupancy and that, if the owner or his successor cease to occupy a housing accommodation in such structure within one year after decontrol of a housing accommodation pursuant to this paragraph, such decontrolled housing accommodation shall be recontrolled, unless for good cause shown, at a maximum rent established on the basis of the last rent collected while such housing accommodation was in the exempt status; and provided, further, that if the administrator shall make a finding that the landlord for the purpose of obtaining such vacancy had harassed the tenant by engaging in a course of conduct proscribed by section 2205.1(b) of this Title (section Y51-10.0d of the Rent Law), no housing accommodation in such structure shall be decontrolled pursuant to this paragraph until a minimum period of three years shall have elapsed since the making of such finding of harassment. Structures containing six or fewer housing accommodations shall be considered to be structures containing six or fewer housing accommodations for the purpose of this paragraph, notwithstanding that such structure shall contain commercial accommodations in addition to such housing accommodations.

(17) Notwithstanding any provision contained in any other paragraph of this subdivision, housing accommodations which become vacant on or after June 30, 1971 by voluntary surrender of possession or pursuant to Part 2204 of this Title; unless the administrator determines or finds, as provided in section 2206.5(e) of this Title, that the housing accommodations become vacant because the landlord or any person acting on his behalf, with intent to cause the tenant to vacate, engaged in any course of conduct (including but not limited to interruption or discontinuance of essential services) which interfered with or disturbed, or was intended to interfere with or disturb, the comfort, repose, peace or quiet of the tenant in his use or occupancy of the housing accommodation.

(18) Housing accommodations not occupied by the

tenant, not including subtenants or occupants, as his primary residence, as determined by a court of competent jurisdiction.

(g) *Housing accommodations subject to rent control, but exempted from control by these regulations.* Notwithstanding the foregoing definition of *housing accommodations,* these regulations shall not apply to the following housing accommodations only so long as they meet the specific requirements hereinafter set forth:

(1) College fraternity or sorority houses. Rooms in a bona fide college fraternity or sorority house certified by the State Rent Commission prior to May 1, 1962, or by the administrator, as exempt. The administrator may so certify if the landlord establishes that the fraternity or sorority is a bona fide organization operated for the benefit of students, and not for profit as a commercial or business enterprise. This exemption shall not apply when the rooms are rented to persons who are not members of the fraternity or sorority.

(2) Nonprofit clubs. Rooms in a bona fide club certified by the State Rent Commission prior to May 1, 1962, or by the administrator, as exempt. The administrator may so certify if, on written request of the landlord, the club establishes that it is a nonprofit organization and is recognized as such by written statement of the Bureau of Internal Revenue; that it rents rooms only to members, bona fide guests of members, and members of bona fide clubs with which the club has reciprocal arrangements for the exchanges of privileges; and that it is otherwise operated as a bona fide club.

(3) Service employees. Dwelling space occupied by domestic servants, superintendents, caretakers, managers or other employees, to whom the space is provided as part or all of their compensation without payment of rent, and who are employed for the purpose of rendering services in connection with the premises of which the dwelling space is a part.

(4) Summer resort housing. Housing accommodations located in a resort community and customarily rented or occupied on a seasonal basis prior to October 1, 1945, which were not rented during any portion of the period

Rent Regulations

beginning November 1, 1943 and ending on February 29, 1944. This exemption shall apply only so long as the housing accommodations continued to be rented on a seasonal basis, and shall be effective only from June 1st to September 30th, inclusive.

(h) *Landlord.* An owner, lessor, sublessor, assignee or other person receiving or entitled to receive rent for the use and occupancy of any housing accommodation, or an agent of any of the foregoing.

(i) *Maximum rent.* The maximum lawful rent for use of housing accommodations. Maximum rents may be formulated in terms of rents and other charges and allowances.

(j) *Person.* An individual, corporation, partnership, association or any other organized group of individuals, or the legal successor representative of any of the foregoing.

(k) *Rent.* Consideration, including any bonus, benefit or gratuity demanded or received for or in connection with the use or occupancy of housing accommodations or the transfer of a lease of such housing accommodations.

(l) *State Enabling Act.* The Local Emergency Housing Rent Control Act, as amended by chapter 403 of the Laws of 1983.

(m) *State Rent Act.* The Emergency Housing Rent Control Law, as amended.

(n) *State Rent Commission.* The Temporary State Housing Rent Commission created by the Emergency Housing Rent Control Law.

(o) *Tenant.* A tenant, subtenant, lessee, sublessee or other person entitled to the possession or to the use or occupancy of any housing accommodation.

2200.3 Additional definitions. (a) *Apartment.* A room or rooms providing facilities commonly regarded in the city as necessary for a self-contained family unit, but not including housing accommodations in a rooming house or a hotel.

(b) *Essential services.* Those essential services which the landlord furnished, or which he was obliged to furnish, on April 30, 1962, and which were included in the maximum rent for the housing accommodation on that date. These may include, but are not limited to, the following: repairs, decorating and maintenance, the furnishing of light, heat, hot and cold water, telephone, elevator service, kitchen, bath and laundry facilities and privileges, maid service, linen service, janitor service, and removal of refuse.

(c) *Final order.* An order shall be deemed to be final on the date of its issuance by the district rent administrator, unless a petition for administrative review (PAR) is filed against such order as provided in section 2208.2 of this Title. Where a PAR is filed, the order of the granting district rent administrator shall not be deemed to be final until the date of issuance of the administrator's order granting or denying the PAR, in whole or in part. Notwithstanding the filing of a PAR by either the landlord or the tenant, an order adjusting, fixing or establishing a maximum rent shall continue to remain in effect until further order of the administrator. An order issued by the administrator pursuant to section 2206.5 of this Title shall be deemed to be final on the date of its issuance.

(d) *Hotel.* Notwithstanding any order, finding, opinion or determination of the State Rent Commission, any establishment which on March 1, 1950 was and still is commonly regarded as a hotel in the city, and which customarily provides hotel services such as maid service, furnishing and laundering of linen, telephone and secretarial or desk use and upkeep of furniture and fixtures, and bellboy service; provided, however, that the term *hotel* shall not include any establishment which is commonly regarded in the city as a rooming house, nor shall it include any establishment not identified or classified as a hotel, transient hotel or residential hotel pursuant to the Federal Act, irrespective of whether such establishment either provides some services customarily provided by hotels, or is represented to be a hotel, or both.

(e) *Hotel tenant.* A tenant, subtenant, lessee, sublessee or other person entitled to possession or to the use or occupancy of any housing accommodation within a hotel, who has resided in such hotel continuously since December 2, 1949.

(f) *District rent administrator.* The person designated by the administrator to administer rent control in the rent district set forth in section 2200.8 of this Part, or such person or persons as may be designated to carry out any of the duties delegated to the district rent administrator by the administrator.

(g) *District rent office.* The Office of the Division of Housing and Community Renewal for a particular rent district, as set forth in section 2200.8 of this Part.

(h) *Rooming house.* In addition to its customary usage, a building or portion of a building, other than an apartment rented for single-room occupancy, in which housing accommodations are rented, on a short-term basis of daily, weekly or monthly occupancy, to more than two occupants for whom rent is paid, not members of the landlord's immediate family. The term shall include boarding houses, dormitories, trailers not a part of a motor court, residence clubs, tourist homes and all other establishments of a similar nature, except a hotel or a motor court.

(i) *Single-room occupancy.* The occupancy by one or two persons of a single room, or of two or more rooms which are joined together, separated from all other rooms within an apartment in a multiple dwelling, so that the occupant or occupants thereof reside separately and independently of the other occupant or occupants of the same apartment.

2200.4 Applicability. These regulations shall apply to all proceedings pending on August 8, 1984.

2200.5 Amendment or revocation. Any provision of these regulations may be amended or revoked by the administrator at any time.

2200.6 Filing of amendments. Any amendment or revocation of these regulations shall be filed with the Department of State.

2200.7 Separability. If any provision of these regulations or the application of such provision to any person or circumstance shall be held invalid, the validity of the remainder of these regulations and the applicability of such provisions to other persons or circumstances shall not be affected thereby.

2200.8 District rent office designations and descriptions of portions of city under their jurisdiction. These regulations shall apply to all housing accommodations located in the City of New York. The rent districts subject to the jurisdiction of the several district rent administrators are described as follows:

District Rent Office Rent District

Bronx	Borough of The Bronx
Brooklyn	Borough of Brooklyn
Lower Manhattan	Borough of Manhattan—south side of 110th Street and below
Queens	Borough of Queens
Staten Island	Borough of Staten Island
Upper Manhattan	Borough of Manhattan—north side of 110th Street and above

2200.9 Conversion after May 1, 1950.

(a)(1) Upon application of the landlord, the administrator shall issue an order decontrolling additional housing accommodations, other than rooming house accommodations, resulting from conversion of housing accommodations on or after May 1, 1950, if there has been a structural change involving substantial alterations or remodeling and such change has resulted in additional housing accommodations consisting of self-contained family units; provided, however, that such order of decontrol shall not apply to that portion of the original housing accommodations occupied by a tenant in possession at the time of the conversion, but only so long as such tenant continues in occupancy; and provided, further, that any such order of decontrol shall remain effective after April 30, 1962 only so long as the housing accommodations are not occupied for other than single-family occupancy.

(2) The term *self-contained family unit* shall mean a housing accommodation with private access, containing two or more rooms, consisting of at least one bedroom and a living room/dining space area in addition to a kitchen (with cooking and refrigeration facilities and a sink), a private bathroom (with a washbasin, toilet and bathtub or enclosed shower), and at least one closet plus an additional closet for each bedroom. Such accommodation shall contain a minimum total area of 395 square feet, exclusive of the area of bathrooms and closets. In lieu of a kitchen, the accommodation may include an enclosed kitchenette or an area in the living room which is either recessed or semienclosed, provided

Rent Regulations

that all of the above-specified kitchen facilities and equipment are within such recessed or semienclosed area. Where, however, the landlord establishes that either the two-room or total floor area requirement, or both, cannot be complied with because of unique or peculiar circumstances, the administrator may waive this requirement if he finds that such waiver is not inconsistent with the purposes of the Rent Law and these regulations and would not be likely to result in the circumvention or evasion thereof.

(b) No order of decontrol shall be issued under this section unless such conversion occurred after the entire structure, or any lessor portion thereof as may have been thus converted, was vacated by voluntary surrender of possession or in the manner provided by section 5 of this State Act or by Part 2204 of this Title, and unless the administrator shall find that the landlord has satisfied all of the requirements of the authorities having jurisdiction over such conversion and over the occupancy of the newly created housing accommodations.

(c) No order of decontrol shall be issued by the administrator where there is a conversion of occupied housing accommodations, unless and until the landlord obtains an order authorizing subdivision or a certificate of eviction in accordance with provisions of section 2204.7 of this Title.

(d) Notwithstanding any of the foregoing provisions of this section, no order shall be issued by the administrator decontrolling housing accommodations:

(1) of any type resulting from conversion after April 30, 1962 of rooming house accommodations or of single-room occupancy accommodations;

(2) in any multiple dwelling aided by a loan made by the city under article 8 of the Private Housing Finance Law, until controls are no longer required by the provisions of said article 8; or

(3) in any multiple dwelling with respect to which tax abatement and tax exemption beginning after April 30, 1962 is in effect under section J51-2.5 of the Administrative Code of the city, until the date on which such tax abatement or tax exemption terminates, whichever is later.

(e) Any housing accommodation decontrolled under this section shall become subject to control if, while in such decontrolled status, it is certified, by a city agency having jurisdiction, to be a fire hazard or in a continued dangerous condition or detrimental to life or health; and once subject to control, it shall continue to be subject to control, notwithstanding the subsequent removal of the conditions on which such certification was based.

§ 2200.10 Substantial demolition after May 1, 1962.
(a) Upon application of the landlord, the administrator shall issue an order decontrolling all of the housing accommodations resulting from substantial demolition of a building, provided that:

(1) not less than 50 percent of the housing after reconstruction shall consist of apartments suitable for occupancy by larger families, or not less than 50 percent of the total floor area of all of the housing after reconstruction shall be utilized for apartments suitable for occupancy by larger families;

(2) all other housing accommodations in the building shall comply with at least the minimum requirement for a self-contained family unit, as defined in section 2200.9 of this Part; and

(3) all of the housing accommodations meet all of the requirements of law and of the city agencies having jurisdiction thereof, and over the occupancy of such accommodations.

(b) If the building after reconstruction fails to meet the requirements of paragraph (a)(1) of this section, but if all of the housing accommodations in such building shall comply with at least the minimum requirements for a self-contained family unit as defined in section 2200.9 of this Part, and if all of the housing accommodations in such building meet all of the requirements of law and of the city agencies having jurisdiction thereof, and over the occupancy of such accommodations, then only those apartments which are suitable for occupancy by larger families shall be decontrolled, and all other housing accommodations in such building shall remain subject to control.

(c) The term *housing accommodations resulting from substantial demolition,* as used in this section, shall mean any housing accommodation which is created on or after May 1, 1962 as a result of the substantial demolition of a multiple dwelling and the reconstruction of such building in such manner as to retain any portion thereof existing prior to such demolition, and:

(1) which is so created after the issuance of one or more certificates permitting the eviction of any tenant or tenants of such multiple dwelling for the purpose of effecting such demolition where application for such certificates was filed after April 24, 1962; or

(2) where no such certificates were issued, which was created after the former structure, or any lesser portion thereof, was vacated on or after November 22, 1963 by voluntary surrender of possession or in any manner provided in Part 2204 of this Title.

(d) The term *apartment suitable for occupancy by larger families,* as used in this section, shall mean a housing accommodation with private access, containing four or more rooms, consisting of at least two bedrooms, a living room/dining room space area and a kitchen (with cooking and refrigeration facilities and a sink), a private bathroom (with a washbasin, toilet and bathtub or enclosed shower), and at least two closets plus an additional closet for each bedroom. Such accommodations shall contain a minimum total area of 560 square feet, exclusive of the area of the bathrooms and closets.

(e) Notwithstanding any of the foregoing provisions of this section, no order shall be issued by the administrator decontrolling housing accommodations resulting from substantial demolition:

(1) in any building aided by a loan made by the city under article 8 of the Private Housing Finance Law, so long as maximum rents are required to be prescribed by the provisions of said article 8;

(2) in any multiple dwelling with respect to which tax abatement and tax exemption under section J51-2.5 of the Administrative Code begins after April 30, 1962, until the date on which such tax abatement or tax exemption terminates, whichever is later; or

(3) in any building where the former structure, or any lesser portion thereof, was vacated on or after November 22, 1963, other than by voluntary surrender of possession or in the manner provided by Part 2204 of this Title.

(f) Housing accommodations created after May 1, 1962, as a result of the reconstruction of a multiple dwelling which has been substantially demolished, where no certificates permitting the eviction of any tenant or tenants of such multiple dwelling for the purpose of effecting such demolition have been issued, or where application for such certificates was filed on or before April 24, 1962, shall not require an order of the administrator decontrolling them and shall not be subject to control pursuant to section 2200.2(f)(8) of this Part.

(g) Housing accommodations decontrolled under this section shall remain decontrolled only so long as the housing accommodations are not occupied for other than single-family occupancy.

(h) Any housing accommodation decontrolled under this section shall become subject to control if, while in such decontrolled status, it is certified, by a city agency having jurisdiction, to be a fire hazard or in a continued dangerous condition or detrimental to life or health; and once subject to control, it shall continue to be subject to control, notwithstanding the subsequent removal of the conditions on which such certification was based.

2200.11 Commercial or professional renting of controlled housing accommodations on or after May 1, 1955. Any housing accommodation subject to these regulations which, on or after May 1, 1955, was or may be rented for commercial or professional use shall continue to be subject to control, unless the State Rent Commission issued an order exempting it from control during the periods of occupancy by the tenant, or an order is issued by the administrator exempting the housing accommodation from these regulations during the period of occupancy by the tenant. Such order shall be issued by the administrator where he finds the renting complies with the requirements of law and of city agencies having jurisdiction, and was made in good faith without any intent to evade the Rent Law or these regulations, and shall be effective as of the date of the commercial or professional renting, or May 1, 1962, whichever date is later.

2200.12 Withdrawal from rental market. Nothing in these regulations shall be construed to require any person to offer any housing accommodations for rent, but housing accommodations already on the market may be withdrawn only after an order is issued by the administrator under section 2204.9 of this Title, if such withdrawal requires that a tenant be evicted from such accommodations.

2200.13 Effect of these regulations on leases and other rental agreements. The provisions of any lease or other rental agreement shall remain in force pursuant to the terms thereof, except insofar as those provisions are inconsistent with the Rent Law or these regulations.

2200.14 Receipt for rent paid. No payment of rent need be made unless the landlord tenders a receipt for the amount to be paid when so requested by a tenant. The landlord shall issue to every tenant either a rent bill or rent receipt at the time of each rental payment. The receipt may be imprinted on the tenant's check or money order tendered in payment for rent. All statements on such bill or receipt shall be legible, and there shall be printed in ink or stamped thereon, where the premises are a multiple dwelling:

(1) the name and address of the licensed real estate broker or firm in charge of the dwelling, stating that he or the firm is so licensed, or the name and address of the managing agent as recorded in the registration on file with the Office of Code Enforcement;

(2) at the owner's option, a telephone listing at which he or someone acting in his behalf may be reached by the tenant for repairs and service; and

(3) at the owner's option, a statement, if rent is paid by check or money order, that such payment is received subject to collection.

2200.15 Waiver of benefit void. An agreement by the tenant to waive the benefit of any provision of the Rent Law or these regulations is void.

2200.16 Fees. (a) There is hereby imposed on every building containing housing accommodations subject to these regulations a fee of $3 per controlled housing accommodation. For the purposes of this section, the number of controlled housing accommodations is the number of such accommodations shown on the report form R-23 filed by the landlord or, if no such report was filed, as otherwise shown on the records of the Office of Rent Control, less the number of units for which decontrol orders were issued, or reports of decontrol properly filed pursuant to section 2203.2 of this Title, on or before October 1, 1972.

(b) Notwithstanding any other provision of these regulations, if the fee prescribed by this section is not paid on or before December 1, 1972 (or, if a bill for such fee is mailed to the landlord after November 15, 1972, within 17 days of the date of mailing), no increase pursuant to section 2201.6 of this Title in the maximum rent collectible from a tenant shall take effect with respect to any housing accommodation in the building until three months after payment of the fee.

(c) This section shall not apply to any building with eight or fewer housing accommodations if such building was owner-occupied on October 1, 1972.

2200.17 Biennial fees. (a) Every landlord shall pay a fee of $20 for each controlled housing accommodation in every building containing housing accommodations subject to these regulations to obtain an order establishing or adjusting the maximum rent, pursuant to section 2201.4 or 2201.5 of this Title, for each successive two-year period commencing January 1, 1984. For the purposes of this section, the number of controlled housing accommodations is the number of such accommodations shown on the records of the Division of Housing and Community Renewal, less the number of units for which decontrol orders were issued, or reports of decontrol were properly filed pursuant to section 42 of the New York City Rent and Eviction Regulations or section 2203.2 of this Title, on or before October 1, 1981 or October 1st biennially thereafter for each successive two-year period.

(b) The fee for processing and obtaining any order with respect to establishing or adjusting the maximum rent pursuant to section 2201.4 or 2201.5 of this Title shall be paid within 30 days of the date of issuance of the landlord's order of eligibility by the Division of Housing and Community Renewal, which shall in no event be refunded. In addition to complying with every other requirement of these regulations applicable to the establishment or adjustment of the maximum rent, the landlord must pay such fee to be eligible for an order establishing or adjusting the maximum rent.

(c) Where a landlord has not paid the fee as required by this section, the administrator may deny, defer or revoke the order establishing or adjusting the maximum rent and any increase in the maximum collectible rent for the biennial period for which the required fee was not paid.

(d) This section shall not apply to any building with eight or fewer housing accommodations if any housing accommodations in such building were owner-occupied on October 1st of the year immediately preceding the biennial period commencing January 1, 1974.

PART 2201

MAXIMUM RENTS

2201.1 Maximum rents for housing accommodations. (a) The maximum rents for housing accommodations shall be the maximum rents in effect on April 30, 1962 pursuant to the State Rent Act, except as otherwise provided in this section.

(b) For housing accommodations for which there was no maximum rent in effect on April 30, 1962, and which were rented subsequent to April 30, 1962, the maximum rent shall be the first rent charged, subject to adjustment as provided by section 2202.15 of this Title and conditioned upon the filing of a proper registration statement within 15 days from the date of such first renting, except as otherwise provided in this section.

(c) For housing accommodations in any establishment which has been deemed to be a hotel by reason of an order, finding, opinion or determination of the State Rent Commission, and which is found by the administrator not to be a hotel as defined by section 2200.3(d) of this Title, the maximum rent shall be the rent charged on the date six months immediately prior to the date of the issuance of the notice of commencement of proceedings to determine that these regulations shall apply to the housing accommodations in such establishment, or on the date of the first renting, whichever is later; subject, however, to adjustment as provided by section 2202.4 of this Title.

(d) For housing accommodations in an establishment which the administrator finds no longer to be a hotel, where such accommodations were not subject to rent control because such establishment was a hotel on March 1, 1950, the maximum rent shall be the rent charged on the date six months immediately prior to the date of issuance of notice of commencement of proceedings to determine that these regulations shall apply to the housing accommodations in such establishment, or on the date of the first renting, whichever is later; subject, however, to adjustment as provided by section 2202.4 of this Title.

(e) For housing accommodations subject to rent control as provided by section 2200.2(e)(4) of this Title, the maximum rents shall be established or fixed by order of the administrator pursuant to section 2202.22(b) of this Title.

(f) Any tenant in a rooming house or in a single-room occupancy accommodation on a daily term of occupancy, who has resided in such rooming house or single-room occupancy accommodation continuously for a period of more than 14 days, shall thereafter be deemed to be a tenant on a weekly term of occupancy.

(g) For housing accommodations in rooming houses or single-room occupancy no maximum rent shall be established on the basis of renting in excess of the permissible occupancy thereof.

2201.2 Services included in maximum rent. Every landlord shall furnish with housing accommodations the same dwelling space and the same essential services, furniture, furnishings and equipment as were furnished, or required to be furnished, on April 20, 1962 or any subsequent date determining the maximum rent.

2201.3 Compensable rent adjustment effective August 1, 1970. (a) Notwithstanding the provisions of section 2201.1 of this Part, effective August 1, 1970:

(1) the maximum rent in effect on July 31, 1970 shall be increased, for any individual housing accommodation where it is less than $60 per month, by $10 per month for a housing accommodation containing less than four rooms and by $15 per month where the housing accommodation contains four or more rooms; or

(2) the maximum rent in effect on July 31, 1970 for any housing accommodation having a maximum rent on such date of $60 or more per month:

(i) for which one or more but less than two full 15-percent rent increases have been granted since May 1, 1953, pursuant to former section 33.2 of the New York City Rent and Eviction Regulations, the maximum rent shall be increased by eight percent;

(ii) for which no full 15-percent increase has been granted since May 1, 1953, pursuant to such former section 33.2, the maximum rent shall be increased by 15 percent; except that:

(a) if there was no such increase for any individual housing accommodation made subject to these regulations pursuant to section 2200.2(e)(2) or (3) thereof, for which a first rent was established after July 31, 1965 and before August 1, 1968, the maximum rent shall be increased five percent; and

(b) if there was no such increase for any individual housing accommodation made subject to these regulations, pursuant to section 2200.2(e)(2) or (3) thereof, for which a first rent was established on or after August 1, 1968, there shall be no increase in the maximum rent.

(b) On or after August 1, 1970, the landlord may file an application for labor cost rent adjustment pursuant to section 2202.14 of this Title. In lieu of such labor cost rent adjustment, the landlord of a building with 20 or fewer housing accommodations shall have the option of filing for a five-percent increase in maximum rent for any individual housing accommodation for which two or more full 15-percent increases have been granted since May 1, 1953, pursuant to the former section 33.2 of the New York City Rent and Eviction Regulations.

(c) Nothing contained in this section, however, shall have the effect of increasing the maximum rent for a housing accommodation where the maximum rent in effect on July 31, 1970 is less than $60 per month, except as provided in paragraph (a)(1) of this section. The provisions of paragraph (a)(2) and of subdivision (f) of this section shall be inapplicable to such housing accommodations.

(d) Where a lease is in effect for any housing accommodation on August 1, 1970, no adjustment of the maximum rent for such accommodation shall become effective until the expiration of such lease.

(e) Where a housing accommodation becomes vacant on or after August 1, 1970 and before January 1, 1972 by voluntary surrender of possession by the tenant, the maximum rent shall be increased by not more than 15 percent over the maximum rent established for such accommodation at the time that the vacancy occurred, provided that a report is filed with the administrator as prescribed by section 2203.9 of this Title. No more than one such full 15-percent vacancy increase may be obtained for a housing accommodation. If the administrator shall make a finding that the landlord, for the purpose of obtaining such vacancy, had harassed the tenant by engaging in a course of conduct proscribed by section 2205.1(b) of this Title (section Y51-10.0d of the Rent Law), in addition to all other civil or criminal penalties, injunctive relief and enforcement remedies authorized by the Rent Law or these regulations, no housing accommodations in the building shall thereafter be entitled to the benefit of a rent increase as the result of becoming vacant between the aforesaid dates.

(f) The total of (1) the rent increase pursuant to paragraph (a)(2) of this section, (2) any increases granted between January 1, 1970 and December 31, 1971, inclusive, pursuant to section 2202.8, 2202.9 or 2202.10 of this Title, and (3) any increase granted on or after August 1, 1970 pursuant to section 2202.11 of this Title, shall not exceed 15 percent of the 1970 base rent. For the purposes of this subdivision, the *1970 base rent* is the maximum rent on July 31, 1970 minus the amount of any increase granted between January 1, 1970 and July 31, 1970, inclusive, pursuant to section 2202.8, 2202.9 or 2202.10 of this Title. This subdivision shall not operate to decrease any maximum rent existing on July 31, 1970.

(g)(1) The rent increases provided for in this section shall be collectible upon the landlord's filing a report with the administrator as provided in section 2203.9 of this Title, subject to adjustment, however, by order of the administrator which shall prescribe (i) that any excess rent paid by the tenant be credited to the tenant in full commencing with the rental payment following the date of issuance of such order, or (ii) that any rent due landlord by reason of the order shall be paid in installments equal to the number of whole months intervening between August 1, 1970 and the date of issuance of such order. If the initial report is filed on or before October 31, 1970, the increase shall take effect August 1, 1970. If the report is filed thereafter, such increase shall take effect with the first rental following the filing.

(2) The report shall contain a certified statement by the landlord that there is no legally habitable rent-controlled housing accommodation, in the building containing the accommodation for which any rent increase is sought, which has not been rented for a period of six months or more prior to the filing of such report, or that if there is such a housing accommodation, the reason it has not been rented is that it is being altered pursuant to a permit issued by the Department of Buildings no later than three months after the vacancy commenced and that the alteration is of such a nature that the accommodation must be kept vacant while it is being made, or for such other cause found by the administrator not to be inconsistent with the purpose of the Rent law or these regulations; provided, further, that in the case of an alteration, it is commenced within 60 days from the issuance of said permit. A copy of the permit and the plans therefor shall accompany the report. No report shall be accepted for filing, and no rent increase provided for in this section shall be collected, in the absence of any such verified statement by the landlord.

(h) The rent increases provided for in this section shall

not be collectible for the period between April 1, 1971 and December 31, 1971, inclusive, unless the landlord shall have filed with the administrator, on or before March 31, 1971, a certified statement attesting that for every month for which he has received a rent increase pursuant to this section, he has expended on the operation, maintenance and improvements of the housing accommodations from which increases were collected an amount which equals the amount expended per month for such purpose averaged over the preceding five years, or such lesser period that he has been landlord of such property, plus 90 percent of all increased rents so collected. If such certified statement is filed after March 31, 1971, such increases shall be collectible beginning on the first day of the month following the date of such filing.

(i) For the purposes of this section, the term *room* shall not include bathroom, foyer, windowless room, and shall be limited to living room, kitchen (other than an enclosed kitchenette or an area in the living room which is either recessed or semienclosed), dining room (other than a dinette or dining alcove) and bedrooms.

2201.4 Maximum base rents effective January 1, 1972.

(a)(1) Effective January 1, 1972, the administrator shall establish new maximum rents for housing accommodations subject to these regulations. Subject to the provisions of section 2201.6 of this Part governing collectibility, such new maximum rent for each housing accommodation shall be the maximum base rent derived by apportioning the maximum gross building rental computed pursuant to subdivision (b) of this section among the individual housing accommodations in the property in accordance with subdivision (e) of this section.

(2) Except as otherwise provided, the application of this section shall be based upon the reports submitted pursuant to sections 2201.3 and 2203.9 of this Title, as modified or adjusted by the administrator.

(3) This section shall not apply to housing accommodations for which first rents were established pursuant to section 2201.1(b), 2202.3 or 2202.22 of this Title where the rehabilitation or improvement of substan-

dard or deteriorated housing accommodations was financed under a governmental program providing assistance through loans, loan insurance or tax abatement, or has been undertaken under another rehabilitation program not so financed but approved by the administrator.

(b) The maximum gross building rental for a property is the sum of:

(1) the real estate taxes charged to the property on the records of the finance administrator for the fiscal year 1971-72, after any abatement or reduction of tax so recorded;

(2) the water charges and sewer rents recorded against the property by the finance administration for the calendar year 1971, excluding any such rate or charges based on meter readings;

(3) an allowance for operating and maintenance expenses (to provide for the cost of fuel, utilities, payroll, maintenance, repairs, replacement reserves and miscellaneous charges) computed pursuant to subdivision (c) of this section;

(4) an allowance for vacancy and collection losses in the amount of one percent of the maximum gross building rental;

(5) an allowance for return on capital value, to provide for debt service and return on equity, computed pursuant to subdivision (d) of this section;

provided, however, that where a property receives income from sources other than housing accommodations, the computation of the maximum gross building rental shall include only that part of the total real estate taxes, water rates and sewer charges and allowance for return on capital value which bears the same proportion to the total of such items as the maximum gross building rental bears to the sum of such rental plus the total income from the other sources, so that the maximum gross building rental shall be computed as follows:

$$\text{MGBR} = \frac{\text{MGBR}}{\text{MGBR} + \text{CI}} \times (\text{RET} + \text{WS} + \text{RCV}) + \text{OM} + \text{VCL}$$

where MGBR = Maximum gross building rental
CI = Commercial income
RET = Real estate taxes

WS   = Water charges and sewer rents
RCV = Allowance for return on capital value
OM   = Allowance for operating and maintenance expenses
VCL = Allowance for vacancy and collection losses.

(c)(1) For purposes of computing the operating and maintenance expense allowance, a building shall be deemed to be a "normal payroll building" if the expenses for labor, including wages and fringe benefits for all employees engaged in operation, maintenance and service of the building, do not exceed $300 per year times the number of housing accommodations in the building. A building in which such expenses exceed such amount shall be deemed to be a "high payroll building."

(2) The allowance for operating and maintenance expenses for a normal payroll building is the sum of the following four items, multiplied by the number of housing accommodations in the building:

$265.58

>plus $0.36 times the number of housing accommodations in the building,
>plus $73.32 times the average number of rooms per housing accommodation in the building,
>plus $2.15 times the age factor for the building, as defined in paragraph (4) of this subdivision.

(3) The allowance for operating and maintenance expenses for a high payroll building is the sum of the following five items, multiplied by the number of housing accommodations in the building:

$315.11

>plus $0.09 times the number of housing accommodations in the building,
>plus $128.31 times the average number of rooms per housing accommodation in the building,
>plus $2.93 times the age factor for the building, as defined in paragraph (4) of this subdivision,
>plus the amount by which the expenses for labor per housing accommodation per year exceed $300.

(4) As used in this subdivision, the *age factor* for a building is the number of years by which the year of the completion of construction of the building precedes 1967; provided that where the completion of construction occurred prior to 1900, the age factor shall be 67.

For purposes of such calculation, *construction* means original construction, without regard to any subsequent rehabilitation or new certificate of occupancy.

(d) The allowance for return on capital value shall be 8.5 percent of the equalized assessed value obtained by multiplying the assessed value of the property by the 1971-1972 equalized ratio 1.754, as established by the New York State Board of Equalization and Assessment pursuant to article 12-A of the Real Property Tax Law.

(e)(1) For purposes of apportioning the maximum gross building rental to individual housing accommodations, each housing accommodation is assigned a room index value based on the number of rooms therein. A housing accommodation of one room is assigned a room index value of 75, one of two rooms a value of 100, and one of more than two rooms a value of 100 plus an additional 25 for each additional room beyond two. The term *room* has, for purposes of this section, the same meaning as in section 2201.3(i) of this Part.

(2) Where a property contains housing accommodations which are not subject to control under these regulations, the portion of the maximum gross building rental attributable to controlled housing accommodations shall be a sum which bears the same proportion to the total as the sum of the room index values for all controlled housing accommodations bears to the sum of the room index values for all housing accommodations in the property, so that:

$$\frac{\text{MGBR(C)}}{\text{MGBR(T)}} = \frac{\text{RIV(C)}}{\text{RIV(T)}}$$

where MGBR = Maximum gross building rental
RIV = Sum of room index values (as defined above)
(C) = Portion allocated to controlled housing accommodations
(T) = Total.

(3) The room index values assigned to each housing accommodation shall be adjusted for floor location. In a building without an elevator, the value computed in accordance with paragraph (1) of this subdivision shall be reduced by two percent for each floor above the middle floor, and increased by two percent for each floor below the middle floor. In a building with one or more elevators, the value shall be increased by one percent for each floor above the middle floor and re-

duced by one percent for each floor below the middle floor. As used in this paragraph, the *middle floor* is, in a building with an odd number of floors, the floor midway between the top and bottom floors, and in a building with an even number of floors, the midpoint between two floors so located that it has an equal number of floors above and below it.

(4) The *maximum base rent* for each housing accommodation is that sum which bears the same proportion to the maximum gross building rental (or so much thereof as is attributable to controlled housing accommodations) as the room index value of the housing accommodations, adjusted for floor location, bears to the total of such adjusted values for all controlled housing accommodations in the property, so that:

$$\text{MBR} = \text{MGBR} \times \frac{R(F)}{\text{Total } R(F)}$$

Where MBR = Maximum base rent (for an individual housing accommodation)
MGBR = Maximum gross building rental (as adjusted, if necessary, pursuant to paragraph (2) of this subdivision
R(F) = Room index value, adjusted for floor located, of the individual housing accommodation
Total R(F) = Sum of room index values, adjusted for floor location.

(5) The administrator may make an appropriate adjustment to the maximum base rent for any housing accommodation with respect to which the landlord pays for gas or electricity or both.

(f) Except as otherwise provided, the term *housing accommodation,* as used in this section, refers to every housing accommodation in a property, whether or not it is subject to or exempt from control under these regulations.

2201.5 Biennial adjustment of maximum rents. (a) Effective January 1, 1974 and biennially thereafter, the administrator shall adjust the maximum rent for each housing accommodation subject to these regulations to reflect the changes, if any, in the components of the maximum gross building rental defined in section 2201.4(b) of this Part. Such adjustment shall be made whether or not the property, or any housing accommodation therein, received or was eligible for maximum base rents under section 2201.4 of this Part.

(b) On or after January 1, 1974, the administrator may require landlords of properties containing housing accommodations subject to control under these regulations to report the actual operating and maintenance expenses for such properties, in such form and manner as he may prescribe, and may adjust the allowance for operating and maintenance expenses in accordance with such data.

2201.6 Collectibility.

(a)(1) No new maximum rent established pursuant to section 2201.4 of this Part, or adjustment pursuant to section 2201.5, 2202.7, 2202.8, 2202.9 or 2202.10 of this Title, or any combination thereof, shall increase the rent collectible from a tenant in occupancy by more than 7½ percent in any one calendar year, except as provided in section 2202.7 of this Title.

(2) The base for computation of the limitation provided in paragraph (1) of this subdivision shall be:

(i) as of January 1, 1972, the maximum rent on December 31, 1971 (including any conditional increases then in effect), less the amount of any rent exemption under section 2202.20 of this Title in effect on December 31, 1971; and

(ii) after January 1, 1972, the maximum rent collectible pursuant to this section.

(b) Where the maximum rent for a housing accommodation on December 31, 1971 exceeds the maximum base rent established pursuant to section 2201.4 of this Part, such prior maximum rent shall continue in effect until the maximum base rent, as adjusted from time to time pursuant to these regulations, shall equal or exceed such prior maximum rent; at which time the maximum base rent as so adjusted shall become the maximum rent for such housing accommodation.

(c) No increase in maximum rent pursuant to this section, in any year other than a year in which a maximum rent, established pursuant to section 2201.4 of this Part or adjusted pursuant to section 2201.5, takes effect, shall be collectible until the landlord shall have given notice thereof to the tenant on a form prescribed by the administrator. A copy of such form shall be filed with the administrator within 30 days of its transmittal to the tenant. Failure to comply with the provisions of this paragraph shall authorize the administrator to revoke the landlord's entitlement to any such increase.

ADJUSTMENTS; DETERMINATION OF RENTS AND SERVICES

Section 2201.1 Maximum rents. Maximum rents may be increased or decreased only by order of the administrator.

2202.2 Effective date of orders adjusting rents. No order increasing or decreasing a maximum rent previously established pursuant to these regulations shall be effective prior to the date on which the order is issued, except as hereinafter provided. If an application for an increase pursuant to section 2202.8 of this Part is submitted on or after August 1, 1970 and is accompanied by a certified statement of expenditures with all required documentation, and no order is issued thereon within four months of the date of filing of an application based on assessed valuation (or on equalized assessed valuation on or after January 1, 1972), or eight months of the date of filing of an application based upon sales price, the increased rent requested shall be collectible by the landlord and shall be placed in an interest-bearing escrow account with a banking organization until the final determination of such application. The order of the district rent administrator shall be made effective as of the date on which the landlord is entitled to collect such requested rent increase for any housing accommodation in the building, pursuant to the permission granted by this section, and, notwithstanding any other provision of these regulations, shall be in accordance with the regulations in effect on such date. Where such order grants a rent increase which is less than the rent collected by the landlord as herein permitted, or denies the application, the excess rent collected shall be refunded to the tenants entitled thereto within 30 days from the date such order shall become final, together with interest from the date of each excessive payment of rent at the prevailing rate of interest paid by the banking organization in which such deposit is made. Any person serving as escrow agent shall not be liable except for fraud or misfeasance.

2202.3 Grounds for increase of maximum rent.

(a)(1) This section and sections 2202.4 to 2202.12, inclusive, of this Part set forth specific standards for the increase of a maximum rent. In applying these standards and issuing an order adjusting a maximum rent, the administrator shall take into consideration all factors bearing on the equities involved, subject to the general limitation that the adjustment can be put into effect without dislocation and hardship inconsistent with the purposes of the Rent Law. On or after November 22, 1963, where any housing accommodations were vacated other than by voluntary surrender of possession or in the manner provided by Part 2204 of this Title, the administrator may, after having due regard to the equities involved, bar adjustments of maximum rents for any and all accommodations in such structure, pursuant to subdivisions (b) and (c) of section 2202.4 of this Part, except for work which:

(i) is necessary in order to remove violations against the property;

(ii) is necessary to obtain a certificate of occupancy, if such certificate is required by law; or

(iii) could have been performed with a tenant in physical possession of the housing accommodation at the time that the work was performed.

(2) The administrator shall have the power to revoke or modify any adjustment granted hereunder if there has been a substantial change in the basis upon which such adjustment was granted.

(b)(1) No application for an increase in any maximum rent may be filed under section 2202.8, 2202.9 or 2202.10 of this Part, unless:

(i) a report of search issued by a city agency having jurisdiction is annexed to such applications, stating either that no violations against such property are recorded or that all violations recorded against such property have been cleared, corrected or abated, or a receipt (or photocopy thereof) issued by such agency attesting to the payment of the fee for the report of search; and

(ii) the landlord certifies that he is maintaining all essential services required to be furnished, and that he will continue to maintain such services so long as such increase in the maximum rent continues in effect.

(2) No new maximum rent shall be established pursuant to section 2201.4 of this Title, and no adjustment shall be made pursuant to subdivision (a) of section 2201.5, unless the landlord has certified that he is maintaining all essential services required to be maintained with respect to the housing accommodations covered by such certification, and that he will continue to maintain such services so long as the new maximum rent or the adjustment is in effect. For purposes of this paragraph, *essential services* shall be defined as: heat during that part of the year when required by law, hot water, cold water, superintendent services, maintenance of front or entrance door security (including but not limited to lock and buzzer), garbage collection, elevator service, gas, electricity and other utility services to both public and required private areas, and such other services wherein failure to provide and/or maintain such would constitute a danger to the life or safety of, or would be detrimental to the health of, the tenant or tenants. Upon a determination that such essential services are not, or were not, being maintained, the Division of Housing and Community Renewal may revoke or modify the new maximum rent established pursuant to section 2201.4 of this Title and/or an adjustment made pursuant to subdivision (a) of section 2201.5, and may direct a refund to the tenants of all or part of the increase paid by the tenants as a result of any such order or orders. Each such certification filed in connection with an adjustment pursuant to section 2201.5 of this Title shall be accompanied by a certification by the landlord that he has actually expended or incurred 90 percent of the total amount of the allowance for operating and maintenance expenses, including the rents collectible from housing accommodations in the property.

(c) Except as provided in subdivision (g) of this section and section 2202.19 of this Part, no landlord shall be entitled to an increase in the maximum rent on any ground unless he certifies that he is maintaining all essential services furnished or required to be furnished as of the date of the issuance of the order adjusting the maximum rent, and that he will continue to maintain such services so long as the increase in such maximum rent continues in effect; nor shall any landlord be entitled to any increase in maximum rent on any ground where an agency of the city having jurisdiction certifies that the housing accommodation is a fire hazard, or is in a continued dangerous condition or detrimental to life or health or is occupied in violation of law; nor shall any landlord be entitled to any increase where the landlord has not removed the violation recorded against such property as shown in the report of search required under subdivision (b) of this section.

(d)(1) No more than one order adjusting the maximum rent for any housing accommodation under section 2202.8 of this Part may be issued in any 24-month period and, except as provided in section 2202.8 of this Part, the adjustment granted by any such order shall not exceed 15 percent.

(2) Any adjustment pursuant to section 2220.8, 2202.9 or 2202.10 of this Part, shall be collectible only to the extent permitted by section 2201.6 of this Title; provided that, in ordering an adjustment pursuant to section 2202.8, the administrator may waive such limitation where a greater increase is necessary to make the earned income of the property equal to its operating expenses.

(e) That portion of the amount of increase computed under sections 2202.8 through 2202.11 of this Part, as is properly attributable to the controlled housing accommodations, shall be apportioned among them in the manner prescribed in section 2201.4 of this Title for the apportionment of the maximum gross building rental. Each controlled housing accommodation shall bear no more than that portion of the amount of increase as is properly attributable to such housing accommodation, whether or not the amount so attributed shall be fully collectible by reason of an existing lease or, in the case of an adjustment pursuant to section 2202.8, 2202.9 or 2202.10 of this Part, by reason of the limitations provided in section 2201.6 of this Title.

(f)(1) Any landlord may file an application to increase the maximum rent otherwise allowable, on forms prescribed by the administrator, only on one or more of the grounds stated in sections 2202.4 through 2202.12 of this Part.

(2) Any landlord may file an application to establish the maximum rents to be effective January 1, 1972, pursuant to section Y51-5.0a(3) of the Rent Law, on forms provided by the administrator, on or before the date prescribed by the administrator, and provided that such application shall be accompanied by a fee in the sum of $5 per rent-controlled housing accommodation, based on the number of such accommodations stated in the city report form R-23 filed for the subject building or, if the owner failed to provide this data in the form filed, on the basis of the number of housing accommodations (whether or not subject to control pursuant to these regulations) shown on the records of the Department of Buildings.

(g) Where an application for an increase in any maximum rent is filed under subdivision (b) and/or (c) of section 2202.4, and section 2202.8, 2202.9 or 2202.10 of this Part, and the landlord is not entitled to any increase by reason of the provisions of subdivision (b) of this section, the administrator may waive such provision and issue orders increasing the maximum rent effective as of the date of issuance of such orders; provided, however, that the landlord agrees in writing to deposit the entire amount of such increase in maximum rent into an escrow or trust account administered by the administrator in accordance with procedures adopted by the administrator for the purpose of obtaining compliance with the provisions of subdivision (b) of this section, and further agrees to obtain and submit to the administrator, within one year from the date of issuance of such orders, a report of search issued by the city agency having jurisdiction, stating that the violations shown in the report of search required under subdivision (b) of this section have been removed, cleared, corrected or abated, and his own certification that he is maintaining and will continue to maintain all essential services in accordance with the provisions of subdivision (c) of this section. In the event the landlord fails to fully comply with such provision within one year from the date of the issuance of the orders increasing the maximum rent, the administrator may, having due regard for the equities involved, revoke such orders and direct full refund to the tenants of the entire increase paid by the tenants as a result of such orders.

(h) If, at least six months before the effective date of the establishment of new maximum rents pursuant to section 2201.4 of this Title, or an adjustment of maximum rents pursuant to section 2201.5(a), the landlord has not certified to the Department of Rent and Housing Maintenance that (1) all rent-impairing violations (as defined in section 302-a of the Multiple Dwelling Law), and (2) at least 80 percent of all other violations of the Housing Maintenance Code or Multiple Dwelling Law that were recorded against the property one year prior to such effective date have been cleared, corrected or abated, such new maximum rents or such adjustment shall not take effect until he shall have entered into a written agreement with such department to deposit income derived from the property into an escrow or trust account as prescribed in such agreement for the purpose of correction of such violations.

2202.4 Increased services or facilities, substantial rehabilitation, major capital or other improvements. The administrator may grant an appropriate adjustment of a maximum rent where he finds that:

(a) the landlord and tenant, by mutual voluntary written agreement, subject to the approval of the administrator, agree to a substantial increase in dwelling space or a change in the services, furniture, furnishings or equipment provided in the housing accommodation; or the tenant has accepted and is obtaining the benefit of increased services, furniture, furnishings or equipment; or

(b) there has been, since March 1, 1959, an increase in the rental value of the housing accommodations as a result of a substantial rehabilitation of the building or housing accommodations therein which materially adds to the value of the property or appreciably prolongs its life, excluding ordinary repairs, maintenance and replacements; or

(c) there has been, since July 1, 1970, a major capital improvement required for the operation, preservation or maintenance of the structure; or

(d) there has been, since March 1, 1959, in structures containing more than four housing accommodations, other improvements made with the express consent of the tenants in occupancy of at least 75 percent of the housing accommodations; provided, however, that whenever the administrator has determined that the improvements proposed are part of a plan designed for overall improvement of the premises or increases in services, the administrator may order increases in maximum rents for all housing accommodations affected upon the express consent of the tenants in occupancy of at least 51 percent of the housing accommodations; and provided further, however, that no adjustment granted under this paragraph shall exceed 15 percent unless the tenants have agreed to a higher percentage of increase, as herein provided; and

(e) the landlord has incurred, since January 1, 1970, in connection with and in addition to a concurrent major capital improvement, other expenditures to improve, restore or preserve the quality of the structure. An adjustment pursuant to this section shall be granted by the administrator only if such improvements represent an expenditure equal to at least 10 percent of the total operating and maintenance expenses for the most recent full calendar year or the landlord's most recent fiscal year, or any 12 consecutive months ending not more than 90 days prior to the filing of the application for an increase pursuant to this subdivision. The adjustment pursuant to this subdivision shall be in addition to any adjustment granted for the concurrent major capital improvement, and shall be in an amount sufficient to amortize the cost of the improvements pursuant to this subdivision over a five-year period.

2202.5 Voluntary written agreements. (a) The landlord and tenant in occupancy may voluntarily enter into a valid written lease, on or after August 1, 1970, in good faith with respect to any housing accommodation, which provides for an increase in the maximum rent on the basis of specified increased services, furniture, furnishings or equipment having a market value commensurate with the increased rent, which is not in excess of 15 percent of the maximum rent in effect on the date of execution of such lease, and the lease is for a term of not less than two years. No increase pursuant to this section shall be authorized with respect to a housing accommodation for which an increase has been effected, pursuant to section 2201.3(c) of this Title, on the basis of a vacancy of the housing accommodation until January 1, 1972, or one year after such increase has become effective as a result of such vacancy, whichever date comes later. No increase shall be authorized unless a report of lease is filed as required by subdivision (d) of this section, or such report has been otherwise accepted by the administrator. Such lease or such lease report:

(1) contains a certification by the landlord that he is maintaining all essential services furnished or required to be furnished as of the date determining the maximum rent, and will continue to maintain such services so long as the increase in maximum rent continues in effect;

(2) gives the landlord no right of cancellation of said lease inconsistent with the provisions of these regulations;

(3) does not provide for the payment by the tenant of any rent in excess of the amount therein provided, unless the maximum rent is thereafter increased:

(i) by order of the administrator pursuant to section 2202.4(a) of this Part; or

(ii) pursuant to subdivision (b), (c), (d) or (e) of such section, where the improvement or substantial rehabilitation of the building or housing accommodations therein was either completed or in progress when such lease was executed; or

(iii) pursuant to a pending application for a financial adjustment of the maximum rents for the subject building pursuant to section 2201.3 of this Title, or section 2202.8, 2202.9, 2202.10 or 2202.11 of this Part; or

(iv) pursuant to a deferred financial adjustment order which was not fully effective; and

(4) gives the tenant the right to cancel such lease at

any time after the expiration of the first two years thereof, by giving the landlord at least 30 days' notice in writing, by registered or certified mail of his intention to cancel such lease and surrender possession of the housing accommodations.

(b) Where a maximum rent was established by the execution of a lease pursuant to the provisions of this section, it may not thereafter be increased by a subsequent lease executed with the same tenant pursuant to this section, except:

(1) by a subsequent written lease in accordance with subdivision (a) of this section, where the rent provided by such subsequent lease does not result in an increase of more than 15 percent over the maximum rent in effect prior to the execution of the original lease, exclusive of adjustments ordered by the administrator; or

(2) where, after the expiration of the term of the original lease, or in a case where the original lease is terminated after the expiration of the first two years of its term, a new written lease may be entered into in accordance with such subdivision (a); or

(3) where the original lease is terminated after the expiration of the first year of its term, in which event a new written lease in accordance with such subdivision (a) may be entered into for a term of not less than the unexpired remainder of the first two years of the original lease plus two years, and providing for an increase commencing with the expiration of the first two years of the original lease, which increase shall not exceed 15 percent over the maximum rent in effect on the effective date of such new lease.

(c) Where the entire structure, or any lesser portion thereof, was vacated by order of a city department having jurisdiction on or after November 22, 1963, and any tenants therein were relocated by the Department of Relocation or such structure was boarded up by the Department of Real Estate, such lease increases in subsequently executed leases shall not become effective for any housing accommodations in the structure, notwithstanding any provision of subdivision (a) of this section to the contrary, until such departments have been reimbursed for expenses necessarily incurred in connection with the foregoing; provided, however, that such reimbursement shall not be required where the vacating was caused by fire or accident not resulting from any unlawful act or omission on the part of the landlord.

(d) Within 60 days following the date of execution of the lease, or within 60 days after the effective date of this amendment, whichever date is later, the landlord shall file a report of such lease, upon forms prescribed by the administrator, which shall also include a statement of additional services or equipment furnished as a consideration of the execution of the lease.

(e) Notwithstanding any other provision of this section to the contrary, where a maximum base rent is established pursuant to section 2201.4 of this Title, during the term of any lease entered into on or after August 1, 1970 pursuant to the provisions of this section, such maximum base rent shall be collectible up to the 7½ percent limitation provided for by section 2201.6 of this Title, even though such lease provides for the payment of a lesser amount.

2202.6 Increase in subtenants or occupants. The administrator may grant an appropriate adjustment of a maximum rent where he finds that there has been, since March 1, 1959, a subletting without written consent from the landlord or an increase in the number of adult occupants who are not members of the immediate family of the tenant, and the landlord has not been compensated therefor by adjustment of the maximum rent by lease, or by order of the administrator, or pursuant to the State Rent Act or the Federal Act. Such adjustment shall be effective only during the period of subletting or increase in the number of tenants.

2202.7 Unique or peculiar circumstances. The administrator may grant an appropriate adjustment of a maximum rent where he finds that the presence of unique or peculiar circumstances materially affecting the maximum rent has resulted in a maximum rent which is substantially lower than rents generally prevailing in the same area for substantially similar housing accommodations; provided that the adjustment shall not result in a maximum rent higher than the rents generally prevalent in the same area of substantially similar housing accommodations.

2202.8 Return on capital value. (a) A landlord may file an application for an increase in maximum rents on the ground that the current maximum gross building rental established pursuant to section 2201.4 or 2201.5 of this Title does not equal the sum of:

(1) the real estate taxes, water charges and sewer rents on the property;

(2) the operating and maintenance expenses of the property;

(3) an allowance for the vacancy and collection losses on the property; and

(4) a return of 8½ percent on capital value which, except as provided in subdivisions (b) and (c) of this section, shall be the equalized assessed value obtained by multiplying the current assessed value of the property by the current equalization ratio established by the New York State Board of Equalization and Assessment pursuant to article 12-A of the Real Property Tax Law.

Increases or decreases in real estate taxes, water charges, sewer rents, and wages currently in effect may be projected in making such computation.

(b) The administrator may make a determination that:

(1) capital value is an amount different from that prescribed in subdivision (a) of this section, where there has been a reduction in assessed valuation for the year next preceding the effective date of the assessed valuation in effect at the time of the filing of the application; or

(2) capital value is equal to five times the equalized assessed value of the buildings, where the assessed valuation of the land exceeds four times the assessed valuation of the buildings thereon.

(c) The administrator may make a determination that capital value is an amount different from that prescribed in subdivision (a) of this section, where there has been a bona fide sale of the property since February 1, 1961, as the result of a transaction at arm's length, on normal financing terms, at a readily ascertainable price, and unaffected by special circumstances such as, but not limited to, a forced sale, exchange of property, package deal, wash sale or a sale to a cooperative. In determining whether a sale was on normal financing terms, the administrator shall give due consideration to the following factors:

(1) the ratio of the cash payment received by the seller to the sales price of the property and the annual gross income from the property;

(2) the total amount of the outstanding mortgages which are liens against the property (including purchase money mortgages), as compared with the equalized assessed value of the property;

(3) the ratio of the sales price to the annual gross income of the property, with consideration given to the total amount of rent adjustments previously granted, exclusive of rent adjustments because of changes in dwelling space, services, furniture, furnishings or equipment, major capital improvements or substantial rehabilitation;

(4) the presence of deferred amortization in purchase money mortgages, or the assignment of such mortgages at a discount; and

(5) any other facts and circumstances surrounding such sale which, in the judgment of the administrator, may have a bearing upon the question of financing.

(d) No increase in maximum rent shall be granted under this section where there is pending, without final disposition, a judicial proceeding to correct the final determination of the Tax Commission with respect to the assessed valuation of such property for the city fiscal year in which the landlord filed the application for such increase, or for the city fiscal year immediately preceding the filing of the application for such increase.

(e) No application for an increase in any maximum rent under this section may be filed with respect to any property if (1) on the date that the application is sought to be filed, less than two years have elapsed since the date of filing of the last prior application for an increase under this section, which application resulted in the granting of an increase, or (2) less than two years have elapsed since the last sale of the property and the application is based upon a sales price in excess of the equalized assessed valuation. This latter limitation shall not apply, however, when the application is based upon a sale, within such two-year period, at a price in excess of the equalized assessed valuation, if such price is less than the price in the last sale which meets the criteria heretofore specified in subdivision (c) of this section occurring prior to two years before the application is sought to be filed.

(f) For the purposes of this section, the test year shall be the most recent full calendar year or the landlord's most recent fiscal year, or any 12 consecutive months ending not more tha 90 days prior to the filing of the application for an increase.

2202.9 Unavoidable increases in operating costs in small structures. (a) A landlord may file an application for an adjustment of maximum rents on the ground that he owns a building containing no more than 19 housing accommodations (whether or not subject to control) and has incurred unavoidable increases in property taxes, fuel, utilities, insurance, and repairs and maintenance, excluding mortgage interest and amortization, and excluding allowances for depreciation, obsolescence and reserves, which have occurred since the Federal date determining the maximum rent. If, as determined by the administrator, the landlord has not been fully compensated by increases in rental income sufficient to offset such increases in operating costs, the administrator shall grant an adjustment of the maximum rents.

(b) Where the administrator finds, in considering the application under this section, that a present tenant is paying a rent less than the maximum rent, the administrator, upon request of the landlord, may reduce the maximum rent of the housing accommodation to the amount actually being paid, or to the highest maximum rent for comparable controlled housing accommodations in the structure, whichever is higher.

(c) A further application may not be filed under this section sooner than one year from the date of filing of the last prior application for an increase with respect to such property under this section, where such prior application resulted in the granting of an increase.

2202.10 Unavoidable increases in operating costs in other specified structures.

(a) A landlord may file an application for an increase in maximum rents on the ground that he operates a hotel or rooming house, or owns a cooperative apartment, and has incurred unavoidable increases in property taxes and other costs, including costs of operation of such hotel or rooming house, but excluding mortgage interest and amortization and excluding allowances for obsolescence and reserves and building depreciation, which have occurred since the Federal date determining the maximum rent or the date the landlord commenced the operation of the property, whichever is later. If, as determined by the administrator, the landlord has not been fully compensated by increases in rental income from the controlled housing accommodations sufficient to offset such increases in operating costs as are allowable to such controlled housing accommodations, the administrator shall grant an adjustment of the maximum rents.

(b) Where the administrator finds, in considering an application under this section, that a present tenant is paying a rent less than the maximum rent, the administrator, upon request of the landlord, may reduce the maximum rent of the housing accommodation to the amount actually being paid, or to the highest maximum rent for comparable controlled housing accommodations in the structure, whichever is higher.

(c) A further application may not be filed under this section sooner than one year from the date of filing of the last prior application for an increase with respect to such property under this section, or under the provisions of section 4(4)(a)(3) of the State Rent Act, where such prior application resulted in the granting of an increase.

2202.11 Labor costs in excess of maximum base rent allowance.
The administrator may make an appropriate adjustment of a maximum rent where he finds that the actual labor expenses incurred or to be incurred (pursuant to a collective agreement or other obligation

actually entered into by the landlord) exceed the provision for payroll expenses in the currently applicable operating and maintenance expense allowance under section 2201.4 or 2201.5 of this Title. No adjustment pursuant to this section may be made within one year from the most recent adjustment in maximum rent pursuant to this section or section 2202.8 of this Part.

2202.12 Rehabilitation or improvement under government-financed program or other approved program. The administrator may grant an appropriate adjustment where he finds that there has been a rehabilitation or improvement of substandard or deteriorated housing accommodations which has been financed under a governmental program providing assistance through loans, loan insurance or tax abatement, or which has been undertaken under any other rehabilitation program not so financed but approved by the administrator.

2202.13 Fuel cost adjustments. (a) Increases or decreases in heating fuel costs, based on findings promulgated by the Division of Housing and Community Renewal for heating fuel price increases and decreases, inclusive of sales and excise taxes and standards for consumption thereof for all types of heating fuels, shall be the bases for rent adjustments; provided, however, no increase shall be authorized unless a report, certification and notice, upon forms prescribed by the administrator, have been served upon the tenant, and the report, with prescribed schedules and proof of service, filed with the Division of Housing and Community Renewal. No increase shall be effective or collectible prior to January 1, 1980.

(b) Such report shall contain a certified statement by the landlord:

(1) of the amount of heating fuel delivered in the calendar year immediately prior to the filing of the report;

(2) of the type of fuel used, and the total number of rooms in the building;

(3) that he has been maintaining and will continue to maintain all essential services provided;

(4) that no rent reduction order based upon landlord's

failure to provide heat or hot water has been in effect during the prior 12 months;

(5) listing any funds received with respect to housing accommodations from any governmental grant program compensating such landlord for fuel price increases during the period for which an adjustment is obtained pursuant to this section;

(6) that the landlord shall provide such other information as the agency may require; and

(7) in order to qualify for rent increases for any individual housing and accommodations, where the maximum collectible rent, plus the cumulative rent adjustments pursuant to this section, is equal to or exceeds the maximum base rent, plus the cumulative amounts calculated as the annual fuel cost adjustments for such housing accommodations, pursuant to the applicable provisions of paragraphs (c)(1)-(2), (d)(1)-(2) of this section, a separate certification that, on information and belief, he will not be earning an amount in excess of the statutory 8½ percent return, computed in accordance with section Y51-5.0g(1)(a) of the Rent Law, after collection of the rent increase prescribed under this section for that housing accommodation, with respect to one or more buildings serviced by a single heating plant.

(c) The basis for the 1980 rent increases shall be as follows:

(1) The heating fuel price increase for the period April 9, 1979 through December 31, 1979 for the particular type of fuel used by the landlord in the building, multiplied by 75 percent of the lesser of:

(i) the amount of heating fuel actually delivered for the building between January 1 and December 31, 1979, divided by the number of rooms in the building to determine the annual fuel consumed per room; or

(ii) the annual maximum fuel consumption standard per room for such particular type of fuel, as promulgated by the city in 1980.

(2) Such 1979 fuel consumption standard shall not exceed 230 gallons per room in buildings using heating oils for heat, with comparable unit limitations to be

established by the Division of Housing and Community Renewal for other types of heating fuels.

(3) The annual fuel cost increase per room shall be divided by 12 to determine the monthly fuel cost increase per room, and that amount shall be multiplied by the number of rooms in each apartment to determine the monthly rent increase.

(4) In determining the number of rooms in the entire building for the purposes of this section, stores, offices and other commercial units shall be assigned the same room count as an equivalent area of residential space. Only living rooms, kitchens over 59 square feet in area, dining rooms and bedrooms shall be considered rooms. Bathrooms, foyers, kitchenettes, kitchens 59 square feet or less in area, alcoves, pantries and closets shall not be considered rooms.

(d) The basis for rent adjustment for 1981 and each year subsequent thereto for the period January 1, 1980 to and including December 31, 1980, and annually thereafter, shall be as follows:

(1) The heating fuel price increase or decrease promulgated by the Division of Housing and Community Renewal for the particular type of heating fuel for the year immediately preceding the service and filing of the report required under this section, multiplied by the amount of fuel actually delivered to the building during that particular year, and divided by the number of rooms determined in the manner set forth in paragraph (c)(4) of this section.

(2) Commencing January 1, 1981, the 1980 annual standard of fuel consumption for buildings using heating oils for heat shall be no more than 225 gallons per room per year, with comparable unit limitations for other types of heating fuels. Such consumption standards for heating oils, with comparable unit limitations for other types of heating fuels, shall be further reduced as follows:

(i) commencing January 1, 1982, by five gallons per room per year for heating oils;

(ii) commencing January 1, 1983, by 10 gallons per room per year for heating oils; and

(iii) commencing January 1, 1984, by 10 gallons per room per year for heating oils.

(3) Seventy-five percent of the annual fuel cost increase per room shall be allocated among the apartments in the manner set forth in paragraph (c)(3) of this section.

(e) If the report is served and filed within 60 days of the date of promulgation of the findings of fuel price increase and standards of consumption by the Division of Housing and Community Renewal, the rent adjustment shall be retroactive to and shall become effective as of January first of the calendar year in which the report is filed. If the report is not served and filed within such period, the rent increase shall become effective on the first day of the month immediately following the service and filing. No more than one report may be served or filed within any calendar year. Where a landlord has obtained one or more rent adjustments under this section and there is a finding of fuel price of the promulgation of findings, the landlord shall lose all right to collect any rent adjustments granted under this section for a period of 12 months, and the rent decrease shall be retroactive and effective January first of the calendar year in which the finding was promulgated.

(f) A landlord who filed a report under this section containing a false certification shall not be authorized nor eligible to collect any rent adjustment under this section for two years following the date of the order of determination of a false certification and, in addition, any rent adjustment obtained within two years prior to such determination shall not be effective nor collectible for the same two-year period following the date of the determination. Such landlord shall also be subject to any additional penalties imposed by law, including but not limited to the refund of any increases obtained by a false certification under this section.

(g) No increase provided for in this section shall be collectible from a tenant to whom there has been issued a currently valid senior citizen rent increase exemption order, insofar as it exceeds one third of the tenant's monthly disposable income. A senior citizen who applies for a rent increase exemption shall receive an order retroactive to the effective date of the annual fuel cost increase adjustment immediately preceding such application.

(h) In the event a rent reduction order, based upon the landlord's failure to provide heat or hot water to housing accommodations for which a landlord is collecting a rent adjustment provided for in this section, is issued by the Division of Housing and Community Renewal, such rent adjustment shall not be authorized nor collected for the time such rent reduction order remains in effect. In addition, the landlord shall not be authorized nor eligible to collect (1) such rent adjustment and (2) any subsequent rent adjustment provided for in this section, until 12 months after the effective date of the order restoring the maximum rent and terminating the rent reduction.

(i) The increase provided pursuant to this section shall not be incorporated into the maximum base rent or the maximum collectible rent for purposes of calculating percentage adjustments to such rents.

(j) A landlord demanding or collecting a rent adjustment provided for in this section shall, at the time of either the demand or collection of rent, issue to the tenant a rent bill or receipt setting forth the amounts of any fuel cost adjustments separate from the amount of rent otherwise demanded or collected. If the tenant has been issued a currently valid senior citizen rent increase exemption order, the landlord shall also state the amount actually payable by the senior citizen after crediting the exemption.

(k) Any rent adjustment granted pursuant to this section shall be reduced by an amount equal to any governmental grant received by the landlord compensating him for any fuel price increase, prorated for all rental space for which the grant was given or limited; provided, however, that such grant is not required, by the city, the agency or any governmental entity, to be expended for fuel-related repairs or improvements.

2202.14 Grounds for decrease of maximum rent. The administrator at any time, on his own initiative or on application of the tenant, may order a decrease of the maximum rent otherwise allowable, on the grounds stated in sections 2202.15 through 2202.18 of this Part.

2202.15 Decrease of first rents. Where a maximum rent has been established for a housing accommodation:

(a) pursuant to section 4(3) of the State Rent Act, and a proper and timely registration statement had been filed as had been required by the Federal Act or by the State Rent Commission; or

(b) pursuant to section 2201.1(b) or (c) of this Title, and a proper and timely registration statement has been filed as required by section 2203.3;

the administrator may order a decrease in the maximum rent where such maximum rent is substantially higher than the maximum rents for comparable housing accommodations, giving due consideration to any other factors bearing on the equities involved, consistent with the purposes of the Rent Law, including but not limited to the factors that such housing accommodations were created from housing accommodations which were vacated on or after November 22, 1963 other than by voluntary surrender of possession or in the manner provided by Part 2204 of this Title. Where the housing accommodations were created from such accommodations, the administrator may give due consideration to the limitation on the amount of the rent adjustment which may be ordered, pursuant to the provisions of section 2202.3(a)(1) of this Part, in considering the equities involved.

2202.16 Rent decrease for reduction of services, etc. (a) The administrator may order a decrease of the maximum rent otherwise allowable, or take action as provided in section 2202.19 of this Part, where there has been a substantial deterioration of the housing accommodations because of the failure of the landlord to properly maintain the same, or there has been a decrease in the dwelling space, essential services, furniture, furnishings or equipment required under section 2201.2 of this Title. It shall be no defense, to an application to decrease the maximum rent, that furniture or furnishings were removed on or after May 1, 1955 from a furnished housing accommodation with the consent of the tenant. The maximum rent for the housing accommodation shall be decreased by that amount which the administrator finds to be the reduction in the rental value of the housing accommodation because of the substantial deterioration or decrease in dwelling space, essential services, furniture, furnishings or equipment. The administrator may, however, take into consideration all factors bearing on the equities involved.

(b) In any proceeding where the landlord has complied with the requirements to paint and decorate the housing accommodation, the order terminating this proceeding shall set forth the date when the apartment shall again be due for a painting.

(c) The administrator may order a decrease of the maximum rent, where there had been a previous increase of the maximum rent on the basis of a prior tenant's installation or use of a television antenna, and a new tenant has not availed himself of this service, by the amount of rent increase formerly granted for such service; provided, however, that the present tenant file an application for the decrease of the maximum rent within 90 days from the date of taking possession of the housing accommodation.

(d) The administrator may order an appropriate decrease of the maximum rent, where there has been a previous increase of the maximum rent on the basis of the installation or use of cable television services, and there is no lease or rental agreement, executed prior to January 1, 1973 specifically providing for such installation or use, presently in force, or such lease or rental agreement has terminated or expired.

2202.17 Rent decrease based on hazardous conditions. The administrator may order a decrease of the maximum rent otherwise allowable, or take action as provided in section 2202.19 of this Part, where a city agency having jurisdiction certifies that the housing accommodation is a fire hazard, or is in a continued dangerous condition or detrimental to life or health, or is occupied in violation of law. In such case, the maximum rent for the housing accommodation may be decreased in such amount as the administrator deems to be necessary or proper.

2202.18 Decrease of inequitable rents for rooming house and single-room occupancy accommodations. Notwithstanding any other provision of these regulations, where a maximum rent has been established for a housing accommodation in a rooming house, or for a single-room occupancy accommodation, the administrator may order a decrease in the maximum rent, having regard for any factors bearing on the equities involved, consistent with the purposes of the Rent Law, to correct speculative, abnormal and unwarranted increases in rent.

2202.19 Alternative provision in lieu of rent decrease. (a) Whenever in the judgment of the administrator such action is necessary or proper in order to effectuate the purpose of the Rent Law, the administrator may, in lieu of decreasing the maximum rents as provided in sections 2202.16 and 2202.17 of this Part, enter into a contract wherein the landlord agrees in writing to deposit all income derived from the property, including income from spaces and accommodations not controlled, into an escrow or trust account supervised by the administrator, in accordance with the conditions imposed by the administrator, for use in maintaining or restoring essential services and equipment, for removing violations against the property or housing accommodations therein, for making such repairs as are necessary to remove a certification, from any city agency having jurisdiction thereof, that the housing accommodation is a fire hazard, or is in a continued dangerous condition or detrimental to life or health, or is occupied in violation of law, and/or for such other uses as the administrator deems necessary or proper for the preservation, repair or maintenance of the property.

(b) Where the landlord has entered into an escrow agreement as provided in subdivision (a) of this section, the administrator shall issue orders adjusting all controlled rents to the appropriate maximum rent, effective as of the first day of the month following the execution of such agreement; provided, however, that in the event the administrator shall determine that the landlord has breached such agreement, the administrator may issue orders:

(1) decreasing the maximum rent pursuant to such agreement;

(2) containing a directive that rent collected by the

landlord in excess of the rent thus decreased be refunded to the tenants; and

(3) containing such other determinations and directives as are necessary to effectuate the purposes of this section.

(c) Notwithstanding any provision of these regulations to the contrary, whenever, in the judgment of the administrator, action as provided in sections 2202.16 and 2202.17 of this Part is necessary or proper in order to effectuate the purposes of the Rent Law or of these regulations, the administrator may, in lieu of decreasing the maximum rents, issue orders adjusting all controlled rents and directing that rents be paid into an escrow account supervised by the administrator for the uses stated in subdivision (a) of this section, where:

(1) the landlord fails to take corrective action after notice by the administrator of proposed action to decrease the maximum rents pursuant to sections 2202.16 and 2202.17 of this Part;

(2) the administrator has notified all mortgagees who have filed with the administrator a declaration of interest in such property and in such proposed action; and

(3) the landlord has failed for three consecutive months to collect any controlled rents or to commence court proceedings for their collection or, if such proceedings have been commenced, the landlord has not diligently prosecuted them or such proceedings have not resulted in judgment in favor of such landlord.

(d) Where the essential services, furnishings, furniture or equipment of any individual housing accommodation are reduced, impaired, mutilated or made unworkable as a result of neglect, failure to exercise due care or failure of the tenant to take practical precautions to prevent such condition, the landlord shall restore such services, furniture, furnishings or equipment and may make application for a temporary increase in the maximum rent based upon cost of such restoration. In the event of the failure of the tenant to make restitution within a reasonable time, as determined by the administrator, an order shall be issued adjusting the maximum rent for such tenant in an amount sufficient to recover the cost over 12 monthly installments or until the tenant surrenders possession, whichever is sooner. The provisions of this paragraph shall be in addition to all other rights and remedies of the landlord.

2202.20 Senior citizen rent increase exemption. (a) No increase in maximum rent, pursuant to section 2201.3, 2201.4, 2201.5, 2201.6, 2202.8, 2202.9, 2202.10, 2202.11 or 2202.13 of this Title, shall be collectible from a tenant to whom there has been granted a rent increase exemption order, pursuant to this section, which became effective prior to the effective date of such increase, except as provided in such exemption order or as modified by subsequent exemption order.

(b) No increase in the legal regulated rent of housing accommodations subject to the provisions of title YY of the New York City Administrative Code, and the Rent Stabilization Code promulgated thereunder, shall be collectible from a tenant to whom there has been issued a currently valid exemption order pursuant to said Administrative Code or pursuant to this section, except as provided in such order or as modified by subsequent exemption order, where such increase is a lawful increase provided under a two-year lease executed pursuant to title YY of the New York City Administrative Code and Rent Stabilization Code, or under such other terms as regards housing accommodations subject to the hotel stabilization provisions of title YY51 of the New York City Administrative Code:

(1) pursuant to an order of the New York City Rent Guidelines Board; or

(2) based upon an owner hardship rent increase order issued by the Conciliation and Appeals Board.

(c) The city, upon application by the tenant on forms prescribed by HPD, shall issue a rent increase exemption order where it finds that the tenant is eligible for such order. A tenant shall be entitled to a rent increase exemption if:

(1) the aggregate disposable income of all members of the household residing in the housing accommodation does not exceed $10,000 per year;

(2) the maximum rent, including rent increases described in subdivisions (a) and (b) of this section, for the

housing accommodation exceeds one third of the aggregate disposable income of all members of the household;

(3) the tenant is entitled to reside in the housing accommodation; and

(4) the head of the household or spouse residing in the housing accommodation was 62 years of age or older on or before the date the application hereunder is filed, and is not a recipient of public assistance pursuant to the Social Services Law. However, persons receiving supplemental security income or additional State payments, or both, under a program administered by the United States Department of Health and Human Services solely or in combination with the New York State Department of Social Services shall not be rendered ineligible thereby.

(d) For the purpose of this section:

(1) The term *aggregate disposable income* shall mean the total income, from whatever source derived (whether or not subject to Federal income taxation), including but not limited to all compensation for personal services, wages, salaries, commissions, tips and earnings from self-employment, inclusive, social security and supplemental security income benefits, interest and dividends, pension payments, unemployment, disability and workers' compensation benefits, rents, royalties, payments from roomers, boarders or subtenants, alimony and support payment pursuant to agreement or court order, other than gifts and voluntary assistance payments from relatives and friends of members of the household not required to provide maintenance or support, received by any member of the household subject to the following adjustments:

(i) all Federal, State and city income taxes and social security taxes shall be deducted;

(ii) union dues withheld from wages or salaries shall be deducted; and

(iii) payments for maintenance or support, made pursuant to a written agreement or order of a court of competent jurisdiction by a member of the household to a person not a member of the household, shall be deducted.

(2) Disposable income to be reported shall be the income received in the last calendar year prior to the filing of the application, except that where the applicant retires between the commencement of such year and the date of filing the application, the income for such year may be adjusted by excluding employment earnings and projecting expected annual retirement income.

(3) The term *head of household* shall mean the person who customarily pays the rent (or his spouse, if older).

(4) The term *member of household* shall mean any person permanently residing in the housing accommodation who is not a bona fide roomer, boarder or subtenant.

(e) The rent increase exemption order shall provide that the landlord may not collect from a tenant, to whom it is issued, rent at a rate in excess of the greater of the following:

(1) one third of the aggregate disposable income;

(2) the maximum rent for rent-controlled housing in effect on December 31st of the calendar year immediately preceding the year in which the initial exemption is effective; or

(3) the legal regulated rent for rent-stabilized housing accommodations in effect on June 30, 1974 or the date immediately preceding eligibility, whichever is later.

Such order shall expire upon termination of occupancy by the tenant to whom it is issued, except as provided in subdivision (j) of this section. The landlord shall file a report of termination of occupancy of such tenant, on a form prescribed by the city, within 30 days.

(f) The effective date of any senior citizen rent increase exemption order issued pursuant to this section shall be:

(1) for rent-controlled housing accommodations, the first day of the month following the month in which the application is filed or the applicant becomes eligible, whichever is later. However, where such tenant could not qualify for senior citizen rent increase exemption between July 1, 1980 and December 31, 1980, due to the sole reason that the aggregate disposable income

of all members of the household exceeded $6,500 per year and did not exceed $8,000 per year, but filed for an exemption on or before December 31, 1980, pursuant to New York City Local Law 61 for 1980, the effective date of that portion of the exemption applicable solely to the fuel cost adjustment collectible pursuant to section 2202.13 of this Part shall be July 1, 1980, including any retroactive adjustments authorized by said section;

(2) for rent-stabilized housing accommodations, the first day of the month in which the application is filed or the applicant becomes eligible, whichever is later. However, where such tenant could not qualify for senior citizen rent increase exemption between July 1, 1980 and December 31, 1980, due to the sole reason that the aggregate disposable income of all members of the household exceeded $6,500 per year and did not exceed $8,000 per year, but filed for an exemption on or before December 31, 1980, the effective date of the exemption order shall be July 1, 1980, including any retroactive adjustments collectible thereby;

(3) for rent-controlled and rent-stabilized tenants, the effective date of any increase described in subdivisions (a) and (b) of this section, including any retroactive adjustments collectible thereby, provided the tenant has filed an application within 90 days after:

(i) any such order was issued increasing the tenant's rent; or

(ii) in the event no order was issued, any notice or report prescribed by the city to increase the tenant's rent was served upon the tenant.

(g) A rent exemption order shall be renewable annually upon application by the tenant, upon forms prescribed by the city, which may include a certification of the tenant's continued eligibility in lieu of the detailed statement of income and other qualifications. Upon the filing of the renewal application, the prior rent exemption order shall remain in effect until an order is issued determining the tenant's renewal application, but in no event for more than six additional months.

(h) The city may audit and review applications made pursuant to this section, and may cause an order issued pursuant to this section to be amended, terminated or revoked, and the city may direct the payment of back rent where it finds that:

(1) the tenant did not qualify for such order;

(2) the tenant no longer qualifies for such order due to a change of circumstances; or

(3) the tenant has submitted materially false statements or has willfully omitted or neglected to make any required material statement, in violation of subdivision (d) of section 2205.1 of this Title.

(i) Orders increasing or establishing maximum rents, pursuant to sections 2202.4-2202.7, 2202.12, 2202.19 and 2202.22 of this Part, are not subject to the provisions of this section, and exemption orders for rent-stabilized tenants shall provide that landlord may collect increases based on an electrical inclusion or an increase in dwelling space, services, equipment or major capital improvement.

(j) When a tenant holding a senior citizen rent increase exemption order granted under these rent regulations, title YY of the New York City Administrative Code or article II, IV, V or VI of the Private Housing Finance Law, moves into a dwelling unit subject to the title YY or these rent regulations on or after March 28, 1977, he may apply to the city to carry the exemption from paying that portion of the maximum rent of the original dwelling unit over to the dwelling unit into which he moves; provided, however, that the exempt amount shall be limited to the lowest of the following:

(1) the amount by which the rent for the subsequent dwelling unit exceeds the rent the tenant was required to pay for the original dwelling unit, after giving effect to the senior citizen rent increase exemption;

(2) the most recent monthly deduction in the original dwelling unit pursuant to senior citizen's exemption issued under the City Rent and Rehabilitation Law, title YY of the New York City Administrative Code, or the Private Housing Finance Law; or

(3) the amount by which the maximum rent of the subsequent housing accommodation exceeds one third of the aggregate disposable income of all members of the household.

Such exemption certificate shall be effective the first day of the month in which the application is filed, or the date the tenant took occupancy of the subsequent dwelling unit, whichever is later, provided both the application is filed and the tenant takes occupancy of the subsequent dwelling unit on or after March 28, 1977.

2202.21 Decrease of services; application, order or report. (a) Until the accommodations become vacant, the landlord shall maintain the same dwelling space, essential services, furniture, furnishings and equipment as are required under section 2201.2 of this Title, unless and until he has filed an application to decrease the dwelling space, essential services, furniture, furnishings or equipment and an order permitting such decrease has been entered thereon by the administrator.

(b) On or after May 1, 1955, the removal of furniture or furnishings from housing accommodations rented as furnished, whether or not such removal is consented to by the tenant, shall constitute a decrease in service.

(c) When the accommodations become vacant, the landlord may, prior to renting to a new tenant, decrease the dwelling space, essential services, furniture, furnishings or equipment. Within 10 days after so renting, the landlord shall file a written report with the district rent administrator showing such decrease.

(d) The order on any application under subdivision (a) of this section may require an appropriate decrease in the maximum rent. Any maximum rent for which a report is required by subdivision (c) of this section may be decreased in accordance with the provisions of section 2202.16 of this Part.

(e) If the landlord shall have failed to file an application or a proper and timely report, as required by subdivision (a) or (c) of this section, the maximum rent shall be deemed in doubt and the administrator may issue an order fixing the maximum rent pursuant to section 2202.22 of this Part.

2202.22 Orders where maximum rent or other facts are in dispute, in doubt or not known, or where maximum rents must be fixed or established. (a) Where the maximum rent or any fact necessary to the determination of the maximum rent, or the dwelling space, essential services, furniture, furnishings or equipment required to be furnished with the accommodation, is in dispute between the landlord and tenant, or is in doubt, or is not known, or is required by section 2201.1(d) or (e) of this Title to be fixed or established, the administrator at any time, upon written request of either party or on his own initiative, may issue an order determining the facts, including the amount of the maximum rent, the dwelling space, essential services, furniture, furnishings and equipment required to be furnished with the accommodations. Where the administrator determines that the accommodations are subject to control, he shall also fix or establish the maximum rent therefor, together with the dwelling space, essential services, furniture, furnishings and equipment required to be furnished with the accommodations, unless such maximum rent had been previously fixed or established by the State Rent Commission or by the administrator.

(b) Where:

(1) no registration statement has been filed under the Federal Act, or the State Rent Act, or the City Rent Law, as required by these regulations; or

(2) no proper or timely registration statement has been filed as required by these regulations; or

(3) no statement has been filed as required by section 2203.9 of this Title; or

(4) no proper or timely statement has been filed as required by said section; or

(5) the administrator in a proceeding pursuant to subdivision (a) of this section is unable to otherwise determine the maximum rent; or

(6) the maximum rent must be fixed or established by the administrator;

he may issue an order fixing or establishing the maximum rent, having regard for the maximum rents for comparable housing accommodations or any other factors bearing on the equities involved, consistent with the purpose of the Rent Law, including but not limited to the factor that such housing accommodations were created from housing accommodations which were vacated, on or after November 22, 1963, other than by voluntary surrender of possession or in the manner provided by Part 2204 of this Title. Where the housing accommodations were created from such accommodations, the administrator may give due consideration to the limitation on the amount of the rent adjustment which may be ordered, pursuant to the provisions of section 2202.3(a)(1) of this Part, in considering the equities involved. Such order shall fix or establish the maximum rent as of May 1, 1950, or the date of first renting, whichever is later, and may contain a directive that all rent collected in excess of the maximum rent fixed or established under this subdivision during the period beginning no earlier than two years prior to the date of the filing of the tenant's statement of violations, if any, or the date of the commencement of the proceeding to fix or establish the maximum rent, whichever date is earlier, shall be refunded to the tenant, together with six percent interest from the date of each such excessive payment of rent, within 30 days after such order shall become final.

(c) Where the landlord has failed to file an application or report required by the State Rent Commission or by either section 2202.21(a) or (c) of this Part or section 35(a) or (c) of the New York City Rent and Eviction Regulations, the administrator at any time, upon written request of the tenant or on his own initiative, may issue an order establishing the maximum rent by decreasing the previous maximum rent for the housing accommodation by that amount which the administrator finds to be the reduction in rental value of the housing accommodation because of the decrease in dwelling space, essential services, furniture, furnishings or equipment. The administrator may take into consideration all factors bearing on the equities involved, consistent with the purposes of the Rent Law. Such order shall establish the maximum rent as of the date of such decrease of dwelling space, essential services, furniture, furnishings or equipment, and may contain a directive that all rent collected in excess of the maximum rent fixed or established under this subdivision, during the period beginning no earlier than two years prior to the date of the filing of the tenant's statement of violations, if any, or the date of the commencement of the proceeding to fix or establish the maximum rent, whichever date is earlier, shall be refunded to the tenant, together with six percent interest from the date of each such excessive payment of rent, within 30 days after such order shall become final.

2202.23 Order where apartment is rented to more than one tenant. (a) On and after February 1, 1952, where an apartment, in whole or in part, is rented or sought to be rented to more than one tenant, the landlord shall file an application with the administrator to fix maximum rents for the units or portions of such apartment. Such application shall set forth the present maximum rent for the apartment, the furniture, furnishings, facilities, equipment and other services added or proposed to be added, the number of occupants and the space to be occupied by each tenant in such apartment, the terms and conditions of occupancy, and all other data which may be required by the administrator. In fixing the maximum rent, the administrator shall apportion the previous maximum rent for the entire apartment among the tenants in proportion to the space they occupy, and shall add thereto the increased rental value of any furniture, furnishings, facilities and equipment added by the landlord. Where the landlord has satisfied all of the requirements of the authorities having jurisdiction over the physical conversion and over the occupancy of the changed housing accommodations, the administrator, in fixing maximum rents for individual tenants, shall also take into consideration all factors bearing on the equities involved, including the cost of any physical conversion or alteration. If there was no previous maximum rent for the entire apartment, the administrator, prior to making the apportionment and fixing a maximum rent for each tenant as hereinabove required, shall establish a maximum rent for the entire apartment, having regard for the maximum rents for comparable housing accommodations, or any factors bearing on the equities involved, consistent with the purposes of the Rent Law. Unless and until an order is issued by the administrator fixing maximum rents for the individual tenants of the apartment, the aggregate maximum rent for all of the tenants in the apartment shall be the maximum rent previously established for the apartment. All orders issued under this section shall be effective as of the date of first renting.

(b) Where no application has been made under this section, the administrator at any time, upon written request of a tenant or on his own initiative, may issue an order pursuant to this section fixing or establishing a maximum rent for each of the individual tenants in the apartment, effective as of the date of such renting. In fixing such maximum rents for the individual tenants, the administrator shall use the standards prescribed in subdivision (a) of this section. Such order may contain a directive that all rent collected in excess of the maximum rent established under this subdivision, during the period beginning no earlier than two years prior to the date of the filing of the tenant's statement of violations, if any, or the date of the commencement of the proceeding to fix or establish the maximum rent, whichever date is earlier, shall be refunded to the tenant, together with six percent interest from the date of each such excessive payment of rent, within 30 days after such order shall become final.

2202.24 Retroactive adjustments. Where an order establishing or adjusting a maximum rent, or the portion thereof collectible from a particular tenant, is effective as of a date prior to the date of its issuance:

(a) Any rent to which the landlord shall be entitled for such prior period shall be payable by the tenant in installments, except that a tenant who vacates the premises when rent for such prior period has not been fully paid shall be obligated to pay the balance forthwith. The installment of back rent payable for each month (or other rental payment period) shall not exceed the difference per month (or other rental payment period) between the rent established by the order and the prior rent.

(b) Any excess rent paid by the tenant for such prior period shall be credited to the tenant in full, commencing with the rental payment immediately following the issuance of the order.

PART 2203

REGISTRATION AND RECORDS

Section 2203.1 Registration of housing accommodations. (a) Except as otherwise specifically provided by these regulations, every landlord of housing accommodations rented or offered for rent shall file a written statement, on the form provided therefor, containing such information as the administrator may require, to be known as a registration statement, unless a registration statement was filed under the Federal Act or the State Rent Act, or unless the maximum rent for such housing accommodations is required, by section 2201.1(d) or (e) of this Title, to be fixed or established by the administrator.

(b) Notwithstanding subdivision (a) of this section, every landlord of a building or property containing dwelling units subject to title YY of the New York City Administrative Code, and housing accommodations subject to these regulations, shall file a registration statement, no later than September 21, 1984, for each housing accommodation subject to these regulations, on a form prescribed by the administrator containing such information as the administrator may require.

(c) Every landlord, of a building or property in which all residential units are subject to these regulations on April 1, 1984, but thereafter one or more of said residential units becomes subject to title YY of the New York City Administrative Code, shall file a registration statement for each residential unit which remains subject to these regulations by September 21, 1984, or within 90 days from the date the first residential unit becomes subject to title YY of the New York City Administrative Code, whichever is later, on a form prescribed by the administrator containing such information as the administrator may require.

(d) The registration required in subdivisions (b) and (c) of this section shall not establish the legal maximum rent unless an order setting forth the legal maximum rent is issued by the Division of Housing and Community Renewal.

2203.2 Report on decontrol of certain housing accommodations. (a) The landlord of a housing accommodation specified in section 2200.2(f)(11), (12) and (17) of this Title shall file a report of such decontrol, upon forms prescribed by the administrator, within 30 days following the date of vacancy on or after June 30, 1971, or the date of first rental of such accommodations after decontrol (whichever date shall be prescribed in such form), or June 1, 1962, whichever date is later, unless a decontrol report was heretofore filed as required by the State Rent Commission.

(b) The landlord of a housing accommodation specified in section 2200.2(f)(13) of this Title shall file a report of such decontrol, upon forms prescribed by the administrator, within 30 days following the date of first rental of such accommodation after decontrol, or June 1, 1962, whichever date is later, unless a decontrol report was heretofore filed as required by the State Rent Commission; and shall file such additional reports, upon forms prescribed by the administrator, as may be required, showing changes in the rental of, and the essential services, furniture, furnishings and equipment provided for, such accommodation.

(c) The landlord of a housing accommodation specified in section 2202.2(f)(14) of this Title shall:

(1) file a report of the eligibility of a housing accommodation for decontrol under such section no later than April 30, 1964;

(2) file a report of decontrol within 30 days after decontrol; and

(3) file an additional report prior to December 30, 1965, or within 30 days after the anniversary date of decontrol, whichever shall be the later, showing changes in the rental of, and the essential services, furniture, furnishings and equipment provided for, such accommodation, and any change or rearrangement of living space. Such reports are to be filed upon forms prescribed by the administrator.

(d) The landlord of a housing accommodation specified in section 2200.2(f)(15) of this Title shall:

(1) file a report of the eligibility of a housing accommodation for decontrol under such section no later than April 1, 1968; and

(2) file an additional report, within 30 days after the anniversary date of decontrol, showing changes in the rental of, and the essential services, furniture, furnishings and equipment provided for, such accommodation, and any change or rearrangement of living space. Such reports are to be filed upon forms prescribed by the administrator.

(e) The landlord of a housing accommodation specified in section 2200.2(f)(16) of this Title shall file a report of such decontrol, upon forms prescribed by the administrator, within 30 days following the date of first rental of such accommodations.

2203.3 First rent. For housing accommodations first rented after April 15, 1962, unless a registration statement was filed with the State Rent Commission on or before April 30, 1962, a registration statement, upon forms prescribed by the administrator, shall be filed by May 15, 1962, or within 15 days after first renting, whichever is later.

2203.4 Change of ownership. Where, since the filing of the registration statement for any housing accommodation, there has been a change in the identity of the landlord, by transfer of title or otherwise, and no notice of such change has been filed, the successor landlord shall file a notice, on a form provided for that purpose, on or before June 1, 1962, or within 15 days after the change, whichever is later.

2203.5 Service of papers. Any notice, order or other process or paper directed to the person named in the registration statement as the landlord at the address given therein or, where a notice of change in identity has been filed, to the person named as landlord and at the address given in the most recent such notice, shall constitute notice to the person who is then the landlord.

2203.6 Notices to attorneys at law. (a) Whenever a person is involved in a proceeding before the administrator, and an attorney at law has filed a notice of appearance for such person in such proceeding, all subsequent written communications or notices to such person (other than subpoenas) shall be sent to such attorney at law at the address designated in such notice of appearance. The notice of appearance to be filed by an attorney at law who represents a party in a proceeding before the administrator shall be on a form prescribed by the administrator, unless proceedings are instituted before the administrator by formal application pursuant to these regulations and the representation of such attorney at law and his mailing address are stated in such application in the space allotted for the mailing address of the represented party. The service of written communications and notices upon such attorney at law shall be deemed full and proper service upon the party or parties so represented.

(b) Whenever an attorney at law shall represent the same party or parties in more than one proceeding before the Division of Housing and Community Renewal, separate notices of appearance shall be filed in each proceeding. For the purposes of this section, a protest against an order of the district rent administrator shall be deemed a separate proceeding.

(c) This section shall not apply to preliminary investigations conducted by the administrator.

2203.7 Failure to file. Where the landlord has failed to file a proper and timely registration statement as required by this Part, the administrator may establish the maximum rent pursuant to section 2202.22 of this Title, and if such maximum rent has been established, no rent increase may be obtained under any provision of these regulations until compliance with this Part.

2203.8 Records and recordkeeping. (a) Every landlord of a rooming house or hotel subject to these regulations, rented or offered for rent, shall keep, preserve, and make available for examination by the administrator, records showing the rents received for each housing accommodation, the particular term and number of occupants for which such rents were charged, and the name and address of each occupant.

(b) Every landlord shall keep, preserve, and make available for examination by the administrator, records of the same kind as he has customarily kept relating to the rents received for housing accommodations.

2203.9 Other reports required to be filed. (a) *Compensable adjustment of maximum rent.*

(1) The landlord of a building wherein the maximum rents for housing accommodations therein are subject to adjustment, as provided in sections 2201.3 and 2202.11 of this Title, shall file a report of such adjustment upon forms prescribed by the administrator.

(2) Prior to filing such report, the landlord shall give the tenants at least five days' written notice of such rent increase, upon forms prescribed by the administrator, as a condition to the collection of such rent adjustment effective on the date of commencement of the next rent payment period following the date of service of such notice.

(3) No report may be accepted by the administrator unless the landlord shall certify compliance with the notice requirement of paragraph (2) of this subdivision.

(b) *Change in tenancy with statutory rent increase.* (1) Where a housing accommodation becomes vacant on or after August 1, 1970 and before January 1, 1972, by voluntary surrender of possession by the tenant, and the maximum rent is increased as provided in section 2201.3(e) of this Title, the landlord shall file a report of such rent increase upon forms prescribed by the administrator.

(c) *Filing of reports in general.* The landlord shall file any report prescribed by sections 2201.3 and 2202.11 of this Title no later than August 31, 1971, whether or not the filing of such report would result in any increase in the maximum rent for the housing accommodations involved. No maximum rent established pursuant to section Y51-5.0a(3) of the Rent Law shall take effect, with respect to any housing accommodation for which such report, or such alternative report as the administrator may prescribe, is not filed by such date, until March 31, 1972 or 90 days after the date of filing, whichever is later.

(d) *Miscellaneous provisions for signing and filing forms prescribed by section 2201.3.*

(1) All forms filed pursuant to the provisions of section 2201.3 of this Title must be filed simultaneously.

(2) Notwithstanding any instructions contained on such forms to the contrary, the landlord may, in lieu of signing copies of city report form R-23 and the original and copies of city application form A-23, affix his facsimile signature to all copies of city report form R-23 and the original and all copies of city application form A-23, provided that he shall attach an affirmation to the original city report form R-23, which shall contain a duplicate of such facsimile signature used by him, together with the statement that he affixed such facsimile signature to such forms with the same force and effect as if he had personally signed each of said forms. The affirmation shall also identify the housing accommodations and the property involved, and state the date when such facsimile signature was affixed to such forms.

2203.10 Certification concerning alteration or demolition of buildings. The landlord shall submit a certified statement to the Division of Housing and Community Renewal, upon forms prescribed by the administrator, before filing plans and applying for a building permit to alter or demolish all or part of a building containing housing accommodations subject to these regulations. Such certified statement shall be submitted at the earliest of the following dates:

(a) not less than 30 days before commencement of any work for which the filing of plans and obtaining of permits is required;

(b) at least 30 days and not more than 120 days prior to filing any such plans or applying for such permit; or

(c) within 30 days after the first communication, written or oral, to any tenant or occupant of such building, of the landlord's intention to alter or demolish.

PART 2204

EVICTIONS

Section 2204.1 Restrictions on removal of tenants, including hotel tenants.

(a) No tenant, so long as he continues to pay the rent to which the landlord is entitled, shall be removed from any housing accommodation by action to evict or to recover possession, by exclusion from possession or otherwise, nor shall any person attempt such removal or exclusion from possession, notwithstanding that the tenant has no lease or that his lease, or other rental agreement, has expired or otherwise terminated, and notwithstanding any contract, lease agreement or obligation heretofore or hereafter entered into which provides for surrender of possession, or which otherwise provides contrary hereto, except one or more of the grounds specified in section 2204.2 of this Part, or unless the landlord has obtained a certificate of eviction as hereinafter provided.

(b) It shall be unlawful for any person to remove or attempt to remove any tenant or occupant from any housing accommodations, or to refuse to renew the lease or agreement for the use of such accommodations, because such tenant or occupant has taken, or proposes to take, action authorized or required by the Rent Law, or any provision of the Administrative Code of the City of New York, the Multiple Dwelling Law, or the Health Code of the City of New York, or any regulation, order or requirement thereunder.

(c)(1) No tenant of any housing accommodations (as defined in subdivision [f] or [g] of section 2200.2 of this Title) shall be removed or evicted, unless and until such removal or eviction has been authorized by a court of competent jurisdiction.

(2) Except as hereinafter provided, this subdivision shall not apply where the removal or eviction is for nonpayment of rent and involves a hotel tenant or an occupant of one or more rooms in a rooming house (which meets all requirements of law and the city agencies having jurisdiction thereof) who has not been in possession for 30 consecutive days or longer, and who occupies his accommodations on a daily or weekly basis, provided the landlord shall give written notice thereof to the tenant at least three days prior to the date specified therein for surrender of possession and prior to any action for removal or eviction. In computing the three-day period, the date of service and any intervening Sunday shall be excluded. Every such notice shall include therein a statement of the rent due and the rental period or periods for which said rent is due. An exact copy of any such notice, together with an

affidavit of service, shall be filed with the district rent office within 48 hours after such notice is given to the tenant. Should the tenant tender the rent due within the three-day period, the landlord may not remove or evict the tenant. The service of a three-day notice for the removal or eviction for nonpayment of rent shall not be required where the landlord institutes judicial proceedings to remove or evict the tenant.

(d) Any statutory tenant who vacates the housing accommodations, without giving the landlord at least 30 days' written notice by registered or certified mail of this intention to vacate, shall be liable to the landlord for the loss of rent suffered by the landlord, but not exceeding one month's rent, except where the tenant has been removed or vacates pursuant to the provisions of this Part. Such notice shall be postmarked on or before the last day of the rental period immediately prior to such 30-day period.

(e) Notwithstanding any provision of this Part, the State, the city, or the New York City Housing Authority may recover possession of any housing accommodations operated by it where such action or proceeding is authorized by statute or regulations under which such accommodations are administered.

2204.2 Proceedings for eviction without certificate. (a) Except as provided in sections 2204.1 and 2204.4 of this Part, an action or proceeding to recover possession of any housing accommodation shall be maintainable, after service and filing of the notice by section 2204.3, only upon one or more of the following grounds:

(1) The tenant is violating a substantial obligation of his tenancy, other than the obligation to surrender possession of such housing accommodation, and has failed to cure such violation after written notice by the landlord that the violation cease within 10 days; or within a three-month period immediately prior to the commencement of the proceeding, the tenant has willfully violated such an obligation inflicting serious and substantial injury upon the landlord.

(2) The tenant is committing or permitting a nuisance in such housing accommodations; or is mali-

ciously or by reason of gross negligence substantially damaging the housing accommodation; or his conduct is such as to interfere substantially with the comfort and safety of the landlord or of other tenants or occupants of the same or another adjacent building or structure.

(3) Occupancy of the housing accommodation by the tenant is illegal because of the requirements of law, and the landlord is subject to civil or criminal penalties therefor, or both; provided, however, that such occupancy shall not be considered illegal by reason of violations placed against the housing accommodations or the building in which same are located by any department or agency of the city having jurisdiction, unless such department or agency has issued an order requiring the tenants to vacate said accommodations or building, or unless such occupancy for such building or such violations relied on by the landlord result from an act, omission or situation caused or created by the tenant.

(4) The tenant is using or permitting such housing accommodation to be used for an immoral or illegal purpose.

(5) The tenant who had a written lease or other written rental agreement, which terminated or shall terminate on or after May 1, 1950, has refused upon demand of the landlord to execute a written extension or renewal thereof for a further term of like duration not in excess of one year, but otherwise on the same terms and conditions as the previous lease, except insofar as such terms and conditions are inconsistent with the Rent Law.

(6) The tenant has unreasonably refused the landlord access to the housing accommodation for the purpose of making necessary repairs or improvements required by law or for the purpose of inspection or of showing the accommodation to a prospective purchaser, mortgagee or prospective mortgagee, or other person having a legitimate interest therein; provided, however, that in the latter event such refusal shall not be grounds for removal or eviction if such inspection or showing of the accommodation is contrary to the provisions of the tenant's lease or other rental agreement.

(7) The eviction is sought by the owner of a dwelling unit or the shares allocated thereto where such dwelling unit is located in a structure owned as a cooperative or as a condominium, and an offering prospectus for the conversion of such structure pursuant to an eviction plan shall have been submitted to and accepted for filing by the Attorney General and declared effective in accordance with section 352-eeee of the General Business Law, provided that:

(i) no eviction proceedings under this subdivision shall be commenced against a nonpurchasing tenant who is either an eligible senior citizen or an eligible disabled person, as defined in accordance with section 352-eeee of the General Business Law:

(ii) no eviction proceeding under this paragraph shall be commenced against a nonpurchasing tenant in occupancy of a dwelling unit until:

(a) such tenant's lease or rental agreement has expired; or

(b) three years after the eviction plan has been declared effective in accordance with section 352-eeee of the General Business Law, whichever is later;

(iii) the owner of such dwelling unit or the shares allocated thereto seeks in good faith to recover possession of a dwelling unit for his own personal use and occupancy or for the use and occupancy of his immediate family; and

(iv) the eviction plan was accepted for filing by the Attorney General on or after July 21, 1982.

(8) The administrator may by order waive the requirements for a certificate of eviction, where:

(i) housing accommodations were vacant at the time when the landlord made application for such waiver;

(ii) where vacated by reason of the last tenant's voluntary surrender thereof; and

(iii) the landlord, in good faith, intends to demolish or substantially rehabilitate the building in which the housing accommodations are located, within the period specified by the administrator in such order.

Rent Regulations

(b) The failure of the landlord to comply with the conditions established by the administrator for granting such waiver shall subject the housing accommodations to all the provisions of the Rent Law and these regulations to the same extent as if no such waiver was granted.

2204.3 Notices required in proceedings under section 2204.2. (a) Except where the ground for removal or eviction of a tenant is nonpayment of rent, no tenant shall be removed or evicted from a housing accommodation by court process, and no action or proceeding shall be commenced for such purpose upon any of the grounds stated in section 2204.2 of this Part, unless and until the landlord shall have given written notice to the tenant and to the district rent office as hereinafter provided.

(b) Every such notice to a tenant to vacate or surrender possession of a housing accommodation shall state the ground under section 2204.2 of this Part upon which the landlord relies for removal or eviction of the tenant, the facts necessary to establish the existence of such ground, and the date when the tenant is required to surrender possession.

(c) Within 48 hours after the notice is served upon the tenant, an exact copy thereof, together with an affidavit of service, shall be filed with the district rent office. In computing such 48-hour period, any intervening Saturday, Sunday or legal holiday shall be excluded.

(d) Every such notice shall be served upon the tenant within the period of time hereinafter set forth prior to the date specified therein for the surrender of possession, and prior to the commencement of any proceeding for removal or eviction:

(1) Where the notice specifies one or more of the grounds stated in paragraphs (a)(2)-(4) of section 2204.2 of this Part as the basis for such removal or eviction, not less than 10 days, unless the tenant is a weekly tenant in which case the notice required shall not be less than two days.

(2) Where the notice specifies one or more of the grounds stated in paragraphs (a)(1), (5) and (6) of section 2204.2 of this Part as the basis for such removal or eviction, not less than one month, unless the tenant is a weekly tenant in which case the notice required shall not be less than seven days.

2204.4 Proceedings for eviction with certificate. (a) No tenant who continues to pay the rent to which landlord is entitled shall be removed or evicted on grounds other than those stated in section 2204.2 of this Part, unless on application of the landlord (provided that where the housing accommodations are located in a structure or building owned by a two or more persons not constituting a cooperative corporation or association, the application shall be consented to by all the coowners), the administrator shall issue a certificate permitting the landlord to pursue his remedies at law at the expiration of the applicable waiting period specified in subdivision (b) of this section. The administrator shall issue an order granting a certificate if the removal or eviction meets the requirements of section 2204.5, 2204.6, 2204.7, 2204.8 or 2204.9 of this Part. The administrator may also issue orders granting certificates in other cases if the requested removal or eviction is not inconsistent with the purposes of the Rent Law or these regulations, and would not be likely to result in the circumvention or evasion thereof, and may impose such terms and conditions, including provisions for relocation and the payment of stipends to the tenants, as the administrator may determine to be necessary or appropriate.

(b)(1) Certificates issued pursuant to these regulations shall authorize the landlord to commence proceedings to remove or evict the tenant after the expiration of the applicable waiting period hereinafter specified in this subdivision. Any waiting period prescribed or fixed pursuant to this subdivision shall commence upon the date of the issuance of the certificate by the administrator. Except as otherwise provided in paragraph (2) of this subdivision, the applicable waiting period shall be as follows:

(i) where relocation is not required, three months; or

(ii) where relocation is required, four months.

(2) In any case where the administrator determines to issue a certificate, and the tenant, because of the provisions of paragraph (e)(2) of this section, is not entitled to the benefit of the relocation requirements of paragraph (e)(1) of this section, the applicable waiting

period with respect to such certificate shall be four months.

(3) Where the administrator finds (i) that suitable accommodations are available for renting into which the tenant can move without substantial hardship or loss, and (ii) that undue hardship would result to the landlord from delay in acquiring possession, the certificate may authorize the landlord to pursue his remedies for removal or eviction of the tenant at the expiration of a period shorter than the minimum waiting period which would otherwise be applicable under the foregoing provisions of this subdivision.

(c) No certificate (including any certificate of eviction issued by the State Rent Commission and enforceable on and after May 1, 1962 under the Rent Law) shall be used in connection with any action or proceeding to remove or evict a tenant, unless such removal or eviction is sought for the purpose specified in the certificate.

(d) In the event that the landlord's intentions or circumstances have so changed that the premises, possession of which is sought, will not be used for the purpose specified in any such certificate mentioned in subdivision (c) of this section, such certificate shall thereupon be null and void. The landlord shall immediately notify the district rent administrator in writing and surrender the certificate for cancellation.

(e)(1) Except as otherwise provided in paragraph (2) of this subdivision, whenever compliance with the relocation requirements of this section is directed by or required pursuant to these regulations as a condition for the granting of a certificate of eviction, the landlord shall provide suitable relocation for the tenant.

(i) Where the landlord and tenant are unable to agree as to the suitability of a housing accommodation offered to a tenant for relocation, the administrator, in determining whether such offered accommodation is suitable, shall give due consideration to the following factors:

(a) the physical condition and facilities of the offered housing accommodation and the adequacy of neighborhood facilities. No accommodation shall be found to be suitable unless:

(1) it is located in an area reasonably accessible to the tenant's place of employment or business and generally not less desirable in regard to community and commercial facilities than the area in which the tenant then resides;

(2) the building containing such accommodation:

(i) is free from violations of law, recorded by a city agency having jurisdiction, which constitute fire hazards or conditions dangerous or detrimental to life or health or which affect the maintenance of essential services; and

(ii) has central heat and central hot water;

(3) such accommodation is decent, safe and sanitary and generally not less desirable than the housing accommodation then occupied by the tenant;

(4) such accommodation contains:

(i) kitchen facilities for the exclusive use of the tenant's family; and

(ii) a fully enclosed bathroom equipped with a washbasin, toilet facilities and a bathtub or shower; and

(5) such accommodation:

(i) has adequate light and ventilation, with a window in all rooms except where approved mechanical ventilation is a lawful substitute; and

(ii) contains adequate space for the occupants without overcrowding.

Notwithstanding the foregoing provisions of this clause where a tenant to be relocated is the sole occupant of a rooming house accommodation of a single-room occupancy accommodation, an accommodation in a licensed rooming house offered to such tenant may be deemed to be suitable, provided such rooming house accommodation meets the requirements of subclauses *(1)*, *(2)*, *(3)* and *(5)* of this clause; and

(b) the tenant's ability to pay the rent for the offered accommodation. No accommodation shall be found to be suitable unless the rent therefor is reasonably within the financial means of the tenant. In general, a gross annual rental for an offered accommodation shall be presumed to

be reasonably with the tenant's financial means if such rental does not exceed the tenant's then rental, or 20 percent of the tenant's gross family income, whichever is higher; provided, however, that:

(1) where the tenant establishes that a gross annual rental below such 20-percent standard is in excess of his financial means, the administrator may determine that the offered accommodation is not suitable for the tenant unless, in addition to any stipend payable to the tenant pursuant to these regulations, the landlord pays to the tenant a sum equal to the amount by which the gross annual rental for the offered accommodation, over a period of two years, exceeds 125 percent of the gross annual rental, over a period of two years, for the tenant's then accommodations; and

(2) the administrator may determine that the offered accommodation is suitable, notwithstanding that the gross annual rental therefor is in excess of such 20-percent standard, if the administrator finds, after due consideration of the tenant's circumstances, that such rental is reasonably within the financial means of the tenant.

(ii) No housing accommodation shall be found to be suitable unless the administrator determines:

(a) that the building containing such accommodation is not located in an area which is being formally considered or has been approved as the site of a proposed public improvement or publicly assisted project, whether public or private, by any city agency authorized to make reports or recommendations or act with respect to the approval of such site for such purposes; or

(b) that such building, although located in such an area, will not be required, for the purpose of constructing or carrying out such improvement or project, to be demolished or to be altered or improved in such manner as to interfere with occupancy by the tenant.

(2) Notwithstanding any provision of paragraph (1) of this subdivision to the contrary, there shall be no relocation requirement where:

(i) the tenant is a single person under the age of 60 years who is the sole occupant of a rooming house accommodation or a single-room occupancy accommodation, and such occupancy has continued for less than six months prior to the date of the filing of the application for a certificate of eviction;

(ii) the tenant's housing accommodation is occupied by three persons or less and the maximum monthly rent therefor, as of January 1, 1961, was $200 or more; or

(iii) the tenant's housing accommodation is occupied by four persons or more and the maximum monthly rent therefor, as of January 1, 1961, was $250 or more.

(3) Whenever compliance with the stipend requirements of this section is directed by or required pursuant to these regulations, the landlord shall pay the applicable stipend hereinafter provided for in this paragraph to each tenant who moves or rents another accommodation after the date of the filing of the application, and prior to the withdrawal or final denial of such application, and such payment shall be made within five days from the date of the tenant's removal. The payment of such stipend shall be made on the basis of the following schedule:

(i) For other than rooming house tenants or single room occupants (except as provided in subparagraphs [iii] and [iv] of this paragraph):

Number	Self-relocated	Landlord-relocated
1-3	$450	$200
4	$600	$300
5 or more	$750	$400

(ii) For rooming house tenants or single-room occupants (except as otherwise provided in subparagraph [v] of this paragraph):

	Self-relocated	Landlord-relocated
(a) sole occupant under 60 years of age	$100	$ 50
(b) sole occupant 60 years of age or over	$150	$ 75
(c) family with no children under 16 years of age	$150	$ 75
(d) family with one or more children under 16 years of age	$450	$200

(iii) For three-person or less family units whose monthly rent as of January 1, 1961 was from $200 to $249.99, inclusive, the stipend is $300. No stipend is required to be paid where such rent was $250 per month or more.

(iv) For four-person or more family units whose monthly rent as of January 1, 1971 was from $250 to $299, inclusive, the stipend is $400. No stipend is required to be paid where such rent was $300 per month or more.

(v) Notwithstanding any provision in this section to the contrary, where a tenant under the age of 60 years is the sole occupant of a rooming house accommodation or of a single-room occupancy accommodation, and such occupancy has not continued for more than six months prior to the date of the filing of the application, he shall not be entitled to the payment of any stipend.

(vi) Tenants who, with or without landlord assistance, move into public housing or publicly aided housing are deemed to be self-relocated for the purpose of this paragraph.

(4) Where a housing accommodation is occupied by more than one tenant, the stipend required to be paid pursuant to paragraph (3) of this subdivision shall be paid to each tenant in proportion to the space personally occupied by him and members of his household.

(5) Where a housing accommodation is sublet, the stipend or stipends required to be paid pursuant to paragraph (3) of this subdivision shall be allocated between the prime tenant and the subtenants, on such basis as the administrator shall determine to be appropriate, with due regard for such factors as space personally occupied by the prime tenant and the subtenants and the duration of the unexpired term of the subtenants' tenancy.

(f) Whenever compliance with stipend requirements of this section is directed by or pursuant to these regulations, the landlord shall deposit in escrow with his attorney a sum of money sufficient to pay the prescribed stipend to:

(1) each tenant in the building or structure who is still in occupancy on the 10th day prior to the expiration of the applicable waiting period; and

(2) each tenant who had previously vacated after the application was filed by the landlord and who has not already received payment of the stipend.

The escrow deposit shall be conditioned upon the payment of the stipend within five days from demand for payment after the tenant's removal from the premises. Proof of payment of the applicable stipends and/or compliance with the requirements of the foregoing provisions of this subdivision shall be filed no later than five days before the expiration of the waiting period.

(g) No application for a certificate of eviction shall be granted under sections 2204.7, 2204.8 and 2204.9(a)(2) and (4) of this Part, unless the administrator determines, after a hearing, that:

(1) there is no reasonable possibility that the landlord can make a net annual return of 8½ percent of the assessed valuation of the subject property without recourse to the eviction sought; and

(2) neither the landlord nor immediate predecessor in interest has intentionally or willfully managed the property to impair the landlord's ability to earn such return.

(h) The effectiveness of any certificate of eviction or of any order granting a certificate of eviction pursuant to sections 2204.7, 2204.8 and 2204.9(a)(2) and (4) of this Part, shall be suspended, and no tenant may be evicted pursuant to such certificate or order, unless and until the requirements of subdivision (g) of this section have been complied with and the commissioner issues an order reinstating the effectiveness of any certificate of eviction or any order granting a certificate of eviction suspended by chapter 1022 of the Laws of 1974, as amended by chapter 360 of the Laws of 1975. The relief granted in this subdivision shall take effect notwithstanding the pendency of any judicial proceeding or appeal.

(i) The provisions of subdivisions (g) and (h) of this section shall not apply to an application under section 2204.7 or 2204.8 of this Part where the alteration, remodeling or construction of a new building is to be aided by interest reduction payments under section 236 of the National Housing Act.

(j) The provisions of this section shall apply to all certificates of eviction issued pursuant to these regulations, unless otherwise specified.

2204.5 Occupancy by landlord or immediate family. (a) A certificate shall be issued where the landlord seeks in good faith to recover possession of a housing accommodation because of immediate and compelling necessity for his own personal use and occupancy, or for the use and occupancy of his immediate family; provided, however, that this section shall not apply where a member of the household lawfully occupying the housing accommodation is 62 years of age or older, has been a tenant in a housing accommodation in that building for 20 years or more, or has an impairment which results from anatomical, physiological or psychological conditions, other than addiction to alcohol, gambling or any controlled substance, which are demonstrable by medically acceptable clinical and laboratory diagnostic techniques, and which are expected to be permanent and which prevent the tenant from engaging in any substantial gainful employment. As used in this subdivision, the term *immediate family* includes only a son, daughter, grandson, granddaughter, stepson, stepdaughter, father, mother, father-in-law, mother-in-law, grandfather, grandmother, stepfather or stepmother.

(b) Where the housing accommodation is located in a structure or premises which contains more than two housing accommodations, and the housing accommodations or structure or premises are owned by two or more persons not constituting a cooperative corporation or association (husband and wife as owners being considered one owner for this purpose), no certificate can be issued under this section for occupancy of any housing accommodation in such structure or premises where two housing accommodations are already owner-occupied as a result of certificates of eviction issued pursuant to this Part or section 5 of the State Rent Act. The prohibition contained in this subdivision shall not apply where the coowners stand in the relationship of *immediate family* as defined in subdivision (a) of this section.

(c)(1) In the case of a housing accommodation in a structure or premises owned by a cooperative corporation or association, a certificate shall be issued by the administrator to a purchaser of stock where:

(i) the tenant originally obtained possession of the housing accommodation by virtue of a rental agreement with the tenant-owner;

(ii) the stock was acquired by the purchaser prior to July 1, 1955, and more than two years prior to the date of the filing of the application;

(iii) the stock was acquired by the purchaser on or after July 1, 1955, and more than two years have expired since the date of filing of the notice of sale with the district rent office, as hereinafter provided in subparagraph (3)(v) of this subdivision;

(iv) the stock was acquired less than two years prior to the date of filing of the application, and on that date stock in the cooperative has been purchased by persons who are tenant-owners of at least 80 percent of the housing accommodations in the structure or premises, and are entitled by reason of stock ownership to proprietary leases of housing accommodations in the structure or premises; or

(v) the cooperative was organized and acquired its title or leasehold interest in the structure or premises before February 17, 1945, and on that date stock in the cooperative allocated to 50 percent or more of the housing accommodations in the structure or premises was held by individual tenant-owners, who are or whose assignees or subtenants are in occupancy of such housing accommodations in the structure or premises at the date of the filing of the application.

(2) No certificate of eviction shall be issued under paragraph (1) of this subdivision, unless the applicant shall establish that he has complied with the requirements of subdivisions (a) and (d) of this section.

(3) No certificate of eviction shall be issued under paragraph (1) of this subdivision, except as provided in paragraph (4) hereof, unless the applicant shall also establish that the cooperative corporation or association has complied with the following requirements:

(i) On the date the cooperative plan was first presented to the tenants, each tenant in occupancy of a controlled housing accommodation in the premises was furnished with a copy of the plan and notified in writing that he had the exclusive right, for a period of 60 days, to purchase the stock allocated to his housing accommodation at the specified price, and that the plan would not be declared effective unless, on or before December 31, 1955, or within six months from the time the cooperative plan was presented to such tenants, whichever date is later, stock in the cooperative had been sold in good faith, without fraud or duress, and with no discriminatory repurchase agreement or other discriminatory inducement, to at least 35 percent of the tenants in occupancy of controlled housing accommodations at the time of the presentation of the plan. Housing accommodations vacant on the date the plan is presented, or subsequently vacated, shall not be included in the computation of the 35-percent requirement, except when the vacant housing accommodation is purchased for personal occupancy of a tenant of a controlled housing accommodation.

(ii) Subsequent to the date the cooperative plan had been declared effective, the tenants of the controlled housing accommodations had been served with a written notice that the plan had been declared effective, setting forth the terms of sale and the names of the tenants of the controlled housing accommodations who had purchased the stock allocated to their own housing accommodations or to vacant housing accommodations, and the names and addresses of other purchasers of vacant housing accommodations; and that the tenants of controlled housing accommodations who had not as yet purchased still had the exclusive right, for a period of 30 days from the date of service of the notice, to purchase the stock allocated to their housing accommodations on the terms previously offered to the tenants; except where:

(a) the cooperative plan had been declared effective prior to July 1, 1955;

(b) prior to that date the tenant of a controlled

housing accommodation in the premises had received written notice or notices that, for a period of not less than 30 days, he had the right to purchase the stock allocated to his housing accommodation at the price and terms specified in said plan;

(c) on July 1, 1955, such stock was held or was thereafter reacquired by the cooperative or by a sponsor, nominee of the cooperative or by any other person associated with the formulation of the plan; and

(d) such stock was offered, after July 1, 1955, for sale for personal occupancy at the same or different terms than previously offered to the tenant of such controlled housing accommodation, the latter was given a written notice of the offer to sell and the right, for a period of 30 days, to purchase the stock on the terms specified in such offer.

(iii) Within 10 days from the date of service of the notice provided by subparagraph (ii) of this paragraph, the cooperative had filed with the district rent office having jurisdiction at that time, either under the State Rent Act or under these regulations, as the case may be, a copy of the cooperative plan; a copy of the first notice served upon all tenants of controlled housing accommodations; a copy of notice required by subparagraph (ii) of this paragraph; and a statement duly verified by an officer of the cooperative and, where the sale was made on or after July 1, 1955, a statement duly verified by each purchaser, that the sale had been made in good faith pursuant to the terms set forth in the cooperative plan, without fraud or duress, and with no discriminatory repurchase agreement or other discriminatory inducement and whether for personal occupancy by the purchaser. A duplicate set of the above-specified papers shall also be kept available in the building for inspection by any tenant of controlled housing accommodations or his authorized representative.

(iv) In the event that the stock allocated to a controlled housing accommodation shall be offered for sale, by the cooperative, its sponsor, nominees or other persons associated with the formulation of the plan, to a purchaser in good faith for his personal occupancy at terms more favorable than those previously offered to the tenant of such controlled housing accommodation, the latter must first be given a written notice of the new terms and 15 days within which to elect to purchase stock at such new terms.

(v) Within 10 days after any sale or resale of stock subsequent to the effective date of the plan, all tenants who had not yet purchased had been served with written notices by the cooperative, setting forth the names and addresses of each of the purchasers, the designation of the housing accommodations and, in those cases where the stock had been sold for personal occupancy of the purchaser, the terms of the sales. Copies of these notices, together with proof of service upon each such tenant, must be filed with such district rent office, as the case may be, within five days of the date of service. Copies of these notices shall also be kept available in the building for inspection.

(4) Where the cooperative plan was declared effective prior to July 1, 1955, the administrator shall issue a certificate of eviction to a purchaser who acquired the stock prior to July 1, 1955 if he finds that the requirements of the former section 55(3) of the State Rent and Eviction Regulations, as in effect immediately prior to July 1, 1955, have been met and that the purchaser had served the tenant of the controlled housing accommodation, before December 31, 1955, with a written notice setting forth the name and address of the purchaser, designation of the housing accommodation and the terms of the sale. A copy of this notice, together with proof of service upon such tenant, must be filed with such district rent office within five days of the date of service. Where, however, stock allocated to a controlled housing accommodation occupied by a tenant has not in fact been sold, prior to July 1, 1955, to a purchaser in good faith for personal occupancy, no certificate of eviction shall be issued unless such tenant had been afforded the rights conferred by subparagraphs (3)(ii)-(v) of this subdivision. The cooperative must file all documents required by such subparagraphs

no later than December 31, 1955, or such later date as is applicable.

(5) As used herein, the term *tenant-owner* includes only:

(i) a person who purchased the stock allocated to a vacant housing accommodation; excluding, however, any housing accommodations which had been vacated after the filing of an application for a certificate of eviction or an order of subdivision, pursuant to these regulations, within the one-year period preceding the presentation of the cooperative plan to the tenants;

(ii) a person who, while he was a tenant in occupancy in the building, purchased the stock allocated to his housing accommodation;

(iii) a person who purchased the stock allocated to a housing accommodation which was occupied by a tenant who obtained his possession from said purchaser of the stock;

(iv) a person who purchased the stock allocated to a housing accommodation from an owner of such stock who was in occupancy of such housing accommodation; or

(v) a person who purchased the stock allocated to a housing accommodation while it was occupied by a tenant, and which thereafter became vacant after voluntary removal by the tenant.

(6) As used herein, the term *housing accommodation* shall not include servants' rooms which are nonhousekeeping and located in the service portion of the building, or apartments not subject to these regulations.

(7) As used herein, the term *stock* shall also include other evidence of interest in the cooperative corporation or association with the right to possession of a housing accommodation by virtue of a proprietary lease or otherwise.

(8) As used herein, the term *cooperative corporation or association* shall also include the sponsor of a cooperative plan.

(9) Where a cooperative plan, and any amendments thereof, presented to the tenants of controlled housing accommodations, is not declared effective and filed with

Rent Regulations

the district rent office, as the case may be, pursuant to subparagraphs (3)(ii) and (iii) of this subdivision, a period of 18 months from the date of the presentation of the first plan must elapse before another cooperative plan may be presented to the tenant of the structure.

(d) Where the landlord purchased and thereby acquired title to the premises on or after September 17, 1947, no certificate shall be issued under this section unless the landlord, on or before the date of the filing of the application, has made a payment or payments totaling at least 20 percent of the purchase price or the assessed valuation of the premises, whichever is the greater; provided, however, that where the administrator finds:

(1) that equivalent accommodations are available for rent into which the tenant can move without substantial hardship or loss; or

(2) that undue hardship would result to the landlord;

a certificate may be issued although less than 20 percent has been paid. The requirements of this subdivision shall not apply where the landlord is a former member of the Armed Forces of the United States of America who obtained a loan for use in purchasing housing accommodations guaranteed in whole or part by the Veterans Administration.

(e) *[Reserved]*

(f)(1) In the case of a housing accommodation or unit in a property submitted to the provisions of the Condominium Act, a certificate shall be issued to the unit owner where: (i) the tenant originally obtained possession by virtue of a rental agreement with the unit owner; (ii) more than two years have expired since the date of recording the deed of such unit to the applicant; or (iii) the date of recording of the deed of such unit to the applicant is less than two years prior to the date of filing of the application, and on that date units in such property have been purchased by persons who were tenants of at least 80 percent of the housing accommodations in the property on the date the declaration was duly recorded, who are or were assignees or tenants in occupancy of such housing accommodations or units in such property on the date of the filing of the application.

(2) No certificate of eviction shall be issued under paragraph (1) of this subdivision unless the applicant shall establish that he has complied with the requirements of subdivisions (a) and (d) of this section.

(3) No certificate of eviction shall be issued under paragraph (1) of this subdivision unless the applicant shall establish compliance with the following requirements:

(i) Within 60 days after the date of the recording of the declaration, an offering statement and offering plan shall be formally filed with the Department of Law of the State of New York, which shall comply with the requirements of the rules and regulations promulgated by the Attorney General of the State of New York, and with section 352-eeee of the General Business Law.

(ii) Within five days after the date of such formal filing of the offering statement and offering plan with the Department of Law of the State of New York, each tenant in occupancy of a controlled housing accommodation in the premises on the date of recording the declaration was:

(a) furnished with a copy of the declaration, any amendment or amendments thereof, and any other instrument required to be recorded under the provisions of sections 339-s and 339-u of the Condominium Act;

(b) furnished with a copy of the offering statement and offering plan; and

(c) notified in writing, by registered or certified mail, that:

(1) he has the exclusive right to purchase the unit occupied by him for a period of 60 days after the date of mailing such advice, or until such tenant shall remove from the accommodations, whichever date shall be earlier; and

(2) no public offering for the sale of any unit in the premises will be made until at least 35 percent of the tenants in occupancy on the date of recording the declaration have agreed to purchase the unit then occupied by the individual tenant.

Housing accommodations vacant on the date of recording the declaration, or subsequently vacated, shall not be included in the computation of the 35-percent requirement, except when the vacant housing accommodation is purchased for personal occupancy by a tenant of a controlled housing accommodation in the premises.

(iii) Within 30 days after at least 35 percent of the units in the premises have been sold in good faith, without fraud or duress, and with no discriminatory repurchase agreement or other discriminatory inducement, the tenants of all other controlled housing accommodations in the premises have been notified in writing, by registered or certified mail, that at least 35 percent of the tenants in occupancy have agreed to purchase the units occupied by them. Such notification shall separately state for each unit the name of the tenant who agreed to purchase, the unit identification and terms of the sale. With respect to vacant units, such notification shall separately state for each of such units the name and address of the purchaser, the unit identification and terms of the sale. Such notification shall also advise the tenants of controlled housing accommodations, who had not as yet purchased, that they still had the exclusive right, for a period of 30 days from the date of service of the notification, to purchase the unit on the previously offered terms.

(iv) Where such unit is offered for sale, after July 1, 1964, at more favorable terms than previously offered to the tenant of such controlled housing accommodations, the tenant shall be given a written notice, by registered or certified mail, of such offer and given the right for a period of 30 days after the date of the mailing of such notice to purchase such unit on the terms specified in such offer.

(v) Within 10 days from the date of mailing the notice required by subparagraph (iii) of this paragraph, the following shall be filed with the district rent office having jurisdiction:

(*a*) a copy of the offering statement and offering

plan, together with proof of filing with the Department of Law of the State of New York;

(b) a copy of the notices required by subparagraphs (ii), (iii) and (iv) of this paragraph; and

(c) a statement, duly verified by a party executing the declaration or an officer of such party where the declaration is made by a corporation, and further duly verified by each purchaser, that the purchase had been made in good faith pursuant to the terms set forth in the offering plan, without fraud or duress, and with no discriminatory repurchase agreement or other discriminatory inducement, and whether for personal occupancy by the purchaser. A duplicate set of above-specified papers shall also be kept available in the building for inspection by any tenant of controlled housing accommodations or his authorized representative.

(vi) In the event that a unit shall be offered for sale to purchaser in good faith for his personal occupancy while the tenant remains in occupancy, if such tenant was in occupancy on the date when the offering statement and offering plan were filed with the Department of Law of the State of New York, at terms more favorable than those previously offered to such tenant, the latter must first be given a written notice, by registered or certified mail, of the new terms and 15 days within which to elect to purchase the unit at such new terms.

(vii) Within 10 days after any sale or resale of any unit, all tenants who had not yet purchased had been served with written notices, by registered or certified mail, setting forth the names and addresses of each of the purchasers, the designation of the housing accommodations and, in those cases where the sale of the unit was for personal occupancy of the purchaser, the terms of the sale. Copies of these notices, together with proof of service upon each such tenant, must be filed with such district rent office within five days of the date of service. Copies of these notices shall also be kept available in the building for inspection.

(4) As used in paragraph (1) of this subdivision, the

term *purchased by persons who were tenants* includes only:

(i) a person who purchased a vacant unit or housing accommodation; excluding, however, any unit or housing accommodation which had become vacant after the filing of an application for a certificate of eviction or an order of subdivision pursuant to these regulations within the one-year period preceding the filing of the offering statement and offering plan with the Department of Law of the State of New York;

(ii) a person who, while he was a tenant in occupancy in the building, purchased the unit occupied by him;

(iii) a person who purchased a unit or housing accommodation which was occupied by a tenant who obtained his possession from the owner of the unit;

(iv) a person who purchased a unit from an owner of such unit who was in occupancy; or

(v) a person who purchased a unit while it was occupied by a tenant who thereafter voluntarily removed therefrom.

(5) As used herein, the term *housing accommodation* shall not include servants' rooms which are nonhousekeeping and located in the service portion of the building, or apartments not subject to these regulations; and the term *tenant* shall not include the persons occupying servants' rooms or apartments not subject to these regulations.

(6) Where an offering plan and offering statement which was presented to the tenants of controlled housing accommodations is not filed with the district rent office as required by clause (3)(v)(*a*) of this subdivision, or where at least 35 percent of the housing accommodations are not sold, within six months from the date of the formal filing of the offering statement and offering plan with the Department of Law of the State of New York, to tenants in occupancy on the date of recording the declaration, a period of 18 months from the date of such formal filing must elapse before another offering plan and offering statement may be presented to the tenants of the building. Where 35 percent of housing

accommodations are not sold to such tenants within such six-month period, the tenants who have not purchased shall be notified in writing, by registered or certified mail, that the offering statement and offering plan has been withdrawn because 35 percent of the tenants in occupancy have not agreed to purchase.

(7) Copies of all notices required by this subdivision to be served on the tenants shall be filed within five days of the date of mailing with the district rent office, together with proof of service upon the tenants.

(g) No certificate of eviction shall be issued under this section where the offering plan for conversion to cooperative or condominium ownership was accepted for filing by the Attorney General on or after July 21, 1982 in accordance with section 352-eeee of the General Business Law.

2204.6 Tenant not using premises for own dwelling. (a) A certificate shall be issued for the eviction of the tenant and subtenants where the landlord seeks in good faith to recover possession of housing accommodations for which the tenant's lease or other rental agreement has expired or otherwise terminated, and at the time of termination the occupants of the housing accommodation are subtenants or other persons who occupied under a rental agreement with the tenant, and no part of the accommodations is used by the tenant as his dwelling.

(b) No tenant shall be evicted under this section where the premises are operated as a rooming house and the eviction of the tenant will result in the removal of the furniture and furnishings used by the occupants, unless the landlord establishes that substantially similar furniture and furnishings will be provided at the time of the removal and that arrangements will be made for the occupants to remain in occupancy under substantially the same terms and conditions as those existing on the date of the issuance of the certificate.

(c) No occupant of housing accommodations, other than the tenant, shall be evicted under this section where the rental agreement between the landlord and tenant contemplated the subletting by the tenant of the entire accommodations or a substantial portion thereof or the portion occupied by the subtenant.

RENT REGULATIONS

(d) No occupant of housing accommodations shall be evicted under this section where the occupant is either the surviving spouse of the deceased tenant or some other member of the deceased tenant's family who has been living with the tenant.

2204.7 Alteration or remodeling. (a) A certificate or an order authorizing subdivision shall be issued where the landlord seeks in good faith to recover possession of a housing accommodation for the immediatee purpose of substantially altering or remodeling it, provided that the landlord shall have secured such approval therefor as is required by law, and the administrator determines that the issuance of the order granting the certificate of eviction is not inconsistent with the purpose of the Rent Law or these regulations. No certificate or order authorizing subdivision involving alteration or remodeling shall be granted under this section unless the administrator shall find that such alteration or remodeling is for the purpose of subdividing an under-occupied housing accommodation containing six or more rooms, exclusive of bathrooms and kitchen, into a greater number of housing accommodations consisting of self-contained family units which meet the requirements of section 2200.9 of this Title. An apartment may be deemed under-occupied when there is less than one occupant for each room, exclusive of bathrooms, kitchen and three additional rooms. Roomers or boarders who are not members of the tenant's family shall not be counted as occupants.

(b) Upon approval of plans by the city agency having jurisdiction thereof, where such approval is required, and before proceeding with such alteration or remodeling, application shall be made to the administrator for an order directing the tenant occupying such housing accommodation to remain in possession of an adequate portion thereof, as determined by the administrator, and to surrender possession of the remainder of said housing accommodation, with a time to be fixed by the administrator. Where it is not practicable for the tenant to remain in possession of a portion of the housing accommodation during the alteration, the administrator may require the landlord to furnish a suitable temporary housing accommodation to the tenant, not unreasonably distant from the premises being altered, and available at a rent not greater than the rent then being paid by the tenant, unless the tenant requests permanent relocation in his answer to the landlord's application. Unless the tenant requests permanent relocation, the order so granted shall be conditioned on the right of such tenant to first occupancy of any housing accommodation resulting from such alteration.

(c) Where the tenant has requested relocation as provided in subdivision (b) of this section, or where the tenant cannot be adequately housed in any portion of the housing accommodation after alteration, a certificate or order authorizing subdivision may only be issued on condition that the landlord comply with the relocation requirements of section 2204.4(e) of this Part. Such order shall also require the landlord to comply with the stipend requirements of subdivisions (e) and (f) of such section.

(d) The administrator shall establish the terms and conditions under which such alteration or remodeling may be made, and shall establish the maximum rent to be paid by the tenant occupying such suitable portion of such housing accommodation during the alteration, and shall establish the maximum rent to be paid by such tenant for the first occupancy of any housing accommodation selected by him in such subdivided housing accommodation after it has been altered or remodeled. The administrator shall, pursuant to section 2202.22(a) of this Title, establish the maximum rent on the basis of the maximum rents for comparable housing accommodations, after taking into consideration all other factors bearing on the equities involved. The landlord shall file an application under section 2200.9 of this Title for an order of decontrol; provided, however, that such order of decontrol shall not apply to that portion of the original housing accommodations occupied by a tenant in possession at the time of the conversion, but only so long as such tenant continues in occupancy.

(e) In the case of housing accommodations in a structure or premises owned by a cooperative corporation or association, where the landlord is the individual owner of stock allocated to a housing accommodation, no certificate or order shall be granted under this section unless the administrator shall also find that the landlord has met the requirements of section 2204.5(c) of this Part.

(f) The order in all such cases shall grant the landlord permission to recover possession of the housing accommodations without further application, should the tenant fail to abide by the order of subdivision issued by the administrator.

2204.8 Demolition. (a) Subject to the provisions of subdivision (b) of this section, a certificate shall be issued where the landlord seeks in good faith to recover possession of housing accommodations for the immediate purpose of demolishing them, provided that the landlord shall have secured such approval therefor as is required by law, and the administrator finds:

(1) that the demolition is to be made for the purpose of constructing a building or structure containing at least 20 percent more housing accommodations, consisting of self-contained family units (as defined in section 2200.9 of this Title), than there are apartments contained in the structure to be demolished, unless violations have been filed against the structure containing the housing accommodations, by city agencies having jurisdiction thereof, as a result of fire hazards or conditions dangerous or detrimental to life or health of the tenants, and the costs of removing such violations would substantially equal or exceed the assessed valuation of the structure. In the latter case, the new buildings or structures shall only be required to make provision for a greater number of self-contained family units than there are apartments contained in the structure to be demolished;

(2) that such demolition is to be made for the purpose of constructing other than housing accommodation; or

(3) that such demolition is to be made for the purpose of carrying out a program of clearance, replanning, reconstruction and neighborhood rehabilitation of substandard and unsanitary areas pursuant to and under the conditions imposed by article XV of the General Municipal Law, and the landlord is required to relocate tenants under the supervision of the New York City Division of Real Property or any other public agency having jurisdiction.

(b) Where application is made pursuant to either paragraph (1) or (2) of subdivision (a) of this section, an order granting a certificate of eviction may only be issued on condition that the landlord comply with the relocation requirements of section 2204.4(e) of this Part. Such order shall also require the landlord to comply with the stipend requirements of subdivisions (e) and (f) of such section.

2204.9 Withdrawal of occupied housing accommodations from rental market.

(a) A certificate shall be issued where the landlord establishes that he seeks in good faith permanently to withdraw occupied housing accommodations from both the housing and nonhousing markets, without any intent to rent or sell all or any part of the land or structure; and:

(1) that he requires the entire structure containing the housing accommodations or the land for his own immediate use in connection with a business which, at the time of the filing of the application for a certificate of eviction, he owns and operates in the immediate vicinity of the property in question;

(2) that substantial violations which constitute fire hazards or conditions dangerous or detrimental to the life or health of the tenants have been filed against the structure containing the housing accommodations, by city agencies having jurisdiction over such matters, and that the cost of removing such violations would substantially equal or exceed the assessed valuation of the structure;

(3) where the landlord is a hospital, convent, asylum, public institution, college, school or any institution operated exclusively for charitable or educational purposes on a nonprofit basis, that the landlord requires the housing accommodations or the land, or any part thereof, for its own immediate use in connection with its charitable, religious or educational purposes, provided that no certificate shall be issued for purposes of withdrawing accommodations for the immediate and personal use and occupancy as housing accommodations by employees, students or members of its staff; or

(4) that the continued operation of the housing ac-

commodations would impose other undue hardship upon the landlord.

(b) Where application is made pursuant to paragraphs (1) and (3) of subdivision (a) of this section, an order granting a certificate of eviction may only be issued on condition that the landlord comply with the relocation and stipend requirements of section 2204.4 of this Title.

PART 2205

PROHIBITIONS

Section 2205.1 General prohibitions. (a) It shall be unlawful, regardless of any contract, lease or other obligation heretofore entered into, for any person to demand or receive any rent for any housing accommodations in excess of the applicable maximum rent established therefor by the State Rent Commission or the Division of Housing and Community Renewal, or otherwise to do or omit to do any act, in violation of any regulation, order or requirement of such administration under the State Enabling Act or under the Rent Law, or to offer, solicit, attempt or agree to do any of the foregoing.

(b) It shall be unlawful for any person, with intent to cause any tenant to vacate housing accommodations, or to surrender or waive any rights of such tenant under the Rent Law or these regulations, to engage in any course of conduct (including but not limited to interruption or discontinuance of essential services) which interferes with or disturbs, or is intended to interfere with or disturb, the comfort, repose, peace or quiet of such tenant in his use or occupancy of the housing accommodations.

(c) The term *rent,* as defined in section 2200.2(k) of this Title, shall also include the payment by a tenant of a fee or rental commission to a landlord or to any person or real estate broker, where such person or real estate broker is an agent or employee of the landlord or is employed by the landlord in connection with the operation of the building, or where such person or real estate broker manages the building in which the housing accommodation is located, or where the landlord or his employee refers the tenant to such person or real estate broker for the purpose of renting the housing accommodation. Where the landlord has listed the housing accommodation with such person or real estate broker for rental purposes, such fact shall be prima facie evidence of the existence of an agency relationship between such other person or real estate broker and the landlord for the purposes of this section.

(d) It shall be unlawful for any person to make any statement or entry false in any material respect in any document or report submitted in any proceeding before the administrator, or required to be kept or filed under the Rent Law or any regulation, order or requirement thereunder, or to willfully omit or neglect to make any material statement or entry required to be made in any such document or report.

(e) It shall be unlawful for a landlord or a successor in interest to use housing accommodations, or the site on which same were located, for purposes other than that specified in the certificate of eviction.

2205.2 Evasion. The maximum rents and other requirements provided in these regulations shall not be evaded, either directly or indirectly, in connection with the renting or leasing or the transfer of a lease of housing accommodations by requiring the tenant to pay, or obligate himself for membership or other fees, or by modification of the practices relating to payment of commissions or other charges, or by modification of the services furnished or required to be furnished with the housing accommodations, or otherwise.

2205.3 Purchase of property as condition of renting. (a) No person shall require a tenant or prospective tenant to purchase or agree to purchase furniture or any other property as a condition of renting housing accommodations.

(b) The term *person* as used in this section shall include an agent or any other employee of a landlord, acting with or without the authority of his employer.

(c) The term *person* as used in this section shall also include a tenant in occupancy of housing accommodations who attempts to sell furniture or any other property to any incoming tenant.

2205.4 Term of occupancy. No tenant shall be required to change his term of occupancy; for example, a tenant on a monthly basis shall not be required to change to a weekly basis, and a tenant on a weekly basis shall not be required to change to a daily basis.

2205.5 Security deposits. Regardless of any contract, agreement, lease or other obligation heretofore or hereafter entered into, no person shall demand, receive or retain a security deposit for or in connection with the use and occupancy of housing accommodations, except:

(a) if the demand, collection or retention of such security deposit was permitted under the rent regulations promulgated pursuant to the Federal Act, the State Rent Law or the local laws of the City of New York, and said security deposit does not exceed the rent for one month in addition to the authorized collection or rent; or

(b) if the demand, collection or retention of such security deposit was pursuant to a rental agreement with the tenant, and said security deposit does not exceed the rent for one month (or for one week where the rental payment period is for a term of less than one month) in addition to the authorized collection of rent, provided in all cases:

(1) that said security deposit shall be deposited in a banking organization no later than July 15, 1960, or within 15 days after receipt thereof, whichever is later, which shall be placed in an interest-bearing account on or before October 1, 1974 or the date of any deposit made thereafter;

(2) the person depositing such security money shall be entitled to receive, as reimbursement for administrative expenses, a sum equivalent to one percent per annum upon the security money so deposited;

(3) the balance of the interest paid by the banking organization shall be held in trust until applied for the rental of the housing accommodations, or until paid to the tenant not less often than annually by check or cash;

and provided further, with respect to properties or building containing six or more family dwelling units, nothing set forth in this section shall be construed to relieve any person receiving or retaining any rent security deposit for or in connection with the use or occupancy of any dwelling unit therein from complying and continuing to comply with the requirements of article 7 of the General Obligations Law.

2205.6 Lease with option to buy. Where a lease of housing accommodations is entered into on or after May 1, 1962, and the tenant, as a part of such lease or in connection therewith, is granted an option to buy the housing accommodations which are the subject of the lease, the landlord, prior to the exercise by the tenant of the option to buy, shall not demand or receive, nor shall the tenant offer, payments in excess of the maximum rent, whether or not such lease allocates such portion or portions of the periodic payments therein provided for as payment on or for the option to buy.

2205.7 Disclosure by employees. It shall be unlawful for any officer or employee of the Division of Housing and Community Renewal, or for any official advisor or consultant to the Division of Housing and Community Renewal, to disclose, otherwise than in the course of official duty, any information obtained under the Rent Law, or to use any such information for personal benefit.

PART 2206

ENFORCEMENT

Section 2206.1 Criminal penalties. Any person who willfully violates any provision of section Y51-10.0 of the Rent Law shall be guilty of and punishable for a crime as specified in section 1(10) of the State Enabling Act, namely, such person shall be subject to a fine of not more than $5,000, or to imprisonment for not more than two years in the case of a violation of subdivision c of section Y51-10.0 of the Rent Law, and for not more than one year in all other cases, or to both such fine and imprisonment. The administrator may certify such facts, which in his opinion constitute such violation, to the district attorney having jurisdiction thereof.

2206.2 Injunctions. The administrator may, whenever in his judgment any person has engaged in or is about to engage in acts or practices which constitute or will constitute a violation of any provision of section Y51-10.0 of the Rent Law, apply to the Supreme Court for an order (a) enjoining such acts or practices, (b) enforcing compliance with such provision of said section or with an order issued by the administrator, or (c) directing the landlord to correct such violation of such provision; and upon sufficient showing, the Supreme Court may issue a temporary or permanent injunction, restraining order or other order, all of which shall be granted without bond. Jurisdiction shall not be deemed lacking in the Supreme Court because a defense is based upon order of an inferior court.

2206.3 Civil penalties. The administrator may, whenever any person has engaged in acts or practices which constitute a violation of any provision of section Y51-10.0 of the Rent Law or Part 2205 of this Title, or where more than six months have elapsed since the landlord's failure to use a certificate of eviction for the purpose for which it was issued, and either the administrator has not waived such failure to use such certificate for the designated purpose or the tenant has not commenced civil action against the landlord as provided in section 2206.7 of this Part, impose a civil penalty by order after a hearing by reason of such violation and bring an action to recover same in any court of competent jurisdiction. Such penalty, in the case of a violation of subdivision d of section Y51-10.0 of the Rent Law or section 2206.5 of this Part, shall be in the amount of $500 for a first such offense and $1,000 for each subsequent offense or, for a violation consisting of conduct directed at the tenants of more than one housing accommodation, and in the case of any other violation of such provisions of the Rent Law or these regulations, in the amount of $100 for the first offense and $500 for each subsequent offense. Such order shall be deemed a final determination for the purposes of judicial review as provided in section Y51-9.0 of the Rent Law and section 2208.12 of this Title. Such action shall be brought on behalf of the city, and any amount recovered shall be paid into the city treasury. Such right of action may be released, compromised or adjusted by the administrator at any time subsequent to the issuance of such administrative order.

2206.4 Civil action by administrator. The administrator may, whenever in his judgment any person has engaged in acts or practices which constitute a violation of any provision of section Y51-10.0 of the Rent Law, commence an action to recover damages, as provided for in section 2206.8 of this Part, in the event that (a) the tenant has not previously commenced such an action as therein provided, and (b) more than six months have elapsed since the occurrence of the violation or issuance of the order. An action instituted by the administrator shall constitute a bar to an action by the person aggrieved. The administrator shall pay over one half of the sum recovered in such action to the person aggrieved and one half to the city treasury, exclusive of costs and disbursements.

2206.5 Finding of harassment. (a) The administrator may, subject to the provisions of subdivision (c) of this section, make a finding of harassment whenever he determines the existence of a violation of section 2205.1(b) of this Title (section Y51-10.0d of the Rent Law), in which event the administrator may:

(1) dismiss any pending application for a certificate of eviction, and grant any subsequent application for such certificate only upon such terms and conditions as he deems necessary to prevent the circumvention or evasion of provisions of this Title;

(2) determine that such housing accommodations or any replacement or subdivision thereof (whether or not by demolition, alteration or substantial rehabilitation) shall constitute housing accommodations subject to control under these regulations, notwithstanding any definition of that term to the contrary; and

(3) refuse to credit any adjustments increasing rent mandated by Part 2202 of this Title (section Y51-5.0 of the Rent Law), and dismiss any application for an adjustment pursuant to said section for such time and under such terms and conditions as the Division of Housing and Community Renewal deems necessary to prevent circumvention or evasion of the Rent Law and these regulations.

(b) After a landlord has evidenced an intent to cause a

building, or individual housing accommodation therein, to become or to remain vacant, or has certified his intention to alter or demolish a structure pursuant to section 2203.10 of this Title, a failure to secure vacant housing accommodations in said premises, or public portions of said premises, or a decrease, discontinuance, interruption or interference with or of any of the following services at said premises, shall constitute presumptive evidence of intent and conduct in violation of section 2205.1(b) of this Title:

(1) garbage collection;

(2) elevator service;

(3) heat during that part of the year when same is required by law;

(4) hot or cold water;

(5) superintendent;

(6) front or entrance door security systems, including but not exclusive of lock and buzzer; and

(7) gas, electricity and other utility services to either public or private areas.

(c) Where the administrator makes a finding of harassment with respect to housing accommodations in which the affected tenant or tenants have not vacated, the landlord may, no sooner than one year after such harassment order is issued, apply for an order terminating such finding by submitting affirmative proof that the proscribed course of conduct has not been engaged in since the issuance of such order. In the event the tenant or tenants of housing accommodations affected by such order vacate at any time after the commencement of the harassment proceeding, the landlord may, no sooner than two years after the issuance of such order, apply for an order terminating the finding of harassment by submitting affirmative proof of the voluntary surrender of the vacated housing accommodation by the tenants in occupancy when the harassment order was issued and the discontinuance of the proscribed course of conduct from the date of such order.

(d) No proceeding to determine whether housing accommodations have become vacant as a result of harassment may be commenced later than 30 days after the entire structure shall have been vacated, unless the landlord failed to certify his intent to alter or demolish the premises as provided in section 2203.10 of this Title, or has used the housing accommodation or the site for purposes other than those specified in a certificate of eviction as provided in section 2205.1(e) of this Title. No proceeding shall be maintained for acts performed in good faith and in a reasonable manner for the purposes of operating, maintaining or repairing any building or part thereof. A finding of harassment shall be attached to and noted upon the registration of the housing accommodations affected by such findings, and a copy thereof shall be filed and docketed in the manner of a notice of mechanic's lien affecting the property. The provisions of this subdivision shall bind all persons or parties who succeed to the landlord's interest in said housing accommodations.

(e) The administrator may make a finding of harassment whenever he determines the existence of conditions which bar decontrol otherwise permitted pursuant to provisions of section 2200.2(f)(17) of this Title. A decrease, discontinuance, interruption or interference with any essential service, resulting in an order decreasing the maximum legal rent for a housing accommodation pursuant to section 2202.16 or 2202.17 of this Title, shall constitute presumptive evidence of intent and conduct constituting harassment. Housing accommodations affected by an order decreasing the maximum legal rent, pursuant to section 2202.16 or 2202.17 of this Title, shall not be decontrolled pursuant to section 2200.2(f)(17) unless the landlord obtains an order either restoring the rent previously reduced pursuant to section 2202.4(a) or terminating the presumptive finding of harassment as provided for in subdivision (c) of this section without regard to the time limitation therein contained.

2206.6 Revocation of orders. (a) The administrator may revoke any order or determination based upon any statement or entry false in any material respect in any document or report submitted in any proceeding before the Division of Housing and Community Renewal, or required to be kept or filed under the Rent Law or these regulations or any requirements thereunder.

(b) Where after the State Rent Commission or the

administrator has granted a certificate of eviction and a tenant voluntarily removes from a housing accommodation, or has been removed therefrom by action or proceeding to evict from or recover possession of a housing accommodation, and the landlord or any successor landlord of the premises does not use the housing accommodation for the purpose specified in such certificate of eviction, the vacated accommodation or any replacement or subdivision thereof shall, unless the administrator approves such different purpose, be deemed a housing accommodation subject to control, notwithstanding any definition of that term in these regulations to the contrary. Such approval shall be granted whenever the administrator finds that the failure or omission to use the housing accommodation for the purpose specified in such certificate was not inconsistent with the purposes of the Rent Law and these regulations, and would not be likely to result in the circumvention or evasion thereof.

2206.7 Civil action by tenant where landlord fails to use certificate of eviction for purposes specified therein. Where after the administrator has granted a certificate of eviction authorizing the landlord to pursue his remedies pursuant to law to acquire possession, and a tenant voluntarily removes from a housing accommodation or has been removed therefrom by action or proceeding to evict from or recover possession of a housing accommodation upon the ground that the landlord seeks in good faith to recover possession:

(a) for his immediate and personal use, or for the immediate and personal use by a member or members of his immediate family, and such landlord or members of his immediate family shall fail to occupy such accommodation within 30 days after the tenant vacates;

(b) for the immediate purpose of withdrawing such housing accommodation from the rental market, and such landlord shall lease or sell the housing accommodation or the space previously occupied thereby, or permit use thereof in a manner other than contemplated in such eviction certificate within a period of one year after such removal of the tenant;

(c) for the immediate purpose of altering or remodeling

such housing accommodation, and the landlord (who required possession for the purpose of effecting such alteration or remodeling) shall fail to start the work of alteration or remodeling of such housing accommodation within 90 days after the removal of the last tenant whose removal is necessary to enable the landlord to effect such alteration or remodeling of such accommodation or, if after having commenced such work, shall fail or neglect to prosecute the work with reasonable diligence;

(d) for the immediate purpose of demolishing such housing accommodations and constructing a new building in accordance with approved plans, or reasonable amendment thereof, and the landlord has failed to complete the demolition within six months after the removal of the last tenant or, having demolished the premises, has failed or neglected to proceed with the new construction within 90 days after the completion of such demolition or, having commenced such construction work, has failed or neglected to prosecute such work with reasonable diligence; or

(e) for some purpose other than those specified above for which the removal of the tenant was sought and the landlord has failed to use the vacated premises for such purposes; such landlord shall, unless for good cause shown, be liable to the tenant for three times the damages sustained on account of such removal, plus reasonable attorney's fees and costs as determined by the court, provided the tenant commences such action within three years from the expiration of the applicable time period as set forth in this section. The damages sustained by the tenant under this section shall be the difference between the rent paid for the housing accommodation from which the tenant was evicted and the rental value of a comparable housing accommodation on the open market. In addition to any other damage, the cost of removal of the tenant's property shall be a lawful measure of damages. The remedy herein provided for shall be in addition to those provided for in any other section of these regulations. Such acts and omissions on the part of a landlord after issuance of a certificate of eviction are hereby declared to be inconsistent with the purposes for which such certificate of eviction was issued.

2206.8 Civil action by tenant. (a) A tenant may bring an action against his landlord, in any court of competent jurisdiction, for a violation of subdivision a of section Y51-10.0 of the Rent Law:

(1) within two years from the date of occurrence of an *overcharge,* defined to mean the amount by which the consideration paid by a tenant to a landlord exceeds the applicable maximum rent;

(2) within one year after the landlord fails to pay a refund as ordered by the Division of Housing and Community Renewal, such time to be calculated from 33 days after the date of the issuance of the order or when the order becomes final, whichever is later; or

(3) in the case of an act proscribed by subdivision e of section Y51-10.0 of the Rent Law, within two years after knowledge of such statement or omission and consequent violation has been made known to the tenant or to the Division of Housing and Community Renewal.

(b) The landlord shall be liable for reasonable attorney's fees and costs, as determined by the court, plus whichever of the following sums is the greater:

(1) such amount, not more than three times the amount of the overcharge or overcharges upon which the action is based, as the court in its discretion may determine; or

(2) an amount not less than $25; provided, however, that such amount shall be the amount of the overcharge or overcharges, or $25, whichever is greater;

if the defendant proves that the violation of the regulation or order in question was neither willful nor the result of failure to take practicable precautions against the occurrence of the violation.

2206.9 Civil action by tenant for unlawful eviction or for surrender of possession as result of harassment. (a) A tenant or occupant who is unlawfully removed by a landlord from any housing accommodation may, within two years from the date of the occurrence, bring a civil action against the landlord by reason of such unlawful removal. In such action, the landlord shall be liable to the tenant for three times the damages sustained on account of such removal, plus reasonable attorney's fees and costs as determined by the court. The damages sustained by the tenant under this subdivision shall be the difference between the rent paid for the housing accommodation from which the tenant was evicted and the rental value of a comparable housing accommodation on the open market. In addition to any other damage, the cost of removal of the tenant's property shall be a lawful measure of damages.

(b) Any tenant who has vacated his housing accommodations, because the landlord or any person acting on his behalf, with intent to cause the tenant to vacate, engaged in any course of conduct (including but not limited to interruption or discontinuance of essential services) which interfered with or disturbed, or was intended to interfere with or disturb, the comfort, repose, peace or quiet of the tenant in his use and occupancy of the housing accommodations, may, within 90 days after vacating, apply to the administrator for a determination that the housing accommodations were vacated as a result of such conduct and, within one year after determination of such fact by the administrator as provided in section 2206.5(e) of this Part, institute a civil action against the landlord by reason of such conduct. In such action the landlord shall be liable to the tenant for three times the damages sustained on account of such conduct, plus reasonable attorney's fees and costs as determined by the court. The damages sustained by the tenant under this subdivision shall be the difference between the rent paid for the housing accommodation from which the tenant was evicted and the rental value of a comparable housing accommodation on the open market. In addition to any other damages, the cost of removal of the tenant's property shall be a lawful measure of damages.

2206.10 Miscellaneous provisions. (a) Any court shall advance on the docket or otherwise expedite the disposition of any action or proceeding brought before it under subdivision 10 of section 1 of the State Enabling Act.

(b) Except as otherwise provided therein, the provisions of sections 2206.2 through 2206.9 of this Part are cumulative. The enforcement of one provision herein shall not constitute a bar to the enforcement by action, proceeding or by making a finding or determination pursuant to other provisions of these regulations.

(c) The administrator may direct that a refund payment to the tenant, for rent collected in violation of subdivision a of section Y51-10.0 of the Rent Law, include interest from the date of each excessive payment of rent. Where the administrator has revoked an order or determination premised on a false statement or entry, he may withhold issuance of an order granting increase in maximum rent for such housing accommodations until the landlord has complied with the refund directive, if any, provided for in such order of revocation.

(d) No person (including but not limited to any officer or employee of the Division of Housing and Community Renewal) shall be held liable for damages or penalties in any court, on any grounds for or in respect of anything done or omitted to be done in good faith pursuant to any provision of the State Rent Act or the Rent Law, or any regulation, order or requirement thereunder, notwithstanding that subsequently such provision, regulation, order or requirement may be modified, rescinded, or determined to be invalid. In any action or proceeding wherein a party relies for ground of relief or defense or raises issue or brings into question the construction or validity of any provision of the Rent Law, or any regulation, order or requirement thereunder, the court having jurisdiction of such action or proceeding may at any stage certify such fact to the Division of Housing and Community Renewal. The administrator may intervene in any such action or proceeding.

2206.11 Inspection and records. (a) Any person who rents or offers for rent or acts as a broker or agent for the rental of any housing accommodations shall, as the administrator may from time to time require, furnish information under oath or affirmation or otherwise, permit inspection and copying of records and other documents, and permit inspection of any such housing accommodations.

(b) Any person who rents or offers for rent, or acts as a broker or agent for the rental of any housing accommodations, shall, as the administrator may from time to time require, make and keep records and other documents and make reports.

PART 2207

PROCEEDINGS BEFORE DISTRICT RENT ADMINISTRATOR

Section 2207.1 Proceedings instituted by landlord or tenant in district rent office.

A proceeding is instituted in a district rent office by a landlord or a tenant with the filing of an application for adjustment of rent, for a certificate of eviction, or for other relief provided by the Rent Law or these regulations. Such application shall be verified by the applicant and filed with the district rent administrator for the district within which the housing accommodation is located, upon the appropriate form issued by the administrator in accordance with the instructions contained in such forms.

2207.2 Proceedings instituted by district rent administrator on his own initiative.

The district rent administrator may institute a proceeding on his own initiative whenever he deems it necessary or appropriate pursuant to the Rent Law or these regulations.

2207.3 Notice to parties affected. (a) Where the application is made by a landlord or tenant, the district rent administrator shall forward, as promptly as possible, a copy of such application by mail to the person or persons affected thereby.

(b) Where the proceeding is instituted by the district rent administrator on his own initiative, he shall forward to all parties affected thereby a notice setting forth the proposed action.

2207.4 Answer. A person who has been served with a copy of an application or a notice of a proceeding shall have seven days from the date of mailing within which to answer, except as otherwise provided in this section. Where the application was made pursuant to section 2202.8 of this Title, a tenant shall have 15 days from the date of mailing within which to answer. Where a proceeding is commenced by the issuance of an order to show cause by the district rent administrator, a person who has been served with a copy of such order to show cause shall file his answer within the period specified in such order to show cause. Every answer must be affirmed, and an original and one copy shall be filed with the district rent administrator.

2207.5 Action by district rent administrator. At any stage of a proceeding, the district rent administrator may:

(a) reject the application if it is insufficient or defective;

(b) make such investigation of the facts, hold such conferences, and require the filing of such reports, evidence, affidavits or other material relevant to the proceeding, as he may deem necessary or appropriate;

(c) forward to or make available for inspection by either party any relevant evidence, and afford an opportunity to file rebuttal thereto;

(d) for good cause shown, accept for filing any papers, even though not filed within the time required by these regulations;

(e) require any person to appear or produce documents, or both, pursuant to a subpoena issued by the administrator;

(f) consolidate two or more applications or proceedings which have at least one ground in common;

(g) forward to either party a notice of action proposed to be taken by the district rent administrator;

(h) grant or order a hearing, except that no multiple-tenant-initiated proceedings for reduction of rents in a building may be determined without a hearing, unless such hearing is waived:

(1) by the landlord by reason of his failure to request same at the time of his answer; or

(2) by the tenants by reason of their failure to request same at the time they reply to the landlord's answer.

2207.6 Final determination by district rent administrator. The district rent administrator, on such terms and conditions as he may determine, may:

(a) dismiss the application if it fails substantially to comply with the provisions of the Rent Law or these regulations;

(b) grant or deny the application, in whole or in part; or

(c) issue an appropriate order in a proceeding instituted on his own initiative.

A copy of any order issued shall be forwarded to all parties to the proceeding.

2207.7 Pending proceedings. (a) Any matter, application, proceeding or protest, undertaken, filed or commenced by, with or before the State Rent Commission, and transferred to the administrator as provided by section 1(11) and (13) of the State Enabling Act and sections Y51-14.0 and Y51-15.0 of the Rent Law, shall be completed or determined by the administrator in conformity with these regulations; except that, where any application for a rent increase pursuant to section 4(4)(a)(1) of the State Rent Act is transferred to the administrator for determination:

(1) such application, solely for the purpose of applying thereto section 2202.8(c) of this Title, shall be treated as if it were sought to be filed on May 1, 1962, provided that if the two-year minimum period prescribed by such section terminates on any date between May 1, 1962 and September 1, 1962, both dates inclusive, the administrator, notwithstanding any other provisions of these regulations, shall treat such application, solely for the purpose of applying such section thereto, as having been filed on the date next succeeding such date of termination, and shall withhold determination of such application until the next succeeding date; and

(2) any such application shall be denied unless the landlord shall file with the administrator, on or before May 31, 1962, a certificate of the Department of Buildings and a certification by the landlord setting forth with respect to the property the matters specified in section 2202.3(b) of this Title.

(b) Where a regulation is amended during the pendency of a proceeding before the district rent administrator, the determination shall be in accordance with the amended regulation.

2207.8 Modification or revocation of orders. (a) Except as provided in subdivision (b) or (c) of this section, or except pursuant to an order of remand issued by the administrator, the district rent administrator or the authorized supervisor of any component of the Division of Housing and Community Renewal may not modify, supersede or revoke any order issued under these or previous regulations unless he finds that such order was the result of illegality, irregularity in vital matters, or fraud, or unless he shall make such finding as is required by subdivision (c) of section 2202.20 of this Title. Where an order is modified, superseded or revoked by the district rent administrator, he may also direct that rent collected by the landlord in excess of the maximum rent be refunded to the tenant, together with six percent interest from the date of each such excessive payment of rent, within 30 days after his action shall become final. Where a rent exemption order issued pursuant to section 2202.20 of this Title is revoked as provided by section 2202.20(h)(2) or (3), such revocation order may also direct the payment of back rent.

(b) The district rent administrator, on his initiative or on application of a tenant, may revoke or cancel an order granting a certificate of eviction (whether issued by the State Rent Commission or under these regulations) at any time prior to the execution of a warrant in a summary proceeding to recover possession of real property by a court, whenever he finds that:

(1) the certificate of eviction was obtained by fraud or illegality; or

(2) the landlord's intentions or circumstances have so changed that the premises, possession of which is sought, will not be used for the purpose specified in the certificate.

(c) The district rent administrator, on his own initiative or on application of a tenant, may revoke or cancel an order granting a certificate of eviction where:

(1) the payment of a stipend is required or is imposed as a condition in an order granting a certificate of eviction pursuant to any section of these regulations and the landlord has willfully failed either to:

(i) pay the prescribed stipend to all tenants in the building who have voluntarily vacated their housing accommodations after the date of filing of the application; or

(ii) deposit the prescribed stipend in escrow, as provided in subdivision (f) of section 2204.4 of this Title, and file proof of compliance with the requirements of such subdivision with the district rent administrator no later than five days prior to the expiration of the waiting period; or

(2) after the issuance of any order granting a certificate of eviction where relocation or the payment of a stipend is required, the landlord willfully engages in a course of conduct which is proscribed by subdivision (b) of section 2205.1 of this Title.

(d) The district rent administrator, on his own initiative or on application of a tenant, may revoke or cancel an order granting a certificate of eviction (whether issued by the State Rent Commission or under these regulations) at any time prior to the date of the issuance of a final order in a summary proceeding to recover possession of real property by a court, whenever he finds that there has been a change of circumstances due to the fact that other suitable housing accommodations subject to the landlord's control have become vacant since the date of the order granting the certificate of eviction.

(e) The commencement of a proceeding by the district rent administrator to revoke or cancel an order granting a certificate of eviction shall stay such order until the final determination of the proceeding, regardless of whether the waiting period in the order has already expired.

(f) The district rent administrator, or the authorized supervisor of any component of the Division of Housing and Community Renewal, shall give notice to the persons affected of his intention to modify, supersede or revoke an order issued by him, in which event the provisions of sections 2207.2 through 2207.6, inclusive, of this Part shall apply.

(g) Whenever the administrator shall have revoked an order premised on fraudulent or materially false representations, the administrator, notwithstanding any other provision of these regulations to the contrary, may withhold the issuance of any order granting an increase in maximum rent for such housing accommodation until the landlord has complied with the refund directive, if any, provided for in such order of revocation.

PART 2208

ADMINISTRATIVE REVIEW

2208.1 Persons who may file a petition for administrative review (PAR). (a) Any person aggrieved by these regulations, or by an order issued by a district rent administrator, may file a PAR with the administrator in the manner provided in these regulations.

(b) A joint PAR, affirmed by each person joining therein, may be filed by two or more landlords or tenants, where at least one ground is common to all persons so filing. The administrator, in his discretion, may treat such PAR as joint or several.

(c) The administrator may, in his discretion, consolidate two or more PAR's which have at least one ground in common.

2208.2 Time for filing a PAR. (a) A PAR against any provision of these regulations may be filed at any time after the effective date thereof.

(b) A PAR against an order of a district rent administrator must be filed with the administrator within 33 days after the date such order is issued, unless subdivision (c) of this section is applicable. A PAR served by mail, postmarked not more than 33 days after the date of such order, shall be deemed compliance with this paragraph.

(c) Where a certificate of eviction has been granted pursuant to section 2204.5 of this Title, a PAR may be filed by a tenant after the expiration of the 33-day period provided for in subdivision (b) of this section, and prior to the date of the issuance of a final order in a summary proceeding to recover possession of real property by a court, where there has been a change of circumstances due to the fact that other suitable housing accommodations subject to the landlord's control have become vacant since the date of the order granting the certificate of eviction.

2208.3 Form and content of a PAR against these regulations or portion thereof. No printed form of a PAR is provided or prescribed. Each PAR against these regulations or portion thereof must be clearly designated "Petition for Administrative Review to the Commissioner of the Division of Housing and Community Renewal re: Section _____ (or Sections _____) of the Rent and Eviction Regulations of the City of New York," and shall set forth the following:

(a) the name and post-office address of the party filing the PAR, and whether he is a landlord or tenant, or representative;

(b) a complete identification of the provision or provisions for which the PAR is being filed, citing the section or sections or these regulations to which the objection is made;

(c) a simple, concise statement of the objections to these regulations or portion(s) thereof; and

(d) a specific statement of the relief requested.

Each PAR shall be affirmed by the party filing the PAR.

2208.4 Form and content of a PAR against an order of the district rent administrator. A person aggrieved by an order issued by the district rent administrator may file a PAR against such order only on a form prescribed by the administrator.

2208.5 Service and filing of a PAR. (a) Each PAR shall be filed in an original and one copy at the Division of Housing and Community Renewal, Office of Rent Administration, 10 Columbus Circle, New York, NY 10019, unless otherwise provided on the form prescribed by the administrator for such PAR.

(b) Where the PAR is against an order issued by the district rent administrator, a copy of the PAR shall also be served on the district rent administrator issuing the order and upon each party affected by the PAR.

(c) A PAR under section 2208.4 of this Part will not be accepted for filing unless accompanied by an affidavit or other proof of such service.

2208.6 Time of filing answer to a PAR. Any person served with a PAR, as provided in section 2208.5 of this Part, may, within 15 days from the date of service, file an affirmed answer thereto by filing the same with the Division of Housing and Community Renewal, Office of Rent Administration, together with proof of service of a copy thereof upon the party filing the PAR. The administrator may, in his discretion and for good cause shown, extend the time within which to answer.

2208.7 Action by administrator. Within a reasonable time after the filing of the PAR and the answers, if any, the administrator may:

(a) reject the PAR if it is insufficient or defective;

(b) make such investigation of the facts, hold such conferences, and require the filing of such reports, evidence, affidavits, or other material relevant to the proceeding, as he may deem necessary or appropriate;

(c) forward to or make available for inspection by either party any relevant evidence, and afford an opportunity to file rebuttal thereto;

(d) for good cause shown, accept for filing any papers, even though not filed within the time required by these regulations;

(e) require any person to appear or produce documents, or both, pursuant to a subpoena issued by the administrator; and

(f) grant or order a hearing.

2208.8 Final determination by administrator. The administrator, on such terms and conditions as he may determine, may:

(a) dismiss the PAR if it fails substantially to comply with the provisions of the Rent Law or these regulations; or

(b) grant or deny the PAR, in whole or in part, or remand the proceeding to the district rent administrator for further action.

In the event that the administrator grants or denies any such PAR, in whole or in part, the administrator shall inform the party or parties filing the PAR of the grounds upon which such decision is based, and of any economic data and other facts of which the administrator has taken official notice.

2208.9 Pending PAR's. Where a regulation is amended during the pendency of a PAR, the determination shall be in accordance with the amended regulation.

2208.10 Time within which administrator shall take final action. (a) If the administrator does not act finally within a period of 90 days after a PAR is filed, or within such extended period as may be fixed by the administrator, the PAR shall be deemed to be denied. The administrator may, however, grant one such extension, not to exceed 30 days, with the consent of the party filing the PAR; any further extension may only be granted with the consent of all parties to the PAR. Final action on a PAR filed against a regulation shall be governed by section 204 of the State Administrative Procedure Act.

2208.11 Stays. (a) The filing of a PAR against an order, other than an order adusting, fixing or establishing a maximum rent, within 33 days after the date of the issuance of such order, shall stay such order until the final determination of the PAR by the administrator. However, nothing herein contained shall limit the administrator from granting or vacating a stay under appropriate circumstances. Where the PAR is against an order granting a certificate of eviction, it shall stay such order as herein provided, regardless of whether the waiting period provided in the order has already expired.

(b) The commencement of a proceeding by the administrator to revoke or cancel an order granting a certificate of eviction shall stay such order until the final determination of the proceeding, regardless of whether the waiting period in the order has already expired.

2208.12 Judicial review. The filing and determination of a PAR is a prerequisite to obtaining judicial review of any provision of these regulations or any order issued thereunder, except as provided by section Y51-8.0 of the Rent Law. A proceeding for review may be instituted under article 78 of the Civil Practice Law and Rules, provided the petition in the Supreme Court is filed within 60 days after the final determination of the order. Service of the petition upon the Division of Housing and Community Renewal shall be made by leaving a copy thereof with the counsel's office at the division's principal office.

2208.13 Modification or revocation of orders on a PAR. (a) The administrator, or application of either party or on his own initiative, and upon notice to all parties affected, may, prior to the date that a proceeding for judicial review has been commenced in the Supreme Court, pursuant to article 78 of the Civil Practice Law and Rules, modify, supersede or revoke any order issued by him under these or previous regulations where he finds that such order was the result of illegality, irregularity in vital matters, or fraud. Where an order is modified, superseded or revoked by the administrator, he may also direct that appropriate rent adjustments be made in accordance with the order issued.

(b) Whenever the administrator shall have revoked an order premised on fraudulent or materially false representations, the administrator, notwithstanding any other provision of these regulations to the contrary, may withhold the issuance of any order granting an increase in maximum rent for such housing accommodation until the landlord has complied with the refund directive, if any, provided for in such order of revocation.

PART 2209

MISCELLANEOUS PROCEDURAL MATTERS

2209.1 When a notice or paper shall be deemed served. (a) Notices, orders, petitions for administrative review, answers and other papers may be served personally or by mail. When service is made personally or by mail, an affidavit by the person making the service or mailing shall constitute sufficient proof of service. When service is by registered or certified mail, the return post-office receipt shall constitute sufficient proof of service.

(b) In any proceedings under these regulations, any notice, order or other process or paper directed to the person named as landlord on the registration statement on file in the district rent office, at the mailing address given thereon, or where a notice of change of identity has been filed in the district rent office, at the mailing address given thereon, or where a notice of address given in such notice of change of identity most recently filed, shall constitute notice to such landlord.

(c) Where a notice of appearance has been filed by an attorney, service on the attorney shall be deemed proper service as if made on the party or parties represented.

2209.2 Power of subpoena. The administrator, or any officer or agent designated by the administrator, may administer oaths and affirmations and may, whenever necessary, by subpoena require any person to appear and testify, or to appear and produce documents, or both, at any designated place. Any person subpoenaed under this section shall have the right to make a record of his testimony and to be represented by counsel.

2209.3 Production of documents. The production of a person's documents at any place other than his place of business shall not be required in any case in which, prior to the return date specified in the subpoena issued with respect thereto, such person either has furnished the administrator with a copy of such documents, certified by such person under oath to be a true and correct copy, or has entered into a stipulation with the administrator as to the information contained in such documents.

2209.4 Action by administrator on failure to obey subpoena. In case of contumacy or refusal to obey a subpoena served upon any person, the Supreme Court, in or for any judicial district in which such person is found or resides or transacts business, upon application by the administrator, shall have jurisdiction to issue an order requiring such person to appear and give testimony or to appear and produce documents, or both; and any failure to obey such order of the court may be punished by such court as a contempt thereof.

2209.5 Privilege against self-incrimination. No person shall be excused from attending and testifying or from producing documents or other evidence in obedience to the subpoena of the administrator, or of any duly authorized officer or agent thereof, on the ground that the testimony or evidence required of him may tend to incriminate him or subject him to a penalty or forfeiture, but no person shall be prosecuted or subjected to any penalty or forfeiture for or on account of any transaction, matter or thing concerning which he is compelled, after having claimed his privilege against self-incrimination, to testify or produce evidence; except that such person so testifying shall not be exempt from prosecution and punishment for perjury committed in so testifying. The immunity herein provided shall extend only to natural persons so compelled to testify.

2209.6 Disclosure of information by the administrator. The administrator shall not publish or disclose any information obtained under the Rent Law or these regulations that the administrator deems confidential, or with reference to which a request for confidential treatment is made by the person furnishing such information, unless the administrator determines that the withholding thereof is contrary to the public interest.

2209.7 Delegation of authority. The administrator may delegate in writing, to the district rent administrator or any other person or persons, the authority to carry out any of the duties and powers granted to him by the Rent Law or these regulations.

2209.8 Opinions and official interpretations. (a) Official interpretations of general applicability with respect to the provisions of the Rent Law or these regulations shall be issued only by the administrator. No interpretation shall be given in response to any hypothetical question.

(b) Any person desiring an opinion, as to the applicability of the Rent Law or these regulations to a specific factual situation, shall make a request in writing for such opinion to the district rent administrator for the locality within which the housing accommodations involved are situated. Such request shall set forth in full the facts out of which the question arises, and shall state the name and post-office address of the person or persons making the request and the location of the housing accommodations involved. If there is a pending or closed proceeding in the particular office, or if the inquirer has previously requested an opinion of the same or substantially the same facts, his request shall so indicate. No opinion shall be given in response to any hypothetical question.

(c) Any opinion or official interpretation shall remain in full force and effect unless and until revoked or modified in writing by the official issuing it or by the administrator.

2209.9 Administrative proceedings pending before Department of Housing Preservation and Development of the City of New York. (a) Any matter, application, proceeding or protest undertaken, filed or commenced by, with or before the city, relating to the regulation and control of residential rents and evictions within the city and pending on April 1, 1984, shall be transferred to, conducted by, and completed or determined by the administrator. In discharging such responsibilities, the administrator shall act and shall determine and complete any such matter, application, proceeding or protest pursuant to and in conformity with the provisions of the Rent Law and these regulations governing such matters, applications, proceedings or protests.

(b) Any protest filed against an order of the city which may be undetermined on March 31, 1984 shall, for the purposes of section 2208.10(a) of this Title, be deemed to have been filed on April 1, 1984.

2209.10 Administrative proceedings on application by interested party for decontrol on the basis of vacancy rate.

(a)(1) All requests for decontrol pursuant to section Y51-12.0 of the Rent Law must be made by application supported by adequate proof pursuant to the provisions of this and subsequent sections.

(2) The burden rests upon the applicant to clearly establish the existence of the five-percent vacancy rate in all or any alleged class of housing accommodations claimed to be eligible for decontrol. The vacancy rate shall mean the net rental vacancy rate. Notwithstanding the class of housing accommodations alleged by the applicant to be eligible for decontrol, the administrator shall make the final determination as to what constitutes a particular class of housing accommodations involved.

(b) No printed form of application is provided or prescribed. Each application must be clearly designated "Application to the Division of Housing and Community Renewal pursuant to section Y51-12.0 of the Rent Law," and shall set forth the following:

(1) the name and post-office address of the party filing the application;

(2) a simple and concise statement showing the nature of the interest of the applicant in the outcome of the proceeding;

(3)(i) a complete statement of the data relied upon for the vacancy rate claimed for the class of housing accommodation for which the applicant claims eligibility for decontrol. Such statement shall include a description of the methods, procedures and qualifications of the personnel used to gather the data submitted in support of the application.

(ii) The survey shall be of the entire universe of housing accommodations within the class claimed to be eligible for decontrol, or shall be based upon a scientific sampling by accepted random sampling techniques to include a comprehensive cross-section of the universe to be surveyed. The sampling used in conducting the survey shall be based on standard social-research data-gathering methodology. Based upon sampling of the data introduced, the standard error for the vacancy rate shall be not more than one quarter of one percent (0.25%) at one standard error, assuming an estimated vacancy rate of five percent; and

(4) a specific statement of the relief requested.

The application shall be verified by the party filing the application.

(c) Service of the application upon the administrator shall be made by filing the original and one copy thereof with the Division of Housing and Community Renewal, Office of Rent Administration, 10 Columbus Circle, New York, NY 10019, or such other address as provided on the application.

2209.11 Action by administrator. After the filing of the application for decontrol on the basis of vacancy rate, the administrator may:

(a) reject the application if it is insufficient or defective;

(b) make such other and further studies and investigations as he deems necessary to make a finding as to whether the percentage of vacancies in all or any particular class of housing accommodation is five percent or more (such studies and investigations shall include, but not be limited to, data gathered by the United States Bureau of the Census or any public or quasi-public agency, or studies made by independent consultants under contract with the Division of Housing and Community Renewal or by its own staff); investigate the facts presented in the application; conduct such conferences as are necessary; require the filing of such other and additional reports, or other evidence relevant to the proceedings;

(c) suspend determination of application until completion of such studies and investigations as the administrator deems necessary to make a finding as to whether the percentage of vacancies in all or any particular class of housing accommodation is five percent or more. In the event that the administrator so suspends his determination, he shall advise the applicant, in writing, of the reasons for such suspension, including the identification of the studies and investigations deemed necessary by him;

(d) require any person to appear or produce documents, or both, pursuant to a subpoena issued by the administrator;

(e) grant or order a hearing.

2209.12 Final determination by administrator. All orders issued pursuant to section Y51-12.0 of the Rent Law shall be deemed to be final administrative determinations, subject to judicial review as provided by section Y51-9.0 of the Rent Law. The administrator, on such terms and conditions as he may determine, may issue a final order:

(a) dismissing the application if it fails substantially to comply with the provisions of section 2209.10 *et seq.* of this Part; or

(b) granting or denying the application, in whole or in part, provided that before he may grant the application, in whole or in part, he shall have first held a public hearing as provided by section Y51-12.0 of the Rent Law.

PART 2210

HOUSING ACCOMMODATIONS COVERED BY TITLE YY OF NEW YORK CITY ADMINISTRATIVE CODE

2210.1 Scope. Notwithstanding any provision of the City Rent and Rehabilitation Law or of these regulations, housing accommodations covered by title YY of the New York City Administrative Code shall be subject to the City Rent and Rehabilitation Law and these regulations as and when title YY, the Rent Stabilization Code and regulations adopted thereunder shall provide.

2210.2 Maximum rent. The maximum rent for such housing accommodations, for the purposes of these regulations, shall be the rent charged on May 31, 1968 or June 30, 1974, whichever is applicable.

2210.3 Registration requirements. Within 90 days after any such housing accommodation shall become subject to these regulations, the landlord thereof shall file a registration statement, on the form provided therefor, containing such information as the administrator may require pursuant to Part 2203 of this Title.

NEW YORK CITY RENT AND REHABILITATION LAW[1]

Section 14 of L 1985, ch 907, provides as follows: "(a) An act of the legislature of the state of New York or local law of the city council of the city of New York for nineteen hundred eighty-five or thereafter which, in form, amends or repeals or purports to amend or repeal any provision or provisions of the former administrative code of the city of New York as in force immediately prior to the date that this act shall take effect, shall be legally effective notwithstanding the repeal of such former administrative code by this act and shall be construed as an amendment or repeal, as the case may be, of the corresponding provision or provisions of this act irrespective of whether such provision or provisions are contained in this act in one or more titles, chapters, subchapters, articles, sections, subdivisions, or other parts thereof and such corresponding provision or provisions shall be deemed and construed to be amended or repealed as though the same had been expressly so amended or repealed.

"(b) An act of the legislature of the state of New York or local law of the city council of the city of New York for nineteen hundred eighty-five or thereafter which adds or purports to add a new section, subsection or other provision of law to the former administrative code as in force and effect immediately prior to the date that this act

[1] The Administrative Code of the City of New York was recodified by L 1985, Ch 907, effective September 1, 1986. Title 26, Ch 3, of the new Code (comprising §§ 26-401 through 26-415), corresponds to the provisions of Title Y (comprising §§ Y51-1.0 through Y51-18.0) of the former Code, as follows:

Former Code sections	New Code sections
Y51-1.0	26-401
Y51-2.0	26-402
Y51-3.0	26-403
Y51-4.0	26-404
Y51-5.0	26-405
Y51-5.1	26-406
Y51-5.2	26-407
Y51-6.0	26-408
Y51-7.0	26-409
Y51-8.0	26-410
Y51-9.0	26-411
Y51-10.0	26-412
Y51-11.0	26-413
Y51-12.0	26-414
Y51-16.0	26-415
Y51-17.0	Omitted
Y51-18.0	Omitted

shall take effect, shall be legally effective notwithstanding the repeal of such former administrative code by this act and shall be construed as having been added to this act and shall be given full effect according to its context as if the same had been added expressly and in terms to this act and shall be deemed and construed to have been inserted in this act in juxtaposition to and as modifying the effect of the corresponding provision or provisions of this act."

Residential Rent Control was extended to March 28, 1988 by Resolution No. 1312, passed by the New York City Council on March 28, 1985.

§ 26-401. Declaration and findings.
§ 26-402. Short title.
§ 26-403. Definitions.
§ 26-404. City rent agency; division of housing and community renewal.
§ 26-405. General powers and duties of the city rent agency.
§ 26-406. Tax abatement for property subject to rent exemption orders.
§ 26-407. Labor cost pass-along.
§ 26-408. Evictions.
§ 26-409. Investigations; records; reports.
§ 26-410. Procedure.
§ 26-411. Judicial review.
§ 26-412. Prohibitions.
§ 26-413. Enforcement and penalties.
§ 26-414. Decontrol on basis of vacancy rate.
§ 26-415. Surveys of need for rent control.

§ 26-401. Declaration and findings

a. The council hereby finds that a serious public emergency continues to exist in the housing of a considerable number of persons in the city, which emergency was created by war, the effects of war and the aftermath of hostilities; that such emergency necessitated the intervention of federal, state and local government in order to prevent speculative, unwarranted and abnormal increases in rents; that there continues to exist an acute shortage of dwellings; that unless residential rents and evictions continue to be regulated and controlled, disruptive practices and abnormal conditions will produce serious threats to the public health, safety and general welfare; that to prevent such perils to health, safety and welfare, preventive action through enactment of local legislation by the council continues to be imperative; that such action, as a temporary measure to be effective until it is determined by the council that such emergency no longer exists, is necessary in order to prevent exactions of unjust, unreasonable and oppressive rents and rental agreements and to forestall profiteering, speculation and other disruptive practices tending to produce threats to the public health; that the transition from regulation to a normal market of free bargaining between landlord and tenant, while still the objective of state and city policy, must be administered with due regard for such emergency; that in order to prevent uncertainty, hardship and dislocation, the provisions of this chapter are declared to be necessary and designed to protect the public health, safety and general welfare.

b. The council further declares that it is city policy to utilize the powers conferred by this chapter, in a manner consistent with the purposes and provisions thereof, to encourage and promote the improvement and rehabilitation of the housing accommodations subject to control hereunder, for the purpose of protecting the public health, safety and general welfare.

§ 26-402. Short title

This chapter shall be known and may be cited as the city rent and rehabilitation law.

§ 26-403. Definitions

When used in this chapter, unless a different meaning clearly appears from the context, the following terms shall mean and include:

a. Administrator. The commissioner of the state division of housing and community renewal.

b. City rent agency. The state division of housing and community renewal.

c. "Documents." Records, books, accounts, correspondence, memoranda and other documents, drafts and copies of any of the foregoing.

d. "Federal act." The Emergency Price Control Act of nineteen hundred forty-two, and as thereafter amended and as superseded by the Housing and Rent Act of nineteen hundred forty-seven, and as the latter was thereafter amended prior to May first, nineteen hundred fifty, and regulations adopted pursuant thereto.

e. "Housing accommodation." 1. Except as otherwise provided in paragraph two of this subdivision e, any building or structure, permanent or temporary, or any part thereof, occupied or intended to be occupied by one or more individuals as a residence, home, sleeping place, boarding house, lodging house or hotel, together with the land and buildings appurtenant thereto, and all services, privileges, furnishings, furniture and facilities supplied in connection with the occupation thereof, and any plot or parcel of land (as distinguished from any building constructed or placed thereon) which is not owned by the city and which was rented prior to May first, nineteen hundred fifty, for the purpose of permitting the tenant thereof to construct his or her own private dwelling (as such term "private dwelling" is defined in subdivision six of section four of the multiple dwelling law) thereon and on which there exists such a private dwelling owned and occupied by a tenant of such plot or parcel, or on or after July first, nineteen hundred seventy-one such private dwelling is owned or occupied by a member of the tenant's immediate family regardless of whether the member of the tenant's immediate family was in occupancy of the private dwelling with the tenant prior to the transfer of title or possession or thereafter took occupancy of the private dwelling pursuant to such transfer of title or possession, including:

(a) Entire structures or premises as distinguished from the individual housing accommodations contained therein, wherein twenty-five or less rooms are rented or offered for rent by any lessee, sublessee, or other tenant of such entire structure or premises; and

(b) Housing accommodations which, under subparagraph (i) of paragraph two of this subdivision e, are or at any time become exempt from or not subject to control and which, while in such status, are certified by a city agency having jurisdiction to be a fire hazard or in a continued dangerous condition or detrimental to life or health; and the subsequent removal of the conditions on which such certification is based shall not cause any such housing accommodation to become exempt from or not subject to control; and

(c) Notwithstanding any other provision of this chapter, all housing accommodations in any multiple dwelling aided by a loan made by the city under article eight of the private housing finance law; provided that where any such housing accommodation, if this subparagraph (c) were not applicable thereto, would not be subject to rent control under this chapter and the regulations thereunder prior to the date on which rent control with respect to such multiple dwelling is required by the provisions of such article eight to begin, this subparagraph (c) shall operate to make such housing accommodation subject to rent control under this chapter and the regulations thereunder only on and after such date; and provided further that if any such housing accommodation, on the date on which rent control with respect thereto ceases to be required by such article eight, would not be subject to rent control, or would be eligible for decontrol on the landlord's application, under the provisions of this chapter and the regulations thereunder, if this subparagraph (c) were not applicable thereto, then such housing accommodation, after such date, shall not be subject to rent control, or shall be eligible for decontrol, as the case may be, in the same manner as if this subparagraph (c) had not been applicable to such housing accommodation.

2. The term "housing accommodation" shall not include:

(a) structures in which all of the housing accommodations are exempt or not subject to control under this chapter or any regulation issued thereunder; or

(b) a hospital, convent, monastery, asylum, public institution, or college or school dormitory or any institution operated exclusively for charitable or educational purposes on a non-profit basis; or

(c) notwithstanding any previous order, finding, opinion or determination of the state rent commission, housing accommodations in any establishment which on March first, nineteen hundred fifty, was and still is commonly regarded as a hotel in the community in which it is located and which customarily provides hotel services such as maid service, furnishing and laundering of linen, telephone and secretarial or desk service, use and upkeep of furniture and fixtures and bellboy service, provided, however, that the term "hotel" shall not include any establishment which is commonly regarded in the community as a rooming house, nor shall it include any establishment not identified or classified as a "hotel", "transient hotel" or "residential hotel" pursuant to the federal act, irrespective of whether such establishment either provides some services customarily provided by hotels, or is represented to be a hotel, or both; and provided further that housing accommodations in hotels which have been and still are occupied by a tenant who has resided in such hotel continuously since December second, nineteen hundred forty-nine, so long as such tenant occupies the same, shall continue to remain subject to control under this chapter; or

(d) Any motor court, or any part thereof; any trailer or trailer space used exclusively for transient occupancy or any part thereof (provided that nothing herein contained shall be construed as legalizing or authorizing any use or occupancy of a trailer or trailer space where prohibited by law); or any tourist home serving transient guests exclusively, or any part thereof; or

(e) Nonhousekeeping, furnished housing accommodations, located within a single dwelling unit not used as a rooming or boarding house, but only if: (1) no more than two tenants for whom rent is paid (husband and wife being considered one tenant for this purpose), not members of the landlord's immediate family, live in such dwelling unit; and (2) the remaining portion of such dwelling unit is occupied by the landlord or his or her immediate family; or

(f) Housing accommodations owned and operated by the United States, the state of New York, or the New York city housing authority; or owned by the city and under the jurisdiction of the city department of housing preservation and development pursuant to the New York city charter; or owned and operated by the city; or housing accommodations in buildings in which rentals are fixed by or subject to the supervision of the state commissioner of housing and community renewal;

(g) Housing accommodations in buildings operated exclusively for charitable purposes on a non-profit basis; or

(h) Except as otherwise provided in item six of subparagraph (i) of this paragraph two, housing accommodations which were completed on or after February first, nineteen hundred forty-seven, provided, however, that, the former structure or any lesser portion thereof, was not vacated, on or after the effective date of this first provision of this subparagraph (h), other than by voluntary surrender of possession or in the manner provided in this chapter, and provided further that maximum rents established under the veterans' emergency housing act, for priority constructed housing accommodations completed on or after February first, nineteen hundred forty-seven, shall continue in full force and effect, if such accommodations are being rented to veterans of world war II or their immediate families who, on June thirtieth, nineteen hundred forty-seven, either occupied such housing accommodations or had a right to occupy such housing accommodations at any time on or after July first, nineteen hundred forty-seven, under any agreement whether written or oral; or

(i) Except as otherwise provided in subparagraphs (b) and (c) of paragraph one of this subdivision e: (1) Housing accommodations created by a change from a non-housing use to a housing use on or after February first, nineteen hundred forty-seven, but only if the space comprising such accommodations was devoted to a non-housing use on February first, nineteen hundred forty-seven; or

(2) Additional housing accommodations, other than rooming house accommodations, created by conversion on or after February first, nineteen hundred forty-seven; provided, however, that any housing accommodations created as a result of any such conversion on or after May first, nineteen hundred fifty, shall continue to be subject to rent control as provided for herein unless the state rent commission, prior to May first, nineteen hundred sixty-two, issued an order decontrolling them, or the city rent agency, on or after such date, issues an order decontrolling them; and the city rent agency shall issue such an order if there has been a structural change involving substantial alterations or remodeling and such change has resulted in additional housing accommodations consisting of self-contained family units as defined by regulations issued by the city rent agency, with due regard for the shortage of housing accommodations suitable for family occupancy and for the purposes of this chapter in relation thereto; and provided further, that

Rent and Rehabilitation Law

any such order of decontrol of the state rent commission or the city rent agency shall remain effective after April thirtieth, nineteen hundred sixty-two only so long as the housing accommodations are not occupied for other than single family occupancy; and provided further, that any such order of decontrol shall not apply to that portion of the original housing accommodations occupied by a tenant in possession at the time of the conversion, but only so long as that tenant continues in occupancy; and provided further, that no such order of decontrol shall be issued unless such conversion occurred after the entire structure, or any lesser portion thereof as may have been thus converted, was vacated by voluntary surrender of possession, or in the manner provided in this chapter, or (where vacated prior to May first, nineteen hundred sixty-two) in the manner provided by section five of the state rent act; and provided further that notwithstanding any of the foregoing provisions of this item two, no such order of decontrol shall be issued with respect to housing accommodations of any type resulting from conversion, after April thirtieth, nineteen hundred sixty-two, to rooming house accommodations or to single room occupancy accommodations, and such resulting accommodations shall continue to be housing accommodations subject to rent control under this chapter and the regulation thereunder; or

(3) Housing accommodations rented after April first, nineteen hundred fifty-three, which were or are continuously occupied by the owner thereof for a period of one year prior to the date of renting; provided, however, that this item three shall not apply where the owner acquired possession of the housing accommodation after the issuance of a certificate of eviction under subdivision two of section five of the state rent act or under subdivision b of section 26-408 of this chapter within the two year period immediately preceding the date of such renting, and provided further that this item three shall not apply to any such housing accommodation rented on or after May first, nineteen hundred sixty-two, where an exemption of any housing accommodation in the same building was obtained under paragraph (h) of subdivision two of section two of the state rent act or has been previously obtained

under this item three; and provided further, that this exemption shall remain effective only so long as the housing accommodations are not occupied for other than single family occupancy; or

(4) Housing accommodations in one or two family houses which were or shall become vacant on or after April first, nineteen hundred fifty-three; provided, however, that this exemption shall remain effective only so long as the housing accommodations are not occupied for other than single family occupancy; or [so in original; no paragraph (5) enacted]

(6)(i) Such housing accommodations resulting from substantial demolition (as such accommodations are defined in this item six), as are decontrolled by order of the city rent agency pursuant to this item six; provided that all housing accommodations resulting from substantial demolition which are not so decontrolled shall continue to be housing accommodations subject to rent control under this chapter and the regulations thereunder.

(ii) The term "housing accommodation resulting from substantial demolition", as used herein, shall mean any housing accommodation (a) which is created on or after May first, nineteen hundred sixty-two, as a result of the substantial demolition of a multiple dwelling and the reconstruction of such building in such manner as to retain any portion thereof existing prior to such demolition, and (b) which is so created after the issuance of one or more certificates permitting the eviction of any tenant or tenants of such multiple dwelling for the purpose of effecting such demolition.

(iii) No order shall be issued under this item six decontrolling any housing accommodation resulting from substantial demolition unless, after such reconstruction, all housing accommodations in the building are self-contained family units as defined by regulations issued by the city rent agency, with due regard for the shortage of housing accommodations suitable for family occupancy and for the purposes of this chapter in relation thereto.

(iv) The city rent agency shall issue regulations, with due regard for such shortage and purposes, specifying minimum requirements for qualifying any housing accommodation resulting from substantial demolition as suitable for occupancy by larger families (including, with respect to the individual unit, but not limited to, number of rooms, space suitable for sleeping purposes and total floor area) and likewise prescribing, subject to such variations and classifications as such agency may determine to be reasonably necessary, the ratio between the total number of housing accommodations resulting from substantial demolition in the building, and the number of such accommodations which must meet such requirements for larger family occupancy, in order that a decontrol order may be granted hereunder.

(v) The city rent agency shall issue an order decontrolling all of the housing accommodations resulting from substantial demolition in the building, if such accommodations meet the requirements of sub-item (iii) of this item six, and if the prescribed proportion thereof meets the requirements of sub-item (iv) of this item six for larger family occupancy; provided that (a) if all such accommodations meet the requirements of such sub-item (iii), but less than the prescribed proportion thereof meet the requirements of such sub-item (iv), then the city rent agency shall issue an order decontrolling only those accommodations which meet the requirements of both such sub-items; and (b) any order of decontrol issued under this item six shall remain effective only so long as the accommodations decontrolled by such order are not occupied for other than single family occupancy.

(vi) In the case of any housing accommodations vacated on or after March twenty-sixth, nineteen hundred sixty-four, no order of decontrol shall be issued under this item six for any housing accommodations resulting from substantial demolition thereof unless such reconstruction occurred after the structure was vacated by voluntary surrender of possession, or in the manner provided in this chapter; or

(7)(i) Individual housing accommodations having unfurnished maximum rents of two hundred and fifty dollars or more per month as of April first, nineteen hundred sixty, or furnished maximum rents of three hundred dollars or more per month as of April first, nineteen hundred sixty, which are or become vacant on or after the effective date of this item seven; or

(ii) On and after October first, nineteen hundred sixty-four individual housing accommodations having unfurnished maximum rents of three hundred dollars or more per month as of April first, nineteen hundred sixty, or furnished maximum rents of three hundred and sixty dollars or more per month as of April first, nineteen hundred sixty; provided, however, that where any such housing accommodation is occupied by a tenant whose household contains one or more children attending an elementary or secondary school, such housing accommodation shall continue to remain subject to control under this chapter and the regulations thereunder until June thirtieth, nineteen hundred sixty-five; and provided further, that where such housing accommodation on March twenty-sixth, nineteen hundred sixty-four is occupied by a tenant whose household contains four or more related persons, it shall continue to remain subject to control under this chapter and the regulations thereunder so long as such tenant remains in occupancy; or

(iii) On and after April first, nineteen hundred sixty-five individual housing accommodations having unfurnished maximum rents of two hundred and fifty dollars to two hundred ninety-nine dollars and ninety-nine cents, inclusive, per month as of April first, nineteen hundred sixty, or furnished maximum rents of three hundred dollars to three hundred fifty-nine dollars and ninety-nine cents inclusive, per month as of April first, nineteen hundred sixty; provided, however, that where any such housing accommodation is occupied by a tenant whose household contains one or more children attending an elementary or secondary school, such housing accommodation shall continue to remain subject to control under this chapter and the regulations thereunder until June thirtieth, nineteen hundred sixty-five; and provided further, that where such housing accommodations on March twenty-sixth, nineteen hundred sixty-four is occupied by a tenant whose household contains four or more related persons, it shall continue to remain subject to control under this chapter and the regulations thereunder so long as such tenant remains in occupancy.

(iv) The exemptions provided for in this item seven shall remain effective only so long as the housing accommodations are not occupied for other than single family occupancy.

(v) The term "related persons", as used in this item seven, shall be limited to the tenant and a parent, grandparent, child, stepchild, grandchild, brother or sister of the tenant or of the tenant's spouse or the spouse of any of the foregoing, who customarily occupied the housing accommodation on and before the effective date of this item seven. The tenant's spouse or an unmarried child or grandchild of the tenant who temporarily resided elsewhere on the effective date of this item seven because of attendance at an educational institution or service in the armed forces of the United States shall be deemed to be a related person in occupancy.

(8) No more than two housing accommodations in any one year period in an owner-occupied structure containing six or fewer housing accommodations which are or become vacant on or after August first, nineteen hundred seventy, by voluntary surrender or pursuant to section 26-408 of this chapter; provided, however, that this exemption shall remain effective only so long as the housing accommodations are not occupied for other than residential dwelling purposes; and provided further, that if the city rent agency shall make a finding of harassment in violation of subdivision d of section 26-412 of this chapter with respect to a housing accommodation in a structure containing six or less housing accommodations, in addition to all other criminal or civil fines, penalties, injunctive relief and enforcement penalties and remedies authorized by section 26-413 of this chapter, no housing accommodation in such structure shall be decontrolled pursuant to this item eight until a minimum period of three years has elapsed since the making of such finding of harassment by the city rent agency. Structures containing six or fewer housing accommodations shall be considered to be structures containing six or fewer housing accommodations for the purposes of this item eight, notwithstanding that such structures shall contain commercial accommodations in addition to such housing accommodations.

(9) Housing accommodations which became vacant on or after June thirtieth, nineteen hundred seventy-one,

provided, however, that this exemption shall not apply or become effective with respect to housing accommodations which the commissioner determines or finds became vacant because the landlord or any person acting on his or her behalf, with intent to cause the tenant to vacate, engaged in any course of conduct (including but not limited to, interruption or discontinuance of essential services) which interfered with or disturbed or was intended to interfere with or disturb the comfort, repose, peace or quiet of the tenant in his or her use or occupancy of housing accommodations and provided, further, however, that nothing contained herein shall be deemed to preclude the applicability to such housing accommodations of the emergency tenant protection act of nineteen seventy-four.

(10) Housing accommodations not occupied by the tenant, not including subtenants or occupants, as his or her primary residence, as determined by a court of competent jurisdiction. No action or proceeding shall be commenced seeking to recover possession on the ground that a housing accommodation is not occupied by the tenant as his or her primary residence unless the owner or lessor shall have given thirty days notice to the tenant of his or her intention to commence such action or proceeding on such grounds.

f. "Landlord." An owner, lessor, sublessor, assignee, or other person receiving or entitled to receive rent for the use or occupancy of any housing accommodation or an agent of any of the foregoing.

g. "Maximum rent." The maximum lawful rent for the use of housing accommodations. Maximum rents may be formulated in terms of rents and other charges and allowances.

h. "Person." An individual, corporation, partnership, association, or any other organized group of individuals or the legal successor or representative of any of the foregoing.

i. "Rent." Consideration, including any bonus, benefit or gratuity demanded or received for or in connection with the use or occupancy of housing accommodations or the transfer of a lease of such housing accommodations.

j. "State Enabling Act." The local emergency housing rent control act.

k. "State Rent Act." The emergency housing rent control law.

l. "State rent commission." The temporary state housing rent commission created by the emergency housing rent control law.

m. "Tenant." A tenant, subtenant, lessee, sublessee, or other person entitled to the possession or to the use or occupancy of any housing accommodation.

§ 26-404. City rent agency; division of housing and community renewal

The division of housing and community renewal shall have charge of and conduct through its own counsel any proceeding under this chapter of the code, except for the provisions of subdivision n of section 26-405 and section 26-406 of this chapter which shall remain under the jurisdiction of the department of housing preservation and development.

§ 26-405. General powers and duties of the city rent agency

a. (1) At the time this chapter shall become effective, the city rent agency shall establish maximum rents which, subject to the provisions of subdivision (b) of this section, shall be the maximum rents in effect on April thirtieth, nineteen hundred sixty-two pursuant to the state rent act and the regulations thereunder.

(2)(a) Notwithstanding the foregoing provision of this subdivision, and except as provided in subparagraph (b) of this paragraph two, effective August first, nineteen hundred seventy, the maximum rent in effect on July thirty-first, nineteen hundred seventy shall be adjusted as follows: (i) For any individual housing accommodation for which one or more but less than two full fifteen per centum rent increases has been granted since May first, nineteen hundred fifty-three pursuant to former subparagraph (d) of paragraph one of subdivision g of this section the maximum rent shall be increased by eight per centum.

(ii) For any individual housing accommodation for

which no full fifteen per centum rent increase has been granted since May first, nineteen hundred fifty-three pursuant to former subparagraph (d) of paragraph one of subdivision g of this section the maximum rent shall be increased by fifteen per centum, except that if there was no such increase for any individual housing accommodation for which a first rent was established pursuant to former subdivision m of this section after July thirty-first, nineteen hundred sixty-five and before August first, nineteen hundred sixty-eight, the maximum rent shall be increased by five per centum, and except that if there was no such increase for any individual housing accommodation for which a first rent was established pursuant to such subdivision on or after August first, nineteen hundred sixty-eight there shall be no increase in maximum rent. On or after August first, nineteen hundred seventy, a landlord may file application for labor cost rent adjustment pursuant to subparagraph (1) of paragraph (1) of subdivision g of this section. In lieu of such labor cost rent adjustment, the landlord of a building with twenty or fewer housing accommodations shall have the option of filing for a five per centum increase in maximum rent for any individual housing accommodation for which two or more full fifteen per centum increases have been granted since May first, nineteen hundred fifty-three pursuant to former subparagraph (d) of paragraph one of subdivision g of this section.

Nothing contained in this subparagraph (a) however, shall have the effect of establishing the maximum rent in an amount less than the maximum rent in effect on July thirty-first, nineteen hundred seventy nor of increasing by more than fifteen per centum the maximum rent for any housing accommodation.

(2)(b) Where the maximum rent in effect on July thirty-first, nineteen hundred seventy for any individual housing accommodation is less than sixty dollars per month such rent shall be increased effective August first, nineteen hundred seventy by ten dollars per month where the housing accommodation is comprised of three rooms or less and by fifteen dollars per month where the housing accommodation is comprised of more than three rooms.

(2)(c) Where a lease is in effect for any housing accommodation on August first, nineteen hundred seventy, no adjustment of maximum rent for such accommodation shall become effective until the expiration of such lease. Where a housing accommodation becomes vacant on or after August first, nineteen hundred seventy and before January first, nineteen hundred seventy-two by voluntary surrender of possession by the tenant the maximum rent shall be increased by no more than fifteen per centum over the maximum rent established for such accommodation at the time the vacancy occurred, provided that a report is filed with the city rent agency as prescribed by its regulations. If the city rent agency shall make a finding of harassment in violation of subdivision d of section 26-412 of this chapter for the purpose of obtaining such a vacancy, in addition to all other civil or criminal penalties, injunctive relief and enforcement remedies authorized by section 26-413 of this chapter, no housing accommodation in the building shall thereafter be entitled to the benefit of a rental increase as a result of becoming vacant between the aforesaid dates.

(2)(d) The total of (i) the increase pursuant to subparagraph (a) of this paragraph, or (ii) any increases granted between December thirty-first, nineteen hundred sixty-nine and December thirty-first, nineteen hundred seventy-one pursuant to subparagraph (a), (b), or (c) of paragraph one of subdivision g of this section and (iii) any increase granted on or after the effective date of this paragraph pursuant to subparagraph (1) of paragraph one of subdivision g of this section shall not exceed fifteen per centum of the "1970 base rent". For purposes of this subparagraph, the "1970 base rent" is the maximum rent on July thirty-first, nineteen hundred seventy minus the amount of any increase granted between December thirty-first, nineteen hundred sixty-nine and July thirty-first, nineteen hundred seventy pursuant to subparagraph (a), (b), or (c) of paragraph one of subdivision g of this section. This subparagraph shall not operate to decrease any maximum rent existing on its effective date.

(2)(e) The rent increases provided for in this paragraph two shall be collectible upon the landlord's filing a report with the city rent agency on forms to be prescribed by such agency, including simplified forms for landlords of buildings with twelve or fewer housing accommodations, and giving such notice to the tenant as such agency may prescribe, subject to adjustment upon order of the city rent agency. The report shall contain a certified statement by the landlord that there is no legally habitable rent controlled housing accommodation in the building which has not been rented for a period of six months or more on the date of the filing of such report, or that if there is such a housing accommodation, the reasons it has not been rented is that it is being altered pursuant to a permit issued by the department of buildings no later than three months after the vacancy commenced and that the alteration is of such a nature that the accommodation must be kept vacant while it is being made or for such other cause found by the city rent agency not to be inconsistent with the purpose of this chapter, provided further that in the case of an alteration it is commenced within sixty days from the issuance of said permit. A copy of the permit and the application therefor shall accompany the report. No report shall be accepted for filing and no rent increase provided for in this paragraph two shall be collected in the absence of any such certified statement by the landlord. Any excess shall be credited to the tenants in full commencing with the rental payment following the receipt by the landlord of such order of adjustment. If such report is filed on or before October thirty-first, nineteen hundred seventy, the increase shall take effect August first, nineteen hundred seventy. If the report is filed thereafter, such increase shall take effect with the first rental payment following filing.

(2)(f) The rent increases provided for in this paragraph two shall not be collected for the period between March thirty-first, nineteen hundred and seventy-one and December thirty-first, nineteen hundred seventy-one until the landlord shall have filed with the city rent agency a certified statement attesting that for every month for which he or she has received a rent increase pursuant to subparagraphs (a) and (b) of this paragraph two, he or she has expended or incurred in the operation, maintenance and improvements of the housing accommodations from which increases were collected an amount which equals the amount expended per month for such purpose averaged over the preceding five years, or such lesser period that he or she has been landlord of such properties, plus ninety per centum of all increased rents so collected.

(3) The city rent agency shall establish maximum rents to be effective January first, nineteen hundred seventy-two by dividing the maximum gross building rental from all housing accommodations in the property whether or not subject to or exempt from control under this chapter by the number of such accommodations, after giving consideration to such factors as may be prescribed by formula, such as size and location of housing accommodations and number of rooms. Such maximum gross building rental shall be computed on the basis of real estate taxes, water rates and sewer charges and an operation and maintenance expense allowance, a vacancy allowance not in excess of two per cent, and a collection loss allowance, both as prescribed by such agency, and an eight and one-half per centum return on capital value. The operating and maintenance expense allowance shall include provision for the cost of fuel, utilities, payroll, maintenance repairs, replacement reserves and miscellaneous charges attributed to the property, excluding mortgage interest and amortization, and may be varied by the agency for different types of properties depending upon such factors as the year of construction, elevator or non-elevator buildings, the average number of rooms per individual housing accommodations in the building. Capital value shall be equalized assessed valuation as established pursuant to article twelve-A of the real property tax law. Where the property receives income from sources other than such housing accommodations, the taxes, water and sewer charges and the capital value attributed to the portion consisting of housing accommodations shall be in the same ratio of the total taxes, water and sewer charges (where not computed separately) and the total capital value as the gross income from such portion consisting of housing accommodations bears to the total gross income from the property, as prescribed by the agency.

The agency shall report to the council on or before October fifteenth, nineteen hundred seventy-one as to the status of preparation of the formulas necessary to implement the rent adjustments to be effective January first, nineteen hundred seventy-two.

(4) The city rent agency shall establish maximum rents effective January first, nineteen hundred seventy-four and biennially thereafter by adjusting the existing maximum rent to reflect changes, if any, in the factors which determine maximum gross building rental under paragraph three of this subdivision except that commencing January first, nineteen hundred eighty-two, said maximum rent shall no longer recognize or reflect the adjustment allocable to changes in heating costs after April ninth, nineteen hundred seventy-nine.

Notwithstanding any other provisions in this paragraph to the contrary, commencing January first, nineteen hundred seventy-four, the city rent agency shall require each owner to make available for examination his or her books and all other financial records relating to the operation of each building under his or her ownership containing accommodations subject to this chapter at least once every three years for the purpose of determining whether the maximum formula rent is appropriate for each building in light of actual expenditures therefor and shall also alter such formula rent to take into account significant variations between the formula and actual cost experience. The agency shall also establish maximum costs for the factors under paragraph three of this subdivision which determine maximum gross building rental to preclude increases which would otherwise result from excessive expenditures in the operation and maintenance of the building. The return allowed on capital may be revised from time to time by local law.

(5) Where a maximum rent established pursuant to this chapter on or after January first, nineteen hundred seventy-two, is higher than the previously existing maximum rent, the landlord may not collect more than seven and one-half percentum increase from a tenant in occupancy on such date in any one year period, provided however, that where the period for which the rent is established exceeds one year, regardless of how the collection thereof is averaged over such period, the rent the landlord shall be entitled to receive during the first twelve months shall not be increased by more than seven and one-half percen-

tum over the previous rent and additional annual rents shall not exceed seven and one-half percentum of the rent paid during the previous year. Notwithstanding any of the foregoing limitations in this paragraph five, maximum rent shall be increased if ordered by the agency pursuant to subparagraphs (d),(e),(f),(g),(h),(i),(k), (l), (m) or (n) of paragraph one of subdivision g of this section. Commencing January first, nineteen hundred eighty, rent adjustments pursuant to subparagraph (n) of paragraph one of subdivision g of this section shall be excluded from the maximum rent when computing the seven and one-half percentum increase authorized by this paragraph five. Where a housing accommodation is vacant on January first, nineteen hundred seventy-two, or becomes vacant thereafter by voluntary surrender of possession by the tenants, the maximum rent established for such accommodations may be collected.

(6) Where a new maximum rent has been established pursuant to former subdivision m of this section or, following the repeal of such subdivision, pursuant to subparagraph (m) of paragraph one of subdivision g of this section, a new maximum rent shall not be established pursuant to paragraph three of this subdivision. Except with respect to a housing accommodation to which the preceding sentence applies, where the maximum rent on December thirty-first, nineteen hundred seventy-one is higher than the maximum rent established pursuant to paragraph three of this subdivision, such prior maximum rent shall continue in effect until the maximum rent under paragraph three, as adjusted from time to time pursuant to the provisions of this chapter, shall equal or exceed such prior maximum rent, at which time the maximum rent for such housing accommodations shall be as prescribed in this chapter.

(7) Section eight housing assistance.

(a) Notwithstanding any provision of this chapter, if during a rental period in which the landlord is eligible for an adjustment or establishment of rents pursuant to paragraph three or four of this subdivision, housing assistance payments are being made pursuant to section eight of the United States housing act of nineteen hundred thirty-seven, as amended, with respect to any housing accommodation covered by this chapter, the maximum rent collectible from the tenant in occupancy shall be the lesser of: (1) the maximum rent established pursuant to paragraph three of this subdivision as adjusted pursuant to this chapter, computed without regard to the limitations of paragraph five of this subdivision (provided that in any case the rent paid by the tenant pursuant to this chapter without regard to this paragraph is higher than such rent, the rent paid shall be substituted for such rent), or (2) the contract or fair market rent approved for the housing accommodation pursuant to federal law or regulation.

(7)(b) Prior to the collection of any increase in maximum rent pursuant to this paragraph, the landlord shall advise the city rent agency of his or her intent to compute the maximum rent pursuant to this paragraph.

(7)(c) If a housing accommodation to which this subdivision applies ceases for any reason to be governed by this paragraph, the maximum rent collectible from the tenant shall be computed as if this paragraph had not applied and any adjustments thereto which would have been permitted pursuant to this chapter during the period such rent was set by this paragraph shall be proper rental adjustments.

(8) Notwithstanding the provisions of this chapter, upon the sale in any manner authorized by law of a multiple dwelling which was previously subject to the provisions of such chapter and which was acquired by the city in a tax foreclosure proceeding or pursuant to article nineteen-A of the real property actions and proceedings law, for a dwelling unit which was subject to this chapter pursuant to the local emergency housing rent control act at the time the city so acquired title, is occupied by a tenant who was in occupancy at the time of acquisition and remains in occupancy at the time of sale, the maximum rent shall be the last rent charged by the city, or on behalf of the city, for such dwelling unit, which rent shall not exceed the rent computed pursuant to paragraph three of this subdivision, computed as of the time of such sale. This paragraph shall not apply to redemptions from

city ownership pursuant to chapter four of title eleven of the code.

(9) The city rent agency, prior to establishing biennially maximum base rents pursuant to this chapter and before establishing a maximum base rent which is different from the previously existing maximum base rent for dwellings covered by this law, shall hold a public hearing or hearings for the purpose of collecting information the city rent agency may consider in establishing maximum base rents. Notice of the date, time, location and summary of subject matter for the public hearing or hearings shall be published in the City Record for a period of not less than fourteen days, and at least once in one or more newspapers of general circulation at least fourteen days immediately preceding each hearing date, at the expense of the city of New York, and the hearing shall be open for testimony from any individual, group, association or representative thereof who wants to testify.

b. Such agency, to effectuate the purposes of this chapter, and in accordance with the standards set forth in paragraph two of subdivision c of this section, may set aside and correct any maximum rent resulting from illegality, irregularity in vital matters or fraud, occurring prior to or after May first, nineteen hundred sixty-two.

c. (1) Whenever such agency determines that such action is necessary to effectuate the purposes of this chapter, it may also establish maximum rents for housing accommodations to which this chapter applies, where no maximum rent with respect thereto was in effect on April thirtieth, nineteen hundred sixty-two, or where no registration statement had been filed with respect thereto as required by the state rent act, or where for any other reason the provisions of subdivision a of this section are not susceptible to application to any such housing accommodations.

(2) Such rents shall be established, having regard for the maximum rents for comparable housing accommodations or any other factors bearing on the equities involved, consistent with the purposes of this chapter.

d. Where any housing accommodations, which are decontrolled (including those decontrolled by order) or exempted from control pursuant to the provisions of subparagraph (i) of paragraph two of subdivision e of section 26-403 of this chapter, are certified by any city agency having jurisdiction to be a fire hazard or in a continued dangerous condition or detrimental to life or health, the city rent agency shall establish maximum rents for such housing accommodations, having regard for the maximum rents for comparable housing accommodations or any other factors bearing on the equities involved, consistent with the purposes of this chapter.

e. Notwithstanding any other provision of this chapter, and subject to the provisions of subdivision f of this section, provision shall be made pursuant to regulations prescribed by the city rent agency for the establishment, adjustment and modification of maximum rents with respect to rooming house and single room occupancy accommodations, which shall include those housing accommodations subject to control pursuant to the provisions of subparagraph (c) of paragraph two of subdivision e of section 26-403 of this chapter (other than those accommodations subject to control under the last proviso of such subparagraph (c)), having regard for any factors bearing on the equities involved, consistent with the purposes of this chapter, to correct speculative, abnormal and unwarranted increases in rent.

f. On or before June thirtieth, nineteen hundred sixty-two, the city rent agency shall undertake a survey and investigation of all factors affecting rents, rental conditions and rental practices with respect to rooming houses and single room occupancy accommodations within the city for the purpose of determining whether the provisions of this chapter and the regulations thereunder relating to the establishment and adjustment of maximum rents for rooming house and single room occupancy accommodations are reasonably designed to prevent exaction of unreasonable and oppressive rents. Not later than January fifteenth, nineteen hundred sixty-three, such agency shall submit to the council a report setting forth the results of such survey and investigation, together with the findings and recommendations of such agency and any amendments to this chapter and the regulations thereunder which such agency may deem necessary or desirable for the accomplishment of the purposes of this chapter in relation to such accommodations. During the period between May first, nineteen hundred sixty-two and the thirtieth day next succeeding the date of the submission of such report to the council (1) no application for an increase in any maximum rent for any rooming house or single room occupancy accommodations may be filed on any ground other than those specified in subparagraphs (f) and (g) of paragraph one of subdivision g of this section, and (2) no maximum rents for any rooming house or single room occupancy accommodations shall be increased on any grounds other than those specified in such subparagraphs (f) and (g); provided that where the maximum rents for any such accommodations were or are decreased prior to or during such period because of the landlord's reduction of living space, essential services, furniture, furnishings or equipment, and such reduction has been corrected, an application for restoration of the rent decrease may be filed and such rents may be adjusted so as to fix maximum rents which the city rent agency may determine to be proper, pursuant to the provisions of subdivision e of this section, but which shall not in any event exceed the maximum rents for such accommodations in effect immediately prior to such rent decrease.

g. (1) The city rent agency may from time to time adopt, promulgate, amend or rescind such rules, regulations and orders as it may deem necessary or proper to effectuate the purposes of this chapter, including practices relating to recovery of possession; provided that such regulations can be put into effect without general uncertainty, dislocation and hardship inconsistent with the purposes of this chapter; and provided further that such regulations shall be designed to maintain a system of rent controls at levels which, in the judgment of such agency, are generally fair and equitable and which will provide for an orderly transition from and termination of emergency controls without undue dislocations, inflationary price rises or disruption. Provisions shall be made, pursuant to regulations prescribed by such agency, for individual adjustment of maximum rents where:

(a) The rental income from a property yields a net annual return of less than six per centum of the valuation of the property.

(1) Such valuation shall be the current assessed valuation established by the city, which is in effect at the time of the filing of the application for an adjustment under this subparagraph (a); provided that:

(i) The city rent agency may make a determination that the valuation of the property is an amount different from such assessed valuation where there has been a reduction in the assessed valuation for the year next preceding the effective date of the current assessed valuation in effect at the time of the filing of the application; and

(ii) Such agency may make a determination that the value of the property is an amount different from the assessed valuation where there has been a bona fide sale of the property within the period February first, nineteen hundred sixty-one, and the time of filing of the application, as the result of a transaction at arm's length, on normal financing terms, at a readily ascertainable price, and unaffected by special circumstances such as but not limited to a forced sale, exchange of property, package deal, wash sale or sale to a cooperative; provided, however, that where an application was filed under this subparagraph (a) on or before the effective date of this sub-item (ii), the city rent agency may determine the value of the property on the basis that there has been a bona fide sale of the property within the period between March fifteenth, nineteen hundred fifty-eight, and the time of the filing of the application. In determining whether a sale was on normal financing terms, such agency shall give due consideration to the following factors:

(a) the ratio of the cash payment received by the seller to (1) the sales price of the property and (2) the annual gross income from the property;

(b) the total amount of the outstanding mortgages which are liens against the property (including purchase money mortgages) as compared with the assessed valuation of the property;

(c) the ratio of the sales price to the annual gross income of the property, with consideration given to the total amount of rent adjustments previously granted, exclusive of rent adjustments because of changes in dwelling space, services, furniture, furnishings or equipment, major capital improvements, or substantial rehabilitation;

(d) the presence of deferred amortization in purchase money mortgages, or the assignment of such mortgage at a discount;

(e) Any other facts and circumstances surrounding such sale which, in the judgment of such agency, may have a bearing upon the question of financing; and

(iii) Where the assessed valuation of the land exceeds four times the assessed valuation of the buildings thereon, the city rent agency may determine a valuation of the property equal to five times the assessed valuation of the buildings, for the purposes of this subparagraph (a).

(2) An application for an increase in any maximum rent under this subparagraph (a) of this paragraph one may not be filed with respect to any property if, on the date when the application is sought to be filed:

(i) Less than two years have elapsed since the date of the filing of the last prior application for an increase under this subparagraph (a) of this paragraph one with respect to such property, which application resulted in the granting of an increase; or

(ii) Less than two years have elapsed since the last sale of the property, and the application is based upon a sale price in excess of the assessed valuation. This subitem shall not apply, however, where less than two years have elapsed since the last sale of the property and the application is based upon a sale within such two-year period at a price in excess of the assessed valuation, if such price is less than the price in the last sale which meets the criteria heretofore specified in this subparagraph (a) occurring prior to two years before the application is sought to be filed and since February first, nineteen hundred sixty-one.

(3) No increase in maximum rents shall be granted under this subparagraph (a) by the city rent agency while there is pending without final disposition any judicial proceeding to correct the final determination of the tax commission with respect to the assessed valuation of such property, (a) for the city fiscal year in which the landlord filed the application for such increase or (b) for the city

fiscal year immediately preceding the filing of the application for such increase.

(4) For the purposes of this subparagraph (a): (i) Net annual return shall be the amount by which the earned income exceeds the operating expenses of the property, excluding mortgage interest and amortization, and excluding allowances for obsolescence and reserves, but including an allowance for depreciation of two per centum of the value of the buildings exclusive of the land, or the amount shown for depreciation of the buildings in the latest required federal income tax return, whichever is lower; provided, however, that no allowance for depreciation of the buildings shall be included where the buildings have been fully depreciated for federal income tax purposes or on the books of the owner; and

(ii) Test year shall be the most recent full calendar year or the landlord's most recent fiscal year or any twelve consecutive months ending not more than ninety days prior to the filing of the application for an increase;

(b) Where a building contains no more than nineteen rental units and the landlord has not been fully compensated by increases in rental income sufficient to offset unavoidable increases in property taxes, fuel, utilities, insurance and repairs and maintenance, excluding mortgage interest and amortization, and excluding allowance for depreciation, obsolescence and reserves, which have occurred since the federal date determining the maximum rent; or

(c) The landlord operates a hotel or rooming house or owns a cooperative apartment and has not been fully compensated by increases in rental income from the controlled housing accommodations sufficient to offset such unavoidable increases in property taxes and other costs as are allocable to such controlled housing accommodations, including costs of operation of such hotel or rooming house, but excluding mortgage interest and amortization, and excluding allowances for depreciation, obsolescence and reserves, which have occurred since the federal date determining the maximum rent or the date the landlord commenced the operation of the property, whichever is later; or

(d) The landlord and tenant in occupancy voluntarily

enter into a valid written lease in good faith with respect to any housing accommodation, which lease provides for an increase in the maximum rent on the basis of specified increased services, furniture, furnishings, or equipment, provided the city rent agency determines that the specified increased services, furniture, furnishings or equipment have a market value commensurate with the increased rent, the increase maximum rent is not in excess of fifteen per centum and the lease is for a term of not less than two years, provided further that a report of lease is filed as prescribed by regulations issued by the city rent agency or has been otherwise accepted by such agency, and provided further, that where the entire structure, or any lesser portion thereof was vacated by order of a city department having jurisdiction, on or after November twenty-second, nineteen hundred sixty-three and any tenants therein were relocated by the department of relocation, or such structure was boarded up by the department of real estate, such lease increases in subsequently executed leases shall not become effective for any housing accommodations in the structure until such departments have been reimbursed for expenses necessarily incurred in connection with the foregoing; provided further, however, that the landlord may obtain such lease increases without making such reimbursement where the vacating was caused by fire or accident not resulting from any unlawful act or omission on the part of the landlord; or

(e) The landlord and tenant by mutual voluntary written agreement, subject to the approval of the city rent agency, agree to a substantial increase or decrease in dwelling space or a change in the services, furniture, furnishings or equipment provided in the housing accommodations; or

(f) There has been since March first, nineteen hundred fifty-nine, an increase in the rental value of the housing accommodations as a result of a substantial rehabilitation of the building or housing accommodation therein which materially adds to the value of the property or appreciably prolongs its life, excluding ordinary repairs, maintenance and replacements; or

(g) There has been since July first, nineteen hundred

seventy, a major capital improvement required for the operation, preservation or maintenance of the structure; or

(h) There has been since March first, nineteen hundred fifty-nine, in structures containing more than four housing accommodations, other improvements made with the express consent of the tenants in occupancy of at least seventy-five per centum of the housing accommodations; provided, however, that whenever the city rent agency has determined that the improvements proposed were part of a plan designed for overall improvement of the structure or increases in services, it may authorize increases in maximum rents for all housing accommodations affected upon the express consent of the tenants in occupancy of at least fifty-one per centum of the housing accommodations, and provided further that no adjustment granted hereunder shall exceed fifteen per centum unless the tenants have agreed to a higher percentage of increase, as herein provided; or

(i) There has been, since March first, nineteen hundred fifty-nine, a subletting without written consent from the landlord or an increase in the number of adult occupants who are not members of the immediate family of the tenant, and the landlord has not been compensated therefor by adjustment of the maximum rent by lease or order of the city rent agency or pursuant to the state rent act or the federal act; or

(j) The presence of unique or peculiar circumstances materially affecting the maximum rent has resulted in a maximum rent which is substantially lower than the rents generally prevailing in the same area for substantially similar housing accommodations.

(k) The landlord has incurred, since January first, nineteen hundred seventy, in connection with and in addition to a concurrent major capital improvement pursuant to subparagraph (g) of this paragraph, other expenditures to improve, restore or preserve the quality of the structure. An adjustment under this subparagraph shall be granted only if such improvements represent an expenditure equal to at least ten per centum of the total operating and maintenance expenses for the preceding year. An adjustment under this subparagraph shall be in addition to any adjustment granted for the concurrent major capital improvement and shall be in an amount sufficient to amortize the cost of the improvements pursuant to this subparagraph over a five-year period.

(*l*) (1) The actual labor expenses currently incurred or to be incurred (pursuant to a collective agreement or other obligation actually entered into by the landlord) exceed the provision for payroll expenses in the current applicable operating and maintenance expense allowance under subdivision a of this section. No application pursuant to this subparagraph may be granted within one year from the granting of an adjustment in maximum rent pursuant to this subparagraph (1), or pursuant to subparagraph (a) of this paragraph. Any rent increase the applicant would be entitled to, or such portion thereof, shall not exceed a total increase of seven and one-half per centum per annum of the maximum rent as provided in paragraph five of subdivision a of this section.

(2) Any adjustment in the maximum rents pursuant hereto shall be subject to:

(i) The adjustment in maximum rent for any twelve-month period for any housing accommodation shall not exceed four percent of the maximum rent in effect on December thirty-first, nineteen hundred seventy-three.

(ii) Where the increase in labor costs compensable herein is the result of an industry-wide collective bargaining agreement or a specific agreement in anticipation of, or subsequent to, an industry-wide collective bargaining agreement, the adjustment shall be in such amount (subject to the above limitation) that the increased rental income from January first, nineteen hundred seventy-four to December thirty-first, nineteen hundred seventy-six shall reflect the increased labor costs for the period from April thirtieth, nineteen hundred seventy-three to April thirtieth, nineteen hundred seventy-six.

(3) For the purpose of this subparagraph (1) the increase in labor costs shall be the amount by which the labor costs (a) actually in effect and paid, or (b) actually in effect and paid or payable and fixed and determined pursuant to agreement on the date of the filing of the application and projected over the period ending April thirtieth, nineteen hundred seventy-six, exceed the labor

costs for the twelve calendar months immediately preceding the last day of the month in which the wage agreement became effective.

(4) Notwithstanding any other provision of this chapter, the adjustment pursuant to this subparagraph shall be collectible upon the landlord's filing of a report with the city rent agency, subject to the provisions of subparagraph (e) of paragraph two of subdivision a of this section.

(5) No increase in the maximum rent for any housing accommodation may be granted under this subparagraph (1) if on the date when the application is sought to be filed, less than the full term of such agreement has elapsed since the date of the filing of the last prior application for an increase with respect to such property under this subparagraph (1), which application resulted in the granting of an increase. Where, however, the landlord establishes the existence of unique or peculiar circumstances affecting an increase in labor costs for the property, the agency may accept such application where it determines that such acceptance is not inconsistent with the purposes of this local law.

(6) The increase authorized herein shall be apportioned equitably among all the housing accommodations in the property whether or not subject to control under this chapter.

(m) Where the rehabilitation or improvement of substandard or deteriorated housing accommodations has been financed under a governmental program providing assistance through loans, loan insurance or tax abatement or has been undertaken under another rehabilitation program not so financed but approved by the commissioner.

(n)(1) The city rent agency shall hereafter promulgate in January of each year;

(i) findings regarding the price increase or decrease, respectively, for all types of heating fuel, including numbers two, four and six home heating oils, utility supplied steam, gas, electricity and coal, together with the sales and excise taxes thereon, on December thirty-first as compared to January first in any year; and

(ii) standards for consumption of heating fuel, which

shall be no more than two hundred twenty-five gallons per year per room commencing January first, nineteen hundred eighty-one, for buildings using heating oils for heat with comparable unit limitations to be established by the city rent agency for utility supplied steam, gas, electricity, coal and any other types of heating systems, provided that such consumption standards for heating fuels shall be reduced by five gallons per room per year for heating oils and a comparable amount for other heating fuels for the next succeeding year and ten gallons per room per year for heating oils and a comparable amount for other heating fuels for two succeeding years thereafter.

Such findings and consumption standards shall be published in the City Record.

(2) To obtain a rental adjustment pursuant to this subparagraph (n), the landlord shall file a report with the agency on forms prescribed by the agency and shall:

(i) certify the amount of heating fuel consumed in the calendar year immediately prior to the filing of the report;

(ii) state the type of fuel used and the number of rooms in the building;

(iii) certify that (a) all essential services required to be provided have been and will continue to be maintained and (b) there has been no rent reduction order issued pursuant to this chapter based on the landlord's failure to provide heat or hot water during the prior twelve months;

(iv) certify on information and belief, in order to qualify for an additional rent increase pursuant to this subparagraph (n), that for an individual housing accommodation, if the maximum rent collectible pursuant to paragraph five of subdivision a of this section plus actual rent adjustments pursuant to this subparagraph (n) and such additional rent increase, is equal to or exceeds the maximum rent established pursuant to paragraphs three and four of subdivision a of this section plus the amount calculated pursuant to subitem (i) of item three and subitem (i) of item four of this subparagraph (n), each to be allocated to such housing accommodation pursuant to subitem (ii) of item four of this subparagraph (n), that the landlord will not be earning an amount in excess of the statutory return specified in subparagraph (a) of paragraph one of subdivision g of this section after collection of a rent increase pursuant to this subparagraph (n), with respect to a building or buildings serviced by a single heating plant;

(v) report any funds received with respect to the housing accommodations from any governmental grant program compensating such landlord for fuel price increases during the period for which an adjustment is obtained pursuant to this subparagraph (n);

(vi) provide such other information as the agency may require.

(3) Rent adjustments for controlled housing accommodations for annual heating fuel cost increases or decreases experienced after December thirty-first, nineteen hundred seventy-nine, shall be determined as follows:

(i) the increase or decrease in heating fuel prices found by the agency for that year shall be multiplied by the actual consumption, not to exceed that year's consumption standard established pursuant to subitem (ii) of item one of this subparagraph; and

(ii) seventy-five percentum of such amount shall be allocated among all rental space in the building, including commercial, professional and similar facilities, provided, for the purposes of this subparagraph (n), that living rooms, kitchens over fifty-nine square feet in area and bedrooms shall be considered rooms and that bathrooms, foyers and kitchenettes shall not be considered rooms.

(4) Rent adjustments for controlled housing accommodations for heating fuel cost increases or decreases experienced from April ninth, nineteen hundred seventy-nine, through and including December thirty-first, nineteen hundred seventy-nine, shall be determined as follows:

(i) the increase or decrease in heating fuel prices found by the agency for that period shall be multiplied by seventy-five percentum of the actual heating fuel consumption during the period from January first, nineteen hundred seventy-nine, through and including December thirty-first, nineteen hundred seventy-nine, which consumption shall not exceed seventy-five percentum of that year's consumption standard established by the agency; and

(ii) such amount shall be allocated among all rental space in the building, including commercial, professional and similar facilities, provided, for the purposes of this subparagraph (n), that living rooms, kitchens over fifty-nine square feet in area and bedrooms shall be considered rooms and that bathrooms, foyers and kitchenettes shall not be considered rooms.

The city rent agency shall promulgate findings for heating fuel price increases or decreases and standards for consumption for the periods set forth in this item four thirty days after this local law is enacted. The standard for consumption shall be no more than seventy-five percentum of two hundred thirty gallons per room for buildings using heating oils for heat with comparable unit limitations to be established by the city rent agency for utility supplied steam, gas, electricity, coal and any other types of heating systems.

(5) A landlord who files a report pursuant to this subparagraph and who falsely certifies shall not be eligible to collect any rent adjustment pursuant to this subparagraph for two years following a determination of a false certification and, in addition, any adjustments obtained pursuant to this subparagraph for up to two years prior to such determination shall not be collectible for that same two year period. Such landlord shall also be subject to any additional penalties imposed by law.

(6) A landlord annually may file a report pursuant to this subparagraph (n) after promulgation by the agency of the findings and consumption standards set forth in item one of subparagraph (n). A rent adjustment pursuant to such report shall be prospectively collectible upon the landlord's serving and filing the report, provided, however, that if a landlord files such report within sixty days of the promulgation of such findings and consumption standards, such rent adjustment shall be retroactive to and shall be effective as of the January first of the year in which the report is filed.

(7) A landlord demanding or collecting a rent adjustment pursuant to this subparagraph (n) shall at the time

of either the demand or collection issue to the tenant either a rent bill or receipt separately setting forth the amount of the adjustment pursuant to this subparagraph (n) and the amount of the maximum rent otherwise demanded or collected. If the tenant has been issued a valid senior citizen rent exemption order, the owner shall also separately state the amount payable by the senior citizen after the exemption.

(8) In the event that a rent reduction order is issued by the city rent agency based upon the landlord's failure to provide heat or hot water to housing accommodations for which the landlord is collecting a rent adjustment pursuant to this subparagraph (n), the rent adjustment shall not be collected during the time such rent reduction order is in effect and for twelve months following the date of the restoration of the rent reduction. In addition, the landlord shall not be eligible to collect any subsequent rent adjustment pursuant to this subparagraph (n) until twelve months following the date of the restoration of the rent reduction.

(9) In the event that the city rent agency promulgates a finding of a price decrease, if any landlord who has obtained a rent adjustment pursuant to this subparagraph (n) does not file a report for a rent adjustment pursuant to this subparagraph (n) within sixty days of the promulgation of such findings, then all rent adjustments obtained pursuant to this subparagraph (n) shall not be collectible for a period of twelve months.

(10) Any rent adjustment obtained pursuant to this subparagraph (n) shall not be included in the maximum rent established pursuant to paragraph four or five of subdivision (a) of this section.

(11) The city rent agency shall have the power to promulgate such regulations as it may consider necessary or convenient to implement and administer the provisions of this subparagraph (n). The regulations shall also require that any rent adjustment granted pursuant to this subparagraph (n) be reduced by an amount equal to any governmental grant received by the landlord compensating the landlord for any fuel price increases, but not required by the city, the agency or any granting govern-

ment entity to be expended for fuel related repairs or improvements.

(o) (1) There has been an increase in heating and heating fuel expenditures in a property resulting from a city-wide rise in heating fuel costs such that the verifiable expenditures for heating or heating fuel in a property for nineteen hundred seventy-four exceeds the verifiable expenditures for such heating or heating fuel during nineteen hundred seventy-three.

(2) To obtain a rental adjustment pursuant to this subparagraph (o), the landlord must certify that he or she is presently maintaining all essential services required to be furnished with respect to the housing accommodations covered by such certification, and that he or she will continue to so maintain such essential services for the period of any such adjustment.

(3) To obtain a rental adjustment pursuant to this subparagraph (o), the landlord must certify on information and belief that he or she will not be earning an amount in excess of the statutory return specified in subparagraph (a) of paragraph one of subdivision g of this section after collection of such rental adjustment, with respect to the building or buildings serviced by a single heating plant; and where the building, or buildings serviced by a single heating plant, contains forty-nine or fewer housing accommodations, the landlord must certify that the amount expended directly for heating or heating fuel in nineteen hundred seventy-four equalled or exceeded ten per cent of the total rental income which was derived from the property during nineteen hundred seventy-four; and, where the building, or buildings serviced by a single heating plant, contains fifty or more housing accommodations the landlord must certify that the amount expended directly for heating or heating fuel in nineteen hundred seventy-four equalled or exceeded seven and one-half percentum of the total rental income which was derived from the property during nineteen hundred seventy-four.

(4) The total rental adjustments for a property to be allocated or deemed allocated pursuant to this subparagraph (o) shall not exceed one-half of the gross amount by which the total verifiable expenditures for heating or

heating fuel for nineteen hundred seventy-four exceeds the total verifiable expenditures for such heating or heating fuel for nineteen hundred seventy-three.

(5) Such total rental adjustments shall be allocated or deemed allocated pursuant to this subparagraph *(o)* to all housing accommodations subject to this chapter, to all other housing accommodations, and to all commercial, professional and similar facilities in or associated with the property in a manner to be determined by the agency. In no event shall any adjustment in maximum rent pursuant to this subparagraph *(o)* for any housing accommodations subject to this chapter exceed a monthly increase of two dollars per room, as defined by item eight below. In any apartment containing five or more rooms, any increase shall not exceed the total of nine dollars.

(6) Any adjustment pursuant to this subparagraph *(o)* shall be effective for all or part of the period July first, nineteen hundred seventy-five through June thirtieth, nineteen hundred seventy-six. Any adjustment pursuant to this subparagraph shall automatically expire no later than June thirtieth, nineteen hundred seventy-six.

(7) The rental increases provided for herein shall be effective and collectible upon the landlord's filing a report with the agency on forms prescribed by the agency and upon giving such notice to the tenants as the agency shall prescribe, subject to adjustments upon order of the agency.

(8) In determining the amount of an adjustment allocation of an adjustment pursuant to this subparagraph *(o)*, only living rooms, kitchens over fifty-nine square feet in area, dining rooms and bedrooms shall be considered rooms; bathrooms, foyers and kitchenettes shall not be considered rooms.

(2) In any case where any housing accommodation was vacated on or after the effective date of this paragraph two, other than by voluntary surrender of possession or in the manner provided in this chapter, the city rent agency may, by regulations having due regard for the equities involved, bar adjustments pursuant to subparagraphs (f) and (g) of paragraph one of this subdivision g, except for work which:

(a) is necessary in order to remove violations against the property;

(b) is necessary to obtain a certificate of occupancy if such certificate is required by law; or

(c) could have been performed with a tenant in physical possession of the housing accommodation.

(3) Any adjustment pursuant to subparagraph (a), (b), or (c) of paragraph one of this subdivision shall be subject to the limitation set forth in paragraph five of subdivision a of this section; provided:

(a) that in ordering an adjustment pursuant to such subparagraph (a), the city rent agency may waive such limitation where a greater increase is necessary to make the earned income of the property equal to its operating expenses; and

(b) that where due to such limitation the landlord will not receive the full amount of the rent increase to which he or she would otherwise be entitled, the order of the city rent agency shall increase the maximum rent by a further additional amount during each succeeding twelve-month period, not to exceed seven and a half percentum of the maximum rent in effect on the date of the filing of the application for an adjustment, under the maximum rent shall reflect the full increase to which the landlord is entitled.

(4) Any increase in maximum rent shall be apportioned equitably among all the controlled housing accommodations in the property. In making such apportionment and in fixing the increases in maximum rents, the city rent agency shall give due consideration (a) to all previous adjustments or increases in maximum rents by lease or otherwise; and (b) to all other income derived from the property, including income from space and accommodations not controlled, or the rental value thereof if vacant or occupied rent-free, so there is allocated to the controlled housing accommodations therein only that portion of the amount of increases necessary pursuant to subparagraph (a), (b), (c) or (k) of paragraph one of this subdivision g, as is properly attributable to such controlled accommodations.

(5) The city rent agency shall compile and make avail-

able for public inspection at reasonable hours at its principal office and at each appropriate local office, the manual of accounting procedures and advisory bulletins applicable to applications under subparagraphs (a), (b) and (c) of paragraph one of this subdivision g, and all amendments to such manual and bulletins.

(6)(a) No application for an increase in any maximum rent may be filed under subparagraph (a), (b) or (c) of paragraph one of this subdivision g with respect to any property unless there is annexed to such application:

(1) A report of search issued by the agency of the city having jurisdiction stating either that no violations against such property are recorded or a receipt (or photocopy thereof) issued by that agency attesting to the payment of the fee for the report of search or that all violations recorded against such property have been cleared, corrected or abated; and

(2) A certification by the landlord of such property that he or she is maintaining all essential services required to be furnished and that he or she will continue to maintain such services so long as any such increase in the maximum rent continues in effect.

(b) Except as provided in subparagraph (c) of this paragraph six and paragraph four of subdivision h of this section, no landlord shall be entitled to an increase in the maximum rent on any ground unless he or she certifies that he or she is maintaining all essential services furnished or required to be furnished as of the date of the issuance of the order adjusting the maximum rent and that he or she will continue to maintain such services so long as the increase in such maximum rent continues in effect; nor shall any landlord be entitled to any increase in the maximum rent on any ground where an agency of the city having jurisdiction certifies that the housing accommodation is a fire hazard or is a continued dangerous condition or detrimental to life or health or is occupied in violation of law; nor shall any landlord be entitled to any increase where the landlord has not removed the violations recorded against such property as shown in the report of search required under subparagraph (a) of this paragraph six.

(c) Where an application for an increase in any maximum rent is filed under subparagraph (f) and/or (g) of paragraph one of this subdivision g, and the landlord is not entitled to any increase by reason of the provisions of subparagraph (b) of this paragraph six, the city rent agency may waive such provisions and issue orders increasing the maximum rent effective as of the date of the issuance of the orders provided, however, that the landlord agrees in writing to deposit the entire amount of such increase in maximum rent into an escrow account administered by the city rent agency in accordance with rules and regulations to be promulgated by such agency for the purpose of obtaining compliance with such provisions and further agrees to obtain and submit to the city rent agency within one year from the date of issuance of such orders; a report of search issued by the agency of the city having jurisdiction stating that the violations shown in the report of search required under subparagraph (a) of this paragraph six have been removed, cleared, corrected or abated, and his or her own certification that he or she is and will continue to maintain all essential services in accordance with the provisions of subparagraph (b) of this paragraph six. In the event the landlord fails to fully comply with such provisions within one year from the date of the issuance of the order increasing the maximum rent, the city agency may, having due regard for the equities involved, revoke such orders and direct full refund to the tenants of the entire increase paid by the tenants as a result of such orders. Any person serving as escrow agent shall not be liable except for fraud or misfeasance.

(d) No new maximum rent shall be established pursuant to paragraph three or four of subdivision a of this section unless not more than one hundred fifty days nor less than ninety days prior to the effective date thereof, the landlord has certified that he or she is maintaining all essential services required to be furnished with respect to the housing accommodations covered by such certification, and that he or she will continue to maintain such services so long as such new maximum rent pursuant to paragraph four of subdivision a of this section shall be accompanied by a certification by the landlord that he or she has actually expended or incurred ninety per centum of the total amount of the cost index for operation and maintenance established for his or her type of building.

(e) The city rent agency shall establish a counseling service to provide assistance to tenants and to landlords of buildings containing nineteen or fewer housing accommodations, by way of instruction in the management, maintenance and upkeep of housing accommodations, their respective responsibilities thereto, the programs and enforcement remedies available in the agency and from other city agencies, and assistance in the preparation of applications and other forms.

(7) Before ordering any adjustment in maximum rents, the city rent agency shall accord a reasonable opportunity to be heard thereon to the tenant and the landlord.

h. (1) Whenever in the judgment of the city rent agency such action is necessary or proper in order to effectuate the purposes of this chapter, such agency may, by regulation or order, regulate or prohibit speculative or manipulative practices or renting or leasing practices, including practices relating to recovery of possession, which in the judgment of such agency are equivalent to or are likely to result in rent increases inconsistent with the purposes of this chapter.

(2) Whenever in the judgment of such agency such action is necessary or proper in order to effectuate the purposes of this chapter, such agency may provide regulations to assure the maintenance of the same living space, essential services, furniture, furnishings and equipment as were provided on the date determining the maximum rent, and such agency shall have power by regulation or order to decrease the maximum rent or take action as provided in paragraph four of this subdivision h for any housing accommodation with respect to which a maximum rent is in effect, pursuant to this chapter, if it shall find that the living space, essential services, furniture, furnishings or equipment to which the tenant was entitled on such date have been decreased.

(3) Whenever any agency of the city having jurisdiction certifies that any housing accommodation is a fire hazard or is in a continued dangerous condition or detrimental to life or health, or is occupied in violation of law, the city

rent agency may issue an order decreasing the maximum rent or take action as provided in paragraph four of this subdivision h for such housing accommodation in such amount as it deems necessary or proper, until the agency issuing such certification has certified that such housing accommodation is no longer a fire or other hazard and is not in a condition detrimental to life and health and is not occupied in violation of law.

(4)(a) Whenever in the judgment of the city rent agency such action is necessary or proper in order to effectuate the purposes of this chapter, such agency may, in lieu of decreasing the maximum rents as provided in paragraphs two and three of this subdivision h, enter into a contract wherein the landlord agrees in writing to deposit all income derived from the property, including income from spaces and accommodations not controlled, into an escrow or trust account for use in maintaining or restoring essential services and equipment, for removing violations against the property or housing accommodations therein, making such repairs as are necessary to remove a certification from any city agency having jurisdiction thereof that the housing accommodation is a fire hazard or is in a continued dangerous condition or detrimental to life or health, or is occupied in violation of law, and/or for such other uses as the city rent agency deems necessary or proper for the preservation, repair or maintenance of the property. The city rent agency may adopt such rules and regulations and orders as it may deem necessary or proper to effectuate the purposes of this paragraph, including but not limited to the issuance of orders adjusting all controlled rents to the appropriate maximum rent effective as of the first day of the month following the execution of the contract provided, however, that in the event the city rent agency shall determine that the landlord has breached such contract, such agency may issue orders (1) decreasing the maximum rents pursuant to such contract; (2) containing a directive that rent collected by the landlord in excess of the rent thus decreased be refunded to the tenants; and (3) containing such other determinations and directives as are necessary in order to effectuate the purposes of this paragraph four.

(b) Notwithstanding any provision of this chapter to the

contrary, whenever in the judgment of the city rent agency action as provided in paragraph two or three of this subdivision h is necessary or proper in order to effectuate the purposes of this chapter, such agency may in lieu of decreasing the maximum rents thereof issue orders adjusting all controlled rents and directing that rents be paid into an escrow account for the uses stated in subparagraph (a) of this paragraph four where:

(1) The landlord fails to take corrective action after notice by the city rent agency of proposed action to decrease the maximum rents pursuant to paragraph two or three of this subdivision h, and,

(2) The city rent agency has notified all mortgagees who have filed with the city rent agency a declaration of interest in such property and in such proposed action, and,

(3) The landlord has failed for three consecutive months to collect any controlled rents or to commence court proceedings for their collection or if such proceedings have been commenced, the landlord has not diligently prosecuted them or such proceedings have not resulted in judgment in favor of such landlord.

(c) The city rent agency shall promulgate rules and regulations for the administration of escrow and trust accounts set forth in this paragraph four. Any person serving as escrow agent or trustee shall not be liable except for fraud, breach of fiduciary duties or misfeasance.

(5) Whenever the essential services, furnishings, furniture or equipment of any individual housing accommodation are reduced, impaired, mutilated, or made unworkable as the result of the neglect, failure to exercise due care, or failure of the tenant to take practicable precautions to prevent such condition, the landlord shall restore such services, furniture, furnishings or equipment and pursuant to regulations to be prescribed by the city rent agency may make application for a temporary increase in the maximum rent based upon the cost of such restoration. In the event of the failure of the tenant to make restitution within a reasonable time, as determined by the city rent agency an order shall be issued adjusting the maximum rent for such tenant in an amount suffi-

cient to recover the cost over twelve monthly installments, or until the tenant surrenders possession, whichever is sooner. The provisions of this paragraph shall be in addition to all other rights and remedies of the landlord.

(6) If at least six months before the effective date of any adjustment or establishment of rents pursuant to paragraph three or four of subdivision a of this section, the landlord has not certified to the agency having jurisdiction that (a) all rent impairing violations (as defined by section three hundred two-a of the multiple dwelling law), and (b) at least eighty per centum of all other violations of the housing maintenance code or other state or local laws that impose requirements on property that were recorded against the property one year prior to such effective date have been cleared, corrected, or abated, no increase pursuant to such paragraphs shall take effect until he or she shall have entered into a written agreement with the city rent agency to deposit all income derived from the property into an escrow or trust account pursuant to subparagraph (a) of paragraph four of this subdivision, in addition to the procedures set forth in this paragraph and all other applicable penalties and procedures under this chapter, such violation shall also be subject to repair or removal by the city pursuant to the provisions of article five of subchapter five of the housing maintenance code, the landlord to be liable for the cost thereof.

i. Any regulation or order issued pursuant to this section may be established in such form and manner, may contain such classifications and differentiations, and may provide for such adjustments including the establishment of new or adjusted maximum rents in whole dollar amounts, and such reasonable exceptions as in the judgment of the city rent agency are necessary or proper in order to effectuate the purposes of this chapter.

j. No increase or decrease in maximum rent shall be effective prior to the date on which the order therefor is issued, except as hereinafter provided. If an application for an increase pursuant to subparagraph (a) of paragraph one of subdivision g of this section submitted on or after August first, nineteen hundred seventy is accompanied by a certified statement of expenditures and no order is issued thereon within four months of the filing of an application based on assessed value or equalized assessed value, or eight months of the filing of an application based on sale price, with all required documentation the increased rent requested shall thereafter be placed in an interest bearing escrow account until a final determination is made upon such application by the city rent agency. Upon initial determination by the agency an order shall be issued providing for the payment of the increased amount, if any, due to the landlord from the date of first deposit of rent in said escrow account with interest, and the excess amount, if any, be paid the tenants entitled thereto, with an appropriate amount of interest. The city rent agency shall promulgate rules and regulations for the administration of such escrow accounts. Any person serving as escrow agent shall not be liable except for fraud or misfeasance.

k. Regulations, orders, and requirements under this chapter may contain such provisions as the city rent agency deems necessary to prevent the circumvention or evasion thereof.

l. The powers granted in this action shall not be used or made to operate to compel changes in established rental practices, except where such action is affirmatively found by the city rent agency to be necessary to prevent circumvention or evasion of any regulation, order, or requirement under this chapter.

m. Findings. The council finds that there is an acute and continuing housing shortage; that this shortage has and continues to have an adverse effect on the population and especially on inhabitants of the city who are sixty-two years of age or older and of limited means, who cannot pay enough rent to induce private enterprise to maintain decent housing at rents they can afford to pay; that this condition is and continues to be particularly acute in a time of rising costs such as the present; that present rising costs and the continuing increase in rents pursuant to amendments to the New York City rent and rehabilitation law may result in such persons being unable to pay their rent, thus making them subject to eviction; that such hardships fall with particular severity upon older persons in the population because of their particular inability to find alternative accommodations within their means, because of the trauma experienced by many older persons who have to relocate and because they may endanger their health by paying additional sums for shelter and thereby deprive themselves of other necessities; that hardships imposed upon such people adversely affect their health and welfare and the general welfare of the inhabitants of the city. The council is aware of the provisions set forth in chapter three hundred seventy-two and chapter one thousand twelve of the laws of nineteen hundred seventy-one. It is our considered opinion that this legislation extending the rent exemption to cover the resultant rent increases due to the maximum rents established January first, nineteen hundred seventy-two, is not more stringent or restrictive than those presently in effect. It is, therefore, found and declared to be necessary for the health, welfare and safety of such persons and of inhabitants of the city that the city continue a system of special rent adjustments for such persons as hereinafter provided.

(1) No increase in maximum rent pursuant to paragraph two or paragraph three, four or five of subdivision a of this section, or subparagraph (a), (b), (c), (*l*) or (n) of paragraph one of subdivision g of this section, shall be collectible from a tenant to whom there has been issued a currently valid rent exemption order pursuant to this subdivision, except as provided in such order.

(2) A tenant is eligible for a rent exemption order pursuant to this subdivision if:

(i) the head of the household residing in the housing accommodation is sixty-two years of age or older and is entitled to the possession or to the use or occupancy of a dwelling unit.

Nothing herein contained shall render ineligible for benefits persons receiving supplemental security income or additional state payments, or both, under a program administered by the United States department of health and human services or by such department and the New York state department of social services.

(ii) The aggregate disposable income (as defined by regulation of the department of housing preservation and development) of all members of the household residing in the housing accommodation does not exceed twelve thousand twenty-five dollars per year, after deduction of federal, state and city income and social security taxes; and

(iii)(a) in the case of a head of the household who does not receive a monthly allowance for shelter pursuant to the social services law, the maximum rent for the housing accommodations exceeds one-third of the aggregate disposable income or if any expected increase in the maximum rent pursuant to paragraph two, three, four or five of subdivision a of this section, or subparagraph (a), (b), (c), (l) or (n) of paragraph one of subdivision g of this section would cause such maximum rent to exceed one-third of the aggregate disposable income; or

(b) in the case of a head of the household who receives a monthly allowance for shelter pursuant to the social services law, the maximum rent for the housing accommodations exceeds the maximum allowance for shelter which the head of the household is entitled to receive pursuant to the social services law or if any expected increase in the maximum rent pursuant to paragraph two, three, four or five of subdivision a of this section, or subparagraph (a), (b), (c), (l) or (n) of paragraph one of subdivision g of this section would cause such maximum rent to exceed the maximum allowance for shelter which the head of the household is entitled to receive.

(3)(a) A rent exemption order pursuant to this subdivision shall provide:

(i) in the case of a head of the household who does not receive a monthly allowance for shelter pursuant to the social services law, that the landlord may not collect from the tenant to whom it is issued rent at a rate in excess of one-third of the aggregate disposable income, or the maximum collectible rent in effect on December thirty-first of the year preceding the effective date of the order, whichever is greater: or

(ii) in the case of a head of the household who receives a monthly allowance for shelter pursuant to the social services law, that the landlord may not collect from the tenant to whom it is issued rent at a rate in excess of either the maximum allowance for shelter which the head of the household is entitled to receive, or the maximum collectible rent in effect on December thirty-first of the year preceding the effective date of the order, whichever is greater: except

(iii) that the landlord may collect from the tenants described in items (i) and (ii) of this subparagraph increases in rent pursuant to subparagraphs (d), (e), and (i) of paragraph one of subdivision g of this section.

(b) Each such order shall expire upon termination of occupancy of the housing accommodation by the tenant to whom it is issued. The landlord shall notify the city rent agency, on a form to be prescribed by such agency, within thirty days of each such termination of occupancy.

(4) Any landlord who collects, or seeks to collect or enforce, rent from a tenant in violation of the terms of a rent exemption order shall, for the purposes of all remedies, sanctions and penalties provided in this chapter, be deemed to have collected or attempted to collect or enforce, a rent in excess of the legal maximum rent.

(5) A rent exemption order shall be issued to each tenant who applies to the New York City department of housing preservation and development in accordance with its regulations and who is found to be eligible under this subdivision. Such order shall take effect on the first day of the first month after receipt of such application, except that where the aggregate disposable income of all members of the household residing in the housing accommodation is greater than five thousand dollars per year but does not exceed twelve thousand twenty-five dollars per year pursuant to subparagraph (ii) of paragraph two of this subdivision m of this section on orders issued on applications received before July first, nineteen hundred seventy-five, the effective date of such order shall be the later of (1) June thirty, nineteen hundred seventy-four or (2) the last day of the month in which a person becomes an eligible head of household in the housing accommodation in which such person resides at the time of filing the most recent application for a rent exemption order, and further, except that where any other application has been received within ninety days of the issuance of the order increasing the tenant's maximum rent pursuant to paragraph three, four or six of subdivision (a) of this section, or subparagraph (a), (b), (c) or (1) of paragraph (1) of

subdivision (g) of this section or pursuant to court order, whichever is later, the rent exemption order shall without further order take effect as of the effective date of said order increasing the tenant's rent including any retroactive increments collectible pursuant to such orders.

(6) A rent exemption order shall be valid for a period of one year and may be renewed for further one year periods upon application by the tenant; provided, that upon any such renewal application being made by the tenant, any rent exemption order then in effect with respect to such tenant shall be deemed renewed until such time as the department of housing preservation and development shall have found such tenant to be either eligible or ineligible for a rent exemption order but in no event for more than six additional months. If such tenant is found eligible, the order shall be deemed to have taken effect upon expiration of the exemption. In the event that any such tenant shall, subsequent to any such automatic renewal, not be granted a rent exemption order, such tenant shall be liable to his or her landlord for the difference between the amounts he or she has paid under the provisions of the automatically renewed order and the amounts which he or she would have been required to pay in the absence of such order. Any rent exemption order issued pursuant to this subdivision shall include provisions giving notice as to the contents of this paragraph relating to automatic renewals of rent exemption orders. Any application or renewal application for a rent exemption order shall also constitute an application for a tax abatement under such section. The department of housing preservation and development may, with respect to renewal applications by tenants whom it has found eligible for rent exemption orders, prescribe a simplified form including a certification of the applicant's continued eligibility in lieu of a detailed statement of income and other qualifications.

(7) Notwithstanding the provisions of this chapter, a tenant who resides in a housing accommodation which becomes subject to this chapter upon the sale by the city of New York of the building in which such housing accommodation is situated may be issued a rent increase

exemption order for increases in rent which occurred during ownership of such building by the city of New York provided that such tenant would have been otherwise eligible to receive a rent increase exemption order at the time of such increase but for the fact that such tenant occupied a housing accommodation owned by the city of New York and was therefore not subject to this chapter. Application for such rent increase exemption orders shall be made within one year from the date such building is sold by the city of New York or within one year of the effective date of this provision, whichever is later.

(8) Notwithstanding the provisions of this chapter or chapter four of this title, when a dwelling unit is subject to regulation under this chapter or chapter four of this title is reclassified by a city rent agency order subject to the other chapter, the tenant, who holds a senior citizen rent increase exemption order at the time of the reclassification or is otherwise eligible and entitled to an exemption order from one or more rent increases but for the reclassification of the dwelling unit, may be issued a rent increase exemption order under the chapter to which the unit is thereafter subject by virtue of the reclassification continuing the previous exemption notwithstanding the reclassification of the dwelling unit or, where no previous rent increase exemption order has been granted, issuing an initial order exempting the tenant from paying the rent increase to the extent for which he or she would have been eligible and entitled to be exempted at the time of the increase and reclassification but for the fact of reclassification of the dwelling unit including exemption from the rent increase granted pursuant to subparagraph (m) of paragraph one of subdivision g of this section to the extent that it is not predicated upon any improvement or addition in a category as provided for in subparagraph (d), (e), (f), (g), (h) or (i) of paragraph one of subdivision g of this section. Application for such rent increase exemption order shall be made within ninety days from the date of reclassification or within ninety days of the effective date of this paragraph, whichever is later. The rent increase exemption order shall take effect as of the effective date of reclassification including any retroactive increments pursuant to such rent increase.

§ 26-406. Tax abatement for properties subject to rent exemption orders

a. Tax abatement, pursuant to the provisions of section four hundred sixty-seven-b of the real property tax law, shall be granted with respect to any real property for which a rent exemption order is issued under subdivision n of section 26-405 of this chapter to the tenant of any housing accommodation contained therein. The rent exemption order shall also constitute the tax abatement certificate.

b. The real estate tax imposed upon any real property for which a rent exemption order is issued, shall be reduced and abated by an amount equal to the difference between (1) the sum of the maximum rents collectible under such orders, and (2) the sum of rents that would be collectible from the tenants of such housing accommodations if no exemption had been granted pursuant to subdivision n of section 26-405 of this chapter.

c. For any individual housing accommodation, the tax abatement computed pursuant to subdivision b of this section shall be available with respect to a period commencing on the effective date of the initial rent exemption order, or January first, nineteen hundred seventy-two, whichever is later, and ending on the expiration date of such order or on the effective date of an order terminating the rent exemption. Notwithstanding any other provision of law, when a head of a household to whom a then current, valid tax abatement certificate has been issued under this chapter, chapter four or chapter seven of this title moves his or her principal residence to a subsequent dwelling unit subject to regulation under this chapter, the head of the household may apply to the city rent agency for a tax abatement certificate relating to the subsequent dwelling unit, and such certificate may provide that the head of the household shall be exempt from paying that portion of the maximum rent for the subsequent dwelling unit which is the least of the following:

(1) the amount by which the rent for the subsequent dwelling unit exceeds the last rent, as reduced, which the head of the household was required to actually pay in the original dwelling unit;

(2) the last amount deducted from the maximum rent

or legal regulated rent meaning the most recent monthly deduction for the applicant in the original dwelling unit pursuant to this section, section 26-508 or section 26-605 of this title; or

(3) where the head of the household does not receive a monthly allowance for shelter pursuant to the Social Services law, the amount by which the maximum rent or legal regulated rent of the subsequent dwelling unit exceeds one-third of the combined income of all members of the household.

Such certificate shall be effective as of the first day of the month in which the tenant applied for such exemption or as of the date the tenant took occupancy of the subsequent dwelling unit, whichever is later, provided both occur after the effective date of this law.

d. Prior to the commencement of each fiscal year, the department of housing preservation and development shall notify the department of finance of the total amount of taxes to be abated under this section with respect to each property for which rent exemption orders were in effect for all or any part of the preceding calendar year. The commissioner of finance shall make the appropriate adjustment in the real estate tax payable in such fiscal year.

e. Tax abatement pursuant to this section shall be in addition to any other tax abatement authorized by law, but shall not reduce the tax for any fiscal year below zero. In the event that the tax abatement certificate authorizes an amount of deduction in excess of the real estate installment, then the balance may be applied to any subsequent installment until exhausted. In such a case the owner shall submit with his or her real estate tax bill and remittance, a verified statement in such form as prescribed by the commissioner of finance setting forth the carry over amount and the amounts previously applied; provided, however, that at the request of the owner such balance shall be paid to the owner by the commissioner of finance in lieu of being applied to any subsequent installment, except where the owner is in arrears in the payment of real estate taxes on any property. For the purposes of this subdivision, where the owner is a corporation, it shall be deemed to be in arrears when any of the officers, directors or any person holding an interest in more than ten percent of the issued and outstanding stock of such corporation is in arrears in the payment of real estate taxes on any property; where title is held by a nominee, the owner shall be deemed to be in arrears when the person for whose benefit such title is held is in arrears in the payment of real estate taxes on any property.

§ 26-407. Labor cost pass-along

a. Notwithstanding any provisions of this chapter, any labor cost pass-along rent increase requested of, or received from, any tenant on or after July first, nineteen hundred seventy-two, pursuant to the provisions of subparagraph (1) of paragraph one of subdivision g of section 26-405 of this title, shall not exceed the maximum rent adjustment as provided under this chapter after the effective date of this section.

b. All such increases in excess of such maximum rent are hereby declared null and void and of no effect. A tenant who paid any such excess increase shall be repaid by a cash refund or credit, to be applied against future rent, in equal installments for the same number of months for which such increase was actually collected, commencing on January first, nineteen hundred seventy-eight.

§ 26-408. Evictions

a. No tenant, so long as he or she continues to pay the rent to which the landlord is entitled, shall be removed from any housing accommodation which is subject to rent control under this chapter by action to evict or to recover possession, by exclusion from possession, or otherwise, nor shall recover possession, by exclusion from possession, or otherwise, nor shall any person attempt such removal or exclusion from possession notwithstanding the fact that the tenant has no lease or that his or her lease, or other rental agreement, has expired or otherwise terminated, notwithstanding any contract, lease agreement, or obligation heretofore or hereafter entered into which provides for surrender of possession, or which otherwise provides contrary hereto, except on one or more of the following grounds, or unless the landlord has obtained a certificate of eviction pursuant to subdivision b of this section:

(1) The tenant is violating a substantial obligation of his or her tenancy other than the obligation to surrender possession of such housing accommodation and has failed to cure such violation after written notice by the landlord that the violation cease within ten days, or within the three month period immediately prior to the commencement of the proceeding the tenant has wilfully violated such an obligation inflicting serious and substantial injury to the landlord; or

(2) The tenant is committing or permitting a nuisance in such housing accommodation; or is maliciously or by reason of gross negligence substantially damaging the housing accommodation; or his or her conduct is such as to interfere substantially with the comfort and safety of the landlord or of other tenants or occupants of the same or other adjacent building or structure; or

(3) Occupancy of the housing accommodation by the tenant is illegal because of the requirements of law, and the landlord is subject to civil or criminal penalties therefor, or both, provided, however, that such occupancy shall not be considered illegal by reason of violations placed against the housing accommodations or the building in which same are located by any department or agency of the city having jurisdiction unless such department or agency has issued an order requiring the tenants to vacate said accommodation or building or unless such occupancy for such building or such violations relied on by the landlord result from an act, omission or situation caused or created by the tenant; or

(4) The tenant is using or permitting such housing accommodation to be used for an immoral or illegal purpose; or

(5) The tenant who had a written lease or other written rental agreement which terminated or shall terminate on or after May first, nineteen hundred fifty, has refused upon demand of the landlord to execute a written extension or renewal thereof for a further term of like duration not in excess of one year but otherwise on the same terms and conditions as the previous lease except in so

far as such terms and conditions are inconsistent with this chapter; or

(6) The tenant has unreasonably refused the landlord access to the housing accommodation for the purpose of making necessary repairs or improvements required by law or for the purpose of inspection or of showing the accommodation to a prospective purchaser, mortgagee or prospective mortgagee, or other person having a legitimate interest therein; provided, however, that in the latter event such refusal shall not be ground for removal or eviction if such inspection or showing of the accommodation is contrary to the provisions of the tenant's lease or other rental agreement.

(7) The eviction is sought by the owner of a dwelling unit or the shares allocated thereto where such dwelling unit is located in a structure owned as a cooperative or as a condominium and an offering prospectus for the conversion of such structure pursuant to an eviction plan shall have been submitted to the attorney general pursuant to section three hundred fifty-two-eeee of the general business law and accepted for filing by the attorney general, and been declared effective in accordance with such law, and any right of continued occupancy granted by such law to a non-purchasing tenant in occupancy of such dwelling unit shall have expired; provided that the owner of the dwelling unit or the shares allocated thereto seeks in good faith to recover possession of a dwelling unit for his or her own personal use and occupancy or for the use and occupancy of his or her immediate family.

b. No tenant shall be removed or evicted on grounds other than those stated in subdivision a of this section unless on application of the landlord the city rent agency shall issue an order granting a certificate of eviction in accordance with its rules and regulations designed to effectuate the purposes of this title, permitting the landlord to pursue his or her remedies at law. The city rent agency shall issue such an order whenever it finds that:

(1) The landlord seeks in good faith to recover possession of a housing accommodation because of immediate and compelling necessity for his or her own personal use and occupancy or for the use and occupancy of his or her immediate family provided, however, that this subdivision

shall not apply where a member of the household lawfully occupying the housing accommodation is sixty-two years of age or older, has been a tenant in a housing accommodation in that building for twenty years or more, or has an impairment which results from anatomical, physiological or psychological conditions, other than addiction to alcohol, gambling, or any controlled substance, which are demonstrable by medically acceptable clinical and laboratory diagnostic techniques, and which are expected to be permanent and which prevent the tenant from engaging in any substantial gainful employment; or

(2) The landlord seeks in good faith to recover possession of a housing accommodation for which the tenant's lease or other rental agreement has expired or otherwise terminated, and at the time of termination the occupants of the housing accommodation are subtenants or other persons who occupied under a rental agreement with the tenant, and no part of the accommodation is used by the tenant as his or her dwelling; or

(3) The landlord seeks in good faith to recover possession of a housing accommodation for the immediate purpose of substantially altering or remodeling it, provided that the landlord shall have secured such approval therefor as is required by law and the city rent agency determines that the issuance of the order granting the certificate of eviction is not inconsistent with the purpose of this chapter; or

(4) The landlord seeks in good faith to recover possession of housing accommodations for the immediate purpose of demolishing them, and the city rent agency determines that such demolition is to be effected for the purpose of constructing a new building, provided that:

(a) If the purpose of such demolition is to construct a new building containing housing accommodations, no certificate of eviction shall be granted under this paragraph unless such agency determines that such new building will contain at least twenty per centum more housing accommodations consisting of self-contained family units (as defined by regulations issued by such agency, with due regard for the shortage of housing accommodations suitable for family occupancy and for the purposes of this chapter in relation thereto) than are contained in the structure to be demolished; except, however, that where as a result of conditions detrimental to life or health of the tenants, violations have been placed upon the structure containing the housing accommodations by any agency of the city having jurisdiction over such matters and the cost of removing such violations would be substantially equal to or would exceed the assessed valuation of the structure, the new building shall only be required to make provision for a greater number of housing accommodations consisting of self-contained family units (as so defined by regulation) than are contained in the structure to be demolished; and

(b) The city rent agency shall, by regulation, as a condition to the granting of certificates of eviction under this paragraph, require the relocation of the tenants in other suitable accommodations, provided that the city rent agency may, by regulation, authorize the granting of such certificates as to any tenants or classes of tenants without such requirement of relocation, where such exemption will not result in hardship to such tenants or classes of tenants and will not be inconsistent with the purposes of this chapter; and

(c) The city rent agency may, by regulation, in order to carry out the purposes of this chapter, impose additional conditions to the granting of certificates of eviction under this paragraph, including, but not limited to, the payment of stipends to the tenants by the landlord in such amounts and subject to such variations and classifications as such agency may determine to be reasonably necessary; and

(d) No certificate of eviction shall be issued pursuant to this paragraph unless the landlord shall have secured such approval as is required by law for the construction sought to be effected, and the city rent agency determines that the issuance of such certificate is not inconsistent with the purpose of this chapter.

(5) Notwithstanding any provisions to the contrary contained in this subdivision or in subdivision d of section 26-410 of this chapter or in the local emergency housing rent control act:

(a) no application for a certificate of eviction under paragraph three or four of this subdivision and no application for a certificate of eviction under paragraph one of subdivision j or under subdivision c of this section for the purpose of withdrawing a housing accommodation from the housing market on the grounds that the continued operation of such housing accommodation would impose undue hardship upon the landlord, pending or made on or after the effective date hereof shall be granted by the city rent agency unless the city rent agency finds that there is no reasonable possibility that the landlord can make a net annual return of eight and one-half per centum of the assessed value of the subject property without recourse to the remedy provided in said paragraph three or four or said subdivision c or j and finds that neither the landlord nor his or her immediate predecessor in interest has intentionally or willfully managed the property to impair the landlord's ability to earn such return; and

(b) the effectiveness of any certificate of eviction or of any order granting a certificate of eviction pursuant to paragraphs three and four of this subdivision shall be suspended, and no tenant may be evicted pursuant to any such certificate or order, unless the city rent agency:

(i) finds that there is no reasonable possibility that the landlord can make a net annual return of eight and one-half per centum of the assessed value of the subject property without recourse to the remedy provided in said paragraphs three and four and finds that neither the landlord nor his or her immediate predecessor in interest has intentionally or willfully managed the property to impair the landlord's ability to earn such return; and

(ii) issues an order reinstating the effectiveness of any certificate of eviction suspended pursuant to this paragraph. The pendency of any judicial proceeding or appeal shall in no way prevent the taking effect of the relief granted in this subparagraph.

(c) the provisions of this paragraph shall not apply to an application for a certificate of eviction from a housing accommodation when the landlord seeks in good faith to recover possession thereof for the immediate purpose of substantially altering or remodelling it or for the immediate purpose of demolishing it for the purpose of constructing a new building when such altering or remodelling or the construction of such new building is to be aided by interest reduction payments under section two hundred thirty-six of the national housing act.

c. The city rent agency may from time to time, to effectuate the purposes of this chapter, adopt, promulgate, amend or rescind such rules, regulations or orders as it may deem necessary or proper for the control of evictions. Any such rules, regulations or orders may include, in addition to any other provisions authorized by this subdivision, provisions restricting the filing of applications for, or the issuance of orders granting, certificates of eviction where such agency finds that a course of conduct has been engaged in which is proscribed by subdivision d of section 26-412 of this chapter. The agency shall also require, prior to the filing of plans with the department of buildings for a new building or alteration on the site of controlled housing accommodations and prior to the filing of an application for a permit for the demolition or removal of an existing multiple dwelling which contains controlled housing accommodations, that the applicant certify to and file with the agency such information and give such notice to tenants as it deems necessary to prevent evasion of the law and regulations governing evictions. It may also require that an order granting a certificate of eviction be obtained from it prior to the institution of any action or proceeding for the recovery of possession of any housing accommodation subject to rent control under this chapter upon the grounds specified in subdivision b of this section or where it finds that the requested removal or eviction is not inconsistent with the purposes of this chapter and would not be likely to result in circumvention or evasion thereof; provided, however, that no such order shall be required in any action or proceeding brought pursuant to the provisions of subdivision a of this section.

d. (1) The city rent agency, on its own initiative or on application of a tenant, may revoke or cancel an order granting a certificate of eviction at any time prior to the execution of a warrant in a summary proceeding to recover possession of real property by a court whenever it finds that:

(a) The certificate of eviction was obtained by fraud or illegality; or

(b) The landlord's intentions or circumstances have so changed that the premises, possession of which is sought, will not be used for the purpose specified in the certificate.

(2) The commencement of a proceeding by the city rent agency to revoke or cancel an order granting a certificate of eviction shall stay such order until the final determination of the proceeding regardless of whether the waiting period in the order has already expired. In the event the city rent agency cancels or revokes such an order, the court having jurisdiction of any summary proceeding instituted in such case shall take appropriate action to dismiss the application for removal of the tenant from the real property and to vacate and annul any final order or warrant granted or issued by the court in the matter.

e. Notwithstanding the preceding provisions of this section, the state, the city, or the New York city housing authority may recover possession of any housing accommodations operated by it where such action or proceeding is authorized by statute or regulations under which such accommodations are administered.

f. Any order of the city rent agency under this section granting a certificate of eviction shall be subject to judicial review only in the manner prescribed by subdivision eight of section one of the state enabling act and sections 26-410 and 26-411 of this chapter.

g. (1) Where after the city rent agency has granted a certificate of eviction authorizing the landlord to pursue his or her remedies pursuant to law to acquire possession and a tenant voluntarily removes from a housing accommodation or has been removed therefrom by action or proceeding to evict from or recover possession of a housing accommodation upon the ground that the landlord seeks in good faith to recover possession of such accommodation:

(a) For his or her immediate and personal use, or for the immediate and personal use by a member or members of his or her immediate family, and such landlord or members of his or her immediate family shall fail to occupy such accommodation within thirty days after the tenant vacates, or such landlord shall lease or rent such space or permit occupancy thereof by a third person within a period of one year after such removal of the tenant; or

(b) For the immediate purpose of withdrawing such housing accommodation from the rental market and such landlord shall lease or sell the housing accommodation or the space previously occupied thereby, or permit use thereof in a manner other than contemplated in such eviction certificate within a period of one year after such removal of the tenant; or

(c) For the immediate purpose of altering or remodeling such housing accommodation, and the landlord shall fail to start the work of alteration or remodeling of such housing accommodation within ninety days after the removal, on the ground that he or she required possession for the purpose of effecting such alteration or remodeling, of the last tenant whose removal is necessary to enable the landlord to effect such alteration or remodeling of such accommodation, or if after having commenced such work shall fail or neglect to prosecute the work with reasonable diligence; or

(d) For the immediate purpose of demolishing such housing accommodations and constructing a new building in accordance with approved plans, or reasonable amendment thereof, and the landlord has failed to complete the demolition within six months after the removal of the last tenant or, having demolished the premises, has failed or neglected to proceed with the new construction within ninety days after the completion of such demolition, or having commenced such construction work has failed or neglected to prosecute such work with reasonable diligence; or

(e) For some purpose other than those specified above for which the removal of the tenant was sought and the landlord has failed to use the vacated premises for such purpose; such landlord shall, unless for good cause shown, be liable to the tenant for three times the damages sustained on account of such removal plus reasonable attorney's fees and costs as determined by the court. In addition to any other damage, the cost of removal of property shall be a lawful measure of damage. The remedy herein provided for shall be in addition to those provided for in subdivision h of this section, paragraph (a) of subdivision ten of section one of the state enabling act and subdivision a of section 26-413 of this chapter.

(2) The acts and omissions mentioned in subparagraphs (a), (b), (c), (d) and (e) of paragraph one of this subdivision, on the part of a landlord after issuance of a certificate of eviction, are hereby declared to be inconsistent with the purposes for which such certificate of eviction was issued.

h. Where after the city rent agency has granted a certificate of eviction authorizing the landlord to pursue his or her remedies pursuant to law to acquire possession for any purpose stated in subdivision b or j of this section or for some other stated purpose, and a tenant voluntarily removes from a housing accommodation or has been removed therefrom by action or proceeding to evict from or recover possession of a housing accommodation and the landlord or any successor landlord of the premises does not use the housing accommodation for the purpose specified in such certificate of eviction, the vacated accommodation or any replacement or subdivision thereof shall, unless the city rent agency approves such different purpose, be deemed a housing accommodation subject to control, notwithstanding any definition of that term in this chapter to the contrary. Such approval shall be granted whenever the city rent agency finds that the failure or omission to use the housing accommodation for the purpose specified in such certificate was not inconsistent with the purpose of this chapter and would not be likely to result in the circumvention or evasion thereof. The remedy herein provided for shall be in addition to those provided for in subdivision g of this section, paragraph (a) of subdivision ten of section one of the state enabling act and subdivision a of section 26-413 of this chapter.

i. Any statutory tenant who vacates a housing accommodation without giving the landlord at least thirty days' written notice by registered or certified mail of his or her intention to vacate, shall be liable to the landlord for the loss of rent suffered by the landlord, but not exceeding one month's rent, except where the tenant has been removed or vacates pursuant to the provisions of this section. Such notice shall be postmarked on or before the last day of the rental period immediately prior to such thirty-day period.

j. (1) Nothing in this chapter shall be construed to require any person to offer any housing accommodations for rent, but housing accommodations alread; on the rental market may be withdrawn only after prio, written approval of the city rent agency, if such withdrawal requires that a tenant be evicted from such accommodations.

(2) The city rent agency, in order to carry out the purposes of this chapter, may issue regulations providing for issuance of certificates of eviction in any case where the landlord seeks such approval in order to use the premises (including the building or land) (a) for the purpose of conducting a business, or (b) where the landlord is a hospital, convent, asylum, public institution, college, school or any institution operated exclusively for charitable, religious or educational purposes on a nonprofit basis and the landlord seeks such approval in order to use the premises (including the building or land) or any part thereof in connection with the landlord's charitable, religious or educational purposes; such agency, if it grants approval, shall condition same upon compliance by the landlord with designated requirements which may consist of any conditions that such agency would have authority to prescribe by regulation under subparagraphs (b) and (c) of paragraph four of subdivision b of this section with respect to applications for certificates of eviction under such paragraph four provided, however, that such agency shall not condition any such approval granted to a hospital, convent, asylum, public institution, college, school, or any institution operated exclusively for charitable, religious or educational purposes upon compliance with requirements exceeding or less than those applicable to any private owner in similar circumstances. Nothing contained in this paragraph shall be construed as authorizing or requiring such agency to approve the withdrawal of any housing accommodations from the rental market by any landlord for the purpose of using the premises for any business other than one in existence and conducted by such landlord at the time such withdrawal is sought. No certificate of eviction shall be issued to a nonprofit school, college, hospital, or other charitable institution, including without limitation, any organization

exempt from taxation under the Federal Internal Revenue Code, which seeks to recover possession of the housing accommodations or to withdraw such accommodations from the rental or non-rental housing market, for immediate and personal use and occupancy as housing accommodations by its employees, students or members of its staff.

k. The city rent agency by order issued pursuant to its regulations may waive the requirements of subdivision b of this section where (1) the housing accommodations were vacant at the time when landlord made application for such waiver, and (2) were vacated by reason of the last tenant's voluntary surrender thereof, and (3) the landlord, in good faith, intends to demolish or substantially rehabilitate the building in which the housing accommodations are located within a period approved by the city rent agency. The failure of the landlord to comply with the conditions established by the city rent agency for the granting of the application shall subject the housing accommodations to all the provisions of this chapter.

§ 26-409. Investigation; records; reports

a. The city rent agency is authorized to make such studies and investigations, to conduct such hearings, and to obtain such information as it deems necessary or proper in prescribing any regulation or order pursuant to this chapter or in administering and enforcing this chapter and the regulations and orders thereunder or the state rent act and the regulations and orders thereunder.

b. The city rent agency is further authorized, by regulation or order, to require any person who rents or offers for rent or acts as broker or agent for the rental of any housing accommodations to furnish any such information under oath or affirmation, or otherwise, to make and keep records and other documents, and to make reports, including, but not limited to, reports with respect to decontrolled or exempt housing accommodations, and the city rent agency may require any such person to permit the inspection and copying of records and other documents and the inspection of housing accommodations. Any officer or agent designated by the city rent agency for such purposes may administer oaths and affirmations and may, whenever necessary, by subpoena, require any such person to appear and testify or to appear and produce documents, or both, at any designated place.

c. For the purpose of obtaining any information under this section, the city rent agency may by subpoena require any other person to appear and testify or to appear and produce documents, or both, at any designated place.

d. The production of a person's documents at any place other than his or her place of business shall not be required under this section in any case in which, prior to the return date specified in the subpoena issued with respect thereto, such person either has furnished the city rent agency with a copy of such documents certified by such person under oath to be a true and correct copy, or has entered into a stipulation with the city rent agency as to the information contained in such documents.

e. In case of contumacy by, or refusal to obey a subpoena served upon, any person referred to in this section, the supreme court in or for any judicial district in which such person is found or resides or transacts business, upon application by the city rent agency, shall have jurisdiction to issue an order requiring such person to appear and give testimony or to appear and produce documents, or both; and any failure to obey such order of the court may be punished by such court as a contempt thereof. The provisions of this subdivision e shall be in addition to the provisions of paragraph (a) of subdivision nine of section one of the state enabling act and subdivision a of section 26-412 of this chapter.

f. Witnesses subpoenaed under this section shall be paid the same fee and mileage as are paid witnesses pursuant to the civil practice law and rules.

g. Upon any such investigation or hearing, the city rent agency, or an officer duly designated by the city rent agency to conduct such investigation or hearing, may confer immunity in accordance with the provisions of the criminal procedure law.

h. The city rent agency shall not publish or disclose any information obtained under this chapter that the city rent agency deems confidential or with reference to which a request for confidential treatment is made by the person furnishing such information, unless the city rent agency determines that the withholding thereof is contrary to the public interest.

i. Any person subpoenaed under this section shall have the right to make a record of his or her testimony and to be represented by counsel.

j. Without limiting any power granted by this section or any other provision of law, the city rent agency may by regulation require the owner of a building or property containing both housing accommodations subject to this chapter and housing accommodations subject to chapter four of this title to execute and file registration statements with respect to the housing accommodations subject to this chapter along with those filed pursuant to such chapter four. Notwithstanding any other provisions of law, such agency may promulgate regulations, and take other necessary or appropriate actions, pursuant to this subdivision prior to April first, nineteen hundred eighty-four, to take effect on or after such date.

§ 26-410. Procedure

a. After the issuance of any regulation or order by the city rent agency, any person subject to any provision of such regulation or order may, in accordance with regulations to be prescribed by such agency, file a protest against such regulation or order specifically setting forth his or her objections to any such provisions and affidavits or other written evidence in support of such objections. Statements in support of any such regulation or order may be received and incorporated in the record of the proceedings at such times and in accordance with such regulations as may be prescribed by such agency. Within a reasonable time after the filing of any protest under this section, such agency shall either grant or deny such protest in whole or in part, notice such protest for hearing, or provide an opportunity to present further evidence in connection therewith. In the event that such agency denies any such protest in whole or in part, it shall inform the protestant of the grounds upon which such decision is based, and of any economic data and other facts of which it has taken official notice.

b. In the administration of this chapter, the city rent

agency may take official notice of economic data and other facts, including facts found by it as a result of action taken under section 26-405 of this chapter.

c. Any proceedings under this section may be limited by the city rent agency to the filing of affidavits, or other written evidence, and the filing of briefs, except that no multiple-tenant initiated proceeding for the reduction of rents in a building may be determined without a hearing.

d. Any protest filed under this section shall be granted or denied by the city rent agency, or granted in part and the remainder of it denied, within a reasonable time after it is filed. If such agency does not act finally within a period of ninety days after the protest is filed, the protest shall be deemed to be denied. However, such agency may grant one extension not to exceed thirty days with the consent of the party filing such protest; any further extension may only be granted with the consent of all parties to the protest. No proceeding may be brought pursuant to article seventy-eight of the civil practice law and rules to challenge any order or determination which is subject to such protest unless such review has been sought and either (1) a determination thereon has been made or (2) the ninety-day period provided for determination of the protest (or any extension thereof) has expired. If such agency does not act finally within a period of ninety days after the entry of an order of remand to such agency by the court in a proceeding instituted pursuant to subdivision eight of section one of the state enabling act or section 26-411 of this chapter, the order previously made by such agency shall be deemed reaffirmed. However, such agency may grant one extension not to exceed thirty days with the consent of the petitioner; any further extension may only be granted with the consent of all parties to the petition.

e. The city rent agency shall compile and make available for public inspection at reasonable hours at its principal office and at each appropriate local office a copy of each decision rendered by it upon granting, or denying, in whole or in part, any protests filed under this section and shall have available at each appropriate local office a register of properties concerning which a vacate order was issued by a city department having jurisdiction or proceedings have been brought to determine whether any housing accommodations therein became vacant as a result of conduct proscribed by subdivision d of section 26-412 of this chapter.

§ 26-411. Judicial review

a. (1) Any person who is aggrieved by the final determination of the city rent agency in an administrative proceeding protesting a regulation or order of such agency may, in accordance with article seventy-eight of the civil practice law and rules, within sixty days after such determination, commence a proceeding in the supreme court. The petition shall specify his or her objections and pray that the regulation or order protested be enjoined or set aside in whole or in part. Such proceeding may at the option of the petitioner be instituted in the county where the city rent agency has its principal office or where the property is located. The city rent agency shall file with such court the original or a transcript of such portions of the proceedings in connection with its final determination as are material under the petition. Such return shall include a statement setting forth, so far as practicable, the economic data and other facts of which the city rent agency has taken official notice. Upon the filing of such petition the court shall have jurisdiction to set aside the regulation or order protested, in whole or in part, to dismiss the petition, or to remit the proceeding to the city rent agency, provided, however, that the regulation or order may be modified or rescinded by the city rent agency at any time notwithstanding the pendency of such proceeding for review.

(2) No objection to such regulation or order, and no evidence in support of any objection thereto, shall be considered by the court, unless such objection shall have been presented to the city rent agency by the petitioner in the proceedings resulting in the determination or unless such evidence shall be contained in the return. If application is made to the court by either party for leave to introduce additional evidence which was either offered and not admitted or which could not reasonably have been offered or included in such proceedings before the city rent agency, and the court determines that such evidence should be admitted, the court shall order the

evidence to be presented to the city rent agency. The city rent agency shall promptly receive the same, and such other evidence as the city rent agency deems necessary or proper, and thereupon the city rent agency shall file with the court the original or a transcript thereof and any modification made in such regulation or order as a result thereof; except that on request by the city rent agency, any such evidence shall be presented directly to the court. Upon final determination of the proceeding before the court, the original record, if filed by the city rent agency with the court, shall be returned to the city rent agency.

b. No regulation or order of the city rent agency shall be enjoined or set aside, in whole or in part, unless the petitioner shall establish to the satisfaction of the court that the regulation or order is not in accordance with law, or is arbitrary or capricious. The effectiveness of an order of the court enjoining or setting aside, in whole or in part, any such regulation or order shall be postponed until the expiration of thirty days from the entry thereof. The jurisdiction of the supreme court shall be exclusive and its order dismissing the petition or enjoining or setting aside such regulation or order, in whole or in part, shall be final, subject to review by the appellate division of the supreme court and the court of appeals in the same manner and form and with the same effect as provided in the civil practice law and rules for appeals from a final order in a special proceeding. Notwithstanding any provision of paragraph one of subdivision (b) of section five thousand seven hundred one of the civil practice law and rules to the contrary, any order of the court remitting the proceeding to the city rent agency may, at the election of the city rent agency, be subject to review by the appellate division of the supreme court and the court of appeals in the same manner and form and with the same effect as provided in the civil practice law and rules for appeals from a final order in a special proceeding. All such proceedings shall be heard and determined by the court and by any appellate court as expeditiously as possible and with lawful precedence over other matters. All such proceedings for review shall be heard on the petition, manuscript and other papers, and on appeal shall be heard on the record, without requirement of printing.

c. Within thirty days after arraignment, or such additional time as the court may allow for good cause shown, in any criminal proceeding, and within five days after judgment in any civil or criminal proceeding, brought pursuant to subdivision ten of section one of the state enabling act or section 26-413 of this chapter involving alleged violation of any provision of any regulation or order of the city rent agency, the defendant may apply to the court in which the proceeding is pending for leave to file in the supreme court a petition setting forth objections to the validity of any provision which the defendant is alleged to have violated or conspired to violate. The court in which the proceeding is pending shall grant such leave with respect to any objection which it finds is made in good faith and with respect to which it finds there is reasonable and substantial excuse for the defendant's failure to present such objection in an administrative proceeding before the city rent agency. Upon the filing of a petition pursuant to and within thirty days from the granting of such leave, the supreme court shall have jurisdiction to enjoin or set aside in whole or in part the provision of the regulation or order complained of or to dismiss the petition. The court may authorize the introduction of evidence, either to the city rent agency or directly to the court, in accordance with subdivision a of this section. The provisions of subdivision b of this section shall be applicable with respect to any proceedings instituted in accordance with this subdivision.

d. In any proceeding brought pursuant to subdivision ten of section one of the state enabling act or section 26-413 of this chapter involving an alleged violation of any provision of any such regulation or order, the court shall stay the proceeding:

(1) During the period within which a petition may be filed in the supreme court pursuant to leave granted under subdivision c of this section with respect to such provision;

(2) During the pendency of any protest properly filed under section 26-410 of this chapter prior to the institution of the proceeding under subdivision ten of section

one of the state enabling act or section 26-413 of this chapter, setting forth objections to the validity of such provision which the court finds to have been made in good faith; and

(3) During the pendency of any judicial proceeding instituted by the defendant under this section with respect to such protest or instituted by the defendant under subdivision c of this section with respect to such provision, and until the expiration of the time allowed in this section for the taking of further proceedings with respect thereto.

e. Notwithstanding the provisions of subdivision d of this section, stays shall be granted thereunder in civil proceedings only after judgment and upon application made within five days after judgment. Notwithstanding the provisions of subdivision d of this section, in the case of a proceeding under paragraph (a) of subdivision ten of section one of the state enabling act or subdivision a of section 26-413 of this chapter, the court granting a stay under subdivision d of this section shall issue a temporary injunction or restraining order enjoining or restraining, during the period of the stay, violations by the defendant of any provision of the regulation or order involved in the proceeding. If any provision of a regulation or order is determined to be invalid by judgment of the supreme court which has become effective in accordance with subdivision b of this section, any proceeding pending in any court shall be dismissed, and any judgment in such proceeding vacated, to the extent that such proceeding or judgment is based upon violation of such provision. Except as provided in subdivisions c and d of this section and as heretofore provided in this subdivision e, the pendency of any protest under section 26-410 of this chapter before the city rent agency or judicial proceeding under this section, shall not be grounds for staying any proceeding brought pursuant to subdivision ten of section one of the state enabling act or section 26-413 of this chapter; nor, except as provided in this subdivision e, shall any retroactive effect be given to any judgment setting aside a provision of a regulation or order.

f. The method prescribed herein for the judicial review

of a regulation or order of the city rent agency shall be exclusive.

§ 26-412. Prohibitions

a. It shall be unlawful, regardless of any contract, lease or other obligation heretofore or hereafter entered into, for any person to demand or receive any rent for any housing accommodations in excess of the applicable maximum rent established therefor by the city rent agency or otherwise to do or omit to do any act, in violation of any regulation, order or requirement of the city rent agency under the state enabling act or under this chapter, or to offer, solicit, attempt or agree to do any of the foregoing.

b. It shall be unlawful for any person to remove or attempt to remove from any housing accommodations the tenant or occupant thereof or to refuse to renew the lease or agreement for the use of said accommodations, because such tenant or occupant has taken, or proposes to take, action authorized or required by the state rent act or by this chapter or any provision of this code, the multiple dwelling law, or the health code of the city of New York, or any regulation, order or requirement thereunder.

c. It shall be unlawful for any officer or employee of the city rent agency or for any official adviser or consultant to the city rent agency to disclose, otherwise than in the course of official duty, any information obtained under this chapter, or to use any such information for personal benefit.

d. It shall be unlawful for any person, with intent to cause any tenant to vacate housing accommodations or to surrender or waive any rights of such tenant under this chapter or the regulations promulgated thereunder, to engage in any course of conduct including, but not limited to, interruption or discontinuance of essential services which interferes with or disturbs or is intended to interfere with or disturb the comfort, repose, peace or quiet of such tenant in his or her use or occupancy of the housing accommodations.

e. It shall be unlawful for any person to make any statement or entry false in any material respect in any document or report submitted in any proceeding before the city rent agency or required to be kept filed under this chapter or any regulation, order or requirement thereunder, or to wilfully omit or neglect to make any material statement or entry required to be made in any such document or report;

f. It shall be unlawful for a landlord or a successor in interest to use housing accommodations or the site on which same were located for any purposes other than that specified in the certificate of eviction.

§ 26-413. Enforcement and penalties

a. Any person who wilfully violates any provision of section 26-412 of this chapter shall be guilty of and punishable for a crime as specified in subdivision ten of section one of the state enabling act, namely such persons shall be subject to a fine of not more than five thousand dollars, or to imprisonment for not more than two years in the case of a violation of subdivision c of section 26-412 of this chapter and for not more than one year in all other cases, or to both such fine and imprisonment. The city rent agency, may certify such facts, which in its opinion constitute such violation, to the district attorney having jurisdiction thereof.

b. (1) The city rent agency may, whenever in its judgment any person has engaged in or is about to engage in acts or practices which constitute a violation of any provision of section 26-412 of this chapter, apply to the supreme court for an order (a) enjoining such acts or practices, (b) enforcing compliance with such provision of said section or with an order issued by the city rent agency, or (c) directing the landlord to correct such violation of such provision; and upon sufficient showing, the supreme court may issue a temporary or permanent injunction, restraining order or other order, all of which shall be granted without bond. Jurisdiction shall not be deemed lacking in the supreme court because a defense is based upon an order of an inferior court.

(2) The city rent agency may, whenever in its judgment any person has engaged in acts or practices which constitute a violation of any provision of section 26-412 of this chapter:

(a) Impose by administrative order after hearing, a civil penalty for any violation of said section and bring an action to recover same in any court of competent jurisdiction. Such penalty in the case of a violation of subdivision d of such section shall be in the amount of five hundred dollars for a first such offense and one thousand dollars for each subsequent offense or for a violation consisting of conduct directed at the tenants of more than one housing accommodation; and in the case of any other violation of such section in the amount of one hundred dollars for the first such offense and five hundred dollars for each subsequent offense. Such order by the city rent agency shall be deemed a final determination for the purposes of judicial review as provided in section 26-411 of this chapter. Such action shall be brought on behalf of the city and any amount recovered shall be paid into the city treasury. Such right of action may be released, compromised or adjusted by the city rent agency at any item subsequent to the issuance of such administrative order.

(b) Commence an action to recover damages, as provided for in paragraph two of subdivision d of this section in the event that (i) the tenant has not previously commenced such an action as therein provided and (ii) more than six months have elapsed since the occurrence of the violation or issuance of the order. An action instituted by the city rent agency shall constitute a bar to an action by the person aggrieved. The city rent agency shall pay over one-half of the sum recovered in such action to the person aggrieved and one-half to the city treasury, exclusive of costs and disbursements.

(3)(a) Subject to the provisions of subparagraph (b) of this paragraph, make a finding of harassment whenever it determines the existence of a violation of subdivision d of section 26-412 of this chapter in which event the city rent agency may (i) dismiss any pending application for a certificate of eviction and grant any subsequent application for such certificate only upon such terms and conditions as it deems necessary to prevent the circumvention or evasion of provisions of this chapter; (ii) determine that such housing accommodations or any replacement or subdivision thereof (whether or not by demolition, alteration or substantial rehabilitation) shall constitute housing accommodations subject to control under the provisions of this chapter, notwithstanding any definition of that term to the contrary; and (iii) to refuse to credit any adjustments increasing rent mandated by section 26-405 of this chapter and dismiss any applications for an adjustment pursuant to said section for such time and under such terms and conditions as the city rent agency deems necessary to prevent circumvention or evasion of the provisions of this chapter.

(b) No proceeding to determine whether housing accommodations have become vacant as a result of harassment may be commenced later than thirty days after the entire structure shall have been vacated, unless the landlord failed to certify his or her intent to alter or demolish the premises as provided by subdivision c of section 26-408 of this chapter. No proceeding shall be maintained for acts performed in good faith and in a reasonable manner for the purposes of operating, maintaining or repairing any building or part thereof. A finding of harassment shall be attached to and noted upon the registration of the housing accommodations affected by such findings, and a copy thereof shall be filed and docketed in the manner of a notice of mechanic's lien affecting the property. The provisions of this paragraph shall bind all persons or parties who succeed to the landlord's interest in said housing accommodations.

(4) Revoke any order or determination based upon any statement or entry false in any material respect in any document or report submitted in any proceeding before the city rent agency or required to be kept or filed under this chapter or any requirements thereunder.

c. (1) Any court shall advance on the docket or otherwise expedite the disposition of any action or proceeding brought before it pursuant to the provisions of subdivision b of this section.

(2) The provisions of subdivision b of this section are cumulative. The enforcement of one provision thereof shall not constitute a bar to the enforcement by action, proceeding or by making a finding or determination pursuant to other provisions of said subdivision.

(3) The city rent agency may direct that a refund payment to the tenant for rent collected in violation of subdivision a of section 26-412 include interest from the date of each excessive payment of rent. Where the city

rent agency has revoked an order or determination premised on a false statement or entry, it may withhold issuance of an order granting increase in maximum rent for such housing accommodations until the landlord has complied with the refund directive, if any, provided for in such order of revocation.

d. (1) Where after the city rent agency has granted a certificate of eviction authorizing the landlord to pursue his or her remedies pursuant to law to acquire possession and a tenant voluntarily removes from a housing accommodation or has been removed therefrom by action or proceeding to evict from or recover possession of a housing accommodation upon the ground that the landlord seeks in good faith to recover possession of such accommodation:

(a) For his or her immediate and personal use, or for the immediate and personal use by a member or members of his or her immediate family, and such landlord or members of his or her immediate family shall fail to occupy such accommodation within thirty days after the tenant vacates; or

(b) For the immediate purpose of withdrawing such housing accommodation from the rental market, and such landlord shall lease or sell the housing accommodation or the space previously occupied thereby, or permit use thereof in a manner other than contemplated in such eviction certificate within a period of one year after such removal of the tenant; or

(c) For the immediate purpose of altering or remodeling such housing accommodation, and the landlord (who required possession for the purpose of effecting such alteration or remodeling) shall fail to start the work of alteration or remodeling of such housing accommodation within ninety days after the removal of the last tenant whose removal is necessary to enable the landlord to effect such alteration or remodeling of such accommodation, or if after having commenced such work shall fail or neglect to prosecute the work with reasonable diligence; or

(d) For the immediate purpose of demolishing such housing accommodations and constructing a new building in accordance with approved plans, or reasonable amendment thereof, and the landlord has failed to complete the demolition within six months after the removal of the last tenant or, having demolished the premises, has failed or neglected to proceed with the new construction within ninety days after the completion of such demolition, or having commenced such construction work, has failed or neglected to prosecute such work with reasonable diligence; or

(e) For some purpose other than those specified above for which the removal of the tenant was sought and the landlord has failed to use the vacated premises for such purposes; such landlord shall, unless for good cause shown be liable to the tenant for three times the damages sustained on account of such removal plus reasonable attorney's fees and costs as determined by the court provided that the tenant commences such action within three years from the expiration of the applicable time period as set forth in this subdivision. The damages sustained by the tenant under this subdivision shall be the difference between the rent paid for the housing accommodation from which such tenant was evicted, and the rental value of a comparable housing accommodation on the open market. In addition to any other damage, the cost of removal of the tenant's property shall be a lawful measure of damages. The remedy herein provided shall be in addition to those provided for in subdivisions a and b of this section. Such acts and omissions on the part of a landlord after issuance of a certificate of eviction are hereby declared to be consistent with the purposes for which such certificate of eviction was issued.

(2) A tenant may bring an action against his or her landlord in any court of competent jurisdiction for a violation of subdivision a of section 26-412 of this chapter within: (a) two years from the date of occurrence of an overcharge, defined to mean the amount by which the consideration paid by a tenant to a landlord exceeds the applicable maximum rent, or (b) within one year after the landlord fails to pay a refund as ordered by the city rent agency, such time to be calculated from thirty-three days after the date of the issuance of the order or when the order becomes final, whichever is later, or (c) in the case of an act proscribed by subdivision e of section 26-412 of this chapter, within two years after knowledge of such

statement or omission and consequent violation has been made known to the city agency. The landlord shall be liable for reasonable attorney's fees and costs as determined by the court, plus whichever of the following sums is the greater: (i) such amount not more than three times the amount of the overcharge, or the overcharges, upon which the action is based as the court in its discretion may determine or (ii) an amount not less than twenty-five dollars, provided, however, that such amount shall be the amount of the overcharge or overcharges or twenty-five dollars, whichever is greater, if the defendant proves that the violation of the regulation or order in question was neither wilful nor the result of failure to take practicable precautions against the occurrence of the violation.

(3) A tenant or occupant who is unlawfully removed by a landlord from any housing accommodation may, within two years from the date of occurrence, bring a civil action against the landlord by reason of such unlawful removal. In such action, the landlord shall be liable to the tenant for three times the damages sustained on account of such removal plus reasonable attorney's fees and costs as determined by the court. The damages sustained by the tenant under this paragraph shall be the difference between the rent paid for the housing accommodation from which such tenant was evicted and the rental value of a comparable housing accommodation on the open market. In addition to any other damage the cost of removal of the tenant's property shall be a lawful measure of damage.

e. No person (including, but not limited to any officer or employee of the city rent agency) shall be held liable for damages or penalties in any court, on any grounds for or in respect of anything done or omitted to be done in good faith pursuant to any provision of the state rent act or of this chapter, or any regulation, order, or requirement thereunder, notwithstanding that subsequently such provision, regulation, order or requirement may be modified, rescinded, or determined to be invalid. In any action or proceeding wherein a party relies for ground of relief or defense or raises issue or brings into question the construction or validity of any provision of this chapter or any regulation, order, or requirement thereunder, the court having jurisdiction of such action or proceeding may at any stage certify such fact to the city rent agency. The city rent agency may intervene in any such action or proceeding.

§ 26-414. Decontrol on basis of vacancy rate

Whenever the city rent agency shall find, after making such studies and investigations as it deems necessary for such purpose, or for processing an application supported by adequate proof filed by an interested party pursuant to regulation that the percentage of vacancies in all or any particular class of housing accommodations in the city, as such class is determined by the city rent agency, is five per centum of more, the controls imposed on rents and evictions by and pursuant to this chapter, with respect to the housing accommodations as to which such finding has been made, shall be forthwith scheduled for orderly decontrol, with due regard to preventing uncertainty, hardship and dislocation, by order of such agency; provided, however, that notwithstanding any provision of this section to the contrary, such agency shall not order the decontrol of any particular class of housing accommodations as to which it shall find that the percentage of vacancies is less than five per centum; provided, further, that no such order shall be made unless such agency shall hold a public hearing on such proposal at which interested persons are given a reasonable opportunity to be heard. Notice of such hearing shall be provided by publication thereof, on at least five days during the period of fifteen days next preceding the date of the commencement of such hearing, in the City Record and in at least two daily newspapers having general circulation in the city.

§ 26-415. Surveys of need for rent control

As provided in subdivision three of section one of the local emergency housing rent control act, the mayor shall cause to be made, and shall present to the council a report of the results of, a survey of the supply of housing accommodations within the city, the condition of such accommodations and the need for continuing the regulation and control of residential rents and evictions within the city.

RENT ADMINISTRATOR'S INTERPRETATIONS

The references in the following Administrator's Interpretations, Advisory Sheets, and Operational Bulletins to the sections of the Regulations are to the Regulations before their having been filed with the Secretary of State. Upon such filing, the Regulations were given new section numbers. The following chart gives the corresponding section numbers in the filed Regulations with the section numbers in these Interpretations, Advisory Sheets and Bulletins.

Filed section numbers	*Pre-filed section numbers*
2200.1	1
2200.2	2
2200.3	3
2200.4	4
2200.5	5
2200.6	6
2200.7	7
3300.8	8
2200.9	11
2200.10	12
2200.11	13
2200.12	14
2200.13	15
2200.14	16
2200.15	17
2200.16	19
2200.17	20
2201.1	21
2201.2	22
2201.3	23
2201.4	24
2201.5	25
2201.6	26
2202.1	31
2202.2	32

Administrator's Interpretations

Filed section numbers	Pre-filed section numbers
2202.3	33
2202.4	33.1
2202.5	33.2
2202.6	33.3
2202.7	33.4
2202.8	33.5
2202.9	33.6
2202.10	33.7
2202.11	33.8
2202.12	33.9
2202.13	33.10
2202.14	34
2202.15	34.1
2202.16	34.2
2202.17	34.3
2202.18	34.4
2202.19	34.5
2202.20	34.6
2202.21	35
2202.22	36
2202.23	37
2202.24	38
2203.1	41
2203.2	42
2203.3	43
2203.4	44
2203.5	45
2203.6	46
2203.7	47
2203.8	48
2203.9	49
2203.10	50
2204.1	51
2204.2	52
2204.3	53
2204.4	54
2204.5	55
2204.6	56
2204.7	57
2204.8	58
2204.9	59
2205.1	61

Administrator's Interpretations

Filed section numbers	Pre-filed section numbers
2205.2	62
2205.3	63
2205.4	64
2205.5	65
2205.6	66
2205.7	67
2206.1	70
2206.2	71
2206.3	72
2206.4	73
2206.5	74
2206.6	75
2206.7	76
2206.8	77
2206.9	78
2206.10	79
2206.11	80
2207.1	81
2207.2	82
2207.3	83
2207.4	84
2207.5	85
2207.6	86
2207.7	87
2207.8	88
2208.1	91
2208.2	92
2208.3	93
2208.4	94
2208.5	95
2208.6	96
2208.7	97
2208.8	98
2208.9	99
2208.10	100
2208.11	101
2208.12	102
2208.13	103
2209.1	110
2209.2	111
2209.3	112
2209.4	113

ADMINISTRATOR'S INTERPRETATIONS

Filed section numbers	*Pre-filed section numbers*
2209.5	114
2209.6	115
2209.7	116
2209.8	117
2209.9	118
2209.10	119
2209.11	120
2209.12	121
2210.1	130
2210.2	131
2210.3	132

INTERPRETATION NO. 1
(Revised December 27, 1968)

§ 33.1c—*Rewiring of an Inadequately Wired Building by Landlord as Basis for Increase of Maximum Rent Under Section 33.1c of the Regulations; rewiring subsequent to prior rewiring rent increases.*

A landlord requests advice from a District Rent and Rehabilitation Office as to whether the rewiring of an inadequately wired building would constitute a major capital improvement within the contemplation of Section 33.1c of the Rent, Eviction and Rehabilitation Regulations for which the consent of the tenants of the building would not be required. He also asks the amount of rent increase which would be granted for such rewiring.

The rewiring of an inadequately wired building is a major capital improvement required for the preservation and maintenance of a building, and it is not necessary for the landlord to obtain the consent of his tenants for such improvement and the resulting increase in rent. The tremendous and continuously accelerating increase in tenants' use of electric current has rendered rewiring necessary for the operation, preservation, and maintenance of many structures. Wiring systems installed relatively recently, as well as earlier installations, have become inadequate to supply needed electricity. Since inadequate wiring reduces voltage, appliances frequently give unsatisfactory performance and are often damaged. Far more serious, however, are the fire hazards which exist in inadequately wired buildings. These hazards increase as tenants resort to dangerous expedients in order to plug in more attachments and appliances than existing wiring can safely accommodate.

Administrator's Interpretations

At the request of the Administrator a thorough study of the problem of inadequate wiring has been made by the Department of Water Supply, Gas and Electricity. This study confirms the necessity for the rewiring of inadequately wired buildings and that such rewiring should make provision for immediate and reasonably foreseeable anticipated needs of the tenants for a safe and adequate supply of electric current. The Administrator has determined that rewiring of a building will, therefore, be deemed to be a major capital improvement within the meaning of Section 33.1c of the Regulations, but only where the installations, including the present wiring and installations, meet the minimum standards of the Basic Rewiring Requirements.

BASIC REWIRING REQUIREMENTS

a. The minimum size service entrance conductors shall be No. 2 B & S gauge copper or the equivalent in capacity. Feeders shall be computed on the basis of three watts per square foot of floor area plus 3,000 watts for small appliance load, for which three appliance circuits are required. An additional 1500 watts shall be added for each appliance circuit over three. A minimum of four appliance circuits shall be computed for each apartment. The computed load of an individual appliance branch circuit shall be the connected load, but shall in no case be less than 1500 watts. Calculations shall be based on a permissible demand of 100 per cent for the first 15,000 watts and 60 per cent for the balance.

b. Three No. 8 sub-feeder (riser) wires (or wiring of equivalent capacity) producing a usable capacity at the apartment panel of not less than 64 amperes, at 120 volts, terminating in a panel containing at least six branch circuit positions.

c. At least one 3-wire or two 2-wire appliance branch circuits with two duplex receptacle outlets of the double contact parallel blade type for kitchen use exclusively and located at a place which is readily accessible to a work area or table, approximately 44 inches above the floor and not installed over a sink or stove, or behind a refrigerator. If space, as described, is not available in the kitchen, these outlets may be installed, subject to the approval of the Borough Superintendent of the Department of Water Supply, Gas and Electricity, immediately adjacent to the kitchen. Appliance circuits, except those provided in the kitchen, shall be individual appliance branch circuits.

d. Where there is only one branch circuit for more than ten outlets in an apartment, such circuit shall be split so as to provide two branch circuits in addition to the new circuits and outlets installed. Such split shall result in a reasonable division of the outlets on each circuit.

e. A minimum of two duplex receptacle outlets connected to a general purpose circuit in each living room. Where such outlet is required to be added, it shall be spaced approximately 15 feet away from any other outlet, where practicable, but in no event less than 12 feet measured horizontally.

f. At least one duplex receptacle outlet connected to a general purpose circuit in each bedroom. Such receptacle outlet shall be in a convenient location and readily accessible for use by the tenant.

In addition to the installations described in the Basic Rewiring work is in progress in the building, shall install for each rewiring, the landlord, at the written request of the tenant, which may be made at any time while the rewiring work is in progress in the building, shall install appliance outlets and all needed wiring within the apartment from the panel box to the tenant's air-conditioning units, or to the place where the tenant proposes to install such units.

In addition to the installations described in the Basic Rewiring Requirements, which shall be required as a minimum for each rewiring, the landlord, at the written request of the tenant, which may be made at any time while the rewiring work is in progress in the building, shall install additional electrical receptacle outlets or wall switches on a general purpose circuit.

In no case shall a tenant be compelled to pay an additional rental increase for the installation of additional electrical receptacle outlets above the minimum requirements of the Basic Rewiring Requirements unless by written consent.

Administrator's Interpretations

It has been determined that the cost of installation of the rewiring bears a direct relation to the type and height of the structure. Therefore, the following schedule of rental values shall be applicable to electrical rewiring:

BASIC REWIRING REQUIREMENTS

	Monthly Charge
For buildings less than seven stories in height	
(a) with 8 apartments or less	$3.75
(b) with 9 apartments or more	3.25
For buildings of seven or more stories in height	4.75
For each air-conditioner circuit and outlet in a building less than seven stories in height installed at tenant's written request, or where required for an existing air-conditioning unit	$ .90
For each air-conditioner circuit and outlet in a building of seven stories or more in height installed at tenant's written request, or where required for an existing air-conditioning unit	1.20
For each duplex receptacle outlet installed in a living room or bedroom to comply with the Basic Rewiring Requirements, and for each additional electrical receptacle outlet or wall switch installed at tenant's written request	.35
Where there is only one existing circuit in an apartment containing ten or more outlets and the single circuit is split so as to provide two branch circuits in addition to any new circuits and outlets installed as provided under "Basic Rewiring Requirments, subdivision d"	.20

Where a landlord undertakes the rewiring work herein described and secures the written consent of 51 per cent of the tenants thereto, he may apply for the rent increases agreed to by the tenants for such work pursuant to Section 33.1d of the Regulations; in such instance, the rental schedule herein shall not apply but the landlord will be required to comply with all other requirements hereof.

The rental schedule herein will be applicable to all buildings except where it is found that because of unique conditions, the foregoing allowances may not be appropriate. In all such cases, the facts must be submitted to the Administrator for a prior opinion before the commencement of the rewiring.

The rewiring contemplated herein is expected to be of a capacity at the apartment panel sufficient to permit the installation of air-conditioner circuits in any apartment in the building. Such rewiring implies the consent of the landlord to the installation of air-conditioning units by the tenant. When the building is being rewired, the landlord must comply with the tenant's request to install air-conditioner circuits and outlets and additional electrical outlets up to the capacity of the minimum rewiring required herein to supply such circuits. If such request is made at any time after the building is rewired and the landlord does not elect to make such installation, the tenant must be permitted to have such installation made by a licensed electrician at his own expense and without being obligated to pay any additional increase to the landlord for the installation of such air-conditioner circuits and outlets and/or additional electrical outlets.

Where the landlord installs the necessary wiring and outlets within the apartment for the purpose of connecting the tenant's air-conditioning units with the panel box, the additional monthly charge of $.90 or $1.20 (whichever is applicable) permitted herein, in addition to the rent increase for the Basic Rewiring Requirements, will be granted after completion of such work, even though the tenant has not actually made the installation of the air-conditioning unit. In no case, however, shall a tenant be compelled to pay the said additional monthly charge of $.90 or $1.20 a month for the installation of an air-conditioner circuit and outlet in the absence of his written consent to such installation except, however, where the tenant has previously installed an air-conditioning unit and connected it to a general purpose circuit, the landlord shall be required to install the necessary wiring and outlet for the connection of such air-conditioning unit with the panel box without obtaining tenant's consent and shall be entitled to collect the additional monthly charge therefor.

Where a tenant installs an air-conditioner subsequent to the completion of the rewiring of the building and illegally connects it to a general purpose outlet, the landlord may give the tenant a ten days' notice in writing by certified mail requesting the tenant to remove the air-conditioner. The failure of the tenant to remove the air-conditioner within ten days from the date of the notice shall be deemed to be a consent by the tenant for the landlord to install the requisite electrical wiring for the air conditioner. An appropriate increase of the maximum rent will be granted on the landlord's application for each legal air-conditioner circuit so installed by him.

Administrator's Interpretations

PROCEDURES

It will not be necessary for a landlord to request a prior opinion in rewiring applications where the rental schedule herein is applicable. Before proceeding with the rewiring a preliminary application shall be submitted for approval to the borough office of the Bureau of Gas and Electricity of the Department of Water Supply, Gas and Electricity, by a licensed electrical contractor or a licensed professional engineer, indicating the plan of rewiring.

After such preliminary approval has been granted, an application for a certificate of electrical inspection shall be filed by a licensed electrical contractor before the work begins.

After completion of the rewiring, a landlord may file his application for rental increases pursuant to Section 33.1c of the Regulations, an affidavit of the electrical contractor (Report Form R-33.1(c)RE) attesting to completion of the work in accordance with the approved plan and indicating the charge to the owner therefor, and a list of tenants identified by apartment designation, who have consented in writing to pay an additional rent increase for the installation of air-conditioner circuits and outlets and/or for additional electric outlets over the minimum requirements set forth herein.

The application must be accompanied by a sworn statement of the landlord that all tenants were given the opportunity of requesting that air-conditioner circuits and outlets and additional electrical outlets be installed in their apartments at the time of rewiring.

In his application the landlord will be required to describe briefly the type of wiring which had previously been in the building and the type of heavier wiring now installed. This description must include a specific statement as to the capacity formerly available and the capacity available as a result of the rewiring.

The landlord will also be required to set forth his total costs and expenses for the work and whether any part of the cost was financed by a loan. If any part of the cost was financed, the landlord shall be required to state from whom or what source the loan was obtained and the terms and conditions thereof.

Where the tenant, with the permission of the landlord, has already installed a proper circuit and outlet for air-conditioning at his own expense, he will not be required to pay any additional charge for reconnecting the air-conditioner circuit or for any air-conditioner circuit and outlet which may be installed as a replacement.

The Administrator deems it proper to note that a landlord who has rewired a building and desires to receive rent adjustments pursuant to this opinion cannot unreasonably deny any tenant in the building the right to install air-conditioning units. The landlord may not demand, as a condition of his permission, that the tenant sign a lease increasing the maximum rent pursuant to Section 33.2 of the Regulations.

As a condition of filing an application for and receiving orders increasing maximum rents, the landlord must certify and establish that he is maintaining essential services and must at the time of filing the application for a rental increase furnish a report of search issued by the Office of Code Enforcement of the Department of Rent and Housing Maintenance of the Housing and Development Administration stating either that no violations against the property are recorded or that all violations recorded against the property have been complied with or a receipt (or photocopy thereof) issued by the Borough Office of the Department of Buildings attesting to the payment of the fee for a report of search. Such report of search will not be acceptable unless issued by such agency within 45 days prior to the date of filing the application, or in lieu thereof, such receipt may not be dated more than 14 days prior to the date of filing the application.

No order of increase with respect to any housing accommodation shall be issued unless the landlord has restored all areas in such accommodations disturbed by the rewiring installation, including painting and plastering, where necessary and until a Certificate of Electrical Inspection of the Department of Water Supply, Gas and Electricity has been submitted to the District Rent Office.

Administrator's Interpretations

REWIRING SUBSEQUENT TO PRIOR RENT INCREASES FOR ADEQUATE REWIRING

A landlord may make application for a so-called "second round" of adequate rewiring rent increases where at least ten years have expired since the date of issuance of the previous orders increasing the maximum rents on the basis of an adequate wiring. The granting of such additional rent increases will be conditioned upon the landlord complying with all of the requirements stated in this Interpretation as well as establishing that there is a necessity for such rewiring and that such rewiring will afford the tenants an additional supply of current commensurate with their current requirements for the foreseeable future.

Such necessity may be established by evidence from the Bureau of Gas and Electricity of the Department of Water Supply, Gas and Electricity or by a licensed Professional Engineer.

The rewiring standards and schedule of rental values will apply to all installations where a contract was entered into between the landlord and a licensed electrical contractor or where an application for a Certificate of Electrical Inspection was filed on or after November 1, 1968.

Supplement No. 1

(Issued November 30, 1965)

§ 33.1—*Installation of air conditioner or other outlets in a building previously adequately rewired; elimination of necessity for Certificate of Electrical Inspection as a condition to filing application for increase of maximum rent under Section 33.1 of the Regulations.*

Where a landlord adequately rewired a building pursuant to the requirements of either the Temporary State Housing Rent Commission or of the City Rent and Rehabilitation Administration and orders increasing the maximum rents were granted by the appropriate agency on the basis of such rewiring, the filing of a Certificate of Electrical Inspection from the Department of Water Supply, Gas and Electricity with the application for a further rent increase based upon the subsequent installation of air conditioner or other outlets will not be required provided that the landlord or his agent submits with the consent application for further rent adjustment (1) a copy of the application filed with the New York City Department of Water Supply, Gas and Electricity setting forth the scope of the proposed work and (2) an affidavit from the licensed electrical contractor stating that he has complied with the terms of the application filed with such City Department and that the completed installation complies with all local laws, rules and regulations.

INTERPRETATION NO. 2

(Issued June 25, 1962)

§ 2 g (3) and § 52 a—*Partial Payment of Rent by Performance of Janitorial Services; Obligation of Such Tenant To Continue With the Performance of Such Services.*

The landlord of a small multiple dwelling rented a housing accommodation having a maximum rental of $50.00 per month to a tenant pursuant to an agreement whereby the tenant was given a monthly allowance of $20.00 in return for which the tenant agreed to perform the following janitorial services: washing and sweeping the vestibules, stairs and hallways at least once each week, and oftener during inclement weather, and arranging for garbage collection 5 days each week. The tenant paid the balance of $30.00 to the landlord in cash each month.

The tenant undertook to perform these services on a permanent basis. However, he has now advised the landlord that he does not desire to continue performing these janitorial services after the expiration of the current month and is willing to forego the monthly allowance of $20.00 and pay the entire $50.00 per month to the landlord in cash.

The landlord seeks advice whether the tenant's apartment is subject to the Rent, Eviction and Rehabilitation Regulations; and, if it is subject to control, what remedy is offered him by reason of the tenant's refusal to continue with the performance of the janitorial services.

The housing accommodations occupied by the tenant is subject to control. Section 2 g (3) of the Regulations exempts from control "dwelling space occupied by domestic servants, superintendents, caretakers, managers, or other employees to whom the space is provided as part or all of their compensation *without payment of rent* and who are employed for the purpose of rendering services in connection with the premises of which the dwelling space is apart." (emphasis supplied). Since the tenant receives an allowance for the janitorial services performed and pays the difference between the maximum monthly rent and such allowance in cash to the landlord, such cash payment is payment of rent and the janitor-tenant is considered to be a tenant within the meaning of Section 2 o of the Regulations.

Section 52 a of the Regulations permits a landlord to maintain an action or proceeding to recover possession of a housing accommodation without obtaining a certificate of eviction from the Administrator where "the tenant is violating a substantial obligation of his tenancy other than the obligation to surrender possession of such housing accommodation and has failed to cure such violation after written notice by the landlord that the violations cease within 10 days." Therefore, upon compliance with the requirements of Section 53 of the Regulations, the landlord may institute a summary dispossess proceeding against a janitor-tenant who refuses to perform janitorial services upon the ground that the tenant is violating a substantial obligation of his tenancy if the tenant has failed to cure such violation after written notice by the landlord that the violation cease within 10 days. The landlord's right to evict the tenant will then be determined in the summary dispossess proceeding.

INTERPRETATION NO. 3

(Revised January 31, 1969)

§ 33.2 and § 33.5—*Increase of Maximum Rent Pursuant to Sections 33.5, 33.6, 33.7 and 33.8 of the Regulations Where a Statutory Lease is Executed After the Filing of the Application.*

An application was filed by a landlord pursuant to the provisions of Section 33.5 of the Rent and Eviction Regulations for an increase in maximum rents. Subsequent to the filing of the application the landlord requests advice from the District Rent Director whether he may properly provide in a lease executed with a tenant in possession or a new tenant pursuant to the provisions of Section 33.2 of the Regulations that the lease rent will be increased during its term by such amount as may be ordered by the

Office of Rent Control in the pending Section 33.5 proceeding.

The inclusion of the proposed provision violates subparagraph (3) of paragraph a of Section 33.2 of the Regulations which permits a further increase in a lease rent only where it is based on an order for increases in service, equipment, etc., to which the tenant has consented or an order increasing the maximum rent on the basis of a major capital improvement or a substantial rehabilitation of the building or the housing accommodations therein which was either completed or in progress when the lease was executed. A rent increase granted pursuant to Section 33.5 of the Regulations (or similarly pursuant to Sections 33.6, 33.7 and 33.8 of the Regulations) does not come within the above exception.

However, where a lease, executed on or after January 1, 1963 and prior to the effective date of this revision of Administrator's Interpretation No. 3, recites that at the time of its execution the tenant was advised by the landlord that an application described by docket number or date of filing the application with the District Rent Office, was pending before the Office of Rent Control for an increase of the maximum rent in effect prior to the execution of such lease pursuant to Section 33.5 of the Regulations (or to Sections 33.6, 33.7 or 33.8, whichever section is applicable), the lease may provide for a consent by the tenant to an increase in the maximum rent over the rent fixed by the lease, to be effective upon the expiration date of the lease, or other termination date thereof, whichever date is the earlier, and in an amount equal to the rent increase granted to the landlord in the said application. In the absence of such provision in a lease executed on or after January 1, 1963 and prior to the effective date of this revision, any rent increase to which the landlord may be entitled in an application pursuant to the above specified sections of the Regulations pending at the time of the execution of such lease shall not increase the maximum rent upon the expiration or other termination of such lease except to the extent that such increase when added to the maximum rent in effect on the date of filing of the application for such increase would result in a maximum rent in excess of the

Administrator's Interpretations

maximum rent fixed by such lease. In the latter case such new maximum rent shall take effect upon the expiration or other termination of the lease.

Where the lease was executed on or after the effective date of this revision of Administrator's Interpretation No. 3, the lease need not recite the advice referred to in the preceding paragraph of this revised Interpretation provided that the Lease Report filed with the District Rent Office specifically states that the landlord has informed the tenant prior to the execution of the lease that such application(s) was pending before the Office of Rent Control and that it may result in an increase of the maximum rent, payable upon the expiration or other termination of the lease and that it contain the tenant's acknowledgment that such information was given to him by the landlord.

INTERPRETATION NO. 4

(Issued August 1, 1962)

§ 33b—*Certificates of the Department of Buildings That There Are No Violations of Record; Date of Issuance of Acceptable Certificate.*

Paragraph b of Section 33 of the Rent, Eviction and Rehabilitation Regulations provides that "no application for an increase in any maximum rent may be filed under paragraphs (b), (c) or (d) of Section 33.1 or under Sections 33.5, 33.6 or 33.7 of these Regulations unless (1) a certificate of the Department of Buildings is annexed to such application stating either that no violations against such property are recorded in the index maintained by the Central Violations Bureau of such department or that all violations therein recorded against such property have been cleared, corrected or abated * * *." A landlord seeks advice as to how long prior to the application for rent increase such certificate may be dated.

The Administrator has determined that the filing of a Certificate of "no violations" issued by the Department of Buildings within 45 days prior to the date of filing an application complies with the requirements of paragraph b of Section 33 of the Regulations.

It should be noted, however, that any violation affecting essential services which was placed against the property after the date of issuance of such Certificate must be cleared, corrected or abated before a rent increase may be ordered. A dismissal card dated after the date of such certificate will be accepted as proof that the violation has been corrected. A dismissal card dated prior to the date of such certificate will not be accepted even if dated subsequent to the date of the violation contained in such certificate.

INTERPRETATION NO. 5
(Issued August 1, 1962)

§ 33 b, § 33.1 and § 54—*Failure To Obtain "No Violation" Certificate From the Department of Buildings Because of Tenant's Unreasonable Refusal of Access to the Housing Accommodation; Refusal of Tenant To Permit Landlord To Make Major Capital Improvements or a Substantial Rehabilitation; When a Conditional Certificate of Eviction May Be Issued.*

A landlord states that he is unable to comply with the requirements of paragraph b of Section 33 of the Rent, Eviction and Rehabilitation Regulations due to the tenant's refusal to permit access to the housing accommodation to correct a violation and seeks advice as to the proper procedure under such circumstances in order that he may make application for a rent increase.

Paragraph b of Section 33 of the Regulations provides that applications for certain types of rent increases may not be filed unless a Certificate of "No Violations" from the Department of Buildings is annexed to the application. However, where a landlord cannot obtain such Certificate due to the existence of a violation or violations affecting the tenant's housing accommodation which cannot be cleared, corrected or abated solely because the tenant unreasonably refuses access to the apartment to the landlord. An affidavit by the landlord stating such facts will be accepted by the Administrator together with the Certificate showing the existence of the violation.

If it appears from the record that the tenant is in fact preventing the landlord from correcting the conditions which caused the violation to be placed against the property, the Administrator may permit the application to be filed and accept the affidavit as justification for failure to cure the violation and obtain its dismissal. In the event that it appears that the tenant did not unreasonably refuse access to the landlord the application will be dismissed.

Administrator's Interpretations

The landlord also states that he is desirous of making major capital improvements to and a substantial rehabilitation of a building owned by him for which the consent of the tenants is not required, and that several of the tenants refuse to give his contractor access to their respective apartments. As a result the contractor is unable to complete the major capital improvements and the rehabilitation of the building. The landlord proposes to make application for eviction certificates in order to gain access to these apartments.

Applications for rent increases pursuant to the provisions of paragraphs b and c of Section 33.1 of the Regulations provide for non-consent rent increases based upon substantial rehabilitation of or major capital improvements to a property. If the completion of the improvement or substantial rehabilitation is prevented solely by the unreasonable refusal of access by a tenant, the Administrator may issue a Certificate permitting eviction of the tenant pursuant to Section 54 of the Regulations conditioned upon the continued refusal of the tenant to make the apartment accessible to the landlord during the waiting period provided for in such certificate.

It is to be noted that the foregoing would not be applicable to rent increases sought pursuant to paragraph a of Section 33.1 of the Regulations where the tenants' consent would be required for the increase.

INTERPRETATION NO. 6

(Revised January 31, 1969)

§ 33.1b, § 33.1c and § 33.2—*Provision in a statutory lease for payment of rent in excess of the permissible 15% increase where a major capital improvement or substantial rehabilitation was either completed or in progress when the lease was executed.*

A landlord states that he had just completed the rewiring of the electrical circuit in his building and is about to file an application with the District Rent Office for rent increases pursuant to Section 33.1b of the Rent and Eviction Regulations. An apartment has just become vacant in the structure and the landlord proposes to enter into a statutory lease with a new tenant. He seeks advice as to whether it would be proper for him to include a provision in the statutory lease which would permit him to collect the rent increase which may be ordered in the pending application.

Section 33.2a(3) of the Regulations permits a statutory lease to provide for the payment of rent by the tenant in excess of the amount provided in the lease where the maximum rent is thereafter increased by order of the Administrator pursuant to Section 33.1b or Section 33.1c of the Regulations, where a major capital improvement or substantial rehabilitation of the building or the housing accommodations therein is either completed or in progress when the lease was executed.

Accordingly, a lease may recite (1) that at the time of its execution the tenant was advised by the landlord that a specified major capital improvement or a substantial rehabilitation of the building or housing accommodations therein was either completed or in progress when the lease was executed, (2) that the landlord has either made application, or will, upon completion of the major capital improvement or substantial rehabilitation, make application for rent increases on the basis thereof, and (3) that the tenant consents to an increase in the maximum rent above the rent fixed in the lease and agrees to pay the amount of the rent increase ordered as additional rent payable under the lease. It should be noted, however, that the tenant's liability for the payment of additional rent is measured by the rent adjustment to be ordered by the District Rent Director.

The foregoing shall also apply to cases where the maximum rent was decreased prior to the execution of the lease and the landlord subsequently restores the services, etc., which was the basis for such rent decrease. Under such circumstances the lease may contain recitals similar to those hereinabove provided for in the preceding paragraph in order to put the tenant on notice of the possibility of a further rent increase after such restoration of services, etc. However, it is to be noted that the restoration work need not be completed or in progress at the time of the execution of the lease.

Where the lease does not contain the recitals referred to above, the maximum rent will nevertheless be increased effective as of the date of issuance of the order granting the rent increase on the basis of a major capital

Administrator's Interpretations

improvement, substantial rehabilitation or restoration of services, whichever is applicable. The landlord may not be able to enforce collection of such rent increase until the expiration or other termination of the lease unless such recitals are incorporated in the lease or the advice contemplated in the lease clause is stated in the Lease Report filed with the District Rent Office and the tenant acknowledges that such information was given to him by the landlord and further agrees to pay the amount of the rent increase ordered as additional rent payable under the lease.

INTERPRETATION NO. 7
(Issued March 21, 1975)

Section 35a—Change from rent inclusion of electric current to direct payment by tenant to the public utility company, subject to Agency approval; rent decrease to be ordered.

Tenants of many multiple dwellings receive unmetered electric current as a service included in the rent, usually because it was a service supplied to the tenants on March 1, 1943 (the Federal Maximum Rent Date) or thereafter became an obligatory service, or because the landlord elected to supply such service as a result of the prohibition by the State Public Service Commission in 1952 against the continuance of the practice of submetering electric current.

Where the service was supplied on the "freeze date" (March 1, 1943) the agreement to supply unmetered electric current to the tenant was made prior to rent control and at a time when there were few electrical appliances on the market and household kitchen appliances consisted largely of electric irons, toasters, radios, refrigerators and vacuum cleaners. Consequently, the landlord had some understanding as to what the tenants' demand for current would be. Subsequent to the "freeze date" landlords elected to obligate themselves to provide electrical current with some ability to estimate the amount of power consumption in exchange for scheduled rent increases.

At the time of the landlord's election to discontinue submetering electric service due to the prohibition of such practice by the State Pulic Service Commission in

1952, landlords were permitted to request the utility company to supply electric current directly to the tenants and bill each accordingly, or do away with the meters and have the cost of the electric service absorbed in the monthly rent. Where the latter option was chosen by the landlord, orders were issued by the State Rent Commission increasing the maximum rents in conformity with the formula set up at that time, and the landlord was required to furnish unlimited electric current to the tenants.

The growing number of electrical appliances and equipment presently available to the tenant has caused demands for increased electric current beyond all previous contemplation and in many instances in excess of the capacity of the existing electrical wiring system. Even some wiring systems installed relatively recently, as well as earlier installations, have become inadequate to supply the needed electricity.

It is the policy of the Administrator to encourage the preservation and maintenance of the City's existing housing supply, and in keeping with that policy, the rewiring of a building to deliver adequate electric current to meet ever increasing demands has uniformly been held to be a major capital improvement required for the operation, preservation or maintenance of a structure. Inadequate wiring reduces voltage, causes unsatisfactory performance of appliances and results in increased fire hazards.

However, considering the greatly increased usage of electrical appliances, the probability of further increase in usage and the accelearating increase in cost of electric current, some landlords no longer find it economically feasible to install adequate wiring in a building where the electric current is included in the rent. Further, even where a building was previously rewired, the landlord may find that the present cost of supplying electric service to the tenants has made this arrangement uneconomical. In any event the costs index for electricity has increased markedly since the date on which the original rental value was established and the substantially higher level of present day costs of electric current requires updated schedules.

Therefore, in order to foster the installation of adequate wiring and to encourage the maintenance and upgrading of such systems, the Administrator deems it appropriate to permit termination of rent inclusion of electric current where the entire structure has been rewired in accordance with the provisions of Administrator's Interpretation No. 1, provided the landlord complies with all of the conditions set forth in this Interpretation.

PROCEDURES

Where a landlord wishes to change from rent inclusion to direct payment by tenants to public utility, he must fully comply with the requirements set forth below and obtain an order from the Office of Rent Control termininating rent inclusion of electric current before switching to the tenants' accounts. The rental decreases in such order to become effective the date of the switchover to the tenants' accounts which date is to be reported to the appropriate District Rent Office by letter in such time as set forth in the order. The order will also specify the amount of rent decrease reflecting the adjusted value of the service previously supplied by landlord.

The landord shall submit to the appropriate District Rent Office:

1. A master copy of Application Form TRI-A-35a, Combination Application for Rent Decrease, Notice and Order, in duplicate, and four copies for each controlled apartment.

2. An affidavit stating:

   a. that the building has been rewired in accordance with the provisions of Administrator's Interpretation No. 1;

   b. that he will pay, or has paid all costs attentent to the installation of meters and the transfer of service from the public utility to the tenants, on a metered basis; and

   c. that he consents to the reduction of the maximum legal rents (Maximum Collectible Rents and Maximum Base Rents) in accordance with this Interpretation.

3. The Certificate(s) of Electrical Inspection issued by the Bureau of Gas and Electricity.

4. In the event that the rewiring of the building predates the application for termination of rent inclusion by

more than three years, the landlord shall be required to obtain and supply to the District Rent Office, written verification from a Licensed Professional Engineer or Licensed Electrical Contractor stating that the existing wiring system affords the tenants an adequate supply of electricity and meets all current demands in accordance with this Interpretation. In addition, the application must be accompanied by a sworn statement of the landlord that, within six months prior to the date of filing of the application, all tenants in rent controlled apartments were given the opportunity of requesting additional air-conditioning circuits and outlets as well as additional electrical outlets in their apartments, and that all such requests were complied with prior to the filing of the application to terminate rent inclusion of electric current.

RENT DECREASE SCHEDULE

	Monthly Adjustment
(a) Rent Inclusion on March 1, 1943:	
For *each* room as per Registration	$2.25
plus one bathroom	2.25
For each additional full or partial bathroom	1.10
For operation of refrigerator	2.80
(b) Rent Inclusion granted by order:	
For each room as per registration	$2.05
plus one bathroom	2.05
For each additional full or partial bathroom	1.00
(c) Where additional rent increases were previously granted for applicances or equipment:	
Electric current for refrigerator	$2.55
Electric current for television	1.05
Electric current for washing machine	1.05
Electric current for dishwasher	
installed by landlord	1.55
installed by tenant	1.05
Electric current for "air conditioners"	.45 per 1,000 BTU's

Where prior increase was predicated upon amount of horsepower in lieu of BTU's, use the following schedule:

⅓ H.P.	$2.60
½ H.P.	3.40
¾ H.P.	5.15
1 H.P.	6.70

Any other appliances, the amount granted by an earlier increase order of the Rent Agency multiplied by 1.4 of such amount.

Any increase in maximum base rent in existing MBR orders for electrical inclusion will be revoked.

ADMINISTRATOR'S INTERPRETATIONS

This Interpretation supersedes Administrator's Interpretation No. 7 (revised December 27, 1968) as of the date of publication of this revision in THE CITY RECORD. [Published in City Record on March 26, 1975]

INTERPRETATION NO. 8 (Revised)

(Effective November 6, 1972)

§ 33.1—*Modernization or conversion of an existing oil-, gas-, or coal-fired central heating system or upgrading or modification of existing residual oil burning equipment as the basis for the increase of maximum rents pursuant to Section 33.1 of the Regulations.*

Uninterrupted service of heat and hot water has long been considered essential to public health and well-being. In recent years the importance of air pollution control to life and property has received national recognition. Properly functioning heating equipment is basic to maintenance of these services and the control of air pollution. Further, specific legislation has been passed establishing standards for residual oil burning equipment.

In many older buildings using grades of oil and types of fuel, there are frequent breakdowns because the equipment has deteriorated or has become obsolete. Defective or poorly functioning heating systems are the basis for thousands of complaints of insufficient heat filed annually with the Office of Code Enforcement, Central Complaint Bureau and the placement of smoke violations by the Department of Air Resources. In addition, malfunctioning heating equipment also constitutes a serious fire hazard.

The Administrator has therefore determined that (1) the modernization or conversion of a heating system involving the replacement or installation of a new burner, boiler, and/or fuel storage tank, where necessary to improve the operation of deteriorated or obsolete equipment; and (2) the upgrading or modification of existing residual oil burning equipment as hereinafter set forth shall be considered an increase in service and or equipment within the meaning of Section 33.1 of the Regulations. Such heating improvements must meet the specified minimum standards and must comply with the procedures set forth below.

It should be noted that upgrading or modification of existing residual oil burning equipment differs from heating system modernization or conversion in that no replacement of equipment is contemplated. (By definition fuel oil grades Nos. 5 and 6 are considered residual oil.) Conversion of such heating equipment to use No. 4 or No. 2 fuel oil, gas, or a combination of gas and No. 2 fuel oil is an acceptable alternative to upgrading, as is conversion to purchase steam service.

All installations and/or replacements must be made with new equipment and have a capacity to satisfy both heat and hot water service obligations of the landlord. Further, every heating system improvement must result in a fully automatic heating system and be in compliance with all applicable requirements of law.

The basic modernization and upgrading requirements which follow are the result of ongoing study in which various City officials, heating equipment manufacturers and contractors, fuel suppliers, and other organizations provide technical advice and information. Accordingly, it has been determined that boilers which have been in operation 25 years or more, and burners (other than those firing residual fuel oil) and fuel storage tanks which have been in use 20 years or more shall be considered eligible for replacement under the terms of this Interpretation. Where, because of unique and peculiar circumstances, as determined by the Administrator, such equipment needs replacement even though the 20 or 25 year period, whichever is applicable, has not expired their replacement under such circumstances may also warrant rent increases under this Interpretation.

An exception has been made with regard to existing burners firing No. 6 grade fuel oil, in that the replacement interval has been liberalized in furtherance of the City's air pollution control program. The Administrator finds that the replacement of an existing No. 6 burner with a new and improved model designed to fire residual oil, or the installation of a new gas conversion or gas/oil firing burner will be eligible for the rent increase indicated provided that landlord has not been granted a prior rent adjustment for a burner installation made subsequent to January 1964 in connection with a heating system improvement. However, where the landlord has received a prior rent adjustment for upgrading residual oil burning equipment pursuant to Local Law No. 14, he will not be eligible for a subsequent adjustment based on burner replacement within five years of the date of upgrading.

BASIC MODERNIZATION REQUIREMENTS

Separate requirements have been established for the installation or replacement of major heating system components, namely, boilers, burners and tanks. Landlord may elect to install or replace any one or a combination of these items provided that the installation meets the following requirements. For example, in the event of an oil-burning modernization, the landlord may replace an existing boiler and burner, while retaining the existing fuel storage tank. Where the modernization involves gas-fired equipment, the landlord may elect to install a new gas conversion burner in the existing boiler, or replace both boiler and burner with a gas-designed boiler. Similarly, where the modernization involves the conversion of an existing coal-burning system, the landlord may install an oil or gas burner if existing boiler is in good operating condition; in the case of conversion to oil, a fuel storage tank would also be required.

Boiler Replacement

The installation shall include a new boiler with either a tankless hot water coil or a separate new hot water heater, new boiler controls and electrical wiring, reconditioning and re-installation of existing burner.

Gas-Designed Boiler

The installation shall include a new boiler with either a tankless hot water coil or a separate new hot water heater, and a new gas-fired burner. It shall also include all new controls and electrical wiring.

Burner Replacement or Conversion

The installation shall include one of the following units:

No. 2 or No. 4 burner—including a new burner, controls, and electrical wiring and a combustion chamber, where necessary; or

No. 6 oil burner—a new burner designed to fire residual oil in conjunction with new auxiliary equipment and electrical wiring as specified by the Department of Air Resources together with necessary modifications to existing boiler and fuel storage tank as shall comply with all requirements of Local Law No. 14 of 1966; or

Gas/oil burner—a new dual fuel burner designed to fire gas or No. 2 oil on a temperature controlled basis including all new controls and electrical wiring; or

Gas conversion burner—a new gas burner including all new controls and electrical wiring.

Fuel Storage Tank Replacement or Installation

The fuel storage tank shall be of sufficient capacity to contain a minimum oil reserve equivalent to one week's usage.

BASIC UPGRADING REQUIREMENTS

Pursuant to The Air Pollution Control Code of 1971 all residual oil fired equipment must be upgraded to conform with standards established by the Department of Air Resources. The work performed in upgrading of existing residual oil burning equipment and modification of existing equipment to fire a lighter grade fuel must comply with the provisions of the Code and/or current criteria established by the Department of Air Resources and the various City departments having jurisdiction.

RENT ADJUSTMENTS

Rent adjustments will be granted based on a seven-year amortization of the actual cost, exclusive of interest and/or financial charges, allocated on the basis of total number of rooms in the structure. Where two or more buildings share a common heating system, the "number of rooms in the structure" shall be the aggregate room count for all buildings tied into the heating system.

Inasmuch as the schedule of rental values has been eliminated for modernization or conversion of an existing heating system and none has been established for upgrading of residual oil burning equipment due to wide variance of job requirements, individual cost will be closely scrutinized as to reasonableness. Where the claimed cost appears excessive, or where the landlord fails to support his claim adequately, the Administrator reserves the right to adjust such claimed cost to reflect an amount that the Administrator shall find to be reasonable for such modernization or upgrading.

Administrator's Interpretations

It should also be noted that any person who willfully makes any false statement or entry or omits to disclose discounts, refunds, rebates, etc., shall be guilty of a crime punishable by law. In addition, submission of fraudulent cost information may result in denial of an application for rent increases, or in the revocation—retroactive to date of orders—of rent increases already issued, and may preclude any subsequent adjustment in rents for this improvement.

PROCEDURES

Where a landlord "modernizes" or "upgrades" a heating system he may file an application for rent increases pursuant to Section 33.1 of the Regulations on Application Form A-33.1HSI. In his application landlord shall briefly state the nature and extent of the work performed. The landlord shall file a master copy of the application in duplicate and four copies for each controlled apartment. All of the following documents shall be submitted together with the application. Failure to submit one or more of the required documents may result in rejection of the application.

1. A copy of the signed contract for the heating system improvement which is the basis of this application.

2. A certification by the heating contractor, Report Form R-33.1H (Revised 1972), in duplicate, which shall contain all requested information relative to the completed improvement including dates on which work permits were issued by and certificates of approval were requested from City agencies having jurisdiction over heating system improvements; or in the alternative the specific approvals or certificates required for the type of work done as listed on reverse side of Report Form R-33.1H (Revised 1972) "Heating Contractor's Statement and Certification."

3. A copy of Application Form APC5-0 or APC5-G processed by the Department of Air Resources to show Combustion Application number and date of filing for all improvements involving fuel burning equipment having a BTU input of more than 350,000 BTU per hour. NOTE: The applicant should enter initials "RCS" on upper right hand corner of Form APC 5-0 or APC 5-G before filing with the Department of Air Resources.

4. A certification by an independent or certified public accountant, in duplicate, which shall contain the information set forth in the "Suggested Form of Accountant's Certification." In the alternative, the landlord may submit the original and one duplicate copy of invoices or bills, and the original cancelled checks together with the one duplicate copy of both sides of such checks; these should be submitted with Application Form A-33.1 HSI.

5. A total room count for the entire structure(s), including professional or commercial space and accommodations occupied by the landlord and service employees, and stores, if any. Also included in this count are decontrolled and exempt accommodations.

Include in the room count the following:

a. Kitchens, bedrooms, dining rooms, finished basement or attic rooms, recreation rooms, and other rooms suitable for use as living quarters. A kitchenette or "half-room" which is partitioned off from floor to ceiling should be counted as a separate room; but, a combined kitchenette and dinette, separated only by shelves or cabinets; should only be counted as one room.

b. Rooms used for office purposes.

c. Substitute for area of store space the room count for residential space above store.

The following are not to be included in the room count: Bathrooms, strip or pullman kitchens, halls, foyers, alcoves, pantries, laundries, closets, storage space, and basement or attic rooms which are not suitable for living quarters.

6. Unless work involves modernization or upgrading of residual oil burning equipment in compliance with Local Law No. 14 of 1966 as incorporated in the Air Pollution Code of 1971, a report of search issued by the Office of Code Enforcement of the Department of Rent and Housing Maintenance of the Housing and Development Administration stating either that no violations against the property are recorded or that all violations recorded against the property have been complied with, or a receipt (or copy thereof) issued by the Borough office of the Department of Buildings attesting to the payment of the fee for a report of search. Such report of search will

not be acceptable unless issued by such agency within 45 days prior to the date of filing the application, or in lieu thereof, such receipt may not be dated more than 14 days prior to the date of filing the application. See Operational Bulletin No. C-9, revised April 25, 1968, for further details.

The above procedures will apply to all heating system improvements except where such work involves: (a) unique and peculiar circumstances; or (b) conversion to steam service for which the landlord should apply for a prior opinion approval before commencing the work. In his application for prior opinion, the landlord should give full particulars about the proposed installation including the estimated cost and number of rooms in structure.

Suggested Form For Accountant's Certification

Re: Premises ....
....

TO: The Office of Rent Control
Department of Rent and Housing Maintenance
Housing and Development Administration

I am an independent (or certified) public accountant, registered as such by and in good standing with the New York State Education Department. My number is ....

I have examined the accompanying application for rent increases under Section 33.1 of the Rent Regulations based upon an increase in service and/or equipment required by law, to wit, the heating system improvement submitted by .... (insert name of individual or corporate owner), and all original invoices or bills and original cancelled checks relating to such installation. Attached hereto is a copy of my original worksheets showing the documents examined by me.

My examination was made in accordance with generally accepted auditing standards.

I hereby certify that the Owner's Application is supported by the owner's records and the invoices or bills and the original cancelled checks examined by me.

I further certify that $........ not yet paid but due under the terms of the contract does not represent any interest, finance charges, rebates, discounts or refunds to the landlord but is being withheld until all of the terms of the contract relating to the upgrading or modification of the heating system have been fulfilled.

As an independent (or certified) public accountant, I have no direct or indirect interest in the success of the accompanying application. I have placed my initials and the date, for identification, in the lower right hand corner of the face of the application.

I have read this certification and I hereby affirm under the penalties provided by law that the contents thereof are true of my own knowledge.

....
(Signature of Accountant)
Dated: .... 19....

ADMINISTRATOR'S INTERPRETATION No. 9
(Revised)

(Effective November 6, 1972)

§ 33.1—*Replacement of Plumbing as Basis for Increase of Maximum Rent Under Section 33.1c of the Regulations.*

A landlord requests advice from a District Rent Office whether the replacement of existing plumbing consisting of galvanized iron piping by a new brass plumbing system would be considered a major capital improvement within the contemplation of Section 33.1c of the Rent and Eviction Regulations. He further inquires as to how much he could expect by way of rent increases if such plumbing improvement is considered to be a major capital improvement.

Faulty plumbing accelerates the deterioration of buildings because of the frequency of leaks and even though repairs are promptly made, water seeps through floors, plaster and walls. The dampness thus created causes rotting of the exposed parts of the building and is conducive to infestation. Galvanized iron being susceptible to corrosion, the installation of long lasting, rust resisting, brass or copper piping has become an accepted practice in modern building construction. Therefore, the Administrator finds that the installation of new brass or copper piping in place of existing galvanized iron piping is

Administrator's Interpretations

required for the operation, preservation or maintenance of buildings and accordingly is a major capital improvement within the meaning of Section 33.1c of the Regulations where made as a part of a comprehensive plan to preserve the structure. Rigid copper tubing may be substituted for brass or copper piping in buildings with less than seven stories (levels of elevation-basements, sub-basements, and cellars are counted as stories), if such use otherwise conforms to the rule and regulation established by the Department of Buildings. Thin wall tubing is not acceptable. To qualify as a major capital improvement plumbing installation must be a part of a coordinated building wide, consecutively timed project. Piecemeal repairs will not so qualify. This determination conforms with the Administrator's general policy of encouraging landlords to take affirmative steps to preserve and improve the existing housing supply.

The Administrator has recognized the following plumbing installations to be major capital improvements. Consideration has also been given to the current costs for making such improvements and has determined that the following Rent Values shall be applicable:

NEW BRASS OR COPPER PLUMBING IMPROVEMENT

	Monthly
(a) for housing accommodations with single bathroom—	
Basement Piping without new Water Service installation	$1.00
Basement Piping with new Water Service installation	1.30
Risers (concealed)[1]	2.60
(exposed replacing exposed)	1.30
Branches to Four Fixtures (concealed)[2]	3.00
(exposed replacing exposed)	1.00
Trim in Kitchen and one Bathroom (includes modern faucets for all sinks and tub): including shower (consisting of new head, body, arm with concealed brass supply and faucets) in connection with:	
installation of shower including curtain rod over tub (none before)	2.05
replacement of existing shower having exposed piping	1.80
replacement of existing shower having concealed piping	1.65

[1] The term "concealed" as it refers to risers shall be interpreted to mean covering by new matching wall construction extending from floor to ceiling. This will normally require furring and plastering; ordinary box enclosures will not be acceptable.

[2] Normal adjustment of $3 covers seven concealed branches connecting four fixtures to risers: two branches to each of the following: kitchen sink, bathtub and wash basin; one branch to toilet. The value of concealed branches per fixture is $.75.

Administrator's Interpretations

	Monthly
where no shower exists and none is installed	.60
Flushometer Replacement[3]	.35

(b) additional allowances for housing accommodations which have a bathroom, toilet or wash basin in addition to the single bathroom contemplated in (a)—

Set of concealed risers (hot and cold water)[1, 4]	1.30
Basement Piping (with set of additional risers)	.25
Concealed branches (per fixture)[2]	.75
In lieu of branches[5]	.25
New Trim:	
wash basin faucets	.15
bathtub faucets	.25
kitchen sink faucets	.25
shower—requires new head, body, arm with concealed brass supply and faucets in connection with:	
installation of shower including curtain rod over tub (none before)	1.45
replacement of existing shower having exposed piping	1.20
replacement of existing shower having concealed piping	1.05

(c) Where an order has been issued less than 6 years ago for a rent increase for the installation of a kitchen sink, wash basin or bathtub or where simultaneous application is being made for the installation of these fixtures, the allowance for trim relating to such fixtures shall be reduced by the applicable rental value specified in (b).

(d) Where an order has been issued 6 or more years ago for a rent increase for the installation of a kitchen sink, wash basin or bathtub, the allowance for trim relating to such equipment shall be the full rental value specified in (b).

The above rental values includes costs for the proper restoration of floors, walls and ceilings incidental to such improvements.

The rental schedule herein will apply to all buildings except where it is found that because of a unique and

---

[3] Flushometer replacement on a building-wide basis for which no rent increase was granted for at least twenty years.

[4] Normal installation is considered to include two complete sets of risers. Therefore $1.30 additional allowance is provided for one additional set of risers. No allowance for additional risers is warranted where there is a common wall between two plumbing installations (i.e. back to back). Basement piping is adjusted by $.25 per set of risers. New water service adjustment is not affected.

[5] Allowance is made in lieu of branch for any single fixture backing on an existing riser which requires less than three feet of piping.

peculiar combination of factors the foregoing allowance may not be appropriate and such facts are submitted to the Administrator for a prior opinion before the commencement of the plumbing improvement.

PROCEDURES

It will not be necessary for a landlord to request a prior opinion in plumbing improvement applications where the rental schedule herein is applicable. After the completion of such improvement, a landlord should file his application for rental increases pursuant to Section 33.1c of the Regulations, which does not require the consent of the tenants. In his application the landlord will briefly describe the type of plumbing which was previously supplied to the building and a description of the plumbing improvement which is the basis for the application. In addition the landlord will be required to file Form R-33.1(c)P (Plumbing Contractor's Statement) in duplicate after completion of the work which states that "the installation of the improvements referred to herein complies with all of the requirements of the City agencies having jurisdiction and that application has been filed or made to the appropriate City agencies for the required approvals[6] by the plumbing contractor and a report of search issued by a City agency having jurisdiction annexed to such application stating either that no violations against such property are recorded or that all violations recorded against such property have been cleared, corrected or abated or a receipt (or photocopy thereof) issued by such agency attesting to the payment of the fee for the report of search. See Operational Bulletin No. C-9, revised April 25, 1968.

The Administrator deems it proper to note that as a condition of receiving orders increasing maximum rents the landlord must certify and establish that he is maintaining essential services.

INTERPRETATION NO. 10
(Revised October 8, 1965)

§ 2e—*Termination of Business Space Rent Control Law; recontrol of housing accommodations exempt from control by reason of the definition of "Business Space" in such law; maximum rent.*

---

[6] Failure to obtain such approvals within 90 days, after the issuance of any order increasing the maximum rent, may result in the revocation of such order.

A tenant states that an emergency rent was fixed by the Court for his residential apartment pursuant to the provisions of the Emergency Business Space Rent Control Law even though his apartment was used solely for residential purposes. The rent fixed by the Court was $150.00 per month. He seeks advice as to what rent his landlord may properly demand since the Business Space Rent Control Law expired on December 31, 1963.

Prior to its expiration, the definition of "Business Space" in the Emergency Business Space Rent Control Law [Section 2(a)] read as follows:

"All rental space in any city other than . . . dwelling space and meeting rooms in hotels, and dwelling space in rooming houses, apartment houses, dwelling and other housing accommodations, except, on and after March first, nineteen hundred fifty-two, a building in which at least sixty per centum of the total rentable area and sixty per centum of the total number of units formerly used as dwelling space, is lawfully occupied as business space on such date . . . ."

When the Court fixed the rental for the tenant's apartment, it also determined that the accommodation was subject to the provisions of the Emergency Business Space Rent Control Law, thereby divesting the Administrator of authority to regulate or control apartments found by the Court to be "business space" within the meaning of the then Emergency Business Space Rent Control Law.

The expiration of such law on December 31, 1963 did not have the effect of re-imposing residential rent control over apartments which had previously been subject to the former Business Space Rent Control Law (850 Co. v. Schwartz, 15 N. Y. 2d 899, 258 N. Y. S. 2d 428; Viro Realty Corp'n v. Gabel, Sup. Ct., N. Y. Co., McCaffrey, J., N. Y. L. J. 2/2/65, p. 17, cols. 5 & 6).

INTERPRETATION NO. 11
(Revised June 23, 1964)

§ 33.1—*Installation of Air-Conditioning Unit by Tenant as Basis for Increase of Maximum Rent.*

(1) A tenant who pays for the electricity supplied to his apartment directly to the utility company wishes to in-

stall an air-conditioning unit which will rest on part of the window sill. The unit will not be entirely within the window line but will protrude beyond the window sill, or if it does not protrude, it will be attached to the outside of the building, rather than being secured from the inside. Will an order increasing the maximum rent pursuant to Section 33.1 of the Regulations be issued by the District Rent Director on the landlord's application by reason of the installation of the air-conditioning unit by the tenant in the manner described?

Yes. The air-conditioning unit, if installed in the manner described by the tenant, will not be incidental to the tenant's enjoyment of his housing accommodation since the air-conditioner as installed by the tenant will protrude beyond the confines of the space rented to the tenant under his rental agreement with his landlord. Where a landlord has consented to the utilization of such additional facility by the tenant, he may properly apply for a $2.00 per month rent adjustment pursuant to Section 33.1 of the Regulations on the basis of such increase in services, etc. The increase will remain effective so long as the tenant referred to in the order remains in occupancy.

For the purpose of this interpretation the term "window line" shall mean the outside facing of the building wall unless the window sill protrudes beyond the building wall. In the latter case the "window line" shall mean the outer edge of the window sill.

(2) Where the landlord furnishes unmetered and unlimited electric service to the tenant under a rent inclusion plan, the District Rent Director will approve increases in maximum rent for each air-conditioning unit installed on the basis of a monthly allowance of $.33 per 1000 BTUs (British Thermal Units) of cooling capacity per hour.

The foregoing allowance takes into account the average normal use of a window-type air conditioner in New York City during the period from May through September allocated on an equal year-round monthly basis.

The BTU capacity of an individual air conditioner is specified on the name-plate attached to the unit. In order to determine the proper rental value all that will be required is to multiply $.33 by the number of 1000 BTUs designated on the name-plate. For example, the nameplate designated a 9,000 BTU capacity. All that would be required in order to ascertain the rental value would be to multiple $.33 by 9. In the given example the rental value is $2.97 per month.

The order which will be issued by the District Rent Director will include an additional allowance for the privilege of maintaining the air-conditioning unit in the window where such allowance is proper. Where the installation is made in a "through-the-wall" sleeve which is constructed by the landlord, an allowance of $1.25 per month will be granted.

All orders granting increases of the maximum rent on the basis of the installation by the tenant of air-conditioning units will remain in effect only so long as the tenant referred to in the order remains in occupancy. Where such tenant removes from the apartment and a new tenant takes possession, the maximum rent will be reduced automatically by the amount of adjustment provided for in such order.

The tenant further states that she inquired of one of her neighbors who was friendly with the former tenant of her apartment and was informed that the rental was only $60.00 a month and not $69.00, as shown by the records of the District Rent Office. Upon the tenant's confronting her landlord with this information, she was informed by the landlord that he had collected $60.00 as the rent for the first twenty-three months of the lease term and had collected $69.00 as rent for the last or twenty-fourth month of the lease. The landlord further stated that the rent ceiling for the apartment became $69.00 per month as a result of the execution of this voluntary lease agreement with the prior tenant. The tenant seeks advice as to what the maximum rent for her apartment is in view of the foregoing.

Section 33.2 of the Rent, Eviction and Rehabilitation Regulations provides for an automatic increase in the maximum rent where a voluntary lease agreement is executed which meets the requirements of the Regulations.

Administrator's Interpretations

INTERPRETATION NO. 12

(Issued June 5, 1964)

§ 33.2—*Voluntary Lease Agreement Providing for Graduated Rentals; Computation of Maximum Rents Resulting Therefrom.*

A tenant states that he moved into an apartment on October 1, 1963 after having executed a voluntary lease agreement with his landlord for a two-year term commencing October 1, 1963 at a monthly rental of $79.35. Upon inquiry at the District Rent Office the tenant was advised that a Lease Report had been filed by the landlord indicating that the prior tenant had executed a voluntary lease agreement for a term commencing October 1, 1961 and ending on September 30, 1963 at a monthly rental of $69.00, being 15% above the $60.00 maximum rent in effect at the time the former tenant executed the lease.

While the lease must provide for an increase in rent, with a 15% limitation, it would ordinarily provide for the same monthly rent throughout the lease term. However, where the rent is only increased for the last month of the lease term it would be proper for the Rent Director, either on his own initiative or on application of an interested party, to institute a proceeding pursuant to Section 36 a of the Regulations to establish the maximum rent for the accommodation by prorating the total rent collected for the lease term. Under the facts presented the maximum rent would be fixed at $60.37 per month. Where the 15% lease increase was collected for a period of less than six months of the lease term, it would also be proper to prorate the rent collected over the entire lease period for the purpose of determining the maximum rent.

However, where the lease provides for a full 15% increase for at least the last six months of its term, even though the lease provides for no increase or less than a full 15% increase for the other period, the lease will be deemed proper to increase the maximum rent by 15% effective on the date when the lease provides for such 15% increase.

INTERPRETATION NO. 13

(Issued June 5, 1964)

§ 2 f (14)—*Meaning of term "attending elementary school"; decontrol schedule for occupied accommodations.*

A tenant seeks advice from a District Rent and Rehabilitation Office as to whether the apartment occupied by him would become decontrolled pursuant to the provisions of the newly enacted "High Rent Decontrol Law" provision of the Rent Law. He states that for the past five years his monthly rent has been $325.00 for his unfurnished apartment and that it is occupied by his household which consists of his wife, a child attending kindergarten and himself.

Under the provisions of Section 2 f (14) of the Rent, Eviction and Rehabilitation Regulations and Section Y51-3.0 e(2)(i)(7) of the Rent Law individual housing accommodations having unfurnished maximum rents of $250.00 or more per month as of April 1, 1960 shall continue to remain subject to control until they become vacant or until the date specified in such decontrol provision.

The decontrol of occupied housing accommodations is staggered, the date of decontrol depending upon the amount of rental and the nature of the occupancy. The following table sets forth the decontrol schedule for occupied accommodations.

	Maximum Monthly Rents As Of April 1, 1960		Effective Date
	Unfurnished	Furnished	Of Decontrol
1. occupied by 4 or more related persons	$250.00 or more	$300.00 or more	on vacancy
2. occupied by less than 4 related persons	$250.00 to $299.99	$300.00 to $359.99	
a. no school children			April 1, 1965
b. with children attending elementary or secondary school			June 30, 1965
3. occupied by less than 4 related persons	$300.00 or more	$360.00 or more	
a. no school children			October 1, 1964
b. with children attending elementary or secondary school			June 30, 1965

The term "related persons" is defined by Section 2 f (14) of the Regulations to mean the tenant and a parent, grandparent, child, step-child, grandchild, brother or sister of the tenant or of the tenant's spouse or the spouse of any of the foregoing, who customarily occupied the apartment on the effective date of Local Law No. 13 for the year 1964. Subparagraph (14) of Section 2 f also provides that "the tenant's spouse or unmarried child or grandchild of the tenant who temporarily resided elsewhere on the effective date of this" subparagraph "because of attendance at an educational institution or service in the armed forces of the United States shall be deemed to be a related person in occupancy."

Where the tenant's household contains one or more children attending elementary or secondary school the accommodations continue to remain subject to control until June 30, 1965 even though the accommodations may otherwise qualify for decontrol at an earlier date.

Under the facts presented the apartment would become decontrolled on October 1, 1964 since the maximum rent on April 1, 1960 was $325.00 (unfurnished) and the apartment was occupied by less than four related persons. The occupancy by a child attending kindergarten does not postpone the effective date of decontrol to June 30, 1965. The report of the Committee on General Welfare of the City Council in recommending the adoption of the proposed local law decontrolling "high rents" states:

"Uprooting during the school year of families with children attending elementary or secondary school presents an unwarranted hardship on such families and unnecessary dislocation for the children. We believe it should be avoided. The bill provides, therefore, that where decontrol would otherwise take place at an earlier date, housing accommodations containing one or more children attending an elementary or secondary school shall continue to remain subject to control until June 30, 1965."

In enacting this proviso it was the intent of the City Council to avoid disrupting elementary and secondary education. It is clear that a child attending kindergarten does not attend a school dealing with the fundamentals of education. A disruption of such attendance does not entail the kind of hardship contemplated by the City Council.

INTERPRETATION NO. 14

(Issued June 5, 1964)

§ 2 f (14)—*Execution of voluntary agreements increasing rents effective as of the date decontrol becomes effective.*

A landlord states that several housing accommodations in a building owned by him will become eligible for decontrol under the provisions of the newly enacted "High Rent Decontrol Law" provisions of the Rent Law. He seeks advice whether it would be proper for him to enter into agreements with his tenants which would provide for rent increases which shall become effective on the effective date of decontrol.

Since the agreements which the landlord contemplates entering into with his tenants will become effective upon the termination of rent control it would be proper for the landlord to negotiate and consummate a voluntary agreement with his tenants governing their continued right of occupancy at any rental agreed upon by them. Decontrol of so-called "high rents" under the provisions of Section Y51-3.0e(2)(i)(7) of the Rent Law and Section 2f(14) of the Rent, Eviction and Rehabilitation Regulations was staggered in order to afford landlords and tenants an opportunity to negotiate mutually satisfactory rental agreements. The consummation of such agreements during this twilight period is desirable and is consistent with the purpose for phasing decontrol in stages.

INTERPRETATION NO. 15

(Issued December 15, 1964)

§ 52 e—*Tenant's refusal to renew lease as a basis for eviction; date of demand for renewal or extension of lease.*

A lease for a housing accommodation expired on October 31, 1964. On November 1, 1964 the landlord submitted a renewal lease to the tenant for a term of one year, but otherwise on the same terms and conditions as the lease which had just expired. The tenant refused to sign such lease even though the execution of the lease was demanded by the landlord. Thereupon, the landlord served the tenant with the written notice provided for by Section 53 of the Rent, Eviction and Rehabilitation Regulations alleging the refusal of the tenant to sign the one-year renewal lease as demanded by the landlord as the basis for the tenant's eviction and requiring the tenant to surrender possession no later than December 31, 1964. In the event that the tenant refuses to surrender possession by December 31, 1964, may the landlord properly commence proceedings for the eviction of the tenant without a Certificate of Eviction?

No. The landlord has not made a timely demand for the tenant to execute the renewal lease and, therefore, may not now commence a court action to remove or evict the tenant. Where a landlord desires to invoke the provisions of paragraph e of Section 52 of the Rent, Eviction and Rehabilitation Regulations he must make such demand prior to the expiration of the lease which he seeks to be renewed or extended.

Where such demand is made prior to the expiration of the lease at an unreasonably early stage, the tenant may refuse to sign and no ground for eviction under Section 52 e of the Regulations would exist through such refusal. Where the lease provides for monthly payment of rent, a demand made one or two months prior to expiration of lease would ordinarily be a reasonable period for this purpose. It is to be noted that the demand should also include a statement that "the tenant's refusal to execute the offered lease may result in the landlord's termination of the tenancy and bringing a Court action or proceeding to recover possession of the housing accommodations".

INTERPRETATION NO. 16

(Revised May 14, 1968)

§ 33.1c—*Effect of Tax Abatement on Rent Increases Otherwise Allowable for the Installation of Improvements; Restoration of Offset Allowance Given Tenants Upon Expiration of Tax Abatement; Procedure for Obtaining Recoupment of Such Offset Allowances.*

A landlord filed an application for rent increases pursuant to Section 33.1c of the Rent, Eviction and Rehabilitation Regulations on the basis of his having installed a central heating and hot water system in a multiple dwelling owned by him. He further states in his application that he will apply for tax abatement and tax exemption relief as provided in Section J51-2.5 of the Administrative Code. He now seeks advice as to the effect tax abatement, if allowed, would have on any rent increases which may be granted for the improvement made by him.

In order to encourage the elimination of unhealthy and dangerous conditions in existing dwellings or the replacement of inadequate and obsolete sanitary facilities in such dwelling, the City has made provision in the Administrative Code for a tax exemption for improvements (defined in the Code to be physical changes in an existing dwelling other than painting, ordinary repairs, normal replacement of maintenance items) for a 12-year period and for tax abatement which will permit the recovery of

75 per cent of the cost of the improvement over a nine-year period. This tax abatement provision applies not only to central heating and hot water systems, but to other improvements for which the City will allow such relief. In order to obtain this relief, the landlord is required by such Section J51-2.5 of the Code to do the following:

(1) obtain a certificate from the City Planning Commission that the improvement "will not interfere with projected public improvements or the clearance and rebuilding of substandard and insanitary areas;"

(2) obtain a certificate from the Department of Buildings that the building is structurally sound;

(3) if the building is in an area for which a preliminary or final plan has been approved pursuant to Section 72-m of the General Municipal Law (now covered by Article 15 of the General Municipal Law), obtain a certificate by the Project Board or the Department of Development—Office of Rehabilitation for the area that the building is to be or has been improved in conformity with such plan;

(4) if the building is in an area where a program of local neighborhood improvement or housing maintenance is being carried out, obtain a certificate by the Department of Development—Office of Rehabilitation stating such fact;

(5) obtain a certificate from the Department of Development—Office of Rehabilitation of the reasonable cost of the alterations and improvements; and

(6) file an application with the City Tax Commission for such benefits between February 1st and March 15th for the relief afforded by Section J51-2.5 of the Administrative Code.

In a proper case the City will allow the landlord a tax abatement of 75 per cent of the reasonable cost of the improvement amortized over a period of nine years. That means that for every $1,000 found to be reasonable cost of the improvement the City will yield the landlord $750 in tax abatement via annual tax remissions of $83.33 each year. The Administrator will, however, allow two-thirds of this tax abatement to be used to offset any rent increase which would otherwise be allowable for the improvement. Concretely, assume a situation were presented to the District Rent Director where a building consisting of ten five-room apartments qualifies for tax abatement and the landlord was granted such abatement in the sum of $360 for each year. This translated into monthly rents for each of the ten apartments would indicate that the monthly tax abatement allocable to each apartment would be $3. Two-thirds of this amount, or $2 per month, would be deducted from the amount the tenant would be required to pay in the absence of tax abatement.

It is to be noted that the tax abatement offset provided for herein is computed on the basis of the City's granting tax abatement for a nine-year period. In cases where the City may provide for tax abatement over a greater period, the tax abatement offset will be appropriately modified to reflect such extended period.

Where tax abatement has been granted by the City and the landlord is already receiving the benefits thereof, the rent increase orders will reflect a rent increase which is modified by tax abatement. Where tax abatement has been granted by the City which will become effective after the rent increase, the rent increase orders will be modified to reflect the tax abatement allowance.

In cases where it would be proper for the landlord to register the housing accommodations as "first rents," rather than to file an application pursuant to Section 33.1 of the Regulations, similar consideration to the receipt of tax abatement by the landlord will be given by the District Rent Director. Where a "first rent" has been accepted or reduced pursuant to Section 34.1 of the Regulations prior to the receipt of tax abatement by the landlord, the maximum rent will be modified pursuant to Section 33 a(2) of the Regulations to reflect that fact.

RESTORATION OF THE AMOUNT OF THE OFFSET ALLOWANCE UPON EXPIRATION OF TAX ABATEMENT

Since the tenants have been given an offset of two-thirds of the tax abatement benefits which the City allowed because the City intended that tax abatement be shared by the landlord and his tenants, it follows that when those benefits expire the landlord has no fund to share with his tenants. Accordingly, the continuation of the offset allowance to the tenants when the landlord no longer receives tax abatement would in effect be a rent reduction which was never contemplated by the Rent Law or the Regulations. Such a result is clearly inconsistent with the purpose for allowing the tax abatement offset to the tenants.

In the meantime, landlords who received tax abatement benefits were not given the full rental value for the improvements since the tenants were only required to pay the portion of the rent increase which represented the difference between the full rent increase allowable for the improvements and the amount of tax abatement which the landlord received. Where the tax abatement period is terminated the landlords are required to pay full taxes upon their properties. Since they are no longer receiving tax abatement, these landlords are equitably and legally entitled to a restoration of maximum rents which would reflect the full rental value for the improvements.

PROCEDURES

Where tax abatement benefits are still being obtained on the effective date of this revision of Administrator's Interpretation No. 16, before a landlord may make application for restoration of maximum rents by way of recoupment of the tax abatement offset, he will be required to give the tenants at least three months', and not more than six months' notice, in writing prior to the expiration of such benefits that tax abatement benefits will shortly cease and that on a specified date nine years (or such other period allowed by the City for tax abatement benefits) will have elapsed since the date of issuance of the order by the Rent Agency which granted the tenants an offset allowance based upon the City's granting tax abatement to the property. The notice must also advise the tenants that after such date, the landlord will make application to the District Rent Office for an order increasing the maximum rent by the amount previously allowed the tenant as his share of such tax abatement.

Administrator's Interpretations

Where such tax abatement has already expired and the full tax abatement period has already elapsed since the date of issuance of the order by the Rent Agency providing such offset allowance to the tenants, no notice to the tenants shall be required as a condition to filing the application.

The application shall be made on Application Form A-33.1C (Rev. 1-68). Item 8 of such form shall be completed by inserting an "x" in box "h" and in the space provided for in the "Statement of Landlord" make the following or similar statement setting forth the basis for the application:

"Landlord was granted an increase in maximum rent (see Docket No. ....) for improvements which qualified the landlord to receive a tax abatement allowance, two-thirds of which was used to offset any rent increase which would otherwise be allowable for the improvement. The tax abatement benefits have now expired and the landlord makes application to increase the maximum rent by the amount of such offset."

INTERPRETATION NO. 17
(Revised November 30, 1965)

§ 52 a—*Installation of peephole by tenant in entrance door without landlord's permission as a basis for eviction.*

A tenant states that he has installed a peephole in the entrance door to his apartment without his landlord's permission. His landlord, upon learning of the installation of the peephole, has requested him to restore the door to its original condition. In view of the tenant's refusal to comply with such request, the landlord has served a written notice on the tenant giving him 10 days to restore the door, claiming that the tenant has violated a provision of their rental agreement that "the tenant will not drive nails, drill into, disfigure or deface any part of the building . . . and not make any alterations". The notice further advises him that his "failure to cure such violation will compel the landlord to terminate the lease and to commence Court action to evict" him. The tenant seeks advice as to whether his conduct is a breach of a substantial obligation of his tenancy which would be the basis for his eviction.

Section 52 of the Rent, Eviction and Rehabilitation Regulations reads in part as follows:

"Section 52. *Proceedings for eviction without certificate.* Except as provided in Sections 51 and 54 of these Regulations, an action or proceeding to recover possession of any housing accommodation shall be maintainable, after service and filing of the notice required by Section 53, only upon one or more of the following grounds:

"a. The tenant is violating a substantial obligation of his tenancy other than the obligation to surrender possession of such housing accommodation and has failed to cure such violation after written notice by the landlord that the violation cease within 10 days; . . .."

The Administrator is of the opinion that under the related statement of facts the breach of the lease prohibition referred to would not be a breach of a "substantial obligation" of the tenancy within the meaning and scope of paragraph a of Section 52 of the Regulations. The installation of a peephole or window-type viewer in the entrance door of the apartment at a location in the door which is consistent with the purpose for which such installation was made (i.e. to identify callers) serves a legitimate purpose and is not within the ambit of the proscription provided for in the rental agreement.

INTERPRETATION NO. 18

(Issued February 18, 1977, Effective February 28, 1977)

Section 33.1a. Upgrading or Conversion of Existing Incinerators as the Basis for Rent Increases Pursuant to Section 33.1 of the Regulations.

In view of the serious problem that air pollution presents to the health and well-being of the public, the City Council enacted Local Law No. 14 for the year 1966 and Local Law No. 14 for the year 1968, and amended the Administrative Code of the City of New York in relation to air pollution control. As a result of this legislation, the Department of Air Resources and other City agencies directly concerned with this problem have issued rules and criteria for implementing these laws.

All buildings and structures subject to the City Rent Law are mandated by those laws to comply with their provisions relating to air pollution control. Likewise, the landlords are required to comply with the various rules and regulations promulgated by the City agencies having jurisdiction. This means that the owner must either: (a) upgrade the existing incinerator in compliance with criteria issued by the Department of Air Resources, or (b) convert the incinerator installation to a refuse chute and refuse room with a compacting machine which is certified to the Department of Buildings by the Department of Sanitation as being approved. However, where the landlord has been authorized by the Department of Air Resources to discontinue incinerator operation, the landlord may convert the discontinued incinerator to a refuse chute room without being required to install a compacting system. Such conversion of the incinerator, with or without a compacting system, must comply with the pertinent rules and regulations of the Department of Buildings. Where, however, the landlord discontinues incinerator service, and does not convert the discontinued incinerator to a refuse chute and refuse room, the landlord shall provide an acceptable substitute method of refuse collection and/or disposal, e.g., which if on the same floor may be an acceptable substitute.

The upgrading of an existing incinerator, or the conversion of an incinerator to a refuse chute and refuse room with compacting system, or the conversion to a refuse chute and refuse room without a compacting system where authorized, shall be considered to be an increase in service and/or equipment within the meaning of Section 33.1a of the Regulations with the implied consent of the tenants due to the requirements of such local laws.

MINIMUM REQUIREMENTS

1. Incinerator upgrading:

   a. An auxiliary gas or oil burner regulated by automatic firing clocks.

   b. An overfire air fan and nozzle system.

   c. Control apparatus such as a scrubber or such equivalent or additional control apparatus as may be determined by the Department of Air Resources.

2. Conversion to refuse chute and refuse rooms with compacting system:

   a. Conversion of an existing incinerator must comply with rules relating to the construction and maintenance of refuse chutes and refuse rooms as issued by the Department of Buildings.

b. Compacting machines shall be of make and model approved by the Department of Sanitation and certified to the Department of Buildings. Approval of compacting system will be implicit in Building Department sign-off or letter of completion.

3. Conversion of refuse chute and refuse room without compacting system.

As in 2a above.

RENT ADJUSTMENTS

Rent adjustments will be granted based on a seven-year amortization of the verified reasonable cost, exclusive of interest and/or financial charges, allocated on the basis of total number of rooms in the structure. Where the claimed cost appears excessive, or where the landlord fails to support his claim adequately, the Administrator reserves the right to adjust such claimed cost to reflect an amount that the Administrator shall find to be reasonable for such upgrading or conversion.

In buildings having two or more existing incinerators, rent increases shall be computed by dividing the total verified costs for all incinerator upgrading and/or conversion by the total number of rooms in the building irrespective of the number of apartments serviced by each individual incinerator, thereby assuring that each tenant will receive the same per room rent adjustment.

In the case of incinerator upgrading, a fuel usage allowance of $0.10 per room per month will be granted in addition to the indicated rent adjustment provided that the landlord submits the following documentary evidence in addition to that specified under Procedures:

Gas Usage: A copy of the Certification of Adequate Supply of Natural Gas (Form AR439) filed with the Department of Air Resources; said document must bear date stamp of that Department indicating date copy was obtained. *A certification which does not bear this stamp will not be considered acceptable evidence.*

No. 2 Fuel Oil: Copies of Building Department Oil Burning Equipment Application (Form 15), and Certificate of Approval (Form 16A) attesting to satisfactory installation of new equipment.

Where an order had previously been issued for incinerator modernization pursuant to Administrator's Interpretation No. 18 (issued December 30, 1964, revised and effective May 20, 1971), the indicated rent increases for subsequent upgrading with scrubbers or other similar device as provided for in this revision shall be reduced by the amount of the previous grant.

Where the landlord is granted tax abatement by the City for this improvement, then two-thirds of the amount abated will be regarded as an appropriate allowance which will reduce the indicated tenant rent increases allowable for the improvement.

PROCEDURES

Where a landlord "upgrades" or "converts" an existing incinerator he may file an application for rent increases pursuant to Section 33.1a of the Regulations on Application Form A-33.1 IM (Combination (Revised 11-76)). The landlord shall file a master copy of the application in duplicate and four copies for each controlled apartment. All of the following documents shall be submitted together with the application. Failure to submit one or more of the required documents may result in rejection of the application.

For All Applications—

1. A copy of the contract for incinerator upgrading or conversion.

2. The original invoices or bills itemized to show cost breakdown of components and identifying finance charges, if any, together with photocopy duplicates of such invoices and bills.

3. The original cancelled checks identifying payment of specific invoices together with photocopy duplicates of both sides of such checks.

4. A total unit count for the premises, together with the room count for each apartment, including professional or commercial space and accommodations occupied by the landlord and service employees. Also included in this count are decontrolled or exempt accommodations. Include in the room count the following:

a. Kitchens, bedrooms, dining rooms, finished basement or attic rooms, recreation rooms, and other rooms suitable for use as living quarters. A kitchenette or "half-room" which is partitioned off from floor to ceiling should be counted as a separate room. A cooking area measuring less than 59 square feet adjoining a dining area less than 55 square feet where the combined area is 59 square feet or more, contains a window is clearly separated from the remainder of the apartment but not each other by permanent construction effectively enclosing the combined area allowing access through a door or permanent framed doorway shall be counted as one room. Decorative dividers, railings, steps, shelves or cabinets do not satisfy this requirement.

b. Rooms used for office purposes.

The following are not to be included in the room count: Bathroom, strip or pullman kitchens, halls, foyers, alcoves, pantries, laundries, closets, storage space, and basement or attic rooms which are not suitable for living quarters.

AND

For Incinerator Upgrading—

1. A copy of the application (Form APC-5R, including specifications) filed with and approved by the Department of Air Resources.

2. Department of Air Resources Certificate of Operation (Form EPA-22.6).

3. A copy of the Building Notice Application (Form 21) or Alteration Application (ALT) filed with and approved by the Department of Buildings.

4. Department of Buildings Letter of Completion.

5. Bureau of Gas and Electricity Certificate of Electrical Inspection (Form G and E 16A) bearing the Bureau seal of approval.

For Conversion With Compacting System—

1. A copy of the Building Notice Application (Form 21) or Alteration Application (ALT) filed with and approved by the Department of Buildings.

2. Department of Buildings Letter of Completion.

3. Bureau of Gas and Electricity Certificate of Electrical

ADMINISTRATOR'S INTERPRETATIONS

Inspection (Form G and E 16A) bearing the Bureau seal of approval.

For Conversion Without Compaction—

1. Department of Air Resources Authorization to Discontinue Incinerator (Form APC-172).

2. A copy of the Building Notice Application (Form 21) or Alteration Application (ALT) filed with and approved by the Department of Buildings.

3. Department of Buildings Letter of Completion.

4. Bureau of Gas and Electricity Certificate of Electrical Inspection (Form G and E 16A) bearing the Bureau seal of approval. This form is required only where sprinklers are electrically operated.

AMENDATORY INTERPRETATION NO. 1
(Issued May 27, 1976)

Anything to the contrary in Administrator's Interpretation No. 1 (effective January 2, 1969), No. 8 and No. 9 (both effective November 6, 1972) and Operational Bulletin No. C-14 (revised December 1, 1964), No. C-15, Supplement No. 15 (effective September 22, 1971) Nos. C-9 and C-9, Supplement No. 1 (both revised April 25, 1968) notwithstanding, landlords are not required to submit a report of search nor a receipt (or photocopy thereof) issued by the Borough Office of the Department of Buildings attesting to the payment of the fee for a report of search to obtain rent increases for substantial rehabilitation or major capital improvements. (Effective June 4, 1976)

SCHEDULE OF RENTAL VALUES OF THE CITY RENT AND REHABILITATION ADMINISTRATION
(In effect on March 1, 1977)

Cost to be amortized includes price of item, sales tax, delivery and installation charges but **DOES NOT** include finance charges.

	Monthly Increase
AIR CONDITIONERS (new)	
installed by tenant with protrusion beyond window line or attached to exterior of building (see Administrator's Interpretation No. 11)	$2.00
installed by landlord in compliance with requirements of Electrical Code—no allowance for protrusion	1/40 of cost[1,2]

Administrator's Interpretations

circuit (including heavy duty outlet and wiring) applicable to tenant or landlord installed air conditioner where circuit is installed in conjunction with or subsequent to installation of adequate wiring. (See Administrator's Interpretation No.1) .... 1/40 of cost
"through-the-wall" sleeve constructed by landlord for installation of air conditioner, additional allowance (See Administrator's Interpretation No. 11) 1.50
current—(See Electric Current)

AIR CONDITIONER (used)
No rent increase will be granted for a used air conditioner.

ARCHES .... None

BATHROOMS—(See Operational Bulletin No. C-15, Supplement No. Flushometers (See Administrator's Interpretation No. 9) new low tank and toilet bowl (with new toilet seat).................. 1/40 of cost[1]

BATHROOM VANITIES—(See Advisory Sheet No. 3) .... 1/40 of cost[1,3]

BATHTUB EQUIPMENT
Bathtub Enclosures (with shatter proof doors made of tempered glass or plastic and anodized aluminum frame) .... 1/40 of cost[1]
Shower—Installation (See Advisory Sheet No. 7) (none before)
Bathtub—Replacement of bathtub on legs with sunken tub (See Advisory Sheet No. 7)

BELL, BUZZER AND INTERCOMMUNICATIONS SYSTEMS (See Operational Bulletin No. C-15)

BOILER ROOM ENCLOSURE (See Operational Bulletin No. C-15, Supplement No. 11)

BURGLAR, HOLD-UP AND FIRE ALARM SYSTEMS (See Operational Bulletin No. C-15, Supplement No. 14)

CELLAR STAIR ENCLOSURE (See Operational Bulletin No. C-15, Supplement No. 11)

CHAIN DOOR GUARD—(See Advisory Sheet No. 6)

CLOSED CIRCUIT TELEVISION (Apartment Security Systems) (See Operational Bulletin No. C-15)

CLOTHES CLOSETS [built-in] .... 1/40 of cost[1]

CLOTHES HAMPERS .... None

CONGO WALL LINOLEUM .... None

COOKING STOVES see "Gas Ranges"

DISHWASHER (installed by landlord)......................... 1/40 of cost[1]

DISHWASHER (installed by tenant) (See Operational Bulletin No. C-15, Supplement No. 6)
permanently attached to plumbing or floor 1.00
not permanently attached to plumbing or floor................. None

DOOR LOCKS [Apartment Entrance]—(See Advisory Sheet No. 6)

Item of Equipment	Federal Specifications	
Auxiliary Lock*		
Horizontal Bolt	Type 196	$.20
Vertical Bolt	Segal 666 or equivalent**	.25
Mortise Lock (number installed)	Series 86A	
1–9		.75
10–49		.70
50 or more		.65

* Where required, an auxiliary lock may be installed as a supplement to an existing heavy duty latch set; when installed in one building in quantities of 50 or more, reduce the rental values by $.05.

** No Federal Specifications available.

Administrator's Interpretations

DOORS
    Apartment entrance, fireproof Kalamein (new) complete installation with or without frame (See Operational Bulletin No. C-15, Supplement No. 16)
    Vestibule Entrance (See Operational Bulletin No. C-15)

ELECTRIC CURRENT supplied by landlord (rent inclusion)
    Conversion from DC to AC type current . . . amortize .... 7 years
    Lighting and miscellaneous (small appliances) by number of rooms in apartment (new service only):

Efficiency apartment (including bathroom)	$4.10
2 room apartment (including bathroom)	6.15
Each additional room	2.05
Each additional full or partial bathroom	1.00
Refrigerator (none before)	2.55
Television	1.05
Washing Machine	1.05
Dishwasher	1.55
Air Conditioner per 1,000 BTU	.45

    (See Advisory Sheet No. 8)

ELECTRICAL OUTLETS
    per duplex outlet receptacle, provided that the distance between all receptacles is not less than 12 feet, measured horizontally along the wall at the floor of the room .... .35
    Note—Where additional outlets are provided in connection with the rewiring of an inadequately wired building, the rental values specified in Administrator's Interpretation No. 1 are applicable.

ELECTRICAL REWIRING—(See Administrator's Interpretation No. 1)

ELECTRICAL WALL SWITCHES (per room, none before) .... .35
    Note—Whether installed separately or in conjunction with Administrator's Interpretation No. 1

ELEVATOR IMPROVEMENTS
    Conversion (manual to automatic)—file under Section 35 of the Rent Regulations
    Modernization & Mandatory Upgrading (See Operational Bulletin No. C-14, Advisory Sheet No. 5)

EXTERIOR LIGHTS—(See Operational Bulletin No. C-28, Supplement Nos. 1 & 2)

GAS supplied by landlord (included in rent) for operation of range (none before) 2.50

GAS RANGES (installed)
    new modern free-standing domestic model gas range with heat control .... 1/40 of cost[1,2]

HEAT AND HOT WATER (none before) (See Operational Bulletin No. C-15, Supplement No. 9)

HEATING SYSTEM IMPROVEMENTS—(See Administrator's Interpretation No. 8)

INCINERATORS (upgrading or conversion)—(See Administrator's Interpretation No. 18)

INLAID LINOLEUM OR VINYL ASBESTOS TILE (either ⅛" or 1⁄16") .... 1/40 of cost[1]

KITCHEN CABINETS..................................... 1/40 of cost[1]

KITCHEN COMBINATION, SINGLE UNIT (refrigerator, sink and gas range)—(See Operational Bulletin No. C-15, Supplement No. 4)

KITCHEN MODERNIZATION—(See Operational Bulletin No. C-13)

Administrator's Interpretations

KITCHEN SINK (installed and not part of Kitchen Modernization).	1/40 of cost[1,2]
LIGHTING FIXTURES [new (none before)—per room] including complete installation with wall switch or combination wall switch and outlet..	1/40 of cost[1]
LINOLEUM RUG..	None
MAIL BOXES—(See Operational Bulletin No. C-15) for mail boxes installed in connection with installation of bell and buzzer systems	
MEDICINE CABINETS......................................	None
PEEPHOLES (entrance door window type viewers) (none before) with mechanical door-chime	
where there is an existing door bell	.10
where there is no existing door bell	.15
without mechanical door-chime............................	.10
(See Operational Bulletin No. C-15)	
PLUMBING REPLACEMENTS—(See Administrator's Interpretation No. 9)	
RANGE HOOD	
Plain (shell) or Ductless (with filter and blower), baked enamel or stainless steel with or without outlet (installation must comply with requirements governing electrical outlets)...............	1/40 of cost[1]
REFRIGERATORS (installed)	
Used mechanical refrigerator (none before)....................	$2.00
New mechanical refrigerator	1/40 of cost[1,2]
SCREENS, STORM WINDOWS AND STORM DOORS	
screens (new and full length only—none before)................	1/40 of cost[1,2]
combination screen, storm window or storm door	1/40 of cost[1,2]
SECURITY SYSTEMS—(See Operational Bulletin No. C-15 and Operational Bulletin No. C-15, Supplement No. 14)	
SHOWERS	
installed over tub (See "Bathtub Equipment")	
stall showers (none before)—(See Advisory Sheet No. 7)	
TELEPHONE/DOOR RELEASE AND INTERCOMMUNICATION SYSTEM—(See Operational Bulletin No. C-15)	
TELEVISION SIGNAL RECEPTION	
Where a previous order has been issued increasing the maximum rent on the basis of the installation of any of the below Television Signal Reception systems, the subsequent replacement of one system by another, or the installation of an additional system shall have no additional rental value.	
Tenant installed television antenna (any part of landlord's property)	2.00
Master antenna hook-up (landlord-owned system)	2.00
Community antenna terminal (attached to tenant's apartment from any part of landlord's property)......................	None
See Section 828 of the Executive Law.	
TOILET BOWL (See "Bathrooms")	
VESTIBULE DOORS—(See Operational Bulletin No. C-15)	
WASH BASIN exclusive of vanities (installed and not part of bathroom modernization)	1/40 of cost[1,3]
WASHING MACHINE (installed by tenant)	
permanently attached to plumbing or floor	1.00
not permanently attached to plumbing or floor.................	None
WASHING MACHINE (installed by landlord)....................	1/40 of cost[1]
WINDOW GRILLES—(See Operational Bulletin No. C-15, Supplement No. 13)	

Administrator's Interpretations

WINDOWS (replacement in whole or in part)—(See Advisory Sheet No. 4)
WINDOW SHADES AND VENETIAN BLINDS................ None

RENT CONTROL ADVISORY SHEETS
ADVISORY SHEET NO. 1-33.1 e
(Issued August 11, 1971)

§ 33.1 e—Meaning of the terms "in addition to a concurrent major capital improvement" and "other expenditures to improve, restore or preserve the quality of the structure"; Procedure for Obtaining Rent Increases; Computation of the Rent Increase.

A landlord requests advice as to whether he would qualify for rent increases pursuant to Section 33.1 e of the Regulations under the following circumstances:

In addition to the installation of a new boiler and oil burner equipment, the landlord states that he proposes to make other expenditures for the installation of a new roof, painting and puttying all exterior windows, pointing-up the exterior brick walls, the repavement of the sidewalks, courtyards and paved rear yards, the painting and decorating of lobby walls and ceiling, the installation of carpeting in the lobby, the installation of new lobby entrance doors, and to refurbish the planters in front of the building.

He also states that the estimate for these "other expenditures" will be at least 10% of the total operating and maintenance expense for his most recent fiscal year.

The City in its deep concern for the preservation and upgrading of its present rental housing stock amended the Rent Law by adding a new provision for the adjustment of maximum rents where an owner demonstrates that in addition to making a major capital improvement to a property he has undertaken to "concurrently" make other expenditures to "improve, restore or preserve the quality of the structure." The motivating purpose behind the enactment of this new provision was to provide the

---
[1] Rental Value revised to 1/40 of cost by Advisory Sheet No. 8.
[2] The full amortized cost shall apply to "None Before" and to replacement of equipment which has been in use for a period of at least 8 years. Where the replaced equipment was in use for a shorter period, the monthly increase for the new equipment shall be prorated to reflect such fact.
[3] The full amortized cost shall apply to "None Before" and to replacement of equipment which has been in use for a period of at least 12 years. Where the replaced equipment was in use for a shorter period, the monthly increase for the new equipment shall be prorated to reflect such fact.

stimulus for the infusion of capital investment for the correction of conditions arising from years of neglect of residential housing and for the installation of major capital improvements as a concurrent component of a program for upgrading the quality of the building. Section 33.1 e of the Regulations was adopted by the Administrator in order to provide for regulatory implementation of this provision of the Rent Law. The construction given to this provision and its companion Regulation is being made in the light of the legislative consideration for the enactment of this provision.

Section 33.1 e of the Regulations reads as follows:

"e. The landlord has incurred, since January 1, 1970, in connection with and in addition to a concurrent major capital improvement, other expenditures to improve, restore or preserve the quality of the structure. An adjustment pursuant to this section shall be granted by the Administrator only if such improvements represent an expenditure equal to at least 10 percent of the total operating and maintenance expenses for the most recent full calendar year or the landlord's most recent fiscal year or any twelve consecutive months ending not more than 90 days prior to the filing of the application for an increase pursuant to this paragraph. The adjustment pursuant to this paragraph shall be in addition to any adjustment granted for the concurrent major capital improvement and shall be in an amount sufficient to amortize the cost of the improvements pursuant to this paragraph over a five-year period."

The above section makes references to "other expenditures to improve, restore or preserve the quality of the structure." These expenditures cover improvements made concurrently with a major capital improvement which will enhance the physical appearance of the exterior as well as that of the public area within the building. The restoration intended is broad enough to include delayed maintenance and repairs which should be restored as a component of a comprehensive program for upgrading the quality of the building. The preservation intended would include work which would stem the attrition of the structure resulting from normal wear and tear. In the

Administrator's Interpretations

latter category, we might have such items as weather-proofing the exterior, pointing-up the exterior bricks, puttying windows, repair and painting fire-escapes. This provision will provide an incentive to owners to keep and maintain their properties as decent and desirable places of abode. The guideline to be used is that the net result must be one from which it clearly appears from the nature of the work done or to be done that the quality of the housing has been or would be materially upgraded.

The Rent Law and Section 33.1 e of the Regulations specify that such "other expenditures" be made in connection with and in addition to a "concurrent major capital improvement" to qualify for rent increases. The Administrator is of the opinion that a practical construction of the word "concurrent" must be given in order to effectuate the purpose and legislative intent for enacting this new provision, and has therefore determined that expenditures for the major capital and other improvements need not be simultaneously incurred provided that the landlord demonstrates that both are part of a building-wide, consecutively timed program, and that no previous rent adjustment had been granted for the same improvement. The program may consequently be divided into two phases; namely, major capital improvements and "other expenditures." Thus, upon completion of *either* the concurrent major capital improvement *or* the other related improvements the landlord may file an application for rent increases covering the specific phase of the program which has been completed. The remaining phase must then be completed and a subsequent application filed within an interval not to exceed one year. Piecemeal improvements will not qualify.

As used in Section 33.1 e of the Regulations the term "operating and maintenance expenses" includes the cost of fuel, utilities, payroll, maintenance and repairs, but excludes taxes, water rates, sewer charges, debt service, mortgage interest and amortization, as well as cost of improvements and replacement of equipment.

It is to be noted that the "concurrent major capital improvement" contemplated by Section 33.1 e of the Regulations is limited to the following:

Administrator's Interpretations

a. Building-wide bathroom modernization;

b. Bell, buzzer and intercommunication systems, telephone/door release intercommunications systems, closed circuit television systems;

c. Cellar stair enclosure;

d. Electric rewiring;

e. Installation of central heat and hot water system (none before);

f. Upgrading or modification of existing residual oil burning system;

g. Modernization or conversion of existing heating system;

h. Incinerator upgrading or conversion with compactor;

i. Installation of brass plumbing water supply system; and

j. Elevator modernization.

Where the contemplated major capital improvement does not encompass any of the above, the landlord must obtain a prior opinion pursuant to Section 117 of the Rent and Eviction Regulation concerning feasibility of proposed major capital improvement for this Section 33.1 e program.

PROCEDURES

Where a landlord desires or contemplates relief pursuant to the provisions of Section 33.1 e of the Regulations and proposes to complete the work in two separate phases he is *required* to file a Report Form R-33.1e Supplement simultaneously with any application which he may make under Section 33.1 for that phase of the program which has already been completed. The supplement shall include a detailed description of the scheduled program which the landlord commits himself to complete within one year from the date of issuance of the order increasing the rent on the basis of the completed first phase. *Failure to include this schedule will result in the denial of the application for other related improvements since no rent increase would be warranted unless they are made concurrently with the type of major capital improvement specified in this Advisory Sheet.*

Thus, where "other related improvements" constitute

the first phase of a given program, any rent increase granted under Section 33.1 e will be conditional upon completion of the proposed major capital improvement(s) within the indicated time interval. *The failure of the landlord to comply with this commitment may result in the revocation of the increase for the other related improvements since it is conditioned upon the making of a concurrent major capital improvement.*

Conversely, where completion of the major capital improvement(s) is the first step, with the other related improvements to be performed at a later date, *any rent increase subsequently granted under Section 33.1 e will be conditioned upon substantial compliance with the schedule outlined by the landlord.* This means that only those scheduled "other improvements" which have been completed within the specified one-year interval will be eligible for rent increases, *provided* that the total amount expended on the *completed* other improvements represents an expenditure equal to at least 10 percent of the total operating and maintenance expenses for the year reported on the Report Form R-33.1e Supplement. Any item of improvement which appears on landlord's proposed schedule, but has not been completed within the prescribed time limit, will be considered a piecemeal improvement not qualifying for a rent adjustment.

Where a landlord simultaneously completes both the major capital and other related improvements he must file applications for both types of improvements on the appropriate agency forms and submit them as one composite application in accordance with filing instructions set forth in item 3 below.

Upon completion of either or both phases of the projected program, the landlord may file an application for rent increases on the appropriate agency form(s) submitting therewith all required documentation as follows:

Where Work Is To Be Completed In Two Phases

Note: Irrespective of the sequence in which work is performed, Report Form R-33.1e Supplement must be submitted simultaneously with the application for rent increases based on completion of the first phase, and the following legend must be endorsed at the top of the face side of the accompanying application: "REPORT FORM R-33.1e SUPPLEMENT IS BEING FILED SIMULTANEOUSLY WITH THIS APPLICATION." The application submitted upon completion of the *second phase* must bear the following legend at the top of face side of the application form: "THIS IS BEING FILED IN CONNECTION WITH CLOSED DOCKET NO. ....." *(Enter docket number under which the rent increase was granted based on completion of phase one.)*

1. Major capital improvement(s) only:

    a. Application Form A-33.1 must be used unless there is a special application form for the given major capital improvement.

    b. Proof of compliance with agency requirements and those of governmental agencies having jurisdiction as set forth in appropriate directives and/or regulations.

    c. Proof of payment (except in those instances where there are established rental values) consisting of either the original and duplicate copies of bills, invoices and cancelled checks, or a certification by an independent or certified public accountant, in duplicate, which shall contain the information set forth in the "Suggested Form for Accountant's Certification."

The rent adjustment will be granted in accordance with the "Schedule of Rental Values," if any, for the improvement. If there is no schedule, it will be based upon the amortization of the verified cost thereof over such period as the Administrator may find to be appropriate.

2. Other related improvements only:

    a. Application Form A-33.1e must be used. In such application the landlord must describe in detail all of the related improvements, the date the same were completed or furnished, and the actual cost thereof exclusive of finance charges. If an increase in the maximum rent had previously been granted based on any of the included improvements, no further adjustment is warranted.

    b. Proof of compliance with agency requirements and those of governmental agencies having jurisdiction where required.

    c. Proof of payment as in 1 c above.

Administrator's Interpretations

The rent adjustment pursuant to Section 33.1 e of the Regulations is limited to a five-year amortization of the verified cost of the other improvements.

Where Work Is Completed In A Single Phase

3. Both major capital and other related improvements:

    a. As for 1a and 2a above.

    b. As for 1b and 2b above.

    c. As for 1c and 2c above.

    d. Attach rider showing "operating and maintenance expenses" as heretofore defined for the most recent full calendar or fiscal year, or any twelve consecutive months ending not more than 90 days prior to the date of filing the application.

    e. Endorse following legend at the top of the face side of the application form for the major capital improvement: "THIS IS SUPPLEMENTARY TO THE ATTACHED APPLICATION FORM A-33.1e WHICH IS BEING FILED SIMULTANEOUSLY WITH THIS FORM."

Rent adjustments will be granted in accordance with the terms set forth in items 1 and 2 above.

Suggested Form for Accountant's Certification

                                    Re: Premises ....
                                                ....

To: The Office of Rent Control
      Department of Rent and Housing Maintenance
      Housing and Development Administration

I am an independent (or certified) public accountant, registered as such by and in good standing with the New York State Education Department. My number is

I have examined the accompanying application for rent increases under Section 33.1 of the Rent Regulations based upon an increase in service and/or equipment, to wit (list improvements which are based for application), submitted by.....................................
.... (insert names of individuals or corporate owners), and all original invoices or bills and original checks relating to such installation. Attached hereto is a copy of

my original worksheets showing the documents examined by me.

My examination was made in accordance with generally accepted auditing standards.

I hereby certify that the Owner's Application is supported by the owner's records and invoices or bills and the original cancelled checks examined by me.

I further certify that $ .... not yet paid but due under the terms of the contract does not represent any interest, finance charges, rebates, discounts or refunds to the landlord but is being withheld until all of the terms of the contract relating to the upgrading or modification of the heating system have been fulfilled.

As an independent (or certified) public accountant, I have no direct or indirect financial interest in the success of the accompanying application. I have placed my initials and the date, for identification, at the lower right hand corner of the face of the application.

I have read this certification and I hereby affirm under the penalties provided by law that the contents thereof are true of my own knowledge.

....
(Signature of Accountant)
Dated:......................

ADVISORY SHEET NO. 2-32

(Issued August 11, 1971)

§ 32—Landlord's option to collect rent requested where no order has been issued by the District Rent Director on application for relief pursuant to Section 33.5 within the period prescribed in Section 32 of the Regulations; Procedure to be complied with by landlord as a condition to collecting the rent requested pending the issuance of the order determining the application.

This advisory sheet sets forth special instructions to be followed by the landlord who elects to collect the increased rent requested in his application pursuant to Section 33.5 of the Regulations during the pendency of his application.

Certification Requirement *(Optional)*

Section 32 of the Rent and Eviction Regulations provides that no order increasing or decreasing a maximum

Administrator's Interpretations

rent previously established pursuant to these Regulations shall be effective prior to the date on which the order is issued except as hereinafter provided. If an application for an increase pursuant to Section 33.5 of these Regulations is submitted on or after August 1, 1970 and is accompanied by a certified statement of expenditures with all required documentation and no order is issued thereon within four months of the date of filing of an application based on assessed valuation (or on equalized assessed valuation on or after January 1, 1972), or eight months of the date of filing of an application based upon sales price, the increase in rent requested shall be collectible by the landlord and shall be placed in an interest bearing escrow account with a banking organization until the final determination of such application. The order of the District Rent Director shall be made effective as of the date on which the landlord is entitled to collect such requested rent increase for any housing accommodation in the building pursuant to the permission granted by this section in said escrow account. Where such order grants a rent increase which is less than the rent collected by the landlord as herein permitted or denies the application, the excess rent collected shall be refunded to the tenants entitled thereto within 30 days from date such order shall become final together with interest at the prevailing rate of interest paid by the banking organization in which such deposit is made. Any person serving as escrow agent shall not be liable except for fraud or misfeasance.

Where the owner elects to file his application offering the Certification specified in Section 32, the Certification should be presented and prepared in compliance with the following instructions.

A—Certifying Agent

An Independent Accountant's Certificate and a duplicate thereof are to be submitted with the application filed at the District Rent Office.

To be acceptable, an Independent Accountant's Certificate must be prepared by a person registered by and in good standing with the Education Department of the

University of the State of New York as a Certified Public Accountant or Enrolled Public Accountant, or a person licensed by and/or in good standing with a similar agency enforcing comparable requirements in another State. The accountant offering such Certification may not be a salaried employee of the owner of the property.

The Certification, properly dated and prepared on the accountant's professional stationery, shall be addressed to the appropriate District Rent Office and should indicate the accountant's license or certificate number and bear his signature.

B—Suggested Form

The Certification to be filed should be substantially in the following form:

Re:
Premises: ....
....

To the District Rent Office:

I am an Independent Certified Public Accountant/Enrolled Public Accountant registered as such by and in good standing with the New York State Education Department. My license number is ....

I have reviewed the accompanying application for rent increase under Section 33.5 of the Regulations submitted by .... In this respect and in accordance with generally accepted auditing standards, I have examined the owner's books of account and find that the items of Income and Expenses presented in the application fairly and accurately reflect such records or, where specifically indicated, constitute projections permitted and allowances computed in accordance with instructions in Instruction Sheet No. 2.

The application and accompanying schedules are mathematically correct and, in my opinion, report Income and Operating Expenses applicable to the subject property. I have initialled and dated the original of Application Form A-33.5 or A-33.5LO in the lower righthand corner of the first page.

C—Amended Filing Requirements and Notification to Tenants

Applications are still to be filed with the District Rent Office in accordance with Instruction 23 of Instruction Sheet No. 2 with the following additional requirements:

Administrator's Interpretations

1. The original and copy of the Certification should accompany the original and copy of Form A-33.5 or Form A-33.5LO.

2. Completed Notice Form N-2 (33.5) for each controlled unit eligible for Section 33.5 rent increases must be affixed to the tenant's copy of Form A-33.5 or Form A-33.5LO. Notice Form N-2 (33.5) should contain the same name and mailing address and apartment number indicated in Item 2 on Form A-33.5 or Form A-33.5LO and should also specify the monthly rent increase requested, to be placed in escrow in the event final orders are not issued by the District Rent Director prior to the applicable statutory four or eight month period.

D—Instructions for Claiming Monthly Increases

Rent increases to be collected in escrow may *only* be claimed from *controlled apartments*. In requesting same the owner should be aware of the following restrictions and limitations:

1. Increases may *not* be claimed from units which received 15% compensatory rent adjustments under Section 23 of the Regulations, since August 1, 1970.

2. Units which, since August 1, 1970 have received compensatory and/or labor recoupment increases (Sections 23 and 33.8), totaling less than 15% can only be required, at maximum, to pay an amount in escrow which, when added to the adjustments previously received, would establish an aggregate of not more than 15% over the "base rent" on July 31, 1970.

3. Where, an apartment is under lease on the date escrow collection is to begin, no increase can be claimed until expiration of such lease.

4. Where, an apartment received a 15% rent increase in a previous Section 33.5 action, no escrow collection of any further increase can be claimed until two years have elapsed since the date of the prior 33.5 order.

5. Where, under a previous Section 33.5 action, an adjustment of less than 15% to any unit had been ordered, escrow collection as to any further increase can only be claimed to the extent that the aggregate of the

amount previously ordered and that currently collectible should not be more than 15% over the maximum rent acknowledged in the prior 33.5 application. After two years from the date the prior 33.5 order has elapsed, any balance calculated as due may be additionally collected.

E—Instruction for Calculation of Monthly Increases

It is suggested that monthly increases, *not to exceed 15%* to be collected in escrow, should be established in the same percentage for all controlled apartments eligible to pay same, subject to the restrictions and limitations outlined in "D" above. To establish such percentage the method of calculation should be as follows:

1. Determine the total annual rent for *controlled units only* as included in Item 8, Annual Rental, of your application. Deduct from this sum the annual rents of controlled units which received a 15% compensatory increase under Section 23 of the Regulations since August 1, 1970. The remaining balance represents the annual rental income for those controlled apartments from which there may be eligibility to collect increases in escrow.

2. Divide the rent adjustment being claimed in your application, Item 26, by the controlled rental income balance established in "1" above. The resulting percentage should be used to calculate the monthly increases claimed. If such percentage exceeds 15%, increases claimed should be limited to 15%.

3. Apply the percentage determined in "2" above to the monthly rents as listed in Schedule A, Rental Income, of your application for each unit eligible to pay escrow increases. The monthly increase so determined should be inserted on Notice Form N-2 (33.5).

It should be recognized that the increases so calculated are based upon an unaudited review of your application. The appropriate monthly increase will be established after audit examination by order from the District Rent Director. Where such order grants a rent increase less than that collected under escrow, the excess rent shall be refunded to the tenant within 30 days from the date of the District Director's order together with interest at the prevailing rate of interest paid by the banking organization in which such deposit was made.

Administrator's Interpretations

F—Escrow Procedure

An escrow agent must be an attorney duly admitted to practice in the State of New York. Within three days after the first collection of any increase in rent collected for any housing accommodation affected by the application, the escrow agent shall open an interest bearing escrow account in any banking organization licensed to do business in the City of New York. Such account shall be designated as an escrow or trust account for the benefit of the tenants of the premises affected by the proceeding. All rent increases paid to the landlord on the basis of such application shall be deposited in such bank account within three days of the date of payment by the tenant and shall remain on deposit until the final determination of the application.

Where the landlord elects to avail himself of the privilege of collecting the rent increase requested during the pendency of the application, the rent bill must indicate the total rent requested with an allocation showing present maximum rent and the rent increase requested. The bill should also contain a legend stating that "The additional rent requested is being collected subject to refund with interest in the event that such refund is ordered by the District Rent Director. Such additional rent will be deposited in escrow as provided by Section 32 of the Rent and Eviction Regulations in the . . . . Bank (Account No. . . . .)." The escrow agent is . . . . Esq. of . . . .

ADVISORY SHEET NO. 3

(Revised March 1, 1977)

The Collation of the Schedule of Rental Values in effect on February 28, 1977 is hereby amended as hereinafter indicated. In addition to stating the appropriate rental values for the item enumerated, this Advisory Sheet also specifies minimum standards for the installation and any other pertinent requirements relative to the improvement. Where the procedure to be followed for obtaining rent increases is different than that which is usually prescribed, the appropriate procedure is set forth in this Advisory Sheet.

Monthly Increase

BATHROOM VANITIES* . amortize cost over 40 months

---

* Where waste and water lines are changed as a result of the installation of the bathroom vanity, a permit must be obtained from the Plumbing Division of

Minimum Standards

a. Minimum Size Limits—22" wide by 20" deep; Back splash—3" high;

b. Made of durable mica material including a mica kick base or legs;

c. Post Form Top and Back Splash—made of one piece of molded mica;

d. Two Door Cabinet—full length doors, or with apron —may or may not have an etched design;

e. Outside hinges and decorative door pulls;

f. Cast Iron Sink—Minimum Dimensions: Round, diameter 18"; Oval, 16" × 19";

g. Stainless Steel Rim around Sink;

h. Faucets—one piece with mixer and pop-up waste.

Procedure

Consent of the tenant in occupancy must be obtained. This scheduled increase will be granted only for those vanities which meet the above specifications.

ADVISORY SHEET NO. 4

(Issued November 30, 1971)

WINDOWS (Replacement in Whole or in Part)

Operational Bulletin No. C-15, Supplement No. 8 (as revised September 9, 1969) and the Collation of Schedule of Rental Values (dated March 1, 1970) relative to window replacement are hereby revised as hereinafter indicated. In addition to stating appropriate rental values for various types of window replacement, this Advisory Sheet also specifies minimum standards for the installation and other pertinent requirements relative to the replacement, as well as procedures to be followed for obtaining rent

---

the Department of Buildings and the installation must be made by a licensed plumber.

Where an order had been issued twelve or more years ago for the installation of a bathroom sink, the full rental value indicated above shall be granted for the installation of an approved vanity.

Where an order had been issued less than twelve years ago for the installation of a bathroom sink, the amount of rent increase provided for in that order shall be prorated and this prorated allowance shall be added to the difference between the allowance for the vanity and the bathroom sink.

increases upon completion of the improvement. The minimum installation requirements and the Schedule of Rental Values which are hereinafter set forth shall apply to all window replacements except those involving casement windows or other unique and peculiar circumstances.

BASIC INSTALLATION REQUIREMENTS

Separate requirements have been established covering both material standards and minimum specifications for each type of window replacement included in the following Schedule of Rental Values. However, all installations shall include such restoration, repairs, and painting as are necessary to insure a complete workmanlike window replacement.

WOOD WINDOW REPLACEMENTS

All wood window replacements shall be constructed of Ponderosa Pine or an equivalent with minimum sash thickness of 1⅜ inches complete with necessary hardware including locking device. Size of new frame shall be governed by existing masonry window opening.

Sashes (Traditional): The installation shall include new pre-primed sashes complete with glass, a lock, lower sash lifts, and weatherstripping and/or weatherstripping stops; as well as such replacement of chains with new chains or other operating mechanism, frame and incidental repairs, as is required to maintain a complete draft-free, sound and operable window.

Frame and Sashes: The installation shall include a new pre-primed frame, weatherstripping, and operating mechanism in addition to all sash items listed above.

Prime Window Unit: The installation shall include a prefabricated unit of wood construction which incorporates new sashes of traditional, tilt-in, or snap-out design enclosed by a squared frame whose sides contain the operating mechanisms, and which—being sized to fit the space previously occupied by traditional wood sashes—is set within the existing wood window frame. The term "prime" refers to a permanent installation as opposed to a storm window which is merely ancillary window equipment.

ALUMINUM WINDOW REPLACEMENT

Prime Window Unit: The installation shall include a prefabricated unit of aluminum construction which incorporates all of the items listed above and which meets or exceeds the performance requirements of ANSI (American National Standards Institute) Standard A 134.1 and/or Window Classification DH-A2 as established by AAMA (Architectural Aluminum Manufacturers Association).

Exterior Frame Cover: The installation shall include a trim cover of heavy siding quality aluminum with a baked enamel finish which shall completely cover the exterior surface of existing wood window frame.

SCHEDULE OF RENTAL VALUES

The rent adjustments granted will be computed upon the following (per month—per window) schedule of increases:

Type of Replacement	Monthly Increase
Wood	
Sashes (traditional)	$ .75
Frame and Sashes	1.85
Prime Window Unit	1.10
Aluminum	
Prime Window Unit	1.15
Exterior Frame Cover*	.35

* Allowance granted only when installed in conjunction with an aluminum prime window unit.

PROCEDURES

The rental schedule indicated above will apply to all window replacements except where such work involves:

    a. Casement windows; or

    b. Unique and peculiar circumstances

for which the landlord should apply for *a prior opinion approval before commencing work.* In his application for the prior opinion, the landlord should give full particulars about the proposed window replacement including the estimated cost and the number of windows involved in a given apartment.

When work is completed the landlord may file an application for rent increases pursuant to Section 33.1a of the Regulations. *All applications for rent increases, including cases where a prior opinion had been issued,*

ADMINISTRATOR'S INTERPRETATIONS

must include the written consent of the individual tenant in occupancy and be accompanied by a signed statement from the installer or supplier of the claimed window replacement which shows his name, address and telephone number, and certifies that the complete improvement complies with the basic installation requirements herein set forth.

ADVISORY SHEET NO. 5

(Issued November 30, 1971)

MANDATORY ELEVATOR UPGRADING

Operational Bulletin No. C-14 (Revised December 1, 1964), relating to elevator modernization, is hereby supplemented to include appropriate rent adjustment for compliance with mandated requirements set forth in Section C26-1801.1 of the Administrative Code, pursuant to which all existing elevators in residential and commercial structures must comply with retroactive provisions of the law, effective as of December 1, 1970. Those provisions which relate to elevators in residential structures are applicable to car switch (i.e., manually operated) elevators intended for both "passenger" and/or "service" use, and involve the following items of equipment: elevator hoistway door interlocks, emergency interlock release switches, car gate switches, and signal systems. *It should, however, be noted that only those items need be installed or upgraded which do not already comply with current requirements.*

Accordingly, where the required upgrading of a manual elevator—whether for passenger or service use—involves the installation of approved type interlocks to remove a violation, or is made in anticipation of the issuance of a violation notice relating to such requirement, the landlord will be eligible for a rent increase based on a 10-year amortization of the verified cost of expenditures directly related to compliance with Section C26-1801.1. *No application for rent increases based on the upgrading of an existing car switch elevator will however be entertained unless it includes the installation of hoistway door interlocks.* Rent adjustments shall therefore be limited to expenditures reflecting the installation of hoistway door interlocks *and* the installation and/or upgrading of those aforementioned items of equipment which do not meet current Building Department standards.

PROCEDURES

When the upgrading has been completed the landlord should file an application for rent increases on Application Form A-33.1EM, describing therein the scope and cost of the work which is the basis for the requested rent adjustment. He must also state whether the upgrading was performed to remove a pending violation. His statement should include a listing of all existing elevators in structure, identifying each elevator according to type of operation (manual, automatic, or dual control) and intended use (regularly operated for passenger, service, or passenger/service), and clearly indicating which elevators were upgraded in compliance with Section C26-1801.1. The landlord is also required to submit the following documents with his application:

1. A signed copy of the contract for elevator upgrading.

2. The original invoices or bills *itemized to segregate those items of cost which represent compliance with Section C26-1801.1 of the Administrative Code,* together with one photocopy duplicate of such invoices or bills.

3. The original cancelled checks together with one photocopy duplicate of both sides of such checks.

4. One photocopy each of the approved Building Notice Application (Form 21), and the Work Permit (Form 20) issued by the Building Department.

5. An original and one copy of the Elevator Contractor's Certification (Form R-33.1EM Interlocks).

Rent increases will be computed based on a 10-year amortization of the verified cost of the upgrading equally allocated among all units (whether or not subject to rent control) in the structure, including ground and first floor apartments.

NOTE: The above procedures are applicable only to cases involving elevator *upgrading*. Cases relating to elevator *modernization* will continue to be processed in accordance with the provisions of Operational Bulletin No. C-14. UNDER NO CIRCUMSTANCE MAY THE CONVERSION OF AN ELEVATOR FROM MANUAL TO AUTOMATIC

Administrator's Interpretations

SERVICE BE CONSIDERED OR APPROVED WITHIN THE CONTEXT OF OPERATIONAL BULLETIN NO. C-14 OR THIS ADVISORY SHEET. SUCH CONVERSION MAY ONLY BE CONSIDERED WITHIN THE PURVIEW OF SECTION 35 OF THE RENT AND EVICTION REGULATIONS.

ADVISORY SHEET NO. 6

(Issued November 30, 1971)

APARTMENT ENTRANCE DOOR LOCKS AND CHAIN DOOR GUARDS

According to Local Law No. 8 of the Year 1971 which became effective on March 31, 1971, Section D-26-20.05 of the Housing Maintenance Code pertaining to apartment door locks was amended and now requires that all apartment entrance doors in a Class A multiple dwelling must be equipped with a heavy duty latch set and a heavy duty dead bolt operable by a key from the outside and a thumb-turn from the inside and must also be equipped with a chain door guard to permit partial opening of the door. The Federal Supply Service of the General Services Administration has established standards for various types of heavy duty locks which appear in detail in the Federal Specifications Bulletin No. FF-H-106a. These and other standards were considered in determining which locks meet the requirements of the law.

In most cases the existing locks in apartment doors may be retained; even where they do not have a heavy duty dead bolt they could be made to comply with the law by installing a secondary or auxiliary lock with a horizontal bolt of the Type 196 according to Federal Specifications or with a vertical bolt such as the Segal 666 lock or its equivalent. As an alternative, the mortise type lock which meets the Federal Specifications of Series 86A can replace the existing non-complying lock at the primary lock.

The *monthly rental increases* which are applicable for the installation of approved locks and/or chain door guards are listed below with specific references to the Federal Specifications to which they relate:

ADMINISTRATOR'S INTERPRETATIONS

Item of Equipment	Federal Specifications	Monthly Rent Increase
Auxiliary Lock*		
Horizontal Bolt	Type 196	$.20**
Vertical Bolt	Segal 666 or equivalent***	.25**
Mortise Lock (By number installed)	Series 86A	
1–9		.75
10–49		.70
50 or more		.65
Chain Door Guard	***	.05

The installation of locks and chain door guards in compliance with the provisions of Local Law No. 8 of the Year 1971 is an increase in service and/or equipment within the meaning of Section 33.1a of the Regulations, with the implied consent of the tenant, due to the requirements of the local law.

To qualify for an increase in rent, the following conditions *must* be met:

(1) Locks must meet the indicated standards in the Federal Specifications Bulletin FF-H-106a for the particular lock type. The Vertical Bolt Lock, for which no standards have been established, must be of the Segal 666 or equivalent in material and type, and not diecast.

(2) Two keys must be furnished to each tenant.

(3) Chain door guard must be of extruded brass or equivalent, the *minimum* thickness of the jamb plate must be .075″ with chain of hardened steel and welded links. Where possible, screws 7/8″ or longer should be used.

(4) Date of installation or replacement must be January 22, 1971 or later.

With his application for a rent increase, the landlord must submit a paid bill or invoice which identifies the manufacturer and model number of the lock and/or door chain and must certify that the equipment meets the standards set forth in this Advisory Sheet.

Where, due to unusual circumstances, scheduled rental increases are inadequate because of more costly installa-

---

  * Where apartment entrance door is presently equipped with a heavy duty latch set lock, compliance with the law may be effected by the installation of a second or auxiliary lock.

  ** For auxiliary locks installed in one building, in quantities of 50 or more, reduce the rental values by $.05.

  *** No federal specifications available.

tion charges or more expensive equipment, a landlord may file a prior opinion application submitting complete and detailed specifications to permit the determination of the appropriate rental value for the particular instance.

ADVISORY SHEET NO. 7

(Issued October 31, 1972)

The Collation of the Schedule of Rental Values in effect on January 1, 1972 is hereby amended to include the installation of a shower, (none before) and the replacement of a bathtub on legs with a sunken tub when each of these is performed separately (not in conjunction with bathroom modernization or building-wide adequate plumbing improvements).

	Monthly Rent Increase
Shower—Installation (none before) over tub including new shower head, body, arm with concealed brass supply, faucets and curtain rod	$1.75*
Bathtub—Replacement of bathtub on legs with sunken tub . . . . Where there is no overhead shower, set in 4' tile around tub Where there is an overhead shower, set in 6' around tub	$5.65*

Where the shower installation is performed as part of an adequate plumbing improvement, the rental values listed in Administrator's Interpretation No. 9 will apply. Where the bathtub and shower are replaced or installed as part of a bathroom modernization, the rental values in Operational Bulletin No. C-15, Supplement No. 15 will be applicable.

Where a custom or prefabricated shower installation is contemplated in apartments where there is no bathroom, a landlord may file a prior opinion application submitting complete and detailed design diagrams and specifications of the shower and shower room enclosure including floor diagrams to permit the determination of the appropriate rental value for a legally approved installation.

ADVISORY SHEET NO. 8

(Issued March 1, 1977)

The Collation of the Schedule of Rental Values in effect on February 28, 1977 is hereby revised as of

---

* Written consent of the tenant in occupancy must be obtained. The installation or replacement must be made by a licensed plumber and meet the requirements of the City departments having jurisdiction.

ADMINISTRATOR'S INTERPRETATIONS

the date of issuance of this bulletin in the following respects:

NOTE: Cost to be amortized includes price of item, sales tax, delivery and installation charges but **DOES NOT** include finance charges.

Monthly Increase

AIR CONDITIONER (new)
    installed by landlord in compliance with requirements of Electrical Code—no allowance for protrusion .... amortize cost over 40 months[1]
    circuit (including heavy duty outlet and wiring)..................................... amortize cost over 40 months

BATHROOMS
    new low tank and toilet bowl (with new toilet seat)................................... amortize cost over 40 months

BATHROOM VANITIES.......................... amortize cost over 40 months[2]

BATHTUB EQUIPMENT
    Bathtub Enclosures (with shatter proof doors made of tempered glass or plastic and anodized aluminum frame) .... amortize cost over 40 months

CLOTHES CLOSETS (built in) .... amortize cost over 40 months

DISHWASHER (installed by landlord) .... amortize cost over 40 months

ELECTRIC CURRENT supplied by landlord (rent inclusion)
    Conversion from DC to AC type current . . . amortize............................... 7 years
    Lighting and miscellaneous (small appliances) by number of rooms in apartment (new service only):
        Efficiency apartment (including bathroom) $4.10
        2 room apartment (including bathroom).. 6.15
        Each additional room 2.05
        Each additional full or partial bathroom . 1.00
        Refrigerator (none before) 2.55
        Television............................... 1.05
        Washing Machine 1.05
        Dishwasher 1.55
        Air conditioner per 1,000 BTU............. .45

GAS RANGES (installed)
    new modern free-standing domestic model gas range with heat control .... amortize cost over 40 months[1]

INLAID LINOLEUM OR VINYL ASBESTOS TILE (either 1/8″ or 1/16″)....................... amortize cost over 40 months

KITCHEN CABINETS .... amortize cost over 40 months

KITCHEN SINK (installed and not part of Kitchen Modernization)....................... amortize cost over 40 months[1]

LIGHTING FIXTURES (new, none before)—including complete installation of wall switch or combination wall switch and outlet............ amortize cost over 40 months

RANGE HOOD
    Plain (shell) or Ductless (with filter and blower), baked enamel or stainless steel with or without outlet (Installation must comply with requirements governing electrical outlets) .... amortize cost over 40 months

REFRIGERATORS (installed)
    new mechanical refrigerator................ amortize cost over 40 months[1]

SCREENS, STORM WINDOWS AND STORM DOORS
    screens (new and full length only—none before) .... amortize cost over 40 months[1]
    combination screen, storm window or storm door .... amortize cost over 40 months[1]

532

Administrator's Interpretations

WASH BASINS
    exclusive of vanities (installed and not part of
      bathroom modernization)................. amortize cost over 40 months[2]
WASHING MACHINE (installed by landlord) .... amortize cost over 40 months

ADVISORY SHEET NO. 9

(Issued May 24, 1978)

Schedule of Rental Value

Window Guard For Each Apartment Window
  Mandated by Law: $0.25 per month.

MANDATORY WINDOW GUARDS

Where the landlord of multiple dwellings provides and installs window guards on windows of each apartment in which a child or children 10 years or under reside and on windows in the public halls of such buildings except openings onto fire escapes and secondary means of egress in ground floors of non-fireproof buildings in compliance with Section 131.15 of the New York City Health Code, as amended August 12, 1976, the tenant's consent is not required. Applications for rental increases based upon such installation may be made only on Application Form A-33.1C **(Rev. 7/72).** The landlord will check item "i. other" and explain on the reverse side that the installation of window guards is a mandated improvement and set forth the number of windows upon which window guards were installed. If the tenant's signature is not obtained, landlord should check item k. in that form stating the tenant had impliedly consented to such an increase in service or equipment. The following requirements must be met as a condition of obtaining any order granting a rent increase:

1. Landlord must submit an original and four (4) copies of Application Form A-33.1C **(Rev. 7/72)** fully completed and executed for each tenant along with two (2) copies of Department of Health Form HE (10/76) entitled "Children Can't Fly" signed, dated and completed for each tenant.

---

[1] The full amortized cost shall apply to "None Before" and to replacement of equipment which has been in use for a period of at least 8 years. Where the replaced equipment was in use for a shorter period, the monthly increase for the new equipment shall be prorated to reflect such fact.

[2] The full amortized cost shall apply to "None Before" and to replacement of equipment which has been in use for a period of at least 12 years. Where the replaced equipment was in use for a shorter period, the monthly increase for the new equipment shall be prorated to reflect such fact.

2. Landlord must submit a certification in the form hereafter set forth that the window guards approved by the Department of Health were installed in accordance with the Department of Health's specifications and meet the requirements of all other agencies having jurisdiction.

3. Landlord must submit paid invoice or receipted bill with name of manufacturer and model number of window guards actually installed in the subject building for which rental adjustments are being requested.

4. Landlord must purchase and install window guards which bear the approval of the Window Guard Acceptance Board of the New York City Department of Health, 125 Worth Street, New York, New York.

5. The installation must be in conformity with the Department of Health's specifications which also can be obtained from the Department of Health located at 125 Worth Street, New York, New York.

In addition it should be noted that:

6. The rental increase is subject to revocation if it is determined that the equipment or installation does not conform to NYC Department of Health's standards.

7. No additional increase will be granted for window guards that may be required in the public areas.

(Certificate to be filed with each building application for rental adjustments for window guards. See 2 above.):

CERTIFICATE OF INSTALLATION

RE: _____ _____
         Address of Building

I am the landlord or _____ of the subject
                         (indicate appropriate title)
building where window guards have been installed and have personal knowledge of the equipment used and its installation.

I certify that each and every window guard installed is of the make, model and manufacture approved by the Department of Health, to wit:

MANUFACTURER'S NAME   _____
MODEL # _____

Administrator's Interpretations

DEPARTMENT OF HEALTH
APPROVAL # _____

I further certify that each and every installation of such window guards was in accordance with the specifications of the NYC Department of Health appropriate for such make, model and manufacture and meets the requirements of all other agencies having jurisdiction. The installations are as follows:

Number of Guards

Apt. #

Apt. #

Apt. #

I have read this certification and I hereby affirm under the penalties provided by law that the contents thereof are true of my own knowledge.

DATED:

_____
Landord or _____
of Landlord
(Designate Title)

_____
Address

_____
Telephone Number

OPERATIONAL BULLETIN NO. C-30

Operational Bulletin No. C-30—Sound Housing Procedures (Issued August 13, 1979).

Under the provisions of Chapter 1022 of the Laws of 1974, as amended by Chapter 360 of the Laws of 1975, no certificate of eviction pursuant to Section 57, 58, 59a(2) or 59a(4) of the Rent and Eviction Regulations may be granted or remain effective unless the City Rent Agency after a hearing, finds:

(1) there is no reasonable possibility that the landord can make a net annual return of 8½ per cent of the assessed value of the property; and

(2) neither the landlord nor his immediate predecessor intentionally or wilfully managed the property to impair his ability to earn such return.

No such finding is required, however, where alteration,

Administrator's Interpretations

remodeling or construction of a building is aided by interest reduction payments under Section 236 of the National Housing Act.

In order to meet the above requirements, the landlord, in applying for a certificate of eviction under Sections 57, 58, 59a(2) or 59a(4) of the Rent and Eviction Regulations, must complete and return a verified and duplicate copy of "Statement of Building's Economic Viability" (Form R-1022, R-1022A) with all required schedules, attachments, exhibits and affidavit of service to the appropriate District Rent Office within 60 days of receipt of a form N-21 notice from the Division of Rent Control, to avoid rejection of his application or revocation of certificates already issued. The landlord must serve a copy of his Statement and Schedule (Forms R-1022, R-1022A) with attachments and exhibits upon each attorney appearing on behalf of any tenant(s) and upon each rent controlled tenant who is not represented by an attorney at or prior to submission to the Rent Control Division.

Where the landlord fails to return the completed Statement of Building's Economic Viability, schedule and attachment within the time required, orders rejecting or denying the application will be issued.

Upon receipt of the Building's Economic Viability Report Forms, the processing unit will immediately forward the package to the Accounting Division for an audit.

Landlord and tenant may be required to submit additional material at any time and failure to do so within the time designated may result in denial of the application or issuance of Relocation Notices initiating relocation procedures.

Sound Housing Audit

Review of the question whether the owner could have realized 8½ per cent return on the assessed valuation of the property under "normal" operating conditions necessitates a review of the economic status of the building.

The landlord is required to submit data of *all* income from the property. In addition, registration and other rent records will be reviewed to develop the amounts of rents which would have been collectible had the owner availed itself of all applicable maximum rent and other adjustments. For apartments and commercial units neither of which are rent controlled, the owner must submit leases and other rent and income records. The appropriate rental value to be assigned vacant units will be determined by inspection conducted by the Division of Rent Control, where necessary.

The landlord must also submit a statement of his operating expenses for the property and, if deemed necessary, corroborative data including managing agent's statements, vendors' bills, cancelled checks, payroll records, contracts, books of account, etc., to be audited by the Division of Rent Control accountants.

In addition to submitting financial statements for the first year after acquisition of the property and the current year prior to filing the statement, the landlord may be required to submit financial statements for intervening years to provide a basis for a more comprehensive judgment as to feasibility of the 8½ per cent return position.

An audit report will be prepared by the City Rent Agency's Accounting Division, taking into consideration the maximum potential imputed income for the property and recognition of the operating costs for each of the periods reviewed, indicating whether an 8½ per cent return could have been earned under "normal" operating conditions.

Processing Unit

Where the Sound Housing Audit Report, upon analysis by the Processing Unit results in a finding that the building could have earned an 8½ per cent return under "normal" operating conditions or that the landlord and its immediate predecessor in interest has intentionally or wilfully managed the building so as to impair the landlord's ability to earn such return, the case will be closed with an order denying certificates of eviction.

Where no such finding is made, the City Rent Agency will conduct a hearing to give the landlord and tenants opportunity to establish their respective claims with respect to the economic status of the building and take testimony regarding any alleged mismanagement of the property. Copies of the Accounting Review together with notification that the Accounting Worksheets are available for examination, will be sent to each of the attorneys for the parties or the persons not represented by attorney for comment and rebuttal in the time designated. (effective August 17, 1979)[1]

OPERATIONAL BULLETIN NO. 84-1

New procedures for instituting a proceeding for administrative review of an order issued by a District Rent Administrator
(Issued June 1984, revised October, 1984)

Any person aggrieved by an order issued by a District Rent Administrator may file a petition for administrative review (PAR) to the Commissioner.

A joint PAR, verified by each person joining therein, may be filed by two or more landlords or tenants, where at least one ground is common to all persons so filing. At the Commissioner's discretion, the PAR may be treated as joint or several.

At the Commissioner's discretion, two or more PAR's which have at least one ground in common may be consolidated.

A PAR against an order of a District Rent Administrator must be filed with the Commissioner within thirty-three days after the date such order is issued. A PAR served by mail, postmarked not more than thirty-three days after the date of such order, shall be deemed timely filed.

A person aggrieved by an order issued by the District Rent Administrator may file a PAR against such order on a form prescribed by the Commissioner or on a reasonable facsimile thereof. Such forms are available at the District Rent Offices and at the Office of Rent Administration, 10 Columbus Circle, New York, New York 10019.

Each PAR shall be filed in an original and one copy at the Division of Housing and Community Renewal, Office of Rent Administration, 10 Columbus Circle, New York,

---

[1] Operational Bulletin No. C-30 is issued to reflect the processing required to implement Chapter 1022 of 1974 as amended by Chapter 360 of the Laws of 1975, commonly referred to as the Sound Housing Law. To secure a certificate of eviction under Sections 57, 58, 59a(2) and 59a(4) of the Rent and Eviction Regulations, the landlord must establish (1) there is no reasonable opportunity to earn 8½ per cent of assessed valuation and (2) neither he nor his predecessor intentionally or wilfully managed the property so as to impair his earning ability before tenant(s) may be evicted.

Administrator's Interpretations

New York 10019, unless otherwise provided on the form prescribed by the Commissioner for such PAR.

Where the PAR is against an order issued by the District Rent Administrator, a copy of the PAR shall also be served on the District Rent Administrator issuing the order and upon each party affected by the PAR.

A PAR will not be accepted for filing unless accompanied by an affidavit or other proof of service upon the District Rent Administrator and each party affected by the PAR.

Any person served with a PAR may, within fifteen days from the date of service, file a verified answer thereto, by filing the same with the Commissioner, together with proof of service of a copy thereof upon the party filing the PAR. At the Commissioner's discretion, and for good cause shown, the time within which to answer may be extended.

Within a reasonable time after the filing of the PAR and the answer, if any, the Commissioner may:

(a) Reject the PAR if it is insufficient or defective.

(b) Make such investigation of the facts, hold such conferences, and require the filing of such reports, evidence, affidavits, or other material relevant to the proceeding as the Commissioner may deem necessary or appropriate to determine whether the District Rent Administrator's order is correct.

(c) Forward to or make available for inspection by either party any relevant evidence and afford an opportunity to file rebuttal thereto.

(d) For good cause shown, accept for filing any papers, even though not timely filed.

(e) Require any person to appear or produce documents or both pursuant to a subpoena issued by the Commissioner.

(f) Grant or order a hearing.

The Commissioner, on such terms and conditions as may be determined, may:

(a) Dismiss the PAR if it fails substantially to comply with the provisions of this Operational Bulletin.

(b) Grant or deny PAR, in whole or in part, or remand the proceeding to the District Rent Administrator for further action.

(c) In the event that the Commissioner grants or denies any such PAR in whole or in part, the Commissioner shall inform all parties of the grounds upon which such decision is based.

Where a relevant statute or regulation is amended during the pendency of a PAR, the determination shall be in accordance with the amended law or regulation.

If the Commissioner does not act finally within a period of ninety days after a PAR is filed, or within such extended period as may be fixed by the Commissioner, the PAR shall be deemed to be denied. The Commissioner may, however, grant one such extension not to exceed thirty days with the consent of the party filing the PAR; any further extension may only be granted with the consent of all parties to the PAR.

The filing of a PAR against an order, other than an order adjusting, fixing or establishing a maximum rent, within thirty-three days after the date of the issuance of such order shall stay such order until the final determination of the PAR by the Commissioner. On application by an aggrieved party, the Commissioner, at the Commissioner's discretion, may stay any other order on such terms and conditions as the Commissioner may determine during the pendency of the PAR. However, nothing herein contained shall limit the Commissioner from granting or vacating a stay under appropriate circumstances.

The filing and determination of a PAR is a prerequisite to obtaining judicial review of any order or determination issued by a District Rent Administrator. A proceeding for judicial review may be instituted under Article 78 of the Civil Practice Law and Rules provided the petition in the Supreme Court is filed within sixty days after the issuance date of the order of the Commissioner. Service of the petition upon the Division of Housing and Community Renewal shall be made by leaving a copy thereof with Counsel's Office at the Division's Principal Office located at 2 World Trade Center, New York City. In addition, the Attorney General must be served at 2 World Trade Center, New York City.

ADMINISTRATOR'S INTERPRETATIONS

The Commissioner, on application of either party or on the Commissioner's own initiative, and upon notice to all parties affected, may, prior to the date that a proceeding for judicial review has been commenced in the Supreme Court pursuant to Article 78 of the Civil Practice Law and Rules, modity, supersede or revoke any order issued by the Commissioner under these or previous Regulations where the Commissioner finds that such order was the result of illegality, irregularity in vital matters, or fraud. Where an order is modified, superseded or revoked by the Commissioner, the Commissioner may also direct appropriate rent adjustments be made in accordance with the order issued.

OPERATIONAL BULLETIN NO. 84/3*

New procedures for the Implementation of the Freedom of Information Law (FOIL)
AND
Procedures for Responding to Subpoenas Duces Tecum for Legal Files and Records
(Issued October 1, 1984)

1. J. Seldon - Loach is hereby designated as the records Access Officer of the Office of Rent Administration, Division of Housing and Community Renewal, 10 Columbus Circle, New York, New York 10019.
2. All FOIL requests to review files, documents, etc. must be in writing, on at least five (5) days prior notice, and addressed to the Records Access Officer at the above address.
3. The FOIL request must specifically describe the item requested and, if known, its location.
4. Within five (5) business days of receipt of the FOIL request, the Records Access Officer will notify the requestor, in writing, whether the request has been granted or denied.
5. If the FOIL request has been denied, the requestor may appeal such denial to the designated Appeals Officer within thirty (30) days of issuance of the denial.

---

* Operational Bulletin No. 84-2, will be found under State Tenant Protection Bulletins, infra.

Administrator's Interpretations

6. Nathaniel Geller, Assistant Deputy Counsel, Office of Rent Administration, Division of Housing and Community Renewal, 10 Columbus Circle, New York, New York 10019, is hereby designated Appeals Officer.
7. The appeal must be determined within seven (7) business days of receipt of the appeal.
8. If the FOIL request has been granted, the requestor will be advised, in writing, within five (5) days of making such request that the requested records may be inspected in accordance with the procedure set forth in item "9" herein.
9. The Records Access Officer will ascertain and/or confirm the location of the file or other documents requested and advise the requestor, in writing, of the location thereof, the name of the person who has possession of the documents, and that such documents may be reviewed from Monday through Friday between the hours of 9:00 A.M. and 4:00 P.M. or at a specified date and time.
10. A requestor who wishes to obtain copies of the requested documents shall be charged $.25 per page.
11. Prior to inspecting the requested documents, the requestor must complete and sign the Division's form OS-97, Application for Public Access to Records.
12. If copies of the requested documents are sought, the person receiving payment for such copies must complete the Division's Receipt, form OS-97a, and give the requestor a copy of the Receipt.
13. Parties to a pending proceeding or their legal representatives, who wish to inspect their file, should give the Division seventy-two hours advance notice. "Parties" are defined as the owner, tenant or an attorney of either who has filed a Notice of Appearance with the Division.
14. Parties to a pending proceeding should direct requests to inspect their file to the Public Information Unit of the District Rent Office at which their file is located.

Administrator's Interpretations

15. The addresses and telephone numbers of the District Rent Offices are attached.

1. The following named persons have been appointed this agency's Subpoena Officers for Legal Files and Records:

Lower Manhattan 2 Lafayette Street 12th Floor	= Lucy Coruzzi	− 566-6953
Upper Manhattan 215 West 125th St. New York, N.Y. 5th Floor	= Lena Garner	− 678-2190
Bronx 260 East 161st St. Bronx, N.Y. 8th floor	= Edwin Martin	− 585-2600, Ext 51
Brooklyn 91 Lawrence Street Brooklyn, NY 2nd floor	= Ethel Martin	− 643-2272
Queens 164-19 Hillside Avenue Jamaica, N.Y. 11432 Ground Floor	= Pam Zaffuto (Vergy Boling)	−
Staten Island (No records. Records for this office are located at 2 Lafayette St.)	= Morty Zweifler Ann Annicharico	816-0277
Nassau 50 Clinton St. 2nd Fl.	= Wm. Robert Balalaos	516-481-8887
Westchester 99 Church Street 2nd floor	= Milton Blumenthal	918-948-4434
Rockland 94 96 North Main Street	= John Timmeny (Tues. & Thurs. At other times call Harry Sach)	− 914-425-6575
10 Columbus Circle	= Barbara Butler	− 307-5760 Ext. 729
17 John Street	= Josephine Massi	− 566-5112
2 World Trade Center Room #5880	= Zhetora Parks	− 488-7146
2 World Trade Center Room #5880	= Jocelyn Francis	− 488-7146

2. Persons seeking to serve subpoenas on this agency should be directed to the appropriate District Rent Office and subpoena officer.

3. This agency will not respond to a subpoena unless it is marked "So Ordered" and signed by a Judge of the court issuing the subpoena; the subpoena fee of $5.00 is paid; and the subpoena describes with specificity the files and/or records requested.

4. Subpoenas must be issued at least 24 hours before the return date so as to enable the agency to locate the requested files and/or records; process the files and/or records for delivery to the appropriate courthouse; and make delivery to the appropriate courthouse.

5. Subpoenas should be responded to by photocopying the contents of the file and/or record; comparing the copy with the original; certifying the copy; delivering the certified copy of the file and/or record to the record room of the appropriate courthouse on the return date.

6. For the purposes of certifying copies of original documents, as stated in paragraph 5, the Subpoena Officers have been appointed certifying officers.

7. If the subpoena officer is unable to comply with the record requested, a letter shall be sent to the court advising the judge of that fact, requesting additional time to comply.

8. All questions which may arise concerning the validity of the subpoena that cannot be resolved by the subpoena officer shall be determined by either of the Assistant Deputy Counsels. If neither of them are available and time is of the essence, then the Deputy Counsel or a Bureau Chief may be consulted.

OPERATIONAL BULLETIN NO. 84-3

(Revised February 14, 1986)

New procedures for the Implementation of the Freedom of Information Law (FOIL)

AND

Procedures for Responding to Subpoenas Duces Tecum for Legal Files and Records

1. Ms. Peggy Shepard is hereby designated as the records Access Officer of the Office of Rent Administration, Division of Housing and Community Renewal, 92-31 Union Hall Street, Jamaica, New York, 11433.

2. All FOIL requests to review files, documents, etc. must be in writing, on at least five (5) days prior

Administrator's Interpretations

notice, and addressed to the Records Access Officer at the above address.

3. The FOIL request must specifically describe the item requested and, if known, its location.

4. Within five (5) business days of receipt of the FOIL request, the Records access officer will notify the requestor, in writing, whether the request has been granted or denied.

5. If the FOIL request has been denied, the requestor may appeal such denial to the designated Appeals Officer within thirty (30) days of issuance of the denial.

6. Nathaniel Geller, Assistant Deputy Counsel, Office of Rent Administration, Division of Housing and Community Renewal, 92-31 Union Hall Street, Jamaica, New York 11433, is hereby designated Appeals Officer.

7. The appeal must be determined within seven (7) business days of receipt of the appeal.

8. If the FOIL request has been granted, the requestor will be advised, in writing, within five (5) days of making such request that the requested records may be inspected in accordance with the procedure set forth in item "9" herein.

9. The Records Access Officer will ascertain and/or confirm the location of the file or other documents requested and advise the requestor, in writing, of the location thereof, the name of the person who has possession of the documents, and that such documents may be reviewed from Monday through Friday between the hours of 9:00 A.M. and 4:00 P.M. or at a specified date and time.

10. A requestor who wishes to obtain copies of the requested documents shall be charged $.25 per page.

11. Prior to inspecting the requested documents, the requestor must complete and sign the Division's form OS-97R, Application for Public Access to Records.

12. If copies of the requested documents are sought, the person receiving payment for such copies must com-

plete the Division's Receipt, form OS-97R, and give the requestor a copy of the Receipt.

13. Parties to a pending proceeding or their legal representatives, who wish to inspect their file, should give the Division seventy-two hours advance notice. "Parties" are defined as the owner, tenant or an attorney of either who has filed a Notice of Appearance with the Division.

14. Parties to a pending proceeding should direct requests to inspect their file to the Public Information Unit of the District Rent Office at which their file is located.

15. The addresses and telephone numbers of the District Rent Offices are attached.

1. The following named persons have been appointed this agency's Subpoena Officers for Legal Files and Records:

Lower Manhattan 2 Lafayette Street 12th Floor	Laurina Seignious (Seymour Zuckerman)	566-6969
Upper Manhattan 215 West 125th St. 5th Floor	Lena Garner (A. Mahoney)	678-2190
Bronx 260 E. 161st St 8th Floor	Henrietta Costello (B. Bernstein)	585-2613
Brooklyn 91 Lawrence St. Second Fl.	Julius Pinkowitz (M. Pizzaro)	(718) 643-7824
Queens 164-19 Hillside Avenue Ground Floor	Rosyln Krzeminski (A. Chazin)	(718) 526-2040 Ext. 13
Staten Island (No records. Records for this office are located at 2 Lafayette St.	Elizabeth Hegy (A. Annicharico)	(718) 816-0277
Nassau 50 Clinton Street 2nd Fl.	Wm. Robert Balalaos (B. Moffett)	(516) 481-8887
Westchester 99 Church Street 2nd Floor	Harry Sack (S. Weir)	(914) 948-4434
Rockland 94 96 North Main Street	John Timmeny (Tues. & Thurs. At other times call Harry Sack)	(914) 425-6575
Queens-Central 92-31 Union Hall Street, 4th Fl.	Peggy Shepard	(718) 739-6400
2 World Trade Center, Room 5880 Litigation	Zhetora Parks	(212) 488-7146
2 World Trade	Michael Robinson	(212) 488-3154

ADMINISTRATOR'S INTERPRETATIONS

Center, Room 5880
Litigation
10 Columbus Circle   Daniel Frament   (212) 307-5760
11th Floor

2. Persons seeking to serve subpoenas on this agency should be directed to the appropriate District Rent Office and subpoena officer.

3. This agency will not respond to a subpoena unless it is marked "So Ordered" and signed by a Judge of the court issuing the subpoena.

4. Subpoenas must be issued at least 24 hours before the return date so as to enable the agency to locate the requested files and/or records; process the files and/or records for delivery to the appropriate courthouse; and make delivery to the appropriate courthouse.

5. Subpoenas should be responded to by photocopying the contents of the file and/or record; comparing the copy with the original; certifying the copy; delivering the certified copy of the file and/or record to the record room of the appropriate courthouse on the return date.

6. For the purposes of certifying copies of original documents, as stated in paragraph 5, the Subpoena Officers have been appointed certifying officers.

7. If the subpoena officer is unable to comply with the record requested, a letter shall be sent to the court advising the judge of that fact, requesting additional time to comply.

8. All questions which may arise concerning the validity of the subpoena that cannot be resolved by the subpoena officer shall be determined by either of the Assistant Deputy Counsels. If neither of them are available and time is of the essence, then the Deputy Counsel or a Bureau Chief may be consulted.

OPERATIONAL BULLETIN NO. 84-4

Major Capital Improvements/Substantial
Rehabilitation/Increased Services and Equipment
(Issued November 13, 1984)

This Operational Bulletin relates to the processing of rent increase applications filed by landlords based upon building-wide major capital improvements, substantial rehabilitation and increased services and new equipment pursuant to the provisions of Section 33.1 (9NYCRR2202.3A and 9NYCRR2102.3) of the Rent and Eviction Regulations, Section 34.1 (NYCRR 2502.4) of the Tenant Protection Regulations and Sections 41 and 20C(1) of the Rent Stabilization Code.

The District Rent Administrator shall grant a rent adjustment pursuant to appropriate regulations if it is determined that:

1. a. The landlord and tenant by mutual voluntary agreement, subject to approval by the Division, agree to a substantial increase of dwelling space or an increase in the services, new furniture, new furnishings or new equipment provided in the housing accommodations; which agreement may be established by the signatures of landlord and tenant on the prescribed application form or by corroborative proof of such earlier agreement.

    b. there has been an increase in the rental value of the housing accommodations as a result of a substantial rehabilitation of the building or housing accommodations therein which materially adds to the value of the property or appreciably prolongs its life, excluding ordinary repairs, maintenance and replacements; and that the legal regulated rent has not been adjusted prior to the application based in whole or part upon the grounds set forth in the application; or

    c. there has been a major capital improvement required for the operation, preservation or maintenance of the structure; and that the legal regulated rent has not been adjusted prior to the application based in whole or part upon the grounds set forth in the application.

2. the cost of such work has been adequately substantiated by submission of copies of contracts, invoices, cancelled checks, and other pertinent documents which might be required; and

3. that all other requirements for the granting of such rent increases have been met.

Administrator's Interpretations

The District Rent Administrator shall determine:

(A) That an installation constitutes a major capital improvement if it is (1) building-wide, (2) deemed depreciable under the Internal Revenue Code, (3) structural in nature, (4) an improvement to the building or to the building stock, (5) and required for the operation, preservation or maintenance of the structure.

(B) That an installation constitutes a substantial rehabilitation of a building or housing accommodation if it will materially add to the value of the property or appreciably prolong its life, exclusive of ordinary repairs, maintenance, and replacements.

(C) That there has been a substantial increase of dwelling space or an increase in services, new furniture, new furnishings, or new equipment provided to the housing accommodation on written consent of the tenant (in occupancy). However, the landlord shall be entitled to collect the increase for new equipment when installed subject to the approval of the District Rent Administrator. Increases for improvements or new equipment in vacant apartments do not require prior approval by the District Rent Administrator, but may be challenged or objected to by a tenant at any time after occupancy.

Computation of rent adjustment

A. 60-Month Period of Amortization
(Building-Wide)

The rent adjustment granted by the District Rent Administrator applicable to rent stabilized and rent controlled apartments shall be computed based upon a 5 year (60 months) period of amortization of the verified reasonable cost of the major capital improvement(s) or substantial rehabilitation.

B. 40-Month Period of Amortization
(Apartment only)

The rent adjustment granted by the District Rent Administrator applicable to rent stabilized and rent controlled apartments shall be computed based upon a 40 month period of amortization of the verified reasonable cost, including cost of installation, for an increase in the services, new furniture, new furnishings, new equipment or improvements provided to the housing accommodation.

Limitation on Amount of Rent Increase Collectible in a 12-month period

In order to carry out the mandate of the Statute, Regulations, and Code against unreasonably high rent increases, the District Rent Administrator shall limit the amount of building-wide rent increases based upon major capital improvement(s) and substantial rehabilitation *to be collected* in any 12-month period commencing on the effective date of the rent increase to 15% of the rent. In such cases as the *District Rent Administrator* deems appropriate, the 15% limitation may be waived.

In a case where the appropriate rent increase is determined to be an amount greater than 15% of the rent, the District Rent Administrator shall order the owner to collect 15% of the rent in the first 12-month period, and defer collection of the balance to subsequent 12-month periods depending on the amount of the rent increase granted.

In rent stabilized apartments in New York City, as required by Section 40 of the Rent Stabilization Code, major capital improvement increases are retroactive to 30 days after the completion of the filing of the application. Any arrears which accrued as a result of the issuance of an order after the 30-day effective period, shall be spread forward in future years so as not to exceed the 15% limitation in any 12-month period.

Lease renewals which include the major capital improvement increase shall be based upon the total increase granted exclusive of arrears.

However, such lease agreement may contain language which provides that in addition to the rent required in the lease the tenant shall pay any arrears not to exceed 15% in any 12-month period and when such arrears have been repaid, the rent reserved in the lease shall be the only collectible rent. In the event that a vacancy occurs prior to the full collection of the major capital improvement increase, the new tenant shall pay the full amount of the increase in addition to any vacancy or guideline increase ordered by the New York City Rent Guidelines Board.

ADMINISTRATOR'S INTERPRETATIONS

Installation of New Prime Windows

The installation of new prime windows (not just the addition of storm windows), building-wide, constitutes a major capital improvement pursuant to appropriate regulations warranting a rent increase. In cases where the old windows were more than 25 years old, the District Rent Administrator shall grant a rent increase based upon the full substantiated cost of the new windows.

In those cases where the old windows were between 15 and 25 years old, the District Rent Administrator may grant a rent increase based upon the full substantiated cost of the new windows if the District Rent Administrator determines that the replacement windows were necessary; or, regardless of the age of the windows the District Rent Administrator shall grant a rent increase based on 50% of the substantiated cost of the new windows if the replacements were for energy conservation purposes.

Cosmetic Improvements

The District Rent Adminstrator shall allow the reasonable substantiated cost of a cosmetic improvement in the computation of a rent increase based upon a major capital improvement only if the cosmetic improvement was done within 6 months and was directly related to the major capital improvement included in the owner's application. For example, if an owner installs new mailboxes in the inner lobby and a new intercom system in the vestibule, then the District Rent Administrator shall allow the substantiated cost of painting and plastering the inner lobby and vestibule provided that the cost of such work was included in the owner's application. As seen from this example, the *major capital improvement must be completed prior to or contemporaneous with, the commencement of the work for the cosmetic improvement.*

The cosmetic improvement must:

A. Improve, restore or preserve the quality of the structure;

B. represent an expenditure equal to at least 10% of the total operating and maintenance expenses for the most recent full calendar year or the most recent fiscal year or any 12 consecutive months ending not more than 90 days prior to the filing of the application; and

C. must have been completed within 6 months of the completion of the major capital improvement.

SUPPLEMENT NO. 1 TO OPERATIONAL BULLETIN 84-4

(January 30, 1986)

Introduction

On November 13, 1984, the State Division of Housing and Community Renewal (DHCR) issued Operational Bulletin No. 84-4 which related to rent adjustments based upon a Major Capital Improvement (MCI). Since the issuance of the Bulletin, the DHCR has decided to implement changes in MCI procedures in accordance with its authority under Section 33 of the State Rent and Eviction Regulations (9NYCRR 2102.3), Section 33 of the Rent and Eviction Regulations for New York City (9NYCRR 2202.3), Section 34(a)(2)(iv) of the Tenant Protection Regulations [9NYCRR 2502.4(a)(2)(iv)], and Section 35A of the Code of the Rent Stabilization Association of New York City, Inc.

These sections of the Regulations and Code require the DHCR to take into consideration all factors bearing on the equities involved when it orders rent adjustments. The changes in MCI procedures are as follows:

A. *Application For Prior Opinion of the DHCR*

An owner may, at his or her option, apply for the DHCR's prior opinion in all cases where the owner contemplates filing an application for a rent increase based upon the installation of an MCI or a substantial rehabilitation of the premises. Owners are not required to obtain the DHCR's approval of the proposed work prior to applying for an MCI increase.

The prior opinion would permit the owner to know with certainty, prior to making any financial commitment or expenditure, whether the proposed work qualifies for a rent increase as an MCI or substantial rehabilitation. Such factors as the useful life of the existing sub-system, the structural nature of the proposed work and its necessity for the operation, preservation, and maintenance of the building will be considered by the District Rent Administrator or Director of Processing. If an owner files an application for a prior opinion, tenants will be permitted to challenge the proposed cost and propriety of the planned installation. If a Prior Opinion order is issued, it will be subject to administrative review by any aggrieved party.

Where the MCI installation or substantial rehabilitation will be financed through the proceeds of a government sponsored loan program, such as the Article 8A Program, the Prior Opinion proceeding will be expedited for processing and approval will be based upon certification to the DHCR by the government agency involved that the projected work is in accordance with its standards and qualifications and conforms to code requirements.

Upon obtaining prior approval or upon completing the installation of the MCI or the substantial rehabilitation, the owner will file with the District Rent Administrator or Director of Processing an application to increase the rents based upon the actual cost incurred, and submit the required documentation in order to substantiate such cost, including a copy of the Prior Opinion order, if any. Municipal certificates must be submitted where required. An application for a rent increase based upon an MCI or substantial rehabilitation of the premises previously approved in a prior opinion will be examined only as to actual cost expended for the improvement.

B. *Permissible Charges for the Installation of an Air Conditioner for Both Rent Controlled and Rent Stabilized Apartments in New York City.*

An owner may charge a tenant the following amounts for the installation of an air conditioner between October 1, 1985 and September 30, 1986:

   (1) $222.48* per annum per air conditioner ($18.54 per month), where the tenant installs his own air conditioner, and "free" electricity is included in the rent.

---

* The 1985 charge (estimated average operating cost) per air conditioner of $233.07 per annum ($19.43 per month) reduced to reflect a 4.6% decline in the price of electricity for electrical inclusion buildings. See *1985 Price Index of Operating Cost for Rent Stabilized Apartment Houses in New York City,* Urban Systems Research and Engineering, Inc., Page 30, May, 1985.

This initial charge is subject to adjustment on October 1, 1986 and each subsequent October 1st thereafter. It will be adjusted either upward or downward depending upon whether the "Price Index of Operating Costs for Rent Stabilized Apartment Houses in New York City," prepared for the New York City Rent Guidelines Board by the Urban Systems Research and Engineering, Inc., shows an increase or decrease in the cost of electricity for electrical inclusion buildings.

(2) $222.48 per annum air conditioner ($18.54 per month) plus one-fortieth (1/40th) of the cost of the new air conditioner, where "free" electricity is included in the rent and the owner, with the tenant's written consent, installs a new air conditioner for the tenant.

(3) $5.00 per month per air conditioner, where the tenant installs his own air conditioner, which protrudes beyond the window line, and pays for his own electricity, and the installation of the air conditioner will result in damage to the owner's property.

These charges will apply to both Rent Controlled and Rent Stabilized apartments in New York City, for air conditioners installed on and after October 1, 1985, regardless of any prior, differing charges and procedures. Neither of these charges shall be part of the base rent for the purpose of computing any guidelines or other increases under the Rent Stabilization Law or Code.

C. *Restrictions on the Use of Reserve Funds*

Rent increases based on an MCI are made available to owners as an incentive for them to invest in their property. Accordingly, money from the reserve fund of a building converted to cooperative or condominium ownership should not be used as the basis for an MCI rent increase adjustment. To encourage such investment, the adjustment will be allowed only if the funds used for the MCI are contributed previously by the sponsor prior to the conversion or are obtained by a special assessment of the shareholders or the owners of condominium units.

Administrator's Interpretations

It has, therefore, been determined that where an MCI has been paid for after conversion, out of a cash reserve fund deposited by the owner/sponsor/landlord, such MCI will not be the basis for a rent increase. Likewise, if an MCI is installed subsequent to transfer of title to a cooperative corporation, the corporation will not be eligible for a rent increase unless the MCI is paid for by a special assessment of *all* the shareholders (proprietary lessees), or the sponsor or holder of unsold shares pays for the MCI without removing funds from the cash reserve fund. It should be noted that if a cooperative corporation is eligible to file for an MCI increase, the application must be filed by the managing agent of the corporation on behalf of the corporation and all proprietary lessees, including the sponsor. This will avoid multiple applications for the same MCI.

D. *Individual Apartment Improvements or Installation of New Equipment*

Operational Bulletin 84-4 is amended to the extent of no longer requiring the approval of the DHCR for individual apartment improvements, including the installation of new equipment, based upon tenant consent, or completed or installed while the apartment is vacant. However, increased apartment services continue to require DHCR approval, as for example, a master television antenna, or cable TV. Owners will be required to note on the Annual Registration Form that such improvements or equipment were installed and the rent increased as a result. Tenants would then have 4 years to challenge such increase.

E. *6% Limitation On Major Capital Improvements, Substantial Rehabilitation and Hardship Increases For Rent Stabilized Apartments In New York City*

It has been determined that the 6% annual limitation contained in Section YY51-6.0.c. of the New York City Administrative Code applies to all increases for MCI's, substantial rehabilitations and hardships, whether alternative or comparative, and must be imposed in the processing of such applications for rent stabilized apartments in New York City.

In addition to the 6% annual limitation, an additional

Administrator's Interpretations

6% increase will be allowed towards arrears arising from any delay in the processing of applications for such increases.

Any rent increases in the above categories which exceed 6% may be collected in future years in a similar manner as the 15% limitation contained in Operational Bulletin 84-4, which continues to apply to rent controlled apartments statewide and rent stabilized apartments outside New York City.

ANNUAL UPDATE OF SECTION B OF SUPPLEMENT NO. 1 TO OPERATIONAL BULLETIN 84-4

B. *Permissible Charges for the Installation of an Air Conditioner for Both Rent Controlled and Rent Stabilized Housing Accommodations in New York City.*

An owner may charge a tenant the following amounts for the installation of an air conditioner between October 1, 1986 and September 30, 1987:

(1) $219.14* per annum per air conditioner ($18.26 per month), where the tenant installs his own air conditioner, and "free" electricity is included in the rent. This initial charge is subject to adjustment on October 1, 1987 and each subsequent October 1st thereafter. It will be adjusted either upward or downward depending upon whether the "Price Index of Operating Costs for Rent Stabilized Apartment Houses in New York City," prepared for the New York City Rent Guidelines Board by the Urban Systems Research and Engineering, Inc., (or such other research company as the Rent Guidelines Board may choose), shows an increase or decrease in the cost of electricity for electrical inclusion buildings.

For air conditioners previously installed between October 1, 1985 and September 30, 1986, the allowable charge of $222.48 per annum is hereby reduced to $219.14 per annum, per air conditioner ($18.26 per month), effective October 1, 1986.

---

* The 1986 charge (estimated average operating cost) per air conditioner of $222.48 per annum ($18.54 per month) reduced to reflect a 1.5% decline in the price of electricity for electrical inclusion buildings. See *1986 Price Index of Operating Cost for Rent Stabilized Apartment Houses in New York City*, Urban Systems Research and Engineering, Inc, Page 43, May, 1986.

(2) $219.14 per annum per air conditioner ($18.26 per month) plus one-fortieth (1/40th) of the cost of the new air conditioner, where "free" electricity is included in the rent and the owner, with the tenant's written consent, installs a new air conditioner for the tenant.

(3) $5.00 per month per air conditioner, where the tenant installs his own air conditioner, which protrudes beyond the window line, and pays for his own electricity, and the installation of the air conditioner will result in damage to the owner's property.

These charges will apply to both Rent Controlled and Rent Stabilized housing accommodations in New York City, for air conditioners installed on and after October 1, 1986, regardless of any prior, differing charges and procedures. Except as to the rent increase for the new air conditioner (Item (2) above), none of these charges shall be part of the base rent for the purpose of computing any guidelines or other increases under the Rent Stabilization Law or Code.

OPERATIONAL BULLETIN 85-1

Rent Stabilization Rider for Apartment
House Tenants in New York City
(Issued July, 1985)

Introduction

Pursuant to Section YY51-6.0d of the New York City Rent Stabilization Law (RSL), the State Division of Housing and Community Renewal (DHCR), has promulgated a rent stabilization lease rider (Rider) which describes the rights and duties of owners and tenants as provided for under the RSL and other laws. The Rider also informs rent stabilized tenants of the rent paid by the previous tenant. The Rider is only informational and its provisions do not modify or become part of the lease. The Rider does not replace or modify the RSL, the Rent Stabilization Code, or any order of DHCR or the New York City Rent Guidelines Board. The Rider must be in larger type than the lease. Upon the face of each lease the following language must appear in bold type "Attached to this lease are the pertinent rules and regulations governing tenants' and landlords' rights under the rent stabilization law."

1. SERVICE OF RIDER

   Owners must provided every rent stabilized tenant with a copy of the Rider, as follows:

   A. No later than October 4, 1985, a copy of the Rider must be served on every tenant who signed a vacancy or renewal lease which commenced before or after April 1, 1984, but prior to October 4, 1985. Owners may serve the Rider personally or by mail;

   B. An owner must attach a copy of the Rider to every vacancy lease signed by a new tenant which commences on or after October 4, 1985.

   C. A copy of the Rider must be attached to every renewal lease (or short form renewal) which commences on or after October 4, 1985.

2. PENALTIES

   A. A tenant who is not served with a copy of the Rider by October 4, 1985, if applicable, or who signs a vacancy or renewal lease (or short form renewal) thereafter, to which a copy of the rider is not attached, may file form RA-90 with DHCR. This form is called "Tenants Complaint Of Owner's Failure To Renew Lease And/Or Failure To Furnish A Copy Of A Signed Lease." Tenants should use the reverse side of this form (the additional comments section), specifying the complaints.

   B. Upon complaint by the tenant, DHCR will notify the owner to serve the Rider by certified mail. Noncompliance by the owner within 10 days thereafter will result in the denial of any rent increases commencing on or after October 4, 1985, resulting from a lease renewal, a hardship, or a Major Capital Improvement, until the Rider is served. In addition, an owner who fails to serve a tenant with a rider after being ordered to do so by DHCR may be fined $250.00.

Administrator's Interpretations

3. "STATUS OF APARTMENT AND LAST TENANT" SECTION OF RIDER

This section of the Rider contains three boxes:

A. If the last tenant after April 1, 1980 was rent stabilized, the owner must check this box and fill in the last tenant's final monthly rent;

B. If the tenant receiving the Rider is the first rent stabilized tenant in the apartment, and the apartment was rent controlled when the last prior tenant vacated, the owner must check this box, but does not need to fill in such last prior tenant's rent;

C. If the last tenant living in the apartment received a special rent reduction, such as a resident superintendent, owners should check the box marked "other". If the current tenant's occupancy of the apartment commenced prior to April 1, 1980, owners should also check this box, but do not have to fill in any rent information.

AVAILABILITY OF RIDER

Copies of the Rider are available from Blumberg's Law Products and any legal stationery store, the Rent Stabilization Association, and the Real Estate Board of New York, Inc.

Copies of the Rider are *not* available either from DHCR's District Rent Offices or DHCR's Office of Rent Administration at 10 Columbus Circle, New York City.

FORM OF RIDER

Rent Stabilization Rider, 4-85
Use with new or renewal leases

Rent Stabilization Rider For Apartment House Tenants In New York City

Prepared by: Rent Stabilization Association of NYC, Inc
1500 Broadway, New York, NY 10036 · 212-944-4720

FAILURE TO ATTACH A COPY OF THIS RIDER TO A TENANT'S LEASE WITHOUT CAUSE MAY RESULT IN A FINE OR OTHER SANCTIONS

Introduction

This Rider generally informs tenants and owners about their basic rights and responsibilities under the Rent Stabilization Law. The Rent Stabilization Law protects tenants by regulating rents, services, and evictions. It also provides property owners with rent increases and remedies so that owners may meet increased maintenance costs, obtain increases for new services and equipment and otherwise properly maintain the property.

This Rider does not contain every rule applicable to rent stabilized apartments. The Appendix lists organizations which can provide assistance to tenants and owners who have inquiries, complaints or requests relating to subjects covered in this Rider.

This Rider is only informational. Its provisions are not part of the lease. However, it must be attached to the lease. The Rider does not modify the lease. It does not replace or modify the Rent Stabilization Law, the Rent Stabilization Code, any order of the New York State Division of Housing and Community Renewal (DHCR), or any order of the New York City Rent Guidelines Board.

A tenant should keep a copy of this Rider and of any lease the tenant signs.

Increases for Renewal and Vacancy Leases

Provided that the tenant's apartment is registered with DHCR, the owner is entitled to increase the rent when a tenant renews a lease (a "renewal lease") or when a new tenant enters into a lease upon moving into an apartment (a "vacancy lease"). Each year, effective October 1, the New York City Rent Guidelines Board sets the percentage of maximum permissible increase over the September 30 rent for leases which will begin during the year that the guidelines order is in effect. The date a lease starts determines which guidelines order applies.

Guidelines orders provide increases for:

(a) **Renewal Leases:** Different percentages are set for rent increases for leases for 1 or 2 years. The renewing tenant has the choice of the length of the lease.

(b) **Vacancy Leases:** In addition to the percentage increase permitted the owner for a renewal lease, the owner may charge to a new tenant a vacancy allowance if set by the Rent Guidelines Board. The tenant has the choice of whether a vacancy lease will be for 1 or 2 years.

Security Deposits

The general rule is that an owner may collect a security deposit no greater than one month's rent. However, if the present tenant moved into an apartment prior to the date the apartment first became rent stabilized and the owner collected more than one month's rent, the owner may continue to retain a security deposit of up to two month's rent for that tenant only. When the rent is increased, the owner may charge an additional amount to bring the security deposit up to the full amount to which the owner is entitled.

Security deposits must be deposited in an interesi-bearing trust account. Owners may deduct a 1% service fee and must credit the balance of the interest annually, or on request of the tenant, pay the tenant the balance of the interest earned.

Other Rent Increases

In addition to guidelines increases, the rent may be permanently increased where:

(a) **Improvements, New Services or Equipment to Apartment:** While a tenant may demand serviceable used equipment at no increase in rent, an owner is generally permitted to add 1/40th of the cost of improvements, new services or equipment and its installation, such as a new stove or refrigerator, to the monthly rent. However, if a tenant is in occupancy of the apartment, the increase may be charged immediately for new equipment only with the written consent of the tenant and the subsequent approval of DHCR. Increases for new services or improvements are only permitted after approval by DHCR. An increase for improvements, new services or equipment installed when an apartment is vacant does not require the consent of the next tenant or an order of DHCR. However, the tenant may challenge all or part of the increase after occupancy.

(b) **Building-Wide Major Capital Improvements or Substantial Rehabilitation:** An owner is permitted a rental increase for certain types of building-wide substantial rehabilitation or major capital improvements such as the replacement of a boiler, or new plumbing. The owner must receive approval from DHCR which will permit the owner to amortize the cost over 5 years. The owner is not required to obtain tenant consent. Tenants are served with a copy of an owner's application and have a right to respond to the application.

(c) **Hardship:** An owner may apply for a rental increase for hardship when:

(1) the rent is not sufficient to enable the owner to maintain approximately the same average annual net income for a current three-year period as compared with the annual net income which prevailed on the average over the period 1968 through 1970, or for the first three years of operation if the building was completed since 1968, or for the first three years the owner owned the building if he cannot obtain records for the years 1968-1970; or

(2) where the annual gross rental income does not exceed the annual operating expenses by a sum equal to at least 5% of such gross income.

If an application for a rent increase based on a building-wide major capital improvement, substantial rehabilitation, or hardship is granted, the owner may charge the increase during the term of an existing lease only if the lease contains a clause specifically authorizing the owner to do so.

An increase based on a building-wide major capital improvement or substantial rehabilitation may not exceed 15% in any 12-month period. In appropriate circumstances, DHCR may waive the 15% limitation and authorize an increase in excess of 15%. An increase based on hardship may not exceed 6% in any 12-month period. Any increase authorized by DHCR which exceeds these annual limitations may be collected in future years.

Status of Apartment and Last Tenant (Owner to Check Box 1, 2 or 3)

1. ☐ The last tenant after April 1, 1980 was a rent stabilized tenant and had a final rent of $ ______________________ per month.

—OR—

2. ☐ This apartment was subject to rent control until the last tenant moved out. The tenant to whose lease this Rider is attached is the first rent stabilized tenant.

—OR—

3. ☐ Other (please specify) ______________________

____

____

If the owner checked Box 2, the owner was entitled to bring the rent up to the "market rent" before renting it to the first stabilized tenant. That first rent charged to the first stabilized tenant becomes the initial base rent for the apartment under the rent stabilization system. If the tenant believes this rent exceeds a "fair market rent" the tenant may file a "fair market rent appeal" with DHCR. The owner is required to give the tenant a notice of the right to file such an appeal on an official form. The notice must be served personally or by certified mail. A tenant has only 90 days after receiving the notice or 90 days from the date he or she is served with a copy of the apartment registration form, to file such an appeal. Otherwise, the rent sent forth on the notice or registration form becomes final.

The "fair market rent" is computed based upon a "special guideline" established annually by the Rent Guidelines Board, or by averaging this "special guideline" with decontrolled rents charged for similar apartments (called "comparables") on June 30, 1974, updated by annual guidelines increases.

No matter which Box is checked, the owner is not entitled to a rent which is more than the legal regulated rent. That amount is the rent registered with DHCR as set forth below, or a rent established after a "fair market rent appeal," plus increases in rent permitted to be added to the first stabilization rent.

Rent Registration

Owners are required to register the rents and services of apartments with DHCR. To complete the rent registration process, the owner must also serve a copy of the apartment registration form upon the tenant. The tenant may challenge the correctness of the apartment's rental as stated in the registration statement within 90 days of the date that the tenant is served by the owner. Challenge forms may be obtained at any District Rent Office listed on the Appendix to this Rider.

Failure to file a timely tenant challenge results in the rent, which is specified in the registration statement, being conclusively deemed to be the lawful rent for the apartment. However, the tenant's failure to challenge any data other than rent shall not be conclusive as to the correctness of such other data, and shall not prevent the tenant from challenging such other data at a future time. An annual update of this registration must be served on the tenant and filed with DHCR no later than September 3rd of each year.

Renewal Leases

Between 120 and 150 days before the end of a lease, the owner is required to notify the tenant in writing that the lease will soon expire. That notice must also offer the tenant the choice of a 1- or 2-year lease at the permissible guidelines increase. After receiving the notice, the tenant always has 60 days to accept the owner's offer, whether or not the offer is made within the above time period.

Any renewal lease, except for the increased rent and its length, is required to be on the same terms and conditions as the expired lease. Unless a fully executed copy of same is provided to the tenant within 30 days from the owner's receipt of the lease signed by the tenant, the owner may not collect a rent increase under the lease until such lease is provided. However, an owner may add to a renewal lease the following clauses, even if such clauses were not included in the tenant's prior lease:

(a) the rent may be adjusted by the owner on the basis of Rent Guidelines Board or DHCR orders;

(b) the owner may charge a vacancy allowance for a subtenant or assignee if the owner or the lease grants permission to sublet or assign provided the prime lease is a renewal lease. (Subletting will be discussed later in this Rider);

(c) (1) if the building in which the apartment is located is receiving tax abatement benefits pursuant to Section 421-a of the Real Property Tax Law, a clause may be added providing that the owner will be permitted to charge a free market rent upon the expiration of the tax abatement period. (Such clause must state the date on which the tax abatement period is scheduled to expire, and must be in at least 12 point type);

(2) if the building in which the apartment is located is subject to Rent Stabilization solely because the owner is receiving benefits pursuant to Section J51-2.5 of the Administrative Code of the City of New York, a clause may be added providing that the owner will be permitted to charge a free market rent upon the termination of such benefits;

(d) if the Attorney General, pursuant to Section 352-eeee of the General Business Law, has accepted for filing an eviction plan to convert the building to cooperative or condominium ownership, a clause may be added providing that the lease may be cancelled upon expiration of a 3-year period after the plan is declared effective. (The owner must give the tenant at least 90 days notice that the 3-year period has expired or will be expiring.)

If a tenant wishes to remain in occupancy beyond the expiration of the lease, the tenant may not refuse to sign a proper renewal lease.

An owner may refuse to offer a tenant a renewal lease only under certain conditions explained later in this Rider under the heading "When An Owner May Refuse To Renew A Lease."

Services

The owner may not decrease services which were provided or required on the date the apartment first became subject to the Rent Stabilization Law or which were added or required after that date.

Required services include building-wide services such as heat, hot water, janitorial service, maintenance of locks and security devices, and repair and maintenance, and may include elevators, air conditioning and other amenities. Upon a finding by DHCR that services are not being maintained on complaint of a tenant, a rent reduction shall be imposed and future rent increases shall be barred until the rent is restored.

Ancillary services provided by the owner, such as garage space or recreational facilities, whether provided with or without additional charge, may also not be decreased. Required services may also include services within the apartment, such as maintenance and repair of appliances and painting every 3 years.

Laws other than the Rent Stabilization Law also govern physical maintenance, health, safety, habitability, and sanitation standards. These laws include the Multiple Dwelling Law of the State of New York and the New York City Housing Maintenance Code. Housing code violation complaints may be made to the New York City Central Complaint Bureau.

Subletting and Assignment

A tenant may have the right to sublet his or her apartment, even if subletting is prohibited in the lease, provided that he or she complies strictly with the provisions of Real Property Law Section 226-b. To comply with Real Property Law Section 226-b, the tenant must do all of the following to assert his or her right to sublet:

(a) Notify the owner by certified mail, return receipt requested, that he or she intends to sublet. The request to sublet must contain all of the following information:

1. The term of the sublease;
2. The name of the proposed subtenant;
3. The business and permanent home address of the proposed subtenant;
4. The tenant's reason for subletting;
5. The tenant's address for the term of the sublease;
6. The written consent of any co-tenant or guarantor of the lease; and
7. A copy of the proposed sublease, to which a copy of the tenant's lease should be attached if available, acknowledged by both the tenant and proposed subtenant as a true copy of the sublease.

(b) If within 10 days after the mailing of the tenant's request to sublet, the owner asks for additional information about the proposed subletting, the tenant must provide the additional information if the owner's request is not unduly burdensome.

(c) The owner must respond in writing to the tenant's request to sublet within 30 days after the mailing of tenant's request or after the mailing of the additional information asked for by the owner. If the owner does not send a written response within the 30-day period, the owner is deemed to have consented to the proposed subletting, and the tenant may proceed to sublet.

(d) If the owner has reasonable objections to the subletting and notifies the tenant in writing of his objections within the required 30 day period, the tenant cannot sublet, and the owner is not required to release the tenant from his or her lease.

(e) If the tenant believes that the owner's objections to subletting are unreasonable, the tenant may proceed to sublet in accordance with his or her request. A lawsuit may result from such action. If the court finds that the owner acted in bad faith by withholding consent, the tenant may recover court costs and attorney's fees.

If a tenant in occupancy under a renewal lease sublets his or her apartment, the owner may charge the tenant the rent the owner could have charged had the renewal lease been a vacancy lease. Thus, the rent increase is tied to the vacancy allowance available when the tenant's renewal lease commenced, but takes effect when the subletting takes place. If a tenant in occupancy under a vacancy lease sublets, the owner is not entitled to any rent increase during the subletting.

Additional Rules Which Apply When a Subletting Has Occurred:

(1) A tenant who sublets his or her apartment is entitled to the rent permitted under the Rent Stabilization Law, plus a 10% surcharge payable to the tenant if the apartment sublet is fully furnished with the tenant's furniture. Any additional rent, above such surcharge which the tenant charges the subtenant, shall be considered an overcharge which may subject the tenant to civil liability to the subtenant for three times the rent overcharge plus interest and attorney's fees.

(2) A tenant who sublets must maintain the apartment as his or her primary residence and must intend to reoccupy it as a primary residence when the sublease expires.

(3) A tenant who sublets his or her apartment retains the right to renew the lease. The subtenant does not have a right to renew the lease. A tenant may sublet his or apartment for a term which extends beyond the end of the lease. It is unreasonable for an owner to refuse to consent to a sublease solely because it extends beyond the end of the tenant's lease.

(4) A tenant who sublets his or her apartment retains the right to purchase the shares of the apartment if the building is converted to cooperative or condominium ownership.

(5) The subletting may not be for more than a total of two years out of the four-year period preceding the expiration of the sublease, (for sublets occurring on or after July 1, 1983).

(6) Any provision in a tenant's lease which prohibits subletting or waives the tenant's right to sublet is illegal and unenforceable.

(7) A tenant who sublets his apartment remains the one primarily responsible to the owner for the payment of rent, and all obligations of the lease.

A tenant who does not comply with the rules regarding subletting may forfeit the right to a renewal lease or even be subject to eviction by the owner.

Assignment of Leases

In an assignment, a tenant transfers the entire remainder of his or her lease to another person (the assignee), and gives up all of his or her rights to reoccupy the apartment.

Pursuant to the provisions of Real Property Law Section 226-b, a tenant may not assign his or her lease without the written consent of the owner, unless the lease expressly provides otherwise. An owner is not required to have reasonable grounds to refuse to consent to the assignment. However, if the owner unreasonably refuses consent, the owner must release the tenant from the remainder of the lease, if the tenant, upon 30 days notice to the owner, requests to be released.

If the owner refuses to consent to an assignment and does have reasonable grounds for withholding consent, the tenant cannot assign and the owner is not required to release the tenant from the lease.

When An Owner May Refuse To Renew a Lease

So long as a tenant pays the lawful rent to which the owner is entitled, the tenant, except for the specific instances set forth herein, is entitled to remain in the apartment. An owner may not harass a tenant by engaging in an intentional course of conduct intended to make the tenant move from his or her apartment.

However, the owner may refuse to renew a lease and bring an action in Civil Court at the expiration of the lease on the following grounds:

(a) the tenant refuses to sign a proper renewal lease offered by the owner;

(b) the owner seeks the apartment in good faith for personal use or the personal use of members of the owner's immediate family.

However, if the tenant or the tenant's spouse is 62 years of age or older, or the tenant or the tenant's spouse is handicapped, the owner must offer to provide, and if requested provide, an equivalent or superior dwelling unit at the same or lower stabilized rent in a closely proximate area;

(c) the apartment is owned by a hospital, convent, monastery, asylum, public institution, college, school dormitory or any institution operated exclusively for charitable or educational purposes on a non-profit basis and the institution requires the apartment for its charitable or educational purposes. The institution must first send a 120-day notice of intention not to renew the tenant's lease.

(1) If the institution seeks the apartment for related residential purposes the following limitations apply:

(A) the institution may not refuse to renew the lease if the tenant took occupancy before the institution acquired the property;

(B) even if the tenant took occupancy after the institution acquired the property, the institution may not refuse to renew the lease of a tenant who took occupancy before July 1, 1978, unless the tenant received notice at the time he or she signed his or her original lease that the tenancy was subject to non-renewal.

(2) If the institutional owner requires the apartment for related non-residential use, then the limitations set forth in c(1) A & B above do not apply.

(d) The tenant does not occupy the apartment as his or her primary residence. However, an owner may not require, unless the tenant wishes to do so voluntarily, that as a condition of renewal, the tenant execute an affidavit of primary residence.

Grounds for Refusing to Renew a Lease Which Require Prior Approval From DHCR:

There are additional grounds for refusing to renew a lease which require approval from DHCR. A tenant will be served with a copy of the owner's application and have a right to object. These grounds include:

(a) where the owner seeks in good faith to recover possession of the apartments for the purpose of demolishing them and constructing a new building, or

(b) where the owner requires the apartment or the land for his or her own use in connection with a business which he or she owns and operates.

If the owner's application is granted, the owner may bring an action in Civil Court after sending a 30 day notice to the tenant, provided the tenant's lease has already expired.

Eviction While the Lease is in Effect

If an action is brought in Civil Court to evict a tenant during the term of the lease, the tenant will receive notice of the action and of the tenant's right to answer and appear in court.

The owner may only bring such an action in court to evict a tenant because a tenant:

(a) does not pay rent.
(b) is violating a substantial obligation of the tenancy.
(c) is committing or permitting a nuisance.
(d) is illegally using or occupying the apartment.
(e) has unlawfully refused the owner access.
(f) is occupying an apartment in a cooperative or condominium under an eviction plan. A non-purchasing tenant in a non-eviction plan may not be evicted except on the grounds set forth in (a)—(e) above. *(See subdivision (d) of the paragraph titled "Renewal Leases.")*

Tenants are cautioned that causing violations of health, safety or sanitation standards of housing maintenance laws, or permitting such violations by a member of the family or household or by a guest may be the basis for such a court action by the owner.

Cooperative and Condominium Conversion

Any cooperative or condominium plan accepted for filing by the New York State Attorney General's Office will include specific information about tenant rights and protections. An information booklet about the general subject of conversion is available from the New York State Attorney General's Office.

Senior Citizens' and Disabled Persons' Benefits

Tenants or their spouses who are 62 years of age, or older and whose "net" household income is not over $10,000 per year may qualify for an exemption from guidelines rent increases or hardship increases. The exemption will be only from that portion of the increases which causes the tenant's rent to exceed one-third of the "net" household income.

The exemption is not available for increases based on new services or equipment within the apartment or for any rent increase based upon a major capital improvement. When renewing a lease, a senior citizen eligible for an exemption or eligible to renew an existing exemption has to request a 2-year lease. When a senior citizen is granted a rent increase exemption, the owner may obtain a real estate tax credit from New York City equal to the tenant's exemption.

Notwithstanding any of the above, a senior citizen who receives a rent increase exemption is still required to pay a full month's rent as a security deposit.

Senior citizens and disabled persons in buildings which are being converted to cooperative or condominium ownership may also be eligible for exemption, in an eviction plan, from any requirement that tenants must purchase their apartment to remain in occupancy. This exemption is available to senior citizens or to disabled persons with impairments expected to be permanent, which prevent the tenant from engaging in any substantial gainful employment. A conversion plan accepted for filing by the New York State Attorney General's Office will contain specific information on this right.

Special Cases and Exceptions

Some special rules relating to stabilization rents and required services may apply to newly constructed buildings which receive tax abatement or exemption and to buildings rehabilitated under certain New York City, New York State or federal financing or mortgage insurance programs. The rules mentioned in this Rider specifically do not apply to hotel units or units subject to the hotel stabilization system.

Appendix

Some Agencies Which Can Provide Assistance

New York State Division of Housing and Community Renewal (DHCR)

The DHCR is a state agency empowered to administer and enforce the Rent Stabilization Law and the Rent Control Law. Tenants should contact the District Rent Offices for assistance.

All telephone numbers are area code 212 unless otherwise designated.

Office of Rent Administration

10 Columbus Circle, 11th Floor, New York, New York 10019	903-9550
Registration Hot Line	488-3746
Small Business Owner Assistance Unit	903-9555

District Rent Offices:

Lower Manhattan
(South side of 110 St. and below):
2 Lafayette Street, 12th Floor
New York, New York 10007
Tel. 566-7970

Upper Manhattan
(North side of 110 St. and above):
215 West 125th Street, 5th Floor
New York, New York 10027
Tel. 678-2201

Bronx:
260 East 161 Street, 8th Floor
Bronx, New York 10451
Tel. 585-2600

Brooklyn:
91 Lawrence Street, 2nd Floor
Brooklyn, New York 11201
Tel. (718) 643-7570

Queens:
164-19 Hillside Avenue, Ground Floor
Jamaica, New York 11432
Tel. (718) 526-2040

Staten Island:
350 St. Mark's Place, Ground Floor
Staten Island, New York 10301
Tel. (718) 816-0277

Attorney General of the State of New York—Two World Trade Center, New York, New York 10047

Consumer Frauds and Protection Bureau 488-7530
—investigates and enjoins illegal or fraudulent business practices, including the overcharging of rent and mishandling of rent security deposits by owners.

Real Estate Financing Bureau 488-3310
—administers and enforces the laws governing cooperative and condominium conversions. Investigates complaints from tenants in buildings undergoing cooperative or condominium conversion, concerning allegations of improper disclosure, harassment and misleading information.

New York City Department of Housing Preservation and Development (HPD):

Office of Rent and Housing Maintenance
100 Gold Street, Room 8170, New York, New York 10038
—provides owners with assistance on housing matters. 566-3918
—provides tenants considering court action to enforce housing maintenance standards with assistance at 125 Church Street, 3rd Floor, New York, NY 10007 566-6222

Senior Citizen Rent Increase Exemption Program (SCRIE)
17 John Street, 4th Floor, New York, NY 10038 566-5414 or 5413
—administers SCRIE Program

New York City Central Complaint Bureau
215 West 125th Street, New York, New York 10027 960-4800
—receives telephone complaints relating to physical maintenance, health, safety and sanitation standards, including emergency heat and hot water service.

New York City Rent Guidelines Board (RGB)
51 Chambers Street, Room 201, New York, New York 10007 349-2262
—promulgates annual percentage of rent increases for rent stabilized apartments and provides information on guidelines orders.

Copies of New York State and New York City rent laws are available in the business section of some public libraries. Telephone or write to a public library to determine the exact library which has such legal material.

Administrator's Interpretations

EMERGENCY OPERATIONAL BULLETIN 85-1

(Issued December 10, 1985)

Succession—Right to Renew A Lease
In A Rent Stabilized Housing Accommodation

Introduction

This Operational Bulletin has been prepared to establish the conditions under which tenants of Rent Stabilized housing accommodations are entitled to renew leases or rental agreements for Rent Stabilized accomodations located inside New York City.

1. An owner of a rent stabilized housing accommodation is required to offer a tenant and his or her immediate family the automatic right to renew his or her lease for one or two years. The owner may charge a Rent Guidelines Board Increase based on the length of the renewal lease term which the tenant selects, but the renewal lease must be on the same terms and conditions as the expiring lease, except for the special clauses which the Stabilization Law or Code permits the owner to add.

2. An owner of a rent stabilized housing accommodation is required to offer a non-immediate family member as defined herein, who has continuously resided in the dwelling unit as a primary resident since the commencement of the tenancy, or the beginning of the relationship, the right to first refusal of a new lease. In the event the non-immediate family member accepts a lease, the owner may charge the maximum legal rent allowed.

3. At the owner's option, a new lease may be offered at the maximum legal rent to an occupant of a rent stabilized housing accommodation other than the tenant, immediate family, or non-immediate family member as herein defined, in the event the tenant listed on the initial lease is no longer in occupancy.

Definitions

Tenant

For housing accommodations other than hotels, the named tenant on the lease or rental agreement, or any member of the tenant's immediate family who has continuously resided in the dwelling unit as a primary resident since the commencement of the tenancy or the beginning of the relationship as a member of the immediate family.

Notwithstanding the foregoing, where the named tenant or member of his or her immediate family is a senior citizen or disabled person a tenant shall also include a member of the immediate family as defined herein, provided that such family member has maintained his or her primary residence at the dwelling unit for the purpose of providing health care to such individual, for one year prior to the date that such individual either dies or permanently vacates such dwelling unit and has no legal right to occupy another rent regulated dwelling unit in the State of New York. A tenant shall also include a senior citizen of disabled person who establishes residence with a member of his or her immediate family, provided that such senior citizen or disabled person has maintained his or her primary residence at the dwelling unit of such family member, for the purpose of receiving health care from such family member, for one year prior to the date that such family member either dies or permanently vacates such dwelling unit, and has no legal right to occupy another rent regulated dwelling unit in the State of New York.

Renewal Lease

For housing accommodations other than hotels upon the expiration of a prior lease or rental agreement, the tenant shall have the right of one or two years, except that where a mortgage or a mortgage commitment existing as of April 1, 1984, prohibits the granting of one year lease terms or the tenant is the recipient of a Senior Citizen Rent Increase Exemption pursuant to Sections YY51-4.1 and 4.1.1 of the Administrative Code of the City of New York, the tenant may not select a one year lease.

Immediate Family

A husband, wife, son, daughter, stepson, stepdaughter, father, mother.

Non-Immediate Family Member

A brother, sister, nephew, niece, uncle, aunt, grandfather, grandmother, grandson, granddaughter, father-in-law, mother-in-law, son-in-law, daughter-in-law.

ADMINISTRATOR'S INTERPRETATIONS

Senior Citizen

A person who is sixty-two years of age or older.

Disabled Person

A person who has an impairment which results from anatomical, physiological or psychological conditions, other than addiction to alcohol, gambling, or any controlled substance, which are demonstrable by medically acceptable clinical and laboratory diagnostic techniques, and which are expected to be permanent.

OPERATIONAL BULLETIN 85-2

Rent Increases for Rent Stabilized Housing Accommodations Based Upon Owner Hardship-Guidelines and Procedures.
(Issued September 9, 1985)

INTRODUCTION

This Operational Bulletin relates to increases in the legal regulated rents of rent stabilized housing accommodations located inside and outside New York City which may be available to owners who file hardship applications with the New York State Division of Housing and Community Renewal (DHCR). The DHCR may grant such increases pursuant to the Emergency Tenant Protection Act of 1974 (ETPA), or Title YY of the New York City Administrative Code, which constitutes the New York City Rent Stabilization Law (RSL).

A. DEFINITION OF HARDSHIP

The ETPA and RSL provide a mechanism for adjusting rents pursuant to orders issued by the Local Rent Guidelines Boards, which determine, on an annual basis, the rent increase, if any, to which an owner is entitled upon execution of new or renewal leases. Both the ETPA and RSL also provide, in the unusual situation, where the guidelines rent adjustments are insufficient to permit a particular property to keep up with increased operating costs, that the onwer can file with the DHCR, an application for building-wide rent increases based upon a hardship. Both the ETPA and RSL contain provisions for a "comparative hardship" pursuant to which an owner may obtain a rent increase sufficient to maintain the same postiion with respect to certain income and operating expenses as it experienced in defined base years. The precise statutory formulas are markedly different inside, as opposed to outside, New York City. The procedures for processing these applications are of long standing and have been established through usage and practice.

Chapter 403 of the Laws of 1983, which amended both the ETPA and RSL, provides an alternative method for determining a hardship increase based essentially on an owner's maintaining certain gross rent income, as later defined, at a level which exceeds reasonable operating expenses by five percent.

B. COMPARATIVE HARDSHIP OUTSIDE OF NEW YORK CITY

The comparative hardship formula is stated in Section 6(4) of the ETPA.

It essentially provides that: 1) an owner must establish, by application, the existence of a hardship as further defined, and 2) the DHCR must determine whether additional rent increases are needed to maintain approximately the same average ratio (as defined by usage and upheld by applicable appellate case law) between operating expenses and gross rents for the preceding five year period. The criteria for determining such an application are detailed in Section 34(c), [2502.4(c)], of the Tenant Protection Regulations, Tenant Protection Bulletin No. 20 and Supplement 1 thereto.

C. COMPARATIVE HARDSHIP INSIDE NEW YORK CITY

Inside New York City the comparative hardship formula is set forth in Section YY51-6.0 c (6) of the Administrative Code of the City of New York, and is administered primarily through the Rent Stabilization Code. Pursuant thereto DHCR will, in essence, grant an appropriate rent adjustment where:

1. The owner has not maintained the same average net income in a current three year period when compared with the average net income during a three year base period, generally defined as 1968 through 1970;

2. The circumstances and accuracy of the information provided in the owner's application has been adequately substantiated by submission of copies of certified financial statements or federal income tax returns

Administrator's Interpretations

and other pertinent documents which might be required; and

3. All other requirements of the granting of such rent increases have been met.

To restore the onwer's average net income in the current period to the average net income in the base period, the rent adjustment granted by the DHCR, in order to conform with the Rent Stabilization Code, is computed as follows:

1. Subtract the average net income in the current period from the average net income in the base period (after adjustments).

2. The result represents the dollar amount of annual gross rent adjustment.

3. To convert the dollar amount into a percentage rent increase, divide the dollar amount by the annual gross rent roll of the stabilized apartments submitted with the application. (The rent roll should be dated within two (2) months of the date of the filing of the application).

The collection of any increase in the stabilized rent for any apartment cannot exceed six (6) percent in any year from the effective date of the order granting the increase, over the rent set forth in the schedule of gross rents. The collectibility of any dollar excess above said sum is spread forward in similar increments and added to the stabilized rents as established or set in future years. No more than one order adjusting any stabilization rent because of hardship may be issued in any thirty-six (36) month period.

D. ALTERNATIVE HARDSHIP

Rent increase applications may be filed by owners based upon alternative hardship applications pursuant to Section 6(5) of the Emergency Tenant Protection Act, (EPTA) and Section YY51-6.9c. (6-a) of the New York City Administrative Code. Section 6(5) of the ETPA is directly implemented by Section 34(d), [2502.4(d)], of the Tenant Protection Regulations. The alternative hardship enables an owner of a building not owned as a cooperative or condominium, acquired by the same owner or a related entity three years prior to any application, to receive an appropriate rent adjustment where the DHCR finds (subject to the definitions and restrictions stated in the regulations) that such an increase is necessary because the annual operating expenses are not less than 95 per cent of the annual gross rent income (the actual income receivable per annum arising out of the operation and ownership of the property). The new total gross annual rent income is determined by dividing the annual operating expenses by 95 percent. The nature and source of annual gross rent income is set forth in Section 34 (d)(1)(a), [2502.4 d(1)(i)], of the Tenant Protection Regulations. The instructions and application forms previously issued by the DHCR reflect these regulations.

ALTERNATIVE HARDSHIP FORMS AND PROCEDURES

The following is designed to give further guidance as to the DHCR policy and procedure in processing these applications after the forms are completed by owners in accordance with the instructions and the applicable Regulations. Instructions which accompany the forms referred to in this operational bulletin, provide further details.

The DHCR has broad discretion under the applicable regulations to, *inter alia,* accept or reject applications, extend time for filing, hold hearings, and require production of documents. See Sections 85 and 86, [2507.5], [2507.6], of the Tenant Protection Regulations. In the absence of a Rent Stabilization Code containing Alternative Hardship Provisions, the DHCR has authority and discretion in accordance with Chapter 403 of the Laws of 1983 to utilize reasonable procedures in carrying out its statutory mandate. Nothing herein should be construed as a waiver of that discretion. This bulletin advises on how that discretion will ordinarily be exercised.

A. APPLICABLE FORMS

RTP45, RTP45A-G Owner's Application for Rent Increase Based on Alternative Hardship
RTP 45.1 Notice to Tenant of Commencement of Proceeding for Rent Increase based on an Alternative Hardship
RTP 45.2 Instructions for filing an owner's

Administrator's Interpretations

	Application for Rent Increase based on Alternative Hardship
RTP 45.3	Owner's Certification of Service of Notice to Tenant; Re Commencement of Proceeding for Rent Increase based on Alternative Hardship RTP 45.5
RTP 45.4	Instructions for Notifying the tenants that a Proceeding for a Rent Increase based on an Alternative Hardship has been commenced.
RTP 3	Tenant's Answer
RAR 1, RAR 2 (PAR)	Petition for Administrative Review

B. PROCEDURE

I. *Docketing:*

An owner shall file three copies of the application form including appropriate schedules (RTP45, RTP45A through G) with the District Rent Office (DRO) in the district in which the building is located. The DRO will assign the application a docket number.

II. *Preliminary Review:*

The DHCR will then perform a preliminary review of the application to determine whether the application on its face indicates eligibility for an alternative hardship increase. To affirmatively pass such review:

(1) the building, as evidenced by the application, must be experiencing a hardship as defined in Section 34(d)(1), [2502.4(d)(1)], of the Tenant Protection Regulations. (See RTP45D of the application forms);

(2) the owner must answer a series of threshold questions which further determine if the onwer has met all the requirements which otherwise may bar the owner from filing or receiving increase (See Section 34(d)(2), [2502.4(d)(2)], of the Tenant Protection Regulations entitled Restrictions; see also RTP 45A, B, and C of the application forms); and

(3) all the forms must be completed and all relevant supporting schedules attached.

If the application is not complete, the DHCR will reject it and return two copies of the submission to the owner. Such a rejection is a Final Order subject to review by the

Administrator's Interpretations

Commissioner. (PAR) (See Sections 131-142, [2510 *et seq.*], of the Tenant Protection Regulations, and Part XI of this Operational Bulletin) However, the rejection is without prejudice to refiling a completed application with the DRO, as a new application with a new filing date, provided the owner is still eligible to use the same test year as defined in Section 34(d)(1)(g), [2502.4(d)(1)(vii)], of the Tenant Protection Regulations. For good cause shown, the DHCR may, in exceptional cases, provide a reasonable cure period in its rejection which would enable an owner to preserve his right to use a particular test year. See section 85(d), [2507.5(d)], of the Tenant Protection Regulations. If the application passes preliminary review the owner shall be notified on Form RTP45.5, that he may thereafter notify the affected tenants that an alternative hardship proceeding has been commenced.

III. *Restrictions:*

The restrictions against filing or receiving an alternative hardship increase are fully set forth in Section 34(d)(2), [2502.4(d)(2)] of the Tenant Protection Regulations. They are listed below, with further explanations where appropriate.

a) Maintenance of Services.

Section 34(d)(2)(b), [2502.4(d)(2)(ii)], of the Tenant Protection Regulations sets forth the DHCR's broad discretionary authority with respect to alternative hardship and the requirement of maintenance of services. That discretion is limited by § YY51-6.0.3 which specifically bars an owner from applying for or collecting further rent increases upon a determination by the DHCR that an owner has failed to maintain services as defined therein. Thus, where the DHCR has issued an order determining that an owner has failed to maintain services as defined in the applicable law and regulations, the DHCR may not grant an alternative hardship application pending service complaints or tenant answers which raise lack of maintenance of services as an issue do not, in and of themselves bar the hardship application or the granting of an increase. The DHCR will act with respect to those applications in accordance with its discretionary authority and may issue an order granting the increase conditioned on the removal of violations or conditions affecting services.

b) Pending tax certiorari proceedings or objections: Section 34(d)(2)(a)(v), [2502.4(d)(2)(i)(e)], of the Tenant Protection Regulations provides for the resolution of legal objections to real estate taxes and water and sewer charges for the test year. This restriction is derived from the requirement that the applicable increase be based on expenses that are both actual and reasonable, as well as the DHCR's authority to safeguard tenants from practices which would otherwise subvert the levels of rent adjustment as provided by the applicable law. In lieu of an absolute bar, the DHCR as a reasonable alternative, will accept submission by an owner, of applicable proof of taxes based upon the proposed assessed value (as set forth in its certiorari petition or duly field objection to such tax), together with proof of actual payment in accordance with applicable law. If after such tax objection is resolved, the owner's actual and reasonable tax expense allocable to the test year exceeds the amount the DHCR used in determining the application, an additional increase may be granted prospectively, if warranted. Similar reasonable alternatives will be entertained as to unresolved water and sewer charges.

c) Ownership by the same or related entity for 36 months: Section 34(d)(2)(a)(ii), [2502.4(d)(2)(i)(b)], of the Tenant Protection Regulations sets forth the requirement that an owner or an entity related to the owner must have acquired the building at least 36 months prior to the date of the application in order to be eligible for alternative hardship increases. A cooperative corporation or the Board of Managers of a condominium will not be considered the owner of the building, nor are individual shareholders or unit owners building owners for the purpose of eligibility for the alternative hardship, and as such will be unable to file alternative hardship applications.

d) Five percent equity in the property: Owners' equity is defined in Section 34(d)(1)(e), [2502.4(d)(1)(v)], of the Tenant Protection Regulations. That equity must exceed five per cent of the sum of the amounts listed in Section 34(d)(2)(a)(iii), [2502.4(d)(2)(i)(c)] of the Tenant Protection Regulations. (See Form RTP 45B.) Owners will generally

Administrator's Interpretations

satisfy this requirement and avoid the more complex statutory calculations required, if the arms length purchase price of their property, less the unrepaid principal of any loan or mortgage used to finance the purchase of the property exceeds five percent of the arms length purchase price. (The precise formulation is set forth in Form RTP 45A, question 5 though 9 and the applicable instructions therefor).

e) The grant of a previous hardship increase: Section 34(d)(2)(a)(iv), [2502.4(d)(2)(i)(d)], of the Tenant Protection Regulations has the effect of prohibiting the filing or granting of an application where the building had been granted a hardship increase within 36 months of the effective date of the issuance of a previous hardship application order, or if a six percent increase is still in effect based on a prior application.

IV. *Owner Notification to Affected Tenants:*

Within twenty days of receipt of the RTP45.4, the owner must hand deliver or mail a complete set of the application forms submitted to the DHCR, to the affected tenants, plus a DHCR notice of the Proceeding (RTP45.1) and 3 copies of the DHCR answer form (RTP3).

A complete copy of the owner's submission to the DHCR including all required schedules and all supporting documentation plus a copy of the DHCR's Instruction Booklet (RTP45.2) must be made available at the DRO and at the subject building or complex in the office of the resident manager, managing agent or superintendent during normal working hours. If such office is not available on site, these documents must be made available at a near-by alternative location. If such location is not available, as attested to by affidavit of the owner, such documents may be inspected at the DRO.

V. *Filing of the Application with the DHCR:*

After completing notification to the affected tenants, the owner must then complete and file with the appropriate DRO the DHCR's form "Owner's Certification of Service" (RTP-45.3). The date that this form is received by the appropriate DRO will be considered the date of completion of filing with the DHCR. The DHCR will, where necessary, take appropriate action to verify the accuracy of the owner's certification of service. At the time of filing the RTP-45.3, the owner must also submit a certified rent roll as of the date of the filing of the application.

VI. *Tenant Answer:*

Tenants shall submit two copies of their answers, if any, to the appropriate DRO within twenty days of receipt unless, for good cause shown, an extension is granted by the District Rent Office.

VII. *Mortgage interest as an includable expense and its impact on processing:*

The alternative hardship, unlike the two comparative hardship formulas, allows for the inclusion of interest on a bona fide mortgage as an allowable expense in computing the appropriate rent adjustment. (See Section 34(d)(1) (b), (c), and (d), [2502.4(d)(1)-(ii)(iii) and (iv)], of the Tenant Protection Regulations; Form RTP45E and instructions therefor.) Even where the mortgage is "bona fide", as defined by Sections 34(d)(1)(c) and (d), [2502.4(d)(1)(iii) and (iv)], of the Tenant Protection Regulations, the DHCR on its own initiative where warranted, or in the face of a meaningful tenant objection, will also ascertain whether the claimed mortgage interest expense is reasonable, actual, applicable to the operation and maintenance of property, reasonably allocable to the test year and in keeping with the general legislative purposes and intent.

Because mortgage interest, as an allowable expense, is a new feature belonging solely to this hardship, adjudication of mortgage interest expense issues can only be further defined by a case by case determination. Where a unique and unprecedented issue regarding claimed mortgage interest expense is raised in a meaningful manner it will be reviewed by a mortgage interest committee established by the DHCR to aid the District Rent Administrator (DRA) or the Director of Processing in his determination. However, two general examples of proposed adjudications by the DHCR are set forth below:

Example 1

Where there has been a change in mortgage debt since the effective date of the addition of the alternative hardship provisions to the applicable law, the

Administrator's Interpretations

DHCR will make appropriate adjustments to the claimed mortgage interest expense, to disallow interest on that portion of the principal balance of the current mortgage which exceeds the expiring balance of the previous mortgage. This will assure that the mortgage interest expense reflects the actual and reasonable cost of maintenance of the property. Monies otherwise utilized from refinancing for the operation and maintenance of the property, to the extent compensable by application, is covered by Operational Bulletin 84-4, issued November 13, 1984, entitled "Major Capital Improvements/Substantial Rehabilitation/Increased Services and Equipment" and the applicable law, code and regulations cited therein.

Example 2

Points and other charges payable during the test year which represent prepayment of interest (and are therefore a non-recurring expense) will be allocated over the term of the mortgage, or a reasonable period, to more accurately reflect the reasonable and actual expenses of the operation and maintenance of the property. In addition, they will be adjusted to reflect that portion of the mortgage expense allowed for mortgage interest computations.

VIII. *Issuance of the Order:*

The DRA or the Director of Processing, after taking all necessary and appropriate action, shall issue a determination either dismissing the application if it fails to substantially comply with the provisions of the Regulations, or granting the application, in whole or in part.

In the event an application is granted, the collection of any rent increase shall not exceed six percent of the legal regulated rent in effect on the filing of the application. The collectibility of any amount above that sum shall be spread forward in similar increments and added to the rent as established or set in future years. In buildings containing residential apartment units subject to Rent Control or otherwise exempt from regulation, adjustments for both income and expenses will be made to calculate the appropriate share for those apartments subject to this application. No application may be made for any hardship until such time as the increase based on a prior hardship application falls below six per cent for a given year. In no event may an application for hardship be made within thirty-six months of the effective date of the issuance of a previous hardship application order.

IX. *Effective Date of the Order:*

In New York city, the DHCR will use the Rent Stabilization Code to ascertain the effective dates of any order granting an increase, with due consideration to all factors bearing on the equities involved, as required by the Rent Stabilization Code.

The effective date of the rent increase for buildings located outside of New York City is governed by Section 32, [2502.2], of the Tenant Protection Regulations, which provides that adjustments of legal regulated rents are effective as of the date of the issuance of the order unless the order itself provides otherwise. Rent increases shall be expressed on a percentage basis.

X. *Petition for Administrative Review (PAR):*

A PAR is the method of review of a DRA or Director of Processing order and is a prerequisite in order to obtain judicial review.

Any person aggrieved by an order of a DRA or a Director of Processing may file a PAR (Forms RAR-1 and 2) within 33 days after the date of such order. A PAR served by mail, postmarked not more than thirty-three days after the date of such order, shall be deemed in compliance with this paragraph. See Tenant Protection Bulletin 84-1 and Sections 8 and 131-143, [2500.8, 2510 *et seq.*], of the Tenant Protection Regulations for the relevant procedure by the DHCR upon administrative review.[1]

OPERATIONAL BULLETIN NO. 86-1

(January 14, 1986)

Summary Of Guideline Rates Of Maximum Rent Increases Filed By County And New York City Rent Guide-

---

[1] Pursuant to Chapter 888 of the Laws of 1985, the DHCR has been authorized to amend the Rent Stabilization Code for New York City. At such time as the amended Code is promulgated, the DHCR will issue a supplement to this Bulletin providing cross references for the new Code to the ETPA Regulations contained in this Bulletin.

Administrator's Interpretations

lines Boards For Leases Commencing Between October 1, 1985 and September 30, 1986

	*Rockland County	**Nassau County	***Westchester County	****New York City
1. One-Year Lease	4.5%	4.5%	6%	4.0%
2. Two-Year Lease	7.0%	6.5%	10%	6.5%

The guidelines shall be applied to the base rent without tax or cost escalating factors, unless stated otherwise in the specific guidelines order.

All counties outside New York City require that owners file operating expense statements for eligibility to collect any guideline rent increases.

Rockland County

When a vacancy occurs, the owner shall be allowed to increase the rent level for that housing accommodation to the highest legal regulated rent as of October 1, 1985, of a housing accommodation in the same building or complex having the same number of rooms or by a factor of 5% *whichever is lower.*

This base rent is then established for housing accommodations in this building or complex having the same number of rooms *for the balance of the guideline year.*

The allowable guideline rent increase shall be added to this base rent provided further that the owner shall fully recite in the lease the designation and location of the housing accommodation having the same number of rooms and the highest legal regulated rent.

** Nassau County

Where a vacant apartment is rented to a new tenant, an additional guideline, not to exceed *one month's prior legal regulated rent,* may be charged, to be paid by the tenant in equal monthly installments over the term of the lease selected by the tenant. This additional guideline may still be taken if the landlord has filed or files an application with the State Division of Housing and Community Renewal (DHCR) or otherwise obtains a rent adjustment based upon the installation of new equipment to replace existing equipment.

In order for the vacancy allowance to be collectible, the owner must file a certification with DHCR affirming that at least one month's prior rent has been spent preparing the apartment for the incoming tenant. The affirmation part of the certification should conform substantially to the certification used on the owner survey schedule filed with the DHCR; and a copy of this certification must be attached to the incoming tenant's lease.

In general, all expenses associated with the rental to a new tenant may be included in the cost of preparing the apartment. Thus, the cost of painting, cleaning, replacing and refinishing wood floors, venetian blinds, kitchen floors and bathroom tiles, window washing, and exterminating are includable. Other non-includable expenses are lease preparation, rental expense, rental agent, advertising, and any labor of the owner's own employees performed as part of their regular job. Loss of rent, however, is not an includable expense unless the owner can demonstrate that the prior tenant did not vacate in time for the owner to prepare the apartment before the expiration of the lease or tenancy; and that the new tenant's rent was proportionately reduced based on the days lost due to preparation of the apartment.

Only one permanent vacancy allowance may be charged for an apartment in the twelve (12) month guidelines period. A temporary vacancy allowance of one (1) month's prior legal regulated rent may be surcharged a subsequent vacancy tenant notwithstanding that a permanent vacancy allowance was collected within the 12 months guidelines period but only when a new certification of expenditures is filed with the DHCR, and a copy is attached to the incoming tenant's lease. This temporary vacancy allowance shall only be collectible during the term of the lease and shall not become part of the legal regulated rent for purposes of computing subsequent rent increases.

Where the legal regulated rent includes *electric and gas* service, the owner may charge an additional 2% guideline rate, which shall not become part of the legal regulated rent. This rate is only applicable to accommodations in solely residential buildings.

Administrator's Interpretations

Where the tenant pays for heat, the guideline authorized shall be reduced by 1% for one year leases and 1.5% for two year leases.

*** *Westchester County*

No additional guideline rent increase when renting a vacant apartment to a new tenant.

**** *New York City* (Rent Guidelines Board Order Number 17)

The following is a summary of orders established by the New York City Rent Guidelines Board for leases commencing between October 1, 1985 and September 30, 1986.

1. *ADJUSTMENTS* These guidelines are also applicable to buildings receiving partial tax exemption pursuant to Sections 421 and 423 of the Real Property Tax Law.

For the purposes of these guidelines, any lease or tenancy for a period of less than one year shall be deemed a one year lease or tenancy; any lease or tenancy for a period in excess of one year and up to and including two years, shall be deemed a two year lease or tenancy.

A. *FOR RENEWAL LEASES*

   1. One-year lease .... 4.0% over 9/30/85 lawful rents.
   2. Two-year lease .... 6.5% over 9/30/85 lawful rents.

B. *FOR VACANCY LEASES*

The same adjustment as for renewal leases (A. above) plus 7½%, except no vacancy allowance is permitted:

(1) where there was a new tenancy during the 10/1/84–9/30/85 guidelines year (Guidelines 16), unless no vacancy allowance was permitted pursuant to Guidelines 16; or

(2) in a building of over 50 units in which 10% or more of the units were vacant for the 60 days preceding the commencement of the lease.

No more than one vacancy lease allowance may be collected during the term of this guidelines order (October 1, 1985 to September 30, 1986).

C. *SUPPLEMENTARY ADJUSTMENT*

For a lease for a housing accommodation with a lawful monthly rent of less than $300.00 on 9/30/85, the levels of rent increase shall be the same as for a renewal or vacancy lease (as in 1A and B above) plus $15.00 per month, provided that the resulting monthly rental does not exceed:

1) for a renewal lease or a vacancy lease where the 7.5% allowance does not apply

    for a one-year lease $312.00

    for a two-year lease $319.50

2) for a vacancy lease where the 7.5% vacancy allowance applies

    for a one-year lease $334.59

    for a one-year lease $342.00

D. ELECTRICAL INCLUSION ADJUSTMENT

For the lease of a housing accommodation in which the rent includes electrical service, no additional increase shall be allowed

E. ARTICLE 7-C OF THE MULTIPLE DWELLING LAW

For renewal and vacancy leases, the rate of rent increase above the base rent (as defined by Section 286, paragraph 4 of the Multiple Dwelling Law (MDL) shall be the same as those above (1A and B) for renewal and vacancy leases, except that for purposes of the provision prohibiting the 7.5% vacancy allowance in buildings of more than 50 units in which more than 10% of the units were vacant for the 60 days preceding the commencement of the lease, only residential units covered by Article 7-C of the MDL or those that have had a residential certificate of occupancy issued for the unit shall be counted.

F. SPECIAL GUIDELINE (FAIR MARKET RENT)

For housing accommodations subject to the Rent and Rehabilitation Law on 9/30/85, which subsequently become vacant, and where the tenant has filed a Fair Market Rent Appeal, the special guideline's criterion is 20% above the sum of the 1984-1985 maximum base rent as it existed or would have existed, plus the current allowable fuel adjustments as established on Rent Control forms pursuant to Section 33.10 of the Rent and Eviction Regulations for New York City (9 NYCRR 2202.13), beginning in 1980.

G. DECONTROLLED UNITS

The permissible rent for decontrolled units as defined in Order 3a, which become decontrolled after 9/30/85, shall not exceed the formula outlined in (F) above.

Administrator's Interpretations

H. *FUEL*

No fuel cost adjustment is warranted for leases which commenced during the 10/1/82-9/30/83 guideline year (R.G.B.O. #14), the 10/1/83-9/30/84 guideline year (R.G.B.O. #15), or the 10/1/84-9/30/85 guideline year (R.G.B.O. #16).

I. *HOTELS* (Hotel Order #15)

The level of fair rent increases over the lawful rent actually charged and paid on June 30, 1985 shall be 2% for a new or renewal tenancy. If no lease is in effect, the effective date of the increase shall be the later of one year from the date the tenant commenced occupancy or one year from the date of the last level of fair rent increase charged to the tenant. Any resultant retroactive increase shall be collectible in monthly installments not exceeding one-half of the monthly increase permitted under the Order (if the rental period is other than monthly, the retroactive portion of the increase shall be prorated accordingly). In no event shall there be more than one guidelines increase during one guideline period.

The 2% increase is not applicable, however, to units in buildings of more than 30 units where more than 5% of the units are vacant for the 60 days preceding the effective date of Hotel Order Number 15, unless the owner can prove to the satisfaction of the DHCR that he has attempted in good faith to rent said units.

2. *ESCALATOR CLAUSES*

Where a lease which was in effect on 5/31/68 or, for a unit which became subject to the Rent Stabilization Law of 1969 pursuant to ETPA, which was in effect on 6/30/74, contained an escalator clause for increased costs of operation and which is still in effect, the lawful rent on 9/30/85 shall include the increased rental, if any, due under such clause except those charges which accrued within one year of the commencement of the renewal lease. Where a lease contains an escalator clause that the owner may validly renew under the Code, the increased rental, if any, due under such escalator clause shall be offset against the amount of increase authorized in Guidelines Order 17 unless such clause is deleted from the lease commencing during the Guidelines Order 17 period.

3. *STABILIZER*

The ½% "stabilizer" charged in leases pursuant to previous orders shall remain in effect until the expiration of such lease and shall be included in the base rent for the purpose of computing subsequent rents.

4. *CREDITS*

Rentals paid in excess of the rent increases established in these orders shall be fully credited against the next month's rent.

RENT ADMINISTRATOR'S OPERATIONAL BULLETINS

Operational Bulletin No. C-5 Supplement No 1—Expediting Proceedings before the District Rent Director
(Issued April 22, 1965)

In order that there be uniformity with respect to expediting proceedings pending in the several District Rent Offices, the following rules have been promulgated:

1. Cases which the rent examiner may expedite without prior clearance by the District Rent Director or his Deputy:

　a. Dangerous or hazardous conditions reported as a referral case by a City Code Enforcement Agency.

　b. Failure to provide heat or hot water during the cold weather months.

　c. Landlord's applications for rent increase due to tenant's installation of air-conditioner during summer months.

　d. Defective stoves.

　e. Applications for restoration of rents where repairs are made by a mortgagee in possession, receiver or a new owner.

　f. Applications for restoration of rents or for rehabilitation improvements where the New York City Department of Real Estate is receiver.

　g. Applications for first rents where rehabilitation aid loans have been granted to the owner by the New York City Housing and Redevelopment Board.

　h. Refrigerator complaints during warm weather months.

　i. Fires in rent controlled buildings.

　j. Rat infested buildings.

　k. Buildings vacated upon order of municipal authorities as a result of some emergency.

　l. Instances where a tenant has rented a vacant apartment and upon landlord's refusal to paint and decorate the apartment, the tenant has painted it at his own expense.

m. "Horror" cases in general. [Unit supervisor's approval shall be noted on Progress Sheet (Form N-7).]

2. Cases which the rent examiner may *not* expedite without prior clearance by the District Rent Director or his Deputy:

a. Any other type of action in which the District Rent Director or his Deputy considers to merit expedition. The prior written approval of the District Rent Director or his Deputy shall be noted on the case Progress Sheet (Form N-7) together with a notation indicating the basis for such action.

Operational Bulletin No. C-7—Electrical Rewiring; Administrator's Interpretation No. 1; Differences between Administrator's Opinion No. 117 and Administrator's Interpretation No. 1; Procedure where Administrator's Opinion No. 117 applies.

(Issued June 5, 1962)

On May 22, 1962 the Administrator issued "Administrator's Interpretation No. 1" concerning rewiring of an inadequately wired building as a basis for increase of maximum rents under Section 33.1(c) of the Rent, Eviction and Rehabilitation Regulations. The rewiring standards and schedule of rental values set forth in Administrator's Interpretation No. 1 will apply to all installations where a contract was entered into between the landlord and a licensed electrical contractor or where an application for a certificate of electrical inspection was filed with the Department of Water Supply, Gas and Electricity on or after May 22, 1962. In all other cases Opinion No. 117 of the State Rent Administrator will govern.

Applications filed with the State Rent Commission prior to May 1, 1962 pursuant to Section 33(1) of the State Regulations and applications filed with the Rent and Rehabilitation Administration after May 1st where the contract for the work was executed and an application for certificate of electrical inspection filed on or before May 21, 1962 will be processed under Section 33.1(c) of the City Regulations by applying State Rent Administrator's Opinion No. 117. However, the landlord will be required to file an additional statement setting forth his total costs and expenses for the work and whether any part of the cost was financed by a loan. If

OPERATIONAL BULLETINS

any part of the cost was financed, the landlord will also be required to state from whom or what source the loan was obtained and the terms and conditions thereof.

In all cases where Opinion No. 117 of the State Rent Administrator applies, the application, unless filed prior to May 1, 1962, shall be filed on Application Form A-33(1). The landlord will also file the "Electrical Contractor's Statement", State Form 33(1) Supplement, and the additional statement of costs and financing referred to in the preceding paragraph.

Where the application was filed with the State Rent Commission prior to May 1, 1962 a certificate of the Department of Buildings stating either that no violations against the property are recorded in the index maintained by the Central Violations Bureau of the department or that all violations therein recorded against the property have been cleared, corrected or abated, should be filed by the landlord and Form N-21 requesting such certificate should be served upon the landlord. No orders shall be issued increasing maximum rents in any housing accommodations unless such certificate is obtained and filed with the application.

Where the application is filed with the Rent and Rehabilitation Administration on or after May 1, 1962, the certificate of the Department of Buildings must be annexed to the application as required by Section 33(b) of the Regulations.

It is contemplated that new application forms and a new "Electrical Contractor's Statement" will be issued in the immediate future which will be designed for use in cases where Administrator's Interpretation No. 1 is applicable.

Operational Bulletin No. C-7—Completion of Application Form A-33.1 RE Supplement No. 1
(Issued December 1, 1964)

Application Form A-33.1 RE has been designed for use in connection with applications for rent increases based upon the rewiring of the electrical wiring system of a building in accordance with the provisions of Administrators Interpretation No. 1. Since the increases allowed are determined on the basis of a fixed rental value schedule, the cost of the work and whether such cost was financed are not matters which must be disclosed to the tenants. Accordingly, items 3 and 4 of the "Statement of Landlord" need not be completed on the copies of the application which are to be mailed to the tenants. However, the original master application and one copy of such master application must be completed in all respects before the application will be acceptable for docketing.

Operational Bulletin No. C-8—Action to be taken by District Director upon certification of hazardous conditions, etc. by City Department; disconnecting electrical current by Department of Water Supply, Gas and Electricity; procedure for decreasing maximum rents.
(Issued July 20, 1962)

In furtherance of the Administrator's policy of cooperating with other City departments the following procedures have been designed to meet the problem of compelling certain landlords to remedy serious violations concerning defective electrical rewiring.

The Department of Water Supply, Gas and Electricity after having exhausted routine procedure necessary to have owners remove such violations has no alternative other than to disconnect the electrical current. Before taking final action thereon the Department of Water Supply, Gas and Electricity gives the landlord (owner) written notice of its intention to disconnect the electric current on a specified date.

A copy of the above "disconnect notice" will be forwarded by the Department to the District Rent and Rehabilitation Office having jurisdiction. Immediately upon receipt of such advice, the District Office will cause a Notice of Commencement of Proceedings for Decrease of Maximum Rent—Section 34.3 [Notice Form N-2T (34.3)] to be served upon the landlord indicating that the maximum rent will be reduced by 50% by reason of the conditions certified to this Administration.

No final action may be taken by the District Office in such proceeding until the District Office has been notified by the Department of Water Supply, Gas and Electricity that the electrical current has actually been disconnected. Upon receipt of such advice orders shall be forthwith issued decreasing the maximum rents as proposed, unless the landlord's time to answer has not expired. Where the violations have been removed the City Department will so advise the District Office and the proceedings may then be terminated on that basis.

Operational Bulletins

Operational Bulletin No. C-9—§§ 33b and c; Report of Search or Receipt Attesting to Payment of Fee for Report of Search; Proof of the Correction or Removal of City Agency Violations
(Revised April 25, 1968)

Under the provisions of paragraph b of Section 33 of the Regulations no application for an increase in any maximum rent may be filed under Sections 33.1b, 33.1c, 33d, 33.5, 33.6, 33.7 or 33.8a unless (1) a report of search issued by the Office of Code Enforcement of the Department of Rent and Housing Maintenance of the Housing and Development Administration is annexed to such application stating either that no violations against such property are recorded or that all violations recorded against such property have been complied with, *or* (2) a receipt (or photocopy thereof) issued by the Borough Office of the Department of Buildings is annexed to such application attesting to the payment of the fee for a report of search. Such report of search will not be acceptable unless issued by such agency within 45 days prior to the date of filing the application, or in lieu thereof, such receipt may not be dated more than 14 days prior to the date of filing the application.

The application may be dismissed if no report of search is received by the Office of Rent Control within 45 days after submission of the application with receipt (or photocopy thereof) of payment of fee for such report.

Where the report of search issued by the Office of Code Enforcement certifies that violations have been placed against a property; or where an agency of the City having jurisdiction certifies that the housing accommodation is a fire hazard or is in continued dangerous condition or detrimental to life or health or is occupied in violation of law, proof of the correction of any violation recorded against such property as of the filing date of the application must be made unless

 (1) the violations are in the judgment of the District Rent Director tenant caused e.g. bars on windows, overcrowding, fire escape obstructed; or

 (2) the tenant has refused access to the owner for the purpose of correcting the violations after notice in accordance with the regulations of the Office of Code Enforcement or has refused access to the Office of Code Enforcement for re-inspection; or

(3) the violation does not affect an essential service to which the housing accommodation is entitled; or

(4) the violations are, in the judgment of the District Rent Director, of such nature that the failure to correct them should not bar the rent increase for which application has been made.

Proof of correction of any violation may be made by submitting a "Dismissal Card" issued by the Office of Code Enforcement.

Such "Dismissal Card" will only be acceptable as proof if it is dated after the date of the certification by the Office of Code Enforcement.

Where the "Dismissal Card" is dated prior to the date of such certificate even though it is dated after the date of the violations recorded on such certificate, it will not be acceptable and the landlord should be requested to obtain a new report of search or a new "Dismissal Card".

In lieu of a "Dismissal Card" any other evidence of dismissal issued on an official form by the Office of Code Enforcement which indicates by violation order and date of dismissal the necessary decertification may be submitted and accepted as proof of the correction of any violation of record.

It is to be noted that the above is applicable to all applications filed pursuant to the sections of the Regulations referred to above. However, for applications relating to major capital improvements and/or substantial rehabilitation where the landlord elects to deposit the rent increase in an escrow account, the procedures set forth in Operational Bulletin No. C-9, Supplement No. 1, will also be applicable.

Operational Bulletin No. C-9, Supplement No. 1—Filing of Application for Major Capital Improvement or Substantial Rehabilitation Where There Are Violations of Record or There is a Submission of a Receipt of Payment for Report of Search.

(Revised April 25, 1968)

Applications may now be filed, while violations of record are outstanding, under the provisions of Section 33.1b and c of the Regulations for substantial rehabilitations and major capital improvements.

The following procedures are adopted to facilitate such filing, and to expedite the issuance of orders, and to establish an escrow program to be administered by the Office of Rent Control of the Department of Rent and Housing Maintenance of the Housing and Development Administration.

The landlord may file an application for substantial rehabilitation, Section 33.1b, or major capital improvement, Section 33.1c, by annexing:

1. A report of search of the Office of Code Enforcement of the Department of Rent and Housing Maintenance of the Housing and Development Administration, issued no more than 45 days prior to the filing of the application and stating either that there are no recorded violations against such property or that all violations recorded against such property have been complied with; or

2. A receipt (or photocopy thereof) indicating payment to the cashier in the Borough Office of the Department of Buildings for a report of search. Such receipt may not be dated more than 14 days prior to the date of filing the application; or

3. A report of search from the Office of Code Enforcement issued no more than 45 days prior to the filing of the application which shows outstanding violations of record.

When the application is accompanied by such receipt or report of search showing outstanding violations, the landlord is required to agree that within 30 days after the issuance of an appropriate notice, the landlord will file forms prescribed by the Office of Rent Control in duplicate which (1) designate the escrow agent, (2) set forth the terms and conditions of the escrow agreement and (3) provide that the landlord will comply with such other terms and conditions as may be required by the Office of Rent Control. The landlord will also be given an opportunity during this 30-day period to submit evidence that violations of record on the property have been cleared, corrected or abated.

Upon return by the landlord of the said executed escrow agreement within 30 days, the District Rent Director shall issue orders conditioned on compliance with the escrow agreement. If the landlord fails to return the executed escrow agreement within 30 days, the District Rent Director may issue an order terminating the proceeding. If the landlord submits evidence that there are no violations of record or that violations of record placed against the property on or prior to the date of filing the application have been dismissed, orders may be issued by the District Rent Director increasing the maximum rents without provision for an escrow agreement.

Where tenants' answers to the landlord's application under Sections 33.1b and 33.1c of the Regulations indicate service complaints, and the landlord submits an executed Escrow Agreement to remove violations of record, the District Rent Director shall forward copies of tenants' answers to the landlord and shall provide the tenants with appropriate service complaint applications at the time of issuance of orders of rental adjustment.

The landlord may elect to withdraw the application for one or more housing accommodations where violations would bar the issuance of orders without provision for an Escrow Account.

To successfully comply with the escrow agreement, the landlord must obtain and submit to the District Rent Director, no later than one year from the date of issuance of any orders increasing the maximum rent pursuant to his application, except for good cause shown, a report of search or acknowledgment by the Office of Code Enforcement stating that the violations recorded on or prior to the date of the filing of the application have been dismissed, corrected or abated.

Failure of the landlord to fulfil his obligations under the escrow agreement may cause the District Rent Director to commence a proceeding to revoke the orders previously issued and direct full refund to the tenants of the entire increase paid by the tenants as a result of such orders.

Violations of record placed against the property for which applications for rental increases have been submitted on or prior to the date of filing the application must be complied with prior to the issuance of orders increasing the maximum rent without provision for an escrow

OPERATIONAL BULLETINS

agreement or prior to the termination of an escrow agreement unless

1. the violations or service conditions are in the judgment of the District Rent Director tenant caused e.g. bars on windows, overcrowding, fire escape obstructed: or
2. the tenant has refused access to the owner for the purpose of correcting the violation or service condition after notice or has refused access to the Office of Code Enforcement for re-inspection; or
3. the violation or service condition does not affect an essential service to which the housing accommodation is entitled; or
4. the violations or service conditions are, in the judgment of the District Rent Director, of such nature that the failure to correct them should not bar the rent increase for which application has been made.

Operational Bulletin No. C-10—Co-operation with other City agencies; violations of laws administered by Health Dept. or Dept. of Buildings.
(Issued October 1, 1962)

In many cases inspections made by our Inspectors uncovers conditions which may be a violation of the laws which are administered by either the Health Department or the Department of Buildings. While our inspectors are not always knowledgeable of such laws, there are a great many cases where by the very nature of the conditions which exist in a building, it may be assumed that violations do exist and the appropriate City agency should be alerted to the conditions.

The Borough office of such agency should be notified by letter. It is suggested that the letter take the following form:

"RE: Premises—
Our Docket No.

Dear Sir:

In making a recent inspection of the above premises our inspector found the following conditions to exist:

Since the existence of these conditions may be in violation of the law administered by your department, we are forwarding this information to you for such action as may be warranted.

Yours truly,
District Rent and
Rehabilitation Director"

A copy of the letter written to the City department should be placed in the docket.

Operational Bulletin, No. C-11—§ 13 of the Regulations; Home Occupations which may be conducted in apartments which require no approval from the City Department of Buildings; permissive occupancy by doctors, dentists or osteopaths.

(Revised May 12, 1965)

Section 13 of the Rent, Eviction and Rehabilitation Regulations permits the Administrator to exempt a housing accommodation rented for commercial or professional purposes only where he finds that the renting complies with the requirements of law and of City agencies having jurisdiction.

The Department of Buildings has advised that home occupations may be conducted in a residential building when the individual conducting such home occupation resides in the apartment used for such purpose.

Under Section 12-10 of the Zoning Resolution the definition of "Home Occupations" includes, but is not limited to:

(a) Fine arts (painting, drawing, architecture, sculpturing and commercial art) studios;

(b) Professional offices (as listed by the New York State Department of Education and by the Judiciary Law), viz:

Architecture
Certified Public Accountancy
Dental Hygiene
Dentistry
Law
Licensed Practical Nursing
Medicine
Optometry
Osteopathy
Physiotherapy
Podiatry
Psychology
Professional Engineering & Land Surveying
Public Accountancy
Registered Professional Nursing

(c) Teaching of not more than four pupils simultaneously, or, in the case of musical instruction, of not more than a single pupil at a time.

However, under Section 12-10 of the Zoning Resolution (as revised 1/28/65) home occupations shall not include:

(a) Advertising or public relations agencies

(b) Barber shops

(c) Beauty Parlors

(d) Commercial stables or kennels

(e) Depilatory, electrolysis, or similar offices

(f) Interior decorator's offices or work shops

(g) Ophthalmic Dispensing

(h) Pharmacy

(i) Real estate or insurance offices

(j) Stockbroker's offices

(k) Veterinary medicine.

The above specified uses, subject to the limitations set forth in Section 12-10 of the Zoning Resolution, require no approval from the Department of Buildings unless such home occupation requires a change in partitions or arrangement of the rooms.

It is to be noted however that under Section 22-14 of the Zoning Resolution community facilities may appropriately be located in residential areas to provide recreational, religious, health or other essential services for the residents. Included in the definition of community facilities such Resolution defines community facilities to be "medical offices or group medical centers, including the practice of dentistry or osteopathy, limited to a location below the level of the first story ceiling, except that in multiple dwellings such uses may be located on the second floor, if

(a) separate access to the outside is provided, or

(b) such use existed on January 1, 1948."

However, it should be noted that even where such use is permitted by the Zoning Resolution, it is still necessary that this type of occupancy be approved by the Department of Buildings by the filing of an application and plans. Even where the second floor was used on January 1, 1948 for such professional purposes such approval would be required. For instance a second floor apartment was used as a doctor's office on January 1, 1948. Where the apartment has since become vacant, the landlord can legally rent this space to a different doctor for office use, only if such use was approved by the Department of Buildings. The most satisfactory evidence of the legality of an existing use is generally the approved plans and application showing such use.

Business or occupational changes other than for "Home Occupations" are considered as changes in use and will require the filing of an alteration application and plans for approval by the Department of Buildings. These applications to the Department of Buildings are filed by registered architects or professional engineers.

The main difference between community facilities and home occupations is that in community facilities there is no requirement that the practitioner live in the apartment and that the facilities be restricted to his personal use. Community facilities are independent of the residents requirement and may be used by a number of practitioners.

Since the Department of Buildings cannot grant approval without first examining the plans and checking for all the requirements of both the Administrative Code and the Zoning Resolution, prior opinion as to the possibility of approving such changes cannot be given by the Department of Buildings. Therefore, in all such cases specific approval of the use must be obtained by the landlord from the Department of Buildings before a Section 13 application may be granted.

Operational Bulletin No. C-12—§ 33.5 applications; projection of payroll increases; dual orders, effective date of orders granting increases on subsequent application.

(Issued December 13, 1962)

Wage increases provided for in union wage agreements executed prior to the date of the filing of § 33.5 applications may be projected where such wage increase becomes effective within one year from the date of filing the fair return application. Where the application is granted prior to the date that the projected wage increase becomes effective, orders shall be issued, where required, providing for dual increases in the maximum rents. The first part of such order shall be effective on the date of issuance. Any further adjustment resulting from consideration of the

Operational Bulletins

projected wage increase shall take effect on the date when the wage increase itself is effective.

Where the union agreement provides for more than one increase in wages although each wage increase will become effective within one year from the date the § 33.5 application is filed, projection will only be allowed on the first of such increases.

Orders increasing the maximum rents in a subsequent § 33.5 application may not become effective sooner than 24 months after the effective date of the second part of the dual order.

Where a dual order issued, the total increase in maximum rents provided for in such order shall not exceed 15% of the rent in effect on the date the application was filed.

Operation Bulletin No. C-13—Kitchen modernizations—cabinets and appliance inserts; rental values
(Revised July 27, 1966)

Operational Bulletin No. C-13, revised February 1, 1965, is hereby clarified by the issuance of this revision which is primarily concerned with minimum requirements for metal kitchen cabinets with baked-enamel finish.

Our attention has been called to the fact that in many cases recent installations have included metal cabinets of lesser cost and quality than those considered in establishing current rental values. The cabinets used in the 1962 study which developed standards for rent adjustments were all of heavy guage furniture steeel with insulated doors and a minimum depth of 13 inches. The minimum 12-inch depth quoted in the previous bulletin revisions was intended as an absolute minimum and reflected an industry practice of referring to "12-inch" cabinets although the units were in fact 13 inches deep. Accordingly, the Administrator has directed the following clarification of the Schedule of Rental Values relating to Metal Kitchen Cabinets in order to insure that the grade and quality of the installations shall be commensurate with the rental values assigned to such installations.

Since there is no evidence that installations involving other than baked-enamel metal kitchen cabinets have deviated from the standards of grade and quality intended for such installations, provisions for **Other Kitchen Cabinets** and **Kitchen Cabinet Appliance Inserts** as promulgated in the revision of February 1, 1965 remain unchanged. It should be noted, however, that there will be no deviation permitted from the minimum specifications set forth in the Operational Bulletin.

It is to be noted that no additional allowance will be given for the demolition or removal of existing equipment nor for the installation of new equipment or for the restoration of ceilings and walls, where required, since these costs are included in the rental values indicated herein. The indicated rental values also include the installation of necessary filler(s).

METAL KITCHEN CABINETS
(Baked-enamel finish)

All metal cabinets with baked-enamel finish shall be made of cold-rolled furniture steel, free from imperfections, of tensile strength or sufficient guage—ranging from 16 through 24 or more, depending on function—to store articles usually placed in kitchen cabinets by tenants. Hardware and trim, including hinges, handles and catches, shall be of rustproof materials.

Base cabinets shall be constructed with plastic tops and shall be of a minimum height of 36 inches and have a minimum backsplash of 4 inches. Minimum depth of wall cabinets shall be 13 inches. All cabinets shall have insulated doors.

Size and Type	Doors	Shelves	Monthly Rental Value
Wall Cabinets			
30" high			
12"-18" wide	1	2	$ .35
21"-42" wide	2	1	.45
18" high			
18"-30" wide	1 or 2	1	.35
33"-42" wide	2	1	.45
Base Cabinets 24" deep		Drawers	
9"-18" wide	1	1	$.50
21"-33" wide	2	1	.70
36"-42" wide	2	2	.90
15"-24" wide	0	3 or 4	.80
Full Length Cabinets			
84" high			
(min. 13" deep)			
18"-21" wide		varies	$.55

OPERATIONAL BULLETINS

OTHER KITCHEN CABINETS*

[Laminated with wood, metal with plastic, unfinished wood (see below for "Minimum Specifications")]

TYPE OF CABINET, COUNTER AND SOFFIT	Hardwood	Laminate With Wood	Metal With Plastic	Unfinished Wood
		Per Linear Foot		
Base Cabinets				
Standard[6]	$ .25	$ .30	$ .30	$ .15
Undersink[7]	.20	.20	.20	.10
Sink front	.15	.15	.15	.10
All drawer	.30	.35	.35	.20
Wall Cabinets[8]				
30" or more high	.20	.25	.20	.10
Less than 30" high	.15	.20	.15	.10
Counter (formica or equivalent with 4" backsplash)	.10	.10	.10	.10
Soffit (dropped ceiling)	.03	.03	.03	.03
84" Full Length Cabinets		Per Cabinet		
Utility (15" min. width)[9]				
13" deep	$ .75	$ .90	$ .90	$ .45
24" deep	.90	1.10	1.05	.55
Oven[10]	1.05	1.20	1.20	.65

* Where depth of a cabinet is less than standard due to structural problems such as jutting beams there must be proof of necessity. Established rental values will apply in these instances. However, no adjustments will be allowed if a wall cabinet is less than 6" deep, a base cabinet less than 18" deep, or a full length utility cabinet less than 12" deep. A utility cabinet 18" or more in depth will be granted the indicated allowance for a 24" deep cabinet, those less than 18" will receive the 13" standard increase. Oven cabinets must be of standard dimensions.

[6] A standard base cabinet shall be at least 24" deep and 34"-35" high with one or more top drawers and one or more doors depending upon the width of the cabinet. It shall also have a full back, sides, and base with a storage compartment containing one or two shelves.

[7] An undersink cabinet, or the backless portion of a combination under sink cabinet, or a sink front shall not exceed 30" in width when used with a single sink insert 24" × 21", nor 36" in width when used with a single sink insert 30" × 21", nor 42" in width when used with a double sink insert 32" × 21" or larger.

[8] Wall cabinets shall be 12" or more deep and have full backs and sides, with the exception of softwood cabinets which are ordinarily made without backs. The height of a cabinet shall be measured by its open portion, open shelves are not to be considered as part of the overall height.

[9] Utility cabinets 12" or more in width, but less than 15" wide, will be allowed ⅘ths of the monthly allowance indicated. No rent increase will be allowed for utility cabinets which are less than 12" wide.

[10] Oven cabinets shall have doors and cabinet space above and below the oven cut-out.

NOTE—Where an order had previously been issued, either by the Federal authorities or by the State Rent Commission, on the basis of kitchen cabinet installation, and an order, or the most recent order, if there is more than one such order, was issued more than 10 years ago, a subsequent replacement shall have the full rental value indicated above. Where the last

MINIMUM SPECIFICATIONS

1. Minimum specifications for cabinets manufactured from different materials are as follows:

   A. *Hardwood cabinets* shall have fronts consisting of exterior frame, doors and drawer front of ⅝" or more thickness constructed of woodbase core with hardwood veneer of a minimum ⅛" thickness affixed to both inner and outer surfaces; the frames shall be of reinforced hardwood construction. They shall have baked factory or custom finish both inside and out, and all exposed sides shall have fully finished returns.

   B. *Unfinished wood cabinets* shall include all hardwood cabinets which do not have baked factory or custom finish inside and out, and all softwood cabinets regardless of finish. Softwood cabinets shall have fronts consisting of exterior frame, doors and drawer fronts of ⅝" or more thickness.

   C. *Laminate with wood cabinets* shall have fronts consisting of exterior frame, doors and drawer fronts of ⅝" or more thickness constructed of either solid plastic or a woodbase core with laminated facing affixed to both inner and outer surfaces; the frames shall be of reinforced hardwood construction. They shall have baked factory or custom finish inside. All exposed sides shall have laminated returns.

   D. *Metal with plastic cabinets* shall be of heavy gauge steel construction; front panels shall have plastic inserts, or plastic facing, or shall have door and drawer fronts of solid laminate or laminated wood. Doors and drawer fronts shall be of ⅝" or more thickness.

2. All cabinet models other than undersink, unfinished wood wall units, or the cut-out portion of oven cabinets shall have complete backs of hardboard, plywood, particleboard, solid wood, or metal. Interior sides, except in metal cabinets, shall be of 5-layer plywood or particleboard construction.

order was issued less than 10 and more than 5 years prior to such replacement, the rental value thereof shall be the difference between such full rental value and the rent increase provided for in such order. Where the last order was issued less than 5 years prior to such replacement, no rent adjustment for such replacement shall be warranted.

OPERATIONAL BULLETINS

3. There shall be no additional allowances granted for special purpose cabinets or accessories such as rotating shelves, fitted drawers, open or dropped shelves; or for full counter backsplashers, or for counter top length in excess of the combined measurements for base cabinets and under-the-counter appliances.

KITCHEN CABINET APPLIANCE INSERTS

(The allowances indicated are applicable only if the installation is a part of a total kitchen cabinet installation)

	Monthly Increase
KITCHEN SINK (with swinging mixing faucet and waste strainer)	
Single bowl (24" × 21" minimum)	
porcelain	$1.25
stainless steel	1.40
Double bowl (32" × 24" minimum)	
porcelain	1.40
stainless steel	1.60
RANGE HOODS—see "Operational Bulletin No. C-15, Supplement No. 6"	
WALL OVEN AND BURNER PLATE	3.50

NOTE—Where an order had previously been issued, either by the Federal authorities or by the State Rent Commission, on the basis of the installation of any kitchen sink and/or cooking stove, and an order, or the most recent order, if there is more than one order, was issued more than the number of years indicated herein for such appliance, a subsequent replacement shall have the full rental value indicated above. Where the last order was issued less than the number of years indicated herein prior to such replacement, the rental value thereof shall be the difference between such full rental value and the rent increase provided for in such order.

Appliance	Number of Years
a. kitchen sink	12
b. wall oven and burner plate replacing free-standing gas range or cooking stove	10

PROCEDURES

With Application Form A-33.1C (KM), the landlord shall submit the following:

1. Written consent of the tenant.
2. An itemized copy of the contract or invoice which shall include full particulars of the installation, giving name of manufacturer and model number of each cabinet and appliance insert; description, dimensions as per manufacturer's specifications; net price with installation (e.g. XYZ Kitchen Cabinets Co., Model No. BC 21 base cabinet, hardwood, 42" W × 35" H × 24" D, $75.00, including delivery and sales tax).

3. Affidavit by contractor that the cabinets and appliance inserts referred to in the attached invoice were actually installed in the housing accommodations (identify as in the application). If not installed by the contractor, the affidavit should be made by the landlord.
4. A rough sketch showing exact dimensions of area and kitchen layout, including exact measurements of cabinet components.
5. Proof from City Departments having jurisdiction that electrical and plumbing installations have been made in compliance with local ordinances, rules and regulations.

Operational Bulletin No. C-14—Elevator Modernization; rental values; procedures.

(Revised December 1, 1964)

The Administrator has completed a study relating to the modernization of elevators and has tentatively formulated the policies and procedures hereinafter set forth. The matters contained herein shall apply to all cases where such work has been started on or after January 1, 1963.

The Administrator has determined that the following elevator rehabilitation only will be considered a major capital improvement within the meaning of Section 33.1 c of the Regulations for which rent increases may be granted.

I. Complete Elevator Modernization

A complete elevator modernization must include the installation of a complete new controller-selector, a new cab and all new hoistway doors.

The rental value for such modernization will be based upon the recoupment of the actual cost thereof over a period of 10 years, except that the *maximum* monthly rental increase per apartment shall not exceed

$2.50 in buildings containing 40-59 apartments

$2.00 in buildings containing 60 or more apartments.

II. Partial Elevator Modernization

A partial elevator modernization must include the installation of a complete new controller-selector and

Operational Bulletins

refinishing the cab with a multiple spray enamel and lacquer coating, or its equivalent. A partial modernization may include additional work providing that the foregoing minimum standards have been complied with.

The rental value for such modernization will be based upon the recoupment of the actual cost thereof over a period of 10 years, except that the *maximum* monthly rental increase per apartment shall not exceed

$.80 in buildings containing 40-59 apartments

$.55 in buildings containing 60 or more apartments.

III. Replacement of Open Grille Elevator Car Gates

The following schedule of rent increases will be allowed, except where it is part of a complete or partial elevator modernization, for replacement of open grille elevator cab gates with new one- or two-speed solid panel doors including new door operator, securing floating platform where one exists, installing all necessary wiring, refinishing the cab (multiple spray enamel and lacquer coating, or its equivalent).

Number of Units in Structure	Monthly Increase Per Unit
25 units or fewer	$.50
26-40 units	.40
41-64 units	.25
65 units or more	.15

IV. Procedures

The landlord must file Application Form A-33.1EM—Landlord's Application for Increase of Maximum Rent—Major Capital Improvement—Elevator Modernization. The landlord is also required to submit the following information and documents:

1. Copy of contract for elevator modernization.

2. Cancelled checks and other evidence of expenditure for elevator modernization.

3. Photostat of approved permit from Building Department to alter elevator (Form 21) or elevator alteration specification sheet and approved permits (Forms 12 and 20).

4. Building Department Final Certificate of Compliance (Form 73).

5. Previous and present elevator maintenance contract history.

6. "Elevator Contractor's Statement of Modernization" [Report Form R-33.1(c)EM] (a detailed questionnaire describing the modernization and containing a check list of new parts and components included with the installation and the extent of repairs and replacements made with used parts or equipment).

7. Certificate of "No Violations" from the Central Violations Bureau of the Department of Buildings.

V. Miscellaneous

1. Buildings with fewer than 40 units will be handled on a prior opinion basis.

2. Where structure has more than one elevator, the average number of apartments served per elevator will determine the appropriate maximum grants.

3. The above applies to buildings with 6 or 7 stops (6 stories and basement). Rent adjustments in buildings with more than 7 stops per elevator or with unique and peculiar circumstances will be handled by prior opinion.

4. Ten-year period of amortization does not apply to elevator modernization installed as part of an over-all building-wide rehabilitation program.

5. Where landlord makes application for a prior opinion he is required to submit three estimates covering the work which he proposes to do.

6. The total rent adjustment for elevator modernization shall be allocated equally among all units including ground and first floor apartments.

7. The amortized cost used as a basis for rent adjustment may not exceed the amount claimed in the Building Department Permit Application.

Operational Bulletin No. C-15—Rental Values; Installation of Conventional Bell and Buzzer Systems; Installation of Telephone/Door Release and Intercommunication Systems; Installation of Peepholes or Door Interviewers; Vestibule Doors; Closed Circuit Television.

(Revised June 30, 1969 and effective July 1, 1969)

(Operational Bulletin No. C-15 (Revised August 30, 1968) and Operational Bulletin No. C-26 (Revised August 31, 1965) are superseded by this revision of Operational Bulletin No. C-15, effective on the date of filing with the City Clerk.)

OPERATIONAL BULLETINS

The Administrator, having completed his study of the various home security systems which are presently being installed in New York City apartment houses as well as new systems which the industry is offering to install, has adopted the minimum standards and rental values which are set forth in this bulletin.

The request or written consent in writing of a majority of the tenants in occupancy (51% to the installations described in Schedule B or C will not make it mandatory for the landlord to make such installations. However, where the landlord has made such installation after first obtaining the consent of a majority of the tenants in occupancy to the type of installation described in either Schedule B or C, rent increases will be granted in accordance with the provisions of the appropriate schedule.

Where less than 51 percent of such tenants have consented to the installation described in either schedule A, B or C, but the cumulative total under all schedules is equal to a majority of the tenants in occupancy, the Administrator shall deem such cumulative total to be a request or consent in writing for the installations described in Schedule A.

The rental values for the installation of conventional bell, buzzer and voice intercommunication systems (Schedule A); telephone activated door release and intercommunication systems (Schedule B); closed circuit television and intercommunication systems (Schedule C), and the procedures to be followed in obtaining rent increases based on such installations are as follows:

SCHEDULE A

Conventional Type Bell, Buzzer and Intercommunication Systems

	Monthly Rental Value
(1) Installation of a bell and buzzer system equipped with automatic self-closing and self-locking doors (none before) with each tenant receiving two keys	$ .50
(2) Installation of a bell and buzzer system equipped with automatic self-closing and self-locking doors with voice communication (none before) with each tenant receiving two keys	
with new U.S. Government approved mail boxes	1.25[a]
without new U.S. Government approved mail boxes because previously installed	1.05[a]
(3) Installation of new intercom (none before) with an existing bell and buzzer system	.55[a]

601

(4) Installation of new U.S. Government approved mail boxes... .20[b]
(5) Replacement of existing system containing items referred to in (1) with all new equipment .... .50[c]
(6) Replacement of existing system containing items referred to in (2) with all new equipment[c]
    with mail boxes.. 1.25
    without mail boxes because previously installed........ 1.05

Minimum Standards

All splices must be made in approved junction boxes which shall be installed at accessible locations. The bell panels in the building vestibule must be constructed of non-corrosive and non-combustible material and stamped in a permanent manner with the apartment designation. Provision shall also be made in the bell panel for the insertion of a plastic card containing the tenant's name. The bell panel shall be installed flush with the building structure. The bell and buzzer buttons shall be of standard type and readily replaceable for periodic maintenance.

SCHEDULE B

(The written consent of 51 per cent of the tenants in occupancy required.) Dial or combination Push Button Telephone Activated Door Release and Intercommunication Systems

Minimum Standards

Furnish and install:

A. A lobby combination push-button panel or dial telephone box which shall be flush mounted 63 inches from the floor surface to top box or panel. The telephone box shall be constructed of heavy gauge (not less than .09 inches) brushed stainless steel (or equivalent) security locked cover plate;

B. A handset telephone made of cycolac (or its equivalent in durability) which shall have non-removable transmitter and receiver caps, and shall be equipped with vandal resistant (metal clad) cord;

C. Conduit of suitable diameter, which shall be run from lobby box to terminal relay box in basement or other convenient location;

---

[a] Consent of 51 per cent of the tenants in occupancy is required.

[b] Where mail boxes are installed as a substitute for mail distribution to the tenants, no rent increase will be allowed for the mail boxes.

[c] Where existing, inoperable system is ten or more years old.

Operational Bulletins

D. A suitable directory which can be kept current, listing tenant names and appropriate dial or pushbutton code numbers or letters, which shall be mounted in a well-lit and convenient location in the lobby;

E. A standard handset telephone at a convenient location in each apartment and which will provide tenant with a system of private voice communication with the lobby, and from which (only after such communication has been established) the occupant may then activate the door releasing mechanism by dialing or pushing a button located on the instrument.

Rental Values for Schedule B Installations:

Number of Units in Structure	Monthly Increase per Apartment
20	$4.45
21	4.30
22	4.15
23— 24	3.95
25— 26	3.75
27— 28	3.55
29— 31	3.35
32— 35	3.10
36— 39	2.90
40— 44	2.70
45— 49	2.55
50— 59	2.35
60— 69	2.15
70— 79	2.00
80— 89	1.90
90— 99	1.80
100—124	1.70
125—149	1.60
150—174	1.50
175—224	1.45
225—274	1.40
275—324	1.35
325 or more	1.30

SCHEDULE C (The written consent of 51 per cent of the tenants in occupancy required.) Homes Security Systems (Closed Circuit Television)[d]

Minimum Standards

All work shall comply with the New York City Electrical Code and all applicable rules and regulations of other City Departments having jurisdiction, if any. Cables shall be securely fastened and not subject to mechanical injury.

---

[d] All doors leading to the residential area of the building (including basement, garage and roof-bulkhead doors) which are not monitored by a video camera must be equipped with a locking device which does not permit free ingress to such residential area.

OPERATIONAL BULLETINS

All splices shall be enclosed in suitable junction boxes and installed in locations accessible for maintenance and repair. Power supply to the equipment shall be installed in an approved wiring method. Cameras shall be mounted in tamper proof cabinets. Spotlights, if any, shall also be tamper proof.

	Monthly Increase per Apartment, by Number of Units in Building				
	24 or less	25-34	35-44	45-69	70 or more
1. Individual Apartment Videos:[e]					
a. in buildings with existing bell, buzzer and intercommunication system	$2.95	$2.65	$2.45	$2.20	$2.10
b. in buildings with bell and buzzer needing intercommunication system	3.30	3.00	2.80	2.55	2.45
c. unlocked buildings, needing bell, buzzer and intercommunication system	3.80	3.50	3.30	3.05	2.95
2. Elevator Security System[f]	2.30	1.65	1.25	.85	.55
3. Service Entrance Security[f]	2.15	1.55	1.15	.80	.50
4. Elevator and Service Entrance Security Systems Combined[f]	4.30	3.10	2.30	1.60	1.00

Procedures to be followed for all Schedules

After completion of the work, the landlord may file an application with the Administrator for rent increases pursuant to Section 33.1 of the Regulations. In addition the landlord is required to file an affidavit from the contractor(s) attesting to the completion of the work and setting forth in detail the work performed and the material supplied. Where any type of voice intercommunication system is installed, the written consent of 51 percent of the tenants in occupancy is required, and such consent must refer specifically to the amount of increase for installations listed under either Schedule A, Schedule B or Schedule C.

It is to be noted that all installations described in Schedules A, B and C must comply with the Department of Buildings "Rules Relating to Entrance Doors, Locks and Intercommunication Systems," filed with the City Clerk on September 11, 1967 and published in The City

---

[e] $1.00 per month additional for transistorized equipment.

[f] 24-hour door man service required unless there is another employee assigned to observe the viewer or monitor during such 24-hour period.

OPERATIONAL BULLETINS

Record on September 12, 1967, and/or any revision or amendment of such rules.

The rental value specified in either Schedule A, Schedule B, or Schedule C will apply except where it is found that because of unique and peculiar circumstances, the foregoing allowances may not be appropriate. Such conditions should be submitted to the Administrator for a prior opinion and approval before commencement of the installation, along with three independent cost estimates of the proposed improvement, and the written consent of a majority of the tenants in occupancy as to the specific amount of rent increase requested.

All tenant consent signatures for scheduled or above scheduled rent increases must appear on Office of Code Enforcement Form RC-1 (Revised 11-68), and the dates of the individual tenant's consent shall not extend over more than a three month period. The original petition should be filed in the Borough Code Enforcement Office where the building is located. One copy should be filed with the District Rent Office at the time the application for rent increases is filed; one copy shall be retained by the tenants' representative and another copy by the landlord. See Instructions on Form RC-1 (Revised 11-68) Applications for rent increases must be made on Form A-33.1 BSS. The following items shall also be submitted with the application:

1. Copy of contract for the installation of any security system, Schedules A, B or C.

2. Maintenance and service contract for a minimum period of five years for installations under Schedules B or C.

3. Where an elevator security system is installed, a Building Permit (Form 20) from the Elevator Division of the Department of Buildings must be obtained and submitted to the District Rent Office.

As a condition of filing an application and prior to receiving orders increasing maximum rents, the landlord must certify and establish that he is maintaining essential services.

OPERATIONAL BULLETINS

PEEPHOLES—(entrance door interviewers)—(none before) [g]

Window-type viewer: (any device having no distinct reverse vision).[h] Unless there is a clearly marked apartment designation and a name plate at the apartment entrance, the viewer must also include the apartment designation and contain a slot for the insertion of a name plate. Where there is no door bell at the apartment entrance door, the installation of a mechanical chime is required. The viewer must have the approval of the Office of Rent Control as well as the approval of the Board of Standards and Appeals and the installation shall also comply with the rules and requirements of the Department of Buildings. It is to be noted that the approval of the Board of Standards and Appeals and/or any other City Department will not be binding on the Administrator. No allowance will be given in cases where the tenant had previously installed a window-type viewer at his own expense. The monthly allowances for landlord-installed peepholes is as follows:

with mechanical door-chime
    where there is an existing door bell .... $.10
    where there is no existing door bell .... .15
without mechanical door-chime .... .10

VESTIBULE DOORS—

If in conjunction with the installation of any of the above intercommunication systems (none before) the replacement of existing vestibule doors is required, the following additional monthly allowances per apartment for hollow aluminum doors (or its equivalent) may be granted, without further tenant consent.

Number of units in Building	Monthly Rent Increase Per Apt. 1 Door	2 Doors
20-29	$.15	$.20
30-49	.10	.15
50-69	.05	.10
70 or more	—	.05

Operational Bulletin No. C-15 (Revised September 26, 1966) and Operational Bulletin No. C-26 (Revised August 31, 1965) are superseded by this revision of Operational Bulletin No. C-15, effective on the date of filing with the City Clerk.

Operational Bulletin No. C-15—Rental Values; subsequent replacement of mechanical refrigerators.
    Supplement No. 1 (Issued July 12, 1963)

---

[g] The tenant's consent is implied where the installation is required by Chapter 493 of the Laws of 1965.

[h] Mirrored surface viewer will be accepted only where application for a rent increase is filed prior to November 1, 1966.

OPERATIONAL BULLETINS

(NOTE: The subject matter of this supplement was previously contained in Operational Bulletin No. C-15, issued on February 11, 1963. This supplement does not change the rental value schedule heretofore in effect. However, the matter contained in the footnote was clarified.)

The rental values for mechanical refrigerators installed is as follows:

	Monthly Rental Value
Used mechanical refrigerator (none before)	$2.00

Replacement of old refrigerator with a new mechanical refrigerator [according to National Electrical Mfgrs. Ass'n. (NEMA) standards] [a]

Net Capacity (in cubic feet)—

	Conventional or Semi-Automatic Defroster	Fully Automatic Defroster	Zero-Degree Freezer
up to and including 7.5	$3.00	$4.00	—
7.6-8.9	3.50	4.50	—
9.0-10.9	4.00	5.00	—
10.0-12.4	—	—	$5.75
11.0-12.9	4.50	5.50	—
12.5 and over	—	—	6.25
New mechanical refrigerator (none before)			$2.00[b]

Operational Bulletin No. C-15—Rental Values; subsequent replacement of kitchen sinks.
Supplement No. 2 (Issued July 12, 1963)

(NOTE: The subject matter of this supplement was previously contained in Operational Bulletin No. C-15, issued on February 11, 1963. This supplement does not change the rental value schedule heretofore in effect. However, the matter contained in the foot-note was clarified.)

The rental values for the replacement of kitchen sinks is as follows:

	Monthly Rental Value
SINKS—(a) kitchen[c]	
Combination sink and tub (porcelain enamel on iron or steel)	$2.50
Combination sink and tub with metal cabinet (porcelain enamel on iron or steel)	3.00
Combination sink and drain board (porcelain enamel on iron or steel) with drawers and metal cabinet	$3.00

---

[a] Where an order had previously been issued, either by the Federal authorities or by the State Rent Commission, on the basis of the replacement of a mechanical refrigerator and an order, or the most recent order, if there is more than one such order, was issued more than eight years prior to the date of installation, a subsequent replacement shall have the full rental value indicated above. Where the last order was issued within an eight-year period prior to such replacement, the rental value thereof shall be the difference between such full rental value and the rent increase provided for in such previous order.

[b] Plus the rental value specified above for a replacement.

Operational Bulletin No. C-15—Rental Values; Electrical Rewiring; Revision of Administrator's Interpretation No. 1.

Supplement No. 3 (Issued July 12, 1963)

Administrator's Interpretation No. 1, revised May 10, 1963, is hereby revised by changing the schedule of rental values in the following respects:

(a) The monthly charge of $2.75 shall apply to buildings less than seven stories in height.

(b) The monthly charge of $4.00 shall apply to buildings of seven or more stories in height.

Administrator's Interpretation No. 1 is hereby further revised by changing the last paragraph of such Interpretation to read as follows:

"The rewiring standards and schedule of rental values herein will apply to all installations where a contract was entered into between the landlord and a licensed electrical contractor or where an application for a certificate of electrical inspection was filed on or after May 22, 1962. Where such contract was entered into and where the application for a certificate of electrical inspection was filed prior to May 22, 1962, the State Administrator's Opinion #117 will continue to be applicable provided that such rewiring shall have been commenced in good faith prior to August 1, 1963 and thereafter the work was diligently prosecuted to completion."

Except as hereinabove provided, Administrator's Interpretation No. 1 shall continue to be in effect as revised on May 10, 1963.

Operational Bulletin No. C-15—Air-Conditioner Installations: Rental Values for "direct connection" and "through-the-wall sleeves"; revision of Interpretation No. 11.

Supplement No. 3A (Issued June 23, 1964)

The Basic Rewiring Requirements set forth in Administrator's Interpretation No. 1 (revised November 1, 1963) provides for a rent increase of $.75 or $1.00 per month for each air-conditioner circuit and outlet installed by the landlord. Where no outlet is installed, but, the air-condi-

---

[c] Where an order had previously been issued, either by the Federal authorities or by the State Rent Commission, on the basis of the installation of a kitchen sink, and an order, or the most recent order, if there is more than one such order, was issued more than twelve years after the date of issuance of such order, a subsequent replacement shall have the full rental value indicated above. Where the last order was issued within a twelve-year period prior to such replacement, the rental value thereof shall be the difference between such full rental value and the rent increase provided for in such previous order.

OPERATIONAL BULLETINS

tioner is directly connected from the apartment fuse panel box to the junction box of the air-conditioner, the Administrator deems such installation to be the equivalent to the installation of an "air-conditioner circuit and outlet," as such term is used in Administrator's Interpretation No. 1, which would entitle the landlord to a rent increase of either $.75 or $1.00, whichever amount would be appropriate under the circumstances.

In cases where the air-conditioner is installed in a "through-the-wall" sleeve which is constructed by the landlord an additional allowance of $1.25 per month will be granted. The next to the last paragraph of Administrator's Interpretation No. 11 is hereby revised in order to provide for such additional allowance. The revised paragraph shall read as follows:

> "The order which will be issued by the District Rent Director will include an additional allowance for the privilege of maintaining the air-conditioning unit in the window where such allowance is proper. Where the installation is made in a "through-the-wall" sleeve which is constructed by the landlord, an allowance of $1.25 per month will be granted."

Operational Bulletin No. C-15—Rental Values; Combination Kitchen Units (refrigerator, sink and gas range).
Supplement No. 4 (Revised May 21, 1964)

The rental values for combination kitchen units for (a) apartments consisting of 2½ rooms or less and (b) apartments consisting of 3 rooms with a kitchen having less than 70 square foot area and no separate dining area shall be as indicated in this bulletin. Heretofore, rent adjustments pursuant to § 33.1 of the Regulations were granted on a prior opinion basis. With the issuance of this bulletin it will not be necessary for a landlord to file an application for a prior opinion. The rental values indicated herein shall be applied to all pending applications where the installation was made subsequent to January, 1962.

The application for the rent increase must include the written consent of the tenant and be accompanied by the following documents:

> (a) An affidavit in duplicate, made by the landlord, stating that the apartment consists of 2½ rooms or less or that the apartment consists of 3 rooms with a

Operational Bulletins

kitchen having less than 70 sq. ft. area and that the apartment does not have a separate dining area; that the unit has a one-piece body and a one-piece top of either porcelain or stainless steel; and that over-head cabinets, if included, are joined to body by matching wall splasher.

(b) A detailed bill from seller which states make, model, cost, over-all width of unit, and exact description of component parts of combination unit.

(c) Proof from the Department of Buildings that the installation complies with the Multiple Dwelling Code and regulations where the combination unit includes a cooking component or sink which did not replace an existing cooking component or sink.

The rental values for combination kitchen units are as follows:

RENTAL VALUES FOR SINGLE UNIT KITCHEN COMBINATION
(refrigerator, sink and gas range)

Components of Combination Unit	Rental Value[1]
STOVE	
Complete Range with Oven	$2.00
2-Burner Cooking Plate	.75
3 or 4 Burner Cooking Plate	1.00
REFRIGERATOR	
8.9 Cubic Feet and Under, Net Capacity (NEMA)	$3.25
SINK	
Without Undersink Cabinet	$2.00
With Undersink Cabinet	3.00
OVERHEAD CABINETS[2]	
With Connecting Wall (Back) Splasher	
34" to 59.9"	$1.00
60" to 72.9"	1.25

[1] Replacement and "none before" adjustments for individual components will have the same rental value. Where a previous order increasing the maximum rent had been issued, either by the Federal authorities or the State Rent Commission, on the basis of the replacement of a mechanical refrigerator, a gas range or cooking stove, or a kitchen sink and an order, or the most recent order if there is more than one such order, was issued more than ten years prior to the date of installation, a subsequent replacement of such component shall have the full rental value indicated above. Where the last order was issued within a ten year period prior to such replacement, the rental value thereof shall be the difference between such full rental value and the rent increase provided for in such previous order.

[2] Adjustment is allowed only for overhead cabinets which are joined as an integrated part of unit by means of back splasher, and are the same overall width as body of unit. There are at present no overhead cabinets with wall splashers made in the 24" to 34.9" category.

OPERATIONAL BULLETINS

RENTAL VALUE

ALLOWANCE FOR OVER-ALL WIDTH OF UNIT[3]	3-Unit Combination (Range with Oven)	All other Units (2 or 3 Components)
24" to 34.9"	None	None
35" to 46.9"	$1.00	$ .25
47" to 59.9"	1.50	.50
60" to 72.9"	2.00	1.00

Operational Bulletin No. C-15—Rental Values; sunken bathtubs replacing tub with legs; showers.
Supplement No. 5 (Issued June 23, 1964)

The Schedule of Rental Values (April 1, 1964) is hereby revised as of the date of issuance of this bulletin in the following respects:

	Monthly Increase
BATHTUBS	
replacement of tub on legs with sunken tub	$1.50*

*Consent of tenant in occupancy *must* be obtained.

SHOWERS
| pipes concealed (none before) | .75* |
| (replacing existing exposed shower) | .45* |

Operational Bulletin No. C-15—Rental values for dishwashers and range hoods; revision of Schedule of Rental Values
Supplement No 6 (Issued February 1, 1965)

The Schedule of Rental Values (April 1, 1964) is hereby revised as of the date of issuance of this bulletin in the following respects:

DISHWASHERS (installed by landlord)
| portable | None |
| under-counter (24") (not to exceed $4.50 per month) amortize | 7 years |

DISHWASHER (installed by tenant)
| permanently attached to plumbing or floor | $1.00 |
| not permanently attached to plumbing or floor | None |

DUCTLESS RANGE HOODS—See "Range Hoods"

INCINERATOR MODERNIZATION—see "Administrator's Interpretation No. 18"

KITCHEN CABINETS—see "Operational Bulletin No. C-13" (revised February 1, 1965)

KITCHEN CABINET APPLIANCE INSERTS—see "Operational Bulletin No. C-13" (revised February 1, 1965)

KITCHEN MODERNIZATIONS—See "Operational Bulletin No. C-13" (revised February 1, 1965)

---

*These rental values are only applicable where such installation is made in connection with the installation of plumbing replacements contemplated by Administrator's Interpretation No. 9. *See appendix.*
in new law tenant where there is no bathroom................ 2.00**
**Consent of tenant in occupancy *must* be obtained. In addition the installation must be legal and approved by the Department of Buildings.

[3] "Allowance for overall width of unit" has been added to compensate for variations in cost of unit.

OPERATIONAL BULLETINS

PEEPHOLES (entrance door window-type viewers)—see "Administrator's Interpretation No. 17"

	Monthly Increase
RANGE HOODS*	
Plain (shell)	
baked enamel (including metal tones)	$ .25
stainless steel	.30
Ductless (with filter and blower)	
baked enamel (including metal tones) with outlet"	1.00
without outlet	.85
stainless steel with outlet**	1.10
without outlet	.95

WINDOW-TYPE ENTRANCE DOOR VIEWERS—see "Administrator's Interpretation No. 17"

Operational Bulletin No. C-15—Rental values for inlaid linoleum and vinyl asbestos tile; revision of Schedule of Rental Values
Supplement No. 7 (Revised December 15, 1965)

The Schedule of Rental Values (April 1, 1964) is hereby revised as of the date of issuance of this bulletin in the following respects:

The Administration has reviewed its rental values for kitchen floor coverings in light of the definition of the term "kitchen" in the Multiple Dwelling Law. Section 33 of such law states that "any space designed for cooking or warming of food, that is 59 square feet or more, shall be considered a kitchen." The rental values hereinafter specified accordingly apply only to installations that utilize at least 59 square feet of floor covering.

The indicated rental values shall apply to installations made on or after the date of issuance of this bulletin.

	Monthly Increase
INLAID LINOLEUM OR VINYL ASBESTOS TILE (Installed) ***	
none before—inlaid linoleum	$1.00
—vinyl asbestos (either ⅛" or ¹⁄₁₆")	1.25
replacement after 8 years of existing floor covering	
—inlaid linoleum	.50
—vinyl asbestos tile (either ⅛" or ¹⁄₁₆")	.65

---

* Where an order had previously been issued, either by the Federal authorities or by the State Rent Commission, on the basis of the installation of a range hood, and an order, or the most recent order, if there is more than one such order, was issued more than 10 years ago, a subsequent replacement shall have the full rental value indicated above. Where the last order was issued within a 10 year period prior to such replacement, the rental values thereof shall be the difference between such full rental value and the rent increase provided for in such order.

** Installation must comply with requirements governing electrical outlets.

*** In all cases, landlord should submit the following with the application:

Operational Bulletins

Operational Bulletin No. C-15—Subsequent Replacement of Gas Ranges; Replacement of Prime Double-Hung Windows with Tilt-Out or Snap-Out Windows; Revision of Schedule of Rental Values
Supplement No. 8 (Revised September 9, 1969)

The Schedule of Rental Values (April 1, 1964) is hereby revised as of the date of publication in the City Record of this Bulletin in the following respects:

GAS RANGES (installed)

	Monthly Increase
New modern free-standing domestic model gas range (none before)	$3.60*
New modern free-standing domestic model gas range (replacing existing equipment)	2.60*

WINDOWS (replacement)

	Monthly Increase
Prime double-hung windows replaced with tilt-out or snap-out windows (with consent of tenant)	$.75

Operational Bulletin No. C-15—City department certificates required for installation of heating and hot water systems (none before)
Supplement No. 9 (Revised September 9, 1969)

The certificates of approval required as a condition to granting rent increases based on the installation of central heating and hot water systems (none before), are as follows:

---

1. Affidavit (or building plan) attesting to size of kitchen area and amount of flooring material installed.
2. Copy of bill stating the thickness of tile if vinyl is installed.
3. Written consent of tenant.

* plus $.35 for each $15 (inclusive of Sales Tax) or fraction thereof (minimum $5.00) actual cost above $110 (inclusive of Sales Tax).

All gas ranges must meet the specifications of the U.S. of America Standards Institute (except for automatic oven pilot) and must contain oven heat controls.

NOTE—Where no previous order had been issued, during the past 10 years, increasing the maximum rent for replacement of a gas range or cooking stove, a subsequent replacement shall have the full rental value indicated above. Where replacement is made in a shorter period of time (less than 10 years), the amount of the basic increase ($2.60) shall be prorated. For example, if a new range costing $110 or less replaces one that is only 8 years old, the monthly rental increase allowable will be eight-tenths of $2.60, or $2.08. When the cost of the new range, replacing one that is less than ten years old, is higher than $110 and increases above the basic $2.60 are indicated, those additions or $.35 will be prorated which represent the corresponding additional units of $15 cost above the basic cost ($100) in the previous rental grant. To illustrate, a new range costing $140 is installed, replacing a range which had been in use for 8 years and for which a rental increase of $2.25 had been granted. Since the previous grant incorporated one additional unit of $15 above the basic cost for which an addition of $.25 to the previous basic allowance of $2.00 was made, the present allowance requires prorating one of the $.35 additions and the basic $2.60 e.g. 8/10 ($2.60 + .35) + $.35 so that the rental increase in this instance is $2.71.

For Installation of Central Heating System (none before)
1. Certificates for the appropriate type of equipment installed:
   a. Oil burning equipment
      (1) Department of Buildings Application for Certificate of Approval for Oil Burning Installation including Owner's Application to the Fire Department for a permit to Store Fuel Oil (Form 16) [a]
      (2) Department of Building Certificate of Approval. (Form 16A) [b]
      (3) Department of Air Resources Certificate of Operation. [c]
   b. Gas burning equipment
      (1) Department of Buildings Gas Certificate.
      (2) Department of Air Resources Certificate of Registration. [d]

For Installation of Central Hot Water System (none before)
1. Department of Buildings Final Plumbing Approval. (Form 105—Plumbing Card)

This Bulletin is solely applicable to original installations of central heating and hot water systems. For a listing of certificates of approval required by City departments for the improvement and/or replacement of existing heating equipment pursuant to Operational Bulletin No. C-15, Supplement No. 12, or Administrator's Interpretation No. 8 see Report Form R-33.1H (Heating Contractor's Statement).

Operational Bulletin No. C-15—Rental Values for Television Signal Reception; Revision of Schedule of Rental Values
Supplement No. 10 (Issued August 8, 1966)

The Schedule of Rental Values (April 1, 1964) is hereby revised as of the date of issuance of this bulletin in the following respect:

---

[a] In lieu of the indicated form, a fuel storage permit may be filed.

[b] In lieu of the indicated form, a "Letter of Completion" from the Department of Buildings attesting to the satisfactory completion of the installation may be submitted.

[c] Department of Air Resources Certificate of Operation will not be required for oil burning equipment firing not more than 2½ GPH of #2 fuel oil and having a maximum input capacity of less than 350,000 BTU per hour.

[d] Department of Air Resources Certificate of Registration will not be required for gas burning equipment having a maximum input capacity of less than 350,000 BTU per hour.

OPERATIONAL BULLETINS

The category of Television Antenna is amended to read *Television Signal Reception* as follows:

	Monthly Increase
TELEVISION SIGNAL RECEPTION*	
a. Tenant installed television antenna (any part of landlord's property)	$2.00
b. Master antenna hook-up (landlord-owned system)	2.00
c. Community antenna terminal (attached to tenant's apartment from any part of landlord's property)	2.00**

Operational Bulletin No. C-15, Supplement No. 11—Rental Values; Enclosing of Boiler Room and/or Cellar Stairs.

(Issued May 29, 1968)

The Administrator has determined that enclosure of a boiler room in any multiple dwelling having central heat regardless of size of structure or year built, and the enclosure of cellar stairs in new law tenements containing three or four apartments shall be considered an increase in service and/or equipment within the meaning of Section 33.1a of the Regulations for which rent increases may be granted. Both situations represent compliance with provisions in the Multiple Dwelling Law from which specific groups of structures had previously been exempt, and accordingly the consent of the tenants to such increase is implied.

The following schedules of rental values reflect a ten-year amortization of the average price charged by local contractors for boiler room and/or cellar stair enclosures, and shall apply to all installations, except as herein otherwise stated, without the necessity for a landlord to submit documentary evidence in substantiation of his actual cost. Where, however, a landlord claims that he is entitled to higher rent adjustments because an expenditure in excess of the established cost was incurred due to unique and peculiar circumstances, both the landlord and contractor will be required to submit detailed and persuasive proof of such expenditure as hereinafter shown under *Procedures*. In such instances, rent increases will be granted based on a ten-year amortization of verified

---

* Where a previous order has been issued increasing the maximum rent on the basis of the installation of any of the above Television Signal Reception systems, the subsequent replacement of one system by another, or the installation of an additional system, shall have no additional rental value.

** This is exclusive of any charges which may be allowed by the Board of Estimate of the City of New York for installation and service.

reasonable cost equally allocated among all units in structure.

I. Boiler Room Enclosure

Number of Units in Structure	Monthly Increase Per Unit
3	$1.00
4	.75
5-6	.55
7-9	.40
10-12	.30
13-16	.25
17-20	.20
21-25	.15
Over 25	.10

II. Cellar Stair Enclosure in New Law Tenements Containing No More Than Four (4) Dwelling Units

Number of Units in Structure	Monthly Increase Per Unit
3	$1.00
4	.75

III. Combined Boiler Room and Cellar Stair Enclosure in New Law Tenements Containing No More Than Four (4) Dwelling Units

Number of Units in Structure	Monthly Increase Per Unit
3	$1.75
4	1.30

Note—The above rental values shall apply where: (a) both enclosures are installed simultaneously; or (b) installations are made in compliance with dual orders contained on the same Building Department "Notice of Violation" whether or not enclosures are constructed simultaneously; or (c) installations are made within six months of each other. In the case of (b) or (c) combined total rent adjustments may not exceed the above allowances.

IV. Procedures

Where a landlord installs a boiler room enclosure in any multiple dwelling regardless of the size of the structure or year built, or where a landlord installs a boiler

Operational Bulletins

room enclosure and/or cellar stair enclosure in any new law tenement containing three (3) or four (4) dwelling units he may file an application for rent increases pursuant to Section 33.1a of the Regulations. However, to be eligible for rent adjustments, landlord must establish that no boiler room enclosure and/or cellar stair enclosure had existed prior to instant installation.

It is to be noted that no increases will be permitted for boiler room enclosure where a landlord has been granted rent increases under Administrator's Interpretation No. 8 for a heating system modernization which was completed after January 1, 1966. Nor will rent adjustments be granted for cellar stair enclosure where subject structure is classified as other than a new law tenement containing three or four dwelling units.

Landlord must submit the following documentary evidence with his application *in every instance:*

1. Proof of eligibility—
    a. Copy of Building Department "Notice of Complaint" or "Notice of Violation" directing landlord to *provide* a fireproof boiler room (Order No. 226) and/or cellar stair enclosure (Order No. 222); OR
    b. Inspector's Preliminary Report of Violation Form No. 194PR given by the Department of Buildings Inspector; OR
    c. An affidavit signed by landlord and contractor stating that no enclosure(s) had existed prior to the present installation.
2. Copy of contract(s) for installation of enclosure(s).
3. A total count of dwelling units including decontrolled, never controlled, and exempt accommodations.
4. Copy of Building Department Notice(s) describing classification and size of structure, and scope of work to be done.
5. Building Department Letter of Completion establishing that the work completed complies with all rules, regulations, and requirements of law.

Additional evidence to be submitted where rent adjustments in excess of established rental values are requested:

1. Cancelled checks and/or other evidence of expenditure such as copies of paid invoices or bills.
2. An affidavit signed by contractor itemizing all construction costs such as total square feet of walls, roof, and flooring, number of feet of ductwork, and number of doors installed, as well as any additional work performed in connection with instant installation(s).
3. Supplemental Statement of Landlord in Support of Application for Rent Adjustment(s) Pursuant to Section 33.1 of the Regulations (Report Form R-33.1).

Note—Applications submitted under Operational Bulletin No. C-15, Supplement No. 11 may be filed on either Form A-33.1C or Form A-33.1; to facilitate the processing of the application it is preferred that Form A-33.1C (revised 1-68) be used with an original and three (3) copies of each Form filed for each accommodation for which a rent increase is requested.

Operational Bulletin No. C-15—Upgrading or Modification of Existing Residual Oil Burning Equipment; Rental Increase and Procedures
Supplement No. 12 (Revised June 30, 1969, Effective July 1, 1969)

Pursuant to Local Law No. 14 of the Year 1966 all residual oil fired equipment must be upgraded to conform with standards established by the Department of Air Resources (formerly Department of Air Pollution Control). By definition fuel oil grades Nos. 5 and 6 are considered to be residual oil. Conversion of heating equipment to use No. 4 or No. 2 fuel oil, gas, or a combination of gas and No. 2 fuel oil is an acceptable alternative to upgrading, as is conversion to purchased steam service.

This Operational Bulletin shall be applicable to upgrading of existing residual oil burning equipment and modification of existing equipment to fire a lighter grade of fuel where the work performed complies with the provisions of Local Law No. 14 of 1966 and/or current criteria established by the Department of Air Resources and the various City departments having jurisdiction. Where, however, such compliance involves replacement of an existing heating system or any of its component parts (namely burner, boiler and/or fuel storage tank), regardless of grade or type of fuel to be used subsequent to installation, the provisions of Administrator's Interpretation No. 8 (revised June 30, 1969) shall be applicable.

The Administrator has determined that upgrading or modification of existing residual oil burning equipment shall be considered an increase in service and/or equipment within the meaning of Section 33.1a of the Regulations with the implied consent of the tenants due to the requirements of local law.

It should be noted that upgrading or modification of existing residual oil burning equipment differs from heating system modernization or conversion as defined in Administrator's Interpretation No. 8 in that no replacement of equipment is contemplated.

Rent Adjustments

Rent adjustments will be granted based on a nine-year amortization of the actual cost, exclusive of interest and/or financial charges, allocated on the basis of total number of rooms in the structure. Where two or more buildings share a common heating system the "number of rooms in structure" shall be the aggregate room count for all buildings tied into the heating system.

Because no schedule of rental values has been established for upgrading or modification of residual oil burning equipment due to the wide variance of job requirements, individual cost will be closely scrutinized as to reasonableness. Where the claimed cost appears excessive, or where the landlord fails to support his claim adequately, the Administrator reserves the right to adjust such claimed cost to reflect an amount that the Administrator shall find to be reasonable for such upgrading or modification.

It should also be noted that any person who wilfully makes any false statement or entry or omits to disclose discounts, refunds, rebates, etc., shall be guilty of a crime punishable by law. In addition, submission of fraudulent cost information may result in denial of an application for rent increases, or in the revocation—retroactive to date of orders—of rent increases already issued, and may preclude any subsequent adjustment in rents for this improvement.

Procedures

Where a landlord "upgrades" or "modifies" existing residual oil burning equipment he may file an application for rent increases pursuant to Section 33.1a of the Regulations on Application Form A-33.1 OBU. In his application the landlord shall state the nature and extent of the work performed.

The following shall be included with the application:

1. A copy of the signed contract for upgrading or modification of residual oil burning equipment.

2. A certification by the heating contractor (Report Form R-33.1H), in duplicate, which shall contain all requested information relative to the completed improvement including dates on which work permits were issued and certificates of approval were requested from City agencies having jurisdiction over heating system upgrading or modification; or, in the alternative, the specific approvals or certificates required for the type of work done, as listed on reverse side of Report Form R-33.1H "Heating Contractor's Statement and Certification."

3. A copy of Application Form APC 5-0 processed by the Department of Air Resources to show Combustion Application number and date of filing. **NOTE**—the applicant should enter the initials "RCS" on upper right hand corner of Form APC 5-0 before filing with the Department of Air Resources.

4. A certification by an independent or certified public accountant, in duplicate, which shall contain the information set forth in the "Suggested Form of Accountant's Certification." In the alternative, the landlord may submit the original and one duplicate copy of invoices or bills, and the original cancelled checks together with one duplicate copy of both sides of such checks; these should be submitted with Application Form A-33.1 OBU.

5. A total room count for the entire structure(s), including professional or commercial space and accommodations occupied by the landlord and service employees, and stores, if any. Also included in this count are decontrolled and exempt accommodations.

Include in the room count the following:

a. Kitchens, bedrooms, dining rooms, finished basement or attic rooms, recreation rooms, and other rooms suitable for use as living quarters. A kitchenette or "half-room" which is partitioned off from floor to ceiling should be counted as a separate room; but, a combined kitchenette and dinette, separated only by shelves or cabinets, should only be counted as one room.

b. Rooms used for office purposes.

c. Substitute for area of store space the room count for residential space above store.

The following are not to be included in the room count: Bathrooms, strip or pullman kitchens, halls, foyers, alcoves, pantries, laundries, closets, storage space, and basement or attic rooms which are not suitable for living quarters.

Suggested Form for Accountant's Certification

Re: Premises ....
....

To: The Office of Rent Control
Department of Rent and Housing Maintenance
Housing and Development Administration

I am an independent (or certified) public accountant, registered as such by and in good standing with the New York State Education Department. My number is ....

I have examined the accompanying application for rent increases under Section 33.1 of the Rent Regulations based upon an increase in service and/or equipment required by law, to wit, the upgrading or modification of existing residual oil burning equipment submitted by .... (insert name of individual or corporate owner), and all original invoices or bills and original cancelled checks relating to such installation. Attached hereto is a copy of my original worksheets showing the documents examined by me.

My examination was made in accordance with generally accepted auditing standards.

I hereby certify that the Owner's Application is supported by the owner's records and the invoices or bills and the original cancelled checks examined by me.

I further certify that $........ not yet paid but due

under the terms of the contract does not represent any interest, finance charges, rebates, discounts or refunds to the landlord but is being withheld until all of the terms of the contract relating to the upgrading or modification of the heating system have been fulfilled.

As an independent (or certified) public accountant, I have no direct or indirect financial interest in the success of the accompanying application. I have placed my initials and the date, for identification, in the lower right hand corner of the face of the application.

I have read the certification and I hereby affirm under the penalties provided by law that the contents thereof are true of my own knowledge.

....
(Signature of Accountant)

Dated: ....

Operational Bulletin No. C-15—Rental Values; Window Grilles
Supplement No. 13 (Issued February 25, 1970)

The Administrator has determined that the installation of window grilles which bear the approval of the New York City Board of Standards and Appeals and which conform with the requirements of all other City agencies having jurisdiction over this type of installation, would provide a means of protection from burglary and at the same time would permit easy egress in the event of fire or other emergency.

Applications for rental increases based upon such installations may be made on Application Form A-33.1C. The following requirements must be met as a condition of obtaining any order granting a rent increase:

a. Tenant's written consent must be obtained prior to installation.

b. Installation is limited to those windows which are readily accessible from the outside. These would normally include windows in street level apartments, windows leading to fire escapes and adjoining thereto, and windows easily accessible from hallways, corridors and roofs.

c. Landlords must submit the invoice with the name of the manufacturer, model number and dimensions of the grille, when applying for the increase.

Operational Bulletins

d. A rental increase will be granted for the installation of only those grilles which bear the approval of the Board of Standards and Appeals which has set up the following specifications:

1. Operating instructions shall be printed on a durable label attached to the visible face of the latch box cover door.

2. Maximum size of the grille frame shall be 40" wide × 72" high.

3. No key operated lock, padlock or chain shall be used.

4. The maximum uplift force required to disengage the latch shall not exceed four pounds.

5. All moving parts shall be covered with a heavy lubricant at all times.

The rental values for approved window grilles having a height of 50" to 72", both dimensions inclusive, are as follows:

Width of Grille	Monthly Rent Value Per Window Grille
24"–33"	$.75
34"–39"	.80

Where a landlord proposes to make an installation of a window grille of smaller dimensions in height and/or width than those provided for in the above Schedule of Rental Values, the landlord will be required to make application for a prior opinion and obtain approval before commencement of the installation.

Operational Bulletin No. C-15—Rental Values; Combination Burglar, Hold-up and Fire Alarm Systems.
Supplement No. 14 (Issued February 25, 1970)

The Administrator has determined that the installation of a burglar alarm system hereinafter described is a substantial increase in services and facilities which would warrant an adjustment in rent under Section 33.1a of the Rent and Eviction Regulations.

The burglar alarm system, for which the Schedule of Rental Values has been established, is a combination burglar, hold-up and fire alarm system consisting of an electronically activated burglar alarm (with stand-by batteries in case of power failure) to which the apartment door, appropriate windows* and other points of entry are wired; a panic or hold-up toggle switch to activate the alarm when a hold-up is taking place, or shortly thereafter; and a thermostate heat detector, which sets off the alarm at or above a given level or smoke or heat. Normally, these devices once set off, continue to ring until turned off by key. It may be possible to install a timing device which could shut off the alarm automatically, after a specified interval.

The following Schedule of Rental Values will be applicable under the conditions noted below.

Schedule of Rental Values for Combination Burglar, Hold-up and Fire Alarm Systems

	Monthly Rental Values
For installations involving wiring *one* entrance door, *one* toggle (panic) switch, and *one* thermostat	$3.15
For wiring each additional opening (door or window), add	.15
For each additional thermostat, add	.10
For each additional toggle (panic) switch, add	.15

Illustration of the Computation of the Rental Value

For an apartment that requires wiring one entrance door, three windows, five thermostats and a toggle (panic) switch, to the basic $3.15 should be added $.45 for three windows and $.40 for four additional thermostats, for a total monthly rental value of $4.00.

Landlord's Obligations and Minimum Equipment Standards

Landlord's Obligations:

1. To obtain consent of tenant in occupancy as a precondition to installation.

2. To assume responsibility for proper maintenance and operation of the equipment. Minimum Equipment Standards:

a. The system installed should be a comprehensive one covering all areas accessible from the outside.

b. 18 gauge steel cabinet (or its equivalent) approximately 12" wide by 15" high and 4" deep, containing burglar, fire and hold-up alarm equipment.

---

* This refers only to those windows which are *readily accessible from the outside*. Whereas these might include all windows at street level or close to the roof, for apartments on upper floors, they would most frequently involve only two windows; i.e., those opening or adjacent to a fire escape or public hall.

Operational Bulletins

c. Unit supplied with a combination AC-DC power supply with provision for standby battery in case of power failure.

d. Alarm bell made of cast aluminum with an 8" har steel shell (or equivalent).

e. Protective contacts for window switches in non-conductive material.

f. Toggle switch (used as hold-up or panic switch) mounted in case.

g. One thermostate heat detector per room except the bathroom.

h. The thermostate heat sensing device and wiring must be listed with any recognized testing laboratory and should be installed on the ceiling, or at a height of not less than 7 feet from the floor, for maximum protection.

i. Shunt lock at apartment door to permit tenant to enter without activating alarm.

j. Two control keys.

k. All work shall comply with the New York City Electrical Code and all applicable rules and regulations of the City departments having jurisdiction, if any.

In unique situations involving the installation of a more sophisticated system, a prior opinion application must be filed, and approval obtained, before the installation is undertaken.

Operational Bulletin No. C-15—Modernization of Existing Bathrooms and Installation of Bathrooms (None Before); Rental Values, Minimum Requirements and Procedures.
Supplement No. 15 (Issued September 17, 1971)

The Administrator has established as of the date of issuance of this bulletin the following rental values for modernization of existing two-and three-fixture bathrooms and installation of bathrooms (none before) pursuant to Section 33.1 of the Regulations. Heretofore, rent adjustments for such improvements were granted on a prior opinion basis. In the future, the filing of an application for a prior opinion will not be required except as hereinafter specified.

To be eligible for a rent increase the modernization or installation must comply with the following minimum bathroom requirements:

Minimum Bathroom Requirements*

1. *New piping:* shall include soil, waste and vent branches, trap and concealed water supply branches for each fixture; and a lead bend for water closet.

2. *Three new bathroom fixtures:* shall include

a. Built-in bathtub with overhead shower; bathtub to be a minimum of 4'6" long or 4' square and to have an acid-resistant finish.**

b. Washbasin of cast iron or vitreous china with mixing faucets and pop-up waste, the bowl to have minimum dimensions of 19 × 17 inches.***

c. Water closet of vitreous china.

3. *Ceramic tile floor and wainscoting* to a minimum height of 4' on all walls, except 6' from floor around bathtub area.

4. *New accessories:* shall include a recessed medicine cabinet with mirror to be located above lavatory, shower curtain rod, 2 towel bars, toilet paper holder, soap dish with grab bar at tub, soap dish at basin and a marble door saddle.

5. *A new electric fixture* above medicine cabinet, an *outlet* either above or beside medicine cabinet and a *light switch* convenient to door.

6. *Heat riser or radiator.*

7. *Window or ventilator* in compliance with Building Department specifications.

8. *Bathroom door with lock*

Rent Adjustments

The following Schedule of Rental Values will be applicable to all buildings except for specific situations hereinafter noted.

---

* Where an apartment contains an existing water closet, but not a two or three-fixture bathroom and the water closet is to be retained in its present location, but the enclosure cannot be enlarged due to structural or other valid reasons, a partial bathroom constructed in a separate location will be eligible for a rent increase provided it meets all basic requirements other than the water closet and items pertaining thereto.

** Where it can be proved that structural problems prevent installation of either abovementioned size, a bathtub 39" square or a tiled stall shower may be permitted. A tiled stall shower may be installed in addition to a bathtub on a prior opinion basis. However, except in the event of proved structural problems a tiled stall shower may only be installed in place of a bathtub where apartment contains a second bathroom, one of which contains a bathtub.

*** A bathroom vanity may be installed in lieu of wash basin.

OPERATIONAL BULLETINS

Schedule of Rental Values

	Monthly Rent Increase
Single Bathroom Installation	
Modernization of an existing three-fixture bathroom[1]	$14.50
Modernization of an existing two- to three-fixture bathroom including enlargement of partitions[1]	17.50
Installation of new bathroom—in lieu of water closet[2]	20.50
Installation of partial bathroom—existing water closet and enclosure[2]	17.50
Building-Wide Bathroom Installation With Complete New Drainage System *	
Modernization of an existing three-fixture bathroom[1]	16.00
Modernization of an existing two- or three-fixture bathroom including enlargement of partitions	19.00
Installation of new bathroom—in lieu of water closet[2]	22.00
Installation of partial bathroom—existing water closet and enclosure to be retained[2]	19.00

Note: Rent Increases include a cast iron bathtub. Deduct $.60 for installation of a steel bathtub.

An additional allowance of $2.00 will be granted where tiling on all walls is extended from floor to ceiling.

Deduct $2.75 where brass or copper plumbing is installed simultaneously.

Where building-wide bathroom modernization or installation is planned on a line basis and landlord proposes to

---

* Where complete vertical drainage system is retained deduct $3.00 from monthly rent increase. If soil stack is retained, but new waste and vent lines are installed, deduct $1.50.

1. a. Where an order had previously been issued for installation or replacement of wash basin, low tank toilet, flushometer, shower or other bathroom component, the following deductions shall be made from the above schedule: If order was issued 12 or more years ago no deductions shall be made; if last order was issued 6 or more years ago but less than 12 years previous to present date deduct one-half of the allowance granted; if last order was issued less than 6 years ago deduct full amount granted. However, an existing fixture installed less than 6 years previous to present alteration may be retained, and be so noted on Report Form R-33.1B (Plumbing Contractor's Statement and Certification).
   b. Where an order had previously been issued for installation of brass plumbing the following amount reflecting the value of bathroom branches and a portion of the trim shall be deducted: $2.75 if grant involved concealed plumbing, $1.25 if exposed.
   c. Where the area of an existing two-fixture bathroom is adequate to accommodate the addition of the third fixture without the enlargement of partitions, the allowance for modernization of a three-fixture bathroom will apply.
2. a. Where an order had previously been issued for exclusive use of a hall water closet, a minimum of $2.00 shall be deducted from the above schedule. Where a further adjustment had been granted for a low tank toilet see 1a for additional deduction.
   b. Where an order had previously been issued for installation of a private water closet within subject apartment, $2.00 shall be deducted from the above schedule if order was issued 6 or more years ago, or $2.75 if order was issued less than 6 years ago.
   c. Where a bathroom is installed in what was previously a small bedroom, $3.00 shall be deducted from the above schedule to compensate for loss of living space.

apply for rent adjustments as each line of apartments is completed, landlord should apply for a prior opinion submitting therewith a comprehensive and consecutively timed program for the entire structure.

Procedures

The rental schedule indicated above will apply to all bathroom modernizations and installations (none before) except where the landlord claims that he has experienced substantially higher than average costs and submits documentary evidence in support of his claim. In such instances the monthly rent increase will be based on a 7-year amortization of verified costs, limited to a maximum of 50 percent above the scheduled value.

Where, however, the landlord claims that due to unique circumstances an excessive expenditure is indicated, or where a complete and a partial bathroom or two complete bathrooms are to be modernized in a single apartment, the landlord should apply for a prior opinion before commencing work. In his application for the prior opinion, the landlord should give full particulars about the proposed scope of work including complete cost information.

Written consent of the tenant will be required where bathroom modernization or installation (none before) is performed in one or more, but less than all, apartments in a given building. However, where a single bathroom installation would complete a line of apartments, the landlord may submit evidence of such fact in lieu of written tenant consent. Where bathroom modernization on a building-wide or line basis is involved, written consent of 51 percent of the *tenants in occupancy* will be required except where such work is done in connection with a complete building-wide rehabilitation. No tenant consent will be necessary where there is a building-wide installation (none before) to replace existing water closets.

When work is completed the landlord may file for rent increases pursuant to Section 33.1 of the Regulations. A separate Application Form A-33.1BMI Combination must be filed for each apartment for which a rent increase is requested, and should include a brief description of the previous plumbing fixtures and facilities, as well as the

Operational Bulletins

nature and extent of the completed improvement. In addition, a Master Application Form A-33.-1BMI must be filed where the scope of work involves two or more apartments.

The following shall be submitted with the applications:

1. A certification by the plumbing contractor (Report Form R-33.1B, in duplicate) which shall contain all requested information relative to the completed installation including dates on which work permits were issued by and certificates of approval were requested from City agencies having jurisdiction over bathroom modernization or installation: or, the specific approvals and certificates required for the type of work done as listed on reverse side of Report Form R-33.1B "Plumbing Contractor's Statement and Certification."

2. For building-wide bathroom modernization or installation: a report of search issued by the Office of Code Enforcement of the Department of Rent and Housing Maintenance of the Housing and Development Administration stating either that no violations against the property are recorded or that all violations recorded against the property have been complied with, or a receipt (or copy thereof) issued by the Borough Office of the Department of Buildings attesting to the payment of the fee for a report of search. Such report of search will not be acceptable unless issued by such agency within 45 days prior to the date of filing the application, or in lieu thereof, such receipt may not be dated more than 14 days prior to the date of filing the application. See Operational Bulletin No. C-9, revised, for further details.

3. Where an appropriate rent increase is to be computed based on a 7-year amortization of verified costs due to higher than average costs, or is to be determined on the basis of a prior opinion order, the landlord shall submit the following additional documents:

   a. A copy of the signed contract for bathroom modernization or installation. (Attach to Report Form R-33.1—Supplemental Statement of Landlord) and either b or c.

   b. A certification by an independent or certified public accountant, in duplicate, which shall contain the information set forth in the "Suggested Form for Accountant's Certification"; or

c. If the landlord does not desire to submit a certification by an accountant, he may in lieu thereof submit the original invoices or bills together with one duplicate copy of such invoices and bills, and the original cancelled checks together with one duplicate copy of both sides of such checks.

No rent increase order will be issued unless the landlard has submitted to the Office of Rent Control all of the aforementioned documents relating to the specific installation made, including either a statement by the Plumbing Contractor (Report Form R-33.1B) certifying that the work has been completed and that certificates of approval have been officially requested from the City departments having jurisdiction, or copies of the appropriate permits and certificates of approval required by City departments having jurisdiction, as shown on the reverse side of Report Form R-33.1B.

Suggested Form for Accountant's Certification
Re: Premises ....

To: The Office of Rent Control
   Department of Rent and Housing Maintenance
   Housing and Development Administration

I am an independent (or certified) public accountant, registered (as such by and in good standing) with New York State Education Department. My number is .....

I have examined the accompanying application for rent increases under Section 33.1 of the Rent Regulations based upon an increase in service and/or equipment, to wit, the bathroom modernization(s) or installation(s) submitted by .... (insert name of individual or corporate owner) and all original invoices or bills and original cancelled checks relating to such installation. Attached hereto is a copy of my original worksheets showing the documents examined by me.

My examination was made in accordance with generally accepted auditing standards.

I hereby certify that the owner's application is supported by the owner's records and the invoices or bills and the original cancelled checks examined by me.

I further certify that $.... not yet paid but due under the terms of the contract does not represent any interest, finance charges, rebates, discounts or refunds to the landlord but is being withheld until all of the terms of the contract relating to the bathroom modernization(s) or installation(s) have been fulfilled.

As an independent (or certified) public accountant, I have no direct or indirect financial interest in the owner-applicant or the success of the accompanying application upon which I have placed my initials, and the date, for identification, in the lower right hand corner of the face of the application.

I have read this certification and I hereby affirm under the penalties provided by law that the contents thereof are true of my own knowledge.

....
Signature of Accountant
Dated ....197..

OPERATIONAL BULLETINS

Operational Bulletin No. C-15—Rental Values, Doors (apartment entrance) Fireproof Kalamein. Supplement No. 16

(Supersedes Operational Bulletin No. C-15, Supplement No. 15, issued September 17, 1971.)

Monthly Rent Increase

DOORS *(apartment entrance)* fireproof Kalamein *(new)*
  complete installation with frame............................ $2.75
  complete installation without frame......................... 2.00
Complete installation includes painting and plastering where required.

To qualify for the monthly rental increase, the following conditions must be met:

(a) door must be self-closing, kalamein with a minimum one hour fire resistance rating, bearing affixed to the jamb thereof, a metal tag or stamp issued by the Board of Standards and Appeals or the Department of Buildings;

(a) door must be equipped with new hinges, knob, a heavy duty latch set with a heavy duty dead bolt lock according to standards of Federal General Services Administration specifications FF-H-106a Series 86A*, extruded brass (or its equivalent) chain door guard, minimum thickness of jamb plate .075", with welded hardened steel link chain an approved peephole with name plate and chime where there is no bell and buzzer;

(c) two keys must be provided.

Where the landlord of an old law tenement four stories or more in height is replacing an apartment door opening into any stairs or public hall unprotected by an approved sprinkler system that does not meet the required minimum one hour fire resistance rating mandated by Section D26-20-07 subdivision b of the New York City Administrative Code, as amended by Local Law No. 17 for the Year 1973, tenant consent is not required except as hereinafter set forth. It is not a violation of such law to continue existing apartment entrance doors not meeting the one hour fire resistance rating below the fourth floor until an application for an alteration permit for alterations to such an apartment is made. Where the installa-

---

* Detailed specifications are available upon request of the Research Division.

tion of the fireproof apartment door is not required to bring the building into compliance with the law, the freely given consent of the tenant both to the installation and to the resulting monthly increase must be obtained. Increases will be granted only for those doors which meet the above specifications. For doors of unusual size and/or where it is necessary to use additional equipment, due to unusual circumstances, landlord would have to file a prior opinion application and obtain approval before the installation is undertaken.

Operational Bulletin No. C-16—Certification of costs by landlord in making applications pursuant to § 33.1 of the Regulations; Use of Report Form R-33.1.

(Issued June 20, 1963)

Where an application is made by a landlord for a rent increase pursuant to the provisions of Section 33.1 of the Regulations, it may be necessary that the actual cost to the landlord be substantiated in cases where there is no prescribed rental value.

In connection with this substantiation, it will be necessary for the landlord to execute a supplemental statement [Report Form R-33.1 (7-63)] which will attest the fact of the actual cost, exclusive of financial charges, rebates, discounts or refunds, if any. The landlord will be required to submit not only the actual paid bills or invoices; but, also to attach photocopy duplicates of such bill or invoices to the original supplemental statement.

This supplemental statement will not necessarily be required to be filed with the application. Where the District Director deems such statement and evidence to be necessary for the proper determination of the application, Notice Form N-21 (Notice of Opportunity to Present Further Information and Evidence) should be mailed to the landlord, together with three copies of blank Report Form R-33.1, requesting the landlord to file the supplemental statement and to submit the original invoices or bills.

THE CITY OF NEW YORK   Docket
CITY RENT and REHABILITATION ADMINISTRATION   No.
SUPPLEMENTAL STATEMENT OF LANDLORD IN SUPPORT OF
APPLICATION FOR RENT ADJUSTMENT(S) PURSUANT
TO § 33.1 OF THE REGULATIONS

STATE OF NEW YORK
CITY OF NEW YORK   } SS:
COUNTY OF ....

........, being duly sworn, deposes and says that (s)he is (one of) (the .... of .... Corp.), the owner(s) of the property mentioned and described in the application heretofore filed with and now pending before the City Rent and Rehabilitation Administration and is making this affidavit, knowing that said City Rent and Rehabilitation Administration may rely upon the truth of the statements herein made by me in granting the relief requested by me in said application.

That the increased services, improvements, substantial rehabilitation or work specifically set forth in said application were provided by the landlord for a total cost, excluding financial charges, and without any rebates, discounts or refunds, of $......

That as evidence of such payment deponent hereby submits the original invoices or bills for the above and attaches photocopy duplicates of such invoices and bills, which deponent states are true copies of the originals thereof.

That deponent further states that the amounts set forth on such bills or invoices are in fact the amounts actually paid by the landlord.

Sworn to before me this
....day of........, 196..

Signature of Landlord

Operational Bulletin No. C-17—Administration of oaths by employees of the City Rent and Rehabilitation Administration; Form of oath
(Issued February 26, 1964)

Section Y51-7.0b of the Rent Law provides that ". . . Any officer or agent designated by the city rent agency . . . may administer oaths and affirmations . . . ." Pursuant to such authority granted to her by the aforesaid provision of the Rent Law, the Administrator has duly designated several persons in each of the District Rent Offices as persons who may administer oaths in connection with making affidavits, applications and any other documents or papers which may be filed in connection with proceedings before the City Rent and Rehabilitation Administration.

The administration of a formal oath to the party executing the document is an absolute necessity in all cases. Without compliance with this formality the deposition is only an unsworn statement which cannot form the basis of a prosecution for perjury.

Accordingly, all persons who are so designated to administer oaths must administer the following oath after first requesting the party who has made the statement to raise his or her right hand:

"Do you solemnly swear (or affirm) that the statements contained in this document are the truth, the whole truth and nothing but the truth, so help you God?"

After obtaining an affirmative answer, the party taking the oath shall sign the document in the presence of the employee who shall then complete the jurat by inserting the date, signing his name and affixing the official stamp of his authority.

Where any employees of the Principal Office have been designated to administer oaths, the same procedure shall be followed.

Operational Bulletin No. C-18—"High Rent" Decontrol; Local Law No. 13; Amendment No. 9; Report of Eligibility for Decontrol; Report of Decontrol. (Issued March 26, 1964)

The amendment of the City Rent Law by Local Law No. 13 for the Year 1964, decontrols certain housing accommodations renting for $250.00 or more per month as of April 1, 1960. The Regulations have been amended to conform to the Rent Law by adding Section 2 f (14). In addition Section 42 of the Regulations was amended by adding paragraph c which requires the filing of (1) a Report of Eligibility for Decontrol no later than April 30, 1964, (2) a Report of Decontrol within 30 days after decontrol, and (3) a Supplementary Report of Decontrol one year later.

Housing accommodations having unfurnished maximum rents of $250.00 or more per month, or having furnished maximum rents of $300.00 or more per month, as of April 1, 1960 which are or become vacant on or after the effective date of Local Law No. 13 are decontrolled immediately.

The decontrol of occupied housing accommodations is staggered, the date of decontrol depending upon the amount of rental and the nature of the occupancy. The following table sets forth the decontrol schedule for occupied accommodations.

Maximum Monthly Rents As Of April 1, 1969

	Unfurnished	Furnished	Effective Date Of Decontrol
1. occupied by less than 4 related persons	$300.00 or more	$360.00 or more	
a. no school children			October 1, 1964
b. with school children			June 30, 1965
2. occupied by 4 or more related persons	$300.00 or more	$360.00 or more	on vacancy
3. occupied by less than 4 related persons	$250.00 to $299.99	$300.00 to $359.99	
a. no school children			April 1, 1965
b. with school children			June 30, 1965
4. occupied by 4 or more related persons	$250.00 to $299.99	$300.00 to $359.99	on vacancy

The term "related persons", as defined by Section 2 f (14) of the Regulations means the tenant and a parent, grandparent, child, step-child, grandchild, brother or sister of the tenant or of the tenant's spouse or the spouse of any of the foregoing, who customarily occupied the apartment on the effective date of Local Law No. 13 for the year 1964. Subparagraph (14) of Section 2 f also provides that "the tenant's spouse or unmarried child or grandchild of the tenant who temporarily resided elsewhere on the effective date of this" subparagraph "because of attendance at an educational institution or service in the armed forces of the United States shall be deemed to be a related person in occupancy."

In addition such decontrol remains effective only so long as the housing accommodation is not occupied for other than single-family occupancy.

Amendment No. 9 to the Regulations adds paragraph c to Section 42. As indicated above various reports must be filed by the landlord. Appropriate forms are being prepared by the Administrator and should be ready for public distribution within the next 15 days.

PROCEDURE

Section 42 c requires the landlord to file a Report of Eligibility for Decontrol. Report Form R-42ED is designed to supply the District Director with the information which will show whether the housing accommodation will qualify for decontrol under the provisions of Section 2 f (14) of the Regulations. An original and three copies of this report must be filed with the District Rent Office no later than April 30, 1964. These reports will be screened for completeness and reviewed by the District Office.

After varifying the maximum rent indicated in item 1 of the report, Part B should be reviewed on the basis of the information supplied in Part A. If the applicable box is not marked with an "X", the examiner should make the appropriate notation on the original and all copies in red. The report should then be docketed and the docket number noted on the original and all copies. The original will be retained by the District Office and one copy mailed to the landlord, tenant and Research and Survey Division at the Principal Office of the Administrator. The tenant should also be given two copies of Answer Form N-4.

In the cases where the tenant files an answer which prima facie shows that the accommodation is not eligible for decontrol as stated by the landlord in his report, proceedings should be instituted by the District Rent Director pursuant to Section 36 a of the Regulations and his finding and determination of the issue raised by the tenant should be finalized by the issuance of a formal order (O-36).

It is to be noted that the filing of the report is subject to examination and review at anytime even though the Report Form advises the tenant to file an answer to the report within 7 days. Accordingly, there can be no "late" application by the tenant for a review of the report by the District Rent Director. The above procedure relative to Report Form R-42ED will ordinarily dispose of all issues relative to decontrol pursuant to Local Law No. 13 prior to decontrol.

Within 30 days after decontrol the landlord will file a decontrol report (Report Form R-42HR). This report will be screened and processed in the same manner that the District Rent Office processes reports of decontrol under the other decontrol provisions of the Rent Law.

Operational Bulletin No. C-19—§ 33.1 Application based upon restoration of services, etc.; Refusal by tenant to permit restoration; Sub-item k of item 8 of Application Form A-33.1C clarified.
(Issued May 19, 1964)

Sub-item k of Item 8 of Application Form A-33.1C now reads:

"Landlord has restored or offered to restore services, equipment, etc. which was the basis of an order reducing maximum rent. (See Docket No. . . . .)"

It is urged that a landlord's mere offer to restore services, equipment, etc. will be a sufficient basis for the restoration of a reduced maximum rent. Such strained construction of sub-item k was never contemplated. The offer to restore must be genuine and will only be the basis for the restoration of a decreased maximum rent where the tenant has unreasonably refused to permit the landlord to restore such services, etc. What is reasonable depends upon the facts which are peculiar to the individual case. Where it is put in issue, a conference should ordinarily be held at which both landlord and tenant can submit their proof.

Application Form A-33.1C is being revised in order to incorporate the above construction of sub-item k. The present forms may be used until the present inventory is exhausted. However, where the current form is used on applications filed after the revision of the form, the application should not be rejected for the reason that the form is obsolete.

The revised form will read:

"k. Landlord has restored services, equipment, etc. which was the basis of an order reducing maximum rent, or the Tenant has unreasonably refused to permit the Landlord to restore such services. (See Docket No. . . . .)".

Operational Bulletin No. C-20—Certification of Rent-Rolls; Application Form A-1RR

(Issued September 29, 1964)

Application Form A-1RR has been designed to facilitate the certification of rent-roll requests. Heretofore, such requests were honored only when made by the owner or some other party who was authorized by him to obtain such information. Upon reconsideration of this policy, the Administrator has determined that there are others who have a legitimate interest in obtaining this information. The new form indicates which parties may properly request rent-roll certifications.

In all cases a copy of the application and certification will be mailed to the landlord in order that he may be apprised of the fact that the District Rent Office has certified the rent-roll for the property. This will insure that the applicant has a legitimate interest in obtaining the information and at the same time give the landlord an opportunity of knowing whether there are any discrepancies between his records and that of the District Rent Office.

Where the records of the District Rent Office do not disclose that the landlord indicated in item 1 is the same as the owner indicated on the Registration Statement or the last Report of Change in Identity of Landlord, blank Report Form R-44 should be mailed to the indicated landlord with a request that the form be completed and returned to the District Rent Office. However, the rent-roll certification should be completed without waiting for the filing of Report Form R-44.

It is to be noted that in item 6 of Application Form A-1RR there is a blank space for the insertion of a date. If no date is filled in, it should be assumed that the date is the date of the certification. No application may be rejected due to the failure of the applicant to insert such date.

APPLICATION FOR CERTIFICATION OF RENT-ROLL

1. MAILING ADDRESS OF LANDLORD:
Name............... Tel.No.....
Number and Street..........................
City, Zone No., and State ....

2. MAILING ADDRESS OF APPLICANT. *[complete if applicant is not the landlord.]*
Name............... Tel. No.....
Number and Street..........................
City, Zone No., and State ....

(Number and Street) (Apt. No.) (Borough and Zone No.)
3. Address of housing accommodations:

4. Name and Address of Applicant's Attorney, if any:

5. The applicant is (check the appropriate box)
   a. ☐ the owner of the above premises.
   b. ☐ the contract vendee of the above premises.
   c. ☐ a savings bank, insurance company or other lending institution which has issued a mortgage commitment affecting the above premises.
   d. ☐ a holder of a mortgage lien on the above premises.
   e. ☐ the attorney for the party checked above.
   f. ☐ the attorney for a party in pending litigation in which the rent-roll for the above premises is in issue. (Attach rider in duplicate identifying the litigation by stating the title of the action, the Court, Docket or Index No. of the action, and the names and addresses of all attorneys appearing in the action. **An additional copy of Application Form A-1RR should be submitted for each attorney appearing in the action.**)
   g. ☐ Other *(explain).*

6. The District Rent and Rehabilitation Director is hereby requested to certify whether the attached rent-roll or rent-list correctly states the maximum rents in effect on .... 196.. for the indicated housing accommodations in accordance with the records of the District Rent Office. (**Submit in triplicate unless item 5 f applies.**)

....
(Signature of applicant)

NOTE—In all cases a copy of this application and the requested certification will be mailed to the landlord indicated in item 1.

Operational Bulletin No. C-21—*Notice of Commencement of Proceedings to reduce rents to be served upon mortgagees when requested; Report Form R-44* [Supplement]

(Issued October 15, 1964)

OPERATIONAL BULLETINS

Several financial institutions which hold mortgages on rent-controlled properties have requested this Administration to advise them when proceedings have been commenced by District Rent Directors to reduce rents on a building-wide basis due to violations and/or multiple tenants complaints concerning the substantial deterioration of a property. These mortgagees state that after having received notice of such action, they will be in a position to bring pressure to bear upon the owner to remedy the condition and lend their financial assistance, if needed, for that purpose.

The Administrator has accordingly designed Report Form R-44 [Supplement] which shall be used by such mortgagees for the purpose of making the request and filed in duplicate with the District Rent Office having jurisdiction over the property involved. The form is printed in buff color and is of a size which will permit its filing with the registration statements. Whenever action to reduce rents is to be initiated a notation should be made on the Progress Sheet that the form has been filed and that a copy of the notice must be mailed to the indicated party. It is to be noted that *only* the initial Notice of Commencement of Proceedings need be mailed to the mortgagee. There is no requirement for the filing of the form by the mortgagee or that due process requires service upon the mortgagee. However, it is anticipated that this cooperative procedure will result in the acceleration of restoration activity by landlords. Your narrative reports should contain comments concerning the advisability of continuing this program.

REPORT FORM R-44 [SUPPLEMENT]

(Number and Street)   Borough and Zone No.

1. Address of housing accommodations:

The undersigned, being the holder of a mortgage which is now a lien on the above premises, hereby requests the District Rent Director to serve a copy of any Notice of Commencement of Proceedings to reduce the maximum rents for the entire premises indicated above on the basis of a multiple tenants' complaint or on the basis of the certification of building-wide violations by a City Department having jurisdiction.

....
(Signature of applicant-mortgagor)

Mailing Address:
Number and
Street.....................................
City, Zone No.,
and State ....

Dated .... 19..

OPERATIONAL BULLETINS

Operational Bulletin No. C-22—District Director's Orders and Order and Opinions of the Administrator; Date of Issuance and Mailing
(Issued February 15, 1965)

It has been the practice of this Administration to mail all orders on the date of their issuance. However, in order to insure that there be no exceptions to this procedure the following directive is hereby promulgated:

> No order of the District Rent Director or order and opinion of the Administrator may be date-stamped as being issued unless such order or order and opinion can also be mailed on such date. Where it is not possible to both issue and mail such order or order and opinion on the same date, the issuance shall be deferred until such date when it can be both issued and mailed.

Operational Bulletin No. C-23—Affirmation by attorney in lieu of affidavit
(Issued February 15, 1965)

Rule 2106 of the Civil Practice Law and Rules provides:

> "R. 2106. Affirmation of truth of statement by attorney. The statement of an attorney admitted to practice in the courts of the state and appearing in an action as attorney of record or as of counsel with the attorney of record, when subscribed and affirmed by him to be true under the penalties of perjury, may be served or filed in the action in lieu of and with the same force and effect as an affidavit."

Accordingly, wherever provision is made in the Regulations for the filing of an affidavit of service, if the party making such service is an attorney appearing in the proceeding before the Rent Administration, such attorney may, in lieu of executing an affidavit of service, file an affirmation of service which need not be sworn to before a notary public or other person authorized to administer oaths. Such affirmation shall follow the attorney's statement and shall read as follows:

> "The undersigned, attorney of record [of counsel with the attorney of record] for ...., one of the parties to this proceeding, affirms that the foregoing statement is true under penalty of perjury."

Where a formal application is filed and the applicant-landlord or applicant-tenant is also an attorney and affirmation may be executed in lieu of an affidavit. However, it must be noted, that the statement to which the affirmation refers must contain all the elements contained in the affidavit which is incorporated in the official application form.

Operational Bulletin No. C-24—Additional allowance where bathrooms, etc. are installed in rooming houses or in single room occupancy accommodations
(Issued April 22, 1965)

The Administrative Code requires that there be provided in rooming houses (a) at least one water-closet on each floor containing any room used for "class B occupancy"; and (b) at least one water-closet, one bath or shower and one wash basin (i) for each six persons who may lawfully occupy any room or rooms used for "class B occupancy", and (ii) for any remainder of less than six persons. (Section D26-6.1)

With respect to apartments used for single room occupancy, the Administrative Code requires that there shall be provided in each such apartment, at least one water-closet, one bath or shower and one wash basin for each six persons who may lawfully occupy rooms in such apartment, and for any remainder of less than six such persons.

Thus, where an additional water-closet, bath or shower and wash basin are required to be installed, the existing sanitary facilities will be utilized by a fewer number of tenants who will thereby in effect be afforded an increase in services within the meaning of Section 33.1 of the Regulations. In cases where the new facilities are installed in space which was formerly rentable, it would be equitable to consider the resulting loss of income as a factor in determining the rental value of such increase in service. Thus it would be proper to allocate such expense to all rooms which had used the existing facilities and add such amount to the rent increase otherwise allowable for the new improvement or increase in service provided to the tenants using the old facilities.

Operational Bulletin No. C-25—§ 34.2 MD applications; notice to Tenants' Representative of Landlord's cross-application for rent increase or of Landlord's application for restoration of rents after rent decreases ordered for reduction in services, etc.
(Issued July 27, 1965)

Where a tenants' multiple application for rent reduction pursuant to § 34.2 is filed by a Tenants' Representative, the representative's interest in the matter does not terminate with the filing of the application at the District Rent Office. Nor does such interest terminate with the reduction order. The representative, as well as the District Director, is primarily concerned with the restoration of service. The rent reduction removes the profit motive from a continued elimination of service; but, the maintenance of service remains our objective. This may be achieved in one of two ways. During the pendency of the proceedings to reduce the rent, the landlord may restore the service or replace it with improvements which would qualify him for a rent increase rather than a rent reduction. For example, where the tenants complain of a defective bell and buzzer system as the basis for a rent reduction, the landlord may rewire the existing system and obtain a rent increase as provided in Operational Bulletin No. C-15. In such situations it would be proper to advise the Tenants' Representative that the landlord has made application for rent increases based upon the complete rewiring of the existing bell and buzzer system.

Similarly, where the landlord claims that he has restored the services which were the basis for the rent reduction orders and has filed an application for the restoration of the rents, the Tenants' Representative should also be notified that the application has been filed.

In a great many cases the Tenants' Representative has been very helpful in clarifying the issues. Such assistance should continue to be utilized until the tenants' complaint has been finally resolved.

Operational Bulletin No. C-26—Home security systems; minimum standards and rental values
This Operational Bulletin is superseded by 1968 revision of Operational Bulletin No. C-15, supra.
Operational Bulletin No. C-27—Emergency and Expeditious Section 34.2 Proceedings Based Upon a Total Decrease in Heating and/or Hot Water Service.

(Issued February 8, 1966)

The following expeditious procedures have been adopted by the Administrator for processing complaints of no heat and/or hot water:

Complaints concerning the total elimination of heat and/or hot water must be personally instituted and expeditiously terminated by District Rent Directors whether such complaints originate by telephone, by correspondence, by delivery in person or from the filing of a formal

OPERATIONAL BULLETINS

application for rent decrease. Such complaint from one tenant in the building (or from any other reliable source) will be sufficient to cause the District Director to initiate the expeditious action provided for in this Bulletin.

Whenever a telephone complaint is made or a complaint is delivered in person, inquiry should be made of the complainant to obtain pertinent information identifying the housing accommodation by street, address, apartment number, the name of the landlord or agent, the address of the landlord or agent, the telephone number of the landlord or agent, and the name of the complainant as well as his telephone number. Interdepartmental Referral Form 75M should be used for memoranda of receipt of such complaints by the District Office.*

Whenever there is a telephone complaint or a letter complaint, or a complaint delivered in person, the District Director shall cause an immediate inspection to be made in order to verify the allegation of no heat and/or hot water. A similar expedite inspection should be made when a formal application for rent reduction for reason of no heat and/or hot water has been received.

The inspector will report, by telephone, to the District Director, the name and address of the landlord or agent, the number of apartments in the building and the extent of the breakdown in heating service, as well as what steps, if any, are being taken by the landlord to restore heat and/or hot water.

Where the inspection shows that there is *no* heat and/or hot water being furnished, the District Director shall, within 24 hours, institute an Administrative proceeding under Section 34.2. The District Director shall immediately issue a notice, Form N-34.2H, to the landlord of record and to any mortgagee of record, requiring the landlord, within 3 days from the date of the mailing of the notice,** to show cause why the rentals of the apartments in the building should not be reduced, based upon inspection evidence that no heat and/or hot water is being provided in the building.

---

* NOTE: Copies of Form 75M will also serve as a "request" for expedite inspection, outlined below, and for advice of the Building Dept. where there is evidence, upon inspection, that the landlord has chronically failed to provide "adequate" heat.

** (Certified Mail—Return Receipt Requested)

Where the complaint of no heat and/or hot water has been received by

In all instances where a formal application for rent decrease due to no heat and/or hot water has been received, notice and final orders of disposition shall be mailed to both landlord and tenants.

Upon the expiration of the 3 day time limitation given to the landlord to respond to the notice issued, a re-inspection should be ordered to ascertain the facts as to the situation regarding heat and hot water.

The District Director should take immediate appropriate final action, to reduce rents to as low as $1.00 or to dismiss the proceeding, based upon the telephoned report of reinspection.

The inspector's written reports, covering both the initial inspection and the re-inspection, should be inserted into the file within a reasonable period of time after the inspector's return to the District Office.

The District Director shall notify the Dept. of Buildings of any rent reduction action taken, by forwarding a copy of the master form 0-30 to the Borough Superintendent of the Dept. of Buildings.

Operational Bulletin No. C-28—Amendments to Multiple Dwelling Law; Department of Buildings Rules relating to such amendments; addenda to Operational Bulletin No. C-15 (peepholes); rental values; procedure.
(Issued May 2, 1966)

The Multiple Dwelling Law was amended in 1965 by requiring an owner of a multiple dwelling to

1. provide increased illumination for all public areas (Chapter 1013 Laws of 1965);

2. provide "night time heating" (Chapter 839 Laws of 1965);

3. provide peepholes in the entrance door to each housing unit in a multiple dwelling (Chapter 493 Laws of 1965);

4. provide lights at entrance-way (Chapter 496 Laws of 1965), rear yards, side yards, front yards and courts (Chapter 1020 Laws of 1965); and

---

telephone, by letter or has been delivered in person and the initial inspection report shows that heat and/or hot water *is being provided* at time of inspection, an Administrative action under Section 34.2 will be opened and terminated with notice to the complainant. [Order Form 0-86]

Operational Bulletins

5. provide viewing mirrors in self-service elevators (Chapter 1014 Laws of 1965).

In order to implement the above requirements, the Department of Buildings promulgated "Rules for Enforcement of Amendments to Multiple Dwelling Law" (filed with the City Clerk on November 17, 1965) which relate, among other things, to items 3, 4 and 5 above. Where provision is hereinafter made for any rent increases based upon the furnishing of any of the mandated service increases, no order granting a rent increase will be issued unless the landlord has established compliance with the requirements of the above amendments to the Multiple Dwelling Law. It is also to be noted that applications filed for rent increases relating to items 3 and 4 above, if made subsequent to the date of issuance of this bulletin, may be deemed to be an application for rent increases allowable for both items 3 and 4. If rent increases have already been granted for item 3 (peepholes), the application should so state. In the exceptional case where rent increases may be granted due to the increased cost of providing janitorial service, the application should also include that item as a basis for rent increases.

This Administration has caused a study to be made with respect to the propriety of granting rent increases due to the above requirements of the Multiple Dwelling Law and the enforcement rules promulgated by the Department of Buildings. As indicated herein some of these studies could not be completed due to the lack of sufficient operating experience by the affected landlords. Under the circumstances the promulgation of any rental values for such services would be arbitrary and subject the Administrator to an indefensible Court challenge. Therefore, no rental values are presently being established for those items. Nevertheless the landlord is not without relief, since such increased operating expenses may properly be considered by the Administrator in an application for rent increases pursuant to Section 33.5 of the Regulations. However, after a sufficient body of experience has been culled, the study will be continued on the basis of such additional information.

A review of the Administrator's policy with respect to each of the above items of mandated increase services follows:

1. INCREASED INTERIOR ILLUMINATION.

The required increase to a minimum 60 watt or equivalent for vestibule, entrance-hall, public stairways, etc. does not warrant any increase in the maximum rent for the individual housing accommodations unless compliance with such requirement would necessitate the installation of additional fixtures. In such cases the landlord should file an application for a Prior Opinion on Application Form A-33.1PO. In such application he should establish the need for such additional fixtures and submit an estimate from a licensed electrician or electrical contractor of the cost thereof.

2. HEATING.

The study which the Administrator has already completed indicates that "landlords who had previously adhered to minimum standards will experience little, if any, additional expense." As noted above, the Administrator will cause a continuing study to be made and will re-examine his position after there has been sufficient operating experience by affected landlords to warrant the formulation of another policy.

The Administrator, does however, recognize that landlords may find the burden of supplying "night time heating" too onerous where the heating system is a hand-fire coal burning system. Under such circumstances the landlord will be permitted to apply for rent increases which will compensate him for the increased cost of supplying additional janitorial service to fire the heating system on a 24-hour basis. The application should be made on Application Form A-33.1C (indicating the implied consent of the tenants since the service is mandated by law). The landlord should establish the cost of supplying janitorial service for a three-year period ending September 30, 1965 together with such cost for the current year commencing October 1, 1965. Any rent increase granted will not reflect any fuel cost and will be limited to the cost of supplying increased janitorial service required to comply with "night time heating law".

3. PEEPHOLES.

Operational Bulletin No. C-15 (revised January 31, 1966) makes provision for rent increases for the installation of peepholes. The rental values provided for therein

OPERATIONAL BULLETINS

will continue to remain in effect. However, said bulletin is hereby clarified in the following respects:

a. Where there are two entrance-doors which require the installation of a peephole, the indicated rental value shall apply to each door.

b. Where the present entrance-door has a glass panel which must be replaced before a peephole may be installed in the door, the rental value will be an additional $.10 above the amount otherwise provided for, provided that the new panel is of a fire-resistant material which is approved by City agencies having jurisdiction.

c. Where the landlord replaces the existing door with a new fire-resistant door with the tenant's consent, the new door must include an approved peephole. The rent increase which may be granted for the installation of such new entrance-door will be limited to $1.00 per month.

4. *EXTERIOR LIGHTS.*[a]

4. Exterior Lights[a] No. of Units in Building[c]	Monthly Increase per Apartment[b] (1) 3 Fixtures	(2) Each Fixture Over 3
3	$1.40	$.45
4	1.05	.35
5	.85	.25
6	.70	.20
7	.60	.20
8	.55	.15
9	.45	.15
10	.40	.15
11-15	.35	.10
16-25	.25	.05
26-40	.15	.05
41-60[d]	.10	—
61-90[d]	.05	—

---

[a] No rent increase will be granted unless all requirements or rules of the Department of Buildings with respect to exterior lights have been complied with and certificates of approval of all City departments having jurisdiction have been issued.

[b] The indicated rental values are based upon the installation of exterior lights which comply with the minimum requirements of the Rules of the Department of Buildings and will apply to all installations of the Rules of the Department of buildings and will apply to all installations made on and after June 28, 1965. Where such installation was completed, or substantially completed, on or after June 28, 1965 but prior to the date of issuance of this bulletin, the rental values will be computed on the basis of the recoupment of the verified cose thereof over a period of ten years, not to exceed 50% above the amount specified in the above schedule. Where partial electrical facilities already exist, the above schedule will be prorated to reflect the reduced cost of installation.

OPERATIONAL BULLETINS

5. *ELEVATOR MIRRORS.*

The installation of the required mirrors in elevators does not warrant any increase in the maximum rent for the individual housing accommodations. The installation is mandated for multiple dwellings containing self-service elevators. The allocation of the cost thereof over a reasonable period would result in an amount so small that it can readily be absorbed by the landlord as a normal operating expense.

It is contemplated by the Administrator that the landlord will file a master application seeking rent increases on the basis of the total compliance with the above requirements of the Multiple Dwelling Law and the Department of Buildings. The filing of individual applications would serve no useful purpose and would merely place an added burden on the landlord without affording him any compensating benefits. In filing a master application, the landlord should leave the tenant's name blank and insert "see attached rent-roll" in the space reserved for the tenant's name. A separate copy of the application should be prepared for each tenant with the name of the tenant and address inserted in each copy in such space. Only the original application need be notarized by the landlord.

Operational Bulletin No. C-28—Exterior Lights; Rental Values.
Supplement No. 1 (Revised January 19, 1967)

The Department of Buildings has recently amended their regulations relating to the installation of mandated exterior lights, and now base the entrance-way lighting

---

Where the landlord proposes to install decorative entrance-way lights which are substantially similar to the decor of the building with concealed installation, or where there are unique or peculiar circumstances, application may be made for a Prior Opinion on Application Form A-33.1PO. In such case the rental value for such installation may not be more than 50% above the amounts specified in the above schedule.

Where the landlord has made an installation which is superior to that contemplated by the previous paragraph with the tenant's consent in writing of 75 per cent of the tenants in occupancy, the landlord may file Application Form A-33.1C for rent increases which will reflect the rental value of such installation.

[c] The total unit count of the building must include professional or commercial space accommodations occupied by the landlord and all other decontrolled or exempt units, if any. In buildings with commercial units, the unit count for such space will be the unit count for the residential space directly above such commercial space.

[d] Structures containing 41-90 units, inclusive, will be granted increases on the basis of multiples of three fixtures only. For example, where 6 fixtures are installed, the increases will be twice those shown in column (1).

OPERATIONAL BULLETINS

fixtures required on the frontage of a building. For example: where a building front is 22 feet or less, one 50 watt entrance-way fixture is sufficient. Buildings with more than 22 feet of frontage—where the combined width of the entrance doors are 5 feet or less—may install one 100 watt fixture at the entrance. Buildings over 22 feet with entrance doors having a combined width in excess of 5 feet—must install two entrance-way lights having 150 watts in the aggregate.

Operational Bulletin No. C-28, Supplement No. 1 (Issued August 8, 1966) is accordingly revised, in order to make provision for rental values related to installations complying with the current Department of Buildings regulations. The Schedule of Rental Values is therefore revised to read as follows:

4. Exterior Lights[a]

No. of Units in Building[c]	1 Fixture 50 watts	1 Fixture 100 watts	2 Fixtures 150 watts (Aggregate)	Each Rear, Side or Courtyard Fixture 40 watts
3	$.55	$.85	$1.30	$.45
4	.40	.65	1.00	.35
5	.35	.50	.80	.30
6	.30	.45	.65	.25
7	.25	.35	.55	.20
8	.20	.30	.50	.15
9	.20	.30	.45	.15
10	.15	.25	.40	.15
11-15	.15	.20	.30	.10
16-25	.10	.15	.20	.05
26-40	.05	.10	.15	.05
41-60	—	.05	.10	[d]
61-90	—	—	.05	[d]

[a] No rent increase will be granted unless all requirements or rules of the Department of Buildings with respect to exterior lights have been complied with and certificates of approval of all City departments having jurisdiction have been issued, except that the District Rent Director may waive such requirements in cases where the building contains no more than 12 housing accommodations. As a condition for granting such waiver the landlord must file an affidavit made by a duly licensed electrician or electrical contractor stating that the installation was made in compliance with all rules and regulations of the Department of Buildings with respect to the installation of exterior lights and with the pertinent provisions of the Electrical Code; that the actual installation was made either by him or under his personal supervision; and that he has made application to the Department of Water Supply, Gas and Electricity for a certificate of approval. The affidavit should also acknowledge that it is being made by him in order to induce the District Rent Director to waive the requirement for obtaining such certificate of approval prior to granting rent increases based upon such installation.

It should be noted that in the event departmental violations are placed against the property with respect to such installation, orders may be issued revoking any rent increase granted on the basis of such installation.

[b] The indicated rental values are based upon the installation of exterior lights which comply with the minimum requirements of the Rules of the

OPERATIONAL BULLETINS

Operational Bulletin No. C-29—§ 35 orders permitting elevator conversion and eviction certificates pursuant to §§ 58 and 59; establishment of a record book at District Rent Office of such orders or eviction certificates; certification of rent-rolls to contain notice of such register book.
(Issued May 23, 1966)

As an added public service, District Rent Offices will henceforth maintain a record book in which entries of all order *issued on and after the date of this bulletin* with respect to (a) the permissive conversion of manually-operated elevators to automatic operation and (b) the issuance of eviction certificates pursuant to §§ 58 and 59 of the Regulations. It is to be noted that conditions specified in § 35 orders permitting the conversion of such elevators not only bind the landlord-applicant, but also must be complied with by any subsequent owner(s). It is important that a new owner be apprised of any orders of the Administrator which he is required to comply with. In the case of elevator conversions, the cost of such compliance may seriously affect the transaction to such extent that the new owner would not have consummated the purchase of the property if he knew of such conditions. Similarly, where eviction certificates are issued pursuant to §§ 58 and 59 there may be conditions which would also affect the purchase of the property. The new procedures, put into effect by this bulletin, will alert prospective purchasers to the fact that there are outstanding orders which may affect properties in which they may be interested.

Where a docket is submitted to a landlord or a prospective buyer, or his representative, for examination, a

---

Department of Buildings and will apply to all installations made on and after August 2, 1966.

Where the landlord proposes to install decorative entrance-way lights which are substantially similar to the decor of the building with concealed installation, or where there are unique or peculiar circumstances, application may be made for a Prior Opinion on Application Form A-33.1PO. In such case the rental value for such installation may not be more than 50% above the amounts specified in the above schedule.

Where the landlord has made an installation which is superior to that contemplated by the previous paragraph with the tenant's consent in writing of 75 per cent of the tenants in occupancy, the landlord may file Application Form A-33.1C for rent increases which will reflect the rental value of such installation.

[c] The total unit count of the building must include professional or commercial space accommodations occupied by the landlord and all other decontrolled or exempt units, if any. In buildings with commercial units, the unit count for such space will be the unit count for the residential space directly above such commercial space.

[d] Buildings with multiple rear or courtyard lights may qualify for a minimum grant.

notation must be made on the Progress Sheet (Notice Form N-7) for the docket with a notation of the name and address of such party and his interest in the matter. In addition the party requisitioning the docket will be required to sign his name on the Progress Sheet.

The application for certification of rent-roll (Application Form A-1RR) has been revised to provide for a notice to the applicant that a record book is maintained at the District Rent Office which contains the information referred to above. The revised form will contain the following legend:

> "THE APPLICANT IS PUT ON NOTICE that orders issued pursuant to § 35 of the Regulations permitting the conversion of manually operated elevators to self-service operation and eviction certificates granted pursuant to §§ 58 and 59 of the Regulations may contain conditions and/or provisions which are binding, not only upon the landlord named therein, but also upon any new owner(s). A record book of such orders is maintained at the District Rent Office which also maintains a separate record book of vacate orders issued by City Departments and of harassment proceedings. SUCH ORDERS ARE AVAILABLE FOR INSPECTION AT THE DISTRICT RENT OFFICE."

RENT ADMINISTRATOR'S INFORMATION AND INSTRUCTION SHEETS

INFORMATION SHEET NO. 1

(Revised January 31, 1969)

Voluntary Lease Agreements—Section 33.2 of the Regulations

Under Section 33.2 of the Rent and Eviction Regulations landlords and tenants are permitted to enter into voluntary leases which may provide for an increase in rent not in excess of 15% above the maximum rent in effect *on the effective date of such lease* for a controlled housing accommodation where the conditions specified in Section 33.2 of the Regulations are met.

The tenant, by executing such a lease, secures himself against having to pay more than the amount agreed upon during the term of the lease. Similarly, by executing such a lease, the landlord commits himself to charging no more than the amount agreed upon during the term of the lease.

As a condition for the increase in the maximum rent, the landlord must certify "that he is maintaining all essential services furnished or required to be furnished," including any additional services which the tenant may secure in his bargaining for the lease, "and will continue to maintain such services so long as the increase in maximum rent continues in effect."

The maximum rent is automatically increased by the execution of such a voluntary lease, *provided that the landlord files a Lease Report* (Report Form R-33.2) *within 60 days after the date of delivery of such lease to the landlord* by the tenant. A tenant who signs a voluntary lease, in addition to the protection afforded by the lease, will continue to have the protection of the Rent Law and the Regulations.

The following questions and answers will clarify many of the problems presented to the Office of Rent Control concerning voluntary lease agreements.

Information Sheets

1. Q. A landlord requests a tenant in occupancy to enter into a two-year lease providing for an increase of not more than 15% in the maximum rent. Must the tenant sign such a lease?

   A. No. The tenant need not sign a lease providing for a rent increase unless he wishes to. The maximum rent cannot be increased merely because the tenant does not sign a lease. Nor may the tenant be evicted on the basis of his refusal to sign a lease providing for an increase in rent.

2. Q. Upon what grounds may a landlord obtain an increase in the maximum rent if the tenant does not have the protection of a lease?

   A. In the absence of a lease the landlord may under the Regulations obtain a rent increase on application to the District Director with the tenant's consent for increased services or facilities and without the tenant's consent where he makes a major capital improvement or a substantial rehabilitation of the premises. The Regulations also provide for rent increases based upon increased occupancy or subletting of the tenant's apartment, for financial adjustment of the rents on the basis of a 6% fair return on the valuation of the property, for increased costs of operation of buildings containing no more than four residential units, for an alternative equalization adjustment of maximum rents in a property or offset and recoupment of increased labor costs.

3. Q. If a tenant declines to accept the landlord's terms for a lease, or does not enter into any lease, may the landlord decrease the essential services which he gave, or which he was required to give, for the maximum rent?

   A. No. Should the landlord for any reason refuse to provide such services, the tenant may file a complaint with the District Rent Director. Where the landlord refuses to restore the services, the maximum rent may be reduced.

4. Q. I signed a two-year lease which just expired. Can my landlord evict me?

A. Tenants who continue to remain in possession after the expiration of voluntary lease agreement are statutory tenants and are entitled under the Regulations to the same protection against eviction as any tenant who had not signed a statutory lease.

5. Q. A landlord proposes to include a so-called "escalator clause" in the lease to provide for an additional increase in rent during the term of the lease in the event that such increase is permitted by the Rent Regulations, or in the event that rent control terminates. Is such a clause proper under the Rent and Eviction Regulations?

A. No. A lease containing such a clause does not ordinarily comply with the requirements of Section 33.2 of the Regulations. Should such a clause be included in a lease it will be excluded from any consideration and not have the force and effect intended. The maximum rent will be adjusted by 15% (or such lesser percentage as may be provided in the lease) above the maximum legal residential rent in effect on the effective date of the lease.

6. Q. If a landlord enters into a voluntary lease agreement while an application for a rent increase is pending on the basis of the rewiring of the electrical system in the building, will the lease rent be increased during the term of the lease if the application is granted?

A. Yes. Administrator's Interpretation No. 6 and Section 33.2a(3) of the Regulations permits a statutory lease rental to be increased where the maximum legal residential rent is thereafter increased (a) by order of the Administrator pursuant to Section 33.1a of the Regulations (including restoration of rents previously reduced) or (b) pursuant to Section 33.1b or Section 33.1c of the Regulations, where the major capital improvement or substantial rehabilitation of the building or the housing accommodations therein was either completed or in progress when such lease was executed.

INFORMATION SHEETS

7. Q. If a landlord enters into a voluntary lease agreement and subsequently a major capital improvement or substantial rehabilitation is commenced and completed, will the lease rent be increased during the term of the lease agreement?

A. No. Although the maximum legal rental for the apartment will be adjusted by an order, the landlord will not be permitted to collect a rental in excess of the amount provided for in the lease until its expiration or other termination.

8. Q. If a landlord enters into such a lease while a net annual return Section 33.5, unavoidable increases in operating costs in small structures Section 33.6, unavoidable increases in operating costs in other specific structures Section 33.7, alternative equalization adjustment of maximum rents in a property or offset or recoupment of increased labor costs Section 33.8 application is pending, or is subsequently filed, will the lease rent be increased during the term of the lease if the application is granted?

A. No. Any written lease still in effect which provides for the payment of a rent less than the maximum rent fixed by an order adjusting the rental pursuant to any one of the sections of the regulations indicated above will govern the rent for the housing accommodation until the expiration or other termination of the lease. Upon expiration or termination of the lease the landlord will be permitted to collect the dollar amount of increase fixed by the order above the lease rental.

9. Q. What does a tenant gain by signing such a voluntary lease agreement?

A. By signing a voluntary lease agreement, the tenant obtains the contractual right to remain in the leased premises, subject to the conditions in the lease, at the rent agreed upon in the lease for the duration of its term. Also, if the landlord becomes eligible for a greater increase in rent during the term of the lease through certain adjustment sections of the Regulations, he will not be able to compel the tenant to pay the increase during the lease term without the tenant's written consent unless the lease is executed under the circumstances described in Question No. 6 or that the tenant has consented to pay such increase in the Lease Report filed with the District Rent Office.

10. Q. The tenant is agreeable to having a lease, but prefers a three-year lease instead of a two-year lease. Would this be proper under the Regulations?

   A. Yes. The lease may be for as long a period as the landlord and tenant may agree upon, provided it is at least for a two-year period. However, the Regulations provide that if the lease is with a new tenant and is for longer than a two-year term, the new tenant must be given the right to cancel the lease at any time after the expiration of the first two years of the lease by giving the landlord at least 30 days' notice in writing by registered or certified mail of his intention to cancel the lease and surrender possession of the apartment. If the tenant elects to cancel his lease in such case, he must vacate the apartment.

11. Q. The tenant would like to have the right to cancel the lease upon 30 days' notice to the landlord at any time prior to the expiration of the lease. Is this permissible?

   A. Yes. The lease may give the tenant the right to cancel or terminate the lease at any time.

12. Q. The tenant wishes to pay a 10% increase and the landlord is willing to accept this. Is this permissible?

   A. Yes. The rent increase may be in any amount not exceeding 15%.

13. Q. The tenant is willing to sign a lease but he wishes a new stove, or a new refrigerator, or the right to put up a television antenna, or some other increase or improvement in the services as a consideration for the execution of the lease. May this be part of the lease agreement?

   A. Yes. This is a matter of bargaining between landlord and tenant. It is important to remember that

INFORMATION SHEETS

the lease should specifically include a statement of such additional services and state that they are included in the lease rent and are being provided by the landlord on the effective date of the lease term. The lease may also provide that the tenant consents to an increase in rent for such increase in service in addition to the permissible 15% statutory lease increase. (See answer to Question No. 17.)

14. Q. If a tenant signs a lease which provides for additional services or equipment, and the landlord fails to furnish such additional services or equipment, what may the tenant do?

A. He may file a complaint with the District Rent Director and the new maximum rent may be reduced.

15. Q. Will the housing accommodations be decontrolled if the tenant signs such a lease?

A. No. The tenant continues to receive the protection of the Rent Law and of the Regulations as well as the benefits of the lease.

16. Q. A tenant is not agreeable to entering into a voluntary lease agreement, but he does want a new refrigerator, or a new stove, or a new service. How may he obtain it?

A. The tenant and the landlord must come to an agreement about the additional service. Application Form A-33.1C is provided on which the landlord can apply for an increase based upon this agreement. The amount of the increase of the maximum rent for the additional service will be determined by the District Rent Director in accordance with the rental value prescribed by the Administrator.

17. Q. Is it possible for a landlord to obtain an increase in the maximum rent for an increase in services, etc. in addition to the permissible 15% statutory lease increase?

A. Yes. It is permissible for a statutory lease to provide for a further rent increase where the tenant has consented to the increase in services, etc. and the Administrator has issued an order increasing the maximum rent on the basis of such increase in services, etc. Where the consent to the increase in services, etc., is a part of the same agreement which provided for the statutory lease increase, it would be proper for the landlord to file a combination form (Application Form A-33.1C) which reports the lease increase and makes application for a further rent adjustment based upon the increased services, etc.

18. Q. If the landlord and tenant sign such a voluntary lease agreement, what remains to be done for it to become effective?

    A. The new maximum rent takes effect automatically in accordance with the terms of the lease if the lease complies with the requirements of Section 33.2 of the Regulations. Within sixty days after the date of delivery of the lease to the landlord by the tenant, the landlord must file a Lease Report (Report Form R-33.2) of it upon prescribed forms with the District Rent Director. This must include a statement of any additional services or equipment furnished to the tenant as a consideration for the execution of the lease.

19. Q. When may the landlord and the tenant enter into a voluntary lease agreement?

    A. The landlord and tenant may enter into and execute a voluntary lease at any time. However, Section 33.2 provides that where a voluntary lease has not expired a subsequent lease may be entered into provided that at least twelve months of the prior lease had already expired. The new voluntary lease must be for a period including the unexpired portion of the first two years of the prior lease plus at least two years. Where the prior lease provided for a full 15% increase, the new lease may not provide for a further rent increase before the expiration of the original two years of the earlier lease.

    For instance, if a housing unit had a maximum rent of $100 per month and it was increased by a voluntary lease to $115 per month with a term which began on January 15, 1962 and was to terminate on January 14, 1964, no new statutory lease could be obtained prior to January 15, 1963. On or after January 15, 1963, a landlord could enter into a new lease for a term expiring no sooner than January 14, 1966 with the rent remaining at $115 per month until January 14, 1964, and the further 15% increase, or whatever lesser amount the tenant agreed to pay, would become effective on January 15, 1964. If the prior lease did not provide for a full 15% increase, but only for a 10% increase, and increased the maximum rent from $100 per month to $110 per month, the landlord and tenant can enter into a new voluntary lease which would increase the maximum rent, effective upon the execution of the new lease, to $115 per month until January 14, 1964 and then provide for an additional increase of not more than 15% above the $110 maximum rent for the two years commencing January 15, 1964. If the prior lease did not provide for a full 15% increase, but only a 10% increase, and increased the maximum rent from $100 per month to $110 per month, the only voluntary lease that the landlord and tenant could enter into before the expiration of the first year of the original lease (January 14, 1963) would be one which would increase the maximum rent from $110 per month to $115 per month and which would provide for a minimum term of two years.

20. Q. May a lease validly provide that during the first year the maximum rent is increased by 10% and during the second year by an additional 5% over the original maximum rent?

A. Yes. Such a clause is valid under the Regulations since it does not require the payment of more than 15% over the former maximum rent at any time during the term of the lease.

INFORMATION SHEET NO. 2

(Revised February 25, 1969 and effective April 1, 1969)

Painting and Decorating Complaints

Painting and decorating service where required to be supplied by your landlord is considered to be an essential service included in the maximum rent for your apartment. Generally, this means that your landlord must under the Rent Law paint your apartment at two-year intervals, or at three-year intervals if it was his practice to paint every third year. However, if your landlord never supplied this service, the Rent Law does not require him to do so now. Effective August 3, 1967, the Housing Maintenance Code of The City of New York was amended to require an owner of a multiple dwelling to paint occupied dwelling units every three years and more often when required by contract or other provision of law.

Where painting is not an essential service under the Rent Regulations and the landlord paints for the first time in order to comply with the requirements of the Housing Maintenance Code, the painting is considered to be an increase in services under the provisions of Section 33.1 of the Rent Regulations. Upon completion of the painting the landlord may make application to the District Rent Office for a rent increase, limited to the customary 10% rental value of such service. Upon the issuance of a rent increase order, the landlord will then be obligated to paint the apartment at no more than three-year intervals.

If your landlord does not meet his obligation to paint, you may file an application with the District Rent Office for a rent reduction under the provisions of Section 34.2 of the Rent Regulations upon the expiration of the two- or three-year interval, whichever applies, since the last painting. Application Form A-34.2P (Tenant's Application for a Decrease in Rent Based on Failure to Paint) should be filed in duplicate at the District Rent Office servicing your neighborhood. However, it is advisable for you to remind your landlord that painting is due before filing a complaint with your District Rent Office.

The purpose of this Information Sheet is to answer a variety of questions concerning painting and decorating service which are frequently asked. If your particular problem is not covered, it is suggested that you write or call at your District Rent Office.

INFORMATION SHEETS

Questions and Answers

1. Q. Should I ask my landlord to paint my apartment before I file an application with the District Rent Office?

   A. Yes. The landlord cannot be said to have decreased your essential services except upon failure to comply with the request that he paint and decorate. You may advise him at a reasonable time before your apartment is due to be painted, and then make application thereafter unless the landlord and you agree upon a mutually agreeable date for the painting of your apartment.

2. Q. Has the tenant the same right to painting service that he had under the State Law?

   A. Yes. Your landlord must continue to provide the same painting and decorating service as he was required to provide on April 30, 1962. This will not require your landlord to paint any more frequently than was the custom in the period immediately prior to March 1, 1943, the Federal maximum rent date, nor will your landlord in any case be required to paint more frequently than at two-year intervals. While there is a presumption of a two-year painting practice, your landlord may submit evidence of his actual painting practice for the ten-year period preceding the date of the filing of the tenant's application.

3. Q. My apartment hasn't been painted in over two years. Am I entitled to have my apartment painted?

   A. Yes, unless your landlord can establish a practice of painting at greater intervals.

4. Q. The two-year painting practice applies to my apartment. My apartment was due for a painting on January 1, 1965. However, my landlord refused to paint and I had to apply to the Rent Office. A proceeding was then instituted to reduce the maximum rent because of my landlord's failure to paint and decorate. Before an order could be issued reducing my maximum rent the landlord painted and on the basis of the restoration of

painting services, the Rent Office issued an order terminating the rent reduction proceeding. When is my next painting due?

A. If the order which determined the rent reduction proceeding fixed a date when the next painting will be due, the landlord will be required to paint on that due date. If the order did not fix the date when the next painting will become due then the apartment is required to be painted either two or three years from the date the apartment was last painted, unless the tenant in occupancy consents to another date.

5. Q. My apartment was painted every three years prior to April 30, 1962. Only two years have elapsed since the last painting. Can I now demand that my landlord paint my apartment?

A. On April 30, 1962, there was a three-year painting practice. Accordingly, your landlord may continue painting at three-year intervals without being in violation of the Rent Regulations.

6. Q. Prior to April 30, 1962 my landlord had a practice of painting the entire apartment every two years and the kitchen and the bathroom every year. My apartment was last completely painted and decorated 1½ years ago. Can I make the landlord paint the kitchen and the bathroom now?

A. No. The painting of the kitchen and bathroom alone cannot be compelled. It must be done as a part of the entire painting of the apartment which is due at the end of two years.

7. Q. My landlord has always painted one or two rooms at a time. Can I now make him paint the entire apartment at one time?

A. No. In this particular case the obligation of the landlord is to continue the same painting service that was provided or required to be provided on April 30, 1962 or any subsequent date determining the maximum rent.

8. Q. What steps must a tenant take in order to get his apartment painted?

A. Ask your landlord to paint your apartment. If you claim that closets are in need of painting or that

Information Sheets

floors need cleaning and shellacking you should call that fact to your landlord's attention when you ask him to paint. If he fails to do so, you may obtain two copies of Application Form A-34.2P from your District Rent Office. These forms may be obtained by requesting them through the mail. After carefully reading the instructions, complete each copy of the form making certain to answer all questions. If the tenant also has a complaint about a reduction in related services such as window shades or venetian blinds, he should clearly set forth that fact in his application. These services are only required to be furnished when needed and not at any regular interval. Unless specific complaint is made concerning these service decreases, no consideration will be given to such service decreases until painting and decorating again become due because these services are deemed to be a part of your landlord's decorating obligation. File two copies of the Application Form with your District Rent Office.

9. Q. What happens after that?

A. The District Rent Office will forward a copy of your application to your landlord, together with a notice that the maximum rent may be reduced because of your landlord's alleged failure to comply with his obligation to paint and decorate. Should your landlord not dispute that painting is due he will be given one month to paint and decorate your apartment and file proof of the completion of the work. If he does not restore this service within one month, an order reducing the maximum rent will be issued. However, if your landlord disputes the obligation to paint and decorate he is required to reply within seven days of the mailing of the tenant's application and submit evidence to support his contention. Should the District Rent Office, after a study of the record, determine that your landlord has an obligation to paint and decorate and that he has failed to comply with this obligation, a notice will be sent

INFORMATION SHEETS

to both you and your landlord stating that unless your landlord restores the service within seven days of the date of the notice, and submits written proof thereof with the District Rent Office within that period, an order reducing the maximum rent will be issued by the District Director. This proof may be in the form of an affidavit of the painter or the tenant's written admission that the apartment was properly painted.

10. Q. My landlord had a practice of painting a particular apartment every two years. He painted the apartment three years ago. I moved into this apartment a year ago and at that time paid for my own painting. I now claim that the two-year interval had run when I moved in and that my landlord is now obligated to paint and decorate. My landlord advised me that since my apartment was painted only a year ago he will not paint for another year. May I file an application for a rent reduction based upon my landlord's failure to paint?

A. Yes. In computing the time period, the date when your landlord last painted the apartment determines whether or not he is in default of his obligation of maintaining the painting and decorating service.

11. Q. I rented a vacant apartment last month and upon my landlord's refusal to paint and decorate the apartment, I painted it at my expense. Can I get my rent reduced?

A. If less than one year has expired since the tenant rented the apartment, he can file an application on Application Form A-34.2P for a rent reduction pursuant to Section 34.2 of the Regulations. If the landlord claims that at the time of the renting the painting was not due, the landlord will be required to produce his books and records. Should the landlord fail to establish that the painting was not due at that time, the landlord will be given an opportunity to promptly refund to the tenant the actual cost of the painting and decorating provided that the cost is reasonable. Where

Information Sheets

the tenant has provided himself with decorating which is not usually supplied by landlords, the landlord will be given an opportunity of establishing his usual cost for supplying such service and his obligation to refund will be limited to that amount. If the landlord refuses to make the refund, it will be determined that there has been a reduction in painting and decorating service and an appropriate rent reduction will be ordered. Where the refund is made to the tenant, the interval governing the landlord's obligation to paint runs from the date when the tenant painted. However, in cases where the tenant painted when renting, the landlord will not be given an opportunity to paint in lieu of a rent reduction. In such cases the landlord can satisfy his obligation to paint and decorate only by making a proper refund to the tenant.

12. Q. I have been living in my apartment for over six years. My apartment was painted at two-year intervals by my landlord. The last painting was due at the beginning of my seventh year of occupancy. I requested my landlord to paint at that time. Upon his refusal to paint, I painted the apartment myself. Can I now file an application for a rent reduction?

    A. Yes. The District Rent Office will give your landlord an opportunity of establishing his usual cost of supplying such service and permit him to reimburse you by an amount determined by the District Rent Office after taking into consideration reasonable painting costs and other equities involved.

13. Q. My landlord last painted my apartment two years ago. He now refuses to paint, however, I don't want a rent reduction, I want my apartment painted.

    A. File Application Form A-34.2P with your District Rent Office. The landlord will be notified of his obligation to paint. If he fails to do so an order will be issued reducing the rent. Since your landlord has 33 days for filing a protest against an order reducing the maximum rent, it is suggested that you wait until this period expires before making arrangements for doing the job at your own expense. After you have painted your apartment, the landlord will not be permitted to obtain a restoration of the rent unless he refunds an amount agreeable to you for the cost of painting. Otherwise, he will be required to wait two or three years dependent upon the painting practice from the date you had the apartment painted before he may obtain a restoration of the rent. If after the rent reduction is ordered, your landlord agrees to paint before you arrange for your own painting, he may paint and make application for rent restoration.

14. Q. Do I have to remove my furniture from the walls and place it in the middle of each room to be painted?

   A. While you do not have to remove heavy pieces of furniture, such as a piano or a very heavy combination radio-phonograph, your landlord's request that you place other pieces of furniture in the middle of the room is a reasonable one which you must comply with. It then becomes the obligation of your landlord to properly cover and protect your furniture while he is having the apartment painted.

15. Q. I have wall to wall carpeting. My landlord insists that I must lift my carpeting and roll it to the center of the room, or otherwise remove it.

   A. You are not obligated to do this.

16. Q. Some of the rooms in my apartment have wallpaper. My landlord does not want to give me new wallpaper but is willing to paint these rooms instead. Must he give me wallpaper?

   A. No. Your landlord has the option of either giving you new wallpaper or painting those rooms.

17. Q. Are there circumstances under which my landlord could place wallpaper over existing wallpaper?

   A. The amended Housing Maintenance Code provides as follows: "Neither the owner nor a tenant of a

Information Sheets

dwelling unit shall place wallpaper or wall covering upon a wall or ceiling in the public or tenant-occupied parts of a dwelling unless existing wallpaper or wall covering is first removed and such wall or ceiling is cleaned and repaired. However, if wallpaper or wall covering is in good condition, free from vermin and a coat of acceptable paint or sizing is applied, one additional layer of wallpaper or wall covering may be applied."

18. Q. My landlord insists that I must remove the wallpaper, and also that I must then prepare the surface of the walls for painting by "sizing" the walls. Must I do this?

    A. That depends upon the facts. Where the landlord previously either hung the wallpaper or paid for the wallpaper, it is his obligation to both remove the wallpaper and "size" the walls if he now wishes to paint. If the tenant paid for the wallpaper and either paid for the hanging of the wallpaper or hung the wallpaper himself, the tenant will be required to remove same and size the walls.

19. Q. My landlord is willing to paint my apartment; but, insists that all of the woodwork and walls shall be painted a buff color since he wants uniformity of colors in his building. My apartment was last painted by my landlord with a variety of colors and the colors used in each room blends in with the decorative scheme for each of the rooms. For that reason, I have refused to permit my landlord to paint my apartment. I have requested him to repaint with the existing colors. Do I have to permit my landlord to change the color scheme of the rooms in my apartment?

    A. No. The landlord must repaint with the existing color scheme unless he obtains the consent of the tenant.

20. Q. What is the landlord's obligation in repainting my apartment where previously various color schemes were applied by myself or a prior tenant after the landlord painted the apartment?

    A. The landlord's painting obligation will be met when he paints the entire apartment in a neutral shade and in a workmanlike manner.

21. Q. My landlord insists that I sign a paper or a release, agreeing to free both him and his painters from any damage done to my furniture which may occur as a result of the painting of my apartment. Do I have to sign such a paper?

   A. No. You are under no obligation to sign such a paper. Should your landlord refuse to proceed with the painting and decorating unless a release is executed, the District Rent Director will consider there has been a failure to provide the customary painting and decorating service.

22. Q. Must a tenant permit his landlord to provide painting and decorating service on week-ends, holidays or after 5:00 P.M.?

   A. This service should be provided by your landlord during normal working hours during the day and not on week-ends or holidays. However, it would be permissible for you and your landlord to arrange for the performance of these services at any time that is otherwise agreeable to you.

23. Q. Prior to April 30, 1962 my landlord had the practice of supplying me with paint every two years and I did the painting and decorating. I have now asked my landlord to furnish me with paint since it is over two years since I had last painted my apartment. If my landlord continues to refuse to supply me with paint, may I apply for a rent reduction?

   A. Yes. Where your landlord had the practice of supplying you with paint in lieu of painting, his refusal to supply paint in accordance with this custom will be deemed to be a reduction of painting and decorating service.

24. Q. My landlord has just painted and decorated my apartment. However, the job is substandard and was done in an unworkmanlike manner. If my landlord refuses to redo the painting, may I apply for a rent reduction?

   A. Yes. In order for your landlord to meet his obligation to supply painting and decorating service, the service must be performed in a workmanlike manner.

Information Sheets

INSTRUCTION SHEET NO. 1

(Revised February 25, 1969 and effective April 1, 1969)

[To be used for the preparation and filing of green OPTIONAL APPLICATION FORM A-33.5SO]

Landlord's Application for Increase of Maximum Rent (Fair Return)

(Section 33.5 of the Regulations)

The information set forth in this instruction sheet should be carefully read and followed. Before filing any application pursuant to Section 33.5, special note should be taken of the following:

a—No application may be filed unless
  (1) A report of search issued by the Department of Rent and Housing Maintenance, Office of Code Enforcement, is annexed to the application stating either that no violations against such property are recorded or that all violations recorded against such property have been cleared, corrected or abated or a receipt *(or photocopy thereof)* issued by that agency attesting to the payment of the fee for the report of search (**Note:** The landlord is required to file the report of search with the District Rent Office upon receipt of such report. No rent increase will be granted until all violations existing on or before the date of filing the application have been cleared, corrected or abated); **and**

  (2) More than two years have elapsed since the date of filing the last "Fair Return" application which resulted in an order granting a rent increase.

b—If the property was acquired since February 1, 1961, the purchase price may be claimed as your "Valuation Basis." However, where such purchase price is greater than the current assessed valuation, it will generally be considered for use as the valuation basis, if more than two years have elapsed between the date of the sale and the date of filing your application.

Green OPTIONAL APPLICATION FORM A-33.5SO is to be used by owners of properties containing twelve or less residential units who desire to accept a standard allowance of 16.5 per cent of the Annual Rental Income (Item 8) as representing the combined annual total cost for Repairs and Maintenance and Replacements and Improvements Expenses (Items 17 and 18) of the property. The acceptance of such allowance will eliminate the necessity for the preparation of any schedule detailing these expenses or the presentation of any bills and cancelled checks proving such costs.

Where a substantial portion of the Annual Rental Income (Item 8) is derived from commercial tenants, the Administrator reserves the right to review the acceptability of the 16.5 per cent allowance claimed.

INSTRUCTIONS FOR PREPARATION OF OPTIONAL APPLICATION FORM A-33.5SO

The following instructions will explain how to properly complete Items 1 through 6.

Schedules required to support "Test Year" Income and Expense (Items 7 through 26) should be prepared in accordance with those instructions found on Application Form A-33.5SO, and the specific instructions detailed below for Item 13 *(Janitorial Allowance)*, Items 17 and 18 (Allowance for *"Repairs and Maintenance"* and for *"Replacements and Improvements"*), Item 20 *(Depreciation Allowance)*, Items 23 and 24 *(Valuation Basis)*, and Item 25 *(Net Annual Return)*.

Item 1—Name and mailing address of landlord

Enter name of landlord and that of his representative, if any. Address and telephone number of landlord or his representative should also be shown.

Item 2—Name and mailing address of tenant

On the original and duplicate, this item is to be left blank. See Filing Instructions—for the manner in which those copies to be served upon individual tenants are to be completed.

Item 3—Address of Subject Building(s)

Enter the address of the property for which the application is being filed.

INFORMATION SHEETS

Item 4—Building Data

Enter separately the number of dwelling units *(including those units occupied by landlord or superintendent, or occupied rent-free)*, the number of stores, units for professional or business use, garages and the total of all units. Also, enter the total number of rooms, exclusive of bathrooms.

Item 5—Acquisition Data

Enter the date the property was acquired by the present owner and the cost. Also indicate the manner of acquisition by checking either "Purchase" or "Otherwise." If the latter, attach explanation.

Item 5A—Type of fuel used

State the type of fuel currently in use or supplying heat and/or hot water and also the full storage capacity of the fuel tank or bin.

Item 6—Assessment Data

(a) Enter the total assessed valuation in effect at the time of filing application and the specific amounts for "Land" and "Building" in the appropriate spaces. The breakdown of such total into "Land" and "Building" can be obtained from the office of the Real Property Assessment Department of the Borough in which the property is located.

(b) and (c) This information should be copied from the tax bill.

(d) Proceedings are considered to be "pending" for any of the two indicated tax years, where a protest of the assessed valuation has been filed with the Tax Commission and the time for filing writs or appeals has not expired; or where writ(s) of certiorari have been filed with no final disposition in such actions yet determined.

(e) Where reductions were secured in any of the two indicated tax years, this information should be taken from the notice of final settlement with the Tax Commission or any Court order directing same. (Attach copies of such notice or order.)

Item 6A—Prior Rent Increases

It is important that the information with regard to prior rent increases be accurately stated.

INFORMATION SHEETS

SPECIFIC INSTRUCTIONS

Item 13—Janitorial Allowance

Any landlord who personally performs the janitorial services (such as cleaning halls, attending to heating system, cleaning of walks, etc.) may claim an allowance for such services computed at the rate of $6.10 per month for each residential unit including any apartment occupied by the owner. Claim for such allowance **must** be accompanied by a written statement from the owner, describing the janitorial services he performs.

Where the janitorial functions are performed by an employee, the amount of salaries and wages and related payroll costs paid to such employee for the "test year" plus the rental allowance for any apartment occupied by the employee, should be entered under this item. The schedule of this expense (designate as Schedule E) should show the following:

Employee's Name	Regular or Part-Time	Wage Rate (Monthly or Weekly)	Amount Paid for Test Year $

The following evidence **must** be submitted to substantiate the claimed expense of salaries and related costs paid to an employee for the "test year":

(a) Cancelled checks in payment of wages, or if payments were made in cash, present an affidavit signed by the employee specifying his wage rate, the amount of cash and any rental or other allowances received by him.

(b) Copies of quarterly Social Security Tax Returns.

(c) Copies of quarterly State Unemployment Insurance Tax Returns.

(d) Current Workmen's Compensation Insurance policy.

(e) Current Disability Benefits Insurance policy.

Items 17 and 18—Allowance for "Repairs and Mainttenance for "Replacements and Improvements"

This allowance is normally to be computed at 16.5 per cent of Annual Rental Income (Item 8). However, if the rents in Item 8 include increases granted to the present owner for Major Capital Improvements (such as electrical rewiring, plumbing, exterior lights, peepholes, etc.) it will

Information Sheets

be advantageous to the applicant to utilize the following alternate method of computation:

(a) Determine the amount of annual rent increase received for the Major Capital Improvement.

(b) Deduct this sum from the Rental Income shown in Item 8.

(c) Your normal "Repairs and Maintenance" and "Replacements and Improvements" allowance should be computed at 16.5 per cent of the resultant figure in (b) above.

(d) In addition, the annual rent increase determined in (a) above may be claimed as the write-off for the cost of the Major Capital Improvement.

Example—Assume the annual rental in Item 8 is $8,460.00. In a period prior to the filing of this application the owner rewired the building at a cost of $2,500.00 and was granted an annual rent increase of $360.00 under Section 33.1c of the Regulations. Based upon these facts, the applicant's presentation for expense to be claimed should be as follows:

(a) Annual MCI increase	$ 360.00
(b) Rental Income (Item 8) of $8,460.00 minus amount shown in (a) above	$8,100.00
(c) Normal R & M and R & I allowance 16.5 per cent of (b) above	$1,336.50
(d) Add write-off for MCI cost	360.00
Total allowance to be claimed in application	$1,696.50

The alternate method described above cannot be used, if on the date the application is filed the owner had recouped 140 per cent of his cost for the Major Capital Improvement by virtue of the amount of rental increases already collected. In the example given above, 140 per cent of the $2,500.00 rewiring cost would amount to $3,500.00.

NOTE: If applicant uses the alternate method of computation, he will be required to substantiate the cost of the M.C.I.

Item 20—Depreciation Allowance

The allowance to be claimed should be the lower of the following:

(a) The total amount claimed as depreciation in your latest Federal Income Tax Return (including the depreciation allowance(s) claimed for improvements, additions and/or replacements)

As compared to

(b) 2 per cent of the assessed valuation of the Building exclusive of the Land.

OR

2 per cent of that portion of the total purchase price of the property (if acquired since February 1, 1961) representing Building value, if such purchase price is being claimed as the Valuation Basis.

That part of the purchase price to be assigned as Building value should be determined by applying the ratio relationship found in the assessed valuation of the property. Example: Assume the total assessed valuation of the property to be $10,000.00 of which the Building valuation is $8,000.00. Thus it is found that the Building Assessed Valuation is 80 per cent of the total. Assume further that the property was purchased since February 1, 1961 for a price of $15,000.00. Accordingly the 80 per cent ratio as applied to the $15,000.00 total purchase cost of the property, would establish $12,000.00 as that portion representing the value of the Building alone. The 2 per cent depreciation allowance is to be computed on this amount.

The schedule to be prepared for this item (designate as Schedule L) should indicate your computation of the depreciation allowance claimed in the application. An exact transcript of the schedule of depreciation as shown in your latest Federal Income Tax Return should also be included. Where no deduction for depreciation has been made in your latest Federal Income Tax Return, submit reason why none was claimed.

Items 23 and 24—Valuation Basis

If the property was purchased by the present owner before February 1, 1961 entry should only be made in Item 23. If the property was purchased since February 1, 1961, fill in both Items 23 and 24.

Enter in Item 23, the assessed valuation of the property in effect at the time of filing the application. This amount should be the same as the total shown in Sub-item a of Item 6 on the front of the application.

INFORMATION SHEETS

If the property was acquired since February 1, 1961, as a result of a bona fide sales transaction, enter the purchase price in Item 24.

Item 25—Net Annual Return Claimed

Compute this item as 6 per cent of amount shown in either Item 23 or 24, in accordance with the following instructions.

(a) Where only the assessed valuation, Item 23, is entered because the property was purchased before February 1, 1961, the 6 per cent computation should be made on this amount.

(b) Where Item 24 shows the purchase price since February 1, 1961, and this amount is greater than the assessed valuation shown in Item 23, you may compute your 6 per cent return on such purchase price, only if you have owned the property for more than two years at the time of filing this application. If two years have not elapsed since the date of the sale, the 6 per cent return should be determined on the assessed valuation shown in Item 23.

(c) where the purchase price in Item 24 is less than the assessed valuation shown in Item 23, the two-year ownership requirement does not apply and the 6 per cent return computation should be based on this lower purchase price.

INSTRUCTIONS FOR FILING

An original and one copy of Forms A-33.5SO and A-33.5A, together with an original and one copy of all required schedules, must be filed with the District Rent Office by delivery or mailing. The landlord is also required to file an additional copy of Forms A-33.5SO and A-33.5A for each housing accommodation affected by the application, with the name and mailing address of the tenant inserted in Item 2 of Form A-33.5SO. These copies will be served upon the tenants by the District Rent Director.

Where the present owner acquired title to the property since February 1, 1961, the owner is also required to file a supplemental statement, Form A-33.5 Supplement, with the application. An original and two copies of this form must be filed together with two copies of the contract of sale, closing statement, assignment agreements and other documents relative to the sales transaction.

Before filing the application be sure to sign the original and at least one copy. It is not necessary that the application be sworn to but false statements may subject you to the penalties provided by law. The application must be signed by the individual owner or a partner or corporate officer if the building is owned by a partnership or corporation. The required additional copies may be signed by facsimile signature.

INSTRUCTION SHEET NO. 2

(Revised February 25, 1969 and effective April 1, 1969)

To be used for the preparation and filing of

Landlord's Application for Increase of Maximum Rent (Fair Return)

(Section 33.5 of the Regulations)

The information set forth in this instruction sheet should be carefully read and followed. Before filing any application pursuant to Section 33.5, special note should be taken of the following:

a—No application may be filed unless

(1) A report of search issued by the Department of Rent and Housing Maintenance, Office of Code Enforcement, is annexed to the application stating either that no violations against such property are recorded or that all violations recorded against such property have been cleared, corrected or abated or a receipt *(or photocopy thereof)* issued by that agency attesting to the payment of the fee for the report of search (Note: The landlord is required to file the report of search with the District Rent Office upon receipt of such report. No rent increase will be granted until all violations existing on or before the date of filing the application have been cleared, corrected or abated.); and

(2) More than two years have elapsed since the date of filing the last "Fair Return" application which resulted in an order granting a rent increase.

Information Sheets

b—If the property was acquired since February 1, 1961, the purchase price may be claimed as your "Valuation Basis." However, where such purchase price is greater than the current assessed valuation, it will generally be considered for use as the valuation basis, if more than two years have elapsed between the date of the sale and the date of filing your application.

PART A—Instructions For Preparation of Application Preparation of Form A-33.5 and Form A-33.5LO

Instruction 1—**Name and mailing address of landlord —Item 1.**

Enter name of landlord and that of his representative, if any. Address and telephone number of landlord or his representative should also be shown.

Instruction 2—**Name and mailing address of tenant— Item 2.**

On the original and duplicate, this item is to be left blank. See Instruction 23 for the manner in which those copies to be served upon the individual tenants are to be completed.

Instruction 3—**Address of subject building(s)—Item 3.**

Enter the address of the property for which the application is being filed.

Instruction 4—**Building Data—Item 4.**

Enter separately the number of dwelling units (including those units occupied by landlord or superintendent, or occupied rent-free), the number of stores, units for professional or business use, garages and the total of all units. Also, enter the total number of rooms, exclusive of bathrooms.

Instruction 5—**Acquisition Data—Item 5.**

(a) Enter the date the property was acquired by the present owner and the cost. Also indicate the manner of acquisition by checking either "Purchase" or "Otherwise." If the latter, attach explanation. Also indicate year of construction.

(b) Enter the number of stories; check "Yes" or "No" whether there are any elevators on the premises. If

"Yes," indicate number of automatic and of manual elevators.

(c) State the type of fuel currently in use for supplying heat and/or hot water and also the full storage capacity of the fuel tank or bin.

Instruction 6—**Assessment Data—Item 6.**

(a) Enter the total assessed valuation in effect at the time of filing application and the specific amounts for "Land" and "Building" in the appropriate spaces. The breakdown of such total into "Land" and "Building" can be obtained from the office of the Real Property Assessment Department of the Borough in which the property is located.

(b) and (c) This information should be copied from the tax bill.

(d) Proceedings are considered to be "pending" for any of the two indicated tax years, where a protest of the assessed valuation has been filed with the Tax Commission and the time for filing writs or appeals has not expired; or where writ(s) of certiorari have been filed with no final disposition in such actions yet determined.

(e) Where reductions were secured in any of the two indicated tax years, this information should be taken from the notice of final settlement with the Tax Commission or any Court order directing same. (Attach copies of such notice or order.)

Instruction 6A—**Prior Rent Increases—Item 6A.**

It is important that the information with regard to prior rent increases be accurately stated.

Instruction 7—**Test Year—Item 7.**

You may select as your "Test Year" one of the following:

(a) The most recent calendar year (January 1st to December 31st).

(b) Your most recent fiscal year (year ending at a date other than December 31st, provided that books of account are maintained and closed accordingly and Income Tax Returns are filed for this period.)

(c) Any 12 consecutive months ending within 90 days

Information Sheets

prior to the date of filing of this application. Such period must end on the last day of a month.

Instruction 8—Rental Income Items 8, 8a and 8b.

Enter in Item 8 the total annual rental income from Column 5 of Form A-33.5A, preparation of which is covered by Instruction 22. It is to be noted that this total should include the annual rental income from all sources, i. e., dwelling units, stores, units for professional or business use and garages. A vacancy allowance of 1 per cent of the total annual rental income, Item 8, may be claimed in Item 8a. Net Annual Rental 8b, should reflect the difference between Items 8 and 8a.

Instruction 9—Miscellaneous Income (Other Than Rents)—Item 9.

List in a separate schedule and enter in Item 9 income received from the operation of washing machines and other laundry equipment, vending machines, sign rentals, etc., during the "test year" (designate as Schedule B). Indicate the types of machines, the number of each, and the charges for the use of same. Receipts or reimbursements for the use of water, gas, electricity, telephone, fuel or other services should not be included in this Item, but should be reflected as credits in reduction of the costs incurred to provide such services. Where there is no "Miscellaneous Income," enter "None" in Item 9.

Instruction 10—Total Income—Item 10.

Enter total of Items 8b plus 9.

Instruction 11—Fuel—Item 11.

Enter the cost of all fuel used during the "test year" for the operation of the property. Attach to the application a schedule (designate as Schedule C) showing the following:

Date of Delivery   Vendor   Tons or Gallons   Type   Amount

Instruction 12—Utilities—Item 12.

Enter the cost for the "test year" of water and sewer charges and of all gas and electric service applied to the tenants. Water and sewer charges may be claimed per bill in effect at the time of filing the application. Costs for electricity, gas or telephone paid for building employees should be reflected in "Payroll and Related Costs"—Item

13. The schedule to be prepared should show the following for each type of expense (designate as Schedule D):

Period		
From To	Type of Service	Amount

Instruction 13—Payroll and Related Costs; or Owner's Janitorial Allowance—Item 13.

Salaries and wages and related payroll costs for employees, or janitorial allowance claimed by the owner for his own services, should be entered under this item.

For any landlord who personally performs the janitorial services (such as cleaning halls, attending to heating system, cleaning of walks, etc.), in buildings containing 12 residential units or less the amount that will be allowed is $6.10 per month per residential unit including any apartment occupied by the owner. This computed claim for "Owner's Janitorial Allowance" should be accompanied by a statement describing the nature of the janitorial services that he performs (designate as Schedule E).

Where a property has a payroll of one or more employees required for its servicing and operation (such as superintendent, elevator operators, doormen, porters and handymen), the amount of salaries and wages paid to such employees for the "test year," plus the amount of rental allowance for apartments occupied by employees should be entered under this item and set forth in the schedule in the following manner (designate as Schedule E):

Employee's Name	Regular or Part-Time	Services Performed	Wage Rate (Monthly or Weekly)	Amount Paid for Test Year

Expenditures directly related to the amount of salaries and wages paid for the "test year" such as social security and unemployment taxes, welfare and pension payments, and Disability and Workmen's Compensation Insurance expenses are to be added to the salaries and wages scheduled.

Salaries and wages and related costs paid for the "test year" period for repair and maintenance work (such as wages of painters, carpenters, etc.) or for executive or administrative services should not be entered under this item.

INFORMATION SHEETS

Payroll and related costs may also be claimed in a "projected" amount. Computation can be made to adjust the "test year" experience to new wage rates or other payroll changes prescribed by written agreement in effect at the time of filing the application. Where such projected expense is presented such costs may not be claimed in any subsequent action filed under Section 33.8b of the Regulations.

Instruction 14—**Real Estate Taxes—Item 14.**

Set forth in a schedule and enter the amount of real estate taxes payable for the tax-year in effect at the time the application is filed (designate as Schedule F).

Instruction 15—**Insurance—Item 15.**

Enter the annual costs of premiums for policies in effect at the time of filing the application for insuring the building and contents for fire, tornado, sprinkler leakage, boiler, plate glass and public liability, etc.

The gross annual premium costs are to be reduced by all credits which have been or may be received, such as dividends, rate adjustments, etc.

This schedule (designate as Schedule G) should show the following:

Type of Insurance	Amount of Coverage	From: (Date)	To: (Date)	Term No. of Years	Total Premium	Annual Cost

Instruction 16—**Standard Management Allowance—Item 16.**

Where the landlord claims expenses for the management of the property such claim will usually be allowed pursuant to the schedule of percentages hereinafter set forth which have been developed by the Administrator after a review of the Standard Management Fees adopted by the Real Estate Boards for the several Boroughs of the City. The usual allowable expense will be based upon the following percentages (designated as Schedule H).

(1) For properties with Total Income (Item 10) of less than $100,000.00
    (a) containing 12 or fewer residential units:
        7 per cent of Total Income with a minimum annual allowance of $240.00;
    (b) containing more than 12 residential units:
        5 per cent of Total Income.
(2) For properties with Total Income (Item 10) of more than $100,000.00:
    (a) 5% on the first $100,000.00.
    (b) On excess over $100,000.00;

3%—From $100,000.01 to $200,000.00,
2%—From $200,000.01 to $500,000.00,
1%—From $500,000.01 up. (Instruction 16 am February 25, 1970)

Instruction 17—**Repairs and Maintenance—Item 17.**

Annual cost to be entered under this item should be that amount computed as the average of repair and maintenance expenses incurred for a four-year period ending with the last month of the "test year."

This average of a four-year cycle of "repair and maintenance" expenses is for the purpose of establishing for the "test year" an annual amount which would be normally recurrent. Where the applicant is unable to present such costs for a four-year period he should submit an explanation.

Where the applicant has been the owner of the property for less than four years, the bills and data of the previous owner of the property should be used to complete the four-year experience.

Expenditures for repairs and maintenance to be considered under this category are such items as painting and decorating, plumbing repairs, carpentry, electrical and general repairs and supplies. Wages and related costs paid to employees performing repair services and the costs of service contracts for oil burner, refrigeration and elevator maintenance, should also be included. Do not include items of the nature described in Instruction 18.

In presenting repair and maintenance expenses, separate schedules should be prepared for **each** of the four years, listing in detail all invoices for those costs incurred in **each** year (designate as Schedule I). Totals should be taken for **each** of the four years and these totals should then be **separately** stated and the one-year average entered in Item 17. The schedules prepared to show the itemization for each of the four years should be arranged as follows:

Invoice	Vendor	Type of Repair	Location (Apt. No. Lobby, Etc.)	Amount

Any credits received (such as allowances in price, returns of merchandise, reimbursements from tenants, payments from insurance carriers for damages, etc.) are to be noted and deducted from the total costs for the period covered.

Information Sheets

For buildings containing 251 or more residential units, where books of account are maintained in which all transactions of the property during the year are recorded and said transactions are properly totaled and summarized at the end of each year, repair and maintenance expenses may be set forth in Schedule I in the following fashion:

Invoices covering expenses for those years required may be listed in detail in the manner described above, or if the applicant elects, he may present the general ledger totals of each category of repair and maintenance costs which made up the total of repair and maintenance expense, for the required years. This presentation of book totals should follow the same classifications reflected in the books of account, such as painting (within apartments), painting (within building-lobby, halls, etc.), exterior painting (windows, sashes, fire escapes, etc.), carpentry repairs, plumbing repairs, electrical repairs, mechanical repairs, supplies, misc. repairs, etc.

OPTIONAL ALLOWANCE FOR PROPERTIES CONTAINING 12 OR LESS RESIDENTIAL ACCOMMODATIONS

(the green Application Form A-33.5SO must be used)

Where a building contains 12 or less residential units, the landlord may use 16.5 per cent of the "annual Rental Income," Item 8, for the combined Items 17 and 18 ("Repairs and Maintenance," and "Replacements and Improvements") in lieu of preparing and substantiating Schedules "I" and "J" in detail. Where a substantial portion of the "Annual Rental Income," Item 8, is derived from commercial tenants, the Administrator reserves the right to review the acceptability of the 16.5 per cent allowance claimed. Complete details with respect to the preparation of this form is contained in Instruction Sheet No. 1.

OPTIONAL ALLOWANCES FOR PROPERTIES CONTAINING 13 to 39 OR 40 to 250 RESIDENTIAL ACCOMMODATIONS

(the buff Application Form A-33.5LO must be used)

Where the property contains 13 to 250 residential units, inclusive, in lieu of scheduling and substantiating expenses for "Repairs and Maintenance" and "Replacements and Improvements" (Items 17 and 18), the owner may claim a combined percentage allowance for such Items. The percentage of Annual Rental Income (Item 8) that may be claimed as the allowance is set forth in the Table below. Where a substantial portion of the Annual Rental Income (Item 8) is derived from commercial tenants, the Administrator reserves the right to review the acceptability of the allowance claimed.

It should be noted that the percentages in the Table below not only relate to type and size of property, but also to length of ownership by the applicant. In selecting the appropriate percentage, length of ownership is to be determined as being that period of time **between the date the property was acquired by the present owner to the end of the "Test Year" of the application.** In instances only where the property has been owned ten years or more, two copies of the Deed recording conveyance of title should be submitted. If it is claimed that the property has been held ten years or more despite the fact that the Deed records conveyance on a date which would indicate a period of less than ten years, an affidavit (two copies) specifying the original date of acquisition and detailing the history of ownership subsequent thereto should also be presented.

Type of Property:	% Allowance to be used if Applicant has owned the property:	
	Less than 10 Years	10 Years or more
Containing 13 to 39 Residential Units		
Walk-up	11.5%	14.5%
Elevator	9.0%	12.0%
Containing 40 to 250 Residential Units		
Walk-up	10.5%	14.0%
Elevator	8.0%	11.5%

Special Note: Where the applicant elects to file claiming the "standard allowance" prescribed above, he may use the following alternate method in calculating "Repairs and Maintenance" and "Replacements and Improvements" if the rents in Item 8 include increases granted to the **present owner** under Sections 33.1b or 33.1c of the

Information Sheets

Regulations, such as Rewiring, Plumbing, Exterior Lights, Peepholes, etc.

(a) Determine the amount of annual rent increase received for the Major Capital Improvement.

(b) Deduct this sum from Rental Income shown in Item 8.

(c) Your normal "Repairs and Maintenance" and "Replacements and Improvement" allowance should be computed at the applicable per cent of the resultant figure in (b) above.

(d) In addition, the annual rent increase determined in (a) above may be claimed as the write-off for the cost of the Major Capital Improvement.

Example: Assume the annual rental in Item 8 for a 10-family house in $8,460. In a period prior to the filing of this application the owner rewired the building at a cost of $2,500 and was granted an annual rent increase of $360 under Section 33.1c of the Regulations.

Based upon these facts, the applicant's presentation for expense to be claimed should be as follows:

(a) Annual MCI increase .... $ 360.00
(b) Rental Income, Item 8 of $8,460 minus amount shown above... $8,100.00
(c) Normal R & M and R & I allowance 16.5 per cent of (b) $1,336.50
(d) Write-off for MCI Cost 360.00
Total allowance to be claimed in application $1,696.50

The alternate method described above cannot be used, if on the date the application is filed the owner had recouped 140 per cent of his cost for the Major Capital Improvement by virtue of the amount of rental increases already collected. In the example given above, 140 per cent of the $2,500 rewiring cost would amount to $3,500.

Note: If applicant uses the alternate method of computation, he will be required to substantiate the cost of the M.C.I.

Instruction 18—Replacements and Improvements—Item 18.

Enter one year's proration of the cost of all improvements and replacements made since the date the property was acquired by the present owner and not fully depreciated. This should be computed in accordance with the

Information Sheets

average useful lives prescribed by the U. S. Treasury Department, examples of which are listed below:

Item	Useful Life
Cooking Ranges	8 yrs.
Sinks	20 yrs.
Kitchen Cabinets	20 yrs.
Roofing	10 yrs.
Boilers	10 yrs.
Refrigerators	10 yrs.

These will be used unless the landlord can establish, on the basis of his own experience, useful lives which differ.

The schedule for this item (designate as Schedule J) should show the following:

Date Acquired	Vendor	Item	Where Used (Apt. No.)	Cost	Useful Life	Charge to Test Year

Cost of Rehabilitation or Major Capital Improvements for which rental increases were received prior to May 1, 1962, pursuant to § 33(1)(b) (substantial rehabilitation) or § 33(1)(c) (major capital improvement) of the State Rent and Eviction Regulations, or since May 1, 1962 under § 33.1b or § 33.1c of the City Rent Regulations, may be considered in the following manner: A write-of of such costs may be charged to the "test year" in an amount equal to the annual increase in rents received. Where the rental increase granted compensated the owner not only for the cost of the improvement but also for an attendant additional operating expense (such as installation of a central heating system, necessitating a new or additional cost of fuel) the annual charge to be reflected in the "test year" should be that amount which will permit recoupment of the cost of the improvement only. (The new or additional cost of fuel will be reflected in the application as "fuel" expense.)

The above write-off procedure should not be used, if on the date the application is filed the owner had recovered 140 per cent of his cost by virtue of the amount of rental increases already collected. In such instance the "test year" charge should be computed based upon the normal life expectancy of the improvement.

Instruction 19—**Miscellaneous—Item 19.**

Enter all expenses incurred in the "test year" necessary to the operation of the property and not otherwise classified (such as legal and accounting fees, exterminat-

Information Sheets

ing, upkeep of uniforms, permit and inspection fees, etc.). Mortgage interest and amortization are not to be included as operating expenses of the building.

Legal and accounting fees may be included as they apply to the operation of the building rather than to the financial or personal affairs of the ownership. Legal costs should be shown for a three-year period ending with the last month of the "test year" and the one-year average entered under this item. Where fees claimed were paid for professional services rendered in connection with prior applications, the amounts to be included in the three-year average shall be the amounts actually paid but not to exceed 25 per cent of the actual amount of the increases ordered in the prior applications. The schedule (designate as Schedule K) should show the following:

Date of Invoice   Vendor   Type of Expense   Amount

Instruction 20—Depreciation—Item 20.

Enter the lower of the following:

(1) The total amount of depreciation claimed in the latest Federal Income Tax Return (including the depreciation allowance(s) claimed for improvements, additions and/or replacements); or

(2) 2 per cent of the assessed valuation of the building exclusive of the land; or, where the purchase price is being claimed as the "valuation basis" 2 percent on that part of the purchase price which represents the building value. To establish such building value one must apply to the total purchase price the same ratio that the assessed valuation of the building bears to the total of the current assessed valuation. Example: Assume the property's total assessed valuation to be $10,000.00 of which the building valuation is $8,000.00. This establishes 80 per cent as the ratio of the building's valuation. Accordingly 80 per cent would be the ratio applied to whatever purchase price is claimed as the "valuation basis." The 2 per cent depreciation allowance is to be computed on the amount thus determined.

The schedule for this item (designate as Schedule L) should show the applicant's computation for the depreciation allowance claimed. Also submit an exact copy of the depreciation schedule shown on the Federal Income Tax Return followed by this statement: "This schedule has been transcribed from the latest Federal Income Tax Return covering the tax year ending on

.... (Day) ....
(Month) .... (Year)

Instruction 21—**Computation of Net Annual Return and Rent Adjustment Indicated—Items 23, 24, 25 and 26.**

Part A—Enter in Item 23 the assessed valuation of the property, in effect at the time of filing the application (Sub. Item a of Item 6). Such amount will be considered as the "valuation basis" except as otherwise provided in paragraph b of Section 33.5 of the Regulations.

Part B—Where the property was acquired since February 1, 1961, in a bona fide sales transaction (as defined in paragraph b of Section 33.5 of the Regulations) enter this amount in Item 24. If such sale was for an amount greater than the assessed valuation in Part A above, such purchase price may be used as the "valuation basis" if on the date of filing the application, more than two years will have elapsed since the sale. Where a purchase price since February 1, 1961 was less than the assessed valuation in Part A above, the two-year ownership requirement does not apply and such purchase price may be used as the "valuation basis."

Preparation of Form A-33.5A

Instruction 22—**Rental Income—Schedule A.**

All controlled, decontrolled, uncontrolled and commercial units in the property are to be listed at the rent in effect at the time the application is filed. For any units that are vacant or occupied in whole or in part rent-free, the rental value must be listed. If such unit is a controlled housing accommodation, the amount to be shown should be the maximum rent in effect, even if rented for less. If such space is decontrolled housing, commercial or business, its full rental value should be entered on this schedule. This includes any units occupied by the landlord or his employees.

In Column 2, place a check-mark next to all uncontrolled, decontrolled, business and commercial space. Attach a separate schedule listing all units so indicated, stating the rents collected from each unit on March 1, 1943 or on the earliest known date thereafter.

Filing Application

Instruction 23—**Filing.**

An original and one copy of Form A-33.5 or Form A-33.5LO and Schedule A-Rental Income (Form A-33.5A), together with an original and one copy of all required schedules, must be filed with the District Rent Office by delivery or mailing. The landlord is also required to file an additional copy of the above forms for each housing accommodation affected by the application, with the name and mailing address of the tenant inserted in Item 2 on Form A-33.5 or Form A-33.5LO. These copies will be served upon the tenants by the District Director.

Where the present owner acquired title to the property since February 1, 1961, the owner is also required to file a supplemental statement (Form A-33.5 Supplement) with the application. An original and two copies of this form must be filed together with two copies of the contract of sale, closing statement, assignment agreements and other documents relative to the sales transaction.

Where a property contains more than 40 residential units the requirement to serve a copy of the rent roll (Form A-33.5A) upon each tenant may be waived upon application to the District Director. If a waiver is granted, the landlord must be prepared to make the rent roll available to the tenants at such places and at such times as the District Director deems to be reasonable. The application for a waiver of individual service of Form A-33.5A should be made by letter addressed to the District Director, giving the address of the property, the total number of rental units, and the number of controlled residential units.

Before filing the application be sure to sign the original and at least one copy. It is not necessary that the application be sworn to but false statements may subject you to the penalties provided by law. The application must be signed by the individual owner or a partner or corporate officer if the building is owned by a partnership or corporation. The required additional copies may be signed by facsimile signature.

PART B—Instructions for the Submission of Evidence Introduction

At a date subsequent to the filing of the application, written notice will be sent for the submission of evidence. The evidence which will be required, is detailed in the Specific Instructions that follow.

To facilitate the processing of your case, it is suggested that all data necessary to fully substantiate all items claimed in your application, be presented to the Accounting Division in the following fashion:

(a) Assemble all bills and cancelled checks for same, and other supporting data, by category of expense. Arrange each invoice and cancelled check in the same sequence in which the items to which they refer are listed in the schedule of your application. It is suggested that each cancelled check be fastened to the invoice which it paid. Bookkeeping records such as General Ledgers and books of original entry are also required for those years for which operating expenses are claimed in your application.

(b) After arranging data as described above, place such evidence into separate envelopes or packages for each category.

(c) Identify each envelope or package with the docket number of the application, the address of the property and the "Item" to which it relates, and place same into a secure package to be mailed or delivered to the Accounting Division. Be sure that the docket number and address of the property are clearly marked on the outside of this package.

Specific Instructions

The following specific instructions for submission of evidence are identified by the relevant Item number in Application Form A-33.5 or Form A-33.5LO.

INFORMATION SHEETS

Item 7—Test Year

Where the test year selected ends on a date other than December 31st, submit an explanation stating:

(a) Whether your books are kept and closed on the basis of such fiscal year.

(b) Whether your Federal Income Tax was filed, or will be filed (if not due yet) with such fiscal year as its basis.

Item 8—Rental Income

Submit leases and other data to support present rentals of stores and business units. Also submit information as to the amount of rent being collected from each of these units on March 1, 1943 or on the earliest known date thereafter.

Item 9—Miscellaneous Income

Submit copies of contracts with vendors or concessionaires. If machines are owner operated, present records to support income received during the "test year."

Item 11—Fuel

Submit invoices and delivery tickets for all fuel deliveries listed in your Schedule. Where invoices or tickets are missing, obtain duplicates from vendors. The vendor's statement listing all individual deliveries made, by date, quantity and amount, may be submitted instead.

Item 12—Utilities

Submit the bills listed in Schedule D of your application for electricity, gas, water and sewer. Note and comment as to any amounts which apply to personal use by the landlord.

Item 13—Payroll and Related Costs, or Owner's Janitorial Allowance

Where one or more persons are employed in the operation of the property, payroll records must be submitted to substantiate the amount claimed in Schedule E. The evidence to be presented must support the expense of salaries and wages and other related costs incurred during the "test year" period. Where, however, the expense claimed reflects an annual amount which projects wage rates in effect at the time of filing the application, payroll data for the period from the beginning of the "test year" to date should be submitted. The following payroll records are required covering the period specified above:

(a) Original weekly, bi-weekly or monthly payroll sheets.

(b) Copies of the quarterly returns for Social Security Taxes.

(c) Copies of the quarterly State Unemployment Insurance Tax Returns.

(d) Copy of prevailing union contract, if any.

(e) Receipts for payments to union pension and welfare funds.

Also submit the following:

(f) Copy of latest Federal Unemployment Tax Return.

(g) Current Workmen's Compensation Insurance Policy and last audit report.

(h) Current Disability Benefits Insurance Policy.

(i) Cancelled checks in payment of wages to employees and for the related costs listed above.

Item 14—Real Estate Taxes

Submit the tax bill in effect at the time of filing the application.

Item 15—Insurance

Submit all policies listed in Schedule G of your application plus all policies currently in force. If there has been any cancellation of insurance since the date of filing, explain same. Prepare a list of amounts, refunds or credits received from insurance companies, brokers, adjusters, or received as a result of claims, during or since the "test year." Describe the nature of each.

Item 17—Repairs and Maintenance

Submit the following:

(a) All the invoices listed in Schedule I of your application and cancelled checks in payment, arranged in the same order as in that Schedule.

(b) All credit memos for merchandise returned, or for allowances received, relating to invoices listed in Schedule I.

(c) Prepare a listing of payments received as refunds or

Information Sheets

allowances from vendors, reimbursements from tenants, or adjustments due to fire or other losses. Where recoveries have been received for fire or other damage, submit copy of settlement statement from insurer and a full explanation as to when and where damage was sustained, also specific costs incurred to repair same.

Item 18—Replacements and Improvements

Submit the following:

(a) All invoices listed in Schedule J of your application and cancelled checks in payment.

(b) A list of payments or allowances received on the trade-in or sale of equipment.

Item 19—Miscellaneous

Submit bills and cancelled checks for all costs listed in Schedule K.

Item 20—Depreciation

A transcript of the Depreciation Schedule in the latest Federal Income Tax Return should be submitted as part of Schedule L of the application. Where depreciation allowance is being claimed and no deduction for this item is made in your latest Federal Income Tax Return, submit an explanation.

Items 23 and 24—Valuation Basis

Tax bill to confirm the assessed valuation entered in Item 23 will have been presented in support of Real Estate Tax Expense claimed in Item 14.

Where the property was acquired since February 1, 1961, contracts of sale, closing statements, assignment agreements and other documents relative to the sales transaction are to be submitted at the time of filing the application.

SPECIAL INSTRUCTIONS FOR HOTELS

Owners and operators of hotels applying under Section 33.5 of the Regulations must file their applications in accordance with the special instructions set forth below.

Form A-33.5—Complete all "Items" except Items 8, 8a and 8b in the manner prescribed in this Instruction Sheet. Item 8, Rental Income, should reflect the actual income earned in the test year selected. Accordingly, no

Vacancy Allowance, Item 8a, should be claimed. Therefore the amount to be entered in Item 8b should be the same as that shown in Item 8.

Operating expenses that cannot be classified into those categories listed on Form A-33.5, should be included in Item 19, Miscellaneous, and detailed in a supporting schedule.

Submit a statement reconciling the amount shown as the Net Return Earned In Test Year, Item 22, with that amount indicated as your Net Profit or Loss, as per your accountant's report or books of account for the same period.

In lieu of Form A-33.5A (Schedule A—Rental Income) submit the following supporting schedules:

Schedule A-1—**Listing of Controlled Tenants.** This list is to be prepared with columnar headings as follows:

(1) Unit number or designation

(2) Number of rooms

(3) Name of present tenant

(4) Term of occupancy (i. e., "D"-Day, "W"-Week, "M"-Month)

(5) Present maximum rent

Schedule A-2—**Rooms—Income Earned for the Test Year.**

From permanent tenants, including rentals from controlled tenants per Schedule A-1 .... $

From transient tenants .... $

    Total Rooms—Income Earned for Test Year............................. $

The total amount appearing on this schedule is to be transferred to Form A-33.5, Items 8 and 8b.

Schedule A-3—**Schedule of Present Occupancy.** This schedule is to be prepared as of the date of the application and is to show the following information:

	Number of Units	Number of Rooms
Controlled Tenants, per "Schedule A-1"		
Other Permanent Tenants..................		
Transient		
For Employees' or Hotel's Own Use		
Unoccupied...............................		
TOTAL—Entire Hotel......................		

INFORMATION SHEETS

INSTRUCTION SHEET NO. 5

(Issued December 1, 1963)

Increase of Maximum Rent (Increased Costs—Small Structures) (Section 33.6 of the Regulations)

Section 33.6 of the Rent, Eviction and Rehabilitation Regulations is designed to give relief to the so-called "non-professional" landlord who owns no more than four rental units (excluding any unit(s) personally occupied by him) within the City, and who for lack of detailed records may not be in a position to establish his right to rent increases based upon a return on the valuation of the property under Section 33.5 of the Regulations, Application Form A-33.6 has been issued by the Administrator for use by landlords wishing to file for rent increases under Section 33.6.

Instructions for preparing and filing an application under this section are printed on Application Form A-33.6 and should be read in conjunction with this Instruction Sheet before completing the application and filing it with the District Rent Office.

On the face of the application form general information is required concerning the property and the rental income derived therefrom. On the reverse side, information should be presented concerning those items of expense which are to be considered. Bills and checks for all expenses shown must accompany the application.

Adjustments granted under this section will be determined by computing the total increased costs sustained by the applicant (i.e. the difference between the expenses presented for the current period and those of the base period, reduced by compensating rent increases received from the tenants since the base period). The base period is either 1943, the year when Federal rent control took effect, or the calendar year in which the landlord acquired the property, whichever is later.

Adjustments factors for Heating Fuel and various types of Repair and Maintenance expenses have been established showing the change in the cost for each year since Federal rent control took effect. By applying same to current expenses, the increase in the cost of the various items can be determined. For example, if a landlord has spent $200.00 for heating fuel during the current year and the base period factor is 40, it would indicate that 40% of the $200.00 current expense, or $80.00, represents the increase in cost sustained. The base period expense for heating fuel would thus be recognized as $120.00. **For items of Real Estate Taxes, Insurance, and Utilities, bills must be presented for both base and current periods to establish the actual increase in costs sustained.**

The amount representing the increase in expenses in excess of compensating rental increases received will constitute the adjustment to which a landlord will be entitled under this section.

In no event will a landlord be entitled to an adjustment under this section where he is not maintaining all essential services required to be provided with the housing accommodations.

NO APPLICATION MAY BE FILED UNLESS A CERTIFICATE OF THE DEPARTMENT OF BUILDINGS IS ANNEXED TO THE APPLICATIONS STATING THAT NO VIOLATIONS AGAINST SUCH PROPERTY ARE RECORDED IN THE INDEX MAINTAINED BY THE CENTRAL VIOLATIONS BUREAU OF SUCH DEPARTMENT.

INSTRUCTION SHEET NO. 6

Landlord's Application for Increase in Maximum Rent (Partial Labor Cost Recoupment)

(See Section 33.8b of the Regulations)

CAUTION: Where additional wage increase(s) have been granted by the owner after the date of filing this application, such additional wage increase(s) may not be the subject of another application under § 33.8b of the Regulations for a period of three years from the date of a filing which results in a grant of the application. No application under § 33.8b may be filed if there is an application under § 33.8a (Landlord's Application for Equalization Adjustment of Maximum Rent) pending or if a rental increase under § 33.8a was granted within the past three years.

The application form and all attachments must be filled

Information Sheets

out completely and accurately. An application which is incomplete or incorrect may be rejected.

1. GENERAL INSTRUCTIONS

A. Application May Be Filed.

These instructions are to be used for a building employing either union or non-union building service employees where the owner has granted wage increase(s) to such employees since April 21, 1967. These instructions are to be used only for building service employees, i.e., for use in a building employing union or non-union building service employees whose duties are that of superintendent, janitors, handymen, elevator operators, doormen and porters. The listing in Part III may only include individual employees who perform services in the above categories and who represent the normal complement of *service* employees regularly employed throughout the year. Building service employees *do not* include employees hired for temporary purposes, those hired as vacation replacements, or those hired as repair and maintenance personnel, i.e., painters, plumbers, carpenters, etc. and management or office personnel.

Recoupment of labor costs pursuant to § 33.8b of the Regulations is limited to Labor Cost Increases sustained or to be sustained on or after April 21, 1967. Accordingly, before filing this application special note should be taken of the following:

(1) An application may only be filed on or after a date (on or after April 21, 1967) which is prescribed by the union agreement as the effective date for the wage increase(s); or

(2) Where non-union service employees are affected, an application may only be filed on or after the date on which the wage increase was first paid.

(3) You may initiate your application for rent increase under § 33.8b of the Regulations (Partial Labor Cost Recoupment) by filing Application Form A-33.8b (10-67). This application form is known as a "short form" application.

B. No Applications May Be Filed.

Where an order was issued less than three years ago under either § 33.8a or § 33.8b or if there is a pending

697

application under § 33.8a (Landlord's Application For Equalization Adjustment of Maximum Rent). This form is not to be used where owner-services are being performed. Use Application Form A-33.8b OS in such cases.

C. Union and Non-Union Building Service Agreements.

Union

Where the union agreement was signed prior to April 21, 1967 and such agreement also includes a provision for a wage rate increase to be paid effective as of a date on or after April 21, 1967, the application may only be filed on or after the date such increase becomes effective. If the agreement specifies that additional wage increases are to be paid subsequently, the landlord may also claim recoupment of additional wage adjustments to be incurred in not more than two succeeding years.

Where building service employees are covered by a union agreement, signed by the owner on or after April 21, 1967, this application may be filed to recoup a wage increase effective on or after this date. Where the contract includes provision for more than one annual increase, claim may be made in this application for recoupment of an aggregate Labor Cost Increase reflecting not more than three successive annual increases.

Non-Union

If the building is staffed by "non-union" employees only, recoupment will only be permitted for wage adjustments paid on or after April 21, 1967 and prior to the date of filing Application Form A-33.8b DS. Recoupment may be claimed for all wage adjustments paid on or after April 21, 1967 to the date of filing the application. No consideration will be given to wage increases paid on or after the date of filing such application form where such application results in an order increasing the maximum rents.

Buildings with both Union and Non-Union Service Employees

Where a building is staffed with both "union" and "non-union" building service employees, complete the application in accordance with the above instructions for each category.

D. Separate Applications Must Be Filed for Each Property.

A property shall include any structure or group of structures including the land containing housing accommodations having either common facilities, or which are contiguous, or which are operated as a single enterprise and which the District Rent Director shall, in his discretion find appropriate to be considered as a single operation for the purpose of this section.

2. FORMS TO BE COMPLETED

A—Application Form A-33.8b DS [Landlord's Application for Increase in Maximum Rent (Partial Labor Cost Recoupment) (Detailed Supplement)] in quadruplicate;

B—Part IIA of Application Form A-33.8b DS (Schedule of Rental Income) in quadruplicate;

C—Master Order Form O-33.8b in duplicate;

D—Notice of Determination Form N-33.8b in duplicate for each controlled tenant named in Part IIA of Application Form A-33.8b DS; and

E—Certificate of Independent Accountant in triplicate.

3. COMPLETION OF FORMS

Part I of Application Form A-33.8b DS—

Enter name and address of landlord and name and address of landlord's representative, if any, in the box designated "Mailing Address of Landlord". Also fill in the "Address of Property".

Item 2. Insert x in either "YES" or "NO" box. If "YES" is indicated specify the section of the Regulations under which the increase was granted, i.e., § 33.5, § 33.6 or § 33.7, by entering 5, 6 or 7 in the blank space. Also enter the "Docket No." and the "Date of Issuance of Order".

Item 3. Insert the number of controlled apartments, the number of uncontrolled apartments and the total number of apartments. "Semi-professional" apartments and apartments occupied by the landlord or his employees are considered to be "controlled" apartments. Decontrolled and exempt apartments are considered to be "uncontrolled" apartments. Where a maximum rent for an apartment has been established as a result of a filing of a "first rental registration statement" after a substantial rehabilitation, or, where as a result of a substantial rehabilitation, a new maximum rent for a housing accommodation has been established based upon either an Advisory Opinion or an Order Granting A Prior Opinion, such apartment may be listed as an "uncontrolled" apartment for the purpose of this proceeding. This option shall be uniformly applied to all such apartments in the property. Where the landlord has exercised this option, such apartment shall be designated by an asterisk in column 1 of Part IIA, Schedule of Rental Income.

Item 4. Insert the total number of building service employees who represent the normal complement regularly employed throughout the year in servicing the property.

Item 5. Insert the number of "union" building *service* employees and the number of "non-union" building *service* employees.

Item 6. Insert the "Union Local No."; date of signing current agreement; and effective date(s) of wage increase(s) therein.

Item 7. Insert the date(s) for each wage increase paid to "non-union" employees on or after April 21, 1967.

Item 8. Insert x in either the "YES" or "NO" box. If you insert "x" in the "YES" box, state Docket No. ..... These proceedings normally relate to applications dealing with reduction of doormen, switchboard, etc., employees or elevators conversions under Section 35 of the Regulations.

Part IIA. Schedule of Rental Income.

Column 1—Enter apartment designation.

Column 2—Enter name of present tenant. If vacant, write "VACANT".

Column 3—See instructions on top of the form for mean-

Information Sheets

ing of "controlled" and "uncontrolled" and instructions for completing item 3 of Part I. All controlled and uncontrolled units in the property are to be listed under either sub-column "a" or "b", whichever is applicable at the rent in effect at the time the application is filed. For any apartments that are vacant or occupied in whole or in part rent-free, the rental value must be listed. If such apartment is a "controlled" housing accommodation, the amount to be shown should be the maximum rent in effect, even if rented for less. If such space is "uncontrolled", its full rental value should be entered on this schedule. This includes any units occupied by the landlord or his employees.

Column 4—Enter the number of rooms under either "a" or "b", whichever is applicable.

Column 5—This column, representing the amount of monthly rent adjustment to each tenant cannot be computed until the percentage of such adjustment is determined under Part IV of this application. The percentage entered on line 13 of Part IV must then be entered in the heading for column 5 of Part IIA. To compute the amount of monthly increase payable by each tenant, multiply the tenant's current monthly rent by the indicated percentage and enter the result in column 5.

Where more than one sheet is used for the Schedule of Rental Income be sure to number each sheet consecutively in the space provided in the upper right hand corner. Columns 3a, 3b, 4a, 4b and 5 should be totalled separately for each sheet and entered on Part II—Summary Schedule of Rental Income.

Part II. Summary Schedule of Rental Income.

The totals from each of the individual Part IIA sheets (Schedule of Rental Income) should be entered in the appropriate columns (3a, 3b, 4a, 4b and 5) of Part II—Summary Schedule of Rental Income. Enter sheet numbers in numerical order.

Line 1—Total columns 3a, 3b, 4a, 4b and 5, individually and enter in the appropriate spaces on line 1.

Line 2—Line 2 is the annual total of columns 3a, 3b and 5. Complete the indicated computation.

Line 3—Line 3 is the total annual rents from all apartments, both controlled and uncontrolled.

Computation of Allocation Factor

Where the total annual rent as shown on line 3 is derived solely from controlled apartments, enter 0% on line 6 and omit lines 4 thru 5c without further computation.

Where the total annual rent as shown on line 3 includes income from uncontrolled apartments, lines 4, 5 and 6 must be completed in accordance with instructions indicated on the form.

Determination of § 33.5, 33.6 or 33.7 Offset Rate

Complete lines 7, 8 and 9 where an order has been issued since May 1, 1966 granting a rent increase under § 33.5, § 33.6 or § 33.7.

Enter the section of the Regulations (33.5, 33.6 or 33.7) in the space following "Section 33. . ." and the total annual amount of rent increase ordered. If you do not know whether such an order was issued or the amount of the rent increase, you may write to the Accounting Division at the Principal Office, 280 Broadway, New York, New York 10007 for such information.

Part III. Computation of Base Year Payroll and Aggregate Labor Cost Increase.

Wage recoupment will only be granted for increases effective or paid on or after April 21, 1967 to building *service* employees *only.* Building service employees are generally those whose duties are that of superintendents, janitors, handymen, elevator operators, doormen and porters. The listing in Part III may only include individual employees who perform services in the above categories and who represent the normal complement of *service* employees regularly employed throughout the year. Do *not* include building service employees hired for temporary purposes, nor those hired as vacation replacements, or those hired as repair and maintenance personnel, i.e., painters, plumbers, carpenters, etc. and management or office personnel.

INFORMATION SHEETS

Column 1—Enter names of building service personnel currently employed at the property. List only those individuals who comprise the normal complement of permanent service employee. Insert check (✓) mark if the employee is a member of a building service union.

Column 2—Enter the job title of each employee, e.g., superintendent, handyman, elevator operator, doorman, porter, etc.

Column 3—Enter for each employee the number of hours that constitutes his regular work-week. The employee's normal work-week is the number of hours he is regularly required to work. For example, although there may be a union agreement which prescribes a standard 40-hour week for an individual employee, where he consistently works 48 hours a week and is paid accordingly, his normal work-week shall be considered to be 48 hours. Conversely, where the building service staff includes a "part time" employee who regularly works less than the standard week, his work-week listed in column 3 should specify the "part-time" weekly hours he is regularly in attendance.

Column 4—Enter for each employee the weekly wage he received or which was paid to the person(s) holding his job title for the normal scheduled work-week (listed in column 3) prior to wage increase(s). The amount inserted should be the *gross* weekly amount then earned by the employee before any deductions. It should not include the rental value or allowances for an apartment or other living spaces occupied by the employee wholly or partially rent-free; monies paid by the employer on behalf of the employee for gas, electricity, telephone; or for additional payments for making repairs, painting or performing extra work on or off the property. *The weekly wage reported should be limited to the employee's normal duties at the subject property.* Where the employee's services are also performed off the property, only the wages for the time actually spent at the property should be entered.

Wages entered in column 4 must be on the basis of a weekly salary. Where the employer's method of payment is other than weekly, convert the payment to a weekly rate. This conversion should be made by computing the annual wage for the employee and dividing the annual wage by 52. The employee's annual wage should be calculated as follows: if the employee is paid bi-weekly (every two weeks) multiply the gross amount paid by 26. Where the employee is paid semi-monthly (twice a month) multiply the gross amount paid by 24. Where the employee is paid monthly, multiply the gross amount paid by 12.

Normal Weekly Increases—Paid or To Be Paid

Columns 5, 6, 7, 8 & 9—These columns should list the weekly wage increases paid or effective on or after April 21, 1967. Indicate the calculations of the Labor Cost Increase sustained or to be sustained. The *weekly* increases to be entered in the appropriate columns are those which the employer has paid or will be obligated to pay on or after April 21, 1967 additional to the weekly wages shown in column 4.

For Union Agreements

Where wage adjustments are stipulated by union agreement, entries in column 5 should reflect the first of such weekly increases prescribed on or after April 21, 1967. If the agreement also provides for additional weekly wage increases to be paid in successive second or third years, the second year increase should be entered in column 6 and the third year increase should be entered in column 8. Indicate the effective date of each increase in the heading of the appropriate column. The totals to be entered into column 7 should be computed only where the additional wage increase is prescribed by union agreement in a second succeeding year. Likewise, the totals to be entered in column 9 should be computed only where additional wage increases are prescribed by union agreement for successive second and third years.

For Non-Union Agreements

Where wage adjustments are stipulated by non-union agreement, entries in column 5 should reflect the total of all such weekly increases paid on or after April 21, 1967. Columns 6, 7, 8 and 9 should be left blank.

Base Year Payroll and Related Costs

The Base Year Payroll and Related Costs is determined by multiplying the weekly total in column 4 (item A) by 61 (item B in column 4). This computed Base Year Payroll reflects additional expenditures for holidays and vacations and for payroll taxes and Workmen's Compensation Insurance. Where the employer was also required to make contribution to Union Welfare and Pension Funds, the annual amount of such cost *paid,* should be added under column 4. The total computed Base Year Payroll should be entered at the bottom line of column 4. Where there is no additional annual payment to Welfare and Pension Funds, the computed Base Year Payroll and Related Costs should be entered at the bottom line of column 4.

Total Aggregate Labor Cost Increase

The Total Aggregate Labor Cost Increase is determined by multiplying the aggregate weekly total shown in item C of column 10 by 61 (the Annualization Factor, item B in column 10). This computation reflects a Labor Cost Increase to be sustained which includes the recognition of increases applicable to holiday and vacation wage payments as well as additional related expenditures for payroll taxes and Workmen's Compensation Insurance. If the employer is obligated by wage agreement to make *increased* contributions for employees to a Welfare and Pension Plan, such *increased* payments to be incurred during the periods involved should be added. *No increased expense for Welfare and/or Pension contributions may be claimed unless there is provision in the union agreement which requires that such contributions be greater than those previously paid.* For example, assume that the union agreement provides that the owner is required to increase his Welfare and/or Pension contribution by $10.00 per employee per year. If the labor increase for which recoupment is being requested in Part IV is a one year increase, the additional to be added as increased expense for Welfare and/or Pension payments would be $10.00 annually times the number of employees for which such additional payment is required. Likewise, where the labor increase for which recoupment is being requested in Part IV is for a two-year period, the additional to be added as an increased expense for Welfare and/or Pension payments would be $20.00 times the number of such employees; and where the labor increase for which recoupment is being requested in Part IV is for a three-year period, the additional to be added as an increased expense for Welfare and/or Pension payments would be $30.00 times the number of such employees.

Part IV. Determination of Adjusted Aggregate Labor Cost Increase.

Transpose information in accordance with the specific instructions set forth in the application form with regard to items 1, 2 and 3b (if any). Complete all other items in accordance with the specific instructions set forth on the form.

4. APPLICATION PENDING UNDER SECTION 33.5
(Net Annual Return)

A. Landlord's Option and Its Effects.

If an application under Section 33.5 of the Regulations is pending, you may, in lieu of filing an application under Section 33.8b, exercise your option to include your increased labor costs as part of the Section 33.5 application. If you exercise this option:

1. Your increased labor costs may be projected as an additional expense item in your pending Section 33.5 application;
2. Your rental income will be revised to reflect rents in effect on the date you request such projection;
3. In no event will the overall rent increase granted for the property under Section 33.5 exceed 15%; and
4. No application under Section 33.8 may be filed for three years from the date of making such request where the Section 33.5 application is granted.

B. Requirements Where Landlord Exercises Option.

If you exercise this option, you are required to send each tenant written notice of the amendment of your pending Section 33.5 application specifying the amount of the additional labor costs to be incurred. Two copies of the notice sent to the tenants together with two copies of an affidavit of service upon the tenants must be furnished to the appropriate District Rent Office.

5. FILLING OUT MASTER ORDER FORM O-33.8b (Rev. 1-68)

Fill in name and address of landlord as set forth in the application and the address of the housing accommodations in spaces provided. No further entries should be made by the landlord on this form.

6. FILLING OUT NOTICE OF DETERMINATION FORM N-33.8b (Rev. 1-68)

Notice of Determination Form N-33.8b should only be prepared for "controlled" tenants. Fill in name of tenant, address of housing accommodation, apartment or room number in spaces provided. Enter the amount of monthly rent increase from column 5 of Part IIA of the application form in the blank spaces provided.

7. REQUIREMENTS FOR ACCOUNTANTS CERTIFICATE

An Independent Account's Certificate must be completed in triplicate for each application. The original is to be submitted with the notarized copy of Application Form A-33.8b DS filed with the District Rent Office. The other two copies are to be affixed to the copies of Application Form A-33.8b DS that are to be made available for tenants' inspection at the property.

To be acceptable, an Independent Account's Certificate must be prepared by a person registered by and in good standing with the Education Department of the University of the State of New York as a Certified Public Accountant or Enrolled Public Accountant, or a person licensed by and/or in good standing with a similar Government agency enforcing comparable requirements in another state. The accountant offering such certification may not be a salaried employee of the owner of the property.

The certification, properly dated, prepared on the accountant's professional stationery, shall be addressed to the appropriate District Rent Office and should indicate the accountant's license or certificate number and bear his signature.

The certification to be filed shall be substantially in the following form:

"Re: Premises: ....
....

To the District Rent Office:

I am an Independent Public Accountant registered as such by and in good standing with the New York State Education Department. My license number is ....

I have reviewed the accompanying application for rent increases under Section 33.8b of the Regulations submitted by .... In this regard and in accordance with generally accepted auditing standards, I have examined the owner's Books of Account and Payroll Records and find that the application fairly and accurately reflects the owner's Books of Account and Payroll Records with respect to the following:

(a) The building and service employees listed in Part III of the application are the employees shown to be currently employed at the property.

(b) That the weekly scheduled hours are those indicated to be the employees' normal work-week.

(c) That the weekly wage for each employee (Base Year Rate) is the salary indicated to have been paid to person(s) holding such job title prior to the wage increase(s) for which recoupment is being requested in this application.

(d) The listing of employees in Part III is consistent with the normal complement of permanent building service employees regularly employed at the property.

(e) The weekly wage increase(s) claimed in Part III is in conformity with those prescribed by union agreement and/or indicated as having been paid. The effective date(s) of such increase(s) or the date(s) when such increase(s) were paid are correctly stated in items 6 and 7 of Part I of the application.

(f) Wage increases for which recoupment is being requested in this application, are those which become effective or were paid on or after April 21, 1967.

INFORMATION SHEETS

(g) All rents presented in Part IIA of the application are in accordance with the amounts shown in the landlord's Books of Account.

In my opinion all parts of the application are consistent with each other and are mathematically correct and prepared in accordance with instructions. I have initialed and dated the original Application Form A-33.8b DS in the lower right hand corner of the first page."

8. NOTICE AND INFORMATION REQUIREMENTS

NOTE: Both of the requirements set forth in A and B of this item must be met before the landlord files his application with the District Rent Office.

A. Posting.

The landlord must post one of the copies of the completed Application Form A-33.8b DS (including all of the Part IIA sheets) and a copy of the Certificate of the Independent Accountant in the lobby or vestibule of the premises involved. These copies must be placed in a prominent and readily accessible area.

Application Form A-33.8b DS will be deemed to have been "posted" if the landlord reproduces it at his own expense and furnishes each tenant with a completed copy, except that Part IIA may omit all information except such information as would pertain to a specific tenant to whom it is furnished. In such instances, the landlord must attach to his own application filed with the District Rent Office an Affidavit of Service indicating this fact.

B. Information.

The landlord must make one of the copies of the complete Application Form A-33.8b DS including all of the Part IIA sheets available for inspection by the tenants at the office or residence in the building of the building manager or superintendent between the hours of 10 A.M. and 9 P.M., accompanied by a copy of the Accountant's Certificate.

9. FILING INSTRUCTIONS

A. File The Following With The District Rent Office:

1. The original and one copy of Application Form A-

33.8b DS and the original and one copy of Part IIA of the application form.

2. The original and one copy of the Master Order Form O-33.8b (Rev. 1-68).

3. The original and one copy of the Notice of Determination Form N-33.8b (Rev. 1-68) for each controlled tenant.

4. The original Certificate of the Independent Accountant.

B. Who Must Sign and Swear.

Before filing an Application Form A-33.8b DS be sure to sign all copies and have the original sworn to before a Notary Public or other person authorized to administer oaths. The application form must be signed by the individual owner, or by a partner or corporate officer, if the building is owned by a partnership or corporation, or by the managing agent of the property.

10. NEW RENTS AND LEASES

A. When Rent Increases Are Collectible.

The landlord may collect the increased rents after the date of issuance of the Master Order Form O-33.8b by the District Rent Office effective as of the effective date indicated thereon.

B. Effect of Lease.

The following information is intended to answer questions that might arise concerning the relationship between existing leases and an application under Section 33.8b, and the effect of leases signed subsequent to the filing of an application in which an order has been issued, or which is still pending.

1. *Existing Leases.*

Present regulations cover this situation and indicate that any rent increases to which the landlord may be entitled under an application *do not* increase the maximum rent of an apartment until the expiration of the existing lease. In other words, if there is an existing lease at the time the application is filed, the landlord continues to collect the lease rent until the expiration of the lease. Any increases awarded under Section 33.8b during the

Information Sheets

term of the lease become effective upon the expiration of the lease.

Example:

Existing lease from December 1, 1966 to November 30, 1968 at $100 per month. The landlord files an application under Section 33.8b on September 1, 1967, and, pursuant to Section 33.8b, three increases are granted, effective as follows:

> $2.00 per month on October 1, 1967
> $2.00 per month on October 1, 1968
> $2.00 per month on October 1, 1969

Through November 30, 1968 (the expiration date of the lease), the landlord would continue to collect $100 per month. On December 1, 1968, the landlord may collect the legal maximum rent of $104 per month (the October 1, 1967 and October 1, 1968 increases having gone into effect). On October 1, 1969 the landlord may begin collecting $106 per month.

2. *New Leases Signed Subsequent to the Filing of an Application under Section 33.8b*

   (a) Any rent increases ordered under this provision, but not effective until some future date, shall not increase the rent payable during the term of a new lease.

   (b) The increases in maximum rent pursuant to Section 33.8b may go into effect after the expiration of a new lease, only where such lease specifies the amount or amounts, together with the corresponding date or dates, which, by order of the Office of Rent Control, the legal maximum rent shall have been changed. If the orders have not been issued at the time the lease is executed then the lease must include a clause specifying the docket number (if known) or the date of filing the application under Section 33.8b of the Regulations.

   (c) Conversely, if the landlord does not put such a clause in a new lease, the rent increases ordered under this provision, but not yet effective, will *not* increase the maximum rent for that apartment upon the expiration of the lease.

Example A:

The legal maximum rent for an apartment is $100 per month. Landlord is granted rent increases for this apartment pursuant to Section 33.8b of the Regulations, effective as follows:

$2.50 per month on September 1, 1967
$2.50 per month on September 1, 1968
$2.50 per month on September 1, 1969

The landlord may execute a lease on October 1, 1967 stipulating a rental of $117.88 per month for the period October 1, 1967 through September 30, 1969 (15% above $102.50). The lease indicates that the additional increases granted, effective as of September 1, 1968 and September 1, 1969, totaling $5.00, are effective October 1, 1969. The landlord would continue to collect $117.88 per month until the expiration of the lease on September 30, 1969. On October 1, 1969, the maximum rent for that apartment would increase to $122.88 per month. In the absence of such a clause indicating that the increases granted, effective September 1, 1968 and September 1, 1969, are to go into effect on October 1, 1969, the maximum rent for the apartment would continue at $117.88 per month at the termination of the lease.

Example B:

The legal maximum rent for an apartment is $100 per month. Landlord executes a lease on August 1, 1967 for a term of two years at a monthly rental of $115. The lease contains a provision which advises the tenant that an application is pending for rent increases under Section 33.8b and that such application was filed with the District Rent Office on .... 196.... (or that the Docket No. of such application is ....) and that upon the expiration of the lease, the rent for the accommodations will be increased by the amount(s) which may be ordered by the District Rent Director. In the latter case, any rent increase granted under such application and effective during the term of the lease will *not* have the effect of increasing the maximum rent until the termination of the lease.

EXEMPTION FROM RENT INCREASES FOR LOW INCOME ELDERLY PERSONS

NEW YORK CITY RENT INCREASE EXEMPTION FOR LOW INCOME ELDERLY PERSONS[1]

(L 1985, ch 907, 1, effective September 1, 1986)

ADMINISTRATIVE CODE OF THE CITY OF NEW YORK TITLE 26, CHAPTER 7[2]

§ 26-601 Definitions.
§ 26-602 Real property tax exemption.
§ 26-603 Reimbursement for rent exemptions; rent increase exemption fund established.
§ 26-604 Rent increase exemption funding requirement.
§ 26-605 Rent increase exemption orders/tax abatement certificates.
§ 26-606 Applications for exemption orders/abatement certificates; issuance of copies.
§ 26-607 Effective dates of exemption orders/abatement certificates.
§ 26-608 Credit allowances; penalties for overcharge.
§ 26-609 Application for tax benefit; credits.
§ 26-610 Excessive exemption; liens.
§ 26-611 Rules and regulations.
§ 26-612 Violations; penalties.
§ 26-613 Application.
§ 26-614 Certain exemption orders.

[1] L 1985, ch 907, § 14, provides that any act of the state legislature or any local law of the council of the city of New York for 1985 or 1986 which amends, adds, or repeals any provision of the Administrative Code of the city of New York in force immediately prior to September 1, 1986, shall be effective, and shall be construed as an amendment, addition, or repeal of the corresponding provision of the new Administrative Code. For text of this section see note to Administrative Code, Title 26, Chapter 3, supra.

[2] The Administrative Code of the City of New York was recodified by L 1985, Ch 907, effective September 1, 1986. Title 26, Ch 7, of the new Code (comprising §§ 26-601 through 26-614), corresponds to the provisions of Title YYY of the former Code, as follows:

Former Code sections	New Code sections
YYY51-1.0	26-601
YYY51-2.0	26-602
YYY51-3.0	26-603
YYY51-4.0	26-604
YYY51-5.0	26-605
YYY51-6.0	26-606
YYY51-7.0	26-607
YYY51-8.0	26-608
YYY51-9.0	26-609
YYY51-10.0	26-610
YYY51-11.0	26-611
YYY51-12.0	26-612
YYY51-13.0	26-613
YYY51-14.0	26-614

§ 26-601 Definitions

As used in this section:

a. "Commissioner" means the commissioner of housing and community renewal of the state of New York.

b. "Dwelling unit" means that part of a dwelling in which an eligible head of the household resides and which is subject to the provisions of either article II, IV, V, or XI of the private housing finance law, or that part of a dwelling subject to a mortgage insured by the federal government pursuant to section two hundred thirteen of the national housing act, as amended, in which an eligible head of the household resides.

c. "Eligibility date" means the later of (1) January first, nineteen hundred seventy-five, or (2) the last day of the month in which a person became an eligible head of a household in the dwelling unit in which such person resides at the time of filing the most recent application for benefits hereunder, or in the case of a dwelling subject to a mortgage insured by the federal government pursuant to section two hundred thirteen of the national housing act, as amended, "eligibility date" means the later of (1) July first, nineteen hundred seventy-seven, or (2) the last day of the month in which a person became an eligible head of a household in the dwelling unit in which such person resides at the time of filing the most recent application for benefits hereunder.

d. "Eligible head of the household" means a person or his or her spouse who is sixty-two years of age or older and is entitled to the possession or to the use and occupancy of a dwelling unit and whose income when combined with the income of all other members of the household, does not exceed twelve thousand twenty-five dollars for the taxable period.

Nothing herein contained shall render ineligible for benefits persons receiving supplemental security income or additional state payments, or both, under a program administered by the United States department of health and human services or by such department and the New York state department of social services.

e. "Housing company" means any limited-profit housing

company, limited dividend housing company, redevelopment company or housing development fund company incorporated pursuant to the private housing finance law and operated exclusively for the benefit of persons or families of low income, or any corporate owner of a dwelling subject to a mortgage insured by the federal government pursuant to section two hundred thirteen of the national housing act, as amended.

f. "Income" means income received by the eligible head of the household combined with the income of all other members of the household from all sources after deduction of all income and social security taxes and includes without limitation, social security and retirement benefits, supplemental security income and additional state payments, public assistance benefits, interest, dividends, net rental income, salary and earnings, and net income from self-employment, but shall not include gifts or inheritances, nor increases in benefits accorded pursuant to the social security act which take effect after the eligibility date of an eligible head of the household receiving benefits hereunder, whether received by the eligible head of the household or any other member of the household. When the eligible head of the household has retired on or after the commencement of the taxable period and prior to the date of making an application for a rent increase exemption order/tax abatement certificate pursuant to this title, such person's income shall be adjusted by excluding salary or earnings and projecting such person's retirement income over the entire taxable period.

g. "Income tax year" means a twelve month period for which the head of the household filed a federal personal income tax return, or if no such return is filed, the calendar year.

h. "Increase in maximum rent" means any increase in the maximum rent for the dwelling unit becoming effective on or after the eligibility date, excluding any increase in maximum rent attributable to gas or electrical utility charges or an increase in dwelling space, services or equipment.

i. "Maximum rent" means the maximum rent, excluding gas and electric utility charges, which has been authorized or approved by the commissioner or the supervising agency or the legal regulated rent established for the dwelling unit pursuant to the provisions of either article II, IV, V or XI of the private housing finance law, or the rental established for a cooperatively owned dwelling unit previously regulated pursuant to the provisions of article II, IV, V or XI of the private housing finance law, or the rental established for a dwelling unit, in a dwelling subject to a mortgage insured by the federal government pursuant to section two hundred thirteen of the national housing act, as amended.

j. "Members of the household" means the head of the household and any person, permanently residing in the dwelling unit.

k. "Supervising agency" means the department of housing preservation and development.

l. "Taxable period" means the income tax year immediately preceding the date of making application for a rent increase exemption order/tax abatement certificate.

§ 26-602 Real property tax exemption

Real property of a housing company shall be exempt from real property taxes, in an amount equal to the rent increase exemptions actually credited to eligible heads of households pursuant to this chapter. Any such exemption shall be in addition to any other exemption or abatement of taxes authorized by law.

§ 26-603 Reimbursement for rent exemptions; rent increase exemption fund established

In the event that the real property of a housing company containing one or more dwelling units shall be totally exempt from local and municipal real property taxes for any fiscal year as a result of the exemptions from maximum rent credited pursuant to this section or otherwise, the supervising agency may make or contract to make payments to a housing company in an amount not exceeding the amount necessary to reimburse the housing company for the total dollar amount of all exemptions from the payment of maximum rent accorded pursuant to this chapter to eligible heads of the household residing in dwelling units in such real property. A fund to be known as the rent increase exemption fund shall be created and established in order to provide for the payments made pursuant to this section. There may be paid into such fund (1) all of the rental surcharges collected from the housing companies organized and existing pursuant to articles II, IV, V and XI of the private housing finance law and (2) any moneys appropriated or otherwise made available for the purpose of such fund.

§ 26-604 Rent increase exemption funding requirement

In the event that the real property of a housing company containing one or more dwelling units shall be totally exempt from local and municipal real property taxes as a result of the exemption from maximum rent credited pursuant to this chapter or otherwise, the supervising agency shall not issue any rent increase exemption order/tax abatement certificates unless there are monies in the rent increase exemption fund to provide reimbursement to the housing company for the total dollar amount of all exemptions from the payment of maximum rent accorded pursuant to this chapter to eligible heads of the household residing in dwelling units in such real property.

§ 26-605 Rent increase exemption orders/tax abatement certificates

(a) Subject to the provisions of this title an eligible head of the household may obtain a rent increase exemption order/tax abatement certificate entitling him to an exemption from increases in the maximum rent otherwise payable in one of the following amounts:

(1) where the eligible head of the household does not receive a monthly allowance for shelter pursuant to the social services law, the amount by which increases in the maximum rent subsequent to such persons' eligibility date have resulted in the maximum rent exceeding one-third of the combined income of all members of the household for the taxable period, except that in no event shall a rent increase exemption order/tax abatement certificate become effective prior to January first, nineteen hundred seventy-six; or

(2) where the eligible head of the household receives a monthly allowance for shelter pursuant to the social

services law, an amount not exceeding that portion of any increase in maximum rent subsequent to such person's eligibility date which is not covered by the maximum allowance for shelter which such person is entitled to receive pursuant to the social services law.

(b) When a head of a household to whom the then current, valid tax abatement certificate has been issued under this chapter, chapter 3, or chapter 4 of this title moves his or her principal residence to a subsequent dwelling unit subject to this chapter, the head of the household may apply to the supervising agency, subject to the terms and conditions imposed by this chapter, for a tax abatement certificate relating to the subsequent dwelling unit, and such certificate may provide that the head of the household shall be exempt from paying that portion of the maximum rent for the subsequent dwelling unit which is the least of the following:

(1) the amount by which the rent for the subsequent dwelling unit exceeds the last rent, as reduced, which the head of the household was required to actually pay in the original dwelling unit;

(2) the last amount deducted from the maximum rent or legal regulated rent meaning the most recent monthly deduction for the applicant in the original dwelling unit pursuant to this section, section 26-406, or section 26-509 of the administrative code; or

(3) where the head of the household does not receive a monthly allowance for shelter pursuant to the social services law, the amount by which the maximum rent or legal regulated rent of the subsequent dwelling unit exceeds one-third of the combined income of all members of the household.

Such certificate shall be effective as of the first day of the month in which the tenant applied for such exemption or as of the date the tenant took occupancy of the subsequent dwelling unit, whichever is later, provided both occur after the effective date of this law.

(c) Notwithstanding any other provision of law and to the extent applicable to the provisions of this chapter, any renewal application being made by the tenant pursuant to this section, any rent increase order then in effect with respect to such tenant shall be deemed renewed until such time as the department of housing preservation and development shall have found such tenant to be either eligible or ineligible for a rent increase exemption order but in no event for more than six additional months. If such tenant is found eligible, the order shall be deemed to have taken effect upon expiration of the exemption. In the event that any such tenant shall, subsequent to any such automatic renewal, not be granted a rent increase exemption order, such tenant shall be liable to his or her landlord for the difference between the amounts he or she has paid under the provisions of the automatically renewed order and the amounts which he or she would have been required to pay in the absence of such order. Any rent increase exemption order issued pursuant to this chapter shall include provisions giving notice as to the contents of this section relating to automatic renewals of rent exemption orders.

§ 26-606 Applications for exemption orders/tax abatement certificates; issuance and copies.

The eligible head of the household shall apply annually to the supervising agency for a rent increase exemption order/tax abatement certificate on a form to be prescribed and made available by the supervising agency. The supervising agency shall approve or disapprove applications and, if it approves, shall issue a rent increase exemption order/tax abatement certificate. Copies of such order/certificate shall be issued to the housing company managing the dwelling unit of the eligible head of the household, to the eligible head of the household and to the department of finance.

§ 26-607 Effective dates of exemption orders/tax abatement certificates

The effective date of a rent increase exemption order/tax abatement certificate shall be the date of the first increase in maximum rent becoming effective after the applicant's eligibility date, except that in no event shall a rent increase exemption order/tax abatement certificate become effective prior to January first, nineteen hundred seventy-six.

§ 26-608 Credit allowances; penalties for overcharge

Upon receipt of a copy of a rent increase exemption order/tax abatement certificate, the housing company managing the dwelling unit of the eligible head of the household shall promptly accord to the eligible head of the household covered by such order/certificate the appropriate credit against the monthly maximum rent then and thereafter payable. To the extent the full amount of such credit has not been accorded for any past period since the effective date specified in the order/certificate, the housing company shall credit the total aggregate amount not so credited to the monthly maximum rent next payable or to such subsequent monthly maximum rents, as the supervising agency may authorize. It shall be illegal to collect any amount for which a rent increase exemption order/tax abatement certificate provides credit or to withhold credit for any such amounts already collected, and collection or retention of any such amount for a dwelling unit occupied by such eligible head of the household shall be deemed a rent overcharge, and upon conviction therefor the housing company and its directors and any employee responsible therefor shall be guilty of a misdemeanor, punishable by a fine not to exceed one thousand dollars or imprisonment not to exceed six months, or both.

§ 26-609 Application for tax benefit; credits

In order to obtain the tax benefits to which it is entitled under this chapter, a housing company must file with the department of finance a sworn application, in such form as such officer may prescribe, for any period in which the housing company has accorded an eligible head of the household an exemption hereunder from the payment of the maximum rent. Subject to prior or subsequent verification thereof, the department of finance shall credit the total amount of such exemptions actually accorded to occupants of dwelling units contained in the property against the real property taxes next payable with respect to the property, on a prospective basis only. The housing company shall attach to such application copies of all rent increase exemption orders/tax abatement certificates issued to eligible heads of the household residing in dwelling units in such real property.

Low Income Elderly Exemption

§ 26-610 Excessive exemption; liens

If a subsequent audit of taxes payable and exemptions recognized pursuant to this chapter discloses that an exemption previously recognized on the basis of a housing company's verified application is excessive, the amount of tax payable by reason of such disclosure and the statutory penalty thereon, shall be a lien upon the property as of the due date of the tax for which the excessive exemption was claimed, unless after the housing company has filed the tax exemption claims, the supervising agency issues a corrected rent increase exemption order/tax abatement certificate retroactively modifying or revoking the rent increase exemption order/tax abatement certificate based on error in the personal or financial data in the application or based on error in the rent calculation not due to any willful fault of the housing company, in which case the amount of tax payable by reason of the disclosure shall be a lien upon the property as of the date for payment of taxes next following certification of such corrected order by the supervising agency.

§ 26-611 Rules and regulations

The supervising agency may promulgate such rules and regulations as may be necessary to effectively carry out the provisions of this chapter.

§ 26-612 Violations; penalties

It shall be illegal, for any person submitting an application for a rent increase exemption pursuant to this section, to make any false statement or willful misrepresentation of fact, and upon conviction thereof such applicant shall be guilty of a misdemeanor, punishable by a fine not to exceed five hundred dollars or imprisonment not to exceed ninety days, or both.

§ 26-613 Application

This chapter is enacted pursuant to the provisions of section four hundred sixty-seven-c of the real property tax law.

§ 26-614 Certain exemption orders

Notwithstanding the provisions of this chapter, a tenant who resides in a dwelling unit which becomes subject to this chapter upon the sale by the city of New York of the building in which such dwelling unit is situated may be issued a rent increase exemption order for increases in rent which occurred during ownership of such building by the city of New York provided that such tenant would have been otherwise eligible to receive a rent increase exemption order at the time of such increase but for the fact that such tenant occupied a dwelling unit owned by the city of New York and was therefore not subject to this chapter. Application for such rent increase exemption orders shall be made within one year from the date such building is sold by the city of New York or within one year of the effective date of this provision, whichever is later.

PART III: RENT STABILIZATION
Rent Stabilization Law
Rent Stabilization Code for Rent Stabilized
    Apartments in New York City
Rent Stabilization Regulations of the Housing
    and Development Administration
Orders of the Rent Guidance Board
Hotel Orders

PART III

RENT STABILIZATION

RENT STABILIZATION LAW ADMINISTRATIVE CODE OF THE CITY OF NEW YORK[1] TITLE 26, CHAPTER 4

(L 1985, ch 907, § 1, effective September 1, 1985)[2]

§ 26-501 Findings and declaration of emergency.
§ 26-502 Additional findings and declaration of emergency.
§ 26-503 Short title.
§ 26-504 Application.
§ 26-505 Application to multiple family complex.
§ 26-506 Application to hotels.
§ 26-507 Application to certain multiple dwellings purchased from the city.
§ 26-509 Application to department of housing preservation and development for rent increase exemptions and equivalent tax abatement for rent regulated property occupied by certain senior citizens.
§ 26-510 Rent guidelines board.
§ 26-511 Real estate industry stabilization association.

---

[1] The Administrative Code of the City of New York was recodified by L 1985, Ch 907, effective September 1, 1986. Title 26, Ch 4 of the new Code (comprising §§ 26-501 through 26-520), corresponds to the provisions of Title YY (comprising §§ YY51-1.0 through YY51-8.0) of the former Code as follows:

Former Code sections	New Code sections
YY51-1.0	26-501
YY51-1.0.1	26-502
YY51-2.0	26-503
YY51-3.0	26-504
YY51-3.1	26-505
YY51-3.1	26-506
YY51-3.3	26-507
YY51-4.1	omitted
YY51-4.1.1	26-509
YY51-5.0	26-510
YY51-6.0	26-511
YY51-6.0.1	26-512
YY51-6.0.2	25-513
YY51-6.0.3	26-514
YY51-6.0.4	26-515
YY51-6.0.5	26-516
YY51-6.0.6	26-517
YY51-6.1	26-518
YY51-6.2	26-519
YY51-7.0	omitted
YY51-8.0	26-520

[2] L 1985, ch 907, § 14, provides that any act of the state legislature or any local law of the council of the city of New York for 1985 or 1986 which amends, adds, or repeals any provision of the Administrative Code of the city of New York in force immediately prior to September 1, 1986, shall be effective, and shall be construed as an amendment, addition, or repeal of the corresponding provision of the new Administrative Code. (For text of this section, see note to Administrative Code, Title 26, Chapter 3, supra.)

725

§ 26-512 Stabilization provisions.
§ 26-513 Application for adjustment of initial rent.
§ 26-514 Maintenance of services.
§ 26-515 Recovery of possession.
§ 26-516 Enforcement and procedures.
§ 26-517 Rent registration.
§ 26-518 Hotel industry stabilization association.
§ 26-519 Suspension of registration.
§ 26-520 Expiration date.

§ 26-501 Findings and declaration of emergency.

The council hereby finds that a serious public emergency continues to exist in the housing of a considerable number of persons within the city of New York and will continue to exist after April first, nineteen hundred seventy-four; that such emergency necessitated the intervention of federal, state and local government in order to prevent speculative, unwarranted and abnormal increases in rents; that there continues to exist an acute shortage of dwellings which creates a special hardship to persons and families occupying rental housing; that the legislation enacted in nineteen hundred seventy-one by the state of New York, removing controls on housing accommodations as they become vacant, has resulted in sharp increases in rent levels in many instances; that the existing and proposed cuts in federal assistance to housing programs threaten a virtual end to the creation of new housing, thus prolonging the present emergency; that unless residential rents and evictions continue to be regulated and controlled, disruptive practices and abnormal conditions will produce serious threats to the public health, safety and general welfare; that to prevent such perils to health, safety and welfare, preventive action by the council continues to be imperative; that such action is necessary in order to prevent exactions of unjust, unreasonable and oppressive rents and rental agreements and to forestall profiteering, speculation and other disruptive practices tending to produce threats to the public health, safety and general welfare; that the transition from regulation to a normal market of free bargaining between landlord and tenant, while still the objective of state and city policy, must be administered with due regard for such emergency; and that the policy herein expressed is now administered locally within the city of New York by an agency of the city itself, pursuant to the authority

Rent Stabilization Law

conferred by chapter twenty-one of the laws of nineteen hundred sixty-two.

The council further finds that, prior to the adoption of local laws sixteen and fifty-one of nineteen hundred sixty-nine, many owners of housing accommodations in multiple dwellings, not subject to the provisions of the city rent and rehabilitation law enacted pursuant to said enabling authority either because they were constructed after nineteen hundred forty-seven or because they were decontrolled due to monthly rental of two hundred fifty dollars or more or for other reasons, were demanding exorbitant and unconscionable rent increases as a result of the aforesaid emergency, which led to a continuing restriction of available housing as evidenced by the nineteen hundred sixty-eight vacancy survey by the United States bureau of the census; that prior to the enactment of said local laws, such increases were being exacted under stress of prevailing conditions of inflation and of an acute housing shortage resulting from a sharp decline in private residential construction brought about by a combination of local and national factors; that such increases and demands were causing severe hardship to tenants of such accommodations and were uprooting long-time city residents from their communities; that recent studies establish that the acute housing shortage continues to exist; that there has been a further decline in private residential construction due to existing and proposed cuts in federal assistance to housing programs; that unless such accommodations are subjected to reasonable rent and eviction limitations, disruptive practices and abnormal conditions will produce serious threats to the public health, safety and general welfare; and that such conditions constitute a grave emergency.

§ 26-502 Additional findings and declaration of emergency

The council hereby finds that a serious public emergency continues to exist in the housing of a considerable number of persons within the city of New York and will continue to exist after April first, nineteen hundred eighty-five and hereby reaffirms and repromulgates the findings and declaration set forth in section 26-501 of this chapter.

§ 26-503 Short title

This law may be cited as the rent stabilization law of nineteen hundred sixty-nine.

§ 26-504 Application

This law shall apply to:

a. Class A multiple dwellings not owned as a cooperative or as a condominium, except as provided in section three hundred fifty-two-eeee of the general business law, containing six or more dwelling units which:

(1) were completed after February first, nineteen hundred forty-seven, except dwelling units (a) owned or leased by, or financed by loans from, a public agency or public benefit corporation, (b) subject to rent regulation under the private housing finance law or any other state law, (c) aided by government insurance under any provision of the national housing act, to the extent this chapter or any regulation or order issued thereunder is inconsistent therewith, or (d) located in a building for which a certificate of occupancy is obtained after March tenth, nineteen hundred sixty-nine; or (e) any class A multiple dwelling which on June first, nineteen hundred sixty-eight was and still is commonly regarded as a hotel, transient hotel or residential hotel, and which customarily provides hotel service such as maid service, furnishing and laundering of linen, telephone and bell boy service, secretarial or desk service and use and upkeep of furniture and fixtures, or (f) not occupied by the tenant, not including subtenants or occupants, as his primary residence, as determined by a court of competent jurisdiction, provided, however that no action or proceeding shall be commenced seeking to recover possession on the ground that a housing accommodation is not occupied by the tenant as his or her primary residence unless the owner or lessor shall have given thirty days notice to the tenant of his or her intention to commence such action or proceeding on such grounds. For the purposes of this subparagraph where a housing accommodation is rented to a not-for-profit hospital for residential use, affiliated subtenants authorized to use such accommodations by such hospital shall be deemed to be tenants, or (g) became vacant on or after June thirtieth, nineteen hundred

seventy-one, or become vacant, provided however, that this exemption shall not apply or become effective with respect to housing accommodations which the commissioner determines or finds became vacant because the landlord or any person acting on his or her behalf, with intent to cause the tenant to vacate, engaged in any course of conduct (including but not limited to, interruption or discontinuance of essential services) which interfered with or disturbed or was intended to interfere with or disturb the comfort, repose, peace or quiet of the tenant in his or her use or occupancy of the housing accommodations and provided further that any housing accommodations exempted by this paragraph shall be subject to this law to the extent provided in subdivision b of this section; or (2) were decontrolled by the city rent agency pursuant to section 26-414 of this title; or (3) are exempt from control by virtue of item one, two, six or seven of subparagraph (i) of paragraph two of subdivision e of section 26-403 of this title; and

b. Other housing accommodations in class A or class B multiple dwellings made subject to this law pursuant to the emergency tenant protection act of nineteen seventy-four.

c. Buildings or structures, not owned as a cooperative or as a condominium, except as provided in section three hundred fifty-two-eeee of the general business law, or housing accommodation in such buildings or structures eligible to receive the benefits of section 11-243 or section 11-244 of the code or article eighteen of the private housing finance law and not subject to the provisions of chapter three of this title where the owner thereof subjects such buildings and structures to regulation under this chapter.

§ 26-505 Application to multiple family complex

For purposes of this chapter a class A multiple dwelling shall be deemed to include a multiple family garden-type maisonette dwelling complex containing six or more dwelling units having common facilities such as sewer line, water main, and heating plant, and operated as a unit under a single ownership on May sixth, nineteen hundred sixty-nine, notwithstanding that certificates of occupancy were issued for portions thereof as one- or two-family dwellings.

§ 26-506 Application to hotels

a. Notwithstanding the provisions of section 26-504 of this chapter to the contrary, and irrespective of any decontrol pursuant to subparagraph (c) of paragraph two of subdivision e of section 26-403 of the city rent and rehabilitation law, this law shall apply to dwelling units in all hotels except hotels erected after July first, nineteen hundred sixty-nine, whether classified as a class A or a class B multiple dwelling, containing six or more dwelling units, provided that the rent charged for the individual dwelling units on May thirty-first, nineteen hundred sixty-eight was not more than three hundred fifty dollars per month or eighty-eight dollars per week; and further provided that, notwithstanding the foregoing, this law shall apply to dwelling units in any hotel, whether classified as a class A or a class B multiple dwelling, eligible for benefits pursuant to the provisions of section 11-244 of the code.

b. Upon application by a tenant or owner, the division of housing and community renewal, shall determine if such building is a hotel covered by this law, based upon the services provided and other relevant factors. If it is determined that such building is not a hotel, it shall thereafter be subject to this law pursuant to subdivision b of section 26-504 of this chapter.

§ 26-507 Application to certain multiple dwellings purchased from the city

a. Notwithstanding the provisions of any local law or regulation promulgated pursuant to the rent stabilization law of nineteen hundred sixty-nine or the emergency tenant protection act of nineteen seventy-four, upon the sale in any manner authorized by law of a multiple dwelling which was previously subject to the provisions of any such laws or acts which was acquired by the city in a tax foreclosure proceeding or pursuant to article nineteen-A of the real property actions and proceedings law, all dwelling units within the multiple dwelling shall be subject to the rent stabilization law of nineteen hundred

Rent Stabilization Law

sixty-nine, as amended, at the last rent charged by the city, or on behalf of the city, for such dwelling unit.

b. If a unit which was subject to this chapter at the time the city so acquired title is occupied by a tenant who was in occupancy at the time of acquisition and remains in occupancy at the time of sale, such tenant shall be offered a one or two year lease at the rent provided in this section as soon as practical at the sale of the multiple dwelling.

c. This section shall not apply to redemptions from city ownership pursuant to chapter four of title eleven of the code.

[No § 26-508 was enacted]

§ 26-509 Application to department of housing preservation and development for rent increase exemptions and equivalent tax abatement for rent regulated property occupied by certain senior citizens

a. Commencement of department of housing preservation and development jurisdiction.

(1) Notwithstanding any provisions of this chapter to the contrary, on and after October first, nineteen hundred eighty, the department of housing preservation and development shall grant rent increase exemption orders or tax abatement certificates pursuant to this section and applications for such orders and certificates and renewal applications shall be made to the department of housing preservation and development.

(2) The department of housing preservation and development shall have the power, in relation to any application for a rent increase exemption order or tax abatement certificate, to determine the lawful stabilization rent, but it shall not receive applications for adjustment of the initial legal regulated rent pursuant to section 26-513 of this chapter.

(3) The department of finance, and the department of housing preservation and development may promulgate such rules and regulations as may be necessary to effectively carry out the provisions of this section.

b. Rent increase exemptions for certain senior citizens.

(1) No increase in the legal regulated rent shall be collectible from a tenant to whom there has been issued a currently valid rent exemption order pursuant to this

subdivision, except as provided in such order, if such increase is a lawful increase in the monthly legal regulated rent over the rent legally payable on the eligibility date which is provided under a two year lease, or under such other term as regards dwelling units subject to the hotel stabilization provisions of this chapter, for an increase in rent:

(i) pursuant to an order of the New York city rent guidelines board, or

(ii) based upon an owner hardship rent increase order issued by the state division of housing and community renewal.

(2) A tenant is eligible for a rent exemption order pursuant to this section if:

(i) the head of the household residing in the housing accommodation is sixty-two years of age or older and is entitled to the possession or to the use or occupancy of a dwelling unit.

Nothing herein contained shall render ineligible for benefits persons receiving supplemental security income or additional statement payments, or both, under a program administered by the United States department of health and human services or by such department and the New York state department of social services.

(ii) the aggregate disposable income (as defined by regulation of the department of housing preservation and development) of all members of the household residing in the housing accommodation does not exceed twelve thousand twenty-five dollars per year, after deduction of federal, state and city income and social security taxes.

(iii) the maximum rent for the housing accommodation exceeds one-third of the aggregate disposable income.

(3)(i) A rent exemption order pursuant to this subdivision shall provide:

(a) in the case of a head of the household who does not receive a monthly allowance for shelter pursuant to the social services law, that the landlord may not collect from the tenant to whom it is issued rent at a rate in excess of either one-third of the aggregate disposable income, or the rent in effect immediately preceding the eligibility date, whichever is greater; or

Rent Stabilization Law

(b) in the case of a head of the household who receives a monthly allowance for shelter pursuant to the social services law, that the landlord may not collect from the tenant to whom it is issued rent at a rate in excess of either the maximum allowance for shelter which the head of the household is entitled to receive, or the rent in effect immediately preceding the eligibility date, whichever is greater; and

(c) that the landlord may collect from the tenant increases in rent based on an electrical inclusion adjustment or an increase in dwelling space, services or equipment.

(4) Any landlord who collects, or seeks to collect or enforce rent from a tenant in violation of the terms of a rent exemption order shall, for the purposes of all remedies, sanctions and penalties provided in this chapter, be deemed to have collected or attempted to collect or enforce, a rent in excess of the legal regulated rent.

(5) A rent exemption order shall be issued to each tenant who applies to the department of housing preservation and development in accordance with its regulations and who is found to be eligible under this subdivision. Such order shall take effect on the first day of the first month after receipt of such application by the department of housing preservation and development, except that where any other increase in the legal regulated rent within ninety days of the issuance of the order increasing the tenant's maximum rent which a tenant is not exempted from paying the rent exemption order shall without further order of the department of housing preservation and development take effect as of the effective date of said order increasing the tenant's rent including any retroactive increments collectible pursuant to such order.

(6) A rent exemption order shall be valid for a period of one year and may be renewed for further one year periods upon application by the tenant; provided, that upon any such renewal application being made by the tenant, any rent exemption order then in effect with respect to such tenant shall be deemed renewed until such time as the department of housing preservation and development shall have found such tenant to be either

eligible or ineligible for a rent exemption order but in no event for more than six additional months. If such tenant is found eligible, the order shall be deemed to have taken effect upon expiration of the exemption. In the event that any such tenant shall, subsequent to any such automatic renewal, not be granted a rent exemption order, such tenant shall be liable to the owner for the difference between the amounts the tenant has paid under the provisions of the automatically renewed order and the amounts which the tenant would have been required to pay in the absence of such order. Any rent exemption order issued pursuant to this subdivision shall include provisions giving notice as to the contents of this paragraph relating to automatic renewals of rent exemption orders and shall include provisions giving notice that the tenant must enter into a two year renewal lease in order to be eligible for a rent exemption. The notice that each tenant receives from the owner relating to the right to a renewal lease shall contain similar information. Any application or renewal application for a rent exemption order shall also constitute an application for a tax abatement under such section. The department of housing preservation and development may, with respect to renewal applications by the tenants whom it has found eligible for rent exemption orders, prescribe a simplified form including a certification of the applicant's continued eligibility in lieu of a detailed statement of income and other qualifications.

(7) Notwithstanding any other provision of law, when a head of a household to whom a then current, valid rent exemption order has been issued under this chapter, chapter three or chapter seven of this title moves his or her principal residence to a subsequent dwelling unit subject to regulation under this chapter, the head of the household may apply to the city rent agency for a rent exemption order relating to the subsequent dwelling unit, and such order may provide that the head of the household shall be exempt from paying that portion of the legal regulated rent for the subsequent dwelling unit which is the least of the following:

(i) the amount by which the rent for the subsequent dwelling unit exceeds the last rent, as reduced, which the head of the household was required to actually pay in the original dwelling unit;

(ii) the last amount deducted from the maximum rent or legal regulated rent meaning the most recent monthly deduction for the applicant in the original dwelling unit pursuant to this section or section 26-605 of this title; or

(iii) where the head of the household does not receive a monthly allowance for shelter pursuant to the social services law, the amount by which the legal regulated rent of the subsequent dwelling unit exceeds one-third of the combined income of all members of the household.

Such certificate shall be effective as of the first day of the month in which the tenant applied for such exemption or as of the date the tenant took occupancy of the subsequent dwelling unit, whichever is later provided both occur after the effective date of this section.

c. Tax abatement for properties subject to rent exemption order.

(1) Tax abatement, pursuant to the provisions of section four hundred sixty-seven-b of the real property tax law, shall be granted with respect to any real property for which a rent exemption order is issued under subdivision b of this section to the tenant of any housing accommodation contained therein. The rent exemption order shall also constitute the tax abatement certificate.

(2) The real estate tax imposed upon any real property for which a rent exemption is issued, shall be reduced and abated by an amount equal to the difference between:

(i) the sum of the maximum rents collectible under such orders, and

(ii) the sum of rents that would be collectible from the tenants of such housing accommodations if no exemption had been granted pursuant to subdivision b of this section.

(3) For any individual housing accommodation, the tax abatement computed pursuant to this subdivision shall be available with respect to a period commencing on the effective date of the initial rent exemption order, and ending on the expiration date of such order or on the effective date of an order terminating the rent exemption.

(4) Prior to the commencement of each fiscal year, the

department of housing preservation and development shall notify the department of finance of the total amount of taxes to be abated under this section with respect to each property for which rent exemption orders were in effect for all or any part of the preceding calendar year. The commissioner of finance shall make the appropriate adjustment in the real estate tax payable in such fiscal year.

(5) Tax abatement pursuant to this section shall be in addition to any other tax abatement authorized by law, but shall not reduce the tax for any fiscal year below zero. In the event that the tax abatement certificate authorizes an amount of deduction in excess of the real estate installment, then the balance may be applied to any subsequent installment until exhausted. In such a case the owner shall submit with his or her real estate tax bill and remittance, a verified statement in such form as prescribed by the commissioner of finance setting forth the carry over amount and the amounts previously applied; provided, however, that at the request of the owner such balance shall be paid to the owner by the commissioner of finance in lieu of being applied to any subsequent installment, except where the owner is in arrears in the payment of real estate taxes on any property. For the purposes of this paragraph, where the owner is a corporation, it shall be deemed to be in arrears when any of the officers, directors or any person holding an interest in more than ten percent of the issued and outstanding stock of such corporation is in arrears in the payment of real estate taxes on any property; where title is held by a nominee, the owner shall be deemed to be in arrears when the person for whose benefit such title is held is in arrears in the payment of real estate taxes on any property.

d. Notwithstanding the provisions of this chapter, a tenant who resides in a dwelling unit which becomes subject to this chapter upon the sale by the city of New York of the building in which such dwelling unit is situated may be issued a rent increase exemption order for increases in rent which occurred during ownership of such building by the city of New York provided that such tenant would have been otherwise eligible to receive a rent increase exemption order at the time of such increase but for the fact that such tenant occupied a dwelling unit owned by the city of New York and was therefore not subject to this chapter. Application for such rent increase exemption orders shall be made within one year from the date such building is sold by the city of New York or within one year of the effective date of this provision, whichever is later.

§ 26-510 Rent guidelines board

a. There shall be a rent guidelines board to consist of nine members, appointed by the mayor. Two members shall be representative of tenants, two shall be representative of owners of property, and five shall be public members each of whom shall have had at least five years experience in either finance, economics or housing. One public member shall be designated by the mayor to serve as chairman and shall hold no other public office. No member, officer or employee of any municipal rent regulation agency or the state division of housing and community renewal and no person who owns or manages real estate covered by this law or who is an officer of any owner or tenant organization shall serve on a rent guidelines board. One public member, one member representative of tenants and one member representative of owners shall serve for a term ending two years from January first next succeeding the date of their appointment; one public member, one member representative of tenants and one member representative of owners shall serve for terms ending three years from the January first next succeeding the date of their appointment and two public members shall serve for terms ending four years from January first next succeeding the dates of their appointment. The chairman shall serve at the pleasure of the mayor. Thereafter, all members shall continue in office until their successors have been appointed and qualified. The mayor shall fill any vacancy which may occur by reason of death, resignation or otherwise in a manner consistent with the original appointment. A member may be removed by the mayor for cause, but not without an opportunity to be heard in person or by counsel, in his or her defense, upon not less than ten days notice.

b. The rent guidelines board shall establish annually

guidelines for rent adjustments, and in determining whether rents for housing accommodations subject to the emergency tenant protection act of nineteen seventy-four or this law shall be adjusted shall consider, among other things (1) the economic condition of the residential real estate industry in the affected area including such factors as the prevailing and projected (i) real estate taxes and sewer and water rates, (ii) gross operating maintenance costs (including insurance rates, governmental fees, cost of fuel and labor costs), (iii) costs and availability of financing (including effective rates of interest), (iv) over-all supply of housing accommodations and over-all vacancy rates, (2) relevant data from the current and projected cost of living indices for the affected area, (3) such other data as may be made available to it. Not later than July first of each year, the rent guidelines board shall file with the city clerk its findings for the preceding calendar year, and shall accompany such findings with a statement of the maximum rate or rates of rent adjustment, if any, for one or more classes of accommodations subject to this law, authorized for leases or other rental agreements commencing on the next succeeding October first or within the twelve months thereafter. Such findings and statement shall be published in the City Record.

c. Such members shall be compensated on a per diem basis of one hundred dollars per day for no more than twenty-five days a year except that the chairman shall be compensated at one hundred twenty-five dollars a day for no more than fifty days a year. The chairman shall be chief administrative officer of the rent guidelines board and among his or her powers and duties he or she shall have the authority to employ, assign and supervise the employees of the rent guidelines board and enter into contracts for consultant services. The department of housing preservation and development shall cooperate with the rent guidelines board and may assign personnel and perform such services in connection with the duties of the rent guidelines board as may reasonably be required by the chairman.

d. Any housing accommodation covered by this law owned by a member in good standing of an association registered with the department of housing preservation

Rent Stabilization Law

and development pursuant to section 26-511 of this chapter which becomes vacant for any reason, other than harassment of the prior tenant, may be offered for rental at any price notwithstanding any guideline level established by the guidelines board for renewal leases, provided the offering price does not exceed the rental then authorized by the guidelines board for such dwelling unit plus five percent for a new lease not exceeding two years and a further five percent for a new lease having a minimum term of three years, until July first, nineteen hundred seventy, at which time the guidelines board shall determine what the rental for a vacancy shall be.

e. With respect to hotel dwelling units, covered by this law pursuant to section 26-506 of this chapter, the council, after receipt of a study from the rent guidelines board, shall establish a guideline for rent increases, irrespective of the limitations on amount of increase in subdivision d hereof, which guideline shall apply only to permanent tenants. A permanent tenant is an individual or family who at any time since May thirty-first, nineteen hundred sixty-eight, or hereafter, has continuously resided in the same hotel as a principal residence for a period of at least six months. On January first, nineteen hundred seventy-one and once annually each succeeding year the rent guidelines board shall cause a review to be made of the levels of fair rent increases provided under this subdivision and may establish different levels of fair rent increases for hotel dwelling units renting within different rental ranges based upon the board's consideration of conditions in the market for hotel accommodations and the economics of hotel real estate. Any hotel dwelling unit which is voluntarily vacated by the tenant thereof may be offered for rental at the guideline level for vacancies established by the rent guidelines board. If a hotel dwelling unit becomes vacant because the prior tenant was evicted therefrom, there shall be no increase in the rental thereof except for such increases in rental that the prior tenant would have had to pay had he or she continued in occupancy. (No par f has been enacted)

g. From September twenty-fifth, nineteen hundred sixty-nine until the rate of permissible increase is established by the council pursuant to subdivision e of this section, there shall not be collected from any permanent hotel tenant any rent increase in excess of ten percent over the rent payable for his or her dwelling unit on May thirty-first, nineteen hundred sixty-eight, except for hardship increases authorized by the conciliation and appeals board. Any owner who collects or permits any rent to be collected in excess of the amount authorized by this subdivision shall not be eligible to be a member in good standing of a hotel industry stabilization association.

h. The rent guidelines board prior to the annual adjustment of the level of fair rents provided for under subdivision b of this section for dwelling units and hotel dwelling units covered by this law, shall hold a public hearing or hearings for the purpose of collecting information relating to all factors set forth in subdivision b of this section. Notice of the date, time, location and summary of subject matter for the public hearing or hearings shall be published in the City Record daily for a period of not less than eight days and at least once in one or more newspapers of general circulation at least eight days immediately preceding each hearing date, at the expense of the city of New York, and the hearing shall be open for testimony from any individual, group, association or representative thereof who wants to testify.

i. Maximum rates of rent adjustment shall not be established more than once annually for any housing accommodation within the board's jurisdiction. Once established, no such rate shall, within the one-year period, be adjusted by any surcharge, supplementary adjustment or other modification.

§ 26-511 Real estate industry stabilization association

a. The real estate industry stabilization association registered with the department of housing preservation and development is hereby continued.

b. The stabilization code heretofore promulgated by such association, as approved by the department of housing preservation and development, is hereby continued. Such code may be amended from time to time, provided, however, that no such amendments shall be made except by action of the association subject to the approval of the department of housing preservation and development. No provision of such code shall impair or diminish any right or remedy granted to any party by this law or any other provision of law.

c. A code shall not be approved hereunder unless it appears to the department of housing preservation and development that such code:

(1) provides safeguards against unreasonably high rent increases and, in general, protects tenants and the public interest, and does not impose any industry wide schedule of rents or minimum rentals;

(2) requires owners not to exceed the level of lawful rents as provided by this law;

(3) provides for a cash refund or a credit, to be applied against future rent, in the amount of any rent overcharge collected by an owner and any penalties, costs, attorneys' fees and interest from the date of the overcharge at the rate of interest payable on a judgment pursuant to section five thousand four of the civil practice law and rules for which the owner is assessed;

(4) includes provisions requiring owners to grant a one or two year vacancy or renewal lease at the option of the tenant except where a mortgage or mortgage commitment existing as of April first, nineteen hundred sixty-nine, provides that the mortgagor shall not grant a one year lease;

(5) includes guidelines with respect to such additional rent and related matters as, for example, security deposits, advance rental payments, the use of escalator clauses in leases and provision for increase in rentals for garages and other ancillary facilities, so as to insure that the level of fair rent increase established under this law will not be subverted and made ineffective;

(6) provides criteria whereby the commissioner may act upon applications by owners for increases in excess of the level of fair rent increase established under this law provided, however, that such criteria shall provide (a) as to hardship applications, for a finding that the level of fair rent increase is not sufficient to enable the owner to maintain approximately the same average annual net income (which shall be computed without regard to debt

service, financing costs or management fees) for the three year period ending on or within six months of the date of an application pursuant to such criteria as compared with annual net income, which prevailed on the average over the period nineteen hundred sixty-eight through nineteen hundred seventy, or for the first three years of operation if the building was completed since nineteen hundred sixty-eight or for the first three fiscal years after a transfer of title to a new owner provided the new owner can establish to the satisfaction of the commissioner that he or she acquired title to the building as a result of a bona fide sale of the entire building and that the new owner is unable to obtain requisite records for the fiscal years nineteen hundred sixty-eight through nineteen hundred seventy despite diligent efforts to obtain same from predecessors in title and further provided that the new owner can provide financial data covering a minimum of six years under his or her continuous and uninterrupted operation of the building to meet the three year to three year comparative test periods herein provided; and (b) as to completed buildingwide major capital improvements, for a finding that such improvements are deemed depreciable under the Internal Revenue Code and that the cost is to be amortized over a five-year period, based upon cash purchase price exclusive of interest or service charges. Notwithstanding anything to the contrary contained herein, no increase granted pursuant to this paragraph shall, when added to the annual gross rents, as determined by the commissioner, exceed the sum of, (i) the annual operating expenses, (ii) an allowance for management services as determined by the commissioner, (iii) actual annual mortgage debt service (interest and amortization) on its indebtedness to a lending institution, an insurance company, a retirement fund or welfare fund which is operated under the supervision of the banking or insurance laws of the state of New York or the United States, and (iv) eight and one-half percent of that portion of the fair market value of the property which exceeds the unpaid principal amount of the mortgage indebtedness referred to in subparagraph (iii) of this paragraph. Fair market value for the purposes of this paragraph shall be six times the annual gross rent. The collection of any increase in the stabilized rent for any apartment pursuant to this paragraph shall not exceed six percent in any year from the effective date of the order granting the increase over the rent set forth in the schedule of gross rents, with collectability of any dollar excess above said sum to be spread forward in similar increments and added to the stabilized rent as established or set in future years;

(6-a) provides criteria whereby as an alternative to the hardship application provided under paragraph six of this subdivision owners of buildings acquired by the same owner or a related entity owned by the same principals three years prior to the date of application may apply to the division for increases in excess of the level of applicable guideline increases established under this law based on a finding by the commissioner that such guideline increases are not sufficient to enable the owner to maintain an annual gross rent income for such building which exceeds the annual operating expenses of such building by a sum equal to at least five percent of such gross rent. For the purposes of this paragraph, operating expenses shall consist of the actual, reasonable, costs of fuel, labor, utilities, taxes, other than income or corporate franchise taxes, fees, permits, necessary contracted services and noncapital repairs, insurance, parts and supplies, management fees and other administrative costs and mortgage interest. For the purposes of this paragraph, mortgage interest shall be deemed to mean interest on a bona fide mortgage including an allocable portion of charges related thereto. Criteria to be considered in determining a bona fide mortgage other than an institutional mortgage shall include; condition of the property, location of the property, the existing mortgage market at the time the mortgage is placed, the term of the mortgage, the amortization rate, the principal amount of the mortgage, security and other terms and conditions of the mortgage. The commissioner shall set a rental value for any unit occupied by the owner or a person related to the owner or unoccupied at the owner's choice for more than one month at the last regulated rent plus the minimum number of guidelines increases or, if no such regulated rent existed or is known, the commissioner shall impute a rent consistent with other rents in the building. The amount of hardship increase shall be such as may be required to maintain the annual gross rent income as provided by this paragraph. The division shall not grant a hardship application under this paragraph or paragraph six of this subdivision for a period of three years subsequent to granting a hardship application under the provisions of this paragraph. The collection of any increase in the rent for any housing accommodation pursuant to this paragraph shall not exceed six percent in any year from the effective date of the order granting the increase over the rent set forth in the schedule of gross rents, with collectability of any dollar excess above said sum to be spread forward in similar increments and added to the rent as established or set in future years. No application shall be approved unless the owner's equity in such building exceeds five percent of: (i) the arms length purchase price of the property; (ii) the cost of any capital improvements for which the owner has not collected a surcharge; (iii) any repayment of principal of any mortgage or loan used to finance the purchase of the property or any capital improvements for which the owner has not collected a surcharge and (iv) any increase in the equalized assessed value of the property which occurred subsequent to the first valuation of the property after purchase by the owner. For the purposes of this paragraph, owner's equity shall mean the sum of (i) the purchase price of the property less the principal of any mortgage or loan used to finance the purchase of the property, (ii) the cost of any capital improvement for which the owner has not collected a surcharge less the principal of any mortgage or loan used to finance said improvement, (iii) any repayment of the principal of any mortgage or loan used to finance the purchase of the property or any capital improvement for which the owner has not collected a surcharge, and (iv) any increase in the equalized assessed value of the property which occurred subsequent to the first valuation of the property after purchase by the owner.

(7) establishes a fair and consistent formula for allocation of rental adjustment to be made upon granting of an increase by the commissioner;

(8) requires owners to maintain all services furnished by them on May thirty-first, nineteen hundred sixty-eight, or as otherwise provided by law, in connection with the leasing of the dwelling units covered by this law;

(9) provides that an owner shall not refuse to renew a lease except:

(a) where he or she intends in good faith to demolish the building and has obtained a permit therefor from the department of buildings; or

(b) where he or she seeks to recover possession of one or more dwelling units for his or her own personal use and occupancy as his or her primary residence in the city of New York and/or for the use and occupancy of a member of his or her immediate family as his or her primary residence in the city of New York, provided however, that this subparagraph shall not apply where a tenant or the spouse of a tenant lawfully occupying the dwelling unit is sixty-two years of age or older, or has an impairment which results from anatomical, physiological or psychological conditions, other than addiction to alcohol, gambling, or any controlled substance, which are demonstrable by medically acceptable clinical and laboratory diagnostic techniques, and which are expected to be permanent and which prevent the tenant from engaging in any substantial gainful employment, unless such owner offers to provide and if requested, provides an equivalent or superior housing accommodation at the same or lower stabilized rent in a closely proximate area. The provisions of this subparagraph shall only permit one of the individual owners of any building to recover possession of one or more dwelling units for his or her own personal use and/or for that of his or her immediate family. Any dwelling unit recovered by an owner pursuant to this subparagraph shall not for a period of three years be rented, leased, subleased or assigned to any person other than a person for whose benefit recovery of the dwelling unit is permitted pursuant to this subparagraph or to the tenant in occupancy at the time of recovery under the same terms as the original lease. This subparagraph shall not be deemed to establish or eliminate any claim that the former tenant of the dwelling unit may otherwise have against the owner. Any such rental, lease, sublease or assignment during such period to any other person may be subject to a penalty of a forfeiture of the right to any increases in residential rents in such building for a period of three years; or

(c) where the housing accommodation is owned by a hospital, convent, monastery, asylum, public institution, college, school dormitory or any institution operated exclusively for charitable or educational purposes on a non-profit basis and either:

(i) the tenant's initial tenancy commenced after the owner acquired the property and the owner requires the unit in connection with its charitable or educational purposes including, but not limited to, housing for affiliated persons; provided that with respect to any tenant whose right to occupancy commenced prior to July first, nineteen hundred seventy-eight pursuant to a written lease or written rental agreement and who did not receive notice at the time of the execution of the lease that his or her tenancy was subject to non-renewal, the institution shall not have the right to refuse to renew pursuant to this subparagraph; provided further that a tenant who was affiliated with the institution at the commencement of his or her tenancy and whose affiliation terminates during such tenancy shall not have the right to a renewal lease; or

(ii) the owner requires the unit for a non-residential use in connection with its charitable or educational purposes; or

(d) on specified grounds set forth in the code approved by the department of housing preservation and development consistent with the purposes of this law; or

(e) where a tenant violates the provisions of paragraph twelve of this subdivision.

(9-a) provides that where an owner has submitted to and the attorney general has accepted for filing an offering plan to convert the building to cooperative or condominium ownership and the owner has presented the offering plan to the tenants in occupancy, any renewal or vacancy lease may contain a provision that if a building is converted to cooperative or condominium ownership pursuant to an eviction plan, as provided in section three hundred fifty-two-eeee of the general business law, the lease may only be cancelled upon the expiration of three years after the plan has been declared effective, and upon ninety days notice to the tenant that such period has expired or will be expiring.

(10) specifically provides that if an owner fails to comply with any order of the commissioner or is found by the commissioner to have harassed a tenant to obtain vacancy of his or her housing accommodation, he or she shall, in addition to being subject to any other penalties or remedies permitted by law, be barred thereafter from applying for or collecting any further rent increase. The compliance by the owner with the order of the commissioner or the restoration of the tenant subject to harassment to the housing accommodation or compliance with such other remedy as shall be determined by the commissioner to be appropriate shall result in the prospective elimination of such sanctions;

(11) includes provisions which may be peculiarly applicable to hotels including specifically that no owner shall refuse to extend or renew a tenancy for the purpose of preventing a hotel tenant from becoming a permanent tenant; and

(12) permits subletting of units subject to this law pursuant to section two hundred twenty-six-b of the real property law provided that (a) the rental charged to the subtenant does not exceed the stabilized rent plus a ten percent surcharge payable to the tenant if the unit sublet was furnished with the tenant's furniture; (b) the tenant can establish that at all times he or she has maintained the unit as his or her primary residence and intends to occupy it as such at the expiration of the sublease; (c) an owner may terminate the tenancy of a tenant who sublets or assigns contrary to the terms of this paragraph but no action or proceeding based on the non-primary residence of a tenant may be commenced prior to the expiration date of his or her lease; (d) where an apartment is sublet the prime tenant shall retain the right to a renewal lease and the rights and status of a tenant in occupancy as they relate to conversion to condominium or cooperative ownership; (e) where a tenant violates the provisions of subparagraph (a) of this paragraph the subtenant shall be entitled to damages of three times the overcharge and

may also be awarded attorneys fees and interest from the date of the overcharge at the rate of interest payable on a judgment pursuant to section five thousand four of the civil practice law and rules; (f) the tenant may not sublet the unit for more than a total of two years, including the term of the proposed sublease, out of the four-year period preceding the termination date of the proposed sublease. The provisions of this subparagraph shall only apply to subleases commencing on and after July first, nineteen hundred eighty-three; (g) for the purposes of this paragraph only, the term of the proposed sublease may extend beyond the term of the tenant's lease. In such event, such sublease shall be subject to the tenant's right to a renewal lease. The subtenant shall have no right to a renewal lease. It shall be unreasonable for an owner to refuse to consent to a sublease solely because such sublease extends beyond the tenant's lease; and (h) notwithstanding the provisions of section two hundred twenty-six-b of the real property law, a not-for-profit hospital shall have the right to sublet any housing accommodation leased by it to its affiliated personnel without requiring the landlord's consent to any such sublease and without being bound by the provisions of subparagraphs (b), (c) and (f) of this paragraph. Commencing with the effective date of this subparagraph, whenever a not-for-profit hospital executes a renewal lease for a housing accommodation, the legal regulated rent shall be increased by a sum equal to fifteen percent of the previous lease rental for such housing accommodation, hereinafter referred to as a vacancy surcharge, unless the landlord shall have received within the seven year period prior to the commencement date of such renewal lease any vacancy increases or vacancy surcharges allocable to the said housing accommodation. In the event the landlord shall have received any such vacancy increases or vacancy surcharges during such seven year period, the vacancy surcharge shall be reduced by the amount received by any such vacancy increase or vacancy surcharges.

d. (1) Each owner subject to the rent stabilization law shall furnish to each tenant signing a new or renewal lease, a rider describing the rights and duties of owners and tenants as provided for under the rent stabilization law of nineteen hundred sixty-nine. Such publication shall conform to the intent of section 5-702 of the general obligations law and shall be attached as an addendum to the lease. Upon the face of each lease, in bold print, shall appear the following: "Attached to this lease are the pertinent rules and regulations governing tenants and landlords' rights under the rent stabilization law of nineteen hundred sixty-nine".

(2) The rider shall be in a form promulgated by the commissioner in larger type than the lease and shall be utilized as provided in paragraph one of this subdivision.

e. Each owner of premises subject to the rent stabilization law shall furnish to each tenant signing a new or renewal lease, a copy of the fully executed new or renewal lease bearing the signatures of owner and tenant and the beginning an ending dates of the lease term, within thirty days from the owner's receipt of the new or renewal lease signed by the tenant.

§ 26-512 Stabilization provisions

a. No owner of property subject to this law shall charge or collect any rent in excess of the initial legal regulated rent or adjusted initial legal regulated rent until the end of any lease or other rental agreement in effect on the local effective date until such time as a different legal regulated rent shall be authorized pursuant to guidelines adopted by a rent guidelines board.

b. The initial regulated rent for housing accommodations subject to this law on the local effective date of the emergency tenant protection act of nineteen seventy-four or which become subject to this law thereafter, pursuant to such act, shall be:

(1) For housing accommodations which were regulated pursuant to this law or the city rent and rehabilitation law prior to July first, nineteen hundred seventy-one, and which became vacant on or after such date and prior to the local effective date of the emergency tenant protection act of nineteen seventy-four, the rent reserved in the last effective lease or other rental agreement; provided that such initial rent may be adjusted on application of the tenant pursuant to subdivision b of section 26-513 of this chapter.

(2) For housing accommodations which were regulated pursuant to the city rent and rehabilitation law on the local effective date of the emergency tenant protection act of nineteen seventy-four, and thereafter become vacant, the rent agreed to by the landlord and the tenant and reserved in a lease or provided for in a rental agreement; provided that such initial rent may be adjusted on application of the tenant pursuant to subdivision b of section 26-513 of this chapter.

(3) For housing accommodations other than those described in paragraphs one and two of this subdivision, the rent reserved in the last effective lease or other rental agreement.

(4) For any plot or parcel of land which had been regulated pursuant to the city rent and rehabilitation law prior to July first, nineteen hundred seventy-one and which,

(i) became vacant on or after July first, nineteen hundred seventy-one and prior to July first, nineteen hundred seventy-four, the rent reserved in a lease or other rental agreement in effect on June thirtieth, nineteen hundred seventy-four plus increases authorized by the rent guidelines board under this law for leases or other rental agreements commencing thereafter; provided that such initial rent may be adjusted on application of the tenant pursuant to subdivision b of section 26-513 of this chapter or,

(ii) became vacant on or after July first, nineteen hundred seventy-four, the rent agreed to by the landlord and the tenant and reserved in a lease or other rental agreement plus increases authorized by the rent guidelines board under this law for leases or other rental agreements commencing thereafter; provided that such initial rent may be adjusted on application of the tenant pursuant to subdivision b of section 26-513 of this chapter.

(iii) Where the commissioner has determined that the rent charged is in excess of the lawful rents as stated in subparagraph (i) or (ii) hereof, plus lawful increases thereafter, he or she shall provide for a cash refund or a credit, to be applied against future rent, in the amount of any rent overcharge collected by an owner and any penalties, costs, attorneys' fees and interest from the date of the overcharge at the rate of interest payable on a judgment pursuant to section five thousand four of the civil practice law and rules for which the owner is assessed.

c. With respect to accommodations for which the initial legal regulated rent is governed by paragraph two of subdivision b hereof, no increase of such initial legal regulated rent pursuant to annual guidelines adopted by the rent guidelines board shall become effective until the expiration of the first lease or rental agreement taking effect after the local effective date of the emergency tenant protection act of nineteen seventy-four, but in no event before one year after the commencement of such rental agreement.

d. With respect to accommodations, other than those referred to in subdivision c, for which a lease is entered into after the local effective date of the emergency tenant protection act of nineteen seventy-four, but before the effective date of the first guidelines applicable to such accommodations, the lease may provide for an adjustment of rent pursuant to such guidelines to be effective on the first day of the month next succeeding the effective date of such guidelines.

e. Notwithstanding any contrary provisions of this law, on and after July first, nineteen hundred eighty-four, the legal regulated rent authorized for a housing accommodation subject to the provisions of this law shall be the rent registered pursuant to section 26-517 of this chapter subject to any modification imposed pursuant to this law.

§ 26-513 Application for adjustment of initial rent

a. The tenant or owner of a housing accommodation made subject to this law by the emergency tenant protection act of nineteen seventy-four may, within sixty days of the local effective date of this section or the commencement of the first tenancy thereafter, whichever is later, file with the commissioner an application for adjustment of the initial legal regulated rent for such housing accommodation. The commissioner may adjust such initial legal regulated rent upon a finding that the presence of unique or peculiar circumstances materially affecting the initial legal regulated rent has resulted in a rent which is substantially different from the rents generally prevailing in the same area for substantially similar housing accommodations.

b. 1. The tenant of a housing accommodation that was regulated pursuant to the city rent and rehabilitation law or this law prior to July first, nineteen hundred seventy-one and that became vacant on or after January first, nineteen hundred seventy-four may file with the commissioner within ninety days after notice has been received pursuant to subdivision d of this section, an application for adjustment of the initial legal regulated rent for such housing accommodation. Such tenant need only allege that such rent is in excess of the fair market rent and shall present such facts which, to the best of his or her information and belief, support such allegation. The rent guidelines board shall promulgate as soon as practicable after the local effective date of the emergency tenant protection act of nineteen seventy-four guidelines for the determination of fair market rents for housing accommodations as to which any application may be made pursuant to this subdivision. In rendering a determination on an application filed pursuant to this subdivision b the commissioner shall be guided by such guidelines and by the rents generally prevailing in the same area for substantially similar housing accommodations. Where the commissioner has determined that the rent charged is in excess of the fair market rent he or she shall, in addition to any other penalties or remedies permitted by law, order a refund of any excess paid since January first, nineteen hundred seventy-four or the date of the commencement of the tenancy, whichever is later. Such refund shall be made by the landlord in cash or as a credit against future rents over a period not in excess of six months.

2. The provisions of paragraph one of this subdivision shall not apply to a tenant of a housing accommodation for which the initial legal regulated rent is no greater than the maximum rent that would have been in effect under this law on December thirty-first, nineteen hundred seventy-three, or for the period commencing January first, nineteen hundred seventy-four and ending De-

cember thirty-first, nineteen hundred seventy-five as calculated pursuant to the city rent and rehabilitation law (if no such maximum rent has been calculated for a particular unit for the period commencing January first, nineteen hundred seventy-four and ending December thirty-first, nineteen hundred seventy-five, the division of housing and community renewal shall calculate such a rent), as the case may be, if such apartment had not become vacant on or after January first, nineteen hundred seventy-four, plus the amount of any adjustment which would have been authorized under this law for renewal leases or other rental agreement, whether or not such housing accommodation was subject to this law, for leases or other rental agreements commencing on or after July first, nineteen hundred seventy-four.

c. Upon receipt of any application filed pursuant to this section, the commissioner shall notify the owner or tenant, as the case may be, and provide a copy to him or her of such application. Such owner or tenant shall be afforded a reasonable opportunity to respond to the application. A hearing may be held upon the request of either party, or the commissioner may hold a hearing on his or her own motion. The commissioner shall issue a written opinion to both the tenant and the owner upon rendering his or her determination.

d. Within thirty days after the local effective date of the emergency tenant protection act of nineteen seventy-four the owner of housing accommodations as to which an application for adjustment of the initial legal regulated rent may be made pursuant to subdivision b of this section shall give notice in writing by certified mail to the tenant of each such housing accommodation on a form prescribed by the commissioner of the initial legal regulated rent for such housing accommodation and of such tenant's right to file an application for adjustment of the initial legal regulated rent of such housing accommodation.

e. Notwithstanding any contrary provision in this law an application for an adjustment pursuant to this section must be filed within ninety days from the initial registration. This subdivision shall not extend any other time limitations imposed by this law.

§ 26-514 Maintenance of services

In order to collect a rent adjustment authorized pursuant to the provisions of subdivision d of section 26-510 of this chapter an owner must file with the state division of housing and community renewal, on a form which the commissioner shall prescribe, a written certification that he or she is maintaining and will continue to maintain all services furnished on the date upon which the emergency tenant protection act of nineteen seventy-four becomes a law or required to be furnished by any state law or local law, ordinance or regulation applicable to the premises. In addition to any other remedy afforded by law, any tenant may apply to the state division of housing and community renewal, for a reduction in the rent to the level in effect prior to its most recent adjustment and for an order requiring services to be maintained as provided in this section, and the commissioner shall so reduce the rent if it is found that the owner has failed to maintain such services. The owner shall also be barred from applying for or collecting any further rent increases. The restoration of such services shall result in the prospective elimination of such sanctions. The owner shall be supplied with a copy of the application and shall be permitted to file an answer thereto. A hearing may be held upon the request of either party, or the commissioner may hold a hearing upon his or her own motion. The commissioner may consolidate the proceedings for two or more petitions applicable to the same building or group of buildings or development. If the commissioner finds that the owner has knowingly filed a false certification, it shall, in addition to abating the rent, assess the owner with the reasonable costs of the proceeding, including reasonable attorneys' fees, and impose a penalty not in excess of two hundred fifty dollars for each false certification.

§ 26-515 Recovery of possession

a. An owner seeking to recover possession pursuant to subparagraph (c) of paragraph nine of subdivision c of section 26-511 of this chapter shall notify the tenant in occupancy not more than one hundred fifty and not less than one hundred twenty days prior to the end of the tenant's lease term, by mail, of such owner's intention not to renew such lease in order to recover the dwelling unit for its charitable or educational purposes. The owner may give such notice within one hundred twenty days of the expiration of the tenant's lease term, provided it may not commence a summary proceeding to recover the dwelling unit until the expiration of one hundred twenty days from the giving of such notice and, provided, further, that the tenant may remain in occupancy until the commencement of such proceeding at the same rent and upon the same terms and conditions as were provided in his or her expired lease. The notice of intention not to renew the tenant's lease shall be accompanied by a notice on a form prescribed by the division of housing and community renewal setting forth the penalties to which an owner may be subject for his or her failure to utilize the tenant's dwelling unit for the charitable or educational purpose for which recovery of the dwelling unit is sought.

b. If any owner who recovers a dwelling unit pursuant to such subparagraph (c), or any successor in interest, utilizes such unit for purposes other than those permitted under such subparagraph, then such owner or successor shall, unless for good cause shown, be liable to the removed tenant for three times the damages sustained on account of such removal plus reasonable attorney's fees and costs as determined by the court, provided that such tenant commences such action within three years from the date of recovery of the unit. The damages sustained by such tenant shall be the difference between the rent paid by such tenant for the recovered dwelling unit, and the rental value of a comparable rent regulated dwelling unit on the open market. In addition to any other damage, the reasonable cost of removal of the tenant's property shall be a lawful measure of damages.

c. Where a dwelling unit has been recovered pursuant to such subparagraph (c) and within four years of such recovery is rented to a person or entity for purposes other than those permitted pursuant to such subparagraph (c), unless for good cause shown, the rent charged by such owner or any successor in interest for four years following such recovery shall not exceed the last regulated rent payable prior to such recovery.

d. If the owner is found by the commissioner, to have recovered possession of a dwelling unit pursuant to such subparagraph (c) and within four years of such recovery such owner or any successor in interest shall have utilized such unit for purposes other than those permitted pursuant to such subparagraph (c), unless for good cause shown, the commissioner shall impose upon such owner or successor in interest, by administrative order after hearing, a civil penalty for any such violation. Such penalty shall be in an amount of up to one thousand dollars for each offense. Such order shall be deemed a final determination for the purposes of judicial review. Such penalty may, upon the expiration of the period for seeking review pursuant to article seventy-eight of the civil practice law and rules, be docketed and enforced in the manner of a judgment of the supreme court.

§ 26-516 Enforcement and procedures

a. Subject to the conditions and limitations of this subdivision, any owner of housing accommodations who, upon complaint of a tenant, or of the state division of housing and community renewal is found by the state division of housing and community renewal, after a reasonable opportunity to be heard, to have collected an overcharge above the rent authorized for a housing accommodation subject to this chapter shall be liable to the tenant for a penalty equal to three times the amount of such overcharge. If the owner establishes by a preponderance of the evidence that the overcharge was not willful, the state division of housing and community renewal shall establish the penalty as the amount of the overcharge plus interest. (i) Except as to complaints filed pursuant to clause (ii) of this paragraph, the legal regulated rent for purposes of determining an overcharge, shall be the rent indicated in the annual registration statement filed four years prior to the most recent registration statement, (or, if more recently filed, the initial registration statement) plus in each case any subsequent lawful increases and adjustments. (ii) As to complaints filed within ninety days of the initial registration of a housing accommodation, the legal regulated rent shall be deemed to be the rent charged on the date four years prior to the date of the initial registration of the housing accommodation (or, if the housing accommodation was subject to this chapter for less than four years, the initial legal regulated rent) plus in each case, any lawful increases and adjustments. Where the rent charged on the date four years prior to the date of the initial registration of the accommodation cannot be established, such rent shall be established by the division.

Where the rent charged on the date four years prior to the date of initial registration of the housing accommodation cannot be established, such rent shall be established by the division provided that where a rent is established based on rentals determined under the provisions of the local emergency housing rent control act such rent must be adjusted to account for no less than the minimum increases which would be permitted if the housing accommodation were covered under the provisions of this chapter.

(1) The order of the state division of housing and community renewal shall apportion the owner's liability between or among two or more tenants found to have been overcharged by such owner during their particular tenancy of a unit.

(2) Except as provided under clauses (i) and (ii) of this paragraph, a complaint under this subdivision shall be filed with the state division of housing and community renewal within four years of the first overcharge alleged and no award of the amount of an overcharge may be based upon an overcharge having occurred more than four years before the complaint is filed. (i) No penalty of three times the overcharge may be based upon an overcharge having occurred more than two years before the complaint is filed or upon an overcharge which occurred prior to April first, nineteen hundred eighty-four. (ii) Any complaint based upon overcharges occurring prior to the date of filing of the initial rent registration as provided in section 26-517 of this chapter shall be filed within ninety days of the mailing of notice to the tenant of such registration.

(3) Any affected tenant shall be notified of and given an opportunity to join in any complaint filed by an officer or employee of the state division of housing and community renewal.

(4) An owner found to have overcharged may be assessed the reasonable costs and attorney's fees of the proceeding and interest from the date of the overcharge at the rate of interest payable on a judgment pursuant to section five thousand four of the civil practice law and rules.

(5) The order of the state division of housing and community renewal awarding penalties may, upon the expiration of the period in which the owner may institute a proceeding pursuant to article seventy-eight of the civil practice law and rules, be filed and enforced by a tenant in the same manner as a judgment or not in excess of twenty percent thereof per month may be offset against any rent thereafter due the owner.

b. In addition to issuing the specific orders provided for by other provisions of this law, the state division of housing and community renewal shall be empowered to enforce this law and the code by issuing, upon notice and a reasonable opportunity for the affected party to be heard, such other orders as it may deem appropriate.

c. If the owner is found by the commissioner:

(1) to have violated an order of the division the commissioner may impose by administrative order after hearing, a civil penalty in the amount of two hundred fifty dollars for the first such offense and one thousand dollars for each subsequent offense; or

(2) to have harassed a tenant to obtain vacancy of his or her housing accommodation, the commissioner may impose by administrative order after hearing, a civil penalty for any such violation. Such penalty shall be in the amount of up to one thousand dollars for a first such offense and up to twenty-five hundred dollars for each subsequent offense or for a violation consisting of conduct directed at the tenants of more than one housing accommodation.

Such order shall be deemed a final determination for the purposes of judicial review. Such penalty may, upon the expiration of the period for seeking review pursuant to article seventy-eight of the civil practice law and rules, be docketed and enforced in the manner of a judgment of the supreme court.

d. Any proceeding pursuant to article seventy-eight of the civil practice law and rules seeking review of any action pursuant to this chapter shall be brought within sixty days. Any action or proceeding brought by or against the commissioner under this law shall be brought in the county in which the housing accommodation is located.

e. Violations of this law, or of the code and orders issued pursuant thereto may be enjoined by the supreme court upon proceedings commenced by the state division of housing and community renewal which shall not be required to post bond.

f. In furtherance of its responsibility to enforce this law, the state division of housing and community renewal shall be empowered to administer oaths, issue subpoenas, conduct investigations, make inspections and designate officers to hear and report. The division shall safeguard the confidentiality of information furnished to it at the request of the person furnishing same, unless such information must be made public in the interest of establishing a record for the future guidance of persons subject to this law.

g. Any owner who has duly registered a housing accommodation pursuant to section 26-517 of this chapter shall not be required to maintain or produce any records relating to rentals of such accommodation for more than four years prior to the most recent registration or annual statement for such accommodation.

h. The state division of housing and community renewal may, by regulation, provide for administrative review of all orders and determinations issued by it pursuant to this chapter. Any such regulation shall provide that if a petition for such review is not determined within ninety days after it is filed, it shall be deemed to be denied. However, the division may grant one extension not to exceed thirty days with the consent of the party filing such petition; any further extension may only be granted with the consent of all parties to the petition. No proceeding may be brought pursuant to article seventy-eight of the civil practice law and rules to challenge any order or determination which is subject to such administrative review unless such review has been sought and either (1) a determination thereon has been made or (2) the ninety day period provided for determination of the petition for review (or any extension thereof) has expired.

§ 26-517 Rent registration

a. Each housing accommodation which is subject to this law shall be registered by the owner thereof with the state division of housing and community renewal prior to July first, nineteen hundred eighty-four upon forms prescribed by the commissioner. The data to be provided on such forms shall include the following: (1) the name and address of the building or group of buildings or development in which such housing accommodation is located and the owner and the tenant thereof; (2) the number of housing accommodations in the building or group of buildings or development in which such housing accommodation is located; (3) the number of housing accommodations in such building or group of buildings or development subject to this code and the number of such housing accommodations subject to the local emergency housing rent control act; (4) the rent charged on the registration date; (5) the number of rooms in such housing accommodation; and (6) all services provided on the date that the housing accommodation became subject to this chapter.

b. Registration pursuant to this section shall not be subject to the freedom of information law provided that registration information relative to a tenant, owner, lessor or subtenant shall be made available to such party or his or her authorized representative.

c. Housing accommodations which become subject to this chapter after the initial registration period must be registered within ninety days thereafter. Registration of housing accommodations subject to the local emergency housing rent control act immediately prior to the date of initial registration as provided in this section shall include, in addition to the items listed above, where existing, the maximum base rent immediately prior to the date that such housing accommodations become subject to this chapter.

d. Copies of the registration shall be filed with the state division of housing and community renewal in such place or places as it may require. In addition, one copy of that portion of the registration statement which pertains to the tenant's unit must be mailed by the owner to the tenant in possession at the time of initial registration or to the first tenant in occupancy if the apartment is vacant at the time of initial registration.

e. The failure to file a proper and timely initial or annual rent registration statement shall, until such time as such registration is filed, bar an owner from applying for or collecting any rent in excess of the legal regulated rent in effect on the date of the last preceding registration statement or if no such statements have been filed, the legal regulated rent in effect on the date that the housing accommodation became subject to the registration requirements of this section. The filing of a late registration shall result in the prospective elimination of such sanctions.

f. An annual statement shall be filed containing the current rent for each unit and such other information contained in subdivision a of this section as shall be required by the division. The owner shall provide each tenant then in occupancy with a copy of that portion of such annual statement as pertains to the tenant's unit.

g. Each housing accommodation for which a timely registration statement was filed between April first, nineteen hundred eighty-four and June thirtieth, nineteen hundred eighty-four, pursuant to subdivision a of this section shall designate the rent charged on April first, nineteen hundred eighty-four, as the rent charged on the registration date.

§ 26-518 Hotel industry stabilization association

a. Notwithstanding the provisions of section 26-511 of this chapter, a hotel industry stabilization association having as members the owners of no less than two thousand dwelling units covered by this law by virtue of section 26-505 of this chapter may register with the department of housing preservation and development under the terms and for the purposes herein provided by filing with such administration copies of its articles of incorporation or association, copies of its rules, and such other information as the administration may require within thirty days of the effective date of the amendatory local law adding this section.

b. A hotel industry stabilization association shall not be accepted for registration hereunder unless it appears to the department of housing preservation and development that (1) consistent with the provisions of this section membership is open to any owner of a multiple dwelling having dwelling units covered by this law as provided in section 26-505 of this chapter; (2) the association has adopted a code for stabilization of rents covering related terms and conditions of occupancy which is approved by such administration; (3) the association has a firm understanding with a real estate industry stabilization association registered with the department of housing preservation and development to participate in the establishment of a conciliation and appeals board to receive and act upon complaints and applications as provided under this law, and it is further understood that the associations shall share the cost of such board proportionately in relation to the number of dwelling units subject to this law owned by their respective membership; (4) each member is required to agree in writing to comply with the code and to abide by orders of the conciliation and appeals board; and (5) the association is of such character that it will be able to carry out the purposes of this law.

c. A code shall not be approved hereunder unless it appears to the department of housing preservation and development that it provides for a cash refund or a credit to be applied against future rent, in the amount of the excess, if any, of rent paid since January first, nineteen hundred sixty-nine, over the permissible fair increase, and that it gives a hotel tenant the right to request a six month lease at the permissible rent rate within thirty days of the approval of such code, or, if his or her tenancy commences after such thirty day period, within thirty days of the commencement of his or her tenancy, and that is in compliance with the standards set forth in subdivision c of section 26-511 of this chapter to the extent such standards are applicable to the hotel industry, and that it provides specifically that no owner shall refuse to extend or renew a tenancy for the purpose of preventing a hotel tenant from becoming a permanent tenant.

d. (1) Each landlord who is a member of the hotel industry stabilization association shall furnish to each permanent tenant signing a new or renewal lease, a rider describing the rights and duties of owners and tenants as provided under the rent stabilization law of nineteen hundred sixty-nine. Such rider shall conform to the intent of section 5-702 of the general obligation law must be in a print size larger than the print size of the lease which the rider is attached.

(2) The department of housing preservation and development shall prepare a final rider after giving full consideration to proposals submitted by the hotel industry stabilization association and conciliation and appeals board.

§ 26-519 Suspension of registration

The department of housing preservation and development may, after notice and opportunity for hearing, suspend the registration of an association if it finds that the articles, code, rules or other conduct thereof do not conform to the requirements of this law and any such suspension shall remain in effect until such administration issues an order determining that such articles, rules, code or other conduct have been modified to conform with such requirements. For the purposes of this law, the members in good standing of the association shall be deemed to be members in good standing of an association registered with the department of housing preservation and development during and only during, the first sixty days of such period of suspension.

§ 26-520 Expiration date

This chapter shall expire on April first, nineteen hundred eighty-eight unless rent control shall sooner terminate as provided in subdivision three of section one of the local emergency housing rent control law.

RENT STABILIZATION CODE
FOR RENT STABILIZED APARTMENTS
IN NEW YORK CITY*

(Effective May 1, 1987)

TABLE OF CONTENTS

PART 2520 SCOPE   PAGE

Section 2520.1	Statutory authority	766
Section 2520.2	Amendment of Codes	766
Section 2520.3	Construction and implementation	767
Section 2520.4	Delegation of authority	767
Section 2520.5	Designations	767
Section 2520.6	Definitions	769
Section 2520.7	Effective date	775
Section 2520.8	Amendment or revocation	776
Section 2520.9	Filing of amendments	776
Section 2520.10	Separability	776
Section 2520.11	Applicability	776
Section 2520.12	Effect of this Code on leases and other rental agreements	781
Section 2520.13	Waiver of benefit void	781

PART 2521 LEGAL REGISTERED AND REGULATED RENTS

Section 2521.1	Initial legal registered rents for housing accommodations	781
Section 2521.2	Legal regulated rents for housing accommodations	789
Section 2521.3	Classification of buildings	789

PART 2522 RENT ADJUSTMENTS

Section 2522.1	Legal regulated rent adjustments	791
Section 2522.2	Effective date of adjustment of legal regulated rents	791
Section 2522.3	Fair Market Rent Appeal	791
Section 2522.4	Adjustment of legal regulated rent	794
Section 2522.5	Lease agreements	813
Section 2522.6	Orders where the legal regulated rent or other facts are in dispute, in doubt, or not known, or where the legal regulated rent must be fixed	822
Section 2522.7	Consideration of equities	823

---

* Promulgated by the New York State Division of Housing and Community Renewal, One Fordham Plaza, Bronx, New York 10458.

This Code replaces and supersedes the former Code of the Rent Stabilization Association of New York City, Inc. and the Code of the Metropolitan Hotel Industry Stabilization Association, Inc. See § 2520.2 of this new Code.

RENT STABILIZATION CODE

PART 2523 NOTICES AND RECORDS

Section 2523.1	Notice of Initial Legal Registered Rent	824
Section 2523.2	Certification of services	824
Section 2523.3	Failure to file a certification of services	824
Section 2523.4	Failure to maintain services	824
Section 2523.5	Notice for renewal of lease and renewal procedure	825
Section 2523.6	Notices of appearance by attorney or other authorized representative	828
Section 2523.7	Records and record keeping	829
Section 2523.8	Notice of change of ownership	830

PART 2524 EVICTIONS

Section 2524.1	Restrictions on removal of tenant	830
Section 2524.2	Termination notices	831
Section 2524.3	Proceedings for eviction - wrongful acts of tenant	832
Section 2524.4	Grounds for refusal to renew lease, or in hotels, discontinuing a hotel tenancy, without order of the DHCR	835
Section 2524.5	Grounds for refusal to renew lease or discontinue hotel tenancy and evict which require approval of the DHCR	838

PART 2525 PROHIBITIONS

Section 2525.1	General prohibitions	841
Section 2525.2	Evasion	841
Section 2525.3	Conditional rental	842
Section 2525.4	Security deposits	843
Section 2525.5	Harassment	843
Section 2525.6	Subletting; Assignment	844

PART 2526 ENFORCEMENT

Section 2526.1	Overcharge penalties; fines; assessment of costs; attorneys' fees; rent credits	846
Section 2526.2	Orders to enforce the RSL and this Code	849
Section 2526.3	Injunctions by supreme court	850
Section 2526.4	Oaths, subpoenas, hearing officers	850
Section 2526.5	Confidentiality of information	850
Section 2526.6	Inspection and records	851

PART 2527 PROCEEDINGS BEFORE THE DHCR

Section 2527.1	Proceedings instituted by owner or tenant	851
Section 2527.2	Proceedings instituted by the DHCR	851
Section 2527.3	Notice to the parties affected	851
Section 2527.4	Answer	852
Section 2527.5	Preliminary action by the DHCR	852
Section 2527.6	Determination	853
Section 2527.7	Pending proceedings	853
Section 2527.8	Modification or revocation of orders	854
Section 2527.9	When a notice or paper shall be deemed served	854

Section 2527.10 Amendments to complaint or application.... 854
Section 2527.11 Advisory opinions and Operational Bulletins. 855

PART 2528 REGISTRATION OF HOUSING ACCOMMODATIONS

Section 2528.1 Initial registration 855
Section 2528.2 Registration requirements.................. 855
Section 2528.3 Annual registration requirements........... 856
Section 2528.4 Penalty for failure to register.............. 857
Section 2528.5 Confidentiality 857

PART 2529 ADMINISTRATIVE REVIEW

Section 2529.1 Persons who may file 857
Section 2529.2 Time for filing a PAR 858
Section 2529.3 Form and content of a PAR 858
Section 2529.4 Service and filing of a PAR............... 858
Section 2529.5 Time of filing an answer to a PAR 859
Section 2529.6 Scope of review.......................... 859
Section 2529.7 Action by Commissioner 859
Section 2529.8 Final determination by the Commissioner ... 860
Section 2529.9 Modification or revocation of orders by the Commissioner 860
Section 2529.10 Pending PAR proceedings 860
Section 2529.11 Time within which the Commissioner shall take final action 861
Section 2529.12 Stays 861

PART 2530 JUDICIAL REVIEW

Section 2530.1 Commencement of proceeding 861

RENT STABILIZATION CODE
PART 2520 - SCOPE

Section 2520.1 Statutory authority.

These amendments are promulgated and adopted pursuant to the powers granted to the Division of Housing and Community Renewal by Chapter 888 of the Laws of New York for the year 1985.

2520.2 Amendment of Codes.

Sections 1 through 66 inclusive of the Code of the Rent Stabilization Association of New York City, Inc., and sections 1 through 64 inclusive, of the Code of the Metropolitan Hotel Industry Stabilization Association, Inc., as last amended are hereby further amended by deleting such sections in their entirety, and sections 2520.1 through 2530.1 inclusive, are hereby adopted, and this Code shall hereafter be known as the Rent Stabilization Code. Chapter VIII of Subtitle S of Title 9 NYCRR, the

Rent Stabilization Code

Official Compilation of Codes, Rules and Regulations of the State of New York, is hereby redesignated to be known as Rent Stabilization Regulations and divided into Subchapter A - Emergency Tenant Protection Regulations, consisting of existing Parts 2500-2510; and Subchapter B - Rent Stabilization Code, consisting of new Parts 2520-2530.

2520.3 Construction and implementation.

This Code shall be construed so as to carry out the intent of the Rent Stabilization Law to ensure that such statute shall not be subverted or rendered ineffective, directly or indirectly, and to prevent the exaction of unjust, unreasonable and oppressive rents and rental agreements, and to forestall profiteering, speculation and other disruptive practices tending to produce threats to the public health, safety and general welfare; and that the policy herein expressed shall be implemented with due regard for the preservation of regulated rental housing.

2520.4 Delegation of authority.

The Commissioner of Housing and Community Renewal may delegate to a Deputy Commissioner, an Assistant Commissioner, a Rent Administrator or any other person or persons, the authority to carry out any of the duties and powers granted to him by the New York City Rent Stabilization Law or this Code, and the Emergency Tenant Protection Act of 1974, as amended.

2520.5 Designations.

When used in this Code, unless a different meaning clearly appears from the context, the following terms shall mean and include:

(a) RSL. Title 26 of the Administrative Code of the City of New York sections 26-501 through 26-520, as recodified by Chapter 907 of the Laws of New York for the year 1985, constituting the New York City Rent Stabilization Law.

(b) ETPA. The Emergency Tenant Protection Act of 1974.

(c) State Rent Law. The New York State Emergency

RENT STABILIZATION CODE

Housing Rent Control Law, commonly referred to as the State Rent Control Law.

(d) City Rent Law. Title 26 of the Administrative Code of the City of New York sections 26-401 through 26-415, as recodified by Chapter 907 of the Laws of New York for the year 1985, constituting the New York City Rent and Rehabilitation Law, commonly referred to as the City Rent Control Law.

(e) PHFL. The Private Housing Finance Law.

(f) MDL. The Multiple Dwelling Law.

(g) City Rent and Eviction Regulations. Regulations adopted and promulgated by the State Division of Housing and Community Renewal pursuant to the City Rent Law. Parts 2200-2210 of Title 9 NYCRR, officially known as the Official Compilation of Codes, Rules and Regulations of the State of New York.

(h) DHCR. State Division of Housing and Community Renewal in the Executive Department.

(i) Commissioner. Commissioner of the DHCR.

(j) City Rent Agency. DHCR as defined in the City Rent Law.

(k) HPD. New York City Department of Housing Preservation and Development.

(l) Loft Board. The board created in the City of New York pursuant to article 7-C of the MDL, to resolve complaints of owners of interim multiple dwellings and of residential occupants of such buildings qualified for the protection of MDL article 7-C, and to act upon hardship applications made pursuant to such article.

(m) Rent Guidelines Board. The board created in the City of New York pursuant to the RSL to establish guidelines annually for rent adjustments for leases or other rental agreements.

(n) Office of Rent Administration. The office of the DHCR designated by the Commissioner to administer the ETPA, the RSL and the City and State Rent Laws.

(o) District Rent Office. The local rent administration office of the DHCR for a particular rent area in the City of New York.

(p) Rent Administrator. The person designated by the

Commissioner to issue orders based on complaints or applications made to the DHCR.

2520.6 Definitions

(a) Housing Accommodation. That part of any building or structure, occupied or intended to be occupied by one or more individuals as a residence, home, dwelling unit or apartment, and all services, privileges, furnishings, furniture and facilities supplied in connection with the occupation thereof. The term housing accommodation will also apply to any plot or parcel of land which had been regulated pursuant to the City Rent Law prior to July 1, 1971, and which became subject to the RSL after June 30, 1974.

(b) Hotel. Any Class A or Class B Multiple Dwelling which provides all of the services included in the rent as set forth in section 2521.3 of this Title (Classification of Buildings).

(c) Rent. Consideration, charge, fee or other thing of value, including any bonus, benefit or gratuity demanded or received for, or in connection with, the use or occupation of housing accommodations or the transfer of a lease for such housing accommodations.

(d) Tenant. Any person or persons named on a lease as lessee or lessees, or who is or are a party or parties to a rental agreement and obligated to pay rent for the use or occupancy of a housing accommodation.

(e) Initial Legal Registered Rent. The lawful rent for the use and occupancy of housing accommodations under the RSL or the ETPA, as first registered with the DHCR in accordance with the RSL, ETPA and this Code, which has not been challenged pursuant to Part 2526 of this Title (Enforcement), or if challenged, has been determined by the DHCR.

(f) Legal Regulated Rent. The initial legal registered rent as adjusted in accordance with this Code or the rent shown in the annual registration statement filed 4 years prior to the most recent registration statement (or if more recently filed, the initial registration statement), plus in each case, any subsequent lawful increases and adjustments.

(g) Vacancy Lease. The first lease or rental agreement

for a housing accommodation that is entered into between an owner and a tenant.

(h) Renewal Lease. Any extension of a tenant's lawful occupancy of a housing accommodation pursuant to section 2523.5 of this Title (Notice for Renewal of Lease and Renewal Procedure).

(i) Owner. A fee owner, lessor, sublessor, assignee, net lessee, or a proprietary lessee of a housing accommodation in a structure or premises owned by a cooperative corporation or association, or an owner of a condominium unit or the sponsor of such cooperative corporation or association or condominium development, or any other person or entity receiving or entitled to receive rent for the use or occupation of any housing accommodation, or an agent of any of the foregoing, but such agent shall only commence a proceeding pursuant to Section 2524.5 of this Title (Evictions Requiring DHCR Approval), in the name of such foregoing principals.

(j) Permanent Tenant. For housing accommodations located in hotels, an individual or such individual's family members residing with such individual, who have continuously resided in the same building as a principal residence for a period of at least six months. In addition, a hotel occupant who requests a lease of six months or more pursuant to section 2522.5(a)(2) of this Title (Vacancy Lease or Rental), or who is in occupancy pursuant to a lease of six months or more shall be a permanent tenant even if actual occupancy is less than six months. Unless otherwise specified, reference in this Code to "tenant" shall include "permanent" tenant with respect to hotels.

(k) Subtenant or Sublessee. Any person lawfully occupying the housing accommodation pursuant to an agreement with the tenant by authority of the lease or by virtue of rights afforded pursuant to section 226-b of the Real Property Law. Such person shall be entitled to all of the benefits of and be subject to all of the obligations of this Code except the right to renew, and the right to purchase upon conversion to cooperative or condominium ownership.

(l) Occupant. Any person occupying a housing accommodation as defined in and pursuant to section 235-f of the Real Property Law. Such person shall not be considered a tenant for the purposes of this Code.

(m) Hotel Occupant. Any person residing in a housing accommodation in a hotel who is not a permanent tenant. Such person shall not be considered a tenant for the purposes of this Code, but shall be entitled to become a permanent tenant as defined in subdivision (j) of this section, upon compliance with the procedure set forth in such subdivision.

(n) Immediate Family. A husband, wife, son, daughter, stepson, stepdaughter, father, mother, stepfather, stepmother, brother, sister, grandfather, grandmother, grandson or granddaughter of the owner or the tenant.

(o) Family Member. A husband, wife, son, daughter, stepson, stepdaughter, father, mother, stepfather, stepmother, brother, sister, nephew, niece, uncle, aunt, grandfather, grandmother, grandson, granddaughter, father-in-law, mother-in-law, son-in-law, or daughter-in-law of the tenant or permanent tenant.

(p) Senior Citizen. A person who is sixty-two years of age or older.

(q) Disabled Person. A person who has an impairment which results from anatomical, physiological or psychological conditions, other than addiction to alcohol, gambling, or any controlled substance, which are demonstrable by medically acceptable clinical and laboratory diagnostic techniques, and which are expected to be permanent and which prevent such person from engaging in any substantial gainful employment.

(r) Required Services.

(1) That space and those services which the owner was maintaining or was required to maintain on the applicable base dates set forth below, and any additional space or services provided or required to be provided thereafter by applicable law. These may include, but are not limited to, the following: repairs, decorating and maintenance, the furnishing of light, heat, hot and cold water, elevator services, janitorial services and removal of refuse.

(2) For housing accommodations located in hotels in addition to the definition set forth in paragraph (1) of

this subdivision (r), required services shall also include the services set forth in section 2521.3 of this Title (Classification of Buildings), and any other services provided, or required to be provided by applicable law on the applicable base dates set forth below, including, but not limited to, telephone switchboard, bellhop, secretarial, and front desk services.

(3) Ancillary Services.

That space and those required services not contained within the individual housing accommodation which the owner was providing on the applicable base dates set forth below, and any additional space and services provided or required to be provided thereafter by applicable law. These may include, but are not limited to, garage facilities, laundry facilities, receational facilities, and security. Such ancillary services are subject to the following provisions:

(i) No owner shall require a tenant or prospective tenant to lease, rent or pay for an ancillary service, other than security, as a condition of renting a housing accommodation.

(ii) Where an ancillary service is provided to a tenant pursuant to a lease or rental agreement separate and apart from the lease or rental agreement for the housing accommodation occupied by the tenant, the tenant shall not be required to renew such lease, or rental agreement, for the ancillary service upon the expiration of such lease or rental agreement.

(iii) Where an ancillary service is provided to a tenant pursuant to a lease or rental agreement for a housing accommodation, whether at a charge separate and apart from the rental of the housing accommodation, or included in the legal regulated rent, the tenant may be required to renew the rental term for the ancillary service upon the renewal of the lease for the housing accommodation. However, where the owner requires a tenant to continue such ancillary service, the owner may not unreasonably withhold consent to the tenant to sublet for the term of each renewal lease, the space or other facility constituting the ancillary service.

(iv) For housing accommodations located in hotels,

where telephone switchboard service is not provided or required to be provided pursuant to paragraph (2) of this subdivision (r), an owner shall not deny a permanent tenant permission to install a private telephone, provided that such installation shall not cause undue economic hardship to the owner, nor shall an owner cause the removal of a pay telephone from the premises.

(4) The base dates for required services shall be:

(i) For housing accommodations subject to the RSL on June 30, 1974, for building-wide and individual dwelling unit services: May 31, 1968;

(ii) For housing accommodations subject to the RSL pursuant to section 421-a of the Real Property Tax Law, for building-wide and individual dwelling unit services: the date of issuance of the initial Certificate of Occupancy;

(iii) For housing accommodations subject to the RSL on June 30, 1971, and exempted thereafter as a result of a vacancy prior to June 30, 1974, for building-wide services: May 31, 1968; for individual dwelling unit services: May 29, 1974;

(iv) For dwelling units which became subject to the RSL on July 1, 1974, pursuant to section 423 of the Real Property Tax Law, for building-wide and individual unit services: May 29, 1974, except that for housing accommodations in the Riverton Apartments at East 138th Street, Manhattan, which became subject to the RSL on July 1, 1974, pursuant to an initial legal regulated rent date of June 30, 1973, for building-wide and individual dwelling unit services: June 30, 1973;

(v) For housing accommodations which are subject to this Code solely as a condition of receiving or continuing to receive benefits pursuant to section 11-243 (formerly J51-2.5) or 11-244 (formerly J51-5.0) of the Administrative Code of the City of New York, as amended, for building-wide and individual unit services: January 1, 1976, or the date of the issuance of a Certificate of Reasonable Cost, whichever is later;

(vi) For housing accommodations for which rents are established by governmental agencies pursuant to the PHFL, or which are first made subject to this Code pursuant to the PHFL, the building-wide and individual unit services which were required for approval in connection with the establishment of initial rents pursuant to the PHFL: the effective date of the initial rents;

(vii) For housing accommodations whose rentals were previously regulated under the PHFL or any other state or federal law, other than the RSL or the City Rent Law: the date such regulation ends;

(viii) For housing accommodations contained in class B Multiple Dwelling units including single room occupancy facilities, rooming-houses or rooming-units made subject to the ETPA on June 4, 1981, for building-wide and individual dwelling unit services: June 4, 1981;

(ix) For housing accommodations which are first made subject to this Code pursuant to article 7-C of the MDL, for building-wide and individual dwelling unit services: the effective date of the initial rents established by the Loft Board;

(x) For all other housing accommodations not subject to the RSL on June 30, 1974, which become subject to the RSL on or after July 1, 1974 pursuant to the ETPA, for building-wide and individual dwelling unit services: May 29, 1974;

(xi) A service as defined in paragraph (3) of this subdivision (r) for which there is or was a separate charge, shall not be subject to the provisions of this Code where no common ownership between the operator of such service and the owner exists or existed on the applicable base date, or at any time subsequent thereto, and such service is or was provided on the applicable base date and at all times thereafter by an independent contractor pursuant to a contract or agreement with the owner. Where, however, on the applicable base date or at any time subsequent thereto, there is or was a separate charge, and there is or was common ownership, directly or indirectly, between the operator of such service and the owner, or the service was provided by the owner, any increase, other than the charge provided in the initial agreement with a tenant to lease, rent or pay for such service, shall conform to the applicable rent guidelines rate. However, notwithstanding such common ownership, where such service was not provided primarily for the use of tenants in the building or building complex on the applicable base date or at any time subsequent thereto, such increases shall not be subject to any guidelines limitations.

(5) Each housing accommodation must be painted at least once every three years in compliance with title 27 of the Administrative Code of the City of New York (the "Housing Maintenance Code"). In no event shall a tenant be required to pay a painting deposit or to contribute to the cost of the painting except to the extent the owner agrees to provide services in connection with the painting which are not required, and the tenant consents in writing to pay therefor. Any painting deposit previously required shall be returned to the tenant on renewal of his or her lease.

(s) Documents. Records, books, accounts, correspondence, memoranda and other documents, and copies, including microphotographic copies, of any of the foregoing.

(t) Final Order. A final order shall be an order of a Rent Administrator not appealed to the Commissioner within the period authorized pursuant to section 2529.2 of this Title (Time For Filing A PAR), or an order of the Commissioner.

2520.7 Effective Date.

In accordance with the provisions of the State Administrative Procedure Act, this Code shall be effective May 1, 1987, and all amendments to this Code shall become effective in accordance with the State Administrative Procedure Act. Where implementation of a provision would require new or significantly revised filing procedures or notice requirements, the DHCR may postpone implementation of such provision, as required, for up to 180 days after the effective date of this Code, by an advisory opinion issued pursuant to section 2527.11 of this Title (Advisory Opinions and Operational Bulletins), which shall be available to the public on such effective date. Where such postponement is deemed necessary, current filing procedures, notice requirements, or forms, if any, may be utilized until revision thereof.

2520.8 Amendment or revocation.

Any provision of this Code may be amended or revoked at any time in accordance with the procedure set forth in Chapter 888 of the Laws of New York for the year 1985, or as otherwise provided by the State Administrative Procedure Act.

2520.9 Filing of amendments.

Such amendment or revocation shall be filed with the Secretary of State and shall take effect upon the date of filing unless otherwise specified therein or as otherwise provided by the State Administrative Procedure Act.

2520.10 Separability.

If any provision of this Code or the application of such provision to any persons or circumstances shall be held invalid, the validity of the remainder of this Code and the applicability of such provision to other persons or circumstances shall not be affected thereby.

2520.11 Applicability.

This Code shall apply to all or any class or classes of housing accommodations made subject to regulation pursuant to the RSL or any other provision of law, except the following housing accommodations for so long as they maintain the status indicated below:

(a) housing accommodations subject to the City Rent Law;

(b) housing accommodations owned, operated or leased by the United States, the State of New York, any political subdivision, agency or instrumentality thereof, any municipality or any public housing authority;

(c) housing accommodations for which rentals are fixed by the DHCR or HPD, unless, after the establishment of initial rents, the housing accommodations are made subject to the RSL pursuant to applicable law, or housing accommodations subject to the supervision of the DHCR or HPD under other provisions of law or the New York State Urban Development Corporation, or buildings aided by government insurance under any provision of the National Housing Act to the extent the RSL or any regulation or order issued thereunder is inconsistent with such Act. However, housing accommodations in buildings completed or substantially rehabilitated prior to January 1, 1974, and whose rentals were previously regulated under the PHFL or any other state or federal law, other than the RSL or the City Rent Law, shall become subject to the ETPA, the RSL, and this Code, upon the termination of such regulation. An owner of such housing accommodations shall not be eligible for a rent adjustment pursuant to section 2522.4(b) or (c) of this Title (Hardship), for a period of three years, where such owner would not qualify for such rent adjustment in the absence of a voluntary dissolution, termination, or reconstitution pursuant to such PHFL or other state or federal laws.

(d) buildings containing fewer than six housing accommodations on the date the building first became subject to the RSL, unless such buildings are otherwise subject to this Code pursuant to the RSL or other statutes and regulations; for the purposes of this subdivision (d), a building shall be deemed to contain six or more housing accommodations if it was part of a multiple family garden-type maisonette dwelling complex containing six or more housing accommodations having common facilities such as a sewer line, water main or heating plant and was operated as a unit under common ownership on the date the building or complex first became subject to the RSL, notwithstanding that Certificates of Occupancy were issued for portions thereof as one or two-family dwellings;

(e) housing accommodations in buildings completed or buildings substantially rehabilitated as family units on or after January 1, 1974, except such buildings which are made subject to this Code by provision of the RSL or any other statute;

(f) housing accommodations owned, operated, or leased or rented pursuant to governmental funding, by a hospital, convent, monastery, asylum, public institution, or college or school dormitory or any institution operated exclusively for charitable or educational purposes on a non-profit basis, and occupied by a tenant whose initial occupancy is contingent upon an affiliation with such institution; however, a housing accommodation occupied by a non-affiliated tenant shall be subject to the RSL and this Code;

(g) rooms or other housing accommodations in hotels where such housing accommodations (1) are used for transient occupancy; (2) were rented on May 31, 1968 for more than $350.00 per month or $88.00 per week; or (3) are contained in a hotel which was constructed after July 1, 1969;

(h) any motor court, or any part thereof, any trailer, or trailer space used exclusively for transient occupancy or any part thereof; or any tourist home serving transient guests exclusively, or any part thereof. The term tourist home shall mean a rooming house which caters primarily to transient guests and is known in the community as a tourist home;

(i) non-housekeeping, furnished housing accommodations, located within a single dwelling unit not used as a rooming or boarding house, but only if:

(1) no more than two tenants for whom rent is paid (husband and wife being considered one tenant for this purpose), who are not members of the owner's immediate family, live in such dwelling unit; and

(2) the remaining portion of such dwelling unit is occupied by the owner or his or her immediate family; provided that this exemption shall not apply where the tenancy commenced prior to July 1, 1971;

(j) housing accommodations in buildings operated exclusively for charitable purposes on a non-profit basis;

(k) housing accommodations which are not occupied by the tenant, not including subtenants or occupants, as his or her primary residence as determined by a court of competent jurisdiction;

(l) housing accommodations contained in buildings owned as cooperatives or condominiums on or before June 30, 1974; or thereafter, as provided in section 352-eeee of the General Business Law in accordance with section 2522.5(h) of this Title (Leases for Housing Accommodations in Cooperative or Condominium Owned Buildings);

(m) housing accommodations occupied by domestic servants, superintendents, caretakers, managers or other employees to whom the space is provided as part or all of their compensation without payment of rent and who are employed for the purpose of rendering services in connection with the premises of which the housing accommodation is a part;

(n) housing accommodations used exclusively for professional, commercial, or other non-residential purposes;

(o) housing accommodations in buildings completed or substantially rehabilitated as family units on or after January 1, 1974 or located in a building containing less than six housing accommodations, and which were originally made subject to regulation solely as a condition of receiving tax benefits pursuant to section 11-243 (formerly J51-2.5) or section 11-244 (formerly J51-5.0) of the Administrative Code of the City of New York, as amended, or article XVIII of the PHFL; and thereafter receipt of such tax benefits has concluded pursuant to these sections or article XVIII, and:

(1) the housing accommodations which were subject to the RSL pursuant to section 11-243 (formerly J51-2.5) or section 11-244 (formerly J51-5.0) or PHFL article XVIII became vacant; or

(2) for housing accommodations which received benefits pursuant to section 11-243 (formerly J51-2.5) or section 11-244 (formerly J51-5.0) or article XVIII of the PHFL, each lease and each renewal

thereof of the tenant in residence at the time of the expiration of the tax benefit period includes a notice, in at least twelve point type informing such tenant that the housing accommodation shall become deregulated upon the expiration of the last lease or rental agreement entered into during the tax benefit period, and states the approximate date on which such tax benefit period is scheduled to expire.

(p) housing accommodations in buildings completed or substantially rehabilitated as family units on or after January 1, 1974 or located in a building containing less than six housing accommodations, and which were originally made subject to regulation solely as a condition of receiving tax benefits pursuant to section 421-a of the Real Property Tax Law, as amended, and:

(1) the housing accommodations which were subject to the RSL pursuant to section 421-a became vacant; or

(2) for housing accommodations which first became subject to the rent stabilization requirements of section 421-a after July 3, 1984, where each lease and each renewal thereof of the tenant in occupancy at the time the period of tax exemption pursuant to section 421-a expires, contains a notice in at least twelve point type informing such tenant that the housing accommodation shall become deregulated upon the expiration of the last lease or rental agreement entered into during the tax benefit period and states the approximate date on which such tax benefit period is scheduled to expire.

(q) housing accommodations which would otherwise be subject to rent regulation solely by reason of the provisions of article 7-C of the MDL requiring rent regulation, but which are exempted from such provisions pursuant to sections 286(6) and 286(12) of the MDL;

(r) housing accommodations exempted pursuant to any other provision of law.

2520.12 Effect of this Code on leases and other rental agreements.

The provisions of any lease or other rental agreement shall remain in force pursuant to the terms thereof, except insofar as those provisions are inconsistent with the ETPA, the RSL or this Code, and in such event such provisions shall be void and unenforceable. For housing accommodations made subject to the RSL and this Code pursuant to section 2520.11(c) of this Part (Termination of Other Regulation), where such leases or rental agreements are so inconsistent as to render them ineffective in defining the rights and duties of tenants and owners, the DHCR may order the provision of new leases consistent with the ETPA, the RSL and this Code. No renewal lease or vacancy lease offered to a tenant shall contain any right of cancellation or eviction by the owner during the term thereof except as provided for by the ETPA, the RSL or this Code.

2520.13 Waiver of benefit void.

An agreement by the tenant to waive the benefit of any provision of the RSL or this Code is void; provided, however, that based upon a negotiated settlement between the parties and with the approval of the DHCR, or a court of competent jurisdiction where a tenant is represented by counsel, a tenant may withdraw, with prejudice, any complaint pending before the DHCR. Such settlement shall not be binding upon any subsequent tenant, except to the extent that the complaint being settled is subject to the time limitations set forth in the RSL and this Code.

PART 2521 - LEGAL REGISTERED AND REGULATED RENTS

Section 2521.1 Initial legal registered rents for housing accommodations.

(a)(1) For housing accommodations which on March 31, 1984, were subject to the City Rent Law, and became vacant after that date, and which are no longer subject to the City Rent Law, and are rented thereafter subject to the RSL, the initial legal registered rent shall be the rent agreed to by the owner and the tenant and reserved in a lease or provided for in a rental agreement subject to the provisions of this Code, provided that such rent is registered with the DHCR pursuant to Part 2528 of this Title (Registration of Housing Accommodations), and subject to a tenant's right to a Fair Market Rent Appeal to adjust such rent pursuant to section 2522.3 of this Title.

(2) For housing accommodations which on March 31, 1984 were subject to the penalties provided in former section YY51-4.0 of the Administrative Code of the City of New York, and which became vacant thereafter, the initial legal registered rent for the first rent stabilized tenant shall be the rent established by the DHCR for the prior tenant, increased by the guidelines rate of rent adjustments applicable to the new lease plus such other rent increases as are authorized pursuant to section 2522.4 of this Title (Adjustment of Legal Regulated Rent), and shall not be subject to a Fair Market Rent Appeal pursuant to section 2522.3 of this Title.

(b) For those housing accommodations for which the tenant files a timely challenge in accordance with section 2526.1(a)(3)(ii) of this Title (Overcharge Penalties) to the initial legal registered rent, such rent shall be determined by the DHCR as follows:

(1) for housing accommodations other than in hotels, the rent charged and paid on April 1, 1980, plus the lawful increases charged and paid up to March 31, 1984; for housing accommodations not required to be registered by June 30, 1984, the rent charged and paid four years prior to the date the housing accommodation was first required to be registered plus such lawful increases and adjustments charged and paid up to the date immediately prior to the registration date as determined by the DHCR.

(2) for housing accommodations located in hotels, the rent charged and paid on April 1, 1980 plus the lawful increases charged and paid up to March 31, 1984; or for housing accommodations not required to be registered by June 30, 1984, the rent charged and paid four years prior to the date the housing accommodation was first required to be registered plus such

lawful increases and adjustments charged and paid up to the date immediately prior to the registration date as determined by the DHCR, provided, however, that with respect to any vacancy lease or vacancy rental agreement entered into prior to August 15, 1983, following a voluntary vacancy, the initial legal registered rent shall be the rent charged and paid upon such renting, plus subsequent lawful increases and adjustments charged and paid from April 1, 1980, up to March 31, 1984. If any vacant housing accommodation is rented on or after August 15, 1983, the initial legal registered rent shall be the lawful rent paid by the most recent prior tenant plus any subsequent lawful increases and adjustments, or if there has never been a prior tenant, the initial legal registered rent shall be the rent paid by the most recent hotel occupant, plus any subsequent lawful increases and adjustments.

(c) For all other housing accommodations subject to the RSL where a timely challenge was not made as provided for in subdivision (b) of this section, the initial legal registered rent shall be:

(1) for those housing accommodations required to be registered by June 30, 1984, the rent charged and paid as of April 1, 1984; or

(2) for those housing accommodations not required to be registered by June 30, 1984, the rent charged and paid on the date the housing accommodation became subject to the registration requirements of the DHCR.

(d)(1) Notwithstanding the provisions of subdivision (c) of this section, the initial legal registered rent for a housing accommodation for which an overcharge complaint or a Fair Market Rent Appeal was filed by a tenant prior to April 1, 1984, and not finally determined prior thereto, shall be the April 1, 1984 rent as subsequently determined by the DHCR. Such determination will be based upon the law or Code provision in effect on March 31, 1984.

(2) Upon determination of the initial legal registered rent in paragraph (1), legal regulated rents subsequent to April 1, 1984 shall be determined in accordance with

section 2521.2(a) of this Part (Legal Regulated Rents For Housing Accommodations).

(e) The initial legal registered rent for a housing accommodation first made subject to the RSL and this Code pursuant to article 7-C of the MDL shall be the rent established by the Loft Board under section 286(4) of the MDL applicable to a lease offered pursuant to MDL section 286(3). Such rent shall not be subject to the proceedings described in section 2522.3 of this Title (Fair Market Rent Appeal). Notwithstanding that the rent charged and paid during the first lease term may have been less than such initial legal registered rent, the owner may request that the next lease rental be the initial legal registered rent plus the allowable increase established by the Rent Guidelines Board, and such other rent increases as are authorized pursuant to section 2522.4 of this Title (Adjustment of Legal Regulated Rent).

(f) Notwithstanding the provisions of any outstanding lease or other rental agreement, the initial legal registered rent for a housing accommodation in a multiple dwelling for which a loan is made under the PHFL shall be the initial rent established pursuant to such law. Such rent, whether or not the housing accommodation was previously subject to the RSL, shall not be subject to the proceeding described in section 2522.3 of this Title (Fair Market Rent Appeal). Such rent for housing accommodations occupied prior to the granting of the loan made pursuant to the PHFL shall take effect on the date specified in the order establishing the rent. Notwithstanding any other provision of the RSL or this Code, the owner of such housing accommodation shall offer any tenant in occupancy on such effective date or upon initial occupancy a one or two year lease at the tenant's option at such rent, which offer shall be made as soon as practicable after such rent is established, whether or not the rent has taken or is then permitted to take effect; and refusal of such tenant to sign such lease, at such rent, and otherwise upon the same terms and conditions as the expiring lease, if any, shall constitute grounds for an action or proceeding to evict and recover possession of the housing accommodation provided however, that following the tenant's receipt of the offer of such lease at such rent as lawfully established, a tenant in occupancy on such date shall be allowed 30 days to sign such lease and, if during such 30 day period, such tenant gives the owner written notice of an intention to terminate such tenancy and pays the rent established pursuant to law for such month and for any extended period, the tenant shall not be required to surrender the housing accommodation until 60 days after receipt of such offer. Notwithstanding that the rent charged and paid during the first lease term may have been less than such initial legal registered rent, the owner may request that the next lease rental be the initial legal registered rent plus the allowable increase established by the Rent Guidelines Board.

(g) Notwithstanding any other provision of this Code, the initial legal registered rent for a housing accommodation first made subject to the RSL and this Code pursuant to article XIV of the PHFL or section 2429 of article 8 of the Public Authorities Law shall be the rent established pursuant to law which reflects the improvements or rehabilitation and shall be subject to subsequent adjustment by the DHCR. Such rent shall not be subject to the proceedings described in section 2522.3 of this Title (Fair Market Rent Appeal). Notwithstanding any other provision of the RSL or this Code: the owner of such housing accommodation shall offer a tenant in occupancy who first became subject to the RSL and this Code on the effective date of such rent a one or two year lease at the tenant's option at such rent, which offer shall be made as soon as practicable after such rent is effective; and refusal of such tenant to sign such lease at such rent, and otherwise upon the same terms and conditions as the expiring lease, if any, shall constitute grounds for an action or proceeding to evict and recover possession of the housing accommodation, provided, however, that following tenant's receipt of the offer of such lease at such rent, a tenant in occupancy on such effective date shall be allowed 30 days to sign such lease and, if during such 30 day period, such tenant gives the owner written notice of an intention to terminate such tenancy and pays the rent established pursuant to law while in occupancy, the tenant shall not be required to surrender the housing accommodation until 60 days after receipt of such offer.

Notwithstanding that the rent charged and paid during the first lease term may have been less than such initial legal registered rent, the owner may request that the next lease rental be the initial legal registered rent plus the allowable increase established by the Rent Guidelines Board.

(h) If a housing accommodation is rehabilitated pursuant to either article XIV of the PHFL or section 2429 of article 8 of the Public Authorities Law, and article XV of the PHFL, the provisions in subdivision (f) shall apply, rather than the provisions of subdivision (g), if HPD elects to establish rents for the housing accommodation pursuant to article XV of the PHFL.

(i) The initial legal registered rent for a housing accommodation constructed pursuant to section 421-a of the Real Property Tax Law shall be the initial adjusted monthly rent charged and paid but not higher than the rent approved by HPD pursuant to such section for the housing accommodation or the lawful rent charged and paid on April 1, 1984, whichever is later.

(j) The initial legal registered rent for housing accommodations subject this Code solely as a condition of receiving or continuing to receive benefits pursuant to section 11-243 (formerly J51-2.5) or 11-244 (formerly J51-5.0) of the Administrative Code, as amended, shall be the rent charged the initial rent stabilized tenant or the lawful rent charged and paid on April 1, 1984, whichever is later, and shall not be subject to a Fair Market Rent Appeal pursuant to section 2522.3 of this Title. However, as to any housing accommodation which previously received tax benefits pursuant to section 11-243 (formerly J51-2.5) or 11-244 (formerly J51-5.0), was not covered by the provisions of the RSL on June 18, 1985, and was made subject to such law by the provisions of Chapters 288 and 289 of the Laws of New York for the year 1985 (as amended), the initial legal registered rent shall be the rent charged and paid on May 30, 1985, or the maximum rent which could have been charged if the housing accommodation had been continuously subject to the RSL for the entire tenancy of the tenant in occupancy on May 30, 1985, whichever is greater.

(k) Notwithstanding the provisions of the RSL or any other provision of this Code, the initial legal registered rent upon completion of the rehabilitation of a class B multiple dwelling, class A multiple dwelling used for single room occupancy purposes, lodging house or a substantially vacant building intended to be used after rehabilitation for single room occupancy purposes for which a loan is made for such rehabilitation on or after September 1, 1985, under articles VIII or VIII-A of the PHFL shall be the initial rent established by HPD pursuant to such law. Such rent, whether or not the housing accommodation was previously subject to the RSL, shall not be subject to the proceeding described in section 2522.3 of this Title (Fair Market Rent Appeal). Such rent shall take effect on the date specified in the order establishing the rent. Notwithstanding the provisions of the RSL or any other provision of this Code, the owner of such housing accommodation shall offer any tenant in occupancy on such effective date a 1 or 2 year lease, at the tenant's option, at such rent, which offer shall be made as soon as practicable after such rent is established. Refusal of such tenant to sign such lease at such rent, and otherwise upon the same terms and conditions as the expiring lease, if any, shall constitute grounds for an action or proceeding to evict and recover possession of the housing accommodation provided, however, that following the tenant's receipt of the offer of such lease at such rent as lawfully established, a tenant in occupancy on such date shall be allowed 30 days to sign such lease and, if during such 30 day period, such tenant gives the owner written notice of an intention to terminate such tenancy and pay the rent established pursuant to law for such month and for any extended period, the tenant shall not be required to surrender the housing accommodation until 60 days after receipt of such lease offer. Notwithstanding that the rent charged and paid during the first lease term may have been less than such initial legal registered rent, the owner may request that the next lease rental be the initial legal registered rent plus the allowable increase established by the Rent Guidelines Board, and such other rent increases as are authorized pursuant to section 2522.4 of this Title (Adjustment of Legal Regulated Rent).

(1) For housing accommodations whose rentals were previously regulated under the PHFL, or any other state or federal law, other than the RSL or the City Rent Law, upon the termination of such regulation, the initial legal registered rent shall be the rent charged to and paid by the tenant in occupancy on the date such regulation ends. For housing accommodations which are vacant on the date the building first became subject to the RSL and this Code, such rent shall be the rent charged and paid by the most recent tenant, in addition to rental subsidies, if any, which shall be subject to vacancy guidelines increases, and shall not be subject to a Fair Market Rent Appeal pursuant to section 2522.3 of this Title.

(m) Notwithstanding any other provision of this Code, except as provided in paragraph (2) below, governmental agencies or public benefit corporations may enter into an agreement with the DHCR, which shall be incorporated into an order of the DHCR, setting forth the conditions under which:

(1) projects receiving assistance or financing from such agencies may register higher and lower initial legal rents for units subject to occupancy and rent restrictions by such agencies, which rents may then be adjusted pursuant to the RSL and this Code, and shall not be subject to the proceedings described in section 2522.3 of this Title (Fair Market Rent Appeals); or

(2) projects whose rentals were previously regulated under the PHFL or any other state or federal law, other than the RSL or the City Rent Law, upon the date when such regulation ends, may register higher and lower initial legal rents for units which have been subject to occupancy and rent restrictions pursuant to such laws, which rents may then be adjusted pursuant to the RSL and this Code, and shall not be subject to the proceedings described in section 2522.3 of this Title (Fair Market Rent Appeals). Where the DHCR was the agency regulating rentals pursuant to the PHFL, such terms and conditions shall be incorporated into an order of the DHCR.

Such agreement or order shall also set forth the conditions under which the higher and lower legal regulated rents may be charged, with due consideration of equities as set forth in section 2522.7 of this Title (Consideration of Equities).

2521.2 Legal regulated rents for housing accommodations.

(a) The legal regulated rent shall be the initial legal registered rent first established pursuant to section 2521.1 of this Part (Initial Legal Registered Rents for Housing Accommodations), and thereafter shall be the initial legal registered rent as it may be adjusted pursuant to the RSL and this Code, or the rent stated in the annual registration statement filed four years prior to the most recent registration statement as adjusted pursuant to the RSL and this Code, whichever is later.

(b) Where the legal regulated rent is established and a rent lower than the legal regulated rent is charged and paid by the tenant, upon vacancy of such tenant, the legal regulated rent previously established plus the most recent applicable guidelines increases, plus such other rent increases as are authorized pursuant to section 2522.4 of this Title (Adjustment of Legal Regulated Rent), may be charged a new tenant.

2521.3 Classification of buildings.

(a) Upon application by a tenant or owner, the DHCR shall issue an order determining a building's classification based upon the services provided and other relevant factors. Except as provided in subdivisions (c) and (d) of this section, if it is determined that such building is not a hotel, the DHCR shall classify the building as an apartment building unless the owner restores sufficient services to maintain a hotel classification in accordance with subdivision (b) of this section. If the building is reclassified, then the housing accommodations therein shall thereafter be subject to the provisions of this Code applicable to apartment buildings, at the legal regulated rent for each housing accommodation as determined by the order of the DHCR, plus lawful increases and adjustments allowed pursuant to this Code. In order for an owner to retain or continue the building's classification as a hotel, he or she must provide, in addition to any other services he or she is or was providing pursuant to section

2520.6(r) of this Title (Required Services), all four of the following services:
  (1) Maid service, consisting of general house-cleaning at a frequency of at least once a week;
  (2) Linen service, consisting of providing clean linens at a frequency of at least once a week;
  (3) Furniture and furnishings, including at a minimum a bed, lamps, storage facilities for clothing, chair and mirror in a bedroom; such furniture to be maintained by the hotel owner in reasonable condition; and
  (4) Lobby staffed 24 hours a day, seven days a week by at least one employee.

(b) A building's classification as a hotel will not be retained or continued where the DHCR determines that 51% of the permanent tenants are not receiving maid and linen service, except that all tenants receiving such services shall be entitled to receive the services for the duration of their occupancy. Where an owner is providing maid and linen service to 51% of the permanent tenants and the owner wishes to maintain the building's classification as a hotel, the owner shall be afforded 90 days to restore all four hotel services described above, without any additional rent increase for such services, to all of the building's permanent tenants, except that those tenants whose housing accommodations were rented to them as apartment (not hotel) housing accommodations shall have the option of rejecting restoration of hotel services and be subject to the RSL, pursuant to the provisions of this Code applicable to apartment buildings, until they vacate, at which time the owner shall be required to restore hotel services to the housing accommodations.

(c) Notwithstanding the provisions of subdivision (a) of this section, single-room occupancy facilities such as single room occupancy hotels or rooming houses, as defined in the MDL, shall not be subject to reclassification pursuant to this section. However, such housing accommodations shall be included in the definition of hotel as set forth in section 2520.6(b) of this Title for all other purposes of this Code, except that the 4 minimum services enumerated in such section shall not be required to be provided unless such services were provided on the applicable base dates pursuant to section 2520.6(r)(4) of this Title (Required Services).

(d) Notwithstanding the provisions of subdivision (a) of this section, the DHCR may decline to reclassify a hotel to apartment building status if it finds that the owner has reduced any of the 4 hotel services listed in such subdivision (a) for the purpose of reclassification of the building.

PART 2522 - RENT ADJUSTMENTS

Section 2522.1 Legal regulated rent adjustments.

Legal regulated rents may be increased or decreased only as hereinafter specified.

2522.2 Effective date of adjustment of legal regulated rents.

The legal regulated rent shall be adjusted effective the first rent payment date occurring 30 days after the filing of the application, unless otherwise set forth in the order, or as set forth in a Notice of Eligibility pursuant to section 2522.4(a)(3)(ii) of this Part (Adjustment of Legal Regulated Rent), or on the effective date of a lease or other rental agreement providing for the Rent Guidelines Board annual rate of adjustments. No rent adjustment may take place during a lease term unless a clause in the lease authorizes such increase.

2522.3 Fair Market Rent Appeal.

(a) Except as provided in section 2521.1 (a)(2) of this Title (Initial Legal Registered Rents), an appeal of the Initial Legal Registered Rent on the ground that it exceeds the Fair Market Rent for the housing accommodation may be filed with the DHCR by the tenant of a housing accommodation which was subject to the City Rent Law on December 31, 1973. If the housing accommodation was registered in accordance with Part 2528 of this Title (Initial Registration), this right is limited to the first tenant taking occupancy on or after April 1, 1984, except where such tenant had vacated the housing accommodation prior to the service by the owner of the Notice of Initial Legal Registered Rent as required by section 2523.1 of this Title. In such event, any subsequent tenant in occupancy shall also have a right to file a Fair Market Rent Appeal until the owner mails the required Notice and 90 days shall have elapsed without the filing of an appeal by a tenant continuing in occupancy during said 90 day period. Once a Fair Market Rent Appeal is filed, no subsequent tenant may file such appeal. Notwithstanding the above, where the first tenant taking occupancy after December 31, 1973, of a housing accommodation previously subject to the City Rent Law, was served with the notice required by section 26 of the former Code of the Rent Stabilization Association of New York City, Inc., the time within which such tenant may file a Fair Market Rent Appeal is limited to 90 days after such notice was mailed to the tenant by the owner by certified mail.

(b) The tenant need only allege in such appeal:

(1) that the initial legal registered rent is in excess of the Fair Market Rent; and

(2) such facts which, to the best of his or her information and belief, support such allegation.

(c) Such appeal shall be dismissed where:

(1) the housing accommodation was subject to the City Rent Law prior to July 1, 1971, and the initial legal registered rent does not exceed the maximum rent as calculated pursuant to the City Rent Law for the period commencing January 1, 1974 and ending December 31, 1975, whether or not the housing accommodation was subject to the City Rent Law on that date, plus the appropriate guidelines allowance permissible for renewal leases pursuant to Guidelines Board Order No. 6 issued June 28, 1974 and effective July 1, 1974, and Order No. 6C, issued February 7, 1975, and effective July 1, 1974, for any lease or other rental agreement commencing on or after January 1, 1974; or

(2) the appeal is filed more than 90 days after the certified mailing to the tenant of the Initial Apartment Registration, together with the Notice pursuant to section 2523.1 of this Title (Notice of Initial Legal Registered Rent).

(d) The order shall direct the affected owner to make

the refund of any excess rent to the tenant in cash, check or money order, and to the extent the present owner is liable for all or any part of the refund, such present owner may credit such refund against future rents over a period not in excess of six months. If the refund exceeds the total rent due for six months, the tenant at his or her option may continue to abate his or her rent until the refund is fully credited, or request the present owner to refund any balance outstanding at the end of such six month period.

(e) In determining Fair Market Rent Appeals, consideration shall be given to the applicable guidelines promulgated for such purposes by the Rent Guidelines Board and to rents generally prevailing for substantially similar housing accommodations in buildings located in the same area as the housing accommodation involved. The rents for these comparable housing accommodations may be considered where such rents are:

(1) Legal regulated rents, for which the time to file a Fair Market Rent Appeal has expired and no Fair Market Rent Appeal is then pending, or the Fair Market Rent Appeal has been finally determined, charged pursuant to a lease commencing within a 4 year period prior to, or a one year period subsequent to, the commencement date of the initial lease for the housing accommodation involved; and

(2) At the owner's option, market rents in effect for other comparable housing accommodations on the date of the initial lease for the housing accommodation involved as submitted by the owner.

(f) Where the rents of the comparable housing accommodations being considered are legal regulated rents, for which the time to file a Fair Market Rent Appeal has expired, and such rents are charged pursuant to a lease ending more than 1 year prior to the commencement date of the initial lease for the subject housing accommodation, such rents shall be updated by guidelines increases for 1 year renewal leases, commencing with the expiration of the initial lease for the comparable housing accommodation to a date within 12 months prior to the renting of the housing accommodation involved.

2522.4 Adjustment of legal regulated rent.

(a) Increased space and services, new equipment, new furniture or furnishings; major capital improvements; other adjustments.

> (1) An owner is entitled to a rent increase where there has been a substantial increase, other than an increase for which an adjustment may be claimed pursuant to paragraph (2) of this subdivision, of dwelling space or an increase in the services, or installation of new equipment or improvements, or new furniture or furnishings, provided in or to the tenant's housing accommodation, on written tenant consent to the rent increase. In the case of vacant housing accommodations, tenant consent shall not be required.
>
> (2) An owner may file an application to increase the legal regulated rents of the building or building complex on forms prescribed by the DHCR, which the DHCR shall serve upon all affected tenants, on one or more of the following grounds:
>
>> (i) There has been a major capital improvement, including an installation, which must meet all of the following criteria:
>>
>>> (a) deemed depreciable under the Internal Revenue Code, other than for ordinary repairs; and
>>>
>>> (b) is for the operation, preservation, and maintenance of the structure; and
>>>
>>> (c) is an improvement to the building or to the building complex which inures directly or indirectly to the benefit of all tenants, and which includes the same work performed in all similar components of the building or building complex, unless the owner can satisfactorily demonstrate to the DHCR that certain of such similar components did not require improvement; and
>>>
>>> (d) the item being replaced meets the requirements set forth in the useful life schedule, except with DHCR approval of a waiver. Pursuant to sec-

tion 2527.11 of this Title (Advisory Opinions and Operational Bulletins), the DHCR shall issue a useful life schedule in accordance with manufacturing industry standards, which shall also set forth the conditions under which a useful life requirement may be waived.

(ii) There has been other necessary work performed in connection with, and directly related to a major capital improvement, which may be included in the computation of an increase in the legal regulated rent only if such other necessary work was completed within a reasonable time after the completion of the major capital improvement to which it relates. Such other necessary work must:

(a) improve, restore or preserve the quality of the structure; and

(b) have been completed subsequent to, or contemporaneously with, the completion of the work for the major capital improvement.

(iii) With approval by the DHCR, there has been an increase in services or improvement, other than repairs, on a building-wide basis, which the owner can demonstrate are necessary in order to comply with a specific requirement of law.

(iv) With approval by the DHCR, there have been other improvements made or services provided to the building or building complex, other than those specified in subparagraphs (i)-(iii) of this paragraph (2), with the express consent of the tenants in occupancy of at least 75 per cent of the housing accommodations.

(3) An owner who files a complete application with the DHCR for an increase authorized pursuant to subparagraph (i) of paragraph (2) of this subdivision which meets the requirements of such subparagraph may begin to collect such increase in the legal regulated rent prior to the issuance of an order granting the increase provided that:

(i) to be complete, such application must:

(a) contain an itemized list of the work performed;

(b) contain a certification of the cost of such work from the contractor, architect, certified public accountant, engineer or governmental agency; and that the item meets the requirements set forth in the useful life schedule, or a copy of a DHCR approval of a waiver of such useful life requirement is attached;

(c) contain proof of payment for such work the cost of which is certified pursuant to clause (b) above;

(d) contain the owner's sworn affidavit as to the completion of the installation or improvement in accordance with the itemization list and the certified costs, that all applicable governmental codes and regulations have been complied with, the installation or improvement has been properly performed in a workmanlike manner, and the truthfulness of all information submitted with the application;

(e) contain copies of all necessary governmental agency approvals or self-certification by a duly licensed architect or engineer as may be permitted by such governmental agency; and

(f) be for an improvement or installation of an item which is included on the following Schedule, or such other improvement or installation to the building or building complex for the operation, preservation and maintenance of the structure as may be deemed necessary by the DHCR for the continued viability of the building as specified in an Operational Bulletin issued pursuant to section 2527.11 of this Title.

SCHEDULE OF MAJOR CAPITAL IMPROVEMENTS

1. AIR CONDITIONER:

—new central system; or individual units set in sleeves in the exterior wall of every housing accommodation; or, air conditioning circuits and outlets in each living room and/or bedroom (SEE REWIRING).

2. ALUMINUM SIDING:

—installed in a uniform manner on all exposed sides of the building (SEE RESURFACING).

3. BATHROOM MODERNIZATION:

—complete renovation including new sinks, toilets, bathtubs, and/or showers and all required trims in every housing accommodation.

4. BOILER AND/OR BURNER:

—new unit(s) including electrical work and additional components needed for the installation.

5. BOILER ROOM:

—new room where none existed before; or enlargement of existing one to accommodate new boiler.

6. CATWALK:

—complete replacement.

7. CHIMNEY:

—complete replacement, or new one where none existed before, including additional components needed for the installation.

8. COURTYARD AND WALKWAYS:

—concrete resurfacing of entire original area within the property lines of the premises.

9. DOORS:

—new lobby front entrance and/or vestibule doors; or entrance to every housing accommodation, or fireproof doors for public hallways, basement, boiler room and roof bulkhead.

10. ELEVATOR UPGRADING:

—including new controllers and selectors; or new electronic dispatch overlay system; or new elevator where none existed before, including additional components needed for the installation.

11. FIRE ESCAPES:

—complete new replacement including new landings.

12. GAS HEATING UNITS:

—new individual units with connecting pipes to every housing accommodation.

13. HOT WATER HEATER:

—new unit for central heating system.

14. INCINERATOR UPGRADING:

—including a new scrubber.

15. INTERCOM SYSTEM:

—new replacement; or one where none existed before, with automatic door locks and pushbutton speakerbox and/or telephone communication, including security locks on all entrances to the building.

16. KITCHEN MODERNIZATION:

—complete renovation including new sinks, counter tops and cabinets in every housing accommodation.

17. MAILBOXES:

—new replacements and relocated from outer vestibule to an area behind locked doors to increase security.

18. PARAPET:

—complete replacement.

19. POINTING AND WATERPROOFING:

—as necessary on exposed sides of the building.

20. REPIPING:

—new hot and/or cold water risers, returns, and branches to fixtures in every housing accommodation, including shower bodies, and/or new hot and/or new cold water overhead mains, with all necessary valves in basement.

21. RESURFACING OF EXTERIOR WALLS:

—consisting of brick or masonry facing on entire area of all exposed sides of the building.

22. REWIRING:

—new copper risers and feeders extending from property box in basement to every housing accommodation; must be of sufficient capacity (220 volts) to accommodate the installation of air conditioner circuits in living room and/or bedroom.

23. ROOF:

—complete replacement or roof cap on existing roof installed after thorough scraping and leveling as necessary.

Rent Stabilization Code

24. SOLAR HEATING SYSTEM:

—new central system, including additional components needed for the system.

25. STRUCTURAL STEEL:

—complete new replacement of all beams including footing and foundation.

26. TELEVISION SYSTEM:

—new security monitoring system including additional components needed for the system.

27. WASTE COMPACTOR:

—new installation(s) serving entire building.

28. WASTE COMPACTOR ROOM:

—new room where none existed before.

29. WATER TANK:

—new installation(s) serving entire building.

30. WINDOWS:

—new aluminum framed windows. Wood framed windows allowed only for landmark buildings.

(ii) the owner or his or her representative has personally filed the completed application with the DHCR, the DHCR has served such application upon all affected tenants, the owner has thereafter received a Notice of Eligibility from the DHCR stating that the application is complete, and the DHCR has served such Notice of Eligibility upon such tenants. For the purposes of an application filed pursuant to this paragraph (3), the DHCR shall, within 90 days of such filing, fully review such application to insure completion pursuant to subparagraph (i) and shall conduct inspections where appropriate, and thereafter shall provide an owner with a Notice of Eligibility stating that the application is complete, and the effective date of the Notice for the purposes of collecting the increase, or a Notice of Deficiency determining that the application is incomplete, and setting forth the grounds for such determination. A Notice of Eligibility shall be subject to a tenant challenge and subsequent audit by the DHCR. A tenant may file a challenge to the owner's eligibility to collect the rent increase within 60 days after the DHCR has served the tenant with a copy of the Notice of Eligibility by setting forth the grounds of his or her challenge in an answer filed with the DHCR.

(iii) an owner, who on the effective date of this Code, has an application pending before the DHCR for an increase pursuant to subparagraph (i) of paragraph (2) of this subdivision (a), may begin to collect such increase upon compliance with the procedure set forth in subparagraphs (i) and (ii) of this paragraph (3), provided that the retroactive collectibility of the increase shall be no earlier than the first rent payment date one year prior to the filing of an application completed pursuant to such subparagraphs (i) and (ii), and shall not be collected until the DHCR has issued an order granting the increase.

(iv) an owner who is found by the DHCR to have knowingly filed a false affidavit pursuant to clause (d) of subparagraph (i) of this paragraph (3) shall not be entitled to file any future application under this paragraph, and shall be denied the increase for which the owner submitted the application. Any increased rent shall be returned to the tenant and, in addition to any penalty contained in any other provision of law, the DHCR may also impose treble damages for the rent increase collected pursuant to the Notice of Eligibility described in subparagraph (ii) of this paragraph (3).

(4) The increase in the monthly stabilization rent for the affected housing accommodations when authorized pursuant to paragraph (1) of this subdivision (a) shall be 1/40th of the total cost including installation, but excluding finance charges; and any increase pursuant to paragraphs (2) and (3) shall be 1/60th of the total cost including installation but excluding finance charges as allocated in accordance with paragraph (12) of this subdivision (a). For increases pursuant to subparagraphs (iii) and (iv) of paragraph (2) of this subdivision (a), in the discretion of the DHCR, an

appropriate charge may be imposed in lieu of an amortization charge when an amortization charge is insignificant or inappropriate.

(5) Such increases shall not be collectible during the term of a lease then in effect, unless a specific provision in the tenant's lease authorizes an increase during its term pursuant to an order issued by the DHCR, except that increases pursuant to paragraph (1) of this subdivision (a) may be collected upon installation.

(6) The determination of the appropriate adjustment of a legal regulated rent shall take into consideration all factors bearing on the equities involved, subject to the general limitation that the adjustment can be put into effect without dislocation and hardship inconsistent with the purposes of the RSL, and including as a factor a return of the actual cost to the owner, exclusive of interest or other carrying charges, and the increase in the rental value of the housing accommodations.

(7) Except for applications made pursuant to paragraph (3) of this subdivision (a), an owner may apply for the DHCR's advisory prior opinion pursuant to section 2527.11 of this Title (Advisory Opinions and Operational Bulletins), as to whether the proposed work qualifies for an increase in the legal regulated rent.

(8) No increase pursuant to paragraphs (2) and (3) of this subdivision (a) shall be granted by the DHCR, unless an application is filed no later than 2 years after the completion of the installation or improvement unless the applicant can demonstrate that the application could not be made within 2 years due to delay, beyond the applicant's control, in obtaining required governmental approvals for which the applicant has applied within such 2 year period. No increase pursuant to paragraphs (2) and (3) of this subdivision (a) shall be granted within the useful life of an improvement or installation for which an increase was previously granted except with prior DHCR approval for required improvements. In addition, an increase pursuant to paragraphs (2) and (3)

of this subdivision (a) shall not be collectible from a tenant to whom there has been issued a currently valid senior citizen rent increase exemption pursuant to section 26-509 of the Administrative Code of the City of New York, to the extent such increase causes the legal regulated rent of the housing accommodation to exceed one-third of the aggregate disposable income of all members of the household residing in the housing accommodation. The collection of any increase in the legal regulated rent for any housing accommodation pursuant to paragraphs (2) and (3) of this subdivision (a) shall not exceed six percent in any year from the effective date of the Notice of Eligibility or of the order granting the increase over the rent set forth in the schedule of gross rents with collectibility of any dollar excess above said sum to be spread forward in similar increments and added to the legal regulated rent as established or set in future years. In no event shall more than one six percent increase in the legal regulated rent pursuant to paragraphs (2) and (3) be collected in the same year for the permanent, prospective rent increase, and no more than an additional six percent increase for the temporary retroactive portion of such rent increase.

(9) An increase for an improvement made pursuant to paragraphs (2) and (3) of this subdivision (a) shall not be granted by the DHCR to the extent that, after a plan for the conversion of a building to cooperative or condominium ownership is declared effective, such improvement is paid for out of the cash reserve fund of the cooperative corporation or condominium association. Nothing in this paragraph (9) shall prevent an owner from applying for, and the DHCR from granting an increase for such improvement to the extent that the cost thereof is otherwise paid for by an owner.

(10) The DHCR shall not grant an application pursuant to this subdivision (a) for an increase for any improvement made pursuant to paragraphs (2) and (3) of this subdivision (a) to the extent that the cost of such improvement is paid for by an owner with

funds received pursuant to a grant from any governmental agency or entity. A low interest loan or subsidy shall not be considered a grant for the purposes of this paragraph (10). Nothing in this paragraph (10) shall prevent an owner from applying for, and the DHCR from granting an increase for such improvement to the extent that the cost thereof is otherwise paid for by an owner.

(11) An owner who is entitled to a rent increase based upon the installation of new equipment, or new furniture or furnishings pursuant to paragraph (1) of this subdivision (a) shall not be entitled to a further rent increase based upon the installation of similar equipment, or new furniture or furnishings within the useful life of such new equipment, or new furniture or furnishings.

(12) Rent adjustments pursuant to paragraphs (2) and (3) of this subdivision (a) and subdivisions (b) and (c) of this section shall be allocated as follows:

> The DHCR shall determine the dollar amount of the monthly rent adjustment. Such dollar amount shall be divided by the total number of rooms in the building. The amount so derived shall then be added to the rent chargeable to each housing accommodation in accordance with the number of rooms contained in such housing accommodation.

(13) The DHCR shall not grant an owner's application for a rental adjustment pursuant to this subdivision (a), in whole or in part, if it is determined by the DHCR prior to the granting of approval to collect such adjustment that the owner is not maintaining all required services, or that there are current immediately hazardous violations of any municipal, county, state or federal law which relate to the maintenance of such services. However, as determined by the DHCR, such application may be granted upon condition that such services will be restored within a reasonable time, and certain tenant-caused violations may be excepted.

(14) In the case of an improvement constituting a moderate rehabilitation as defined in subdivision 2.1(6) of

the Rules and Regulations Governing Tax Exemption and Tax Abatement pursuant to Title 11 of the Administrative Code of the City of New York, an owner may elect that the total cost for such improvement be deemed to be the amount certified by the Tax Abatement/Tax Exemption Unit of HPD in the certificate of eligibility issued by such office with respect to such improvement. Such election shall be binding on the DHCR and shall waive any claim for a rent increase by reason of any difference between the total cash paid by the owner and such lesser certified amount.

(b) Comparative Hardship.

(1) An owner may file an application on forms prescribed by the DHCR, and the DHCR shall grant, on the application of an owner, appropriate rent adjustments as hereinafter provided, where the gross rental income is insufficient to yield to the owner an average annual net income, (which shall be computed without regard to debt service, financing costs or management fees), for the three year period ending on or within six months of the date of the filing of the owner's application, equal to the annual average net income of the property for:

(i) the period 1968-1970; or

(ii) the first three years of operation, if the building was completed after 1968; or

(iii) the first three fiscal years after a transfer of title to a new owner who acquired title to the building as a result of a bona fide sale of the entire building, and who has been unable to obtain requisite records for the fiscal years between 1968 through 1970, despite diligent efforts to obtain the same from predecessors in title, provided that such new owner submits financial data for not less than six years of continuous and uninterrupted operation of the property under his or her ownership.

(2) Notwithstanding anything to the contrary herein, no increase granted pursuant to this subdivision (b) shall, when added to the annual gross rents as determined by the DHCR, exceed the sum of:

(i) the annual operating expenses; and

(ii) an allowance for management services as determined by the DHCR; and

(iii) actual annual mortgage debt service (interest and amortization) on its indebtedness to a lending institution, an insurance company, a retirement fund or welfare fund under the supervision of the banking or insurance laws of the State of New York or the United States; and

(iv) 8½ percent of that portion of the fair market value of the property which exceeds the unpaid principal amount of the mortgage indebtedness referred to in subparagraph (iii) of this paragraph (2). Fair market value for this subparagraph shall be six times the annual gross rent.

(3) Restrictions.

(i) The collection of any increase in the legal regulated rent for any housing accommodation pursuant to this subdivision (b) shall not exceed six per cent in any year from the effective date of the order granting the increase over the rent set forth in the schedule of gross rents, with collectibility of any dollar excess above said sum to be spread forward in similar increments and added to the legal regulated rent as established or set in future years;

(ii) If the building was previously granted a hardship increase, such increase must have become effective more than 36 months prior to the filing date of the application;

(iii) The owner has resolved all legal objections to any real estate taxes and water and sewer charges for the test period. However, if there is a pending certiorari proceeding relating to the real estate tax expense for the test period, an owner may be permitted to file a hardship application. In such cases, the amount of real estate tax expense that will be recognized for purposes of the test period will be based upon the amount of proposed assessed value set forth by the owner in the certiorari petition; provided, however, that the owner submits proof of actual payment of all taxes due on the owner's proposed assessed value, in accordance with applicable law. If after such tax objection is resolved, the owner's actual and reasonable tax expense allocable to the test period exceeds the amount the DHCR used in determining the hardship application, an additional increase may be granted prospectively by the DHCR in its discretion. The DHCR may also, in its discretion, accept reasonable alternatives as to unresolved water and sewer charges;

(iv) The DHCR shall not grant an owner an increase as provided, in whole or in part, if it is determined prior to the granting of approval to collect an increase pursuant to this subdivision (b) that the owner is not maintaining all required services or there are current immediately hazardous violations of any municipal, county, state, or federal law which relate to the maintenance of such services. However, as determined by the DHCR, where the DHCR determines that insufficient income is the cause of such failure to maintain required services, hardship increases may be granted upon condition that such services will be restored within a reasonable time, and certain tenant-caused violations may be excepted;

(v) In buildings that also contain housing accommodations subject to the City Rent Law, appropriate adjustments for both income and expenses will be made by the DHCR in order to calculate the pro-rata share for those housing accommodations subject to this application;

(vi) The DHCR shall set a rental value for any housing accommodation occupied by the owner or managing agent, a person related to, or an employee of the owner or managing agent, or unoccupied at the owner's choice for more than one month at the last legal regulated rent plus the minimum number of guidelines increases. If no such legal regulated rent existed or is known, the DHCR shall impute a rent equal to the average of rents for similar or comparable housing accommodations subject to this Code in the building during the test period;

(vii) Each owner who files an application for a hardship rent increase shall be required to maintain all records as submitted with the subject application, and further be required to retain same for a period of three years after the effective date of the order; and

(viii) Each application under this subdivision (b) shall

be certified by the owner or his or her duly authorized agent as to its accuracy and compliance with this subdivision (b) under the penalties of perjury.

(ix) The maximum amount of hardship increase to which an owner shall be entitled shall be the difference between the average annual net income for the 3 year base period and the average annual net income for the 3 year current period.

4) Right of tenant to cancel lease where rent increase based upon hardship is granted.

In the event that an order is issued increasing the legal regulated rent because of owner hardship, the tenant may within thirty (30) days of his or her receipt of a copy of the DHCR order, cancel his or her lease on sixty (60) days written notice to the owner. Until such tenant vacates, he or she continues in occupancy at the approved increase in rent.

(c) Alternative Hardship.

As an alternative to the hardship application provided under subdivision (b) of this section, owners of buildings, not owned as cooperatives or condominiums, acquired by the same owner or a related entity owned by the same principals three years prior to the date of application, may apply to the DHCR, on forms prescribed by the DHCR, for increases in excess of the level of applicable guidelines increases established under the RSL, based on a finding by the DHCR that such guidelines increases are not sufficient to enable the owner to maintain an annual gross rent income collectible for such building which exceeds the annual operating expenses of such building by a sum equal to at least five percent of such annual gross rent income collectible, subject to the definitions and restrictions provided for herein.

(1) Definitions.

The following terms shall mean:

(i) Annual gross rental income collectible shall consist of the actual income receivable per annum arising out of the operation and ownership of the property, including but not limited to rental from housing accommodations, stores, professional or business use, garages, parking spaces, and income from easements or air rights, washing machines, vending machines and signs, plus the rent calculated under paragraph (2)(vi) of this subdivision (c). In ascertaining income receivable, the DHCR shall determine what efforts, if any, the owner has followed in collecting unpaid rent;

(ii) Operating expenses shall consist of the actual, reasonable costs of fuel, labor, utilities, taxes (other than income or corporate franchise taxes), fees, (not including attorney's fees related to refinancing of the mortgage), permits, necessary contracted services and non-capital repairs for which an owner is not eligible for an increase pursuant to Part 2522 of this Title (Rent Adjustments), insurance, parts and supplies, reasonable management fees, mortgage interest, and other reasonable and necessary administrative costs applicable to the operation and maintenance of the property;

(iii) Mortgage interest shall be deemed to mean interest on that portion of the principal of an institutional or a bona fide mortgage, including an allocable portion of the charges related to the refinancing of the balance of an existing mortgage or a purchase-money mortgage. Criteria to be considered in determining a bona fide mortgage other than an institutional mortgage shall include, but shall not be limited to, the following: the condition of the property, the location of the property, the existing mortgage market at the time the mortgage is placed, the principal amount of the mortgage, the term of the mortgage, the amortization rate, security and other terms and conditions of the mortgage;

(iv) Institutional mortgage shall include a mortgage given to any insurance company, licensed by the State of New York or authorized to do business in the State of New York, or any commercial bank, trust company, savings bank or savings and loan association (which must be licensed under the laws of any jurisdiction within the United States and authorized to do business in the State of New York). The DHCR may determine in its discretion

that any other mortgage issued by a duly licensed lending institution is an institutional mortgage;
(v) Owner's equity shall mean the sum of:
(a) the purchase price of the property less the principal of any mortgage or loan used to finance the purchase of the property; and
(b) the cost of any capital improvement for which the owner has not collected an increase in rent less the principal of any mortgage or loan used to finance said improvement; and
(c) any repayment of the principal of any mortgage or loan used to finance the purchase of the property or any capital improvement for which the owner has not collected an increase in rent; and
(d) any increase in the equalized assessed value of the property which occurred subsequent to the first valuation of the property after purchase by the owner;
(vi) Threshold income shall mean that annual gross rental income collectible for such building which exceeds the annual operating expense for such building by a sum equal to five percent of such annual gross rental income collectible;
(vii) Test year shall mean any one of the following:
(a) the most recent calendar year (January 1st to December 31st); or
(b) the most recent fiscal year (one year ending on the last day of a month other than December 31st), provided that books of account are maintained and closed accordingly; or
(c) any twelve (12) consecutive months ending within 90 days prior to the date of filing of the hardship application. Such period must end on the last day of a month. Nothing herein shall prevent the DHCR from comparing and adjusting expenses and income during the test year with expenses and income occurring during the three years prior to the date of application in order to determine the reasonableness of such expenses and income.
(2) Restrictions

No owner may file an application, nor may an owner be granted an increase in excess of the level of applicable guidelines increases, unless:
(i) The collection of any increase in the legal regu-

lated rent for any housing accommodation pursuant to this subdivision (c) shall not exceed six per cent in any year from the effective date of the order granting the increase over the rent set forth in the schedule of gross rents, with collectibility of any dollar excess above said sum to be spread forward in similar increments and added to the legal regulated rent as established or set in future years;

(ii) If the building was previously granted a hardship increase, such increase must have become effective more than 36 months prior to the filing date of the application;

(iii) The owner has resolved all legal objections to any real estate taxes and water and sewer charges for the test year. However, if there is a pending certiorari proceeding relating to the real estate tax expense for the test year, an owner may be permitted to file a hardship application. In such cases, the amount of real estate tax expense that will be recognized for purposes of the test year will be based upon the amount of proposed assessed value set forth by the owner in the certiorari petition; provided, however, that the owner submits proof of actual payment of all taxes due on the proposed assessed value, in accordance with applicable law. If after such tax objection is resolved, the owner's actual and reasonable tax expense allocable to the test year exceeds the amount the DHCR used in determining the hardship application, an additional increase may be granted prospectively by the DHCR in its discretion. The DHCR may also, in its discretion, accept reasonable alternatives as to unresolved water and sewer charges;

(iv) The DHCR shall not grant an owner an increase as provided, in whole or in part, if it is determined prior to the granting of approval to collect an increase pursuant to this subdivision (c) that the owner is not maintaining all required services or there are current immediately hazardous violations of any municipal, county, State, or Federal law which relate to the maintenance of such services. However, as determined by the DHCR, where the DHCR determines that insufficient income is the cause of such failure to maintain required services, hardship increases may be granted upon condition that such services will be restored within a reasonable time, and certain tenant-caused violations may be excepted;

(v) In buildings that also contain housing accommodations subject to the City Rent Law, appropriate adjustments for both income and expenses will be made by the DHCR in order to calculate the pro-rata share for those housing accommodations subject to this application;

(vi) The DHCR shall set a rental value for any housing accommodation occupied by the owner or managing agent, or a person related to, or an employee of the owner or managing agent, or unoccupied at the owner's choice for more than one month at the last regulated rent plus the minimum number of guidelines increases or, if no such regulated rent existed or is known, the DHCR shall impute a rent equal to the average of rents for similar or comparable housing accommodations subject to this Code in the building during the test year;

(vii) Each owner who files an application for a hardship rent increase shall be required to maintain all records as submitted with the subject application, and further be required to retain same for a period of three years after the effective date of the order;

(viii) Each application under this subdivision (c) shall be certified by the owner or his or her duly authorized agent as to its accuracy and compliance with this subdivision (c), under the penalty of perjury;

(ix) The annual gross rent income collectible for the test year does not exceed the annual operating expenses of such building by a sum equal to at least five percent of such annual gross rental income collectible;

(x) The owner or a related entity owned by the same principals acquired the building at least 36 months prior to the date of application. A cooperative corporation or the Board of Managers of a condominium association shall not be considered the owner of the building, nor are individual shareholders or unit owners building owners for the purpose of eligibility for the alternative hardship, and as such are not permitted to file alternative hardship applications;

(xi) The owner's equity in the building exceeds five percent of the sum of:

(a) the arm's length purchase price of the property; and

(b) the cost of any capital improvements for which the owner has not collected an increase in rent pursuant to subdivision (a)(2) of this section; and

(c) any repayment of principal of any mortgage or loan used to finance the purchase of the property or any capital improvements for which the owner has not obtained an adjustment in rent pursuant to subdivision (a)(2) of this section; and

(d) any increase in the equalized assessed value of the property which occurred subsequent to the first valuation of the property after purchase by the owner; and

(xii) The maximum amount of hardship increase to which an owner shall be entitled shall be the difference between the threshold income and the annual gross rent income collectible for the test year.

(3) Right of tenant to cancel lease where rent increase based upon hardship is granted. In the event that an order is issued increasing the legal regulated rent because of owner hardship, the tenant may within thirty (30) days of his or her receipt of a copy of the DHCR order, cancel his or her lease on sixty (60) days written notice to the owner. Until such tenant vacates, he or she continues in occupancy at the approved increase in rent.

(d) An owner may file an application to decrease required services for a reduction of the legal regulated rent on forms prescribed by the DHCR on the grounds that:

(1) the owner and tenant by mutual voluntary written agreement, consent to a decrease in dwelling space, or a decrease in the services, furniture, furnishings or equipment provided in the housing accommodation; or

(2) such decrease is required for the operation of the building in accordance with the specific requirements of law; or

(3) such decrease is not inconsistent with the RSL or this Code.

No such reduction in rent or decrease in services shall take place prior to the approval by the DHCR of the owner's application, except that a service decrease pursuant to paragraph (2) of this subdivision (d) may take place prior to such approval.

(e) An owner may file an application to modify or substitute required services, at no change in the legal regulated rent, on forms prescribed by the DHCR on the grounds that:

(1) the owner and tenant by mutual voluntary written agreement, consent to a modification or substitution of the required services provided in the housing accommodation; or

(2) such modification or substitution is required for the operation of the building in accordance with the specific requirements of law; or

(3) such modification or substitution is not inconsistent with the RSL or this Code.

No such modification or substitution of required services shall take place prior to the approval of the owner's application by the DHCR, except that a service modification or substitution pursuant to paragraph (2) of this subdivision (e) may take place prior to such approval.

(f) Pursuant to section 452(7) of the PHFL, as an alternative to the rental adjustments for which an owner may file an application under subdivision (a) of this section, upon the completion of the rehabilitation of a multiple dwelling which is aided by a loan made pursuant to article VIII-A of the PHFL, HPD may adjust the rent for each housing accommodation within the multiple dwelling pursuant to such law. Any work required pursuant to or as a condition of an article VIII-A loan for which a rent adjustment is granted under section 452(7) of the PHFL is not eligible for an increase pursuant to paragraphs (2) or (3) of subdivision (a) of this section.

2522.5 Lease agreements.

(a) Vacancy lease or rental.

(1) For housing accommodations other than hotels,

upon the renting of a vacant housing accommodation, the owner shall provide to the tenant a copy of the fully executed lease for a one or two year term, at the tenant's option (except where a mortgage or mortgage commitment existing as of April 1, 1969, prohibits the granting of one-year lease terms), bearing the signature of the owner and tenant and the beginning and ending dates of the lease term, within 30 days from the owner's receipt of the vacancy lease signed by the tenant. Such lease shall conform to the intent of section 5-702 of the General Obligations Law ("Plain English"). The rent provided therein may not exceed the last legal regulated rent in addition to all increases authorized by this Code. For a housing accommodation subject to the City Rent Law which becomes vacant after March 31, 1984, the owner may not increase the rent charged in the initial lease or other rental agreement pursuant to annual guidelines for a period of one year or until the expiration date of the initial lease or rental agreement, whichever is later.

(2) For housing accommodations in hotels rented to an occupant who has never had a lease, such occupant may at any time during his or her occupancy request a lease and the owner must, within 15 days after such request, grant a lease commencing on the date such request was made at a rent which does not exceed the legal regulated rent, for a term of at least six (6) months. The hotel occupant who requests such a lease becomes a permanent tenant but the lease need not be renewed. Notwithstanding the above, an owner shall not refuse to grant a lease or to extend or continue a tenancy in order to prevent the hotel occupant from becoming a permanent tenant, except to the extent that the owner may be permitted to do so by law pursuant to a warrant of eviction, or other order of a court of competent jurisdiction, or a governmental vacate order.

(3) In addition, where a hotel occupant has not requested a lease, an owner shall not refuse to extend or continue a tenancy solely in order to prevent the hotel occupant from becoming a permanent tenant.

(b) Renewal lease.

(1) For housing accommodations other than hotels, upon such notice as is required by section 2523.5 of this Title (Notice for Renewal of Lease and Renewal Procedure), the tenant shall have the right of selecting at his or her option a renewal of his or her lease for a one or two year term; except that where a mortgage or a mortgage commitment existing as of April 1, 1969, prohibits the granting of one year lease terms or the tenant is the recipient of a Senior Citizen Rent Increase Exemption pursuant to section 26-509 of the Administrative Code of the City of New York, the tenant may not select a one-year lease. The owner shall furnish to the tenant signing a renewal lease form pursuant to section 2523.5 of this Title, a copy of the fully executed renewal lease form, bearing the signatures of the owner and tenant, and the beginning and ending dates of the lease term, within 30 days from the owner's receipt of the renewal lease form signed by the tenant. Such renewal lease form shall conform to the intent of section 5-702 of the General Obligations Law.

(2) Upon complaint by the tenant that he or she was not served with a copy of the fully executed vacancy lease or renewal lease form pursuant to paragraph (1) of subdivision (a) or paragraph (1) of this subdivision (b), the DHCR shall order the owner to furnish the copy of the vacancy lease or renewal lease form. In addition to any other penalties provided under this Code, noncompliance by the owner within 20 days of such order shall result in the denial of any rent guideline increases for vacancy or renewal leases until the fully executed copy of the vacancy lease or renewal lease form is furnished by the owner to the tenant.

(c) Lease Rider and Notice of Rights.

(1) For housing accommodations subject to this Code, an owner shall furnish to each tenant signing a vacancy or renewal lease, a rider in a form promulgated or approved by the DHCR, in larger type than the lease, describing the rights and duties of owners and tenants as provided for under the RSL. Such rider shall conform to the "Plain English" requirements of section 5-702 of the General Obligations Law, shall also be available in Spanish, and shall be attached as an

addendum to the lease. Upon the face of each lease, in bold print, shall appear the following: "ATTACHED RIDER SETS FORTH RIGHTS AND OBLIGATIONS OF TENANTS AND LANDLORDS UNDER THE RENT STABILIZATION LAW". ("LOS DERECHOS Y RESPONSABILIDADES DE INQUILINOS Y CASEROS ESTAN DISPONIBLE EN ESPANOL")

(i) For vacancy leases, such rider shall in addition also include a notice of the prior legal regulated rent, if any, which was in effect immediately prior to the vacancy, an explanation of how the rental amount provided for in the vacancy lease has been computed above the amount shown in the most recent annual registration statement, and a statement that any increase above the amount set forth in such registration statement is in accordance with adjustments permitted by the Rent Guidelines Board and this Code.

(ii) For renewal leases, such rider shall be attached to the form sent to the tenant pursuant to section 2523.5 of this Title (Notice for Renewal of Lease).

(2) For housing accommodations in hotels, each owner shall furnish to each person, at the time of registration, a Notice of Rights in a form promulgated or approved by the DHCR, describing the rights and duties of hotel owners, occupants and tenants as provided for under the RSL and this Code and a hotel occupant's right to become a permanent tenant at a legal regulated rent by requesting a lease for a term of at least 6 months at any time during his or her occupancy. Such notice which shall conform to the "Plain English" requirements of section 5-702 of the General Obligations Law, shall also be available in Spanish. Such notice shall be provided to each hotel occupant in residence on the effective date of this Code no later than 90 days from such effective date. An owner who violates the RSL and this Code by failing to furnish this Notice of Rights, and/or by engaging in any conduct which compels a person to rent as a hotel occupant, prevents a hotel occupant from becoming a permanent tenant, or results in a hotel occupant vacating a housing accommodation, shall be subject to a loss of a guidelines adjustment pursuant to paragraph (3) of this

subdivision (c) as well as penalties pursuant to sections 2526.2(b) and (c)(1) of this Title (Orders to Enforce RSL and Code), and may be subject to a penalty pursuant to section 2526.2(c)(2) of this Title (Harassment Enforcement Orders), in an amount no less than $1000.00.

(3) Upon complaint by the tenant, permanent tenant, or hotel occupant that he or she was not furnished with a copy of the lease rider pursuant to paragraph (1) or the notice pursuant to paragraph (2) of this subdivision (c), the DHCR shall order the owner to furnish the rider or notice. In addition to such other penalties provided for pursuant to section 2526.2 of this Title (Orders To Enforce RSL And Code), if the owner fails to comply within 20 days of such order, the owner shall not be entitled to collect any guidelines lease adjustment authorized for any current lease from the commencement date of such lease. The furnishing of the rider or notice by the owner to the tenant or hotel occupant shall result in the elimination, prospectively, of such penalty. With respect to housing accommodations in hotels, non-compliance by the owner shall not prevent the hotel occupant from becoming a permanent tenant.

(d) Limitations. No provision may be made in any vacancy or renewal lease for adjustment of the legal regulated rent reserved in the lease except as follows:

(1) if the applicable Rent Guidelines rate has not been fixed by the execution date of the vacancy lease or the renewal offer, the lease may make provision for the rent increase, if any, pursuant to the said rate when filed, to become effective as of the commencement date of the lease term, unless the Rent Guidelines Board shall have fixed a later effective date for the said rate, in which event the adjustment may only be effective as of that later date;

(2) where such lease provides that the rental reserved therein may be increased pursuant to an order issued by the DHCR; or

(3) where such lease provides that a rent increase shall be in the amount, if any, authorized by the DHCR in the event an application is filed to establish

a hardship pursuant to section 2522.4 (b) or (c) of this Part; and

(4) in the case of a vacancy lease, where an application for a rent adjustment pursuant to section 2522.4(a) (2) or (3), (b) or (c) of this Part (Major Capital Improvements and Other Adjustments) is pending before the DHCR, such lease also recites that such application is pending before the DHCR and the basis for the adjustment, and that the increase which is the subject of such application, if granted, may be effective during the term of the lease.

(e) Escalator Clauses.

(1) Regardless of whether an escalator clause was contained in the last effective lease or other rental agreement prior to April 1, 1984, no renewal lease or vacancy lease commencing on or after April 1, 1984, shall provide for any escalator clause, except that nothing herein shall prohibit the use of escalator clauses otherwise required by any other statute or regulation affecting the housing accommodation.

(2) For buildings receiving benefits pursuant to section 421-a of the Real Property Tax Law and the regulations promulgated pursuant thereto, such clauses may provide for an annual or other periodic rent increase over the initial rent at an average rate of not more than 2.2 percent of the amount of such initial rent per annum not to exceed the maximum cumulative amount, if any, permitted under the 421-a program rules and regulations. After the tax benefits end, such additional 2.2 percent charges shall no longer be added but the owner may continue to collect the cumulative 2.2 percent increases charged prior to the termination of said tax benefits. Any lease containing the aforementioned provision shall also include a rider with an endorsement signed by the tenant acknowledging the owner's right to include such provision and to collect such rent increase for the tax benefit period. Such rider shall state the approximate date of the expiration of such tax benefits.

(3) Nothing in paragraph (2) of this subdivision (e) shall prohibit the inclusion of a lease provision for an

annual or other periodic rent increase over the legal regulated rent at such rate of rental increase as is provided for and authorized by section 423 of the Real Property Tax Law. Such additional charges pursuant to section 423 of the Real Property Tax Law shall no longer be added after the tax benefits end. Any lease containing the aforementioned provision shall also include a rider with an endorsement signed by the tenant acknowledging the owner's right to include such provision and to collect such rent increase for the tax benefit period. Such rider shall state the approximate date of the expiration of such tax benefits.

(4) No additional charge which became effective on or after November 19, 1982, pursuant to paragraph (2) of this subdivision (e) shall become part of the legal regulated rent.

(f) Vacancy prior to expiration of lease term.

Where the tenant vacates prior to the expiration of the term of the lease, and the housing accommodation is rented to a new tenant pursuant to a lease commencing during the same guidelines period as the prior lease, the rental provided in the new lease shall: (1) be in accordance with and at the guidelines rate of rent adjustment applicable to the new lease; and (2) shall be computed upon the legal regulated rent charged and paid on the last day of the immediately preceding guidelines year; and (3) may include such other rent increases as are authorized pursuant to section 2522.4 of this Part (Adjustment of Legal Regulated Rent).

(g) Same terms and conditions. The lease provided to the tenant by the owner pursuant to subdivision (b) of this section shall be on the same terms and conditions as the expired lease, except where the owner can demonstrate that the change is necessary in order to comply with a specific requirement of law or regulation applicable to the building or to leases for housing accommodations subject to the RSL, or with the approval of the DHCR. Nothing herein may limit the inclusion of authorized clauses otherwise permitted by this Code or by order of the DHCR not contained in the expiring lease. Notwithstanding the foregoing, the tenant shall have the right to have his or her spouse, whether husband or wife, added to the lease or any renewal thereof as an additional tenant where said spouse resides in the housing accommodation as his or her primary residence.

(h) Leases for housing accommodations in cooperative or condominium owned buildings, or in a building for which the Attorney General has accepted for filing a Plan to convert the building to cooperative or condominium ownership.

(1) An owner of one or more housing accommodations subject to this Code may evict the tenant of such housing accommodation and/or refuse to renew a lease therefor, if such housing accommodation is in a building, group of buildings or development which is the subject of an Eviction Plan for conversion to cooperative or condominium ownership under General Business Law section 352-eeee (hereinafter "§ 352-eeee"), provided:

(i) the Attorney General has accepted for filing a Plan to convert the building, group of buildings or development to cooperative or condominium ownership and an amendment declaring the Plan effective as an Eviction Plan has been accepted for filing and a closing has been held thereunder; and

(ii) three years have elapsed from the date on which the Attorney General has accepted for filing an amendment declaring the Plan effective as an Eviction Plan, and at such time or thereafter the tenant's lease has expired or has been cancelled pursuant to paragraph (2) of this subdivision (h).

(2) Until the conditions set forth in paragraph (1) of this subdivision (h) have been met, a tenant in occupancy of a housing accommodation subject to this Code shall have the right to a renewal lease or in the case of a permanent tenant, to continue his or her tenancy on the terms and conditions and at the rent and adjustments thereto as otherwise provided for in this Code. Notwithstanding the foregoing, any vacancy or renewal lease, entered into after the Plan is accepted for filing by

the Attorney General and such Plan has been presented to the tenants in occupancy, may contain a provision authorizing the owner to cancel the lease as of a date not less than three years after the date an Eviction Plan has been declared effective (providing that title has passed to the cooperative corporation or condominium unit owners) on 90 days notice to the tenant. In order to cancel a lease pursuant to such provision, the owner must give the tenant written notice of such election by certified mail no less than 90 days prior to the date upon which the cancellation is to become effective.

(3) For the purposes of this section 2522.5, "filing date" shall mean the date on which a letter was issued by the Attorney General accepting a Plan for filing.

(4) After the filing date, and prior to the Plan being declared effective, if a housing accommodation subject to this Code is vacated, such housing accommodation may only be rented at a rent and upon such terms and conditions as are authorized under this Code for a vacancy lease. Notwithstanding the foregoing, if a vacancy lease herein called an interim lease for such housing accommodation is executed in connection with an agreement to purchase such housing accommodation or the shares allocated thereto, pursuant to any Eviction Plan or Non-eviction Plan, as defined by § 352-eeee, such interim lease:

(i) may provide that once the Plan has been declared effective, if the tenant fails to purchase his or her housing accommodation or the shares allocated thereto on the terms set forth in the subscription or purchase agreement, or otherwise terminates or defaults on the subscription or purchase agreement, such tenant may be evicted: and

(ii) may provide for a rental below the legal regulated rent which may, upon the abandonment or withdrawal of the Plan, be increased to the legal regulated rent, provided the interim lease or other agreement clearly notifies the tenant of what that higher rental will be. If the Plan is abandoned or withdrawn, such tenant remains a rent stabilized tenant.

(5) If a housing accommodation which was subject to this Code is vacated or is rented to a new tenant after any Plan which affects such housing accommodation has been declared effective, and a closing thereunder has occurred, such housing accommodation shall not be subject to this Code.

(6) If a building, group of buildings or development containing units to which this Code applies is converted to cooperative or condominium ownership, whether or not such conversion is pursuant to an Eviction Plan or a Non-eviction Plan as defined by § 352-eeee, the services which shall be required to be maintained under this Code with respect to housing accommodations which remain subject to this Code shall not be diminished or modified without the approval of the DHCR as provided for in section 2522.4(d) or (e) of this Part (Service Decrease or Modification).

(7) The provisions of subdivision (h)(1) of this section, and the right to include a cancellation clause as provided by subdivision (h)(2) of this section, shall not apply to a housing accommodation of which the tenant is a senior citizen or disabled person on the filing date. Until such time as the appropriate agency determines that such tenant is not eligible for such status, such tenant shall continue to be subject to the provisions of this Code.

2522.6 Orders where the legal regulated rent or other facts are in dispute, in doubt, or not known, or where the legal regulated rent must be fixed.

Where the legal regulated rent or any fact necessary to the determination of the legal regulated rent, or the dwelling space, required services or equipment required to be provided with the housing accommodation is in dispute between the owner and the tenant, or is in doubt, or is not known, the DHCR at any time upon written request of either party, or on its own initiative, may issue an order in accordance with the applicable provisions of this Code determining the facts, including the legal regulated rent, the dwelling space, required services, and equipment required to be provided with the housing accommodations.

Such order shall determine such facts or establish the legal regulated rent in accordance with section 2521.2 of this Title (Legal Regulated Rents). Where such order establishes the legal regulated rent, it shall contain a directive that all rent collected by the owner in excess of the legal regulated rent established under this section for such period as is provided in section 2526.1(a) of this Title (Overcharges), or the date of the commencement of the tenancy, if later, either be refunded to the tenant, or be enforced in the same manner as prescribed in section 2526.1(e) and (f) of this Title (Overcharge Recovery and Duty to Refund). Orders issued pursuant to this section shall be based upon the law and Code provisions in effect on March 31, 1984, if the complaint was filed prior to April 1, 1984. However, in the absence of collusion or any relationship between an owner and any prior owner, where such owner purchases the housing accommodations upon a judicial sale and no records sufficient to establish the legal regulated rent were made available to such purchaser, such orders shall establish the legal regulated rent with due consideration of equities pursuant to section 2522.7 of this Part.

2522.7 Consideration of equities.

In issuing any order adjusting or establishing any legal regulated rent, or in determining any applications by tenants pursuant to section 2523.5(f) of this Title (Renewal Lease Rights Determinations), or in determining when a higher or lower legal regulated rent shall be charged pursuant to an agreement between the DHCR and governmental agencies or public benefit corporations, the DHCR shall take into consideration all factors bearing upon the equities involved, subject to the general limitation that such adjustment, establishment, or determination can be put into effect with due regard for protecting tenants and the public interest against unreasonably high rent increases inconsistent with the purposes of the RSL, for preventing imposition upon the industry of any industry-wide schedule of rents or minimum rents, and for preserving the regulated rental housing stock.

PART 2523 - NOTICES AND RECORDS

Section 2523.1 Notice of Initial Legal Registered Rent.

Every owner of housing accommodations previously subject to the City Rent Law, and thereafter rented to a tenant on or after April 1, 1984, shall within 90 days after the housing accommodations become subject to the RSL, give notice in writing by certified mail to the tenant of each such housing accommodation on a form prescribed by the DHCR for that purpose, reciting the Initial Legal Registered Rent for the housing accommodation and the tenant's right to file an application for adjustment of the Initial Legal Registered Rent within 90 days of the certified mailing to the tenant of the notice pursuant to section 2522.3 of this Title (Fair Market Rent Appeal).

2523.2 Certification of services.

Every owner of housing accommodations subject to this Code shall annually file with the DHCR on a form which the DHCR shall prescribe for that purpose, a written certification that he or she is maintaining and will continue to maintain all services as required by section 2520.6(r) of this Title (Required Services), or required to be furnished by any law, or regulation applicable to the housing accommodation. Compliance with section 2528.3 of this Title (Annual Registration Requirements), shall also be compliance with this section.

2523.3 Failure to file a certification of services.

No owner shall be entitled to collect a rent adjustment pursuant to a Rent Guidelines Board Order as authorized under section 2522.5 of this Title (Lease Agreements), until the owner has filed a proper certification as required by section 2523.2 of this Part (Certification of Services), nor shall any owner be entitled to a rent restoration based upon a restoration of services unless such certification is filed together with his or her application for rent restoration. Such restoration shall take effect in accordance with section 2522.2 of this Title (Effective Date of Adjustment of Legal Regulated Rents).

2523.4 Failure to maintain services.

(a) A tenant may apply to the DHCR for a reduction of the legal regulated rent to the level in effect prior to the

Rent Stabilization Code

most recent guidelines adjustment, and the DHCR shall so reduce the rent for the period for which it is found that the owner has failed to maintain required services. The Order reducing the rent shall further bar the owner from applying for or collecting any further increases in rent until such services are restored. If the DHCR further finds that the owner has knowingly filed a false certification, it may, in addition to abating the rent, assess the owner with the reasonable costs of the proceeding, including reasonable attorney's fees, and impose a penalty not in excess of $250.00 for each false certification.

(b) Proceedings pending on the effective date of this Code involving tenant complaints of owners' failure to provide hotel services shall be determined in accordance with the RSL and Hotel Industry Code in effect immediately prior to such effective date of this Code.

2523.5 Notice for renewal of lease and renewal procedure.

(a) On a form prescribed or a facsimile of such form approved by the DHCR, dated by the owner, every owner, other than an owner of hotel accommodations, shall notify the tenant named in the expiring lease not more than 150 days and not less than 120 days prior to the end of the tenant's lease term, by mail or personal delivery, of the expiration of the lease term, and offer to renew the lease or rental agreement at the legal regulated rent permitted for such renewal lease and otherwise on the same terms and conditions as the expiring lease. The owner shall give such tenant a period of 60 days from the date of service of such notice to accept the offer and renew such lease. The tenant's acceptance of such offer shall be entered on the designated part of the prescribed form, or facsimile thereof, and returned to the owner by mail or personal delivery. Pursuant to the provisions of section 2522.5(b)(1) of this Title (Renewal Lease), the owner shall furnish to such tenant a copy of the fully executed renewal lease form bearing the signatures of the owner and tenant within 30 days of the owner's receipt of the renewal lease form signed by the tenant. Upon execution by the owner and delivery to the tenant such form shall constitute a binding renewal lease. Upon failure of the owner to deliver a copy of the fully executed renewal lease form to the tenant within 30 days from the owner's receipt of such form signed by the tenant, such tenant shall not be deprived of any of his or her rights under the RSL and this Code and the owner shall be barred from commencing any action or proceeding against the tenant based upon non-renewal of lease, pursuant to section 2524.3(f) of this Title (Tenant's Refusal to Renew). In the event that such notice is given to the tenant after the expiration of the lease, the provisions of subdivision (c) of this section shall govern.

(b)(1) Except where occupancy is restricted by income limitations pursuant to state or federal law or other requirements of governmental agencies, if an offer is made to the tenant pursuant to the provisions of subdivision (a) and such tenant has vacated the housing accommodation, any member of such tenant's family, as defined in subdivision (o) of section 2520.6 of this Title, who has resided in the housing accommodation as a primary resident from the inception of the tenancy or commencement of the relationship shall be entitled to be named as a party to the renewal lease.

Provided that the tenant's family member has resided in the housing accommodation as a primary resident from the inception of the tenancy or the commencement of the relationship, the residency requirements set forth in this paragraph (1) shall not be deemed to be interrupted by any period during which such family member temporarily relocates from such housing accommodation because he or she:

(i) is engaged in active military duty;

(ii) is enrolled as a full time student;

(iii) is not in residence at the housing accommodation pursuant to a court order not involving any term or provision of the lease, and not involving any grounds specified in the Real Property Actions and Proceedings Law;

(iv) is engaged in employment requiring temporary relocation from the housing accommodation;

(v) is hospitalized for medical treatment; or

(vi) for such other reasonable grounds that shall be

determined by the DHCR upon application by the family member.

(2) In addition to the provisions of paragraph (1) of this subdivision (b), if the tenant is deceased at the expiration of the lease term, such tenant's family member who has not resided in the housing accommodation since the inception of the tenancy or the commencement of the relationship, but who has been residing with such tenant in the housing accommodation as a primary resident for a period of no less than two (2) years immediately prior to the death of the tenant, or where such family member is a senior citizen or disabled person as defined in subdivisions (p) and (q) of section 2520.6 of this Title, for no less than one (1) year prior to the death of the tenant, such family member shall be entitled to a renewal lease. The minimum periods of required residency set forth in this paragraph (2) shall not be deemed to be interrupted where a family member is hospitalized for medical treatment during such minimum period.

(3) The 60 day period from the date of service of the notice for renewal of lease as set forth in subdivision (a) of this section, shall apply to family members.

(c) Where the owner fails to timely offer a renewal lease or rental agreement in accordance with subdivision (a) of this section, the one or two year lease term selected by the tenant shall commence at the tenant's option, either (1) on the date a renewal lease would have commenced had a timely offer been made or (2) on the first rent payment date occurring no less than 120 days after the date that the owner does offer the lease to the tenant. In either event, the effective date of the increased rent under the renewal lease shall commence on the first rent payment date occurring no less than 120 days after such offer is made by the owner, and the guidelines rate applicable shall be no greater than the rate in effect on the commencement date of the lease for which a timely offer should have been made.

(d) Except as provided in Part 2524 of this Title (Evictions), the failure to offer a renewal lease pursuant to this section shall not deprive the tenant of any protections or rights provided by the RSL and this Code and the tenant shall continue to have the same rights as if the expiring lease were still in effect.

(e) On a form prescribed or a facsimile of such form approved by the DHCR, a tenant may, at any time, advise the owner, or an owner may request from the tenant, at the time a renewal lease is offered pursuant to subdivision (a) of this section, the names of all persons other than the tenant who are residing in the housing accommodation, and the following information pertaining to such persons:

  (1) if the person is a family member as defined in subdivision (o) of section 2520.6 of this Title; and
  (2) if the person is a senior citizen or disabled person as defined in subdivisions (p) and (q) of section 2520.6 of this Title.

Failure of the tenant to provide such information to the owner shall place upon all such persons not so made known to the owner, who seek to exercise the right of renewal as provided for in subdivision (b) of this section, the affirmative obligation to establish such right of renewal.

(f) For any family member who is made known to the owner pursuant to subdivision (e) of this section, the DHCR may, upon application by such family member, who is not entitled to a renewal lease as provided for in subdivision (b) of this section, determine with due consideration of equities as set forth in section 2522.7 of this Title (Consideration of Equities), that there are other reasonable grounds pursuant to which such family member shall be entitled to a renewal lease.

2523.6 Notices of appearance by attorney or other authorized representative.

(a) Whenever an attorney or other authorized representative appears for a party who is involved in a proceeding before the DHCR, such person must file a notice of appearance which shall be on a form prescribed by the DHCR, unless the application which instituted the proceeding before the DHCR stated the representation of such person and his or her mailing address in the space allotted for the mailing address of the represented party. An attorney who appears for such party may instead use the letterhead stationery of his or her office as a notice of appearance if the information contained therein substantially conforms to the information required by the form. All subsequent written communications or notices to such party (other than subpoenas) shall be sent to such attorney or other authorized representative at the address designated in such notice of appearance. The service of written communications and notices upon such attorney or other authorized representative shall be deemed full and proper service upon the party or parties so represented. If an authorized representative appears, such notice of appearance must be accompanied by a written authorization, duly verified or affirmed, by the party represented.

(b) Whenever an attorney or other authorized representative shall represent the same party or parties in more than one proceeding before the DHCR, separate notices of appearance and authorizations shall be filed in each proceeding.

(c) Any submission signed by an attorney or other authorized representative must state that such person has personal knowledge of the facts contained in such submission, or if he or she does not have such personal knowledge, the basis for such person's information.

2523.7 Records and record-keeping.

(a) Every owner shall keep, preserve, and make available for examination, records from the date immediately prior to the date the housing accommodation became subject to the RSL, of the same kind as he or she has customarily kept relating to the rents received for housing accommodations, and individual housing accommodation and building-wide services provided or required to be provided on the applicable base date.

(b) Except as provided in subdivision (c) of this section, every owner subject to this Code shall also keep, preserve, and make available for examination, records from the date immediately prior to the date the housing accommodation became subject to the RSL, showing the rents received for each housing accommodation, the particular term and number of tenants for which such rents were charged, and the name of each tenant, and the individual housing accommodation and building-wide services provided or required to be provided on the applicable base date.

(c) Any owner who has duly registered a housing accommodation pursuant to Part 2528 of this Title, shall not be required to maintain or produce any records relating to rentals of such accommodation more than four years prior to the initial or most recent annual registration for such accommodation. Notwithstanding the above, such owner shall continue to maintain records for all housing accommodations for which a complaint of overcharge or a Fair Market Rent Appeal was filed by a tenant prior to April 1, 1984, or a challenge to an initial registration is filed, until a final order of the DHCR is issued.

(d) In the absence of collusion or any relationship between a prior owner and an owner who purchases upon a judicial sale, such purchaser shall not be required to comply with the provisions of subdivisions (a) and (b) of this section for the period prior to such sale, except where records sufficient to establish the legal regulated rent are available to such purchaser. This subdivision (d) shall not be construed to waive the purchaser's obligation to register pursuant to Part 2528 of this Title.

2523.8 Notice of change of ownership.

Within thirty (30) days after a change in ownership, the new owner shall notify the DHCR of such change on a form prescribed by the DHCR. Such form shall be signed by the new owner, listing the address of the building or complex, the name, address and telephone number of the new owner, and the date of the transfer of ownership.

PART 2524 - EVICTIONS

Section 2524.1 Restrictions on removal of tenant.

(a) As long as the tenant continues to pay the rent to which the owner is entitled, no tenant shall be denied a renewal lease or be removed from any housing accommodation by action to evict or to recover possession, by exclusion from possession, or otherwise, nor shall any person attempt such removal or exclusion from possession, except on one or more of the grounds specified in this Code.

(b) It shall be unlawful for any person to remove or attempt to remove any tenant from any housing accommodation or to refuse to renew the lease or rental agreement for the use of such housing accommodation, because such tenant has taken, or proposes to take any action authorized or required by the RSL or this Code, or any order of the DHCR.

(c) No tenant of any housing accommodation shall be removed or evicted unless and until such removal or eviction has been authorized by a court of competent jurisdiction on a ground authorized in this Part or under the Real Property Actions and Proceedings Law.

2524.2 Termination notices.

(a) Except where the ground for removal or eviction of a tenant is non-payment of rent, no tenant shall be removed or evicted from a housing accommodation by court process, and no action or proceeding shall be commenced for such purpose upon any of the grounds permitted in section 2524.3 (Proceedings for Eviction-Wrongful Acts of Tenant) or section 2524.4 (Grounds for Refusal to Renew Lease, or In Hotels, Discontinuing a Hotel Tenancy, Without Order of the DHCR) of this Part, unless and until the owner shall have given written notice to such tenant as hereinafter provided.

(b) Every notice to a tenant to vacate or surrender possession of a housing accommodation shall state the ground under section 2524.3 (Proceedings for Eviction-Wrongful Acts of Tenant) or 2524.4 (Grounds for Refusal to Renew Lease, or In Hotels, Discontinuing a Hotel Tenancy, Without Order of the DHCR) of this Part, upon which the owner relies for removal or eviction of the tenant, the facts necessary to establish the existence of such ground, and the date when the tenant is required to surrender possession.

(c) Every such notice shall be served upon the tenant:

    (1) in the case of a notice based upon subdivision (f) of section 2524.3 of this Part (Refusal To Renew),

at least 15 days prior to the date specified therein for the surrender of possession; or

(2) in the case of a notice on any other ground pursuant to section 2524.3 (Proceedings for Eviction-Wrongful Acts of Tenant) at least 7 calendar days prior to the date specified therein for the surrender of possession or in the case of a notice pursuant to subdivision (c) of section 2524.4 of this Part (Primary Residence), at least 120 and not more than 150 days prior to the expiration of the lease term; or

(3) in the case of a notice pursuant to subdivision (a) of section 2524.4 (Occupancy by Owner or Member Of Owner's Immediate Family), and section 2524.5 of this Part (Grounds For Refusal To Renew Lease Or Discontinue Hotel Tenancy And Evict Which Require Approval Of The DHCR), at least 120 and not more than 150 days prior to the expiration of the lease term, or in the case of a hotel permanent tenant without a lease, at least 120 and not more than 150 days prior to the commencement of a court proceeding; or

(4) in the case of a notice pursuant to subdivision (b) of section 2524.4 of this Part (Recovery By Not-For-Profit Institution), at least 120 and not more than 150 days prior to the expiration of the lease term, or within 120 days of the expiration of the tenant's lease term, provided no summary proceeding can be commenced until the expiration of 120 days from the service of such notice, accompanied by a form prescribed by the DHCR advising the tenant of the penalties set forth in section 2524.4(b) of this Part for failure to use the housing accommodation for the charitable or educational purposes for which recovery is sought.

(d) All notices served pursuant to subdivision (c) of this section shall be in lieu of any notice in any lease or rental agreement providing for a lesser time for termination of tenancy.

2524.3 Proceedings for eviction - wrongful acts of tenant.

Without the approval of the DHCR, an action or pro-

Rent Stabilization Code

ceeding to recover possession of any housing accommodation may only be commenced after service of the notice required by section 2524.2 of this Part (Termination Notices), upon one or more of the following grounds, wherein wrongful acts of the tenant are established as follows:

(a) The tenant is violating a substantial obligation of his or her tenancy other than the obligation to surrender possession of such housing accommodation, and has failed to cure such violation after written notice by the owner that the violations cease within ten days; or the tenant has willfully violated such an obligation inflicting serious and substantial injury upon the owner within the three month period immediately prior to the commencement of the proceeding; or

(b) The tenant is committing or permitting a nuisance in such housing accommodation or the building containing such housing accommodation; or is maliciously, or by reason of gross negligence, substantially damaging the housing accommodation; or the tenant engages in a course of conduct, the primary purpose of which is intended to harass the owner or other tenants or occupants of the same or an adjacent building or structure by interfering substantially with their comfort or safety. The exercise by a tenant of any rights pursuant to any law or regulation relating to occupancy of a housing accommodation, including the RSL or this Code, shall not be deemed a ground for eviction pursuant to this subdivision (b); or

(c) Occupancy of the housing accommodation by the tenant is illegal because of the requirements of law and the owner is subject to civil or criminal penalties therefor, or such occupancy is in violation of contracts with governmental agencies; or

(d) The tenant is using or permitting such housing accommodation to be used for an immoral or illegal purpose; or

(e) The tenant has unreasonably refused the owner access to the housing accommodation for the purpose of making necessary repairs or improvements required by law or authorized by the DHCR, or for the purpose of inspection or showing the housing accommodation to a prospective purchaser, mortgagee or prospective mortgagee, or other person having a legitimate interest therein; provided, however, that in the latter event such refusal shall not be a ground for removal or eviction unless the tenant shall have been given at least 5 days notice of the inspection or showing, to be arranged at the mutual convenience of the tenant and owner so as to enable the tenant to be present at the inspection or showing, and that such inspection or showing of the housing accommodation is not contrary to the provisions of the tenant's lease or rental agreement.

(f) The tenant has refused, following notice pursuant to section 2523.5 of this Title (Notice For Renewal Of Lease And Renewal Procedure), to renew an expiring lease in the manner prescribed in such notice at the legal regulated rent authorized under this Code and the RSL, and otherwise upon the same terms and conditions as the expiring lease. This subdivision (f) does not apply to permanent hotel tenants, nor may a proceeding be commenced based on this ground prior to the expiration of the existing lease term.

(g) For housing accommodations in hotels, the tenant has refused, after at least twenty days written notice to move to a substantially similar housing accommodation in the same building at the same legal regulated rent where there is a rehabilitation as set forth in section 2524.5(a)(3) of this Part (Other Grounds For Eviction), provided:

(1) that the owner has an approved plan to reconstruct, renovate or improve said housing accommodation or the building in which it is located; and

(2) that the move is reasonably necessary to permit such reconstruction, renovation or improvement; and

(3) that the owner moves the tenant's belongings to the other housing accommodation at the owner's cost and expense; and

(4) that the owner offers the tenant the right of reoccupancy of the reconstructed, renovated, or improved housing accommodation at the same legal regulated rent unless such rent is otherwise provided for pursu-

Rent Stabilization Code

ant to section 2524.5(a)(3) of this Part (Other Grounds For Eviction).

(h) In the event of a sublet, an owner may terminate the tenancy of the tenant if the tenant is found to have violated the provisions of section 2525.6 of this Title (Subletting; Assignment).

2524.4 Grounds for refusal to renew lease, or in hotels, discontinuing a hotel tenancy, without order of the DHCR.

The owner shall not be required to offer a renewal lease to a tenant, or in hotels, to continue a hotel tenancy, and may commence an action or proceeding to recover possession in a court of competent jurisdiction, upon the expiration of the existing lease term, if any, after serving the tenant with a notice as required pursuant to section 2524.2 of this Part (Termination Notices) only on one or more of the following grounds:

(a) Occupancy by owner or member of owner's immediate family.

(1) An owner who seeks to recover possession of a housing accommodation for such owner's personal use and occupancy as his or her primary residence in the City of New York and/or for the use and occupancy of a member of his or her immediate family as his or her primary residence in the City of New York, except that tenants in a non-eviction conversion plan pursuant to section 352-eeee of the General Business Law may not be evicted on this ground on or after the date the conversion plan is declared effective.

(2) The provisions of this subdivision (a) shall not apply where a tenant or the spouse of a tenant lawfully occupying the housing accommodation is a Senior Citizen or Disabled Person as previously defined herein, unless the owner offers to provide and, if requested, provides an equivalent or superior housing accommodation at the same or lower regulated rent in a closely proximate area.

(3) The provisions of this subdivision (a) shall only permit one of the individual owners of any building, whether such ownership is by joint tenancy, tenancy

in common, or tenancy by the entirety to recover possession of one or more dwelling units for personal use and occupancy.

(4) No action or proceeding to recover possession pursuant to this subdivision (a) shall be commenced in a court of competent jurisdiction unless the owner shall have served the tenant with a termination notice in accordance with subdivisions (a), (b) and (c)(3) of section 2524.2 of this Part (Termination Notices).

(5) The failure of the owner to utilize the housing accommodation for the purpose intended after the tenant vacates, or to continue in occupancy for a period of three years, may result in a forfeiture of the right to any increases in the legal regulated rent in the building in which such housing accommodation is contained for a period of three years, unless the owner offers and the tenant accepts reoccupancy of such housing accommodation on the same terms and conditions as existed at the time the tenant vacated, or the owner establishes to the satisfaction of the DHCR that circumstances changed after the tenant vacated which prevented the owner from utilizing the housing accommodation for the purpose intended, and in such event, the housing accommodation may be rented at the appropriate guidelines without a vacancy allowance. This paragraph (5) shall not eliminate or create any claim that the former tenant of the housing accommodation may or may not have against the owner.

(b) Recovery by a not-for-profit institution.

(1) The owner is a hospital, convent, monastery, asylum, public institution, college, school dormitory, or any institution operated exclusively for charitable or educational purposes on a non-profit basis, and the owner, upon notice to the tenant in accordance with section 2524.2(c)(4) of this Part (Termination Notices), requires the housing accommodation for its own use in connection with its charitable or educational purposes, and either:

(i) the tenant's initial tenancy commenced after the owner acquired the property, and the owner requires the housing accommodation in connection with its charitable or educational purposes, including, but not limited to, housing for affiliated persons; provided that the owner may not refuse to renew the lease of a tenant whose right to occupancy commenced prior to July 1, 1978 pursuant to a written lease or written rental agreement, and who did not receive notice at the time of the execution of the lease that the tenancy was subject to non-renewal; provided further that a tenant who was affiliated with the owning institution at the commencement of his or her tenancy and whose affiliation terminates during such tenancy shall not have the right to a renewal lease; or

(ii) the owner requires the housing accommodation for a non-residential use in connection with its charitable or educational purposes.

(2) In addition to such penalty provided in section 2526.2 of this Title (Orders to Enforce the RSL and Code), the failure of the owner without good cause to utilize or to continue to use the housing accommodation for the purpose intended after the tenant vacates, and for four years thereafter, shall result in a forfeiture of the right to any increases in the legal regulated rent for the housing accommodation involved for a four year period following the recovery of the housing accommodation from the tenant.

(3) If an owner who recovers a housing accommodation pursuant to this subdivision (b), or any successor in interest, within four years after recovery of the housing accommodation from the tenant, utilizes such housing accommodation for purposes other than those permitted hereunder without good cause, then such owner or successor shall be liable to the removed tenant for three times the damages sustained on account of such removal, plus reasonable attorney's fees and costs as determined by a court of competent jurisdiction, provided that such tenant commences an action to recover such damages within three years from the date of recovery of the housing accommodation. The damages sustained by such tenant shall be the difference between the rent paid by

such tenant for the recovered housing accommodation, and the rental value of a comparable rent regulated housing accommodation, plus the reasonable costs of the removal of the tenant's property.

(c) Primary residence.

The housing accommodation is not occupied by the tenant, not including subtenants or occupants, as his or her primary residence, as determined by a court of competent jurisdiction, provided, however, that no action or proceeding shall be commenced seeking to recover possession on the ground that the housing accommodation is not occupied by the tenant as his or her primary residence unless the owner or lessor shall have given thirty days notice to the tenant of his or her intention to commence such action or proceeding on such grounds. Such notice may be combined with the notice required by section 2524.2(c)(2) of this Title (Termination Notices). For the purpose of this subdivision (c), where a housing accommodation is rented to a not-for-profit hospital for residential use, affiliated subtenants authorized to use such accommodations by such hospital shall be deemed to be tenants for primary residence purposes.

2524.5 Grounds for refusal to renew lease or discontinue hotel tenancy and evict which require approval of the DHCR.

(a) The owner shall not be required to offer a renewal lease to a tenant or continue a hotel tenancy and shall file on the prescribed form an application with the DHCR for authorization to commence an action or proceeding to recover possession in a court of competent jurisdiction after the expiration of the existing lease term, upon any one of the following grounds:

(1) Withdrawal from the rental market.

The owner has established to the satisfaction of the DHCR after a hearing, that he or she seeks in good faith to withdraw any or all housing accommodations from both the housing and non-housing rental market without any intent to rent or sell all or any part of the land or structure and:

(i) that he or she requires all or part of the housing accommodations or the land for his or her own use in connection with a business which he or she owns and operates; or

(ii) that substantial violations which constitute fire hazards or conditions dangerous or detrimental to the life or health of the tenants have been filed against the structure containing the housing accommodations by governmental agencies having jurisdiction over such matters, and that the cost of removing such violations would substantially equal or exceed the assessed valuation of the structure.

(2) Demolition.

The owner has established to the satisfaction of the DHCR after a hearing that he or she seeks in good faith to recover possession of the housing accommodations for the purpose of demolishing them and constructing a new building, provided that either he or she has obtained approved plans for a new building or the DHCR has determined that plans have been submitted to the city agency having jurisdiction over the demolition and new construction. However, a hearing shall not be conducted until the owner has submitted to the DHCR proof of his or her financial ability to complete the undertaking together with copies of the plans that have been submitted to such city agency. No order shall be issued approving the owner's application until said plans have been approved by such city agency, and an order approving the owner's application shall not be granted unless the owner proves that all necessary funding for the proposed construction has been secured.

(3) Other grounds.

The owner will eliminate inadequate, unsafe or unsanitary conditions and demolish or rehabilitate the dwelling unit pursuant to the provisions of article VIII, VIII-A, XIV, XV or XVIII of the PHFL, the Housing New York Program Act, or sections 8 and 17 of the U.S. Housing Act of 1937 (National Housing Act), on the condition that the owner:

(i) proves that it has a commitment for the required financing;

(ii) proves that any rehabilitation requires the temporary removal of the tenant; and

(iii) agrees to offer and will offer the tenants the right of first occupancy following any rehabilitation at an initial rent as determined pursuant to the applicable law and subject to any terms and conditions established pursuant to applicable law and regulations.

(b) Election not to renew.

Once an application is filed under this section, with notification to all affected tenants pursuant to section 2524.2 of this Part (Termination Notices), the owner may refuse to renew the affected tenant's lease until a determination of the owner's application is made by the DHCR. In such event, the owner may not increase the rent charged in excess of the rent provided in the expiring lease. If such application is denied, or withdrawn, prospective renewal leases must be offered to all affected tenants within such time and at such guidelines rates as directed in the DHCR order of denial or withdrawal.

(c) Terms and conditions upon which orders authorizing refusal to offer renewal leases may be based.

The DHCR shall require an owner to pay all reasonable moving expenses and shall further condition the order upon the payment of a reasonable stipend and/or the relocation of the tenant by the owner to a suitable housing accommodation at the same or lower regulated rent in a closely proximate area. If no such housing accommodation is available at the same or lower regulated rent, the owner may be required to pay the difference in rent between the subject housing accommodation and the new housing accommodation to which the tenant is relocated for such period as the DHCR determines, commencing with the occupancy of the new housing accommodation by the tenant.

(d) Any order granting an application pursuant to this section shall not provide for a stay of eviction which exceeds one year. In addition, where the order of the DHCR is conditioned upon the owner's compliance with specified terms and conditions, if such terms and conditions have not been complied with, the order may be modified or revoked.

PART 2525 - PROHIBITIONS

Section 2525.1 General prohibitions.

It shall be unlawful, regardless of any contract, lease or other obligation heretofore or hereafter entered into, for any person to demand or receive, any rent for any housing accommodation in excess of the legal regulated rent, or otherwise to do or omit to do any act, in violation of any regulation, order or requirement under the RSL or this Code, or to offer, solicit, attempt or agree to do any of the foregoing. In addition to the definition contained in subdivision (c) of section 2520.6 of this Title, the term rent, as hereinbefore defined shall also include the payment by a tenant of a fee or rental commission to an owner or to any person or real estate broker where such person or real estate broker is an agent or employee of the owner employed by the owner in connection with the operation or management of the building in which the housing accommodation is located, or where the owner or his or her employee refers the tenant to such person or such real estate broker employed by the owner in connection with the operation or management of the building, for the purpose of renting the housing accommodation, or where there is common ownership, directly or indirectly, or a financial interest between the owner and such person or real estate broker.

2525.2 Evasion.

(a) The legal regulated rents and other requirements provided in this Code shall not be evaded, either directly or indirectly, in connection with the renting or leasing or the transfer of a lease for housing accommodations by requiring the tenant to pay, or obligate himself or herself for membership or other fees, or by modification of the practices relating to payment of commissions or other charges, or by modification of the services furnished or required to be furnished with the housing accommodations, or otherwise.

(b)(1) Upon the receipt of rent in the form of cash or any instrument other than the personal check of the tenant, it shall be the duty of the owner to provide the tenant with a written receipt containing the following:

(1) the date;

(2) the amount;

(3) the identity of the premises and period for which paid; and

(4) the signature and title of the person receiving the rent.

(2) Where a tenant, in writing, requests that an owner provide a receipt for rent paid by personal check, it shall be the duty of the owner to provide the tenant with the receipt described in paragraph (1) of this subdivision (b) for each such request made in writing.

(3) The receipt provided pursuant to this subdivision (b) shall state the name and New York City address of the managing agent or designee thereof, as required by section 27-2105 of the Administrative Code of the City of New York. A failure to comply with the provisions of this subdivision (b) shall constitute an evasionary practice.

2525.3 Conditional rental.

(a) No owner or other person shall require a tenant or prospective tenant to purchase or lease, or agree to purchase or lease, furniture or any other personal property, including, but not limited to, shares to an apartment prior to the acceptance for filing by the Attorney General of a plan of cooperative conversion, as a condition of renting housing accommodations.

(b) No owner or other person shall require a tenant, prospective tenant or a prospective permanent tenant to represent or agree as a condition of renting a housing accommodation that the housing accommodation shall not be used as the tenant's or prospective tenant's primary residence, or the prospective permanent tenant's principal residence.

(c) No owner or other person shall require a tenant or prospective tenant to sign a lease or other rental agreement in the name of a corporation or for professional or commercial use as a condition of renting a housing accommodation when the housing accommodation is to

RENT STABILIZATION CODE

be used as the primary residence of the prospective tenant for residential purposes.

(d) No owner or other person shall engage in any practice including, but not limited to, illusory or collusive rental practices which deprive a tenant in possession of his or her rights under this Code.

(e) The term other person as used in this section shall include an agent, or any other employee of an owner, or any other entity, acting with or without the authority of the owner.

2525.4 Security deposits.

Regardless of any contract, agreement, lease or other obligation heretofore or hereafter entered into, no owner, in addition to the authorized collection of rent, shall demand, receive or retain a security deposit or advance payment for or in connection with the use or occupancy of a housing accommodation which exceeds the rent for one month, provided however, that where a greater security deposit was paid by the tenant in continuous occupancy since the date the housing accommodation became subject to the RSL, such deposit may continue in effect during the term of such lease and any renewals thereof with the same tenant. Such security deposit shall be subject to the following conditions:

(a) the security deposit shall be deposited in an interest-bearing account in a banking organization in New York State; and

(b) the person depositing such security money shall be entitled to receive, as administrative expenses, a sum equivalent to one percent per annum upon the security money so deposited; and

(c) at the tenant's option, the balance of the interest paid by the banking organization shall be applied for the rental of the housing accommodation, or held in trust until repaid, or annually paid to the tenant; and

(d) the owner otherwise complies with the provisions of article 7 of the General Obligations Law (Obligations Relating To Property Received As Security).

2525.5 Harassment.

It shall be unlawful for any owner or any person acting

on his or her behalf, directly, or indirectly, to engage in any course of conduct (including, but not limited to, interruption or discontinuance of required services, or unwarranted or baseless court proceedings) which interferes with, or disturbs, or is intended to interfere with or disturb, the privacy, comfort, peace, repose or quiet enjoyment of the tenant in his or her use or occupancy of the housing accommodation, or is intended to cause the tenant to vacate such housing accommodation or waive any right afforded under this Code.

2525.6 Subletting; Assignment

(a) Housing accommodations subject to this Code rented by a tenant pursuant to an existing lease may be sublet in accordance with the provisions, and subject to the limitations, of section 226-b of the Real Property Law provided that the additional provisions of this section are complied with and provided further that the tenant can establish that at all times he or she has maintained the housing accommodation as his or her primary residence and intends to occupy it as such at the expiration of the sublease.

(b) The rental charged to the subtenant by the tenant shall not exceed the legal regulated rent plus no more than a ten percent surcharge payable to the tenant if the housing accommodation is sublet fully furnished. Where a tenant violates the provisions of this subdivision (b), the subtenant shall be entitled to treble damages.

(c) The tenant may not sublet a housing accommodation for more than a total of two years, including the term of the proposed sublease, out of the four-year period preceding the termination date of the proposed sublease. The term of proposed sublease may, if lawful under this section, extend beyond the term of the tenant's lease, and an owner may not refuse consent to a sublease solely because it extends beyond such term. A sublease which so extends shall be subject to the tenant's right to a renewal lease.

(d) The tenant, rather than the subtenant, retains:

(1) the right to a renewal lease, whether or not the term of the sublease extends beyond the term of the tenant's lease; and

(2) the rights and status of a tenant in occupancy with respect to conversion to condominium or cooperative ownership.

(e) Upon the consent of the owner to a sublet or an assignment of any lease, the legal regulated rent payable to the owner effective upon the date of subletting or assignment may be increased by the vacancy allowance, if any, provided in the Rent Guidelines Board Order in effect at the time of the commencement date of the lease, provided the lease is a renewal lease. Such increase in the case of an assignment shall remain part of the legal regulated rent for any subsequent renewal lease, however, in the case of a subletting, upon termination of the sublease, the legal regulated rent shall revert to the legal regulated rent without the sublet vacancy allowance.

(f) An owner may terminate the tenancy of a tenant who sublets contrary to the terms of this section, or assigns without written consent of the owner, but no action or proceeding to terminate tenancy based upon the non-primary residence of a tenant may be commenced prior to the expiration date of his or her lease.

(g) (1) Notwithstanding the provisions of section 226-b of the Real Property Law, a not-for-profit hospital shall have the right to sublet any housing accommodation leased by it to its affiliated personnel without requiring the owner's consent to any such sublease and without being bound by the provisions of subdivisions (a), (c), (e) and (f) of this section. For the purposes of this section, where a housing accommodation is rented to a not-for-profit hospital for residential use, affiliated subtenants authorized to use such accommodations by such hospital shall be deemed to be tenants.

(2) Whenever a not-for-profit hospital executes a renewal lease for a housing accommodation, the legal regulated rent shall be increased by a sum equal to fifteen percent of the previous lease rental for such housing accommodation, hereinafter referred to as a vacancy surcharge, unless the owner shall have received within the seven-year period prior to the commencement date of such renewal lease any vacancy increases or vacancy surcharges allocable to the said

housing accommodation. In the event the owner shall have received any such vacancy increases or vacancy surcharges during such seven year period, the vacancy surcharge shall be reduced by the amount received by any such vacancy increase or vacancy surcharges.

(h) For housing accommodations which are first made subject to this Code solely by reason of article 7-C of the MDL, nothing herein shall be deemed to prevent or limit the rights of tenants to sell improvements pursuant to MDL section 286(6).

PART 2526 - ENFORCEMENT

Section 2526.1 Overcharge penalties; fines; assessment of costs; attorney's fees; rent credits.

(a) (1) Any owner who is found by the DHCR, after a reasonable opportunity to be heard, to have collected any rent or other consideration in excess of the legal regulated rent shall be ordered to pay to the tenant a penalty equal to three times the amount of such excess, except as provided under subdivision (f) of this section. If the owner establishes by a preponderance of the evidence that the overcharge was not willful, the DHCR shall establish the penalty as the amount of the overcharge plus interest from the date of the first overcharge on or after April 1, 1984, at the rate of interest payable on a judgment pursuant to section 5004 of the Civil Practice Law and Rules, and the order shall direct such a payment to be made to the tenant.

(2) A complaint pursuant to this section must be filed with the DHCR within four years of the first overcharge alleged, and no award of the amount of an overcharge may be based upon an overcharge having occurred more than four years before the complaint is filed, provided that:

    (i) a penalty of three times the overcharge may not be based upon an overcharge having occurred more than two years before the complaint is filed or upon an overcharge which occurred prior to April 1, 1984; and

    (ii) any complaint based upon overcharges occurring prior to the date of filing of the initial rent registration for a housing accommodation pursuant to Part 2528 of this Title (Registration of Housing Accommodations) shall be filed within ninety days of the mailing of notice to the tenant of such registration.

(3) (i) Except as to complaints filed pursuant to subparagraph (ii) of this paragraph (3), the legal regulated rent for purposes of determining an overcharge shall be deemed to be the rent shown in the annual registration statement filed four years prior to the most recent registration statement, (or, if more recently filed, the initial registration statement) plus in each case any subsequent lawful increases and adjustments.

(ii) As to complaints filed within ninety days of the initial registration of a housing accommodation, the legal regulated rent for purposes of determining an overcharge shall be deemed to be the rent charged and paid on April 1, 1980, or for a housing accommodation not required to be registered by June 30, 1984, 4 years prior to the date the housing accommodation was first required to be registered (or if the housing accommodation was subject to the RSL and this Code for less than four years prior to such initial registration, the initial legal regulated rent) plus in each case, any lawful increases and adjustments. Where the rent charged on such dates cannot be established, such rent shall be determined by the DHCR in accordance with section 2522.6 of this Title (Legal Regulated Rent In Dispute).

(4) Complaints filed prior to April 1, 1984, shall be determined in accordance with the RSL and Code provisions in effect on March 31, 1984, except that an overcharge collected on or after April 1, 1984 may be subject to treble damages pursuant to this section.

(b) The DHCR shall determine the owner's liability between or among two or more tenants found to have been overcharged during their particular occupancy of a housing accommodation, and at its discretion, may require the owner to make diligent efforts to locate prior tenants who are not parties to the proceeding, and to make refunds to such tenants or pay the amount of such penalty as a fine.

(c) (1) Any affected tenant shall be given notice of and an opportunity to join in any proceeding commenced by the DHCR pursuant to this section.

(2) Where a complainant pursuant to this section vacates the housing accommodation, and the DHCR continues the proceeding, the DHCR shall give any affected tenant notice of and an opportunity to join in such proceeding.

(d) An owner who is found to have overcharged by the DHCR may be assessed and ordered to pay to the tenant as an additional penalty the reasonable costs and attorney's fees of the proceeding, and except where treble damages are awarded, interest from the date of the overcharge occurring on or after April 1, 1984, at the rate of interest payable on a judgment pursuant to section 5004 of the Civil Practice Law and Rules.

(e) A tenant may recover any overcharge penalty established by the DHCR by deducting it from the rent due to the present owner at a rate not in excess of 20% of the amount of the penalty for any one month's rent. If no such rent credit has been taken, the order of the DHCR awarding penalties may be entered, filed and enforced by a tenant in the same manner as a judgment of the supreme court, on a form prescribed by the DHCR, provided that the amount of the penalty exceeds $1,000 or the tenant is no longer in possession. Neither of these remedies is available until the expiration of the period in which the owner may institute a proceeding pursuant to Part 2530 of this Title (Judicial Review).

(f) Responsibility for overcharges.

(1) For overcharges collected prior to April 1, 1984, an owner will be held responsible only for his or her portion of the overcharges, in the absence of collusion or any relationship between such owner and any prior owners.

(2) For overcharge complaints filed or overcharges collected on or after April 1, 1984, a current owner shall be responsible for all overcharge penalties, includ-

ing penalties based upon overcharges collected by any prior owner. However, in the absence of collusion or any relationship between such owner and any prior owner, where no records sufficient to establish the legal regulated rent were provided at a judicial sale, a current owner who purchases upon such judicial sale shall be liable only for his or her portion of the overcharges, and shall not be liable for treble damages upon such portion resulting from overcharges caused by any prior owner. Such penalties shall be subject to the time limitations set forth in paragraph (2) of subdivision (a) of this section.

(3) This subdivision (f) shall not be construed to entitle a tenant to more than one refund for the same overcharge.

(g) The provisions of this section shall not apply to a proceeding pursuant to section 2522.3 of this Title (Fair Market Rent Appeal).

2526.2 Orders to enforce the RSL and this Code.

(a) Upon notice and reasonable opportunity to be heard, the DHCR may issue orders it deems appropriate to enforce the RSL and this Code.

(b) In addition to any other penalties provided for in this Code, if the DHCR finds that any owner has knowingly violated any provision of the RSL or this Code, it may assess a penalty of up to $250.00 for each such violation against the owner.

(c) If the owner is found by the DHCR:

(1) to have violated an order of the DHCR, the DHCR may impose by administrative order after holding a hearing, a penalty in the amount of $250.00 for the first such offense and $1000.00 for each subsequent offense; or

(2) to have harassed a tenant to obtain a vacancy of a housing accommodation, the DHCR may impose by administrative order after holding a hearing, a penalty in the amount of up to $1000 for a first such offense and up to $2500 for each subsequent offense or for a violation consisting of conduct directed at the tenants of more than one housing accommodation. Such order shall be deemed a final determination for the purposes

of judicial review pursuant to Part 2530 of this Title (Judicial Review). Such penalty may, upon the expiration of the period for seeking review pursuant to article 78 of the Civil Practice Law and Rules, be docketed and enforced in the manner of a judgment of the supreme court.

(3) not to have utilized a housing accommodation for the purpose intended under section 2524.4 (b)(2) of this Title (Recovery By Not-For-Profit Institution), the DHCR shall impose by administrative order after hearing a penalty in the amount of up to $1000 for each such offense.

(d) Any owner who has been found by the DHCR to have refused to comply with an order of the DHCR or to have harassed a tenant shall, in addition to being subject to any other penalties or remedies permitted by law or by this Code, be barred thereafter from applying for or collecting any further rent increase for the affected housing accommodation. The finding by the DHCR that the owner has complied with such order or that the conduct which resulted in the finding of harassment has ceased, shall result in the prospective elimination of the sanctions provided for in this section.

(e) The failure of any owner to pay any fine, penalty or assessment authorized by the RSL or this Code shall, until such fine, penalty or assessment is paid, bar an owner from applying for or collecting any further rent increases for such housing accommodation. The late payment of any fine, penalty or assessment shall result in the prospective elimination of such sanction.

2526.3 Injunctions by supreme court.

The DHCR may commence proceedings in the supreme court to enjoin violations of the RSL, this Code, or orders issued pursuant thereto. In any such proceedings, the DHCR shall not be required to post bond.

2526.4 Oaths, subpoenas, hearing officers.

The DHCR may administer oaths, issue subpoenas, conduct investigations, make inspections and designate officers to hear and report.

2526.5 Confidentiality of information.

The DHCR shall safeguard the confidentiality of information furnished to it at the request of the person furnishing such information, unless such information must be made public or available to a governmental agency in the interest of establishing a record for the future guidance of persons subject to the RSL.

2526.6 Inspection and records.

(a) An owner shall, as the DHCR may from time to time require, furnish information under oath or affirmation or otherwise, permit inspection and copying of records and other documents and permit inspection of any housing accommodations.

(b) An owner shall, as the DHCR may from time to time require, make and keep records and other documents and make reports.

PART 2527 - PROCEEDINGS BEFORE THE DHCR

Section 2527.1 Proceedings instituted by owner or tenant.

A proceeding is instituted by an owner or a tenant with the filing of an application or complaint for adjustment of rent, or for other relief provided by the RSL or this Code. Such application or complaint shall be verified or affirmed by the applicant or complainant and filed upon the appropriate form prescribed by the DHCR.

2527.2 Proceedings instituted by the DHCR.

The DHCR may institute a proceeding on its own initiative whenever the DHCR deems it necessary or appropriate pursuant to the RSL or this Code.

2527.3 Notice to the parties affected.

(a) Where the application or complaint or any answer or reply thereto is made by an owner or tenant, the DHCR shall serve all parties adversely affected thereby with a copy of such application, complaint, answer or reply.

(b) Where the proceeding is instituted by the DHCR, it shall forward to all parties affected thereby a notice setting forth the proposed action.

(c) Except where an attorney or other authorized representative appears for the owner, any notice, order or other process or paper, directed to the person named in the last filed registration statement as the owner at the address given therein, or where a notice of change in identity has been filed, to the person named as owner and at the address given in the most recent such notice, shall constitute notice to the person who is then the owner. In addition thereto, the DHCR shall also serve all parties at the address specified on the application or complaint.

2527.4 Answer.

A person who has been served with a notice of a proceeding accompanied by an application or complaint shall have no less than twenty (20) days from the date of mailing in which to answer or reply, except that in exceptional circumstances, the DHCR may require a shorter period. Every answer or reply shall be verified or affirmed, and an original and one copy shall be filed with the DHCR.

2527.5 Preliminary action by the DHCR.

At any stage of a proceeding the DHCR may:

(a) Reject the application or complaint if it is insufficient or defective.

(b) Make investigations of the facts, conduct inspections, hold conferences, and require the filing of reports, evidence, affidavits, or other material relevant to the proceeding.

(c) Forward to or make available for inspection by either party any relevant evidence and afford an opportunity to file a rebuttal thereto.

(d) For good cause shown, except where prohibited by the RSL, accept for filing any papers, even though not filed within the time required by this Code.

(e) Require any person to appear or produce documents or both pursuant to a subpoena issued by the DHCR.

(f) Consolidate two or more applications, complaints, or proceedings which have at least one ground in common.

(g) Forward to any party a notice of action proposed to be taken.

(h) Grant or order a hearing.

(i) On its own initiative or upon application of any affected owner or tenant, consolidate proceedings applicable to the same building or group of buildings or development, notwithstanding that the housing accommodations affected may be subject to different regulations; in any such consolidated proceedings the determination with respect to any housing accommodation shall be made in accordance with the appropriate law or regulation applicable to such accommodations. Proceedings once consolidated may be severed for good cause shown.

(j) On its own initiative, or at the request of a court of competent jurisdiction, or for good cause shown upon application of any affected party, expedite the processing of a matter.

(k) Sever issues within a proceeding for purposes of issuing an Order and Determination with respect to certain issues while reserving other issues for subsequent determination.

2527.6 Determination.

The DHCR, on such terms and conditions as it shall determine, may:

(a) Dismiss the application or complaint if it fails to substantially comply with the provisions of the RSL or this Code.

(b) Grant or deny the application or complaint in whole or in part.

(c) Issue an appropriate order in a proceeding instituted on DHCR's own initiative.

(d) Issue conditional or provisional orders as may be deemed appropriate under the circumstances. A copy of any order issued shall be forwarded to all parties to the proceeding by the DHCR as the DHCR directs.

(e) Notwithstanding any other provision of this Code, no order shall be deemed final and binding for purposes of judicial review except in accordance with Part 2529 of this Title (Administrative Review).

2527.7 Pending proceedings.

Except as otherwise provided herein, unless undue hardship or prejudice results therefrom, this Code shall apply to any proceeding pending before the DHCR, which proceeding commenced on or after April 1, 1984, or where a provision of this Code is amended, or an applicable statute is enacted or amended during the pendency of a proceeding, the determination shall be made in accordance with the changed provision.

2527.8 Modification or revocation of orders.

The DHCR, on application of either party, or on its own initiative, and upon notice to all parties affected, may issue a superseding order modifying or revoking any order issued by it under this or any previous Code where the DHCR finds that such order was the result of illegality, irregularity in vital matters or fraud.

2527.9 When a notice or paper shall be deemed served.

(a) Except as otherwise provided by section 2529.2 of this Title (Time For Filing A PAR), notices, orders, answers and other papers may be served personally or by mail. When service, other than by the DHCR, is made personally or by mail, an affidavit by the person making the service or mailing shall constitute sufficient proof of service. When service is by registered or certified mail, the stamped post office receipt shall constitute sufficient proof of service. Once sufficient proof of service has been submitted to the DHCR, the burden of proving non-receipt shall be on the party denying receipt.

(b) Where a notice of appearance has been filed by an attorney, in accordance with section 2523.6 of this Title (Notices of Appearance), service on the attorney shall be deemed proper service as if made on the party or parties represented.

2527.10 Amendments to complaint or application.

(a) Right to amend. The DHCR may authorize an amendment to a complaint or application at any time on good cause shown, except that an applicant or complainant shall have the right to amend the application or complaint in writing prior to the time within which an answer may be filed.

(b) Service. Any amendment to an application or complaint shall be served upon all affected parties in the same manner as the original application or complaint.

(c) Amended answer or reply. When an application or complaint is amended after an answer has been filed, all affected parties may file an amended answer or reply within the time provided for the answer or reply.

2527.11 Advisory opinions and Operational Bulletins.

(a) The DHCR may render advisory opinions as to the DHCR's interpretation of the RSL, this Code or procedures, on the DHCR's own initiative or at the request of a party.

(b) In addition to the advisory opinion issued under subdivision (a), the DHCR may take such other required and appropriate action as it deems necessary for the timely implementation of the RSL and this Code, and for the preservation of regulated rental housing in accordance with section 2520.3 of this Title (Construction and Implementation). Such other action may include the issuance and updating of schedules, forms, instructions, and the official interpretative opinions and explanatory statements of general policy of the Commissioner, including Operational Bulletins, with respect to the RSL and this Code.

PART 2528 - REGISTRATION OF HOUSING ACCOMMODATIONS

Section 2528.1 Initial registration.

Each housing accommodation subject to the RSL on April 1, 1984, or thereafter, and not exempted from registration by the DHCR, shall be registered by the owner thereof with the DHCR within 90 days after such date.

2528.2 Initial registration requirements.

(a) The initial registration shall be made on forms prescribed or approved by the DHCR, and shall include:

(1) the address of the building or group of buildings or development in which such housing accommodation is located and the name of the tenant residing therein;

(2) the number of housing accommodations in the building or group of buildings or development;

(3) the number of housing accommodations in the building or group of buildings or development sub-

ject to the RSL and the number of such housing accommodations subject to the City Rent Law;

(4) the rent charged on April 1, 1984, or the rent charged on the date the housing accommodation became subject to the requirements of this Part, and any changes in such rent between such date and the date of registration;

(5) the number of rooms in such housing accommodation; and

(6) all services provided for in the last lease or rental agreement, provided or required to be provided on the applicable base date, or thereafter.

(b) Registration of housing accommodations subject to the City Rent Law immediately prior to the date of filing the initial registration statement shall include, in addition to the items set forth in subdivision (a) of this section, where existing, the maximum rent immediately prior to the date that such housing accommodations became subject to the RSL or the requirements of this Part.

(c) Copies of the registration shall be filed in such manner and in such place or places as the DHCR may designate. In addition, a copy of the Building Services Registration form shall be posted in a public area of the building as prescribed in the DHCR's Instructions for Rent Registration.

(d) One copy of the Initial Apartment Registration form which pertains to the tenant's housing accommodation shall be sent by the owner to the tenant by certified mail. Service of such form pursuant to this subdivision (d) together with the Notice of Initial Legal Registered Rent shall constitute proper service of such Notice of Initial Legal Registered Rent under section 2523.1 of this Title. Provided however, that for registrations served prior to the effective date of this subdivision (d), any method of service permitted by the DHCR at the time of service shall be deemed to have the same effect as service by certified mailing.

2528.3 Annual registration requirements.

In such manner and at such time as shall be determined by the DHCR pursuant to section 2527.11 of this Title (Advisory Opinions and Operational Bulletins):

(a) an annual registration shall be filed containing the current rent for each housing accommodation not otherwise exempt, a certification of services, and such other information as may be required by the DHCR pursuant to the RSL.

(b) upon filing an annual registration, the owner shall provide each tenant then in occupancy with a copy of that portion of such annual registration applicable to the tenant's housing accommodation.

2528.4 Penalty for failure to register.

The failure to properly and timely comply with the initial or annual rent registration as required by this Part shall, until such time as such registration is completed, bar an owner from applying for or collecting any rent in excess of:

a) if no initial registration has taken place, the legal regulated rent in effect on the date that the housing accommodation became subject to the registration requirements of this Part; or

b) the legal regulated rent in effect on April first of the year for which an annual registration was required to be filed, or such other date of that year as may be determined by the DHCR pursuant to section 2528.3 of this Part (Annual Registration Requirements).

The late filing of a registration shall result in the elimination, prospectively of such penalty.

2528.5 Confidentiality.

Registration information filed with the DHCR pursuant to this Part shall not be subject to the Freedom of Information Law, provided that such information relative to a tenant, owner, lessor or subtenant shall be made available to such party or his or her authorized representative.

PART 2529 - ADMINISTRATIVE REVIEW

Section 2529.1 Persons who may file.

(a) A petition for administrative review (PAR) of an order issued by a Rent Administrator may be filed by a party to the proceeding, or other necessary party, in the manner provided in this Part, where such petition alleges the errors upon which such order is based.

(b) (1) A joint PAR, verified or affirmed by each person joining therein, may be filed by two or more owners or tenants, where at least one ground is common to all persons so filing. The Commissioner, in his discretion, may treat such PAR as joint or several.

(2) A PAR may also be filed by a representative of a party, including an attorney at law, provided that said representative duly verifies or affirms the PAR and provided that such representative includes, at the time of the filing of the PAR, written evidence of authorization to act in such representative capacity for the purpose of filing the PAR.

(c) The Commissioner may, in his discretion, consolidate two or more PAR's which have at least one ground in common.

2529.2 Time for filing a PAR.

A PAR against an order of a Rent Administrator must be filed in person or by mail with the DHCR within thirty-five days after the date such order is issued. A PAR served by mail must be postmarked not more than thirty-five days after the date of such order, to be deemed timely filed. If the prepaid postage on the envelope in which the PAR is mailed is by private postage meter, and the envelope does not have an official U.S. Postal Service postmark, then the PAR will not be considered timely filed unless received within the aforementioned thirty-five days or the petitioner submits other adequate proof of mailing within said thirty-five days, such as an official Postal Service receipt or certificate of mailing.

2529.3 Form and content of a PAR.

A PAR may be filed only on a form prescribed by the DHCR, which shall be verified or affirmed by the party filing same, or his or her duly designated representative, and which shall have attached thereto a complete copy of the order to be reviewed.

2529.4 Service and filing of a PAR.

(a) Each PAR shall be filed in an original and one copy at the Division of Housing and Community Renewal,

Rent Stabilization Code

Office of Rent Administration, 92-31 Union Hall Street, Jamaica, New York 11433, unless otherwise provided on the form prescribed by the Commissioner for such PAR.

(b) A copy of the PAR shall be served by the DHCR upon the adverse party.

(c) A PAR will not be accepted for filing unless accompanied by a complete copy of the order to be reviewed.

2529.5 Time of filing an answer to a PAR.

Any person served with a PAR as provided in subdivision (b) of section 2529.4 of this Part (Service And Filing Of A PAR), may, within twenty days from the date of mailing of a copy of the PAR by the DHCR pursuant to section 2529.4(b) of this Part, file a verified or affirmed answer thereto, by filing the same with the DHCR. A copy of such answer to the PAR shall be served by the DHCR upon the adverse party. The Commissioner may, in his discretion, and for good cause shown, extend the time within which to answer.

2529.6 Scope of review.

Review pursuant to this Part shall be limited to facts or evidence before a Rent Administrator as raised in the petition. Where the petitioner submits with the petition certain facts or evidence which he or she establishes could not reasonably have been offered or included in the proceeding prior to the issuance of the order being appealed, the proceeding may be remanded for redetermination to the Rent Administrator to consider such facts or evidence.

2529.7 Action by Commissioner.

Within a reasonable time after the filing of the PAR and the answers, if any, the Commissioner may:

(a) Reject a PAR which is timely filed if it is insufficient or defective, but may provide a specified period of time within which to perfect the PAR.

(b) Make such investigation of the facts, hold such conferences, and require the filing of such reports, evidence, affidavits, or other material relevant to the proceeding as he may deem necessary or appropriate.

(c) Forward to, or make available for inspection by either party, any relevant evidence, and afford an opportunity to file rebuttal thereto.

(d) For good cause shown, accept for filing any papers, other than a PAR, even though not filed within the time required by this Part.

(e) Require any person to appear or produce documents, or both, pursuant to a subpoena issued by the Commissioner.

(f) Grant or order a hearing.

2529.8 Final determination by the Commissioner.

The Commissioner, on such terms and conditions as he determines, shall:

(a) Dismiss the PAR if it fails substantially to comply with the provisions of the RSL or this Code; or

(b) Grant or deny the PAR, in whole or in part, or remand the proceeding to the Rent Administrator for further action;

The Commissioner shall inform all parties to the PAR of the grounds upon which such decision is based.

2529.9 Modification or revocation of orders by the Commissioner.

The Commissioner, on application of either party or on his own initiative, and upon notice to all parties affected, may, prior to the date that a proceeding for judicial review has been commenced in the supreme court pursuant to article 78 of the Civil Practice Law and Rules, issue a superseding order modifying or revoking any order issued by him under this or any previous Code where he finds that such order was the result of illegality, irregularity in vital matters or fraud.

2529.10 Pending PAR proceedings.

Unless undue hardship or prejudice would result therefrom, this Code shall apply to any PAR proceeding pending before the DHCR commenced on or after April 1, 1984, or where a provision of this Code is amended, or an applicable statute is enacted or amended during the pendency of a PAR, the determination shall be in accordance with the changed provision.

Rent Stabilization Code

2529.11 Time within which the Commissioner shall take final action.

If the Commissioner does not act finally within a period of ninety days after a PAR is filed, or within such extended period as provided for herein, the PAR may be "deemed denied" by the Petitioner for the purpose of commencing a proceeding pursuant to section 2530.1 of this Title (Commencement Of Proceeding). The Commissioner may, however, grant one such extension, not to exceed thirty days, with the consent of the party filing the PAR; any further extension may only be granted with the consent of all parties to the PAR. Unless a proceeding for judicial review pursuant to article 78 of the Civil Practice Law and Rules has been commenced, the Commissioner shall determine a PAR notwithstanding that such ninety day or extended period has elapsed.

2529.12 Stays.

The filing of a PAR against an order, other than an order adjusting, fixing or establishing the legal regulated rent, shall stay such order until the final determination of the PAR by the Commissioner. Notwithstanding the above, that portion of an order fixing a penalty pursuant to subdivision (a) of section 2526.1 of this Title (Overcharge Penalties), that portion of an order resulting in a retroactive rent abatement pursuant to section 2523.4 of this Title (Failure To Maintain Services), that portion of an order resulting in a retroactive rent decrease pursuant to section 2522.3 of this Title (Fair Market Rent Appeal), and that portion of an order resulting in a retroactive rent increase pursuant to section 2522.4(a)(2), (3), (b) and (c) of this Title (Adjustment Of Legal Regulated Rent), shall also be stayed by the timely filing of a PAR against such orders until sixty days have elapsed after the determination of the PAR by the Commissioner. However, nothing herein contained shall limit the Commissioner from granting or vacating a stay under appropriate circumstances, on such terms and conditions as the Commissioner may deem appropriate.

PART 2530 - JUDICIAL REVIEW

Section 2530.1 Commencement of proceeding.

A proceeding for judicial review pursuant to article 78 of the Civil Practice Law and Rules may be instituted only to review a final order of the DHCR pursuant to section 2526.2(c)(2) of this Title (Harassment Enforcement Orders); or to review a final order of the Commissioner pursuant to section 2529.8 of this Title (Final Determination by Commissioner); or after the expiration of the 90 day or extended period within which the Commissioner may determine a PAR pursuant to section 2529.11 of this Title (Time Within Which Commissioner Shall Take Final Action), and which, therefore, may be "deemed denied" by the Petitioner. The petition for judicial review shall be brought in the supreme court in the county in which the subject housing accommodation is located and shall be served upon the DHCR and the Attorney General. A proceeding for judicial review of an order issued pursuant to section 2526.2(c)(2), or section 2529.8 of this Title shall be brought within 60 days after the issuance of such order. A party aggrieved by a PAR order issued after the 90 day or extended period of time within which the petitioner could deem his or her petition "denied" pursuant to section 2529.11 of this Title, shall have sixty days from the date of such order to commence a proceeding for judicial review, notwithstanding that sixty days have elapsed after such 90 day or extended "deemed denial" period has expired. Service of the petition upon the DHCR shall be made by personal delivery of a copy thereof to Counsel's Office at the DHCR's principal office, One Fordham Plaza, Bronx, New York 10458, or such other address as may be designated by the Commissioner, and to an Assistant Attorney General at an office of the New York State Attorney General in the City of New York.

RENT STABILIZATION REGULATIONS OF THE HOUSING AND DEVELOPMENT ADMINISTRATION

[Promulgated August 7, 1969]

Pursuant to the authority vested in the Administrator of the Housing and Development Administration by chapter sixty-one of the New York City Charter and by section YY51-4.0c of the Rent Stabilization Law of nineteen hundred sixty-nine, I do hereby promulgate the following rent stabilization regulations:

These Regulations implement the Code of the Rent Stabilization Association of New York City, Inc. and the Code of the Metropolitan Hotel Industry Stabilization Association, Inc., which are now superseded by the Rent Stabilization Code for Rent Stabilized Apartments in New York City (effective May 1, 1987). See the immediately preceding portion of this Part. These Regulations are expressly retained in the new Rent Stabilization Code § 2520.2.

SECTION 1.

Definitions

When used in these regulations, unless a different meaning clearly appears from the context, the following terms shall mean and include:

a. "Administrator." The Housing and Development Administrator.

b. "Association." A real estate industry stabilization association registered with the Housing and Development Administration as provided in Section YY51-6.0 of the rent stabilization law or a hotel industry stabilization association registered with such administration as provided in Section YY51-6.1 of such law. [Am May 29, 1970]

c. "City rent agency." The Office of Rent Control in the Department of Rent and Housing Maintenance of the Housing and Development Administration.

d. "Conciliation and Appeals Board." A board appointed

by the Mayor with the approval of the City Council to receive and act upon complaints and appeals as provided in Section YY51-6.0 of the rent stabilization law.

e. "Member in good standing." An owner of dwelling units subject to the rent stabilization law who joined an association within 30 days of acceptance of its registration by the Housing and Development Administration or within 30 days after becoming such owner, whichever is later, provided that such dwelling units were not under actual control of the City rent agency when he became the owner thereof, and further provided such owner complies with prescribed levels of fair rent increases established under the rent stabilization law, does not violate any order of a conciliation and appeals board, is not found by such board to have harassed a tenant to obtain vacancy of his dwelling unit and has not been expelled or suspended from such membership.

SECTION 2.

Certification of Membership

An association shall file with the Housing and Development Administration within 35 days after its acceptance for registration a certification, in duplicate, of the membership of the association, indicating the mailing address of each member and identifying each building and dwelling unit owned by such member and subject to the rent stabilization law. Such certification shall be amended by the association from time to time whenever such membership shall be changed by either addition of new members or the expulsion or suspension of existing members.

SECTION 3.

Failure of Owners to Join Association, Suspension and Expulsion

Within ten days after a determination by either a conciliation and appeals board or an association that an owner is not a member in good standing, such board or association, as the case may be, shall transmit a copy of such determination to the administrator. Upon receipt of such a determination or upon a finding by the administrator that the owner of a dwelling unit subject to the rent stabilization law has not joined an association, the administrator shall cause the City rent agency, upon notice to the owner, to establish and register the lawful maximum rent for such dwelling unit pursuant to the provisions of Title Y of Chapter 51 of the Administrative Code based upon the rent charged therefor on May thirty-one, nineteen hundred sixty-eight. Thereafter, said dwelling unit shall remain subject to the provisions of such Title Y until such time, if any, as the owner's membership in good standing in the association with respect to said dwelling unit shall be reinstated in accordance with the terms and conditions of the determination.

SECTION 4.
Records

A record shall be made of every determination by a conciliation and appeals board. It shall consist of a statement of the facts at issue, the board's determination, the reasons therefor, and the terms and conditions of the board's determination including, where applicable, terms for reinstatement as a member in good standing. Such records shall be preserved for five years and shall be available for study by the rent guidelines board created pursuant to Section YY51-5.0 of the rent stabilization law.

SECTION 5.
EXPULSION FROM AND READMISSION TO AN ASSOCIATION.

a. No provision in any code shall be construed as authorizing an association to expel a member from an association or to reinstate a member to an association other than by an order of the Conciliation and Appeals Board, except as provided under this section.

b. An association shall expel a member for non-payment of dues upon the determination that the payment of dues for such member is in arrears in excess of sixty days; after the expiration of forty days of such period, the association shall give the member written notice by certified mail, return receipt requested, to an address indicated for correspondence, of such arrearage and inform the member as to the consequences if such default has not been rectified within twenty days of mailing. If such mail is returned to an association, the association shall mail a similar notice by regular mail to the address indicated for correspondence and in care of any other person and to any other address listed in its current membership records, informing the member of the remaining period to pay such dues. An order of expulsion shall be served by regular mail and an association shall obtain a receipt of mailing. Upon such explusion an association shall certify to the Housing and Development Administration in writing of such action and the grounds therefor.

c. An association shall have the sole power, subject to obtaining the specific prior written approval of the Housing and Development Administration, to grant reinstatement to any former member who has been expelled for non-payment of dues whether by order of the Conciliation and Appeals Board or by action of the association, provided that the applicant has complied with the prescribed levels of fair rent increases and other provisions of the code of such association, and that the re-enrollment application meets the following criteria:

(1) The applicant demonstrates and establishes that one of the following factual circumstances exists:

(a) The property was expelled because of the owner's failure to pay membership dues for dwelling units which became vacant between July 1, 1971, and June 30, 1974, if such was required by an association as an obligation of membership;

(b) The owner or agent of the property, through no fault of his own, was not properly served with written notice of the arrearage of dues or the consequences of failure to pay such dues as required by the provisions of this section applicable at the time of the expulsion;

(c) The applicant has been charged by a court with the responsibility of the management and maintenance of such property as an administrator, executor, trustee, referee, or any other similar capacity;

(d) The applicant acquired title through a foreclosure sale or by deed in lieu of foreclosure, with the result that there has been an actual and permanent transfer of title for value at arm's length, which was based upon an arm's length mortgage for value, and provided that no individual or entity having an ownership interest in the property during the period dues were in arrears or at the time of expulsion currently has any ownership interest in the property;

(e) The property was involved in an actual and permanent transfer of title to a bona fide purchaser for value at arm's length, who had been informed by the association that the property was in a good standing and there was no arrearage of dues with an association within sixty (60) days prior the time the title was transferred when, in fact, the property was no longer in good standing or there was an arrearage of dues at such time, or, if such transfer took place on or before March 31, 1977, that such purchaser had a reasonable belief that the property was in good standing, and provided that no individual or entity having an ownership interest in the property during the period dues were in arrears or at the time of expulsion currently has any ownership interest in the property;

(f) The property was acquired from the City, the State or the United States government or an agency, entity or authority thereof, and provided that no individual or entity having an ownership interest in the property during the period dues were in arrears or at the time of expulsion currently has any ownership interest in the property; or,

(g) The entire property, or all residential portions thereof, was the subject of a lease and the applicant has recovered possession of such property or the residential portion, either by summary proceeding or by the termination of a lease of ten or more years, and provided that the owner had no interest in the operation or management of the property during the period dues were in arrears or at the time of expulsion.

(2) Timely application is made to be readmitted during the following periods:

(a) Such application is made not more than six (6) months after the date the property was expelled from an association and, if pursuant to subsections c(1)(c) through (g), within 30 days of the taking of possession or title by the applicant; or,

(b) Such application is made within sixty (60) days of the effective date of this section by the applicant and such application may also be filed by a successor in interest to an owner who would have qualified as an applicant pursuant to subsection c(1) of this section and provided that, as to such successor, no individual or entity having an ownership interest in the property during the period dues were in arrears or at the time of expulsion currently has any ownership interest in the property, or by a successor lessee of an entire property or all residential portions thereof, provided that no individual or entity having an interest in the operation or management of the property during the period dues were in arrears or at the time of the expulsion has any operational or management interest in the property.

(3) An applicant applying for readmission to an association pursuant to subsections c(1)(c) through (g) or (2)(b) submits to an association the following additional material:

(a) If the application is pursuant to subsection (1)(c), a copy of the court order pursuant to which the application is made;

(b) If the application is pursuant to subsection (1)(d), a certified copy of the mortgage instrument which was the basis for the foreclosure or deed transferring title;

(c) If the application is pursuant to subsection (1)(e), a certified copy of the deed;

(d) If the application is pursuant to subsection (1)(d) through (f) or (2)(b), affidavits sufficient to establish the requirements regarding the nature of the transfer and ownership interests; or,

(e) If the application is pursuant to Subsection 1(g), an affidavit sufficient to establish the required nature of the recovery of possession and, if possession was recovered through a summary proceeding, a copy of the judgment or document filed with the court which terminated possession.

(4) The applicant pays to an association an amount equal to outstanding membership dues, current membership dues, and any processing fee imposed by an association to defray its administrative expenses.

d. Prior to granting their respective approvals, an association and the Housing and Development Administration may require that the applicant submit additional statements, information, documents, affidavits, records or reports as they may consider desirable to assist them in reaching a determination. Prior to Housing and Development Administration granting its approval, the Housing and Development Administration may require that an association certify to it that the applicant has satisfied the requirements of subsection c of this section. [As am by Am No 2 (June 13, 1975), and Am No 3 (July 11, 1977)][1]

SECTION 6.

Other Discipline by Association

a. No association shall fine a member for any violation, as provided in section YY51-6.0(c)(11), in excess of $1,000.

b. A member shall have the right to appeal any disciplinary action taken by an association to a Conciliation and Appeals Board, which Board shall issue regulations governing the form, content and time of such an appeal by a member. Such regulation shall provide for a stay of disciplinary action during the time provided for the disposition of such an appeal. [Added May 29, 1970]

[1] Explanation of amendment. This amendment modifies already existing regulations regarding expulsion from associations based upon a failure to pay dues and readmission to members who were expelled for failure to pay dues.

Experience has indicated that there are a number of specific situations in which there are compelling equitable reasons to grant requests for approval of readmission. This amendment carefully defines those situations and the time and manner in which such applications for readmission may be made.

In addition, because claims have been made by owners that there has been an improper service of an arrearage of dues, the regulations define the manner in which notice of arrearages are to be served and required that associations, both for the protection of themselves and of their members, retain documentary proof of the mailing.

Note should be made of the provisions of subsection c(1)(e), which relate to a bona fide purchaser for value at arm's length who believed that the property involved in the transfer was a member in good standing of an association. These amendments require that after April 1, 1977, such a purchaser will be eligible for re-admission for unpaid dues only if the purchaser was informed improperly by an association that the property was in good standing and that there was no arrearage of dues and that such inquiry is to be made within sixty days of the transfer of title which is also the length of time provided in subsection b for an association to determine that a member is in arrears. This qualification will not become effective until April 1, 1977, in order that the industry become aware that any binding information regarding the status of a property should be obtained from the association involved.

SECTION 7.
Dues

The Administrator on his own motion or upon application of an owner may review the amount of dues charged by an association and, if said dues are found by the Administrator to be excessive, he shall order them reduced to a specified amount. [Added May 29, 1970]

SECTION 8.
Salaries of Conciliation and Appeals Board

Salaries of a Conciliation and Appeals Board in effect as of the effective date of this regulation may not be changed without the approval of the Administrator. [Added May 29, 1970]

SECTION 9.
Budget and Accounts

The Administrator may, on his own motion or on application of an owner, require a review and audit of the accounts of an association and shall have the power to institute such procedures and issue such directives as may be necessary to prevent unreasonable or excessive expenditures. He may also adopt procedures and issue directives to assure that the funds provided for the operation of the Conciliation and Appeals Board are adequate for that purpose. [Added May 29, 1970]

SECTION 10.
Abrogation of Code Provisions

The Administrator may, by written order, abrogate any part of a code of an association, if after appropriate notice of at least 15 days to the association and opportunity for hearing, it appears to the Administrator that such abrogation is necessary or appropriate to effectuate the purposes of the rent stabilization law. No proceeding by an association or member adversely affected by an order of the Administrator abrogating any part of the code may be instituted pursuant to Article 78 of the Civil Practice Law and Rules unless the petition is filed within 30 days after such order, after being made by the Administrator, is mailed to the association. Service upon the Administrator shall be made by leaving a copy thereof with the office of the Assistant Administrator for Legal Affairs of the Housing and Development Administration at his office at 100 Gold Street, New York, New York 10038. [Added May 29, 1970]

ORDERS OF THE RENT GUIDANCE BOARD

Order Number 1—Rent Levels June 1, 1968 Through June 30, 1970

Pursuant to the Authority Vested in it by the Rent Stabilization Law of 1969, the Rent Guidelines Board hereby establishes and adopts the following levels of fair rent increases over rentals charged on May thirty-first, nineteen hundred sixty-eight, for dwelling units covered by such law:

Lease Renewals

For two year lease renewals effective on or after June 1, 1968: 10 per cent;

For three year or longer lease renewals effective on or after June 1, 1968: 15 per cent;

For all one year lease renewals effective on or after June 1, 1968, the permissible level of rent increase shall be 10 per cent above the rent charged on May 31, 1968 provided however that the owner shall grant to the tenant, if still in possession on the date hereof, the right to a further one year renewal at no further increase above such stabilized rent. In the event of a renewal or other extension of tenancy for any period less than one year on or after June 1, 1968, the same permissible level of rent increases as applies to one year renewals shall apply provided that the owner shall grant to the tenant the right to continue his occupancy for such period as will afford the tenant a two year occupancy at no increase in rent above 10 per cent over the rent payable on May 31, 1968.

It is further provided that where a lease which was renewed for one year after May 31, 1968 terminated according to its term, and the tenant thereafter either renewed his lease for three years or entered into a new lease for three years (as hereinafter defined), the stabilized rent shall be 10 per cent above the rent charged on

May 31, 1968 until two full years have expired from the date of the initial renewal after May 31, 1968, and thereafter shall be 15 per cent above the rent charged on May 31, 1968, i.e., the stabilized rent now collectible on three year renewals.

Fractional Terms

For the purpose of these guidelines, any renewal lease or tenancy for a period up to and including one year shall be deemed a one year lease or tenancy; the same for a period over one year and up to and including two years shall be deemed a two year lease; and the same for a period over two years and up to and including three years shall be deemed a three year lease.

Leases on Vacant Apartments

Based on the establishment of the aforesaid levels of permissible increases, and pursuant to Section YY51-5.0e of the Rent Stabilization Law, the permissible increases on any housing accommodation covered by this law which becomes vacant shall be 15 per cent on a full two year lease and 25 per cent on a full three year lease, until July 1, 1970.

Order Number 2—Rent Levels July 1, 1970 Through June 30, 1971

Pursuant to the Authority Vested in it by the Rent Stabilization Law of 1969, the Rent Guidelines Board hereby establishes and adopts the following levels of fair rent increases over lawful rentals actually charged and paid on June 30, 1970 or if vacant on June 30, on the last date on which rent was paid on such unit, for dwelling units covered by such law (other than hotel dwelling units):

Lease Renewals

In addition to a one per cent increase affecting all leases which is subject to adjustment in later years of the lease as explained below:

For one-year leases expiring before July 1, 1972: 6 per cent;

For two-year leases expiring before July, 1973: 8 per cent;

For three-year leases expiring before July 1, 1974: 11 per cent.

The one per cent increase affecting all leases is designed as a stabilizer to equalize changes in the yield on capital invested in real estate governed by the Rent Stabilization Law with changes in the yields paid by other long-term investments. This charge for 1970-71 is subject to adjustment by the Rent Guidelines Board on any anniversary date of this Order. No such adjustment will increase or decrease the rent (including stabilizer) by more than one percent in any year of a lease.

Fractional Terms

Except as to leases on vacant apartments, for the purpose of these guidelines any lease or tenancy for a period up to and including one year shall be deemed a one year lease or tenancy; the same for a period over one year and up to and including two years shall be deemed a two year lease; and the same for a period over two years and up to and including three years shall be deemed a three year lease. As to leases on vacant apartments, for the purpose of these guidelines any lease for a period from one year to less than two years shall be deemed a one year lease; the same for a period from two years to less than three years shall be deemed a two year lease; and the same for a period of three years or more shall be deemed a three year lease.

Leases on Vacant Apartments

Where a dwelling unit becomes vacant, the levels of fair rent increase governing the new tenancy are the same levels over rentals charged on June 30, 1970 as those set forth above for lease renewals, plus 7.5 percent over rentals charged on June 30, 1970 on each vacancy of such unit subsequent to the effective date of this Order.

Escalator Clauses

Where a lease for a dwelling unit in effect on May 31, 1968 contained an escalator clause for increased costs of operation, the lawful rental on June 30, 1970 over which the fair rent increase under this Order is computed shall include the increased rental, if any, due under such clause. Moreover, where a lease contained such an escalator clause, unless the owner elects or has elected in writing to delete such clause effective on later than July 1, 1970 from the existing lease and all subsequent leases for such dwelling unit, the increased rental, if any, due under such escalator clause shall be offset against the amount of increase permissible under this Order.

Credits

Rental charged and paid in excess of the levels of fair rent increase established by this Order shall be fully credited against the next month's rent.

Order Number 2a—Rent Levels for Decontrolled Units
June 1, 1968 Through June 30, 1971

Pursuant to the Authority Vested in it by the Rent Stabilization Law of 1969, the Rent Guidelines Board hereby establishes and adopts the following guidelines for rent levels of certain decontrolled dwelling units:

Applicability

This Order shall apply for the period June 1, 1968 thorough June 30, 1971, to any dwelling unit which was subject to control under the city rent and rehabilitation law on May 31, 1968, was subsequently decontrolled and is now subject to the provisions of the Rent Stabilization Law. This Order establishes guidelines only for the first lease following decontrol; however, where a decontrol lease was entered into pursuant to paragraph (c) or (d) of Section 2(f)(15) of the Rent and Eviction Regulations, this Order does not apply to or modify the terms thereof, but is applicable to the first lease for a term commencing after its expiration or other termination. Any subsequent lease shall be subject to the provisions of Rent Guidelines Board Order Number 1 if a lease for a term commencing on or before June 30, 1970, or Order Number 2 if a lease for a term commencing after such date. In no event may the rent under an existing lease be increased except pursuant to the terms thereof.

Renewal Leases

As used in this Order, "renewal lease" means any lease entered into by a tenant in occupancy, whether such occupancy was pursuant to a lease or a statutory tenancy.

The level of fair rent increase for such a renewal lease over the lawful rent actually charged and paid on May 31, 1968 shall be:

—as to dwelling unit of less than four rooms:

25 percent for a two-year lease; or 35 percent for a three-year lease

—as to dwelling unit of four or more rooms:

35 percent for a two-year lease; or 45 percent for a three-year lease which percentage increases shall be inclusive of the 10 percent of the two 10 percent increases, if any, paid under decontrol leases pursuant to Section 2(f)(15) of the Rent and Eviction Regulations, or any other non-service increases paid since May 31, 1968 pursuant to the Rent and Eviction Regulations. Where a renewal lease to which this Order applies is for a one-year term, the level of fair rent increase shall be that prescribed above for a two-year lease, provided that the owner offers to the tenant a one-year extension of the lease at the same rental.

Fractional Terms

For the purpose of this Order any lease or tenancy; (a) for a period up to and including one year shall be deemed a one-year lease or tenancy; (b) for a period over one year and up to and including two years shall be deemed a two-year lease; (c) and for a period over two years and up to and including three years shall be deemed a three-year lease.

Vacancy Leases

Where a dwelling unit was or is vacant at the time of decontrol or, if occupied at such time, when the first vacancy occurs thereafter, the first rent charged and paid for such dwelling unit under a lease with the new tenant shall be the lawful stabilization rent.

Credits

Rental charged and paid in excess of the levels of fair rent increase established by this Order shall be fully credited against the next month's rent.

Explanatory Statement on Order No. 2a

The Rent Stabilization Law of 1969 was intended to prevent excessive rent increases resulting from a low vacancy rate. Based upon an investigation into rental practices in the non-controlled rental market it was determined that May 31, 1968 would serve as an initial base date for determining future allowable increases. The City concluded that rents were then still being negotiated in a housing market where tenants had some degree of bargaining power.

However, Section YY51-6.0(c)(2) of the Rent Stabilization Law further provided that "nothing herein shall supersede or modify the rent increase permitted by the City rent agency following decontrol pursaunt to Section Y51-12.0 of the City rent and rehabilitation law and the regulations adopted thereunder." Section Y51-12.0, and the Rent and Eviction Regulations of the HDA referred to in Order No. 2a, provided for the decontrol of certain so-called luxury apartments. Order 2a relates exclusively to such decontrolled units.

Insofar as particular units were decontrolled pursuant to those regulations prior to May 31, 1968, they present no problem for this Board as the rents charged on May 31, 1968 were free market rents thereafter subject to the Orders of this Board.

However, because the rent control law deferred effective decontrol of units occupied by certain families as defined by that law, many of the units subject to decontrol under sections 2f(13) and (14) of the rent regulations were still subject to standard rent control on May 31, 1968, and were not effectively decontrolled until a subsequent date or in some cases they still remain subject to control until the characteristics of the occupying family change. Similarly, large numbers of the units subject to decontrol under Section 2f(15) became decontrolled on October 1, 1968 provided that the owners offered the tenants, depending on the size of the apartments, either a 1 year lease with a 10% increase or a 2 year lease with two 10% increases. The one year leases terminated last October 1st and the two year leases will terminate on October 1, 1970. The purpose of these leases was to afford the tenants in occupancy an opportunity to locate other quarters, if desired, before the owners could demand free market rentals following decontrol according to Y51-12.0

of the City rent law and the regulations adopted by the rent agency.

It is clear that in today's market, upon decontrol, owners can easily obtain extremely large increases for these apartments from their occupants. In many instances the rents which existing tenants could be forced by circumstances to agree to pay would be higher than those acceptable to prospective tenants not yet in occupancy. To allow a free market rental would mean that in many instances the rents to be charged to the former rent controlled tenants could entail tremendous hardships, particularly as most of the tenants could not readily locate other acceptable housing. On the other hand, the owners of such apartments anticipated receiving free market rentals for the apartments, as was provided for by the law then in effect and was contemplated by the Court in the case of Campo Corporation v City Rent and Rehabilitation Administration.

This Board has been called upon to balance the needs of those tenants formerly under control who wish to continue their tenancy against the claims of the owners that they should be afforded an opportunity to collect free market or comparable rents, as anticipated by both tenants and owners, before coming under the rates of permissible increase applicable to other stabilized apartments. In the statement accompanying our Order No. 2 this Board indicated its awareness of the problem and stated that it would deal separately with this issue.

The accompanying Order No. 2a of this Board establishes rates of permissible increase over the rent charged on May 31, 1968 for tenants in occupancy where the apartment was still controlled on May 31, 1968 and was or is subsequently decontrolled. Such tenants, of course, must be given the option of renewing for 1, 2, or 3 years.

The rates of increase set out in Order No. 2a are for the first renewal or vacancy lease made either after decontrol, or the expiration or termination of a decontrol lease provided for in Section 2f(15) of the Rent Regulations.

For example, if a tenant paying $300 per month on May 28, 1968 for an apartment of four or more rooms, entered into a two year decontrol lease commencing

October 1, 1968, and terminating on October 1, 1970, he can demand a new two year lease at a rental of $405 or a new three year lease at a rental of $435. It should be noted that with the two 10% increases on his "decontrol lease," the tenants would by October 1, 1970 have already been paying a rent of $363.

The Board concluded that where the first vacancy occurs after decontrol or after the expiration of a decontrol lease, the landlord should be able to obtain a free market first rent, provided that he did not obtain the vacancy by harassing the tenant in occupancy. Once the new tenant, who voluntarily agrees with the owner on the amount of the first rent, has executed a lease, he would be protected by the Rent Stabilization Law on future renewals.

Lastly, many of the leases covered by this Order have already been made and owners have been collecting increases in excess of the permissible rates. We recognize that this occurred because of confusion over the allowable rates and that many owners and tenants had applied to the Conciliation and Appeals Board for rulings on the permissible rate. Our Order requires any excess rent paid to be credited immediately and in full against the tenant's next rent bill(s).

The Housing and Development Administration has recently notified the Rent Stabilization Association of its intention to abrogate that portion of Section 66 of the Association's Code which permits the CAB to establish the rent levels for apartments under rent control on May 31, 1968 but subject to decontrol, based upon an opinion of HDA's General Counsel that such Code provision is in conflict with the statute and the responsibility properly lies with this Board.

Order Number 3—Rent Levels July 1, 1971 through June 30, 1972

Pursuant to the authority vested in it by the Rent Stabilization Law of 1969, the Rent Guidelines Board hereby establishes and adopts the following levels of fair rent increases over lawful rents actually charged and paid on June 30, 1971 (including "stabilizer," if any), or if an apartment was vacant on June 30, on the last date on which rent was paid on such unit, for dwelling units covered by such law (other than hotel dwelling units):

Lease Renewals

In addition to a one per cent increase here referred to as a "stabilizer", which is subject to adjustment in later years of the lease as explained below:

—For one-year leases expiring before July 1, 1973: 7 per cent;

—For two-year leases expiring before July 1, 1974: 9 per cent;

—For three-year leases expiring before July 1, 1975: 12 per cent.

Stabilizer

The one per cent increase affecting all leases to be known as a stabilizer is designed to equalize changes in the yield on capital invested in real estate governed by the Rent Stabilization Law with changes in the yields paid by other long term investments. This charge for 1971-72 is subject to adjustment by the Rent Guidelines Board on any anniversary date of this Order. No such adjustment will increase or decrease the rent (including stabilizer) by more than one per cent in any year of the lease.

The stabilizer governing leases entered into pursuant to Order Number 2 of the Rent Guidelines Board remain in effect for 1971-72.

Leases on Apartments Vacant on June 30

Where a dwelling unit is vacant on June 30, 1971, the levels of fair rent increase governing the new tenancy are the same levels over rental charged on the last date on which rent was paid prior to such vacancy as those set forth above for lease renewals (including stabilizer), plus 10 per cent.

Subleases

Where a dwelling unit is subleased pursuant to a clause which provides that upon the exercise of the privilege of subletting the rent payable to the owner effective upon the date of subletting may be established as if the renewal lease had been a vacancy lease, the levels of fair rent increase governing such tenancy are the same levels over rentals charged on June 30, 1971 as those set forth in this Order for lease renewals (including stabilizer), plus 10 per cent.

Fractional Terms

Except as to leases on vacant apartments, for the purpose of these guidelines any lease or tenancy for a period up to and including one year shall be deemed a one year lease or tenancy; the same for a period over one year and up to and including two years shall be deemed a two year lease; and the same for a period over two years and—Rasch Rent Control (7078) gals 1-300 and inserts up to and including three years shall be deemed a three year lease. As to leases on vacant apartments, for the purpose of these guidelines any lease for a period from one year to less than two years shall be deemed a one year lease; the same for a period from two years to less than three years shall be deemed a two year lease; and the same for a period of three years or more shall be deemed a three year lease.

Escalator Clauses

Where a lease for a dwelling unit in effect on May 31, 1968 contained an escalator clause for increased costs of operation, the lawful rental on June 30, 1971 over which the fair rent increase under this Order is computed shall include the increased rental, if any, due under such clause. Moreover, where a lease contained such an escalator clause, unless the owner elects or has elected in writing to delete such clause effective no later than July 1, 1971 from the existing lease and all subsequent leases for such dwelling unit, the increased rental, if any, due under such escalator clause shall be offset against the amount of increase permissible under this Order.

Credits

Rental charged and paid in excess of the levels of fair rent increase established by this Order shall be fully credited against the next month's rent.

Rent Guidance Board Orders

EXPLANATORY STATEMENT OF THE RENT GUIDELINES BOARD UPON ISSUANCE OF ORDER NUMBER 3—JULY 1, 1971 THROUGH JUNE 30, 1972

This statement describes the methods used by the Rent Guidelines Board in establishing, effective July 1, 1971 the amount of maximum rent increases which will be permitted under renewal leases of differing lengths in dwelling units subject to the Rent Stabilization Law.

Pursuant to Section YY51-5.0(d) the Board has, in establishing the permissible increases, considered thoroughly "the economic condition of the residential real estate industry in New York City". The level of the increases permitted under this order are based, in part on "The Report on the 1971 Price Index of Operating Costs for Uncontrolled Apartment Houses in New York City." This report is a result of a study conducted by the Bureau of Labor Statistics of the U.S. Department of Labor at the request of the City of New York and issued in June 1971. As a basis for their research the Bureau developed a weighted index of prices—as of April 1967, 1968, 1969, 1970, 1971—of the components which, taken together, comprise the operating costs for non-controlled apartment houses. These components are real estate taxes, labor costs, fuel and utilities, contract services, administrative costs, insurance costs, cost of parts and supplies and replacement costs. The selection of items for pricing in the index was based on the relative importance of the item in total operating costs and on the availability of reliable price data over time.

According to the Report "prices paid to operate uncontrolled apartment houses in New York City rose sharply by 13.4% between April 1970 and April 1971. . . . This 13.4% increase was significantly larger than any of the 3 earlier years covered by the index. The index rose by 3.5% between 1967 and 1968, increased by 4.0% in the next year, and the increase more than doubled, rising to 8.4% between 1969 and 1970". In determining that all major components of the index rose in 1971 the Report states that the largest increase was for fuel and utilities, up 43.9% and payroll costs, up 15.0%. The changes in the overall index reflect not only the rates of change but also the relative importance of the various components. Therefore, although fuel and utilities registered a 44% over the year price rise this component accounts for only 16% of operating expenses; while taxes which represent 43% of operating costs rose only 7.8% a figure significantly less than the 1970-71 all items rise of 13.4%.

After consulting mortgage lending institutions, city agencies, economists and other sources of information, the Board concluded that although prices would continue to rise over the next 3 years, the annual change relative to the base year would taper off. In studying past economic trends the Board felt there has begun a stabilizing in real estate taxes and the cost of fuel and utilities would now begin to level off.

In having made our calculation as to the future rate of increase in price index the Board then had to express these findings as a percentage increase in rent which would be required to meet the increase in the prices of operating costs.

In establishing last year's rates of permissible increase the Board operated on the basis that operating costs consumed 53% of total rental income. Therefore, to absorb a 2% increase in operating costs rents had to increase slightly more than 1%. Because of the substantial increase in operating costs we adjusted the figure to 56% in making our projection for the current year.

As the Board noted last year these figures represent only raw amounts for rental increases to which the Board made several adjustments and corrections as it is required by law to do. The Board raised the level of vacancy allowance for apartments vacated prior to June 30, 1971 based in part on the new vacancy decontrol law passed by the State Legislature. This is intended to encourage proper maintenance and allow a reasonable compensation for loss of income due to turnover tenancies. The yield equalization charge has been carried over for leases executed during Order #3, the charge being 1% of June 1971 rentals. The Board also elected to allow the "stabilizer" to remain without change for leases executed during guideline period #2. Although the present uncertainties of the money market hardly support a dogmatic attitude towards future yields it remains clear that some adjustment in yield must still be provided to seek to assist the flow of new capital into habitable buildings either for major improvements or to refinance maturing obligations. Based on the experience of Guideline Order #2 the Board felt that to continue the 1% stabilizer would not work an unreasonable hardship upon tenants and that the charge would evidence to institutional lenders a willingness on the part of the Board to deal realistically with the area of capital investment in housing.

RENT GUIDELINE ORDER NUMBER 3a—Rent Levels for Decontrolled Units—July 1, 1971 through June 30, 1972.

Pursuant to the authority vested in it by the Rent Stabilization Law of 1969, the Rent Guidelines Board hereby establishes and adopts the following guidelines for rent levels of certain decontrolled dwelling units:

Applicability

This Order shall apply for the period July 1, 1971 through June 30, 1972 to any dwelling unit which was subject to control under the City Rent and Rehabilitation Law on May 31, 1968, was subsequently decontrolled and is now subject to the provisions of the Rent Stabilization Law. This Order establishes guidelines only for the first lease following decontrol, however, where a decontrol lease was entered into pursuant to paragraph (c) or (d) of Section 2(f)(15) of the Rent Eviction Regulations, this Order does not apply to or modify the terms thereof, but is applicable to the first lease for a term commencing after its expiration or other termination. Any subsequent lease shall be subject to the provisions of Rent Guidelines Board Order No. 3 if executed after June 30, 1971 and before July 1, 1972. In no event may the rent under an existing lease be increased except pursuant to the terms thereof.

Renewal Leases

As used in this Order, "renewal lease" means any lease entered into by a tenant in occupancy, whether such occupancy was pursuant to a lease or a statutory tenancy.

The level of fair rent increases for such a renewal lease over the lawful rent actually charged and paid on May 31, 1968 shall be:

—as to dwelling unit of less than four rooms:

25 per cent for a two-year lease; or 35 per cent for a three-year lease

—as to a dwelling unit of four or more rooms:

35 per cent for a two-year lease; or 45 per cent for a three-year lease.

—which percentage increases shall be inclusive of the 10 per cent or the two 10 per cent increases, if any, paid under decontrol leases pursuant to Section 2(f)(15) of the Rent and Eviction Regulations, or any other non-service increases paid since May 31, 1968 pursuant to the Rent and Eviction Regulations. Where a renewal lease to which this Order applies is for a one-year term, the level of fair rent increase shall be that prescribed above for a two-year lease, provided that the owner offers to the tenant a one-year extension of the lease at the same rental.

Fractional Terms

For the purpose of this Order any lease or tenancy: (a) for a period up to and including one year shall be deemed a one-year lease or tenancy; (b) for a period over one year and up to and including two years shall be deemed a two-year lease; (c) and for a period over two years and up to and including three years shall be deemed a three-year lease

Credits

Rental charged and paid in excess of the levels of fair rent increase established by this Order shall be fully refunded within 30 days thereafter.

Dated: July 1, 1971   Roger Starr
Chairman,
Filed with City Clerk,   Rent Guidelines Board
July 1, 1971

Order Number 4—Rent Levels July 1, 1972 through June 30, 1973

Pursuant to the Authority Vested in it by the Rent Stabilization Law of 1969, the Rent Guidelines Board hereby establishes and adopts the following levels of fair rent increase over lawful rents charged and paid on June 30, 1972, (including the "stabilizer", if any), for dwelling units covered by such law (other than hotel dwelling units).

Lease Renewals

In addition to a one-half of one per cent increase here referred to as a "stabilizer", which is subject to adjustment in subsequent years of the lease as explained below:

—For one-year leases expiring before July 1, 1974: 6 per cent;

—For two-year leases expiring before July 1, 1975: 8 per cent;

—For three-year leases expiring before July 1, 1976: 10 per cent

Stabilizer

The one-half of one per cent increase affecting all leases to be known as a "stabilizer" is designed to equalize changes in the yield on capital invested in real estate governed by the Rent Stabilization Law with changes in the yields paid by other long term investments. This charge for 1972-73 is subject to adjustment by the Rent Guidelines Board on any anniversary date of this Order. No such adjustment will increase or decrease the rent (including stabilizer) by more than one per cent in any year of the lease.

The stabilizer governing leases entered into pursuant to Orders Number 2 or 3 of the Rent Guidelines Board is hereby decreased by one-half of one per cent effective upon the next succeeding anniversary date of any such lease.

Leases on dwelling units receiving partial tax exemption pursuant to Section 421 of the Real Property Tax Law

Where a dwelling unit is in a structure subject to the Partial Tax Exemption Program, under Section 421 of the Real Property Tax Law, permissible percentage increases for renewal leases will be:

—For one-year leases expiring before July 1, 1974: 4 per cent

—For two-year leases expiring before July 1, 1975: 6 per cent

—For three-year leases expiring before July 1, 1976: 8

per cent However, where such unit is vacated on or after June 30, 1972, the levels of fair rent increase governing the new tenancy are the same levels over the rental charged on the last date on which rent was paid prior to such vacancy as those set forth in this section for lease renewals, plus 5 per cent.

Furthermore, nothing in this Order shall prohibit the inclusion of a lease provision for an annual or other periodic rent increase over the initial rent at an average rate of not more than 2.2% per annum where the dwelling unit is receiving partial tax exemption pursuant to Section 421 of the Real Property Tax Law and the Regulations adopted pursuant thereto. This cumulative but not compounded charge of up to 2.2% per annum is in addition to the amount permitted under this section of the Guideline Order for renewal leases.

Subleases

Where a dwelling unit is subleased pursuant to a clause which provides that upon the exercise of the privilege of subletting, the rent payable to the owner effective upon the date of subletting may be established as if the renewal lease had been a vacancy lease, the levels of fair rent increases governing such tenancy are the same levels over rentals charged on June 30, 1972 as those set forth in this Order for lease renewals (including "stabilizer"), plus 5 per cent.

Fractional Terms

Except as to leases on vacant apartments, for the purpose of these guidelines any lease or tenancy for a period up to and including one year shall be deemed a one year lease or tenancy; the same for a period over one year and up to and including two years shall be deemed a two year lease; and the same for a period over two years and up to and including three years shall be deemed a three year lease. As to leases on vacant apartments subject to the Partial Tax Exemption Program, for the purpose of these guidelines any lease for a period from one year to less than two years shall be deemed a one year lease; the same for a period from two years to less than three years shall be deemed a two year lease; and the same for a period of three years or more shall be deemed a three year lease.

Escalator Clauses

Where a lease for a dwelling unit in effect on May 31, 1968 contained an escalator caluse for increased costs of operation and such clause is still in effect, the lawful rental on June 30, 1972 over which the fair rent under this Order is computed shall include the increased rental, if any, due under such clause.

Decontrolled Units

The permissible percentage increases for decontrolled units under Order 3A remains in effect for units covered by such order.

Credits

Rental charged and paid in excess of the levels of fair rent increase established by this Order shall be fully credited against the next month's rent.

Order Number 5—Rent Levels July 1, 1973 through June 30, 1974

Pursuant to the Authority Vested in it by the Rent Stabilization Law of 1969, the Rent Guidelines Board hereby establishes and adopts the following levels of fair rent increase over lawful rents charged and paid on June 30, 1973 (including the "stabilizer", if any) for dwelling units covered by such law (other than hotel dwelling units).

Lease Renewals

—For one-year leases expiring before July 1, 1975: 6½ per cent

—For two-year leases expiring before July 1, 1976: 8½ per cent

—For three-year leases expiring before July 1, 1977: 10½ per cent

Stabilizer

The ½% "stabilizer" established under Order #4 shall remain in effect on leases entered into before July 1, 1973 until the expiration of such leases.

Leases on dwelling units receiving partial tax exemption pursuant to Section 421 of the Real Property Tax Law

Where a dwelling unit is in a structure subject to the Partial Tax Exemption Program under Section 421 of the

Real Property Tax Law, permissible percentage increases for renewal leases will be:

—For one-year leases expiring before July 1, 1975: 4 per cent

—For two-year leases expiring before July 1, 1976: 6 per cent

—For three-year leases expiring before July 1, 1977: 8 per cent

However, where such unit is vacated on or after June 30, 1973, the levels of fair rent increase governing the new tenancy are the same levels over the rental charged on the last date on which rent was paid prior to such vacancy as those set forth in this section for lease renewals, plus 5 per cent.

Furthermore, nothing in this Order shall prohibit the inclusion of a lease provision for an annual or other periodic rent increase over the initial rent at an average rate of not more than 2.2% per annum where the dwelling unit is receiving partial tax exemption pursuant to Section 421 of the Real Property Tax Law and the Regulations adopted pursuant thereto. This cumulative but not compounded charge of up to 2.2% per annum is in addition to the amount permitted under this section of the Guideline Order for renewal leases.

Subleases

Where a dwelling unit subleased pursuant to a clause which provides that upon the exercise of the privilege of subletting, the rent payable to the owner effective upon the date of subletting may be established as if the renewal lease had been a vacancy lease, the levels of fair rent increases governing such tenancy are the same levels over rental charged on June 30, 1973 as those set forth in this Order for lease renewals, plus 5 per cent.

Fractional Terms

Except as to leases on vacant apartments, for the purpose of these guidelines any lease or tenancy for a period up to and including one year shall be deemed a one-year lease or tenancy; the same for a period over one year and up to and including two years shall be deemed a two-year lease; and the same for a period over two years and up to and including three years shall be deemed a three-year lease. As to leases on vacant apartments subject to the Partial Tax Exemption program, for the purpose of these guidelines any lease for a period from one year to less than two years shall be deemed a one-year lease; the same for a period from two years to less than three years shall be deemed a two-year lease; and the same for a period of three years or more shall be deemed a three-year lease.

Escalator Clauses

Where a lease for a dwelling unit in effect on May 31, 1968 contained an escalator clause for increased costs of operation and such clause is still in effect, the lawful rental on June 30, 1973 over which the fair rent under this Order is computed shall include the increased rental, if any, due under such clause.

Decontrolled Units

The permissible percentage increases for decontrolled units under Order 3A remains in effect for units covered by such order.

Credits

Rental charged and paid in excess of the levels of fair rent increase established by this Order shall be fully credited against the next month's rent.

RENT GUIDELINE ORDER NUMBER 6—Rent Levels July 1, 1974 through June 30, 1975.

Pursuant to the authority vested in it by the Rent Stabilization Law of 1969 and Chapter 576 of the Laws of 1974, implemented by Resolution Number 276 of the New York City Council, the Rent Guidelines Board hereby establishes and adopts the following levels of fair rent increase over lawful rents charged and paid on June 30, 1974 (including the "stabilizer", if any) for dwelling units continuously subject to the Rent Stabilization Law of 1969 on and before the local effective date of Chapter 576 (other than hotel dwelling units).

Lease Adjustments

—For one year leases expiring before July 1, 1976: 8½ per cent

—For two year leases expiring before July 1, 1977: 10½ per cent

—For three year leases expiring before July 1, 1978: 12 per cent

Stabilizer

the ½ of one per centum "stabilizer" established under Order #4 shall remain in effect on leases entered into before July 1, 1973 until the expiration of such leases.

Leases on dwelling units receiving partial tax exemption pursuant to Sections 421 and 423 of the Real Property Tax Law

Where a dwelling unit is in a structure subject to the Partial Tax Exemption program under Section 421 of the Real Property Tax Law, or in a structure subject to Section 423 of the Real Property Tax Law as a Redevelopment Project, permissible percentage increases for all leases will be:

—For one year leases expiring before July 1, 1976: 6½ per cent

—For two year leases expiring before July 1, 1977: 8½ per cent

—For three year leases expiring before July 1, 1978: 10 per cent

Furthermore, nothing in this Order shall prohibit the inclusion of a lease provision for an annual or other periodic rent increase over the initial rent at an average rate of not more than 2.2% per annum where the dwelling unit is receiving partial tax exemption pursuant to Section 421 of the Real Property Tax Law and the Regulations adopted pursuant thereto or, where applicable, such rate of rental increase as is provided for and authorized by Section 423 of the Real Property Tax Law. The cumulative but not compounded charge of up to 2.2% per annum as provided by Section 421 or the rate provided by Section 423 is in addition to the amount permitted under this section of the Guideline Order for leases.

Fractional Terms

Except as to leases on vacant apartments, for the purpose of these guidelines any lease or tenancy for a period up to and including one year shall be deemed a one year lease or tenancy; the same for a period over one year and up to and including two years shall be deemed a two year lease; and the same for a period over two years and up to and including three years shall be deemed a three year lease. As to leases on vacant apartments, for the purpose of these guidelines any lease for a period from one year to less than two years shall be deemed a one year lease; the same for a period from two years to less than three years shall be deemed a two year lease; and the same for a period of three years or more shall be deemed a three year lease.

Escalator Clauses

Where a lease for a dwelling unit in effect on May 31, 1968 contained an escalator clause for increased costs of operation and such clause is still in effect, the lawful rental on June 30, 1974 over which the fair rent under this Order is computed shall include the increased rental, if any due under such clause. Moreover, where a lease contained such an escalator clause, unless the owner elects or has elected in writing to delete such clause effective no later than July 1, 1970 from the existing lease and all subsequent leases for such dwelling unit, the increased rental, if any, due under such escalator clause shall be offset against the amount of increase permissible under this Order.

Decontrolled Units

The permissible percentage increases for decontrolled units under Order 3A remain in effect for units covered by such order.

Credits

Rental charged and paid in excess of the levels of fair rent increase established by this Order shall be fully credited against the next month's rent. [Dated June 27, 1974, filed with City Clerk June 28, 1974.]

RENT GUIDELINE ORDER NUMBER 6a—Rent Levels July 1, 1974 through June 30, 1975.

Pursuant to the authority vested in it by the Rent Stabilization Law and Chapter 576 of the Laws of 1974, implemented by Resolution No. 276 of the New York City Council, the Rent Guidelines Board hereby establishes and adopts, in conjunction with Order Number 6, the following levels of fair rent increase over lawful rents charged and paid on June 30, 1974 for dwelling units which were subject to the Rent Stabilization Law or the Rent and Rehabilitation Law on June 30, 1971 and which became vacant between July 1, 1971 and June 30, 1974, for dwelling units not previously subject to either the Rent Stabilization Law or the Rent Rehabilitation Law prior to the local effective date of Chapter 576 (other than hotel dwelling units), and for dwelling units previously subject to the Rent and Rehabilitation Law but subsequently decontrolled for a reason other than vacancy.

Lease Adjustments

—For one year leases expiring before July 1, 1976: 8½ per cent

—For two year leases expiring before July 1, 1977: 10½ per cent

—For three year leases expiring before July 1, 1978: 12 per cent

Fractional Terms

Except as to leases on vacant apartments, for the purpose of these guidelines any lease or tenancy for a period up to and including one year shall be deemed a one year lease or tenancy; the same for a period over one year and up to and including two years shall be deemed a two year lease; and the same for a period over two years and up to and including three years shall be deemed a three year lease. As to leases on vacant apartments, for the purpose of these guidelines any lease for a period from one year to less than two years shall be deemed a one year lease; the same for a period from two years to less than three years shall be deemed a two year lease; and the same for a period of three years or more shall be deemed a three year lease.

Electrical Inclusion Adjustment

In addition to the lease adjustment permitted under Rent Guideline Orders Nos. 6 and 6a, a lease for a dwelling unit for which the owner supplies full electrical service for which there is no additional cost charged to the tenant in addition to rent, the applicable lease adjustment as established by such Orders may be increased by no more than 1½ per cent. This provision shall apply only to leases commencing on or after September 1, 1974.

Escalator Clauses

Where a lease for a dwelling unit in effect on May 31, 1968 contained an escalator clause for increased costs of operation and such clause is still in effect, the lawful rental on June 30, 1974 over which the fair rent under this Order is computed shall include the increased rental, if any, due under such clause. Moreover, where a lease contained such an escalator clause, unless the owner elects or has elected in writing to delete such clause, effective no later than July 1, 1974 from the existing lease and all subsequent leases for such dwelling unit, the increased rental, if any, due under such escalator clause shall be offset against the amount of increase permissible under this Order.

Credits

Rental charged and paid in excess of the levels of fair rent increase established by this Order shall be fully credited against the next month's rent.[1]

---

[1] Dated August 27, 1974; filed with the City Clerk August 29, 1974.

Explanatory statement of the Rent Guidelines Board upon issuance of Order Number 6a—July 1, 1974 through June 30, 1975:

The Rent Guidelines Board must establish annually guidelines for rent adjustment relating to vacancy and renewal leases for property subject to the Rent Stabilization Law and Chapter 576 of the Laws of 1974, implemented by Resolution No. 276 of the New York City Council. In establishing such levels of rent adjustments, the Rent Guidelines Board must consider:

(1) the economic condition of the real estate industry in New York City;

(2) relevant current and projected operating cost indices for New York City; and

(3) such other data as is available and required. These guidelines are to be published in THE CITY RECORD upon their adoption.

This Board must issue Guideline adjustments for leases relating to all housing accommodations subject to the Rent Stabilization Law and Chapter 576, unless excepted from such increases by operation of law. These covered categories include:

(a) stabilized units;

(b) previously decontrolled units;

(c) previously destabilized units;

(d) never heretofore regulated units;

(e) redevelopment company units;

(f) Section 421 housing units; and

(g) non-transient hotel units.

Guidelines Order Number 6 of the Board covered categories (a), (e), and (f) above. This present statement describes the methods used by the Rent Guidelines Board in establishing, effective July 1, 1974, except as otherwise indicated as regards the electrical inclusion adjustment, the amount of maximum rent increases which will be permitted under leases of differing lengths in dwelling units falling within categories (b), (c) and (d) above. The remaining category, category (g) relating to non-transient hotel units, will be covered by a subsequent guideline to be issued by the Board. Until such time, Hotel Guidelines Order Number 4, issued December 27, 1973, shall be applicable to all units subject to such guidelines either pursuant to the Rent Stabilization Law or Chapter 576.

Pursuant to Section YY51-5.0(b) of the Administrative Code as amended, the Board has, in establishing the permissible increase, considered thoroughly "the economic condition of the real estate industry in New York City." An examination of the available data by the Board indicated that the entire rent-regulated portion of the City's housing market is being subjected to cost pressures which are broadly similar in nature to those experienced by the rent-stabilized sector. The inflationary nature of these pressures have already been discussed in its Rent Guidelines Order No. 6. This has led the Board to conclude that units which became vacant between July 1, 1971 and through June 30, 1974 should now be subjected to the same maximum rates of increase for all lease purposes as were promulgated for rent-stabilized units under Guidelines Order No. 6. In reaching its decision, the Board recognized the fact that the operations of vacancy decontrol during the period from July 1, 1971 through June 30, 1974 resulted in substantial rental increases for many dwelling units and, at the same time, increased the scope of inequitable treatment of tenants within rent controlled buildings. The Board, however, feels that it cannot appropriately redress these consequences of vacancy decontrol with the instruments at its disposal. It feels very strongly that this is a legislative matter and that the State Legislature should consider broadening the basis for appeals in cases involving such inequitable treatment.

Similar reasoning was applied in establishing the guidelines for maximum rent increases permitted for dwelling units originally subject to the Rent Stabilization Law but which became vacant on or after July 1, 1971, and prior to July 1, 1974, as well as previously decontrolled units where the reason for decontrol was other than vacancy, and for units which had never heretofore been subject to either rent control or rent stabilization.

The Board has continued its consideration as to the effect of rising interest rates on the housing stock. In developing appropriate lease adjustments for leases entered into between July 1, 1974 and June 30, 1975, the Board fully considered such factor and included an adjustment for this factor into Guidelines Orders Nos. 6 and 6a. In reaching this conclusion, the Board considered the steep rising interest rates and the relatively fewer number of owners refinancing during this period. The possibility of additional guidelines adjustments for the few, individualized instances where hardship may result from mandatory or required refinancing continues under investigation as indicated previously.

In making a special allowance for apartments in which the owner includes the provision of full electrical services as a portion of the tenants' rents, the Board recognizes the nature of cost pressures which were not experienced by the owners of other buildings where the tenants paid for their own electrical consumption. Less than 5 per cent of all buildings fall into the category where the owner pays for the electricity consumed by the individual tenants. Guidelines Orders 6 and 6a take into consideration the ordinary costs of electricity which owners incur in operation of buildings. The "electrical inclusion adjustment" provided in this Guideline Order recognizes the unusual cost an owner incurs where the owner pays for the electricity consumed by the individual tenants. This provision shall apply only to leases commencing on or after September 1, 1974.

This Order also corrects a typographical error found in the clause of Order 6 relating to Escalator Clauses.

RENT GUIDELINE SUPPLEMENTAL ORDER NUMBER 6a—Modifying Rent Guideline Order Number 6a In Part.

The Rent Guidelines Board is mandated under the Rent Stabilization Law as amended by Chapter 576, Laws of 1974, to issue annual guidelines for lease rent adjustments.

By statute the Board is established as a temporary body with meetings limited to ten days a year for its membership, fifteen for its Chairman and no funding for full time staff.

Thus, the system contemplates that the Board develop the percentages from studies performed by outside, independent sources based on a sampling of the housing stock under the system and the Board has been fortunate in having been able to contract with the Bureau of Labor Statistics, United States Department of Labor, for annual studies designed expressly for this purpose.

Until now, the stock in the stabilization system was homogeneous, consisting mainly of apartments in post-World War II buildings with a small percentage of pre-war decontrolled higher rent units. Effective July 1, 1974, this was expanded to include a substantial number of pre-war vacancy decontrolled apartments as well as a variety of other, different kinds of housing.

At the same time, a new Rent Guidelines Board was established by a State law amending the Rent Stabilization Law and on June 8, 1974, a new Rent Guidelines Board was appointed pursuant to such amendment.

As indicated, the most comprehensive study of economic conditions of the residential real estate industry in the City of New York available for this new Board's use in fulfilling its obligations to promptly issue guidelines orders for the year July 1, 1974 through June 30, 1975 was the 1973-1974 Bureau of Labor Statistics study of post-war housing. Separate studies compiled for the Temporary State Commission on Living Costs and the Housing and Development Administration were also studied and support the Board's conclusion that the rise in operating expenses reported in the Bureau of Labor Statistics study is substantially applicable to pre-World War II housing. The Rent Guidelines Board, therefore, was and remains satisfied that the 8½, 10½ and 12 per cent percentages derived therefrom properly reflect fair rent adjustments for one, two or three year lease terms if an owner is to meet his service and maintenance requirements under the Rent Stabilization System.

This does not mean that the Board was not cognizant that the increases traditionally developed from Bureau of Labor Statistics studies have been built upon conditions controlled by the Rent Stabilization Law since 1968. Thus, the increases, based on one, two or three year lease terms, are designed to maintain a balance between income and expenses. The Board was aware that the justification for passing along the latest rise in operating expenses is impaired to the extent this balance may have been abandoned by certain owners charging exorbitant increases in rent during the period between July 1, 1971 and June 30, 1974 when vacancy decontrol was in effect. Albeit, the Board believed that it was precluded from considering spiralling rent increases during the period of decontrol and was constrained to start from the June 30, 1974 base date for income and expenses. The Board has since received an opinion from the Corporation Counsel of The City of New York with which the Attorney General of the State of New York concurs, that it could have considered the magnitude of rentals initially charged during the period of vacancy decontrol when promulgating its Guidelines Order No. 6a, and further, that it has the power by law to reconsider, amend and/or modify its previous Order to reflect such factor.

Accordingly, after reviewing the statistics available in reports prepared by the State of New York and The City of New York as to the effects of vacancy decontrol on rents, and mindful of its mandate under the law to take action necessary to preserve rental housing in the City while at the same time preventing speculative, unwarranted and abnormal increases in rent:

Pursuant to the authority vested in it by the Rent Stabilization Law and as amended by Chapter 576, Laws of 1974, the Rent Guidelines Board hereby modifies and amends Rent Guidelines Board Order No. 6a as follows:

Rent Guidance Board Orders

Applicability

This Supplemental Order modifies the provisions of Rent Guidelines Board Order No. 6a as it applies to dwelling units which were subject to the City Rent and Rehabilitation Law or the Rent Stabilization Law on June 30, 1971, were thereafter vacancy decontrolled or destabilized pursuant to Chapter 371, Laws of 1971, and become subject to the jurisdiction of the Rent Stabilization Law on July 1, 1974 or thereafter by virtue of Chapter 576, Laws of 1974 and City Council Resolution No. 276.

Lease Adjustments

—For one year leases expiring before July 1, 1976: 8½ per cent above the Initial Legal Regulated Rent;[1]

—For two year leases expiring before July 1, 1977: 10½ per cent above the Initial Legal Regulated Rent;

—For three year leases expiring before July 1, 1978: 12 per cent above the Initial Legal Regulated Rent;
provided, however, that these increases shall not go into effect to the extent they increase the initial Legal Regulated Rent above the levels defined below:

A. For dwelling units which were subject to the Rent and Rehabilitation Law on June 30, 1971 and which become subject to the Rent Stabilization Law on or after July 1, 1974:

1. Where the tenant elects a one-year lease term, the owner may charge that portion of the 8½ per cent one-year lease increase which does not cause the rent to exceed 27 per cent above the 1972-1973 maximum rent which was or would have been in effect for that dwelling unit pursuant to the City Rent and Rehabilitation Law (hereinafter, the "1972-1973 maximum rent").

Example: The "1972-1973 maximum rent" is $200 per month. The Initial Legal Regulated Rent is $250 per month. The tenant requests a one-year lease term. The owner may charge tenant a rent not exceeding $254 per month or 27 per cent above the "1972-1973 maximum rent" during the term of said one-year lease.

---

[1] The Initial Legal Regulated Rent is the rent charged and paid on June 30, 1974 or the date on which the dwelling unit first becomes subject to the Rent Stabilization Law, whichever is later.

2. Where the tenant elects a two-year lease term:

(a) For the *first* year of the lease, the owner may charge that portion of the 10½ per cent two-year lease increase which does not cause the rent to exceed 27 per cent above the "1972-1973 maximum rent"; and

(b) for the *second* year of the lease, the owner may charge that portion of the 10½ per cent two-year lease increase which does not cause the rent to exceed 8½ per cent above the Initial Legal Regulated Rent or 27 per cent above the "1972-1973 maximum rent", whichever is greater.

Example: The "1972-1973 maximum rent" is $200 per month. The Initial Legal Regulated Rent is $250 per month. The tenant requests a two-year lease term. For the first year of the lease, the owner may charge tenant a rent not exceeding $254 per month or 27 per cent above the "1972-1973 maximum rent". For the second year of the lease, the owner may charge a rent not exceeding $271.25 per month or 8.5 per cent above the Initial Legal Regulated Rent.

3. Where the tenant elects a three year lease term:

(a) for the *first* year of the lease, the owner may charge that portion of the 12 per cent three-year lease increase which does not cause the rent to exceed 27 per cent above the "1972-1973 maximum rent"; and

(b) for the balance of the lease term, the owner may charge that portion of the 12 per cent three-year lease increase which does not cause the rent to exceed 10½ per cent above the Initial Legal Regulated Rent or 27 per cent above the "1972-1973 maximum rent", whichever is greater.

Example: The "1972-1973 maximum rent" is $200 per month. The Initial Legal Regulated Rent is $250 per month. The tenant requests a three-year lease term. For the first year of the lease, the owner may charge tenant a rent not exceeding $254 per month or 27 per cent above the "1972-1973 maximum rent". For the *second and third* years of the lease, the owner may charge a rent not exceeding $276.25 per month or 10½ per cent above the Initial Legal Regulated Rent.

B. For dwelling units which were subject to the Rent

Stabilization Law on June 30, 1971 were destabilized due to a vacancy occurring between July 1, 1971 and June 30, 1974, become and have been placed under the Rent Stabilization Law again effective July 1, 1974:

1. Where the tenant elects a one-year lease term, the owner may charge that portion of the 8½ per cent one-year lease increase which does not cause the rent to exceed 27 per cent above the December 31, 1973 rent which was or would have been in effect for that dwelling unit pursuant to the Rent Stabilization Law (hereinafter, the "December 31, 1973 rent").

Example: The "December 31, 1973 rent" is $300 per month. The Initial Legal Regulated Rent is $375 per month. The tenant requests a one-year lease term. The owner may charge tenant a rent not exceeding $381 per month or 27 per cent above the "December 31, 1973 rent" during the term of said one year lease.

2. Where the tenant elects a two-year lease term:

(a) for the *first* year of the lease, the owner may charge that portion of the 10½ per cent two-year lease increase which does not cause the rent to exceed 27 per cent above the "December 31, 1973 rent"; and

(b) for the *second* year of the lease, the owner may charge that portion of 10½ per cent two-year lease increase which does not cause the rent to exceed 8½ per cent above the Initial Legal Regulated Rent or 27 per cent above the "December 31, 1973 rent", whichever is greater.

Example: The "December 31, 1973 rent" is $300 per month. The Initial Legal Regulated Rent is $375 per month. The tenant requests a two-year lease term. For the first year of the lease, the owner may charge tenant a rent not exceeding $381 per month or 27 per cent above the "December 31, 1973 rent". For the second year of the lease, the owner may charge a rent not exceeding $406.87 per month or 8.5 per cent above the Initial Legal Regulated Rent.

3. Where the tenant elects a three-year lease term:

(a) for the *first* year of the lease, the owner may charge that portion of the 12 per cent three-year lease increase which does not cause the rent to exceed 27 per cent above the "December 31, 1973 rent"; and

(b) for the balance of the lease term, the owner may charge that portion of the 12 per cent three year lease increase which does not cause the rent to exceed 10½ per cent above the Initial Legal Regulated Rent or 27 per cent above the "December 31, 1973 rent", whichever is greater.

Example: The "December 31, 1973 rent" is $300 per month. The Initial Legal Regulated Rent is $375 per month. The tenant requests a three-year lease term. For the first year of the lease, the owner may charge tenant a rent not exceeding $381 per month or 27 per cent above the "December 31, 1973 rent". For the *second and third* years of the lease, the owner may charge a rent not exceeding $414.37 per month or 10½ per cent above the Initial Legal Regulated Rent.

This Supplemental Order shall be effective as of July 1, 1974 the date on which the Rent Guidelines Board Order No. 6a took effect.

The owner shall be required, upon *offering leases* to the category of tenants covered by this Supplemental Order, including those tenants who have already executed leases under Rent Guidelines Board Order No. 6a to furnish the tenant with *a rent computation* reflecting the limitations provided in this Supplemental Order on forms approved by the Conciliation and Appeals Board.

Dated: September 27, 1974.
Filed with City Clerk: September 27, 1974.

RENT GUIDELINE ORDER NUMBER 6b—Rent Levels July 1, 1974 through June 30, 1975.

Pursuant to the authority vested in it by the Rent Stabilization Law and Chapter 576 of the Laws of 1974, implemented by Resolution No. 276 of the New York City Council, the Rent Guidelines Board hereby establishes and adopts, in conjunction with Orders 6 and 6a, the Special Guideline mandated by Section 12 of Chapter 576 of the Laws of 1974 amending Section YY51-6.0.2b.1 of the New York City Administrative Code.

Special Guidelines

In order to aid the Conciliation and Appeals Board in determining fair market rents for housing accommodations as to applications for adjustment of the initial regulated rent as may be requested by tenants, the Rent Guidelines Board hereby establishes as guidelines:

(a) for dwelling units subject to the City Rent and Rehabilitation Law on June 30, 1971 which became vacant after December 31, 1973 and prior to July 1, 1974, and for dwelling units subject to the Rent and Rehabilitation Law on June 30, 1974 which subsequently become vacant, the 1974 maximum rent as it existed or would have existed, plus 15 per cent; and

(b) for dwelling units subject to the Rent Stabilization Law on June 30, 1971, and which became vacant after December 31, 1973 but prior to July 1, 1974, the maximum rent that was or would have been in effect under the Rent Stabilization Law on December 31, 1973 as adjusted by the one year lease adjustment relating to that type of housing accommodation as contained in the Rent Guidelines Orders 6 and 6a, plus 15 per cent.[1]

RENT GUIDELINE ORDER NUMBER 6c—Rent Levels July 1, 1974 through June 30, 1975.

Pursuant to the authority vested in it by the Rent Stabilization Law of 1969 and Chapter 576 of the Laws of 1974, implemented by Resolution Number 276 of the New York City Council, and after reconsideration pursuant to the order of the Supreme Court, New York County, in Associated Builders and Owners of Greater New York,

---

[1] Dated August 27, 1974; filed with the City Clerk August 29, 1974. Explanatory statement of the Rent Guidelines Board upon issuance of Order Number 6b—July 1, 1974 through June 30, 1975:

In arriving at the Special Guidelines, the Board took into account the relationship that had developed between market rents and controlled rents in the period during which vacancy decontrol was in effect. The data that was developed to document this relationship were based upon studies carried on by the Housing and Development Administration and were further based upon reports by other governmental agencies that were submitted to the Rent Guidelines Board. These various studies showed that there was a 15 to 20 per cent difference between market rents and maximum rents in the period between 1971 and 1974. This relationship was adopted as a standard for the Board's determination of Special Guidelines.

This Special Guideline is created to aid the Conciliation and Appeals Board in determining "fair market rents" for housing accommodations as to which tenants may appeal the amount of the initial legal regulated rent.

Inc. v. The Rent Guidelines Board and Blag Holding Co. v. Starr, the Rent Guidelines Board hereby modifies and amends Rent Guidelines Board's Orders Nos. 6, 6a and 6a Supplemental by establishing and adopting the following levels of fair rent increase over lawful rents charged and paid on June 30, 1974 (including the "stabilizer," if any) for dwelling units continuously subject to the Rent Stabilization Law of 1969 on and before the local effective date of Chapter 576 (other than hotel dwelling units) for dwelling units which were subject to the Rent Stabilization Law or the Rent and Rehabilitation Law on June 30, 1971 and which became vacant between July 1, 1971 and June 30, 1974, for dwelling units not previously subject to either the Rent Stabilization Law or the Rent and Rehabilitation Law prior to the local effective date of Chapter 576 (other than hotel dwelling units), and for dwelling units previously subject to the Rent and Rehabilitation Law but subsequently decontrolled for a reason other than vacancy.

Lease Adjustments

In addition to a one-half of one percent increase here referred to as a "stabilizer", which is subject to adjustment in subsequent years of the lease as explained below:

—For one year leases expiring before July 1, 1976: 8½ percent

—For two year leases expiring before July 1, 1977: 10½ percent

—For three year leases expiring before July 1, 1978: 12 percent

Leases on dwelling units receiving partial tax exemption pursuant to Sections 421 and 423 of the Real Property Tax Law

Where a dwelling unit is in a structure subject to the Partial Tax Exemption program under Section 421 of the Real Property Tax Law, or in a structure subject to Section 423 of the Real Property Tax Law as a Redevelopment Project, permissible percentage increases for all leases will be, in addition to a one-half of one percent increase here referred to as a "stabilizer", which is subject to adjustment in subsequent years of the lease as explained below:

—For one year leases expiring before July 1, 1976: 6½ percent

—For two year leases expiring before July 1, 1977: 8½ percent

—For three year leases expiring before July 1, 1978: 10 percent

Furthermore, nothing in this Order shall prohibit the inclusion of a lease provision for an annual or other periodic rent increase over the initial rent at an average rate of not more than 2.2% per annum where the dwelling unit is receiving partial tax exemption pursuant to Section 421 of the Real Property Tax Law and the Regulations adopted pursuant thereto or, where applicable, such rate of rental increase as is provided for and authorized by Section 423 of the Real Property Tax Law. The cumulative but not compounded charge of up to 2.2% per annum as provided by Section 421 or the rate provided by Section 423 is in addition to the amount permitted under this section of the Guideline Order for leases. . . .

Decontrolled Units

The permissible percentage increases for decontrolled units under Order 3A remain in effect for units covered by such order.

Credits

Rental charged and paid in excess of the levels of fair rent increase established by this Order shall be fully credited against the next month's rent.

Supplemental Order Number 6a

The provisions of Rent Guidelines Board Order No. 6c shall apply to leases affected by Supplemental Order No. 6a. Other than as hereinabove provided, the rent increase limitations contained in the Rent Guidelines Board's Order No. 6a Supplement remain in full force and effect.

Dated: February 7, 1975
Filed with City Clerk: February 7, 1975

RENT GUIDELINE ORDER NUMBER 7—Rent Levels July 1, 1975 through June 30, 1976.

Pursuant to the authority vested in it by the Rent Stabilization Law of 1969 and Chapter 576 of the Laws of 1974, implemented by Resolution Number 276 of 1974 of the New York City Council, the Rent Guidelines Board hereby establishes and adopts the following levels of fair rent increase over lawful rents charged and paid on June 30, 1975 (including the "stabilizer", if any) for dwelling units subject to the Rent Stabilization Law of 1969, as amended.

Adjustments for Renewal Leases

—For one year leases expiring before July 1, 1977: 7½ percent

—For two year leases expiring before July 1, 1978: 9½ percent

—For three year leases expiring before July 1, 1979: 12½ percent

Adjustments for Renewal Leases on dwelling units receiving partial tax exemption pursuant to Sections 421 and 423 of the Real Property Tax Law

Where a dwelling unit is in a structure subject to the Partial Tax Exemption program under Section 421 of the Real Property Tax Law, or in a structure subject to Section 423 of the Real Property Tax Law as a Redevelopment Project, permissible percentage increases for renewal leases are, as follows:

—For one year leases expiring before July 1, 1977: 6 percent

—For two year leases expiring before July 1, 1978: 7½ percent

—For three year leases expiring before July 1, 1979: 10½ percent

Furthermore, nothing in this Order shall prohibit the inclusion of a lease provision for an annual or other periodic rent increase over the initial rent at an average rate of not more than 2.2% per annum where the dwelling unit is receiving partial tax exemption pursuant to Section 421 of the Real Property Tax Law and the Regulations adopted pursuant thereto or, where applicable, such rate of rental increase as is provided for and authorized by Section 423 of the Real Property Tax Law. The cumulative but not compounded charge of up to 2.2% per annum as provided by Section 421 or the rate provided by

Section 423 is in addition to the amount permitted under this section of the Guideline Order for leases.

Leases on Vacant Apartments

Where a dwelling unit becomes vacant, the levels of rent increase governing a new tenancy commencing on or after July 1, 1975, and before June 30, 1976, are the same levels over rentals charged on June 30, 1975 as those set forth above for lease renewals, plus 5 percent over the rentals charged on June 30, 1975 on each vacancy of such unit during the effective period of this Order.

Fractional Terms

Except as to leases on vacant apartments, for the purpose of these guidelines any lease or tenancy for a period up to and including one year shall be deemed a one year lease or tenancy; the same for a period over one year and up to and including two years shall be deemed a two year lease; and the same for a period over two years and up to and including three years shall be deemed a three year lease. As to leases on vacant apartments, for the purpose of these guidelines any lease for a period from one year to less than two years shall be deemed a one year lease; the same for a period from two years to less than three years shall be deemed a two year lease; and the same for a period of three years or more shall be deemed a three year lease.

Electrical Inclusion Adjustment

In addition to the lease adjustment permitted under this Order No. 7, a lease for a dwelling unit for which the owner supplies full electrical service for which there is no additional cost charged to the tenant in addition to rent, the applicable lease adjustment as established by this Order is increased by 3½ percent.

Escalator Clauses

Where a lease for a dwelling unit in effect on May 31, 1968 contained an escalator clause for increased costs of operation and such clause is still in effect, the lawful rental on June 30, 1975 over which the fair rent under this Order is computed shall include the increased rental, if any, due under such clause. Moreover, where a lease contained such an escalator clause, unless the owner elects or has elected in writing to delete such clause, effective no later than July 1, 1975 from the existing lease and all subsequent leases for such dwelling unit, the increased rental, if any, due under such escalator clause shall be offset against the amount of increase permissible under this Order.

Stabilizer

The one-half percent "stabilizers" charged in leases pursuant to previous Orders of this Board shall remain in effect until the expiration of such leases.

Special Guidelines to Update Special Guidelines 6b

In order to aid the Conciliation and Appeals Board in determining fair market rents for housing accommodations as to applications for adjustment of the initial regulated rent as may be requested by tenants, the Rent Guidelines Board hereby establishes a special guideline as mandated by Section 12 of Chapter 576 of the Laws of 1974 amending Section YY51-6.02b(1) of the New York City Administrative Code for dwelling units subject to the Rent and Rehabilitation Law on June 30, 1975 which subsequently become vacant after June 30, 1975, the 1974 maximum rent as it existed or would have existed, plus 22½%.

Limitations on Adjustments for Renewal Leases

The limitations on adjustments for renewal leases provided herein shall be effective for such types of dwelling units listed below for which no leases have commenced between July 1, 1974 and June 30, 1975.

A. For dwelling units which were subject to the Rent and Rehabilitation Law on June 30, 1971 and which become subject to the Rent Stabilization Law on July 1, 1974:

1. Where the tenant elects a one-year lease term, the owner may charge that portion of the 7½ percent one-year lease increase which does not cause the rent to exceed 22½ percent above the 1974-1975 maximum rent which was or would have been in effect for that dwelling unit pursuant to the City Rent and Rehabilitation Law (hereinafter, the "1974-1975 maximum rent").

2. Where the tenant elects a two-year lease term:

(a) for the *first* year of the lease, the owner may charge that portion of the 9½ percent two-year lease increase which does not cause the rent to exceed 22½ percent above the "1974-1975 maximum rent"; and

(b) for the *second* year of the lease, the owner may charge that portion of the 9½ percent two-year lease increase which does not cause the rent to exceed 9½ percent above "the 1974-1975 maximum rent" plus 22½ percent.

3. Where the tenant elects a three-year lease term:

(a) for the *first* year of the lease, the owner may charge that portion of the 12½ percent three-year lease increase which does not cause the rent to exceed 22½ percent above the "1974-1975 maximum rent"; and

(b) for the balance of the lease term, the owner may charge that portion of the 12½ three-year lease increase which does not cause the rent to exceed 12½ percent above "the 1974-1975 maximum rent" plus 22½ percent.

B. For dwelling units which were subject to the Rent Stabilization Law on June 30, 1971, were destabilized due to a vacancy occurring between July 1, 1971 and June 30, 1974, and have been placed under the Rent Stabilization Law again effective July 1, 1974:

1. Where the tenant elects a one-year lease term, the owner may charge that portion of the 7½ percent one-year lease increase which does not cause the rent to exceed 30 percent above the December 31, 1973 rent which was or would have been in effect for that dwelling unit pursuant to the Rent Stabilization Law (hereinafter, the "December 31, 1973 rent").

2. Where the tenant elects a two-year lease term:

(a) for the *first* year of the lease, the owner may charge that portion of the 9½ percent two-year lease increase which does not cause the rent to exceed 30 percent above the "December 31, 1973 rent"; and

(b) for the *second* year of the lease, the owner may charge that portion of the 9½ percent two-year lease increase which does not cause the rent to exceed 9½% percent 30% above "the December 31, 1973 rent".

3. Where the tenant elects a three-year lease term:

(a) for the *first* year of the lease, the owner may charge that portion of the 12½ percent three-year lease increase which does not cause the rent to exceed 30 percent over the "December 31, 1973 rent" and

(b) for the balance of the lease term, the owner may charge that portion of the 12½ percent two-year lease increase which does not cause the rent to exceed 12½ percent over 30% above "the December 31, 1973 rent".

The owner shall be required, upon offering leases to the categories of tenants covered by this provision, to furnish such tenants with a rent computation reflecting the limitations provided in this provision on forms approved by the Conciliation and Appeals Board. Nothing contained in this provision shall be construed to authorize increases in excess of those otherwise established by this Order No. 7.

Decontrolled Units

The permissible percentage increases for decontrolled units under Order 3A remain in effect for units covered by such order.

Credits

Rental charged and paid in excess of the levels of fair rent increase established by this Order shall be fully credited against the next month's rent.[2]

---

[2] Dated July 1, 1975; filed with City Clerk July 1, 1975.

Explanatory statement of the Rent Guidelines Board upon issuance of Order Number 7:

The Rent Guidelines Board must establish annually guidelines for rent adjustment relating to vacancy and renewal leases for property subject to the Rent Stabilization Law and Chapter 576 of the Laws of 1974, implemented by Resolution Number 276 of the New York City Council. The Board must file its findings for the preceding calendar year with the City Clerk by July 1 of each year. The Board shall also file an Order with the City Clerk establishing a level of fair rent increases as the guideline for leases entered into during the next 12-month period. In establishing such levels of fair rent increase, the Rent Guidelines Board must consider:

(1) the economic condition of the real estate industry in New York City;

(2) relevant current and projected operating cost indices for New York City; and

(3) such other data as is available and required. These guidelines are to be published in the City Record upon their adoption.

The Rent Guidelines Board has the power to issue orders with a single rate of adjustment or for rent adjustments varying by class of housing accommodations.

This Board must issue Guideline adjustments for leases relating to all housing accommodations subject to the Rent Stabilization Law and Chapter 576, unless excepted from such increases by operation of law.

These covered categories include: a) stabilized units; b) previously decontrolled units; c) previously destabilized units; d) never heretofore regulated units; e) redevelopment company units; f) Section 421 housing units; and g) non-transient hotel units.

This present statement describes

Rent Guidance Board Orders

the methods used by the Rent Guidelines Board in establishing, effective July 1, 1975, the amount of maximum rent increases which will be permitted under leases of differing lengths in dwelling units covering all units listed above except non-transient hotel units.

Pursuant to Section YY51-5.0(b) of the Administrative Code, as amended, the Board has, in establishing the permissible increases, considered thoroughly, "the economic condition of the residential real estate industry in New York City." The level of the increases permitted under this Order are based, in part on "The Report on the 1975 Price Index of Operating Costs for Rent Stabilized Apartment Houses in New York City." This report is a result of a study conducted by the Bureau of Labor Statistics of the United States Department of Labor for this Board at the request of the City of New York and issued in June 1975. As a basis for its research the Bureau developed a weighted index of prices, as of April, for the years 1967 through 1975 inclusive—of the components which, taken together, comprise the operating costs for rent stabilized apartment houses. The components are real estate taxes, labor costs, fuel and utilities, contract services, administrative costs, insurance costs, cost of parts and supplies, and replacement costs. The selection of items for pricing in the index was based on the relative importance of the item in total operating costs and on the availability of reliable price data over time.

The Bureau of Labor Statistics reported that from April, 1974 to April, 1975 its price index rose 6.5 percent. This increase was considerably lower than the 15.5 percent increase found by the Board to have occurred from 1973 to 1974 mainly because of a steep decline in the rate of increase in the price of energy. Since most leases coming due in the period covered by Guideline No. 7 were entered into prior to last year their rents have not yet reflected the enormous 1974 cost increases attributable in the main to the energy crisis. The basic one year allowance granted by the Rent Guidelines Board this year includes a factor which adjusts for the effects of the 1973-74 cost increase as well as last year's experience. Two and three year increase allowances include these factors as well as an additional factor reflecting the Board's forecast of operating and maintenance cost trends for the next two years.

In recognition of continued high interest rates, the Board also decided to include a "stabilizer" of one-half of one percent in the permissible rent increase.

In making its determinations of allowable increases the Board also considered information submitted by a number of groups and individuals such as hardship application data from the Conciliation and Appeals Board, a study conducted for the Rent Stabilization Association, studies prepared by the New York Owners Committee for Better Housing, Inc., and the Associated Builders and Owners of Greater New York, a report commissioned by the Coalition to Save New York and prepared by the Real Estate Research Corporation and information submitted by interested tenant groups such as the Flatbush and Fresh Meadows Tenants Councils and the Metropolitan Council on Housing.

The Rent Guidelines Board carefully considered the propriety of reinstituting a special allowance for vacancy leases as opposed to renewal leases and found pressing economic justification for such practice. All available evidence indicates that rent stabilized buildings have entered a period of narrowing cash flow. Unusual operating and maintenance cost increases, rising financing costs and vacancy losses could cause severe hardship for buildings currently operating on small margins with increasing risk of negative cash flow. A special allowance for vacancy leases should help to ameliorate this situation.

Last year the Board granted a special increase allowance of 2.5 percent for a dwelling unit for which the owner supplies full electrical service for which there is no cost charged to the tenant in addition to rent. The allowance of 3.5 percent this year reflects both the Board's determination that consumption of electricity in

RENT GUIDELINE ORDER NUMBER 8—Rent Levels July 1, 1976 through June 30, 1977.

Pursuant to the authority vested in it by the Rent Stabilization Law of 1969 and Chapter 576 of the Laws of 1974, implemented by Resolution Number 276 of 1974 of the New York City Council, the Rent Guidelines Board hereby establishes and adopts the following levels of fair rent increase over lawful rents charged and paid on June 30, 1976 (including the "stabilizer," if any) for dwelling units subject to the Rent Stabilization Law of 1969, as amended.

Adjustments for Renewal Leases

Together with such adjustments for unusual fuel costs as may be authorized by the Board, as explained below:

these units has returned to pre-crisis levels, as well as its finding of a relatively small increase in electric rates experienced last year.

The Board also made provision, within its Order, for the inclusion of buildings receiving the benefits of the partial Tax Exemption program promulgated pursuant to Section 421 of the Real Property Tax Law and for the inclusion of buildings receiving benefits pursuant to Section 423 of the Real Property Tax Law as redevelopment company units. Since these buildings are largely unaffected by increases in real estate tax rates, the Board has promulgated a separate guideline to reflect the smaller increase in operating costs experienced by them.

In arriving at Special Guidelines to aid the Conciliation and Appeals Board in determining "fair market rents" for housing accommodations for which tenants may appeal the amount of the initial legal regulated rent, the Guidelines Board took into account the relationship that had developed between market rents and controlled rents in the period during which vacancy decontrol was in effect. The data that was developed to document this relationship were based upon studies carried on by the Housing and Development Administration and were further based upon reports by other governmental agencies that were submitted to the Rent Guidelines Board. These various studies showed that there was a 20 to 25% difference between market rents and maximum rents in the period between 1971 and 1975. This relationship was adopted as a standard for the Board's determination of Special Guidelines.

The guidelines set for dwelling units which were subject to the City Rent and Rehabilitation Law or the Rent Stabilization Law on June 30, 1971, were thereafter vacancy decontrolled or destabilized, and became subject to the jurisdiction of the Rent Stabilization Law on July 1, 1974 or thereafter, have been changed from those issued last year to account for economic trends and to simplify both the administration of these guidelines and their comprehensibility. The Board has received an opinion from the Corporation Counsel of the City of New York with which the Attorney General of the State of New York concurs, that it may consider the magnitude of rentals initially charged during the period of vacancy decontrol when promulgating its guidelines.

The working material and detailed data which went into the Rent Guidelines Board's consideration will be compiled into a final report which will be released not later than August 1, 1975.

—For one year leases expiring before July 1, 1978: 6½ percent

—For two year leases expiring before July 1, 1979: 8 percent

—For three year leases expiring before July 1, 1980: 11 percent

The Board may convene to consider an adjustment for unusual rentals charged on June 30, 1976 as those set forth above for lease renewals, plus 5 percent over the rentals charged on June 30, 1976 on each vacancy of such unit during the effective period of this Order.

Fractional Terms

Except as to leases on vacant apartments, for the purpose of these guidelines any lease or tenancy for a period up to and including one year shall be deemed a one year lease or tenancy; the same for a period over one year and up to and including two years shall be deemed a two year lease; and the same for a period over two years and up to and including three years shall be deemed a three year lease. As to leases on vacant apartments, for the purpose of these guidelines any lease for a period from one year to less than two years shall be deemed a one year lease; the same for a period from two years to less than three years shall be deemed a two year lease; and the same for a period of three years or more shall be deemed a three year lease.

Electrical Inclusion Adjustment

In addition to the lease adjustment permitted under this Order No. 8, a lease for a dwelling unit for which the owner supplies full electrical service for which there is no additional cost charged to the tenant in addition to rent, the applicable lease adjustment as established by this Order is increased by 3½ percent. However, this allowance shall not apply to any dwelling unit as to which an increase for electrical inclusion was collected under Guideline Order No. 6a (et seq.) or 7.

Escalator Clauses

Where a lease for a dwelling unit in effect on May 31, 1968, or where a lease in effect on June 30, 1974 for a dwelling unit which became subject to the Rent Stabilization Law of 1969, by virtue of Chapter 576, Laws of 1974 and Resolution No. 276 of the New York City Council, contained an escalator clause for the increased costs of operation, and such clause is still in effect, the lawful rental on June 30, 1976 over which the fair rent under this Order is computed shall include the increased rental, if any, due under such clause except those charges which accrued within one year of the commencement of the renewal lease. Moreover, where a lease contained an escalator clause which the owner may validly renew under the code, unless the owner elects or has elected in writing to delete such clause, effective no later than July 1, 1976 from the existing lease and all subsequent leases for such dwelling unit, the increased rental, if any, due under such escalator clause shall be offset against the amount of increase authorized under this Order.

Stabilizer

The one-half percent "stabilizers" charged in leases pursuant to previous Orders of this Board shall remain in effect until the expiration of such leases.

Special Guidelines to Update Special Guidelines 6b

In order to aid the Conciliation and Appeals Board in determining fair market rents for housing accommodations as to applications for adjustment of the initial regulated rent as may be requested by tenants, the Rent Guidelines Board hereby establishes a special guideline as mandated by Section 12 of Chapter 576 of the Laws of 1974 amending Section YY51-6.02b(1) of the New York City Administrative Code for dwelling units subject to the Rent and Rehabilitation Law on June 30, 1976 which subsequently become vacant after June 30, 1976, the 1976 maximum rent as it existed or would have existed, plus 15%.

Limitations on Adjustments for Renewal Leases

The limitations on adjustments for renewal leases provided herein shall be effective for such types of dwelling units listed below for which no leases have commenced between July 1, 1974 and June 30, 1976.

A. For dwelling units which were subject to the Rent and Rehabilitation Law on June 30, 1971 and which become subject to the Rent Stabilization Law on July 1, 1974:

1. Where the tenant elects a one-year lease term, the owner may charge that portion of the 6½ percent one-year lease increase which does not cause the rent to exceed 15 percent above the 1976-1977 maximum rent which was or would have been in effect for that dwelling unit pursuant to the City Rent and Rehabilitation Law (hereinafter, the "1976-1977 maximum rent").

2. Where the tenant elects a two-year lease term:

(a) for the *first* year of the lease, the owner may charge that portion of the 8 percent two-year lease increase which does not cause the rent to exceed 15 percent above the "1976-1977 maximum rent"; and

(b) for the *second* year of the lease, the owner may charge that portion of the 8 percent two-year lease increase which does not cause the rent to exceed 15 percent above "the 1976-1977 maximum rent" plus 8 percent.

3. Where the tenant elects a three-year lease term:

(a) for the *first* year of the lease the owner may charge that portion of the 11 percent three-year lease increase which does not cause the rent to exceed 15 percent above the "1976-1977 maximum rent"; and

(b) for the balance of the lease term, the owner may charge that portion of the 11 percent three-year lease increase which does not cause the rent to exceed 15 percent above "the 1976-1977 maximum rent" plus 11 percent.

B. For dwelling units which were subject to the Rent Stabilization Law on June 30, 1971, were destabilized due to a vacancy occurring between July 1, 1971 and June 30, 1974, and have been placed under the Rent Stabilization Law again effective July 1, 1974:

1. Where the tenant elects a one-year lease term, the owner may charge that portion of the 6½ percent one-year lease increase which does not cause the rent to exceed 36 percent above the December 31, 1973 rent which was or would have been in effect for that dwelling unit pursuant to the Rent Stabilization Law (hereinafter, the "December 31, 1973 rent").

2. Where the tenant elects a two-year lease term:

(a) for the *first* year of the lease, the owner may charge that portion of the 8 percent two-year lease increase which does not cause the rent to exceed 36 percent above the "December 31, 1973 rent"; and

(b) for the *second* year of the lease, the owner may charge that portion of the 8 percent two-year lease increase which does not cause the rent to exceed 8 percent over 36 percent above "the December 31, 1973 rent."

3. Where the tenant elects a three-year lease term:

(a) for the first year of the lease, the owner may charge that portion of the 11 percent three-year lease increase which does not cause the rent to exceed 36 percent over the "December 31, 1973 rent" and

(b) for the balance of the lease term, the owner may charge that portion of the 11 percent three-year lease increase which does not cause the rent to exceed 11 percent over 36 percent above "the December 31, 1973 rent."

The owner shall be required, upon offering leases to the categories of tenants covered by this provision, to furnish such tenants with a rent computation reflecting the limitations provided in this provision on forms approved by the Conciliation and Appeals Board. Nothing contained in this provision shall be construed to authorize increases in excess of those otherwise established by this Order No. 8.

Decontrolled Units

The permissible percentage increases for decontrolled units under Order 3A remain in effect for units covered by such order.

Credits

Rental charged and paid in excess of the levels of fair rent increase established by this Order shall be fully credited against the next month's rent.

Dated: June 30, 1976
Filed with City Clerk: July 30, 1976

RENT GUIDELINE ORDER NUMBER 8a—Modification of the Terms of Order No. 8 Governing Rent Levels for Leases commencing between July 1, 1976 and June 30, 1977

Pursuant to the authority vested in it by the Rent Stabilization Law of 1969, and Chapter 576 of the Laws of 1974, as implemented by Resolution No. 276 of the New York City Council and extended by Chapter 203 of the Laws of 1977 and Rent Guidelines Order No. 8, the Rent Guideline Board hereby modifies the terms of its Order No. 8, which governs the levels of fair rent increases over lawful rents charged and paid on June 30, 1976 (including the "stabilizer," if any) for leases commencing between July 1, 1976 and June 30, 1977, for dwelling units subject to the Rent Stabilization Law as amended.

The Board has determined that although the weighted average delivery price of heating fuel for New York City reported in the Journal of Commerce had increased by a factor of more than 25 per cent over the price on April 2, 1978, the operating and maintenance cost increases experienced for stabilized apartment units from 1976 through 1978 were such that no adjustments of the levels of fair rent increases set forth in Order No. 8 are warranted at this time.

The Board may again convene to consider a further adjustment for unusual fuel costs should the weighted average price of heating fuel for New York City reported in the Journal of Commerce change by a factor of 15 per cent or more of the reported price in such publication on April 2, 1979.

Dated: April 27, 1979
Filed with the City Clerk: April 27, 1979

FRANCES LEVENSON, Chairperson

RENT GUIDELINE ORDER NUMBER 9—Rent Levels July 1, 1977 through June 30, 1978.

Pursuant to the authority vested in it by the Rent Stabilization Law of 1969, and Chapter 576 of the Laws of 1974, as implemented by Resolution Number 276 of 1974 of the New York City Council and extended by Chapter

204 of the Laws of 1977, the Rent Guidelines Board hereby establishes and adopts the following levels of fair rent increases over lawful rents charged and paid on June 30, 1977 (including the "stabilizer", if any) for dwelling units subject to the Rent Stabilization Law of 1969, as amended.

Adjustments for Renewal Leases

Together with such further adjustments as may be authorized by the Board, as explained below:

—For one year leases expiring before July 1, 1979: 6½ percent

—For two year leases expiring before July 1, 1980: 8½ percent

—For three year leases expiring before July 1, 1981: 11½ percent

The Board shall convene within 60 days of the date of this Order to consider special guidelines for dwelling units in a structure receiving tax abatement or exemption benefits pursuant to Section J51-2.5 of the Administrative Code of the City of New York and may, at such meeting, adopt guidelines for adjustments for leases for such units pursuant to this Order which shall be effective as of July 1, 1977. Until such determination, the adjustments for renewal leases as set forth above shall be utilized and be subject to further adjustment.

The Board may convene to consider an adjustment for unusual fuel costs should the weighted average delivery price of heating fuel for New York City reported in the Journal of Commerce change by a factor of 25 per cent or more of the reported price in such publication on the same date during the period of July 1, 1976 through June 30, 1977. The Board may also consider, at its annual meetings, any catastrophic change in the Operating and Maintenance Cost Index, and order appropriate supplementary adjustments. The Board reserves the right to modify this Order during its terms pursuant to this paragraph provided that any further adjustments as described in this paragraph may impact on all existing leases effective under this Order where the lease permits the rental reserved therein to be adjusted pursuant to subsequent determinations of the Rent Guidelines Board during the term of such lease.

Adjustments for Renewal Leases on dwelling units receiving partial tax exemption pursuant to Sections 421 or 423 of the Real Property Tax Law

Where a dwelling unit is in a structure subject to the partial tax exemption program under Section 421 of the Real Property Tax Law, or in a structure subject to Section 423 of the Real Property Tax Law as a Redevelopment Project, permissible percentage increases for renewal leases are as follows for the structures in which the exemption is 100 to 80 per cent of the real property taxes otherwise payable:

—For one year leases expiring before July 1, 1979: 5 per cent

—For two year leases expiring before July 1, 1980: 7 per cent

—For three year leases expiring before July 1, 1981: 10½ per cent

Where a dwelling unit is in a structure subject to such partial tax exemption programs in which the exemption is 40 to 79 per cent of the real property taxes otherwise payable, permissible percentage increases for renewal leases are as follows:

—For one year leases expiring before July 1, 1979: 5½ per cent

—For two year leases expiring before July 1, 1980: 7½ per cent

—For three year leases expiring before July 1, 1981: 11 per cent

Where a dwelling unit is in a structure subject to such partial tax exemption programs in which the exemption is 20 to 39 per cent of the real property taxes otherwise payable, permissible percentage increases for renewal leases are as follows:

—For one year leases expiring before July 1, 1979: 6 per cent

—For two year leases expiring before July 1, 1980: 8 per cent

—For three year leases expiring before July 1, 1981: 11½ per cent

Furthermore, nothing in this Order shall prohibit the

inclusion of a lease provision for an annual or other periodic rent increase over the initial rent at an average rate of not more than 2.2% per annum where the dwelling unit is receiving partial tax exemption pursuant to Section 421 of the Real Property Tax Law and the Regulations adopted pursuant thereto or, where applicable, such rate of rental increase as is provided for and authorized by Section 423 of the Real Property Tax Law. The cumulative but not compounded charge of up to 2.2% per annum as provided by Section 421 or the rate provided by Section 423 is in addition to the amount permitted under this section of the Guideline Order for leases.

For such renewal leases under this Order, the percentage of the real property tax exemption shall be determined on the basis of the tax exemption rate in effect on July 1, 1977.

Leases on Vacant Apartments

Where a dwelling unit becomes vacant, the levels of rent increase governing a new tenancy commencing on or after July 1, 1977, and before June 30, 1978, are the same levels over rentals charged on June 30, 1977 as those set forth above for lease renewals, plus 5 per cent over the rentals charged on June 30, 1977 on each vacancy of such unit during the effective period of this Order.

Fractional Terms

Except as to leases on vacant apartments, for the purpose of these guidelines any lease or tenancy for a period up to and including one year shall be deemed a one year lease or tenancy; the same for a period over one year and up to and including two years shall be deemed a two year lease; and the same for a period over two years and up to and including three years shall be deemed a three year lease. As to leases on vacant apartments, for the purpose of these guidelines any lease for a period from one year to less than two years shall be deemed a one year lease; the same for a period from two years to less than three years shall be deemed a two year lease; and the same for a period of three years or more shall be deemed a three year lease.

Electrical Inclusion Adjustment

In addition to the lease adjustment permitted under this Order No. 9, a lease for a dwelling unit for which the owner supplies full electrical service for which there is no additionl cost charged to the tenant in addition to rent, the applicable lease adjustment as established by this Order is increased by 4 per cent. However, this allowance shall not apply to any dwelling unit as to which an increase for electrical inclusion was collected under Guideline Order No. 6 (et. seq.), 7 or 8.

Escalator Clauses

Where a lease for a dwelling unit in effect on May 31, 1968, or where a lease in effect on June 30, 1974 for a dwelling unit which became subject to the Rent Stabilization Law of 1969, by virtue of Chapter 576 of the Laws of 1974 and Resolution No. 276 of the New York City Council and extended by Chapter 204 of the Laws of 1977, contained an escalator clause for the increased costs of operation and such clause is still in effect, the lawful rental on June 30, 1977 over which the fair rent under this Order is computed shall include the increased rental, if any, due under such clause except those charges which accrued within one year of the commencement of the renewal lease. Moreover, where a lease contained an escalator clause which the owner may validly renew under the Code, unless the owner elects or has elected in writing to delete such clause, effective no later than July 1, 1977 from the existing lease and all subsequent leases for such dwelling unit, the increased rental, if any, due under such escalator clause shall be offset against the amount of increase authorized under this Order.

Stabilizer

The one-half percent "stabilizers" charged in leases pursuant to previous Orders of this Board shall remain in effect until the expiration of such leases.

Special Guidelines to Update Special Guidelines 6b

In order to aid the Conciliation and Appeals Board in determining fair market rents for housing accommodations as to applications for adjustment of the initial regulated rent as may be requested by tenants, the Rent Guidelines Board hereby establishes a special guideline as mandated by Section 12 of Chapter 576 of the Laws of 1974, and as extended by Chapter 204 of the Laws of

1977, amending Section YY51-6.02b(1) of the New York City Administrative Code for dwelling units subject to the Rent and Rehabilitation Law on June 30, 1977 which subsequently become vacant after June 30, 1977, the 1976-77 maximum rent as it existed or would have existed, plus 20 percent.

Decontrolled Units

The permissible percentage increases for decontrolled units under Order 3A remain in effect for units covered by such order.

Credits

Rental charged and paid in excess of the levels of fair rent increase established by this Order shall be fully credited against the next month's rent.

Dated: June 30, 1977
Filed with City Clerk: June 30, 1977

RENT GUIDELINE ORDER NUMBER 9a—Modification of the Terms of Order No. 9 Governing Rent Levels for Leases Commencing Between July 1, 1977 and June 30, 1978.

Pursuant to the authority vested in it by the Rent Stabilization Law of 1969, and Chapter 576 of the Laws of 1974, as implemented by Resolution No. 276 of the New York City Council and extended by Chapter 203 of the Laws of 1977 and Rent Guidelines Order No. 9, the Rent Guidelines Board hereby modifies the terms of its Order No. 9, which governs the levels of fair rent increases over lawful rents charged and paid on June 30, 1977 (including the "stabilizer," if any) for leases commencing between July 1, 1977 and June 30, 1978, for dwelling units subject to the Rent Stabilization Law as amended.

The Board has determined that although the weighted average delivery price of heating fuel for New York City reported in the Journal of Commerce had increased by a factor of more than 25 per cent over the price on April 22, 1977, the operating and maintenance cost increases experienced for stabilized apartment units from 1977 through 1979 were such that no adjustments of the levels of fair rent increases set forth in Order No. 9 are warranted at this time.

The Board may again convene to consider a further adjustment for unusual fuel costs should the weighted average price of heating fuel for New York City reported in the Journal of Commerce change by a factor of 15 per cent or more of the reported price in such publication on June 1, 1979.

Dated: June 18, 1979
Filed with the City Clerk June 18, 1979

FRANCES LEVENSON, Chairperson

RENT GUIDELINE ORDER NUMBER 9b—Modification of the Terms of Order No. 9 Governing Rent Levels for Leases Commencing Between July 1, 1977 and June 30, 1978.

Pursuant to the authority vested in it by the Rent Stabilization Law of 1969, and Chapter 576 of the Laws of 1974, as implemented by Resolution No. 276 of the New York City Council and extended by Chapter 203 of the Laws of 1977 and Rent Guidelines Order Nos. 9, and 9a, the Rent Guidelines Board hereby modifies the terms of its Order No. 9a for dwelling units subject to the Rent Stabilization Law as amended.

The Board has determined that although the weighted average delivery price of heating fuel for New York City reported in the Journal of Commerce had increased by a factor of more than 15 per cent over the price on June 1, 1979, the operating and maintenance cost increases experienced for stabilized apartment units from 1977 through 1980 were such that no adjustments of the levels of fair rent increases set forth in Order No. 9 are warranted.

Dated: June 27, 1980
Filed with the City Clerk June 30, 1980

RENT GUIDELINE ORDER NUMBER 10—Rent Levels July 1, 1978 through June 30, 1979.

Adjustments for Renewal Leases

Together with such further adjustments as may be authorized by the Board, as "explained below:

—For one year leases expiring before July 1, 1980: 3½ per cent

—For two year leases expiring before July 1, 1981: 5½ per cent

—For three year leases expiring before July 1, 1982: 7½ per cent

These adjustments shall also apply to dwelling units in a structure subject to the partial tax exemption program under Section 421 of the Real Property Tax Law, or in a structure subject to Section 423 of the Real Property Tax Law as a Redevelopment Project.

The Board may convene to consider an adjustment for unusual fuel costs should the weighted average delivery price of heating fuel for New York City reported in the Journal of Commerce change by a factor of 25 per cent or more of the reported price in such publication on the same date during the period of July 1, 1977 through June 30, 1978. The Board may also consider, at its annual meetings, any catastrophic change in the Operating and Maintenance Cost Index and order appropriate supplementary adjustments. The Board reserves the right to modify this Order during its terms pursuant to this paragraph provided that any further adjustments as described in this paragraph may impact on all existing leases effective under this Order where the lease permits the rental reserved therein to be adjusted pursuant to subsequent determinations of the Rent Guidelines Board during the term of such lease.

Leases on Vacant Apartments

Where a dwelling unit becomes vacant, the levels of rent increase governing a new tenancy commencing on or after July 1, 1978, and on or before June 30, 1979, are the same levels over rentals charged on June 30, 1978 as these set forth above for lease renewals, plus 5 per cent over the rentals charged on June 30, 1978 on each vacancy of such unit during the effective period of this Order.

Rent Guidance Board Orders

Fractional Terms

Except as to leases on vacant apartments, for the purpose of these guidelines any lease or tenancy for a period up to and including one year shall be deemed a one year lease or tenancy; the same for a period over one year and up to and including two years shall be deemed a two year lease; and the same for a period over two years and up to and including three years shall be deemed a three year lease. As to leases on vacant apartments, for the purpose of these guidelines any lease for a period from one year to less than two years shall be deemed a one year lease; the same for a period from two years to less than three years shall be deemed a two year lease; and the same for a period of three years or more shall be deemed a three year lease.

Electrical Inclusion Adjustment

In addition to the lease adjustment permitted under this Order No. 10, a lease for a dwelling unit for which the owner supplies full electrical service for which there is no additional cost charged to the tenant in addition to rent, the applicable lease adjustment as established by this Order is increased by ½ per cent.

Escalator Clauses

Where a lease for a dwelling unit in effect on May 31, 1968, or where a lease in effect on June 30, 1974 for a dwelling unit which became subject to the Rent Stabilization Law of 1969, by virtue of Chapter 576 of the Laws of 1974 and Resolution No. 276 of the New York City Council and extended by Chapter 203 of the Laws of 1977, contained an escalator clause for the increased costs of operation and such clause is still in effect, the lawful rental on June 30, 978 over which the fair rent under this Order is computed shall include the increased rental, if any, due under such clause except these charges which accrued within one year of the commencement of the renewal lease. Moreover, where a lease contained an escalator clause which the owner may validly renew under the Code, unless the owner elects or has elected in writing to delete such clause, effective no later than July 1, 1978 from the existing lease and all subsequent leases for such dwelling unit, the increased rental, if any, due under such escalator clause shall be offset against the amount of increase authorized under this Order.

Stabilizer

The one-half per cent "stabilizers" charged in leases pursuant to previous Orders of this Board shall remain in effect until the expiration of such leases.

Special Guidelines to Update Special Guideline 6b

In order to aid the Conciliation and Appeals Board in determining fair market rents for housing accomodations as to applications for adjustment of the initial legal regulated rent as may be requested by tenants, the Rent Guidelines Board hereby establishes a special guideline as mandated by Section 12 of Chapter 576 of the Laws of 1974, as extended by Chapter 203 of the Laws of 1977, amending Section YY51-6.0.2(b)(1) of the New York City Administrative Code, for dwelling units subject to the Rent and Rehabilitation Law on June 30, 1978 which subsequently become vacant after June 30, 1978, the 1978 maximum base rent, as it existed or would have existed, plus 15 per cent.

Decontrolled Units

The permissible increase for decontrolled units as defined in Order 3a which become decontrolled after June 30, 1978, shall not exceed the 1978 maximum base rent, as it existed or would have existed, plus 15 per cent of such maximum base rent, but in no event shall the increase for each year of the first stabilized lease exceed 15 per cent of the last maximum collectible rent paid by the tenant. Order 3a shall otherwise remain in effect for such units.

Credits

Rental charged and paid in excess of the levels of fair rent increase established by this Order shall be fully credited against the next month's rent

Dated: June 30, 1978
Filed with the City Clerk: June 30, 1978

RENT GUIDELINE ORDER NUMBER 10a—Rent Levels July 1, 1978 through June 30, 1979

Rent Guidance Board Orders

Adjustments for Renewal Leases

Together with such further adjustments as may be authorized by the Board, as explained below:

—For one year leases expiring before July 1, 1980: 4½ per cent

—For two year leases expiring before July 1, 1981: 6½ per cent

—For three year leases expiring before July 1, 1982: 8½ per cent

These adjustments shall also apply to dwelling units in a structure subject to the partial tax exemption program under Section 421 of the Real Property Tax Law, or in structure subject to Section 423 of the Real Property Tax Law as a Redevelopment Project.

The Board may convene to consider an adjustment for unusual fuel costs should the weighted average delivery price of heating fuel for New York City reported in the Journal of Commerce change by a factor of 25 per cent or more of the reported price in such publication on the same date during the period of July 1, 1977 through June 30, 1978. The Board may also consider, at its annual meetings, any catastrophic change in the Operating and Maintenance Cost Index and order appropriate supplementary adjustments. The Board reserves the right to modify this Order during its terms pursuant to this paragraph provided that any further adjustments as described in this paragraph may impact on all existing leases effectively under this Order where the lease permits the rental reserved therein to be adjusted pursuant to subsequent determinations of the Rent Guidelines Board during the term of such lease.

Leases on Vacant Apartments

Where a dwelling unit becomes vacant, the levels of rent increase governing a new tenancy commencing on or after July 1, 1978, and on or before June 30, 1979, are the same levels over rentals charged on June 30, 1978 as those set forth above for lease renewals, plus 5 per cent over the rentals charged on June 30, 1979 on each vacancy of such unit during the effective period of this Order.

Rent Guidance Board Orders

Fractional Terms

Except as to leases on vacant apartments, for the purpose of these guidelines any lease or tenancy for a period up to and including one year shall be deemed a one year lease or tenancy; the same for a period over one year and up to and including two years shall be deemed a two year lease; and the same for a period over two years and up to and including three years shall be deemed a three year lease. As to leases on vacant apartments, for the purpose of these guidelines any lease for a period from one year to less than two years shall be deemed a one year lease; the same for a period from two years to less than three years shall be deemed a two year lease; and the same for a period of three years or more shall be deemed a three year lease.

Electrical Inclusion Adjustment

In addition to the lease adjustment permitted under this Order No. 10a, a lease for a dwelling unit for which the owner supplies full electrical service for which there is no additional cost charged to the tenant in addition to rent, the applicable lease adjustment as established by this Order is increased by ½ per cent.

Escalator Clauses

Where a lease for a dwelling unit in effect on May 31, 1968, or where a lease in effect on June 30, 1974 for a dwelling unit which became subject to the Rent Stabilization Law of 1969, by virtue of Chapter 576 of the Laws of 1974 and Resolution No. 276 of the New York City Council and extended by Chapter 204 of the Laws of 1977, contained an escalator clause for the increased costs of operation and such clause is still in effect, the lawful rental on June 30, 1978 over which the fair rent under this Order is computed shall include the increased rental, if any, due under such clause except those charges which accrued within one year of the commencement of the renewal lease. Moreover, where a lease contained an escalator clause which the owner may validly renew under the Code, unless the owner elects or has elected in writing to delete such clause, effective no later than July 1, 1978 from the existing lease and all subsequent leases for such dwelling unit, the increased rental, if any, due under such escalator clause shall be offset against the amount of increase authorized under this Order.

Stabilizer

The one-half per cent "stabilizers" charged in leases pursuant to previous Orders of this Board shall remain in effect until the expiration of such leases.

Special Guidelines to Update Special Guideline 6b

In order to aid the Conciliation and Appeals Board in determining fair market rents for housing accommodations as to applications for adjustment of the initial legal regulated rent as may be requested by tenants, the Rent Guidelines Board hereby establishes a special guideline as mandated by Section 12 of Chapter 576 of the Laws of 1974, as extended by Chapter 204 of the Laws of 1977, amending Section YY51-6.0.2(b)(1) of the New York City Administrative Code, for dwelling units subject to the Rent and Rehabilitation Law on June 30, 1978 which subsequently become vacant after June 30, 1978, the 1978 maximum base rent, as it existed or would have existed, plus 15 per cent.

Decontrolled Units

The permissible increase for decontrolled units as defined in Order 3a which become decontrolled after June 30, 1978, shall not exceed the 1978 maximum base rent, as it existed or would have existed, plus 15 per cent of such maximum base rent, but in no event shall the increase for each of the first stabilized lease exceed 15 per cent of the last maximum collectible rent paid by the tenant. Order 3a shall otherwise remain in effect for such units.

Credits

Rental charged and paid in excess of the levels of fair rent increase established by this Order shall be fully credited against the next month's rent.

Retroactivity

This Order 10a shall be effective as of July 1, 1978. Additional rental payments charged retroactively pursuant to this Order 10a in excess of rentals permissable under Order 10 may, at the tenant's option, be paid by a tenant in occupancy, who remains in occupancy, in equal monthly installments for the same number of months for which such increase is due or the number of months remaining in the lease, whichever is less, and as to any other tenant, including tenants who vacate or have already vacated prior to the expiration of the lease term, such amount or any remaining unpaid portion thereof shall be immediately due and owing.

Dated: April 6, 1979.
Filed with the City Clerk: April 6, 1979.

RENT GUIDELINE ORDER NUMBER 10b—April 1979 Fuel Adjustment for Rent Levels July 1, 1978 through June 30, 1979.

April 1979 Fuel Adjustment

In addition to the lease adjustment or adjustments permitted under Order No. 10a, together with such further adjustments which may be authorized by the Board pursuant to Order No. 10a or by this Order, the permissible stabilization rental on March 1, 1979, shall be separately supplemented and adjusted as follows:

—For one year leases expiring before July 1, 1980: 2½ per cent.

—For two year leases expiring before July 1, 1981: 2 per cent.

—For three year leases expiring before July 1, 1982: ½ per cent.

As to all existing leases which are fully executed under Order No. 10a as of the date of this Order, the "April 1979 fuel adjustment" shall be effective only where such lease permits the rental reserved to be adjusted pursuant to subsequent determinations of the Board during the term of such lease.

Any "April 1979 fuel adjustment" charged pursuant to this Order No. 10b shall not be included in the rent to which a lease adjustment or adjustments set forth in Order No. 10a (i.e. the June 30, 1978 rent, including the "stabilizer," if any) are applied and, unless so provided by subsequent orders of the Board, the "April 1979 fuel adjustment" shall not merge with such base rent for the purpose of computing any subsequent rent or lease. In no event shall more than one "April 1979 fuel adjustment" be charged to any dwelling unit.

The Board may convene to consider a further adjustment for unusual fuel costs should the weighted average delivery price of heating fuel for New York City reported in the Journal of Commerce change by a factor of 15 per cent or more of the reported price in such publication on April 2, 1979. The Board reserves the right to modify this Order during its terms pursuant to this paragraph provided that any further adjustments as described in this paragraph may impact on all existing leases effective under this Order where the lease permits the rental reserved therein to be adjusted pursuant to subsequent determinations of the Rent Guidelines Board during the term of such lease.

Retroactivity

This Order No. 10b shall be effective as of March 1, 1979.
Dated: April 12, 1979.
Filed with the City Clerk: April 12, 1979.

RENT GUIDELINE ORDER NUMBER 10c—January 1980 Fuel Adjustment for Rent Levels and February 1980 Fuel Adjustment for Vacancy Allowances.

January 1980 Fuel Adjustment for Rent Levels

Where heat is provided or required to be provided to a dwelling unit by an owner from a central or individual system at no charge to the tenant, in addition to the lease adjustment or adjustments permitted under Order Nos. 10a and 10b, for leases commencing between July 1, 1978 and June 30, 1979, together with such further adjustments which may be authorized by the Board pursuant to this Order, the permissible stabilization rental on January 1, 1980 shall be separately supplemented and adjusted by a charge of twelve dollars ($12.00) per month per dwelling unit, which charge shall remain in effect until June 30, 1980.

This "January 1980 fuel adjustment for rent levels" shall be effective only where such lease permits the rental reserved to be adjusted pursuant to subsequent determinations of the Board during the term of such lease.

Any "January 1980 fuel adjustment of rent levels" charged pursuant to this Order No. 10c shall not be included in the rent to which a lease adjustment or adjustments set forth in Orders are applied and shall not merge with the base rent for the purpose of computing any subsequent adjustment or lease. In no event shall more than one "January 1980 fuel adjustment of rent levels" be charged to any dwelling unit.

February 1980 Fuel Adjustment for Vacancy Allowances

Where heat is provided or required to be provided to a dwelling unit by the owner from a central or individual system at no charge to the tenant, in addition to the vacancy allowance permitted for leases commencing between February 1, 1980 and June 30, 1980, together with such further adjustments which may be authorized by the Board pursuant to this Order, where a dwelling unit becomes vacant, the levels of fair rent increase governing a new tenancy commencing on or after February 1, 1980 shall be supplemented and adjusted by an additional ten percent (10%) over the rents charged on June 30, 1979 (including the "stabilizer" and excluding the "April 1979 fuel adjustment," if any) on each vacancy of such unit.

Dated: December 27, 1979
Filed with the City Clerk: December 27, 1979

RENT GUIDELINES ORDER NUMBER 10d—July 1980 Fuel Adjustment for Rent Levels.

July 1980 Fuel Adjustment of Rent Levels and Modification of January 1980 Fuel Adjustment For Rent Levels

Where heat is provided or required to be provided to a dwelling unit by an owner from a central or individual system at no charge to the tenant, in addition to the lease adjustment or adjustments permitted under Order Nos. 10a and 10b for leases commencing between July 1, 1978 and June 30, 1979, together with such further adjustments which may be authorized by the Board pursuant to this Order, the permissible stabilization rental on July 1, 1980 shall be separately supplemented and adjusted by a charge of eight dollars ($8.00) per month per dwelling unit, which charge shall remain in effect until June 30, 1981.

Where the permissible stabilization rental on June 30, 1980 had been separately supplemented and adjusted by a charge of twelve dollars ($12.00) per month per dwelling unit pursuant to Order 10c (the January 1980 Fuel Adjustment for Rent Levels), that twelve dollars ($12.00) per month shall be reduced to eight dollars ($8.00) per month per dwelling unit.

This July 1980 fuel adjustment of rent levels shall be effective only where such lease permits the rental reserved to be adjusted pursuant to subsequent determinations of the Board during the term of such lease.

Any July 1980 fuel adjustment of rent levels charged pursuant to this Order No. 10d, shall not merge with the base rent established pursuant to Order No. 10a for the purpose of computing any adjustment for leases commencing under the terms of subsequent Orders of the Board.

Dated: June 27, 1980
Filed with the City Clerk, June 30, 1980

RENT GUIDELINE ORDER NUMBER 10e—Modification of the Terms of Order No. 10d Governing Rent Levels for Leases Commencing on or after July 1, 1978 and on or before June 30, 1979.[1]

July 1981 Fuel Adjustments for Rent Levels

Where heat is provided or required to be provided to a dwelling unit by an owner from a central or individual system at no charge to the tenant, in addition to the lease adjustment or adjustments permitted under Order Nos. 10a, and 10b for leases commencing on or after July 1, 1978 and on or before June 30, 1979, together with such further adjustments which may be authorized by the Board pursuant to this Order, the separate supplemental

[1] Explanatory Statement of the Rent Guidelines Board in Relation to the Modification of the Terms of Order No. 10d Governing Rent Levels for Leases Commencing on or after July 1, 1978 and on or before June 30, 1979 for Apartments under the Jurisdiction of the Rent Stabilization Law.

charge of eight dollars ($8.00) per month per dwelling, as authorized by Order No. 10d and which was to expire on June 30, 1981 by the terms of said Order, shall continue to be authorized as a separate supplemental charge to the permissible stabilization rental, until the expiration of the lease.

This fuel adjustment shall be effective only where such lease permits the rental reserved to be adjusted pursuant to subsequent determinations of the Board during the term of such lease.

Any fuel adjustment charged pursuant to this Order No. 10e shall not merge with the base rent established pursuant to Order No. 10a for the purpose of computing any adjustment for leases commencing under the terms of subsequent Orders of the Board.

Rent Guidelines Board Order No. 10e, adopted at the June 25, 1981 public meeting of the Board, authorizes a continuation of the supplementary adjustment of the levels of fair rent increases over lawful rents for dwelling units subject to the Rent Stabilization Law of 1969, as amended, for leases entered into between July 1, 1978 and June 30, 1979.

Order 10e authorizes continuation of a separate supplemental increase in the permissible stabilized rent on July 1, 1981 of $8.00 (eight dollars) per month, per dwelling unit to remain in effect until June 30, 1982 or until the expiration of the lease, whichever occurs first. This adjustment shall apply only where heat is provided or required to be provided to a dwelling unit by an owner from a central or individual heating system at no charge to the tenant.

In no event shall more than one Fuel Adjustment for Rent Levels authorized pursuant to this Order be charged to any dwelling unit. This Fuel Adjustment for Rent Levels shall not merge with the base rent for the purpose of computing future adjustments.

This adjustment increases the permissible rents for stabilized apartments with a lease that was fully executed under Order Number 10a and that permits the rental reserved to be adjusted pursuant to subsequent Orders of the Rent Guidelines Board during the term of such lease.

This adjustment does not apply to leases which were signed as the first stabilized lease following a vacancy in a previously rent controlled apartment, which are governed by the provision for decontrolled units in the Order Number 10a, or to the first lease of a unit entering the stabilization system pursuant to Section J51-2.5 of the Administrative Code or Section 421-a of the Real Property Tax Law or any similar program.

Dated: June 29, 1981
Filed with the City Clerk, June 30, 1981

RENT GUIDELINE ORDER NUMBER 11—Rent Levels July 1, 1979 through June 30, 1980.

(Dated June 29, 1979; filed with city clerk, June 29, 1979)

Adjustments for Renewal Leases

Together with such further adjustments as may be authorized by the Board, as explained below:

—For one year leases expiring before July 1, 1981: 8½ per cent

—For two year leases expiring before July 1, 1982: 12 per cent

—For three year leases expiring before July 1, 1983: 15 per cent

These adjustments shall also apply to dwelling units in a structure subject to the partial tax exemption program under Section 421 of the Real Property Tax Law, or in a structure subject to Section 423 of the Real Property Tax Law as a Redevelopment Project.

The Board may convene to consider a further adjustment for unusual fuel costs should the weighted average delivery price of heating fuel for New York City reported in the Journal of Commerce change from the reported price in such publication on April 13, 1979 by the following factors:

—By June 30, 1980: by a factor of 25 per cent or more

—By June 30, 1981: by a factor of 45 per cent or more

—Thereafter, for any leases remaining in effect pursuant to this Order: by a factor of 55 per cent or more.

The Board may also consider any catastrophic change in the Operating and Maintenance Cost Index and order appropriate supplementary adjustments. The Board reserves the right to modify this Order during its term pursuant to this paragraph provided that any further adjustments described in this paragraph shall apply to existing leases only where the lease permits the rental reserved therein to be adjusted pursuant to subsequent determinations of the Rent Guidelines Board during the term of such lease.

Leases on Vacant Apartments

Where a dwelling unit becomes vacant, the levels of rent increase governing a new tenancy commencing on or after July 1, 1979 and on or before June 30, 1980 are the same levels over rentals charged on June 30, 1979 as those set forth above for lease renewals, plus 5 per cent over the rentals charged on June 30, 1979 on each vacancy of such unit during the effective period of this Order.

Fractional Terms

Except as to leases on vacant apartments, for the purpose of these guidelines any lease or tenancy for a period up to and including one year shall be deemed a one year lease or tenancy; the same for a period over one year and up to and including two years shall be deemed a two year lease; and the same for a period over two years and up to and including three years shall be deemed a three year lease. As to leases on vacant apartments, for the purpose of these guidelines any lease for a period from one year to less than two years shall be deemed a one year lease; the same for a period from two years to less than three years shall be deemed a two year lease; and the same for a period of three years or more shall be deemed a three year lease.

Electrical Inclusion Adjustment

For a lease for a dwelling unit for which the owner supplies full electrical service for which there is no additional cost charged to the tenant in addition to rent, the applicable lease adjustments as established by this Order are to be in effect without an additional adjustment for electrical inclusion.

Rent Guidance Board Orders

Escalator Clauses

Where a lease for a dwelling unit in effect on May 31, 1978 or where a lease in effect on June 30, 1974 for a dwelling unit which became subject to the Rent Stabilization Law of 1969, by virtue of Chapter 576 of the Laws of 1974 and Resolution Number 276 of the New York City Council and extended by Chapter 203 of the Laws of 1977, contained an escalator clause for the increased costs of operation and such clause is still in effect, the lawful rental on June 30, 1979 over which the fair rent under this Order is computed shall include the increased rental, if any, due under such clause except those charges which accrued within one year of the commencement of the renewal lease. Moreover, where a lease contained an escalator clause which the owner may validly renew under the Code, unless the owner elects or has elected in writing to delete such clause, effective no later than July 1, 1979 from the existing lease and all subsequent leases for such dwelling unit, the increased rental, if any, due under such escalator clause shall be offset against the amount of increase authorized under this Order.

Stabilizer

The one-half per cent "stabilizers" charged in leases pursuant to previous Orders of this Board shall remain in effect until the expiration of such leases and shall be included in the base rents for the purpose of computing subsequent rents or leases adjusted pursuant to this Order.

Special Guideline to Update Special Guideline 6b

In order to aid the Conciliation and Appeals Board in determining fair market rents for housing accommodations as to applications for adjustment of the initial legal regulated rent as may be requested by tenants, the Rent Guidelines Board hereby establishes a special guideline as mandated by Section 12 of Chapter 576 of the Laws of 1974, as extended by Chapter 203 of the Laws of 1977, amending Section YY51-6.0.2(b)(1) of the New York City Administrative Code, for dwelling units subject to the Rent and Rehabilitation Law on June 30, 1979 which subsequently become vacant after June 30, 1979, the

1978-1979 maximum base rent, as it existed or would have existed, plus 20 per cent.

Decontrolled Units

The permissible increase for decontrolled units as defined in Order 3a which become decontrolled after June 30, 1979, shall not exceed the 1978-1979 maximum base rent, as it existed or would have existed, plus 20 per cent of such maximum base rent, but in no event shall the increase for each year of the first stabilized lease exceed 15 per cent of the last maximum collectible rent paid by the tenant. Order 3a shall otherwise remain in effect for such units.

April 1979 Fuel Adjustment

Any "April 1979 fuel adjustment" charged pursuant to Order 10b shall not be included in the rent to which a lease adjustment set forth in this Order is applied and it shall not merge with the base rent for the purpose of computing a subsequent rent or lease adjusted pursuant to this Order.

Any "April 1979 fuel adjustment" charged pursuant to Order 10b shall only remain in effect for a rent or lease adjusted pursuant to Order 10b and such charge shall be extinguished when a lease to which it applies expires.

Credits

Rental charged and paid in excess of the levels of fair rent increase established by this Order shall be fully credited against next month's rent.

RENT GUIDELINE ORDER NUMBER 11a—Fuel Adjustment for Leases Commencing Between July 1, 1979 and June 30, 1980 to go into Effect One Year from the Date of Commencement of the Lease.

Fuel Adjustment for Rent Levels

Where heat is provided or required to be provided to a dwelling unit by an owner from a central or individual system at no charge to the tenant, in addition to the lease adjustment or adjustments permitted under Order No. 11, for leases commencing between July 1, 1979 and June 30, 1980, together with such further adjustments which may be authorized by the Board pursuant to this Order, the permissible stabilization rental shall be separately supplemented and adjusted by a charge of eight dollars ($8.00) per month per dwelling unit, effective one year from the date of commencment of the lease.

This fuel adjustment shall be effective only where such lease permits the rental reserve to be adjusted pursuant to subsequent determinations of the Board during the term of such lease.

Any fuel adjustment charged pursuant to this Order No. 11a shall not merge with the base rent established pursuant to Order No. 11 for the purpose of computing any adjustment for leases commencing under the terms of subsequent Orders of the Board.

Date: June 27, 1980
Filed with the City Clerk, June 30, 1980

RENT GUIDELINE ORDER NUMBER 11b—Continuation of the Fuel Adjustment for Leases Commencing Between July 1, 1979 and June 30, 1980 Effective One Year from the Date of Commencement of the Lease.[1]

[1] Explanatory Statement of the Rent Guidelines Board in Relation to the Continuation of the Fuel Adjustment for Leases Commencing Between July 1, 1979 and June 30, 1980 To Go Into Effect One Year From The Date of Commencement of the Lease.
Order No. 11b

Rent Guidelines Board Order No. 11b, adopted at the June 25, 1981 public meeting of the Board, authorizes a continuation of the supplementary adjustment of the levels of fair rent increase over lawful rents for dwelling units subject to the Rent Stabilization Law of 1969, as amended, for leases commencing between July 1, 1979 and June 30, 1980. This separate supplemental adjustment of $8.00 (eight dollars) per month per dwelling unit to go into effect one year from the commencement date of the lease, was authorized by Rent Guidelines Board Order No. 11a, and this Order No. 11b authorizes continuation of this supplemental adjustment. This adjustment shall apply only where heat is provided or required to be provided to a dwelling unit by an owner from a central or individual system at no charge to the tenant.

In no event shall more than one fuel adjustment pursuant to Order Nos. 11a and 11b be charged to any dwelling unit. This fuel adjustment shall not merge with the base rent for the purpose of computing future adjustments.

This adjustment increased the permissible rents for stabilized apartments with a lease that was fully executed under Order Number 11 and that permits the rental reserved to be adjusted pursuant to subsequent Orders of the Rent Guidelines Board during the term of such lease.

This adjustment does not apply to leases which were signed as the first stabilized lease following a vacancy in a previously rent controlled apartment, which are governed by the provision for decontrolled units in Order 11, or to the first lease of a unit

Fuel Adjustment for Rent Levels

Where heat is provided or required to be provided to a dwelling unit by an owner from a central or individual system at no charge to the tenant, in addition to the lease adjustment or adjustments permitted under Order No. 11 for leases commencing between July 1, 1979 and June 30, 1980, together with such further adjustments which may be authorized by the Board pursuant to this Order, the separate supplemental charge of eight dollars ($8.00) per month per dwelling unit which was to be effective one year from the date of commencement of the lease, as authorized pursuant to Order Number 11a, shall continue to be authorized as a separate supplemental charge to the permissible stabilization rental, until the expiration of the lease.

This fuel adjustment shall be effective only where such lease permits the rental reserved to be adjusted pursuant to subsequent determinations of the Board during the term of such lease.

Any fuel adjustment charged pursuant to this Order No. 11b shall not merge with the base rent established pursuant to Order No. 11 for the purpose of computing any adjustment for leases commencing under the terms of subsequent Orders of the Board.

Date: June 29, 1981
Filed with the City Clerk, June 30, 1981

RENT GUIDELINE ORDER NUMBER 11c—Continuation of the Fuel Adjustment for Leases Commencing on or after July 1, 1979 and on or before June 30, 1980 Effective One Year From The Date of Commencement of Lease.

Fuel Adjustment for Rent Levels

Where heat is provided or required to be provided to a dwelling unit by an owner from a central or individual system at no charge to the tenant, in addition to the lease adjustment or adjustments permitted under Order Nos.

entering the stabilization system pursuant to Section J51-2.5 of the Administration Code or Section 421-a of the Real Property Tax Law or any similar program.

11, 11a and 11b for leases commencing on or after July 1, 1979 and on or before June 30, 1980, together with such further adjustments which may be authorized by the Board pursuant to this Order, the separate supplemental charge of eight dollars ($8.00) per month per dwelling unit which was to be effective one year from the date of commencement of the lease, as authorized pursuant to Order Number 11a, and was authorized to be continued, pursuant to Order Number 11b, shall continue to be authorized as a separate supplemental charge to the permissible stabilization rental, until the expiration of the lease.

This fuel adjustment shall be effective only where such lease permits the rental reserved to be adjusted pursuant to subsequent determinations of the Board during the term of such lease.

Any fuel adjustment charged pursuant to this Order No. 11c shall not merge with the base rent established pursuant to Order No. 11 for the purpose of computing any adjustment for leases commencing under the terms of subsequent Orders of the Board.

Dated: June 30, 1982
Filed with the City Clerk, June 30, 1982

RENT GUIDELINE ORDER NUMBER 12—Rent Levels July 1, 1980 Through September 30, 1981.

Adjustments for Renewal Leases

Where heat is provided or required to be provided to a dwelling unit by an owner from a central or individual system at no charge to the tenant, the adjustments are as follows:

—For one year lease expiring before October 1, 1982: 11 per cent

—For two year leases expiring before October 1, 1983: 14 per cent

—For three year leases expiring before October 1, 1984: 17 per cent

These adjustments shall also apply to dwelling units in a structure subject to the partial tax exemption program under Section 421 of the Real Property Tax Law, or in a structure subject to Section 423 of the Real Property Tax Law as a Redevelopment Project.

Where heat is not provided or not required to be provided to a dwelling unit by an owner from a central or individual system, the adjustments are as follows:

—For one year leases expiring before October 1, 1982: 5 per cent

—For two year leases expiring before October 1, 1983: 7 per cent

—For three year leases expiring before October 1, 1984: 9 per cent

It is not expected that the Board will convene to discuss fuel costs in the coming year. The Board will discuss the fuel situation at its annual meetings in June as it affects leases signed pursuant to this Order. The Board may also consider any catastrophic change in the Operation and Maintenance Cost Index and order appropriate supplementary adjustments. The Board reserves the right to modify this Order during its term pursuant to this paragraph provided that any further adjustments described in this paragraph shall apply to existing leases only where the lease permits the rental reserved therein to be adjusted pursuant to subsequent determinations of the Rent Guidelines Board during the term of such lease.

Leases on Vacant Apartments

Where a dwelling unit becomes vacant, the levels of rent increase governing a new tenancy commencing on or after July 1, 1980 and on or before June 30, 1981 are the same levels over rentals charged on June 30, 1980 as those set forth above for lease renewals, plus five per cent over the rentals charged on June 30, 1980 on each vacancy of such unit during the effective period of this Order where there has been a change in tenantry in the apartment since July 1, 1975, and plus ten percent over the rentals charged on June 30, 1980 on each vacancy of such lease renewals, plus five per cent over the rentals charged on June 30, 1980 on each vacancy of such unit during the effective period of this Order where there has been a change in tenantry in the apartment since July 1, 1975, and plus ten percent over the rentals charged on June 30, 1980 on each vacancy of such unit during the effective period of this Order where there has been no change in tenantry in the apartment since July 1, 1975.

Fractional Terms

Except as to leases on vacant apartments, for the purpose of these guidelines any lease or tenancy for a period up to and including one year shall be deemed a one year lease or tenancy; the same for a period over one year and up to and including two years shall be deemed a two year lease; and the same for a period over two years and up to and including three years shall be deemed a three year lease. As to leases on vacant apartments, for the purpose of these guidelines any lease for a period from one year to less than two years shall be deemed a one year lease; the same for a period from two years to less than three years shall be deemed a two year lease; and the same for a period of three years or more shall be deemed a three year lease.

Electrical Inclusion Adjustment

For a lease for a dwelling unit for which the owner supplies full electrical service for which there is no additional cost charged to the tenant in addition to rent, the applicable lease adjustments as established by this Order are to be 1.5 per cent in addition to the adjustments for renewal and vacancy leases heretofore stated.

Escalator Clauses

Where a lease for a dwelling unit in effect on May 31, 1978 or where a lease in effect on June 30, 1974 for a dwelling unit which became subject to the Rent Stabilization Law of 1969, by virtue of Chapter 576 of the Laws of 1974 and Resolution Number 276 of the New York City Council and extended by Chapter 203 of the Laws of 1977, contained an escalator clause for the increased costs of operation and such clause is still in effect, the lawful rental on June 30, 1980, or June 30, 1981, over which the fair rent under this order is computed shall include the increased rental, if any, due under such clause except those charges which accrued within one year of the commencment of the renewal lease. Moreover, where a lease contained an escalator clause which the owner may validly renew under the Code, unless the owner elects or has elected in writing to delete such clause, effective no later than July 1, 1980 from the existing lease and all subsequent leases for such dwelling unit, the increased rental, if any, due under such escalator clause shall be offset against the amount of increase authorized under this Order.

Stabilizer

The one-half per cent "stabilizers" charged in leases pursuant to previous Orders of this Board shall remain in effect until the expiration of such leases and shall be included in the base rents for the purpose of computing subsequent rents or leases adjusted pursuant to this Order.

Special Guideline to Update Special Guideline 6b

In order to aid the Conciliation and Appeals Board in determining fair market rents for housing accommodations as to applications for adjustments of the initial legal regulated rent as may be requested by tenants, the Rent Guidelines Board hereby establishes a special guideline as mandated by Section 12 of Chapter 576 of the Laws of 1974, as extended by Chapter 203 of the Laws of 1977, amending Section YY51-6.0.2(b) (1) of the New York City Administrative Code: for dwelling units subject to the Rent and Rehabilitation Law on June 30, 1979 which subsequently become vacant after June 30, 1980, the 1980–1981 maximum base rent, as it existed or would have existed, plus 15 per cent.

Decontrolled Units

The permissible increase for decontrolled units as defined in order 3a which become decontrolled after June 30, 1980, shall not exceed the 1980–81 maximum base rent, as it existed or would have existed, plus 15 per cent of such maximum base rent.

April 1979 Fuel Adjustment

Any "April 1979 fuel adjustment" charged pursuant to Order 10b shall not be included in the rent to which a lease adjustment set forth in this Order is applied and it shall not merge with the base rent for the purpose of computing a subsequent rent or lease adjusted pursuant to this Order.

Any "April 1979 fuel adjustment" charged pursuant to

Order 10b shall only remain in effect for a rent or lease adjusted pursuant to Order 10b and such charge shall be extinguished when a lease to which it applies expires.

Credits

Rental charged and paid in excess of the levels of fair rent increase established by this Order shall be fully credited against the next month's rent.

Dated: July 27, 1980
Filed with the City Clerk June 30, 1980

RENT GUIDELINE ORDER NUMBER 12a—Modification of the Terms of Order No. 12 Governing Rent Levels For Leases Commencing on or After July 1, 1980 and on or before September 30, 1981 and Vacancy Adjustments for Leases Commencing on or After July 1, 1981 and on or before September 30, 1981.

Fuel Adjustments for Rent Levels

The Rent Guidelines Board, having considered all revelant information and data, hereby determines that no fuel cost adjustments for leases commencing on or after July 1, 1980 and on or before September 30, 1981 are warranted at this time.

It is not expected that the Board will convene to discuss fuel costs in the coming year. The Board will discuss the fuel situation at its annual meetings in June as it affects leases signed pursuant to this Order. The Board reserves the right to modify this Order during its term pursuant to this paragraph provided that any further adjustments described in this paragraph shall apply to existing leases only where the lease permits the rental reserved therein to be adjusted pursuant to subsequent determinations of the Rent Guidelines Board during the term of such lease.

Leases on Vacant Apartments

Where a dwelling unit becomes vacant, the levels of rent increase governing a new tenancy commencing on or after July 1, 1981 and on or before September 30, 1981 are the same levels over rentals charged on June 30, 1981 as those set forth for lease renewals pursuant to the adjustments for renewal leases as set forth in Order

Number 12, plus 15 per cent over the rentals charged on June 30, 1981 on each vacancy of such unit during the effective period of this Order.

Dated: June 30, 1981
Filed with the City Clerk June 30, 1981

RENT GUIDELINE ORDER NUMBER 12b—Modification of the Terms of Order No. 12 Governing Rent Levels For Leases Commencing on or After July 1, 1980 and on or before September 30, 1981.

Fuel Adjustment for Rent Levels

The Rent Guidelines Board, having considered all relevant information and data, hereby determines that no fuel cost adjustments for leases commencing on or after July 1, 1980 and on or before September 30, 1981 are warranted at this time.

It is not expected that the Board will convene to discuss fuel costs in the coming year. The Board will discuss the fuel situation at its annual meetings in June as it affects leases signed pursuant to this Order. The Board reserves the right to modify this Order during its term pursuant to this paragraph provided that any further adjustments described in this paragraph shall apply to existing leases only where the lease permits the rental reserved therein to be adjusted pursuant to subsequent determinations of the Rent Guidelines Board during the term of such lease.

Dated: June 30, 1982
Filed with the City Clerk: June 30, 1982

RENT GUIDELINE ORDER NUMBER 12c—Modification of the Terms of Order No. 12 Governing Rent Levels for Leases Commencing on or After July 1, 1980 and on or before September 30, 1981.

Fuel Adjustment for Rent Levels

The Rent Guidelines Board, having considered all relevant information and data, hereby determines that no fuel cost adjustments for leases commencing on or after

July 1, 1980 and on or before September 30, 1981 are warranted at this time.

Dated: June 29, 1983
Filed with the City Clerk: June 29, 1983

RENT GUIDELINE ORDER NUMBER 13—Rent Levels October 1, 1981 Through September 30, 1982.

Adjustments for Renewal Leases

Where heat is provided or required to be provided to a dwelling unit by an owner from a central or individual system at no charge to the tenant, the adjustments are as follows:

—For one year leases expiring before October 1, 1983:
10 per cent

—For two year leases expiring before October 1, 1984:
13 per cent

—For three year leases expiring before October 1, 1985:
16 per cent

These adjustments shall also apply to dwelling units in a structure subject to the partial tax exemption program under Section 421 of the Real Property Tax Law, or in a structure subject to Section 423 of the Real Property Tax Law as a Redevelopment Project.

Where heat is not provided or not required to be provided to a dwelling unit by an owner from a central or individual system, the adjustments are as follows:

—For one year leases expiring before October 1, 1983:
6.5 per cent

—For two year leases expiring before October 1, 1984:
9.5 per cent

—For three year leases expiring before October 1, 1985:
12.5 per cent

It is not expected that the Board will convene to discuss fuel costs in the coming year. The Board will discuss the fuel situation at its annual meetings in June as it affects leases signed pursuant to this Order. The Board may also consider any catastrophic change in the Operation and Maintenance Cost Index and order appropriate supplementary adjustments. The Board reserves the right to modify this Order during its term pursuant to this paragraph provided that any further adjustments described in this paragraph shall apply to existing leases only where the lease permits the rental reserved therein to be adjusted pursuant to subsequent determinations of the Rent Guidelines Board during the term of such lease.

Leases on Vacant Apartments

Where a dwelling unit becomes vacant, the levels of rent increase governing a new tenancy commencing on or after October 1, 1981 and on or before September 30, 1982 are the same levels over rentals charged on September 30, 1981 as those set forth above for lease renewals, plus 15 per cent over the rentals charged on September 30, 1981 on each vacancy of such unit during the effective period of this Order.

Fractional Terms

Except as to leases on vacant apartments, for the purpose of these guidelines any lease or tenancy for a period up to and including one year shall be deemed a one year lease or tenancy; the same for a period over one year and up to and including two years shall be deemed a two year lease; and the same for a period over two years and up to and including three years shall be deemed a three year lease. As to leases on vacant apartments, for the purpose of these guidelines any lease for a period from one year to less than two years shall be deemed a one year lease; the same for a period from two years to less than three years shall be deemed a two year lease; and the same for a period of three years or more shall be deemed a three year lease.

Electrical Inclusion Adjustment

For a lease for a dwelling unit for which the owner supplies full electrical services for which there is no additional cost charged to the tenant in addition to rent, the applicable lease adjustments as established by this Order are to be 4 per cent in addition to the adjustments for renewal and vacancy leases heretofore stated.

Escalator Clauses

Where a lease for a dwelling unit in effect on May 31, 1968 or where a lease in effect on June 30, 1974 for a dwelling unit which became subject to the Rent Stabilization Law of 1969, by virtue of Chapter 576 of the Laws of 1974 and Resolution Number 276 of the New York City Council and extended by Chapter 203 of the Laws of 1977, contained an escalator clause for the increased costs of operation and such clause is still in effect, the lawful rental on September 30, 1981, over which the fair rent under this Order is computed shall include the increased rental, if any, due under such clause except those charges which accrued within one year of the commencement of the renewal lease. Moreover, where a lease contained an escalator clause which the owner may validly renew under the Code, unless the owner elects or has elected in writing to delete such clause, effective no later than October 1, 1981 from the existing lease and all subsequent leases for such dwelling unit, the increased rental, if any, due under such escalator clause shall be offset against the amount of increase authorized under this Order.

Stabilizer

The one-half per cent "stabilizers" charged in leases pursuant to previous Orders of this Board shall remain in effect until the expiration of such leases and shall be included in the base rents for the purpose of computing subsequent rents or leases adjusted pursuant to this Order.

Special Guideline to Update Special Guideline 6b

In order to aid the Conciliation and Appeals Board in determining fair market rents for housing accommodations as to applications for adjustments of the initial legal regulated rent as may be requested by tenants, the Rent Guidelines Board hereby establishes a special guideline as mandated by Section 12 of Chapter 576 of the Laws of 1974, as extended by Chapter 203 of the Laws of 1977, amending Section YY51-6.0.2(b) (1) of the New York City Administrative Code: for dwelling units subject to the Rent and Rehabilitation Law on September 30, 1980 which subsequently become vacant after September 30, 1981 the 1980–1981 maximum base rent, as it existed or would have existed plus 20 per cent.

Decontrolled Units

The permissible increase for decontrolled units as defined in Order 3a which become decontrolled after September 30, 1981, shall not exceed the 1980–81 maximum base rent, as it existed or would have existed, plus 20 per cent of such maximum base rent.

April 1979 Fuel Adjustment

Any "April 1979 fuel adjustment" charged pursuant to Order 10b shall not be included in the rent to which a lease adjustment set forth in this Order is applied and it shall not merge with the base rent for the purpose of computing a subsequent rent or lease adjusted pursuant to this Order.

Any "April 1979 fuel adjustment" charged pursuant to Order 10b shall only remain in effect for a rent or lease adjusted pursuant to Order 10b and such charge shall be extinguished when a lease to which it applies expires.

Credits

Rental charged and paid in excess of the levels of fair rent increase established by this Order shall be fully credited against the next month's rent.

Dated: June 29, 1981
Filed with the City Clerk: June 30, 1981

RENT GUIDELINE ORDER NUMBER 13a—Modification of the Terms of Order No. 13 Governing Rent Levels for Leases Commencing on or After October 1, 1981 and on or before September 30, 1982.

Fuel Adjustments for Rent Levels

The Rent Guidelines Board, having considered all relevant information and data, hereby determines that no fuel cost adjustments for leases commencing on or after October 1, 1981 and on or before September 30, 1982 are warranted at this time.

It is not expected that the Board will convene to discuss fuel costs in the coming year. The Board will discuss the fuel situation at its annual meetings in June as it affects leases signed pursuant to this Order. The Board reserves the right to modify this Order during its term pursuant to this paragraph provided that any further adjustments described in this paragraph shall apply to existing leases only where the lease permits the rental reserved therein to be adjusted pursuant to subsequent determinations of the Rent Guidelines Board during the term of such lease.

Dated: June 30, 1982
Filed with the City Clerk: June 30, 1982

RENT GUIDELINE ORDER NUMBER 13b—Modification of the Terms of Order No. 13 Governing Rent Levels for Leases Commencing on or After October 1, 1981 and on or before September 30, 1982.

Fuel Adjustments for Rent Levels

The Rent Guidelines Board, having considered all relevant information and data, hereby determines that no fuel cost adjustments for leases commencing on or after October 1, 1981 and on or before September 30, 1982 are warranted at this time.

It is not expected that the Board will convene to discuss fuel costs in the coming year. The Board will discuss the fuel situation at its annual meetings in June as it affects leases signed pursuant to this Order. The Board reserves the right to modify this Order during its term pursuant to this paragraph provided that any further adjustments described in this pargraph shall apply to existing leases only where the lease permits the rental reserved therein to be adjusted pursuant to subsequent determinations of the Rent Guidelines Board during the term of such lease.

Dated: June 29, 1983
Filed with the City Clerk: June 29, 1983

RENT GUIDELINE ORDER NUMBER 13c—Modification of the Terms of Order No. 13 Governing Rent Levels for Leases Commencing on or After October 1, 1981 and on or before September 30, 1982.

Fuel Adjustment for Rent Levels

The Rent Guidelines Board, having considered all relevant information and data, hereby determines that no fuel cost adjustments for leases commencing on or after

October 1, 1981 and on or before September 30, 1982 are warranted at this time.

Dated: June 27, 1984
Filed with the City Clerk: June 27, 1984

RENT GUIDELINE ORDER NUMBER 14—Rent Levels October 1, 1982 Through September 30, 1983.

Adjustments for Renewal Leases

Together with such further adjustments as may be authorized by the Board, as explained below:

—For one year leases expiring before October 1, 1984:
4 per cent

—For two year leases expiring before October 1, 1985:
7 per cent

—For three year leases expiring before October 1, 1986:
10 per cent

These adjustments shall also apply to dwelling units in a structure subject to the partial tax exemption program under Section 421 of the Real Property Tax Law, or in a structure subject to Section 423 of the Real Property Tax Law as a Redevelopment Project.

It is not expected that the Board will convene to discuss fuel costs in the coming year. The Board will discuss the fuel situation at its annual meetings in June as it affects leases signed pursuant to this Order. The Board may also consider any catastrophic change in the Operation and Maintenance Cost Index and order appropriate supplementary adjustments. The Board reserves the right to modify this Order during its term pursuant to this paragraph provided that any further adjustments described in this paragraph shall apply to existing leases only where the lease permits the rental reserved therein to be adjusted pursuant to subsequent determinations of the Rent Guidelines Board during the term of such lease.

Leases on Vacant Apartments

Where a dwelling unit becomes vacant, the levels of rent increase governing a new tenancy commencing on or after October 1, 1982 and on or before September 30, 1983 are the same levels over rentals charged on September 30, 1982 as those set forth above for the lease renewals.

Rent Guidance Board Orders

Fractional Terms

Except as to leases on vacant apartments, for the purpose of these guidelines any lease or tenancy for a period up to and including one year shall be deemed a one year lease or tenancy; the same for a period over one year and up to and including two years shall be deemed a two year lease; and the same for a period over two years and up to and including three years shall be deemed a three year lease. As to leases on vacant apartments, for the purpose of these guidelines any lease for a period from one year to less than two years shall be deemed a one year lease; the same for a period from two years to less than three years shall be deemed a two year lease; and the same for a period of three years or more shall be deemed a three year lease.

Electrical Inclusion Adjustment

For a lease for a dwelling unit for which the owner supplies full electrical services for which there is no additional cost charged to the tenant in addition to rent, the applicable lease adjustments as established by this Order are to be the adjustments for renewal and vacancy leases heretofore stated, less one per cent.

Escalator Clauses

Where a lease for a dwelling unit in effect on May 31, 1968 or where a lease in effect on June 30, 1974 for a dwelling unit which became subject to the Rent Stabilization Law of 1969, by virtue of Chapter 576 of the Laws of 1974 and Resolution Number 276 of the New York City Council, extended by Chapter 203 of the Laws of 1977, and further extended by Chapter 383 of the Laws of 1981, contained an escalator clause for the increased costs of operation and such clause is still in effect, the lawful rental on September 30, 1982, over which the fair rent under this Order is computed shall include the increased rental, if any, due under such clause except those charges which accrued within one year of the commencement of the renewal lease. Moreover, where a lease contained an escalator clause which the owner may validly renew under the Code, unless the owner elects or has elected in writing to delete such clause, effective no later than October 1, 1982 from the existing lease and all subsequent leases for such dwelling unit, the increased rental, if any, due under such escalator clause shall be offset against the amount of increase authorized under this Order.

Stabilizer

The one-half per cent "stabilizer" charged in leases pursuant to previous Orders of this Board shall remain in effect until the expiration of such leases and shall be included in the base rents for the purpose of computing subsequent rents or leases adjusted pursuant to this Order.

Special Guideline to Update Special Guideline 6b

In order to aid the Conciliation and Appeals Board in determining fair market rents for housing accommodations as to applications for adjustments of the initial legal regulated rent as may be requested by tenants, the Rent Guidelines Board hereby establishes a special guideline as mandated by Section 12 of Chapter 576 of the Laws of 1974, as extended by Chapter 203 of the Laws of 1977, and further extended by Chapter 383 of the Laws of 1981, amending Sections YY51-6.02(b)(1) of the New York City Administrative Code: for dwelling units subject to the Rent and Rehabilitation Law on September 30, 1982, which subsequently become vacant after September 30, 1982, 15% above the sum of the 1982–1983 maximum base rent, as it existed or would have existed, plus the current allowable fuel cost adjustments as established on Rent Control forms, pursuant to Section 33.10 of the Rent Regulations, beginning in 1980.

Decontrolled Units

The permissible increase for decontrolled units as defined in Order 3a which become decontrolled after September 30, 1982, shall not exceed 15% above the sum of the 1982–1983 maximum base rent, as it existed or would have existed plus the current allowable fuel cost adjustments as established on Rent Control forms, pursuant to Section 33.10 of the Rent Regulations, beginning in 1980.

Rent Guidance Board Orders

Credits

Rental charged and paid in excess of the levels of fair rent increase established by this Order shall be fully credited against the next month's rent.

Dated: June 30, 1982
Filed with the City Clerk: June 30, 1982

RENT GUIDELINE ORDER NUMBER 14a—Modification of the Terms of Order No. 14 Governing Rent Levels for Leases Commencing on or After October 1, 1982 and on or before September 30, 1983.

Fuel Adjustments for Rent Levels

The Rent Guidelines Board, having considered all relevant information and data, hereby determines that no fuel cost adjustments for leases commencing on or after October 1, 1982 and on or before September 30, 1983 are warranted at this time.

It is not expected that the Board will convene to discuss fuel costs in the coming year. The Board will discuss the fuel situation at its annual meetings in June as it affects leases signed pursuant to this Order. The Board reserves the right to modify this Order during its term pursuant to this paragraph provided that any further adjustments described in this paragraph shall apply to existing leases only where the lease permits the rental reserved therein to be adjusted pursuant to subsequent determinations of the Rent Guidelines Board during the term of such lease.

Dated: June 29, 1983
Filed with the City Clerk: June 29, 1983

RENT GUIDELINE ORDER NUMBER 14b—Modification of the Terms of Order No. 14 Governing Rent Levels for Leases Commencing on or After October 1, 1982 and on or before September 30, 1983.

Fuel Adjustment for Rent Levels

The Rent Guidelines Board, having considered all relevant information and data, hereby determines that no fuel cost adjustments for leases commencing on or after October 1, 1982 and on or before September 30, 1983 are warranted at this time.

It is not expected that the Board will convene to discuss fuel costs in the coming year. The Board will discuss the fuel situation at its annual meetings in June as it affects leases signed pursuant to this Order. The Board reserves the right to modify this Order during its term pursuant to this paragraph provided that any further adjustments described in this paragraph shall apply to existing leases only where the lease permits the rental reserved therein to be adjusted pursuant to subsequent determinations of the Rent Guidelines Board during the term of such lease.

Dated: June 27, 1984
Filed with the City Clerk: June 27, 1984

RENT GUIDELINE ORDER NUMBER 14c—Modification of the Terms of Order No. 14 Governing Rent Levels for Leases Commencing on or After October 1, 1982 and on or before September 30, 1983.

Fuel Adjustment for Rent Levels

The Rent Guidelines Board, having considered all relevant information and data, hereby determines that no fuel cost adjustments for leases commencing on or after October 1, 1982 and on or before September 30, 1983 are warranted at this time.

Dated: June 28, 1985
Filed with the City Clerk: June 28, 1985

RENT GUIDELINE ORDER NUMBER 15—Rent Levels for Leases Commencing October 1, 1983 Through September 30, 1984.

Adjustments for Renewal Leases

Together with such further adjustments as may be authorized by the Board, as explained below:

—For one year leases expiring before October 1, 1985:
4 per cent

—For two years leases expiring before October 1, 1986:
7 per cent

Rent Guidance Board Orders

—For three year leases expiring before October 1, 1987:
10 per cent

These adjustments shall also apply to dwelling units in a structure subject to the partial tax exemption program under Section 421 of the Real Property Tax Law, or in a structure subject to Section 423 of the Real Property Tax Law as a Redevelopment Project.

It is not expected that the Board will convene to discuss fuel costs in the coming year. The Board will discuss the fuel situation at its annual meetings in June as it affects leases signed pursuant to this Order. The Board may also consider any catastrophic change in the Operation and Maintenance Cost Index and order appropriate supplementary adjustments. The Board reserves the right to modify this Order during its term pursuant to this paragraph provided that any further adjustments described in this paragraph shall apply to existing leases only where the lease permits the rental reserved therein to be adjusted pursuant to subsequent determinations of the Rent Guidelines Board during the term of such lease.

Leases on Vacant Apartments

Where a dwelling unit becomes vacant, the levels of rent increase governing a new tenancy commencing on or after October 1 1983 and on or before September 30, 1984 are as follows:

—the same as those set forth herein for renewal leases commencing during the effective period of this Order over rentals charged on September 30, 1983, where additional levels of rent increase (vacancy allowances) totaling 15% or more have been charged for that unit pursuant to provisions of the Rent Guidelines Board Orders governing new tenancies commencing on or after July 1, 1979, or;

—the same as those set forth herein for renewal leases commencing during the period of this Order plus 5% over rentals charged on September 30, 1983, where additional levels of rent increases (vacancy allowances) totaling more than 0% but less than 15% have been charged for that unit pursuant to provisions of the Rent Guidelines Board Orders governing new tenancies commencing on or after July 1, 1979, or;

—the same as those set forth herein for renewal leases commencing during the effective period of this Order plus 10% over rentals charged on September 30, 1983, where additional levels of rent increases (vacancy allowances) were last charged for that unit pursuant to provisions of the Rent Guidelines Board Orders governing new tenancies commencing July 1, 1975 through June 30, 1979, or;

—the same as those set forth herein for renewal leases commencing during the effective period of this Order plus 15% over rentals charged on September 30, 1983, where no additional levels of rent increase (vacancy allowances) have been charged for that unit pursuant to provisions of any Rent Guidelines Board Orders governing new tenancies commencing on or After July 1, 1975.

Any level of rent increase for a vacancy in excess of the level set forth herein for renewal leases may be collected no more than once pursuant to this provision governing a new tenancy commencing from October 1, 1983 through September 30, 1984.

Electrical Inclusion Adjustment

For a lease for a dwelling unit for which the owner supplies full electrical services for which there is no additional cost charged to the tenant in addition to rent, the applicable lease adjustments as established by this Order are to be the adjustments for renewal and vacancy leases heretofore stated, less one per cent.

Supplementary Adjustment of Up to $10 Per Month for Renewal and Vacancy Leases for Apartments Renting for Less Than $200 Per Month on September 30, 1983.

For a lease for a dwelling unit with a lawful rent of less than $200 per month on September 30, 1983, the levels of rent increase for renewal and vacancy leases commencing October 1, 1983 through September 30, 1984 are the same as those set forth hereinabove plus $10 per month, provided the rent resulting from application of this level of increase does not exceed the rent that would result from application of the allowable levels of rent increase for renewal and vacancy leases to an apartment renting for $200 per month on September 30, 1983.

Rent Guidance Board Orders

Adjustments for Units In the Category of Buildings Covered By Article 7-C of The Multiple Dwelling Law

Pursuant to Chapter 349 of the Laws of 1982, Section 286 paragraph 7 of The Multiple Dwelling Law, The Rent Guidelines Board hereby establishes that the allowable levels of rent increase above the "base rent," as defined in Section 286 paragraph 4, for units where residential renewal leases are offered pursuant to Section 286, paragraph 3 of The Multiple Dwelling Law, and commence from October 1, 1983 through September 30, 1984 shall be the same as those set forth hereinabove for renewal leases, provided there shall be no supplementary adjustment of up to $10 per month for units in this category of buildings renting for less than $200 per month on September 30, 1983.

Where a dwelling unit in this category of buildings becomes vacant the levels of rent increase governing a new tenancy commencing on or after October 1, 1983 and on or before September 30, 1984 are the same levels over the "base rent," as defined in Section 286, paragraph 4, as set forth above for renewal leases for units in this category unless pursuant to paragraph 6, Section 286 of The Multiple Dwelling Law the owner purchases improvements and thereby the unit is either exempted from the provisions of Article 7-C requiring rent regulation or may be rented at market value subject to subsequent rent regulation.

Fractional Terms

Except as to leases on vacant apartments, for the purpose of these guidelines any lease or tenancy for a period up to an including one year shall be deemed a one year lease or tenancy; the same for a period over one year and up to and including two years shall be deemed a two year lease; and the same for a period over two years and up to and including three years shall be deemed a three year lease. As to leases on vacant apartments, for the purpose of these guidelines any lease for a period from one year to less than two years shall be deemed a one year lease; the same for a period from two years to less than three years shall be deemed a two year lease; and the same for a period of three years or more shall be deemed a three year lease.

Escalator Clauses

Where a lease for a dwelling unit in effect on May 31, 1968 or where a lease in effect on June 30, 1974 for a dwelling unit which became subject to the Rent Stablilization Law of 1969, by virtue of Chapter 576 of the Laws of 1974 and Resolution Number 276 of the New York City Council, extended by Chapter 203 of the Laws of 1977, further extended by Chapter 383 of the Laws of 1981, and applicable Laws of 1983, contained an escalator clause for the increased costs of operation and such clause is still in effect, the lawful rental on September 30, 1983, over which the fair rent under this Order is computed shall include the increased rental, if any, due under such clause except those charges which accrued within one year of the commencement of the renewal lease. Moreover, where a lease contained an escalator clause which the owner may validly renew under the Code, unless the owner elects or has elected in writing to delete such clause, effective no later than October 1, 1983 from the existing lease and all subsequent leases for such dwelling unit, the increased rental, if any, due under such escalator clause shall be offset against the amount of increase authorized under this Order.

Stabilizer

The one-half per cent "stablizer" charged in leases pursuant to previous Orders of this Board shall remain in effect until the expiration of such leases and shall be included in the base rents for the purpose of computing subsequent rents or leases adjusted pursuant to this Order.

Special Guideline to Update Special Guideline 6b

In order to aid the Conciliation and Appeals Board in determining fair market rents for housing accommodations as to applications for adjustments of the initial legal regulated rent as may be requested by tenants, the Rent Guidelines Board hereby establishes a special guideline as mandated by Section 9 of Chapter 576 of the Laws of 1974, as extended by Chapter 203 of the Laws of 1977, further extended by Chapter 383 of the Laws of 1981, and applicable Laws of 1983 amending Sections YY51-6.02(b)(1) of the New York City Administrative Code: for dwelling units subject to the Rent And Rehabilitation Law on September 30, 1983, which subsequently become vacant after September 30, 1983, 20% above the sum of the 1982–83 maximum base rent, as it existed or would have existed, plus the current allowable fuel cost adjustments as established on Rent Control forms, pursuant to Section 33.10 of the Rent Regulations, beginning in 1980.

Decontrolled Units

The permissible increase for decontrolled units as defined in Order 3a which become decontrolled after September 30, 1983, shall not exceed 20% above the sum of the 1982–1983 maximum base rent, as it existed or would have existed plus the current allowable fuel cost adjustments as established on Rent Control forms, pursuant to Section 33.10 of the Rent Regulations, beginning in 1980.

Credits

Rental charged and paid in excess of the levels of fair rent increase established by this Order shall be fully credited against the next month's rent.

Dated: June 29, 1983
Filed with the City Clerk: June 29, 1983

RENT GUIDELINE ORDER NUMBER 15a—Modification of the Terms of Order No. 15 Governing Rent Levels for Leases Commencing on or After October 1, 1983 and on or before September 30, 1984.

Fuel Adjustment for Rent Levels

The Rent Guidelines Board, having considered all relevant information and data, hereby determines that no fuel cost adjustments for leases commencing on or after October 1, 1983 and on or before September 30, 1984 are warranted at this time.

It is not expected that the Board will convene to discuss fuel costs in the coming year. The Board will discuss the fuel situation at its annual meetings in June as it affects leases signed pursuant to this Order. The Board reserves the right to modify this Order during its term pursuant to this paragraph provided that any further adjustments described by this paragraph shall apply to existing leases only where the lease permits the rental reserved therein to be adjusted pursuant to subsequent determinations of the Rent Guidelines Board during the term of such lease.

Dated: June 27, 1984
Filed with the City Clerk: June 27, 1984

RENT GUIDELINE ORDER NUMBER 15b—Modification of the Terms of Order No. 15 Governing Rent Levels for Leases Commencing on or After October 1, 1983 and on or before September 30, 1984.

Fuel Adjustment for Rent Levels

The Rent Guidelines Board, having considered all relevant information and data, hereby determines that no fuel cost adjustments for leases commencing on or after October 1, 1983 and on or before September 30, 1984 are warranted at this time.

Dated: June 28, 1985
Filed with the City Clerk: June 28, 1985

RENT GUIDELINE ORDER NUMBER 16—Rent Levels for Leases Commencing October 1, 1984 Through September 30, 1985.

Adjustments for Renewal Leases

Together with such further adjustments as may be authorized by the Board, as explained below:

—For one year leases expiring before October 1, 1986:
6 per cent
—For two years leases expiring before October 1, 1987:
9 per cent

These adjustments shall also apply to dwelling units in a structure subject to the partial tax exemption program under Section 421 of the Real Property Tax Law, or in a structure subject to Section 423 of the Real Property Tax Law as a Redevelopment Project.

It is not expected that the Board will convene to discuss fuel costs in the coming year. The Board will discuss the fuel situation at its annual meetings in June as it affects leases signed pursuant to this Order. The Board may also consider any catastrophic change in the Operation and Maintenance Cost Index and order appropriate supplementary adjustments. The Board reserves the right to modify this Order during its term pursuant in this paragraph provided that any further adjustments described in this paragraph shall apply to existing leases only where the lease permits the rental reserved therein to be adjusted pursuant to subsequent determinations of the Rent Guidelines Board during the term of such lease.

Leases on Vacant Apartments

Where a dwelling unit becomes vacant, the levels of rent increase governing a new tenancy commencing on or after October 1, 1984 and on or before September 30, 1985 are the same levels over rentals charged on September 30, 1984 as those set forth above for lease renewals, plus seven and one-half percent (7½%) over the rental charged on September 30, 1984, with the following exception:

—for those units in which there had previously been a new tenancy commencing on or after October 1, 1983 and on or before September 30, 1984, where a dwelling unit becomes vacant the levels of rent increase governing a new tenancy commencing on or after October 1, 1984 and on or before September 30, 1985 are the same levels over rentals charged on September 30, 1984 as those set forth above for renewal leases without any additional allowance for the vacancy.

Any level of rent increase pursuant to this provision relating to leases on vacant apartments may be applied no more than once for leases commencing October 1, 1984 through September 30, 1985.

Supplementary Adjustment of up to $10 Per Month for Renewal and Vacancy Leases for Apartments Renting for Less than $250 Per Month on September 30, 1984.

For a lease for a dwelling unit with a lawful rent of less than $250 per month on September 30, 1984, the levels of rent increase for renewal and vacancy leases commencing October 1, 1984 through September 30, 1985 are the same as those set forth hereinabove plus $10 per month, provided the monthly rent resulting from application of this level of increase or any portion thereof does not exceed:

—$265 for a one year renewal lease;
—$272.50 for a two year renewal lease;
—$283.75 for a one year vacancy lease;
—$291.25 for a two year vacancy lease.

Electrical Inclusion Adjustment

For a lease for a dwelling unit for which the owner supplies full electrical services for which there is no additional cost charged to the tenant in addition to rent, the applicable lease adjustments as established by this Order are to be the adjustments for renewal and vacancy leases heretofore stated.

Adjustments for Units In the Category of Buildings Covered By Article 7-C of the Multiple Dwelling Law

Pursuant to Chapter 349 of the Laws of 1982, Section 286 paragraph 7 of The Multiple Dwelling Law, The Rent Guidelines Board hereby establishes that the allowable levels of rent increase above the "base rent," as defined in Section 286 paragraph 4, for units where residential renewal leases are offered pursuant to Section 286, paragraph 3 of The Multiple Dwelling Law, and commence from October 1, 1984 through September 30, 1985 shall be the same as those set forth hereinabove for renewal leases, provided there shall be no supplementary adjustment of up to $10 per month for units in this category of buildings renting for less than $250 per month on September 30, 1984.

Where a dwelling unit in this category of buildings becomes vacant the levels of rent increase governing a new tenancy commencing on or after October 1, 1984 and on or before September 30, 1985 are the same levels over the "base rent," as defined in Section 286, paragraph 4, as set forth above for renewal leases for units in this category unless pursuant to paragraph 6, Section 286 of The Multiple Dwelling Law the owner purchases improvements and thereby the unit is either exempted from the provisions of Article 7-C requiring rent regulation or may be rented at market value subject to subsequent rent regulation.

Fractional Terms

For the purpose of these guidelines any lease or tenancy for a period up to and including one year shall be deemed a one year lease or tenancy, and the same for a period over one year and up to and including two years shall be deemed a two year lease.

Escalator Clauses

Where a lease for a dwelling unit in effect on May 31, 1968 or where a lease in effect on June 30, 1974 for a dwelling unit which became subject to the Rent Stabilization Law of 1969, by virtue of Chapter 576 of the Laws of 1974 and Resolution Number 276 of the New York City Council, extended by Chapter 203 of the Laws of 1977, further extended by Chapter 383 of the Laws of 1981 and Chapter 403 of the Laws of 1983, contained an escalator clause for the increased costs of operation and such clause is still in effect, the lawful rental on September 30, 1984, over which the fair rent under this Order is computed shall include the increased rental, if any, due under such clause except those charges which accrued within one year of the commencement of the renewal lease. Moreover, where a lease contained an escalator clause that the owner may validly renew under the Code, unless the owner elects or has elected in writing to delete such clause, effective no later than October 1, 1984 from the existing lease and all subsequent leases for such dwelling unit, the increased rental, if any, due under such escalator clause shall be offset against the amount of increase authorized under this Order.

Stabilizer

The one-half per cent "stabilizer" charged in leases pursuant to previous Orders of the Board shall remain in effect until the expiration of such leases and shall be included in the base rent for the purpose of computing subsequent rents or leases adjusted pursuant to this Order.

Special Guideline to Update Special Guideline 6b

In order to aid the State Division of Housing and Community Renewal in determining fair market rents for housing accommodations as to application for adjustments of the initial legal regulated rent as may be requested by tenants, the Rent Guidelines Board hereby establishes a special guideline as mandated by Section 9 of Chapter 576 of the Laws of 1974, as extended by Chapter 203 of the Laws of 1977, further extended by Chapter 383 of the Laws of 1981 and Chapter 403 of the Laws of 1983 amending Section YY51-6.02(b) (1) of the New York City Administrative Code: for dwelling units subject to the Rent and Rehabilitation Law on September 30, 1984, which subsequently become vacant after September 30, 1984, 15% above the sum of the 1984–85 maximum base rent, as it existed or would have existed, plus the current allowable fuel cost adjustments as established on Rent Control forms, pursuant to Section 33.10 of the Rent Regulations, beginning in 1980.

Decontrolled Units

The permissible increase for decontrolled units as defined in Order 3a which become decontrolled after September 30, 1984, shall not exceed 15% above the sum of the 1984–85 maximum base rent, as it existed or would have existed, plus the current allowable fuel cost adjustments as established on Rent Control forms, pursuant to Section 33.10 of the Rent Regulations, beginning in 1980.

Credits

Rental charged and paid in excess of the levels of fair rent increase established by this Order shall be fully credited against the next month's rent.

Dated: June 27, 1984
Filed with the City Clerk: June 27, 1984

Clarification of Order Number 16—Rent Levels for Leases Commencing October 1, 1984 through September 30, 1985

Order No. 16 of the New York City Rent Guidelines Board, filed with the City Clerk on June 27, 1984 and published in The City Record on July 3, 1984 is hereby clarified as follows:

1. With respect to the section on Leases for Vacant Apartments: Any provision apparently to the contrary notwithstanding, for those units in which there had previously been a new tenancy commencing on or after October 1, 1983 and on or before September 30, 1984 and where the allowable level of rent increase governing a new tenancy pursuant to Order 15 of the Rent Guidelines

Board was the same as for renewal leases, the levels of rent increase governing a new tenancy commencing on or after October 1, 1984 and on or before September 30, 1985 are the same levels over rentals charged on September 30, 1984 as those set forth in Order 16 for lease renewals, plus seven and one-half percent (7½%) over the rental charged on September 30, 1984.

2. With respect to the provision on the Supplementary Adjustment of Up To $10 Per Month for Renewal and Vacancy Leases for Apartments Renting for Less Than $250 Per Month on September 30, 1984: It was the intent of the Board that the application of the supplementary adjustment of up to $10 per month for units renting for under $250 per month on September 30, 1984 not result in a higher rent than would result from the application of the allowable levels of rent increase for renewal and vacancy leases for those units renting at $250 per month on September 30, 1983, just above the maximum rent level for a unit to which this supplementary adjustment may be applied. Therefore, for those units with a lawful rent of less than $250 per month on September 30, 1984 in which a vacancy lease commences October 1, 1984 through September 30, 1985 and where there is no additional allowance for the vacancy authorized under the provision for leases on vacant apartments in Order 16, the monthly rent resulting from the application of the supplementary adjustment of up to $10 per month or any portion thereof may not exceed the limits stated in Order 16 for renewal leases in such units, viz:

—$265.00 for a one year lease

—$272.50 for a two year lease.

Dated: August 8, 1984
Filed with the City Clerk: August 8, 1984

Explanatory Statement of the Rent Guidelines Board in Relation to 1984–85 Lease Increase Allowances For Apartments Under the Jurisdiction of the Rent Stabilization Law.*

Order No. 16

The Rent Guidelines Board (RGB) by Order No. 16 has set the following maximum rent increases for leases entered on or after October 1, 1984 and on or before September 30, 1985 in apartments under its jurisdiction:

Rent Guidance Board Orders

	1 Year	2 Years
Lease Renewal	6%	9%
Lease Renewal for units renting for less than $250/month	6%+ $10/mo.	9%+ $10/mo.
to a maximum monthly rent:	$265	$272.50
Lofts Lease Renewal and New Leases	6%	9%

New Leases For Apartments—same percentages as above for lease renewals plus:

	Vacancy Allowance
−Where there had not previously been a new tenancy on or after 10/1/83, or where there had previously been a new tenancy 10/1/83 or after and the applicable vacancy allowance under Order 15 was zero:	7.5%
or	
−Where there had previously been a new tenancy on or after 10/1/83, provided the vacancy allowance applicable to such new tenancy under Order 15 was not zero:	0.0%

plus an additional $10/mo. where the unit was renting for less than $250 a month provided the resulting rent does not exceed:

Where the vacancy allowance under this Order is	For A 1 Year Lease	For A 2 Year Lease
7.5%	$283.75	$291.25
0.0%	$265.00	$272.50

Note: *This Explanatory Statement explains the action taken by the Board members on individual points and reflects the general views of those voting in the majority. It is not meant to summarize all of the viewpoints expressed.

The guidelines do not apply to non-transient hotel units which are covered by separate Hotel Orders.

The Board indicated that any increase pursuant to the vacancy allowance provision of Order 16, as well as any increase for a renewal lease, may be collected no more than once during the period governed by Order 16.

Leases for units subject to rent control on September 30, 1984 which subsequently become vacant and then enter the stabilization system are not subject to the above adjustments. Such rentals are subject to review by the State Division of Housing & Community Renewal (DHCR). In order to aid the State Division of Housing & Community Renewal (DHCR), the Rent Guidelines Board has set a special guideline at 15 per cent above the sum of the 1984-85 Maximum Base Rent plus the current allowable fuel cost adjustments pursuant to Section 33.10 of the Rent Regulations.

The "April 1979 Fuel Adjustment" charged pursuant to Order No. 10b, the "January 1980 Fuel Adjustment for Rent Levels" charged pursuant to Order No. 10c, "July 1980 Fuel Adjustment for Rent Levels" charged pursuant to Order No. 10d, "Modification of the terms of Order No. 10d Covering Rent Levels" charged pursuant to Order No. 10e, the "Fuel Adjustment for Leases Commencing Between July 1, 1979 and June 30, 1980 To Go Into Effect One Year From The Date of Commencement of the Lease" charged pursuant to Order 11a, the "Continuation of the Fuel Adjustment for Leases Commencing Between July 1, 1979 and June 30, 1980" charged pursuant to Order No. 11b, and the "Continuation of Fuel Adjustments for Leases Commencing Between July 1, 1979 and June 30, 1980" charged pursuant to Order No. 11c shall not be included in the base rent to which the adjustments set forth in this Order No. 16 apply.

RENT GUIDELINE ORDER NUMBER 16a—Modification of the Terms of Order No. 16 Governing Rent Levels for Leases Commencing on or After October 1, 1984 and on or before September 30, 1985.

Fuel Adjustment for Rent Levels

The Rent Guidelines Board, having considered all relevant information and data, hereby determines that no fuel cost adjustments for leases commencing on or after October 1, 1984 and on or before September 30, 1985 are warranted at this time.

It is not expected that the Board will convene to discuss fuel costs in the coming year. The Board will discuss the fuel situation at its annual meetings in June as it affects leases signed pursuant to this Order. The Board reserves the right to modify this Order during its term pursuant to this paragraph provided that any further adjustments described in this paragraph shall apply to existing leases only where the lease permits the rental reserved therein to be adjusted pursuant to subsequent determinations of the Rent Guidelines Board during the term of such lease.

Dated: June 28, 1985
Filed with the City Clerk: June 28, 1985

RENT GUIDELINE ORDER NUMBER 17—Rent Levels for Leases Commencing October 1, 1985 Through September 30, 1986.

Adjustments for Renewal Leases

Together with such further adjustments as may be authorized by the Board, as explained below:

—For one year leases expiring before October 1, 1987:
4.0 per cent

—For two year leases expiring before October 1, 1988:
6.5 per cent

These adjustments shall also apply to dwelling units in a structure subject to the partial tax exemption program under Section 421 of the Real Property Tax Law, or in a structure subject to Section 423 of the Real Property Tax Law as a Redevelopment Project.

It is not expected that the Board will convene to discuss fuel costs in the coming year. The Board will discuss the fuel situation at its annual meetings in June as it affects leases signed pursuant to this Order. The Board may also consider any catastrophic change in the Operation and Maintenance Cost Index and order appropriate supplementary adjustments. The Board reserves the right to modify this Order during its term pursuant to this paragraph provided that any further adjustments described in this paragraph shall apply to existing leases only where the lease permits the rental reserved therein to be adjusted pursuant to subsequent determinations of the Rent Guidelines Board during the term of such lease.

Leases on Vacant Apartments

Where a dwelling unit becomes vacant, the levels of rent increase governing a new tenancy commencing on or after October 1, 1985 and on or before September 30, 1986 are the same levels over rentals charged on September 30, 1985 as those set forth above for lease renewals, plus seven and one-half percent (7.5%) over the rental charged on September 30, 1985, with the following exception:

—for those units in which there had previously been a new tenancy commencing on or after October 1, 1984 and on or before September 30, 1985, unless the allowable level of increase for that new tenancy pursuant to Order 16 of the Board was the same as for renewal leases, the levels of rent increase governing a new tenancy are the same levels over rentals charged on September 30, 1985 as those set forth above for renewal leases without any additional allowance for the vacancy.

This provision for leases on vacant apartments notwithstanding, for units in buildings of over 50 units in which more than 10% of the units were vacant for the 60 days preceding the commencement of the lease, the allowable level of rent increase governing a new tenancy shall be the same as for renewal leases, i.e. no vacancy increase is permitted.

Any level of rent increase pursuant to this provision relating to leases on vacant apartments may be applied no more than once for leases commencing October 1, 1985 through September 30, 1986.

Supplementary Adjustment of up to $15 Per Month for Renewal and Vacancy Leases for Apartments Renting for Less than $300 Per Month on September 30, 1985.

For a lease for a dwelling unit with a lawful rent of less than $300 per month on September 30, 1985, the levels of rent increase for renewal and vacancy leases commencing October 1, 1985 through September 30, 1986 are the same as those set forth hereinabove plus $15 per month, provided the monthly rent resulting from application of this level of increase or any portion thereof does not exceed the rent that would result from application of the allowable levels of rent increase for renewal and vacancy leases to an apartment renting for $300 per month on September 30, 1985. This limitation is as follows:

For renewal leases of:
    —one year .... $312.00 per month.
    —two years .... $319.50 per month.

Where the 7.5% vacancy allowance applies, for vacancy leases of:
    —one year .... $334.50 per month.
    —two years .... $342.00 per month.

Where the 7.5% vacancy allowance does not apply, for vacancy leases of:
    —one year .... $312.00 per month.
    —two years .... $319.50 per month.

Electrical Inclusion Adjustment

For a lease for a dwelling unit for which the owner supplies full electrical services for which there is no additional cost charged to the tenant in addition to rent, the applicable lease adjustments as established by this Order are to be the adjustments for renewal and vacancy leases heretofore stated.

Adjustments for Units In the Category of Buildings Covered By Article 7-C of The Multiple Dwelling Law

Pursuant to Chapter 349 of the Laws of 1982, Section 286 paragraph 7 of The Multiple Dwelling Law, The Rent Guidelines Board hereby establishes that the allowable levels of rent increase above the "base rent," as defined in Section 286 paragraph 4, for units where residential renewal leases are offered pursuant to Section 286, paragraph 3 of The Multiple Dwelling Law, and commence from October 1, 1985 through September 30, 1986, shall be the same as those set forth hereinabove for renewal leases.

Where a dwelling unit in this category of buildings becomes vacant the levels of rent increase governing a new tenancy commencing on or after October 1, 1985 and on or before September 30, 1986 are the same levels over the "base rent," as defined in Section 286, paragraph 4, as set forth hereinabove for vacancy leases, unless pursuant to paragraph 6, Section 286 of The Multiple Dwelling Law the owner purchases improvements and thereby the unit is either exempted from the provisions of Article 7-C requiring rent regulation or may be rented at market value subject to subsequent rent regulation; however, for purposes of the provision prohibiting the 7.5% vacancy allowance in buildings of more than 50 units in which more than 10% of the units were vacant for the 60 days preceding the commencement of the lease, only residential units covered by Article 7-C of the Multiple Dwelling Law or those that have had a residential certificate of occupancy issued for the unit shall be counted.

Fractional Terms

For the purpose of these guidelines any lease or tenancy for a period up to and including one year shall be deemed a one year lease or tenancy, and the same for a period over one year and up to and including two years shall be deemed a two year lease.

Escalator Clauses

Where a lease for a dwelling unit in effect on May 31, 1968 or where a lease in effect on June 30, 1974 for a dwelling unit which became subject to the Rent Stabilization Law of 1969, by virtue of Chapter 576 of the Laws of 1974 and Resolution Number 276 of the New York City Council, extended by Chapter 203 of the Laws of 1977, further extended by Chapter 383 of the Laws of 1981, by Chapter 403 of the Laws of 1983, and by Chapter 248 of the Laws of 1985, contained an escalator clause for the increased costs of operation and such clause is still in effect, the lawful rental on September 30, 1985, over which the fair rent under this Order is computed shall include the increased rental, if any, due under such clause except those charges which accrued within one year of the commencement of the renewal lease. Moreover, where a lease contained an escalator clause that the owner may validly renew under the Code, unless the owner elects or has elected in writing to delete such clause, effective no later than October 1, 1985 from the existing lease and all subsequent leases for such dwelling unit, the increased rental, if any, due under such escalator clause shall be offset against the amount of increase authorized under this Order.

Stabilizer

The one-half per cent "stabilizer" charged in leases pursuant to previous Orders of the Board shall remain in effect until the expiration of such leases and shall be included in the base rent for the purpose of computing subsequent rents or leases adjusted pursuant to this Order.

Special Guideline to Update Special Guideline 6b

In order to aid the State Division of Housing and Community Renewal in determining fair market rents for housing accommodations as to applications for adjustments of the initial legal regulated rent as may be requested by tenants, the Rent Guidelines Board hereby establishes a special guideline as mandated by Section 9 of Chapter 576 of the Laws of 1974, as extended by Chapter 203 of the Laws of 1977, further extended by Chapter 383 of the Laws of 1981, and Chapter 403 of the Laws of 1983 amending Section YY51-6.0.2.b(1) of the New York City Administrative Code, and Chapter 248 of the Laws of 1985: for dwelling units subject to the Rent and Rehabilitation Law on September 30, 1985, which subsequently become vacant after September 30, 1985, 20% above the sum of the 1984-85 maximum base rent, as it existed or would have existed, plus the current allowable fuel cost adjustments as established on Rent Control forms, pursuant to Section 33.10 of the Rent Regulations, beginning in 1980.

Decontrolled Units

The permissible increase for decontrolled units as defined in Order 3a which become decontrolled after September 30, 1985, shall not exceed 20% above the sum of the 1984-85 maximum base rent, as it existed or would have existed, plus the current allowable fuel cost adjustments as established on Rent Control forms, pursuant to Section 33.10 of the Rent Regulations, beginning in 1980.

Credits

Rental charged and paid in excess of the levels of fair rent increase established by this Order shall be fully credited against the next month's rent.

Dated: June 28, 1985
Filed with the City Clerk: June 28, 1985

RENT GUIDELINE ORDER NUMBER 18—Rent Levels for Leases Commencing October 1, 1986 Through September 30, 1987

Adjustments for Renewal Leases

Together with such further adjustments as may be authorized by the Board, as explained below:

—For one year leases expiring before October 1, 1988:
6.0 per cent

—For two year leases expiring before October 1, 1989:
9.0 per cent

These adjustments shall also apply to dwelling units in a structure subject to the partial tax exemption program under Section 421 of the Real Property Tax Law, or in a structure subject to Section 423 of the Real Property Tax Law as a Redevelopment Project.

It is not expected that the Board will convene to discuss fuel costs in the coming year. The Board will discuss the fuel situation at its annual meetings in June as it affects leases signed pursuant to this Order. The Board may also consider any catastrophic change in the Operation and Maintenance Cost Index and order appropriate supplementary adjustments. The Board reserves the right to modify this Order during its term pursuant to this paragraph provided that any further adjustments described in this paragraph shall apply to existing leases only where the lease permits the rental reserved therein to be adjusted pursuant to subsequent determinations of the Rent Guidelines Board during the term of such lease.

Leases on Vacant Apartments

Where a dwelling unit becomes vacant, the levels of rent increase governing a new tenancy commencing on or after October 1, 1986 and on or before September 30, 1987 are the same levels over rentals charged on September 30, 1986 as those set forth above for lease renewals, plus seven and one-half percent (7.5%) over the rental charged on September 30, 1986, with the following exception:

—for those units in which there had previously been a new tenancy commencing on or after October 1, 1985 and on or before September 30, 1986, unless the allowable level of increase for that new tenancy pursuant to Order 17 of the Board was the same as for renewal leases, the levels of rent increase governing a new tenancy are the same levels over rentals charged on September 30, 1986 as those set forth above for renewal leases without any additional allowance for the vacancy.

Any level of rent increase pursuant to this provision relating to leases on vacant apartments may be applied no more than once for leases commencing October 1, 1986 through September 30, 1987.

Supplementary Adjustment of up to $15 Per Month for Renewal and Vacancy Leases for Apartments Renting for Less than $350 Per Month on September 30, 1986.

For a lease for a dwelling unit with a lawful rent of less than $350 per month on September 30, 1986, the levels of rent increase for renewal and vacancy leases commencing October 1, 1986 through September 30, 1987 are the same as those set forth hereinabove plus $15 per month, provided the monthly rent resulting from application of this level of increase or any portion thereof does not exceed the rent that would result from application of the allowable levels of rent increase for renewal and vacancy leases to an apartment renting for $350 per month on September 30, 1986. This limitation is as follows:

Westchester   3%   5%

Vacancy Rate - Rent may be raised to highest comparable rent for same sized apartment.

Rent Guidance Board Orders

<u>Rockland</u>   3%   4½%

Vacancy Rate - 5% or same rent as comparable apartment, whichever is lower.

For renewal leases of:
—one year .... $371.00 per month.
—two years .... $381.50 per month.

Where the 7.5% vacancy allowance applies, for vacancy leases of:
—one year .... $397.25 per month.
—two years .... $407.75 per month.

Where the 7.5% vacancy allowance does not apply, for vacancy leases of:
—one year .... $371.00 per month
—two years .... $381.50 per month.

The Board also provided, that in the event that a tenant was charged with a supplementary adjustment of up to $15 for rents below $300 under Order 17, the tenant may not be charged the supplementary adjustment under Order 18.

Electrical Inclusion Adjustment

For a lease for a dwelling unit for which the owner supplies full electrical services for which there is no additional cost charged to the tenant in addition to rent, the applicable lease adjustments as established by this Order are to be the adjustments for renewal and vacancy leases heretofore stated.

RENT GUIDELINES	October 1, 1986 (to) September 30, 1987	
New York City	One (1) Year	Two (2) Year
	6%	9%
	(+) 15% if rent is under $350 Vacancy Rate - 7½%	
Nassau	4%	5½%
	Vacancy Rate - One (1) months rent over term of the lease, or part of rent to cover costs of re-renting apartment, i.e., painting, advertising, brokers fees, vacancy loss.	

Adjustments for Units In the Category of Buildings Covered By Article 7-C of The Multiple Dwelling Law

Pursuant to Chapter 349 of the Laws of 1982, Section 286 paragraph 7 of The Multiple Dwelling Law, The Rent

Guidelines Board hereby establishes that the allowable levels of rent increase above the "base rent," as defined in Section 286 paragraph 4, for units where residential renewal leases are offered pursuant to Section 286, paragraph 3 of The Multiple Dwelling Law, and commence from October 1, 1986 through September 30, 1987, shall be the same as those set forth hereinabove for renewal leases.

Where a dwelling unit in this category of buildings becomes vacant the levels of rent increase governing a new tenancy commencing on or after October 1, 1986 and on or before September 30, 1987 are the same levels over the "base rent," as defined in Section 286, paragraph 4, as set forth hereinabove for renewal leases, unless pursuant to paragraph 6, Section 286 of The Multiple Dwelling Law the owner purchases improvements and thereby the unit is either exempted from the provisions of Article 7-C requiring rent regulation or may be rented at market value subject to subsequent rent regulation.

Fractional Terms

For the purpose of these guidelines any lease or tenancy for a period up to and including one year shall be deemed a one year lease or tenancy, and the same for a period over one year and up to and including two years shall be deemed a two year lease.

Escalator Clauses

Where a lease for a dwelling unit in effect on May 31, 1968 or where a lease in effect on June 30, 1974 for a dwelling unit which became subject to the Rent Stabilization Law of 1969, by virtue of Chapter 576 of the Laws of 1974 and Resolution Number 276 of the New York City Council, extended by Chapter 203 of the Laws of 1977, further extended by Chapter 383 of the Laws of 1981, by Chapter 403 of the Laws of 1983, and by Chapter 248 of the Laws of 1985, contained an escalator clause for the increased costs of operation and such clause is still in effect, the lawful rental on September 30, 1986, over which the fair rent under this Order is computed shall include the increased rental, if any, due under such clause except those charges which accrued within one year of the commencement of the renewal lease. Moreover, where a lease contained an escalator clause that the owner may validly renew under the Code, unless the owner elects or has elected in writing to delete such clause, effective no later than October 1, 1986 from the existing lease and all subsequent leases for such dwelling unit, the increased rental, if any, due under such escalator clause shall be offset against the amount of increase authorized under this Order.

Stabilizer

The one-half per cent "stabilizer" charged in leases pursuant to previous Orders of the Board shall remain in effect until the expiration of such leases and shall be included in the base rent for the purpose of computing subsequent rents or leases adjusted pursuant to this Order.

Special Guidelines to Update Special Guideline 6b

In order to aid the State Division of Housing and Community Renewal in determining fair market rents for housing accommodations as to applications for adjustments of the initial legal regulated rent as may be requested by tenants, the Rent Guidelines Board hereby establishes a special guideline as mandated by Section 9 of Chapter 576 of the Laws of 1974, as extended by Chapter 203 of the Laws of 1977, further extended by Chapter 383 of the Laws of 1981, and Chapter 403 of the Laws of 1983 amending Section YY51-6.0.2.b(1) of the New York City Administrative Code, and Chapter 248 of the Laws of 1985: for dwelling units subject to the Rent and Rehabilitation Law on September 30, 1986, which subsequently become vacant after September 30, 1986, 20% above the sum of the 1986-87 maximum base rent, as it existed or would have existed, plus the current allowable fuel cost adjustments as established on Rent Control forms, pursuant to Section 33.10 of the Rent Regulations, beginning in 1980.

The permissible increase for decontrolled units as defined in Order 3a which become decontrolled after September 30, 1986, shall not exceed 20% above the sum of the 1986-87 maximum base rent, as it existed or would have existed, plus the current allowable fuel cost adjustments as established on Rent Control forms, pursuant to Section 33.10 of the Rent Regulations, beginning in 1980.

Credits

Rental charged and paid in excess of the levels of fair rent increase established by this Order shall be fully credited against the next month's rent.

Rent Stabilization Code

In the event that the New York State Division of Housing and Community Renewal promulgates a revised Rent Stabilization Code, with provisions conflicting with the language of this Order, the provisions of the Code shall apply to all leases entered into subsequent to the promulgation of the Code during the term of this Order.

Dated: June 27, 1986

Filed with the City Clerk: June 30, 1986

Explanatory Statement and Findings of the Rent Guidelines Board in Relation to 1986-87 Lease Increase Allowances For Apartments Under the Jurisdiction of the Rent Stabilization Law. (Except when the tenant signed a lease under RGB Order #17 and was charged a supplementary adjustment of up to $15 for apartments renting for less than $300.)

Order No. 18

The Rent Guidelines Board (RGB) by Order No. 18 has set the following maximum rent increases for leases entered on after October 1st, 1986 and on or before September 30th, 1987 in apartments under its jurisdiction:

	1 Year	2 Years
Lease Renewal	6%	9%
Lease Renewal for Units Renting for less than $350	6% + $15/Mo.	9% + $15/Mo.
to a maximum monthly rent*	$371	$381.50

---

* This Explanatory Statement explains the actions taken by the Board members on individual points and reflects the general views of those voting in the majority. It is not meant to summarize all the viewpoints expressed.

Rent Guidance Board Orders

New Leases For Apartments-same percentage as above for lease renewals plus:

	Vacancy Allowance (Subject to the limitation discussed below on the applicability of the vacancy allowance)
-Where there had not previously been a new tenancy on or after 10/1/85, or where there had previously been a new tenancy 10/1/85 or after and the applicable vacancy allowance under Order 17 was zero:	7.5%
or	
-Where there had previously been a new tenancy on or after 10/1/85, provided the vacancy allowance applicable to such new tenancy under Order 17 was not zero:	0.0%

Plus an additional $15/mo. where the unit was renting for less than $350 a month provided the resulting rent does not exceed:

Where the vacancy allowance under this order is	For A 1 Year Lease	For A 2 Year Lease
7.5%	$397.25	$407.75
0.0%	$371	$381.50

For Loft units that have met the legalization requirements under Article 7-C of the Multiple Dwelling Law, the Board established the same guidelines as above for renewal leases. For loft units no additional vacancy allowance for vacancy leases was authorized and the allowable level of rent adjustment is the same as for renewal leases.

The guidelines do not apply to non-transient hotel units which are covered by separate Hotel Orders.

The Board indicated that any increase pursuant to the vacancy allowance provisions of Order No. 18, as well as any increase for a renewal lease, may be collected no more than once during the guideline period governed by Order 18.

Leases for units subject to rent control on September 30th, 1986 which subsequently became vacant and then enter the stabilization system are not subject to the above adjustments. Such renewals are subject to review by the State Division of Housing Community Renewal (DHCR). In order to aid the State Division of Housing Community Renewal (DHCR), the Rent Guidelines Board has set a special guideline at 20 percent above the sum of the 1986-

87 Maximum Base rent plus the current allowable fuel cost adjustments pursuant to Section 33.10 of the Rent Regulations.

The "April 1979 Fuel Adjustment" charged pursuant to Order No. 10b, the "January 1980 Fuel Cost Adjustment for Rent Levels" charged pursuant to Order No. 10c, "July 1980 Fuel Adjustment for Rent Levels" charged pursuant to Order 10d, "Modification of the Terms of Order No. 10d Covering Rent Levels" charged pursuant to Order No. 10e, the "Fuel Adjustment for Leases Commencing Between July 1, 1979 and June 30, 1980 To Go Into Effect One Year From The Commencement of the Lease" charged pursuant to Order 11a, the "Continuation of the Fuel Adjustment for Leases Commencing Between July 1, 1979 and June 30, 1980" charged pursuant to Order No. 11b and the "Continuation of Fuel Adjustments for Leases Commencing Between July 1, 1979 and June 30, 1980" charged pursuant to Order No. 11c shall not be included in the base rent to which the adjustments set forth in this Order No. 18 apply.

HOTEL ORDERS*

Hotel Order Number 12—Rent Levels for Hotel Units July 1, 1982 Through June 30, 1983.

Applicability

This Order shall apply to all units in buildings subject to the Hotel Section of the Rent Stabilization Law, as amended, or Chapter 576 of the Laws of 1974 and occupied by a non-transient hotel tenant. The level of fair rent increase granted herein shall be effective as of the anniversary of the tenant's commencing occupancy with respect to any such tenants who have no lease or rental agreement. This anniversary date will also serve as the effective date for all subsequent Rent Guidelines Board Hotel Orders, unless the Board shall specifically provide otherwise in the Order. Where a lease or rental agreement is in effect, this Order shall govern the rent increase collectible on or after July 1, 1982 upon expiration of such lease or rental agreement, unless the parties have contracted to be bound by this Order as of July 1, 1982, or a subsequent date. But, in no event shall there be more than one guidelines increase during the term of one guideline period.

As regards any unit for which an increase pursuant to this Order is collectible, demand for such increase shall be made within 90 days of the date of this Order or its effective date, whichever is later, or the increase may only be collected prospectively. That portion of the increase that is to be collected retroactively shall be collectible from a tenant in monthly installments, each installment not to exceed one-half of the monthly increase permitted under this Order. Where the rental period is other than monthly, installments for rental periods prior to the date the increase was demanded shall be prorated accordingly.

* Collected here are Hotel Order Numbers 12-15, pertaining to New York City hotel unit rent levels from July 1, 1982-June 30, 1986. Subsequent Hotel Orders will be reflected in the supplement to this material.

Guideline For Rent Increases

The level of fair rent increases over the lawful rent actually charged and paid on June 30, 1982, shall be two (2) per cent.

Additional Charges

It is expressly understood that the rents increased under the terms of this Order are intended to compensate in full for all services provided without extra charge to the statutory date for the particular hotel dwelling unit or at the commencement of the tenancy if subsequent thereto. No additional charges may be made to a tenant for such services, however such charges may be called or identified.

Excluded Units

This increase shall not apply where forty (40) per cent or more of the dwelling units in a hotel are vacant and unoccupied on June 30, 1982. In such case the owner will not be allowed the increase unless he can prove to the statisfaction of the Conciliation and Appeals Board that he has attempted in good faith to rent said units.

Special Guidelines

Pursuant to Section YY51-5.0e of the Rent Stabilization Law and Chapter 576 of the Laws of 1974, special guidelines relating to adjustment of initial legal regulated rents are inapplicable to hotel dwelling units.

Dated: June 30, 1982
Filed with the City Clerk: June 30, 1982

Hotel Order Number 13—Rent Levels for Hotel Units, July 1, 1983 through June 30, 1984.

Applicability

This Order shall apply to all units in buildings subject to the Hotel Section of the Rent Stabilization Law, as amended, or Chapter 576 of the Laws of 1974 and occupied by a non-transient hotel tenant. With respect to any tenants who have no lease or rental agreement, the level of fair rent increase granted herein shall be effective as of one year from the date of the tenant's commencing occupancy, or as of one year from the date of the last level of fair rent increase charged to the tenant, whichever is later. This anniversary date will also serve as the effective date for all subsequent Rent Guidelines Board Hotel Orders, unless the Board shall specifically provide otherwise in the Order. Where a lease or rental agreement is in effect, this Order shall govern the rent increase collectible on or after July 1, 1983 upon expiration of such lease or rental agreement, but in no event prior to one year from the commencement date of the expiring lease, unless the parties have contracted to be bound by this Order as of July 1, 1983, or a subsequent date. In no event shall there be more than one guidelines increase during the term of one guideline period.

As regards any unit for which an increase pursuant to this Order is collectible, demand for such increase shall be made within 90 days of the date of this Order or its effective date, whichever is later, or the increase may only be collected prospectively. That portion of the increase that is to be collected retroactively shall be collectible from a tenant in monthly installments, each installment not to exceed one-half of the monthly increase permitted under this Order. Where the rental period is other than monthly, installments for rental periods prior to the date the increase was demanded shall be prorated accordingly.

Guideline For Rent Increases

The level of fair rent increases over the lawful rent actually charged and paid on June 30, 1983, shall be four (4) per cent.

New Tenancies

The Rent Guidelines Board provisionally adopted the following for new tenancies subject to the implementation of new legislation enacted but not signed into law as of the date of this Order.

Where a hotel dwelling unit becomes vacant, the level of rent increase governing a new tenancy commencing on or after the effective date of the new legislation through June 30, 1984 is:

—for those units which have had a new tenancy commencing on or after July 1, 1978, the same level over rentals charged on June 30, 1983 as that set forth above for levels of fair rent increases.

—for those units which have had no new tenancy commencing on or after July 1, 1978, the same plus 5% over rentals charged on June 30, 1983.

Additional Charges

It is expressly understood that the rents increased under the terms of this Order are intended to compensate in full for all services provided without extra charge to the statutory date for the particular hotel dwelling unit or at the commencement of the tenancy if subsequent thereto. No additional charges may be made to a tenant for such services however such charges may be called or identified.

Excluded Units

This increase shall not apply where forty (40) per cent or more of the dwelling units in a hotel are vacant and unoccupied on June 30, 1983. In such case the owner will not be allowed the increase unless he can prove to the satisfaction of the Conciliation and Appeals Board that he has attempted in good faith to rent said units.

Special Guidelines

Pursuant to Section YY51-5.0e of the Rent Stabilization Law and Chapter 576 of the Laws of 1974, special guidelines relating to adjustment of initial legal regulated rents are inapplicable to hotel dwelling units. However, this provision may be modified by the appropriate agency subject to the implementation of new legislation enacted but not signed into law as of the date of this Order.

Dated: June 29, 1983
Filed with the City Clerk: June 29, 1983

Hotel Order Number 14—Rent Levels for Hotel Units, July 1, 1984 Through June 30, 1985.

Applicability

This Order shall apply to all units in buildings subject to the Hotel Section of the Rent Stabilization Law, as amended, or Chapter 576 of the Laws of 1974 and occupied by a non-transient hotel tenant. With respect to any tenants who have no lease or rental agreement, the level of fair rent increase established therein shall be effective as of one year from the date of the tenant's commencing occupancy, or as of one year from the date of the last level of fair rent increase charged to the tenant, which ever is later. This anniversary date will also serve as the effective date for all subsequent Rent Guidelines Board Hotel Orders, unless the Board shall specifically provide otherwise in the Order. Where a lease or rental agreement is in effect, this Order shall govern the rent increase applicable on or after July 1, 1984 upon expiration of such lease or rental agreement, but in no event prior to one year from the commencement date of the expiring lease, unless the parties have contracted to be bound by this Order as of July 1, 1984, or a subsequent date.

Guidelines for Rent Increases

The level of fair rent increases over the lawful rent actually charged and paid on June 30, 1984 shall be zero (0) per cent.

New Tenancies

For any hotel dwelling unit which is voluntarily vacated by the tenant thereof, the level of rent increase governing a new tenancy shall be the same as the guideline for rent increases set forth above.

Additional Charges

It is expressly understood that the rents collectible under the terms of this Order are intended to compensate in full for all services provided without extra charge to the statutory date for the particular hotel dwelling unit or at the commencement of the tenancy if subsequent thereto. No additional charges may be made to a tenant for such services however such charges may be called or identified.

Special Guidelines

Pursuant to Section YY51-5.0e of the Rent Stabilization Law and Chapter 576 of the Laws of 1974, special guidelines relating to adjustment of initial legal regulated rents are inapplicable to hotel dwelling units, subject to

Chapter 448 of the Laws of 1983 as administered by the appropriate agency.

Dated: June 27, 1984
Filed with the City Clerk: June 27, 1984

Hotel Order Number 15—Rent Levels for Hotel Units, July 1, 1985 through June 30, 1986.

Applicability

This Order shall apply to all units in buildings subject to the Hotel Section of the Rent Stabilization Law, as amended, or Chapter 576 of the Laws of 1974 and occupied by a non-transient hotel tenant. With respect to any tenants who have no lease or rental agreement, the level of fair rent increase established herein shall be effective as of one year from the date of the tenant's commencing occupancy, or as of one year from the date of the last level of fair rent increase charged to the tenant, whichever is later. This anniversary date will also serve as the effective date for all subsequent Rent Guidelines Board Hotel Orders, unless the Board shall specifically provide otherwise in the Order. Where a lease or rental agreement is in effect, this Order shall govern the rent increase applicable on or after July 1, 1985 upon expiration of such lease or rental agreement, but in no event prior to one year from the commencement date of the expiring lease, unless the parties have contracted to be bound by this Order as of July 1, 1985, or a subsequent date. In no event shall there be more than one guidelines increase during the term of one guideline period.

As regards any unit for which an increase pursuant to this Order is collectible, demand for such increase shall be made within 90 days of the date of this Order or its effective date, whichever is later, or the increase may only be collected prospectively. That portion of the increase that is to be collected retroactively shall be collectible from a tenant in monthly installments, each installment not to exceed one-half of the monthly increase permitted under this Order. Where the rental period is other than monthly, installments for rental periods prior to the date the increase was demanded shall be prorated accordingly.

Guideline for Rent Increases

The level of fair rent increases over the lawful rent actually charged and paid on June 30, 1985 shall be two (2) per cent.

New Tenancies

For any hotel dwelling unit which is voluntarily vacated by the tenant thereof, the level of rent increase governing a new tenancy shall be the same as the guideline for rent increases set forth above.

Excluded Units

For buildings of more than 30 units this increase shall not apply where more than 5% of the units are vacant for the 60 days preceding the effective date of this Order. In such case the owner will not be allowed the increase unless he can prove to the satisfaction of the State Division of Housing and Community Renewal that he has attempted in good faith to rent said units.

Additional Charges

It is expressly understood that the rents collectible under the terms of this Order are intended to compensate in full for all services provided without extra charge to the statutory date for the particular hotel dwelling unit or at the commencement of the tenancy if subsequent thereto. No additional charges may be made to a tenant for such services however such charges may be called or identified.

Special Guidelines

Pursuant to Section YY51-5.0e of the Rent Stabilization Law and Chapter 576 of the Laws of 1974, special guidelines relating to adjustment of initial legal regulated rents are inapplicable to hotel dwelling units, subject to Chapter 448 of the Laws of 1983 as administered by the appropriate agency.

Dated: June 28, 1985
Filed with the City Clerk: June 28, 1985

HOTEL ORDER NO. 16—Rent Levels for Hotel Units, July 1, 1986 through June 30, 1987

Applicability

This Order shall apply to units in buildings subject to the Hotel Section of the Rent Stabilization Law, as amended, or Chapter 576 of the Laws of 1974 and occupied by a non-transient hotel tenant. With respect to any tenants who have no lease or rental agreement, the level of fair rent increase established herein shall be effective as of one year from the date of the tenant's commencing occupancy, or as of one year from the date of the last level of fair rent increase charged to the tenant, whichever is later. This anniversary date will also serve as the effective date for all subsequent Rent Guidelines Board Hotel Orders, unless the Board shall specifically provide otherwise in the Order. Where a lease or rental agreement is in effect, this Order shall govern the rent increase applicable on or after July 1, 1986 upon expiration of such lease or rental agreement, but in no event prior to one year from the commencement date of the expiring lease, unless the parties have contracted to be bound by this Order as of July 1, 1986, or a subsequent date. In no event shall there be more than one guidelines increase during the term of one guidelines period.

Guideline for Rent Increases

The level of fair rent increase over the lawful rent actually charged and paid on June 30, 1986 shall be zero (0) per cent.

New Tenancies

For any hotel dwelling unit which is voluntarily vacated by the tenant thereof, the level of rent increase governing a new tenancy shall be the same as the guideline for rent increases set forth above.

Additional Charges

It is expressly understood that the rents collectible under the terms of this Order are intended to compensate in full for all services provided without extra charge to the statutory date for the particular hotel dwelling unit or at the commencement of the tenancy if subsequent thereto. No additional charges may be made to a tenant for such services however such charges may be called or identified.

HOTEL ORDERS

Special Guidelines

Pursuant to Section YY51-5.0e of the Rent Stabilization Law and Chapter 576 of the Laws of 1974, special guidelines relating to adjustment of initial legal regulated rents are inapplicable to hotel dwelling units, subject to Chapter 448 of the Laws of 1983 as administered by the appropriate agency.

Dated: June 27, 1986
Filed with the City Clerk: June 30, 1986

Explanatory Statement and Findings of the Rent Guidelines Board Concerning Increase Allowances for Hotel Units Under the Jurisdiction of the Rent Stabilization Law, Pursuant to Hotel Order No. 16, Effective July 1, 1986 Through and Including June 30th, 1987.[*]

Hotel Order No. 16 provides for an allowable increase of zero (0) percent over the lawful rent actually charged and paid on June 30th, 1986. Said increase allowance shall be effective for a twelve month period commencing July 1st, 1986 and ending on June 30th, 1987. The order does not limit rental levels for commercial space, non-stabilized residential units, or transient units in hotel stabilized buildings during the guideline period. The order also provides that for any hotel dwelling unit which is voluntarily vacated by the tenant thereof, the level of rent increases governing a new tenancy shall be the same as the guideline for rent increases set forth above, that is zero (0) percent vacancy.

Background

The Board conducted two public hearings, after full notice, on May 29th, 1986 and June 2nd, 1986 to gather testimony from the public on the issue of rent increases for stabilized hotel units. The hearing held on June 2nd, 1986 was held in the evening to permit working people to speak. Approximately 61 persons testified at the hearings on the subject of stabilized hotel rent increases. Public meetings of the Board were held on April 16 May 20, 27,

---
[*] This Explanatory Statement explains the actions taken by the Board members on individual points and reflects the general views of those voting in the majority. It is not meant to summarize all of the viewpoints expressed.

June 4th and 17th following public notice. At the meeting of June 4th, data concerning the stabilized hotel sector was presented and discussed. On June 17th, 1986 the guidelines set forth in Hotel Order No. 16 were adopted.

Of the 61 persons who testified at the public hearings on the subject of stabilized hotel rent increases, forty represented tenants and twenty-one represented owners. The Hotel Industry was represented by the Metropolitan Hotel Industry Stabilization Association, Inc. and others. In addition the Board received written testimony from 32 individuals and groups writing on behalf of hotel tenants and owners.

Hotel Order No. 11-Rent Levels for Hotel Units
July 1, 1981 Through June 30, 1982

PURSUANT TO THE AUTHORITY VESTED IN IT BY THE RENT STABILIZATION law of 1969 and Chapter 576 of the Laws of 1974, implemented by Resolution No. 276 of 1974 of the New York City Council and extended by Chapter 203 of the Laws of 1977, the Rent Guidelines Board hereby establishes and adopts the following guidelines for levels of fair rent increase over lawful rents charged and paid on April 30, 1981.

Applicability

This Order shall apply to any hotel unit subject to the Rent Stabilization Law, as amended, or Chapter 576 of the Laws of 1974 and occupied by a non-transient hotel tenant. The level of fair rent increase granted herein shall be effective as of July 1, 1981 with respect to any such tenants who have no lease or rental agreement. Where a lease or rental agreement is in effect, unless the parties have contracted to be bound by an Order as of May 1, 1981, or a subsequent date, this Order shall govern the rent increase collectible on or after July 1, 1981 upon expiration of such lease or rental agreement on or after May 1, 1981. Where the parties to the lease or rental agreement have contracted to be bound by an Order as of May 1, 1981, or a subsequent date, this Order shall govern the rent increase to be collected as of July 1, 1981 or as of such subsequent date as is specified in the terms of the affected lease or rental agreement.

As regards any unit for which an increase pursuant to

this Order is collectible for a period commencing prior to the date upon which an owner demands such increase, the rental increase relating to such period shall be collectible from a tenant in monthly installments, each installment not to exceed the monthly increase authorized by this Order No. 11. Where the rental period is other than monthly, installments for rental periods prior to the date the increase was demanded shall be paid each rental period and each installment shall not exceed the difference in rent permitted by this Order for such rental period. This provision shall not be deemed to create or diminish any substantive right of the owner to retroactive increases and only affects collectibility by installments of the increase authorized by this Order.

Guideline for Rent Increases

The level of fair rent increases over the lawful rent actually charged and paid on April 30, 1981, shall be ten (10) per cent. This increase shall not apply to any tenant who was not in occupancy on April 30, 1981.

Temporary Surcharge For Units Where Owners Have Postponed the Effective Date of REnt Adjustments During the Period May 1, 1981 Through June 30, 1981

A surcharge of 1.67 percent of the lawful rent actually charged and paid on April 30, 1981 shall be authorized in addition to the fair rent increase authorized by this Order, where an increase otherwise authorized or collectible during the period May 1, 1981 through May 31, 1981 was postponed pursuant to the Memorandum of Understanding entered into between the Rent Guidelines Board and the Metropolitan Hotel Industry Stabilization Association on January 22, 1981.

A surcharge of .83 percent of the lawful rent actually charged and paid on April 30, 1981 shall be authorized in addition to the fair rent increase authorized by this Order, where an increase otherwise authorized or collectible during the period June 1, 1981 through June 30, 1981 was postponed pursuant to the Memorandum of Understanding entered into between the Rent Guidelines Board and the Metropolitan Hotel Industry Stabilization Association on January 22, 1981.

Any temporary surcharge collected pursuant to this provision may remain in effect through June 30, 1982 or through the termination of the tenancy, whichever occurs first, and shall not merge with the base rent established pursuant to this Hotel Order No. 11 for the purpose of computing any rental adjustments under the terms of subsequent Orders of the Board.

Additional Charges

It is expressly understood that the rents increased under the terms of this Order are intended to compensate in full for all services provided without extra charge to the statutory date for the particular hotel dwelling unit or at the commencement of the tenancy if subsequent thereto. No additional charges may be made to a tenant for such services however such charges may be called or identified.

Excluded Units

This increase shall not apply where forty (40) per cent or more of the dwelling units in a hotel are vacant and unoccupied on June 30, 1981. In such case the owner will not be allowed the increase unless he can prove to the satisfaction of the Conciliation and Appeals Board that he has attempted in good faith to rent said units.

Special Guidelines

Pursuant to Section YY51-5.0e of the Rent Stabilization Law and Chapter 576 of the Laws of 1974, special guidelines relating to adjustment of initial legal regulated rents are inapplicable to hotel dwelling units.

Dated: June 30, 1981
Filed with the City Clerk: June 30, 1981

PART IV: EMERGENCY TENANT PROTECTION
Emergency Tenant Protection Act of 1974
State Tenant Protection Regulations
State Tenant Protection Bulletins

PART IV EMERGENCY TENANT PROTECTION

Emergency Tenant Protection Act of 1974
State Tenant Protection Regulations
(NYS Tenant Protection Regulations)

PART IV
EMERGENCY TENANT PROTECTION

EMERGENCY TENANT PROTECTION ACT OF 1974

[Enacted by L 1974, ch 576, § 17 of which, as am L 1976, ch 486, am L 1977, ch 203, § 1, L 1981, ch 383, § 1, L 1983, ch 403, § 58, and L 1985, ch 248, § 1, provides:

§ 17. Effective date. This act shall take effect immediately and shall remain in full force and effect until and including the fourteenth day of May, nineteen hundred eighty-seven; except that sections two and three shall take effect with respect to any city having a population of one million or more and section one shall take effect with respect to any other city, or any town or village whenever the local legislative body of a city, town, or village determines the existence of a public emergency pursuant to section three of the emergency tenant protection act of nineteen seventy-four, as enacted by section four of this act, and provided that the housing accommodations subject on the effective date of this act to stabilization pursuant to the New York city rent stabilization law of nineteen hundred sixty-nine shall remain subject to such law upon the expiration of this act.]

Laws 1985, ch 248, § 5, provides as follows:

§ 5. Regardless of the date on which it shall have become a law, any provision of a chapter of the laws of nineteen hundred eighty-five amending the emergency tenant protection act of nineteen seventy-four, which expires in accordance with chapter five hundred seventy-six of the laws of nineteen hundred seventy-four, as last extended by chapter four hundred three of the laws of nineteen hundred eighty-three, chapter eighty-one of the laws of nineteen hundred eighty-five or chapter one hundred seventy-two of the laws of nineteen hundred eighty-five, shall be subject to the provisions of this act and the expiration provisions of such chapter of the laws of nineteen hundred eighty-five shall be deemed to refer to chapter five hundred seventy-six of the laws of nineteen hundred seventy-four as last extended by the provisions of this act.

§ 1. Short title. This act shall be known and may be cited as the "emergency tenant protection act of nineteen seventy-four".

§ 2. Legislative finding. The legislature hereby finds and declares that a serious public emergency continues to exist in the housing of a considerable number of persons in the state of New York which emergency was at its inception created by war, the effects of war and the aftermath of hostilities, that such emergency necessitated the intervention of federal, state and local government in order to prevent speculative, unwarranted and abnormal increases in rents; that there continues to exist in many areas of the state an acute shortage of housing accommodations caused by continued high demand, attributable in part to new household formations and decreased supply, in large measure attributable to reduced availability of federal subsidies, and increased costs of construction and other inflationary factors; that a substantial number of persons residing in housing not presently subject to the provisions of the emergency housing rent control law or the local emergency housing rent control act are being charged excessive and unwarranted rents and rent increases; that preventive action by the legislature continues to be imperative in order to prevent exaction of unjust, unreasonable and oppressive rents and rental agreements and to forestall profiteering, speculation and other disruptive practices tending to produce threats to the public health, safety and general welfare; that in order to prevent uncertainty, hardship and dislocation, the provisions of this act are necessary and designed to protect the public health, safety and general welfare; that the transition from regulation to a normal market of free bargaining between landlord and tenant, while the ultimate objective of state policy, must take place with due regard for such emergency; and that the policy herein expressed shall be subject to determination of the existence of a public emergency requiring the regulation of residential rents within any city, town or village by the local legislative body of such city, town or village.

§ 3. Local determination of emergency; end of emergency. a. The existence of public emergency requiring the regulation of residential rents for all or any class or classes of housing accommodations including any plot or parcel of land which had been rented prior to May first, nineteen hundred fifty, for the purpose of permitting the tenant thereof to construct or place his own dwelling thereon and on which plot or parcel of land there exists a dwelling owned and occupied by a tenant of such plot or parcel, heretofore destabilized; heretofore or hereafter decontrolled, exempt, not subject to control, or exempted from regulation and control under the provisions of the emergency housing rent control law, the local emergency housing rent control act or the New York city rent stabiliziation law of nineteen hundred sixty-nine; or subject to stabilization or control under such rent stabilization law, shall be a matter for local determination within each city, town or village. Any such determination shall be made by the local legislative body of such city, town or village on the basis of the supply of housing accommodations within such city, town or village, the condition of such accommodations and the need for regulating and controlling residential rents within such city, town or village. A declaration of emergency may be made as to any class of housing accommodations if the vacancy rate for the housing accommodations in such class within such municipality is not in excess of five percent and a declaration of emergency may be made as to all housing accommodations if the vacancy rate for the housing accommodations within such municipality is not in excess of five percent. [as amended L 1980, ch 69, § 4, which amendment shall be deemed to have been in full force and effect on and after July 1, 1974]

b. The local governing body of a city, town or village having declared an emergency pursuant to subdivision a of this section may at any time, on the basis of the supply of housing accommodations within such city, town or village, the condition of such accommodations and the need for continued regulation and control of residential rents within such municipality, declare that the emergency is either wholly or partially abated or that the regulation of rents pursuant to this act does not serve to abate such emergency and thereby remove one or more classes of accommodations from regulation under this act. The emergency must be declared at an end once the vacancy rate described in subdivision a of this section exceeds five percent.

c. No resolution declaring the existence or end of an emergency, as authorized by subdivisions a and b of this section, may be adopted except after public hearing held on not less than ten days public notice, as the local legislative body may reasonably provide.

§ 4. **Establishment of rent guidelines boards; duties.**
a. In each county wherein any city having a population of less than one million or any town or village has determined the existence of an emergency pursuant to section three of this act, there shall be created a rent guidelines board to consist of nine members appointed by the commissioner of housing and community renewal upon recommendation of the county legislature which recommendation shall be made within thirty days after the first local declaration of an emergency in such county; two such members shall be representative of tenants, two shall be representative of owners of property, and five shall be public members each of whom shall have had at least five years experience in either finance, economics or housing. One public member shall be designated by the commissioner to serve as chairman and shall hold no other public office. No member, officer or employee of any municipal rent regulation agency or the state division of housing and community renewal and no person who owns or manages real estate covered by this law or who is an officer of any owner or tenant organization shall serve on a rent guidelines board. One public member, one member representative of tenants and one member representative of owners shall serve for a term ending two years from January first next succeeding the date of their appointment; one public member, one member representative of tenants and one member representative of owners shall serve for terms ending three years from the January first next succeeding the date of their appointment and three public members shall serve for terms ending four years

from January first next succeeding the dates of their appointment. Thereafter, all members shall serve for terms of four years each. Members shall continue in office until their successors have been appointed and qualified. The commissioner shall fill any vacancy which may occur by reason of death, resignation or otherwise in a manner consistent with the original appointment. A member may be removed by the commissioner for cause, but not without an opportunity to be heard in person or by counsel, in his defense, upon not less than ten days notice. Compensation for the members of the board shall be at the rate of one hundred dollars per day, for no more than twenty days a year, except that the chairman shall be compensated at the rate of one hundred twenty-five dollars a day for no more than thirty days a year. The board shall be provided staff assistance by the division of housing and community renewal. The compensation of such members and the costs of staff assistance shall be paid by the division of housing and community renewal which shall be reimbursed in the manner prescribed in section four of this act. The local legislative body of each city having a population of less than one million and each town and village in which an emergency has been determined to exist as herein provided shall be authorized to designate one person who shall be representative of tenants and one person who shall be representative of owners of property to serve at its pleasure and without compensation to advise and assist the county rent guidelines board in matters affecting the adjustment of rents for housing accommodations in such city, town or village as the case may be. [Subd a am L 1976, ch 486, L 1979, ch 349]

b. A county rent guidelines board shall establish annually guidelines for rent adjustments which, at its sole discretion may be varied and different for and within the several zones and jurisdictions of the board, and in determining whether rents for housing accommodations as to which an emergency has been declared pursuant to this act shall be adjusted, shall consider among other things (1) the economic condition of the residential real estate industry in the affected area including such factors as the prevailing and projected (i) real estate taxes and sewer and water rates, (ii) gross operating maintenance costs (including insurance rates, governmental fees, cost of fuel and labor costs), (iii) costs and availability of financing (including effective rates of interest), (iv) over-all supply of housing accommodations and over-all vacancy rates, (2) relevant data from the current and projected cost of living indices for the affected area, (3) such other data as may be made available to it. As soon as practicable after its creation and thereafter not later than July first of each year, a rent guidelines board shall file with the state division of housing and community renewal its findings for the preceding calendar year, and shall accompany such findings with a statement of the maximum rate or rates of rent adjustment, if any, for one or more classes of accommodation subject to this act, authorized for leases or other rental agreements commencing during the next succeeding twelve months. The standards for rent adjustments may be applicable for the entire county or may be varied according to such zones or jurisdictions within such county as the board finds necessary to achieve the purposes of this subdivision. [Subd b am L 1976, ch 486 ch am L 1983, ch 403, § 53, effective June 30, 1983]

The standards for rent adjustments established annually shall be effective for leases commencing on October first of each year and during the next succeeding twelve months whether or not the board has filed its findings and statement of the maximum rate or rates of rent adjustment by July first of each year. If such lease is entered into before such filing by the board, it may provide for the rent to be adjusted by the rates then, in effect subject to change by the applicable rates of rent adjustment when filed, such change to be effective as of the date of the commencement of the lease. Said lease must provide that, if the new rates of rent adjustment differ for leases of different terms, the tenant has the option of changing the original lease term to any other term for which a rate of rent adjustment is set by the board, with the rental to be adjusted accordingly. [Added to subd b, L 1979, ch 348, eff June 28, 1979, and am L 1980, ch 330, § 1, eff Jan. 1, 1980]

Where a city, town or village shall act to determine the existence of public emergency pursuant to section three of this act subsequent to the establishment of annual

Tenant Protection Act

guidelines for rent adjustments of the accommodations subject to this act, the rent guidelines board as soon as practicable thereafter shall file its findings and rates of rent adjustment for leases or other rental agreements for the housing accommodations in such a city, town or village, which rates shall be effective for leases or other rental agreements commencing on or after the effective date of the determination. [Added to subd b, L 1979, ch 348, eff June 28, 1979, L 1980, ch 330, § 1]

c. In a city having a population of one million or more, the rent guidelines board shall be the rent guidelines board established pursuant to the New York city rent stabilization law of nineteen hundred sixty-nine as amended, and such board shall have the powers granted pursuant to the New York city rent stabilization law of nineteen hundred sixty-nine as amended.

d. Maximum rates of rent adjustment shall not be established more than once annually for any housing accommodation within a board's jurisdiction. Once established, no such rate shall, within the one-year period, be adjusted by any surcharge, supplementary adjustment or other modification. [Subd d added L 1983, ch 403 § 54, effective June 30, 1983][1]

§ 5. Housing accommodations subject to regulation.

a. A declaration of emergency may be made pursuant to section three as to all or any class or classes of housing accommodations in a municipality, except:

(1) housing accommodations subject to the emergency housing rent control law, or the local emergency housing rent control act, other than housing accommodations subject to the New York city rent stabilization law of nineteen hundred sixty-nine;

(2) housing accommodations owned or operated by the United States, the state of New York, any political subdi-

---

[1] L 1983, ch 403, § 16, eff June 30, 1983, provides: "All of the functions and powers possessed by and all the obligations and duties of the conciliation and appeals board, are hereby transferred and assigned to, assumed by and devolved upon the division of housing and community renewal in the executive department."

L 1983, ch 403, § 17, provides for classification of positions of the rent control division of the department; § 18 provides for the transfer of assets and records; § 19 provides for the continuance of rules and regulations; and § 20 provides for the continuity of proceedings.

vision, agency or instrumentality thereof, any municipality or any public housing authority;

(3) housing accommodations in buildings in which rentals are fixed by or subject to the supervision of the state division of housing and community renewal under other provisions of law or the New York city department of housing preservation and development or the New York state urban development corporation, or, to the extent that regulation under this act is inconsistent therewith aided by government insurance under any provision of the National Housing Act [Am L 1978, ch 655, § 137, eff July 25, 1978.]

(4) (a) housing accommodations in a building containing fewer than six dwelling units, other than any plot or parcel of land in cities having a population of one million or more which had been rented prior to May first, nineteen hundred fifty, for the purpose of permitting the tenant thereof to construct or place his own dwelling thereon and heretofore or hereafter decontrolled, exempt, not subject to control or exempted from regulation and control under the provisions of the emergency housing rent control law or the local emergency housing rent control act and on which plot or parcel of land there exists a dwelling owned and occupied by a tenant of such plot or parcel [subpar (a) of par 4 of subd a amended L 1980, ch 69, § 5, which amendment shall be deemed to have been in full force and effect on and after July 1, 1974]

(b) for purposes of this paragraph four, a building shall be deemed to contain six or more dwelling units if it is part of a multiple family garden-type maisonette dwelling complex containing six or more dwelling units having common facilities such as a sewer line, water main or heating plant and operated as a unit under common ownership, notwithstanding that certificates of occupancy were issued for portions thereof as one- or two-family dwellings.

(5) housing accommodations in buildings completed or buildings substantially rehabilitated as family units on or after January first, nineteen hundred seventy-four;

(6) housing accommodations owned or operated by a hospital, convent, monastery, asylum, public institution,

or college or school dormitory or any institution operated exclusively for charitable or educational purposes on a non-profit basis other than those accommodations occupied by a tenant on the date such housing accommodation is acquired by any such institution, or which are occupied subsequently by a tenant who is not affiliated with such institution at the time of his initial occupancy; [Par 6 am L 1983, ch 403, § 55, effective June 30, 1983]

(7) rooms or other housing accommodations in hotels, other than hotel accommodations in cities having a population of one million or more not occupied on a transient basis and heretofore subject to the emergency housing rent control law, the local emergency housing rent control act or to the New York city rent stabilization law of nineteen hundred sixty-nine;

(8) any motor court, or any part thereof, any trailer, or trailer space used exclusively for transient occupancy or any part thereof; or any tourist home serving transient guests exclusively, or any part thereof;

The term "motor court" shall mean an establishment renting rooms, cottages or cabins, supplying parking or storage facilities for motor vehicles in connection with such renting and other services and facilities customarily supplied by such establishments, and commonly known as motor, auto or tourist court in the community.

The term "tourist home" shall mean a rooming house which caters primarily to transient guests and is known as a tourist home in the community.

(9) non-housekeeping, furnished housing accommodations, located within a single dwelling unit not used as a rooming or boarding house, but only if:

(a) no more than two tenants for whom rent is paid (husband and wife being considered one tenant for this purpose), not members of the landlord's immediate family, live in such dwelling unit, and

(b) the remaining portion of such dwelling unit is occupied by the landlord or his immediate family.

(10) housing accommodations in buildings operated exclusively for charitable purposes on a non-profit basis;

(11) housing accommodations which are not occupied by the tenant, not including subtenants or occupants, as his

primary residence, as determined by a court of competent jurisdiction. For the purposes of this paragraph, where a housing accommodation is rented to a not-for-profit hospital for residential use, affiliated subtenants authorized to use such accommodations by such hospital shall be deemed to be tenants. No action or proceeding shall be commenced seeking to recover possession on the ground that a housing accommodation is not occupied by the tenant as his primary residence unless the owner or lessor shall have given thirty days notice to the tenant of his intention to commence such action or proceeding on such grounds. [Par 11 am L 1983, ch 403, § 55, L 1984, ch 940, § 3.]

(12) Notwithstanding any other provision of this section, nothing shall prevent the declaration of an emergency pursuant to section three of this act for rental housing accommodations located in buildings or structures which are subject to the provisions of article eighteen of the private housing finance law. [Added L 1985, ch 67, § 5]

§ 6. Regulation of rents. a. Notwithstanding the provisions of any lease or other rental agreement, no owner shall, on or after the first day of the first month or other rental period following a declaration of emergency pursuant to section three, which date shall be referred to in this act as the local effective date, charge or collect any rent in excess of the initial legal regulated rent or adjusted initial legal regulated rent until such time as a different legal regulated rent shall be authorized pursuant to guidelines adopted by a rent guidelines board pursuant to section four.

b. The initial legal regulated rents for housing accommodations in a city having a population of less than one million or a town or village as to which a declaration of emergency has been made pursuant to this act shall be:

(1) For housing accommodations subject to the emergency housing rent control law which become vacant on or after the local effective date of this act, the rent agreed to by the landlord and the tenant and reserved in a lease or provided for in a rental agreement; provided that such initial legal regulated rent may be adjusted on applica-

Tenant Protection Act

tion of the owner or tenant pursuant to subdivision a of section nine of this act; and provided further that no increase of such initial regulated rent pursuant to annual guidelines adopted by the rent guidelines board shall become effective until the expiration of the first lease or rental agreement taking effect after the local effective date, but in no event before one year from the commencement of such rental agreement.

(2) For all other housing accommodations, the rent reserved in the last effective lease or other rental agreement; provided that an initial rent based upon the rent reserved in a lease or other rental agreement which became effective on or after January first, nineteen hundred seventy-four may be adjusted on application of the tenant pursuant to subdivision b of section nine of this act or on application of either the owner or tenant pursuant to subdivision a of such section; and further provided that if a lease is entered into for such housing accommodations after the local effective date, but before the effective date of the first guidelines applicable to such accommodations, the lease may provide for an adjustment of rent pursuant to such guidelines, to be effective on the first day of the month next succeeding the effective date of such guidelines.

c. The initial legal regulated rents for housing accommodations in a city having a population of one million or more shall be the initial rent established pursuant to the New York city rent stabilization law of nineteen hundred sixty-nine as amended.

d. Provision shall be made pursuant to regulations under this act for individual adjustment of rents where:

(1) the owner and tenant by mutual voluntary agreement, subject to approval by the state division of housing and community renewal, agree to a substantial modification of dwelling space, or a change in the services, furniture, furnishing, or equipment provided in the housing accommodations, or

(2) there has been since January first, nineteen hundred seventy-four an increase in the rental value of the housing accommodations as a result of a substantial rehabilitation of the building or the housing accommodation therein which materially adds to the value of the

property or appreciably prolongs its life, excluding ordinary repairs, maintenance, and replacements, or

(3) there has been since January first, nineteen hundred seventy-four a major capital improvement required for the operation, preservation or maintenance of the structure, or [where]

(4) an owner by application to the state division of housing and community renewal for increases in the rents in excess of the rent adjustment authorized by the rent guidelines board under this act establishes a hardship, and the state division finds that the rate of rent adjustment is not sufficient to enable the owner to maintain approximately the same ratio between operating expenses, including taxes and labor costs but excluding debt service, financing costs, and management fees, and gross rents which prevailed on the average over the immediate preceding five year period, or for the entire life of the building if less than five years, or

(5) as an alternative to the hardship application provided under paragraph four of this subdivision, owners of buildings acquired by the same owner or a related entity owned by the same principals three years prior to the date of application may apply to the division for increases in excess of the level of applicable guideline increases established under this law based on a finding by the commissioner that such guideline increases are not sufficient to enable the owner to maintain an annual gross rent income for such building which exceeds the annual operating expenses of such building by a sum equal to at least five percent of such gross rent. For the purposes of this paragraph, operating expenses shall consist of the actual, reasonable, costs of fuel, labor, utilities, taxes, other than income or corporate franchise taxes, fees, permits, necessary contracted services and non-capital repairs, insurance, parts and supplies, management fees and other administrative costs and mortgage interest. For the purposes of this paragraph, mortgage interest shall be deemed to mean interest on a bona fide mortgage including an allocable portion of charges related thereto. Criteria to be considered in determining a bona fide mortgage other than an institutional mortgage shall include; condition of the property, location of the property, the existing

mortgage market at the time the mortgage is placed, the term of the mortgage, the amortization rate, the principal amount of the mortgage, security and other terms and conditions of the mortgage. The commissioner shall set a rental value for any unit occupied by the owner or a person related to the owner or unoccupied at the owner's choice for more than one month at the last regulated rent plus the minimum number of guidelines increases or, if no such regulated rent existed or is known, the commissioner shall impute a rent consistent with other rents in the building. The amount of hardship increase shall be such as may be required to maintain the annual gross rent income as provided by this paragraph. The division shall not grant a hardship application under this paragraph or paragraph four of this subdivision for a period of three years subsequent to granting a hardship application under the provisions of this paragraph. The collection of any increase in the rent for any housing accommodation pursuant to this paragraph shall not exceed six percent in any year from the effective date of the order granting the increase over the rent set forth in the schedule of gross rents, with collectability of any dollar excess above said sum to be spread forward in similar increments and added to the rent as established or set in future years. No application shall be approved unless the owner's equity in such building exceeds five percent of: (i) the arms length purchase price of the property; (ii) the cost of any capital improvements for which the owner has not collected a surcharge; (iii) any repayment of principal of any mortgage or loan used to finance the purchase of the property or any capital improvements for which the owner has not collected a surcharge; and (iv) any increase in the equalized assessed value of the property which occurred subsequent to the first valuation of the property after purchase by the owner. For the purposes of this paragraph, owner's equity shall mean the sum of (i) the purchase price of the property less the principal of any mortgage or loan used to finance the purchase of the property, (ii) the cost of any capital improvement for which the owner has not collected a surcharge less the principal of any mortgage or loan used to finance said improvement, (iii) any repayment of the principal of any mortgage or loan used to finance the purchase of the property or any capital improvement for which the owner has not collected a surcharge, and (iv) any increase in the equalized assessed value of the property which occurred subsequent to the first valuation of the property after purchase by the owner.

This subdivision shall apply to accommodations outside a city of one million or more. [Subd d, am L 1983, ch 403, § 55-a, effective June 30, 1983, Amd L 1984, ch 102 § 1, eff April 1, 1984]

e. Notwithstanding any contrary provisions of this act, on and after July first, nineteen hundred eighty-four the legal regulated rent shall be the rent registered pursuant to section twelve-a of this act subject to any modification imposed pursuant to this act. [Added L 1983, ch 403, § 2, eff April 1, 1984]

§ 7. **Maintenance of services.** a. In order to collect a rent adjustment authorized pursuant to the provisions of subdivision b of section four, the owner of housing accommodations subject to this act located in a city having a population of less than one million or a town or village must file with the state division of housing and community renewal on a form which it shall prescribe, a written certification that he is maintaining and will continue to maintain all services furnished on the date upon which this act becomes a law or required to be furnished by any law, ordinance or regulation applicable to the premises. In addition to any other remedy afforded by law, any tenant may apply to the state division of housing and community renewal for a reduction in the rent to the level in effect prior to its most recent adjustment, and the state division of housing and community renewal may so reduce the rent if it finds that the owner has failed to maintain such services. The owner shall be supplied with a copy of the application and shall be permitted to file an answer thereto. A hearing may be held upon the request of either party, or the state division of housing and community renewal may hold a hearing upon its own motion. The state division of housing and community renewal may consolidate the proceedings for two or more petitions applicable to the same building. If the state division of housing and community renewal finds that the owner has knowingly filed a false certification, it shall, in addition to abating the rent, assess the owner with the reasonable costs of the proceeding, including reasonable attorneys' fees, and impose a penalty not in excess of two hundred fifty dollars for each false certification.

b. In order to collect a rent adjustment authorized pursuant to the provisions of subdivision c of section four, the owner of housing accommodations located in a city having a population of more than one million shall comply with the requirements with respect to the maintenance of services of the New York city rent stabilization law of nineteen hundred sixty-nine.

§ 8. Administration. a. Whenever a city having a population of less than one million, or a town or village has determined the existence of an emergency pursuant to section three of this act, the state division of housing and community renewal shall be designated as the sole administrative agency to administer the regulation of residential rents as provided in this act. The costs incurred by the state division of housing and community renewal in administering such regulation shall be paid by such city, town or village. Such local resolution shall forthwith be transmitted to the state division of housing and community renewal and shall be accompanied by an initial payment in an amount previously determined by the commissioner of housing and community renewal as necessary to defray the division's anticipated first year cost. Thereafter, annually, after the close of the fiscal year of the state, the commissioner of housing and community renewal shall determine the amount of all costs incurred and shall certify to each such city, town or village its proportionate share of such costs, after first deducting therefrom the amount of such initial payment. The amount so certified shall be paid to the commissioner by such city, town or village within ninety days after the receipt of such certification. In the event that the amount thereof is not paid to the commissioner as herein prescribed, the commissioner shall certify the unpaid amount to the comptroller, and the comptroller shall withhold such amount from the next succeeding payment of per capita assistance to be apportioned to such city, town or village.

b. The legislative body of any city, or of any town or village acting to impose regulation of residential rents pursuant to the provisions of this act may impose on the owner of every building containing housing accommodations subject to such regulation an annual charge for each such accommodation in such amount as it determines to be necessary for the expenses to be incurred in the administration of such regulation.

c. Whenever a city having a population of one million or more has determined the existence of an emergency pursuant to section three of this act, the provisions of this act and the New York city rent stabilization law of nineteen hundred sixty-nine shall be administered by the state division of housing and community renewal as provided in the New York city rent stabilization law of nineteen hundred sixty-nine, as amended, or as otherwise provided by law. The costs incurred by the state division of housing and community renewal in administering such regulation shall be paid by such city. All payments for such administration shall be transmitted to the state division of housing and community renewal as follows: on or after April first of each year commencing with April, nineteen hundred eighty-four, the commissioner of housing and community renewal shall determine an amount necessary to defray the division's anticipated annual cost, and one-quarter of such amount shall be paid by such city on or before July first of such year, one-quarter of such amount on or before October first of such year, one-quarter of such amount on or before January first of the following year and one-quarter of such amount on or before March thirty-first of the following year. After the close of the fiscal year of the state, the commissioner shall determine the amount of all actual costs incurred in such fiscal year and shall certify such amount to such city. If such certified amount shall differ from the amount paid by the city for such fiscal year, appropriate adjustments shall be made in the next quarterly payment to be made by such city. In the event that the amount thereof is not paid to the commissioner as herein prescribed, the commissioner shall certify the unpaid amount to the comptroller, and the comptroller shall, to the extent not otherwise prohibited by law, withhold such amount from

Tenant Protection Act

the next succeeding payment of per capita assistance to be apportioned to such city. In no event shall the amount imposed on the owners or certified by the division to the city exceed ten dollars per unit per year. [Am L 1983, ch 403, § 3, eff April 1, 1984]

d. The failure to pay the prescribed assessment not to exceed ten dollars per unit for any housing accommodation subject to this act or the New York city rent stabilization law of nineteen hundred sixty-nine shall, until such assessment is paid, bar an owner from applying for or collecting any further rent increases. The late payment of the assessment shall result in the prospective elimination of such sanctions. The city of New York shall certify to the division such information as the division shall deem necessary to comply with the provisions of this subdivision. [Am L 1983, ch 403 § 3]

e. The division shall maintain at least one office in each county which is governed by the rent stabilization law of nineteen hundred sixty-nine or this act. [Am L 1983, ch 403 § 3, eff April 1, 1984]

§ 9. Application for adjustment of initial legal regulated rent. a. The owner or tenant of a housing accommodation described in paragraph one or two of subdivision b of section six may, within sixty days of the local effective date of this act or the commencement of the first tenancy thereafter, whichever is later, file with the state division of housing and community renewal an application for adjustment of the initial legal regulated rent for such housing accommodation. The state division of housing and community renewal may adjust such initial legal regulated rent upon a finding that the presence of unique or peculiar circumstances materially affecting the initial legal regulated rent has resulted in a rent which is substantially different from the rents generally prevailing in the same area for substantially similar housing accommodations.

b. The tenant of a housing accommodation described in paragraph two, subdivision b, of section six may file with the state division of housing and community renewal, within ninety days after notice has been received pursuant to subdivision c of this section, an application for adjustment of the initial legal regulated rent for such housing accommodation. Such tenant need only allege that such rent is in excess of the fair market rent and shall present such facts which, to the best of his information and belief, support such allegation. The rent guidelines board shall promulgate as soon as practicable after its creation guidelines for the determination of fair market rents for housing accommodations as to which an application may be made pursuant to this subdivision. In rendering a determination on an application filed pursuant to this subdivision b, the state division of housing and community renewal shall be guided by such guidelines. Where the state division of housing and community renewal has determined that the rent charged is in excess of the fair market rent it shall order a refund, of any excess paid since January first, nineteen hundred seventy-four or the date of the commencement of the tenancy, whichever is later. Such refund shall be made by the landlord in cash or as a credit against future rents over a period not in excess of six months.

c. Upon receipt of any application filed pursuant to this section nine, the state division of housing and community renewal shall notify the owner or tenant, as the case may be, and provide a copy to him of such application. Such owner or tenant shall be afforded a reasonable opportunity to respond to the application. A hearing may be held upon the request of either party, or the division may hold a hearing on its own motion. The division shall issue a written opinion to both the tenant and the owner upon rendering its determination.

d. Within thirty days after the local effective date of this act the owner of housing accommodations described in paragraph two of subdivision b of section six, as to which an emergency has been declared pursuant to this act, shall give notice in writing by certified mail to the tenant of each such housing accommodation on a form prescribed by the state division of housing and community renewal of the initial legal regulated rent for such housing accommodation and of such tenant's right to file an application for adjustment of the initial legal regulated rent of such housing accommodation.

e. The initial legal regulated rents for housing accommodations in a city having a population of one million or more shall be subject to adjustment in accordance with the provisions of the New York city rent stabilization law as amended.

§ 10. Regulations. a. For cities having a population of less than one million and towns and villages, the state division of housing and community renewal shall be empowered to implement this act by appropriate regulations. Such regulations may encompass such speculative or manipulative practices or renting or leasing practices as the state division of housing and community renewal determines constitute or are likely to cause circumvention of this act. Such regulations shall prohibit practices which are likely to prevent any person from asserting any right or remedy granted by this act, including but not limited to retaliatory termination of periodic tenancies, and shall require owners to grant a new one or two year vacancy or renewal lease at the option of the tenant, except where a mortgage or mortgage commitment existing as of the local effective date of this act provides that the owner shall not grant a one-year lease; and shall prescribe standards with respect to the terms and conditions of new and renewal leases, additional rent and such related matters as security deposits, advance rental payments, the use of escalator clauses in leases and provision for increase in rentals for garages and other ancillary facilities, so as to insure that the level of rent adjustments authorized under this law will not be subverted and made ineffective. Any provision of the regulations permitting an owner to refuse to renew a lease on grounds that the owner seeks to recover possession of the housing accommodation for his own use and occupancy or for the use and occupancy of his immediate family shall require that an owner demonstrate immediate and compelling need and shall not apply where a member of the housing accommodation is sixty-two years of age or older, has been a tenant in a housing accommodation in that building for twenty years or more, or has an impairment which results from anatomical, physiological or psychological conditions, other than addiction to alcohol, gambling, or any controlled substance, which are demonstrable by medically acceptable clinical and laboratory diagnostic techniques, and which are expected to be permanent and which prevent the tenant from engaging in any substantial gainful employment. [Subd a Am L 1983, Ch 403, § 56, applicable to leases and renewals commencing on and after October 1, 1983. The concluding sentence of subd a of § 10 was added by L 1984, ch 234, § 3; shall take effect June 19, 1984, shall apply to any tenant in possession at or after the time it takes effect regardless of whether the landlord's application for an order, refusal to renew a lease or refusal to extend or renew a tenancy took place before June 19, 1984; and this amendment shall expire on the same date as the Emergency Tenant Protection Act shall expire, and shall not affect the expiration of such Law as enacted by L 1974, ch 576, as last extended by L 1983, ch 403.]

b. For cities having a population of one million or more, this act may be implemented by regulations adopted pursuant to the New York city rent stabilization law of nineteen hundred sixty-nine, as amended, or as otherwise provided by law.

c. Each owner of premises subject to this act shall furnish to each tenant signing a new or renewal lease, a copy of the fully executed new or renewal lease bearing the signatures of owner and tenant and the beginning and ending dates of the lease term, within thirty days from the owner's receipt of the new or renewal lease signed by the tenant. [Subd c, added 1984, ch 439, eff July 19, 1984, shall apply to all new or renewal leases subject to the Emergency Tenant Protection Act of 1974, or the Rent Stabilization Law, bearing the signature of the tenant which are received by the owner on or after July 19, 1984.]

§ 10-a. Right to sublease.

Units subject to this law may be sublet pursuant to section two hundred twenty-six-b of the real property law provided that (a) the rental charged to the subtenant does not exceed the legal regulated rent plus a ten percent surcharge payable to the tenant if the unit sublet was furnished with the tenant's furniture; (b) the tenant can establish that at all times he has maintained the unit as his primary residence and intends to occupy it as such at the expiration of the sublease; (c) an owner may terminate the tenancy of a tenant who sublets or assigns contrary to the terms of this section but no action or proceeding based on the non-primary residence of a tenant may be commenced prior to the expiration date of his lease; (d) where an apartment is sublet the prime tenant shall retain the right to a renewal lease and the rights and status of a tenant in occupancy as they relate to conversion to condominium or cooperative ownership; (e) where a tenant violates the provisions of subdivision (a) of this section the subtenant shall be entitled to damages of three times the overcharge and may also be awarded attorneys fees and interest from the date of the overcharge at the rate of interest payable on a judgment pursuant to section five thousand four of the civil practice law and rules; (f) the tenant may not sublet the unit for more than a total of two years, including the term of the proposed sublease, out of the four-year period preceding the termination date of the proposed sublease. The provisions of this subdivision (f) shall only apply to subleases commencing on and after July first, nineteen hundred eighty-three; (g) for the purposes of this section only, the term of the proposed sublease may extend beyond the term of the tenant's lease. In such event, such sublease shall be subject to the tenant's right to a renewal lease. The subtenant shall have no right to a renewal lease. It shall be unreasonable for an owner to refuse to consent to a sublease solely because such sublease extends beyond the tenant's lease; and (h) notwithstanding the provisions of section two hundred twenty-six-b of the real property law, a non-for-profit hospital shall have the right to sublet any housing accommodation leased by it to its affiliated personnel without requiring the landlord's consent to any such sublease and without being bound by the provisions of subdivisions (b), (c), and (f) of this section. Commencing with the effective date of this subdivision [August 6, 1984], whenever a not-for-profit hospital executes a renewal lease for a housing accommodation, the legal regulated rent shall be increased by a sum equal to fifteen percent of the previous lease rental for such housing accommodation, hereinafter referred to as a vacancy surcharge, unless the landlord shall have received within the seven year period prior to the commencement date of such renewal lease any vacancy increases or vacancy surcharges allocable to the said housing accommodation. In the event the landlord shall have received any such vacancy increases or vacancy surcharges during such seven year period, the vacancy surcharge shall be reduced by the amount received by any such vacancy increase or vacancy surcharges. (§ 10-a added L 1983, ch 403, § 57, eff June 30, 1983; subd (h) added L 1984, ch 940, § 4, eff August 6, 1984, and applicable to all actions and proceedings pending August 6, 1984, or commenced thereafter.)

§ 11. Non-waiver of rights. Any provision of a lease or other rental agreement which purports to waive a tenant's rights under this act or regulations promulgated pursuant thereto shall be void as contrary to public policy.

§ 12. Enforcement and procedures. [Section heading Am L 1984, ch 102, § 2, eff April 1, 1984] a. (1) Subject to the conditions and limitations of this paragraph, any owner of housing accommodations in a city having a population of less than one million or a town or village as to which an emergency has been declared pursuant to section three, who, upon complaint of a tenant or of the state division of housing and community renewal, is found by the state division of housing and community renewal, after a reasonable opportunity to be heard, to have collected an overcharge above the rent authorized for a housing accommodation subject to this act shall be liable to the tenant for a penalty equal to three times the amount of such overcharge. If the owner establishes by a preponderance of the evidence that the overcharge was neither willful nor attributable to his negligence, the state division of housing and community renewal shall establish the penalty as the amount of the overcharge plus interest at the rate of interest payable on a judgment pursuant to section five thousand four of the civil practice law and rules. (i) Except as to complaints filed pursuant to clause (ii) of this paragraph, the legal regulated rent for purposes of determining an overcharge, shall be deemed to be the rent indicated in the annual

Tenant Protection Act

registration statement filed four years prior to the most recent registration statement, (or, if more recently filed, the initial registration statement) plus in each case any subsequent lawful increases and adjustments. (ii) As to complaints filed within ninety days of the initial registration of a housing accommodation, the legal regulated rent for purposes of determining an overcharge shall be deemed to be the rent charged on the date four years prior to the date of the initial registration of the housing accommodation (or, if the housing accommodation was subject to this act for less than four years, the initial legal regulated rent) plus in each case, any lawful increases and adjustments. Where the rent charged on the date four years prior to the date fo the initial registration of the accommodation cannot be established, such rent shall be established by the division.

(a) The order of the state division of housing and community renewal shall apportion the owner's liability between or among two or more tenants found to have been overcharged by such owner during their particular tenancy of a unit.

(b) (i) Except as provided under clauses (ii) and (iii) of this subparagraph, a complaint under this subdivision shall be filed with the state division of housing and community renewal within four years of the first overcharge alleged and no award of the amount of an overcharge may be based upon an overcharge having occurred more than four years before the complaint is filed.

(ii) No penalty of three times the overcharge may be based upon an overcharge having occurred more than two years before the complaint is filed or upon an overcharge which occurred prior to April first, nineteen hundred eighty-four.

(iii) Any complaint based upon overcharges occurring prior to the date of filing of the initial rent registration as provided in subdivision b of section twelve-a of this act shall be filed within ninety days of the mailing of notice to the tenant of such registration.

(c) Any affected tenant shall be notified of and given an opportunity to join in any complaint filed by an officer or employee of the state division of housing and community renewal.

(d) An owner found to have overcharged shall, in all cases, be assessed the reasonable costs and attorney's fees of the proceeding, and interest from the date of the overcharge at the rate of interest payable on a judgment pursuant to section five thousand four of the civil practice law and rules.

(e) The order of the state division of housing and community renewal awarding penalties may, upon the expiration of the period in which the owner may institute a proceeding pursuant to article seventy-eight of the civil practice law and rules, be filed and enforced by a tenant in the same manner as a judgment or, in the alternative, not in excess of twenty percent thereof per month may be offset against any rent thereafter due the owner.

(f) Unless a tenant shall have filed a complaint of overcharge with the division which complaint has not been withdrawn, nothing contained in this section shall be deemed to prevent a tenant or tenants, claiming to have been overcharged, from commencing an action or interposing a counterclaim in a court of competent jurisdiction for damages equal to the overcharge and the penalty provided for in this section, including interest from the date of the overcharge at the rate of interest payable on a judgment pursuant to section five thousand four of the civil practice law and rules, plus the statutory costs and allowable disbursements in connection with the proceeding. Such action must be commenced or counterclaim interposed within four years of the date of the alleged overcharge but no recovery of three times the amount of the overcharge may be awarded with respect to any overcharge which had occurred more than two years before the action is commenced or counterclaim is interposed.

(2) In addition to issuing the specific orders provided for by other provisions of this act, the state division of housing and community renewal shall be empowered to enforce this act and its regulations by issuing, upon notice and a reasonable opportunity for the affected party to be heard, such other orders as it may deem appropriate.

(3) If the owner is found by the commissioner:

(i) to have violated an order of the division the commis-

Tenant Protection Act

sioner may impose by administrative order after hearing, a civil penalty in the amount of two hundred fifty dollars for the first such offense and one thousand dollars for each subsequent offense; or

(ii) to have harassed a tenant to obtain vacancy of his housing accommodation, the commissioner may impose by administrative order after hearing, a civil penalty for any such violation. Such penalty shall be in the amount of up to one thousand dollars for a first such offense and up to twenty-five hundred dollars for each subsequent offense or for a violation consisting of conduct directed at the tenants of more than one housing accommodation.

Such order shall be deemed a final determination for the purposes of judicial review. Such penalty may, upon the expiration of the period for seeking review pursuant to article seventy-eight of the civil practice law and rules, be docketed and enforced in the manner of a judgment of the supreme court.

(4) Any proceeding pursuant to article seventy-eight of the civil practice law and rules seeking review of any action pursuant to this act shall be brought within sixty days. Any action or proceeding brought by or against the commissioner under this act shall be brought in the county in which the housing accommodation is located.

(5) Violations of this act or of the regulations and orders issued pursuant thereto may be enjoined by the supreme court upon proceedings commenced by the state division of housing and community renewal or the tenant or tenants who allege they have been overcharged. The division shall not be required to post bond.

(6) In furtherance of its responsibility to enforce this act, the state division of housing and community renewal shall be empowered to administer oaths, issue subpoenas, conduct investigations, make inspections and designate officers to hear and report. The division shall safeguard the confidentiality of information furnished to it at the request of the person furnishing same, unless such information must be made public in the interest of establishing a record for the future guidance of persons subject to this act.

(7) In any action or proceeding before a court wherein a party relies for a ground of relief or defense or raises

issue or brings into question the construction or validity of this act or any regulation, order or requirement hereunder, the court having jurisdiction of such action or proceeding may at any stage certify such fact to the state division of housing and community renewal. The state division of housing and community renewal may intervene in any such action or proceeding.

(8) Any owner who has duly registered a housing accommodation pursuant to section twelve-a of this act shall not be required to maintain or produce any records relating to rentals of such accommodation more than four years prior to the most recent registration or annual statement for such accommodation.

b. Within a city having a population of one million or more, the state division of housing and community renewal shall have such powers to enforce this act as shall be provided in the New York city rent stabilization law of nineteen hundred sixty-nine, as amended, or as shall otherwise be provided by law. [§ 12 am L 1983, ch 403, § 4, eff April 1, 1984]

c. The state division of housing and community renewal may, by regulation, provide for administrative review of all orders and determinations issued by it pursuant to this act. Any such regulation shall provide that if a petition for such review is not determined within ninety days after it is filed, it shall be deemed to be denied. However, the division may grant one extension not to exceed thirty days with the consent of the party filing such petition; any further extension may only be granted with the consent of all parties to the petition. No proceeding may be brought pursuant to article seventy-eight of the civil practice law and rules to challenge any order or determination which is subject to such administrative review unless such review has been sought and either (1) a determination thereon has been made or (2) the ninety-day period provided for determination of the petition for review (or any extension thereof) has expired. [Subd c added L 1984, ch 102, § 3, eff April 1, 1984]

§ 12-a. Rent registration. a. Each housing accommodation in a city having a population of less than one million or a town or village as to which an emergency has been declared pursuant to section three of this act which is subject to this act shall be registered by the owner thereof with the state division of housing and community renewal prior to July first, nineteen hundred eighty-four upon forms prescribed by the commissioner of such division. The data to be provided on such forms shall include the following: (1) the name and address of the building or group of buildings or development in which such housing accommodation is located and the owner and the tenant thereof; (2) the number of housing accommodations in the building or group of buildings or development in which such housing accommodation is located; (3) the number of housing accommodations in such building or group of buildings or development subject to this act and the number of such housing accommodations subject to the emergency housing rent control law; (4) the rent charged on the registration date; (5) the number of rooms in such housing accommodation; and (6) all services provided in the last lease or rental agreement commencing at least six months prior to the local effective date of this act.

b. Registration pursuant to this section shall not be subject to the freedom of information law, provided that registration information relative to a tenant, owner, lessor or subtenant shall be made available to such party or his authorized representative.

c. Housing accommodations which become subject to this act after the initial registration period must be registered within ninety days thereafter. Registration of housing accommodations subject to the emergency housing rent control law immediately prior to the date of filing the initial registration statement as provided in this section shall include, in addition to the items listed above, where existing, the maximum rent immediately prior to the date that such housing accommodations became subject to this act.

d. Copies of the registration shall be filed with the state division of housing and community renewal in such place or places as it may require. In addition, one copy of that portion of the registration statement which pertains to the tenant's unit must be mailed by the owner to the tenant in possession at the time of initial registration or to the first tenant in occupancy if the apartment is vacant at the time of initial registration.

e. The failure to file a proper and timely initial or annual rent registration statement shall, until such time as such registration is filed, bar an owner from applying for or collecting any rent in excess of the legal regulated rent in effect on the date of the last preceding registration statement or if no such statements have been filed, the legal regulated rent in effect on the date that the housing accommodation became subject to the registration requirements of this section. The filing of a late registration shall result in the prospective elimination of such sanctions.

f. An annual statement shall be filed containing the current rent for each unit and such other information contained in subdivision a of this section as shall be required by the division. The owner shall provide each tenant then in occupancy with a copy of that portion of such annual statement as pertains to the tenant's unit.

g. Within a city having a population of one million or more, each housing accommodation subject to this act shall be registered with the state division of housing and community renewal as shall be provided in the New York city rent stabilization law of nineteen hundred sixty-nine. [§ 12-a added L 1983, ch 403, § 5, eff April 1, 1984]

h. Each housing accommodation for which a timely registration statement was filed between April first, nineteen hundred eighty-four and June thirtieth, nineteen hundred eight-four, pursuant to subdivision a of this section shall designate the rent charged on April first, nineteen hundred eighty-four, as the rent charged on the registration date. [Subd h added L 1984, ch 102, § 4, eff April 1, 1984]

§ 13. Cooperation with other governmental agencies. The state division of housing and community renewal and any rent guidelines board may request and shall receive cooperation and assistance in effectuating the purposes of this act from all departments, divisions, boards, bureaus, commissions or agencies of the state and political subdivisions thereof. [Am L 1983, ch 403, § 6, eff April 1, 1984]

§ 14. Application of act. The provisions of this act shall only be applicable:

a. in the city of New York; and

b. in the counties of Nassau, Westchester and Rockland and shall become and remain effective only in a city, town or village located therein as provided in section three of this act.

Outside of N.Y.C.
(Rent Stabilization)

STATE TENANT PROTECTION REGULATIONS

[Section numbers refer to the designation of these Regulations as published in the State of New York Official Compilation of Codes, Rules and Regulations, Vol. 9, Executive (C), Subtitle S Housing, Chapter 8, Part 2500. Section numbers in parentheses refer to the unofficial numerical designation of these Regulations.]

PART 2500 SCOPE

§ 2500.1 (§ 1) Statutory Authority

These Regulations are adopted and promulgated pursuant to the powers granted to the State Division of Housing and Community Renewal by the Emergency Tenant Protection Act of Nineteen Seventy-four, Chapter 576 of the Laws of New York for the year 1974, as amended by Chapter 486, Laws of 1976, Chapter 203, Laws of 1977, Chapter 383, Laws of 1981, Chapter 403, Laws of 1983, Chapter 102, Laws of 1984, and Chapter 234, Laws of 1984. As used in these Regulations the term "Act" shall mean the Emergency Tenant Protection Act of Nineteen Seventy-four.

§ 2500.2 (§ 2) Definitions. When used in these Regulations, unless a different meaning clearly appears from the context, the following terms shall mean and include:

(a) "Division." The State Division of Housing and Community Renewal.

(b) "County Rent Guidelines Board." The board created in each county pursuant to the Emergency Tenant Protection Act of 1974 to establish annually guidelines for rent adjustments under the Act and these Regulations.

(c) "Housing accommodation." Any building or structure, permanent or temporary, or any part thereof, occupied or intended to be occupied by one or more individuals as a residence, home, sleeping place, boarding house, lodging house or hotel, together with the land and buildings appurtenant thereto, and all services, privileges, furnishings, furniture and facilities supplied in connection with the occupation thereof.

(d) "Rent." Consideration, including any bonus, benefit or gratuity demanded or received for or in connection with the use or occupancy of housing accommodations or the transfer of a lease of such housing accommodations.

(e) "Legal regulated rent." The lawful rent for the use of housing accommodations. Under the Emergency Tenant Protection Act of 1974 rents may be formulated in terms of rents and other charges and allowances.

(f) "Person." An individual, corporation, partnership, association, or any other organized group of individuals or the legal successor or representative of any of the foregoing.

(g) "Landlord." An owner, lessor, sublessor, assignee, proprietary lessee of a housing accommodation in a structure or premises owned by a cooperative corporation or association, or other person receiving or entitled to receive rent for the use or occupancy of any housing accommodation or an agent of any of the foregoing.

(h) "Tenant." A tenant, sub-tenant, lessee, sub-lessee, or other person entitled to the possession or to the use or occupancy of any housing accommodation.

(i) "Documents." Records, books, accounts, correspondence, memoranda and other documents, and drafts and copies of any of the foregoing.

(j) "Municipality." A city, town or village.

(k) "Local legislative body."

(1) In the case of a city, the council, common council or board of aldermen and the board of estimate, board of apportionment or board of estimate and contract, if there be one.

(2) In the case of a town, the town board.

(3) In the case of a village, the board of trustees.

(l) "Final order." An order shall be deemed to be final on the date of its issuance.

(m) "Immediate family." Husband, wife, son, daughter, grandson, granddaughter, stepson, stepdaughter, father, mother, father-in-law, mother-in-law, grandfather, grandmother, stepfather or stepmother.

§ 2500.3 (§ 3) Additional definitions.

(a) "Commissioner." The Commissioner of Housing and Community Renewal.

(b) "Office of Rent Administration." The office of the Division of Housing and Community Renewal designated by the Commissioner of Housing and Community Renewal to administer the Emergency Tenant Protection Act of 1974 under these Regulations.

(c) "District Rent Administration Office." The office of the Division for a particular rent area as set forth in Section 2500.8. The Division shall maintain at least one such office in each county subject to the Act.

(d) "Essential services." Those services which the landlord was maintaining, or which he was obligated to maintain, on May 29, 1974. These may include, for example, any or all of the following: repairs, decorating and maintenance, the furnishing of light, heat, hot and cold water, telephone, elevator service, janitor service, removal of refuse, and garage and parking facilities.

(e) "Apartment." A room or rooms providing facilities commonly regarded in the community as necessary for a self-contained family unit but not including housing accommodations located in a rooming house or hotel.

§ 2500.4 (§ 4) Effective date and local effective date.

(a) These Regulations shall become effective May 29, 1974, the effective date of the Act, and all amendments to these regulations shall be effective on the effective date of such amendments.

(b) These Regulations shall apply to housing accommodations on the local effective date for the city, town, or village wherein the housing accommodations are situated. Such local effective date shall be the first day of the month, or the first rent payment date following the declaration of an emergency by the local legislative body of the city, town or village wherein the housing accommodations are situated.

§ 2500.5 (§ 5) Amendment or revocation. Any provision of these Regulations may be amended or revoked at any time by the Division.

§ 2500.6 (§ 6) Filing of amendments. Such amendment or revocation shall be filed with the Secretary of State

TENANT PROTECTION REGULATIONS

and shall take effect upon the date of filing unless otherwise specified therein.

§ 2500.7 (§ 7) Separability. If any provision of these Regulations or the application of such provisions to any persons or circumstances shall be held invalid, the validity of the remainder of these Regulations and the applicability of such provisions to other persons or circumstances shall not be affected thereby.

§ 2500.8 (§ 8) Local areas subject to control. Except as hereinafter provided in Section 2500.9 of these Regulations, these Regulations shall apply to housing accommodations located in the counties of Nassau, Rockland and Westchester, which are subject to the Emergency Tenant Protection Act of 1974 pursuant to a determination of the existence of an emergency thereunder by the local legislative body of the city, town or village wherein the accommodations are situated. Notwithstanding the above, until the Rent Stabilization Code and Hotel Stabilization Code applicable to New York City are amended to implement the provisions of Chapters 102, 439 and 940 of the Laws of 1984 and Chapter 403 of the Laws of 1983, Sections 2502.4(d), 2502.5(c)(9), 2504.4(d) except as to the filing requirements, 2505.7, 2506.1, 2506.2(c), 2507, 2508, 2509 and 2510 of these Regulations shall also apply to those housing accommodations subject to the provisions of Title YY of the Administrative Code of the City of New York.

§ 2500.9 (§ 9) Housing accommodations subject to regulation. These Regulations shall apply to all or any class or classes of housing accommodations in a city, town or village for which a declaration of emergency has been made except the following:

(a) housing accommodations subject to the emergency housing rent control law;

(b) housing accommodations owned or operated by the United States, the state of New York, any political subdivision, agency or instrumentality thereof, any municipality or any public housing authority;

(c) housing accommodations in buildings in which rentals are fixed by or subject to the supervision of the state division of housing and community renewal under other provisions of law or the New York state urban development corporation, or, to the extent that regulation under this Act is inconsistent therewith aided by government insurance under any provision of the National Housing Act;

(d)(1) housing accommodations in a building containing fewer than six dwelling units;

(2) for purposes of this paragraph (d), a building shall be deemed to contain six or more dwelling units if it is part of a multiple family garden-type maisonette dwelling complex containing six or more dwelling units having common facilities such as a sewer line, water main or heating plant and operated as a unit under common ownership, notwithstanding that certificates of occupancy were issued for portions therefor as one- or two-family dwellings.

(e) housing accommodations in buildings completed or buildings substantially rehabilitated as family units on or after January first, nineteen hundred seventy-four;

(f) housing accommodations owned or operated by a hospital, convent, monastery, asylum, public institution, or college or school dormitory or any institution operated exclusively for charitable or educational purposes on a non-profit basis other than accommodations occupied by a tenant on the date such housing accommodation is acquired by such institution, or which are occupied subsequently by a tenant who is not affiliated with such institution at the time of his initial occupancy;

(g) rooms or other housing accommodations in hotels;

(h) any motor court, or any part thereof, any trailer, or trailer space used exclusively for transient occupancy or any part thereof; or any tourist home serving transient guests exclusively, or any part thereof;

(1) The term "motor court" shall mean an establishment renting rooms, cottages or cabins, supplying parking or storage facilities for motor vehicles in connection with such renting and other services and facilities customarily supplied by such establishments, and commonly known as motor, auto or tourist court in the community.

(2) The term "tourist home" shall mean a rooming housing which caters primarily to transient guests and is known as a tourist home in the community.

(i) non-housekeeping, furnished housing accommodations, located within a single dwelling unit not used as a rooming or boarding house, but only if:

(1) no more than two tenants for whom rent is paid (husband and wife being considered one tenant for this purpose), not members of the landlord's immediate family, live in such dwelling unit, and

(2) the remaining portion of such dwelling unit is occupied by the landlord or his immediate family.

(j) housing accommodations in buildings operated exclusively for charitable purposes on a non-profit basis;

(k) housing accommodations which are not occupied by the tenant in possession as his primary residence.

§ 2500.10 (§ 10) Effect of these Regulations on leases and other rental agreements. The provisions of any lease or other rental agreement shall remain in force pursuant to the terms thereof, except insofar as those provisions are inconsistent with the Act or the Regulations.

§ 2500.11 (§ 11) Receipt for rent paid. No payment of rent need be made unless the landlord tenders a receipt for the amount to be paid when so requested by a tenant.

§ 2500.12 (§ 12) Waiver of benefit void. An agreement by the tenant to waive the benefit of any provision of the Act or these Regulations is void.

PART 2501 LEGAL REGULATED RENTS

§ 2501.1 (§ 21) Initial legal regulated rents for housing accommodations.

(a) For housing accommodations which on the local effective date of the Act were under rent control pursuant to the Emergency Housing Rent Control Law, and on or after that date become vacant and are no longer under rent control, and which are rented thereafter and subject to the Act, the initial legal regulated rent shall be the rent agreed to by the landlord and the tenant and reserved in a lease or provided for in a rental agreement.

(b) For all other housing accommodations subject to the Act, the initial legal regulated rent shall be the rent reserved in the last effective lease or other rental agreement prior to the local effective date of the Act.

§ 2501.2 (§ 22) Legal regulated rents for housing accommodations. The legal regulated rent shall be the initial legal regulated rent first established pursuant to section 2501.1, and thereafter shall be the said initial legal regulated rent as it may be adjusted pursuant to the Act and these Regulations, provided, however, that on or after July first, 1984, the legal regulated rent for any housing accommodation registered pursuant to Part 2509 of these Regulations shall be the registered rent subject to any modification made pursuant to the Act or these Regulations.

§ 2501.3 (§ 23) Redetermination of initial legal regulated rent which includes payments reserved under a tax escalation clause for housing accommodations located in a property becoming subject to reduction of real property taxes.

Where the initial legal regulated rent for a housing accommodation includes payments reserved in the lease or other rental agreement under a tax escalation clause, whenever there is a reduction in the amounts of increases in the real property taxes which were previously in effect, the initial legal regulated rent shall be subject to redetermination to exclude such payments or such part thereof as is warranted, as provided for in sections 2503.9 and 2503.10 of these Regulations.

PART 2502 ADJUSTMENTS

§ 2502.1 (§ 31) Legal regulated rents. Legal regulated rents may be increased or decreased only as hereinafter specified.

§ 2502.2 (§ 32) Effective date of adjustment of rents. The legal regulated rent shall be adjusted effective the date of issuance of an order by the Division, unless otherwise set forth in the order, or on the effective date of a lease or other rental agreement providing for the Rent Guidelines Board annual rate of adjustment as filed with the Division and as provided for in section 2502.5.

§ 2502.3 (§ 33) Application for adjustment of initial legal regulated rent.

TENANT PROTECTION REGULATIONS

(a) Fair market rent. (1) The tenant of a housing accommodation for which the initial legal regulated rent was established under section 2501.1(b) based upon the rent reserved in a lease or other rental agreement which became effective on or after January 1, 1974 may file within ninety days after notice has been received pursuant to section 2503.1 an application, on forms prescribed by the Division, for adjustment of the initial legal regulated rent on the allegation that such rent is in excess of the fair market rent and presenting facts which to the best of his information and belief support such allegation.
(2) The Division shall be guided by guidelines promulgated by the Rent Guidelines Board for the determination of fair market rents and upon a determination that the initial legal regulated rent is in excess of the fair market rent, shall establish by order a new legal regulated rent, and further order a refund of any excess rent paid since January 1, 1974 or the date of the commencement of the tenancy, whichever is later, provided that no refund order shall relate to a period more than two years prior to the local effective date as defined in section 2500.4. The order shall direct the landlord to make the refund of any excess rent to the tenant in cash or as a credit against future rents over a period not in excess of six months, and that if the landlord does not make the refund, that the order may be enforced or the rent offset by the tenant in the same manner as a Division order awarding penalties pursuant to section 2506.1(e).

(b) Unique or peculiar circumstances. (1) The landlord or tenant of a housing accommodation described in section 2501.1(a) and 2501.1(b) may, within 60 days of the local effective date of the Act or the commencement of the first tenancy thereafter, file an application on forms prescribed by the Division to adjust the initial legal regulated rent on the grounds that the presence of unique or peculiar circumstances materially affecting the legal regulated rent has resulted in a rent which is substantially different from the rents generally prevailing in the same area for substantially similar housing accommodations.
(2) The Division may grant an appropriate adjustment of the initial legal regulated rent upon finding that such

grounds do exist, provided that the adjustment shall not result in a legal regulated rent substantially different from the rents generally prevailing in the same area for substantially similar housing accommodations.

§ 2502.4 (§ 34) Applications for adjustment of legal regulated rent.

(a) Any landlord may file an application to increase the legal regulated rent otherwise allowable, on forms prescribed by the Division, on one or more of the following grounds:

(1) Increased service or facilities, substantial rehabilitation, or major capital improvements.

(2) The Division may grant an appropriate adjustment of a legal regulated rent where it finds that:

(i) The landlord and tenant by mutual voluntary agreement, subject to approval by the Division, agree to a substantial increase of dwelling space or an increase in the services, furniture, furnishings or equipment provided in the housing accommodations; which agreement may be established by the signatures of landlord and tenant on the prescribed application form or by corroborative proof of such earlier agreement.

(ii) there has been since January 1, 1974, an increase in the rental value of the housing accommodations as a result of a substantial rehabilitation of the building or housing accommodations therein which materially adds to the value of the property or appreciably prolongs its life, excluding ordinary repairs, maintenance and replacements; and that the legal regulated rent has not been adjusted prior to the application based in whole or part upon the grounds set forth in the application; or

(iii) there has been since January 1, 1974 a major capital improvement required for the operation, preservation or maintenance of the structure; and that the legal regulated rent has not been adjusted prior to the application based in whole or part upon the grounds set forth in the application.

(iv) The Division, in determining the amount or rate of appropriate adjustment of a legal regulated rent shall take into consideration all factors bearing on the equities involved, subject to the general limitation that the adjustment can be put into effect without dislocation and hardship inconsistent with the purposes of the Act, and including as a factor a return of the actual cost to the landlord, exclusive of interest or other carrying charges, and the increase in the rental value of the housing accommodations.

(v) No adjustment of a legal regulated rent shall be granted for the replacement of equipment required to be maintained in the housing accommodations under the Act or these Regulations, unless the landlord has entered a mutual voluntary agreement to such an adjustment with the tenant as provided for in paragraph (a)(2)(i) of this section.

(b) Any landlord may file an application to decrease the legal regulated rent on forms prescribed by the Division on the ground that the landlord and tenant by mutual voluntary agreement, subject to the approval of the Division, agree to a substantial decrease in dwelling space, or a decrease in the services, furniture, furnishings or equipment provided in the housing accommodations, or that such decrease in required for the operation of the building in accordance with the requirements of law.

(c) Comparative hardship. The Division may grant an appropriate adjustment of the legal regulated rent where the landlord by application for increases in rents in excess of the rent adjustment authorized by the Rent Guidelines Board under the Act and as provided for in section 2502.5 establishes a hardship, and the Division finds that the rate of such rent adjustment is not sufficient to enable the owner to maintain approximately the same ratio between operating expenses (including taxes, and labor costs but excluding debt service, financing costs, and management fees) and gross rents which prevailed on the average over the immediate preceding five year period, or for the entire life of the building if less than five years. No application may be made under this subdivision for an increase if a six percent increase is still in effect based on an application pursuant to this subdivision or pursuant to subdivision (d).

(d) Alternative hardship. As an alternative to the hardship application provided under subdivision (c) of this section, owners of buildings acquired by the same owner or a related entity owned by the same principals three years prior to the date of application may apply to the Division on forms prescribed by the Division for increases in excess of the level of applicable guideline increases established under the Act based on a finding by the Division that such guideline increases are not sufficient to enable the owner to maintain an annual gross rent income collectible for such building which exceeds the annual operating expenses of such building by a sum equal to at least five percent of such annual gross rent income collectible subject to the definitions and restrictions provided for herein.

(1) Definitions.

For this subdivision (d), the following terms shall mean:

a) "Annual Gross Rent Income Collectible"—the actual income receivable per annum arising out of the operation and ownership of the property, including but not limited to rental from housing accommodations, stores, professional or business use, garages, parking spaces, and income from easements or air rights, washing machines, vending machines, and signs plus the rent calculated under paragraph (2) (c) of this subdivision. In ascertaining income receivable, the Division shall determine what efforts, if any, the owner has followed in collecting unpaid rent.

b) "Operating Expenses"—shall consist of the actual, reasonable costs of fuel, labor, utilities, taxes (other than income or corporate franchise taxes), fees (including attorney's fees for services rendered during the test year not related to refinancing of mortgage) permits, necessary contracted services and repairs for which an owner is not eligible for an increase pursuant to Section 2502.4 of these Regulations, insurance, parts and supplies, reasonable management fees, mortgage interest, and other reasonable and necessary administrative costs applicable to the operation and maintenance of the property.

Tenant Protection Regulations

c) "Mortgage interest"—shall be deemed to mean interest on a bona fide mortgage including an allocable portion of the charges related thereto. Criteria to be considered in determining a bona fide mortgage other than an institutional mortgage shall include but shall not be limited to the following: the condition of the property, the location of the property, the existing mortgage market at the time the mortgage is placed, the principal amount of the mortgage, the term of the mortgage, the amortization rate, security and other terms and conditions of the mortgage.

d) "Institutional Mortgage"—shall include a mortgage given to any bank, trust company, bank and trust company, savings bank or savings and loan association (any of which may be licensed under the laws of any jurisdiction within the United States), pension funds, credit unions, insurance companies and governmental entities. The Division may determine that any other mortgage is an institutional mortgage in its discretion.

e) "Owner's Equity"—shall mean the sum of (i) the purchase price of the property less the principal of any mortgage or loan used to finance the purchase of the property, (ii) the cost of any capital improvement for which the owner has not collected an increase in rent less the principal of any mortgage or loan used to finance said improvement, (iii) any repayment of the principal of any mortgage or loan used to finance the purchase of the property or any capital improvement for which the owner has not collected an increase in rent, and (iv) any increase in the equalized assessed value of the property which occurred subsequent to the first valuation of the property after purchase by the owner.

f) "Threshold Income"—shall mean that income for such building which exceeds the annual operating expense for such building by a sum equal to five percent of such threshold income.

g) "Test Year"—shall mean any one of the following: (i) the most recent calendar year (January 1st to December 31st) (ii) the most recent fiscal year (one year ending on the last day of a month other than December 31st), provided that books of account are maintained and closed accordingly, (iii) any twelve (12) consecutive months ending within 90 days prior to the date of filing of the hardship application. Such period must end on the last day of a month. Nothing herein shall prevent the Division from comparing and adjusting expenses and income during the Test Year with expenses and income occurring during the three years prior to the date of application in order to determine the reasonableness of such expenses and income.

(2) Restrictions.

a) No owner may file an application nor may the Division grant such owner an increase in excess of the level of applicable guideline increases unless:

(i) the annual gross rent income collectible for the Test Year does not exceed the annual operating expenses of such building by a sum equal to at least five percent of such annual gross rental income collectible; and

(ii) The owner or an entity related to the owner acquired the building at least 36 months prior to the date of application; and

(iii) the owner's equity in the building exceeds five percent of the sum of:

- (a) the arms length purchase price of the property; and
- (b) the cost of any capital improvements for which the owner has not collected an increase in rent pursuant to Section 2502.4(a) of these Regulations; and
- (c) any repayment of principal of any mortgage or loan used to finance the purchase of the property or any capital improvements for which the owner has not collected an increase in rent pursuant to Section 2502.4(a) of these Regulations; and
- (d) any increase in the equalized assessed value of the property which occurred subsequent to the first valuation of the property after purchase by the owner; and

(iv) the building was last granted a hardship increase more than 36 months prior to the date of application provided that no application may be made for any hardship if a six percent increase is still in effect based on a prior application, and

(v) the owner has resolved all legal objections to any real estate taxes and water and sewer charges for the test year;

(b) The Division may, in its discretion, deny an owner an increase as provided, in whole or in part, if the owner is not maintainting all essential services as required by law, or there are violations of record of any municipal, county, state, or federal law to his knowledge which relates to the maintenance of such services. Any increase granted herein may be conditioned or revoked upon the owner's failure to continue to maintain such services during the period for which the increase is granted, provided that where the Division determines that insufficient income is the cause of such failure to maintain essential services, hardship increases may be granted conditionally provided that such services will be restored within a reasonable time as determined by the Division.

(c) The maximum amount of hardship increase to which an owner shall be entitled shall be the difference between the Threshold Income and the Annual Gross Rent Income Collectible for the Test Year. In buildings that also contain apartments subject to the Emergency Housing Rent Control Law appropriate adjustments for both income and expenses will be made by the Division in order to calculate the pro rata share for those apartments subject to this application.

However, notwithstanding the above, the collection of any increase in the rent for any housing accommodation pursuant to this Section shall not exceed six percent of the legal regulated rent in effect at the time immediately prior to the issuance of the Order. The collectibility of any amount above said sum shall be spread forward in similar increments and added to the rent as established or set in future years. No application may be made for any hardship if a six percent increase is still in effect based on a prior application.

(d) The Division shall set a rental value for any unit occupied by the owner or managing agent or a person related to the owner or managing agent or an employee of the owner or managing agent, or unoccupied at the owner's choice for more than one month at the last regulated rent plus the minimum number of guideline increase or, if no such regulated rent existed or is known, the Division shall impute a rent equal to the average of rents for similar or comparable apartments subject to these Regulations in the building during the test year.

(e) Each owner who files an application for a hardship rent increase shall be required to maintain all records as submitted with the subject application, and further be required to retain same for a period of three years after the effective date of the Order.

(f) Each application under this Section shall be certified by the owner or his duly authorized agent as to its accuracy and compliance with this section, under the penalty or perjury.

§ 2502.5 (§ 35) Lease agreements.

(a) Vacancy lease. Upon the renting of a vacant housing accommodation after the local effective date of the Act, the landlord shall provide to the tenant and execute a valid written lease for a one or two year period at the tenant's option at a rent which may not exceed the legal regulated rent then in effect, provided further that for a housing accommodation subject to the Emergency Housing Rent Control Law which becomes vacant after the local effective date of the Act, the lease shall not provide for any increase in said rent for a period of one year.

(b) Renewal lease. Upon the expiration of a prior lease or rental agreement, the tenant shall have the right of selecting at his option a renewal lease for a term of one or two years, except that where a mortgage or a mortgage commitment existing as of the local effective date of the Act prohibits the granting of one year lease terms, the tenant may not select a one-year lease.

(c) Limitations. No lease fixing a rent pursuant to a guideline issued by the applicable Rent Guidelines Board shall provide for any adjustment during its term pursuant to any surcharge, supplementary adjustment or other modification to such guideline. No provision may be made in any lease for the payment of a rent in excess of the legal regulated rent except on the following conditions:

(1) the legal regulated rent immediately prior to the effective date of the lease may be increased by the appropriate rate of rent adjustment as last filed with the Division by the Rent Guidelines Board for the county wherein the housing accommodation is located, and if the said rate has not been filed by the commencement date of the lease term, the lease may make provision for the rent increase, if any, pursuant to the said rate to become effective when filed as of the commencement date of the lease term, unless the Rent Guidelines Board shall have fixed a later effective date for the said rate, in which event the increase may only be effective as of that later date.

(2) where a lease is entered into after the local effective date, but before the effective date of the first applicable guidelines as provided in section 4 subdivision b of the Act, the lease may provide for an adjustment of rent pursuant to such guidelines, to be effective on the first day of the month next succeeding the effective date of such guidelines.

(3) pursuant to an order of the Division, where the lease recites that

(i) an application for a rent increase pursuant to sections 2502.4(a)(2)(i), (ii) or (iii) is pending before the Division.

(ii) a rent increase shall be payable in the amount authorized by the Division in the event an application is filed pursuant to section 2502.4(a)(2)(ii) or (iii) based upon work having been completed to comply with new or additional requirements of law.

(iii) a rent increase shall be payable in the amount, if any, authorized by the Division in the event an application is filed to establish a hardship pursuant to section 2502.4(c).

(4) Escalator clauses. Regardless of whether an escalator clause was contained in the last effective lease or other rental agreement prior to the local effective date of the Act, no renewal lease or vacancy lease becoming effective on or after the local effective date shall provide for any escalator clause except as authorized in paragraph (c)(2) of this section.

(5) Prior executed lease.

(i) Where a lease for a one, two or three year term was executed before the local effective date and the term commences on or after the local effective date, the lease shall not be effective to increase the initial legal regulated rent, except that effective on the first day of the month next succeeding the date of filing of guidelines with the Division by the Rent Guidelines Board for the county wherein the property is located, which guidelines are applicable to the class of housing accommodations within the building, the initial legal regulated rent may be increased to the lower of the following rents:

(a) the rent reserved in the lease, or

(b) the initial legal regulated rent increased by the applicable rate of rent adjustment for the lease term pursuant to the guidelines.

provided the landlord first serves on the tenant a written notice setting forth the new legal regulated rent and the method of computation thereof pursuant to this section.

(ii) Where a lease was executed before the local effective date for a term of one, two or three years commencing before the local effective date but providing for one or more rent increases to commence on or after the local effective date, no such increases shall be effective to increase the initial legal regulated rent, except that effective on or after the first day of the month next succeeding the date of filing of the guidelines with the Division by the Rent Guidelines Board for the county wherein the property is located, which guidelines are applicable to the class of housing accommodations within the building, the initial legal regulated rent may then be increased commencing on the date or dates provided for in the lease or on the first of the month next succeeding the date of filing of the guidelines, whichever is the later date, to the lower of the following rents:

(a) the rent in the increased amount provided for in the lease, or

(b) the initial legal regulated rent increased by the applicable rate of rent adjustment for the lease term pursuant to the guidelines,

provided the landlord first serves on the tenant a written notice setting forth the new legal regulated rent and the method of computation thereof pursuant to this section.

6. Lease upon vacancy prior to expiration of prior lease term. Where a lease commenced on or after the local effective date, the tenant vacates prior to the expiration of the term of the lease, and the housing accommodation is rented to and occupied by a new tenant prior to the date on which the prior lease would have expired, the landlord shall provide to the new tenant and execute a valid written lease for a one or two year term, at the tenant's option at the applicable guideline rate of rent adjustment; provided, however, that the base for computing such rent adjustment shall be set by adjusting the prior lease rent to the maximum rent that would be permissible if the last lease with the prior tenant had been for a term ending on the date such prior tenant vacated the housing accommodation.

7. Same Terms and Conditions.

The lease provided to the tenant by the landlord pursuant to both paragraphs (1) and (2) of this section shall be on the same terms and conditions as the last lease prior to the local effective date except where a change is required or authorized by a law applicable to the building or to leases for housing accommodations subject to the Act. Where there was no prior lease for the housing accommodations, the lease shall be on the same terms and conditions as the last leases for the other housing accommodations in the building subject to the Act, and shall otherwise provide for the maintenance by the landlord of all services and facilities required by the laws applicable to the building and housing accommodations.

8. Leases for housing accommodations in cooperative or condominium owned buildings or in a building for which the Attorney General has accepted for filing an offering plan to convert the building to cooperative or condominium ownership.

New or renewal leases may contain a clause permitting termination prior to the expiration of the term by a subsequent owner who has purchased the shares allocated to the rented apartment or purchased the rented apartment, if such clause provides—

(i) That the termination clause shall only be effective for the purpose of permitting the rented apartment, following surrender of possession by the tenant, to be occupied immediately by such owner under the cooperative or condominium building ownership, or by a member of that owner's immediate family as defined in the Tenant Protection Regulations;

(ii) That such owner must serve on the tenant a notice in writing by certified mail no less than 90 days prior to the date of termination of the lease, reciting the date of termination and the full name and address of the owner or the member of the owner's immediate family who is to take occupance of the rented apartment, and his or her relationship to the owner; an exact copy of such notice must also be filed with an affidavit of service with the Division within seven days after such service;

(iii) That such increase, if any, in the legal regulated rent collected under the lease pursuant to the applicable County Rent Guidelines Board rate must be refunded by the owner to the tenant on or before the date of surrender of possession, to the following extent:

(a) Where a one year lease is so terminated prior to the expiration of the one year term, the rent increase must be fully refunded.

(b) Where a two year lease is so terminated prior to the expiration of one year, the rent increase must be fully refunded; if one year or more has expired, such amount of the rent increase as exceeded the one year lease guideline rate must be refunded.

(c) Where a three year lease is so terminated prior to the expiration of one year, the rent increase must be fully refunded; if one year but less than two years has expired, such amount of the rent increase as exceeded the one year lease guideline rate must be refunded; if two years or more have expired, such amount of the rent increase as exceeded the two year lease guideline rate must be refunded.

(iv) Where the rented apartment is located in a city, town or village which has filed a resolution with the Attorney General electing to have Section 352-eee of the General Business Law apply to cooperative and condominium conversion plans, and the plan has been declared effective in accordance with its terms and the requirements of such Section 352-eee:

(a) That the plan for conversion to cooperative or condominium ownership is an "Eviction Plan" as defined in Section 352-eee.

(b) That no eviction proceedings shall be commenced against the tenant for a period of three years after the plan has been declared effective as an "Eviction Plan".

(c) That the termination clause shall not apply if the tenant is an "eligible senior citizen" or an "eligible handicapped person" as defined in such section 352-eee.

9. Delivery of lease to tenant. Each owner shall furnish to each tenant signing a new or renewal lease, a copy of the fully executed new or renewal lease bearing the signature of owner and tenant and the beginning and ending dates of the lease term, within thirty days from the owner's receipt of the new or renewal lease signed by the tenant. The failure to do so will result in the noncollectibility of the guidelines increase otherwise authorized for such lease, until the first rent payment date following the receipt by the tenant of the fully executed lease. For renewal of leases, use of the form prescribed under Section 2503.5(a) of these Regulations shall be deemed as compliance herewith.

§ 2502.6 (§ 36) Orders where the legal regulated rent or other facts are in dispute, in doubt, or not known, or where legal regulated rent must be fixed. Where the legal regulated rent or any fact necessary to the determination of the legal regulated rent, or the dwelling space, essential services, furniture, furnishings or equipment required to be provided with the accommodation, is in dispute between the landlord and the tenant, or is in doubt, or is not known, the division at any time upon written request of either party, or on its own initiative, may issue an order determining the facts including the legal regulated rent, the dwelling space, essential services, furniture, furnishings and equipment, required to be provided with the accommodations.

Such order shall determine such facts or establish the legal regulated rent as of the local effective date or the date of commencement of the tenancy, which ever is later. Where such order establishes the legal regulated rent it may contain a directive that all rent collected by the landlord in excess of the legal regulated rent established under this paragraph for a period commencing with the local effective date or the date of the commencement of the tenancy, if later, be refunded to the tenant in cash or as a credit to the rent thereafter payable, and upon the failure to comply with the directive, that the order may be enforced in the same manner as prescribed in section 2506.1(e).

PART 2503 NOTICES AND RECORDS

§ 2503.1 (§ 41) Notice of initial legal regulated rent. Every landlord of housing accommodations subject to these Regulations, which are rented to a tenant on the local effective date, shall within 30 days after the local effective date give notice in writing by certified mail to the tenant of each such housing accommodation on a form provided by the Division for that purpose, reciting the initial legal regulated rent for the housing accommodation and the tenant's right to file an application for adjustment of the initial legal regulated rent within 90 days after receipt of the notice.

§ 2503.2 (§ 42) Certification of services. Every owner of housing accommodations subject to these Regulations shall file with the Division on a form which it shall

Tenant Protection Regulations

provide for that purpose, a written certification that he is maintaining and will continue to maintain all services furnished on May 29, 1974, the effective date of the Act, or required to be furnished by any law, ordinance, or regulation applicable to the premises.

§ 2503.3 (§ 43) Failure to file a certification of services. No landlord shall be entitled to collect a Rent Guidelines Board rent adjustment authorized under section 2502.5 until the owner has filed a proper certification as required by section 2503.2.

2503.4 (§ 44) Failure to maintain services as certified. A tenant may apply to the Division for a reduction of the legal regulated rent to the level in effect prior to the most recent adjustment under section 2502.5 (c)(1) and (2), and the Division may so reduce the rent where it is found that the owner has failed to maintain the services. If the Division further finds that the owner has knowingly filed a false certification, it shall, in addition to abating the rent, assess the owner with the reasonable costs of the proceeding including reasonable attorney's fees, and impose a penalty not in excess of $250.00 for each false certification.

§ 2503.5 (a) Notice of renewal of lease. On a form prescribed by the Division, every landlord shall notify the tenant in occupancy not more than 120 days and not less than 90 days prior to the end of the tenant's lease term, by certified mail, of such termination of the lease term and offer to renew the lease at the legal regulated rent permitted for such renewal lease and otherwise on the same conditions as the expiring lease and shall give such tenant a period of 60 days from the date of mailing of such notice to renew such lease and accept the offer, provided that as to any lease which expires less than 90 days from the local effective date of the Act, the notice shall be deemed complied with so long as the tenant is provided the 60 day period within which to renew after notice is mailed of his options of renewal. The tenant's acceptance of such offer shall be entered on the designated part of the prescribed form, and returned to the landlord by certified mail.

(b) Where the landlord fails to offer a renewal of the lease in accordance with subdivision (a), the tenant shall have the option of choosing (1) whether the one or two year term of such lease whenever it is offered shall commence on the date a renewal lease would have commenced had a timely offer been made or (2) on the first rent payment date commencing 60 days after the date that the landlord does offer the lease to the tenant on the prescribed notice form. The guideline rate applicable in such cases shall be the rate in effect on the past date on which such lease was required or the rate in effect when the lease is renewed; whichever is lower.

(c) Notwithstanding any other provision of these Regulations, the failure to offer a renewal lease shall not deprive the tenant of any benefit under these Regulations.

§ 2503.6 (§ 46) Notices to attorneys at law.

(a) Whenever a person is involved in a proceeding before the Division and an attorney at law has filed a Notice of Appearance in such proceeding, all subsequent written communications or notices to such person (other than subpoenas) shall be sent to such attorney at law at the address designated in such Notice of Appearance. The Notice of Appearance to be filed by an attorney at law who represents a party in a proceeding before the Division shall be on a form prescribed unless proceedings are instituted before the Division by formal application pursuant to these Regulations and the representation of such attorney at law and his mailing address are stated in such application in the space allotted for the mailing address of the represented party. The service of written communications and notices upon such attorney at law shall be deemed full and proper service upon the party or parties so represented.

(b) Whenever an attorney at law shall represent the same party or parties in more than one proceeding before the Division, separate Notices of Appearance shall be filed in each proceeding.

(c) This section shall not apply to preliminary investigations.

§ 2503.7 (§ 47) Records and record-keeping.

(a) Every landlord subject to these Regulations, shall keep, preserve, and make available for examination, records showing the rents received for each housing accommodation, the particular term and number of occupants for which such rents were charged, and the name and address of each occupant.

(b) Every landlord shall also keep, preserve, and make available for examination, records of the same kind as he has customarily kept relating to the rents received for housing accommodations.

(c) Notwithstanding any other provision of these Regulations, any landlord who has duly registered a housing accommodation pursuant to Part 2509 of these Regulations shall not be required to maintain or produce any records relating to rentals of such accommodation more than four years prior to the most recent registration or annual statement for such accommodation.

§ 2503.8 (§ 48) Notice of legal regulated rent for a vacant housing accommodation previously regulated under the Act.

(a) A landlord of a vacant housing accommodation for lease shall make available to prospective tenants a notice in writing of the monthly rent under the offered lease, and of the prior legal regulated rent, if any, which was in effect immediately prior to the vacancy, and that any increase in the prior legal regulated rent under the offered lease does not exceed the applicable rate of rent adjustment in effect pursuant to the guidelines filed with the Division by the Rent Guidelines Board for the county wherein the housing accommodation is located, or as otherwise authorized by the Act.

(b) At the time of renting the vacant housing accommodation, the landlord shall attach this notice in writing to the executed written lease, and deliver a copy of the notice to the tenant with a copy of the lease, or include a written provision in the lease setting forth the prior legal regulated rent, the amount of any rent increase under the lease and showing that such increase does not exceed the applicable rate of rent adjustment in effect pursuant to the Guidelines filed by the Rent Guidelines Board or as otherwise authorized by the Act. In the event the landlord does not comply with this requirement, the lease

TENANT PROTECTION REGULATIONS

shall not be effective to increase the prior legal regulated rent; however, at such time thereafter that the landlord does provide the notice to the tenant with the required information in writing, the otherwise authorized monthly rent increase shall be collectible commencing with the first rent payment date thereafter.

§ 2503.9 (§ 49) Notice of redetermination of initial legal regulated rent which includes payments reserved under a tax escalation clause, based upon reduction of real property tax increases. Every landlord of housing accommodations subject to these Regulations, for which the initial legal regulated rent includes payments reserved under a tax escalation clause in the lease or other rental agreement shall, whenever there is a reduction in the amounts of increases in the real property taxes which were previously in effect, on or before July 31, 1976 or within 60 days after notice of such reduction and receipt of rebates from the taxing authority, which ever is later, give notice in writing by certified mail to the tenant of each such housing accommodation on a form provided by the Division for that purpose, reciting the redetermined initial legal regulated rent for the housing accommodation, and the amount of the payments previously included in the initial legal regulated rent, which are excluded therefrom based upon the reduction of real property tax increases, and that all refunds of excess rent paid since the local effective date will be made in cash to the tenant or as a credit against future rents over a period not in excess of six months. In the event the initial legal regulated rent has been adjusted by the applicable Rent Guidelines Board rate in a one, two or three year lease, the legal regulated rent provided in such lease shall also be redetermined to exclude the tax increase payments, and shall also be recited in the notice. Where the real property tax increases have been reduced as a result of a legal proceeding commenced by the landlord to reduce the assessed valuation of the property, the landlord may offset the amount of rent reduction by such exact amount as is necessary to recoup the expense of reasonable attorney's fees, costs and expenses, if any, actually incurred in said proceeding.

§ 2503.10 (§ 50) Failure to serve notice of redetermination of initial legal regulated rent based upon reduction of real property tax increases. A tenant may apply to the Division for a redetermination of the initial legal regulated rent, and the legal regulated rent if there has been an adjustment by the applicable Rent Guidelines Board rate in a one, two or three year lease, when the landlord has failed to serve the notice required under section 2503.9 of these Regulations. In determining such application, the Division may direct the refund by the landlord to the tenant of excess rent paid since the local effective date, and may further order the landlord to pay to the tenant such penalty as may be found under section 2506.1 of these Regulations.

PART 2504 EVICTIONS

§ 2504.1 (§ 51) Restrictions on removal of tenant.

(a) So long as the tenant continues to pay the rent to which the landlord is entitled, no tenant shall be removed from any housing accommodations by action to evict or to recover possession, by exclusion from possession, or otherwise, nor shall any person attempt such removal or exclusion from possession, except on one or more of the grounds specified in these Regulations.

(b) It shall be unlawful for any person to remove or attempt to remove any tenant or occupant from any housing accommodations or to refuse to renew the lease or agreement for the use of such accommodations, because such tenant or occupant has taken, or proposes to take, action authorized or required by the Act or any regulation, order or requirement thereunder.

(c) No tenant of any housing accommodation shall be removed or evicted unless and until such removal or eviction has been authorized by a court of competent jurisdiction.

(d)(1) In addition to any other limitation imposed by these Regulations, no proceeding to recover possession of any housing accommodation based upon any wrongful acts or omission of a tenant pursuant to Section 2504.2 may be maintained unless (a) the landlord has given the tenant written notice (the "notice to cure") stating the following:

(i) the wrongful acts or omission of the tenant pursuant to Section 2504.2; and

(ii) the facts necessary to establish the existence of said wrongful acts or omission; and

(iii) the date certain by which the tenant must cure said wrongful acts or omission, which date shall be no sooner than ten days following the date such notice to cure is served upon the tenant.

(b) The tenant fails to cure the wrongful acts or omission specified in the notice to cure by or before the date specified in subparagraph (iii) of paragraph (d)(1)(a).

(c) The requirements of paragraphs (a) and (b) of this subdivision (d) (1) shall not apply where the wrongful act or omission:

(i) is, by its nature, not curable; or

(ii) consists of the re-occurance or continuation of a violation or condition which was the subject of a prior notice to cure transmitted to the tenant no more than six months previously; or

(iii) consists of the wilful violation of an obligation of the tenant inflicting serious and substantial injury on the landlord or the property of the landlord.

§ 2504.2 (§ 52) Proceedings for eviction—wrongful acts of tenant. An action or proceeding to recover possession of any housing accommodation shall be maintainable after service and filing of the notice required by section 2504.3 only upon one or more of the following grounds wherein wrongful acts of the tenants are established.

(a) The tenant is violating a substantial obligation of his tenancy other than the obligation to surrender possession of such housing accommodation; or within the three month period immediately prior to the commencement of the proceeding the tenant has wilfully violated such an obligation inflicting serious and substantial injury to the landlord.

(b) The tenant is committing or permitting a nuisance in such housing accommodations; or is maliciously or by reason of gross negligence substantially damaging the housing accommodations; or his conduct is such as to interfere substantially with the comfort or safety of the landlord or of other tenants or occupants of the same or other adjacent building or structure.

Tenant Protection Regulations

(c) Occupancy of the housing accommodations by the tenant is illegal because of the requirements of law, and the landlord is subject to civil or criminal penalties therefor, or both.

(d) The tenant is using or permitting such housing accommodation to be used for an immoral or illegal purpose.

(e) The tenant has unreasonably refused the landlord access to the housing accommodations for the purpose of making necessary repairs or improvements required by law or for the purposes of inspection or of showing the accommodations to a prospective purchaser, mortgagee or prospective mortgagee, or other person having a legitimate interest therein; provided, however, that in the latter even such refusal shall not be ground for removal or eviction if such inspection or showing of the accommodations is contrary to the provisions of the tenant's lease or rental agreement.

(f) The tenant has refused following notice pursuant to section 2503.5 to renew an expiring lease in the manner prescribed in such notice at the legal regulated rent authorized under these Regulations and the Act.

§ 2504.3 (§ 53) Notices required in proceedings under section 2504.2.

(a) Except where the ground for removal or eviction of a tenant is non-payment of rent, no tenant shall be removed or evicted from housing accommodations by court process and no action or proceeding shall be commenced for such purpose upon any of the grounds permitted in section 2504.2 unless and until the landlord shall have given written notice to the tenant and the Division as hereinafter provided.

(b) Every notice to a tenant to vacate or surrender possession of housing accommodations shall state the ground under section 2504.2 upon which the landlord relies for removal or eviction of the tenant, the facts necessary to establish the existence of such ground, and the date when the tenant is required to surrender possession.

(c) Within seven days after the notice is served upon the tenant, an exact copy thereof together with an affidavit of service shall be filed with the Division.

(d) Every such notice shall be served upon the tenant:

(1) in the case of a notice based upon subdivision (f) of Section 2504.2 of these Regulations, at least fifteen days prior to the date specified therein for the surrender of possession; or

(2) in the case of a notice on any other ground, at least one month prior to the date specified therein for the surrender of possession; and, in any event, prior to the commencement of any proceeding for removal or eviction. Such notice may be combined with a notice to cure if required by Section 2504.1 and, in such case, the one-month period provided herein may, if the notice so provides, include the ten-day period specified in the notice to cure.

§ 2504.4 (§ 54) Grounds for refusal to renew lease and proceed for eviction. The landlord shall not be required to offer a renewal lease to a tenant, and may maintain an action or proceeding to recover possession in a court of competent jurisdiction only upon one or more of the following grounds:

(a) Occupancy by owner or immediate family. (1). An owner who is a natural person seeks in good faith and demonstrates an immediate and compelling need to recover possession of a housing accommodation for his own personal use and occupancy or for the use and occupancy of his immediate family.

(2) The provisions of this paragraph (a) shall not apply where a member of the household is sixty-two years of age or older, or has been a tenant in a housing accommodation in that building for twenty years or more, or has an impairment which results from anatomical, physiological or psychological conditions, other than addiction to alcohol, gambling, or any controlled substance, which are demonstrable by medically acceptable clinical and laboratory diagnostic techniques, and which are expected to be permanent and which prevent such person from engaging in any substantial gainful employment.

(3) The provisions of this paragraph (a) shall only permit one of the individual owners of any building to recover possession of not more than two dwelling units for personal use and occupancy, provided that if an owner, or a member of his immediate family, already occupies two or more apartments in the building, he may only obtain another apartment if he offers the tenant a suitable apartment in the building at the same or lower rent and pays for the tenant's relocation.

(4) No action or proceeding to recover possession pursuant to this paragraph (a) shall be commenced in court unless and until the owner shall have made application to the Division and the Division has issued an order permitting the owner to commence such action or proceeding in court and, in addition, where such order is subject to certain conditions and terms, until such conditions and terms have been complied with.

(b) Withdrawal from the rental market. The owner has established, upon application on the prescribed form, to the satisfaction of the Division after a hearing and under such conditions and terms as the Division may set, that he seeks in good faith to withdraw occupied dwelling units from both the housing and non-housing rental markets, without any intent to rent or sell all or any part of the land or structure.

(c) Other grounds. The owner has established upon an application on the prescribed form, after a hearing and under such conditions and terms as the Division may determine to be warranted, that the requested removal or eviction of the tenant is not inconsistent with the purposes of the Act or these Regulations and would not be likely to result in the circumvention or evasion thereof.

No action or proceeding to recover possession shall be commenced in court by the owner where he is proceeding under paragraphs (b) or (c) of this section, until the owner has made application to the Division and the Division has issued an order permitting the owner to commence such action or proceeding in court and, in addition, where the order of the Division is subject to the owner complying with specified conditions and terms, that the said conditions and terms have been complied with.

(d) Primary residence. The housing accommodation is not occupied by the tenant, not including subtenants or occupants, as his primary residence, as determined by a court of competent jurisdiction. For the purpose of this paragraph where a housing accommodation is rented to a not-for-profit hospital for residential use, affiliated subtenants authorized to use such accommodations by such hospital shall be deemed to be tenants. No action or proceeding shall be commenced seeking to recover possession on such ground unless the landlord shall have given thirty days notice to the tenant of his intention to commence such action or proceeding on such ground. Within seven days after the notice is served on the tenant, an exact copy thereof, with an affidavit of service, shall be filed with the Division.

PART 2505 PROHIBITIONS

§ 2505.1 (§ 61) General prohibitions. It shall be unlawful, regardless of any contract, lease or other obligation heretofore or hereafter entered into, for any person to demand or receive, any rent for any housing accommodations in excess of the legal regulated rent, or otherwise to do or omit to do any act, in violation of any regulation, order or requirement under the Act or these Regulations, or to offer, solicit, attempt or agree to do any of the foregoing.

The term "rent" as hereinbefore defined shall also include the payment by a tenant of a fee or rental commission to a landlord or to any person or real estate broker where such person or real estate broker is an agent or employee of the landlord or is employed by the landlord in connection with the operation of the building, or where such person or real estate broker manages the building in which the housing accommodation is located, or where the landlord or his employee refer the tenant to such person or real estate broker for the purpose of renting the housing accommodation. Where the landlord has listed the housing accommodation with such person or real estate broker for rental purposes such fact shall be prima facie evidence of the existence of an agency relationship between such other person or real estate broker and the landlord for the purposes of this section.

§ 2505.2 (§ 62) Evasion. The legal regulated rents and other requirements provided in these Regulations shall

TENANT PROTECTION REGULATIONS

not be evaded, either directly or indirectly, in connection with the renting or leasing or the transfer of a lease of housing accommodations by requiring the tenant to pay, or obligate himself for membership or other fees, or by modification of the practices relating to payment of commissions or other charges, or by modification of the services furnished or required to be furnished with the housing accommodations, or otherwise.

§ 2505.3 (§ 63) Conditional Rental.

(a) No person shall require a tenant or prospective tenant to purchase or lease or agree to purchase or lease furniture or any other personal property, such as shares to an apartment prior to an approved plan of cooperative conversion, as a condition of renting housing accommodations.

(b) No person shall require a tenant or prospective tenant to agree as a condition of renting a housing accommodation that the housing accommodation shall not be used as the tenant's primary residence.

(c) No person shall require a tenant or prospective tenant to sign a lease or other rental agreement in the name of a corporation or for professional or commercial use as a condition of renting a housing accommodation when the apartment is to be used as the primary residence of the prospective tenant for residential purposes.

(d) The term "person" as used in this section shall include an agent or any other employee of a landlord acting with or without the authority of his employer.

(e) The term "person" as used in this section shall also include a tenant in occupancy of housing accommodations who attempts to sell furniture or any other property to an incoming tenant.

§ 2505.4 (§ 64) Security deposits. Regardless of any contract, agreement, lease or other obligation heretofore or hereafter entered into, no person shall demand, receive or retain a security deposit for or in connection with the use or occupancy of housing accommodations which exceeds the rent for one month in addition to the authorized collection of rent; provided, however, that where a lease in effect on December 1, 1983 validly required a greater security deposit, such requirement may continue in effect during the term of such lease and any renewals thereof with the same tenant. Such security deposits shall be subject to the following conditions:

(a) the security deposit shall be deposited in an interest-bearing account in a banking organization;

(b) the person depositing such security deposit shall be entitled to receive, as administrative expenses, a sum equivalent to one percent per annum upon the security money so deposited;

(c) the balance of the interest paid by the banking organization shall be held in trust until repaid or applied for the rental of the housing accommodations, or at the tenant's option annually paid to the tenant; and

(d) the landlord shall comply with the provisions of section 7-103 of the General Obligations Law.

§ 2505.5 (§ 65) Disclosure by employees. It shall be unlawful for any officer or employee of the Division, or for any official advisor or consultant to the Division, to disclose, otherwise than in the course of official duty, any information obtained under the act, or to use any such information for personal benefit.

§ 2505.6 (§ 66) Conduct with intent to cause the tenant to vacate. It shall be unlawful for any landlord or any person acting on his behalf, with intent to cause the tenant to vacate, to engage in any course of conduct (including, but not limited to, interruption or discontinuance of essential services) which interferes with or disturbs or is intended to interfere with or disturb the comfort, peace, repose or quiet of the tenant in his use or occupancy of the housing accommodations.

§ 2505.7 (§ 67) Regulation of subletting.

(a) Housing accommodations subject to these Regulations may be sublet in accordance with the provisions, and subject to the limitations, of section 226-b of the Real Property Law provided that the additional provisions of this Section are complied with and provided further that the prime tenant can establish that at all times he has maintained the housing accommodation as his primary

Tenant Protection Regulations

residence and intends to occupy it as such at the expiration of the sublease.

(b) The rental charged to the subtenant shall not exceed the legal regulated rent plus a ten percent surcharge payable to the prime tenant if the housing accommodation is sublet with the prime tenant's furniture. Where a prime tenant violates the provisions of this subdivision, the subtenant shall be entitled to damages as provided in Section 2506.1 of these Regulations.

(c) The tenant may not sublet a housing accommodation for more than a total of two years, including the term of the proposed sublease, out the the four-year period preceding the termination date of the proposed sublease, but this provision shall not apply to any sublease commencing prior to July first, 1983. The term of proposed sublease may, if lawful under this section, extend beyond the term of the prime tenant's lease, and a landlord may not refuse consent to a sublease solely because it extends beyond such term. A sublease which so extends shall be subject to the prime tenant's right to a renewal lease.

(d) The prime tenant, rather than the subtenant, retains (1) the right to a renewal lease, whether or not the term of the sublease extends beyond the term of the prime tenant's lease, and (2) the rights and status of a tenant in occupancy with respect to conversion to condominium or cooperative ownership.

(e) An owner may terminate the tenancy of a tenant who sublets or assigns contrary to the terms of this section, but no action or proceeding based upon the nonprimary residence of a tenant may be commenced prior to the expiration date of his lease.

(f) A not-for-profit hospital shall have the right to sublet any housing accommodation leased by it to its affiliated personnel without requiring the landlord's consent to any such sublease and without being bound by the provisions of subdivisions (a) and (e). Whenever a not-for-profit hospital executes a renewal lease for a housing accommodation, the legal regulated rent shall be increased by a sum equal to fifteen percent of the previous lease rental for such housing accommodation, hereinafter referred to as a vacancy surcharge, unless the landlord shall have received within the seven year period prior to the commencement date of such renewal lease and vacancy increases or vacancy surcharges allocable to the said housing accommodation. In the event the landlord shall have received any such vacancy increases or vacancy sucharges during such seven year period, the vacancy surcharge shall be reduced by the amount received by any such vacancy increase or vacancy surcharges.

PART 2506 ENFORCEMENT

§ 2506.1 (§ 71) Penalties for overcharges, assessment of costs and attorneys' fees, rent offsets.

(a)(1) Any landlord who is found by the Division, after a reasonable opportunity to be heard, to have collected any rent or other consideration in excess of the legal regulated rent shall be ordered to pay to the tenant a penalty equal to three times the amount of such excess. If the landlord establishes by a preponderance of the evidence that the overcharge was neither wilful nor attributable to his negligence, the Division shall establish the penalty as the amount of the overcharge plus interest at the rate of interest payable on a judgment pursuant to Section 5004 of the Civil Practice Law and Rules, and the order shall direct such a payment to be made to the tenant.

(2) A complaint pursuant to this section must be filed with the Division within four years of the first overcharge alleged, and no award of the amount of an overcharge may be based upon an overcharge having occurred more than four years before the complaint is filed, provided that:

(i) no penalty of three times the overcharge may be based upon an overcharge having occurred more than two years before the complaint is filed or upon an overcharge which occurred prior to April 1, 1984; and

(ii) any complaint based upon overcharges occurring prior to the date of filing of the initial rent registration for a housing accommodation pursuant to Part X of these Regulations shall be filed within ninety days of the mailing of notice to the tenant of such registration.

(3)(i) Except as to complaints filed pursuant to subparagraph (ii) of this paragraph (3), the legal regulated rent for purposes of determining an overcharge shall be deemed to be the rent shown in the annual registration statement filed four years prior to the most recent registration statement, (or, if more recently filed, the initial registration statement) plus in each case any subsequent lawful increases and adjustment.

(ii) As to complaints filed within ninety days of the initial registration of a housing accommodation, the legal regulated rent for purposes of determining an overcharge shall be deemed to be the rent charged on a date four years prior to the date of such initial registration (or, if the housing accommodation was subject to the Act and these Regulations for less than four years prior to such initial registration, the initial legal regulated rent) plus in each case, any lawful increases and adjustments.

Where the rent charged on the date four years prior to the date of the initial registration of the accommodation cannot be established, such rent shall be established by the Division.

(b) The Division shall apportion the landlord's liability between or among two or more tenants found to have been overcharged during their particular occupancy of an accommodation.

(c) Any affected tenant shall be given notice and an opportunity to join in any complaint filed by an officer or employee of the Division.

(d) A landlord who is found to have overcharged by the Division shall be assessed and ordered to pay to the tenant the reasonable costs and attorneys' fees of the proceeding and interest from the date of the overcharge at the rate of interest payable on a judgment pursuant to Section 5004 of the Civil Practice Law and Rules.

(e) A tenant may recover a penalty payable to him by deducting it from the rent payable to the landlord at a rate not in excess of 20% of the amount of the penalty for any one month's rent. If no such offset has been made, the Division order awarding penalties may, upon the expiration of the period in which the landlord may institute a proceeding pursuant to article 78 of the Civil Practice Law and Rules, be filed and enforced by a tenant in the same manner as a judgment.

(f) Unless a tenant shall have filed a complaint of

overcharge with the Division which complaint has not been withdrawn, nothing contained in this section shall be deemed to prevent a tenant or tenants, claiming to have been overcharged, from commencing an action or interposing a counterclaim in a court of competent jurisdiction for damages equal to one overcharge and the penalty provided for in this section including interest from the date of the overcharge at the rate of interest payable on a judgment pursuant to Section 5004 of the Civil Practice Law and Rules, plus the statutory costs and allowable disbursements in connection with the proceeding. Such action must be commenced or counterclaim interposed within four years of the date of the alleged overcharge but no recovery of three times the amount of the overcharge may be awarded with respect to any overcharge which had occurred more than two years before the action is commenced or counterclaim is interposed.

(g) Nothing herein shall be in derogation of administrative proceedings or litigation commenced prior to April 1, 1984 or other rights which may accrue to affected or aggrieved parties due to such administrative proceedings or litigation.

§ 2506.2 (§ 72) Orders to enforce the Act and Regulations.

(a) Upon notice and reasonable opportunity to be heard, the Division may issue orders it deems appropriate to enforce the Act and Regulations.

(b) If the Division finds that any landlord has knowingly engaged in acts prohibited by the Act and Regulations or orders issued thereunder, it may assess the landlord and order it to pay each tenant affected by such acts the reasonable costs and attorney fees of the proceeding plus a penalty not in excess of $250.00 for each such act. If the landlord has not instituted a proceeding pursuant to Article 78 of the Civil Practice Law and Rules and has not paid the assessment and penalties upon the expiration of the time to do so, each affected tenant may offset against any rent thereafter due the landlord the unpaid amount not in excess of 20% thereof per month.

Tenant Protection Regulations

(c) If a landlord is found by the Division:

(1) to have violated an order of the Division, the Division may impose by administrative order after hearing, a civil penalty in the amount of $250 for the first such offense and $1000 for each subsequent offense: or

(2) to have harrassed a tenant to obtain vacancy of his housing accommodation, the Division may impose by administrative order after hearing, a civil penalty for any such violation. Such penalty shall be in the amount of up to $1000 for a first such offense and up to $2500 for each subsequent offense or for a violation consisting of conduct directed at the tenants of more than one housing accommodation.

§ 2506.3 (§ 73) Injunctions by Supreme Court. The Division may commence proceedings in the Supreme Court to enjoin violations of the Act, of these Regulations, or orders issued pursuant. In any such proceedings, the Division shall not be required to post bond. In addition, any tenant or tenants who allege they have been overcharged may commence proceedings to enjoin such overcharge, and for such other relief as may be proper.

§ 2506.4 (§ 74) Oaths, subpoenas, hearing officers. The Division may administer oaths, issue subpoenas, conduct investigations, make inspections and designate officers to hear and report.

§ 2506.5 (§ 75) Confidentiality of information. The Division shall safeguard the confidentiality of information furnished to it at the request of the person furnishing such information, unless such information must be made public in the interest of establishing a record for the future guidance of persons subject to the Act.

§ 2506.6 (§ 76) Inspection and records.

(a) Any person who rents or offers for rent, or acts as a broker or agent for the rental of any housing accommodations shall, as the Division may from time to time require, furnish information under oath or affirmation or otherwise, permit inspection and copying of records and other documents and permit inspection of any such housing accommodations.

(b) Any person who rents or offers for rent, or acts as a broker or agent for the rental of any housing accommodations shall, as the Division may from time to time require, make and keep records and other documents and make reports.

§ 2506.7 (§ 77) Intervention.

In any action or proceeding before a court wherein a party relies for a ground of relief or defense or raises issues or brings into question the construction or validity of the Act, these Regulations, or any order or requirement thereunder, the court having jurisdiction of such action or proceeding may at any stage certify such fact to the Division. The division may intervene in any such action or proceeding.

PART 2507 PROCEEDINGS BEFORE DIVISION

§ 2507.1 (§ 81) Proceedings instituted by landlord or tenant. A proceeding is instituted by a landlord or a tenant with the filing of an application for adjustment of rent, or for other relief provided by the Act or these Regulations. Such application shall be verified or certified by the applicant and filed upon the appropriate form issued by the Division in accordance with the instructions contained in such forms.

§ 2507.2 (§ 82) Proceedings instituted by the Division. The Division may institute a proceeding on its own initiative whenever the Division deems it necessary or appropriate pursuant to the Act or these Regulations.

§ 2507.3 (§ 83) Notice to the parties affected.

(a) Where the application is made by a landlord or tenant the Division shall forward to all parties affected thereby a notice setting forth the proposed action.

(b) Where the proceeding is instituted by the Division, it shall forward to all parties affected thereby a notice setting forth the proposed action.

§ 2507.4 (§ 84) Answer. A person who has been served with a copy of an application or a notice of a proceeding shall have seven days from the date of mailing in which to answer. Every answer must be verified or certified, and an original and one copy shall be filed with the Division.

Tenant Protection Regulations

§ 2507.5 (§ 85) Action by Division. At any stage of a proceeding the Division may:

(a) Reject the application if it is insufficient or defective.

(b) Make such investigation of the facts, conduct such inspections, hold such conferences, and require the filing of such reports, evidence, affidavits, or other material relevant to the proceeding.

(c) Forward to or make available for inspection by either party any relevant evidence and afford an opportunity to file rebuttal thereto.

(d) For good cause shown accept for filing any papers, even though not filed within the time required by these Regulations.

(e) Require any person to appear or produce documents or both pursuant to a subpoena issued by the Division.

(f) Consolidate two or more applications or proceedings which have at least one ground in common.

(g) Forward to either party a notice of action proposed to be taken.

(h) Grant or order a hearing.

(i) On its own motion or upon application of any affected landlord or tenant, consolidate proceedings applicable to the same building or group of buildings or development notwithstanding that the housing accommodations affected may be subject to differing regulations; and in any such consolidated proceedings the determination with respect to any housing accommodation shall be made in accordance with the appropriate law or regulation applicable to such accommodations.

§ 2507.6 (§ 86) Determination. The District Rent Administrator on such terms and conditions as he may determine, may:

(a) Dismiss the application if it fails substantially to comply with the provisions of the Act or these Regulations.

(b) Grant or deny the application, in whole or in part.

(c) Issue an appropriate order in a proceeding instituted on his own initiative.

(d) Issue conditional or provisional determinations as he may deem appropriate under the circumstances.

A copy of any order issued shall be forwarded to all parties to the proceeding.

(e) Notwithstanding any provision of these Regulations, no order shall be deemed final and binding for purposes of judicial review except in accordance with part XI of these Regulations.

§ 2507.7 (§ 87) Pending proceedings. Where a Regulation is amended during the pendency of a proceeding, the determination shall be in accordance with the amended Regulation.

§ 2507.8 (§ 88) Modification or revocation of orders. The Division, on application of either party or on its own initiative, and upon notice to all parties affected, may, prior to the date that a petition for judicial review has been commenced in the Supreme Court pursuant to Article 78 of the Civil Practice Law and Rules, modify, supersede or revoke any order issued by the Division under these or previous Regulations where the Division finds that such order was the result of illegality, irregularity in vital matters, or fraud. Where an order is modified, superseded or revoked by the Division, it may also direct that all rent collected by the landlord and/or by predecessor and successor landlords in excess of the legal regulated rent be refunded to the tenant.

§ 2507.9 (§ 89) Judicial review.

(a) Any proceeding pursuant to Article 78 of the Civil Practice Law and Rules seeking review of any action of the Division pursuant to these Regulations shall be brought within sixty days.

(b) Any action or proceeding brought by or against the Division under the Act shall be brought in the county in which the housing accommodation is located.

PART 2508 MISCELLANEOUS PROCEDURAL MATTERS

§ 2508.1 (§ 110) When a notice or paper shall be deemed served.

(a) Notices, orders, protests, answers and other papers may be served personally or by mail. When service is made personally or by mail an affidavit by the person making the service or mailing shall constitute sufficient proof of service. When service is by registered or certified mail the return post office receipt shall constitute sufficient proof of service.

(b) Where a notice of appearance has been filed by an attorney, service on the attorney shall be deemed proper service as if made on the party or parties represented.

§ 2508.2 (§ 111) Delegation of authority. The Commissioner of Housing and Community Renewal and any officer of the Division designated by the Commissioner to carry out any power of the Commissioner under the Act or these Regulations may delegate the authority to carry out any of the duties and powers granted by the Act or these Regulations.

§ 2508.3 (§ 112) Small building owners assistance unit. The Division shall establish a small building owners assistance unit which shall provide assistance upon request to owners of buildings with rental housing accommodations. Such assistance shall include, but not be limited to, completing applications for adjustments in rents, filing registration statements, maintaining adequate business and financial records, and complying with provisions of law and regulations. For the purposes of this section, a "small building owner" shall mean an owner of a total of fifty housing accommodations or less.

PART 2509 REGISTRATION OF HOUSING ACCOMMODATIONS

§ 2509.1 (§ 121) Initial registration.

(a) Each housing accommodation subject to these Regulations on April 1, 1984 shall be registered by the owner thereof with the Division prior to July 1, 1984.

(b) The registration shall be made on the forms prescribed by the Division, and shall include:

(1) the address of the building or group of buildings or development in which such housing accommodation is located and the tenant thereof;

(2) the number of housing accommodations in the building or group of buildings or development;

(3) the number of housing accommodations in the building or group of buildings or development subject to the Act and the number of such housing accommodations subject to the Emergency Housing Rent Control Law;

(4) the rent charged on April 1, 1984 and any changes in such rent between such date and the date of registration;

(5) the number of rooms in such housing accommodation; and

(6) all services provided in the last lease or rental agreement commencing at least six months prior to the local effective date of the Act.

(c) Housing accommodations which become subject to the Act after the initial registration period must be registered within ninety days thereafter. Registration of housing accommodations subject to the emergency housing rent control law immediately prior to the date of filing the initial registration statement shall include, in addition to the items set out in subdivision (b) of this Section, where existing, the maximum rent immediately prior to the date that such housing accommodations became subject to the Act.

(d) Copies of the registration shall be filed with the Division in such place or places as it may require. In addition, a copy of the Building Services Registration form shall be posted in a public area of the building as prescribed therein, and a copy of each Apartment Registration form must be mailed by the owner to the tenant in possession of the housing accommodation to which it applies at the time of initial registration or to the first tenant in occupancy if the housing accommodation is vacant at the time of initial registration.

§ 2509.2 (§ 122) Annual Statement. An annual statement shall be filed containing the current rent for each housing accommodation and such other information specified in Section 2509.1 of these Regulations as shall be required by the Division. The owner shall provide each tenant then in occupancy with a copy of that portion of such annual statement as pertains to the tenant's housing accommodation.

TENANT PROTECTION REGULATIONS

§ 2509.3 (§ 123) Penalty for failure to register. The failure to file a proper and timely initial or annual rent registration statement as required by this part shall, until such time as such registration statement is filed, bar an owner from applying for or collecting any rent in excess of the legal regulated rent in effect on the date of the last preceding registration statement or, if no such statements have been filed, the legal regulated rent in effect on the date that the housing accommodation became subject to the registration requirements of the Part. The filing of a late registration shall result in the prospective elimination of such sanctions.

§ 2509.4 (§ 124) Confidentiality. Registration pursuant to this Part shall not be subject to the Freedom of Information Law, provided that registration information relative to a tenant, owner, lessor or subtenant shall be made available to such party or his authorized representative.

PART 2510 ADMINISTRATIVE REVIEW

§ 2510.1 (§ 131) Persons who may file.

(a) Any person aggrieved by these Regulations or by an order issued by a District Rent Administrator may file a petition for administrative review (PAR) to the Commissioner in the manner provided in these Regulations.

(b) A joint PAR, verified or affirmed by each person joining therein, may be filed by two or more landlords or tenants, where at least on ground is common to all persons so filing. The Commissioner, in his discretion may treat such PAR as joint or several.

(c) The Commissioner may, in his discretion, consolidate two or more PAR's which have at least one ground in common.

§ 2510.2 (§ 132) Time for filing a PAR.

(a) A PAR against any provision of these Regulations may be filed at any time after the effective date thereof.

(b) A PAR against an order of a District Rent Administrator must be filed with the Commissioner within thirty-three days after the date such order is issued. A PAR served by mail, postmarked not more than thirty-three days after the date of such order, shall be deemed compliance with this paragraph.

§ 2510.3 (§ 133) Form and content of a PAR against these Regulations or portion thereof. No printed form of a PAR is provided or prescribed. Each PAR against these Regulations or portion thereof must be clearly designated "Petition for Administrative Review to the Commissioner of Housing and Community Renewal re Section .... (or Sections .... of the Tenant Protection Regulations", and shall set forth the following:

(a) The name and post-office address of the party filing the PAR, and whether he is a landlord or tenant, or representative.

(b) A complete identification of the provision or provisions for which the PAR is being filed, citing the section or sections of these Regulations to which the objection is made.

(c) A simple concise statement of the obligations to these Regulations or portions thereof.

(d) A specific statement of the relief requested.

(e) Each PAR shall be verified or affirmed by the party filing the PAR.

§ 2510.4 (§ 134) Form and content of a PAR against an order of the District Rent Administrator. A person aggrieved by an order issued by the District Rent Administrator may file a PAR against such order only on a form prescribed by the Commissioner.

§ 2510.5 (§ 135) Service and filing of a PAR.

(a) Each PAR shall be filed in an original and one copy at the Division of Housing and Community Renewal, office of Rent Administration, 10 Columbus Circle, New York, New York 10019, unless otherwise provided on the form prescribed by the Commissioner for such PAR.

(b) Where the PAR is against an order issued by the District Rent Administrator, a copy of the PAR shall also be served on the District Rent Administrator issuing the order and upon each party affected by the PAR.

(c) A PAR under Section 2510.4 will not be accepted for filing unless accompanied by an affidavit or other proof of such service.

Tenant Protection Regulations

§ 2510.6 (§ 136) Time of filing answer to a PAR. Any person served with a PAR as provided in Section 2510.5(b) of these Regulations, may, within fifteen days from the date of service, file a verified or affirmed answer thereto, by filing the same with the Commissioner, together with proof of service of a copy thereof upon the party filing the PAR. The Commissioner may, in his discretion, and for good cause shown, extend the time within which to answer.

§ 2510.7 (§ 137) Action by Commissioner. Within a reasonable time after the filing of the PAR and the answers, if any, the Commissioner may:

(a) Reject the PAR if it is insufficient or defective.

(b) Make such investigation of the facts, hold such conferences, and require the filing of such reports, evidence, affidavits, or other material relevant to the proceeding as he may deem necessary or appropriate.

(c) Forward to or make available for inspection by either party any relevant evidence and afford an opportunity to file rebuttal thereto.

(d) For good cause shown accept for filing any papers, even though not filed within the time required by these Regulations.

(e) Require any person to appear or produce documents or both pursuant to a subpoena issued by the Commissioner.

(f) Grant or order a hearing.

§ 2510.8 (§ 138) Final determination by the Commissioner. The Commissioner, on such terms and conditions as he may determine, may:

(a) Dismiss the PAR if it fails substantially to comply with the provisions of the Act or these Regulations.

(b) Grant or deny the PAR, in whole or in part, or remand the proceeding to the District Rent Administrator for further action.

(c) In the event that the Commissioner grants or denies any such PAR in whole or in part, the Commissioner shall inform the party or parties filing the PAR of the grounds upon which such decision is based, and of any economic data and other facts of which such decision is based, and of any economic data and other facts of which the Commissioner has taken official notice.

§ 2510.9 (§ 139) Pending PAR's. Where a Regulation is amended during the pendency of a PAR, the determination shall be in accordance with the amended Regulation.

§ 2510.10 (§ 140) Time within which the Commissioner shall take final action.

If the Commissioner does not act finally within a period of ninety days after a PAR is filed, or within such extended period as may be fixed by the Commissioner, the PAR shall be deemed to be denied. The Commissioner may, however, grant one such extension not to exceed thirty days with the consent of the party filing the PAR; any further extension may only be granted with the consent of the party filing the PAR; any further extension may only be granted with the consent of all parties to the PAR. Final action on PAR filed against a regulation shall be governed by Section 204 of the State Administrative Procedure Act.

§ 2510.11 (§ 141) Stays.

The filing of a PAR against an order, other than an order adjusting, fixing or establishing a maximum rent, within thirty-three days after the date of the issuance of such order shall stay such order until the final determination of the PAR by the Commissioner. However, nothing herein contained shall limit the Commissioner from granting or vacating a stay under appropriate circumstances.

§ 2510.12 (§ 142) Judicial review. The filing and determination of a PAR is a prerequisite to obtaining judicial review of any provision of these Regulations or any order issued thereunder. A proceeding for review may be instituted under Article 78 of the Civil Practice Law and Rules provided the petition in the Supreme Court is filed within sixty days after the final determination of the order. Service of the petition upon the Division of Housing and Community Renewal shall be made by leaving a copy thereof with Counsel's Office at the Division's principal office.

Tenant Protection Regulations

§ 2510.13 (§ 143) Modification or revocation of orders on a PAR. The Commissioner, on application of either party or on his own initiative, and upon notice to all parties affected, may, prior to the date that a proceeding for judicial review has been commenced in the Supreme Court pursuant to Article 78 of the Civil Practice Law and Rules, modify, supersede or revoke any order issued by him under these or previous Regulations where he finds that such order was the result of illegality, irregularity in vital matters, or fraud. Where an order is modified superseded or revoked by the Commissioner he may also direct that appropriate rent adjustments be made in accordance with the order issued.

STATE TENANT PROTECTION BULLETINS

BULLETIN NO. 6 REVISED

(Issued August 1, 1978)

Standards with respect to the Terms and Conditions of New and Renewal Leases for Rented Apartments in Buildings owned by Cooperative Associations or Condominiums as revised to conform to Chapter 544 Laws of 1978, amending the General Business Law in relation to conversion of residential real estate from rental status to cooperative or condominium ownership.

In connection with the procedures and requirements of the Tenant Protection Regulations adopted pursuant to Section 10 of the Act, concerning owners granting new one, two or three year leases or such renewal lease at the option of the tenant, the following additional enumerated standards are prescribed with respect to the terms and conditions of new and renewal leases for rented apartments located either in a building which is under cooperative or condominium ownership, or in a building for which the Attorney General of the State of New York has accepted from the owner for filing an offering plan to convert the building to cooperative or condominium ownership, or where such plan has been accepted subject to the requirements of Section 352-ee of the General Business Law as added by Chapter 544 Laws of 1978, and the plan is an "Eviction Plan" as defined therein. (Section 352-ee is only applicable to residential buildings in cities, towns and villages in Nassau, Rockland and Westchester Counties which elect to have the section apply.)

New or renewal leases for one, two or three year terms may contain a clause permitting termination prior to the expiration of the term by a subsequent owner who has purchased the shares allocated to the rented apartment or purchased the rented apartment, if such clause provides—

1. That the termination clause shall only be effective for the purpose of permitting the rented apartment,

following surrender of possession by the tenant, to be occupied immediately by such owner under the cooperative or condominium building ownership, or by a member of that owner's immediate family as defined in the Tenant Protection Regulations;

2. That such owner must serve on the tenant a notice in writing by certified mail no less than 90 days prior to the date of termination of the lease, reciting the date of termination and the full name and address of the owner or the member of the owner's immediate family who is to take occupancy of the rented apartment, and his or her relationship to the owner; an exact copy of such notice must also be filed with affidavit of service with the Division within 48 hours after such service;

3. That such increase, if any, in the legal regulated rent collected under the lease pursuant to the applicable County Rent Guidelines Board rate must be refunded by the owner to the tenant on or before the date of surrender of possession, to the following extent:

   a. Where a one year lease is so terminated prior to the expiration of the one year term, the rent increase must be fully refunded.
   b. Where a two year lease is so terminated prior to the expiration of one year, the rent increase must be fully refunded; if one year or more has expired, such amount of the rent increase as exceeded the one year lease guideline rate must be refunded.
   c. Where a three year lease is so terminated prior to the expiration of one year, the rent increase must be fully refunded; if one year but less than two years has expired, such amount of the rent increase as exceeded the one year lease guideline rate must be refunded; if two years or more have expired, such amount of the rent increase as exceeded the two year lease guideline rate must be refunded.

4. Where the rented apartment is located in a city, town or village which has filed a resolution with the Attorney General electing to have Section 352-ee of the General Business Law (Chapter 544, Laws of 1978) apply to cooperative and condominium conversion plans, and

the plan has been accepted for filing by the Attorney General subject to the requirements of Section 352-ee:

   a. That the plan for conversion to cooperative or condominium ownership is an "Eviction Plan" as defined in Section 352-ee.
   b. That no eviction proceedings shall be commenced against the tenant for a period of two years after the plan is declared effective as an "Eviction Plan" as defined in Section 352-ee (when at least 35% of the tenants in occupancy of all dwelling units have consented to purchase).
   c. That the termination clause shall become null and void if the plan is amended to provide that it shall be a "Non-Eviction Plan" as defined in Section 352-ee.
   d. That the termination clause shall become null and void if the plan is deemed abandoned, void and of no effect because it does not become effective within 12 months from the date of issue of the letter of the Attorney General accepting the filing of the plan as provided in Section 352-ee.
   e. That the termination clause shall become null and void if the tenant is sixty-two years of age or older on the date the plan is declared effective under the requirements of Section 352-ee, (when at least 35% of the tenants in occupancy of all dwelling units have consented to purchase).

In any case where a new or renewal lease for such a rented apartment was entered into prior to the date of this Bulletin, if the lease contains a clause permitting termination by the owner prior to the expiration of the lease term, such termination clause may only be effective under the Act and Regulations if written notice is given to the tenant that the clause is amended to conform to the requirements of this Bulletin.

The foregoing additional standards for the leases of rented apartments in buildings owned by cooperative associations or condominiums or for which plans for such ownership have been accepted for filing by the Attorney General are deemed to be consistent with the purpose and intent of the Act to protect tenants; to encourage the renting of vacant apartments in areas where rental housing is in short supply; and to conform with the purpose and intent of the laws relating to cooperative and condominium ownership of apartment buildings.

BULLETIN NO. 6 REVISED

Supplement No. 1

(Issued October 16, 1978)

Municipalities Reported to have Filed Resolutions with the Attorney General Adopting Section 352-ee General Business Law, as added by Chapter 544 Laws of 1978, (Cooperative and Condominium Conversions).

	Adopted
Nassau County	
Great Neck, Village	8/1/78
Great Neck Plaza, Village	7/26/78
Roslyn, Village *	9/19/78
Russell Gardens, Village	8/14/78
Thomaston, Village	8/14/78
Rockland County	
Spring Valley, Village	8/1/78
Westchester County	
Greenburgh, Town	9/13/78
Hastings-on-Hudson, Village *	9/19/78
Mamaroneck, Village	8/3/78
Mount Vernon, City	8/23/78
New Rochelle, City	9/19/78
Tarrytown, Village	8/21/78
White Plains, City	9/5/78
Yonkers, City	8/29/78

* This municipality is not under the Emergency Tenant Protection Act.

BULLETIN NO. 11

(Issued August 1, 1977)

Status of Emergency Tenant Protection Act in Village of Spring Valley by reason of Decision of Supreme Court Justice Kelly in State of New York, etc. v. Nat Mack et al. holding Village Resolution invalid under the Act.

Supplement No. 1 (Issued October 31, 1978)

Decision by Appellate Division, 2d Department, Supreme Court, affirming Order of the Supreme Court,

Rockland County, that the Village of Spring Valley's Resolution determining an emergency was invalid under the Act because the vacancy rate was in excess of five percent. Application for Leave to Appeal filed by the Village of Spring Valley staying this decision.

This decision was reported in the New York Law Journal, October 26, 1978, on page 12, column 3, as follows:

"PEOPLE ex rel. OFFICE OF RENT ADMINISTRATION, plf and THE VILLAGE OF SPRING VALLEY, ap. v. MACK, res—Order of the Supreme Court, Rockland County (Kelly, J.), dated July 29, 1977, affirmed, with $50 costs and disbursements. No opinion.

"Martuscello, J. P., Latham, Damiani and Titone, JJ., concur."

The Village of Spring Valley by the Village Attorney further informed the Division that an application for leave to appeal this decision to the Court of Appeals is being filed, and this stays the decision until the court determines the Village's application for leave to appeal.

Therefore, pending further developments, the Emergency Tenant Protection Act continues to be operative within the Village of Spring Valley under Division administration. Any owner or tenant requiring further information or assistance should communicate with the Division's Tenant Protection Bureau at Two World Trade Center, 58th Floor, New York City, telephone number 212-488-3217, or the Tenant Protection Field Assistant at the Village of Spring Valley office on Tuesdays, telephone number 914-352-1100.

BULLETIN NO. 15

(Issued June 30, 1978)

Guideline Rates of Maximum Rent Increases

Summary of Guideline Rates of Maximum Rent Increase filed by County Rent Guidelines Boards for Leases commencing between July 1, 1978 and June 30, 1979 on

TENANT PROTECTION BULLETINS

regulated apartments in cities, towns and villages covered by the Act on June 30, 1978.

	Nassau County	Rockland* County		Westchester County
1. One Year Lease	6%	5%	6%	
2. Two Year Lease	8%	8%		5% for 1st year
				4% for 2d year (9% Total)
3. Three Year Lease	10%	11%		5% for 1st year
				5% for 2d year (10% Total)
				4% for 3d year (14% Total)

4. *Additional Guideline Rate for Vacant Apartment Leases in Nassau and Westchester Counties.*

Where a vacant apartment is rented to a new tenant an additional Guideline, not to exceed *one-half of one month's rent of the last lease,* may be charged, to be paid by the tenant in equal monthly installments over the term of the one, two or three year lease given to the tenant by the landlord. This additional charge does not continue in the Legal Regulated Rent upon the expiration of the lease term. Also, this additional Guideline may *not* be taken if the landlord is filing an application with the State Division for a rent adjustment based upon the installation of new equipment to replace existing equipment.

Further information and copies of the *Guidelines and Findings* adopted and filed by each County Rent Guidelines Board are available at the office of Rent Administration:

>Two World Trade Center—58th Floor
>New York, N. Y. 10047—Tel. 212/488-7147
>
>50 Clinton Street—2d Floor
>Hempstead, N. Y. 11550—Tel. 516/481-9494
>
>99 Church Street—4th Floor
>White Plains, N. Y. 10601—Tel. 914/948-4434

[In Nassau County, the County Rent Guideline Board Orders apply to the unincorporated areas of Town of North Hempstead, Villages of Cedarhuurst, Floral Park, Flower Hill, Great Neck, Great Neck Plaza, Lynbrook,

---

* In Rockland County, Guideline rates apply to apartments in those buildings for which owners have filed prescribed data with the Guidelines Board.

Mineola, Rockville Centre, Russell Gardens, Stewart Manor, Thomaston, and City of Long Beach; In Rockland County, the Orders apply to the Village of Spring Valley.]

BULLETIN NO. 18

(Issued April 2, 1979)

Legal Regulated Rents for Vacant Apartments

Supplement No. 1   September 2, 1980

Vacancy guideline for apartments in Westchester and Rockland Counties rented under leases commencing between July 1, 1980 and September 30, 1981.

This Bulletin Supplement recites the requirements under the Emergency Tenant Protection Act and Tenant Protection Regulations for the collection of the vacancy guidelines effective July 1, 1980 which have been adopted and filed with the Division by the Westchester County and Rockland County Rent Guidelines Boards.

The Westchester Vacancy Guideline is as follows:

> When a vacancy occurs, the landlord shall be allowed to increase the base rent for that apartment to the highest rent level of an apartment having the same number of rooms within the same building or complex of buildings, as of the time of the vacancy. This base rent is then established for this building or complex, for apartments having the same number of rooms, for the balance of the guideline term. Upon this base rent shall then be added the allowable one, two, or three year increases under the guidelines, provided the landlord/owner shall further fully recite in the lease to the tenant the designation and location of the apartment having the same number of rooms and the highest rent level.

The Rockland Vacancy Guideline is as follows:

> When a vacancy occurs, the landlord shall be permitted to raise the legal regulated rent of the vacated apartment to the highest level of legal regulated rent of apartments with the same room count in the property complex which legal regulated rent shall

Tenant Protection Bulletins

then be the base for rent guidelines lease adjustment rates for the vacated apartment.

The prescribed Notice form (RTP-25) required under Section 48, Tenant Protection Regulations, to be attached to leases for vacant apartments has been revised for use in Westchester and Rockland and a copy is attached to this Bulletin Supplement.

Under the requirements of the Emergency Tenant Protection Act and the Tenant Protection Regulations, and consistent with the purpose and intent of the Act and Regulations, for the landlord to include a rent increase in the lease to a new tenant based upon the authorized vacancy guidelines, the apartment within the same building or complex of buildings having the same number of rooms and the highest rent level must have the same services, equipment and improvements as are provided to the vacant apartment under the lease to the new tenant, or if any of such services, equipment or improvements are not so provided there must be a reduction in the legal requlated rent for the apartment having the highest rent level in order for that rent level to be used as a vacancy guideline. The reduction must be in the amount which the Division approved in an Order and Determination of the legal regulated rent for that apartment, plus subsequent guideline increases thereon, if any.

In order to clarify the foregoing requirement that the same services, equipment and improvements be provided in the vacant apartment as are included in the legal regulated rent for the apartment having the same number of rooms for such a rent to be included in the vacancy guideline, it is to be noted that this requirement is based upon Section 7 of the Act entitled "Maintenance of Services" whereunder, in order to collect a rent adjustment, the owner must file with the Division.

Section 7: ". . . a written certification that he is maintaining and will continue to maintain all services furnished on the date upon which this act becomes a law or required to be furnished by any law, ordinance or regulation applicable to the premises."

Therefore, a variation in a particular service, item of equipment, or an improvement which has a significant effect on the rental value of an apartment or which causes the service, equipment, or improvement in the vacant apartment not to be comparable or similar shall bar the use of the Vacancy Guideline without an appropriate compensating rent adjustment.

Landlords or tenants may obtain further assistance from the nearest Division Office of Rent Administration at:

> Two World Trade Center—58th Floor
> New York City
> Telephone: (212) 488-3217

> 99 Church Street—4th Floor
> White Plains, New York
> Telephone: (914) 948-4434

For use in Westchester and Rockland Counties

LANDLORD'S NOTICE TO NEW TENANT OF LEGAL REGULATED RENT FOR A VACANT HOUSING ACCOMMODATION PREVIOUSLY REGULATED UNDER EMERGENCY TENANT PROTECTION ACT

(Section 48 of the Tenant Protection Regulations)

(Read instructions and extract of the Regulations on page 3)

Mailing Address of Landlord:
Name _____ Tel. No. ( ) _____
Number and Street _____
Post Office, State _____ (Zip) ____

Address of housing
accommodations _____ (No. and Street) _____
(Apt. No.) _____ (City, town or village)
TO: _____

(New Tenant's Name) (complete at time of renting)

PLEASE TAKE NOTICE THAT:

1. The monthly rent(s) under the offered lease shall be $____ or, if applicable, $____ 1st year, $____ 2nd year, $____ 3rd year, which shall be the Legal Regulated Rent(s). (Insert correct amount(s)).

2. The previous Legal Regulated Rent(s) under the last lease or rental agreement was (were) $____ per month or,

1080

if applicable, $____ per month 1st year, $____ 2nd year, $____ 3rd year. (Insert correct amount(s)).

3. The term of the last lease or rental agreement (applicable box is checked):
   a. ☐ Has expired.
   b. ☐ Will expire on _____, 19__. (Complete with exact date).

4. A Vacancy Guideline rent increase (applicable box is checked):
   ☐ Is *not* included in the lease rent.
   ☐ Is included in the lease rent based upon the legal regulated rent for Apartment No. ____, an apartment in the same building or complex with the same number of rooms, at $____ per month, and authorized for use to increase the rent of this vacant apartment.
   ☐ Apartment No. ____ has the same services, equipment and improvements as are included under the offered lease.
   ☐ Apartment No. ____ has additional services, equipment, and/or improvements which are not included under the offered lease consisting of: (Clearly identify)

for which a reduction in the legal regulated rent has been included in the sum of $____ which is the same amount as was approved on _____, 19__, in an Order and Determination of the Legal Regulated Rent by the Division of Housing and Community Renewal plus subsequent guideline increases thereon, if any.

5. Therefore, the new lease term is (applicable boxes are checked):
   a. ☐ one year   ☐ two years   ☐ three years
and the lease rent includes the authorized guideline rate of increase ____% (insert rate) above:
   ☐ the last legal regulated rent for this apartment.
   ☐ the legal regulated rent of Apartment No. ____, or that rent reduced by the amount of $____ as stated in paragraph 4.

b. ☐ And, in addition, if Item 3b. is checked, for the balance of the last least term at the last Legal Regulated Rent—recited in Item 2—without increase except for the authorized vacancy guideline, if any, to a rent of $_____ per month.

c. ☐ Insert other authorized lease rent increase provisions, if any, in this space:

I have read the foregoing and hereby affirm that the contents are true of my own knowledge.
Dated: _____, 19__.
_____
(Signature of Landlord)

It is not necessary that this Notice be sworn to, but false statements may subject you to the penalties provided by law.

INSTRUCTIONS: This Notice complies with the requirements of Section 48, Tenant Protection Regulations, when the landlord has completed it, made it available to prospective tenants, and attached it to the new tenant's copy of the executed written lease at the time of renting the vacant housing accommodation.

Extract of Tenant Protection Regulations

§ 48. (2503.8) Notice of legal regulated rent for a vacant housing accommodation previously regulated under the Act. A landlord of a vacant housing accommodation for lease shall make available to prospective tenants a notice in writing of the monthly rent under the offered lease, and of the prior legal regulated rent, if any, which was in effect immediately prior to the vacancy, and that any increase in the prior legal regulated rent under the offered lease does not exceed the applicable rate of rent adjustment in effect pursuant to the guidelines filed with the Division by the Rent Guidelines Board for the county wherein the housing accommodation is located, or as otherwise authorized by the Act.

At the time of renting the vacant housing accommodation, the landlord shall attach this notice in writing to the executed written lease, and deliver a copy of the notice to the tenant with a copy of the lease, or include a written provision in the lease setting forth the prior legal regulated rent, the amount of any rent increase under the lease and showing that such increase does not exceed the applicable rate of rent adjustment in effect pursuant to the Guidelines filed by the Rent Guidelines Board or as otherwise authorized by the Act. In the event the landlord does not comply with this requirement, the lease shall not be effective to increase the prior legal regulated rent; however, at such time thereafter that the landlord does provide the notice to the tenant with the required information in writing, the otherwise authorized monthly rent increase shall be collectible commencing with the first rent payment date thereafter. (NOTE: Added by Amendment No. 4 issued September 10, 1975, effective October 1, 1975).

Additional information, copies of Guideline Rates, or assistance are available at
NEW YORK STATE DIVISION OF HOUSING AND COMMUNITY RENEWAL RENT ADMINISTRATION OFFICE LOCATIONS:

In Nassau County:	50 Clinton Street—2nd Floor Hempstead	Tel. 516-481-9494
In Rockland-Westchester Counties:	99 Church Street—4th Floor White Plains	Tel. 914-948-4434
In New York City:	Tenant Protection Bureau Two World Trade Center— 58th Floor New York City	Tel. 212-488-3217

BULLETIN NO. 20

(Issued June 8, 1979)

Criteria for determining eligibility for rent increases on the grounds of hardship and reduction in ratio between operating expenses and gross rents.

Applications by landlords for rent increases in addition to those approved by the County Rent Guidelines Board are authorized by Section 6d of the Emergency Tenant Protection Act (ETPA) as implemented by Section 34-3 of the Tenant Protection Regulations (TPR) which provides:

"3. Hardship. The Division may grant an appropriate adjustment of the legal regulated rent where the landlord by application for increases in rents in excess of the rent adjustment authorized by the Rent Guidelines Board under the Act and as provided for in section 35 establishes a hardship, and the Division finds that the rate of such rent adjustment is not sufficient to enable the owner to maintain approximately the same ratio between operating expenses (including taxes, and labor costs but excluding debt service, financing costs, and management fees) and gross rents which prevailed on the average over the immediate preceding five year period, or for the entire life of the building if less than five years."

Thus, a landlord who applies for a rent adjustment under this subdivision of the TPR must establish the existence of a hardship as a prerequisite to having the application processed to determine whether additional rent increases are warranted to maintain approximately the same average ratio between operating expenses and gross rents for the preceding five year period or for the life of the building if less than five years.

Section 6d of the ETPA, while mandating that an owner must establish a hardship in addition to a ratio slippage, spells out only the factors relating to the Division's findings of the ratio slippage and not those required in the establishment of a hardship. However, Section 10 of the ETPA expressly provides that the Division "shall be empowered to implement this act by appropriate regulations."

Pursuant to such statutory delegation of authority, the Division has determined that a landlord establishes a hardship upon showing:

1. That on or before the commencement of the test year adopted in item 2 below, the landlord has paid at least 20 percent of his purchase price and/or cost of construction of the property. In determining the percentage of the landlord's investment, (a) payments for interest or charges incident to the obtaining of title to the property shall be excluded; (b) any money received by the landlord as a result of refinancing the mortgage or mortgages on the property, whether assumed or placed when title was acquired, shall be deducted from the total payments made toward the purchase price in calculating the percentage of the landlord's investment to the extent that the pro-

ceeds of such refinancing was not reasonably thereafter expended in the improvement of the property. For good cause shown, the Division may waive the requirement that the landlord must have paid at least 20 percent of the purchase price of the property.

2. That for the most recent full calendar year or fiscal year or any twelve consecutive months ending not more than ninety days prior to the filing of the application, the landlord earned less than six percent on the amount of his payments toward the purchase price and/or cost of construction. In determining such percentage,

(a) the same exclusions and deductions shall apply in calculating the total of the landlord's payments toward the purchase price as are applicable and set forth in item 1 above;

(b) the income of the property shall be the annualized legal regulated rents from all housing accommodations subject to the ETPA in effect at the time of the filing of the application except that if a new or renewal lease may properly be entered into within twelve months from the filing of the application, the legal regulated rent permitted to be charged during such twelve month period (based on a lease actually entered into or on an assumed renewal for the same term as the previous lease) shall be annualized, plus the current rents on an annual basis from all other housing accommodations in the building not subject to the ETPA, commercial and business space and other rented or rentable space, plus any other income earned from the operation of the property;

(c) operating expenses shall include all expenses necessary in the operation and maintenance of the property and properly allocable to the test year, including debt service, financing costs, management fees and an allowance for depreciation of two percent of the purchase price of the building or the amount shown for depreciation of the building in the latest required Federal income tax return, whichever is lower, except that no allowance for depreciation of the building shall be included where the building has been fully depreciated for Federal income tax purposes or on the books of the owner. Increases or decreases in real estate taxes, water or sewage charges and wages currently in effect may be projected in computing operating expenses.

The Division has prescribed the application form to be used in making an application under this subdivision of the TPR. Where a hardship is not established under the criteria hereinabove set forth, the Division will deny the application. Where a hardship is established, the Division will process the application and make a finding as to whether the applicable rate or ratio of the guideline rent adjustment increases will be sufficient to maintain approximately the same ratio between the expenses and rents which prevailed on the average over the past five years. If the rate of the guideline rent adjustment increases will not be sufficient, an additional rate of rent increase will be granted above the current ratio as necessary, to raise it to the level of the five year ratio.

The applicant building owner is, of course, required upon notice from the Division to substantiate the content of the application and to make available the books and records deemed necessary to corroborate the items as submitted. The Division will adjust all items as found warranted.

The tenants and the applicant will be given notice when the Division has completed its examination of the application and the answers, with the opportunity to see the record and be heard.

Thereafter, the Division's final action will be taken by the issuance of Orders and Determinations with copies mailed to the applicant owner and each tenant.

TENANT PROTECTION BULLETINS

APPLICATION BASED UPON HARDSHIP

STATE OF NEW YORK
DIVISION OF HOUSING AND COMMUNITY RENEWAL
OFFICE OF RENT ADMINISTRATION   File No. _____

APPLICATION BASED UPON HARDSHIP
(Section 6d. of Emergency Tenant Protection Act of 1974)
Section 34-3 of Tenant Protection Regulations -(see text on other side)

1. Mailing Address of Landlord: 2. Mailing Address of Tenant:
   Name _____ Tel. No. ____   Name _____ Tel. No. ____
   Number and Street _____   Number and Street _____
   Post Office, State and Zip _____   Post Office, State and Zip _____

3. Address of housing (Number and Street) _____ (Apt.No.) ___ (No. of Rooms) ___ (Municipality) ___ Total No. of: Apts. ___ Rooms ___
   accommodations
   (Omit all half rooms)
4. The legal regulated rent is $ _____ per _____.
5. The landlord applies for rent increases in excess of the Rent Guidelines Board rent adjustment rates on the grounds of a hardship: Set forth such facts which you claim to establish a hardship in the space below.

6. Complete the following items:

	Last Current Year	Preceding Five Year Period			
	19__	19__	19__	19__	19__
A. Total Gross Rents		X	X	X	X
B. Gross Rents plus projected annual increases(Guidelines) under leases to be renewed in the present calendar year		X	X	X	X
C. Operating Expenses (exclusive of debt service, financing costs, and management fees) Fuel / Utilities / Payroll-Labor / Real Estate Taxes / Repairs and Maintenance / Capital Improvements (Annualized costs) / Other - if any (identify _____)					
Total Operating Expenses					
D. Ratio between Operating Expenses and Gross Rents*					

* (Plus projected guideline annual increases under leases to be renewed in the present calendar year.)

E. Average Ratio between Operating Expenses and Gross Rents for preceding Five Year period _____

Notice: The landlord will be notified to submit the required records to establish a hardship after this application is completed and filed.

I have read the foregoing and hereby affirm that the contents are true of my own knowledge.

Dated: _____, 19____   Signed _____
                                                  Landlord and Title

See instructions and Notice to Tenant on rdverse side.
It is not necessary that the foregoing be sworn to, but false statements may subject you to the penalties provided by law.

RTP-23 (3-79)

INSTRUCTIONS: An original and one copy of this application, naming each tenant, and accompanying documents, if any, must be filed by delivery or mailing to the nearest office of the State Division of Housing and Community Renewal, Office of Rent Administration:

New York City—Two World Trade Center 58th Floor—New York, N.Y. 10047

White Plains—99 Church Street, 2nd Floor— White Plains, N.Y. 10601

Hempstead—50 Clinton Street, 2nd Floor Hempstead, N.Y. 11550

Extract of Regulations
EMERGENCY TENANT PROTECTION ACT OF 1974
Tenant Protection Regulations
* * * * *

§ 34. Applications for adjustment of legal regulated rent.

3. Hardship. The Division may grant an appropriate adjustment of the legal regulated rent where the landlord by application for increases in rents in excess of the rent adjustment authorized by the Rent Guidelines Board under the Act and as provided for in section 35 establishes a hardship, and the Division finds that the rate of such rent adjustment is not sufficient to enable the owner to maintain approximately the same ratio between operating expenses (including taxes, and labor costs but excluding debt service, financing costs, and management fees) and gross rents which prevailed on the average over the immediate preceding five year period, or for the entire life of the building if less than five years.

NOTICE TO TENANT
OF APPLICATION UNDER SECTION 34-3—HARDSHIP

On the reverse side of this Notice is a copy of an application filed by the landlord. You are hereby afforded the opportunity to respond to the application. Your response should be submitted in duplicate on the answer forms enclosed herewith *within seven (7) days* by delivery or mail to the nearest office of the State Division of Housing and Community Renewal, Office of Rent Administration (see above for addresses).

Tenant Protection Bulletins

You will also receive a further notice of any proposed rent increase following the completion of an accounting examination of this application with the opportunity to appear, examine the findings, and submit any further answer for consideration in the proceeding. Thereafter, an Order and Determination may be issued. Any rent increase which is granted will be collectible upon the expiration of the current lease unless there is a provision in the lease for a Hardship rent increase to be collectible during the lease term, in which event the increase may be effective on the first rent payment date following the date of this Notice, or such later date as may be determined to be appropriate if the landlord does not submit records within the prescribed time limits.

Date of Notice: ―――――― ――――――――――――
State Rent Administrator

The State Division of Housing and Community Renewal will issue a written opinion upon rendering its determination of this application, and copies will be mailed to the tenant and landlord.

TENANT PROTECTION BULLETINS

State of New York
Division of Housing and Community Renewal
Office of Rent Administration
Two World Trade Center
New York, N. Y. 10047

Supplement to
Application Based Upon Hardship

(See Section 34-3 Tenant Protection Regulations and Tenant Protection Bulletin No. 20)

Instruction: Complete and attach to each copy of landlord's *Application Based Upon Hardship.*

Address of Property: No. and Street:_____
City, town or village: _____
County: _____

1. This property was purchased on _____, 19__ at the purchase price of $____ and/or the cost of construction of the building(s) was $____ by (insert full name and address of owner and landlord)
_____

2. The landlord has paid at least 20% of the purchase price and/or cost of construction of the building(s), exclusive of payments for interest or charges incident to the obtaining of title to the property, namely $____. This payment is exclusive of
   (a) payments for interest or charges incident to the obtaining of title to the property;
   (b) any money received by the landlord as a result of refinancing the mortgage or mortgages on the property, whether assumed or placed when title was acquired.

NOTE: If this 20% payment has not been made, do not file the Application because a hardship is not established unless you can establish good cause for such payment being less than 20%. Use the space immediately below for this purpose and do not complete item 2 above. Recite the full facts including the amount of the payment made and why it is less than 20%.

Tenant Protection Bulletins

3. The landlord has earned less than six percent on the amount of his payments toward the purchase price and/or cost of construction in the most recent calendar year or fiscal year or twelve consecutive months ending not more than ninety days prior to the filing of the application, and in evidence therefor submits the following:

NOTE: Do not file the Application if this sum is in excess of six percent, because a hardship is not established.

For One Year Period Commencing _____, 19__:
Total: $_____

Income

Apartment Rents subject to ETPA	$_____
Projected Guideline rate increase for next 12 month period	$_____
Rents of Apartments not subject to ETPA	$_____
Rents of commercial, business, professional space	$_____
All other income	$_____
	Total: $_____

Operating Expenses

Debt Service and Financing Costs	$_____
Identify the specific items:	
First Mortgage	$_____
Second Mortgage	$_____
Other, if any	$_____
Management Fee	$_____
Depreciation, if any—use lower of 2% of building cost or Federal Income Tax Return amount	$_____
Fuel	$_____
Utilities	$_____
Payroll—Labor	$_____
Real Estate Taxes	$_____
Repairs and Maintenance	$_____
Capital Improvements (Annualized)	$_____
Insurance	$_____

TENANT PROTECTION BULLETINS

Other, if any - identify $_____
_____ $_____
_____ $_____
Total Income $_____
Less *Total Expenses* $_____
Balance in the sum of $_____ is therefore less than six percent of amount of payment recited in item 2—$_____, and a hardship is submitted to be established.

I am the landlord, and an owner, one of the owners, or an officer of the owner.

I have read the foregoing and hereby affirm that the contents are true of my own knowledge.

Dated: _____, 19__.   Signed: _____
                            Type or print: Name _____
                                          Title _____

It is not necessary that this Notice be sworn to, but false statement may subject you to the penalties provided by law.

BULLETIN NO. 20

(Issued April 15, 1980)

Supplement No. 1

Criteria for determining eligibility for rent increases on the grounds of hardship and reduction in ratio between operating expenses and gross rents.

Use of annualized legal regulated rents collected in the last calendar year, fiscal year, or other authorized 12 month period to determine whether landlord is earning less than six percent and therefore establishes a hardship.

Paragraph Number 2 (b) of this Bulletin is hereby revised as follows:

2 (b) the income of the property shall be the annualized legal regulated rents from all housing accommodations subject to the ETPA collected in the prescribed year, plus the rents collected on an annual basis from all other housing accommodations in the building not subject to the ETPA, commercial and business space and other rented or rentable space, plus any other income earned from the operation of the property;

Tenant Protection Bulletins

Under this revision, the legal regulated rents will not be projected to include adjustments which may occur within the next 12 month period, for the purpose of determining the rate of earnings based upon the operating expenses for the last year.

BULLETIN NO. 21 (Revised-final)

(Issued July 19, 1979)

Summary of Guideline Rates of Maximum Rent Increases filed by County Rent Guidelines Boards for Leases commencing between July 1, 1979 and June 30, 1980

A. For Tenants in Occupancy	Nassau County	Rockland* County	Westchester County
1. One Year Lease	7%	Gas heat- 9 1/2% Oil -11 1/2%	9%
2. Two Year Lease	10%	Gas heat-12 1/2% Oil - 1313 1/2%	11%
3. Three Year Lease	13%	All - 15%	13%

B. *Additional Vacancy Guideline Rate for Leases to New Tenants*

Nassau County: Where a vacant apartment is rented to a new tenant an additional Guideline, not to exceed *one month's rent of the last lease,* may be charged, to be paid by the tenant in equal monthly installments over the term of the one, two or three year lease given to the tenant by the landlord. This additional charge does not continue in the Legal Regulated Rent upon the expiration of the lease term. Also, this additional Guideline may *not* be taken if the landlord is filing an application with the State Division for a rent adjustment based upon the installation of new equipment to replace existing equipment.

Rockland County: Where a vacant apartment is rented under a one year lease to a new tenant an additional *guideline rate of 4%* may be charged, which increase shall become a part of the rent permanently.

Westchester County: Where a vacant apartment is rented to a new tenant an additional Guideline, not to exceed a *six percent rate of increase* above the last lease

---

*In Rockland County, Guideline rates apply to apartments in those buildings for which owners have filed prescribed data with the Guidelines Board.

rent, may be charged, to be paid by the tenant in equal monthly installments over the term of the one, two or three year lease given to the tenant by the landlord. This additional charge shall continue in the Legal Regulated Rent upon the expiration of the lease term. Also, this additional Guideline may *not* be taken if the landlord is filing an application with the State Division for a rent adjustment based upon the installation of new equipment to replace existing equipment.

C. *Other Additional Guideline Rates:*

Nassau County: For apartments in buildings which provide electric service under the legal regulated rent— 1½% additional guideline rate

Rockland County: A fuel cost supplemental guideline rate may further be adopted by the Board to be collectible at the end of the first year of a two year lease or three year lease, or the second year of a three year lease, if the fuel costs increase 20% above the level in effect on July 1, 1979, and the lease incorporates prescribed conditions under which the additional rent increase may become effective. These conditions include the requirement of a 90-day notice to the tenant, and an option to the tenant to cancel the lease and vacate upon a 60-day advance notice in lieu of paying the additional increase for the balance of the lease term.

Westchester County: For apartments in buildings which provide electric service under the legal regulated rent— 1% additional guideline rate.

D. *Guideline Rates for Separate Classes of Housing:*

Nassau County:

1. Classes of housing in the Village of Great Neck consisting of four formerly rent controlled apartments which are occupied by tenants who were in possession at the time the apartments were removed from rent control by Village Resolution:

      $35 per month for two apartments
      $60 " " " one apartment and
      $65 " " " one apartment

2. For leases of apartments in buildings in the City of Long Beach with 60–99 accommodations—the same

guidelines as are applicable to all other apartments in the County (see sections A, B, and C of this Bulletin).

Westchester County:

For leases in apartments in the Village of Hastings-on-Hudson which first came under the Act May 1, 1979—the same guidelines as are applicable to all other apartments in the County (see sections A, B, and C of this Bulletin).

Further information and copies of the Guidelines and Findings adopted and filed by each County Rent Guidelines Board will be availabe at the Office of Rent Administration:

>Two World Trade Center—58th floor
>New York, N.Y. 10047—Tel. 212-488-7147
>
>50 Clinton Street—2d floor
>Hempstead, N.Y. 11550—Tel. 516-481-9494
>
>99 Church Street—4th floor
>White Plains, N.Y. 10601—Tel. 914-948-4434

BULLETIN NO. 21 (REVISED-FINAL)

(Issued October 25, 1979)

Supplement No. 1

Summary of Guideline Rates of Maximum Rent Increase filed by County Rent Guldelines Boards for Leases commencing between July 1, 1979 and June 30, 1980

Westchester County—Guideline Rates for the Class of Housing without Heat and Hot Water

1. *One Year Lease* 6%
2. *Two Year Lease* 7%
3. *Three Year Lease* 9%

These Guideline Rates are applicable to increase the legal regulated rents in leases and lease renewals for apartments within the class of housing where heat and hot water are not included in the rent and are provided by each tenant and not the landlord.

The Westchester County Rent Guidelines Board adopted these Guideline Rates for this class of housing at a public meeting on October 24, 1979 with a specific provision that the Rates were retroactive to July 1, 1979.

Therefore, these Guideline Rates for this class of housing are the maximum increases in the legal regulated rents for the apartments within the class occupied under leases and lease renewals commencing on and after July 1, 1979. Where such a lease or lease renewal was executed or commenced prior to the adoption of these Rates on October 24, 1979, at a rent which was increased by the Guideline Rates applicable to all other classes of housing, such lease rent must be reduced to not exceed the authorized rate of increase. The landlord must further refund to the tenant, all excess rent increases collected prior to October 24, 1979 in cash or by credit to the next rent payment collected from the tenant.

It is to be noted that an additional Guideline Rate of rent increase is applicable to leases on vacant apartments at the rate of 6%, and to apartments which provide electric service under the legal regulated rent at the rate of 1%.

BULLETIN NO. 21 (REVISED-FINAL)

(Issued December 27, 1979)

Supplement No. 2.

Summary of Guideline Rates of Maximum Rent Increase filed by County Rent Guidelines Boards for Leases commencing between July 1, 1979 and June 30, 1980

Westchester County—Guideline Rates for the Class of Housing without Heat

      7% for a one year lease
      8% " " two   "   "
     10% " " three "   "

These Guideline rates are applicable to increase the legal regulated rents in leases and lease renewals for apartments within the class of housing where heat is not included in the rent and is provided by each tenant and not the landlord.

TENANT PROTECTION BULLETINS

The Westchester County Rent Guidelines Board adopted these Guideline rates for this class of housing at a public meeting on December 26, 1979, with a specific provision that the rates were retroactive to July 1, 1979.

Therefore, these Guideline rates for this class of housing are the maximum increases in the legal regulated rents for the apartments within the class occupied under leases and lease renewals commencing on and after July 1, 1979. Where such a lease or lease renewal was executed or commenced prior to the adoption of these rates on December 26, 1979, at a rent which was increased by the Guideline rates applicable to all other classes of housing, such lease rent must be reduced to not exceed the authorized rate of increase. The landlord must further refund to the tenant all excess rent increases collected prior to December 26, 1979 in cash or by credit to the next rent payment collected from the tenant.

It is to be noted that an additional Guideline rate of rent increase is applicable to leases on vacant apartments at the rate of 6%, and to apartments which provide electric service under the legal regulated rent at the rate of 1%.

Further information is available at the Office of Rent Administration located at:

>Two World Trade Center—58th Floor
>New York, N. Y. 10047—Tel. (212) 488-3217
>
>50 Clinton Street—2nd Floor
>Hempstead, N. Y. 11550—Tel. (516) 481-9494
>
>99 Church Street—4th Floor
>White Plains, N. Y. 10601—Tel. (914) 948-4434

BULLETIN NO. 21 (REVISED-FINAL)

(Issued February 1, 1980)

Supplement No. 3

Summary of Guideline Rates of Maximum Rent Increase filed by County Rent Guidelines Board for Leases Commencing between December 1, 1979 and June 30, 1980

Nassau County—Village of Freeport—Guideline Rates

>7% for a one year lease
>10% "   " two   "   "
>13% "   " three "   "

These Guideline rates are applicable to increase the legal regulated rents in leases and lease renewals for apartments within all classes of housing in the Village of Freeport subject to the Act commencing between December 1, 1979 the local effective date of the Act and June 30, 1980, and for determinations of fair market rents under leases commencing prior to December 1, 1979.

The Nassau County Rent Guidelines Board adopted these Guideline rates at a public meeting on January 30, 1980.

Therefore, these Guideline rates for this class of housing are the maximum increases in the legal regulated rents for the apartments within the class occupied under leases and lease renewals commencing on and after December 1, 1979, and for use by the State Division in determining Fair Market Rent upon application by a tenant to have the legal regulated rent reduced on the grounds it was increased in excess of the fair market rent.

An additional Guideline Rate of rent increase is also applicable to leases on vacant apartments not to exceed one month's rent of the last lease and to apartments which provide electric service under the legal regulated rent at the rate of 1½%.

BULLETIN NO. 21 (REVISED-FINAL)

(Issued March 13, 1980)

Supplement No. 4

Summary of Guideline Rates of Maximum Rent Increase filed by County Rent Guidelines Boards for Leases commencing between December 1, 1979 and June 30, 1980 and for determination of Fair Market Rents under prior leases

WESTCHESTER COUNTY:

Villages of Mount Kisco and Pleasantville

Guideline Rates for Leases commencing between December 1, 1979 and June 30, 1980 and determination of fair market rents.

For class of housing wherein the landlord/owner provides heat and hot water:

    1. For one year leases   8%
    2. For two year leases   12%
    3. For three year leases   14%

For class of housing wherein the tenant pays for costs of heat and hot water to a supplier who is not the landlord/owner:

    1. For one year leases   5%
    2. For two year leases   8%
    3. For three year leases   10%

For class of housing wherein the tenant pays for cost of heat to a supplier who is not the landlord/owner and landlord/owner provides hot water:

    1. For one year leases   6%
    2. For two year leases   9%
    3. For three year leases   11%

Additional Guideline for Vacant Apartments:
6%
to be collected in the same manner as adopted in the Guidelines on July 9, 1979

Additional Guideline for apartments receiving electricity as a service included in the rent:

Additional proviso where the last legal regulated rent is in effect under a lease which commenced prior to December 1, 1979 and includes additional rent charges pursuant to escalation clauses based upon increases in taxes, fuel and/or other indices:

The applicable Guideline increase shall be computed upon the amount of the rent excluding the exact dollar amount of such additional rent charges, to establish the rent under the Guidelines.

STATE TENANT PROTECTION BULLETIN NO. 21

(Issued April 10, 1980)

Supplement No. 5.

Summary of Guideline Rates of Maximum Rent Increase Filed by County Rent Guidelines Boards

TENANT PROTECTION BULLETINS

WESTCHESTER COUNTY:

Village of Port Chester

Guideline Rates for Leases commencing between January 1, 1980, (local effective date), and June 30, 1980 and determination of fair market rents, filed on April 9, 1980.

For class of housing wherein the landlord/owner provides that and hot water:

1. For one year leases   9%
2. For two year leases   13%
3. For three year leases   15%

For class of housing wherein the tenant pays for costs of heat and hot water to a supplier who is not the landlord/owner:

1. For one year leases   6%
2. For two year leases   9%
3. For three year leases   11%

For class of housing wherein the tenant pays for cost of heat to a supplier who is not the landlord/owner and landlord/owner provides hot water:

1. For one year leases   7%
2. For two year leases   10%
3. for three year leases   12%

Additional Guideline for Vacant Apartments:
6%
to be collected in the same manner as adopted in the Guidelines on July 9, 1979

Additional Guideline for apartments receiving electricity as a service included in the rent:
1%

Additional proviso where the last legal regulated rent is in effect under a lease which commenced prior to December 1, 1979 and includes additional rent charges pursuant to escalation clauses based upon increases in taxes, fuel and/or other indices:

The applicable Guideline increase shall be computed upon the amount of the rent excluding the exact dollar amount of such additional rent charges, to establish the rent under the guidelines.

Tenant Protection Bulletins

Fair market rent guidelines are applicable to initial legal regulated rents that are the subject of tenant applications under Sec. 9(b) of the ETPA. Only rents in effect within one year before the local effective date of the ETPA in Port Chester may be subject to fair market rent adjustment consideration.

Further information is available at the Office of Rent Administration located at:

>Two World Trade Center—58th Floor
>New York, N. Y. 10047—Tel. (212) 488-3217
>
>50 Clinton Street —2d Floor
>Hempstead, N. Y. 11550—Tel. (516) 481-9494
>
>99 Church Street—4th Floor
>White Plains, N. Y. 10601—Tel. (914) 948-4434

BULLETIN NO. 21 (REVISED-FINAL)

(Issued May 1, 1980)

Supplement No. 6

Summary of Guideline Rates of Maximum Rent Increase filed by County Rent Guidelines Board for Leases commencing between January 1, 1980 and June 30, 1980 and for determination of Fair Market Rents under prior leases.

Nassau County—Village of Baxter Estates—Guideline Rates:

>7% for a one year lease
>10% " " two   "   "
>13% " " three "   "

These Guideline rates are applicable to increase the legal regulated rents in leases and lease renewals for apartments within all classes of housing in the Village of Baxter Estates subject to the Act commencing between January 1, 1980, the local effective date of the Act, and June 30, 1980, and for determinations of fair market rents under leases commencing prior to January 1, 1980.

The Nassau County Rent Guidelines Board adopted these Guideline rates at a public meeting on April 29, 1980.

Therefore, these Guideline rates for this class of housing are the maximum increases in the legal regulated rents for the apartments within the class occupied under leases and lease renewals commencing on and after January 1, 1980, and for use by the State Division in determining Fair Market Rent upon application by a tenant to have the legal regulated rent reduced on the grounds it was increased in excess of the Fair Market Rent.

An additional Guideline rate of rent increase is also applicable to leases on vacant apartments not to exceed one month's rent of the last lease and to apartments which provide electric service under the legal regulated rent at the rate of 1½%.

STATE TENANT PROTECTION BULLETIN NO. 22
and
OPERATIONAL BULLETIN NO. 111
(Issued July 9, 1979)

Schedule of rental values for electric current to operate air conditioners when provided as a new service.

The previous schedule of rental values (September 1, 1975) is hereby changed to authorize the following rent increases for air conditioner electric current. The listed *monthly* amounts are on an annual year round basis for the indicated sizes of air conditioning units where the tenant installs the air conditioning unit and receives electric current therefor as a new service by agreement with the landlord, and the landlord files the prescribed application with the Division for the approval of a monthly increase in the maximum or legal regulated rent:

BTU Size	Seasonal KWHR	Average Seasonal Cost* 700 Hours Operation	Annualized Monthly Increase
4000	520	$ 54.65	$ 4.55
5000	580	60.96	5.00
6000	610	64.11	5.35
8000	910	95.64	8.00
12000	1,345	141.36	11.75
15000	1,630	171.31	14.25
18000	1,890	198.64	16.55

* *Source:* Consolidated Edison, Westchester Division— letter dated June 14, 1979 to Builder's Institute.

Effective this date, all applications for approval of rent increases for the electric current to operate air conditioners as a new service shall be determined to grant the requested monthly rent increases not to exceed the foregoing listed amounts for the size air conditioner recited in the application.

STATE TENANT PROTECTION BULLETIN NO. 22 (REVISED)
and
OPERATIONAL BULLETIN NO. 111 (REVISED)

(Issued July 24, 1981)

Schedule of adjustments to rents for the cost of electricity for newly-installed air conditioners.

This is to authorize revised adjustments to rents previously set on July 9, 1979, to allow for the new installation of air conditioners in buildings which are master-metered and the cost of electricity is included in the rent. Listed below are the monthly year round rates for the indicated size air conditioner installed by the tenant by agreement with the landlord. The landlord must file the prescribed application with the Division for the approval of a monthly increase in the maximum or legal regulated rent.

Air Conditioner BTU Size	Average KWH per Season	Monthly Rent Allowance
4,000	625	$ 6.20
5,000	695	6.90
6,000	730	7.25
8,000	1,090	10.70
12,000	1,615	16.00
15,000	1,955	19.40
18,000	2,265	22.50

Source: Letters dated July 8, 1981 and June 18, 1981, Consolidated Edison Company of New York, Inc., Westchester Division.

This schedule shall take effect immediately.

STATE TENANT PROTECTION BULLETIN NO. 23 and OPERATIONAL BULLETIN NO. 112.

(Issued October 1, 1979)

Present standards for determination of monthly rent adjustments for apartments where the landlord has completed a major capital improvement or a substantial rehabilitation—Sections 34-1(b or c) Tenant Protection Regulations and Sections 33-1 (b or c) Rent and Eviction Regulations.

Where the landlord has filed an application or applications for rent adjustments and establishes the grounds for such rent adjustments under Sections 34-1 (b or c) Tenant Protection Regulations or Section 33-1 (b or c) of the Rent and Eviction Regulations, the rent adjustments are determined as follows:

1. By allocating the actual cash cost to the landlord over a 60 month period, and apportioning such allocated monthly sum based upon the total number of rooms in the building to each apartment excluding half rooms from such count. In determining the actual cash cost, all finance, interest, or other carrying charges are excluded, and the cost is then based upon the contracts, invoices, and checks or other evidence of payment thereof, and

2. In the event, the allocated apartment's adjustment exceeds a 15% rate of rent increase above the maximum rent or legal regulated rent, the rent adjustment may be limited to such rate for any 12 month period, until the entire allocated adjustment has been reached so long as the tenant in possession continues in occupancy, and

3. In the event, the building has or will receive monetary assistance from governmental or other sources to carry out the improvement program, these sums shall be deducted from the actual cash cost in determining the monthly rent adjustments, and the adjustments shall also be subject to any other condition in connection with such assistance.

4. In the event that there are leases or other written rental agreements in effect for the apartments, the rent adjustments shall be subject to such leases or agreements

and such provisions therein as are not in violation with or inconsistent with all applicable laws and regulations thereunder.

5. In the event the improvements consist of equipment intended to alleviate energy shortages and energy cost increases which replaces otherwise adequate equipment, such as the installation of a gas heating system to replace an oil heating system, the rent adjustment otherwise determined based on the costs of the improvement shall be limited to one-half thereof in order to include an offset for the savings in annual operating costs to the landlord and a reasonable rent adjustment for the avoidance of service interruptions because of the energy shortages.

STATE TENANT PROTECTION BULLETIN NO. 27

(Issued March 10, 1980)

Attachment to Notice for Renewal of Lease or to Lease—prescribed for use if County Rent Guidelines Board has not filed the Guideline Rate applicable to the lease term, for compliance with Chapter 348 Laws of 1979

The State Division has printed the attached form (8A-80) which is prescribed for use as an attachment to the Notice for Renewal of Lease or Lease when provided by the Landlord to the Tenant, if the County Rent Guidelines Board has not filed the Guideline Rate applicable to the lease term.

The form is in conformity with the requirements of Chapter 348, Laws of 1979 amending the Emergency Tenant Protection Act. The use of the existent Guideline Rate is authorized, subject to increase or decrease when the new applicable Guideline Rate is filed and to a right of the tenant to change the term of the lease at that time.

Prescribed Form for Landlord's Attachment to Notice for Renewal of Lease or to Lease

—If the County Rent Guidelines Board has not filed the applicable Guideline rates—(Chapter 348 Laws of 1979)

If the County Rent Guidelines Board has not filed the

rate of rent adjustment which is applicable to the term of this Lease Renewal or Lease, the reserved rent is the last Legal Regulated Rent adjusted by an amount not in excess of the existent rent guideline rate. Said adjustment shall be subject to increase or decrease pursuant to the applicable Rent Guideline rate after it is filed, or such lower rate as the landlord may agree to. The increase or decrease in rent shall be effective on the date of the commencment of this Lease Renewal or Lease term. The adjustments shall be payable by the tenant or refundable by the landlord on the first rent payment date of the month next succeeding the date of the filing of the Rent Guideline rate. In addition, on said date, if the new rates of rent adjustment differ for leases of different terms, the tenant shall have the option of changing the original Lease term to any other term for which a rate of rent adjustment has been set, with adjustment of the rent accordingly.

Dated: _____

_____
Signature of Landlord

Dated: _____

_____
Signature of Tenant

TENANT PROTECTION BULLETIN NO. 28
EMERGENCY TENANT PROTECTION ACT

August 15, 1980

Summary of Guidelines for Leases Between July 1, 1980–September 30, 1981

Part I—*NASSAU COUNTY*

Municipalities of:
- Baxter Estates, Village
- Cedarhurst, Village
- Floral Park, Village
- Flower Hill, Village
- Freeport, Village
- Great Neck, Village
- Great Neck Plaza, Village
- Long Beach, City
- Lynbrook, Village
- Mineola, Village
- North Hempstead, Town

Tenant Protection Bulletins

>Rockville Centre, Village
>Russell Gardens, Village
>Steward Manor, Village
>Thomaston, Village

A. *Lease Guideline Rates:*

>One year lease   9%
>Two year lease   13%
>Three year lease   15%

B. *Additional Vacancy Guideline Rate for Leases to New Tenants:*

One month's rent of the last lease legal regulated rent may be charged to be paid in equal monthly installments over the new lease term. This additional charge does *not* continue in the legal regulated rent upon the expiration of new lease term.

C. *Further Guidelines:*
   1. For housing accommodations in Village of Great Neck Plaza and Village of Great Neck which provide gas and electric service in the legal regulated rents—4%.
   2. For housing accommodations without service of heat in the legal regulated rent—3% reduction in Lease Guideline rates.

D. *Reopening of Guidelines:*

The Board may reopen the guidelines for further prospective adjustment upward or downward in the event the unit price of the heating fuel shall change by rate of 20% from the price on June 30, 1980, any such adjustment to be effective only if the lease agreement makes such provision for an adjustment of the lease rent.

Municipality of Manorhaven Village

A. *For class of housing accommodations with services of heat, hot water, and gas included in the legal regulated rents:*

>One year lease   9.5%
>Two year lease   13.5%
>Three year lease   15.5%

Tenant Protection Bulletins

B. *For class of housing accommodations without services of heat and hot water included in the legal regulated rents:*

> One year lease   6%
> Two year lease   10%
> Three year lease 12%

C. *Additional Vacancy Guideline Rate for Leases to New Tenants:*
Same as the other foregoing municipalities.

D. *Reopening of Guidelines:*
Same as the other foregoing municipalities.

Municipality of City of Glen Cove

Leases on housing accommodations subject to the Act in buildings containing 100 or more apartments located in the City of Glen Cove commencing between May 1, 1980, the local effective date of ETPA, and June 30, 1980—and between July 1, 1980 and September 30, 1981—and for determination of fair market rents by the State Division of Housing and Community Renewal.

(1) For one year leases commencing between May 1, 1980 and September 30, 1981   9%
above the legal regulated rent, exclusive of any cost escalators, if any

For two year leases commencing between May 1, 1980 and September 30, 1981   13%
above the legal regulated rent, exclusive of any cost escalators, if any

For three year leases commencing between May 1, 1980 and September 30, 1981   15%
above the legal regulated rent, exclusive of any cost escalators, if any

These guidelines shall be applied to the base rent without tax or other cost escalation factors.

(2) For class of housing accommodations where the service of electricity is included in the legal regulated rents, an additional 1½%.

(3) Additional Vacancy Guideline Rate for Leases to New Tenants:

Where a vacant apartment is rented to a new tenant, an additional guideline, not to exceed *one month's rent* of the last lease, may be charged, to be paid by the tenant in equal monthly installments over the term of the lease given to the tenant by the landlord. This additional charge does not continue in the Legal Regulated Rent upon the expiration of the lease term. Also, this additional Guideline may still be taken if the landlord is filing an application with the State Division of Housing and Community Renewal for a rent adjustment based upon the installation of new equipment to replace existing equipment.

(4) The Board may convene to consider a further adjustment for unusual fuel costs should either the weighted average tank wagon delivery price for Nassau County reported in the Journal of Commerce change from the reported price in such publication on June 30, 1980, which is $1.01 per gallon for No. 2 fuel oil, and the utility charge per cubic foot of gas price on such date by a factor of 20%, provided that the lease contain a clause permitting such adjusted Guideline to be collected prospectively.

PART II—ROCKLAND COUNTY

Village of Spring Valley

For housing accommodations in buildings for which owners filed required data with Rockland County Rent Guidelines Board:

A. *Lease Guideline Rates*

   One year leases: Gas heated buildings   5%
                          Oil   "   "   8%

Further, that the Board reserves the right to adjust (reopen) this rate of increase upward or downward if the bulk cost of *gas* either increases or decreases by more than twenty-five (25%) of the bulk cost of *gas* on July 1, 1980. In this event, upon petition by either landlord or tenant the Board will be required to meet. Upon a finding by the Board that the guideline rate of adjustment in the amount of five percent (5%) should be adjusted upward or downward, the adjustment shall become effective in the first rent payment date following such finding for the remaining term of the lease. The tenant shall have the right to cancel the lease with thirty (30) day written notice to the landlord in the event that the guideline rate is adjusted upward.

Further, that to be eligible for the five percent (5%) increase the one-year lease commencing in the guidelines year beginning July 1, 1980 shall include the reopener clause.

Further, that the Board reserves the right to adjust (reopen) this rate of increase upward or downward if the bulk cost of oil (#2) either increases or decreases by more than twenty-five (25%) of the bulk cost of oil (#2) on July 1, 1980. In this event, upon petition by either landlord or tenant the Board will be required to meet. Upon a finding by the Board that the guideline rate of adjustment in the amount of eight percent (8%) should be adjusted upward or downward the adjustment shall become effective in the first rent payment date following such finding for the remaining term of the lease. The tenant shall have the right to cancel the lease with thirty (30) day written notice to the landlord in the event that the guideline rate is adjusted upward.

Further, that to be eligible for the eight percent (8%) increase the one-year lease commencing in the guidelines year beginning July 1, 1980 shall include the reopener clause.

Two year leases: Gas heated buildings 9%
Oil   "   "   12%

Two year leases in gas and oil heated buildings shall include a reopener clause as did one-year leases.

The Board reserves the right to adjust (reopen) the two (2) year lease rates of increase upward or downward if the bulk cost of oil (#2) or gas either increases or decreases by more than twenty percent (20%) of the costs on July 1, 1980. In this event, upon petition by either landlord or tenant the Board will be required to meet. Upon a finding by the Board that the two-year lease guideline rates of adjustment in the amount of 9% (gas) and 12% (#2 oil) should be adjusted upward or downward, the adjustment shall become effective in the first rent payment following such finding for the remaining term of the lease. The twenty percent (20%) figure is non-cumulative as to each succeeding guideline year beginning July 1 which date shall be the new base from which the figure of twenty percent (20%) is computed, for the remaining term of the lease.

The tenant shall have the right to cancel the lease with thirty (30) days written notice to the landlord in the event that the guideline rate is adjusted upward.

Further, that to be eligible for the guideline rates of increase for two (2) year leases commencing in the guidelines year beginning July 1, 1980 the lease must include both the reopener and cancellation clauses.

Three year leases: Gas heated buildings   12.5%
                       Oil   "   "   15.5%

The Board reserves the right to adjust (reopen) the three (3) year lease rates of increase upward or downward if the bulk cost of oil (#2) or gas either increases or decreases by more than twenty percent (20%) of the costs on July 1, 1980. In this event, upon petition by either landlord or tenant the Board will be required to meet. Upon a finding by the Board that the three-year lease guideline rates of adjustment in the amount of 12½% (gas) and 15½% (oil) should be adjusted upward or downward, the adjustment shall become effective in the first rent payment following such finding for the remaining term of the lease. The twenty percent (20%) figure is non-cumulative as to each succeeding guideline year beginning July 1, which date shall be the new base from which the figure of twenty percent (20%) is computed, for the remaining term of the lease.

The tenant shall have the right to cancel the lease with thirty (30) days written notice to the landlord in the event that the guideline rate is adjusted upward.

Further, that to be eligible for the guideline rates of increase for three (3) year leases commencing in the guidelines year beginning July 1, 1980 the lease must include both the reopener and cancellation clauses.

Additional Reopener:

Using the normal average degree days for the heating season established for the Westchester-Rockland area by the United States Weather Service if the cumulative number of degree days vary plus (+) or (−) 10%, the Guidelines Board reserves the right to adjust (reopen) upward or downward these guideline rates for the guidelines year beginning July 1, 1980 upon petition by either landlord or tenant and this motion also provides that the same terms and conditions as to reopeners and cancelation appear in the apartment lease to be eligible for the guidelines increases adopted for the guidelines beginning July 1, 1980.

B. *Additional Vacancy Guidelines Rate for Leases to New Tenants:*

When a vacancy occurs, the landlord shall be permitted to raise the legal regulated rent of the vacated apartment to the highest level of legal regulated rent of apartments with the same room count in the property complex which legal regulated rent shall then be the base for rent guidelines lease adjustment rates for the vacated apartment.

Part III—WESTCHESTER COUNTY

Municipalities of:
    Dobbs Ferry, Village
    Eastchester, Town
    Greenburgh, Town
    Harrison, Town
    Hastings-on-Hudson, Village
    Irvington-on-Hudson, Village
    Larchmont, Village
    Mamaroneck, Town
    Mamaroneck, Village
    Mount Kisco, Village
    Mount Vernon, City
    New Rochelle, City
    Pleasantville, Village
    Port Chester, Village
    Tarrytown, Village
    White Plains, City
    Yonkers, City

Lease Adjustments Guidelines

Tenant Protection Bulletins

*All Cities, Towns and Villages
County of Westchester
Subject to Emergency Tenant Protection Act*

A. *For the Classes of Housing Accommodations for which the Owners have submitted required data to the Board pursuant to the Board's Resolution adopted December 12, 1979, as implemented by written notices to said owners received by certified mail or personal service at the buildings.*

1. *For that Class wherein the landlord/owner provides heat and hot water:*

    For one year leases commencing on or after July 1, 1980 and prior to September 30, 1981 — 12%

    For two year leases commencing on or after July 1, 1980 and prior to September 30, 1981 — 15%

    For three year leases commencing on or after July 1, 1980 and prior to September 30, 1981 — 16%

2. *For that Class wherein the tenant pays for cost of heat and hot water to a supplier who is not the landlord/owner:*

    For one year leases commencing on or after July 1, 1980 and prior to September 30, 1981 — 9%

    For two year leases commencing on or after July 1, 1980 and prior to September 30, 1981 — 12%

    For three year leases commencing on or after July 1, 1980 and prior to September 30, 1981 — 13%

3. *For that Class wherein the tenant pays for cost of heat to a supplier who is not the landlord/owner and landlord/owner provides hot water:*

    For one year leases commencing on or after July 1, 1980 and prior to September 30, 1981 — 10%

    For two year leases commencing on or after July 1, 1980 and prior to September 30, 1981 — 13%

    For three year leases commencing on or after July 1, 1980 and prior to September 30, 1981 — 14%

B. *Additional Vacancy Guideline for Leases to New Tenants:*

When a vacancy occurs, the landlord shall be allowed to increase the base rent for that apartment to the highest rent level of an apartment having the same number of rooms within the same building or complex of buildings, as of the time of the vacancy. This base rent is then established for this building or complex, for apartments having the same number of rooms, for the balance of the guideline term. Upon this base rent shall then be added the allowable one, two, or three year increases under the guidelines, provided the landlord/owner shall further fully recite in the lease to the tenant the designation and location of the apartment having the same number of rooms and the highest rent level.

The highest legal regulated rent for apartments of each size in a building or complex of buildings is therefore established as of the date of the first such sized vacant apartment's renting to a new tenant.

C. *Additional Guideline of Housing Accommodations Receiving Electricity in the Legal Regulated Rent:* 1½%

Where the Legal Regulated Rent includes electric service, an additional guideline rate of increase may be charged not to exceed 1.5% rate of increase above the last Legal Regulated Rent.

D. *Reopening of Guidelines:*

The Board may reopen the guideline rates for adjustment upward or downward prospectively if there is a change by 20% or more in the July 1, 1980 costs of heating fuel or utilities, and provided that any such adjustment will only be applicable to leases which include a provision authorizing such change in the legal regulated rent to come into effect during the lease term.

Further information and copies of the *Guidelines and Findings* adopted and filed by each County Rent Guidelines Board will be available at the Office of Rent Administration:

>Two World Trade Center—58th Floor
>New York, N. Y. 10047—Tel. 212/488-7147

>50 Clinton Street—2d Floor
>Hempstead, N. Y. 11550—Tel. 516/481-9494

>99 Church Street—4th Floor
>White Plains, N. Y. 10601—Tel. 914/948-4434

TENANT PROTECTION BULLETIN NO. 28
Supplement No. 1

*Summary of Guidelines for Leases
Between July 1, 1980–September 30, 1981*

(Issued April 1, 1981)

Additional Guidelines—Nassau County

Adopted March 9, 1981 and filed by the Nassau County Rent Guidelines Board pursuant to the following section of the Guidelines previously adopted:

"(5) The Board may convene to consider a further adjustment for unusual fuel costs should either the weighted average tank wagon delivery price for Nassau County reported in the Journal of Commerce change from the reported price in such publication on June 30, 1980, which is $1.01 per gallon for No. 2 fuel oil, and the utility charge per cubic foot of gas price on such date by a factor of 20%, provided that the lease contain a clause permitting such adjusted Guideline to be collected prospectively."

". . . Guideline of $2.55 per room surcharge per month on oil heated apartments for the term of the lease, not to become a part of the base rent, with the following structure to apply:

A studio apartment	– 2 rooms
One Bedroom apartment	– 3 rooms
Two Bedroom apartment	– 4 rooms
Three Bedroom apartment	– 5 rooms,

to be effective April 1, 1981, and affecting leases under Guidelines 11 and 12 which commence on or after April 1, 1981, or which commenced between July 1, 1980 and March 31, 1981 and contain a clause permitting an adjusted Guideline to be collected prospectively . . ."

TENANT PROTECTION BULLETIN NO. 28
Supplement No. 2

*Summary of Guidelines for Leases
Between July 1, 1980–September 30, 1981*

(Issued April 1, 1981)

Additional Guidelines—Rockland County

Adopted February 26, 1981 and filed by the Rockland

County Rent Guidelines Board pursuant to the following section of the Guidelines previously adopted:

"The Board reserves the right to adjust (reopen) the . . . lease rates of increase upward or downward if the bulk cost of oil (#2) or gas either increases or decreases by more than twenty percent (20%) of the costs on July 1, 1980. In this event, upon petition by either landlord or tenant the Board will be required to meet. Upon a finding by the Board that the . . . guideline rates of adjustment in the amount of 12-½% (gas) and 15-½% (oil) should be adjusted upward or downward, the adjustment shall become effective in the first rent payment following such finding for the remaining term of the lease. The twenty percent (20%) figure is non-cumulative as to each succeeding guideline year beginning July 1, which date shall be the new base from which the figure of twenty percent (20%) is computed, for the remaining term of the lease.

"*Additional Reopener:*

"Using the normal average degree days for the heating season established for the Westchester-Rockland area by the United States Weather Service if the cumulative number of degree days vary plus (+) or (−) 10%, the Guidelines Board reserves the right to adjust (reopen) upward or downward these guideline rates for the guidelines year beginning July 1, 1980 upon petition by either landlord or tenant and this motion also provides that the same terms and conditions as to reopeners and cancellation appear in the apartment lease to be eligible for the guidelines increases adopted for the guidelines beginning July 1, 1980.

"In buildings which are predominantly heated by oil (over 50%) with leases effective on or after July 1, 1980 which contain "re-opener" clauses may be *further increased *above the existing guidelines lease rent* as follows:

> 1 year lease – 1½%
> 2 year lease – 1%
> 3 year lease – ½%

Leases which hereafter become effective during the Guidelines Year ending September 30, 1981 in buildings which are predominantly heated by oil (over 50%) may be

TENANT PROTECTION BULLETINS

further increased *above the Guidelines lease increases* adopted effective July 1, 1980 as follows:

> 1 year lease – 1½%
> 2 year lease – 1%
> 3 year lease – ½%"

*as provided by the Board's "reserve statement" for Rent Guidelines Adjustments, Minutes of Meetings June 17, 1980 and June 18, 1980.

Tenant Protection Bulletin No. 30
EMERGENCY TENANT PROTECTION ACT
Operational Bulletin No. 113
EMERGENCY HOUSING RENT CONTROL LAW

April 1, 1981.

Cities, towns and villages reported by Attorney General to have adopted and filed as of March 20, 1981 Resolutions making § 352-eee General Business Law applicable to protect tenants where rental buildings are converted to cooperative or condominium ownership—(Re: Section 35-8 Tenant Protection Regulations—ETPA, and Section 55-3 Rent and Eviction Regulations—EHRCL)

ROCKLAND COUNTY:	Date Adopted	Date Effective	ETPA* Adopted	Rent Control In Effect**
Municipality				
Town of Haverstraw	10/10/78	11/15/78	No	No
Village of Nyack	10/31/79	12/1/79	No	No
Village of South Nyack	11/13/79	12/16/79	No	No
Village of Spring Valley	8/1/78	9/6/78	Yes	No
Village of Suffern	2/14/81	2/19/81	No	No
NASSAU COUNTY:				
Village of Baxter Estates	4/15/80	5/21/80	Yes	No
Village of Cedarhurst	9/6/79	10/31/79	Yes	Yes
Village of Freeport	8/4/80	8/11/80	Yes	Yes
City of Glen Cove	4/22/80	9/29/80 (a)	Yes	Yes
Village of Great Neck	8/1/78	9/7/78	Yes	No
Village of Great Neck Estates	8/4/80	8/13/80	Yes	No
Village of Great Neck Plaza	7/26/78	8/30/78	Yes	No
Village of Hempstead	6/17/80	7/11/80	No	Yes
Village of Lawrence	9/11/78	2/7/79	No	Yes
City of Long Beach	12/18/79	1/30/80	Yes	Yes
Town of North Hempstead	3/18/80	4/25/80	Yes	Yes
Village of Port Washington North	4/15/80	5/21/80	No	No
Village of Rockville Centre	5/21/79	6/23/79	Yes	No
Village of Roslyn	9/19/78	11/1/78	No	Yes
Inc. Village of Roslyn	9/19/80	9/19/80	No	Yes
Village of Russell Gardens	8/14/78	9/20/78	Yes	No
Village of Thomaston	8/14/78	9/17/78	Yes	No

WESTCHESTER COUNTY:

Town of Bedford	2/6/79	3/11/79	No	No
Town of Eastchester	10/3/78	11/9/78	Yes	Yes
Town of Greenburgh	11/25/80	12/10/80 (a)	Yes	Yes
Town of Harrison	12/19/80	12/23/80 (a)	Yes	Yes
Village of Hastings-on-Hudson	9/19/78	10/25/78	Yes	No
Village of Irvington	9/21/78	4/25/80 (a)	Yes	No
Village of Irvington	10/16/78	7/9/80	Yes	No
Village of Larchmont	1/7/80	10/17/80	Yes	No
Village of Mamaroneck	6/12/80	7/19/80 (a)	Yes	Yes
Village of Mount Kisco	5/19/80	7/4/80	Yes	No
City of Mount Vernon	8/23/78	9/27/78	Yes	Yes
City of New Rochelle	11/20/79	12/27/79	Yes	Yes
Village of North Tarrytown	11/13/78	12/28/78	No	Yes
Village of Ossining	5/20/80	6/22/80	No	No
City of Peekskill	9/25/78	11/4/78	No	No
Village of Pelham	1/20/81	2/9/81	No	No
Village of Pleasantville	8/28/78	11/17/78	Yes	No
Village of Port Chester	11/21/78	12/28/78	Yes	No
City of Rye	1/17/79	2/22/79	No	No
Village of Scarsdale	5/13/80	6/15/80	No	No
Village of Tarrytown	8/21/78	9/27/78	Yes	Yes
City of White Plains	9/5/78	10/6/80 (a)	Yes	Yes
City of Yonkers	8/29/78	10/15/78	Yes	Yes
Town of Yorktown	8/7/79	8/14/80	No	No
Village of Yorktown Heights	8/7/79	9/12/79	No	No

(a) Amended.
* All buildings completed after January 1, 1974 are excluded from ETPA.
** All buildings completed after February 1, 1947, and all housing units vacated either after June 30, 1957 in certain municipalities (consult DHCR record for listings), or after July 1, 1971, otherwise, are excluded from Rent Control.

For those buildings with rented housing accommodations subject to Rent Control, Section 55-3, Rent and Eviction Regulations, is applicable. For those buildings with rented housing accommodations subject to ETPA, Section 35-8, Tenant Protection Regulations, must be complied with.

Guidelines For Lease Agreements Commencing
Between July 1, 1980 and September 30, 1981
All Cities, Towns and Villages
County of Westchester
Subject to Emergency Tenant Protection Act

For the Classes of Housing Accommodations for which the Owners have submitted required data to the Board pursuant to the Board's Resolution adopted December 12, 1979, as implemented by written notices to said owners received by certified mail or personal service at the buildings.

1. *For that Class wherein the landlord/owner provides heat and hot water:*
   For one year leases commencing on or after July 1, 1980 and prior to September 30, 1981   12%
   For two year leases commencing on or after July 1, 1980 and prior to September 30, 1981   15%
   For three year leases commencing on or after July 1, 1980 and prior to September 30, 1981   16%

2. *For that Class wherein the tenant pays for costs of heat and hot water to a supplier who is not the landlord/owner:*
   For one year leases commencing on or after July 1, 1980 and prior to September 30, 1981   9%
   For two year leases commencing on or after July 1, 1980 and prior to September 30, 1981   12%
   For three year leases commencing on or after July 1, 1980 and prior to September 30, 1981   13%

3. *For that Class wherein the tenant pays for cost of heat to a supplier who is not the landlord/owner and the landlord/owner provides hot water:*
   For one year leases commencing on or after July 1, 1980 and prior to September 30, 1981   10%
   For two year leases commencing on or after July 1, 1980 and prior to September 30, 1981   13%
   For three year leases commencing on or after July 1, 1980 and prior to September 30, 1981   14%

4. *Additional Guideline for that Class which is Vacant:*

   *When a vacancy occurs, the landlord shall be allowed to increase the base rent for that apartment to the highest rent level of an apartment having the same number of rooms within the same building or complex of buildings, as of the time of the vacancy. This base rent is then established for this building or complex, for apartments having the same number of rooms, for the balance of the guideline term. Upon this base rent shall then be added the allowable one, two, or three year increases under the guidelines, provided the landlord/owner shall further fully recite in the lease to the tenant the designation and location of the apartment having the same number of rooms and the highest rent level.

*As recited in letter dated July 29, 1980 by Chairman.

5. *Additional Guideline for that Class receiving electricity as a service included in the rent:*

Where the legal Regulated Rent includes electric service, an additional guideline rate of increase may be charged not to exceed 1.5% rate of increase above the last Legal Regulated Rent.

6. *Reopening of Guidelines:*

The Board may reopen the guideline rates for adjustment upward or downward prospectively if there is a change by 20% or more in the July 1, 1980 costs of heating fuel or utilities, and provided that any such adjustment will only be applicable to leases which include a provision authorizing such change in the legal regulated rent to come into effect during the lease term.

Guidelines for Lease Agreements commencing between July 1, 1980, and September 30, 1981

Unincorporated areas of Town of North Hempstead, Villages of Cedarhurst, Floral Park, Flower Hill, Freeport, Baxter Estates, Great Neck, Great Neck Plaza, Lynbrook, Manorhaven, Mineola, Rockville Centre, Russell Gardens, Stewart Manor, Thomaston, and City of Long Beach (Apartments in buildings of 60 or more accommodations), and City of Glen Cove (Apartments in buildings of 100 or more accommodations).

1. Leases on housing accommodations subject to the Act in buildings located in UNINCORPORATED AREAS OF TOWN OF NORTH HEMPSTEAD, VILLAGES OF CEDARHURST, FLORAL PARK, FLOWER HILL, GREAT NECK, FREEPORT, BAXTER ESTATES, GREAT NECK

Tenant Protection Bulletins

PLAZA, LYNBROOK, MINEOLA, ROCKVILLE CENTRE, RUSSELL GARDENS, STEWART MANOR, THOMASTON, and CITY OF LONG BEACH (Apartments in buildings of 60 or more accommodations).

(1) For one year leases commencing between July 1, 1980 and September 30, 1981   9%
above the legal regulated rent, exclusive of any cost escalators, if any

For two year leases commencing between July 1, 1980 and September 30, 1981   13%
above the legal regulated rent, exclusive of any cost escalators, if any

For three year leases commencing between July 1, 1980 and September 30, 1981   15%
above the legal regulated rent, exclusive of any cost escalators, if any

These guidelines shall be applied to the base rent without tax or other cost escalation factors.

(2) Where a vacant apartment is rented to a new tenant, an additional guideline, not to exceed *one month's rent* of the last lease, may be charged, to be paid by the tenant in equal monthly installments over the term of the lease given to the tenant by the landlord. This additional charge does not continue in the Legal Regulated Rent upon the expiration of the lease term. Also, this additional Guideline may still be taken if the landlord is filing an application with the State Division of Housing and Community Renewal for a rent adjustment based upon the installation of new equipment to replace existing equipment.

(3) Where the legal regulated rent in the Village of Great Neck Plaza includes *electric and gas* service, an additional Guideline rate of *4%* may be

charged. This rate shall also be applicable to such accommodations in the Village of Great Neck.

(4) Where the tenant pays for heat, the Guideline authorized shall be reduced by *3%*.

(5) The Board may convene to consider a further adjustment for unusual fuel costs should either the weighted average tank wagon delivery price for Nassau County reported in the Journal of Commerce change from the reported price in such publication on June 30, 1980, which is $1.01 per gallon for No. 2 fuel oil, and the utility charge per cubic foot of gas price on such date by a factor of 20%, provided that the lease contain a clause permitting such adjusted Guideline to be collected prospectively.

2. Leases on housing accommodations subject to the Act in buildings located in the VILLAGE OF MANORHAVEN commencing between June 1, 1980, the local effective date of ETPA, and June 30, 1980—and between July 1, 1980 and September 30, 1981—and for determination of fair market rents by the State Division of Housing and Community Renewal. The guidelines shall be applicable to that class of accommodations in buildings for which the owners submitted data to the Board.

  A. For class of housing accommodations with services of heat, hot water and gas included in the legal regulated rents:

        One year lease 9.5%
        Two "   "   13.5%
        Three "   "   15.5%

  B. For class of housing accommodations without services of heat and hot water included in the legal regulated rents:

        One year lease 6%
        Two "   "   10%
        Three "   "   12%

  C. Additional Vacancy Guideline Rate for Leases to New Tenants:

        Same as the foregoing municipalities

D. Reopening of Guidelines for further adjustment:

Same as the foregoing municipalities

3. Leases on housing accommodations subject to the Act in buildings containing 100 or more apartments located in the City of Glen Cove commencing between May 1, 1980, the local effective date of ETPA, and June 30, 1980 —and between July 1, 1980 and September 30, 1981—and for determination of fair market rents by the State Division of Housing and Community Renewal.

> (1) For one year leases commencing between May 1, 1980 and September 30, 1981   9%
>   above the legal regulated rent, exclusive of any cost escalators, if any
>
>   For two year leases commencing between May 1, 1980 and September 30, 1981   13%
>   above the legal regulated rent, exclusive of any cost escalators, if any
>
>   For three year leases commencing between May 1, 1980 and September 30, 1981   15%
>   above the legal regulated rent, exclusive of any cost escalators, if any

These guidelines shall be applied to the base rent without tax or other cost escalation factors.

> (2) For class of housing accommodations where the service of electricity is included in the legal regulated rents, an additional 1½%.
>
> (3) Additional Vacancy Guideline Rate for Leases to New Tenants:
>   Where a vacant apartment is rented to a new tenant, an additional guideline, not to exceed *one month's rent* of the last least, may be charged, to be paid by the tenant in equal monthly installments over the term of the lease given to the tenant by the landlord. This additional charge does not continue in the Legal

Regulated Rent upon the expiration of the lease term. Also, this additional Guideline may still be taken if the landlord is filing an application with the State Division of Housing and Community Renewal for a rent adjustment based upon the installation of new equipment to replace existing equipment.

(4) The Board may convene to consider a further adjustment for unusual fuel costs should either the weighted average tank wagon delivery price for Nassau County reported in the Journal of Commerce change from the reported price in such publication on June 30, 1980, which is $1.01 per gallon for No. 2 fuel oil, and the utility charge per cubic foot of gas price on such date by a factor of 20%, provided that the lease contain a clause permitting such adjusted Guideline to be collected prospectively.

Guidelines and Statements of maximum rates of rent adjustment for leases or other rental agreement commencing between July 1, 1980 and September 30, 1981, for the Village of Spring Valley, County of Rockland.

Lease Adjustments:

Leases on housing accommodations subject to the Act in buildings located in the Village of Spring Valley in the County of Rockland, which has heretofore adopted resolutions to place housing accommodations under the Act, in accordance with the limitations, requirements, and classification prescribed by the Board and recited in the Minutes of the Board meetings.

For classes of housing accommodations for which owners have filed with the Board data relating to building income and expenses following receipt of written notice of such required filing:

1. *For one year leases commencing on or after July 1, 1980 and prior to September 30, 1981:* [1]

    In gas heated buildings 5%

"Further, that the Board reserves the right to adjust (reopen) this rate of increase upward or downward if the

[1] Adopted June 17, 1980.

Tenant Protection Bulletins

bulk cost of *gas* either increases or decreases by more than twenty-five (25%) of the bulk cost of *gas* on July 1, 1980. In this event, upon petition by either landlord or tenant the Board will be required to meet. Upon a finding by the Board that the guideline rate of adjustment in the amount of five percent (5%) should be adjusted upward or downward, the adjustment shall become effective in the first rent payment date following such finding for the remaining term of the lease. The tenant shall have the right to cancel the lease with thirty (30) day written notice to the landlord in the event that the guideline rate is adjusted upward.

"Further, that to be eligible for the five percent (5%) increase the one-year lease commencing in the guidelines year beginning July 1, 1980 shall include the reopener clause."

In oil heated buildings 8%

"Further, that the Board reserves the right to adjust (reopen) this rate of increase upward or downward if the bulk cost of oil (#2) either increases or decreases by more than twenty-five (25%) of the bulk cost of oil (#2) on July 1, 1980. In this event, upon petition by either landlord or tenant the Board will be required to meet. Upon a finding by the Board that the guideline rate of adjustment in the amount of eight percent (8%) should be adjusted upward or downward the adjustment shall become effective in the first rent payment date following such finding for the remaining term of the lease. The tenant shall have the right to cancel the lease with thirty (30) day written notice to the landlord in the event that the guideline rate is adjusted upward.

"Further, that to be eligible for the eight percent (8%) increase the one-year lease commencing in the guidelines year beginning July 1, 1980 shall include the reopener clause."

2. *For two year leases commencing on or after July 1, 1980 and prior to September 30, 1981:* [2]

In gas heated buildings 9%
In oil   "   " 12%

[2] Adopted June 18, 1980.

"That *2-year leases* in *gas and oil heated buildings* shall include a reopener clause as did one-year leases.

"The Board reserves the right to adjust (reopen) the two (2) year lease rates of increase upward or downward if the bulk cost of oil (#2) or gas either increases or decreases by more than twenty percent (20%) of the costs on July 1, 1980. In this event, upon petition by either landlord or tenant the Board will be required to meet. Upon a finding by the Board that the two-year lease guideline rates of adjustment in the amount of 9% (gas) and 12% (#2 oil) should be adjusted upward or downward, the adjustment shall become effective in the first rent payment following such finding for the remaining term of the lease. The twenty percent (20%) figure is non-cumulative as to each succeeding guideline year beginning July 1 which date shall be the new base from which the figure of twenty percent (20%) is computed, for the remaining term of the lease.

"The tenant shall have the right to cancel the lease with thirty (30) days written notice to the landlord in the event that the guideline rate is adjusted upward.

"Further, that to be eligible for the guideline rates of increase for two (2) year leases commencing in the guidelines year beginning July 1, 1980 the lease must include both the reopener and cancellation clauses."

3. *For three year leases commencing on or after July 1, 1980 and prior to September 30, 1981:* [3]

   In gas heated buildings 12.5%
   In oil   "   " 15.5%

"That for *3* year leases in *gas* heated buildings the guideline rate shall be *12-½%*.

"That for *3* year leases in *oil* heated buildings the guideline rate shall be *15-½%*.

"That *3 year leases* in gas and oil heated buildings shall include a reopener clause.

"The Board reserves the right to adjust (reopen) the three (3) year lease rates of increase upward or downward

[3] Adopted June 18, 1980.

Tenant Protection Bulletins

if the bulk cost of oil (#2) or gas either increases or decreases by more than twenty percent (20%) of the costs on July 1, 1980. In this event, upon petition by either landlord or tenant the Board will be required to meet. Upon a finding by the Board that the three-year lease guideline rates of adjustment in the amount of 12-½% (gas) and 15-½% (oil) should be adjusted upward or downward, the adjustment shall become effective in the first rent payment following such finding for the remaining term of the lease. The twenty percent (20%) figure is non-cumulative as to each succeeding guideline year beginning July 1 which date shall be the new base from which the figure of twenty percent (20%) is computed, for the remaining term of the lease.

"The tenant shall have the right to cancel the lease with thirty (30) days written notice to the landlord in the event that the guideline rate is adjusted upward.

"Further, that to be eligible for the guideline rates of increase for three (3) year leases commencing in the guidelines year beginning July 1, 1980 the lease must include both the reopener and cancellation clauses."

4. *Vacancy Guideline:* [4]

"That when a *vacancy* occurs, the landlord shall be permitted to raise the legal regulated rent of the vacated apartment to the highest level of legal regulated rent of apartments with the same room count in the property complex which legal regulated rent shall then be the base for rent guidelines lease adjustment rates for the vacated apartment."

5. *Additional Reopener:* [5]

"Using the normal average degree days for the heating season established for the Westchester-Rockland area by the United States Weather Service if the cumulative number of degree days vary plus (+) or (−) 10%, the Guidelines Board reserves the right to adjust (reopen) upward or downward these guideline rates for the guidelines year beginning July 1, 1980 upon petition by either landlord or tenant and this motion also provides that the same terms and conditions as to reopeners and cancella-

[4] Adopted June 18, 1980.   [5] Adopted June 18, 1980.

tion appear in the apartment lease to be eligible for the guidelines increases adopted for the guidelines beginning July 1, 1980."

TENANT PROTECTION BULLETIN NO. 32
EMERGENCY TENANT PROTECTION ACT

Summary of Guidelines Filed by County Rent Guidelines Boards for Lease Agreements Commencing between October 1, 1981 and September 30, 1982

PART I
NASSAU COUNTY

Cities, towns and villages under ETPA excepting Great Neck Estates and Roslyn

A. *Lease Guideline Rates:*

        One year lease - 12%
        Two " " - 15%
        Three " " - 17%

B. *Additional Vacancy Guideline Rate for Leases to New Tenants:*

One month's rent of the last Legal Regulated Rent for lease renewal may be collected in equal monthly installments over new lease term of one, two or three years, and be a permanent increase in the legal regulated rent in addition to the one, two or three year guideline rate above the last legal regulated rent.

C. *Further Guidelines:*

1. For housing accommodations which provide electric service in the legal regulated rents: Additional – 4% increase.

2. For housing accommodations without service of heat and hot water in the legal regulated rent:

  Under one year lease - 1½% decrease in guideline for 10½% increase
  " two " " - 2% " " " " 13% "
  " three" " " - 2½% " " " " 14½% "

Supplement 1 – Village of Great Neck Estates

A. *Lease Guideline Rates:*

        One year lease - 8%
        Two " " - 10%
        Three " " - 12%

Tenant Protection Bulletins

(1) These rates adopted for all leases commencing between September 1, 1981 and September 30, 1982.

(2) No vacancy guideline adopted for new tenants.

(3) No guidelines adopted for leases commencing between November 1, 1980, local effective date of ETPA, and August 31, 1981.

(4) Guidelines adopted for the apartments in class of buildings for which owners filed required income and expense statements with Guidelines Board, consisting of two buildings located as follows:

1 Ascot Ridge
88 Middle Neck Road

(5) No guidelines adopted for apartments in class of buildings for which owners did not file required income and expense statements with Guidelines Board, consisting of one building located as follows:

106 Middle Neck Road

B. *Guidelines adopted for determining tenant applications to State Division for Fair Market Rents under Section 9b, ETPA:*

One year lease	- 8%
Two " "	- 10%
Three " "	- 12%

Supplement 2 – Village of Roslyn

A. *Lease Guideline Rates:*

One year lease	- 12%
Two " "	- 15%
Three " "	- 17%

B. *Additional Vacancy Guideline Rate for Leases to New Tenants:*

When a new tenant leases an apartment which has become vacant, the landlord may collect a vacancy guideline increase equal in amount to one month of the previous legal regulated rent in equal installments over the new lease term of one, two or three years. The vacancy guideline becomes a permanent increase in the legal regulated rent which the landlord may collect in addition to the basic guideline of 12%, 15% and 17% for one, two or three year lease.

For example: If a tenant rents a vacant apartment for which the former tenant was paying $120 as the legal regulated rent, and the new tenant signs a one year lease, the vacancy guideline increase would be $10 per month ($120 ÷ 12 months = $10 per month). In addition the landlord may also collect the one year lease guideline of $14.40. Using the $120 previous legal regulated rent as a base, a 12% lease guideline is added plus the $10 vacancy allowance, which together equal the new legal regulated rent of $144.40 for a one year lease.

Examples for 1, 2 and 3 year leases are outlined below:

Previous Legal Regulated Monthly Rent	Lease Period	Monthly Lease Guideline	Vacancy Guideline	New Legal Regulated Monthly Rent
$120	1 year	$14.40 (12%)	$10.00	$144.40
$120	2 years	$18.00 (15%)	$ 5.00	$143.00
$120	3 years	$20.40 (17%)	$ 3.33	$143.73

C. *Further Guidelines:*

1. For housing accommodations which provide electric service in the legal regulated rents: Additional − 4% increase.

2. For housing accommodations without service of heat and hot water in the legal regulated rent:

Under one year lease - 1½% decrease in guideline for 10½% increase
" two " " - 2% " " " " 13% "
" three " " - 2½% " " " " 14½% "

D. *These Guidelines adopted for all leases commencing between June 1, 1981, the local effective date of ETPA, and September 30, 1982.*

E. *Guidelines adopted for determining tenant applications to State Division for Fair Market Rents under Section 9b, ETPA:*

As set forth in A, B and C.

PART II
ROCKLAND COUNTY

Village of Spring Valley housing accommodations in buildings for which owners filed required data with Board

Tenant Protection Bulletins

A. *Lease Guideline Rates:*

One year lease	Gas Heated Buildings - 9%
	Oil " " - 10½%
Two " "	Gas " " - 12½%
	Oil " " - 13½%
Three " "	Gas " " - 15%
	Oil " " - 16%

B. *Additional Vacancy Guideline Rate for Leases to New Tenants:*

When a vacancy occurs, the landlord shall be permitted to raise the legal regulated rent of the vacated apartment to the highest level of legal regulated rent of apartments with the same room count in the property complex which legal regulated rent shall then be the base for rent guidelines lease adjustment rates for the vacated apartment, with the further provision that the lease guideline on the rent increased by the vacancy guideline shall not exceed an additional 5%. For the purpose of this adjustment during the guideline year, the comparable apartment rent shall be that in effect on October 1, 1981.

C. *Further Guidelines:*

Fuel Cost Reopener

Using the normal average degree days for the heating season established for the Westchester-Rockland area by the United States Weather Service if the cumulative number of degree days vary plus (+) or (−) 10%, the Guidelines Board reserves the right to adjust (reopen) upward or downward these guideline rates for the guidelines year beginning October 1, 1981 upon petition by either landlord or tenant and this motion also provides that the same terms and conditions as to reopeners and cancellation appear in the apartment lease to be eligible for the guidelines increases adopted for the guidelines beginning October 1, 1981.

In the event that the total cost of fuel at any point in 1981 exceeds 20% of the cost of the base figures for the year ending 1980, the board reserves the right to reopen the guidelines using the following standards:

For oil heated buildings, the reference standard shall be the posted rate of #2 oil, as stated in the publication "Realty" using the median of the high and low costs.

For gas heated buildings the reference standard shall be Orange and Rockland Utilities Company price and degree day index, using the median of high and low costs.

PART III
WESTCHESTER COUNTY

Housing accommodations for which owners filed required data with Westchester County Rent Guidelines Board in cities, towns and villages under ETPA excepting tenant-occupied former rent controlled apartments in City of Mount Vernon.

A. *Lease Guideline Rates:*

With heat and hot water:

    One year lease - 12%
    Two   "   "   - 15%
    Three "   "   - 18%

Without heat and hot water:

    One year lease - 9%
    Two   "   "   - 12%
    Three "   "   - 15%

Without heat:

    One year lease - 10%
    Two   "   "   - 13%
    Three "   "   - 16%

B. *Additional Vacancy Guideline for Leases to New Tenants:*

When a vacancy occurs, the landlord is allowed to increase the base rent for that apartment. The new base rent may equal the highest rent for an apartment with same number of rooms within the same building or complex of buildings at the time the vacancy occurs. The increase in the base rent for a vacant apartment is permissible only when the landlord informs the tenant of the specific apartment, including its rent and location (street address) used to establish the base rent. However, the increase in the base rent cannot exceed 6% above the last legal regulated rent where the vacant apartment is rented to a tenant from another apartment in the building or complex. The landlord may also add the increase approved for one-, two- or three-year leases to the new base rent.

Apartments vacated during the guideline period (10/1/81 – 9/30/82), will have a base rent equal to what is established for the first vacancy in apartments in each category according to size. The highest legal regulated rent for various sized apartments is therefore established effective on the date the first apartment in each sized category is vacated and rented to a new tenant.

C. *Additional Guideline of Housing Accommodations Receiving Electricity in the Legal Regulated Rent:*

2.5% above last legal regulated rent and excluding from that base rent for calculating the increase any additional charge for electricity service to tenants with air conditioners (no additional guideline increase on this charge).

D. *Further Guidelines:*

Mortgage Refinancing Reopener:

Board reserves the discretionary right to grant a further guideline rate of increase to a class of housing in a building upon receipt of application to do so based upon mortgage refinancing expense increases sustained in a building during the year October 1, 1981 to September 30, 1982, which application is accompanied by necessary supporting data and confirmed by analysis of Board and its staff assistants from DHCR.

TENANT PROTECTION BULLETIN NO. 34
EMERGENCY TENANT PROTECTION ACT

Summary of Guidelines Filed by County Rent Guidelines Board for Lease Agreements Commencing Between October 1, 1982 and September 30, 1983

NASSAU COUNTY

Guidelines for rental increases for housing accommodations in buildings in all cities, towns and villages under ETPA in Nassau County for which owners have filed required schedules of data with County Rent Guidelines Board.

A. *Lease Guideline Rental Increase Rates:*

One-year lease 6%
Two-year lease 10%
Three-year lease 12%

B. *Additional Vacancy Guideline Rate of Increase for Leases to New Tenants:*

Where a vacant apartment is rented to a *new* tenant, the landlord may collect an additional increase, over and above the Lease Guideline Rate (part A), in the amount of one month's rent at the prior Legal Regulated Rent, collected in equal monthly installments over the term of the new lease. Such additional increase shall then become a permanent part of the new Legal Regulated Rent as follows:

> Prior Monthly Legal Regulated Rent plus *Authorized Percent of Increase* (part A) plus *[One Month's Rent at the Prior Rate* divided by the *Number of Months in the New Lease Term]*= New Monthly Legal Regulated Rent.

Please note, however, that where the new tenant is from the same building or building complex as the apartment to be rented, only half of one month's rent at the prior rate, and not the full amount as shown in the above calculation, may be used for the purpose of establishing a vacancy rate increase.

C. *FURTHER GUIDELINES:*
  1. For housing accommodations in a solely residential building, which include the cost of electric and gas service in the Legal Regulated Rent, an additional 2% of the prior Legal Regulated Rent may be added to the new Legal Regulated Rent for the term of the current lease only. Such additional increase shall *not* become a permanent part of the Legal Regulated Rent.
  2. For housing accommodations which do not include the cost of heat and hot water in the Legal Regulated Rent, guideline rates of increase, as shown in part A, must be reduced as follows:

     One-year lease —1 ½% decrease in guideline rate of 6% for a total 4 ½% increase

     Two-year lease —2% decrease in guideline rate of 10% for a total 8% increase

     Three-year lease —2 ½% decrease in guildeline rate of 12% for a total 9 ½% increase

Tenant Protection Bulletins

D. *Further Information:*

Listings of building addresses for which owners are, or are not, authorized to collect guideline rates of rent increase for lease agreements commencing during the period October 1, 1982 to September 30, 1983 may be examined at either of the following offices of the Division of Housing and Community Renewal:

Nassau

50 Clinton Street, 2nd Floor
Hempstead, N. Y. 11550
Tel. No. (516) 481-9494

New York City

Two World Trade Center, 58th Floor
New York, N. Y. 10047
Tel. No. (212) 488-7147

TENANT PROTECTION BULLETIN NO. 35
EMERGENCY TENANT PROTECTION ACT

Summary of Guidelines Filed by County Rent Guidelines Boards for Lease Agreements Commencing between October 1, 1982 and September 30, 1983

ROCKLAND COUNTY

Guidelines for rental increases for housing accommodations in buildings in the Village of Spring Valley for which owners have filed required schedules of data with Rockland County Rent Guidelines Board.

A. *Lease Guideline Rental Increase Rates:*

> One-year lease   7%
> Two-year lease   10%
> Three-year lease 12.5%

B. *Additional Vacancy Guideline Rate of Increase for Leases to New Tenants:*

When a vacancy occurs, the landlord is permitted to increase the base rent for the vacated apartment. The new base rent *may* equal the highest rent for an apartment, in the same building or building complex, having the same number of rooms as the vacated apartment at the time the vacancy occurs, subject to the following conditions:

1) The rent for an apartment judged comparable to the vacated apartment, under the above criteria, shall be the rent in effect for the comparable apartment as of October 1, 1982.
2) The landlord must inform the tenant or prospective tenant of the specific apartment which is being used to establish the new base rent. Such information must include apartment number, street address and monthly rent.

When the above conditions have been complied with, an additional 5% guideline rate of rental increase may be added to the new base rent, for a one-, two-, or three-year lease, in lieu of the guideline rates shown in part A above.

C. *Further Guidelines (Fuel Cost Reopener):*

If the cumulative number of degree-days vary plus or minus 10%, using the normal average degree-days for the heating season established for the Westchester-Rockland area by the United States Weather Service, the Guidelines Board reserves the right to adjust, upwards or downwards, the guideline rates shown in part A for the guideline year beginning October 1, 1982. Such adjustments may be made upon petition by either landlord or tenant.

In addition, if the total cost of fuel at any point in 1982 exceeds 20% of the cost shown in the base figures for the year ending December 30, 1981, the Board *also* reserves the right to reopen deliberations on guideline rates, as follows:

1) For oil-heated buildings, the reference standard used shall be the posted rate of #2 oil, as stated in the publication "Realty", using the median of high and low costs.
2) For gas-heated buildings, the reference standard used shall be the Orange and Rockland Utilities Company price and degree-day index, using the median high and low costs.

Please note that the terms and conditions concerning adjustments (fuel cost reopener) described herein *must* be included in the lease for any apartment in order for that apartment to be considered eligible for guideline increases adopted for the current guideline year.

D. *Further Information:*

Listings of building addresses for which owners are, or are not, authorized to collect guideline rates of rent increase for lease agreements commencing during the period October 1, 1982 to September 30, 1983 may be examined at either of the following offices of the Division of Housing and Community Renewal.

White Plains

99 Church Street, 4th Floor
White Plains, New York 10601
Tel. No. (914) 948-4434

New York City

Two World Trade Center, 58th Floor
New York, N. Y. 10047
Tel. No. (212) 418-7147

TENANT PROTECTION BULLETIN NO. 36
EMERGENCY TENANT PROTECTION ACT

Summary of Guidelines Filed by County Rent Guidelines Board for Lease Agreements Commencing between October 1, 1982 and September 30, 1983

WESTCHESTER COUNTY

Guidelines for rental increases for housing accommodations for which owners have filed required data with Westchester County Rent Guidelines Board in cities, towns and villages under ETPA, excepting tenant-occupied former rent controlled apartments in the City of Mount Vernon, subject to ETPA on and after October 1, 1982, and accommodations in the Village of North Tarrytown, subject to ETPA July 1, 1982.

A. *Lease Guideline Rental Increase Rates:*

With heat and hot water:
>One-year lease - 4%
>Two-year lease - 6%
>Three-year lease - 9%

Without heat and hot water:
>One-year lease - 3%

>   Two-year lease - 5%
>   Three-year lease - 6%
>
> Without heat:
>   One-year lease - 3%
>   Two-year lease - 5%
>   Three-year lease - 6%

B. *Additional Vacancy Guideline Rate of Increase for Leases to New Tenants:*

When a vacancy occurs, the landlord is permitted to increase the base rent for the vacated apartment. The new base rent *may* equal the highest rent for an apartment, in the same building or building complex, having the same number of rooms as the vacated apartment at the time the vacancy occurs, subject to the following conditions:

1) Once a vacancy has occurred in any group of comparable apartments (same number of rooms) during the guideline period (10/1/82–9/30/83), selection of an apartment for use in establishing a *new* base rent for a newly vacated apartment (in the same group of comparable apartments) shall be limited to that apartment and rental amount which were used to set the base rent for the *first* vacated apartment in the group.

2) The result increased base rent may not be more than 5% higher than the last legal Regulated Rent for the newly vacated apartment.

3) The landlord must inform the tenant or prospective tenant, in writing, of the specific apartment which is being used to establish the new base rent. Such information must include apartment number, street address and monthly rent.

When all of the above have been complied with, rates of increase described in part A may be applied to the newly established base rent for the subject apartment.

C. *Additional Guideline Rate of Increase for Housing Accommodations Which Include the Service of Electricity in the Legal Regulated Rent:*

Where the service of electricity is included in the Legal Regulated Rent, a charge of 2.5% of the *last* Legal Regulated Rent may be added to the new rent (as estab-

Tenant Protection Bulletins

lished by application of guideline rates of increase described above). Please note, however, that electricity charges to tenants with air conditioners may *not* be included in the last Legal Regulated Rent when calculating *this* amount since no additional guideline rate has been established for such charges.

D. *Further Information:*

Listings of building addresses for which owners are, or are not, authorized to collect guideline rates of rent increase for lease agreements commencing during the period October 1, 1982 to September 30, 1983 may be examined at either of the following offices of the Division of Housing and Community Renewal.

White Plains

99 Church Street, 4th Floor
White Plains, N. Y. 10601
Tel. No. (914) 948-4434

New York City

Two World Trade Center, 58th Floor
New York, N. Y. 10047
Tel. No. (212) 488-7147

Tenant Protection Bulletin No. 37 Emergency Tenant Protection Act

Legal Regulated Rents for apartments which are rented to tenants in a building owned on a cooperative or condominium basis.

Section 35-8 of the Tenant Protection regulations, under the Emergency Tenant Protection Act (ETPA), sets forth the requirements for leases for housing accommodations, in buildings containing six or more housing units which are either:

1. Cooperative- or condominium-owned buildings; or
2. Buildings for which the Attorney General has accepted, for filing, an offering plan to convert to cooperative or condominium status.

Under this Regulation, all apartments which are rented to tenants in such buildings are subject to ETPA when

one or more of the housing units in the building is made available for occupancy on a rental basis. This applies whether or not the "landlord" renting the premises is:
1. The purchaser-owner of the apartment in question;
2. The building owner; or
3. The sponsor or other person having legal ownership of the apartment.

The legal regulated rent *which may be collected* for such an apartment is, therefore, subject to determination under ETPA and the Tenant Protection Regulations. According to this determination, the legal regulated rent, *where the apartment was previously subject to ETPA,* shall be:
1. The rent in the *last* lease to the *last* tenant of the apartment, *which was lawful under ETPA,*
2. Increased by an amount not in excess of the guildeline rates of increase which were filed by the County Rent Guidelines Board and which are *authorized for use in a lease for an apartment in the building in question.*

If an apartment does not have a prior legal regulated rent, however, because it was not previously rented under ETPA, the initial rent charged, under a one-, two- or three-year lease term, shall be the *initial* legal regulated rent as defined in Section 21 of the Tenant Protection Regulations.

No increases in the rent, besides those specified above, are lawful, *unless* there is an application filed with the Division of Housing and Community Renewal, establishing the grounds for such additional increase under the Tenant Protection Regulations, *and the Division has issued an Order and Determination approving the application.* The grounds, in the Regulations, for such an additional increase include provision of increased services to tenant, major capital improvements and landord's financial hardship. The prescribed application forms (RTP-24 in the case of increased services and capital improvements; RTP-23 in the case of financial hardship) must be used when applying for such increases.

Tenants renting an apartment in a cooperative or condominium have the same rights, with respect to services, evictions, harassment and rent adjustments, as tenants in buildings, subject to ETPA, which are not owned on a cooperative or condominium basis. Collection of a unlawful rent is subject to assessment of penalties which may include payment to the tenant of three times the overcharge(s), if collection by the owner, landlord, lessor and/or broker/agent was wilful or negligent.

Persons requiring further information, or who wish to obtain copies of the Regulations of Tenant Protection Bulletins for Nassau, White Plains or Rockland, should contact one of the following Division of Housing and Community Renewal offices:

>Two World Trade Center, 58th Floor
>New York, NY 10047
>Tel. (212)488-7147

>50 Clinton Street, 2d Floor
>Hempstead, NY
>Tel. (516)481-9494

>99 Church Street
>White Plains, NY
>Tel. (914)-948-4434

TENANT PROTECTION BULLETIN NO. 38
EMERGENCY TENANT PROTECTION ACT

Initial Legal Regulated Rent under the Emergency Tenant Protection Act (ETPA) for tenanted housing accommodations which are decontrolled from the Emergency Housing Rent Control Law (EHRCL)

WESTCHESTER COUNTY
City of Mt. Vernon

Determination of Initial Legal Regulated Rents under ETPA in Mt. Vernon, after decontrol from EHRCL.

A. *Definition*—The Initial Legal Regulated Rent under ETPA, for accommodations formerly under EHRCL, is the rent agreed to by landlord and tenant and "reserved in a lease or provided for in a rental agreement", prior to the effective date of control for each decontrolled, tenanted housing accommodation. (See Section 21(1), Tenant Protection Regulations.)

B. *Application to Mt. Vernon*—In the City of Mt. Vernon, rental housing accommodations have been regulated, either under EHRCL or ETPA, since August 19, 1974 when the City Council filed its Resolution declaring the existence of a housing emergency and placing all housing accommodations, within the municipality and not otherwise excluded, under ETPA. Among the categories of rental housing units excluded by ETPA are "housing accommodations subject to the emergency housing rent control law." Therefore, such accommodations did not become subject to ETPA, after passage of this Resolution, so long as they remained under EHRCL. However, individual rental housing accommodations under EHRCL were subject to decontrol *when they became vacant and were subsequently rented* (Vacancy Decontrol). Such decontrolled apartments thereafter became subject to the ETPA.

On June 19, 1981, the Mt. Vernon City Council filed a further Resolution for the decontrol of *all* housing accommodations, in the city, subject to EHRCL. On the effective date of such decontrol, all EHRCL-regulated housing accommodations cease to be exempt from the ETPA. There are, however, different effective dates of decontrol for these accommodations, depending on whether landlord has offered a two-year lease, in the prescribed fashion as set forth in Section 12(2-a) of the EHRCL, and whether or not tenant has accepted such lease offer. Initial Legal Regulated Rents for newly decontrolled apartments may also vary based on the different effective dates. The following charts present and explain these differences:

Tenant Protection Bulletins

CHART I — Implementing the Decontrol Process in Mt. Vernon

When Decontrol Occurs:	Effective Date of Decontrol	One Step or First Step of Two-Step Increase	Initial Legal Regulated Rent — Second Step of Two-Step Increase
1) And No Lease is Offered by Landlord to Tenant.	6/19/83 (two years from Mt. Vernon City Council decontrol filing date)	Same as last monthly rental under EHRCL.	If last monthly rental was part of a two-step increase under EHRCL and second step not yet in place, second step to be implemented under ETPA.
2) And Lease is Offered by Landlord and Accepted by Tenant.	Execution date of prescribed two-year lease (any time after 6/19/81)	Old rent under EHRCL, increased by EHRCL—authorized amount.	Increased, one year after implementation of first step, by EHRCL—authorized amount.
3) And Lease is Offered by Landlord but Not Accepted by Tenant.	12/19/81 (six mos. from decontrol filing date) or 30 days from date landlord offered two-year lease, in prescribed fashion, whichever date is later.	Same as monthly rental under EHRCL.	If last monthly rental was part of a two-step increase under EHRCL and second step not yet in place, second step to be implemented under ETPA.

CHART II — Illustrations of Rent Determinations during the Decontrol Process

Status of Lease Offer	Sample Situations with Explanation
1) No Lease Offered	a) If rent paid for 6/83 under EHRCL was $230, then rent due under ETPA for the following month (7/83) will also be $230. b) If part of a two-step process under EHRCL where the second step has not yet been implemented, then applicable rates apply. Commencing 1/83 these were 15% and 5% for the first and second years, respectively. Therefore, second step increase to be implemented equals 5% of $230 (or $11.50) + $230 = $241.50.
2) Lease Offered and Accepted	a) If prior rent under EHRCL was $200, then, applying EHRCL—authorized rates of increase (15% the first year and 5% the second, for the period 11/80 - 10/81), the new rent under ETPA will be: 15% of $200 (or $30) + $200 = $230. b) The second step will be: 5% of $230 (or $11.50) + $230 = $241.50.
3) Lease Offered but Not Accepted	a) If rent paid for 12/81 was $230 and ETPA takes effect 1/82, then new rent will also be $230. b) If part of a two-step process under EHRCL where the second step has not yet been implemented, then applicable rates apply. During 12/80 - 12/81 these were 15% and 10% for the first and second years, respectively. Therefore second step is 10% of $230 (or $23) + $230 = $253.

C. *Grounds for Subsequent Increases in the Legal Regulated Rent*—The Legal Regulated Rent, once established under ETPA, may not, thereafter, be increased, except as set forth in the ETPA and Tenant Protection Regulations (issued pursuant to the ETPA) as follows:

1) By landlord's offer the tenant's acceptance and execution of a lease or lease renewal for a one-, two- or three-year term at a rent increase not in excess of the authorized guideline rates established by the Westchester County Rent Guidelines Board.

2) By application of landlord to the Division of Housing and Community Renewal and approval of such application by the Division. Grounds for application for an increase, under the Regulations, include provision of increased services to tenant, major capital improvements and landlord's financial hardship. The prescribed application forms (RTP-24 in the case of increased services or capital improvements; RTP-23 in the case of financial hardship) must be used.

D. *Enforcement and Penalties*—Any demand or collection of a rent increase in excess of the authorized amount, if wilful or negligent, may subject landlord (or landlord's authorized representative) to an assessment of three times the overcharge and/or a penalty, not in excess of $250, for each violation of the ETPA, Tenant Protection Regulations or relevant Order and Determination of the Division of Housing and Community Renewal.

E. *Further Information*—Persons requiring further information, or who wish to obtain copies of the ETPA, EHRCL or pertinent Regulations, should contact one of the following Division of Housing and Community Renewal offices:

New York City	*—Two World Trade Center, Rm. 5870, New York, N.Y. 10047* *Telephone Number (212) 488-3217*
White Plains	*—99 Church Street, 4th Floor, White Plains, N.Y. 10601* *Telephone Number (914) 948-4434*
Mount Vernon	*—City Hall, Mount Vernon, N.Y. Wednesdays and Thursdays only)* *Telephone Number (914) 668-2200*

TENANT PROTECTION BULLETIN NO. 38
REVISED EMERGENCY TENANT PROTECTION ACT

Initial Legal Regulated Rent under the Emergency Tenant Protection Act (ETPA) for tenanted housing accommodations which are decontrolled from the Emergency Housing Rent Control Law (EHRCL)

WESTCHESTER COUNTY
City of Mt. Vernon

Determination of Initial Legal Regulated Rents under ETPA in Mt. Vernon, after decontrol from EHRCL, and applicable guidelines for ETPA Renewals

This bulletin is issued to modify Bulletin No. 38 as to the initial legal regulated rent and to set forth the rent increases authorized by the Westchester County Rent Guidelines Board for leases to commence on or after July 1, 1983. These guidelines are applicable only to those apartments which were subject to the Emergency Housing Rent Control Law on June 19, 1981, the date the Mount Vernon City Council filed the resolution decontrolling all such apartments with the Division of Housing and Community Renewal. Such apartments will no longer be subject to the Emergency Housing Control Law, but will become automatically subject to the Emergency Tenant Protection Act of 1974, June 19, 1983, if such tenants are living in a building containing six (6) or more housing accommodations and have not previously signed a two year lease with their landlord. Those tenants who have signed a 2 year lease after June 19, 1981 became subject to the ETPA on the date the lease was signed.

The Westchester County Rent Guidelines Board, pursuant to the Authority granted under the ETPA, has established the following guideline rates in the City of Mount Vernon for these two categories of tenants only, effective July 1, 1983:

One year lease, or first year of a two or three year lease	15%
Second year of a two or three year lease, an additional	10%
Third year of a three year lease, an additional	5%

For those tenants who have not received a compensatory rent increase under Section 33(8) (Landlord's Sixty Day Notice of Maximum Rent Adjustment), or by lease, commencing on or after January 1, 1983, the above guidelines will prevail for leases commencing on or after July 1, 1983.

For those tenants in this category who have received a compensatory rent increase or who have received an increase in rent pursuant to a lease on or after January 1, 1983, and who select a two or three-year lease, the rent increase for the first year of the two or three year lease will be 15% above the rent paid in December, 1982. If the tenant has paid a 15% increase above the rent paid in December 1982, that rent will continue until June 30, 1984 when the second year increase of 10% above that rent will go into effect. If a three-year lease is signed, a third increase of 5% will go into effect on or after July 1, 1985.

For those tenants in this category who have received a compensatory increase or who have received a rent increase by lease on or after January 1, 1983, and who select a one year lease only, the rent reserved in the lease will be 15% above the rent paid in June, 1983, with the new lease commencing July 1, 1983, or at the expiration of their present lease term after June 30, 1983.

All future payments to be made by the tenant after July 1, 1983 are to be based upon the tenant's written lease issued in accordance with the ETPA.

If the new lease commencing on or after July 1, 1983 should result in a Legal Regulated Rent in excess of the rent paid for the lowest comparable (by room count) apartment which was subject to the Emergency Tenant Protection Act prior to June 19, 1981 in the same building or complex, the rent reserved in the lease may not exceed the Legal Regulated Rent of the comparable apartment at any time during the lease term.

The designation and the rent of the lowest comparable apartment must be recited in the first lease offer.

Further information—Persons requiring further information, or who wish to obtain copies of the ETPA,

TENANT PROTECTION BULLETINS

EHRCL or pertinent Regulations, should contact one of the following Division of Housing and Community Renewal Offices:

New York City —Two World Trade Center, Rm. 5870, New York 10047
Telephone Number (212) 488-3217

White Plains —99 Church Street, 4th Floor, White Plains, N.Y. 10601
Telephone Number (914) 948-4434

Mount Vernon —City Hall, Mount Vernon, N.Y. (Wednesdays and Thursday only)
Telephone Number (914) 668-2200

Tenant Protection Bulletin No. 39 Emergency Tenant Protection Act

Summary of Guideline Rates of Maximum Rent Increases filed by County Rent Guidelines Boards for leases commencing between October 1, 1983 and September 30, 1984.

	*Nassau County	**Rockland County	***Westchester County
1. *One-Year Lease*	6.5%	4%	No increase
2. *Two-Year Lease*	9%	7.5%	No increase

These guidelines shall be applied to the base rent without tax or tax cost escalating factors.

All counties require the owners to file operating expense statements before they are eligible to collect any guideline rent increases.

Nassau County

(a) Where a vacant apartment is rented to a new tenant, who is *not residing in the same building or complex,* an additional *guideline not to exceed one month of the prior legal regulated rent* may be charged, prorated over the term of the lease *selected by the tenant.*

(b) Where the Legal Regulated Rent includes electric and gas service, an additional guideline rate of 2% may be charged. This does not become part of the Legal Regulated Rent and it is applicable only to accommodations within solely residential buildings or in mixed buildings in which the non-residential units are separately metered.

(c) Where the tenant pays for heat, the guideline authorized shall be reduced by 1.5% for one-year leases and 2% for two-year leases.

**Rockland County*

When a vacancy occurs, the landlord shall be allowed to increase the rent level for that apartment to the highest rent level as of October 1, 1983, for an apartment having the same number of rooms within the same building or complex, or by a factor of 5%, *whichever is lower.*

This base rent is then established for apartments in this building or complex having the same number of rooms for the balance of the guideline year. Upon this base rent shall then be added the allowable one or two-year increases under the guidelines, provided the owner shall further fully recite in the lease the designation and location of the apartment having the same number of rooms and the highest rent level.

***Westchester County*

No additional guideline rent increase when renting a vacant apartment to a new tenant.

Further information and copies of the *Guidelines and Findings* adopted and filed by each County Rent Guidelines Board are available at the Office of Rent Administration:

Two World Trade Center—58th Floor
New York, N.Y. 10047—Tel. (212)488-7147
50 Clinton Street—2nd Floor
Hempstead, N.Y. 11550—Tel. (516)481-9494
99 Church Street—4th Floor
White Plains, N.Y. 10601—Tel. (914)948-4434

**Tenant Protection Bulletin No. 84-2
Emergency Tenant Protection Act**

(Issued October 1, 1984)

Summary of Guideline Rates of Maximum Rent Increases filed by County Rent Guidelines Boards for

Tenant Protection Bulletins

leases commencing between October 1, 1984 and
September 30, 1985

	*Rockland County	**Nassau County	***Westchester County	****New York City
1. One-Year Lease	3%	6%	0%	6%
2. Two-Year Lease	6%	8%	3%	9%

The guidelines shall be applied to the base rent without tax or cost escalating factors.

All counties outside New York City require the owners to file operating expense statements before they are eligible to collect any guideline rent increases.

Rockland County

When a vacancy occurs, the owner shall be allowed to increase the rent level for that apartment to the highest rent level as of October 1, 1984, for an apartment having the same number of rooms within the same building or complex, or by a factor of 5%, *whichever is lower.*

This base rent is then established for apartments in this building or complex having the same number of rooms *for the balance of the guideline year.*

Upon this base rent the allowable guideline rent increase shall be added, provided that the owner shall further fully recite in the lease the designation and location of the apartment having the same number of rooms and the highest rent level.

**Nassau County*

Where a vacant apartment is rented to a new tenant not then residing in the building or complex, an additional guideline, not to exceed *one month's prior legal regulated rent* may be charged, to be paid by the tenant in equal monthly installments over the term of the lease selected by the tenant. This additional guideline may still be taken if the owner has filed or files an application with the State Division of Housing and Community Renewal for a rent adjustment based on the installation of new equipment to replace existing equipment.

Where the legal regulated rent includes *electric and gas* service, an additional 2% may be charged, which shall not become part of the legal regulated rent. This rent shall only be applicable to accommodations contained in solely residential buildings.

Where the tenant pays for heat, the guideline authorized shall be reduced by 1.5% for one-year leases, and 2% for two-year leases.

***Westchester County*

No additional guideline rent increase when renting a vacant apartment to a new tenant.

****New York City*

The following is a summary of orders established by the New York City Rent Guidelines Board for leases commencing between *October 1, 1984 and September 30, 1985.*

1. ADJUSTMENTS

   A. *FOR RENEWAL LEASES*

1. One-year lease	6%
2. Two-year lease	9%

   These guidelines also apply to dwelling units with partial tax exemption under Sections 421 and 423 of the Real Property Law as a Redevelopment Project.

   Any lease less than one year shall be deemed a one-year lease. Any lease of over one year and up to and including two years, shall be deemed a two-year lease.

   B. *FOR VACANCY LEASES*

   Vacancy leases shall be further increased by 7½%, providing there has been no new tenant during the 10/10/83 - 9/30/84 guideline year. No more than one vacancy lease allowance for leases commencing during this period.

   C. *SUPPLEMENTARY CHARGE*

   For a vacancy or renewal lease for a unit with a lawful rent of less than $250.00 per month on 9/30/84, the levels of rent increase shall be the same as for a renewal lease (as in 1A. above) plus an additional charge of $10.00 provide, however, that the resulting rent does not exceed:

$265.00 per month for a one-year renewal lease;
272.50 per month for a two-year renewal lease;
283.75 per month for a one-year vacancy lease;
291.25 per month for a two-year vacancy lease.

   D. *ELECTRICAL INCLUSION*

   For the lease of a dwelling unit in which the rent includes electrical service, no additional increase shall be allowed.

E. ARTICLE 7-C OF THE MULTIPLE DWELLING LAW

For units where renewal leases are offered pursuant to Section 286, paragraph 3 of the Multiple Dwelling Law (MDL), the rate of rent increase above the base rent (as defined by Section 286 paragraph 4 of the MDL) shall be the same as those above for renewal leases, except that there will be no supplement adjustment of up to $10.00 per month for apartments with a rent of less than $250.00 per month. This also applies to vacancy leases.

F. SPECIAL GUIDELINE (FAIR MARKET RENT)

For dwelling units subject to the Rent and Rehabilitation Law on 9/30/84, which subsequently become vacant, the Fair Market Rent shall be 15% above the 1984-85 maximum base rent, as it existed or would have existed, plus the current allowable fuel adjustments as established on Rent Control forms pursuant to Section 2202.13 [33.10] of the Rent and Eviction Regulations for the City of New York, effective 1980.

G. DECONTROLLED UNITS

The permissible rent increase for decontrolled units as defined in Order 3a, which become decontrolled after 9/30/84, shall not exceed the formula outlined in (F) above.

H. FUEL

No fuel cost adjustment for leases commencing on or after 10/1/83 to 9/30/84 are warranted at this time.

I. HOTELS

The level of fair rent increases over lawful rent actually charged and paid on 6/30/84 shall be zero (0) per cent.

2. ESCALATOR CLAUSES

Where a lease which was in effect on 5/31/68, or in effect on 6/30/74 for a unit which became subject to the Rent Stabilization Law of 1969 pursuant to ETPA, contained an escalator clause for increased costs of operation and which is still in effect, the lawful rental on 9/30/84 shall include the increased rental, if any, due under such clause, except those charges which accrued within one year of the commencement of the renewal lease. Moreover, where a lease contained an escalator clause that the owner may validly renew under the Code, the increased rental, if any, due under such escalator clause shall be offset against the amount of increase authorized under this Order.

3. *STABILIZER*

The ½% "stabilizer" charged in leases pursuant to previous orders shall remain in effect until the expiration of such lease and shall be included in the base rent for the purpose of computing subsequent rents.

4. *CREDITS*

Rentals paid in excess of the rent increases established in these orders shall be fully credited against the next month's rent.

PART V: MISCELLANEOUS LAWS
Rules of Practice for the Office of Rent
   Administration Adjudicatory Proceeding
Omnibus Housing Act of 1983
Private Housing Finance Law (§§ 607, 608, 706-a)
Increase of Rentals, Department of
   HPD Supervisory Agency
Public Authorities Law (§ 2429)
Destabilization Provisions of Real Property
   Tax Law (§§ 421-a, 489) J51 Housing
Unlawful Evictions

PART V

MISCELLANEOUS LAWS

RULES OF PRACTICE FOR THE OFFICE OF RENT ADMINISTRATION ADJUDICATORY PROCEEDINGS

[State of New York Official Compilation of Codes, Rules, and Regulations, Volume 9, Executive (C), Subtitle S Housing, Chapter 7, Subchapter A, Part 2051.]

§ 2051.1 Proceedings Before The Hearings Unit

(a) Preliminary Matters.

After a proceeding has been referred for hearing to the Hearings Unit, a review of the file shall be made to insure that the proceeding was properly instituted and affected parties have received proper notice, with an opportunity to answer, in accordance with the rules governing proceedings before the DHCR as enunciated in the State Rent and Eviction Regulations, the City Rent and Eviction Regulations, and the Tenant Protection Regulations.

(b) Subsequent Pleadings-Amendments to complaint, application or answer.

(1) Right to amend. The DHCR or the parties shall have the right reasonably and fairly to amend the complaint, application or answer.

(2) Applicant's right. (i) The applicant, including a complainant, has the right to amend the proceeding in writing prior to an answer being filed. (ii) The applicant has the right to amend the complaint or application by addition or deletion in writing after an answer has been filed at the discretion of the DHCR. (iii) After a notice of hearing has been served on the parties, amendments to the pleadings are subject to the discretion of the administrative law judge.

(3) Authority to amend. The authority of the DHCR to amend any aspect of the proceeding may be exer-

cised by the Commissioner, Counsel, or a Deputy Counsel, or the Chief or Deputy Chief of the Enforcement/Compliance Bureau, who may add new parties, particulars or charges in their discretion or at the direction of the administrative law judge.

(4) Service. Any amendment to a proceeding shall be served upon all parties unless made upon the record at a public administrative hearing.

(5) Amended Answer. When a complaint is amended after an answer has been filed but before the hearing, each respondent may file an amended answer with the DHCR at least two business days prior to the hearing. If the amendment of the complaint is made during the two-business-day period prior to the scheduled hearing, or at the hearing, the hearing may be adjourned for at least two business days.

§ 2051.2 Action By The Administrative Law Judge.

At any stage of a proceeding after a matter has been referred to the Hearings Unit, an administrative law judge or the chief administrative law judge may:

(a) Recommend rejection of the complaint or application with or without prejudice, at the discretion of the DHCR and without the conduct of a hearing, if it is insufficient or defective.

(b) Direct investigation of the facts including inspections, hold conferences, and require the filing of reports, evidence, affidavits, or other material relevant to the proceeding.

(c) Forward to or make available for inspection by either party any relevant evidence except where protected by privilege and afford an opportunity to file rebuttal thereto.

(d) For good cause shown, accept for filing any papers, even though not filed within the time required by regulation.

(e) Require any person to appear or produce documents or both pursuant to a subpoena issued by the DHCR.

(f) Forward to either party a notice of action proposed to be taken.

(g) On his own motion or upon application of any affected owner or tenant, direct the consolidation of proceedings which have at least one ground in common, or which are applicable to the same building or group of buildings or development, notwithstanding that the housing accommodations affected may be subject to differing regulations; and in any such consolidated proceedings, the determination with respect to any housing accommodation shall be made in accordance with the appropriate law or regulation applicable to such accommodations. Proceedings may be severed subsequent to consolidation for good cause shown.

(h) Sever issues within a proceeding for purposes of recommending the issuance of an Order and Determination with respect to certain issues while reserving other issues for subsequent recommended determination.

(i) Recommend the issuance of conditional or provisional determinations as he may deem appropriate under the circumstances. A copy of any order issued shall be forwarded to all parties to the proceeding by the DHCR and otherwise as the DHCR directs.

(j) Recommend the termination of a proceeding based on the default of an applicant or complainant.

§ 2051.3 Hearings.

(a) Definitions:

(1) The term "administrative law judge" means any person appointed as a hearing officer or examiner to hear proceedings in accordance with the provisions of the law and to conduct such other and further hearings in connection therewith as may be required and to report findings to the Commissioner or the district rent administrator as the case may be.

(2) The term "chief administrative law judge" shall mean that administrative law judge designated to supervise the administrative law judges and designated as the chief of the hearings bureau.

(3) Any word or term which is defined in the law or

regulations shall have the same meaning when used herein.

(4) When used in these rules of practice, unless a different meaning clearly appears from the context, the term "law" shall mean and include any one or more of the following: the Rent Stabilization Law, the Emergency Tenant Protection Act of 1974, the NYC Rent and Rehabilitation Law, the Emergency Housing Rent Control Law, and all amendments thereto. The term "regulations" shall mean and include any one or more of the following: the Rent Stabilization Code, the State and City Rent and Eviction Regulations and the Emergency Tenant Protection Regulations.

(b) When Held: Hearings shall be held in all cases in which they are mandated by law. Additionally, hearings shall be held at the direction of the Commissioner, the Commissioner's designee, a District Rent Administrator, the Counsel, a Deputy Counsel, or a Bureau Chief whenever necessary to determine facts in dispute. A hearing need not be held when the record is complete based on written submissions. Where a hearing has been directed, it shall be scheduled promptly.

(c) Notice of hearing:

All parties shall be given reasonable notice of such hearing, which notice shall include (a) a statement of the time, place, and nature of the hearing; (b) a statement of the legal authority and jurisdiction under which the hearing is to be held; (c) a reference to the particular sections of the statutes and rules involved, where possible; (d) a short and plain statement of matters asserted. Upon application of any party to the administrative law judge, a more definite and detailed statement shall be furnished whenever the administrative law judge finds that the statement is not sufficiently definite or not sufficiently detailed. The finding of the administrative law judge as to the sufficiency of definitiveness or detail of the statement or the failure or refusal to furnish a more definite or detailed statement shall not be subject to judicial review in the first instance.

Any statement furnished shall be deemed, in all respects, to be a part of the notice of hearing.

(d) Powers of Administrative Law Judges and Conduct of Hearing.

(1) Generally

Administrative law judges are authorized to:

(i) Administer oaths and affirmations.

(ii) On their own motion, at the discretion of the administrative law judge or at the request of any party, sign and issue subpoenas requiring attendance and giving of testimony by witnesses and the production of books, papers, documents and other evidence, and said subpoenas shall be regulated by the civil practice law and rules. Nothing herein contained shall affect the authority of an attorney for a party to issue such subpoenas under the provisions of the civil practice law and rules.

(iii) Provide for the taking of testimony by deposition and to fix appropriate terms and conditions therefor.

(iv) Regulate the course of the hearings, set the time and place for continued hearings, and fix the time for filing of briefs and other documents.

(v) Request that the parties appear and confer to consider the simplification of the issues, or direct appearance for the clarification of issues.

(2) Conduct of hearing.

(i) The administrative law judge shall not be bound by common law or statutory rules of evidence or by technical or formal rules or procedure. The administrative law judge shall conduct the hearing in such order and manner and with such methods of proof and interrogation as he deems appropriate to ascertain the substantial rights of the parties. All parties shall be accorded full opportunity to present such testimony and to introduce documentary or other evidence as may be pertinent. At the commencement of the hearing, the administrative law judge shall identify all parties present and may make an opening statement describing the nature of the proceeding, the issues and the manner in which the hearing shall be conducted. No administrative law judge shall participate in any hearing in which he has an interest. If a party files a timely and sufficient affidavit of personal bias or disqualification of an administrative law judge, the matter shall be referred to and decided by the chief administrative law judge, or, in the absence of the chief administrative law judge, by the deputy counsel or an assistant deputy counsel. Challenges to the chief administrative law judge shall be referred to and decided by the deputy counsel for rent administration or by an assistant deputy counsel. The hearing shall generally be conducted in accordance with the New York State Civil Service Commission publication "Revised Manual No. 16" (1972), entitled "Manual For Hearing Officers In Administrative Adjudication In The State Of New York" authored by Louis J. Naftalison.

(ii) Appearances. (a) All parties to the proceeding may be present and/or may appear by attorney, agent or representative and shall be allowed to present testimony in person or by counsel, call, examine and cross-examine witnesses.

(b) If a notice of hearing has not been delivered to a party, the DHCR in its discretion may adjourn a scheduled hearing to determine whether that party expects to attend a hearing, or whether the complaint should be dismissed for administrative convenience, default entered, or other appropriate action taken.

(c) If a respondent fails to appear at the duly noted time and place of the hearing, and the hearing is not adjourned, the hearing shall proceed on the evidence in support of the complaint. If an applicant or complainant fails to appear, the administrative law judge may similarly note the default on the record and go forward with the respondent's case, if any, to contravert any prima facie case made. Upon application in writing or on his own motion, the administrative law judge or chief administrative law judge may for good cause shown, prior to an order, reopen or allow for continuation of the proceeding upon equitable terms and conditions.

(iii) New parties. (a) In the discretion of the administrative law judge, any other person who has a substantial personal interest may be allowed to intervene as a party, in person or by counsel.

(b) The administrative law judge may require that any person not already a party be joined as a necessary party to the proceeding.

(c) In such joinder, the hearing shall be adjourned unless the person ordered to be joined is present and consents to waive service of notice of hearing and pleadings and to proceed as if he or she had been designated as such necessary party in the original complaint or application.

(d) In the event of such adjournment, the DHCR shall serve a new notice of hearing and copy of the complaint or application as amended upon the person so joined and upon all other parties, and shall also serve on the person so joined copies of the previous pleadings and a notice that the prior hearing record may be examined at the offices of the DHCR during normal business hours.

(e) Upon such waiver of notice by a person who is present, or upon service of such new notice of hearing and an amended complaint, the hearing shall proceed as if the party so joined had been designated in the original complaint or application.

(iv) Who shall conduct. Hearings shall be conducted by an administrative law judge designated by the DHCR. No person who shall have previously made the investigation, engaged in a prior formal conciliation proceeding or caused the notice of charges to be issued, shall act as an administrative law judge in such case.

(v) Procedure. (a) The administrative law judge shall have full authority to control the procedure of the hearing, subject to these rules, and to rule upon all motions and objections, except motions to grant or dismiss the application or complaint. Effect shall be given to the rules of privilege recognized by law.

(b) Motions to grant or dismiss will be preserved on the record for the decision of the Commissioner or the district rent administrator in an order after hearing, or in extraordinary circumstances, after leave of the administrative law judge, said motion may be made and decided in the Commissioner's discretion or at the discretion of the district rent administrator in an interlocutory ruling.

(c) The administrative law judge, on motion of a party or on his or her own motion, may call and examine witnesses, direct the production of papers or other matter, and introduce documentary or other evidence. The administrative law judge may exclude from the hearing room a witness, other than a party or complainant, who has not yet testified.

(d) In the interest of the prompt administration of justice and without prejudice to the substantial rights of any party and in the discretion of the administrative law judge, any issue in a case or any other issue related thereto may be heard and decided, though not specifically indicated in the notice of hearing.

(e) All oral testimony shall be given under oath or affirmation, and a record of the proceeding shall be made and kept. Irrelevant or unduly repetitious evidence or cross-examination may be excluded. Evidence supplemental to that introduced at the hearing may be made part of the record.

(f) A determination may not be based on settlement negotiations which do not result in a stipulation of settlement. Unsuccessful attempts at settlement shall not be received in evidence except as to the issue of good faith where good faith is an issue in the proceeding.

(g) Evidence shall not be received in camera except at the discretion of the administrative law judge in extraordinary circumstances. However, where desirable, the administrative law judge in consultation with counsel may provide for the use of devices, such as deletion of names and coding, in order to protect personal privacy or information.

(h) The initial burden of proof shall be upon the party who initiated the proceeding.

> (vi) Stipulations. Written stipulations may be introduced in evidence if signed by the person sought to be bound thereby or by that person's attorney-at-law. Oral stipulations may be made on the

record at open hearing. The entire record may be in the form of a stipulation, submitted to the designated administrative law judge or the chief administrative law judge without the convening of a hearing.

(vii) *Continuations, adjournments and substitutions of administrative law judge.* (a) The DHCR may postpone a scheduled hearing, or continue a hearing from day to day, or adjourn it to a later date or to a different place, by announcement thereof at the hearing or by appropriate notice to all parties. In the discretion and upon such terms and conditions set by the administrative law judge, adjournment of a scheduled hearing may be granted upon affidavit of actual engagement before a higher tribunal or for good cause shown in writing. Except where an adjournment of a hearing is on consent of all other parties to the proceeding, a party's written request for an adjournment of a scheduled hearing must be received at least three business days prior thereto. Applications made thereafter, and which are not on consent must be made by formal motion on the record at the hearing unless the administrative law judge directs otherwise. (b) Whenever a case is assigned to an administrative law judge the hearing or any adjourned hearing thereon shall continue before the same administrative law judge until a final disposition thereof unless the case is transferred pursuant to motion or for good cause by the chief administrative law judge. Good cause shall include, *inter alia,* the absence, disability or disqualification of an administrative law judge. The hearing shall continue upon the previous record unless it can be shown that substantial prejudice will result therefrom.

(c) Each party, or his attorney, shall have the right to inspect the file, to rebut any evidence given, and to cross-examine other parties and witnesses, in person if practicable, inspect the report of the administrative law judge hearing the case and request a copy thereof.

(d) By order of the chief administrative law judge or the administrative law judge, a case may be transferred from one designated place of hearing to another for the convenience of parties or witnesses and as the interests of justice may require.

 (viii) The chief administrative law judge or the administrative law judge may sever a case or may consolidate two or more proceedings which have at least one ground in common where the interests of justice will be served and where there will be no prejudice to the substantial rights of any party. If two or more proceedings are consolidated, any applicable rules set forth herein shall apply.

 (ix) The DHCR and parties, or their duly authorized representatives, may stipulate that a specified case involving an issue affecting in common certain claimants be designated as a test case, and that the parties be bound by any decision in such case, subject to the right of appeal. The stipulation shall be filed with the administrative law judge.

 (x) Information from the DHCR's records may be officially noticed, and the case file, except for privileged items contained therein, shall be made available by the administrative law judge to the parties to the hearing or their attorneys for the necessary preparation and presentation of the case. All parties shall have the right to call, examine and cross-examine other parties and witnesses with regard to such information. The administrative law judge may take official notice of all facts of which judicial notice could be taken and of other facts within the specialized knowledge of the Agency. When official notice is taken of a material fact not appearing in the evidence in the record and of which judicial notice could not be taken, every party shall be given prior notice thereof and afforded an opportunity to dispute the fact or refute its materiality.

 (xi) Motions and objections. Motions made during a hearing and objections with respect to the conduct of a hearing, including objections to the introduction of evidence, shall be stated orally, and shall be included in the record made of the hearing.

(xii) Oral arguments and briefs. The administrative law judge may permit the parties, their attorneys or representatives, the DHCR attorney, if any, and interveners and interested organizations to argue orally and to file briefs within such time limits as the administrative law judge may determine. All such briefs shall be filed in duplicate with the administrative law judge, with proof of service upon all counsel in the proceeding and parties appearing without counsel.

(xiii) Public hearings. Hearings shall be open to the public. The administrative law judge may exclude from the hearing room or from further participation in the proceeding any person who engages in improper conduct at the hearing or otherwise disrupts the proceeding except a party to the proceeding, an attorney of record, or a witness engaged in testifying. In addition, the administrative law judge may take such other actions as are necessary to insure the proper conduct of the hearing.

(xiv) Incomplete record. The Commissioner, the district rent administrator or the administrative law judge may, on a finding that the record is incomplete or fails to provide the basis for an informed decision, direct further hearing sessions for the taking of additional evidence or for other purposes. Such direction may be on the Commissioner's or district rent administrator's or administrative law judge's own motion or on application of a party.

(xv) Ex parte communications. No person shall communicate with the administrative law judge subsequent to the commencement of a hearing on any matter relating to the case, other than a status inquiry, unless a copy of such communication is sent to all parties to the proceeding. If such a communication is made in violation of this rule, a copy of the communication, or a written summary if the communication was oral, shall be sent to all the parties by the administrative law judge.

(xvi) (a) When an attorney represents a party at a hearing, the administrative law judge shall ascertain whether or not such attorney is appearing in a proceeding where attorney fees may be awarded by statute or regulation. If so, the administrative law judge may entertain a motion for an award of attorneys' fees. If such an award is requested, the administrative law judge shall require such attorney to submit an affidavit in support of his claim for fees, setting forth in detail:

(1) the total amount requested;

(2) the time spent in providing representation subdivided into time spent: (i) in case preparation; (ii) at hearing; (iii) in post hearing matters

(3) the legal and factual complexities involved; and

(4) any other factors which may be deemed relevant to determination of the fee that should be allowed including, but not limited to, a statement of the attorney's customary hourly rate, his background and particular qualifications.

When an attorney has ceased to represent a party during the course of a proceeding the DHCR shall have no obligation to notify said attorney of any determination reached in the matter and may refuse to entertain a request for attorney's fees for prior legal services to the party.

(xvii) Whenever any deaf person is a party to a hearing before the DHCR or a witness therein, the DHCR in all instances shall appoint a qualified interpreter of the deaf to interpret the proceedings to and the testimony of such deaf person. The DHCR shall determine a reasonable fee for all such interpreting services which shall be a charge upon the agency.

(xviii) Investigation. Whenever an investigation, inspection, inquiry, or other examination is necessary in deciding a case, the chief administrative law judge or an administrative law judge may request such investigation, inspection, inquiry, or other examination to be made. A hearing may be adjourned pending receipt of the report of such investigation, inspection, inquiry, audit or examination. The provisions of Section 2051.3(d)(2)(x) of this Part shall apply to such report.

(xix) After the hearing is concluded, the administrative law judge shall review the evidence and briefs, if any, submitted by the parties, determine the credibility of the witnesses, and shall propose findings of fact relevant to the issues of the hearing. The administrative law judge shall prepare an official report which includes a summary of the testimony of the hearing as well as proposed findings and conclusions and shall prepare a proposed order for the Commissioner or district rent administrator.

§ 2051.4 Miscellaneous Procedural Matters

(a) Subpoenas and subpoenas duces tecum. (1) Who may issue. The Commissioner, the Commissioner's designee, an administrative law judge, DHCR's counsel, a Deputy Counsel, or an Assistant Deputy Counsel may issue subpoenas and subpoenas duces tecum whenever necessary to compel the attendance of witnesses or to require the production for examination of any books, payrolls, rent rolls, ledgers, correspondence, documents, papers or any other evidence relating to any matter under investigation or in question before the DHCR.

(2) When and where returnable. Subpoenas and subpoenas duces tecum issued by the designated officers and employees of the DHCR may be made returnable at any stage of any investigation or proceeding pending before the division. Documents, books and records required for a public hearing before an administrative law judge may be subpoenaed and made returnable prior to such hearing at such time and place stated in

the subpoena by the issuing officer, or made returnable at the time and place designated for hearing.

(3) Application for a subpoena.

(i) Subpoenas and subpoenas duces tecum may be issued by the designated officers and employees of the DHCR upon the application of a party, his representative or a party's attorney. Issuance of a subpoena duces tecum at the instance of a party shall depend upon a showing of necessity.

(ii) Application for a subpoena may be made at any stage in the proceeding and should be made in writing. The administrative law judge may, at his discretion:

> (a) cause the subpoena requested to be issued; or
>
> (b) by hearing notice or amended hearing notice direct the production of all or some of the witnesses or material sought and within the control of a party to the proceeding at the hearing; or
>
> (c) advise the attorney for a party who has sought the issuance of the subpoena to proceed in accordance with Section 2302 of the Civil Practices Law and Rules (C.P.L.R.). Said advisement shall be in writing and on notice to all other parties or placed on the record.

(iii) Where a party to the proceeding fails to produce evidence and/or witnesses found to be within its control, and which were directed by hearing notice or by the administrative law judge to be produced, the administrative law judge may then cause to be issued and served a subpoena for the production thereof, or the administrative law judge may draw a negative inference from the failure to produce.

(4) Subpoenas by attorneys. (i) An attorney appearing for a party may issue and cause to be served subpoenas or subpoenas duces tecum returnable at a hearing before an administrative law judge in accordance with Section 2302 of the Civil Practice Law and Rules. (ii) Motions to enforce, quash or modify a subpoena issued pursuant to Section 2302 of the Civil Practice Law and Rules shall be made in a court of competent jurisdiction. However, upon an offer of proof, the administra-

tive law judge may cause to be issued a subpoena or direct a party to produce all or any part of the requested matter. Upon failure to comply therewith in whole or in part, the administrative law judge may cause enforcement actions to be undertaken in whole or in part to obtain compliance, and/or the administrative law judge may draw a negative inference from the failure to comply.

(iii) Where the attorney for a party issues a subpoena and thereafter applies for judicial enforcement thereof, the administrative law judge may, at his discretion, continue the hearing to take testimony from other witnesses. At his discretion, or where the issued subpoena relates to a final witness, the administrative law judge may grant an adjournment but shall require that within a period not in excess of ten (10) days the party issuing the subpoena present proof to the administrative law judge that it has instituted a proceeding to compel compliance. The administrative law judge may thereafter require proof of diligent pursuit of the matter and shall continue the hearing within (30) days of notification of resolution of the compliance proceeding.

(5) Depository officer. An officer or employee of the DHCR may be designated as a depository officer, who shall receive and hold documents, books and records subpoenaed and/or produced at said hearing and required for use during the period between the commencement of a public hearing and any adjourned date thereof. Such records shall be made available for inspection and copying during the ordinary business hours of the DHCR. If produced at hearing, the administrative law judge assigned to the matter shall be the depository officer.

(6) Public bodies. Absent a specific statute or rule to the contrary, a subpoena duces tecum directed to another public body or agency does not require approval of the court.

(7) Witness or mileage fees. Where a subpoena or subpoena duces tecum is issued at the instance of a party or by an attorney, the cost of service and witness and mileage fees and the burden of ser-

vice shall be borne by such party or attorney. Such witness and mileage fees shall be the same as are paid at trials in the New York State Supreme Court.

(b) Depositions and telephone testimony. (1) Depositions. An administrative law judge may authorize a deposition to be taken on oral or written questions in accordance with the provisions of C.P.L.R. Section 3117(a)3 and shall admit such deposition into evidence at a hearing in lieu of the personal appearance and testimony of the deponent at the hearing, subject to the following conditions:

(i) All parties and counsel have been offered a reasonable opportunity to participate in the taking of the deposition and to cross-examine thereat.

(ii) The deposition was taken before any person authorized to administer an oath in the place where the deposition is taken and was either subscribed and sworn to by the deponent or certified as accurate by the stenographer.

(iii) The absence of cross-examination shall not be a bar to the admission of such deposition provided, however, that, if justice so requires, the deponent may be subject to further inquiry by additional deposition.

(iv) Any other reasonable condition fixed by the administrative law judge.

(2) Testimony by telephone. With the consent of all parties and where necessary to prevent an otherwise unavoidable adjournment or for other good cause shown, the administrative law judge may permit the testimony of a witness to be taken by telephone subject to the following procedure:

(i) It is practicable to reach the witness by telephone call;

(ii) a person within the hearing room can testify that the voice of the witness is recognized;

(iii) the administrative law judge, reporter, if any, and respective attorneys can hear the questions and answers;

(iv) the witness is placed under oath and testifies that he or she is not being coached by any other person; and

(v) the testimony is limited in scope.

Rent Administration Rules

(c) Settlements and Withdrawals. (1) Stipulation. At any time the parties may stipulate to settle the case subject to the approval of the commissioner or the district rent administrator. Such stipulation shall either be in writing, signed by the parties or their attorneys, or be placed on the record at a public hearing.

(2) Terms. (i) The stipulation should contain precise and unambiguous terms.

(ii) The stipulation should provide that it is subject to the issuance of an order or notice thereon by the commissioner or district rent administrator incorporating its operative terms.

(3) Order after stipulation or withdrawal. (i) An order after stipulation or withdrawal of a proceeding may be signed and issued by the commissioner or district rent administrator without a hearing and without findings of fact.

(ii) Such order may be enforced in the same manner as any order after hearing issued by the commissioner or district rent administrator.

(d) Orders after hearing. (1) Form. An order issued after hearing shall set forth the findings of fact and conclusions of law or reasons for the decision or determination of the commissioner or district rent administrator.

(2) Service. Copies of orders signed by the commissioner or district rent administrator shall be sent to all parties including interveners or to their attorneys or representatives, if represented. A copy of the order may also, where warranted, be delivered to the Attorney General, the Secretary of State or to such public officers as the DHCR deems proper.

(3) Filing. Copies of all orders rendered after a hearing shall be filed at the administrative offices of the DHCR and at the office where the complaint or application was filed.

(e) Compliance investigation. (1) Investigation. At any time after the date of a settlement agreement, an order after hearing, an order after stipulation or otherwise, and at any other times in its discretion, the DHCR may investigate whether the parties are complying with the terms of such agreement or order.

(2) Action. Upon a finding of noncompliance, the DHCR may take appropriate action to assure compliance.

(f) Rules and regulations. (1) Any rule or regulation established governing practice and procedure before administrative law judges and the DHCR may be added to, amended, modified, rescinded or superseded by the DHCR at any time in accordance with the requirements of law.

(2) These rules and regulations shall be construed liberally to effectuate the purposes and provisions of the law.

(3) These rules and regulations and any addition, amendment, modification, rescission or supersedure thereof shall be available to the public at all offices of the DHCR and at the hearings bureau.

(g) Record. (1) The record in a proceeding before the DHCR shall include:

(i) all notices, pleadings, motions, intermediate rulings;

(ii) evidence presented;

(iii) a statement of matters officially noticed except matters so obvious that a statement of them would serve no useful purpose;

(iv) questions and offers of proof, objections thereto, and rulings thereon;

(v) proposed findings and exceptions, if any;

(vi) any decision, determination, opinion, order or report rendered.

(2) The DHCR shall make a complete record of all adjudicatory proceedings conducted before it. For this purpose, the DHCR may use whatever means it deems appropriate, including but not limited to, the use of stenographic transcriptions or electronic recording devices. Upon request made by any party upon the agency within a reasonable

time, but prior to the time for commencement of judicial review, or its giving notice of its decision, determination, opinion or order, the DHCR shall prepare the record together with any transcript of proceedings within a reasonable time and shall furnish a copy of the record and transcript or any part thereof to any party as he may request. The party making the request shall bear full responsibility for the cost of the preparation and furnishing of such transcript or any part thereof, including the cost of an original for the division. Any party requesting a copy of the record and/or any transcript made, or portion thereof, shall be required to pay the costs thereof.

§ 2051.5 Administrative Review.

Persons who may file. Any person aggrieved by an order issued by a District Rent Administrator may file a petition for administrative review (PAR) to the Commissioner in the manner provided in Operational Bulletin Number 84-1 and any supplements thereto.

§ 2051.6 Limitations; Severability.
  (a) These Rules shall not act in any manner so as to limit any powers of the Commissioner or any designated officer or employee of the DHCR as provided for by law or regulation.
  (b) If any provision of these Rules or the application thereof to any persons or circumstances shall be held invalid, the validity of the remainder of these Rules and the applicability thereof to other persons or circumstances shall not be affected thereby.

OMNIBUS HOUSING
ACT OF 1983 [1983, ch 403]

Section 1. **Legislative findings.** The legislature hereby finds and declares that the serious public emergency which led to the enactment of the existing laws regulating residential rents and evictions continues to exist; that extension of such laws is therefore required in the public interest, and that such laws would better serve the public interest if certain changes were made thereto, including the placing of all of the systems of regulation of rents and evictions under a single state agency.

The legislature further recognizes that severe disruption of the rental housing market is threatened as a result of the present state of the law and judicial decisions in relation to the rights of tenants to sublet or to assign leases. The situation, in addition to creating widespread uncertainty on the part of all parties as to their rights, has permitted speculative and profiteering practices on the part of certain holders of apartment leases, leaving many subtenants without protection and removing many housing accommodations from the normal open housing market. Accordingly, the necessity for enactment of strengthened and clarified protections of the legitimate rights of the affected parties is hereby found to be required to protect the public interest.

The legislature further finds and declares that recent judicial decisions refusing to extend the protection of the human rights law to unrelated persons sharing a dwelling will exacerbate this serious problem; that unless corrective action is taken by the legislature, thousands of households throughout this state composed of unrelated persons who live together for reasons of economy, safety and companionship may be placed in jeopardy. The legislature therefore declares that in order to prevent uncertainty, potential hardship and dislocation of tenants living in housing accommodations subject to government regulations as to rentals and continued occupancy as well

Omnibus Housing Act

as those not subject to such regulation, the provisions of this act are necessary to protect the public health, safety and general welfare. The necessity in the public interest for the provisions hereinafter enacted is hereby declared as a matter of legislative determination.

§ 16. Transfer of functions. All of the functions and powers possessed by and all the obligations and duties of the conciliation and appeals board, are hereby transferred and assigned to, assumed by and devolved upon the division of housing and community renewal in the executive department. [Effective April 1, 1984]

§ 17. (a) Notwithstanding any other provision of law, the state shall, no later than January first, nineteen hundred eighty-four, develop a classification plan for all positions necessary to implement the provisions of this act. Such plan shall provide for the classification of positions in accordance with article eight of the civil service law. Such plan shall be specific as to the titles, duties and salary grades of all such positions.

(b) No later than January first, nineteen hundred eighty-four, officers and employees of the division of rent control of the department of housing preservation and development of the city of New York and of the conciliation and appeals board shall be notified of the plan developed pursuant to subdivision (a) of this section; such officers and employees shall be informed as to their individual salary as soon as practicable thereafter.

(c) Subject to subdivisions (d) and (e) of this section, each such officer and employee shall notify the commissioner of the state division of housing and community renewal whether or not he elects to become an employee of the state; in the absence of such notification, an officer or employee shall be deemed to have so elected.

(d) All officers and employees of the division of rent control of the department of housing preservation and development of the city of New York, other than those determined by such department to be necessary to carry out the provisions of title YYY of chapter fifty-one, subdivision n of section Y51-5.0 and sections Y51-5.1 and YY-4.1.1 of the administrative code of the city of New York relating to senior citizen rent increase exemption and tax abatement, shall be transferred to the state division of housing and community renewal. Such transfer shall be in accordance with section seventy of the civil service law, except that all such officers and employees shall be offered employment with the state. Each such transferred officer or employee, subject to the right of election set forth in subdivision (c) of this section, shall become an employee of the state of New York effective April first, nineteen hundred eighty-four. Officers and employees so transferred shall not within a period of two years from the effective date of such transfer be involuntarily assigned to work outside the geographical boundaries of the city of New York.

(e) In accordance with section forty-five of the civil service law, such officers and employees of the conciliation and appeals board as the commissioner of the state division of housing and community renewal deems necessary shall be transferred to such state division. Each such transferred employee, subject to the right of election set forth in subdivision (c) of this section, shall become an employee of the state of New York effective April first, nineteen hundred eighty-four. Officers and employees so transferred shall not within a period of two years from the effective date of such transfer be involuntarily assigned to work outside the geographical boundaries of the City of New York.

(f) Employees in positions established pursuant to subdivision (a) of this section shall be included in one appropriate employer-employee negotiating unit pursuant to article fourteen of the civil service law except that those employees designated managerial or confidential pursuant to such article fourteen prior to the effective date of this act shall continue to be so designated. Upon the termination of the period of unchallenged representation of any employee organization certified or recognized to represent employees of the division of rent control or the conciliation and appeals board, petitions may be filed with the public employment relations board to alter negotiating units in accordance with standards set forth in section two hundred seven of the civil service law; provided, however, that such board shall not alter any such negotiating unit comprised exclusively of such employees or that part of any other negotiating unit comprised of such employees. Nothing herein shall preclude the merger of such negotiating unit and any other unit with which the state negotiates pursuant to article fourteen with the consent of the governor's office of employee relations and the recognized or certified representatives of the negotiating units. Should such merger occur pursuant to this subdivision, the public employment relations board shall have jurisdiction to alter negotiating units in accordance with the standards set forth in section two hundred seven of the civil service law. Notwithstanding any other provision of law, an application to the public employment relations board seeking a designation by the board that certain persons are managerial or confidential may be filed at any time before April first, nineteen hundred eighty-five, and thereafter pursuant to the provisions of the civil service law.

(g) Each officer or employer whose position is allocated to a salary grade pursuant to this section shall continue to receive the salary received by such employee on March thirty-first, nineteen hundred eighty-four or shall receive the hiring rate of that grade whichever is higher. For purpose of this subdivision and subdivision (b) of this section, the term "salary" shall mean the basic annual salary otherwise payable to any officer or employee who becomes a state employee under the provisions of this act exclusive of overtime compensation and any allowance in lieu of maintenance. The salary of the incumbent of a position compensable on an hourly or per diem basis, or any other basis other than at an annual salary rate, shall be deemed to be the salary which would otherwise be payable if the services were required on a full-time annual basis for the number of hours per day and days per week established by law or administrative rules or orders for regular full time employees.

(h) Each officer and employee who becomes a state employee pursuant to this act shall be credited with vacation and sick leave earned and accumulated, but unused at the time he became a state employee, but not in excess of the maximum accumulation permitted for other state employees. The state shall not be responsible for awarding of credit or compensation for any other time or leave credits.

(i) If any officer or employee of the division of rent control is entitled to receive from the city of New York any cash benefits owing as a result of his employment with such city, such cash benefits shall be paid by the city of New York within one year of the date he becomes a state employee pursuant to this act, or as otherwise provided in accordance with the provisions of an applicable collective bargaining agreement. The city of New York shall be liable for the satisfaction of any claims by any such officer or employee arising out of the terms and conditions of his employment prior to the date on which such officer or employee became a state employee pursuant to the provisions of this act.

(j) On and after April first, nineteen hundred eighty-four, officers and employees who become employees of the state pursuant to this act shall become members of the New York state employees' retirement system to the extent permitted or required by the provisions of the retirement and social security law, except that any employee who is a member of the New York city employees' retirement system may elect to continue membership in the New York city employees' retirement system. Any election pursuant to this section shall be made no later than the ninetieth day next succeeding the date on which the provisions hereof become effective, by filing a written notice thereof with the administrative head of the New York state employees' retirement system and the New York city employees' retirement system and, once made and filed, shall be irrevocable. Upon the retirement of an employee who has made such an election, the calculation of final average salary by the New York city employees' retirement system shall be performed as if the salary earned as a state employee on and after such effective date were earned in New York city employment. In the case of an employee who becomes a member of the New York state employees' retirement system pursuant to this section, the New York city employees' retirement system shall make a transfer of reserves, contributions and credits to the New York state employees' retirement system, in the manner required by section forty-three of the retirement and social security law.

(k)(1) Credit for service with the New York city concili-

OMNIBUS HOUSING ACT

ation and appeals board. Notwithstanding any other provisions of law to the contrary, members employed by the New York state division of housing and community renewal on July first, nineteen hundred eighty-six who were employed by the New York city conciliation and appeals board prior to its transfer to the division of housing and community renewal pursuant to this chapter, may obtain credit for such prior service rendered after July first, nineteen hundred seventy-five at the conciliation and appeals board, as hereinafter provided.

(2) To obtain such credit a member shall (a) on or before December thirty-first, nineteen hundred eighty-six, file a request for such credit with the New York state employees' retirement system in the manner prescribed by the state comptroller; and (b) deposit with the retirement system an amount equal to three percent of the employees' salary earned during the period such prior service was rendered, with interest at the rate of five percent per annum, compounded annually. Such deposit must be made on or before May thirty-first, nineteen hundred eighty-seven, provided however, such member may elect to deposit such amount over a period of time no greater than the period for which credit is being claimed, in which case such payments must commence no later than March thirty-first, nineteen hundred eighty-seven. If the full amount of such payments is not paid to the retirement system, the amount of service credited shall be proportional to the total amount of payments made. (subd k added L 1986, ch 471, eff July 21, 1986)[1]

(l) The comptroller of the city of New York shall certify to the state administrator the amount of money required to be paid by the state of New York for pension costs resulting from elections made pursuant to this section. The comptroller of the state of New York shall pay to the New York city employees' retirement system, upon ap-

---

[1] L 1986, ch 471, § 2 provides: The cost of crediting such prior service with the New York city conciliation and appeals board, other than the amounts required to be paid by the members pursuant to the provisions of section one of this act, shall be paid by the state of New York over a ten year period, notwithstanding that past service cost would ordinarily be shared by all participating employers in the New York state employees' retirement system. The amounts of the the state's annual payment in each of the ten years and the manner of making such payments shall be determined by the state comptroller.

proval by the state administrator, the amounts so certified by the comptroller of the city of New York. The comptroller of the city of New York shall also certify to the state administrator the amount of money required to be contributed by each of such employees. The comptroller of the state of New York shall be authorized to withhold the contributions of such employees and pay that amount to the New York city employees' retirement system. The amount so certified shall be the same as the amounts required to be contributed for similarly situated city employees by the city of New York and by employees of the City of New York. [Effective June 30, 1983]

§ 18. **Transfer of assets and records.** All assets and records of such conciliation and appeals board shall become the property of the state division of housing and community renewal, respectively, as of April first, nineteen hundred eighty-four and shall be delivered to the custody of such division as directed by the commissioner. All records of any real estate industry stabilization association or of any hotel industry stabilization association registered pursuant to the New York city rent stabilization law of nineteen hundred sixty-nine, as amended, which relate to the identification of owners who were members of such associations and dwelling units for which dues were paid to such associations by such members shall become the property of the state division of housing and community renewal as of April first, nineteen hundred eighty-four and shall be delivered to the custody of such division as directed by the commissioner thereof. [Effective April 1, 1984]

§ 19. **Continuance of rules and regulations.** a. All rules, regulations, acts, determinations and decisions of the conciliation and appeals board in force on the effective date of this section shall continue in force and effect as rules, regulations, acts, determinations and decisions of the division of housing and community renewal until duly modified or abrogated by the division of housing and community renewal.

b. The code of the rent stabilization association of New York city, Inc. in force on the effective date of this section is continued as the code governing all matters arising under the rent stabilization law of nineteen hundred

OMNIBUS HOUSING ACT

sixty-nine and the emergency tenant protection act of nineteen seventy-four. [Effective April 1, 1984]

§ 20. **Continuity of proceedings.** Any proceeding or other business or matter undertaken or commenced by or before the conciliation and appeals board, and pending on April first, nineteen hundred eighty-four, may be conducted and completed by the division of housing and community renewal in the same manner and under the same terms and conditions and with the same effect, as if conducted and completed by such conciliation and appeals board. [Effective April 1, 1984]

§ 21. **Terms occurring in laws and other documents.** Whenever the conciliation and appeals board is referred to or designated in any law or other document, such reference or designation shall be deemed to refer to the division of housing and community renewal. [Effective April 1, 1984]

§ 27. **Transition provisions.** a. All assets and records of the division of rent control of the department of housing preservation and development of the city of New York, except those required by such department for the administration of title YYY of chapter fifty-one and subdivision n of section Y51-5.0, sections Y51-5.1 and YY51-4.1.1 of the administrative code of the city of New York shall become the property of the state division of housing and community renewal as of the effective date of this section and shall be delivered to the custody of such division as directed by the commissioner thereof. The state division of housing and community renewal and the department of housing preservation and development of the city of New York shall cooperate in maintaining to the extent practicable the existing offices of such department utilized for the operation of the rent control program of the city of New York for the use of the division and where appropriate the joint use of both such division and department subject to an appropriate allocation of costs between them.

b. That portion of any monies collected by the city rent agency prior to April first, nineteen hundred eighty-four as fees or service charges for functions transferred by this act to the division of housing and community renewal, which is applicable to activities to be conducted on or after April first, nineteen hundred eighty-four, shall at the request of the commissioner be transmitted to the division of housing and community renewal.

c. Notwithstanding any other provision of the law, the state shall be required to reimburse the city of New York for services and expenses, including fringe benefits necessary to the operation of the rent control program in accordance with chapter twenty-one of the laws of nineteen hundred sixty-two, from April first, nineteen hundred eighty-two up to and including March thirty-first, nineteen hundred eighty-four after first deducting any fees collected by the city applicable to such period and such operation upon a submission of a claim thereafter by the city of New York, except that payments for fringe benefits shall be paid by the state on or before June thirtieth, nineteen hundred eighty-five, subject to appropriation by the state. [Effective April 1, 1984]

§ 28. Continuance of rules and regulations. All rules, regulations, acts, determinations and decisions of the division of rent control of the department of housing preservation and development of the city of New York, other than those pursuant to title YYY of chapter fifty-one, subdivision n of section Y51-5.0, or sections Y51-5.1 and YY51-4.1.1 of the administrative code of the city of New York, in force on April first, nineteen hundred eighty-four shall continue in force and effect as rules, regulations, acts, determinations and decisions of the division of housing and community renewal until duly modified or abrogated by the division of housing and community renewal. [Effective April 1, 1984]

§ 29. Powers of the department of housing preservation and development. The department of housing preservation and development of the city of New York shall continue to exercise all powers possessed by it for the administration of title YYY of chapter fifty-one, subdivision n of section Y51-5.0, sections Y51-5.1 and YY51-4.1.1 of the administrative code of the city of New York, relating to senior citizen rent increase exemption and tax abatement. [Effective April 1, 1984]

§ 30. **Continuity of proceedings.** Any judicial or administrative proceeding or other business or matter undertaken or commenced by or before the department of housing preservation and development of the city of New York relating to the operation of the rent control or rent stabilization programs of the city of New York, other than those pursuant to title YYY of chapter fifty-one, subdivision n of section Y51-5.0 or sections Y51-5.1 and YY51-4.1.1 of the administrative code of the city of New York, and pending on April first, nineteen hundred eighty-four, may be conducted and completed by the division of housing and community renewal in the same manner and under the same terms and conditions and with the same effect, as if conducted and completed by such department. [Effective April 1, 1984]

§ 31. **Terms occurring in laws, contracts and other documents.** Whenever the city rent agency or the division of rent control of the department of housing preservation and development of the city of New York, other than with respect to title YYY of chapter fifty-one, subdivision n of section Y51-5.0 or section Y51-5.1 or YY51-4.1.1 of the administrative code of the city of New York is referred to or designated in any law, contract or other document, such reference or designation shall be deemed to refer to the division of housing and community renewal. Any provision of any law permitting the city rent agency to charge or collect any fee or service charge shall be deemed to confer the same power upon the division of housing and community renewal. [Effective April 1, 1984]

§ 32. **Consolidated proceedings.** The state division of housing and community renewal may on its own motion or upon application of any affected owner or tenant consolidate proceedings applicable to the same building or group of buildings or development notwithstanding that the housing accommodations affected may be subject to differing regulations. The determination with respect to any housing accommodation in such consolidated proceedings shall be made in accordance with the appropriate law or regulation applicable to such accommodation. [Effective April 1, 1984]

§ 33. The division of housing and community renewal shall establish a small building owners assistance unit which shall provide assistance upon request to owners of buildings with rental housing accommodations. Such assistance shall include, but not be limited to, completing applications for adjustments in rents, filing registration statements, maintaining adequate business and financial records, and complying with provisions of law and regulations. For the purposes of this section "a small building owner" shall mean an owner of a total of fifty housing units or less. [Effective April 1, 1984]

§ 34. Subdivision two of section two hundred thirteen of the civil practice law and rules, as amended by chapter one hundred thirty-eight of the laws of nineteen hundred sixty-six, is amended to read as follows:

2. an action upon a contractual obligation or liability express or implied, except as provided in section two hundred thirteen-a of this article or article 2 of the uniform commercial code; [Effective April 1, 1984, applicable to actions and proceedings commenced after June 30, 1983]

§ 35. Such law and rules is amended by adding a new section two hundred thirteen-a to read as follows:

§ 213-a. Actions to be commenced within four years; residential rent overcharge. An action on a residential rent overcharge shall be commenced within four years of such overcharge. [Effective April 1, 1984, applicable to actions and proceedings commenced after June 30, 1983]

§ 36. Section three hundred twenty-eight of the multiple dwelling law, as added by chapter five hundred forty-seven of the laws of nineteen hundred sixty-one, subdivision three as added by chapter nine hundred eight of the laws of nineteen hundred seventy-six, is amended to read as follows:

§ 328. Central Violations Bureau. 1. In cities having a population of one million or more, the department shall establish a central violations bureau which shall establish and maintain currently an index showing and a file containing, with respect to each building located in the city, the name, address and telephone number of the present owner of the building and whether or not he is a member in good standing of the rent stabilization association or registered pursuant to the emergency tenant protection act of nineteen seventy-four or the rent stabilization law of nineteen hundred sixty-nine where one or more dwelling units therein are subject to the rent stabilization law, each notice and order of the building department, the fire department, the health department, the water supply, gas and electricity department and of every other municipal department or agency having jurisdiction over such building alleging the occupation of such building in violation of law or the existence of a nuisance therein and of each notice, order, rule or certificate showing the clearance, correction or abatement of such violation or nuisance.

2. It shall be the duty of the department and of every other municipal department and agency having jurisdiction over buildings located in the city of New York to file with the central violations bureau established by this section a true copy of each notice and order of such department or agency alleging the occupation of a building in violation of law or the existence of a nuisance therein and of each notice, order, rule or certificate showing the clearance, correction or abatement of such violation or nuisance within seventy-two hours from the date of issuance of such notice, order, rule or certificate.

3. In any action or proceeding before the housing part of the New York city civil court either (a) the visually displayed or (b) the printed computerized violation files of the department responsible for maintaining such files and all other computerized data as shall be relevant to the enforcement of state and local laws for the establishment and maintenance of housing standards, including but not limited to the name, address and telephone number of the present owner of the building and whether or not he is a member in good standing of the rent stabilization association or registered pursuant to the emergency tenant protection act of nineteen seventy-four or the rent stabilization law of nineteen hundred sixty-nine where one or more dwelling units therein are subject to the rent stabilization law, shall be prima facie evidence of any matter stated therein and the court shall take judicial notice thereof as if same were certified as true under the seal and signature of the commissioner of that department. [Effective September 1, 1983]

§ 61. Notwithstanding any provision of this act or other provision of law, the rent stabilization association of New York city, inc. shall submit proposed changes in the rent stabilization code to the department of housing preservation and development for its approval not later than December thirty-first, nineteen hundred eighty-three to implement the provisions of this act. Any reference in the rent stabilization law of nineteen hundred sixty-nine or the emergency tenant protection act of nineteen seventy-four to such code shall be deemed to include the amendments adopted pursuant to this section. [Effective June 30, 1983]

§ 62. The sum of one hundred thousand dollars ($100,000), or so much thereof as may be necessary, is hereby appropriated to the rent stabilization association of New York city, inc. out of any moneys in the state treasury in the general fund to the credit of the state purposes account, not otherwise appropriated, and made immediately available, for the expenses of such association in establishing, amending and promulgating the code of the association consistent with the provisions of this act. Such moneys shall be payable on the audit and warrant of the comptroller on vouchers certified or approved in the manner prescribed by law, providing that no expenditure shall be made from this appropriation until a certificate of approval of availability shall have been issued by the director of the budget and filed with the state comptroller and a copy filed with the chairman of the senate finance committee and the chairman of the assembly ways and means committee. Such certificate may be amended from time to time by the director of the budget and a copy of each amendment shall be filed with the state comptroller, the chairman of the senate finance committee and the chairman of the assembly ways and means committee. [Effective June 30, 1983]

§ 63. **Severability.** The provisions of this act shall be severable, and if the application of any clause, sentence, paragraph, subdivision, section or part of this act to any person or circumstance shall be adjudged by any court of competent jurisdiction to be invalid, such judgment shall not necessarily affect, impair or invalidate the application of any such clause, sentence, paragraph, subdivision, section, part of this act or remainder thereof, as the case may be, to any other person or circumstance, but shall be confined in its operation to the clause, sentence, paragraph, subdivision, section or part thereof directly in-

Omnibus Housing Act

volved in the controversy in which such judgment shall have been rendered. [Effective June 30, 1983]

Private Housing & Finance Law

§ 607. Rent regulation of multiple dwellings rehabilitated with a loan granted pursuant to section three hundred twelve of the housing act of nineteen hundred sixty-four

1. In cities with a population of one million or more, upon completion of rehabilitation of a class A multiple dwelling, which is aided by a loan made pursuant to section three hundred twelve of the housing act of nineteen hundred sixty-four, the agency shall establish the initial rent for each rental dwelling unit within the rehabilitated or converted multiple dwelling notwithstanding the provisions of, or any regulation promulgated pursuant to, the emergency housing rent control law, the local emergency housing rent control act, the emergency tenant protection act of nineteen seventy-four, the local rent stabilization law or any local law enacted pursuant thereto. After the agency has set the initial rents, all rental dwelling units within such rehabilitated or converted multiple dwellings shall become subject to the rent stabilization law of nineteen hundred sixty-nine.

2. The occupant in possession of such a dwelling unit when the multiple dwelling is made subject to the rent stabilization law of nineteen hundred sixty-nine shall be offered a choice of a one or two year lease at the initial rents established by the agency notwithstanding any contrary provisions of, or regulations adopted pursuant to, the rent stabilization law of nineteen hundred sixty-nine and the emergency tenant protection act of nineteen seventy-four.

3. Prior to establishing initial rents the agency shall cause all tenants in occupancy of such multiple dwelling to be notified of, and have an opportunity to comment on, the contemplated rehabilitation. Such notification shall advise such tenants of the approximate expected rent increase and the subsequent availability of a one or two year lease. Such notification and opportunity to comment shall be provided before the rehabilitation and again

after the construction is complete and before the establishment of the initial rents.

4. For the purposes of this section, "multiple dwelling" shall include any class A multiple dwelling having three or more units, and shall include multiple family garden-type maisonette dwelling complexes under single ownership having common facilities such as a sewer line, water main and heating plant notwithstanding the fact that certificates of occupancy were issued for portions thereof as one or two family dwellings.

5. For the purposes of this section, the meaning of the terms "agency", "conversion", "non-residential property" and "rehabilitation" shall be the meaning provided pursuant to section eight hundred one of this chapter.

6. The agency may promulgate supplementary rules and regulations to carry out the provisions of this section, not inconsistent with the provisions of this section. [L 1979, ch 598, effective July 10, 1979]

§ 608. Rent regulations of rehabilitated multiple dwellings aided by certain federal housing assistance programs

1. In cities with a population of one million or more, upon completion of rehabilitation of a class A multiple dwelling which is aided by a mortgage loan entered into in conjunction with a housing assistance payments contract in connection with moderate rehabilitation pursuant to section eight of the United States housing act of 1937, as amended, the agency shall establish the initial rent for each rental dwelling unit within the rehabilitated or converted multiple dwelling notwithstanding the provisions of, or any regulation promulgated pursuant to, the emergency housing rent control law, the local emergency housing rent control act, the emergency tenant protection act of nineteen seventy-four, the local rent stabilization law or any local law enacted pursuant thereto. After the agency has set the initial rents, all rental dwelling units within such rehabilitated or converted multiple dwellings shall become subject to the rent stabilization law of nineteen hundred sixty-nine.

2. The occupant in possession of such a dwelling unit when the multiple dwelling is made subject to the rent stabilization law of nineteen hundred sixty-nine shall be offered a choice of a one or two year lease at the initial

rents established by agency notwithstanding any contrary provisions of, or regulations adopted pursuant to, the rent stabilization law of nineteen hundred sixty-nine, and the emergency tenant protection act of nineteen seventy-four.

3. Prior to establishing initial rents the agency shall cause all tenants in occupancy of such multiple dwelling to be notified of, and have an opportunity to comment on the contemplated rehabilitation. Such notification shall advise such tenants of the approximate expected rent increase and the subsequent availability of a one or two year lease. Such notification and opportunity to comment shall be provided before the rehabilitation and again after the construction is complete and before the establishment of the initial rents.

4. For the purposes of this section, "multiple dwelling" shall include any class of multiple dwelling having three or more units, and shall include multiple family garden-type maisonette dwelilng complexes under single ownership having common facilities such as a sewer line, water main and heating plant notwithstanding the fact that certificates of occupancy were issued for portions thereof as one or two family dwellings.

5. For the purposes of this section, the meaning of the terms "agency", "conversion", "non-residential property" and "rehabilitation" shall be the meaning provided pursuant to section eight hundred one of this chapter.

6. The agency may promulgate supplementary rules and regulations to carry out the provisions of this section, not inconsistent with the provisions of this section. [Added L 1981, ch 20, § 1, eff March 17, 1981]

§ 706-a. Rentals (New York City Rehabilitation Mortgage Insurance Corporation).

Notwithstanding the provisions of, or any regulation promulgated pursuant to, the emergency housing rent control law, the local emergency housing rent control act or local law enacted pursuant thereto, all dwelling units in a multiple dwelling the rehabilitation of which commenced after July first, nineteen hundred seventy-seven and which is financed by a loan insured by the corporation, except for dwelling units occupied by reason of ownership of stock in a cooperative, shall be subject to the rent stabilization law of nineteen hundred sixty nine, beginning immediately after initial rents as established under applicable provisions of law for such dwelling units become effective on the basis of such rehabilitation, provided that any occupant in possession of a dwelling unit that first becomes subject to the rent stabilization law of nineteen hundred sixty-nine pursuant to this section shall be offered a two-year lease notwithstanding any contrary provisions of, or regulations adopted pursuant to, such rent stabilization law, at the initial rent established for such dwelling unit. For purposes of this section a multiple dwelling shall be deemed to include any garden-type maisonette dwelling project consisting of a series of dwelling units which together and in their aggregate were arranged or designed to provide three or more apartments and are provided as a group collectively with all essential services such as, but not limited to, water supply, house sewers and heat, and which are in existence and operated as a unit under single ownership on the date upon which an application for mortgage insurance pursuant to this article, is received by the corporation, notwithstanding that certificates of occupancy were issued for portions thereof as private dwellings. [L 1977, ch 564, am L 1980, ch 848, § 2]

INCREASE OF RENTALS—DEPT H P D SUPERVISING AGENCY

Administrative Code of the City of New York
Title 26, Chapter 26[1]

(L 1985, Ch 907, effective September 1, 1986)

§ 26-530 Increase of rentals. a. Before acting upon any application or motion for an increase in the maximum rental per room to be charged tenants and cooperators of dwellings where the department of housing preservation and development is the "supervising agency" under the provisions of the private housing finance law, a public hearing shall be held. Said hearing shall be held upon no less than twenty days' written notice to the tenants and said notice shall have annexed thereto a copy of the application or motion for increase in rentals and shall set forth the facts upon which the application or motion is based.

b. No application or motion for an increase in the maximum rental per room shall be entertained or acted upon hereunder for a period of two years from the date or any previous order of the "supervising agency" for the increase of maximum rent affecting the same dwelling.

c. No increase in maximum rental per room or surcharge thereto or any other penalty shall be charged to or assessed against any tenant or tenant-cooperator of dwellings, where the department of housing preservation and development is the "supervising agency", for failure to authorize the commissioner of finance to verify to such "supervising agency" the amount of income as it appears on their New York state or New York city income tax returns.

---

[1] The Administrative Code of the City of New York was recodified by L 1985, Ch 907, effective September 1, 1986. Title 26, Ch 6 of the new Code corresponds to § B61.0 of the former Code.

Public Authorities Law

§ 2429. Rentals (State of New York Mortgage Agency Act).

Notwithstanding the provisions of, or any regulation promulgated pursuant to, the emergency housing rent control law, the local emergency housing rent control act or local law enacted pursuant thereto, all dwelling units in a multiple dwelling the rehabilitation of which commenced after July first, nineteen hundred seventy-eight and which is financed by a loan insured by the agency, except for dwelling units occupied by reason of ownership of stock in a cooperative, shall be subject to the rent stabilization law of nineteen hundred sixty-nine, beginning immediately after initial rents as established under applicable provisions of law for such dwelling units become effective on the basis of such rehabilitation, provided that any occupant in possession of a dwelling unit that first becomes subject to the rent stabilization law of nineteen hundred sixty-nine pursuant to this section shall be offered a two-year lease notwithstanding any contrary provisions of, or regulations adopted pursuant to, such rent stabilization law, at the initial rent established for such dwelling unit. [L 1978, ch 788, § 7]

Destabilization Provisions of Real Property Tax Law § 421-a

§ 421-a. Exemption of new multiple dwellings from local taxation

(2). . .

(f) Notwithstanding the provisions of any local law for the stabilization of rents in multiple dwellings or the emergency tenant protection act of nineteen seventy-four, the rents of a unit shall be fully subject to control under such local law or such act, unless exempt under such local law or such act from control by reason of the cooperative or condominium status of the unit, for the entire period during which the property is receiving tax benefits pursuant to this section for the period of any such applicable law or act is in effect, whichever is shorter. Thereafter, such rents shall continue to be subject to such control to the same extent and in the same manner as if this section had never applied thereto, except that such rents shall be decontrolled if:

(i) with respect to units subject to the provisions of this section on the effective date of this subparagraph such a unit becomes vacant after the expiration of such ten year period or applicable law or act; provided, however, the rent shall not be decontrolled for a unit which the commissioner of housing and community renewal or a court of competent jurisdiction finds became vacant because the landlord or any person acting on his behalf engaged in any course of conduct, including but not limited to, interruption or discontinuance of essential services which interfered with or disturbed or was intended to interfere with or disturb the comfort, repose, peace or quiet of the tenant in his use or occupancy of such unit, and, that upon such finding in addition to being subject to any other penalties or remedies permitted by law, the landlord of such unit shall be barred from collecting rent for such unit in excess of that charged to the tenant who vacated such unit until restoration of possession of such tenant, if the tenant so desires, in which case the rent of such tenant shall be established as if such tenant had not vacated such unit, or compliance with such other remedy, including, but not limited to, all remedies provided for by the emergency tenant protection act of nineteen seventy-four for rent overcharge or failure to comply with any order of the commissioner of housing and community renewal, as shall be determined by the commissioner of housing and community renewal to be appropriate; provided, however, that if a tenant fails to accept any such offer of restoration of possession, such unit shall return to rent stabilization at the previously regulated rent; or

(ii) With respect to units which become subject to the provisions of this section after the effective date of this subparagraph, such tax benefit period as provided in the opening paragraph of this paragraph or applicable law or act shall have expired and either each lease and renewal thereof for such unit for the tenant in residence at the time of such decontrol has included a notice in at least twelve point type informing such tenant that the unit shall become subject to such decontrol upon the expiration of such tax benefit period as provided in the opening paragraph of this paragraph or applicable law or act and states the approximate date on which such tax benefit period as provided in the opening paragraph of this paragraph is scheduled to expire; or such unit becomes vacant as provided under subparagraph (i) of this paragraph. [Opening paragraph and paragraph (ii) of paragraph (f) of subd 2, Am L 1985, chs 288, 289]

(g) . . .

(h) . . .

(i) Authority of city to enact local law. Except as otherwise specified in this section, a city to which this section is applicable, may enact a local law to restrict, limit or condition the eligibility, scope or amount of the benefits under this section in any manner, provided that the local law may not grant benefits beyond those provided in this section and provided further that in the city of New York such local law must be approved by the board of estimate and shall not take effect sooner than one year after such approval by the board of estimate. (Paragraph (i) of subd 2 Am L 1985, ch 288)

Destabilization Provisions of Real Property Tax Law § 489 (J51 Housing)

§ 489. Exemption from taxation of alterations and improvements to multiple dwellings to eliminate fire and health hazards; abatement

7. Any local law or ordinance may also provide any or all of the following:

(a) The benefits of this section shall not apply to any multiple dwelling, building or structure as provided in paragraph (a) of subdivision one of this section in which rents, subsequent to alterations and improvements, shall exceed such amount, if any, as may be fixed by the local legislative body or by the municipal agency designated by the local legislative body of the municipality involved, based upon a standard formula.

(b) (1) The benefits of this section shall not apply to any multiple dwelling, building or structure as provided in paragraph (a) of subdivision one of this section which is not subject to the provisions of the emergency housing rent control law or to local law enacted pursuant to the local emergency housing rent control act, where the local legislative body or other governing agency of the municipality involved shall prescribe that the benefits herein provided shall not apply to such multiple dwelling, building or structure as provided in paragraph (a) of subdivision one of this section provided that such local legislative body or other governing agency shall not use the authority conferred in this paragraph (b) to rescind any benefits granted under former section five-h of the tax law prior to July first, nineteen hundred fifty-eight; and further provided that where the benefits provided herein or under such former section five-h of the tax law are granted or had been granted on or after July first, nineteen hundred fifty-eight, to any multiple dwelling, building or structure which is decontrolled subsequent to the granting of such benefits, the local legislative body or other governing agency may withdraw such benefits from such dwelling.

(2) Any dwelling unit subject to rent regulation on or before the effective date of this subparagraph as a result of receiving a tax exemption or abatement pursuant to this section shall be subject to such regulation until the

Real Property Destabilization

occurrence of the first vacancy of such unit after such benefits are no longer being received at which time such unit shall be deregulated or if each lease and renewal thereof for such unit for the tenant in residence at the time of the expiration of the tax benefit period has included a notice in at least twelve point type informing such tenant that the unit shall become subject to deregulation upon the expiration of such tax benefit period and states the approximate date on which such tax benefit period is scheduled to expire, such dwelling unit shall be deregulated as of the end of the tax benefit period; unless such unit would have been subject to regulation under the rent stabilization law of nineteen hundred sixty-nine or the emergency tenant protection act of nineteen seventy-four.

(c) The benefits of this section shall apply to any multiple dwelling building or structure as provided in paragraph (a) of subdivision one of this section occupied, as a rule, for permanent residence purposes and which is not used in whole or in part for single room occupancy and which is not subject to the provisions of the emergency housing rent control law or to local law enacted pursuant to the local emergency housing rent control act, provided that it is located within an area which has been designated by the local planning commission under the provisions of section 72m of article fifteen of the general municipal law or where a program of local neighborhood improvement or housing maintenance is being carried out under the supervision or with the assistance of the local government and provided that the rents or carrying charges, subsequent to alterations and improvements, (1) shall not exceed such amount, if any, as may be fixed by the local legislative body or by the municipal agency designated by the local legislative body of the municipality involved, based upon a standard formula, or (2) where the local legislative body so provides, shall not exceed such amount, if any, as may be fixed for such multiple dwelling, building, or structure as provided in paragraph (a) of subdivision one of this section pursuant to any local law enacted pursuant to the local emergency housing rent control act, and further provided that prior to such alterations and improvements, the multiple dwelling, building or structure as provided in paragraph (a) of subdivision one of this section, if a multiple dwelling, was either a multiple dwelling occupied, as a rule, as a temporary or transient residence or occupied, as a rule, for permanent residence purposes and used in whole or in part for single room occupancy.

(d) The benefits of this section shall apply to any building or structure as provided in paragraph (a) of subdivision one of this section, provided that the rents or carrying charges subsequent to conversion (1) shall not exceed such amount, if any, as may be fixed by the local legislative body or by the municipal agency designated by the local legislative body of the municipality involved, based upon a standard formula, or (2) where the local legislative body so provides, shall not exceed such amount, if any, as may be fixed for such dwelling pursuant to any local law enacted pursuant to the local emergency housing rent control act. (Subparagraph 2 of paragraph b of subd 7, Am L 1985, chs 288, 289)[1]

[1] § 489(7)(b), as am L 1985, ch 288, takes effect June 30, 1985, and shall be deemed to have been in full force and effect on and after June 19, 1985, and shall cover any tenant in physical possession of an apartment covered by the provisions of this section as amended, regardless of whether a proceeding to evict the tenant was begun between June 19 and June 30, 1985, or whether a warrant for his eviction has been issued, and shall also apply to tenancies commencing thereafter and provided further that the legal regulated rent for any unit which is subject to the provisions of such section and which was not covered by the provisions of the rent stabilization law of nineteen hundred sixty-nine on the date prior to the effective date of such section shall be the greater of the rent charged on May thirtieth, nineteen hundred eighty-five or the maximum rent which could have been charged if the unit had been continuously subject to the rent stabilization law of nineteen hundred sixty-nine for the entire tenancy of the tenant in occupancy on the effective date of such section. L 1985, ch 288, § 8.

UNLAWFUL EVICTIONS

Administrative Code of the City of New York
Title 26, Chapter 5[1]

(L 1985, Ch 907, effective September 1, 1986)

§ 26-521 Unlawful eviction. a. It shall be unlawful for any person to evict or attempt to evict an occupant of a dwelling unit who has lawfully occupied the dwelling unit for thirty consecutive days or longer or who has entered into a lease with respect to such dwelling unit or has made a request for a lease for such dwelling unit pursuant to the hotel stabilization provisions of the rent stabilization law except to the extent permitted by law pursuant to a warrant of eviction or other order of a court of competent jurisdiction or a governmental vacate order by:

(1) using or threatening the use of force to induce the occupant to vacate the dwelling unit; or

(2) engaging in a course of conduct which interferes with or is intended to interfere with or disturb the comfort, repose, peace or quiet of such occupant in the use or occupancy of the dwelling unit, to induce the occupant to vacate the dwelling unit including, but not limited to, the interruption or discontinuance of essential services; or

(3) engaging or threatening to engage in any other conduct which prevents or is intended to prevent such occupant from the lawful occupancy of such dwelling unit or to induce the occupant to vacate the dwelling unit including, but not limited to, removing the occupant's possessions from the dwelling unit, removing the door at the entrance to the dwelling unit; removing, plugging or otherwise rendering the lock on such entrance door inoperable; or changing the lock on such entrance door without supplying the occupant with a key.

[1] The Administrative Code of the City of New York was recodified by L 1985, Ch 907, effective September 1, 1986. Title 26, Ch 5 of the New Code (comprising §§ 26-521 through 2-529), corresponds to the provisions of §§ D16-1.01 through D16-1.09 of the former Code.

b. It shall be unlawful for an owner of a dwelling unit to fail to take all reasonable and necessary action to restore to occupancy an occupant of a dwelling unit who either vacates, has been removed from or is otherwise prevented from occupying a dwelling unit as the result of any of the acts or omissions prescribed in subdivision a of this section and to provide to such occupant a dwelling unit within such dwelling suitable for occupancy, after being requested to do so by such occupant or the representative of such occupant, if such owner either committed such unlawful acts or omissions or knew or had reason to know of such unlawful acts or omissions, or if such acts or omissions occurred within seven days prior to such request.

§ 26-522 Definitions. a. For the purpose of this chapter the following terms shall have the following meanings:

(1) "Dwelling unit" means a dwelling unit as such term is defined in subdivision thirteen of section 27-2004 of the housing maintenance code.

(2) "Owner" means an owner as defined in section 27-2004 of the housing maintenance code.

b. For the purposes of this chapter a "person" shall not include a government employee acting within the scope of employment.

§ 26-523 Criminal and civil penalties. a. Any person who intentionally violates or assists in the violation of any of the provisions of this chapter shall be guilty of a class A misdemeanor. Each such violation shall be a separate and distinct offense.

b. Such person shall also be subject to a civil penalty of not less than one thousand nor more than ten thousand dollars for each violation. Each such violation shall be a separate and distinct offense. In the case of a failure to take all reasonable and necessary action to restore an occupant pursuant to subdivision b of section 26-521 of this chapter, such person shall be subject to an additional civil penalty of not more than one hundred dollars per day from the date on which restoration to occupancy is requested until the date on which restoration occurs, provided, however, that such period shall not exceed six months.

Unlawful Evictions

§ 26-524 Enforcement actions or proceedings. The civil penalties prescribed by this chapter shall be recovered by an action or proceeding in any court of competent jurisdiction. All such actions or proceedings shall be brought in the name of the city by the corporation counsel. In addition, the corporation counsel may institute any other action or proceeding in any court of competent jurisdiction that may be appropriate or necessary for the enforcement of the provisions of this chapter, including actions to secure permanent injunctions enjoining any acts or practices which constitute a violation of any provision of this chapter, mandating compliance with the provisions of this chapter or for such other relief as may be appropriate. In any such action or proceeding the city may apply to any court of competent jurisdiction, or to a judge or justice thereof, for a temporary restraining order or preliminary injunction enjoining and restraining all persons from violating any provision of this chapter, mandating compliance with the provisions of this chapter, or for such other relief as may be appropriate, until the hearing and determination of such action or proceeding and the entry of final judgment or order therein. The court, or judge or justice thereof, to whom such application is made, is hereby authorized forthwith to make any or all of the orders above specified, as may be required in such application, with or without notice, and to make such other or further orders or directions as may be necessary to render the same affectual. No undertaking shall be required as a condition to the granting or issuing of such order, or by reason thereof.

§ 26-525 Lien. Every civil penalty imposed by judgment upon an owner pursuant to this chapter shall be a lien upon the dwelling with respect to which such civil penalty is imposed from the time of the filing of a notice of pendency in the office of the clerk of the county in which such dwelling is situated.

§ 26-526 Notice of pendency. a. In any action or proceeding instituted under this chapter, the corporation counsel may file in the county clerk's office of the county where the dwelling affected by such action or proceeding is situated, a notice of the pendency of such action or proceeding. Such notice may be filed at the time of the commencement of the action or proceeding, or at any time afterwards, before final judgment or order. The corporation counsel shall designate in writing the name of each person against whom the notice is filed and the number of each block on the land map of the county which is affected by the notice. The county clerk in whose office the notice of pendency is filed shall record and index such notice against the names and blocks designated.

b. Any such notice may be vacated upon the order of a judge of the court in which such action or proceeding was instituted or is pending, or upon the consent in writing of the corporation counsel. The clerk of the county where such notice is filed shall cancel such notice upon receipt of such consent or of a certified copy of such order.

§ 26-527 Liability for costs. Neither the city nor any officer or employee thereof shall be liable for costs in any action or proceeding brought pursuant to this chapter.

§ 26-528 Monies recovered. All monies recovered under this chapter shall be paid into the general fund of the city.

§ 26-529 Remedies and penalties. The remedies and penalties provided for herein shall be in addition to any other remedies and penalties provided under other provisions of law.

INDEX

References are to pages

RENT CONTROL

Access to premises, evidence of tenant's refusal to permit, 432
Accountant's certification form for major capital improvement, 517, 519
Accounts. Escrow accounts, infra
Acute housing shortage, city rent and rehabilitation counsel's finding of, 422
Additional services or facilities, increase of rent based on, 133-135, 138, 139, 287, 288, 310, 547-552
Adjournments, Office of Rent Administration rules of practice, 1161, 1163
Adjudicatory proceedings, Office of Rent Administration rules of practice, 1155 et seq.
Adjustments
● generally, 284-314, 1030
- advisory bulletins as to, 194, 195
- application for adjustment of initial rent, 751-753
- biennial adjustment of maximum rents, regulations as to, 280, 281
- capital improvements, adjustment of maximum rent granted on basis of, 287, 288, 406
- capital value, adjustments as affected by lack of return on, 292
- emergency tenant protection laws, 1011
- equalization adjustment, infra
- facilities, adjustment of maximum rent for increase of, 287, 288
- federal finance program or other approved program, adjustment of maximum rent based on rehabilitation or improvement under, 296
- fuel cost adjustments, 296-300
- labor costs in excess of maximum base rent allowance, adjustment on basis of, 295, 296
- maximum rents, generally, 68, 246
- orders as to, generally, 310, 313

RENT CONTROL—Cont'd

Adjustments—Cont'd
- real estate industry stabilization association, 740-748
- regulations, generally, 72 et seq., 284-314
- rehabilitation, adjustment of maximum rent on basis of, 287, 288
- Rent Stabilization Code, 791 et seq.
- retroactive adjustments, 314
- senior citizens rent increase exemption, 305-310
- services, adjustment of maximum rent based on increase or decrease of, 287, 288, 310
- small structures, adjustment granted on basis of unavoidable increase in operating costs, 294
- subtenants or occupants, adjustments as affected by increase in, 291
- unique or peculiar circumstances as basis for adjustment of maximum rent, 291
- voluntary written agreements for increase of maximum rents, 288-291
Administrative law judge
- defined, Office of Rent Administration rules of practice, 1157
- rules of practice, Office of Rent Administration adjudicatory proceedings, 1156 et seq.
Administrative review. Appeal and review, infra
Administrator
● generally. Rent administrator, infra
- definition, 247, 380
Advertising agency located in home, 591
Advisory bulletins, State Rent Administrator, 130-200
Advisory opinions, Rent Stabilization Code, 855
Affidavit of service of rent protest, advisory bulletin as to, 193
Aged persons. Elderly persons, infra

INDEX

RENT CONTROL—Cont'd
Agreement
- as to leases, see more specific entries
- increase of rent by mutual agreement between landlord and tenant, 288-291, 405
- renewal of lease, 563

Air conditioning
- administrator's interpretation, 463, 464, 490-492, 507
- amortization costs, 532
- expediting proceedings involving questions as to, 581
- operational bulletin as to rent increase based on installation of, 608, 609
- permissible charges for installation, 553, 554, 556, 557
- tenant protection bulletins, 1102, 1103

Alternative hardship, applications and forms, 566-574

Alternative provision in lieu of rent decrease, 303-305

Aluminum window replacements, 526

Amendment
- filing requirements, rent increase, 520, 521
- New York City rent and eviction regulations, 263
- office of rent administration regulations as to rent and eviction, amendment of, 55
- protests as affected by amendment of rent control regulation, 124, 125
- regulations, generally, 263
- shower installations, amendment of schedule of rental values, 531
- tenant protection regulations, 1026

Ancillary services, defined, 772-775

Annual gross rent income collectible, definition, 1034

Annual return. Net annual return, infra

Answer
- district rent and rehabilitation director, proceedings before, 362, 363
- hardship increase application, answer by tenant, 572
- New York City rent and eviction regulations, proceedings before district rent and rehabilitation director, 362, 363

RENT CONTROL—Cont'd
Answer—Cont'd
- rules of practice, Office of Rent Administration adjudicatory proceedings, 1156
- time of filing answer to protest as to rent control regulations, 122-124

Apartment, definition of, 54, 261

Appeal and review
• generally, 538-541
- alternative hardship increase, 568, 574
- commissioner's actions, 539-540
- Emergency Housing Rent Control Law, judicial review under, 31
- eviction certificate, judicial review of order granting, 25
- judicial review, infra
- Omnibus Housing Act, 1174 et seq.
- orders issued by rent administrator, filing petition against, 538
- protest to rent control regulations, 125, 126
- Rental Stabilization Code, 857-861
- rules of practice, Office of Rent Administration adjudicatory proceedings, 1173
- tenant protection regulations, 1064, 1067 et seq.

Appearances
- notice, 126, 127
- rules of practice, Office of Rent Administration adjudicatory proceedings, 1156, 1159, 1160

Applications
- advisory bulletins of state rent administrator, 132 et seq.
- elderly persons, exemption from rent increases for low income elderly persons, 720, 721
- Emergency Housing Rent Control Law, application for elimination of, 39
- emergency tenant protection laws, 1011
- exception from regulations, application for, 65, 66
- maximum rent, regulations as to filing application for increase, 74, 286, 669, 676
- operational expense increases, standards for determining applications to compensate, 201, 203, 209, 212

References are to pages

INDEX

RENT CONTROL—Cont'd
Applications—Cont'd
- services, application for rent adjustment based on decrease of, 310

Appointment of rent guidelines board officers, 998

Appropriation, request by mayor for, 245, 246

Architect using home for office, 590

Art studio located in home, 590

Asylum as exempt from city rent and rehabilitation law, 382

Attorneys
- argument of counsel, Office of Rent Administration adjudicatory proceedings rules of practice, 1165
- fees. Attorneys' fees, infra
- home used as office, 590
- notice to, generally, 317, 318
- Rent Stabilization Code, notice of appearance, 828
- right to representation, 29, 443
- service of notice on, 92, 93, 127, 317, 318
- subpoenaed persons, right to representation, 29
- tenant protection regulations, notice to attorneys, 1046

Attorneys' fees
- Emergency Housing Rent Control Law, liability of landlord for attorney's fees on violation of, 37
- eviction, recovery of attorney's fees on basis of wrongful, 117
- landlord's liability, 359
- rules of practice, Office of Rent Administration adjudicatory proceedings, 1166
- tenant protection regulations, 1058

Audit to determine return, 536

Barber shop located in home, 591

Base rents, establishment of, 276-280

Bathrooms
- administrator's interpretations, schedule of rental values, 508
- concurrent major capital improvement, 513
- operational bulletin as to modernization as basis for increase of rents, 625-630
- shower installation, amendment of Schedule of Rental Values, 531

RENT CONTROL—Cont'd
Bathrooms—Cont'd
- vanities, amortization costs and guidelines, 523, 524

Beauty parlor located in home, 591

Bell or buzzer installation as concurrent major capital improvement, 514

Biennial adjustment of maximum rents, regulations as to, 280, 281

Boardinghouse. Roominghouse, infra

Broker, inspection of records maintained by, 117, 118

Building viability report form, requirement for obtaining certificate of eviction, 536

Bulletins, State Rent Administrator, 130-200, 581 et seq.

Burden of proof, Office of Rent Administration rules of practice, 1162

Burglar alarm system, operational bulletin as to rent increase based on installation of, 623, 624

Business use. Commercial use, infra

Calculations of adjustments, 522, 549

Cancellation
- certificate of eviction, 25
- fraud, cancellation of certificate of eviction obtained by, 436
- regulations as to landlord's right of, 289, 290

Capital improvement
• generally, 74, 76
- accountant's certification, form, 517, 519
- advisory bulletin as to increase of rent based on capital improvements, 138, 139
- application and form requirements, 514-516, 552, 553
- definition of, 511
- interpretation of administrator as to rent increase based on, 473-475
- maximum rent adjustments, 287, 288, 406
- operational bulletin as to increase of maximum rent for, 586-590
- proof of compliance with agency requirements, 516
- rent increases, generally, 547-552

Capital value, adjustment of maximum rent based on lack of return on, 292

References are to pages

1205

RENT CONTROL—Cont'd
Caretakers of property, exemption from rent controls of accommodations furnished to, 62
Cellar stair enclosure as concurrent major capital improvement, 514
Central heat installation as concurrent major capital improvement, 514
Central Violations Bureau, Omnibus Housing Act, 1184
Certificates and certification
- agents certifying, 517, 519
- cost certification in application for rent increase, operational bulletin, 632, 633
- eviction, infra
- no violations certificate issued by Department of Buildings, administrator's interpretation as to filing of, 471, 472
- rent role certification, operational bulletin as to, 637
- window guards, certificate of installation, 534, 535
Certified public accountant using home as office, 590
Chain door guards to apartment entrances, specifications, 529-531
Change
- adjustments, supra
- amendment, supra
- New York City rent and eviction regulations, modification of orders, 365-367
- ownership, report as to change of, 92, 138, 317
- protest, modification of orders on, 371
- term of occupancy, rent control regulations as to change in, 112
Charges assessable against owner of occupied structure, 246
Charitable institutions, exemption from rent controls, 56-58, 383, 778, 1002, 1003, 1028
Chief administrative law judge, defined, Office of Rent Administration rules of practice, 1157
City Rent Agency (New York City)
- definition of, 247, 380
- enforcement and penalties, 450
- establishment of, 224
- Omnibus Housing Act, 1174 et seq.

RENT CONTROL—Cont'd
City Rent Agency—Cont'd
- powers of, generally, 391
- state rent control functions transferred to, 229
Civil actions for enforcement of rent control laws
• generally, 114-117
- certificate of eviction, action by tenant where landlord fails to use for purposes specified, 357, 358
- harassment, 359, 360
- New York City rent and eviction regulations
- - administrator, action by, 354
- - certificate of eviction, civil action by tenant where landlord fails to use for purposes specified therein, 357, 358
- - harassment, civil action by tenant for unlawful eviction of or surrender of possession as result of, 359, 360
- - tenant, action by, 357-360
Civil service employees as affected by transfer of departmental functions, 242-244
Classification of buildings, Rent Stabilization Code, 789
Closed circuit television system as concurrent major capital improvement, 514
Collectibility of rent, regulations as to, 281, 282
Colleges and universities
- dormitories as not subject to rent control, 57, 382, 1003, 1028
- fraternity or sorority houses as exempt from rent controls, 62, 250, 260
Commercial use
- Business Space Rent Control Law, 489, 490
- controlled housing accommodations as subject to rent controls, 64, 268
- operational bulletin, professional offices in home, 590, 591
- Rent Stabilization Code, 779
Comparative hardship outside or inside New York, definition of, 565
Complaints
• generally, 660 et seq.
- emergency tenant protection laws, 1016

References are to pages

INDEX

RENT CONTROL—Cont'd
Complaints—Cont'd
- heat, lack of, 581, 642-644
- petitions, infra
- Rent Stabilization Code, 846-855

Compromise and settlement, Office of Rent Administration rules of practice, 1171

Computation of adjustments, 522, 549

Concurrent major capital improvement, definition, 511

Conditional certificate of eviction, administrator's interpretations, 472, 473

Conditional rental
- purchase of property as, 111, 112, 154, 155, 350
- Rent Stabilization Code, 842, 843
- tenant protection regulations, 1055

Condominiums
- co-operative apartment, infra
- property tax law, destabilization provisions, 1194 et seq.
- Rent Stabilization Code, applicability of, 779

Confidential information, 236, 1061, 1067

Conflicts of interest, rent guidelines boards, 998

Consolidation of actions, 121, 1063, 1157

Construction and interpretation by Rent Administrator, New York City, 457 et seq.

Contempt for failure to obey subpoena, 28, 29, 136, 442

Convent as exempt property, 382, 775

Converted buildings
• generally, 63, 159
- city rent and rehabilitation law, 384
- Private Housing and Finance Law, 1188 et seq.

Cooperation of government agencies, 244, 245, 1022

Co-operative apartment
- increase of rent, advisory bulletin as to, 176-184
- maximum rent adjustment, 295
- property tax law, destabilization provisions, 1194 et seq.
- Rent Stabilization Code, applicability of, 779

RENT CONTROL—Cont'd
Corporation counsel, unlawful hotel evictions, 1201

Correction of violation, proof of, 585

Corroborative evidence of agreement as to increased service or facilities, 1032

Cosmetic improvements, rent increase, 551

Cost
- certification of cost by landlord in making application for rent increase, operational bulletin as to, 632, 633
- court costs. Costs of actions, infra
- fees, infra
- increase of maximum rent based on increased cost, instruction sheets for completion of information as to, 695
- labor costs, infra
- operating expenses, infra
- unavoidable increase in costs, administrator's advisory bulletin as to rent increase based upon, 174-176

Costs of actions
- attorneys' fees, supra
- hotel, unlawful eviction, 1202
- Rent Stabilization Code enforcement, 846
- tenant protection regulations, 1058
- witness fees, 29

Counsel. Attorney, supra

Counseling services to tenants and landlords, 418

County rent guidelines board, defined, tenant protection regulations, 1024

Credits
- elderly persons, exemption from rent increases for low income elderly persons, 720
- rate of rent increase, 580
- Rent Guidelines Board's orders as to credits on excess rents, 874 et seq.
- Rent Stabilization Code, 846

Crimes and criminal penalties
• generally, 114-117, 121
- advisory bulletins as to violation of rental laws, 153
- Emergency Housing Rent Control Law violations, 36

References are to pages

1207

INDEX

RENT CONTROL—Cont'd
Crimes and criminal penalties —Cont'd
- hotel, eviction, 1200
- New York City rent and eviction regulations, 352

Cross-examination, Office of Rent Administration rules of practice, 1163, 1170

Damages
- eviction of tenant for damaging housing, 21, 431
- treble damages for violations, advisory bulletin as to, 152, 153

Dangerous or hazardous conditions
- decrease of rent based on, 302
- expediting proceedings as to, 581

Deaf persons, Office of Rent Administration rules of practice, 1166

Death, eviction of surviving spouse of deceased tenant, 107

Declaration of emergency, 997

Decontrolled units
- generally, 264-266, 315, 316
- administrative proceedings on application by interested party, 374 et seq.
- advisory bulletin as to, 136, 137
- city rent and rehabilitation law as affected by, 384-387
- New York City rent and eviction regulations, administrative proceedings on application by interested party for decontrol on basis of vacancy rate, 374 et seq.
- permissible rent, 578
- Rent Guidelines Board's orders as to, 874-878, 883 et seq.
- report on, 91, 92
- schedule for decontrol of occupied accommodations, administrator's interpretation as to, 493, 496
- tenant protection bulletins, 1145, 1151
- vacancy rate, 456

Decorating
- office of decorator located in home, 591
- painting, infra

Decrease of maximum rent, grounds for, 84 et seq., 300 et seq.

Decrease of services, rent decrease for, 301, 302, 310

RENT CONTROL—Cont'd
Definitions
- city rent and rehabilitation law, definitions under, 380 et seq.
- elderly persons, exemption from rent increases for low income elderly persons, 714
- Emergency Housing Rent Control Law, definitions under, 4 et seq.
- essential services, 54
- hotels, unlawful eviction, 1200
- maximum rent, 5, 261, 390, 714
- New York City rent and eviction regulations, 247, 248, 261-263
- office of rent administration, definitions as to rent and eviction regulations of, 50-55
- rent, 153
- rules of practice, Office of Rent Administration adjudicatory proceedings, 1157, 1158
- tenant protection regulations, 1024-1029, 1034 et seq.

Delegation of authority by Administrator, 128, 373

Demolition
- eviction, 23, 26, 109, 347, 348, 433
- exemption from city rent and rehabilitation law, 386, 387
- New York City rent and eviction regulations, substantial demolition of structures, 266-268

Dental hygienist using home as office, 590

Dentist using home as office, 590

Depilatory office located in home, 591

Depositions, Office of Rent Administration rules of practice, 1159, 1170

Deposits
- painting, Rent Stabilization Code, 775
- security deposits, infra

Destabilization provisions of Real Property Tax Law, 1194 et seq.

DHCR. Housing and Community Renewal Division, infra

Disabled person defined, Rent Stabilization Code, 771

Disclosure
- administrator or employees, disclosure of information by, 114, 120, 136, 352, 373, 449
- confidential information, 236, 1061, 1067

References are to pages

1208

INDEX

RENT CONTROL—Cont'd
Disclosure—Cont'd
- Freedom of Information Act, 541-547
- inspection of records, infra
- production of documents, infra
- tenant protection regulations, 1056

Discontinuance of service by landlord
- generally, 114
- administrator's advisory bulletin as to, 137
- prohibition as to, 236, 449

Dismissal card as proof of correction of violation, 586

District rent and rehabilitation director, proceedings before, generally, 362 et seq.

District Rent and Rehabilitation Office, definition of, 263

Docketing, alternative hardship, 568

Documents
- definition of, 248, 380, 775
- production of documents, infra
- records and reports, infra

Domestic servants, housing as exempt, 62, 779

Doors
- fireproof Kalamein doors, operational bulletin as to increase of rent based on installation of, 631
- locks to apartment entrances, specifications, 529-531
- peepholes or interviewers, rent increase based on installation of, 501, 502, 606, 647

Dormitories as exempt from rent controls, 57, 1003, 1028

Dwelling unit, defined, hotel's unlawful eviction, 1200

Educational institutions
- colleges and universities, supra
- exemptions from Rent Stabilization Code, 775

Elderly persons
- acute housing shortage for, 422, 423
- definition, 564, 771
- low income elderly persons, exemption from rent increases, 713 et seq.
- rent increase exemptions, generally, 305-310
- tax abatements, 732-736

Electricity
- amortization costs, 532

RENT CONTROL—Cont'd
Electricity—Cont'd
- change of services, administrator's interpretation, 475
- inclusion adjustment, 578
- Rent Guidelines Board's orders as to electrical inclusion adjustment, 892, 893, 905 et seq.
- rewiring as basis for rent increase, 460, 514, 582-584, 608
- schedule of rental values, administrator's interpretations, 509
- tenant protection bulletins, 1102, 1103, 1138

Elevator
- mirrors installed in elevators as basis for rent increase, operational bulletin as to, 648
- upgrading, 527-529, 650

Eligibility to file protests, 121

Eligible head of household defined, exemption from rent increases for low income elderly persons, 714

Emergency
- declaration of emergency, 997
- expediting proceedings as to buildings vacated upon order of municipal authorities as result of, 581
- local determination as to continuation of, 225
- Rent Stabilization Law, findings and declaration of emergency under, 726, 727

Emergency housing rent control
- generally, 1-200
- advisory bulletins, State Rent Administrator, 130-200
- application for abolishment of, 39
- definitions, 4 et seq.
- enforcement of regulations, 35
- evictions under, 21 et seq.
- existing rights preserved, 48
- governmental agency, co-operation with, 29
- intent, 47
- investigations, 28
- judicial review, 31
- New York City, 223 et seq.
- pending proceedings, 47
- procedural matters, 30
- prohibitions, generally, 34, 35
- records and reports, 28

References are to pages

1209

RENT CONTROL—Cont'd

Emergency housing rent control —Cont'd
- rent and eviction regulations, Rent Administration Office of the Division of Housing and Community Renewal, 49-129
- separability of provisions, 48
- short title for, 48
- temporary state housing rent commission, 10, 11

Emergency Tenant Protection Act of 1974, 994 et seq.

Employees
- disclosure of information by employees of Commission, 114, 120, 136, 352, 373, 449
- exemption from Rent Stabilization Code, employee housing, 779

Engineer using home as office, 590

Entrance doors. Doors, supra

Equalization adjustment
- advisory bulletin as to application and computation of, 143-146
- maximum rents, 71

Equalized assessed valuation, tenant protection regulations, 1036

Equity ownership, alternative hardship increase, 570

Escalator clauses
• generally, 873 et seq.
- rate of rent increase guidelines, 579, 580
- Rent Guidelines Board's orders as to, 873 et seq.

Escrow account
- agreement as to deposit of rent in lieu of rent decrease, 303-304
- increase in rent, procedure, 523
- payment of rents into, 417, 419, 420, 422

Essential services, definition of, 54, 261, 262, 523

Estoppel. Waiver and estoppel, infra

Evasive tactics to maximum rent laws, 111, 154, 350

Eviction
• generally, 94 et seq., 320-322, 1199 et seq., and see other specific entries throughout this index
- advisory bulletin as to, 135, 147-151, 195
- alteration, eviction for, 345-347

RENT CONTROL—Cont'd

Eviction—Cont'd
- certificate of eviction
- - application requirements, 535, 536
- - building viability report form, 536
- - cancellation or revocation of, 436
- - conditional certificate, 472, 473
- - Emergency Housing Rent Control Law requirements as to, 21 et seq.
- - eviction of tenant with or without certificate, 95-99
- - judicial review, 25, 437
- - necessity of, 432
- - protest of order granting, 121, 122
- - stay of order granting, 125
- damage to housing as basis for, 21
- demolition purposes, 23, 26, 109, 347, 348, 433
- Emergency Housing Rent Control Law, evictions under, 21 et seq.
- Housing and Community Renewal Division regulations,
- New York City, eviction regulations, 247 et seq., 320 et seq.
- notice requirements, 96, 97, 325
- nuisance, eviction of tenant permitting or committing, 431
- occupancy by landlord or immediate family, eviction based on, 22, 26, 99-106, 333-344, 432, 433
- Omnibus Housing Act, 1174 et seq.
- peephole installed by tenant in entrance door without landlord's permission as basis for eviction, administrator's interpretation as to, 501, 502
- proceedings for eviction with or without certificate, 322-333
- prospective purchaser, eviction for refusal to permit landlord to show premises to, 22
- protest
- - certificate of eviction, protest of order granting, 121, 122
- - prohibition as to eviction of tenant filing, 35, 240
- refusal of tenant to renew lease as basis for, 496, 497
- regulations as to. Rent, eviction and rehabilitation regulations, infra
- remodeling, eviction for, 345-347

References are to pages

INDEX

RENT CONTROL—Cont'd
Eviction—Cont'd
- Rent Stabilization Code, 830-840
- spouse of deceased tenant, 107
- stay of order granting certificate of, 125
- subdividing property by alteration or remodeling, 107-109
- subtenant, 23, 106, 107
- tenant protection bulletins, 1072 et seq., 1105
- tenant protection regulations, 1049 et seq.
- urban renewal, 109
- withdrawal of occupied housing accommodations from rental market, 109, 110, 348, 349

Evidence
- agreement as to increased service or facilities, tenant protection regulations, 1032
- rules of practice, Office of Rent Administration adjudicatory proceedings, 1159
- support of application for increase of rent, advisory bulletin, 169, 170
- witnesses, infra

Excessive exemptions, rent increases for low income elderly persons, 721

Excessive rent, prohibitions against, 35

Exemption from rent controls, generally, 55, 56, 61, 1001; as to particular exemptions see more specific entries throughout this index

Exemption from taxation, property tax law destabilization provisions, 1196 et seq.

Ex parte communications, Office of Rent Administration rules of practice, 1165

Expediting proceedings before District Rent Director, operational bulletin as to, generally, 581

Explanatory statements and clarifications, Rent Guidelines Board orders, 875-878, 881-883, 964-967, 978

Extension of lease, eviction of tenant for refusal as to, 22, 431

Facilities, adjustment of maximum rent on increase of, 287, 288

RENT CONTROL—Cont'd
Factual disputes as to maximum rent, orders as to, 87

Fair market rent, generally, 578, 791, 1096

Fair return rental, administrator's advisory bulletin as to, 275

False reports or statements, prohibition as to, 449

Family
- administrator's advisory bulletin as to renting to, 171
- city rent and rehabilitation law defining related persons, 389
- defined, Rent Stabilization Code, 771
- eviction based on required usage by family of landlord, 99-106, 333-344, 432, 433

Farming tenants as exempt from rent control regulations, 62

Federal Act
- adjustment of maximum rent based on rehabilitation or improvement under, 296
- definition of, 248, 380

Federal government
- Federal Act, supra
- rent control regulations as not applicable to accommodations owned and operated by, 56, 1001
- temporary state housing rent commission co-operating with, 29

Fees
- assessability of fees against owner of occupied structure, 246
- attorneys' fees, supra
- emergency tenant protection laws, operating expenses, 1006
- New York City rent and eviction regulations, 270
- receipt attesting to payment of fee for report of search as to violations, operational bulletin as to, 585
- witnesses subpoenaed under Emergency Housing Rent Control Law, 29

Filing. Records and reports, infra

Final order, defined, 262, 775

Financial grounds, administrator's advisory bulletin for increase of rent on basis of, 135, 136

References are to pages

1211

INDEX

RENT CONTROL—Cont'd
Fines and penalties
- city rent agency, 450
- crimes and criminal penalties, supra
- defined, hotel's unlawful eviction, 1200
- elderly persons, exemption from rent increases for low income elderly persons, 720, 721
- emergency tenant protection laws, 1017
- New York City rent and eviction regulations, civil penalties for violations, 353
- Rent Stabilization Code, 846, 857
- riders, penalties for failure to serve tenant with rent stabilization rider, 558, 559
- tenant protection regulations, 1058, 1065

Fire
- alarm system, operational bulletin as to increase of rent based on installation of, 623, 624
- expediting proceedings as to fires in rent control buildings, 581
- maximum rent decrease, fire hazards, 302, 400, 418
- property tax law, destabilization provisions, 1196 et seq.

Forms
- accountant's certification for major capital improvement, 517, 519
- advisory bulletins of state rent administrator as to use of, 132 et seq.
- alternative hardship, 567-574
- order, form of protest against, 368
- regulations, form and content of protest against, 122, 123, 368
- window guard installation, form for, 534, 535

Fractional terms, Rent Guidelines Board's orders as to, 872 et seq.

Fraternity houses as exempt from rent control laws, 62, 250, 260

Fraud, revocation or cancellation of certificate of eviction obtained by, 25, 436

Freedom of information law, implementation, 541-547

Fuel adjustments
• generally, 296-300

RENT CONTROL—Cont'd
Fuel adjustments—Cont'd
- advisory bulletin, 143-146
- emergency tenant protection laws, operating expenses, 1006
- guidelines, 579
- Rent Guidelines Board's orders as to, 915 et seq.

Furnished room accommodations as exempt from rent controls, 58, 1003

Graduated rentals, administrator's interpretation as to voluntary lease agreement providing for, 493

Guidelines Board. Rent Guidelines Board, infra

Harassment
• generally, 354-356
- civil action by tenant for unlawful eviction or for surrender of possession as result of, 359, 360
- Rent Stabilization Code restrictions, 843, 844

Hardship
- administrator's advisory bulletin, 170-173
- definition, 564
- emergency tenant protection laws, 1006
- tenant protection bulletins, 1083 et seq.
- tenant protection regulations, 1033, 1036

Hazardous conditions. Dangerous or hazardous conditions, supra

Health department, operational bulletin as to co-operation with, 589

Hearings
- maximum rent adjustment, City Rent and Rehabilitation Law, 399
- Private Housing and Finance Law, rent increases, 1192
- Rent Stabilization Code, 850
- rules of practice, Office of Rent Administration adjudicatory proceedings, 1155 et seq.

Heat or heating system
• generally, 613
- complaints of no heat, processing of, 581, 642-644
- enclosure of boiler room as basis for rent increase, operational bulletin as to, 615

References are to pages

1212

INDEX

RENT CONTROL—Cont'd
Heat or heating system—Cont'd
- expediting proceedings for failure to provide, 581
- modernization or conversion of heating system, 475, 514, 618, 619
- night time heating as basis for rent increase, operational bulletin as to, 646

Hold up alarm system, operational bulletin as to increase of rent based on installation of, 623, 624

Hospitals
- exemption, 56, 382, 775, 1002, 1028
- staff housing, sublease regulations per Rent Stabilization Code, 845

Hotel
• generally, 981 et seq.
- advisory bulletin as to increase of rent, 176-184
- ancillary services, defined, 772
- city rent and rehabilitation law applicable to, 382, 383
- defined, 54, 55, 262, 769
- eviction of tenants, restrictions on, 94, 95, 320-322, 835-841, 1199 et seq.
- exemption from rent control, 57, 1003
- factual determination as to whether establishment continues as, 90
- hotel occupant, defined, Rent Stabilization Code, 771
- instructions for completion of information sheets for increase of rent, 693
- maximum rents, 71, 295
- permanent tenant, defined, Rent Stabilization Code, 770
- rate of rent increase, guidelines, 579
- recordkeeping requirements for, 93, 318
- Rent Stabilization Code, generally, 778
- Rent Stabilization Law, generally, 728-730
- required services, defined, 771, 772
- stabilization association for hotel industry, 761-763

Hot water system, installation as improvement, 514, 613

RENT CONTROL—Cont'd
Housing accommodation, defined, 4, 51, 248, 381, 769
Housing and Community Renewal Division
• generally, 49-129
- administrative review, 857-861
- advisory opinions and operational bulletins, 855
- amendment to complaint or application, 854
- emergency tenant protection, rent guidelines boards, 999
- Omnibus Housing Act, 1174 et seq.
- proceedings related to Rent Stabilization Code, 846-855
- refusal to renew lease, Rent Stabilization Code, 835-841
- registration of housing accommodations, 855-857
- Rent Stabilization Code enforcement, generally, 846-851

Housing company, definition, 714
Housing Development Administration, rent stabilization regulations, 863 et seq.
Housing Preservation and Development Department, Private Housing and Finance Law, 1192
Identity of landlord, administrator's advisory bulletin as to report of change of, 138
Illegal purposes of occupancy, basis for eviction of tenant, 22, 431
Illumination increase as basis for rent increase, operational bulletin as to, 646
Immediate family, definition, 333, 563, 771, 1025
Immoral purpose, eviction of tenant using or permitting housing to be used for, 22, 431
Improvements
- administrator's interpretations, schedule of rental values, 507 et seq.
- capital improvement, supra
- definition, 511
- eviction of tenant for refusal to permit entry onto property for making, 22, 26
- property tax law, destabilization provisions, 1196 et seq.
- rehabilitated buildings, infra

References are to pages

RENT CONTROL—Cont'd
Improvements—Cont'd
- tenant protection bulletins, 1104
- tenant protection regulations, 1032

Incinerators, upgrading or conversion of, 502-507, 514

Income tax year, definition, 714

Increase of maximum rent, generally, 73, 138-142; and see more specific entries throughout this index

Increase of services, rent adjustments, 133-135, 138, 139, 287, 288, 310, 547-552

Information and instruction sheets of Rent Administrator
- generally, 652 et seq., 695
- application by landlord for increase of maximum rent (fair return), 669, 676
- labor cost recoupment, instruction sheets for application for increase in maximum rent based on, 696 et seq.
- painting and decorating complaints, 660
- voluntary lease agreements, 652 et seq.

Initial legal registered rent, Rent Stabilization Code, 769, 781-791, 855-857

Injunctions
- city rent agency order or regulation, injunctive relief as to, 445
- Emergency Housing Rent Control Law, 32, 35, 36
- hotel, unlawful eviction, 1201
- New York City rent and eviction regulations, injunctive relief, 352, 353
- tenant protection regulations, 1061

Inspection of records
- generally, 117, 118, 361
- freedom of information law, 541-547
- Rent Stabilization Code requirements, 850

Instructions
- claiming monthly increase, 521
- rent administrator. Information and instruction sheets of rent administrator, supra

Insurance
- advisory bulletin for rent increase based on cost of, 143-146
- emergency tenant protection laws, operating expenses, 1006

RENT CONTROL—Cont'd
Insurance—Cont'd
- office located in home, 591

Intentional conduct by landlord causing tenant to vacate, 114

Intercommunication systems, concurrent major capital improvement, 514

Intergovernmental co-operation, 244, 245, 1022

Interior decorating. Decorating, supra

Interpretations by Rent Administrator, 457 et seq.

Interpreters, Office of Rent Administration adjudicatory proceedings, 1166

Interruption of services. Discontinuance of service by landlord, supra

Intervention
- rules of practice, Office of Rent Administration adjudicatory proceedings, 1161
- tenant protection regulations, 1062

Interviewers
- administrator's interpretations, schedule of rental values, 510
- installation of, 502, 606, 646, 647

Investigations
- city housing rent agency, authority of, 230, 231, 441
- Emergency Housing Rent Control Law, 28
- rules of practice, Office of Rent Administration adjudicatory proceedings, 1156

Janitorial services, administrator's interpretation as to partial payment of rent by performance of, 468

Joinder of parties, Office of Rent Administration rules of practice, 1161

Joint protest as to rent control regulations, 121

Judicial notice, Office of Rent Administration rules of practice, 1164

Judicial review
- certificate of eviction, judicial review of, 437
- city rent agency, judicial review of proceedings of, 231-235, 445
- protest, judicial review of, 370
- Rent Stabilization Code, 861, 862

Jurisdiction of District Rent and Rehabilitation Offices, 263, 264

References are to pages

Index

RENT CONTROL—Cont'd
Kennel located in home, 591
Kitchen
- floor coverings, operational bulletin as to rent increase based on installation of, 612
- modernization, generally, 593-598, 609
- refrigerators, infra
- revised rental values, kitchen equipment, 207
- sinks, operational bulletin as to rent increase based on installation of, 609
- stoves, infra

Knowledge. Notice or knowledge, infra

Labor costs
- emergency tenant protection laws, operating expenses, 1006
- maximum rent adjustment, 295, 296, 391
- pass-along, 430
- recoupment of labor costs, instruction sheet for, 696-712

Landlord, definition under city rent and rehabilitation law, 390

Legal regulated rent defined, Rent Stabilization Code, 769

Liens
- elderly persons, exemption from rent increases for low income elderly persons, 721
- hotel, unlawful eviction, 1201

Lights installed as basis for rent increase, operational bulletin as to, 646, 648-651

Limitation of actions or proceedings
- Emergency Housing Rent Control Law violations, 37
- refund, time limitation as to enforcement for wrongful eviction, 115-117

Limitations
- alternative hardship increase, 569-571
- amount of rent collectible in twelve-month period, 550
- conditional rental, supra
- major capital improvements, rehabilitation, and hardship increases for rent stabilized apartments, 555, 556
- reserve funds, restrictions on use of, 554, 555

RENT CONTROL—Cont'd
Limitations—Cont'd
- tenant protection regulations, 1036

Loans under Private Housing and Finance Law, 1188 et seq.

Local Emergency Housing Rent Control Law, New York City, 223 et seq.

Local rent administrator
- definition of, 53
- proceedings before, 118-121

Local rent office, definition of, 53

Locks to entrance doors in apartments, specifications, 529-531

Low income elderly persons, rent increase exemptions, 713 et seq.

Mail, service of notice or paper by, 126, 127, 289, 290

Major capital improvement. Capital improvement, supra

Malicious damage to property by tenant, eviction based on, 431

Management and managers
- emergency tenant protection laws, fees as operating expenses, 1006
- exemption from rent controls of accommodations furnished to managers, 62

Maximum rent
- generally, 68 et seq.
- adjustments, supra
- city rent agency determining, 390 et seq.
- definition of, 51, 261, 390, 714
- elderly persons, exemption from rent increases for low income elderly persons, 714
- grounds for increase of, 283
- New York City rent and eviction regulations
  - generally, 271-282
  - - biennial adjustment of, 280, 281
  - - collectibility, 281, 282
  - - compensable rent adjustment, 272-276
  - - grounds for increase of, 283
  - - maximum base rents effective January 1, 1972, 276-280
  - - services included in, 272
- prohibitions, generally, 111-114, 235
- rates of maximum rent increase, summary of, 574-580

References are to pages

1215

RENT CONTROL—Cont'd

Maximum rent—Cont'd
- Rent Stabilization Law, maximum rent under, 377

Mileage fees, Office of Rent Administration rules of practice, 1169

Modification. Change, supra

Monastery as exempt from regulations, 382

Mortgage
- interest. Mortgage interest, infra
- notice of commencement of proceedings to reduce rent served upon mortgagees, 638, 639

Mortgage interest
- alternative hardship increase, mortgage interest as includible expense, 572, 573
- defined, tenant protection regulations, 1034
- emergency tenant protection laws, operating expenses, 1006

Motor court
- city rent and rehabilitation law, 383
- exemption from rent controls, 57, 1003

Multiple Dwelling Law, 578, 644, 781, 957 et seq.

Multiple tenants, order where an apartment is rented to, 90

Municipally owned housing accommodations, exemption from rent control, 56, 1001, 1027

Net annual return
- advisory bulletin as to rent increase based on issue of, 141, 142
- determination of, 401, 402
- rent increase as affected by, 80

New dwellings, property tax law destabilization provisions, 1194 et seq.

New equipment installation, guidelines, 555

New York City housing rent control
- as to particular matters, see more specific entries throughout this index
- City Rent Agency, supra
- elderly persons, exemption from rent increases for low income elderly persons, 713 et seq.
- local Emergency Housing Rent Control Law, 223 et seq.

RENT CONTROL—Cont'd

New York City housing rent control —Cont'd
- Rent Administrator's information and instruction sheets, 652 et seq.
- Rent Administrator's interpretations, 457 et seq.
- Rent Administrator's operational bulletins, 581 et seq.
- rent and eviction regulations, 247 et seq.
- Rent Stabilization Association of New York City, infra

Non-housing use changed to housing use as affected by city rent and rehabilitation law, 384

Non-immediate family member, definition, 563

Non-professional landlord, administrator's advisory bulletin as to relief available to, 173-176, 287

Nonprofit
- clubs as exempt from rent controls, 62
- definition of nonprofit clubs, 260
- exemption from rent controls, 57, 62, 382, 778, 1002, 1003, 1028

Non-residential. Commercial use, supra

Notarizing application before filing, administrator's advisory bulletin, 133

Notice and knowledge
- amended filing requirements for rent increase, notice to tenants, 520, 521
- appearance notice, 126, 127
- attorneys at law, notice to, 92, 127, 317, 318, 828
- cancellation of lease, 290, 439
- change of ownership, Rent Stabilization Code, 830
- district rent and rehabilitation director, notice of proceedings before, 362
- eviction notice, 96, 97, 325
- hotel, unlawful eviction, 1201, 1202
- Housing and Community Redevelopment Division proceedings, 851-855
- mortgagees, notice of commencement of proceedings to reduce rent, 638, 639

References are to pages

INDEX

RENT CONTROL—Cont'd
Notice and knowledge—Cont'd
- Private Housing and Finance Law, notice of contemplated rehabilitation, 1188 et seq.
- Rent Stabilization Code, 824-830, 850
- rules of practice, Office of Rent Administration adjudicatory proceedings, 1156, 1158, 1160
- tenant protection regulations, 1044, 1062, 1064

No violation certificate, administrator's interpretation, 472, 473

Nuisance, eviction of tenant permitting or committing, 21, 431

Nurse using home as office, 590

Oath and affirmation
- notarized applications, 133
- Rent Stabilization Code, enforcement of, 850
- rules of practice, Office of Rent Administration adjudicatory proceedings, 1159
- tenant protection regulations, 1061

Occupant defined, Rent Stabilization Code, 770, 771

Offer by landlord to restore services as basis for restoration of reduced maximum rent, operational bulletin as to, 636

Office of rent administration, rent and eviction regulations of
- generally, 49 et seq.
- adjustments, generally, 72 et seq.
- amendment or revocation of regulation of, 55
- application for exception from rent controls, 65, 66
- commercial or professional renting of controlled housing accommodations, 64
- conversion of housing accommodations as factor, 63
- definitions, 50-55
- enforcement of regulations, 114-118
- equalization adjustment as to maximum rents, 71
- evictions, 94-110
- exemption from regulation, 55, 56, 61
- local rent administrator, proceedings before, 118-121
- maximum rents, 68 et seq.

RENT CONTROL—Cont'd
Office of rent administration, rent and eviction regulations of—Cont'd
- miscellaneous procedural matters, 126-129
- primary residence of tenant in possession, rent control laws as applicable to housing accommodations which are not, 65
- procedural matters, generally, 126-129
- prohibited acts as to maximum rent, 111-114
- protests, 121-126
- receipt for rent paid, 65
- registration and records, 91-94
- revocation of, 55
- scope of regulations, 49 et seq.
- waiver of rent control laws by tenant, 65
- withdrawal from rental market, 64

Offset allowance upon expiration of tax abatement, administrator's interpretation of restoration of amount of, 497-501

Oil burning system upgrading as concurrent major capital improvement, 514

Omnibus Housing Act of 1983, 1174 et seq.

One family houses, exemption under city rent and rehabilitation law as to, 383

Operating expenses
- administrator's advisory bulletin as to completion of application concerning operating statement, 161, 162
- defined, tenant protection regulations, 1034
- emergency tenant protection, 999, 1003
- maximum rent adjustment, 294, 295
- rent increases, generally, 80, 82
- standards for determining applications to compensate, 201, 203, 209, 212, 214, 216
- tenant protection bulletins, 1083 et seq.

Operational bulletins
- Rent Administrator, New York City, 581 et seq.
- Rent Stabilization Code, 855

References are to pages

1217

INDEX

RENT CONTROL—Cont'd
Ophthalmologist using home as office, 591
Opinions and official interpretation, New York City rent and eviction regulations, 373, 374
Opinions of State Rent Administrator relating to rent and eviction regulations, generally, 128 et seq.
Option to purchase, lease coupled with, 113, 114, 352
Optometrist using home as office, 590
Order
- adjustments to maximum rents, generally, 310, 313
- alternative hardship increase, 573, 574
- elderly persons, exemption from rent increases for low income elderly persons, 717, 719, 721
- final order, definition of, 262
- form of protest against, 368
- maximum rent adjustments by order of administrator, 282
- modification of, 356, 357, 365-367, 371
- multiple tenants, order where an apartment is rented to, 90
- Rent Guidelines Board, 871 et seq.
- revocation of, 126, 356-357, 365-367, 371
- services, adjustment of maximum rent based on decrease of, 301, 302, 310
- state rent administrator, protest against order of, 126
Osteopath using home as office, 590
Overcharges
- administrator's advisory bulletins as to recovery of, 195, 196
- penalties, Rent Stabilization Code, 720, 846
Ownership, change of, 92, 138, 317, 830
Painting
- administrator's advisory bulletin as to, 155-160
- complaints as to painting and decorating, information and instruction sheets as to, 660
- expediting proceedings involving questions as to, 581, 582
- Rent Stabilization Code, 775

RENT CONTROL—Cont'd
Partial tax exemption, Rent Guidelines Board's orders as to, 885-890, 902-904, 917 et seq.
Peepholes, installation of, 501, 502, 510, 606, 646, 647
Penalties. Fines and penalties, supra
Pending proceedings
• generally, 242
- Emergency Housing Rent Control Law, pending proceedings under, 47
- hotel, unlawful eviction, 1201
- New York City rent and eviction regulations, 364
- protest as to rent control regulations as affected by amendment of regulation, pendency of, 124, 125
- Rent Stabilization Code administrative review, 860
- tax certiorari proceedings, alternative hardship increase, 570
- tenant protection regulations, 1064
- transfer of, 241
Permits as operating expenses, emergency tenant protection laws, 1006
Personal use by landlord, eviction for, 22, 26, 99-106, 333-344, 432, 433
Petition for administrative review, 857-861
Pharmacy located in home, 591
Physician using home as office, 590
Physiotherapist using home as office, 590
Plumbing improvements affecting rental values, 486-489, 514, 531
Podiatrist using home as office, 590
Poor and elderly persons, New York City exemption from rent increases, 713 et seq.
Previous hardship increase, alternative hardship increase, 571
Primary residence of tenant in possession, rent control laws as applicable to, 65
Prime windows, major capital improvement, 551
Private Housing Finance Law, 1188 et seq.
Privilege against self-incrimination, 128, 372, 373
Privileged information, 236, 1061, 1067

References are to pages

1218

INDEX

RENT CONTROL—Cont'd
Production of documents
- generally, 127, 372, 442
- New York City rent and eviction regulations, 372, 373
- rules of practice, Office of Rent Administration adjudicatory proceedings, 1156

Professional renting of controlled housing accommodations, 268
Professional use. Commercial use, supra
Property tax. Taxation, infra
Protest
- generally, 121-126
- alternative hardship increase, petitions, 574
- discrimination against tenant, 449
- Emergency Housing Rent Control Law, protest as to regulations or orders under, 30
- eviction of tenant for filing, 35, 240
- form and content of protest against order of local rent administrator, advisory bulletin as to, 191-193
- judicial review of, 370
- modification of orders on, 371
- New York City rent and eviction regulations
  - generally, 367 et seq., 443 et seq.
  - – action by administrator, 369
  - – answer to protest, time of filing, 368, 369
  - – form and content of protest against regulations or order 368
  - – judicial review, 370
  - – modification or revocation of orders on protest, 371
  - – persons who may file, 367
  - – service and filing of, 368
  - – stay, 370
  - – time for filing, 367, 368, 369
  - – – administrator, time for action by, 370
  - – – answer to protest, 368, 369
- orders issued by rent administrator, filing petition against, 126, 538
- verification of, 192, 193

Psychologist using home as office, 590
Public Authorities Law, 1193
Public relations agency located in home, 591

RENT CONTROL—Cont'd
Purchase of property. Sale, infra
Rat infested buildings, expediting proceedings as to, 581
Real estate industry stabilization association, 740-748
Real estate office located in home, 591
Real Property Tax Law. Taxation, infra
Receipt for rent paid, 65, 269, 841, 842, 1029
Records and reports
- alternative hardship increase application, 571, 572
- city rent agency, 441
- decontrol of certain housing accommodations, regulations governing report on, 315, 316
- Emergency Housing Rent Control Law, requirements under, 28
- inspection of, 117, 118, 361
- New York City rent and eviction regulations, filing of amendments, 263
- office of rent administration, requirements of, 91-94
- rental income, administrator's advisory bulletin as to completion of form for reporting, 169
- Rent Stabilization Code, 824-830, 850
- search issued by Office Code Enforcement, operational bulletin as to increase in maximum rent requiring report of, 585, 586
- services, adjustment of maximum rent based on decrease of, 310
- tenant protection regulations, 1026, 1044

Refrigerators
- complaints, expediting proceedings as to, 581
- operational bulletin as to rent increase based on replacement of, 607
- revised rental values, 207

Refund directive, advisory bulletin as to failure to comply with, 153
Registration
- generally, 49 et seq.
- accommodations, generally, 91-94
- emergency tenant protection laws, rent registration, 1020

References are to pages

1219

INDEX

RENT CONTROL—Cont'd
Registration—Cont'd
- New York City rent and eviction regulations
  • generally, 315-320
  - - change of ownership, 317
  - - decontrol of certain housing accommodations, report on, 315, 316
  - - failure to file, effect of, 318
  - - first rent, 317
  - - notices to attorneys at law, 317, 318
  - - recordkeeping, generally, 318
  - - service of papers, 317
- Rent Stabilization Code requirements, 855-857
- Rent Stabilization Law, registration required under, 377, 760-761
- suspension of association registration under Rent Stabilization Law, 763
- tenant protection regulations, 1065

Rehabilitated buildings
• generally, 74
- adjustment of maximum rent on basis of, 287, 288
- administrator's interpretations, schedule of rental values, 507 et seq.
- advisory bulletin as to, 138, 139
- city rent and rehabilitation law, supra
- eviction, 107-109
- increase in rents, generally, 547-552
- New York City
  • generally, 378 et seq.
  - - administrator's interpretations, schedule of rental values, 507 et seq.
  - - agency. City rent agency, supra
  - - capital value, definition of, 401, 402
  - - decontrol on basis of vacancy rate, 456
  - - definitions, 380 et seq.
  - - evictions, 430-441
  - - investigations, 441
  - - judicial review of proceedings, 445
  - - labor cost pass-along, 430
  - - labor cost rent adjustment application under, 391

RENT CONTROL—Cont'd
Rehabilitated buildings—Cont'd
- New York City—Cont'd
  - - maximum rents, determination of, 391 et seq.
  - - net annual return, determination of, 401, 402
  - - prohibitions, generally, 449
  - - records and reports, 441
  - - tax abatement for properties subject to rent exemption orders, 428-430
- Private Housing and Finance Law, 1188 et seq., 1192, 1193
- public authorities law, 1193
- tenant protection bulletins, 1104
- tenant protection regulations, 1032

Reimbursements, exemption from rent increases for low income elderly persons, 716
Rejection of protest as to rent control regulations, 124
Relative. Family, supra
Religious housing accommodations as not subject to rent control, 56, 775, 1001, 1028
Relocation of tenants upon issuance of certificates of eviction, 434
Remodeling. Rehabilitation, supra
Renewal of lease
- adjustments in lease period, 577
- administrator's interpretation as to effect of tenant's refusal to, 496, 497
- defined, Rent Stabilization Code, 770
- Rent Guidelines Board orders as to, 871 et seq.
- specifications, 562, 563
- tenant protection bulletins, 1105

Rent Administration Office rules of practice, 1155 et seq.
Rent Administrator
- advisory bulletins, 130-200
- information and instruction sheets, New York City, 652 et seq.
- interpretations, New York City, 457 et seq.
- local rent administrator, supra
- operational bulletins, New York City, 581 et seq.
- protest against order of, 126
Rent, definition of, 153

References are to pages

1220

INDEX

RENT CONTROL—Cont'd
Rent Guidelines Board
- generally, 737-740, 871 et seq.
- credits, 874 et seq.
- decontrolled units, 874-878, 883 et seq.
- electrical inclusion adjustment, 892, 893, 905 et seq.
- escalator clauses, 873 et seq.
- explanatory statements and clarifications, 875-878, 881-883, 964-967, 978
- fractional terms, 872 et seq.
- fuel adjustments, 915, 920, 921, 928 et seq.
- lease renewals, 871 et seq.
- orders of. See lines throughout this group
- special guidelines, 900 et seq.
- stabilizer, 879 et seq.
- subleases, 879, 880, 886, 888
- supplemental orders and modifications, 895-900, 903, 915 et seq.
- supplementary adjustments, generally, 956 et seq.
- tax exemption, effect of, 885-890, 902-904, 917 et seq.
- vacant apartments, 872 et seq.

Rent increase exemption fund, low income elderly persons, 716

Rent roll requests, operational bulletin as to certification of, 637

Rent stabilization
- association. Rent Stabilization Association of New York City, infra
- hotel orders, 981 et seq.
- Housing Development Administration's regulations, 863 et seq.
- Rent Guidelines Board, orders of, 871 et seq.

Rent Stabilization Association of New York City
- generally, 377, 725 et seq.
- adjustments, 751-753, 791-823
- administrative review, 857-861
- annual registration of housing accommodations, 856, 857
- appearance by attorney or other authorized representative, 828
- application of, 728, 729
- attorney's fees, 846
- certification of services, 824
- change of ownership, notice of, 830

RENT CONTROL—Cont'd
Rent Stabilization Association of New York City—Cont'd
- classification of buildings, 789
- Commissioner, administrative review by, 857-861
- conditional rental, 842, 843
- confidentiality of information, 850, 857
- costs, assessment of, 846
- credits, 846
- definitions, 769-775
- delegation of authority, 767
- DHCR. Housing and community redevelopment division, supra
- enforcement and procedures, 756-760
- evasion of regulations, 841, 842
- evictions, 754-756, 830-840
- exemptions, 776-781
- findings and declaration of emergency, 726, 727
- fines and penalties, 846, 857
- grounds for refusal to renew lease with or without order or approval of DHCR, Rent Stabilization Code, 835-841
- guidelines board, 737-740
- harassment, 843, 844
- hearing officers, 850
- hotel industry stabilization association, 761-763
- hotels, application to, 728-730
- hotel tenancy, discontinuance of, Rent Stabilization Code, 835-841
- Housing and Community Renewal Division, supra
- injunctions, Supreme Court, 850
- inspection and records related to enforcement, 850
- judicial review, 861, 862
- leases and rental agreements, effect on, 781
- maintenance of services, 754
- multiple family complex, application to, 729, 730
- notices and records, 824-830
- oaths, 850
- orders to enforce Rent Stabilization Code and this Code, 849
- overcharge penalties, 846
- painting, 775

References are to pages

1221

INDEX

RENT CONTROL—Cont'd
Rent Stabilization Association of New York City—Cont'd
- pending proceedings, administrative review, 861
- petition for review, 857-861
- real estate industry stabilization association, 740-748
- receipts, 841, 842
- records and recordkeeping, 776, 829
- registered rents, legal, 769, 781-789
- registration of housing accommodations, 855-857
- renewal of lease, notice and procedure, 825
- rent increase exemptions and tax abatement for property occupied by senior citizens, application for, 731-736
- rent registration, 760-761
- security deposits, 843
- separability clause, 776
- services, discontinuance or interruption, 824, 843, 844
- stabilization of rents, generally, 749-751
- stay of proceedings, administrative review, 861
- subletting, 770, 844-846
- subpoenas, 850
- Supreme Court injunctions, 850
- suspension of association registration, 763
- termination notices, 831
- time and date for filing petition for administrative review, 857-859
- waiver of benefit void, 781

Repairs
- emergency tenant protection laws, operating expenses, 1006
- eviction for refusal to permit entrance for making, 22, 26, 433
- improvements, supra
- property tax law, destabilization provisions, 1196 et seq.

Reports. Records and reports, supra
Request by mayor for appropriations, authority as to, 246
Required services, defined, Rent Stabilization Code, 771-775
Reserve funds, restrictions on use of, 554, 555

RENT CONTROL—Cont'd
Retroactive adjustments of maximum rent, 314
Review. Appeal and review, supra
Revocation
- certificate of eviction, 25
- fraud, revocation of certificate of eviction obtained by, 436
- orders, 126, 365-367, 371, 527, 535, 542
- regulations, revocation of, 55, 263
- rent adjustment laws generally, 73
Rewiring of building as basis for increase of maximum rent, administrator's interpretation or operational bulletin as to, 460, 514, 582-584, 608
Roominghouse
- advisory bulletin as to increase of rent for, 176-184
- decrease of maximum rent, 302, 303
- definition of, 54, 263
- exempt from rent controls, 58, 60, 1003, 1028
- maximum rents, 68, 69, 295
- recordkeeping required of, 93, 318
Rules of practice for the Office of Rent Administration adjudicatory proceeding, 1155 et seq.
Sale
- condition of renting, purchase of property as, 111, 112, 154, 155, 350
- lease with purchase option, 113, 114, 352
- showing of property to prospective purchaser, eviction of tenant for refusal, 22, 26
- tenant protection regulations, purchase price, 1036
Schedules of rental values, 196-200, 507 et seq.
Schools. Educational institutions, supra
Seasonal rent. Summer resort housing, infra
Security deposits
• generally, 112, 113
- New York City rent and eviction regulations, 351
- Rent Stabilization Code, 843
- tenant protection regulations, 1055
Security systems, operational bulletin as to increase of rent on basis of installing, 601, 602

References are to pages

1222

INDEX

RENT CONTROL—Cont'd

Self-contained family unit, rent controls as to, 63
Self-incrimination, privilege against, 128, 372, 373
Self-occupancy by landlord. Family of landlord, supra
Senior citizens. Elderly persons, supra
Servants, exemption from rent controls of accommodations furnished to, 62, 779
Service employees, definition of, 260
Service of process
• generally, 92, 123, 126, 127
- New York City rent and eviction regulations, 317, 368, 371
- rent stabilization rider, 558
- rules of practice, Office of Rent Administration adjudicatory proceedings, 1156
- subpoenas, infra
- tenant protection regulations, 1064, 1068
Severability of provisions
- New York City rent and eviction regulations, 263
- Omnibus Housing Act, 1186
- rules of practice, Office of Rent Administration adjudicatory proceedings, 1173
- tenant protection regulations, 1027
Sewer charges
- emergency tenant protection, rent guidelines boards, 999
- tenant protection regulations, 1037
Shower installations, amendment of Schedule of Rental Values, 531
Single room occupancy
- decrease of rent for, 302, 303
- definition of, 263
Small Building Owners Assistance Unit
- Omnibus Housing Act, 1183
- tenant protection regulations, 1064
Sorority houses as exempt from rent control laws, 62, 250, 260
Spouse of deceased tenant, eviction of, 107
Stabilization. Rent stabilization, supra
Stabilization rider for apartment house tenants, 557-559
Stabilizer charge, rate of rent increase, 580, 879 et seq.

RENT CONTROL—Cont'd

State owned property as not subject to rent control, 56, 1001, 1027
Statute of limitations. Limitation of actions, supra
Statutory lease executed after filing of application for increase in maximum rent, administrator's interpretation as to, 469-471
Stay of proceedings
- administrative review, Rent Stabilization Code, 861
- eviction, 124, 370
- tenant protection regulations, 1070
Stockbroker's office located in home, 591
Stoves
- expediting proceedings involving questions as to defects, 581
- replacement of gas stoves, 611-613
- revised rental values, 207
Sublease
- adjustment of maximum rents as affected by increase in subtenants, 291
- advisory bulletin as to rent increase based on, 140
- definition of subtenant, 55
- emergency tenant protection laws, 1014
- eviction of subtenant, 23, 106, 107
- increase in number of subtenants as based for rent increase, 76
- Rent Guidelines Board's orders as to, 879, 880, 886, 888
- Rent Stabilization Code regulation, 770, 844-846
- tenant protection regulations, 1056
- termination of tenancy by owner, 845
- vacancy increase or surcharge, Rent Stabilization Code, 845, 846
Subpoenas
- city rent agency's authority as to, 442
- contempt for failure to obey, 28, 29, 127, 442
- duces tecum subpoenas, procedures for response, 541-547
- New York City rent and eviction regulations, 372
- powers of administrator, 127
- rent, eviction and rehabilitation regulations, supra

References are to pages

RENT CONTROL—Cont'd

Subpoenas—Cont'd
- Rent Stabilization Code, 850
- rules of practice, Office of Rent Administration adjudicatory proceedings, 1159, 1167-1169
- tenant protection regulations, 1061

Subtenant. Sublease, supra

Summer resort housing
- definition, 260, 261
- exempt from rent control regulations, 62

Superintendent. Management and managers, supra

Supervision, increase of rentals, 1192

Supreme Court injunctions, Rent Stabilization Code, 850

Surveys of need for rent control, 456

Suspension of registration under Rent Stabilization Law, 763

Taxation
- abatement of taxes, 428-430, 497-501, 719
- alternative hardship increase, 570
- destabilization provisions, 1194 et seq.
- elderly persons, exemption from rent increases for low income elderly persons, 714, 716, 719
- maximum rent adjustment, increase of property taxes, 294, 295
- operating expenses, emergency tenant protection laws, 1006
- partial tax exemption, 780, 885-890, 902-904, 917 et seq.
- Private Housing and Finance Law, rent increases, 1192
- Rent Stabilization Code, tax benefits, 779, 780
- tenant protection regulations, 1037

Telephone/door release as concurrent major capital improvement, 514

Telephone testimony, Office of Rent Administration rules of practice, 1170

Television
- antenna, increase of rent based on installation of, 614, 615
- closed circuit security system, increase of rent based on installation of, 508, 514, 603, 604
- signal reception, administrator's interpretations and schedule of rental values, 510

RENT CONTROL—Cont'd

Temporary state housing rent commission, establishment of, 10, 11

Tenant, definition of, 391, 562, 563, 769

Termination notices, Rent Stabilization Code, 831

Term of occupancy, change, 112, 351

Test year, 80, 161, 162

Threats, hotels' unlawful eviction, 1199

Threshold income defined, tenant protection regulations, 1035

Time
- alternative hardship increase, 574
- answer to protest as to rent control regulations, 122-124
- New York City rent and eviction regulations
- - notice or papers deemed served, 371
- - protest, supra
- protests as to rent control regulations, time for, 121, 122, 125
- Rent Stabilization Code, 857-861

Tourist court or home, 58, 383, 778, 1003, 1028

Trailers and trailer spaces, 383, 775

Treble damages for violations, 152, 153

Two-family house, exemption from rent controls, 58, 59, 383

Underlying leases, exemption from rent controls of structures subject to, 58

Unique or peculiar circumstances as basis for adjustment of maximum rent, 170-173, 291

United States. Federal government, supra

Universities. Colleges and universities, supra

Unlawful evictions, generally, 1199 et seq.

Urban renewal, eviction based on, 109

Utilities
- administrator's interpretations, schedule of rental values, 509
- electricity, supra
- emergency tenant protection laws, operating expenses, 1006
- heat or heating systems, supra
- sewer charges, supra
- water, infra

References are to pages

INDEX

RENT CONTROL—Cont'd

Vacancies
- adjustments in lease period, 577
- hotel orders, exclusions, 982, 984, 987, 992
- Rent Guidelines Board's orders as to, 872 et seq.
- Rent Stabilization Code, 769, 845, 846

Value of rentals, advisory bulletin as to schedule of, 196-200

Verification of protest, advisory bulletin as to, 192, 193

Vestibule doors, operational bulletin as to rent increase based on installation of, 606

Veterans' Emergency Housing Act, exemption from rent controls of housing accommodations completed under, 57

Veterinarian's office located in home, 591

Voluntary lease agreements
- increase in rent, 139, 140, 185-191, 288-291
- information and instruction sheets as to, 652 et seq.

Wage increases as affecting increase of maximum rents, operational bulletins as to, 592, 593

Waiver and estoppel
- emergency tenant protection laws, 1016
- New York City rent and eviction regulations, 269
- prohibited acts affecting waiver of rights by tenant, 349
- rent control laws, waiver by tenant, 65
- tenant protection regulations, waiver of benefits, 1029

Water
- complaints as to absence of hot water, processing of, 642-644
- emergency tenant protection, Rent Guidelines Boards, 999
- expediting proceedings for failure to provide, 581
- tenant protection regulations, 1037

Windows
- guards, specifications, 533-535
- operational bulletin as to rent increase based on replacement of, 611

RENT CONTROL—Cont'd

Windows—Cont'd
- prime windows installation, rent increase, 551
- replacement guidelines, 524-527

Withdrawal from rental market
- eviction based on, 109, 110, 348, 349
- New York City rent and eviction regulations, 269
- rent controls as affected by, 64

Witnesses
- fees, 29
- rules of practice, Office of Rent Administration, 1163, 1170
- self-incrimination, 128, 372, 373
- subpoenas, supra
- telephone testimony, 1170

References are to pages

Index

RENT CONTROL—Cont'd

Vacancies,
— adjustments in lease period, 877
— hotel orders' exclusions, 882, 884, 887, 892
— Rent Guidelines Board's orders, as to, 378 et seq.
— Rent Stabilization Code, 760, 855-846
Value of rentals, advisory bulletin as to schedule of, 195-200
Verification of protest, advisory bulletin as to, 193, 198
Vestibule doors, operational bulletin as to rent increase based on installation of, 600
Veterans, Emergency Housing Act, exemption from rent controls of housing "accommodations," completed under, 74
Veterinarian's office located in house, 591
Voluntary lease agreements,
— increase in rent, 139, 140 584-10, 585-551
— information and instruction sheets as to 582 et seq.
Wage increases as affecting increase of maximum rents, operational bulletin as to, 592, 593
Waiver and estoppel,
— emergency tenant protection laws, 1013
— New York City Rent and eviction regulations, 969
— prohibited acts shooting waiver of rights by tenant, 949
— rent control laws, waiver benefits, 95
— tenant protection regulations, waiver of benefits, 1066
Water,
— complaints as to absence of water, processing of, 341-344
— Emergency tenant protection, Rent Guidelines Boards, 429
— expediting proceedings for failure to provide, 531
— tenant protection regulations, 1063
Windows,
— guards, specifications, 593-596
— operational bulletin as to rent increase based on replacement of, 611

RENT CONTROL—Cont'd

Windows—Cont'd
— prime winds as installation increase, 561
— replacement guidelines, 52-521
— Withdrawal from rental market, exemption based on, 109, 110, 844, 845
— New York City rent and eviction regulations, 987
Witnesses,
— rent controls as affected by, 64
— fees, 25
— index of printed volumes of Rent Administration, LRB, 1170
— set purchases on a 158, 373, 375
— subpoenas forms,
— telephone testimony, 1170

References are to pages
1270